FROM JIM CROW TO CIVIL RIGHTS

MICHAEL J. KLARMAN

FROM JIM CROW TO CIVIL RIGHTS

THE SUPREME COURT AND THE STRUGGLE FOR RACIAL EQUALITY

OXFORD
UNIVERSITY PRESS

2004

OXFORD
UNIVERSITY PRESS

Oxford   New York
Auckland   Bangkok   Buenos Aires   Cape Town   Chennai
Dar es Salaam   Delhi   Hong Kong   Istanbul   Karachi   Kolkata
Kuala Lumpur   Madrid   Melbourne   Mexico City   Mumbai   Nairobi
São Paulo   Shanghai   Taipei   Tokyo   Toronto

Copyright © 2004 by Michael J. Klarman

Published by Oxford University Press, Inc.
198 Madison Avenue, New York, New York 10016

www.oup.com

Oxford is a registered trademark of Oxford University Press

Library of Congress Cataloging-in-Publication Data
Klarman, Michael J.
From Jim Crow to civil rights : the Supreme Court and the struggle
for racial equality / by Michael J. Klarman.
    p. cm.
Includes bibliographical references and index.
ISBN 0-19-512903-2
1. Segregation—Law and legislation—United States—History.
2. United States—Race relations—History. 3. United States. Supreme Court.
I. Title.
KF4757.K58 2003
342.73'0873—dc21   2003000515

9 8 7 6 5 4 3 2 1

Printed in the United States of America
on acid-free paper

To my mother, Muriel Klarman,

and to the memory of my father, Herbert E. Klarman

PREFACE

I signed a contract to write this book in the spring of 1998, but in some sense I have been working on it since the first semester that I taught constitutional law at the University of Virginia School of Law—the spring of 1988. Every teacher of constitutional law must ultimately make peace with *Brown v. Board of Education* (1954), which is widely deemed to be the most important Supreme Court decision of the twentieth century. Figuring out what one thinks about *Brown* has two dimensions. Why is the decision right? (Virtually everyone today agrees that it is right, though this was not so in 1954, when it was decided.) How important was the ruling in the history of American race relations?

My first stab at answering the normative question—why *Brown* is right—was a 1991 law review article that considered whether *Brown* could be defended on the ground that the southern political system was antidemocratic: In the 1950s, southern blacks were generally not permitted to vote, and state legislatures were badly malapportioned in favor of rural whites, who were the most committed to maintaining white supremacy. In subsequent scholarship, I turned to the question of impact—how much *Brown* mattered to race relations in the United States. This work situated *Brown* within a host of forces—political, social, economic, demographic, ideological, and international—that were pushing the United States toward greater racial equality in the middle of the twentieth century. I wondered whether these broad background forces might not have rendered *Brown* unnecessary, and I inquired into the connections between *Brown* and the 1960s civil rights movement. As I taught and wrote about American constitutional history through the 1990s, I developed certain perspectives that I thought shed light on the Court's role in American society and governance: the connection between the work of the justices and public opinion, the extent to which the Court protects minority rights, the general indeterminacy of constitutional law, and the unpredictable consequences of Supreme Court decision making.

This book attempts to weave together the various strands of this earlier scholarship. While it is primarily about the constitutional history of race discrimination, I hope that it also furthers our general understanding of the Supreme Court's role in American society.

Though I am first and foremost a law professor, I have had formal training in history, and in this book I have drawn on scholarship from a wide range of disciplines: constitutional law and constitutional theory, history, political science, and sociology. My goal has been to write a book that is not only multidisciplinary but that might also appeal to educated laypersons with an interest in race, the Supreme Court, or the civil rights movement. Parts of the book do contain technical legal discussion; I do not believe that one can really understand Court decisions without paying some attention to legal doctrine. Yet because of my general approach to constitutional history—which is to understand it more as political and social history than as the intellectual history of legal doctrine—most of the book should be accessible even to those with no legal background.

In the course of this project, I have accumulated a huge string of debts, which it gives me great pleasure to acknowledge here. I could not possibly have read and researched as widely as I have for this project without the able and cheerful transcription of my dictation by the following people: Tina Baber, Kathy Burton, Sue DeMasters, Jeanne Gordon, Evelyn Gray, Sharon Hutchinson, Kim Jennings, Dianne Johnson, Lisa Lambert, Pam Messina, Christine Moll, Diane Moss, Susan Simches, and Karen Spradlin. I owe special thanks on this score to Cindy Derrick and on this and every other score to Phyllis Harris.

I am grateful to Beth Marsh at the *Journal of American History* for sharing with me her substantial knowledge of how to illustrate a scholarly work. India Artis at the Crisis Publishing Company was very helpful at coming up with possible illustrations from the *Crisis*, which is the journal of the National Association for the Advancement of Colored People. Susan Armeny edited two of my articles, eight years apart, for the *Journal of American History*, and both times I learned valuable lessons from her work. Lynn Lightfoot copyedited the main body of the text before delivery of the manuscript to Oxford University Press. I am grateful to both Susan and Lynn for making this book more readable than it would otherwise have been. I also want to thank Dedi Felman, my editor at Oxford University Press, who has graciously coped with the paranoia of this first-time book author and been a constant source of encouragement and guidance.

A small army of talented and good-natured law students at the University of Virginia have provided outstanding research assistance: Susan Burgess, Carter Burwell, Kathleen Carignan, Miriam Cho, Lance Conn, Peggy Cusack, Vanessa Horbaly, David Marcus, Laura Mazzarella, Genevieve McCormack, Nicole McKinney, Amy Miller, Catherine Morgen, Michelle Morris, Jim Morse, Dilip Paliath, Joe Palmore, Afi Johnson Parris, Stephene Parry, Terence Rasmussen, Julia Rasnake, Sean Reid, Dimitri Rocha, Reuel Schiller, Josh Segev, Michael Signer, Earnhardt Spencer, Mark Stancil, Joel Straka, Hilary Talbot, and Dana Williams. At Stanford Law School, where I was privileged to spend the academic year of 2001–2002, I benefited from the able research assistance of Jeremiah Frei-Pearson, Sanjay Mody, and Ryan Spiegel. Several other research assistants have made it possible for me to access distant archives without spending the time necessary to travel there: Carlton Currens at the University of Kentucky, Christopher Karpowitz at Princeton University, Daniel London at the University of Michigan, Evan Schultz at the Library of Congress, and Bradley Visosky at the University of Texas.

Another, smaller group of University of Virginia law students spent an entire summer of their careers or a comparable block of time during the academic year helping with this project, and they deserve special thanks: John Blevins, Jay Carey, Rebecca Edwards, Wijdan Jreisat, Elena Lawrence, Melissa Mather, Viva Moffat, Ted Murphy, Stephanie Russek, Andrew Schroeder, Leslie Shaunty, Ryan Sparacino, Cecelia Walthall, and Rai Wilson. Several of these young men and women must have long since assumed that this project had fallen by the wayside. It had not; I am just a slow worker.

The reference librarians at the University of Virginia School of Law are, in a word, fabulous. I have imposed on them in ways too numerous to mention and sometimes hard even to fathom, but they have never yet denied a single request. I could not possibly have researched this book the way I wanted to without their assistance. Thanks to Taylor Fitchett, Micheal Klepper, Xinh Luu, Barbie Selby, and Joe Wynne for their many contributions, and special thanks to Kent Olson and Cathy Palombi. I also want to thank Paul Lomio, the head reference librarian at the Stanford Law School, who was a tremendous help during my year visiting there. I am grateful as well to Deb Brent, Mandana Hyder, and Laura Skinner for helping to collect many thousands of pages of material.

Many friends and colleagues have read and commented on a chapter or more of the book while it was in manuscript form. I am grateful to the following for their valuable comments: Barry Adler, Akhil Amar, Ed Ayers, John Q. Barrett, David Bernstein, Alan Brinkley, Dan Carter, Lance Conn, Matt Dillard, John Donohue, John Hart Ely, Jon Entin, Adam Fairclough, Eric Foner, Barbara Fried, Barry Friedman, David Garrow, Paul Gaston, Howard

Gillman, John Harrison, Sam Issacharoff, John Jeffries, Walter Kamiat, Pam Karlan, Herbert Klarman, Mary Klarman, Muriel Klarman, J. Morgan Kousser, Hal Krent, Andrew Kull, Earl Maltz, Richard McAdams, Chuck McCurdy, Neil McMillen, Dan Ortiz, James Patterson, Rick Pildes, Jack Rakove, Eric Rise, Gerald Rosenberg, Bill Ross, Andrew Schroeder, Bruce Schulman, Stephen Siegel, David Strauss, David Thelen, Mark Tushnet, Stephen Ware, Ted White, Stephen Whitfield, and two sets of anonymous referees for the *Journal of American History*.

I presented various chapters or portions of chapters as lectures or in faculty workshops at the following schools: Case Western Reserve University School of Law, University of Chicago School of Law, Cumberland School of Law, University of Florida College of Law, Florida State University School of Law, Hastings College of Law, University of Illinois College of Law, Marshall Wythe School of Law at the College of William and Mary, University of Miami School of Law, University of Southern California Law School, Stanford Law School, University of Texas School of Law, University of Virginia Corcoran Department of History, University of Virginia School of Law, and Yale Law School. I also presented portions of the manuscript at conferences on various topics at the American Society for Legal History, the University of Colorado School of Law, the University of North Carolina at Greensboro History Department, the Institute for Southern Studies at the University of South Carolina, the University of Sussex in Brighton, England, and the Marshall Wythe School of Law at the College of William and Mary. I wish to thank the participants in all these events for their stimulating comments.

Several chapters or portions of chapters have been published as articles, and I would like to thank the journals that published them for granting me permission to reproduce my work here. An earlier version of chapter 1 was published in the 1998 *Supreme Court Review* as "The *Plessy* Era" (copyright © 1999 by the University of Chicago. All rights reserved), and an earlier version of chapter 2 was published in 1998 in the *Vanderbilt Law Review* as "Race and the Court in the Progressive Era." The criminal procedure material in chapter 3 appeared in a different form as "The Racial Origins of Modern Criminal Procedure," published in 2000 in the *Michigan Law Review*. A revised version of the criminal procedure material in chapters 4 and 5 was published in the *Journal of American History* in 2002 as "Is the Supreme Court Sometimes Irrelevant? Race and the Southern Criminal Justice System in the 1940s" (copyright © Organization of American Historians. Reprinted with permission). Much of the white-primary material in chapters 4 and 5 appeared in the *Florida State University Law Review* in 2001 as "The White Primary Rulings: A Case Study in the Consequences of Supreme Court Decisionmaking" (copyright © Florida State University Law Review). A much earlier and significantly different version of the backlash argument in chapter 7 first appeared in 1994 in the *Journal of American History* as "How *Brown* Changed Race Relations: The Backlash Thesis" (copyright © Organization of American Historians. Reprinted with permission) and in the *Vir-*

ginia Law Review as "*Brown*, Racial Change, and the Civil Rights Movement." I would also like to thank Roy M. Mersky at the University of Texas Law School for granting me permission to quote from the Tom C. Clark Collection and Melissa Jackson for permission to quote from the Robert Jackson Papers.

Two deans at the University of Virginia School of Law—Bob Scott and John Jeffries—have provided all the support that any scholar could wish for. I have repeatedly asked them for favors to which I am not entitled, and they have rarely denied a request. Even more important, both Bob and John have encouraged me to believe that this was a worthwhile project and that I could pull it off. I am enormously grateful for their support. I would also like to thank Dean Kathleen Sullivan of the Stanford Law School for inviting me to spend the 2001–2002 academic year as a visitor there. It was in that wonderful environment that I was able to do most of the writing of the last two chapters.

My good friend Ken Hoge read the entire manuscript and made many helpful suggestions. My former student and research assistant Andrew Schroeder not only devoted an entire summer of his life to working on this project but then, glutton for punishment that he is, read a late version of the manuscript and offered a dozen pages of valuable suggestions for improving it.

Five former students, who later became colleagues and have remained good friends, deserve special mention for their contributions. As a law student nearly a decade ago, Reuel Schiller provided both able research assistance and useful commentary on my initial effort to understand the connections between *Brown* and the civil rights movement. More recently, he has read and provided extremely helpful comments on several chapters. Barry Cushman was my research assistant over a dozen years ago when I first became interested in the topic of race and equal protection. He also provided valuable comments on several chapters and, perhaps more important, has been a constant source of stimulation over the years as we have continued to debate the merits of our respective approaches to constitutional history. (Mine is right, of course, though I have never managed to convince Barry of that or, come to think of it, any of my other legal history colleagues here at Virginia.) Liz Magill also read several chapters in manuscript form, and her comments, especially with regard to the last two chapters, proved instrumental in my revisions. Daryl Levinson and Jim Ryan read virtually the entire manuscript, treated it with the care that they accord to their own scholarship, and provided detailed suggestions on how to improve it. It is students and colleagues such as these who make law teaching and scholarship such rewarding endeavors.

My two largest professional debts are to Mike Seidman and Bill Stuntz. Most of what I think about constitutional law has been influenced by Mike, who is one of the most creative constitutional theorists in America. I twice had the privilege of coteaching a course on constitutional theory with him, and that experience has profoundly shaped my approach to the subject.

Mike has read nearly every word in this book, and he generously provided dozens of pages of detailed, thoughtful, and constructive comments. Bill Stuntz and I began our teaching careers at Virginia one year apart, in 1986 and 1987. During the last fifteen years, he has read and commented on nearly all of the scholarship that I have produced. He has also been a constant source of advice, encouragement, and good cheer (and, he thinks, of baseball wisdom). Not only have Mike and Bill made enormous contributions to this book, but for years they have served as models of excellence — scholarly, pedagogical, and collegial — that I have tried in some small way to emulate.

With all this help, I should have written a perfect book.

My personal debts are fewer but no less substantial. My brother, Seth Klarman, not only took time from a hectic schedule to read the entire manuscript, offering many helpful suggestions, but over the years he has been a dependable source of moral and other support. My mother, Muriel Klarman, has always stressed the importance of academic excellence and the worth of scholarly achievement, and during my childhood she strove to create a home environment that was conducive to both. My children — Muli, Rachael, Ian, and Teymura — made essentially no constructive contribution to this book, nor did I expect them to. Yet they have had to live with the burden of it for much too long. Because of them, the next book will have to wait a while. My greatest debt is to my spouse, Lisa Landsverk, who has had to bear far more than her fair share of the familial load because of my obsession with this project. Without her love and support, I could not have written this book, and I would not have wanted to.

My principal regret about this book is that I could not finish it fast enough for my father, Herbert Klarman, to have read it. I hope he would have liked it.

CONTENTS

FROM JIM CROW TO CIVIL RIGHTS

INTRODUCTION

In the years 1895–1900, an average of 101 blacks were lynched a year—mostly in the South. In 1898, a white supremacist campaign to eliminate black political influence culminated in a race riot in Wilmington, North Carolina, which killed at least a dozen blacks. In 1897, President William McKinley declared that "the north and the south no longer divide on the old [sectional] lines," as he and the Republican party turned an increasingly blind eye to violations of the civil and political rights of southern blacks. In 1895, the acknowledged leader of southern blacks, Booker T. Washington, acquiesced in racial segregation and black disfranchisement and urged blacks instead to pursue education and economic advancement. Segregation spread through most spheres of southern life, and blacks were almost entirely barred from voting and from serving on southern juries. Most scientists agreed that the black race was biologically inferior.[1]

In the years 1950–1955, lynchings of blacks had decreased to nearly zero. President Harry S Truman had recently issued executive orders that desegregated the federal military and the federal civil service. Southern black voter registration rose to roughly 20 percent, up from 3 percent just a decade earlier. The walls of segregation were beginning to crumble, as police forces, minor league baseball teams, juries, public universities, and public accommodations were desegregated in many cities of the border states, the peripheral South, and occasionally even the Deep South. Blacks were serving on the federal judiciary and in Congress; Ralph J. Bunche had won the 1950

Nobel Peace Prize; and black players were starring in professional baseball. Few scientists any longer believed in biological racial differences.

In 1896, the U.S. Supreme Court ruled in *Plessy v. Ferguson* that railroad segregation laws were permissible under the Fourteenth Amendment. In 1954, the Court's decision in *Brown v. Board of Education* held that the same constitutional provision invalidated statutes that segregated public schools. This book addresses three principal questions: What factors explain the dramatic changes in racial attitudes and practices that occurred between 1900 and 1950? What factors explain judicial rulings such as *Plessy* and *Brown*? How much did such Court decisions influence the larger world of race relations?

Many different sorts of factors—political, economic, social, demographic, ideological, international, and legal—account for the transformation in American racial attitudes and practices over time. As blacks moved from southern farms to northern cities, they gained access to the franchise, and they eventually began to wield significant clout in national politics. As blacks secured better jobs and higher incomes, they acquired financial resources and heightened expectations with which to challenge the racial status quo. As blacks moved from farms to cities, they developed social networks that facilitated collective protest, and they escaped the oppressive racial mores of the countryside. As the nation fought wars "to make the world safe for democracy" and to defeat Nazi fascism, millions of white Americans reconsidered the meaning of democracy and whether it was consistent with a racial caste system. As African and Asian nations achieved independence after World War II and the United States competed with the Soviet Union for the allegiance of the Third World, Jim Crow became an albatross around America's neck. Between 1900 and 1950, Supreme Court justices grew more committed to racial equality and invalidated a variety of schemes that had segregated and disfranchised southern blacks. This book analyzes these and other factors behind the nation's racial transformation and evaluates the relative importance of legal and extralegal forces.

Legal scholars and political scientists have long debated how to understand judicial decision making. One school, that of the formalists, argues that judges decide cases by interpreting legal sources, such as texts (statutes and constitutions), the original understanding of such documents, and legal precedents. According to an extreme version of this view, judges engaged in constitutional review "lay the article of the Constitution which is invoked beside the statute which is challenged and . . . decide whether the latter squares with the former." In its more moderate (and more plausible) form, formalism holds that judicial decision making is significantly constrained by legal sources such as text, original understanding, and precedent, even though some room for judicial discretion remains. A competing school, that of the realists or the attitudinalists, argues that judicial interpretation mainly reflects the personal values of judges. In its crudest form, this perspective attributes judicial decision making to what the judge ate for breakfast. In its subtler (and more plausible) form, it is reflected in a famous statement by Justice Oliver Wendell Holmes: "The felt necessities of the time, the prevalent moral and political theories, intuitions of public policy, avowed or unconscious, even the prejudices which judges share with their fellow-men, have had a good deal more to do than the syllogism in determining the rules by which men should be governed."[2]

This book argues that judicial decision making involves a combination of legal and political factors. A legal axis, which consists of sources such as text, original understanding, and precedent, exists along a continuum that ranges from determinacy to indeterminacy. In other words, some legal questions have fairly clear answers, while others do not. A political axis, which consists of factors such as the personal values of judges, the broader social and political context of the times, and external political pressure, exists along a continuum that ranges from very strong preferences to relatively weak ones. In other words, judges feel more strongly, as a matter of personal preference or as a reflection of broader social mores, about some issues than about others. When the law is clear, judges will generally follow it, unless they have very strong personal preferences to the contrary. When the law is indeterminate, judges have little choice but to make decisions based on political factors. Moreover, different judges accord different weights to these two axes, and some judges may deem a particular factor in decision making to be legal, while others will regard that same factor as political. Thus, different judges, even when confronted with the same legal sources and holding the same personal preferences, might reach different legal interpretations because they prioritize the legal and political axes differently.

An important qualification is necessary: This book makes no claim about how judges *should* decide cases. This is not a work of normative constitutional theory. It does not prescribe, but rather it seeks to describe and to interpret how the justices decided cases involving race and the Constitution from *Plessy v. Ferguson* (1896) to *Brown v. Board of Education* (1954). No pejorative connotation is intended by the term "political axis." No conclusion turns on whether particular factors in judicial decision making are labeled "legal" or "political." I have simply tried to sort the various factors into categories in a way that approximates how most justices during this period would have understood their jobs. But I do not mean to suggest that it is illegitimate for judges to consider political factors in their constitutional decision making.

This book argues that because constitutional law is generally quite indeterminate, constitutional interpretation almost inevitably reflects the broader social and political context of the times. "Equal protection of the laws" does not plainly condemn school segregation, and the Fifteenth Amendment's ban on race-based qualifications to the suffrage does not plainly prohibit race-neutral voter qualifications that disparately affect blacks. In the absence of determinate law, constitutional interpretation necessarily implicates the values of the judges, which themselves generally reflect broader social attitudes. At a time when most white Americans deemed the Fifteenth Amendment to be a mistake, the justices were naturally inclined to sustain disfranchisement measures that did not flagrantly violate it. At a time when most whites were intent on preserving "racial purity" and assumed that blacks were inferior, the justices were naturally predisposed to sustain racial segregation, which the Fourteenth Amendment does not plainly proscribe. Once racial attitudes had changed, as a result of the factors to which I have already alluded, the justices reconsidered the meaning of the Constitution.

The notion that the values of judges tend to reflect broader social mores requires qualification: Though judges live in a particular historical and cultural moment, they are not perfect mirrors of public opinion. Judges occupy an elite subculture, which is characterized by greater education and relative affluence. On many constitutional issues, people's opinions are highly correlated with such factors. For example, although most Americans at the beginning of the twenty-first century support voluntary, nondenominational prayer in public schools, most highly educated, reasonably affluent Americans do not. Reflecting such elite views, most justices continue to regard such prayer as unconstitutional, even though 60–70 percent of Americans disagree. Yet the fact that judges occupy an elite subculture does not negate the principal point: Judges are part of contemporary culture, and they rarely hold views that deviate far from dominant public opinion. Thus, the justices did not protect women under the Equal Protection Clause until after the women's movement, and they did not invalidate racial segregation until after public opinion on race had changed dramatically as a result of various forces that originated in, or were accelerated by, World War II.[3]

One implication of this perspective on constitutional interpretation is that the justices are unlikely to be either heroes or villains. Judges who generally reflect popular opinion are unlikely to have the inclination, and they may well lack the capacity, to defend minority rights from majoritarian invasion. It is difficult to treat them as villains, because their rulings simply reflect the dominant opinion of their time and place. Yet neither are their interventions on behalf of minority rights likely to be particularly heroic, as such decisions will usually reflect the views held by a majority or a sizable minority of the population. For the justices to have invalidated racial segregation in 1896 would have been heroic, yet for the most part they were not even tempted to do so. When they finally did invalidate segregation in 1954, their decisions reflected views that were held by roughly half the country. I emphasize again that my purpose in this book is neither to criticize nor to defend decisions such as *Plessy* or *Brown* but only to explain them. I do not argue that Court rulings *ought* to reflect popular opinion, only that they usually do.

Finally, this book investigates the consequences of the Court's constitutional decision making in the race context. Some scholars have contended that Court rulings make little if any difference, while others have claimed that they make a vast difference. At one extreme, we hear that *Brown v. Board of Education* created the civil rights movement and at the other that it had no impact whatsoever. This book argues for a middle ground: Some Court decisions involving race were much more efficacious than were others. By examining which Court rulings mattered and why, we can identify the social and political conditions that influence efficacy—factors such as the intensity of opponents' resistance, the capacity of the beneficiaries of Court decisions to capitalize on them, the ease with which particular rulings are evaded, the availability of sanctions against those who violate rights, the relative attractiveness of particular rights-holders, and the availability of lawyers to press claims. A related question is how important was the role that law played in the subordination of blacks. Court decisions that invalidated statutes that segregated and disfranchised blacks might not have been very consequential if segregation and disfranchisement depended more on social custom and physical force than on law.[4]

Court decisions can have a wide variety of consequences. Analyzing only their direct effects—such as how many schools *Brown* desegregated—misses the possible indirect consequences of Court rulings, which include raising the salience of an issue, educating opinion, motivating supporters, and energizing opponents. None of these indirect consequences is susceptible to precise measurement, but this book tries to say something about the variety of ways in which Court rulings may have influenced the larger world of race relations.[5]

Litigation can also have consequences that are independent of those that result from Court decisions. Litigation is a method of protest that is distinct from alternative methods, such as political mobilization, economic pressure, street demonstrations, and physical resistance. Whether or not it succeeded in securing Court victories, litigation may have had educational, organizational, and motivational consequences for the civil rights movement. This book analyzes litigation as a distinct method of social protest and evaluates its advantages and disadvantages.

Profound changes in American race relations took place between 1895 and 1965. Let us now turn to the questions of why those changes occurred and how much the constitutional rulings of the U.S. Supreme Court had to do with it.

CHAPTER ONE

The *Plessy* Era

In 1890, the Louisiana legislature, following a trend initiated in Florida a few years earlier, passed a law requiring railroads to provide "equal but separate" accommodations for black passengers. A citizens' committee of upper-class Afro-Creoles in New Orleans organized to challenge the law, which was emblematic of the deterioration in the civil and political rights of southern blacks around this time. The committee thought a legal challenge to the statute was important not simply for the immediate effect it might have in stemming the tide of Jim Crow legislation, but also because "the North needs to be educated as to conditions in the South and its disloyalty and rebellious tendencies." Committee members hired a famous Republican advocate of civil rights, Albion Tourgee, to represent them, and selected as their plaintiff Homer Plessy, a working-class Afro-Creole who shared the white physical appearance of the members but not their elite cultural status. The committee arranged with railroad officials for Plessy to be arrested in New Orleans, because once the train left the city, whites would "simply beat and throw him out and there will be no arrest." Because Plessy appeared white, the arrest could not have taken place without the connivance of railroad officials, which was forthcoming because railroads disliked the segregation law, which was both expensive and inconvenient for them. Yet as the litigation wound its way to the Supreme Court in the mid-1890s and as race relations in the South kept getting worse, the leader of the citizens' committee, Louis Martinet, wondered if they were "fighting a hopeless battle—a battle made doubly hopeless by the tyranny and cruelty of the Southern white and the Negro's own lack of appreciation, his want of energy and his submissiveness."[1]

The Supreme Court confronted four main issues involving race and the Constitution in the period 1895–1910—the *Plessy* era, as I shall call it. The first issue was the constitutionality of state-imposed racial segregation. Besides *Plessy v. Ferguson* (1896), which involved railroad segregation, the justices decided *Berea College v. Kentucky* (1908), which involved a constitutional challenge to state-imposed segregation in private higher education. The second issue was the disfranchising of blacks by southern states, which produced numerous high-court challenges. Several times, the justices declined to reach the merits, dismissing challenges on procedural grounds. Other times, the Court narrowly interpreted the Fifteenth Amendment, refusing to invalidate either legislation that was race-neutral on its face but had been adopted for a racially discriminatory purpose, or broad grants of discretion to voter registrars that invited discrimination, or private individuals' interferences with the right of blacks to vote. In one extraordinary case, *Giles v. Harris* (1903), the Court candidly conceded that even if disfranchisement devices were unconstitutional, it was powerless to provide remedies.

The third issue was the exclusion of blacks from juries, which was raised in numerous cases where southern blacks sought to overturn their criminal convictions on this ground. The justices reaffirmed *Strauder v. West Virginia* (1880), which held that barring blacks from jury service, either by statute or discriminatory administration, violated the Fourteenth Amendment. Yet in nearly all of these cases, the Court rejected the jury discrimination challenge by imposing stringent standards of proof and invoking broad deference to state court findings of fact. Only when officials admitted transgressions or denied defendants proof opportunities did the justices find violations and reverse convictions. The fourth issue had to do with the education of blacks. *Cumming v. Richmond County Board of Education* (1899) rejected a Fourteenth Amendment challenge to separate-and-*un*equal education because the justices deemed inequality reasonable under the circumstances.

Scholars today tend to vilify the Court for its performance during this era. They have called *Plessy* "ridiculous and shameful," "racist and repressive," and a "catastrophe." They also have blamed the Court for "invit[ing] the pervasive spread of legally imposed Jim Crow" and for "unleash[ing] forces of ignorance, evil and hate." Yet the *Plessy* Court's race decisions reflected, far more than they created, the regressive racial climate of the era. Moreover, contrary to popular belief, these rulings were not blatant nullifications of post–Civil War constitutional amendments designed to secure racial equality. On the contrary, *Plessy*-era race decisions were plausible interpretations of conventional legal sources: text, original intent, precedent, and custom. The rulings can be criticized, of course, but not on the grounds that they butchered clearly established law or inflicted racially regressive results on a nation otherwise inclined to favor racial equality. It is also unlikely that contrary rulings would have significantly alleviated the oppression of blacks: Such rulings probably could not have been enforced, and, in any event, the oppression of blacks was largely the work of forces other than law.[2]

CONTEXT

Extraordinary changes in racial attitudes and practices occurred in the Reconstruction decade following the Civil War. Slavery was abolished. The 1866 Civil Rights Act and the Fourteenth Amendment guaranteed blacks basic civil rights, such as freedom of contract and property ownership. The Reconstruction Act of 1867 and the Fifteenth Amendment enfranchised blacks for the first time in most of the nation. Additional federal legislation in the 1870s solidified suffrage protection, forbade race discrimination in jury selection, and guaranteed equal access to common carriers and public accommodations. Southern blacks voted in extraordinary numbers, electing hundreds of black officeholders. Black jury service was common; streetcars generally were desegregated; and blacks finally gained access to public education. In the North as well, blacks in most states voted for the first time; restrictions on their legal testimony were removed; and blacks were admitted to public schools, which in some states were integrated.

The end of Reconstruction in the mid-1870s did not immediately halt these advances. Republican politicians mostly remained committed to protecting black suffrage, though northern opinion was increasingly dubious about federal intervention, and military enforcement was no longer politically practicable. Prominent southern Democrats, such as Wade Hampton and L. Q. C. Lamar, still endorsed black suffrage and promised that Redeemer governments that supplanted Republican regimes would protect it.[3] Southern blacks continued to vote in large numbers, and black officeholding persisted well beyond the end of Reconstruction, peaking in some states in the 1880s. Black jury service continued as well, in some places into the 1890s, though in reduced numbers. Some racial integration persisted in southern public accommodations and even more in railroad travel. Although public schools remained completely segregated in the South, the enormous racial disparities in funding that would later develop did not exist in the early 1880s.[4]

By around 1890, race relations in the South had begun what was to be a long downward spiral. The number of blacks lynched each year rose dramatically. The same Democratic politicians who had earlier campaigned for black votes now demanded disfranchisement. States adopted poll taxes and literacy tests to suppress any black voting not already nullified by fraud and violence. Segregation in railway travel increased; soon it was mandated by statute. Blacks seldom sat on juries any longer. Black officeholding waned, then disappeared. Racial disparities in educational funding increased in the 1890s; early in the twentieth century, they became enormous. Legislatures adopted new measures for coercing black agricultural labor. Racial practices unregulated by law were also affected. In New Orleans in the 1880s, there had been interracial labor solidarity, interracial clienteles in brothels, and interracial sporting competitions. Virtually all this integration disappeared in the 1890s.[5]

A renewed interest in emigration to Africa and in establishing separate black cities was one response of southern blacks to their deteriorating situation. Another was the growing popularity of Booker T. Washington's racial accommodationism. Only the absence of genuine alternatives inclined so many southern blacks to acquiesce temporarily in segregation and disfranchisement and to direct their energies instead toward economic advancement and industrial education. Adopting a "policy of self-effacement" was better than suffering white violence, such as the racial slaughter perpetrated by whites in Wilmington, North Carolina, in 1898 and in Atlanta in 1906. One black leader regretted that Washington could not teach his students to become race leaders instilled with "the spirit of true manhood, of manly courage and resistance," because such traits would not be "tolerated in the communities where they are."[6]

The deterioration in race relations grew out of the interplay between regional developments and national ones. The regional changes affected the inclinations of white southerners with regard to race. The national changes relaxed constraints that had kept white southerners from previously implementing their preferred racial policies.[7]

Economic hardship among southern farmers in the 1880s fostered protest movements, such as the Farmers' Alliance. By 1890, the alliance was translating its enormous membership into political power, first within the Democratic party and then in the Populist party, which was influential in some southern elections in the mid-1890s. The growing political power of poor white farmers, whose precarious economic and social status inclined them to treasure white supremacy, did not bode well for blacks. Higher-status whites were more often concerned with class than with race and sometimes displayed paternalistic racial attitudes that were holdovers from the era of slavery. These racial paternalists, who had supported qualified black rights during Redemption, were supplanted around the turn of the century by political demagogues, such as "Pitchfork" Ben Tillman and James Vardaman, who preached unrestrained white supremacy. As governor of South Carolina in 1892, Tillman pledged that he would himself "willingly lead a mob in lynching a negro who had committed an assault upon a white woman."[8]

The political challenge posed by Populism also impelled conservatives to invoke the threat of "Negro domination" to disrupt potential cross-racial alliances among poor farmers. In some states, Populists appealed to black voters in an effort to defeat Democrats. In North Carolina, mostly white Populists joined with mostly black Republicans to seize control of state government in the mid-1890s. Even where such interracial alliances were improbable, though, Democratic appeals to race loyalty and Reconstruction memories effectively coerced white political unity.[9]

The inclination of southern whites to subordinate blacks was a necessary, but not a sufficient, cause of the worsening of race relations in the 1890s. Without northern acquiescence, southern racial practices could not have become so oppressive. Several factors explain white northerners' increasing willingness to permit white southerners a free hand in ordering race relations, to "say of the race problem that it is a Southern question and should be left to the South."[10]

First, growing black migration to the North had heightened the racial anxieties of northern whites. Fears of a southern black exodus had existed during the Civil War, but these fears diminished as black migration tapered off immediately after the war. But black migrants to the North, numbering only 49,000 in the 1870s and 62,000 in the 1880s, increased to 132,000 and 143,000 in the following two decades. The growing numbers of blacks in the North led to discrimination in public accommodations, occasional efforts to segregate public schools, increased lynchings, and deteriorating racial attitudes. Even former bastions of abolitionism, such as Boston and Cleveland, experienced growing racial prejudice and discrimination. When whites rioted against blacks in Springfield, Illinois, in 1908, killing and wounding dozens, William English Walling, one of the founders of the National Association for the Advancement of Colored People (NAACP), warned that southern politicians such as "Vardaman and Tillman [were] transferr[ing] the race war to the North."[11]

Another factor contributing to worsening race relations in the North was the immigration of millions of southern and eastern Europeans, which began in the 1880s and accelerated around 1900. Northerners concerned about the dilution of "Anglo-Saxon racial stock" by Italian Catholics and Russian Jews were attracted to southern racial policies. Henry Cabot Lodge, in 1890 a staunch supporter of the suffrage rights of southern blacks, in 1896 was an enthusiastic defender in the Senate of preserving American racial superiority by adopting literacy tests to restrict European immigration. A southern suffragist nicely captured the linkage:

> [J]ust as surely as the North will be forced to turn to the South for the nation's salvation [on account of the purity of its Anglo-Saxon blood], just so surely will the South be compelled to look to its Anglo-Saxon women as a medium through which to retain the supremacy of the white race over the African.

Racial nativism was strongest in New England, where six of the justices on the *Plessy* Court were raised or educated.[12]

American imperialism also fostered the convergence of northern and southern racial attitudes. Beginning with the clamor for annexation of

Hawaii early in the 1890s and culminating with the acquisition of Puerto Rico and the Philippines after the Spanish-American War of 1898, imperialists argued partly in racial terms of Manifest Destiny, the "white man's burden." Most imperialists rejected full citizenship rights for persons thus incorporated into the United States—a position that the Court quickly accommodated—and they found it hard to reconcile that position with criticism of southern black disfranchisement. One delegate to Alabama's 1901 disfranchisement convention observed that territorial acquisition "has forced the race problem to the attention of the whole country and in the wise solution of this question we have the sympathy instead of the hostility of the North." A Louisiana senator wondered how northerners could justify trying to foist on the South "a government they will not tolerate in the newly acquired territories."[13]

A growing desire for sectional reconciliation also contributed to the deterioration in race relations. The awesome human toll of the Civil War ensured that sectional bitterness would hinder immediate reconciliation. However, long-term forces promoted national unity: The South and the North had a common ancestry, history, and religion. A principal divisive issue was the political and civil status of southern blacks. A pressing postwar question was: Which would ultimately triumph—the desire of both sections for reconciliation or the commitment of northerners to protecting the rights of southern blacks? As Civil War antagonisms faded, the sectional rift gradually healed, often at southern blacks' expense. By the early 1870s, Confederate political leaders were receiving amnesty, and Confederate soldiers were being invited to Memorial Day observances. In 1876, the Republican presidential candidate, Rutherford B. Hayes, won on a platform of sectional reconciliation and then put a white southerner in the Cabinet, while he removed federal troops from the South. In the late 1880s, President Grover Cleveland appointed a former Confederate officer, L. Q. C. Lamar, to the Supreme Court.[14]

The pace of sectional reconciliation accelerated in the 1890s, as northerners acquiesced in southern racial "home rule." National organizations of all sorts, including a bicyclists' league and a women's suffrage association, preserved sectional peace by permitting southern white chapters to exclude or segregate blacks. The sectional issue was less important in 1896 than in any presidential election since the war. After his victory, President William McKinley declared that "the north and the south no longer divide on the old [sectional] lines."[15]

The Spanish-American War, which afforded battlefield opportunities to demonstrate cross-regional solidarity, further advanced reconciliation. The *Atlanta Constitution* proclaimed that the death of the first southern white soldier "seals effectively the covenant of brotherhood between the north and south and completes the work of reconciliation which commenced at Appomattox." A black editor cautioned that "the closer the North and South get together by this war," the more difficult it would become for blacks "to maintain a footing." In 1899, McKinley appeared before the Georgia legislature, where a year earlier he had been denounced for appointing a black postmaster against local white opposition, and affirmed the national government's responsibility for the care of Confederate soldiers' graves. In his second inaugural address, in 1901, McKinley ignored black rights and boasted of sectional reconciliation: "We are reunited. Sectionalism has disappeared."[16]

A final cause in the worsening of race relations was the evisceration of the Republican party's historical commitment to protecting black rights. This factor was especially significant given the party's domination of the national government, including the Court, from 1897 to 1911. During Reconstruction, Republicans had been committed to protecting black rights, partly for ideological reasons and partly for partisan ones: Blacks voted overwhelmingly Republican. The party's commitment to black suffrage had not ended when federal troops were withdrawn from the South in 1877. Although President Hayes pursued a policy of sectional reconciliation, he did not abandon southern blacks. Strategically, Republicans could not yet afford to do so, given that Democrats frequently controlled the House after 1874, and all presidential contests from 1876 to 1888 were decided by razor-thin margins. Several northern states—New York, Connecticut, Ohio, Indiana—were not yet reliably Republican, and party leaders believed that the GOP must remain competitive in the South to ensure national control. Because blacks made up 40–60 percent of the population of most southern states and voted overwhelmingly Republican, the party's best hope for southern political power lay in protecting black suffrage.[17]

Moreover, well past the end of Reconstruction, northern Republicans profited by "waving the bloody shirt" and condemning southern white outrages against blacks. After the mid-1870s, northern opinion no longer countenanced federal military intervention, but many northern whites still condemned the fraud and violence used by southern whites to nullify the Fifteenth Amendment. Republican administrations continued to enforce voting rights legislation after Reconstruction, and President Hayes in 1879–1880 vetoed seven Democratic efforts to repeal it. Well into the 1880s, condemnation of outrageous southern electoral tactics helped unite a Republican party divided over economic and fiscal issues. Republican leaders such as James G. Blaine and James A. Garfield voiced strong support for black suffrage in the late 1870s, as did party platforms throughout the 1880s.[18]

By the 1890s, however, three important factors had undermined the party's commitment to black suffrage. First, Republican efforts to create a viable southern wing had plainly failed. Attempts during Reconstruction to build a southern party principally on black voters succumbed to ferocious white resistance, and efforts by President Hayes to appeal to white conservatives and by President Chester A. Arthur to appeal to white independents had proved no more successful. By the late 1880s, the Republican vote in most southern states was declining, as whites suppressed the black vote and the few remaining white Republicans deserted the party amid rising racial tensions. After winning 40–41 percent of the southern presidential vote between 1876 and 1884, the Republican total fell to 37 percent in 1888 and 30 percent in 1896. In 1894, for the first time since black enfranchisement, all twenty-eight southern congressional districts with majority-black populations elected Democrats.[19]

Second, the electoral dividends of bloody-shirt tactics had declined by the 1890s. A new generation of northern voters was less offended by southern suppression of black voting—a shift that was evident in the fate of the Republican elections bill in 1890–1891. The party platform in the 1880s had promised stronger legislation to protect suffrage. In 1888, Republicans won control of the presidency and both congressional houses for the first time since 1874, and enactment of such legislation seemed possible. Yet the bill was apparently more popular with politicians than with constituents, and Republican congressmen ultimately sacrificed it for legislative action on economic issues deemed more urgent: the tariff and the currency. The elections bill died of insufficient Republican ardor, the last gasp of civil rights for decades.[20]

Finally, Republicans in 1894 won one of the largest congressional victories in history and in 1896 the largest presidential victory in a quarter century. These were transitional elections. Some formerly contested northern states became secure Republican bastions, and a political equilibrium was established that remained largely undisturbed until the presidency of Franklin Roosevelt. Moreover, in the mid-1890s, Republicans proved competitive for the first time in border states such as Kentucky and Maryland. The party now seemed able to maintain national control without southern electoral support, thus removing an important incentive to defend black suffrage in the South. The hegemony of Republicans in the North also eliminated the party's need to bid for the votes of northern blacks, which in earlier decades had sometimes been the deciding factor in closely fought elections.[21]

For these reasons, Republican racial policy changed. In 1896, the *Nation* observed a "striking" shift from four years earlier, in "the entire absence of any allusion" to black political rights in Republican state conventions. The national platform diluted its usual demand for a "free ballot and a fair count" in the South. McKinley, who had voted for the House elections bill in 1890, failed to mention it in his 1896 letter accepting the presidential nomination or in his 1897 inaugural address. In 1898, he declined to criticize the election riot that year of whites in Wilmington, North Carolina, which killed a dozen blacks and destroyed black political power in that city. Republican parties in northern states became less inclined to run black candidates, and black representation at party conventions declined.[22]

That was the extralegal context in which Supreme Court justices had to decide cases involving race and the Constitution in the *Plessy* era. Had such traditional legal sources as text, original understanding, and precedent plainly resolved the issues, then the background context might have been less important to the justices' rulings. But legal sources did not defin-

FIGURE 1.1
John Marshall Harlan, the sole
dissenter in *Plessy v. Ferguson*
(1896), in 1907. (*Library of
Congress, Prints and
Photographs Division, George
Grantham Bain Collection*)

itively resolve the issues. Accordingly, such political factors as the broader
mores of the time and the personal values of the justices were necessarily
instrumental.

The little that is known about the racial views of the justices on the
Plessy Court suggests little deviation from dominant public opinion. Edward
D. White had been a Confederate soldier. He helped redeem Louisiana
from Republican rule during Reconstruction, and it is possible that he had
belonged to Klan-like organizations. Chief Justice Melville W. Fuller had
been a prominent Democratic legislator from Illinois during the war. He had
led legislative opposition to Lincoln's Emancipation Proclamation, had supported state constitutional provisions that rejected black suffrage and barred
black migration, and had helped segregate Chicago schools. David J. Brewer
was the son of an abolitionist minister, a critic of the *Dred Scott* decision, a
proponent of emancipation, and a supporter of black suffrage and of black
education. Yet, as a justice on the Kansas Supreme Court in the early 1880s,
he dissented from a decision that invalidated school segregation on the basis
of state law. Brewer's dissenting opinion made it clear that he believed that

neither state law nor the Fourteenth Amendment forbade the state from seg-regating its public schools.[23]

The performances of these justices in race cases during the *Plessy* era were consistent with the meager evidence we have of their personal views on race. Only John Marshall Harlan, the sole *Plessy* dissenter, seemed to defy his past. Harlan had been a slave owner in Kentucky. Although he fought for the Union, he opposed emancipation. As a postwar politician, he opposed the Thirteenth Amendment and the Civil Rights Acts of 1866 and 1875. Harlan's judicial decisions suggest that his views on race may have changed after he ascended to the Court in 1877, but he plainly was the exception.[24]

CASES

SEGREGATION

Plessy v. Ferguson (1896) involved the constitutionality of a Louisiana statute requiring railroads to provide separate and equal accommodations for black and white passengers. Railroad segregation had first become an issue around 1840 in Massachusetts, when some carriers imposed it by regulation or cus-tom. Abolitionists narrowly failed to convince the state legislature to forbid it, but they did persuade railroad companies to do so. In 1865, Massachusetts became the first state to forbid race discrimination in public accommoda-tions. Prior to legislative regulation, antebellum courts ruled that railroads were subject to common-law requirements that public carriers accept all customers, subject only to reasonable regulations imposed for public con-venience. A few antebellum lawsuits challenged segregation, but the prevail-ing view of courts was that it qualified as a reasonable policy.[25]

Postbellum southern black codes frequently mandated railroad segrega-tion, but they remained in force only a year or two. As southern legislatures came under Republican control in the mid-1860s, several enacted laws that forbade racial distinctions by common carriers. Yet these laws were notori-ously underenforced, and most were repealed once Democrats regained control in the 1870s. In 1875, Congress enacted legislation that was generally understood to forbid segregation by common carriers, but the Court invali-dated it in 1883. In the absence of state or federal statutory regulation, segre-gation on common carriers again became an issue to be resolved by courts applying the common law.[26]

One cannot accurately measure the extent of railway integration in the post-Reconstruction era. However, travelers' accounts, court decisions, and newspaper reports make it clear that there was some integration in first-class travel and a good deal in second-class smoking cars. More integration existed in the seaboard states than in the Southwest, probably owing to deeper paternalistic traditions. Finally, streetcar transportation, integrated in most southern cities soon after the war, generally remained so through 1900.[27]

Yet railroad integration appears to have been declining even before the first segregation statutes were enacted. In other words, what formal segregation replaced for the most part was not integration, but informal segregation. Legislatures passed railroad segregation laws in two waves. Florida enacted the first in 1887; by 1892, eight other states had followed its lead. The eastern seaboard states followed, beginning in 1898. Streetcar segregation laws swept the South between 1900 and 1906. Segregation measures required separate-but-equal accommodations, imposed criminal sanctions, and afforded limited exceptions, such as nurses accompanying patients.[28]

Why did legislatures pass these laws when they did? On one view, the statutes reflect the growing political power of lower-class whites, who favored black subordination to maintain their own precarious status. Many upper-class whites plainly cared more about class segregation than about race segregation. That several segregation laws were adopted by legislatures dominated by the Farmers' Alliance supports this interpretation. Another view is that these laws may have been directed toward a younger generation of blacks, unschooled in traditional racial etiquette. On this view, more aggressive blacks sued railroads over inferior accommodations, and many companies preferred integrating to paying damages or equalizing separate facilities. Legislatures then responded by mandating segregation. Another possibility is that segregation laws reflected changed circumstances more than changed attitudes. As southern railway transportation expanded after the war, black and white strangers came into closer physical proximity, leading to novel legislative efforts at social control. Finally, the statutes may simply have been responses to the removal of external constraints. After the Court in 1883 invalidated the 1875 Civil Rights Act, federal law no longer preempted state segregation measures.[29]

Whatever explains these statutes, the issue in *Plessy* was their constitutionality. The text of the Fourteenth Amendment provides no definitive answer. It does not specifically forbid racial classifications, and "equal protection of the laws" does not plainly bar "equal but separate" facilities. The failure of the Fourteenth Amendment to forbid government race consciousness was no accident. Advocates of abolishing all racial classifications proposed suitable language, but it was rejected. Indeed, some Radical Republicans opposed ratification because they thought the amendment's limited reach rendered it "a party trick designed only for electioneering purposes." Other Republicans favored ratification, while lamenting their inability to marshal enough votes to ban racial classifications.[30]

That Congress would not forbid all such classifications in 1866 is hardly surprising. The ideological implications of a war to end slavery had helped to eradicate northern bans on black migration and black testimony in court, but racism remained strong. Most northern states still disfranchised blacks, either excluded them from public education altogether or segregated them, and forbade interracial marriage. Most northern whites supported only *civil* rights for blacks, such as freedom of contract, property ownership, and court access—rights guaranteed in the 1866 Civil Rights Act, for which the Fourteenth Amendment was designed to provide a secure constitutional foundation. Many northern whites, including some Republicans, still resisted black *political* rights, such as voting or jury service, and *social* rights, such as interracial marriage or school integration. Republican congressmen deliberately refrained from protecting black suffrage in the Fourteenth Amendment, for fear of alienating constituents. School segregation was infrequently discussed during legislative debates in 1866. Democrats occasionally argued that the Civil Rights Act or the Fourteenth Amendment would produce horrible consequences, such as compulsory school integration, but Republicans invariably denied such a possibility.[31]

Segregation in schools and in railway travel were not necessarily the same issue, however. Blacks were almost universally excluded from, or segregated in, public schools when the Fourteenth Amendment was adopted, but railway travel was often integrated. Northern states had largely eliminated segregated transportation, and many southern cities had desegregated streetcars. On the reasonable assumption that constitutional amendments generally reinforce rather than alter predominant social practices, one can plausibly argue that the Fourteenth Amendment barred railroad segregation.[32]

Moreover, in the mid-1860s, Congress showed some support for integrated railroad transportation. The same Congress that wrote the Fourteenth Amendment segregated schools in the District of Columbia, but it also drafted local railroad charters that could be construed as forbidding segregation. In 1873, the Court interpreted one such charter—"no person shall be excluded from the cars on account of race"—to forbid segregation, not just exclusion. Yet the existence of such charters does not prove that the Fourteenth Amendment was intended to bar railroad segregation. Congress frequently imposed racial policies on the District that it would not mandate nationally. Nor is this 1873 Court decision good evidence of what most Republicans thought about railroad integration in 1866, when the Fourteenth Amendment was adopted. Reconstruction was near or at its peak in 1873.[33]

It would be a mistake to regard the 1875 Civil Rights Act as strong evidence of the original understanding of the Fourteenth Amendment. On the one hand, less than a decade after adoption of the Fourteenth Amendment, a substantial majority of Republican congressmen endorsed legislation that required "full and equal enjoyment" of public conveyances, "applicable alike to citizens of every race and color"—language that most supporters believed forbade segregation. On the other hand, Republicans became more egalitarian over the course of Reconstruction, and that fact undermines efforts to infer the amendment's original understanding from legislation adopted many years later. Moreover, in legislative debates, some Republicans stated that Congress had broader power under section 5 of the Fourteenth Amendment, which authorizes congressional enforcement "by appropriate legislation," than courts had under section 1, which forbids states to deny equal protection. Thus, that congressmen believed they had authority to forbid railroad segregation does not prove that they thought courts did. Finally, at least some Republicans believed that "full and equal enjoyment" barred only racial exclusion, not segregation.[34]

The foregoing evidence suggests there was no definitive original understanding of the Fourteenth Amendment with regard to railroad segregation. Judicial precedent, however, strongly supported the practice. It would be wrong to assume that because the justices in *Plessy* had not previously considered the question that they were writing on a blank slate. For three decades, the decisions of lower courts had generally sustained segregation. Two lines of precedent were especially relevant: cases that sustained railroad practices of segregation and those that upheld school segregation laws.[35]

Before the enactment of segregation statutes, railroad policies of segregation were subject to three sorts of legal challenge. First, the common law required carriers to afford access to everyone who could pay the fare but did permit reasonable regulations for public convenience. For example, companies were allowed to establish separate "ladies'" cars, which excluded unaccompanied males. Beginning in the 1850s, common-law decisions generally sustained railroad segregation as reasonable, opining that "repugnancies" between the races arising from natural differences created friction that segregation could minimize. But, to be reasonable, separate facilities had to be equal.[36]

Second, federal courts interpreted the "full and equal enjoyment" provision of the 1875 act to forbid racial exclusion and inequality, but not segregation. Even though legislative debates on the act had revealed greater opposition to segregation than had Fourteenth Amendment debates, courts were reluctant to construe ambiguous language to forbid segregation. These rulings are especially noteworthy because they came around 1880, when public opinion was more supportive of integration than it would later be.

The third sort of legal challenge had to do with the Interstate Commerce Commission. The commission interpreted its enabling act, which barred "undue or unreasonable prejudice or disadvantage," to permit segregation, provided that facilities were equal. The commission reasoned that segregation was reasonable and that public sentiment demanded it. Thus, courts and agencies interpreting three texts dealing generally with equality and ambiguously with segregation overwhelmingly deemed separate but equal to be permissible. No court construing the Equal Protection Clause would have felt compelled to reach a different conclusion.[37]

Because formal segregation was imposed earlier in public schools than on railroads, many lower courts prior to *Plessy* had confronted the Fourteenth Amendment issue in education. These decisions almost unanimously concluded that public school segregation was constitutional. Perhaps, had they been so inclined, the justices in 1896 could have identified reasons that railroad-segregation statutes were constitutionally distinct from school-segregation ones—some version of the rights-privileges distinction, for example.[38] Yet the many lower-court decisions that rejected Fourteenth Amendment challenges to school segregation would have made it difficult to adopt Harlan's "color-blind" approach. Indeed, in 1883, the Court in *Pace v. Alabama*, with Harlan's acquiescence, had squarely rejected color blindness and unanimously sustained an Alabama statute that imposed heavier penalties on fornication when the participating parties were of different races. *Pace* reasoned that so long as both fornicators were subject to similar penalties, the races were being treated equally. Analytically, *Plessy's* endorsement of separate but equal was a straightforward application of *Pace*.[39]

Finally, by 1900, the Court's nonracial Fourteenth Amendment jurisprudence had established that laws that impinged on property and liberty interests were constitutional if reasonable. For example, *Holden v. Hardy* (1898), which rejected a challenge to a maximum-hour law for miners, stated the constitutional question to be "whether the legislature has adopted the statute in exercise of a reasonable discretion, or whether its action be a mere excuse for an unjust discrimination, or the oppression, or spoliation of a particular class." Thus, to find racial segregation permissible because it was reasonable would simply align race with the rest of the Court's Fourteenth Amendment jurisprudence. Given dominant public opinion in the mid-1890s, it would be easy to deem racial separation a valid exercise of the state's power to promote health, safety, and morals.[40]

Thus, the constitutional case for sustaining railroad segregation was strong. Although the original understanding of the Fourteenth Amendment was ambiguous, *Plessy* correctly observed that segregation has been "generally, if not universally, recognized as within the competency of state legislatures." Based on precedent, most contemporary commentators had concluded that racial segregation was permissible. Given the strong legal case for sustaining segregation, the justices were unlikely to resist powerful public opinion endorsing the practice.[41]

Plessy upheld the constitutionality of separate-but-equal railroad accommodations. The justices denied that the purpose of the Fourteenth Amendment was "to abolish distinctions based upon color, or to enforce social, as distinguished from political, equality." Further, they denied that "enforced separation of the two races stamps the colored race with a badge of inferiority" and insisted that if blacks thought otherwise, this was "solely because [they choose] to put that construction upon it."[42]

Traditional sources of constitutional interpretation did not dictate a contrary result in *Plessy*, but given the drastic deterioration in racial attitudes and practices by 1896, one wonders whether the Court would have invalidated segregation even had the legal sources better supported that result. By the 1890s, most southern whites strongly favored segregation. Rising white-on-black violence, including lynchings, made segregation seem "the embodiment of enlightened public policy"—a progressive solution to growing interracial conflict. Northern whites too had become more accepting of segregation. A Boston newspaper, commenting in 1896 on the exclusion of a black bishop from a white hotel, observed that social equality "appears more unthinkable today than ever." Northern whites were increasingly inclined to accommodate the racial preferences of white southerners. The Republican party had become relatively indifferent toward the rights of blacks. The justices are usually not oblivious to such large-scale shifts in social attitudes. *Plessy* simply mirrored the preferences of most white Americans.[43]

This is a point about judicial inclination as well as capacity. We shall see later that even had the *Plessy* justices been inclined to invalidate segregation, they would probably have lacked the power to enforce such a ruling. Yet they almost certainly had no such inclination and probably deemed segregation to be wise policy. If they endorsed the policy and traditional legal sources supported its constitutionality, then *Plessy* was easy.

Two facts complicate this argument and require some explanation. First, John Marshall Harlan dissented in *Plessy*. If he could find railroad segregation unconstitutional, why could not the other justices? Public opinion in the 1890s did not unanimously favor segregation. Some remnants of abolitionist thought continued to nurture integrationist ideals. Not all judges agreed that the common law permitted segregation of common carriers or that the Fourteenth Amendment allowed school segregation. That this recessive strand of integrationist opinion would find some, albeit slender, representation on the Court is hardly astonishing. More surprising is the identity of its representative: Harlan, the former slave owner and opponent of emancipation. That the vote in *Plessy* was 7–1 rather than 8–0 hardly suggests genuine uncertainty.[44]

Second, most northern states had responded to the Court's invalidation of the public accommodations provision in the 1875 Civil Rights Act by enacting similar measures, which courts generally interpreted to bar segregation as well as exclusion. Does the existence of these laws suggest that *Plessy* contravened dominant northern opinion? Probably not. Northern public accommodations statutes were largely symbolic. Writing the principle of nondiscrimination into law was important to many blacks, whose votes were prized by Democrats and Republicans battling for control of closely contested states in the 1880s. Actually enforcing such laws, however, would have alienated larger blocs of whites who were opposed to "social equality" for blacks. For many reasons—the triviality of sanctions, the inability of most blacks to afford litigation, the unwillingness of white jurors to convict or impose significant penalties, and the risk of physical violence to those blacks who tested their rights—these statutes were notoriously underenforced. The unlikelihood of enforcement probably explains why northern Democratic parties, home to the most unreconstructed white supremacists, supported or at least tolerated these statutes.[45]

Moreover, for northerners to desegregate their own railroad travel was very different from imposing integration on fiercely resistant white southerners. Some northern whites candidly conceded that they would have favored segregation had blacks been as large a percentage of populations in the North as they were in the South. Others believed, on federalism grounds, that southerners should be permitted to implement their own racial policies. Thus, without any inconsistency, northerners could support state public accommodations laws while endorsing *Plessy*.[46]

Generally indifferent reaction to *Plessy* in the North confirms that it was consistent with white opinion there. Most northern newspapers gave it routine notice or none at all. The *New York Times*, which reported several other decisions that day on its front page, relegated *Plessy* to a page-three column on railway news. One student of *Plessy* concludes that it "embodied conventional wisdom" and another that it so closely "mirror[ed] the spirit of the age . . . that the country hardly noticed."[47]

During this era, the Court had one other opportunity to consider the constitutionality of segregation. In 1904, Kentucky barred interracial instruction at all schools and colleges. The law was directed at Berea College, which was founded in 1855 to educate Appalachian whites and former slaves. Berea was one of only two integrated southern colleges. The other was Maryville, in Tennessee, which had recently been targeted by similar legislation.[48]

Berea College was more difficult for the justices than *Plessy* was, since the *Plessy* era was also the *Lochner* era. In 1905, *Lochner v. New York* invalidated a state maximum-hour law—one of the century's most (in)famous decisions. The *Lochner* Court was a staunch defender of property and contract rights, yet even it distinguished between government regulation of quasi-public entities, such as common carriers, and regulation of more private enterprises. For example, this Court sustained the regulation of railroad rates, so long as it was nonconfiscatory, but it invalidated price regulation for businesses not "affected with a public interest." These justices thought that regulation of common carriers was easier to justify because of their monopoly position.

The same monopoly status that enabled railroads to set unreasonable rates also permitted them to ignore the segregationist preferences of white travelers. Thus, even libertarians often found railroad segregation statutes justifiable. By contrast, if a private college integrated its student body, segregationists were free to move elsewhere. Thus, for the state to require the segregation of private colleges raised distinct issues of constitutional liberty. Indeed, dicta in *Plessy* had suggested that governments had no business interfering with integration that came about through the "voluntary consent of individuals." The Kentucky law in *Berea College* did just that.[49]

Yet race relations had deteriorated further between *Plessy* (1896) and *Berea College* (1908). Sectional reconciliation promoted by the Spanish-American War and growing black migration promoted northern segregationism. During these years, schools were segregated in Alton, Illinois; East Orange, New Jersey; Wichita, Kansas; and Oxford, Pennsylvania. Whites in

Chicago made several unsuccessful attempts to segregate schools. San Francisco segregated Japanese students. Several midwestern medical schools expelled blacks. In a widely noted speech in 1907, Charles Eliot, the president of Harvard University, stated with regard to Berea College that "perhaps if there were as many Negroes here as there we might think it better for them to be in separate schools." This shift in opinion is reflected in the generally indifferent reaction in the northern press to the Court's validation of the Kentucky statute and in the broadly favorable reaction of law review commentators.[50]

Berea College is hard to interpret. The justices declined to decide whether in general a state could compel the segregation of private schools. Instead, they held that because Berea College was a state-chartered corporation, restrictions could be imposed on it that would violate the Constitution if applied to individuals—a classic application of the rights-privileges distinction. One might have a constitutional right to attend, or to teach at, an integrated school, but there was no constitutional right to a corporate charter. Although Kentucky's law did reach individuals as well, the Court did not address that part of the statute, because the case before it involved only Berea College.

Commentators suggest that the justices' "ducking" of the broader constitutional issue indicates that had they been forced to take a position, they would have invalidated the law as applied to individuals. In support of that argument, such commentators note that the Kentucky court invoked the corporate-charter rationale as an afterthought, that the issue was barely even raised in the Supreme Court, and that the rationale seems contrived, given that the Court had already invalidated numerous state laws for violating the constitutional rights of corporations.[51]

This argument is unpersuasive. If the justices really wanted to invalidate segregation in private education, they could have ruled that the law was nonseverable and thus that its permissible applications to corporations must fall along with its impermissible applications to individuals. This would not have been a stretch. The most one can infer from the contrived rationale of *Berea College* is that the justices preferred to avoid the tough constitutional question.

That the justices might have deemed segregation sufficiently important to justify curtailing individual liberty is entirely conceivable. Even the most libertarian of them acknowledged that the state's interest in regulating health, safety, and morals (the so-called police power) could sometimes trump individual liberty interests. After *Plessy*, one could argue that segregation plainly qualified as such a reasonable police-power objective, because it advanced state interests in reducing interracial violence and preventing miscegenation. President Theodore Roosevelt proclaimed in 1905 that "race purity must be maintained," and many courts concurred, rejecting constitutional challenges to bans on miscegenation. Moreover, the justices probably would have deemed segregation more important in schools than on railroads, given the lengthier interracial contact and the involvement of more impressionable youngsters.[52]

One cannot know for sure how the justices would have ruled on compulsory segregation of private education. But the legal materials would not have compelled them to invalidate it, and if their personal predilections had mirrored public opinion, they would have been inclined to sustain it.

During the *Plessy* era, the Court had no occasion to consider the constitutionality of segregation in *public* schools. Earlier efforts to bring this issue to the Court had failed for lack of funds. The absence of such a case, however, should raise no doubt as to what its outcome would have been. This Court almost certainly would have sustained public school segregation.[53]

Nineteenth-century public education was more segregated than was railroad transportation. Antebellum northern states segregated blacks or excluded them entirely from public schools. Only a few far-northern states, with minuscule black populations, permitted integration, and Massachusetts was alone in forbidding school segregation by law. Three more northern states—Rhode Island, Connecticut, and Michigan—integrated schools after the war, a reflection of the conflict's egalitarian ideology. But most states continued to segregate schools, and a couple excluded blacks entirely. Not until the 1870s and 1880s did most northern states forbid school segregation, and the practice remained prevalent (albeit illegal) in regions where there were many blacks. As black immigration accelerated in the 1890s, some localities resegregated schools.[54]

All antebellum southern states excluded blacks from public education. During Reconstruction, congressional Republicans made a state's readmission to the Union conditional on its providing public education to blacks. Segregation then replaced exclusion. The only school integration in the South during Reconstruction was in New Orleans, where it lasted about six years, involved only 20 percent of all black students, and ultimately succumbed to fierce white opposition. Elsewhere, integration was impractical, given the intensity of white resistance and the shallow roots of public education. Republicans in Louisiana and South Carolina secured constitutional provisions that explicitly barred school segregation, but these were ignored in practice. Although many southern blacks supported integration in principle, they generally pursued equal funding of segregated schools instead, capitulating to staunch white resistance. After Reconstruction, many southern states segregated public schools by law, confirming what already existed in fact. Thus, school segregation was more pervasive than railroad segregation in the South, had been enshrined in law earlier, and generated less resistance among blacks.[55]

What was the legal backdrop for evaluating the constitutionality of public school segregation? The original-intent argument against school segregation is much weaker than it is with regard to railroad segregation. Given the rudimentary status of public education in the 1860s, many contemporaries would have considered it a privilege rather than a right and thus subject to whatever conditions a state chose to attach. By contrast, access to common carriers was a well-established common-law right. Moreover, the Congress that wrote the Fourteenth Amendment segregated schools in the District of Columbia, while forbidding some local railroads from segregating passengers. Most states that ratified the amendment segregated blacks or excluded them altogether from public education and almost certainly believed the amendment permitted those practices. When the issue (infrequently) arose during congressional debates, Democratic opponents, seeking to score rhetorical points, were invariably the ones who argued that school segregation would be prohibited—an interpretation that Republican supporters of the amendment consistently denied.[56]

The original understanding of the Fourteenth Amendment plainly permitted school segregation. For a court to invalidate it would have required rejecting originalism as its theory of constitutional interpretation or focusing its originalist lens at a higher level of generality, attending to the framers' broad conceptions of equality rather than to their narrow views regarding particular social practices. Ultimately, the Court would pursue both strategies in expanding the constitutional rights of blacks. Around 1900, though, strong originalist support for school segregation probably would have influenced most justices.

Lower court precedent was similarly unequivocal. More than a dozen decisions by state supreme courts and lower federal courts had rejected constitutional challenges to school segregation. These decisions invoked original intent as well as natural racial differences. They also reasoned that the Equal Protection Clause could not possibly forbid all group classifications, as gender segregation was unquestionably permissible. Because some group classifications were acceptable, the question had to be whether a particular one was reasonable, and racial classifications plainly qualified as such, given dominant social mores.[57]

It is true that some court decisions ordered blacks admitted to white schools. But all such decisions involved either *state* legal prohibitions on segregation or instances of inequality in black schools. In the entire nineteenth century, only two state trial judges, both in 1881, invalidated school segregation under the Fourteenth Amendment. Precedent was sufficiently uniform that contemporary legal commentators assumed that the federal Constitution permitted school segregation. Congress apparently shared this assumption, as the Blair bill, passed by the Senate three times in the 1880s, would have provided education funding to states apportioned according to illiteracy rates, while it would have explicitly permitted segregation.[58]

Given that both original intent and precedent strongly supported school segregation, only a dramatic shift in public sentiment could have led the Court to invalidate it. Instead, by 1900, opinion had become even more prosegregation. Southern whites had always been hostile to school integration, and by 1900 they were even less supportive than they had formerly been of providing equal education funding for blacks. Northern whites for the most part were uninterested in compelling southern school desegregation, partly because by 1900 fewer of them were committed to integrating their own schools. Northern state laws that barred school segregation, mainly enacted in the 1870s and 1880s, are weak evidence of support in the North for integration in 1900. Those laws were a product of three principal factors: slow growth in northern black populations; highly competitive state politics; and inefficiencies of dual school systems where blacks were few in number and sparsely distributed. All those conditions had changed by 1900.[59]

Black migration to the North was substantial in the 1860s, and it sparked race riots in southern Ohio and Indiana and efforts to enforce black exclusion laws in Indiana and Illinois. But that migration slowed in succeeding decades, fostering greater racial tolerance, which was manifested in the enactment of laws forbidding segregation in public accommodations and in public schools. Increased black migration in the 1890s reignited white prejudices, fostering demands for school segregation.[60]

The intense political competition that had facilitated bans on school segregation also lapsed. From 1874 until 1894, neither political party enjoyed a secure advantage in the lower North. Black populations as low as 1 or 2 percent could tip the balance, and both parties had incentives to bid for black votes. Thus, in some states, it was Republicans and in others, Democrats who enacted civil rights legislation. After the transitional elections of the mid-1890s, however, Republicans held solid majorities in most northern states and no longer needed black votes. Many of the school boards that introduced segregation around 1900 were controlled by Republicans.[61]

Finally, many northern communities had desegregated schools before the enactment of state laws that barred segregation, because operating dual school systems where there were few blacks was inefficient. Rural districts sometimes spent two or three times as much per capita on black students as whites. Those costs were hard to bear in the economic crisis of the 1870s. By 1900, though, migration from South to North and from farm to city had increased black population densities and reduced the economic inefficiencies of segregation.[62]

The commitment of northern whites to school integration had not been strong in the first place. Prohibitions on segregation were largely symbolic and in practice were often ignored without penalty, especially in regions with the most blacks and the least tolerant whites: New York City, Philadelphia, southern New Jersey, and the southern parts of Ohio, Indiana, and Illinois. Antisegregation laws did not show willingness among northern whites to accept school integration for themselves, much less to impose it on resistant white southerners.[63]

The justices in the *Plessy* era almost certainly would have sustained public school segregation. Even Harlan, whom the NAACP later called "one of the best friends of the Negro in this country," probably would have concurred, judging from his *Cumming* opinion, which upheld separate-and-unequal education (discussed below), and his insistence in *Berea College* that segregation in private education raised legal issues very different from those involved in the segregation of public schools.[64]

DISFRANCHISEMENT

The *Plessy* Court also considered constitutional challenges to various aspects of southern schemes for disfranchising blacks.

Antebellum southern states had not permitted slaves to vote. Some had extended suffrage rights to free blacks, but not after the 1830s. The antebellum trend in the North was also toward restricting black suffrage; by 1860, only five states, all of them in New England, allowed blacks to vote without restriction. New York also permitted blacks to vote, but with a property requirement not applicable to whites.[65]

White resistance to black voting did not end with the Civil War. Although the war's egalitarian ideology enhanced support for black suffrage and most Republicans ultimately endorsed it, white southerners generally remained opposed, as did northern Democrats. Between 1865 and 1867, six state referenda in the North rejected black suffrage. Fearing political backlash, Republican congressmen defeated proposed versions of the Fourteenth Amendment that would have enfranchised blacks. The dominant understanding of the amendment ultimately adopted was that it protected civil, not political, rights. Even Republicans who favored black suffrage acknowledged that they lacked the votes to secure it.[66]

Republicans faced a conundrum in the mid-1860s. If they forced black suffrage on resistant constituents, they risked losing their tenuous hold on several northern states. However, if they permitted southern states to continue disfranchising blacks, Republicans had no chance of being competitive in southern politics and risked Democrats regaining national control. In 1866, Republicans, valuing expediency over principle, pressured southern states to enfranchise blacks, while leaving northern states free to disfranchise them. Section 2 of the Fourteenth Amendment provided that states denying the vote to adult males for reasons other than criminal offense should suffer proportionate reductions in congressional representation. As blacks were 40 percent or more of the population in eight southern states, section 2 provided strong inducement to enfranchise them. But the pressure applied only if the amendment passed, which could not happen so long as southern states refused to ratify.[67]

Republicans preserved enormous congressional majorities in the 1866 election, partly by avoiding the suffrage issue, and party leaders in 1867 pursued a different tack. Exercising the war power, Congress forced black suffrage on the South and used federal troops to register blacks to vote for delegates to state constitutional conventions that Congress mandated. Huge numbers of black voters turned out, ensuring Republican domination of the conventions and of newly elected state legislatures. Yet this strategy lacked permanence, as the war power was limited in duration, and Congress did not clearly possess alternative, constitutionally permissible means of mandating black suffrage by statute. Moreover, recently enacted southern state laws and constitutions that protected black suffrage might easily be repealed, should Democrats regain power. Finally, promises that Congress had extracted from southern states seeking readmission not to restrict suffrage were of dubious constitutionality, as they deprived states of equal rights.[68]

Thus, by 1868, most Republicans favored a constitutional amendment to permanently protect black suffrage. Yet, to avoid charges of hypocrisy, such an amendment would have to be national in scope, which simply recreated the party's dilemma, as many northern whites still opposed black suffrage. The party's solution involved deceit. The Republican platform of 1868 endorsed suffrage for southern blacks under the Reconstruction Act, while insisting that "the question of suffrage in the loyal States properly belongs to the people of those States." Immediately after the election, however, Republicans introduced a constitutional amendment to bar racial disfranchisement nationally. Democrats screamed fraud, but Republicans rammed the measure through Congress and state legislatures, often by narrow partisan margins. In a couple of northern states, voters retaliated by returning Democratic majorities at the next election. The Republican-dominated Congress, however, ignored Democratic efforts to rescind these states' earlier ratifications. Four southern states still excluded from congressional representation were forced to ratify as a condition of readmission.[69]

With suffrage rights secured, huge numbers of southern blacks voted, overwhelmingly for Republicans. Given large black populations in all southern states, Republicans won resounding victories. Blacks elected large, though never proportionate, numbers of black officeholders. At times during Reconstruction, blacks were nearly half of the lower-house delegates in Mississippi and Louisiana and a majority in South Carolina. Sixteen southern blacks served in Congress; many held state executive offices; and a black justice sat on the South Carolina Supreme Court. Hundreds of blacks held local offices as sheriffs, magistrates, county councillors, and school board members.[70]

The political power of southern blacks was short-lived, however. Southern whites, even where in the minority, wielded preponderant economic, social, and physical power. Through fraud, intimidation, and violence, whites eventually succeeded in suppressing black voting, which enabled Democrats to "redeem" the South. Whites who were determined to overthrow Republican regimes (for example, in Alabama in 1874, in Mississippi in 1875, and in South Carolina in 1876) murdered large numbers of blacks. The administration of Ulysses S. Grant had sporadically used military intervention to suppress such violence. But in the fall of 1875, the president and his cabinet calculated that intervening in Mississippi, where whites had killed scores of blacks in political violence, would alienate northern voters, many of whom no longer supported military coercion. Freed from external constraint, southern whites did whatever they deemed necessary to regain political control.[71]

Black voting in the South, though reduced, did not end with Reconstruction. A majority of blacks still voted in most southern states in 1880. Blacks continued to sit, often in large numbers, in state legislatures and occasionally in Congress. In state legislatures in 1882, there were nine blacks in South Carolina and eleven in Mississippi; in 1890, there were eighteen in Louisiana. In Tennessee and North Carolina, black officeholding peaked in the 1880s, as blacks demanded their share of political spoils in return for providing the bulk of Republicans' electoral support. Black congressmen represented Mississippi into the 1880s, South Carolina and Virginia into the 1890s, and North Carolina until 1901. Perhaps most important, many blacks continued to hold the local offices that exercised day-to-day control over people's lives. In North Carolina's majority-black congressional district, hundreds of blacks held local office under the Republican-Populist regime of the mid-1890s.[72]

The political participation of southern blacks declined dramatically around 1890. Through fraud and intimidation, Democrats seized control of majority-black counties that previously had voted Republican or independent. Democratic control of the presidency from 1885 to 1889 may partially explain this shift, as southern white disfranchisers were largely immunized from federal prosecution for the first time since voting rights legislation was enacted in 1870. In addition, Republicans, who regained control of the presidency and Congress by 1890, no longer seemed committed to protecting southern black suffrage. Finally, rapid growth in the southern Farmers' Alliance in the late 1880s, which threatened to divide whites along class lines, may have furthered the cause of black disfranchisement.[73]

Though its timing and method varied, the general pattern of black disfranchisement was consistent across states. First, whites reduced black political participation by force and fraud, which they justified as "necessary to prevent the [South] from falling back into the control of the inferior race." Then, Democratic legislatures enacted laws, such as complex voter registration requirements, which further reduced black voting and Republican representation. This facilitated state constitutional changes, such as poll taxes and literacy tests, which consummated black disfranchisement. Generally, black participation had already been drastically reduced before constitutional changes were implemented.[74]

Formal disfranchisement took many forms. Complex registration requirements conferred broad discretion on (white) registrars and created disadvantages for illiterates and itinerants—groups assumed to be disproportionately black. Residency requirements also penalized itinerants. Secret-ballot laws functioned as literacy tests, requiring voters to read and mark ballots themselves. Disfranchisement for crimes was gerrymandered to reflect white perceptions of black criminal propensities—"furtive offenses [rather than] the robust crimes of the whites," explained the Mississippi Supreme Court. Voters were disfranchised for arson, fornication, and wife beating, but not for murder.

Most southern states adopted literacy tests, which would have disproportionately disqualified blacks even if applied fairly, given the higher rates of illiteracy among blacks. But nobody expected registrars appointed by white supremacist Democrats to impartially administer the tests. Moreover, most literacy tests were qualified by "understanding clauses," which permitted registrars to enroll white illiterates who could understand a constitutional provision read to them. Grandfather clauses likewise exempted from literacy tests those eligible to vote before 1867 (when southern blacks were first enfranchised) and their descendants and, sometimes, former soldiers and their descendants. Every southern state adopted a poll tax of one or two dollars, which was sometimes cumulative over years of nonpayment, as a voting restriction. These taxes disparately affected poorer blacks and disfranchised many farm workers, most of whom lived on credit and earned less than one hundred dollars a year. Most states also adopted white primaries, excluding blacks from the only southern elections that mattered after the 1890s: Democratic primaries.[75]

The timing of disfranchisement varied across states. Georgia adopted a poll tax in 1871 and made it cumulative in 1877. In 1882, South Carolina enacted a draconian registration law and an infamous "eight-box" law, which operated as a literacy test by requiring voters to deposit ballots in the correct boxes. Many states adopted secret-ballot laws and complex registration requirements in 1889 and 1890, and Mississippi held a disfranchising convention in 1890. South Carolina followed suit in 1895, but most disfranchising conventions and amendments came later: 1898 in Louisiana, 1900 in North Carolina, 1901 in Alabama, and 1901–1902 in Virginia. Texas, with a smaller black population and less bitter memories of the Civil War and Reconstruction, did not adopt a poll tax until 1903, and Georgia passed its disfranchising amendment in 1908.[76]

The causes of formal disfranchisement were complex, and the electoral dynamics varied from state to state. Most southern whites thought that the Fifteenth Amendment was illegitimate; it "had no moral sanction and is not binding on their conscience." Accordingly, they would probably have supported disfranchisement as soon as it was made possible by the decline of Republican power in the South and the reduced threat of national intervention. Extralegal suppression of black voting in the late 1880s hastened the first condition, and the second soon followed, though national Republicans made one last effort to intervene. In 1888, Republicans regained control of the presidency and Congress for the first time since 1874. The party platform and President Benjamin Harrison's inaugural address promised legislation to supervise federal elections, thus jeopardizing the disfranchisement already accomplished through force and fraud. Southern states responded with registration laws, secret-ballot requirements, and other disfranchisement measures, hoping to obviate the need for extralegal techniques. When the Republicans' elections bill failed, white southerners perceived it as an invitation to extend formal disfranchisement.[77]

Political developments in the South also contributed to disfranchisement, with the rise and fall of Populism in the 1890s playing a role.[78] The high tide of southern Populism between 1892 and 1896 probably explains the relative dearth of disfranchisement activity in those years: Conservatives feared holding constitutional conventions with radical Populism afoot. Moreover, Populism's temporary reinvigoration of partisan competition encouraged all factions to seek black votes, and that inhibited disfranchisement efforts.

Disfranchisement accelerated after the demise of southern Populism. White former Populists often blamed blacks for their electoral defeats and supported disfranchisement. In Georgia, Alabama, Louisiana, and Texas, fraudulent manipulation of black votes probably enabled Democrats to cheat Populists out of victories. Moreover, some former Populists had learned the lesson that competing with Democrats was impossible, so long as black suffrage could be used as a rhetorical whip to maintain white solidarity. Conservative white Democrats, anxious to avoid repetition of the interracial, class-based movement that had triumphed in North Carolina and had nearly done so in several other states, usually led disfranchisement crusades. Fearful of "negro domination," many whites resolved to end forever the threat that black suffrage posed to white supremacy. Conservatives were also eager to disfranchise poor white farmers who had supported Populism.[79]

As a result of formal and informal disfranchisement, black voter registration and turnout fell dramatically in the 1890s. By early in the 1900s, it had been virtually eliminated, except in large cities where a few hundred blacks still voted. In Louisiana, black voter registration fell from 95.6 percent before the 1896 registration law, to 9.5 percent immediately thereafter, and to 1.1 percent in 1904. Alabama's black voter registration plummeted from 180,000 in 1900 to 3,000 in 1903. Registration figures undoubtedly overstated turnout. In Mississippi, black voter turnout was estimated at 29 percent in 1888, 2 percent in 1892, and 0 percent in 1895. After Florida implemented election-law changes in 1888, black voter turnout fell from an estimated 62 percent to 11 percent in 1892 and 5 percent in 1896.[80]

Disfranchisement had calamitous consequences for southern blacks. When blacks could not vote, neither could they be elected to office. No blacks sat in the Mississippi legislature after 1895, down from a high of 64 in 1873. In South Carolina's lower house, which had a black majority during Reconstruction, a single black remained in 1896. The last southern black congressman until the 1970s, George White of North Carolina, relinquished his seat in 1901. More important, disfranchisement meant that almost no blacks held local offices. In the late nineteenth century, sheriffs, justices of the peace, jurors, county commissioners, and school board members were the most important governmental actors. As we shall see, the preferred method of denying constitutional rights to blacks was to vest discretion in local officials and trust them to preserve white supremacy. Disfranchisement was essential to this strategy. During Reconstruction and for a while after, many such local officials were blacks or white Republicans beholden to black voters. After disfranchisement, though, they were almost entirely whites committed to black subordination. Disfranchisement thus facilitated the exclusion of blacks from juries and diversion of their share of public school funds.[81]

The legal question confronting the justices was whether disfranchisement measures violated the Fifteenth Amendment, which provides that the right of citizens to vote "shall not be denied or abridged by the United States or by any State on account of race, color, or previous condition of servitude." Southern whites carefully avoided open contravention of the amendment. They assumed that the implementation of explicit racial conditions on suffrage would prompt federal intervention—either court action or reduction of southern congressional representation under section 2 of the Fourteenth Amendment. Thus, in 1910, southern politicians were alarmed by Maryland's disfranchisement proposal, which denied that the Fifteenth Amendment was binding and expressly qualified the suffrage based on race. Critics thought the nation would "not submit without a protest to the barefaced nullification" of the Fifteenth Amendment and feared that Maryland's scheme would endanger more subtle disfranchisement measures. Even southern state courts might have felt compelled to invalidate laws expressly barring black political participation, much as they reversed convictions of blacks where jury commissioners had deliberately and openly excluded black jurors. In 1904, a Georgia court invalidated a law forbidding blacks from voting in municipal elections.[82]

Yet, most white southerners thought the Fifteenth Amendment was illegitimate. A leading Louisiana disfranchiser stated a prevalent view when he called the amendment "the greatest crime of the Nineteenth Century"; crazed Republicans bent on partisan gain had imposed ignorant "negro domination" on the South. Deterred from explicitly nullifying the amendment, white southerners generally felt "morally justified in evading and defeating [its] admitted purpose." Disfranchisers were not subtle about their objectives. At the Virginia convention, Carter Glass acknowledged that his mission was "to discriminate to the very extremity of permissible action under the limitations of the Federal Constitution, with a view to the elimination of every negro voter who can be gotten rid of, legally."[83]

The original understanding of the Fifteenth Amendment seemed to permit suffrage restrictions that disparately affected blacks. Many Republicans in 1869–1870 had favored a broader amendment that forbade suffrage qualifications based on property and education. One prominent senator had warned that simply banning race-based disfranchisement would permit property and literacy tests that would "cut out forty-nine out of every fifty colored men in those States from voting." At different moments, both houses had passed broader measures. Yet Republicans could not secure consensus in the limited time available to the lame-duck Congress of 1869, and the conference committee adopted the most limited version of the amendment, which plainly seemed to permit property and literacy qualifications. New England Republicans intent on disfranchising illiterate Irish immigrants and California Republicans intent on disfranchising Chinese aliens opposed the broader measures. To the extent that the justices in the *Plessy* era felt constrained by original intent, they could not have invalidated literacy tests or poll taxes based simply on disparate racial impact. With black illiteracy rates of roughly 50 percent and most southern blacks still impecunious tenant farmers and sharecroppers, such voting qualifications, even if fairly administered, would have disfranchised most blacks.[84]

Yet several other grounds for challenging disfranchisement did exist. First, the grandfather clause could be attacked as a surrogate racial classification. This criterion for determining voter eligibility—whether a person or his ancestors had voted before 1867—was simply a stand-in for race. Second, one might challenge voter qualifications based on the discriminatory motive that animated them, which the law today would consider dispositive. Third, the procedure for administering literacy tests might be unconstitutional. Determining the "good character" of prospective voters and the adequacy of their "understanding" conferred vast discretion on registrars. That discretion invited discrimination and, it could be argued, therefore violated the Constitution. Fourth, one might challenge actual (as opposed to merely potential) discrimination in the administration of voter qualifications. Suits challenging disfranchisement in Virginia, South Carolina, Alabama, and Mississippi raised these claims.[85]

The law relevant to resolving these challenges was virtually nonexistent in 1900. No precedents determined whether a statutory classification that on its face made no reference to race was actually a racial surrogate. Still, the grandfather clause was as patent a constitutional evasion as could be imagined. Many contemporaries predicted that courts would invalidate it, and, as we shall see in the next chapter, the justices proved them right, though too late to make much practical difference.

Williams v. Mississippi (1898) raised two challenges to black disfranchisement. A black defendant contested his murder indictment on the ground that Mississippi unconstitutionally excluded blacks from grand juries. Mississippi law required that jurors be qualified voters, and Williams challenged the suffrage qualifications in the 1890 constitution, arguing that they had been adopted for a discriminatory purpose and that they conferred unbridled discretion on registrars.

The decision in *Williams* rejected both challenges. First, the Court invoked the traditional judicial aversion to examining legislative motive. In *Fletcher v. Peck* (1810), Chief Justice John Marshall denied that allegations that legislators had been bribed justified rescission of a land grant, as courts could not properly consider legislative motive. More recently, and closer to

FROM JIM CROW TO CIVIL RIGHTS

the point, the Court in 1885 had unanimously rejected an equal protection challenge to a San Francisco ordinance imposing a curfew on laundries. The city council's animus toward Chinese, who operated most laundries, was no secret. Yet the justices implicitly denied the relevance of legislative motive and considered only whether the ordinance was reasonably related to permissible police-power objectives. Furthermore, nothing in the congressional debates on the Fifteenth Amendment suggested that facially neutral but racially motivated suffrage qualifications were prohibited, and a couple of fleeting references implied the contrary.[86]

Yet the tradition of rejecting motive inquiries was not the only one available to the Court. Marshall seemed to contradict his *Fletcher* views in *McCulloch v. Maryland* (1819), where he expansively defined congressional powers but cautioned that courts would invalidate laws that Congress enacted "under the *pretext* of executing its [enumerated] powers"—apparently a motive inquiry. Similarly, in post–Civil War decisions, the Court invalidated, on ex post facto grounds, laws imposing ironclad oaths as professional qualifications. These decisions are difficult to understand except as motive inquiries. The majority invalidated the oaths as intended to impose punishment on Confederate sympathizers, while dissenters saw a bona fide occupational qualification. Finally, Justice Stephen Field, sitting on circuit, expressly applied motive analysis to invalidate San Francisco's "queue ordinance," which required prisoners to cut their hair short—a measure that had plainly been inspired by anti-Chinese animus.[87]

Thus, in 1898, some precedent existed on both sides of the question of whether legislative motive was relevant to constitutionality. Yet the tradition of rejecting motive inquiries was preponderant, and *Williams* had more law behind it than a contrary ruling would have. Indeed, had it seemed probable that a discriminatory motive could invalidate otherwise constitutional legislation, southern disfranchisers probably would have been more circumspect in their public statements.

As to the constitutionality of delegating broad discretion to registrars, the relevant precedent was *Yick Wo v. Hopkins* (1886), where the Court invalidated a San Francisco ordinance that required persons establishing laundries in wood buildings, but not in stone or brick ones, to secure permits from the board of supervisors. *Yick Wo* had two rationales. First, the ordinance contained no criteria to guide supervisors' discretion. Second, in practice, the board had granted permits to essentially all Caucasian applicants, while denying them to all of the roughly two hundred Chinese petitioners. Both aspects of *Yick Wo* were potentially relevant to black disfranchisement.[88]

The purpose of "good character" and "understanding" clauses was to invite discrimination by registrars. Opponents had criticized such provisions as shams—as authorizing officials "to perform questionable or dishonest acts"—and warned that courts would invalidate them. Yet even these vague standards were more than the ordinance in *Yick Wo* had provided. Moreover, "good character" clauses were consciously patterned after similar federal law requirements for alien naturalization. Whether "good character" and "understanding" are precise enough to constrain administrative discretion is debatable; later Courts have wrestled with whether particular legislative standards are so vague as to be unconstitutional. *Yick Wo* did not dictate a result one way or the other in *Williams*, and the justices distinguished it on the unhelpful ground that it was not this case.[89]

Broad administrative discretion can also be challenged as applied. The *Williams* decision rejected this claim as well, observing that "it has not been shown that their [Mississippi's voter requirements] actual administration was evil, only that evil was possible under them." For the Court to reject an as-applied challenge in the absence of supporting evidence is unremarkable. The more interesting question is what standard of proof the Court would have applied had the issue been appropriately presented. *Yick Wo* would have been the most relevant precedent, but discrimination there was irrefutable. Had the standard been set this high, black litigants who challenged disfranchisement rarely could have met it. The *Plessy*-era justices never resolved this question regarding disfranchisement, though they shed some light on it in the analogous context of jury discrimination, where the standard they applied proved virtually impossible to satisfy.[90]

The Court's failure to resolve the standard-of-proof question was not due to the absence of an appropriate case. In *Giles v. Harris* (1903), the plaintiff alleged race discrimination in the administration of a "good character and understanding" clause and sought an injunction compelling registration of himself and others similarly situated. Writing for the majority, Justice Oliver Wendell Holmes ruled that even if the allegations were proved, plaintiff was not entitled to the requested relief, for two reasons. First, if the allegation of rampant fraud were true, then for the Court to order registration would make it a party to the sham. Second, such an order would be "an empty form" if Alabama whites really had conspired to disfranchise blacks. The Court would be powerless to enforce such an injunction, and therefore the plaintiff's remedy must come from the political branches of the national government. Holmes did not rule out a suit for money damages, but it would have to be heard before a jury, unlike an injunction suit. With blacks excluded from southern juries, such a suit was unlikely to succeed. In any event, when Giles brought a damages action, the Court in *Giles v. Teasley* (1904) rejected his claim on similar grounds. First, if the registration board were patently unconstitutional, then it could do Giles no harm. Second, the Court could provide no effective relief against this sort of state political action.[91]

The extraordinary *Giles* opinions are among the Court's most candid confessions of limited power. The only analogous statements appear in cases where the justices confessed their inability to protect civil liberties during wartime. *Ex parte Milligan* (1866) conceded that the Court had been unable to calmly consider the constitutionality of applying martial law to civilians outside of war zones during the Civil War. In *Korematsu v. United States* (1944), Justice Robert H. Jackson's dissent admitted the Court's inability to interfere with military operations during World War II, including the eviction of Japanese Americans from their homes on the West Coast. The *Giles* decisions suggest that even plain constitutional violations during peacetime may go unredressed in the face of hostile public opinion. The justices had conceded that they would provide no remedy even if Alabama was violating the Fifteenth Amendment.[92]

The Court failed to reach the merits in several other disfranchisement challenges. Suits that sought to enjoin registration and vote tabulations were dismissed as moot because elections had already occurred. These cases, together with the *Giles* decisions, led contemporary observers to remark upon the Court's tendency to dispose of disfranchisement challenges "on some technical or subsidiary point, leaving the merits of the real issue untouched."[93]

The Court issued one other disfranchisement decision during this period. *James v. Bowman* (1903) gave an affirmative answer to the long-standing question of whether a Fifteenth Amendment violation required state action. Specifically, could Congress, under its power to enforce the amendment, criminalize racially motivated interferences with the franchise by private individuals? The constitutional text seems to provide a clear negative answer: "The right of citizens of the United States to vote shall not be denied or abridged by *the United States or by any state* on account of race." Decades earlier, the Court had interpreted similarly explicit language in the Fourteenth Amendment to require state action, invalidating legislation punishing private interferences with the civil rights of blacks.[94]

Conversely, several federal court decisions, mostly from the early 1870s, had rejected constitutional challenges to prosecutions of private individuals for interfering with the political and civil rights of blacks. Justice Joseph P. Bradley, sitting on circuit in *United States v. Cruikshank* (1874), denied in dicta that a Fifteenth Amendment violation required state action. On appeal, the Court in dicta strongly intimated the same, declaring in the context of a prosecution of private individuals that the right to be free of race discrimination in voting was a privilege of U.S. citizenship—and thus within Congress's power to protect. Moreover, other Court decisions had held that Congress, under its Article I power to regulate the time, place, and manner of federal elections, could criminalize individual interferences with the right to vote in congressional elections. Thus, precedent adequately supported, though it hardly compelled, a contrary result in *James v. Bowman*. Other federal court decisions had anticipated *James*, invalidating federal prosecutions of private individuals under the 1870–1871 legislation. In light of those precedents, the text of the Fifteenth Amendment, and the dramatic decline in popular support for black suffrage, the result in *James* was not surprising.[95]

During the *Plessy* era, the Court rejected all constitutional challenges to black disfranchisement. *Giles v. Harris* suggests that one reason was the justices' recognition of their own limited power. Yet, we should not read *Giles* to suggest that they would have invalidated disfranchisement had they simply possessed the power to enforce such a ruling. The justices were probably no more committed to black suffrage than were most white Americans.

By 1900, most white southerners were determined to eliminate black suffrage, even if doing so required violence and murder. In 1898, whites in Wilmington, North Carolina, who were determined to eliminate black political influence, concluded a political campaign fought under the banner of white supremacy by murdering roughly a dozen blacks and driving 1,400 out of the city. Many southern blacks now abandoned politics. Northern and southern Progressives viewed black disfranchisement as an enlightened response to election violence and fraud. Disfranchising blacks, one southern Progressive declared, would remove "the most fruitful source of bitterness between the races." The *New York Times* noted "the determination of the white man to rule the land wherein he lives" and preferred the "more peaceful methods" of disfranchisement to "terrorism."[96]

The commitment of northern whites to black suffrage had greatly eroded since Reconstruction. The ideal of universal manhood suffrage was undermined by concerns about enfranchising millions of southern and eastern European immigrants—concerns that made northern whites increasingly sympathetic to the desire of southern whites to disfranchise blacks. Imperialist adventures of the 1890s further eroded northerners' commitment to universal suffrage. The *Nation* noted the coincidence of *Williams v. Mississippi*, which sanctioned black disfranchisement, with the country's efforts to deal with the "varied assortment of inferior races in different parts of the world, which must be governed somehow, and which, of course, could not be allowed to vote." Sectional reconciliation sentiment further reduced northerners' willingness to contest southern disfranchisement. Finally, Republicans' commitment to protecting black suffrage had dissipated, as is shown by the abandonment of the elections bill in 1890–1891, in favor of action on tariffs and silver purchase. The electoral realignment of the mid-1890s rendered Republicans less dependent on, and thus less motivated to protect, southern black voters.[97]

By 1900, many white northerners shared the view of most white southerners that the Fifteenth Amendment had been a mistake and that black suffrage was "the greatest self-confessed failure in American political history." This opinion shift was evident in Congress's posture toward disfranchisement. In 1893–1894, Democrats took advantage of their simultaneous control of Congress and the presidency for the first time since the 1850s to repeal most of the 1870s voting rights legislation. When Republicans regained national control from 1897 to 1911, they made no effort to reenact these measures. Moreover, Congress failed to remedy patent violations of section 2 of the Fourteenth Amendment, which *requires* reduction of a state's congressional representation if its adult male citizens are disfranchised for any reason other than crime. Because disfranchisement need not be racially motivated to trigger section 2, the difficulty blacks faced in proving Fifteenth

Amendment violations in court should have been no obstacle to congressional enforcement of section 2. Yet Congress took no action on proposed resolutions to reduce southern representation, and few Republicans protested. Presidents McKinley and Roosevelt made it clear that they did not support efforts to penalize the South for disfranchising blacks.[98]

The Court, like Congress, broadly reflects public opinion. If Congress was unwilling to enforce section 2, the reluctance of the justices to order remedies for less transparent violations of the Fifteenth Amendment is unsurprising. The *Giles* decisions raise doubts as to whether the Court would have intervened against even explicitly racial voting qualifications. A contemporary observer concluded that, with the Court and Congress reflecting "the apathetic tone of public opinion," the Fifteenth Amendment, though still part of the Constitution "in the technical sense," was "already in process of repeal . . . as a . . . rule of conduct."[99]

JURY SERVICE

During the *Plessy* era, the Court reviewed nearly a dozen cases in which southern black defendants challenged their criminal convictions on the ground that blacks had been systematically excluded from the juries that indicted or convicted them. The justices reaffirmed an earlier decision forbidding states from excluding blacks from juries and reversed a couple of convictions because defendants had been denied an adequate opportunity to prove race discrimination in jury selection. In most of these cases, however, the Court affirmed convictions, ruling that black defendants had not satisfied the burden of proving discriminatory jury selection and deferring to state court findings of no discrimination.

During the antebellum period, all southern and most northern states excluded blacks from juries. Even after the Civil War, most whites staunchly resisted black jury service. Early in Reconstruction (1865–1866), the laws of many southern states still barred blacks from serving on juries. These laws were soon repealed, as newly enfranchised blacks used political power to secure state and federal laws that forbade racial exclusions from jury service. Later in Reconstruction and occasionally into the 1880s, large numbers of southern blacks served on juries, especially in heavily black counties. However, in former slave states where blacks were not numerous enough to elect Republican governments—Maryland, Kentucky, West Virginia—state laws continued to bar black jury service until the Court intervened in 1880.[100]

As whites suppressed black voting, blacks disappeared from juries. Most southern whites found black jury service, which they conceived as a form of political officeholding, even more objectionable than black suffrage. As segregation spread across southern society, the jury box succumbed to its pressure. Except in North Carolina, where it rebounded in the mid-1890s, black service on southern juries dwindled by the late 1880s and disappeared in the

1890s. For the first three decades of the twentieth century, essentially no blacks sat on southern juries.[101]

The Fourteenth Amendment is less supportive of black jury service than the Fifteenth is of black suffrage. The latter expressly forbids racial restrictions on voting, but the framers of the former refrained from prohibiting all racial classifications and repeatedly denied intending to protect political rights, such as voting and jury service. Democratic opponents charged that the 1866 Civil Rights Act and the Fourteenth Amendment would integrate juries, but Republican supporters demurred.

When the Fifteenth Amendment was proposed in 1869, the question arose whether it should prohibit race discrimination in officeholding as well as in voting. The issue was concrete, as the Georgia legislature had recently excluded duly elected blacks, ostensibly because the state constitution did not sanction officeholding by blacks. An early version of the amendment, which protected officeholding, passed the Senate but not the House. Too many northern Republicans feared that prejudiced constituents, though perhaps willing to tolerate black voters, would never countenance black officials. This legislative history suggests that the original understanding of the Fifteenth Amendment did not cover officeholding, which is how jury service generally was conceived. Even Radical Republican Henry Wilson conceded that states remained free to exclude blacks from juries.[102]

However, Republican attitudes toward black jurors changed during Reconstruction, and legislation that protected the right of blacks to serve on juries did not require the two-thirds majority in both houses that a constitutional amendment did. In 1875, Congress criminalized race discrimination in jury selection. Democrats objected that the Fourteenth Amendment did not authorize protection of political rights. Republicans responded that nondiscriminatory jury selection was a *civil* right of black criminal defendants. Even the 1866 Civil Rights Act, which was limited to civil rights, had guaranteed blacks the same right as whites to the "full and equal benefit of all laws and proceedings for the security of persons and property."[103]

The Supreme Court first confronted race discrimination in jury service in *Strauder v. West Virginia* (1880). Notwithstanding the original understanding of the postwar amendments, the justices, dividing along partisan lines, invalidated a law barring blacks from juries. *Strauder* emphasized that the Fourteenth Amendment, unlike the 1866 Civil Rights Act, was not limited to particular rights. The amendment's purpose, the majority declared, was "to strike down all possible legal discriminations against [blacks]." The justices emphasized the civil rights of black defendants, not the political rights of excluded jurors. *Strauder's* adventurous holding and egalitarian rhetoric confirm that not all Republicans had abandoned black rights by 1880. Indeed, just the previous year, congressional Republicans had repulsed Democratic efforts to repeal the 1875 act's prohibition on race discrimination in jury service. The Hayes administration supported Strauder's appeal, and Republican newspapers praised the decision.[104]

Strauder's holding was of limited significance, as only a few border states still barred blacks from juries by statute in 1880. The typical jury selection statute of the time required that jurors be of "good intelligence, sound judgment, and fair character." *Strauder* did not resolve how to handle allegations that blacks had been excluded from juries by administrative discrimination. In 1881, *Neal v. Delaware*, in dicta, implied that the complete absence of blacks from juries, despite Delaware's sizable black population, constituted prima facie evidence of discrimination. But *Neal's* holding was more limited, as the Court reversed the conviction on the ground that Delaware had conceded discrimination in jury selection. A few years later, *Yick Wo* confirmed that discrimination through administration was just as unconstitutional as discrimination by statute. Yet in *Yick Wo*, the discrimination had been irrefutable. As of 1900, the Court still had not clarified the standards of proof for establishing racially discriminatory administration, with regard to jury selection or any other matter.[105]

In the absence of law on that subject, the Court's resolution was bound to be influenced by public sentiment. By the 1890s, southern whites were intensely opposed to black officeholding, and they largely succeeded in eradicating it. A principal theme in North Carolina's 1898 white supremacy campaign was the need to eliminate black officeholders. The last black (prior to the 1965 Voting Rights Act) was elected to Virginia's legislature in 1891, Mississippi's in 1895, and South Carolina's in 1902. There were no black congressmen from the South between 1901 and 1972. Even federal patronage appointments of blacks as postmasters and customs collectors became intensely controversial, leading to white protests, the lynching of a black postmaster in South Carolina in 1898, and publicized battles between President Theodore Roosevelt and whites in Mississippi and South Carolina in the early years of the twentieth century.[106]

Northern whites, including Republicans, were not committed to protecting southern black officeholding. Most had never been enthusiastic about the practice, which is why the Fifteenth Amendment did not expressly protect it. By 1900, even in the North, fewer blacks were holding office. Blacks were no longer in the legislatures of several states: Indiana after 1897, Massachusetts after 1902, and Ohio after 1906. President McKinley ceased antagonizing southern whites with black patronage appointments after the Spanish-American War. After creating a firestorm over such appointments early in his first term, Theodore Roosevelt largely abandoned the practice. President William Howard Taft completely ended federal patronage for southern blacks and reduced it for northern blacks. There is no reason to doubt that the justices shared most white Americans' aversion to black officeholding or at least their willingness to accommodate the fierce opposition of southern whites.[107]

Despite public opposition to black officeholding, the Court during the *Plessy* era reaffirmed *Strauder's* prohibition on race discrimination in jury service and *Neal's* holding that discrimination could be proved by the admissions of state officials. Indeed, *Carter v. Texas* (1900) slightly extended these rulings, quashing an indictment because black defendants had been denied the opportunity to present evidence of discrimination in jury selection. Other decisions, however, largely nullified *Strauder* by making such discrimination virtually impossible to prove. Once the Court had rejected challenges to disfranchisement, the absence of blacks from juries could be defended, in jurisdictions where jurors were selected from voter lists, on the ground that few blacks were registered to vote. Moreover, *Yick Wo* notwithstanding, the Court refused to invalidate vague jury selection statutes that required "good intelligence, sound judgment, and fair character." Several decisions held that defendants were entitled to hearings on motions to quash indictments only if they produced evidence, not mere allegations, of discrimination. What evidence the justices had in mind is unclear. Rejecting *Neal*'s dicta, the Court ruled that the lengthy absence of blacks from a county's juries raised no inference of discrimination. The justices also rejected as an inadequate proffer of proof an attempt to compel the testimony of jury commissioners. Further, the Court reaffirmed the presumption that state officials have acted constitutionally and allocated to defendants the burden of overcoming that presumption. Yet, as one contemporary commentator observed, "[T]he motives of the county officers in selecting persons for jury service are too subtle, too subjective, to admit of positive proof."[108]

Furthermore, where defendants offered proof that was rejected as inadequate by state courts, the justices deferred, unless the findings were clearly erroneous—the most lenient standard of appellate review. Because the Court had previously interpreted federal law to authorize removal of jury discrimination claims to federal court only when a state *statute* discriminated, and because federal habeas corpus review of state convictions was almost completely unavailable at this time, state trial judges always made the initial findings on jury discrimination. By deferring to those findings, the justices virtually eliminated any possibility that jury discrimination claims would be heard in a forum not openly committed to white supremacy. Although state courts conceded they were bound by *Strauder*, they also denied that administration of the law should be "in the hands of a people assumed to be inferior to the white race." State judges were reluctant to challenge jury commissioners' denials of discrimination and required "very strong and convincing testimony" to rebut them. The absence of blacks from county juries for decades, in spite of the presence of hundreds of qualified black voters, was ruled insufficient to overcome commissioners' denials of discrimination.[109]

These jury discrimination cases illustrate how constitutional rights can be nullified through so-called subconstitutional rules about standards of proof, appellate review, and federal court access. Though consistently reaffirming *Strauder*, the justices left southern courts free to exclude blacks from juries. Conceding that *Strauder* was binding, state courts routinely rejected constitutional challenges to convictions of black defendants secured from all-white juries in counties with large black populations where no black jurors had served for years. Between 1904 and 1935, the Court did not reverse the conviction of even one black defendant on the ground of race discrimination in jury selection, even though blacks were universally excluded from southern juries. The subconstitutional rules changed only when the Court's formal commitment to nondiscrimination in jury service became a substantive resolve. Then, the justices began to infer discriminatory purpose from the long-term absence of blacks from juries and to determine disputed facts independently, rather than deferring to state court findings. Because the subsequent adoption of more efficacious subconstitutional rules reflected the justices' heightened sensitivity to race discrimination, one can only conclude that the *Plessy*-era justices' use of subconstitutional rules that effectively nullified *Strauder* is partially attributable to their indifference to racial injustice.[110]

SEPARATE AND UNEQUAL

Plessy sustained a statute that mandated "equal but separate" railroad accommodations. In practice, however, segregation in public education and in railroad travel afforded blacks nothing like equality. "Scarcely fit for a dog to ride in" is how one black Marylander described Jim Crow railroad cars. During the *Plessy* era, the Court heard just one case contesting inequality in segregation. Blacks in Richmond County, Georgia, challenged the school board's decision to close a black high school, while the white one remained open, and to reallocate funds to black elementary schools.[111]

Antebellum southern states had almost universally excluded blacks from public education. After the war, many southern whites continued to oppose black education. Freedmen's Bureau schools, which educated former slaves, were frequently attacked, as were the northerners who taught in them. Southern states early in Reconstruction and border states which escaped Reconstruction altogether funded black schools from paltry sums collected from taxes paid by blacks. Only pressure from Congress and from southern black voters induced southern whites to fund black education at all.[112]

Reconstruction Republicans wrote state constitutions that extended equal education to blacks while generally avoiding the segregation issue. In practice, however, essentially all public schools in the South were segregated, even in the two states whose constitutions prohibited such segregation. Southern whites were so resistant to school integration that most blacks resigned themselves for the time being to pursuing equality within a segregated system.[113]

Before black political power was nullified in the South, public funding for black and white education remained nearly equal. In South Carolina, per capita spending was equal until about 1880, and in North Carolina and Alabama, blacks actually received more than whites. Under Virginia's Readjusters (1879–1883), the gap between black and white school funding narrowed, only to widen again after their overthrow. Nashville's black teachers received equal pay until disfranchisement. As Congress lost interest and southern blacks lost voting rights, southern whites were liberated to follow their inclinations regarding black education. Most thought that it spoiled good field hands, encouraged competition with white labor, and rendered blacks dissatisfied with their subordinate status.[114]

As southern whites became freer to implement their own views, unfavorable attitudes toward black education were spreading. During Reconstruction, some southern whites had thought blacks should be educated for their new citizenship responsibilities. By 1900, however, most southern whites rejected black voting and saw less need for equal black education. Many concluded that postwar experiments in black education had proved a failure. In 1901, Georgia's governor, Allen D. Candler, stated: "God made them negroes and we cannot by education make them white folks. We are on the wrong track. We must turn back." A few years later, South Carolina's governor, Cole Blease, concluded, "[T]he greatest mistake the white race has ever made was to educate the free Negro." Many whites now accepted "scientific" evidence that purported to show that the black race was losing the Darwinian struggle for survival, that it was deteriorating on the road to extinction, and that ameliorative efforts through education were futile. Many southern whites came to oppose black education entirely, while others supported rudimentary education for literacy and basic industrial and agricultural training; few supported equal educational opportunities.[115]

Yet southern law, independent of federal constitutional constraints, required equal black education. A typical state constitution mandated segregation but forbade racial distinctions in the distribution of public school funds. In 1883, North Carolina enacted legislation permitting localities to supplement state educational funds with taxes segregated by race—that is, taxes raised from whites would be allocated to white schools and taxes paid by blacks would be allocated to black schools. State courts promptly invalidated the law under the state constitution, which forbade "discrimination in favor of or to the prejudice of either race" in public education. Around the same time, state and federal courts invalidated Kentucky's practice of funding black education entirely from taxes paid by blacks.[116]

By 1900, every southern state faced popular demands for formal segregation of public school funds, as whites complained about their taxes subsidizing black education. Yet political campaigns to segregate school funds failed everywhere. Opponents predicted that the courts would invalidate such schemes, which Kentucky and North Carolina decisions suggest was likely. They also warned of congressional intervention and questioned why formal separation was necessary when less direct methods had already achieved the same goal. Beginning in the 1890s, states subverted constitutional mandates for racial equality in education by granting local school boards discretion in allocating public funds. An Alabama law required that state education funds be apportioned to counties according to total numbers of (black and white) schoolchildren and then distributed to township trustees to allocate to schools in a manner they "deem just and equitable." Such statutes frequently required school terms of the same length for blacks and whites but left other issues—teacher salaries and qualifications, student-teacher ratios, grading of schools, spending on physical plants and equipment—to the discretion of local officials, who diverted funds to white schools. This was the same technique that had sabotaged the rights of blacks to vote and serve on juries.[117]

The disfranchisement of blacks removed political constraints on the racially discriminatory administration of public school funds. Progressive educational campaigns, which swept the South from 1900 to 1915, poured much larger sums into public education, which administrators could freely divert to white schools. The temptation to "rape the Negro school fund" was great and was seldom resisted. Enormous racial disparities in educational spending ensued. By 1915, per capita spending on white pupils was roughly three times that on black pupils in North Carolina, six times in Alabama, and twelve times in South Carolina. Incredibly, these disparities were mild in comparison with other inequalities, such as spending on physical plants, equipment, and transportation. Formal segregation of public school funds could hardly have been more effective at diverting educational resources to whites. Yet these disparities were difficult to challenge in court. School officials had broad discretion in allocating public funds, and courts refused to presume discrimination.[118]

The *Plessy*-era Court's only case involving racial inequality in education was *Cumming v. Richmond County Board of Education* (1899). There, a Georgia county had ceased funding a black high school, while continuing to operate a high school for whites, on the ground that the limited funds available for black education were better spent on a larger number of children in primary schools (three hundred) than a much smaller number in secondary education (sixty). The Court rejected the Fourteenth Amendment challenge to this separate-and-*un*equal scheme, reasoning that the board's action was not motivated by racial animus and that redistributing funds among black schools to maximize the educational opportunities of blacks as a group was reasonable. The author of the unanimous opinion was Harlan, the sole dissenter in *Plessy* and the most egalitarian Fuller Court justice.[119]

In analyzing *Cumming*, one should begin by asking whether this Court would have invalidated a *statute* that provided high school education only to whites. Perhaps surprisingly, the answer is not clear. The Fourteenth Amendment forbids states from denying persons "equal protection of the laws." This language cannot mean that everyone must be treated the same, as the very purpose of legislation is to differentiate. At the most, it means that differential treatment must be justified by relevant differences. That formulation, however, empowers courts to determine whether differences among individuals or groups are sufficient to justify differential treatment. In 1899, the justices likely believed that natural racial differences justified different educational opportunities. This approach is not inconsistent with *Plessy*, which did *not* hold that the Constitution required racially separate facilities to be equal. The Louisiana statute, not the Court, imposed the equality requirement. Thus the Court in *Plessy* had no occasion to decide whether separate and *un*equal could be constitutional. Language in the opinion suggested, however, that the Constitution required reasonableness, not equality. In 1899, the justices might easily have thought it unreasonable to provide blacks with inferior railroad accommodations, but not unreasonable to provide inferior educational facilities. They certainly would have thought this with regard to women.[120]

On the other hand, when the Court in 1883 rejected an equal-protection challenge to a statute that punished fornication more severely when the parties were of different races than when they were of the same race, it emphasized that the law treated both parties to interracial fornication the same. Likewise, as we shall see in chapter 2, the Court in 1914 condemned in dicta a statute that authorized racial inequality in luxury railroad accommodations. A much-cited speech by a Republican senator in 1866 declared that the Fourteenth Amendment would forbid a state from supporting white public schools from general taxes and black schools only from a special tax on blacks. Finally, state and federal courts in the 1880s invalidated state laws that expressly authorized racially unequal educational expenditures. These legal sources suggest that the Court might have invalidated a statute that provided high school education for whites only.[121]

Cumming did not have to resolve that question, however, as the inequality there derived from administrative discrimination. Georgia law granted county education boards discretion over establishing high schools. The Court's jury cases refused to presume the discriminatory exercise of administrative discretion or to infer discriminatory purpose from disparate racial impact. Thus, even if this Court would have invalidated a discriminatory statute, it was not bound to overturn Richmond County's unequal expenditures.

Existing law permitted, but it did not compel, the Court to invalidate the discrimination in *Cumming*. With the law indeterminate, the outcome probably depended on the justices' personal views, which likely reflected general societal attitudes. By 1900, most white Americans believed that education for blacks and whites served different purposes. Most southern whites opposed black education altogether or favored only industrial training; few endorsed black secondary schooling. Reflecting hostile white opinion, Booker T. Washington, generally acknowledged to be the leader of southern blacks, stressed industrial education, rather than liberal arts. Public high school education was still virtually nonexistent for southern blacks. In 1890, only 0.39 percent of southern black children attended high school, and in 1910 just 2.8 percent. The black public high school in *Cumming* was the only one in Georgia; there were only four in the whole South. In 1916, Georgia had fifty-four times as many whites as blacks enrolled in public high schools, and Mississippi, South Carolina, and Louisiana still did not have a single four-year black high school.[122]

Northern whites, though more committed to black literacy, generally agreed that southern blacks needed to receive only limited education. Northern philanthropic organizations, such as the Peabody and Rosenwald funds, which heavily subsidized southern black education, supported industrial training to prepare blacks for the same "negro jobs" held by their parents: manual labor and service positions. The Southern Education Board, which combined northern philanthropists and southern educators in a public schools crusade in the early 1900s, declined to endorse equal black education, partly from conviction and partly from fear of alienating southern whites. President McKinley, visiting the Tuskegee Institute, praised its industrial-education mission and its managers, who "evidently do not believe in attempting the unattainable." President Taft also endorsed primarily industrial training for southern blacks: "I am not one of those who believe it is well to educate the mass of Negroes with academic or university education." The justices likely shared this predominant white view of black education and thus found reasonable Richmond County's reallocation of limited black educational funds from the high school to primary schools.[123]

In all four settings considered in this chapter—segregation, disfranchisement, black jury service, and separate-and-unequal education—traditional sources of constitutional law were sufficiently indeterminate to accommodate white supremacist preferences. National opinion had become more sympathetic to the perspective of southern whites, and so did the justices' rulings.

CONSEQUENCES

Except for a few insignificant jury discrimination cases, the Court during the *Plessy* era rejected all civil rights claims. In doing so, the justices eschewed two other options theoretically available to them: either vindicating the claims or declining to rule on them at all. Assessing the significance of decisions that affirm the status quo is rather difficult. When the Court orders existing practices to change, one can observe whether they do. But when a decision approves the status quo, how can one measure its impact?

It can be argued that judicial validation of existing arrangements entrenches them by lending the Court's imprimatur. If Court decisions educate opinion, then sustaining particular practices may legitimize them. Furthermore, a decision that affirms the status quo, by definition, refrains from ordering changes. Measuring the full effect of such decisions requires assessing how efficacious contrary rulings might have been: Could they have been enforced? What changes would their enforcement have entailed? Concretely, one consequence of *Plessy* is that the Court failed to invalidate railroad segregation. A complete accounting of *Plessy*'s consequences must consider what the effects of a contrary decision might have been, though measuring the effects of counterfactual judicial rulings is a daunting task.

SEGREGATION

Did *Plessy*, by legitimizing segregation, encourage its expansion? One historian writes that *Plessy* "invited the pervasive spread of legally imposed Jim Crow" and another that it "gave further impetus to the case for segregation." A federal jurist concludes that *Plessy* "unleashed forces of ignorance, evil and hate" and that segregated schools "were the direct result of *Plessy*." Yet there is no direct evidence that *Plessy* led to an expansion of segregation. Most southern states enacted railroad segregation laws between 1887 and 1892, not awaiting advance judicial approval. Atlantic seaboard states, it is true, only followed suit after *Plessy*: South Carolina in 1898, North Carolina in 1899, Virginia in 1900, and Maryland in 1904. But delay in these states is explicable on other grounds. South Carolina's legislature had considered segregation bills repeatedly since 1890, but the railroad companies were powerful enough to defeat them. North Carolina and Maryland were unlikely to adopt segregation laws in the mid-1890s, when those states were governed by Populist-Republican and Republican regimes, respectively. The spread of segregation to new social contexts is also more plausibly attributable to factors other than *Plessy*. Jim Crow possessed an internal logic that facilitated its expansion. If jails were segregated, why not courtrooms; and if courtrooms, why not have separate Bibles on which witnesses swore? Politicians were disinclined to resist proposed expansions of Jim Crow, for fear of inviting opponents to question their commitment to white supremacy. In sum, white southerners generally codified their racial preferences first and tested judicial receptivity later. They expressed confidence that if constitutional laws could not be written to accomplish their objectives, then "the South will find a way to get around the Constitution."[124]

Even if *Plessy* did not inspire the expansion of segregation, it may have provided legitimacy to the practice and thus delayed its eventual demise. As one historian notes, after *Plessy*, separate but equal "bore the imprimatur of the national government." Measuring the symbolic or educational effects of Court decisions is nearly impossible. But evidence suggests that most Americans make up their own minds on pressing moral issues and are relatively heedless of the Court's instruction. As we shall see, the twentieth century's most famous constitutional ruling, *Brown v. Board of Education*, probably was less educational than is commonly supposed. If relatively few Americans were educated by *Brown* to condemn segregation, why should *Plessy* have convinced them to endorse it?[125]

What if *Plessy* had come out the other way? Court decisions are not self-executing. Southern whites would not have voluntarily complied with a judicial ban on railroad segregation laws. The Fourteenth Amendment, imposed against the will of most white southerners, exerted little moral force upon them, and a judicial interpretation that forbade railroad segregation statutes would have carried little more, especially because it would have been issued by a Republican-dominated Court. Only federal coercion could have enforced such a ruling.

Would the national government have possessed either the inclination or the capacity to overcome southern white resistance? Congress and the president would have probably been disinclined to enforce an antisegregation ruling for the same reasons that the justices were disinclined to issue it. Congress had last passed civil rights legislation in 1875, when Republican commitment to racial equality was near its zenith, and even that law contained ambiguous language that permitted a segregationist interpretation, which is what most courts gave it. By the 1890s, such legislation was inconceivable, making it unlikely that Congress and the president would have eagerly enforced a court decision barring segregation.[126]

Even had the inclination existed, however, the national government probably lacked the capacity to enforce such a ruling. Earlier public accommodations legislation had gone largely unenforced. The 1875 act was essentially a dead letter before the Court invalidated it in 1883, and so were public accommodations laws passed in southern states during Reconstruction. Blacks seeking to enforce their statutory rights of access to public accommodations frequently encountered hostility and violence. If southern public accommodations laws were nullities when Republicans controlled state and federal governments and troops still occupied portions of the South, how could a Court decision barring segregation have been enforced in 1896, when Democrats controlled every southern state but one and troops had long since ceased policing southern race relations?[127]

Even public accommodations laws in northern states had proved inconsequential in practice. Many blacks were intimidated out of exercising their statutory rights to equal access, and those who insisted on their rights were often rebuffed, sometimes violently. Most blacks whose rights were violated were too poor to sue. Even enforcement by public authorities required juries willing to convict and impose penalties, yet regions where the rights of blacks were most likely to be violated yielded the least sympathetic juries. A Court decision barring railroad segregation laws would have been even less enforceable than were public accommodations statutes in northern states. Southern whites were more resistant to integration than were northern whites. Plaintiffs would have been even scarcer, as southern blacks were more economically dependent on whites and thus more vulnerable to reprisal. No NAACP-like organization yet existed to spread the risks and the costs of litigation. By the 1890s, southern black challenges to segregation would have invited physical retaliation and perhaps even lynching. Homer Plessy could bring a legal challenge to segregation in the uniquely tolerant racial environment of New Orleans, but probably nowhere else in the Deep

South. Few southern white lawyers would have taken such cases, and very few black lawyers were practicing in the South. Because southern whites were united in their support of segregation, state judges, jurors, prosecutors, and law enforcement officers would have given no support to a Court ruling invalidating segregation laws. Finally, Congress had even less power to enforce an antisegregation ruling than state governments had to enforce public accommodations laws. Whereas states could criminalize private violations of blacks' access rights, the *Civil Rights Cases* (1883) clearly prevented Congress from doing so. Moreover, in the absence of federal grant-in-aid programs, states exercised greater financial leverage over local governments than Congress did over states.[128]

Even an enforceable Court decision that barred railroad segregation statutes would only have restored the pre-*Plessy* status quo. Yet that was increasingly one of de facto segregation imposed by company policy or custom. Segregation laws were probably unnecessary for segregating railroad travel. In many other contexts, segregation was accomplished without statute. Steamboat travel was more segregated than railroad travel, yet only three states compelled it by law. After 1900, southern courtrooms were universally segregated without statutory mandate, and segregation was pervasive in theaters, hotels, and restaurants, even though it was rarely compelled by law. It is true that some railroad companies resisted segregation statutes because separate accommodations were expensive. Yet even without statutory compulsion, railroads would have faced enormous public pressure to segregate as race relations deteriorated. Thus, after 1900, southern railroads universally segregated *inter*state passengers, even though the Court had ruled that the Dormant Commerce Clause forbade states to compel railroads to segregate such passengers.[129]

Why did legislatures enact such laws if they were unnecessary for segregating passengers? Perhaps they did so for symbolic reasons and because of the political dynamics of white supremacy. Statutes may possess symbolic value quite apart from their functional significance. Even today, most southern states ban adultery, fornication, and sodomy, while declining to enforce such laws. Much of Jim Crow was concerned with symbolism, including rules of sidewalk etiquette, refusals to extend courtesy titles to blacks, and expectations of black submissiveness. Some Jim Crow statutes may have served similar functions, by expressing white political supremacy, regardless of whether the laws were necessary to effect segregation.[130]

After black disfranchisement, politicians had little incentive to resist any segregationist proposal. Just as politicians today compete to demonstrate toughness on crime, candidates under Jim Crow had to constantly affirm their commitment to white supremacy. Once somebody proposed an extension of segregation, any hint of opposition to it could jeopardize one's political future and earn one the label "nigger lover." This political dynamic explains the impassioned campaigns by southern politicians in the early

1900s to repeal the Fifteenth Amendment, when southern blacks were already almost completely disfranchised.[131]

A contrary ruling in *Berea College* would have been inconsequential for similar reasons. In 1900, only two southern private colleges permitted integration, ensuring that such a decision would have had limited consequences. But even for those two colleges, it probably would have been insignificant. Berea's president admitted while the case was pending that its resolution was irrelevant to the college's future, as "the dominant element in Kentucky, though it may be defeated on this special issue, can find other ways to prevent the reestablishment of the ideal conditions of the past, for many years to come."[132]

Berea's experience illustrates how Jim Crow law reflected, more than it produced, segregationist practices. The student body, which had been majority black for much of Berea's history, was about 85 percent white when Kentucky formally segregated it. In recent years, the college on its own initiative had dismissed its only black faculty member, barred interracial dating, and segregated students in dormitories, dining halls, and sports teams. The college president's main public argument against the segregation law was that it was unnecessary, because Berea was already segregated. The enactment of Kentucky's law illuminates the political dynamics of Jim Crow. Once a legislator introduced the segregation bill, even representatives who privately conceded that the state was unjustified in meddling with race relations in a private college could not oppose it without jeopardizing their political careers.[133]

Finally, to imagine the truly unimaginable, what would have been the consequences in 1900 had the Court invalidated segregation of public schools? Because southern whites cared far more about segregating schools than about segregating railroads, resistance would have been ferocious—much more intense even than the massive resistance following *Brown* in the mid-1950s. Indeed, such a ruling, had it been enforceable, probably would have destroyed southern public education. But it would not have been enforceable. Few blacks would have dared to sue for admission to white schools, even in the unlikely event that they could have found lawyers willing to represent them. Blacks willing to become plaintiffs in school desegregation suits were hard to find in the Deep South in the 1950s, when reprisals were usually economic and only occasionally involved physical violence. In the 1890s, the number of southern blacks lynched each year was usually one hundred or more, and many of these victims had sparked white ire by conduct far less insurrectionary than challenging school segregation.[134]

The practical nullification of northern bans on school segregation is illustrative. Most northern states had such prohibitions, and courts in the late 1800s ruled in favor of blacks who could prove official acts of segregation. Yet the rulings made little difference in the face of determined white resistance. Occasional victories entitled black plaintiffs to admission to white schools, but because the suits were not treated as class actions, no significant integration occurred. Pennsylvania experienced only one such suit in the twenty-five years after it banned segregation in 1881, and New Jersey only two in the first thirty years under its law. Most blacks were too poor to sue, and others were deterred by the prospect of white economic reprisals and violence. Moreover, many blacks were ambivalent about integrated schools, which never hired black teachers and often provided hostile learning environments for black students. Finally, prospective black litigants may have appreciated the limited capacity of legal decisions to overcome strong white opposition. Segregationist school boards could nullify integrationist rulings through gerrymandered attendance zones, discriminatory transfer policies, and classroom segregation.[135]

Five times in ten years, beginning in 1899, black parents in Alton, Illinois, appealed adverse jury verdicts in school segregation cases to the state supreme court, each time winning reversal. Yet Alton schools remained segregated until 1950, and no other Illinois blacks challenged school segregation in court. Southern Illinois had much in common with the South. But blacks in the South were poorer and more economically dependent on whites; southern whites were more committed to segregation and prepared to use violence to maintain it; and no state in the South had an analogue to northern Illinois, which was, at least rhetorically, committed to integration. If segregation bans were this inefficacious in the North, how could a Court decision that barred school segregation in the South have made any difference at all? Even during Reconstruction, when Republicans controlled state and federal governments, the two southern state constitutions that expressly barred school segregation were almost completely nullified in practice.[136]

DISFRANCHISEMENT

Court decisions such as *Williams v. Mississippi* (1898) probably played little role in advancing black disfranchisement. Many states had already adopted disfranchising laws; two had held disfranchising conventions; and there was a third under way, before *Williams* signaled judicial approval. The first states to hold disfranchisement conventions were Mississippi (1890) and South Carolina (1895). Probably they were first because they had the largest black populations, the most vivid recollections of "negro domination" during Reconstruction, and the earliest decline of state Republican parties. Disfranchisement elsewhere came later, not because other states required advance Court approval, but because of differing local circumstances, combined perhaps with a copycat effect. Virginia (1901–1902), with a smaller black population and a Reconstruction experience relatively devoid of black political power, was slower to disfranchise blacks. In North Carolina (1900) and Alabama (1901), the rise of Populism in the 1890s delayed disfranchisement. That many southern states attached grandfather clauses to literacy tests, despite widespread doubts about their constitutionality, demonstrates that disfranchisers did not require advance judicial approval before acting.

Nor did *Williams* likely play a significant role in legitimizing disfranchisement. Southern whites did not need the Court's imprimatur to validate their efforts to undermine the Fifteenth Amendment. Most thought the amendment an illegitimate act of external coercion. Had the Court invalidated disfranchisement, most southern whites would have seen that decision as no more legitimate than the amendment. *Williams* may have had a greater effect on northern white attitudes. But the ruling itself was possible only because most northern whites already sympathized with disfranchisement.

Had *Williams* invalidated disfranchisement, it almost certainly would have been inefficacious. The national government would have lacked both the inclination and the capacity to enforce it. Republicans controlled Congress and the presidency from 1897 to 1911, yet they made no effort to reenact voting rights legislation repealed by Democrats in 1893–1894 or to enforce section 2 of the Fourteenth Amendment, which seemed to require reduction in southern congressional representation as a penalty for disfranchising blacks. Section 2 would have been much easier to enforce than a Court decision that invalidated disfranchisement. Implementation lay entirely within the control of Congress, as the Constitution requires Congress to reapportion state representation in that body every ten years. By contrast, enforcement of a Court decision that barred disfranchisement would have required the cooperation of local officials — judges, jurors, prosecutors, sheriffs — who had ample opportunity and incentive to nullify. If Congress was unwilling to remedy disfranchisement by imposing a constitutionally mandated sanction that was entirely within its control, why would it have been inclined to enforce a Court decision invalidating disfranchisement?

Such a ruling would probably have been unenforceable even had Congress supported it. If the Court had invalidated the discriminatory administration of literacy tests and ordered plaintiffs registered, the decision would have had little impact. Few southern blacks had the money to litigate voting rights cases, and in 1900 there was no NAACP or any similar organization to offer support. The willingness of whites to use violence to suppress black suffrage would have deterred most blacks from litigating.[137]

Suppose the hypothetical decision had gone further and facially invalidated literacy tests and poll taxes, either because these measures were adopted with a discriminatory purpose or because they conferred too much discretion on administrators. How could southern whites' defiance of such a ruling have been checked? Civil rights legislation adopted in the 1870s theoretically protected black voting, yet by the late 1880s, force and fraud had disfranchised most southern blacks. When a Democratic Congress repealed most of that legislation in 1893–1894, Republicans pointed out that it had already become a dead letter in the South. Convicting individuals for violating the voting rights of blacks had become almost impossible. In several states, such prosecutions in the early 1870s had suppressed Klan violence against black voters. But successful cases required money, a committed U.S. attorney general (in the early 1870s, it was Amos Akerman), black jurors, and army assistance in rounding up defendants and protecting prosecutors and witnesses. These supportive conditions quickly eroded. Akerman's successor, George H. Williams, was not committed to black suffrage. After the economic panic of 1873, the Justice Department lacked the resources for voting rights prosecutions. Escalating intimidation—sometimes the murder—of witnesses and prosecutors hindered such cases. After Congress in 1879 removed the ironclad oath as a condition of jury service and provided for bipartisan jury selection, securing convictions or even indictments became difficult, given that "almost every Democrat in the [South] approves and sanctions the frauds committed, believing that the end justifies the means." The few convictions obtained resulted in trivial fines of five or ten dollars and no imprisonment.[138]

Even if enforceable, the hypothetical Court decision would have simply restored the status quo ante, which by the 1890s was one of black disfranchisement through force and fraud. Such extralegal methods were sufficiently efficacious that one prominent southerner observed in 1890, when legal disfranchisement had barely begun, that "the Negro as a political force has dropped out of serious consideration." Mississippi, with a majority-black population, had virtually eliminated black voting before it adopted formal suffrage restrictions. Many white southerners admitted that disfranchisement laws were simply a way of "purifying" the electoral system. Rather than disfranchising blacks through force and fraud, which was "debauching the morals and warping the intellect," legal methods would be used to the same end. If the legal methods had been unavailable, though, whites had proved their willingness to kill blacks in order to secure white political supremacy, as they had done in Wilmington, North Carolina, in 1898. A leader of the Wilmington riot conceded that the state's new disfranchising amendment was unconstitutional, but he insisted that "there aren't enough soldiers in the U.S. army" to prevent North Carolina whites from disfranchising blacks. As a Kentucky newspaper pointed out several years later: "Certain it is that the white man will not again submit to his political domination as in the days of the Carpetbagger. The simple expedient of force will doubtless be used if all other means fails."[139]

That fraud and violence played a large role in disfranchising blacks does not mean that the legal restrictions employed to disfranchise them were inconsequential. Extralegal suppression of black voting undermined Republican strength in legislatures enough to enable the enactment of complex registration requirements and secret-ballot laws, which further reduced black suffrage. In some states, these measures had an enormous impact. The South Carolina legislature in 1882 adopted complex registration requirements and an eight-box law, and black turnout fell from roughly 70 percent to 35 percent. Imagining the Court invalidating such measures in the 1890s is difficult, however, given their prevalence throughout the nation. The disfranchisement technique most susceptible to challenge was a literacy test with a grandfather and/or understanding clause. Yet these were evidently the least important instruments of disfranchisement, as most blacks had ceased voting before their adoption. Most South Carolina blacks were disfranchised before the 1895 convention adopted a literacy test, and fewer than 10 percent of Georgia's black male adults were voting when its constitution was amended in 1908.[140]

Black disfranchisement ultimately rested on the discriminatory administration of voter registration requirements and on the threat and reality of white violence. Thus, protecting black suffrage required military intervention, as during the Klan trials of the early 1870s, or federal takeover of the voting apparatus, as under the 1965 Voting Rights Act. The first option ceased to be politically viable after the demise of northern ardor for civil rights by the mid-1870s. The second required a more elaborate national bureaucratic apparatus, not to mention greater political will, than existed around 1900. Federal court review of state administration of the electoral system—the only feasible option at the time—was powerless to constrain the determined resistance of southern whites to black voting.[141]

JURY SERVICE

The only civil rights victories of the *Plessy* era were a few Court reversals of convictions of black defendants who had been denied opportunities to prove race discrimination in jury selection. These rulings had no impact, as blacks remained almost universally excluded from southern juries until after World War II. *Strauder* was easily evaded through the fraudulent exercise of administrative discretion. By refusing to infer discriminatory motives from disparate racial impact or to closely scrutinize findings of fact by state courts, the justices essentially invited nullification.

What if the Court had altered the burdensome subconstitutional rules of the *Plessy* era and made race discrimination in jury selection easier to prove? Southern whites would have resisted such decisions just as staunchly as they would have resisted judicial bans on segregation and disfranchisement. However, in jury selection, the capacity for federal enforcement might have been greater. The Court can better review behavior in courtrooms than behavior in railroad cars or voting booths. Judicial proceedings are recorded, and blacks who challenged jury selection methods did not bear the onus of initiating litigation. Moreover, jury discrimination can be remedied in a fashion not directly requiring the cooperation of state legal officers or the political branches of the national government: The justices can reverse convictions indefinitely until juries have been selected in a nondiscriminatory manner. However, one can scarcely imagine this Court adopting that remedy, given the justices' evident lack of commitment to black jury service. Nor is it inconceivable that southern whites would have defied such a remedy and executed sentences in spite of the Court's reversal. Georgia had defied the Marshall Court in this fashion in the early 1830s on an issue of intense concern to it: the removal of the Cherokees. Ultimately, only the federal executive can suppress state nullification of federal court orders. Whether President Andrew Jackson would have coerced Georgia is unknowable, as the critical case was mooted before he had to decide. President Dwight David Eisenhower did coerce Arkansas in 1957 over school desegregation, but a substantial majority of Americans outside of the South supported *Brown v. Board of Education*. Whether a president in 1900 would have intervened against southern nullification of decisions that protected the right of blacks to serve on juries seems doubtful, given northern indifference.[142]

An extraordinary case from East Tennessee early in the twentieth century confirms that even a greater commitment by the justices to protecting the right of blacks to serve on juries might have been inefficacious. In 1906, a black man, Ed Johnson, was accused of raping a white woman in Chattanooga. He narrowly escaped being lynched, and his trial, before a jury from which blacks had been systematically excluded, occurred in a mob-dominated atmosphere. The trial judge denied the defense team's request for a continuance for fear that delaying the trial would result in a lynching, and the lawyers were pressured not to vigorously cross-examine the alleged victim or to appeal the defendant's conviction. By the time that two black lawyers had entered the case and moved for a new trial, the deadline for filing such a motion under the local court rules had expired. The lawyers then asked the federal district court for a writ of habeas corpus and challenged Johnson's conviction on the grounds of race discrimination in jury selection and mob domination of the trial. The district judge denied the writ but stayed Johnson's execution pending an appeal to the Supreme Court.

Two days before the scheduled execution, the Supreme Court allowed the appeal, informing Sheriff Joseph F. Shipp of Chattanooga and other public officials by telegram. The next evening a mob, with the sheriff's connivance, broke into the jail and lynched Johnson. Members of the mob left a note on Johnson's mutilated body, which read, "To Justice Harlan. Come get your nigger now." Local officials refused to prosecute the lynchers, and leading citizens blamed the lynching on the justices' intervention in local affairs. Sheriff Shipp won a landslide reelection victory a few days later; his supporters warned that a vote against him would be construed as community condemnation of the lynching. The Justice Department refused to prosecute, expressing doubts about its constitutional authority to intercede and about a local jury's willingness to convict. Though Shipp was ultimately convicted of criminal contempt in unprecedented proceedings before the Supreme Court, similar charges brought against most members of the lynch mob were dismissed because witnesses had been intimidated into silence. The few lynch mob members who were found guilty of contempt received sentences of just two to three months in prison, and Shipp was greeted as a hero by a crowd of 10,000 when he returned home from jail. This extraordinary case reveals the lengths to which southern whites were prepared to go in resisting federal interference with local Jim Crow justice. It raises doubts as to whether high-court reversals of the convictions of black defendants on the ground of race discrimination in jury selection would have had much effect in the South at this time.[143]

As we shall see, in 1935, the Court did change the subconstitutional rules regarding race discrimination in jury service, yet blacks remained excluded from southern juries for several more decades. Nondiscriminatory jury selection procedures could place blacks on venires, but prosecutors used peremptory challenges, which enable litigants to remove prospective jurors without cause, to exclude blacks from trial juries. The Court did not remove that obstacle to black jury service until 1986.[144]

SEPARATE AND UNEQUAL

Southern states were shortchanging black public education before *Cumming* endorsed the practice. Southern whites did not need a Court decision to confirm their beliefs that natural racial differences justified inferior black education and that blacks deserved less education money because they paid less in taxes. Growing racial disparities in education funding after 1900 were less a product of *Cumming* than of black disfranchisement and of Progressive school campaigns that raised the stakes of denying blacks proportional shares of public education money.

Racial disparities in education funding resulted not from statutory mandate, but from discriminatory administration. To remedy such inequalities, a Court decision would have had to eliminate discretion or closely supervise its exercise. The political branches of the national government would have been disinclined to enforce such a decision. By 1900, northern whites were generally willing to accommodate the racial preferences of southern whites, and most did not believe southern blacks needed or deserved equal education. Even had the inclination for enforcement existed, the capacity was probably lacking. Local school officials who flouted Court decisions could have been sued, civilly or criminally, but such sanctions require the involvement of prosecutors, judges, and jurors— all of whom would have been white southerners unsympathetic toward the underlying right. Civil litigation, moreover, would have placed the onus on generally impecunious blacks, who were susceptible to economic and physical reprisal. Even blacks able to sue would have had a hard time finding willing lawyers, as shown by the difficulty Cumming had in obtaining counsel in the Supreme Court. For these reasons, white North Carolinians and Kentuckians had successfully evaded and defied state court decisions from the 1880s that barred segregated local school taxes. Southern whites would have resisted even more fiercely a Supreme Court decision in 1900 that barred racial inequality in education, because they would have regarded it as "outside interference" and because white opposition to equal black education had increased appreciably by then. A more efficacious remedy—cutting off federal funds to defiant districts—was unavailable in 1900, when the national government did not subsidize grade school education. The recognition by southern blacks that legal remedies were futile may partially explain the almost complete absence of litigation to challenge the enormous racial disparities in southern education funding that developed in the early 1900s.[145]

By 1910, according to the NAACP, courts had "touched bottom in the race problem," with "the emasculation of the Fourteenth Amendment and the Waterloo of Berea." A northern black newspaper opined in 1913 that "the Supreme Court has never but once decided anything in favor of the 10,000,000 Afro-Americans of this country." The Court had reached "the lowest point yet [in] the receding tide of sentiment in favor of equal civil rights," and there was a risk that blacks would lose their "faith in justice . . . [and] in the judgment of courts." With the NAACP concluding that the Supreme Court "has virtually declared that the colored man has no rights," one could even imagine blacks deciding to abandon litigation. Had that been a consequence of the race decisions of the *Plessy* era, it might have been significant, depending on how critical litigation was to the long-term success of the civil rights movement—an issue addressed in subsequent chapters. Yet, disappointing Court decisions did not deter blacks from litigating. In the absence of viable alternatives—political protest, economic boycotts, street demonstrations, and violent resistance—litigation remained the most promising protest strategy available. Unlike political protest, litigation could be conducted by small numbers of people. Moreover, unlike direct-action protest, litigation was relatively safe, because it took place in courtrooms rather than on the streets—a significant advantage during this era of rampant white-on-black violence. Whatever the explanation, blacks continued to litigate, and from 1909 onward, they frequently had the NAACP's assistance in doing so. As we shall see in the next chapter, Court victories lay just around the corner.[146]

Justices in the *Plessy* era were too immersed in their historical context to spot the oppression that historical hindsight can readily see in racial practices at the turn of the twentieth century. To them, segregation seemed a reasonable response to escalating white-on-black violence and an overwhelming white consensus behind preserving "racial purity." Disfranchisement seemed preferable to racial massacres, like the ones in Wilmington and Atlanta, and most justices probably agreed with most white Americans that the Fifteenth Amendment had been a mistake. Conventional legal sources, such as text, original intent, and precedent, did not plainly bar segregation. Even though the Fifteenth Amendment explicitly forbids disfranchisement based on race, it does not clearly prohibit either literacy tests or poll taxes, regardless of their motivation. In 1900, traditional legal sources did not define the standards for proving racially discriminatory administration. In the absence of clear law, the justices naturally followed their personal preferences and the broader social mores, which led them to sustain segregation, disfranchisement, all-white juries, and unequal educational funding.

In three of the four settings canvassed in this chapter—all but segregation—blacks' rights were nullified, not by statute, but through administrative discrimination. Especially after black disfranchisement, administrative officials could be entrusted with discretion to maintain white supremacy. Thus, subconstitutional rules that governed proof of administrative discrimination—burdens of proof, rules of access to federal court, standards of appellate review—were critical to the enforcement of blacks' constitutional rights. The rules employed by *Plessy*-era justices facilitated nullification of those rights. Judgments about the appropriate content of subconstitutional rules cannot be entirely separated from views about the importance of the underlying rights. Although the *Plessy* Court's use of subconstitutional rules to undermine *Strauder* was not mere pretext, a camouflage for racism, justices more committed to racial equality would have changed the rules.[147]

Even had these justices been more racially egalitarian, their interventions would probably have been inefficacious. In 1900, the political branches of the national government would not have been eager to enforce egalitarian decisions, for essentially the same reasons that the justices were disinclined to render them. Southern whites would have fiercely resisted such rulings, and after disfranchisement, blacks had little political clout with which to enforce them. Moreover, most methods of federal implementation required the cooperation of local officials—judges, jurors, prosecutors, sheriffs—none of whom would have favored more egalitarian decisions. The national government lacked sufficient administrative capacity to bypass the local enforcement apparatus. No Federal Bureau of Investigation existed, and the Justice Department lacked the resources to prosecute most civil rights violations. Few federal grant-in-aid programs existed, eliminating one potential lever for coercing southern compliance with civil rights rulings. The federal government lacked adequate personnel to oversee the administration of elections. The sort of federal bureaucratic power that proved critical to the enforcement of civil rights in the 1960s was inconceivable in 1900.[148]

Finally, even enforceable Court decisions would have had relatively little effect on the lives of southern blacks. Most Jim Crow laws merely described white supremacy; they did not produce it. Legal disfranchisement measures and de jure railroad segregation played relatively minor roles in disfranchising and segregating southern blacks. Entrenched social mores, reinforced by economic power and the threat and reality of physical violence, were primarily responsible for bolstering the South's racial hierarchy. Legal instantiation of these norms was often more symbolic than functional. Thus, more favorable Court rulings, even if enforceable, would not have appreciably alleviated the oppression of southern blacks.[149]

CHAPTER TWO

The Progressive Era

In 1908, Alonzo Bailey, a poor black agricultural laborer, signed a contract in Alabama to work for a white planter for one year at wages of twelve dollars per month. For unknown reasons, Bailey subsequently left the plantation, thus breaching his contract. He was arrested under a state law criminalizing the fraudulent undertaking of a labor contract that paid advance wages. The law made a breach prima facie evidence of fraudulent intent—a presumption that state evidence law did not permit defendants to rebut with their testimony. Bailey was tried, convicted, and sentenced to serve 136 days at hard labor. To avoid the chain gang, he would have had to agree to a much longer period of service to a white planter. Instead, with the assistance of one of the state's ablest white lawyers and behind-the-scenes support from a federal judge and Booker T. Washington, Bailey appealed his conviction to the U.S. Supreme Court. He challenged the state law as a violation of the Thirteenth Amendment's prohibition on slavery and involuntary servitude and the federal antipeonage statute. In *Bailey v. Alabama* (1911), the justices vindicated his claim.[1]

In the 1910s, the Court issued partial civil rights victories in four sets of race cases. One pair involved peonage laws that coerced primarily black labor. In addition to *Bailey*, *United States v. Reynolds* (1914) invalidated on similar grounds an Alabama law criminalizing breach-of-surety agreements, under which private parties paid costs and fines to liberate prisoners in exchange for promised labor. *McCabe v. Atchison, Topeka & Santa Fe Railway Co.* (1914) stated in dicta that an Oklahoma law authorizing railroads to exclude one race from luxury accommodations, rather than providing separate-but-equal facilities, violated the Fourteenth Amendment, notwithstanding disparate per capita racial demand. *Guinn v. Oklahoma* (1915) and *Myers v. Anderson* (1915) invalidated under the Fifteenth Amendment grandfather clauses, which were devices that insulated illiterate whites from disfranchisement by exempting from literacy tests those persons and their descendants who were enfranchised before 1867, when most southern blacks first received the vote. Finally, *Buchanan v. Warley* (1917) invalidated under the Fourteenth Amendment a city ordinance segregating neighborhood blocks by race.[2]

The justices rendered these decisions in a racial context even more oppressive than that of the *Plessy* era, which creates a puzzle. As one commentator has explained, "The challenge for constitutional historians is to understand why these decisions occurred at a time when race relations in law, politics, and general social contemplation hit rock-bottom levels of injustice and callousness." One possibility is that this apparent disjunction between cases and context reveals that the justices possess a significant capacity to defend minority rights from majority oppression. Another possibility is that even in the depths of Progressive Era racism, national opinion still supported formal compliance with constitutional norms, which is all that these rulings really required. Whether the decisions were consistent or inconsistent with national opinion, they may confirm that constitutional law is partly about law, not simply about politics. Even justices from whom the NAACP confessed "little hope" of securing racial justice may have felt bound to invalidate practices that plainly contravened text, original intent, or precedent. Thus, Progressive Era race cases may show that where the law is relatively clear, the Court tends to follow it, even in an unsupportive context.[3]

Whatever their disjunction from popular opinion, Progressive Era race decisions proved inconsequential. Because they were concerned more with form than substance, they were easy to circumvent. For example, the invalidation of grandfather clauses enfranchised no blacks, and American cities became more segregated, despite the invalidation of residential segregation ordinances. This is not to say that decisions addressed more to substance than form would have been efficacious. Southern blacks still lived in an environment too dangerous to permit civil rights protest, and the political branches of the national government possessed neither the inclination nor the capacity to coerce intensely committed white southerners to change their racial practices.

CONTEXT

One can detect in the Progressive Era traces of several of the extralegal forces that would ultimately undermine Jim Crow: the Great Migration of blacks from southern farms to northern cities, the growing political power of northern blacks, urbanization, increasing black literacy, the growth of a black middle class, and the ideological ramifications of America's "war to make the world safe for democracy." Chapter 3 explores these developments in detail, but their impact on the race decisions of the Progressive Era cannot have been substantial. The Great Migration and America's entrance into World War I postdated all Progressive Era race decisions except *Buchanan*. Other factors, such as the growth of a black middle class and the rising political power of northern blacks, were in incipient stages in the 1910s. Even if one believes, as is plausible, that Supreme Court justices are among the first in society to be influenced by such developments, these changes cannot have greatly affected the race rulings of the time. For those living through the Progressive Era, racial attitudes and practices seemed to have reached a post–Civil War nadir. Conditions were worse, not better, than during the *Plessy* period.[4]

The racial context of the Progressive Era can be divided into northern, southern, and national arenas. At all three levels, race relations continued to deteriorate, seemingly caught in an endless downward spiral, as "a wave of hysteria on the color question [swept] over the entire country."[5]

Chapter 1 noted that gradual increases in black migration to the North in the 1890s produced greater discrimination in public accommodations and demands for the segregation of public schools. As that migration expanded in the first decade of the twentieth century and exploded in the second, northern discrimination and segregation proliferated, and the migrants discovered that "the white man of the North is of the same race as the white man of the South, and that in his blood is the virus of domination and power." Many northern public schools became segregated for the first time in decades, even in former abolitionist enclaves such as Boston and Ohio's Western Reserve. Some northern colleges began segregating blacks in dormitories. By 1910, Cleveland's better restaurants and hotels were excluding blacks, and Lake Erie beaches were being segregated. At the other end of Ohio, Cincinnati probate judges were blocking interracial marriages, and public officials were segregating brothels. In 1913, many northern state legislatures debated reenacting antimiscegenation laws that had been repealed decades earlier— a response to the marriage of Jack Johnson, the controversial black boxing champion, to a white woman. On the West Coast, the growing animosity of whites toward Japanese culminated in a 1906 San Francisco ordinance segregating schools and a 1913 California state law forbidding aliens ineligible for citizenship from owning real estate. That animosity helped consolidate a racial alliance between the West and the South. In 1914, Senator Key Pittman of Nevada opposed the women's suffrage amendment "because he realized that its passage would embarrass the South in its treatment of the Negro problem, and . . . he did not care to endanger the chances of future anti-Japanese legislation by alienating the South."[6]

Economic opportunities for working-class northern blacks contracted in the years before World War I. A black Bostonian observed in 1911, "The industrial outlook . . . for the Negro is starker than since the Civil War. . . . The blood . . . of the abolitionists seems to have run out." Though industrial opportunities for blacks had always been scarce, some skilled jobs had been available, such as barber, waiter, coachman, and chef. As European immigration exploded around the turn of the century, however, blacks began losing many of these jobs. They also suffered from the growing power of labor unions, which generally excluded them and sought "black" jobs for white members. The use of black strike breakers by northern industry fed the racial animosities of working-class whites. Increased interracial competition for jobs and housing in the first decade of the century fostered white-on-black racial violence in several northern cities: New York in 1900; Evansville, Indiana, in 1903; Springfield, Ohio, in 1904 and 1906; Greensburg, Indiana, in 1906; and Springfield, Illinois, in 1908. When a black man was lynched in Coatesville, Pennsylvania, in 1911 "under the most hideous circumstances that could possibly be imagined," a correspondent opined in the NAACP's journal, the *Crisis*, that "it could not have taken place in Coatesville or elsewhere, a dozen or even half a dozen years ago." Now, however, "through the sheer power of Southern example, we have come to regard a black criminal as in a different category." Racial tensions grew as the black populations of many northern cities more than doubled in a few years as a result of the Great Migration, beginning in 1916. Massive outbreaks of white-on-black violence erupted in east St. Louis in 1917 and Chicago in 1919, killing an estimated forty-eight and thirty-eight people, respectively, most of them black. More than twenty northern cities experienced race riots in 1919, as working-class whites resolved to take "drastic action" against the "growing menace" posed by the recent influx of southern blacks.[7]

Southern racial attitudes and practices also continued deteriorating in the decades after *Plessy*. Formal disfranchisement campaigns, commencing with Mississippi's constitutional convention in 1890, culminated in the early 1900s, as the remaining southern states disfranchised blacks. At the time of *Plessy*, significant numbers of blacks still voted in many southern states. By 1910, that was no longer true. The last black local officials were evicted from office in the first decade of the twentieth century. With black political power completely nullified in the South, radical racists such as James Vardaman, Hoke Smith, and Cole Blease swept to power. Blease bragged that he would resign as governor of South Carolina and "lead the mob," rather than use his office to protect a "nigger brute" from lynching. Vardaman promised that "every Negro in the state will be lynched," if necessary, to maintain white supremacy.[8]

Racial disparities in education funding became enormous in the early 1900s, as a result of disfranchisement and Progressive school campaigns, and some southern politicians called for eliminating black education entirely. Segregation spread into new spheres, such as streetcars, and into new states, such as Oklahoma and Maryland. Southern streetcars were generally desegregated soon after the Civil War and remained so through 1900. But between

1900 and 1906, streetcar segregation laws swept the South, over the strenuous resistance of blacks and of streetcar companies. Blacks conducted lengthy, though ultimately unsuccessful, boycotts against the changes. Legislatures also segregated restaurants, theaters, public parks, jails, and saloons. White nurses were forbidden to treat black hospital patients, and white teachers were forbidden to work in black schools. Banks established separate deposit windows for blacks. In courts, witnesses were sworn in with Jim Crow bibles. White fraternal organizations, such as the Knights of Pythias, brought lawsuits to prevent black lodges from sharing their names. Much of the South's most oppressive labor legislation—emigrant-agent laws, vagrancy laws, anti-enticement laws, and contract-labor laws (all described below)—was enacted or reenacted during these years. Southern cities adopted the first residential segregation laws in the 1910s, and a movement was afoot to segregate the southern countryside in response to the increasing number of black landowners, whom whites found to be "a menace to the moral and social status of the South." Though the annual number of reported lynchings decreased in that decade, their relative barbarity seemed to increase. Burnings and other forms of mutilation became so common as to "excite . . . hardly a word of public comment."[9]

Economic opportunities were shrinking for skilled black laborers in the South. As in the North, whites repossessed traditionally black jobs: barber, mason, railroad fireman. The growing power of racially exclusionary labor unions also harmed southern blacks. Around 1910, unionized white railway workers struck employers in an effort to have black firemen dismissed. When the strike failed, they simply murdered many of the black workers. Black coal miners in east Tennessee also lost jobs to whites around this time. Black lawyers increasingly found themselves out of work. A more rigid color line forbade their presence in some courtrooms and made them liabilities to clients in others, as white supremacist judges and jurors disdained black lawyers. One house of the Florida legislature passed a bill to prohibit blacks from practicing law in the state's courts. Mississippi, which had as many as twenty-five black lawyers in 1900, had only about five in 1935.[10]

Developments in race relations at the national level are probably most relevant to understanding the justices' decision-making context. In 1911, southern congressmen tried to include in the proposed Seventeenth Amendment, which was to establish popular election of senators, a provision altering Article I, section 4, to confer on state governments final control over the time, place, and manner of Senate elections. Many northerners endorsed this proposal, which was commonly understood to implicitly sanction southern black disfranchisement. In 1912, southerners spearheaded a temporarily successful effort to exclude blacks from the American Bar Association by pressuring the executive committee to cancel the membership of W. H. Lewis, who happened to be assistant attorney general of the United States. In 1913, the famous antilynching crusader Ida Wells-Barnett was asked not to march with the Chicago delegation of a national women's suffrage organization in its annual parade in Washington, D.C., because of southern opposition to integration. After controversial black boxer Jack Johnson lost his heavyweight title in 1915, an informal color line was established, preventing blacks from competing for the boxing championship for a generation. During the Progressive Era, much of the nation accepted as conventional wisdom southern whites' interpretation of the Civil War as a product of Yankee abolitionist fanaticism and of Reconstruction as a result of Republican vindictiveness and partisanship. For example, the *New York Times* in 1915 referred casually to "the legacy of crime and violence left by the misguided 'statesmen' of reconstruction," whose "best intentions had become a curse to the country." The tremendous popularity of D. W. Griffith's epic film *Birth of a Nation* (1915), which glorified the Confederacy, vilified Reconstruction, and portrayed blacks as "women chasers and foul fiends," typified the national racial mood.[11]

The changing racial policies of the national political parties illustrate this continued deterioration in race relations. The racial policies of Theodore Roosevelt's first (1901–1905) and second (1905–1909) administrations were noticeably different. Though Roosevelt was no egalitarian, his behavior during the first two years in office endeared him to blacks and antagonized southern whites. In 1901, he invited Booker T. Washington to the White House for dinner to confer on southern patronage. To white southerners, that connoted social equality, and they roundly condemned it. Roosevelt seemed genuinely puzzled by the intensely critical reaction and later privately regretted the incident. In 1902–1903, Roosevelt battled with southern whites who resisted black patronage appointments in Indianola, Mississippi, and Charleston, South Carolina. Roosevelt was motivated in this fracas more by the principle of national supremacy than by that of racial equality. Though he insisted that he would appoint qualified candidates regardless of race, in fact Roosevelt named many fewer blacks to southern federal offices than had his predecessors, McKinley and Harrison.[12]

By his reelection in 1904, Roosevelt had come to better understand the racial intransigence of southern whites, and he adjusted the tone and emphasis, if not the substance, of his racial policy. He visited the South twice in 1905 and in a public letter boasted of his southern heritage, expressed grief at southern whites' attacks on him, and showed concern for southern welfare. Roosevelt declined to condemn black disfranchisement, remained silent after Atlanta's 1906 race riot, and blamed lynchings primarily on black rapists. He reiterated Booker T. Washington's advice that southern blacks should concentrate on moral and economic uplift, not politics, and insisted that "race purity must be maintained." Learning from experience, Roosevelt largely ceased appointing blacks to southern patronage positions.[13]

The most notorious racial incident of Roosevelt's presidency was the 1906 Brownsville affair, in which he dismissed three companies of black soldiers. The episode involved ten or twenty black soldiers alleged to have gone on a rampage, killing at least one white. When all the blacks refused to incriminate their comrades, Roosevelt, at the army's behest, gave them dishonorable discharges. The incident attracted national attention, including Senate hearings. Black leaders condemned the administration's endorsement of the concept of group guilt, which to many was reminiscent of Roosevelt's blaming blacks for failing to ferret out criminals in their midst and thus bearing responsibility for lynchings. Some black leaders were so disaffected that they voted Democratic in 1908. Southern whites were delighted with Roosevelt's response, which several southern legislatures endorsed.[14]

Republican racial policy continued to deteriorate under Roosevelt's successor, William Howard Taft (1909–1913). As secretary of war, Taft had issued the order to dismiss the Brownsville soldiers, had supported primarily industrial education for blacks, and had endorsed suffrage restrictions. In 1908, Taft became the first Republican presidential candidate to actively campaign in the South, seeking white votes. His inaugural address endorsed southern efforts to avoid domination by an "ignorant, irresponsible electorate," conceded that popular opinion probably no longer supported the Fifteenth Amendment, and reassured white southerners that it was not "the disposition or within the province of the Federal Government to interfere with the regulation by Southern States of their domestic affairs." Taft also promised to defer to local sentiment on patronage appointments in the South, reasoning that to insist on black candidates contrary to community sentiment would simply generate racial antagonism and do "more harm than good." Indeed, the little federal patronage that had still gone to southern blacks under Roosevelt almost completely disappeared during Taft's presidency. The Taft administration supported lily-white factions within southern Republican parties over rival "black and tans," hoping to broaden the party's appeal to whites. It also initially opposed challenging Oklahoma's grandfather clause, for fear of alienating southern whites. That position changed only after an insubordinate U.S. attorney forced the administration's hand, leading ultimately to the Supreme Court's decision in *Guinn*. When a delegation of black leaders petitioned Taft to support federal antilynching legislation, he declared himself powerless to interfere on an issue within the states' jurisdiction.[15]

The political nadir of race relations at the national level may have come in the 1912 presidential election and its aftermath. Taft was the Republican nominee. Many blacks condemned his administration's racial policies, especially on patronage, as well as his failure to criticize disfranchisement or to support federal action against lynching. Taft further alienated blacks during the campaign by declaring that they "ought to come and [are] coming more under the guardianship of the South." The Republican platform abandoned even its nominal support of black voting rights. The Progressive party candidate, Theodore Roosevelt, reiterated Taft's views endorsing southern home rule on the race issue, while opposing the seating of black delegates at the party's national convention. Many blacks still regarded Roosevelt as anathema because of Brownsville, and southern Progressives were openly white supremacist. Facing such unattractive alternatives, many civil rights leaders, including W. E. B. Du Bois, William Monroe Trotter, and Oswald Garrison Villard, endorsed a native Virginia Democrat, Woodrow Wilson. Many blacks were concerned about Wilson's racial views, as he had been president of one of the few northern colleges, Princeton, that completely barred blacks. But during the campaign, Wilson promised blacks justice—"executed with liberality and cordial good feeling"—though he refused to make more specific commitments on racial policy. One black editor characterized black voters' choices in 1912 as "three dishes of crow."[16]

Soon after Wilson's victory, southern cabinet members—Secretary of the Treasury William McAdoo, Postmaster General Albert Burleson, and Secretary of the Navy Josephus Daniels—segregated working, eating, and bathroom facilities in their departments. The president approved this segregation, "a new and radical departure" from a fifty-year tradition of an integrated civil service, as necessary to reduce interracial friction and preserve black jobs. The administration also authorized the Civil Service Commission to require photographs of job applicants, to enable racial identification, and the percentage of blacks holding federal civil service positions declined significantly. Black patronage also fell to new lows, as southern senators such as Vardaman and Tillman "declared open war on all Negro appointees and there [was] no disposition manifested by the President and his advisers to counter their opposition." Even positions customarily allocated to blacks since the Civil War—such as register of the Treasury and minister to Haiti—now went to whites. Du Bois, who had endorsed Wilson in 1912, soon concluded that the president had been "insincere" on the race question and pronounced his record to be one of "the most grievous disappointments that a disappointed people must bear." Southern congressmen took advantage of unusual Democratic control of the federal government to introduce bills nationalizing southern racial policy—segregating federal employees and D.C. streetcars, banning interracial marriage (so much for states' rights!), barring blacks from becoming military officers, and repealing the Fifteenth Amendment. Though these bills had little serious chance of passage, they inspired some of the most racist rhetoric ever heard in Congress and forced the NAACP to divert scarce resources to opposing them.[17]

This was the social and political context in which the justices confronted race cases during the Progressive Era. The South was back "in the saddle" for the first time since the Civil War. Wilson was the first native southern president since Andrew Johnson (1865–1869), and Edward White, elevated to the chief justiceship by Taft, was the first native southern chief since Roger Taney (1835–1864). Once Democrats took control of both congressional houses in 1913, southerners dominated committees; they held eleven of thirteen chairs in the House and twelve of fourteen in the Senate. Josephus Daniels, editor of the *Raleigh News and Observer*, a leader in North Carolina's white supremacy campaign of 1898, and soon-to-be secretary of the navy, had called during the 1912 campaign for the nationalization of southern racial policy. Contemporaries had ample reason to expect Daniels's call to be answered.[18]

CASES

VOTING

Southern disfranchisement of blacks through literacy tests was politically feasible only because illiterate whites were insulated. Two mechanisms accomplished this. Mississippi's trailblazing disfranchisement convention of 1890 adopted an "understanding" clause, which protected the suffrage rights of illiterates who were able to satisfy a registrar that they could understand a state constitutional provision read to them. Proponents of these understanding clauses intended registrars to exercise their discretion in the service of white supremacy. Yet, many southern whites hesitated to confer broad discretion on officials who might use it to favor particular parties or factions. They preferred an alternative mechanism for insulating illiterate whites from disfranchisement: the grandfather clause. Some grandfather clauses exempted from literacy tests those who became qualified to vote before 1867 (the year that most southern blacks were enfranchised) and their lineal descendants. Others provided, in addition or as an alternative, exemption for those who had fought in certain wars and their lineal descendants. A half dozen states adopted some form of grandfather clause.[19]

Relevant precedent was sparse when the Court first confronted a challenge to black disfranchisement in *Williams v. Mississippi* (1898), discussed in chapter 1. *Williams*, which applied precedents from other settings, ruled that a legislature's racially discriminatory purpose was irrelevant to the constitutionality of suffrage qualifications. Yet grandfather clauses were not simply racially motivated. Rather, it could be argued that they were racial surrogates, substituting for race an ostensibly race-neutral criterion that almost perfectly correlated with race: whether one was eligible to vote before black enfranchisement.

Many southern whites appreciated that courts were unlikely to tolerate such blatant circumvention of the Fifteenth Amendment. Louisiana's 1898 constitutional convention was the first to adopt a grandfather clause, and some delegates warned that courts would invalidate it as a "weak and transparent subterfuge." The convention conferred with the state's two U.S. senators, who confirmed that view; one declared the provision to be "grossly unconstitutional." The senators also reported consulting with constitutional lawyer colleagues and being warned that adopting the grandfather clause would likely lead to a reduction in Louisiana's congressional representation under section 2 of the Fourteenth Amendment. The convention ignored this advice, apparently following the chairman's reasoning that so long as voting restrictions disfranchised blacks and not whites, it was irrelevant whether they were "more or less ridiculous." Several other states adopted grandfather clauses, despite doubts about their constitutionality. The North Carolina legislature was sufficiently concerned that it added a nonseverability clause, to reassure those who worried that invalidation of the grandfather clause would leave in place a literacy test with no protection for illiterate whites. Virtually every state that adopted a grandfather clause limited its duration, hoping to accomplish its purpose before litigation began. Only Oklahoma's grandfather clause, at issue in *Guinn*, was permanent. Many contemporary legal scholars who were generally sympathetic to black disfranchisement predicted that courts would invalidate grandfather clauses.[20]

The decisions in *Guinn* and *Myers* vindicated those predictions and struck down grandfather clauses from Oklahoma and Annapolis, Maryland. The issue was easy for justices committed to at least minimalist constitutionalism. The *Washington Post* observed that the grandfather clause "was so obvious an evasion that the Supreme Court could not have failed to declare it unconstitutional." A *Harvard Law Review* commentator queried, "Is it not a trespass on the dignity of a court to expect it to refuse to brush aside so thin a gauze of words?" Of the more than 55,000 blacks who resided in Oklahoma in 1900, only fifty-seven came from states that had permitted blacks to vote in 1866—the relevant date under the grandfather clause. Chief Justice White, writing for the Court, easily concluded that Oklahoma's incorporation of the race-based suffrage standards of 1866 into its modern constitution effectively nullified the Fifteenth Amendment.[21]

The Oklahoma Supreme Court had rejected the challenge to the grandfather clause, noting that some blacks qualified under it, and some whites and Indians did not. The state court opinion does not read like a nullifying decision, as the judges seem genuinely to have believed that the grandfather clause was constitutionally distinguishable from an expressly racial classification. One lesson to draw from these conflicting decisions of the state and federal supreme courts is that constitutional clarity lies in the eye of the beholder. Whether a particular judge thinks relevant legal materials compel a certain outcome depends partly on that judge's situation and political commitments. State judges will often be more inclined to sustain state legislation than will Supreme Court justices, because they are likelier to share the policy sentiments that inspired the legislation and because they are susceptible to social and political pressures from which the justices are more insulated. That Oklahoma judges believed the grandfather clause could be reconciled with the Fifteenth Amendment does not mean the issue was difficult for the Supreme Court.[22]

Northern opinion may well have supported *Guinn*, which made the case even easier. Though northern whites during the Progressive Era were

largely sympathetic to southern disfranchisement of blacks, they did not necessarily countenance nullification of the Constitution. Northerners repulsed
southern efforts to repeal the Fifteenth Amendment and may have seen the
grandfather clause as too transparent an evasion. President Taft, who shared
the prevalent view that the Fifteenth Amendment had been a mistake and
endorsed white political supremacy, decried the grandfather clause as a
repudiation of the Constitution. The *Indianapolis Star* believed that the
issue in *Guinn* was not "the wisdom or unwisdom of Negro suffrage, but . . .
whether a State has the power to overrule the Federal Constitution." The
New York Times, which saw the Fifteenth Amendment as "a blunder in
statesmanship [which] left terrible consequences," thought "no other decision was possible" in *Guinn*, because the grandfather clause "had no reason
for being unless it was for the purpose of nullifying the Fifteenth Amendment, and the court is not there to nullify the Constitution." Thus, *Guinn*, in
addition to being a relatively clear legal result, may have been consonant
with dominant national opinion.[23]

PEONAGE

Though the Civil War and the Thirteenth Amendment had abolished slavery, southern whites were reluctant to replace it with a free-labor system,
which contravened their assumption that blacks would not work without
compulsion. Most northern whites shared this assumption, which explains
the willingness of the army and the Freedmen's Bureau to compel former
slaves to enter agricultural labor contracts. This assumption was also
reflected in the so-called Black Codes that were adopted by southern states
in 1865–1866 and that sought to perpetuate slavery in substance. At their
core, these codes included mandatory contract laws supported by vagrancy
provisions. A typical law required blacks to enter year-long agricultural labor
contracts in January or risk being convicted as vagrants and compelled to
work for planters under criminal-surety arrangements. The market for black
labor was further artificially constrained by criminal antienticement laws,
which forbade employers to hire one another's workers; laws excluding
blacks from nonagricultural pursuits; convict-lease laws; and other measures.
By 1868, the Freedmen's Bureau, military governors, and reconstructed
southern legislatures had nullified the most coercive and transparently discriminatory elements of these codes. Yet because most white Republicans
embraced stereotypes about black labor, some coercive practices, such as
vagrancy and convict-lease laws, remained on the books even during Reconstruction.[24]

Between Redemption and the Progressive Era, southern states resurrected old legal mechanisms for coercing black labor and invented new
ones. The most extreme methods were convict labor (the chain gang) and
convict lease. The latter, which involved leasing convicts to private enter-

prises, such as railroads and mines, was initiated by many states during Reconstruction to raise money and eventually became an important source of public revenue. Over time, it was increasingly limited to blacks. A variant on convict lease was criminal surety, under which indigents convicted of minor offenses, such as vagrancy or petty larceny, had fines and court costs paid by a surety, for whom they contracted to work. Breach of a surety agreement was itself a criminal offense, which generally led to another, longer surety contract. Most southern states also adopted contract-enforcement laws, which, for example, criminalized entering into a contract to cultivate land without providing notice that the party was currently in breach of a similar contract. These laws intersected with antienticement statutes, which criminalized one employer's hiring the contract labor of another. Many states also adopted false-pretenses laws, which criminalized a worker's breach of a labor contract after he had fraudulently accepted advance wages. Finally, southern states restricted labor agents from seeking workers for out-of-state employment, usually through prohibitive licensing fees.[25]

As of 1900, the justices had yet to consider the constitutionality of most coercive labor measures. As none of those adopted after the Black Codes was explicitly racial, no transparent Fourteenth Amendment violation existed. Two southern courts invalidated prohibitive labor-agent taxes, but the justices in *Williams v. Fears* (1900) ruled the other way, finding no unconstitutional interference with Congress's power to regulate interstate commerce. The most promising basis for challenging contract-labor laws was the Thirteenth Amendment, which provides that "[n]either slavery nor involuntary servitude, except as a punishment for crime . . . shall exist within the United States, or any place subject to their jurisdiction." Because of its exception for "punishment for crime," however, convict labor and convict lease were presumably permissible.

Soon after the Civil War, federal courts construed the amendment to invalidate coercive racially discriminatory apprenticeships, which some states used to deprive black parents of custody of their children. Other Court rulings, however, had limited the concept of the "badges and incidents" of slavery. The *Civil Rights Cases* (1883) announced that "it would be running the slavery argument into the ground" to sustain, under Congress's power to enforce the Thirteenth Amendment, a ban on race discrimination in public accommodations. Similarly, *United States v. Hodges* (1906) ruled that the Thirteenth Amendment did not authorize Congress to criminalize physically intimidating blacks into breaching labor contracts. Both decisions emphasized that a ban on slavery was not tantamount to forbidding all race discrimination. Yet these rulings also clarified that the Thirteenth Amendment, unlike the Fourteenth and the Fifteenth, constrained the actions of private individuals as well as those of the state. Slavery and involuntary servitude were forbidden, regardless of whether established by law or by private force. *Clyatt v. United States* (1905) explicitly confirmed this, sustaining the application of the 1867 Peonage Act to private individuals who used physical force, not contract-labor laws, to coerce workers.[26]

As of 1910, high-court precedent on coerced-labor issues was sparse, but lower courts had been more active. Southern state courts and lower federal courts had clarified that legislatures could not constitutionally criminalize the breach of ordinary labor contracts. Some such rulings relied on the Thirteenth Amendment, others on state constitutional prohibitions on imprisonment for debt, which every southern state but Louisiana had. Lower courts treated the federal and state prohibitions as roughly congruent; one judge noted the "kindred purposes" they served. In *Robertson v. Baldwin* (1897), the justices identified exceptional circumstances under which contractual breaches could be criminalized, such as sailors at sea, whose decision to jump ship could endanger crews and impose extreme costs on ship owners. *Robertson* did not reach the question of whether ordinary labor-contract breaches could be criminalized, though the majority intimated, and Harlan's dissent stated, that they could not. Given the virtual unanimity among lower courts, the justices probably would have concluded that the Thirteenth Amendment prohibited criminalizing such behavior.[27]

Against this legal backdrop, *Bailey v. Alabama* (1911), which challenged the constitutionality of a false-pretenses law, was easy. In 1885, Alabama became the first southern state to adopt such a law applying to labor contracts. The statute criminalized entering into a labor agreement that provided advance wages with the fraudulent intent to subsequently breach. Southern agricultural labor contracts typically lasted a year and almost always provided advance wages. Punishing fraud rather than the breach itself was essential, as southern courts were virtually unanimous in rejecting criminalization of ordinary contract breaches. Thus, the Alabama Supreme Court had interpreted this law in 1891 to require proof of fraudulent intent when the contract was signed. A half dozen southern states, including Alabama, responded to this and similar rulings by adopting new false-pretenses laws in the first years of the twentieth century. These statutes created presumptions of fraudulent intent from the fact of breach. Moreover, Alabama evidence law barred accused breachers from testifying about their uncommunicated motives. The decision in *Bailey* invalidated Alabama's revised law under the 1867 Peonage Act and the Thirteenth Amendment and ruled that it effectively criminalized the ordinary breach of a labor contract.[28]

Bailey is analogous to *Guinn*: Both involve fairly minimalist constitutional interpretations. Had the justices done less, they would have essentially acquiesced in southern nullification of the Constitution. Southern courts had already invalidated, on state and federal constitutional grounds, laws criminalizing breach of labor contracts after receipt of advance wages. Yet Alabama's law did little more. Because fraudulent intent was presumed from the breach and the defendant's testimony to the contrary was barred, Alabama had effectively criminalized the breach of any labor contract that paid advance wages—that is, essentially all long-term agricultural labor contracts. Once the justices accepted the nearly universal baseline proposition that the Thirteenth Amendment barred criminalizing ordinary contract breaches, how could they not invalidate Alabama's transparent subterfuge? As one commentator has observed, *Bailey* reads like "an utterly assured Court vindicating a clear command of the Constitution in the face of a brazen legislative effort at subversion."[29]

The vote in *Bailey* was 5–2, Justices Oliver Wendell Holmes and Horace Lurton dissenting, with two vacancies remaining after several recent deaths and resignations. That two justices dissented does not mean that the others found the case difficult or the law unclear. Holmes's dissent rejected the baseline proposition that the Thirteenth Amendment forbids criminalization of ordinary contract breaches; he did not deny that Alabama's law was a transparent evasion of that prohibition. Because Holmes believed that the state could directly criminalize ordinary contract breaches, Alabama's indirect pursuit of that result was naturally permissible. Holmes was usually an unadulterated majoritarian. If most Alabamans, as represented by their state legislators, wished to criminalize contract breaches, Holmes saw no constitutional reason to object. He took a similar view of majorities redistributing wealth, forbidding foreign-language instruction in private schools, imposing criminal punishments that most of his colleagues deemed cruel and unusual, and sterilizing mentally disabled persons. Holmes was not generally committed to even minimal constitutionalism. For justices who were, *Bailey* was easy.[30]

United States v. Reynolds (1914) involved a criminal-surety law, which authorized the state to hire out minor criminals to private parties who paid their fines and court costs in exchange for promises to labor at specified rates (usually for several months) to pay off expenses. Breach of a surety contract was itself a criminal offense, which usually led to another surety contract of longer duration. Those laboring under such agreements often had first been convicted of vagrancy, petty larceny, or some other "Negro crime," such as incitement to insurrection or trespass. One could be convicted and hired out for crimes as minor as using offensive language. For such a crime, one might be fined ten dollars plus twenty-five dollars in court costs, which would take eight months to work off. Local law enforcement officers were frequently in cahoots with planters and conducted "vagrancy roundups" or otherwise "manufactured" petty criminals during harvesting season when labor was in great demand.[31]

The decision in *Reynolds* invalidated Alabama's criminal-surety scheme under the 1867 Peonage Act and the Thirteenth Amendment. *Reynolds* was not as easy as *Bailey*. Convict labor and convict lease seem obviously constitutional, given the Thirteenth Amendment's express allowance of involuntary servitude as punishment for crime. It could be argued that criminal surety was a more humane substitute for convict lease, as it enabled convicts to escape harsh conditions, including armed guards, shackling, and isolation from their families. Thus, invalidating criminal surety seems to have required the justices to take account of the social realities of surety arrangements — a departure from their usual formalistic approach to race cases.[32]

Still, *Reynolds* did not require much greater creativity than *Bailey* had. Criminal surety could appear constitutionally unobjectionable only by ignoring the patent fraud in a system that routinely manufactured black criminals. The Thirteenth Amendment permitted involuntary servitude only as punishment for crime. Thus, for law enforcement officers and magistrates to corrupt the surety system by fraudulently creating black criminals clearly violated the amendment. Moreover, in practice, the surety system invited "an ever-turning wheel of servitude." Breach of surety agreements generally resulted in new surety contracts of greater duration, and convicts often were eventually forced to labor much longer than the original violation warranted. In *Reynolds*, the victim's petty-larceny conviction earned a fine of fifteen dollars plus costs, which translated, because of indigency, into a sixty-eight-day prison sentence. That led to an initial surety contract requiring ten months of labor. When that contract was breached, the new surety agreement lasted fourteen and a half months. Even Holmes, who reiterated that a state should be permitted to criminalize simple contract breaches, thought that the surety system's successive contracts of increasing duration was peonage.[33]

Bailey and *Reynolds* were easy, not only because the law seemed reasonably clear, but also because public opinion supported the results, despite the Progressive Era's regressive racial attitudes. Segregation and disfranchisement were different from peonage, which many racists condemned, for reasons both of interest and humanity. Even southern whites were divided over peonage. Most planters supported coercive labor measures, but other whites, less dependent on black labor, favored mobility, in the hope that blacks would migrate. Divisions among whites explain why anti–emigrant-agent laws were controversial and why southern courts felt free to invalidate them, when they would not have dreamed of condemning segregation and disfranchisement. Divisions among whites also explain the fierce political battles that developed over convict lease, which planters and industrialists supported but organized labor opposed. Some white southerners also opposed peonage for fear that it would inhibit foreign immigration. Several notorious peonage cases involved white European immigrants and elicited complaints from foreign ambassadors. The U.S. assistant attorney general's scathing reports on peonage in 1907–1908 emphasized the luring of European immigrants from New York City to southern turpentine farms and lumber mills more than it did the coercion of black agricultural workers in the South. More than one southern judge invalidating a contract-labor law expressed concern that peonage would deter immigration.[34]

Many white southerners also condemned peonage as a "barbaric atavism." Some peons were held under conditions almost indistinguishable from slavery. They worked under armed guard and were shackled by day and locked up at night; they were routinely beaten and tracked down by dogs if they attempted to escape. Most southern whites thought the Thirteenth Amendment legitimate, unlike the Fourteenth and the Fifteenth. Many were genuinely appalled by peonage conditions. A Georgia federal judge was disgusted at the "lawless and violent men who would seize helpless and pathetic Negroes," and a South Carolina jurist condemned "those brutalities and outrages which have so greatly shocked the public conscience in some of the peonage cases."[35]

These considerations of interest and humanity induced southern whites, including a couple of federal district judges with impeccable white supremacist credentials, to lead the legal assault on peonage. Charles Russell, the assistant attorney general who was appointed in 1906 to investigate and prosecute peonage, was a Virginian of unquestioned loyalty to southern racial policy. Similarly, black leader Booker T. Washington, who was willing to make temporary concessions to segregation and disfranchisement as blacks pursued economic advancement, vigorously fought peonage, which obstructed such efforts. Most northerners, deeply invested in free-labor ideology for a half century, were appalled by southern coercive labor schemes, which one northern newspaper called "sordid, barbarous, and demoralizing." As the *New York Globe* pointed out, "The social mingling of black and white is one affair, the refusal of equal civil and economic rights another. . . . The northerner who . . . has been brought up on the political principles of Abraham Lincoln . . . finds slavery, peonage, or any variation or mitigation thereof extremely distasteful." While the federal government turned a blind eye to most southern racial practices, it was willing to condemn peonage, filing an amicus brief in *Bailey* and bringing a criminal prosecution in *Reynolds*.[36]

In addition, by the time the justices invalidated criminal surety in 1914, every southern state but one had abolished convict lease, which had been used to justify surety arrangements. Since the 1890s, Populist and Progressive reformers had targeted convict lease for extinction. Death rates among leased prisoners were staggering, and public investigations unearthed numerous instances of torture and other abuse. Organized white labor, moreover, was opposed to having to compete with convicts, who cost less to hire and did not strike. Only Alabama still practiced convict lease at the time of *Reynolds*. Thus, invalidation of criminal surety, the little sibling of convict lease, is an instance of the Court's suppressing an isolated practice, not of its frustrating dominant national (or even southern) opinion.[37]

TRANSPORTATION

Every southern state had adopted a railroad segregation law by 1910. Without exception, these required that racially separate facilities be equal. *Plessy* upheld such laws as reasonable. *McCabe v. Atchison, Topeka & Santa Fe*

Railway Co. (1914) involved an Oklahoma statute that permitted railroads to provide luxury accommodations, such as sleeping cars, dining cars, and chair cars, only to whites (or only to blacks). The law required separate but equal for other facilities. Three other southern states had similar laws.[38]

The justices rejected McCabe's challenge on procedural grounds. The plaintiffs had not requested and been denied the relevant services, nor had they shown that an injunction was appropriate because money damages would have been inadequate. In dicta, though, five justices expressed an opinion on the merits, finding an equal protection violation. They rejected the state's defense that requiring railroads to provide equal luxury accommodations for blacks was unreasonable because per capita demand was much lower among blacks than among whites. This argument was flawed, these justices concluded, because the Fourteenth Amendment guarantees "personal" rights, not "group" rights. In other words, an individual black is entitled to equal treatment with an individual white. According to the Court, it was no response to such a claim that blacks *as a group* demanded less of a particular service than did whites.[39]

McCabe's dictum hardly represents a new constitutional departure. It is true that *Plessy* technically did not require that separate be equal to be constitutional. The Louisiana railroad segregation law, not the Court, had mandated equality. *Plessy* had no reason to consider the constitutionality of separate and *un*equal. Still, the dominant contemporary understanding clearly required that racially separate facilities be equal to be constitutional. In the absence of such an understanding, why would every southern state that adopted a railroad segregation statute have required equality? *Pace v. Alabama* (1883) contributed to that understanding, rejecting a Fourteenth Amendment challenge to a statute that punished fornication more severely when the parties were of different races because the races were treated equally. Lower court decisions from the 1880s invalidating state laws that imposed racially separate taxes for segregated schools likewise revealed an understanding that the Fourteenth Amendment permitted racial distinctions but forbade racial inequality. None of this is to suggest that such an interpretation was compelled. The amendment says nothing explicit about racial classifications, and interpreting it to forbid all inequalities would be nonsensical. Yet, by 1900, the assumption that racially separate facilities must be equal to be constitutional was deeply embedded in legal, if not popular, understanding. Against that baseline, *McCabe* was easy.[40]

In this sense, *McCabe* is analogous to *Bailey*. One can easily imagine interpreting the Thirteenth Amendment to permit criminalizing ordinary breaches of contract. As the amendment expressly forbids only *involuntary* servitude, courts could have ruled that obligations arising from initially voluntary undertakings were beyond its purview. Yet by 1900, southern courts themselves had almost universally rejected that interpretation. Starting from a baseline assumption that ordinary breaches of contract could not be criminalized, *Bailey* was easy. Similarly, starting from a baseline understanding that racial classifications, in order to satisfy equal protection, must guarantee equality—an assumption previously embraced by all southern state legislatures—*McCabe* followed automatically.

Yet perhaps this interpretation is too neat. Four justices—Oliver Wendell Holmes, Joseph R. Lamar, James C. McReynolds, and Edward D. White—concurred in *McCabe* without opinion. In all likelihood, they were dissenting from the majority's dicta on the merits. Can *McCabe* have been easy if four justices and two lower courts thought Oklahoma's statute constitutional? Moreover, the decision in *Cumming* (1899) had sustained the constitutionality of separate and *un*equal in public education—apparently a strong precedent in support of Oklahoma's statute. Oklahoma plausibly argued that railroads ought not to be required to operate largely empty luxury accommodations for blacks. That is, the argument that disparate per capita racial demand justified differential treatment of blacks and whites had a factual basis. Thus, *McCabe*'s dictum requiring equality in segregated luxury accommodations arguably departs from *Cumming* and perhaps from *Plessy*, which emphasized reasonableness more than equality.[41]

Yet, one must recall that constitutional clarity lies in the eye of the beholder. Different interpretive communities often construe identical constitutional language differently. We have seen that a southern state court could even reconcile the grandfather clause with the Fifteenth Amendment. Thus, five justices could have found *McCabe* legally easy, while four others did not. Three dissenters on the merits—White, Lamar, and McReynolds—were the only southern justices. That southerners and northerners would sometimes interpret the Constitution's racial prescriptions differently is no surprise. The other dissenter on the merits was Holmes, who barely believed in constitutionalism. Holmes probably thought that if a majority of Oklahomans supported separate and unequal, the justices had no business interfering. Nor is *Cumming* fatal to this minimalist-constitutionalism interpretation of *McCabe*. The racially unequal educational funding in *Cumming* resulted from administrative discrimination, not statute. The Court of this era never seemed willing to challenge the discriminatory exercise of administrative discretion. In 1914, most northerners probably believed that equal protection at least required that statutory racial classifications guarantee equality.

Whether or not *McCabe* was legally compelled, it was politically easy. The majority's dictum in no way questioned the constitutionality of segregation. Moreover, though the logic of the majority's "personal rights" dictum might ultimately doom segregation, in 1914 the justices could not conceivably have embraced those implications. The Court implicitly reaffirmed the constitutionality of school segregation in the 1920s and again in the 1930s.[42]

Finally, *McCabe* was another instance of the justices using the Constitution to suppress outliers. Most southern legislatures required railroads to provide separate-and-equal accommodations. Only Oklahoma and three others expressly permitted unequal luxury accommodations. These aberrant statutes illustrate the continuing deterioration in southern race relations: Segregation was no longer sufficient; it now had to be made formally unequal as well. *McCabe* simply held outliers to the norm accepted by all southern states a decade earlier and still adhered to by most. *McCabe's* dictum was almost certainly consonant with northern public opinion, and possibly with southern as well.

RESIDENTIAL SEGREGATION

Neighborhoods in antebellum southern cities were frequently integrated. Slaves usually lived near their masters, and whites fearful of black insurrection were reluctant to permit large residential districts free of white supervision. Those housing patterns lingered after the war. Older southern cities, such as New Orleans, Charleston, and Savannah, had more residential integration than did newer cities, such as Atlanta and Birmingham. As rural blacks flocked to cities in search of better economic opportunities, education, and physical security, whites began insisting on residential segregation. Black migrants were shunted into low-lying areas on city peripheries, often near railroad tracks or dumps, and residential segregation increased. Black populations in most northern cities were too small before the Great Migration for pervasive housing segregation to develop. Northern whites generally did not demand such segregation until they felt threatened by large black population increases.[43]

Buchanan v. Warley (1917) was a Fourteenth Amendment challenge to a Louisville, Kentucky, residential segregation ordinance, which provided that houses sold on majority-white (or majority-black) blocks could be occupied only by whites (or by blacks). Baltimore enacted the first such ordinance in 1910, and similar laws proliferated over the decade, especially in border states and the peripheral South. Within a few years, similar ordinances were adopted in several Virginia cities; Winston-Salem, North Carolina; Greenville, South Carolina; and Atlanta, Georgia. It was black migration to cities that inspired these ordinances. As black neighborhoods became congested, middle-class blacks sought to escape crime, vice, and substandard ghetto housing by moving into white areas. Whites responded by pressuring city councils to enact these ordinances, which were defended as necessary to preserve social peace, protect racial purity, and safeguard property values from deteriorating as residential patterns destabilized. *Buchanan* invalidated Louisville's ordinance as an interference with property rights protected under the Due Process Clause.[44]

Buchanan was not as legally easy as other race rulings from the Progressive Era. Justices committed only to constitutional minimalism might have sustained Louisville's ordinance based on *Plessy*. Still, the equal protection case against residential segregation ordinances was stronger than that against railway segregation laws. Moreover, even if *Buchanan* were more constitutionally creative, it reflects the justices' robust commitment to property rights more than any shift in racial proclivities. Thus, only to the extent that laissez-faire constitutionalism reliably promotes civil rights is *Buchanan* a significant advance in race-relations jurisprudence.

Buchanan was not constitutional minimalism. Most important, two recent decisions, *Plessy* and *Berea College*, had sustained racial segregation in railroad transportation and, more qualifiedly, in private higher education. If state-mandated segregation was constitutionally permissible in those contexts, why not in others? So long as the state could plausibly justify residential segregation—as preserving peace, racial purity, and property values—precedent seemed to sanction it. Indeed, one could argue that segregation in housing was more important than on railroads, because interracial contact in the former setting was less transient. *Buchanan* failed to convincingly distinguish precedent, and contemporary legal commentators widely criticized it. Indeed, law review commentary, both before and after *Buchanan*, was so overwhelmingly supportive of residential segregation ordinances that they can hardly be portrayed as *obviously* unconstitutional.[45]

Yet the case against residential segregation ordinances, though not compelling, was hardly absurd. Whatever else it was supposed to accomplish, the Fourteenth Amendment was plainly intended to provide a constitutional basis for the 1866 Civil Rights Act, which guaranteed blacks the same rights as whites with regard to property, contracts, court access, and legal protection. The 1866 act responded to southern Black Codes, some of which barred blacks from owning real estate in certain places. Thus, discrimination in property rights was a core concern of the drafters of the Fourteenth Amendment, unlike discrimination in education or transportation. Only the provision for formal equality in residential segregation ordinances kept them from being obviously unconstitutional: Whites could not purchase homes on majority-black blocks any more than blacks could on majority-white ones. Were the justices to look beyond this formal equality and acknowledge that the purpose of the Louisville ordinance was to exclude blacks from white neighborhoods, they would spot a core violation of the Fourteenth Amendment. Thus, in 1890, a California federal judge invalidated under the amendment a San Francisco ordinance that evicted the Chinese from Chinatown. Indeed, the issue appeared so clear-cut that no appeal was taken from that decision, and no other California municipality enacted a similar ordinance, despite rampant hostility toward the Chinese.[46]

Regardless of how constitutionally creative *Buchanan* was, it was not a significant departure with regard to *race*. *Buchanan* was decided during the *Lochner* era, when the justices were most committed to protecting property rights. The ruling's doctrinal hook is due process, not equal protection, as one would have expected if race were the predominant concern. Though Justice William Day's opinion for the Court is muddled, its consistent theme is the importance of property rights. The NAACP argued the case largely in those terms, which was the easiest way to distinguish *Plessy* and *Berea College*. Furthermore, Justice James McReynolds, a notorious racist who dissented from most progressive racial rulings, joined the unanimous opinion in *Buchanan*. McReynolds's vote was almost certainly motivated by concerns about property rights, not racial equality.[47]

Tellingly, three of the five southern courts that considered the issue had invalidated residential segregation ordinances. Though the precise holding varied, these decisions consistently emphasized owners' rights to sell property unimpeded by government regulation. For example, the North Carolina Supreme Court noted an "inalienable right to own, acquire, and dispose of property, which is not conferred by the Constitution, but exists of natural right." Concerns of racial equality played no role in these decisions, and southern courts during the Progressive Era had no constitutional qualms about laws that segregated public schools or railroad passengers. In an era before the culturally elite values of judges translated into egalitarian racial commitments, judges demonstrated, as they have for most of American history, robust support for property rights.[48]

One objection to this interpretation of *Buchanan* is that the Court that same year seemed to silently overrule *Lochner* in *Bunting v. Oregon* (1917), which sustained a maximum-hours law for male industrial workers. Moreover, *Buchanan*'s author, Day, had dissented in *Lochner*. If the Court in 1917 was no longer devoted to substantive due process,* and if Day never had been, then how persuasive can the property rights interpretation of *Buchanan* be? Finally, the contrast between the justices' growing willingness to sustain general zoning restrictions and their invalidation of residential segregation ordinances might suggest that *Buchanan* was more about racial equality than about property rights.[49]

These arguments are plausible but hardly compelling. Though *Bunting* did appear to overrule *Lochner*, the justices in 1917 were far from abandoning substantive due process, as shown by another decision that year, *Adams v. Tanner*, which invalidated a Washington State law restricting employment-agency fees. Moreover, though Day did dissent in *Lochner*, he was not a consistent foe of substantive due process, as shown by his dissent in *Wilson v. New* (1917), a decision that rejected a substantive-due-process challenge to a federal minimum wage for railroad workers. Furthermore, however much their commitment to contractual liberty had eroded by 1917, the justices had always been more protective of property rights.[50]

Finally, although nonracial zoning cases indicate some erosion even in property rights commitments, the justices probably would have distinguished, whether or not doing so makes economic sense, between zoning

---

*Substantive due process was the doctrine frequently used by the justices in the first decades of the twentieth century to extend special protection to property and contract rights.

regulations restricting property *use* and *sale*. Louisville's ordinance prevented owners from selling land to a group of willing buyers (blacks) who probably would have been the bulk of potential purchasers, because the land at issue was in mixed neighborhoods into which few whites would eagerly buy. Even the committed majoritarian, Holmes, could not countenance such a substantial interference with property rights. Moreover, treating *Euclid v. Ambler Realty Co.* (1926), which sustained general-use zoning, as evidence that *Buchanan* (1917), which invalidated racial zoning, must have been principally about race, not property rights, is dubious. Lower court decisions became significantly more permissive of general-use zoning in the 1920s, and we do not know how the justices would have decided *Euclid* in 1917.[51]

In sum, *Buchanan* probably had more to do with property rights than with civil rights. Yet some recent commentators have challenged the coherence of this distinction, arguing that *Lochner*-era commitments to property and contract rights benefited racial minorities. Indeed, some have even suggested that had the justices been more consistently committed to laissez-faire constitutionalism, blacks would not have needed civil rights legislation, as Jim Crow could not have survived in the absence of state support. As one of these commentators has put it, "Mr. Herbert Spencer's Social Statics is just the right antidote to Jim Crow." On this view, *Lochner*-like principles mandated that *Plessy* and *Berea College* come out differently than they did, because the state lacked adequate justification for intervening in the affairs of private railroads and colleges. This perspective celebrates *Buchanan* for demonstrating, contrary to conventional wisdom, that "conservative" property rights decisions can produce "liberal" civil rights outcomes.[52]

These libertarian commentators usefully remind us that in an era of black political powerlessness, state regulation was unlikely to advantage blacks. Jim Crow legislation and the arguments used to defend it did tend to violate libertarian principles. Yet libertarians have overstated their case. Jim Crow legislation was generally more symbolic than functional. Blacks were mostly disfranchised and railroad travel mostly segregated before legislatures had intervened. The same was true of residential segregation. White supremacy depended less on law than on entrenched social mores, backed by economic power and the threat and reality of violence. Invalidating legislation would have scarcely made a dent in this system. Ultimately, federal civil rights legislation was critical to enfranchising blacks, desegregating public education and public accommodations, and eroding race discrimination in private employment. Libertarians understandably have been reluctant to acknowledge this. Not only are they mistaken in claiming that *Lochner*-like principles would have undermined Jim Crow, but those principles themselves condemn the civil rights legislation that has proved transformative. Because such legislation prevents employers and business owners from conducting affairs as they see fit, some libertarians attacked it when it was enacted as embodying "a principle of unsurpassed ugliness."[53]

Whether *Buchanan* was principally about race or about property rights, public opinion outside of the South may well have supported the ruling. When Baltimore adopted the first such residential segregation ordinance, Charles Bonaparte, the former attorney general of the United States, ridiculed it as "petty, impolitic, medieval in conception, injurious to the best interests of the city, worthy, perhaps, of Russia." The *New York Evening Post* considered it "utterly absurd in this day and generation to return to the ghetto of the middle ages, abandoned by Europe long ago." After *Buchanan* invalidated such ordinances, the *Nation* praised the Court for holding "that the most hateful institution of the Russia which has passed away shall not be set up under the American flag."[54]

None of the Progressive Era race decisions shows a significant shift in the justices' racial attitudes. Most were legally easy decisions. (*Buchanan*, one could argue, was not legally easy, but it had more to do with property rights than with civil rights.) The decisions were also politically easy, as public opinion supported formal vindication of constitutional rights, and the justices were mainly suppressing isolated practices.

The most serious objection to this interpretation is that although the substance of most of these rulings is consistent with minimalist constitutionalism, the justices' willingness even to reach the merits is probably not. In three of the four sets of Progressive Era race cases, it could be argued that the Court should have dismissed the suits without even confronting the merits; instead the justices ignored procedural objections and rendered civil rights victories. Their willingness to stretch to reach the merits may reveal a slight shift in their racial predilections.[55]

Oklahoma's grandfather clause may have been obviously unconstitutional, but even to reach the question, *Guinn* had to surmount two obstacles, either of which might have derailed the constitutional challenge. First, *Giles v. Harris* (1903) seemed to reject judicial involvement in "political" questions. It is true that the cases are distinguishable. The justices in *Giles* were troubled that plaintiffs sought injunctive relief without demonstrating the inadequacy of damages, whereas *Guinn*, a criminal prosecution of election officials, posed no remedial difficulty. Moreover, ruling for the plaintiffs in *Giles* would have meant invalidating Alabama's entire voter registration system, whereas striking down the grandfather clause in *Guinn* left Oklahoma's system substantially intact. Though these differences are real, justices intent on avoiding political questions might easily have declined to confront the merits in *Guinn*. As contemporary critics pointed out, the justices "had refused every [prior] opportunity to pass squarely upon . . . disfranchisement." Yet now, "the technicality loving judges . . . have brushed aside the technicalities [and] gone straight to the heart of the case."[56]

Perhaps more significant, constitutional infirmities to one side, one could argue that the grandfather clause was insulated from attack because no federal statute plainly authorized the challenge. Civil rights statutes dating from Reconstruction contained several provisions that expressly protected the right to vote, but these had been invalidated by the Court in the 1870s or repealed by Congress in the 1890s. As of 1910, all that remained of this legislation were catchall provisions. Most pertinent, section 6 of the Civil Rights Act of 1870 punished conspiracies "to injure, oppress, threaten, or intimidate any citizen with intent to hinder his free exercise and enjoyment of any right or privilege granted or secured by the Constitution or laws of the United States." One could argue that this provision was intended to cover neither voting nor state officials administering law but only violent, private interferences with other federal rights. As the voting provisions of these statutes entailed less severe punishment than their catchall sections, Congress may not have intended the latter to incorporate the former. Moreover, because a Democratic Congress had repealed the voting provisions in 1893–1894, it could be argued that the catchall sections, even if originally intended to cover suffrage, did not do so thereafter. Finally, the catchall provisions were probably addressed primarily toward Klan-style intimidation, not state officials administering law, which explains why they began, "if two or more persons shall band or conspire together or go in disguise upon the public highway." In sum, statutory arguments against *Guinn*'s prosecution were substantial. By rejecting them, the justices seem to have stretched to decide a constitutional question that they might easily have avoided.[57]

Similarly, in *McCabe*, five justices plainly strained to condemn Oklahoma's separate-and-unequal railway law. Plaintiffs sought to enjoin the statute's enforcement before it went into effect, leading the Court to unanimously dismiss the suit as unripe. The justices also questioned the propriety of seeking an injunction without a showing that damages would be inadequate. These procedural flaws—the NAACP called them "foolish mistake[s]"—induced the association to stay out of the case. Yet rather than simply dismissing for lack of jurisdiction, the majority reached out to announce that the statute violated equal protection. Perhaps these justices' determination to state a view on the merits shows a heightened concern for racial equality.[58]

Buchanan also involved a potentially fatal procedural flaw. Buchanan, a white real estate agent, had agreed to sell a house on a predominantly white block to Warley, the black head of the local NAACP branch. The contract explicitly authorized Warley's repudiation if the sale proved illegal for any reason. Warley promptly invoked this clause, noting Louisville's residential segregation ordinance. Buchanan then sued, invoking the Fourteenth Amendment in reply to Warley's defense based on the ordinance. *Buchanan* thus had all the markings of a "friendly," nonadversarial suit, which means that jurisdiction was dubious, as Article III of the Constitution empowers federal courts to adjudicate only "cases or controversies." Holmes was initially inclined to dismiss the suit on this ground, but the justices ultimately finessed the procedural hurdle. One could argue that their willingness to do so reveals strong views on the merits.[59]

By contrast, the *Plessy*-era justices' invocation of procedural grounds to avoid confronting the merits invariably disadvantaged civil rights litigants—for example, in *Berea College* and several disfranchisement cases. Indeed, contemporary newspapers observed that "[i]t seems impossible to force the [race] issue squarely upon [the Court]" because "always at the last stage some technicality . . . emerges to prevent the facing of the issue by the impartial and learned justices." Thus, the apparent eagerness of the justices during the Progressive Era to reach the merits and render decisions favorable to civil rights suggests an increased concern for racial equality.[60]

CONSEQUENCES

VOTING

Some contemporaries treated *Guinn* as momentous. One compared it in significance to *Dred Scott*, and another deemed it "one of the most important judgments pronounced by the Court in fifty years." If one focuses strictly on concrete results, such assessments are difficult to fathom. *Guinn*'s implications for black suffrage were utterly trivial. Only Oklahoma had a permanent grandfather clause. Other states had limited the duration of their grandfather clauses, hoping to avoid judicial challenge. By 1915, all other grandfather clauses had achieved their purpose of insulating illiterate whites from the disfranchising effect of literacy tests, and the clauses had been extinguished by sunset provisions. Thus, *Guinn* suppressed a lone outlier. As a Richmond newspaper coolly observed, grandfather clauses already had "served their purpose" and were "no longer vital to the South's protection." The NAACP complained, "To the amazement of the white South itself this illegal, undemocratic and outrageous provision has actually been allowed to stand on the statute books and be enforced for SEVENTEEN YEARS!"[61]

Moreover, *Guinn* ruled the grandfather clause invalid on its face, as a surrogate racial classification, thus avoiding any inquiry into legislative motive. Given the ingenuity and intransigence of southern whites, success in the judicial battle against Jim Crow would require motive inquiries or shifting the focus from purpose to effect. *Guinn* represented no movement in this direction. Indeed, the Court explicitly noted that a literacy test uncorrupted by a grandfather clause was permissible—dicta that ensured that the ruling had no impact on black disfranchisement. Mississippi and South Carolina, disfranchisement pioneers, already had demonstrated that a literacy test without a grandfather clause could nullify black suffrage. So long as registrars committed to white supremacy exercised broad discretion in administering literacy tests, illiterate whites could generally register, while literate blacks could not. As late as the 1950s, Alabama registrars were finding black

Ph.D.'s from Tuskegee to be illiterate. Solving this problem required challenging local officials' discretion—a lesson that Congress eventually learned and effectively applied in the 1965 Voting Rights Act.

Guinn also had no effect on other disfranchisement techniques, such as poll taxes, white primaries, complex registration requirements, fraud, and violence. For these reasons, a New Orleans newspaper confidently concluded that Guinn was "not of the slightest political importance in the South." The *Buffalo Express* observed that Guinn "may end the legal attempts to keep Negroes from voting. But how about the illegal ones?" The *Binghamton* (New York) *Press* thought blacks would likely discover that "getting the right to vote from the Supreme Court in Washington is not exactly the same thing as getting the right from the election board in their own voting district." The *New York Times* assured readers that, Guinn notwithstanding, "The white man will rule his land. The only question left by the Supreme Court's decision is how he will rule it."[62]

In Oklahoma, Guinn had no effect on black voter registration, as the legislature responded by immediately "grandfathering" the grandfather clause. Under the new statute, voters in the 1914 congressional election, when the grandfather clause was in effect, were automatically registered. All other eligible voters, including essentially all blacks, had to register between April 30 and May 11, 1916, or be forever disfranchised. The federal government failed to challenge this patent evasion, and the justices had no opportunity to invalidate it until 1939. Thus, one lesson of Guinn was that, in the absence of subsequent enforcement litigation, judicial rulings to protect civil rights were easily circumvented. Follow-up litigation was hard to come by at a time when the NAACP's annual legal budget was roughly $5,000 and it had fewer than fifteen local branches, almost all of them in the North. In 1915, the association's secretary confessed that lack of resources caused "many splendid test cases to slip through [our] fingers."[63]

PEONAGE

Some contemporaries treated *Bailey* as tremendously significant, again drawing comparisons to *Dred Scott*. Similarly, one legal historian deems the peonage decisions "the most lasting of the White Court's contributions to justice for black people, and among its greatest achievements." This extravagant assessment is difficult to justify.[64]

Bailey and *Reynolds* seem to have had little effect on peonage. The Florida and Georgia legislatures and courts evaded *Bailey* by disingenuously distinguishing it. For thirty more years, these states applied a false-pretenses law with a phony presumption essentially identical to that invalidated in *Bailey*. Yet, after *Reynolds* in 1914, the Court decided no more peonage cases until World War II, when it finally invalidated these evasive measures. As with *Guinn*, Court decisions accomplished little when the justices vacated the field for decades afterward. At a time when appealing civil rights cases to the Court was difficult—because of physical danger, black litigants' poverty, a dearth of willing lawyers, and the NAACP's infancy—isolated litigation victories produced few concrete benefits.[65]

After *Bailey*, some other southern legislatures repealed the statutory presumptions that the Court had condemned, and some courts invalidated them. But these states retained the basic false-pretenses laws which *Bailey* had approved. All-white juries still determined whether black agricultural workers had accepted advance wages with the fraudulent intent to subsequently breach contracts. Removal of the statutory presumption cannot have affected many case outcomes. Moreover, as few blacks would have relished testing their luck in court, most would have simply assumed that contractual breach would lead to prosecution and conviction.[66]

Furthermore, *Bailey* and *Reynolds* left undisturbed many alternative methods of coercing black labor: convict labor, convict lease, vagrancy laws, antienticement laws, and anti–labor-agent laws. Given the capacity and the inclination of southern law enforcement officers to manufacture black criminals for convict labor and convict lease, contract-enforcement laws were unnecessary for coercing black labor. The highly visible, mostly black chain gang was a powerful inducement for blacks to abide by labor contracts rather than risk convictions for loitering or vagrancy.[67]

Finally, many instances of coerced black labor made no pretense of legality. Blacks worked under shotguns, were locked up at night, and were tracked down with hunting dogs if they escaped. Measuring the extent of such extralegal coerced labor is impossible, but it clearly existed. Ironically, it was not plainly prohibited by any federal statute: The 1867 Peonage Act prohibited only coerced labor *for debt*. Indeed, the risk of federal peonage prosecution may have occasionally induced employers to adopt these more direct methods of coercing black labor. The chance of such activity being prosecuted under state law was extremely remote.[68]

At a time when many, perhaps most, southern whites still believed that they had a proprietary interest in black labor and that blacks would work only if coerced, judicial invalidation of a couple of peonage statutes was unlikely to prove efficacious. Illustrating the problem, Mississippi judges, who felt legally obliged to invalidate a contract-labor law, nonetheless expressed sympathy for the legislature's "purpose of requiring the fickle laborers in our cotton country to reasonably observe their contracts." Blacks prosecuted under unconstitutional peonage laws were among the least likely defendants to be able to afford to appeal convictions to a tribunal not under the sway of local planters. In Attala County, Mississippi, local magistrates continued to exercise "absolute authority over the negro[; f]rom their decision there is no appeal if it's a negro." Nor did the NAACP or any similar organization able to render legal or financial assistance operate in the rural South in the 1910s.

Founded in 1909, the NAACP achieved a significant southern presence only around World War I and even then only in cities. Federal prosecutions required the support of U.S. attorneys, judges, and jurors. Though some of these people abhorred peonage, others likely shared the belief of southern planters that black labor had to be coerced. The federal government's enthusiasm for prosecuting peonage did not last long, especially once the southern-sympathizing Wilson administration assumed office in 1913. In any event, successful prosecutions generally required the testimony of black witnesses, who were usually under the control, both economic and physical, of planters. Such witnesses were easy to intimidate. In one infamous Georgia case, a planter who was worried about a federal investigation into his peonage practices simply ordered the murder of eleven of his tenants who were potential witnesses. Letters that reported instances of peonage to the NAACP in the early 1920s frequently noted that witnesses were afraid to say anything publicly because of the likely repercussions. Even those black witnesses who made it into court were unlikely to enjoy much credibility with white jurors. Especially in regions where peonage was prevalent, it was very difficult to empanel a jury that did not include some who sympathized with the view that blacks had to be coerced to work. Accordingly, juries often acquitted peonage defendants who were plainly guilty, sometimes ignoring clear signals from the judge to convict. Even in the few peonage cases that did produce convictions, judges tended to impose lenient sentences, in deference to local white opinion.[69]

Measuring the amount of southern peonage that existed is impossible. Black mobility and the competitive market for agricultural labor limited coercive possibilities. Yet experts agree that southern peonage remained widespread after *Bailey* and *Reynolds*. In a 1921 report, the U.S. attorney general concluded that peonage continued "to a shocking extent" in Georgia. That same year, the NAACP reported that "[t]hroughout the South, . . . Negroes are held today in as complete and awful and soul-destroying slavery as they were in 1860." The association's files for the 1920s are filled with letters from Georgia, Florida, Mississippi, Tennessee, Arkansas, and other southern states that report widespread instances of coerced black labor. These letters describe black workers being whipped and beaten and generally treated like slaves. Some letters report that blacks who showed resistance were killed and their bodies dumped in rivers. In 1927, the great Mississippi River flood revealed the extent to which peonage practices remained prevalent in the delta region, as unaccustomed federal intervention, in the form of refugee camps administered by the Red Cross with assistance from national guardsmen, both exposed and reinforced planters' control over their tenants. When the amount of southern peonage later declined, economic and social changes ignited by the accelerating black migration to the North, the New Deal, and World War II probably played a larger role than did judicial intervention.[70]

TRANSPORTATION

McCabe almost certainly had no effect on railroad accommodations for southern blacks. The Constitution, as interpreted by the Court, only required that state law not authorize inequality. Actual railroad conditions were governed not by the Constitution but by the common law of common carriers, state statutes providing for separate but equal, and the Interstate Commerce Act's prohibition on "undue or unreasonable prejudice or disadvantage." Common-law challenges to racially unequal railroad accommodations had frequently succeeded through the mid-1880s, but such cases virtually disappeared thereafter. Similarly, the Interstate Commerce Commission (ICC) had challenged racial discrimination on railroads in the late 1880s, though the absence of effective enforcement mechanisms meant that railroad practices changed little. By the Progressive Era, the ICC, while still requiring formal equality, largely deferred to denials of discrimination by southern railroads. Finally, black litigants, who rightly suspected an inhospitable forum, apparently never challenged racial inequalities in railroad accommodations under state separate-but-equal statutes. One lesson of *McCabe* was that so long as legislatures refrained from codifying inequality, railroads had great leeway in how they treated black passengers.[71]

Freed from meaningful legal constraints, southern railroads provided black passengers with accommodations that were anything but equal. Blacks willing to pay for first-class Pullman accommodations were frequently denied access. Those who were seated were sometimes later evicted by whites threatening physical violence. Conditions in Jim Crow cars were so vile that their elimination frequently led the list of blacks' demands for racial reform. The NAACP called the cars "a nightmare of discomfort, insecurity and insult." Railroad cars allocated to blacks were "stifling with the odor of decayed fruit," seats were filthy, and the air was "fetid." White passengers entered Jim Crow cars to smoke, drink, and antagonize black passengers. "[C]onvicts and insane people" were relegated to these cars. Such conditions plainly violated state law—and with regard to interstate travel, they violated federal law as well—yet they prevailed throughout the South and generally did not prompt legal challenges.[72]

Several legal historians have treated *McCabe* as important, less for its substantive impact on railroad accommodations than for its doctrinal implications. On this view, the justices' treatment of equal protection rights as "personal" rather than "group" rights logically implied the demise of segregation, not just separate and *un*equal. One leading authority observes that *McCabe's* rationale "had potentially monumental consequences," and another calls it "the first step toward dismantling" *Plessy*. Indeed, subsequent Court decisions did invoke the personal-rights dictum of *McCabe* to invalidate both a state scheme for educating black lawyers out of state and the judicial enforcement of racially restrictive covenants on land.[73]

That subsequent civil rights rulings quoted *McCabe* does not prove that it played any role in their outcome. The personal-rights dictum had logical implications that the justices in 1914 plainly rejected. If equal protection rights belonged to persons rather than to groups, then individual blacks should have been entitled to the same opportunities as individual whites, not just those that were equivalent for the races considered as a whole. Segregation was inconsistent with this understanding, yet the justices in 1914 were not about to reconsider *Plessy*. Though *McCabe* refrained from expressly endorsing *Plessy*, the justices noted that there was "no reason to doubt the correctness" of the lower court's rejection of the segregation challenge on the basis of *Plessy*. As late as 1927, the justices seemed to regard public school segregation as obviously permissible.[74]

For decades after *McCabe*, the justices proved unwilling to accept the logical implications of the personal-rights dictum. Only changes in the social and political context of race relations around World War II induced them to begin viewing segregation as inconsistent with personal rights to equal protection. Perhaps the availability of *McCabe*'s dictum helped later justices translate their more egalitarian inclinations into legal holdings. Alternatively, these more racially progressive justices might have simply invented the personal-rights conception, regardless of *McCabe*. Indeed, as *McCabe* had invented it, why could not subsequent justices have done so? As we shall see, as the justices became more egalitarian, their legal creativity expanded. Civil rights rulings during and after World War II frequently required not just creative reconfiguration of old doctrines but sometimes the flat overruling of prior decisions. The justices rarely hesitated to overrule precedents once they had become sufficiently committed to racial equality.

RESIDENTIAL SEGREGATION

Many contemporaries deemed *Buchanan* momentous. The *Nation* called it "vitally important," and Moorfield Storey, author of the NAACP's brief, considered *Buchanan* "the most important decision" since *Dred Scott*. Many modern commentators have endorsed this view, even suggesting that had *Buchanan* come out the other way, racial apartheid might have swept the South. In support, they note that many southern cities were awaiting the ruling before adopting their own segregation ordinances.[75]

Yet, *Buchanan* notwithstanding, urban housing became vastly more segregated. In the Deep South, legal regulation was plainly unnecessary to maintain residential segregation. Blacks in cities such as Birmingham, Alabama, knew better than to enter white neighborhoods uninvited. As one southern newspaper put it, "There may be no written law saying where a Negro shall live and where a white man shall live, but in a white man's town there need be no law, because the Negroes cannot mix with the whites." In cities in the border states and the peripheral South, where residential segre-

FIGURE 2.1
Moorfield Storey, the first
president of the NAACP, who
argued and briefed some of
the association's first cases in
the Supreme Court. (*Library
of Congress, Prints and
Photographs Division, Visual
Materials from the NAACP
Records*)

gation ordinances had been invalidated, no desegregation occurred. In
northern cities, such as Chicago and New York, where such ordinances were
never seriously contemplated, residential segregation dramatically increased
in the 1910s and 1920s, owing to the Great Migration.

Southern newspapers had predicted after *Buchanan* that residential
segregation would be unaffected, because public sentiment could segregate
as effectively as law. Awareness that legal regulation was unnecessary to
maintain residential segregation may explain why southern courts generally
complied with *Buchanan*. By 1917, white southerners had become adept at
disfranchising blacks despite the Fifteenth Amendment, excluding them
from juries despite *Strauder*, and diverting black education funds despite
state constitutional provisions and court rulings guaranteeing equality.
Small wonder that southern whites could accept *Buchanan* so calmly,
secure in the knowledge that the Court had invalidated "an ordinance, not
a system," and that residential segregation would be maintained "by custom, if not by law."[76]

Why were residential segregation ordinances enacted if they were
unnecessary to maintain segregated housing? To some extent, such ordi-

nances, like disfranchisement amendments and railroad segregation laws, were attributable more to politicians seeking votes than to genuine threats of integration. A single black family's entrance into a white neighborhood could rivet public attention and create an irresistible opportunity for ambitious politicians. Once someone proposed extending segregation to a new sphere of life, the incentives of politicians were skewed toward jumping on the bandwagon. This explains why some of the first cities to adopt these ordinances were already the most segregated. As Booker T. Washington noted:

> After such ordinances have been introduced it is always difficult, in the present state of public opinion in the South, to have any considerable body of white people oppose them, because their attitude is likely to be misrepresented as favoring negroes against white people. They are . . . afraid of the stigma, "nigger lover."[77]

Even to the extent that these ordinances were responsive to genuine threats of integration, alternative methods of maintaining segregation were generally available. Some alternatives involved public action, some private action, and some challenged the coherence of the public-private distinction. Ethnic and racial minorities have historically had good reasons, not just fear of threatened violence, for congregating together in neighborhoods. Yet private choice alone cannot account for failed black efforts to escape ghettos. Racially restrictive covenants may have played some role in segregating the races. Virtually every relevant court decision until 1948 upheld judicial enforcement of such covenants, which appeared in large numbers around the same time as residential segregation ordinances. Formal and informal agreements among real estate agents also prevented blacks from entering white neighborhoods. City-planning officials surreptitiously zoned by race, despite *Buchanan*. Residential segregation was also maintained through use-restriction zoning, urban renewal and relocation, placement of public housing and schools, and use of highways to separate neighborhoods. Litigation challenging racially motivated but facially neutral zoning generally failed. Furthermore, banks would rarely lend to blacks who sought admission to white neighborhoods. Discriminatory federal lending policy also excluded blacks from white neighborhoods, while it encouraged white flight to suburbs.[78]

Working-class whites, more threatened by black job competition and more dependent on home investments, did not resort to legal devices, such as restrictive covenants, to maintain segregation but instead used force. Black families entering white neighborhoods frequently faced mob violence, bombing, and other physical harassment. Between 1917 and 1921, Chicago had fifty-eight such bombings. Overwhelmingly white police forces almost invariably failed to protect black "intruders" or even to investigate such attacks. Blacks who defended themselves from mob assaults frequently faced arrest and prosecution. For blacks to enter white neighborhoods in southern cities was even more dangerous, because they had less political clout, and white violence was less restrained.[79]

Some commentators have suggested that even if *Buchanan* failed to prevent pervasively segregated housing patterns, it may have had broader significance. One scholar argues that *Buchanan* "cool[ed] legislative ardor for additional segregation in other areas of American life," and a respected jurist contends, "*Buchanan* was of profound importance in setting a brake to decelerate what would have been runaway racism in the United States." Yet understanding conceptually why *Buchanan* would have had this effect or showing that it did proves impossible. White southerners were generally uninhibited in pursuing their segregationist impulses, leaving it for courts to sort out which measures were constitutional. Thus, state conventions blithely adopted grandfather clauses, despite pervasive constitutional doubts. Likewise, many southern cities adopted virtually identical segregation ordinances after *Buchanan*, even though judicial invalidation was almost certain. If cities adopted obviously impermissible segregation ordinances after *Buchanan*, why would they have refrained from experimenting with novel Jim Crow measures that had not yet been judicially condemned? Indeed, the statute books reveal no trace of *Buchanan*'s supposed inhibitory effect. Jim Crow legislation expanded throughout the first half of the twentieth century. Segregation extended to new areas of life, such as restaurants, parks, and barbershops, and to new technologies, such as office elevators, taxicabs, and buses. *Buchanan* did not stem the rising tide of white supremacy.[80]

Court decisions can matter in ways other than producing concrete changes in social practices. Perhaps the civil rights victories of the Progressive Era should be seen as "more symbols of hope than effective bulwarks against the racial injustice that permeated American law." Success for any social protest movement requires convincing potential participants that its goals are feasible. Progressive Era Court victories may have been especially important in this regard because other branches of the national government and all southern state governments were so completely unresponsive to blacks' interests. At a time when the oppression of southern blacks seemed immutable, perhaps "the White Court shook the illusion that this arrangement was permanent."

This perspective may help explain why contemporary commentators took such extravagant views of the significance of Court rulings that seemed to have so little practical effect. As Oswald Garrison Villard, the grandson of the great abolitionist William Lloyd Garrison, told NAACP president Moorfield Storey, *Buchanan* was "the most hopeful thing that has happened for some time in this dark period of our country's history." Likewise, a New York newspaper thought that *Bailey* "will put the heart into the colored people." And Booker T. Washington, while conceding that *Guinn* would make no "great difference in the South" politically, thought that "[t]he moral influence of any . . . court decision that guarantees freedom must awaken confidence where [it has] been lacking."[81]

The motivational impact of Court decisions is difficult to confirm or disprove, yet some evidence supports this interpretation. *Buchanan* especially seems to have energized the NAACP, which had been instrumental to the litigation (although disaggregating the impact of *Buchanan* from that of World War I is impossible). After *Buchanan*, NAACP national membership increased from just under 10,000 to roughly 45,000. Membership in the Louisville branch rose from fewer than 100 before the ruling to more than 1,500 afterward. Thus, victories such as *Buchanan* may have both inspired blacks to believe the racial status quo was malleable and concretely benefited the litigation arm of the civil rights movement.[82]

Progressive Era litigation may have advanced civil rights in another way. Regardless of whether lawsuits produced court victories, they may have been an important form of racial protest. One precondition for defeating Jim Crow was empowering southern blacks to overcome the norms of deference and subordination that many had internalized in self-defense. Racial change would not occur without southern blacks fighting for it. Protest had to start somewhere, yet the efforts of blacks to change the caste system were undercut by the system. Political protest was unavailable, given black disfranchisement. Social protest in the form of street demonstrations would likely have incited deadly retaliation at a time when blacks were frequently lynched for less—when "the fear of physical violence brood[ed] in the air of the South." Significantly, the only direct-action protests of the early twentieth century— the boycotts of newly segregated streetcars from 1900 to 1906—were nonconfrontational, and thus protestors were largely insulated from reprisal.[83]

In such an oppressive environment, litigation offered two significant advantages. Unlike social and political protest, litigation does not require mass participation to succeed, only a single party with a winning case and the resources necessary to pursue it. In addition, Progressive Era litigation offered a relatively safe venue for challenging the racial status quo, as it occurred in courtrooms, not on streets. Courtrooms may have been the only feasible arena for civil rights protest in an era when black lynchings remained common. This is not to deny that litigation could be dangerous, but it was safer than street protest. Once undertaken, moreover, litigation could arouse the civil rights consciousness of blacks, educate them about their rights, and convince them that current arrangements were malleable. Whether successful or not, at least black litigants would not be taking their "medicine of insult, discourtesy and prejudice sitting down and saying nothing, [thereby] los[ing their] self-respect."[84]

This perspective helps explain why Progressive Era race cases came from where they did and involved the sorts of suits they did. *Guinn* and *McCabe* were from Oklahoma, *Buchanan* from Kentucky, and *Myers v. Anderson*, *Guinn*'s companion case, from Maryland. These border states had institutionalized Jim Crow, but they also had much smaller black populations than the South, and their race relations were not nearly as antediluvian. The era's only race cases from the real South were *Bailey* and *Reynolds*, and the latter was a federal prosecution of a white man for peonage. Only *Bailey* involved a black litigant challenging racial practices in the real South, and he received financial and legal assistance from prominent whites, including a federal judge. That blacks outside the border states rarely litigated against Jim Crow suggests that street protests would have been inconceivable at this time. In most of the rural Deep South, merely establishing an NAACP branch would have jeopardized lives.[85]

Though Progressive Era litigation may have helped motivate and organize civil rights protest, two possible countervailing effects must not be ignored. First, judicial victories can have the insidious consequence of legitimizing injustice, in two different ways. Just as invalidation of a practice conveys judicial disapproval, so does implicit or explicit validation confer legitimacy. Thus, though *Guinn* condemned grandfather clauses, it explicitly approved literacy tests. Moreover, when the justices purport to solve a constitutional problem, yet the underlying grievance remains unremedied, the legitimacy of the grievance may be diminished. When residential segregation persisted after *Buchanan* had invalidated segregation ordinances, some may have reasoned that the cause could not be any constitutional violation. Had *Buchanan* not "solved" the housing segregation problem by invalidating such ordinances, perhaps more Americans would have been troubled by pervasive residential segregation.[86]

Judicial victories may also have the more concrete deleterious effect of persuading social protestors to channel energy and resources to the method that has already proven successful: litigation. Yet many objectives of the modern civil rights movement were probably beyond the capacity of courts to deliver, in two senses. First, conventional doctrinal tools seemed to constrain courts more than they did legislatures—for example, the "state action" requirement. Justices in the 1960s were unwilling to give sit-in demonstrators what they wanted: a declaration that trespass and breach-of-peace prosecutions of demonstrators protesting segregation in public accommodations were unconstitutional. By contrast, Congress created a federally protected right of access to public accommodations in the 1964 Civil Rights Act. Similarly, the justices lacked ready doctrinal tools to declare that discrimination in private employment was unconstitutional, but Congress in 1964 barred such conduct under its powers to regulate interstate commerce and to enforce the Fourteenth Amendment. Though courts creatively reinterpreted legal doctrine as the civil rights movement gained momentum, limits existed beyond which most judges declined to go. In these areas, legislation, not litigation, was essential to the movement's success.[87]

Second, even litigation victories within the reach of conventional doctrine were generally inefficacious until Congress supplied effective enforcement mechanisms. Thus, the invalidation of state-mandated school segregation in *Brown v. Board of Education* had little effect upon the South until

Congress in 1964 authorized the withholding of federal education funds from districts that continued to segregate their schools. Similarly, neither the Fifteenth Amendment nor Court decisions implementing it secured black suffrage in the Deep South until Congress in 1965 authorized the appointment of federal registrars to ensure nondiscriminatory voter enrollment. To the extent that later Court victories may have diverted scarce resources from political and social mobilization to litigation, they possibly contravened the long-term interests of the civil rights movement. In the 1910s, however, when alternative methods of protest were generally unavailable to southern blacks, litigation did not compete for scarce resources.[88]

Thus, measuring the overall consequences of race decisions from the Progressive Era is extremely complicated. Substantively, they accomplished almost nothing. As symbols of potential racial change and vehicles for mobilizing black protest, they may have been significant. Yet by implicitly legitimizing the unjust arrangements they validated and by encouraging the investment of scarce resources in litigation rather than in alternative protest strategies as they became available, one could argue that these Court victories hindered civil rights protest in the long term.

On the merits, as opposed to willingness even to confront the merits, Progressive Era rulings displayed no significant change in judicial racial attitudes. Nor did they produce significant changes in racial practices. *Guinn* blocked a transparent evasion of the Fifteenth Amendment but had no effect on black disfranchisement. *Bailey* and *Reynolds* invalidated peonage schemes that plainly violated traditional understandings of the Thirteenth Amendment and state constitutional prohibitions on imprisonment for debt, but apparently had no effect on the amount of peonage that existed. *McCabe* barred only statutory mandates of separate-and-*un*equal railroad accommodations but had no impact on actual railroad practices. Finally, *Buchanan* invalidated residential segregation ordinances because they interfered with property rights, not racial equality, and it had no effect on segregated housing patterns.[89]

At a time when white southerners could get away with lynching blacks, disfranchising them, segregating them, and coercing their labor, the Court proved a barrier to schemes that came too close to formal constitutional nullification. Yet because the justices challenged only the form, not the substance, of southern racial practices, nothing significant changed for blacks. Grandfather clauses were unnecessary: It was easy to disfranchise blacks but not illiterate whites without them. Black labor could be coerced without false-pretenses laws backed by phony presumptions. Statutes did not have to authorize separate and unequal for southern blacks to receive inferior railroad accommodations. Residential segregation ordinances were unnecessary to keep neighborhoods segregated.

The justices eventually discovered that they could make a dent in Jim Crow only by penetrating form to deal with substance. Decades later, they

began investigating legislative motive, questioning the fact findings of southern trial courts, piercing the public-private distinction, and generally questioning the good faith of southern whites. Progressive Era justices had no
inclination for such undertakings, which public opinion would not have
supported anyway. Moreover, even when subsequent Courts showed a
greater willingness to penetrate form for substance, their interventions were
only marginally effective until Congress supplied better enforcement mechanisms, including threats to withhold federal funds from those who discriminated based on race, replacing state voter registrars with federal ones, and
extending antidiscrimination rules to private actors. A Congress that would
not even consider antilynching legislation and a president who pioneered
the segregation of the federal civil service were not about to enlist in a judicial crusade against Jim Crow. With race relations reaching a post–Civil War
nadir, minimalist and inconsequential Court rulings on race were hardly a
surprise.[90]

CHAPTER THREE

The Interwar Period

In 1919, black tenant farmers and sharecroppers in Phillips County, Arkansas, tried to organize a union and to hire white lawyers to sue planters for peonage practices. Local whites cracked down with a vengeance. When whites shot into a church where black unionists were meeting, blacks returned the gunfire. A white man was killed. Mayhem quickly ensued. Marauding whites, some from adjoining states, supported by federal troops ostensibly dispatched to quell the disturbance, went on a rampage. They tracked down blacks throughout the countryside and killed dozens of them. Seventy-nine blacks, and no whites, were prosecuted and convicted for their actions during this "race riot," and twelve received the death penalty. The trials of those twelve lasted only an hour or two each, and the juries, from which blacks had been systematically excluded, deliberated for only a few minutes. Huge mobs of angry whites surrounded the courthouse, menacing the defendants and the jurors and threatening a lynching. Six of the defendants appealed their death sentences to the Supreme Court, arguing that mob-dominated trials violate the Due Process Clause of the Fourteenth Amendment.[1]

Between the First and Second World Wars, the justices decided four kinds of cases involving race and the Constitution. In landmark rulings, the Court created new procedural rights in criminal cases and reversed the convictions of blacks who had been egregiously mistreated by the criminal justice system in the South. *Moore v. Dempsey* (1923), the Phillips County case, interpreted the Due Process Clause to forbid convictions obtained through mob-dominated trials. *Powell v. Alabama* (1932) ruled that the Fourteenth Amendment required states to provide lawyers for indigent defendants in capital cases, and it overturned convictions where counsel had been appointed only on the morning of trial. *Norris v. Alabama* (1935) reversed convictions where blacks had been deliberately excluded from juries and revised subconstitutional rules that had previously made such claims nearly impossible to prove. *Brown v. Mississippi* (1936) construed the Due Process Clause to forbid convictions based on confessions extracted through torture.

In the voting rights area, the Court resolved several challenges to southern schemes that barred blacks from participating in Democratic primaries. After invalidating two permutations of the white primary in *Nixon v. Herndon* (1927) and *Nixon v. Condon* (1932), the justices in *Grovey v. Townsend* (1935) upheld the exclusion of blacks by the resolution of a party convention, finding no state action under the Fourteenth Amendment. *Breedlove v. Suttles* (1937) rejected a constitutional challenge to the poll tax.

With regard to housing, the Court twice invalidated residential segregation ordinances, rejecting invitations to limit or overrule *Buchanan v. Warley* (1917). However, *Corrigan v. Buckley* (1926) dismissed a challenge to racially restrictive covenants and strongly hinted that judicial enforcement of such agreements was not state action under the Fourteenth Amendment.

Finally, with regard to education, the decision in *Gong Lum v. Rice* (1927) unanimously rejected a challenge to Mississippi's placement of Chinese-American students in black public schools rather than in white ones. *Missouri ex rel. Gaines v. Canada* (1938) invalidated a state law that provided blacks who wished to pursue graduate or professional education with scholarships to attend universities outside the state.

These interwar race decisions were a mixed bag, and the victories cannot be understood as minimalist constitutionalism. Several decisions made new law in protecting black rights. Yet the advances were limited. The justices were willing to intervene against the worst abuses of Jim Crow, such as the willingness to execute innocent blacks who were convicted on the basis of tortured confessions in farcical trials. They were less inclined to challenge the more routine but fundamental aspects of white supremacy, such as segregation and disfranchisement, which emerged from this period mostly unscathed. The Court also made only slight advances in state-action doctrine, which ultimately would prove a formidable obstacle to transforming the constitutional law of race.

The interwar Court advanced at roughly the same pace as the rest of the nation. The 1930s marked a racial turning point, as attitudes and practices became more progressive for the first time since Reconstruction. Yet progress was minimal as compared with the forward movement that would occur during and after World War II.

Extralegal forces connected with World War I helped transform American race relations, but their impact was gradual, not immediate. One momentous factor was southern black migration, which had been increasing slowly in the last decade of the nineteenth century and the first decade of the twentieth but which exploded in 1916 as a result of the war. Forces pushing blacks from the South—boll weevils, falling cotton prices, disfranchisement, peonage, and lynchings—had long been present. World War I added a crucial pull factor. The Wilson administration's preparedness campaign created industrial labor shortages just as submarine warfare curtailed European immigration, which declined from 1.2 million in 1914 to 111,000 in 1918. For the first time, blacks enjoyed significant industrial employment opportunities in northern cities. A half million southern blacks migrated in the 1910s, and another million in the 1920s, aided by the enactment of restrictive immigration legislation soon after the war. Between 1910 and 1930, New York's black population increased from 91,000 to 327,000, Chicago's from 44,000 to 233,000, and Detroit's from 5,700 to 120,000.[2]

It is true that the Great Migration had some deleterious consequences for race relations. Northern whites tended to become more prejudiced as black numbers increased, as shown by the numerous urban race riots during and after World War I. Yet the migration's contribution to progressive racial change was substantial. As the NAACP noted, "[T]he greatest significance of this migration is the increased political power of black men in America," as they relocated from a region of pervasive disfranchisement to one that extended the suffrage without racial restriction. Moreover, northern blacks often held the balance of power between competitive political parties, especially after the New Deal electoral realignment reinvigorated northern Democrats and liberated blacks from historical tendencies to vote solidly Republican. In Chicago, blacks reaped rewards from providing the margin of victory for Republican mayor "Big Bill" Thompson, including civil service positions proportionate to their share of the population, black police officers, integration of public schools, and mayoral criticism of discrimination in public accommodations. Chicago elected a black state senator in 1914 and a black alderman in 1915. The growing political power of blacks in New York City translated into black policemen and firemen, access for black doctors to Harlem Hospital and a training school for black nurses, the first black National Guard unit, playgrounds and parks for the black community, and black legislators and judges.[3]

Not long thereafter, blacks began influencing national politics, often supporting civil rights bills designed to improve conditions for southern blacks. The first such instance was in 1918 when a Republican congressman from St. Louis, Leonidas C. Dyer, who represented a large black constituency, introduced antilynching legislation, which passed the House in 1922 but was filibustered to death in the Senate. By 1928, Chicago had a black congressman, Oscar DePriest. In 1930, black political power contributed to the Senate's defeat of Judge John Parker's nomination to the U.S. Supreme Court. Blacks opposed Parker because of statements he had made opposing black suffrage in a North Carolina gubernatorial contest ten years earlier. Contemporaries viewed Parker's defeat as "the first national demonstration of the Negro's power since Reconstruction days." After the New Deal's reconfiguration of national politics, both parties aggressively pursued black votes in 1936, leading *Time* to call that year's presidential election the most "Negro-minded" since 1860.[4]

The principal inspiration for the Great Migration was better job opportunities in the North. Rising economic status facilitated social protest. A larger black population provided a broader economic base for black entrepreneurs and professionals, such as teachers, ministers, lawyers, and doctors—groups that later supplied resources and leadership for civil rights protest. Participation in protest movements generally requires some economic independence—which most southern blacks lacked—as well as disposable income and leisure time. Improved economic status also enabled blacks to use boycotts as levers for social change, beginning with the "don't shop where you can't work" campaigns of the 1930s. Finally, black economic advancement helped break the vicious circle of race discrimination, whereby poverty fueled prejudice, which reinforced poverty.[5]

Northern migration resulted in better education, which also facilitated subsequent social protest. Educated people can better discover or imagine different social arrangements, and most successful protest movements have had an educated leadership. In the South, white opinion opposed equal black education; black schools were obscenely underfunded; and black secondary education was almost nonexistent. In the North, by contrast, political and business elites valued education for everyone, and black migrants took advantage of greater educational opportunities.[6]

In addition, more flexible racial mores in the North permitted challenges to the status quo that would not have been tolerated in the South. Northern blacks voted and ordinarily enjoyed basic civil rights, such as protection from lynching. In the North, a "[black] man could feel more like a man," and thus blacks were less likely to internalize racist norms of black subordination and inferiority, which posed major obstacles to creating a racial protest movement in the South. Southern whites did not tolerate black militancy, such as that voiced in the *Chicago Defender*, the nation's leading black newspaper. Only in the North could a protest organization such as the NAACP develop and thrive. The association had virtually no southern branches until World War I and even then only in the largest cities, where vicious postwar violence quickly shut them down. Only a national organization could force southern racial change—through legislation or litigation—

as southern white supremacy was too pervasive and ruthless to permit effective internal challenge.[7]

Northern migration also brought blacks to the attention of national elites. In an era of relatively primitive communications — no radio or television and few national news magazines — rural southern blacks could be disfranchised, coerced in their labor, cheated out of public school funds, and even lynched — all without most northern whites even being aware of what was happening. As northern black populations grew, race became more salient to national policy makers. Riots in northern cities from 1917 to 1919, resulting from increased racial tension over jobs and housing, forced race issues upon the national consciousness to the highest degree since Reconstruction. James Weldon Johnson of the NAACP thought the riots, though "regrettable, . . . mark[ed] the turning point in the psychology of the whole nation regarding the Negro problem." After the Great Migration, most Americans recognized, as President Warren G. Harding reminded them in 1921, that race was now a national issue, no longer merely a sectional one.[8]

Finally, northern migration may have marginally tempered the oppression of southern blacks. Most southern whites were happy to see blacks go, but some — especially planters — were not. Thus, the black exodus induced southern cities and states to promise, and occasionally deliver, ameliorative policies, such as antilynching laws, increased educational spending, higher agricultural wages, and fairer legal treatment. One observer reported, with some exaggeration, that "[c]olored people in those states had never experienced such collective good will, and many of them were so grateful and happy that they actually prayed for the prolongation of the war."[9]

Before southern blacks migrated north, they moved from farms to cities within the South, also largely for economic reasons. (So did whites.) Black migration to southern cities was also at an early stage in the 1910s, though it was further advanced than was migration to the North. The populations of Atlanta and Richmond — black and white — doubled between 1900 and 1920, and Birmingham's increased nearly fivefold. Although the South remained predominantly rural, its urbanization rate was greater than that of the rest of the country. The percentage of southern blacks who lived in cities rose from 6.7 percent in 1860 to 22 percent in 1910 and to 37.3 percent in 1940.[10]

Southern black urbanization greatly affected race relations. Better economic opportunities eventually fostered a black middle class, which capitalized on the segregated economy to develop sufficient wealth and leisure time to participate in social protest. Many urban blacks were economically independent of whites and thus could challenge the racial status quo without endangering their livelihoods. Economic clout could be leveraged into social change, as when thousands of blacks in Jacksonville, Florida, in 1920 canceled insurance policies with a company whose agents had led a lynch mob. Urban blacks were better educated, because employers and merchants valued black literacy. Into the 1930s, almost all black high schools in the South were in large cities.[11]

Urbanization also enhanced black political power, as suffrage restrictions were less stringently applied in the cities. Even at the peak of disfranchisement, several hundred blacks voted in Richmond and Atlanta. By the late 1930s, thousands were registered in the large cities of the peripheral South, such as Miami. Even though the white primary excluded them from state and national contests, blacks voted in and occasionally influenced the outcome of nonpartisan municipal elections and bond referenda. Urban blacks were also freer to participate in other forms of protest. Racial etiquette in the cities was somewhat less oppressive, partly because close personal supervision and discipline were difficult to maintain. Lynchings had always been mainly a rural phenomenon. Southern NAACP branches were almost entirely restricted to larger cities until World War II. Finally, urbanization reduced collective-action barriers to social protest. Urban blacks lived closer to one another, enjoyed better communication and transportation, and shared social networks—such as black colleges and churches—that helped overcome the organizational obstacles confronting any social protest movement.[12]

Southern blacks had made huge educational advances by World War I. Illiteracy rates for southern blacks aged ten and over fell from 76.2 percent in 1880 to 26 percent in 1920. Moorfield Storey, the Boston Brahmin who served as NAACP president and appellate advocate, observed, with regard to black literacy, that "[n]o race in the history of the world to my knowledge has made such progress from such beginnings in so short a time." After World War I, black secondary and college education in the South continued to progress "at a breath-taking rate." The number of public high schools for blacks in the South rose from about 100 in 1915 to 1,000 in 1930. In 1900, only about 1,000 blacks attended college in the United States, but by 1930 roughly 20,000 did. Black literacy was important for several reasons: Effective social protest usually requires educated leadership; educated people are likelier to resist subordinate caste status; literacy facilitates the coordination of social protest; and black education reduced observable racial differences that had been used to justify segregation and disfranchisement.[13]

The South's transition from a rural, preindustrial, premodern society fueled other forces for racial change. By the 1910s, the annual number of southern lynchings had decreased significantly, and the number of politicians and newspapers condemning the practice had increased. On one view, lynchings depended on weak social controls—a condition that was inconsistent with the urbanization and industrialization slowly penetrating the South. Reduced violence opened greater space for social protest. In addition, whereas in 1900 no regionwide organization of whites committed to ameliorating the plight of blacks existed, in 1912 the Southern Sociological Congress (SSC) was founded in Nashville with the goals, among others, of promoting interracial understanding and securing "fair play and fair dealing" for blacks. The SSC, composed mostly of liberal whites, conducted interracial meetings, condemned lynching and peonage, and advocated improvements in black education and legal treatment. Some thought its founding "the inauguration of a new era in the history of the South." The better-known spiritual descendant of the SSC, the Commission on Interracial Cooperation (CIC), sought to educate whites about the atrocious living conditions endured by most southern blacks without challenging segregation or disfranchisement. The CIC was founded in 1919, and within a year roughly 500 interracial committees operated in the South under its auspices.[14]

World War I also had more immediate implications for race relations, including the ideological ramifications of a "war to make the world safe for democracy." W. E. B. Du Bois of the NAACP wrote in 1919: "Make way for Democracy! We saved it in France, and by the Great Jehovah, we will save it in the United States of America, or know the reason why." Black journalist William Monroe Trotter urged Americans to focus less on making Europe safe for democracy and more on "making the south safe for the Negroes." Black soldiers serving in France were accepted and esteemed in ways alien to Jim Crow America, and some demanded better treatment upon their return. Military service also afforded blacks greater economic opportunities, as did wartime labor scarcity for those who remained at home.[15]

The war inspired civil rights militancy. Blacks who had set aside their "special grievances" and "closed ranks" with whites, borne arms for their country, and faced death on the battlefield were not hesitant about asserting their rights. Du Bois wrote, "[W]e are cowards and jackasses if now that that war is over, we do not marshal every ounce of our brain and brawn to fight a sterner, longer, more unbending battle against the forces of hell in our own land." A black journalist noted, "The men who did not fear the trained veterans of Germany will hardly run from the lawless Ku Klux Klan." Black troops in Houston refused to be segregated in streetcars or restaurants, and their unwillingness to suffer insults and brutality from white police officers triggered a bloody race riot in 1917. Returning black soldiers were treated as heroes in the black community, spoke to NAACP branches about their experiences, and demanded voting rights. If they were good enough to risk their lives on the battlefield, why were they not good enough to vote?[16]

Heightened black militancy proved an enormous boon to the NAACP. National membership increased from roughly 10,000 in April 1917 to 44,000 in 1918 and 91,000 in 1919. Many new southern branches were formed. The war provided the occasion for the NAACP to urge (successfully) that President Wilson condemn lynching and (unsuccessfully) that the national government abolish railroad segregation for black servicemen. Several branches outside of the South convinced cities to ban the white supremacist film *Birth of a Nation*, and others—mainly in peripheral South cities but also in Atlanta and Birmingham—conducted successful voter registration drives. The extent of black militancy was evident in the ferocity of the southern white backlash, which included an increase in the number of lynchings— from thirty-six in 1917 to sixty in 1918 and to seventy-six in 1919.[17]

Although the forces just described eventually created background conditions that facilitated civil rights protest, the changes were neither rapid nor unidirectional. The Great Migration eventually enhanced black political and economic power, but in the short term it generated interracial friction over jobs and housing, greater discrimination in public accommodations and schools, frequent bombings of black homes in white neighborhoods, and several deadly race riots during and after World War I. Moreover, as late as 1940, more than three-fourths of American blacks still lived in the South, where they were subject to formal segregation, disfranchisement, Jim Crow justice, and occasional lynchings. The urbanization of southern blacks, which eventually facilitated social protest, immediately aggravated interracial tension over housing and employment and produced white demands for residential segregation ordinances and efforts to recapture "black jobs." Moreover, despite the accelerated pace of urbanization, three-fourths of all southerners were still rural dwellers in 1920. Finally, though the First World War had egalitarian ideological and material consequences, it also incited a furious white backlash. Fearful that returning black soldiers would launch a social revolution, southern whites prepared for a race war. The Ku Klux Klan began riding again through the South, warning blacks not to "get any new-fangled ideas about democracy." Black soldiers were assaulted, forced to shed their uniforms, and sometimes lynched. In Orange County, Florida, thirty blacks were burned to death in 1920 because one black man had attempted to vote. White violence succeeded in suppressing incipient black protest and quickly restored racial "normalcy" to the South.[18]

Whatever the long-term trends, the immediate prospects for American blacks were bleak in the 1920s, as revealed by snapshots of American race relations in the North, in the South, and at the national level. Black migration to the North fed the racial prejudice of northern whites. Northern blacks were more likely to be excluded from public accommodations in the 1920s than previously, and in 1925 the NAACP noted "a distinct movement towards segregation in public schools in Northern states." Even formerly egalitarian institutions, such as Oberlin and Harvard, now segregated black students in dormitories. Most northern whites did not easily tolerate blacks moving into their neighborhoods, and they resisted through racially restrictive covenants, hostile neighborhood associations, economic pressure, and violence. The NAACP's biggest case in the 1920s involved defending Dr. Ossian Sweet, a black doctor from Detroit, and several family members, who were charged with murder for allegedly killing a member of a mob that was attacking their home in a white neighborhood. Whether attributable to legal or extralegal causes, northern residential segregation increased dramatically in the 1920s. Housing segregation meant school segregation, even if authorities did not gerrymander attendance zones or use discriminatory transfer policies, as they frequently did. The influx of white southerners to northern cities exacerbated racial tensions, contributing to the political successes of the Ku Klux Klan in several northern and western states in the early 1920s. Klan members on the Springfield, Ohio, school board succeeded in securing segregation. In Indianapolis, a Klan-dominated city council segregated schools in 1922 and neighborhoods in 1926. The Klan tried to persuade several northern legislatures to pass antimiscegenation laws.[19]

Northern blacks also faced pervasive economic discrimination. Many blacks retained industrial jobs first opened to them during the war, but these remained the least skilled and lowest paying, with little opportunity for advancement. Outside of industries such as meatpacking, iron and steel, and automobile production, most decent jobs remained unavailable. Telephone and other utility companies generally refused to hire blacks, and department stores rejected black clerks. Most northern labor unions continued to exclude blacks.[20]

Southern blacks had it much worse. Agriculture was in severe crisis in the 1920s. Cotton prices collapsed after the war and remained low for the next decade. Black sharecroppers and tenant farmers, usually dependent on cotton production, were hit the hardest. Black farm ownership peaked around 1910 and declined steadily thereafter. Skilled black laborers also lost ground. Most southern unions, which became more powerful in the 1920s, excluded blacks. Unions secured legislation that required that plumbers and electricians be licensed—measures that proved effective at excluding blacks. On the railroads, black firemen lost jobs through a terrorist campaign that killed dozens. Whites also reclaimed traditionally black occupations, such as waiter, barber, elevator operator, and hotel bellman. Technological advances eliminated other job opportunities, partly because blacks were excluded from skills training. As garage mechanics replaced blacksmiths, and commercial laundries and home washing machines replaced laundresses, blacks lost jobs. New industries, such as textiles, oil and gas, and furniture production excluded blacks from the outset, except for the most menial tasks.[21]

The civil rights outlook for southern blacks was equally bleak. At a time when racial disparities within a supposedly separate-but-equal system were enormous and went largely unchallenged, litigation against segregation seemed all but inconceivable. Many southern counties with large black populations did not provide black high schools until the 1930s, and the huge racial disparities in per capita educational spending that arose during the Progressive Era remained constant or even increased slightly in the 1920s. In 1925–1926, South Carolina spent $80.55 per capita for white students and $10.20 for blacks; for school transportation, the state spent $471,489 for whites and $795 for blacks. With regard to parks, playgrounds, and beaches, separate but equal frequently meant blacks got nothing. Southern white "liberals" limited their racial agenda to enacting state (but not federal) antilynching legislation, making the legal system fairer for blacks, reducing disparities in education spending, and securing minimal public services for blacks. Almost no southern whites were yet prepared to challenge segregation. Indeed, segregation legislation proliferated in the 1920s.[22]

The NAACP was anemic in the South. The postwar white backlash destroyed many new southern branches and drastically curtailed membership. When the national secretary, John Shillady, traveled to Austin, Texas, in 1919 to defend a beleaguered branch from state legal harassment, a white mob, which included public officials, "beat him nearly into unconsciousness," causing injuries severe enough to force him to resign. NAACP membership in the state declined from 7,700 in 1919 to 1,100 in 1921, and all but seven of thirty-three branches closed. Even southern branches that survived this postwar onslaught frequently became dormant later. At one point in the 1920s, every Alabama branch was declared inactive. The Birmingham secretary attributed his branch's dormancy to the "reign of terrorism" inflicted by the Ku Klux Klan, which had an estimated 15,000 members in that city. In parts of the South, black leaders were still afraid to be seen talking with NAACP officials. Yet, even in more tolerant Virginia, national secretary Walter White found the Richmond branch "absolutely dead" in 1929, and Norfolk's black newspaper that same year decried as "cause for shame" the "scant support" black Virginians gave the NAACP.[23]

The outlook for blacks was little better at the national level. The racial policies of Republican administrations in the 1920s were no improvement on Woodrow Wilson's. Although President Harding urged federal anti-lynching legislation in 1921 and the House passed such a bill in 1922, Republicans abandoned the notion after the bill was killed "by the determined filibuster of Southern senators and the apathy and cowardice of certain Republicans." Nor did Republican administrations try to enforce section 2 of the Fourteenth Amendment to remedy black disfranchisement. They did not curtail segregation and discrimination in the federal civil service; they did not appoint blacks to patronage positions from which Wilson had removed them; they did not support black factions in struggles for control of southern Republican parties; and they did not fulfill campaign promises to remove federal troops from the black nation of Haiti. Early on, Harding gave a publicized speech in Birmingham in which he unequivocally rejected social equality among the races—that is, integration. At least Harding was cordial to black leaders and reasonably friendly in public remarks. His successor, Calvin Coolidge, was neither. Of the three main presidential candidates in 1924, only Coolidge declined to repudiate the Ku Klux Klan. The NAACP's journal, the Crisis, told readers that year, "Republican presidents are just about as bad as Democratic and Democratic presidents are little better than nothing." Robert La Follette and his Progressive party, though adopting "one of the best programs ever laid down by a political party in America," had "inexcusabl[y] . . . dodg[ed] two tremendous issues—the Ku Klux Klan and the Negro." The year 1928 was no better, as both major parties and their candidates maintained an "intense and dramatic silence" on the race issue. The NAACP called it "the most humiliating presidential campaign" that blacks had endured. Republican racial policy had become so regressive that five southern states voted Republican that year for the first time in decades, in reaction against a Democrat, Al Smith, who was Catholic, urban, ethnic, and anti-Prohibition. Some black leaders concluded that it did not matter "a tinker's damn" who won that election. The victor, Herbert Hoover, was even more aggressive in bolstering the lily-white factions of southern Republican parties in an effort to exclude blacks. In 1930, he nominated to the Supreme Court North Carolinian John Parker, who had endorsed black disfranchisement ten years earlier. During his presidency, Hoover never spoke out against disfranchisement, peonage, or lynching. When he ran for reelection, Du Bois called him "the man in the lily white house."[24]

As the 1930s began, prospects for progressive racial change were about as bleak as at any time since the Civil War. By 1940, however, significant change appeared to be in the offing. The decade that began with black hopelessness ended with an optimism unmatched since Reconstruction.[25]

The Great Depression left blacks, who occupied the bottom rung on the economic ladder, in worse condition than ever. Whites reclaimed more "black jobs," such as street cleaning and garbage collecting. With white unemployment high, no black job was safe. In 1930, Atlanta whites proclaimed, "No Jobs for Niggers until Every White Man Has a Job." The terrorist campaign against black railroad firemen intensified, and at least ten more were murdered in the early 1930s. Roughly half of all urban blacks, South and North, were unemployed in 1932. Even on the relief rolls, southern blacks faced systematic discrimination. Black banks and other businesses failed at alarming rates. Economic turmoil among whites exacerbated racial tensions, and the number of southern blacks lynched increased significantly in the early 1930s.[26]

The NAACP was nearly bankrupt and vulnerable to criticism from the Left. As most blacks struggled to put food on the table, the association's traditional focus on desegregating streetcars and theaters seemed frivolous. Black intellectuals, such as Ralph Bunche and E. Franklin Frazier, criticized the NAACP for ignoring most blacks' concerns and urged greater attention to interracial labor organizing. The National Negro Congress and the Communist party threatened to coopt the NAACP's northern urban constituency by supporting direct action, including rent strikes and economic boycotts designed to pressure ghetto shopkeepers to hire blacks. In response, the association began to emphasize economic issues, devoting greater attention to black jobs, fair administration of relief programs, and interracial unionism through the Congress of Industrial Organizations (CIO). The NAACP's financial turmoil resulted from its dependency on membership dues, which about half its members stopped paying during the depression. A Garland Fund grant of $100,000 to the association in 1930 largely evaporated in the stock market crash. Financial conditions were so dire that NAACP officials considered suspending publication of its journal, the *Crisis*. Funding shortages and staff cutbacks curbed litigation efforts. The association suffered from such "severe financial strain" that it had to condition involvement in litigation upon lawyers reducing their usual fees and to insist that local branches finance their own lawsuits.[27]

The 1932 presidential election offered little reason for optimism. Fewer black delegates attended this Republican National Convention than any in the century, and the party platform made no pledges regarding race, abandoning even nominal support for federal antilynching legislation. Democrats were even worse. No regular black delegates attended their convention; the party platform ignored race entirely; and most black leaders were wary of the party's presidential nominee, Franklin D. Roosevelt. Roosevelt's personal and political background showed no solicitude for the interests of blacks, and he had alienated many blacks with his boast as vice-presidential candidate in 1920 that he had written Haiti's constitution. Roosevelt had strong southern ties as a result of his long stays at Warm Springs, Georgia, for polio treatment. His vice-presidential running mate, John Nance Garner of Texas, was anathema to blacks. Despite widespread disaffection among blacks, Hoover won roughly 70 percent of black votes in 1932, as the lesser of two evils. Democrats won huge majorities in Congress, which put southerners in charge of committees, as they had been during Wilson's first term. Roosevelt had neither the inclination nor the capacity to challenge southern Democrats on civil rights issues, such as antilynching legislation, because he required their support on economic matters. His Justice Department refused to investigate lynchings or to support challenges by southern blacks to their exclusion from Democratic primaries. Most cabinet members, except Interior secretary Harold Ickes, were preoccupied with economic recovery and uninterested in race.[28]

Race discrimination pervaded the first New Deal. Recovery programs, though facially nondiscriminatory, were administered locally, which in the South meant by whites who generally ignored the interests of disfranchised blacks. The minimum-wage and maximum-hour provisions of the National Industrial Recovery Act benefited blacks little, as traditionally black occupations, such as domestic work, were excluded from coverage. Where blacks were included, many of them lost jobs, because whites generally would not hire blacks if they were legally required to pay equal wages. Black farmers were denied their fair share of crop-reduction benefits under the Agricultural Adjustment Act (AAA), because white planters dominated local administrative committees, and the Agriculture Department refused to challenge them. Tens of thousands of southern blacks were driven from farms by the AAA, which provided incentives for planters to reduce workforces. Southern blacks were shortchanged in the administration of relief projects and were segregated in the southern work camps of the Civilian Conservation Corps and in workers' housing at Tennessee Valley Authority job sites. Public housing built with funds from the Public Works Administration (PWA) maintained segregated residential patterns.

An administration critic noted in 1934 that "[w]hatever the New Deal has done for the white workman, it seems to have done less than nothing for the Negro."[29]

Yet, quite unintentionally, the New Deal proved a turning point in American race relations. Its objective was to help poor people, and blacks, as the poorest of the poor, benefited disproportionately. Perhaps more important was its racial symbolism. However discriminatory its administration, the New Deal at least included blacks within its pool of beneficiaries—a development sufficient to raise black hopes and expectations after decades of malign neglect from Washington. Another important symbol was Roosevelt's appointment of a "black cabinet" of advisors within departments and agencies. Although lacking in governing authority, these appointees exercised moral suasion on behalf of the nondiscriminatory administration of programs and fair employment within agencies. They also symbolized black accomplishment and political influence. Moreover, one prominent cabinet member, Harold Ickes, was the former head of the NAACP branch in Chicago and brought progressive racial views with him to Washington. Ickes ended segregation in Interior Department cafeterias and restrooms, engineered the appointment of southern liberal Clark Foreman as a special advisor on blacks' economic status, and implemented hiring quotas in PWA construction projects.[30]

Eleanor Roosevelt was another important symbol of progressive racial change. She entered the White House without much concern for racial issues but was quickly educated through friendships with black leaders Walter White and Mary McLeod Bethune. Mrs. Roosevelt spoke to black organizations, mingled socially with blacks, served as an intermediary between black leaders and the administration, and wrote newspaper columns criticizing discrimination and supporting civil rights legislation. Even the president, though unwilling to support such legislation, occasionally spoke out against lynching and the poll tax, which is more than most of his predecessors had done. He also displayed an unprecedented openness to blacks, inviting them to the White House, speaking at black colleges, and allowing himself to be photographed with blacks.[31]

Moreover, a few New Deal programs were generally fair to blacks. Racial quotas in PWA housing projects ensured fair job allocations, and blacks received roughly one-third of new housing units. The National Youth Administration, headed by liberal white southerner Aubrey Williams, paid equal wages and included blacks in skills training. Although blacks were cheated out of a fair share of AAA crop-reduction benefits, they voted with surprisingly little white resistance in referenda on cotton-marketing quotas—another symbolic breakthrough at a time of almost universal black disfranchisement in the South. The New Deal employed unprecedented numbers of black professional and white-collar workers. Finally, the vast expansion of national power during the New Deal would eventually enhance the federal government's ability to protect the rights of southern blacks. Yet one must not overstate the New Deal's racial progressivism. Had it posed too great a threat to the racial status quo, white southerners would never have supported the New Deal.[32]

The combination of economic inclusion and racial symbolism made Roosevelt the most popular president among blacks since Lincoln. In the 1934 congressional elections, a majority of blacks voted Democratic for the first time. With some northern states electorally competitive for the first time in a generation, and blacks no longer dependably voting Republican, both parties had incentives to appeal for black votes, which sometimes held the balance of power in critical industrial states. In 1936, national Democrats made a novel and concerted bid for black votes. Senator Robert Wagner of New York described Roosevelt as the second great emancipator, while Harold Ickes spoke of a "New Deal for Negroes." An unprecedented thirty black delegates attended the Democratic National Convention. A black minister gave the invocation, and the only black congressman, Arthur Mitchell of Chicago, delivered the welcoming address. Republicans bid for black votes with a more progressive civil rights platform, and their presidential candidate, Alf Landon, endorsed federal antilynching legislation and criticized Roosevelt's dependence on southern race-baiters. *Time* predicted that the result in several northern states would turn on black voters. A Gallup poll after the election revealed that roughly 75 percent of blacks had supported Roosevelt. This dramatic shift from 1932 confirmed the mobility of black voters, thereby strengthening both parties' incentive to woo them in the future.[33]

The Democratic party of 1936 differed fundamentally from that of 1932. Labor unions were more prominent, as were racial and religious minorities, such as Jews, Catholics, and blacks. These groups supported the New Deal primarily for economic reasons, but they shared a commitment to using national power to defend civil rights and civil liberties. Jews had essentially the same reason as blacks to oppose restrictive covenants, which often excluded them as well, and to condemn lynching, which had claimed the life of a prominent Atlanta Jew, Leo Frank, in 1915. Unions that sought to organize unskilled workers in industries that employed many blacks had obvious incentives to support civil rights, and CIO unions in the 1930s generally did so. This transformation of the Democratic coalition was evident in Roosevelt's 1936 pledge of "no forgotten men and no forgotten races." As other groups gained influence within the party, white southerners lost it. The national convention in 1936 repealed the two-thirds rule for nominating presidential candidates, which had secured southern interests for a century. After the election, southerners were less than half of the party's congressmen for the first time since the 1890s. Southerners provided 90 percent of the party's electoral votes in 1920 and 1924, but only about 25 percent in 1932 and 1936. Votes on antilynching legislation illustrate the changed Democratic coalition: In 1922, only 8 House Democrats supported it, but in 1937, 171 of 185 northern and western Democrats did so.[34]

By the second half of the 1930s, black prospects no longer seemed so bleak. Significant changes were afoot at the national level, in the North, and even in the South. The strategic importance of black voters in the North translated into federal patronage, such as Roosevelt's appointment in 1937 of the first black federal judge in U.S. history, William Hastie. Blacks began to receive more federal relief funds during Roosevelt's second term, and black journalists who had earlier criticized discrimination in relief programs seemed generally satisfied after 1936. Northern Democrats fought harder to overcome the southern filibuster against antilynching legislation in 1937–1938, as compared with the "gentlemanly tea party" of 1935.[35]

The number of black college graduates approximately doubled during Roosevelt's first administration. Elite institutions such as Harvard and less elite ones such as Howard produced many talented black lawyers in the 1920s and 1930s—for example, Charles Houston and William Hastie from the former, and Thurgood Marshall, Oliver Hill, and Spotswood Robinson from the latter. Black lawyers were symbolically important to black spectators witnessing courtroom performances, and they were more reliably committed to civil rights causes than were most white lawyers, especially in the South. In the 1910s, the NAACP had criticized "half prepared" black lawyers who argued its cases locally, and through the 1920s the association had always been represented in the Supreme Court by eminent whites, such as Moorfield Storey and Louis Marshall.[36]

Organized labor's greater support for interracial organizing and civil rights was another important force for racial progress in the 1930s. Unions, widely seen as dangerous, alien, irresponsible forces during the Progressive Era, had gained legitimacy by the time of the Roosevelt administration. The New Deal bolstered the social and economic status of organized labor by legally protecting the right to unionize. Unions affiliated with the American Federation of Labor (AFL) had traditionally excluded or segregated blacks, and the national organization deferred to member unions on race issues. A competitor appeared in 1935, the CIO, which was committed to organizing industries rather than crafts. The CIO's different focus required appealing to unskilled workers, who were disproportionately black. Excluding blacks from industrial unions would have made them a perpetual strikebreaking threat. Moreover, the few unions historically committed to racial equality, such as the United Mine Workers and the International Ladies' Garment Workers, were CIO affiliates. Several CIO leaders were ideologically committed to interracial labor organization. Most CIO affiliates did not exclude blacks, and few even segregated them into separate locals. Landmark CIO efforts to organize steelworkers, auto workers, and meatpackers in the late 1930s included interracial appeals. The CIO strongly supported civil rights initiatives, such as anti–poll-tax and antilynching legislation. The CIO's appeal to black workers forced the AFL to become more egalitarian.

Although white working-class racism remained an obstacle to progressive racial change, the rise of interracial unionism in the 1930s provided an important boost to civil rights.[37]

The demise of "scientific" theories of inherent racial differences was another important development of the 1930s. Around 1900, the vast majority of scientists believed in natural racial differences and white superiority, but those views came under attack after World War I. Within two decades, they had been almost entirely repudiated in favor of a new paradigm, which attributed racial differences to culture and environment. The changing demography of scientists partially explains this shift in perspective, as many younger researchers came from the ethnic and racial groups purportedly shown to be inferior by the older science. The Great Migration may also have been significant, as the development of a northern black middle class, educated and acculturated, altered researchers' expectations. The Great Depression, destroyer of so many paradigms, helped undermine the supposition that economic and social rank were attributable to natural ordering rather than circumstance and luck. The New Deal's reformist ideology inclined sympathetic scientists to eschew biological determinism, which denied the possibility of transformative social change. In the late 1930s, revulsion against genetic experiments by Nazi scientists bolstered the new paradigm. By 1940, few respectable scientists espoused biological explanations for observable differences in the behavior of racial groups. It is true that shifts in scientific paradigms do not immediately affect mass opinion, and even among elites, belief is not tantamount to action. Yet the groundwork had been laid for a fundamental rethinking of racial differences. Among the intellectual elite, which includes Supreme Court justices, the ideology of white supremacy had been thoroughly undermined by 1940.[38]

Southern racial attitudes and practices were also becoming slightly more progressive for the first time since Reconstruction. Black voter registration in the South increased during and after the 1936 election campaign, growing in Atlanta from roughly 1,000 in 1936 to more than 2,000 in 1939, and in Miami from 50 in 1920 to 2,000 in 1940. In a few peripheral South cities, blacks ran for local offices—and sometimes won—for the first time in generations. Some universities in North Carolina, Texas, Oklahoma, and Maryland began allowing their football teams to compete against northern schools with integrated squads, and Dallas hosted an integrated collegiate track-and-field contest. Defunct branches of the NAACP came back to life, further evidence of "a new awakening of interest in the Association in the South." Black schoolteachers in several cities, guided by the NAACP, brought pay-equalization suits. Racial disparities in education funding began slowly declining outside the Deep South, partly as a result of threatened litigation and partly because whites now had a harder time morally justifying denying equal education to blacks. By the late 1930s, many southern newspapers and the majority of white southerners, according to a Gallup poll, supported federal antilynching legislation. Several states began debating poll-tax repeal, a crucial reform for a New Deal political coalition that wished to enfranchise its natural constituency: the poor. In 1937, the CIO began an interracial unionization campaign in the South. Blacks held leadership positions in CIO locals, and white workers struck on behalf of blacks and helped them register to vote.[39]

The growing attentiveness of national Democrats to northern black voters and incipient changes in southern racial practices generated a backlash among southern whites. A few southern politicians, such as Senators Josiah Bailey of North Carolina and Harry Byrd and Carter Glass of Virginia, had always opposed the New Deal, but most had supported it, with the implicit understanding that race relations were off limits to reform. By 1936, southern political opposition to Roosevelt was growing, because of racial concerns and conservative discomfort with Roosevelt's tilt to the left in 1936. The first evidence of racial backlash was Senator "Cotton" Ed Smith's walkout from the Democratic convention in protest against the large number of black delegates and the delivery of the invocation by a black minister. The convention's revocation of the two-thirds rule for nominating presidential candidates contributed to the growing unease among white southerners. One southern newspaper declared that the New Deal had "absolved southerners from any further obligation of loyalty to a party that has betrayed its most loyal adherents." The *Charleston News & Courier* observed that Walter White of the NAACP "has the northern Democrats on their knees." Senator Glass warned of a second Reconstruction being forced upon the South, this time by Democrats. The solid support of northern Democrats for antilynching legislation in 1937–1938 confirmed these fears and inspired warnings from southern politicians that voting rights legislation would be next. When Roosevelt intervened in several southern Senate primaries in 1938 to target conservative New Deal foes, they defended themselves by playing the race card, which led to a "recrudescence of anti-Negro feeling" in those states.[40]

The anxiety of southern whites at incipient racial changes should not be exaggerated. Many criticized Smith's antics and denied anything new or sinister in northern Democrats' appeals to black voters. These skeptics charged that conservatives were manipulating race to generate opposition to the second New Deal and its redistributive tendencies. Indeed, white southerners' perceptions of racial threat do seem highly correlated with economic attitudes. Still, some southern whites sensed a genuine challenge to the established racial order—something not experienced since Populism in the 1890s—and the racial backlash was responsive to real, albeit limited, changes in racial attitudes and practices.[41]

Northern race relations were also changing in the 1930s. The New Deal inspired northern blacks to register in record numbers, which amplified the parties' incentives to respond to the concerns of blacks. Black voter registration in Philadelphia increased from roughly 70,000 in 1932 to 135,000 in 1940, even though black population growth in the city was less than 15 percent. Increased black political power produced more black officeholders and stronger public accommodations laws. Northern blacks also engaged in collective economic protest, as they organized boycotts in roughly thirty-five cities against ghetto shopkeepers who refused to hire blacks; some were successful. Blacks in several northern cities boycotted segregated schools, sometimes leading to integration. In the late 1930s, some northern churches began criticizing racial segregation and discrimination; previously exclusionary Catholic universities began admitting blacks; and New York's Catholic parochial schools began to integrate.[42]

By 1940, blacks had greater reason for optimism than at any time since Reconstruction. The psychological and the material benefits of the New Deal, the racial symbolism of the black cabinet and Eleanor Roosevelt's progressivism, and the ineluctable forces of urbanization, industrialization, and expanded black education had created a favorable environment for racial progress. In practice, however, changes had been minor. President Roosevelt continued to oppose civil rights bills, the most rudimentary of which, anti-lynching, still could not survive Senate filibuster. Southern black disfranchisement remained nearly universal outside the largest cities, and segregation was as deeply entrenched as ever. Fundamental racial change would require the cataclysmic intervention of World War II.

Supreme Court justices sitting between 1920 and 1937, when Roosevelt made his first appointment, often divided over the constitutionality of economic regulation. Conservatives generally triumphed in the 1920s. Outcomes became less predictable after President Hoover appointed Charles Evan Hughes and Owen Roberts in 1930. In race cases, the justices were occasionally unanimous. When they divided, it was often along the same conservative-liberal axis that characterized their economic rulings. Some contemporary commentators suggested a correlation between economic and racial liberalism, observing after Hoover's appointments that the Court was more "fairly disposed toward colored people than at any time in its history." Yet even more liberal justices were not racially egalitarian in any strong sense; they neither opposed segregation nor endorsed black political and social equality. Most grew up at a time when white supremacy went largely unchallenged, making them unlikely candidates to champion racial equality from the bench. Only a younger generation of justices, who came of age when racial attitudes were changing and who were beholden to a New Deal political coalition more responsive to the interests of blacks, would effect a fundamental shift in race-relations jurisprudence.[43]

The little that is known about these justices' racial views suggests no strong egalitarian bent. James McReynolds, who served the entirety of this period, was an open and notorious racist—"perhaps the most bigoted justice to sit on the Supreme Court in this century." He openly described blacks as ignorant, immoral, and lazy, and in 1938 insultingly turned his back on black lawyer Charles Houston, who was arguing the Missouri law school equalization case. William Howard Taft, chief justice from 1921 to 1930, was not a racist in the McReynolds mold, but when he was the president, he had sympathized with disfranchisement and favored lily-white southern Republican parties. White southerners enthusiastically supported his nomination to the Court, which the NAACP called "almost disastrous." Oliver Wendell Holmes, who served until 1932, was a Social Darwinist who probably accepted prevailing scientific theories of racial difference and white supremacy and showed little humanitarian sympathy toward anyone, let alone blacks. Louis Brandeis, this Court's most liberal justice, privately displayed some sympathy for blacks but publicly—as a justice or otherwise—voiced no position on any significant race issue; racial equality was not an important component of the interwar liberal agenda. Only Charles Evans Hughes, chief justice from 1930 to 1941, seems to have held progressive racial views relative to his era. Hughes was the son of an abolitionist preacher, and he consistently denounced racial and religious bigotry. As an associate justice in the 1910s, he had authored "several of the best [race] decisions that the reluctant Supreme Court has ever handed down," and in the 1930s he defended the right of blacks to use the Court's cafeteria. The racial views of the other justices are unknown, though we have no reason to believe that they differed significantly from those of the general populace.[44]

Race was generally not salient enough for a Court nominee's views on the subject to garner attention at Senate confirmation hearings, and blacks rarely had the political power to force the issue. The defeat of John Parker's nomination to the Court in 1930 is not to the contrary. The NAACP opposed Parker, who a decade earlier had publicly opposed black suffrage. Given the narrowness of his defeat—41–39—that opposition may have been dispositive. But Parker was defeated because of an unusual confluence of factors; the Senate rejected no other Court nomination between 1894 and 1968. The stock market crash in 1929 and the ensuing depression sapped President Hoover's political strength. Many southern Democrats, who would have typically supported the nomination of a conservative southerner—especially when he would have been the only southern justice—opposed Parker because they spied another Hoover effort to expand southern Republicanism. Southern Democrats were especially alert to such incursions after Hoover's unprecedented triumph in five southern states in 1928. Finally, progressive Republican senators, such as Hiram Johnson and William Borah, who tended to be hostile to the NAACP's agenda, opposed their party's nominee because of his appeals-court rulings that they deemed antiunion. The AFL criticized the nomination for similar reasons, and its opposition was far more influential than the NAACP's. That race was not sufficiently salient to generally influence Court nominations is confirmed by Roosevelt's success at appointing white southerners Hugo Black, Stanley Reed, and Jimmy Byrnes. Indeed, the Senate easily approved Black, despite rumors—publicly confirmed just after the vote—that he had belonged to the Klan in the 1920s.[45]

CASES

CRIMINAL PROCEDURE

The most striking Court victories for civil rights in the interwar years came in southern criminal cases that revealed Jim Crow at its worst. Impoverished, illiterate black defendants, probably or certainly innocent of the charges made against them, were railroaded to the death penalty in egregiously unfair trials. Appalling facts made these cases attractive for Court intervention, but the justices had to manufacture new constitutional law to reverse convictions.

Moore v. Dempsey (1923), a progenitor of modern American criminal procedure, involved six blacks sentenced to death for a murder allegedly committed during the Phillips County race riot, described at the beginning of this chapter. The justices reversed the convictions on the ground that mob-dominated trials violate the Due Process Clause.[46]

The second and third criminal procedure cases, *Powell v. Alabama* (1932) and *Norris v. Alabama* (1935), involved the famous Scottsboro Boys episode. Nine black youths, aged thirteen to twenty—impoverished, illiterate, and transient—were charged with raping two white women on a freight train in northern Alabama in 1931. They were tried in a mob-dominated atmosphere, and eight of the nine received death sentences. The state supreme court reversed one sentence because the defendant was too young to be executed under state law and affirmed the other seven. The Supreme Court twice reversed the convictions—first, because the right to counsel had been denied, and second, because of race discrimination in jury selection.[47]

In the fourth case, *Brown v. Mississippi* (1936), the Court reversed the death sentences of three black sharecroppers who had been convicted of murdering their white landlord. The confessions of the defendants constituted the principal inculpatory evidence, and they had been extracted through torture. The Court ruled that such convictions violated the Due Process Clause of the Fourteenth Amendment.[48]

These four cases arose from three similar episodes. Southern blacks were charged with serious crimes against whites: rape or murder. The defendants were nearly lynched before trial. Mobs consisting of hundreds or thousands of whites surrounded the courthouses, demanding that the defendants be turned over for execution. No change of venue was granted, except in the Scottsboro retrial. Lynchings were avoided only because state militiamen armed with machine guns surrounded the courthouses. Serious doubt existed—at the time of the trials, not just in retrospect—as to the guilt of the defendants. The defendants in *Moore* and *Brown* were tortured into confessing. Lawyers were appointed only a day or even less before trial, without adequate opportunity to consult clients, interview witnesses, or prepare defense strategy. Trials took place soon after the crimes to avoid lynchings—less than a week in *Brown*, twelve days in *Powell*, and a month in *Moore*. Trials lasted only a few hours—forty-five minutes in *Moore*—and juries, from which blacks were intentionally excluded, deliberated only a few minutes before imposing death sentences.[49]

Prior to *Moore*, the justices had reversed state convictions on federal constitutional grounds in only a few cases of race discrimination in jury selection. The Court had frequently denied that the Fourteenth Amendment converted Bill of Rights guarantees into protections against *states* and had narrowly construed the Due Process Clause of that amendment, which expressly constrains states.[50] That the justices would use these interwar cases as occasions for novel constitutional interpretations is unsurprising. Judges are naturally tempted to wait for sympathetic cases to announce new rights. These southern criminal cases involved appalling injustices. Much as lynching was a convenient issue upon which to mobilize politically, lynch law was an attractive vehicle for legal mobilization. Even justices who usually showed little solicitude for the interests of blacks were offended by such farcical trials. Segregating or disfranchising southern blacks was one thing. Railroading possibly innocent defendants to the death penalty through tortured confessions and mob-dominated trials was another: It was legal lynching.[51]

Not one of these defendants was plainly guilty; it is possible that all of them were innocent. Yet guilt or innocence was often beside the point when southern blacks were accused of killing white men or sexually assaulting white women. Mere allegations generally sufficed for conviction. One white southerner, defending Alabama's treatment of the Scottsboro defendants, explained: "If a white woman is prepared to swear that a Negro either raped or attempted to rape her, we see to it that the Negro is executed." White supremacy norms did not permit white jurors to believe a black man over a white woman. Existing gender norms did not allow defense counsel to closely interrogate white women over allegations involving sex. A southern white newspaper observed around the time of Scottsboro that a white woman's honor was more important than a black man's life. Whites sometimes defended lynchings for rape on the ground that white women should not have to "appear in court and become known, disgraced forever." Because most southern white men believed that black males secretly lusted after "their" women, they generally found rape allegations credible. Similarly, in black-on-white murder cases that inflamed local passions, "accusation [was] equivalent to condemnation." The function of trials in such cases was less to establish guilt or innocence than to forestall a lynching.[52]

The defendants in these four Court cases would likely have been lynched before World War I. The peak of southern lynchings was around 1890, when well over one hundred were reported annually, and in some years over two hundred. Lynchings were primarily, though not exclusively, southern and racial phenomena. Over time, lynchings outside the South and of persons not black became rarer. Lynchings were most common in sparsely populated areas, and especially in those experiencing rapid population growth and containing transient black populations. Many more blacks were lynched in the Deep South than in the peripheral South or the border states. Most lynchings were linked to allegations of crime, though, contrary to popular myth, usually not rape (which was alleged in only about 20 percent of lynchings). More often, the crime charged was murder—nearly 40 percent of lynchings—though occasionally the offense was much less serious, such as breach of racial etiquette, general uppityness, or "talk[ing] big." Some lynchings are best understood as the dispensation of populist justice, though others can only be interpreted as efforts to subordinate blacks. Prior to 1920, local communities usually supported lynchings. Efforts to prosecute even known lynchers were rare, and convictions virtually nonexistent. Public lynchings witnessed by hundreds or thousands of people, many of whom brought their families to the lynching and took home souvenirs from the victim's tortured body, were not uncommon.[53]

By the 1920s, however, the number of lynchings reported annually had declined dramatically—from an average of 187.5 in the 1890s, to 92.5 in the first decade of the twentieth century, to 61.9 in the second decade, to 46.2 in the first half of the 1920s, to 16.8 in the second half of that decade. There are many possible explanations for this steady decline: the threat of federal anti-lynching legislation; the growing public repugnance toward lynching, which increased the risk of state prosecution; diminishing southern insularity resulting from improvements in transportation and communication; more professional law enforcement; better education; and perhaps more settled race relations, which rendered obsolete the social-control function of lynchings. Yet the decline probably also depended on replacing lynchings with quick trials that could be counted on to produce guilty verdicts, death sentences, and swift executions. Arkansas adopted a law designed to prevent lynchings by providing for special court terms within ten days in cases of rape or other crimes likely to arouse community passions. Defense counsel in cases such as *Moore*, *Brown*, and Scottsboro generally refrained from requesting continuances, because trial delays enhanced the likelihood of a lynching. In these cases and many others, law enforcement officers promised mobs that the defendants would be quickly tried and executed if the mob would refrain from lynching them. Prosecutors urged juries to convict in order to reward mobs for good behavior and thus encourage future restraint. Opponents of leniency urged governors not to commute death sentences if they expected mobs to desist from lynching, and some governors justified allowing death sentences to stand on this basis. Incredibly, lawyers occasionally made similar arguments to appellate courts that were reviewing convictions from mob-dominated trials.[54]

If all of this seems extraordinary, one must recall that for southern whites defending mob-dominated trials, the relevant comparison was to lynchings, not to elaborate court proceedings with all the trappings of due process. In the early 1930s, a Georgia newspaper warned that challenging a conviction that resulted from a mob-dominated trial was "playing with fire," as a hasty trial was better than a lynching and indeed was "a first step, and a very important one." Local newspapers frequently bragged when a lynching was averted and congratulated citizens on their self-restraint. White Alabamans seemed genuinely puzzled at outside criticism of the Scottsboro proceedings. Avoiding a lynching was "a genuine step forward" and thus deserved commendation, not condemnation. The state supreme court lauded the speed of the Scottsboro trials, which it thought was likely to instill greater respect for the law. Some white southerners considered it ironic that Alabama should be criticized for delivering exactly what racial progressives had been seeking: the substitution of trials for lynchings. Several southern newspapers warned that if outsiders continued to assail Alabama after juries returned guilty verdicts for the Scottsboro defendants, there would be little incentive to resist a lynching next time.[55]

State-imposed death sentences in these cases were little more than formalizations of the lynching process. A dissenting state justice in *Brown* explained that the trial was simply a "fictitious continuation of the mob which originally instituted and engaged in the admitted tortures." The function of mob-dominated trials was to avoid lynchings, and the purpose of lynchings was more to subordinate blacks than to punish guilty parties. Thus, the result of these trials was essentially foreordained. Of the relatively few defendants who were acquitted in mob-dominated trials, several were shot dead before they could leave the courthouse.[56]

Mob-dominated proceedings were appealing occasions for intervention by justices who believed that criminal trials were supposed to determine guilt, not simply prevent lynchings. Had the injustices been less obvious, this Court might have been reluctant to interfere. Federal courts were restrained by long tradition, grounded in federalism concerns, from supervising state criminal trials. Prior to *Moore*, a federal constitutional law of state criminal procedure did not exist. All four decisions discussed here created new law; none qualify as minimalist constitutionalism. Thus, these rulings must reveal increased judicial sensitivity regarding race, though the facts were so egregious that perhaps no large shift in attitudes was necessary.

That the justices had become more solicitous of the rights of blacks is confirmed by the Court's refusal eight years earlier to intervene in state criminal proceedings, even on appalling facts. In 1913, Leo Frank, superintendent of an Atlanta pencil factory, was charged with murdering a thirteen-year-old employee, Mary Phagan. The evidence presented against Frank at trial was suspect, and modern authorities have concluded that he was probably innocent. But Frank was a transplanted northerner, a Jew, and an industrialist—an alien in the South's predominantly rural, agricultural, Protestant culture. Frank's arrest unleashed a torrent of anti-Semitism. Each day, trial participants could hear a mob screaming "hang the Jew" through the ground-floor courtroom's open windows. In the presence of the jury, the trial judge consulted with the police chief and a state militia colonel on security measures. At the judge's initiative, neither Frank nor his lawyers were present when the jury returned its verdict, to avoid a lynching in the unlikely event of acquittal or mistrial. After Frank had exhausted state court appeals, he sought a federal writ of habeas corpus, which enables detainees to challenge the legality of their detention in court. In 1915, the Supreme Court rejected his appeal from a denial of the writ, ruling that the Due Process Clause required only that state defendants be afforded an opportunity to raise a mob-domination claim in a forum other than the one allegedly under mob influence. Because the state supreme court had considered his claim, Frank had no federal constitutional grievance. Invoking federalism concerns, the justices declined to second-guess the state court's determination that the mob had not influenced the trial outcome. Georgia's governor, John M. Slaton, after reviewing the evidence and concluding that Frank was probably innocent, commuted his sentence to life imprisonment, explaining, "Feeling as I do about this case, I would be a murderer if I allowed this man to hang." Apparently unpersuaded by the governor's reasoning, a mob seized Frank from the state prison farm at Milledgeville, carried him back to Marietta, Phagan's home town, and lynched him.[57]

By contrast, in *Moore*, the Court ordered a federal district judge to conduct a hearing on whether the defendants' convictions violated due process because they had been generated by mob-dominated trials. *Frank* and *Moore* can be reconciled. Holmes's majority opinion in *Moore* can be read two ways—one consistent with *Frank* and the other not. Holmes at one point deems it irrelevant whether the state provided adequate corrective process, if the federal court determines that mob domination made the trial a farce— the same point he had made in his *Frank* dissent and one that is obviously inconsistent with the majority opinion there. Yet elsewhere in *Moore*, Holmes states that the corrective process afforded by the Arkansas Supreme Court was flawed—a determination that would permit reversal even within the bounds of *Frank*. The state court apparently refused to make its own finding on mob domination, noting that "no attempt is made [by the appellants] to show that a fair and impartial trial was not had," and refusing to conclude "that this must necessarily have been the case."[58]

The decisions may be technically consistent, but the justices in *Moore* were probably simply more solicitous of defendants' rights. This shift in disposition probably cannot be attributed to the changes in Court composition, which, if anything, were disadvantageous to litigants who challenged mob-dominated trials. One of the two *Frank* dissenters, Charles Evan Hughes, had resigned from the Court in 1916 to run for president. Moreover, in the interim, President Harding had made several conservative Court appointments: William Howard Taft, George Sutherland, and Pierce Butler. One could not have easily predicted that these new justices would jettison traditional federalism constraints on the Court's supervision of state criminal proceedings.[59]

FIGURE 3.1
The lynching of Leo Frank in Marietta, Georgia, in 1915.
(*Underwood & Underwood*/CORBIS)

Extralegal changes best explain the shift from *Frank* to *Moore*. The nation and the justices took a dimmer view of lynching—and lynch law—after World War I. Before the war, the NAACP was largely unsuccessful at focusing national attention on lynching. President Theodore Roosevelt criticized lynchings, while blaming them mainly on black criminals. President Taft refused comment because he thought lynchings beyond the federal government's jurisdiction. President Wilson repulsed repeated efforts to secure his condemnation, until an alarming increase in lynchings during and after the war: from 36 in 1917, to 60 in 1918, to 76 in 1919. This resurgence in lynchings inspired the NAACP's massive publicity campaign in favor of a federal antilynching statute. Widespread race riots during and after the war also helped focus national attention on interracial violence and lawlessness. President Wilson finally condemned lynchings in the summer of 1918. The NAACP circulated 50,000 copies of the president's statement and in 1919 convened an antilynching conference endorsed by many national figures. After that conference, the NAACP issued an address to the nation on lynching, signed by 130 prominent citizens, including former president Taft, who would be chief justice by the time of *Moore*. The Republican party platform in 1920 urged Congress to consider antilynching legislation, and in a special message to Congress in 1921, President Harding endorsed such a measure, declaring, "Congress ought to wipe the stain of barbaric lynching from the banners of a free and orderly representative democracy." The House passed an antilynching bill in 1922. The NAACP then submitted to the Senate memorials in support of the bill; they were endorsed by half of the nation's governors, many big-city mayors, leading church officials, state court judges, and college presidents. The association also ran full-page ads in national newspapers, proclaiming lynching "The Shame of America." The lobbying campaign failed; southern Democratic senators filibustered the bill to death. Yet the vast majority of Republican congressmen supported antilynching legislation in 1922; their sentiments were likely shared in 1923 by a majority of the justices, who were also Republicans. Just as Republican congressmen were motivated by the recent epidemic of antiblack violence to condemn lynching, so may the justices have been prompted to condemn lynching's close cousin: mob-dominated trials.[60]

The Scottsboro cases presented the justices with similarly appealing facts for creating novel constitutional law. The trials of the nine black youngsters accused of rape were mob-dominated; defense counsel was not appointed until the morning of the trial; and the record raised substantial doubts about their guilt. The Scottsboro defendants raised three constitutional claims in their first Court appeal, *Powell v. Alabama* (1932): mob domination of trial, race discrimination in jury selection, and violation of the right to counsel. The justices reversed their convictions on the last ground, declining to address the others. Why they chose this rationale is impossible to know. Either of the others would have required making less new law. *Moore* had already established a right against mob-dominated trials, and numerous cases dating back to *Strauder* (1880) had barred race discrimination in jury selection.[61]

Possibly the justices selected the rationale they thought would prove least controversial. Overturning Powell's conviction because of mob domination would have required extending *Moore*, as the Scottsboro trials were not quite as farcical as those of the Phillips County defendants. Powell received some defense; his trial lasted several hours, not forty-five minutes; his jury deliberated more than the five minutes in *Moore*; his case did not raise the broader implications of an alleged black uprising; and he had not been tortured into confessing. Thus, reversing convictions in *Powell* on the basis of *Moore* would have required more significant changes in Jim Crow justice. Moreover, *Powell*'s author, George Sutherland, was one of two dissenters in *Moore*, and thus unlikely to favor extending it. Overturning Powell's conviction because of race discrimination in jury selection would also have been more controversial, because white supremacy in the legal system depended on preserving all-white juries. By contrast, reversing convictions on the basis of a violation of the right to counsel would probably affect neither the outcome of retrials nor southern criminal justice generally.[62]

FIGURE 3.2
The Scottsboro defendants, 1931. (*Bettmann*/CORBIS)

Prior to *Powell*, the Court had never overturned a state conviction because of a violation of the right to counsel, though neither had it expressly rejected such an interpretation of the Fourteenth Amendment. Every state court that confronted the issue had interpreted its own constitution to guarantee appointed counsel for indigent defendants in capital cases. Powell had received a court-appointed lawyer. He made two arguments why that appointment violated the federal Constitution. First, the state had denied him adequate opportunity to hire counsel of his choice. Second, the court appointment was made the morning of the trial, and thus counsel did not have adequate opportunity to consult clients, interview witnesses, and prepare a defense.[63]

The Alabama Supreme Court deemed this last-minute appointment sufficient to satisfy the state constitution. Supreme Court justices have no authority, barring exceptional circumstances, to review state court interpretations of state law. Thus, to reverse Powell's conviction, they had to expand the federal Constitution, which justices seem most willing to do when it involves simply applying consensus national norms to a few outliers. No state denied appointed counsel to indigent defendants in capital cases. One reason that state courts had yet to consider whether the federal Constitution guaranteed such a right is that all of them had interpreted state constitutions to do so.

Having identified a federal constitutional right to appointed counsel in capital cases, reversing Powell's conviction was easy. Not only had Powell been denied adequate opportunity to hire his own lawyer, but the judge's appointment of counsel was obviously inadequate. At a preliminary hearing, Judge Alfred E. Hawkins had casually appointed all seven lawyers in Scottsboro to look after the defendants' interests until trial. This diffusion of responsibility ensured that nobody really represented them, and it violated state law, which limited the number of court-appointed lawyers to two. The day of the trial, Hawkins appointed a Tennessee lawyer, Stephen Roddy, whom the defendants' families had sent to Scottsboro to protect the defendants' interests. Roddy told the judge that he did not want the assignment because he was unfamiliar with Alabama criminal procedure, and Hawkins then appointed a local lawyer to assist him. Defense counsel did cross-examine prosecution witnesses but made only feeble efforts to change the trial venue, presented neither opening nor closing arguments, and called no witnesses other than the defendants, who implicated each other in desperate efforts to avoid death sentences. The trials were not quite the sham affairs of *Moore*, but the Scottsboro defendants had clearly not been adequately represented. Several southern courts had previously reversed convictions under state law when counsel had been granted only *a few days* to prepare.[64]

In addition, the trial record disclosed a high probability of the defendants' innocence—a fact likely to influence justices reviewing convictions, even if technically irrelevant. Criminal procedure safeguards often shield the guilty and thus are inevitably controversial. The justices are naturally more inclined to create new criminal procedure rights when defendants may be innocent. Medical evidence in the Scottsboro trials raised serious doubts about whether the two women, Victoria Price and Ruby Bates, had been raped, and their testimonies contradicted each other. The women also had clear motives for lying, as they wished to avoid possible Mann Act prosecutions for crossing state lines for immoral purposes (prostitution). By the time *Powell* reached the Court, many across the nation had concluded that the defendants were innocent. Northern newspapers that endorsed the Court's reversal of the Scottsboro convictions noted substantial doubts regarding guilt. The *Washington Post* concluded, "Public opinion doubtless will approve of the decision."[65]

Alabama retried the defendants beginning in 1933. Clarence Norris appealed his second conviction to the Court on the ground of race discrimination in jury selection. Precedents dating from the *Plessy* era made such claims nearly impossible to prove. Relying on these precedents, the Alabama Supreme Court rejected the claim, denying any affirmative duty on the state to place blacks on juries, refusing to presume discrimination by jury commissioners, and deferring to commissioners' denials of discriminatory motive. In the Supreme Court, Alabama invoked *Thomas v. Texas* (1909) for the proposition that federal courts must defer to state court findings of fact regarding jury discrimination.[66]

The Court overturned Norris's conviction—its first such reversal on the grounds of jury discrimination since 1904—and implicitly repudiated the precedents and altered the subconstitutional rules that had doomed most such claims. The justices reinvigorated dicta from *Neal v. Delaware* (1881), which authorized drawing inferences of discrimination from the lengthy absence of blacks from juries. If no blacks had served for years in a county where many were qualified, the state bore the burden of explaining the absence. Otherwise, the constitutional safeguard "would be but a vain and illusory requirement." Further, federal courts had to determine for themselves disputed facts regarding race discrimination in jury selection, rather than deferring to state court findings.[67]

Norris was an attractive case for reconsidering jury discrimination precedents. Not only had blacks been absent from juries for decades in counties with large black populations—this was true in *Plessy*-era precedents as well—but local officials were caught in embarrassing lies. Seeking to deflect charges of race discrimination in jury selection, court officials had forged black names on jury rolls prior to Norris's retrial. Uncontradicted trial testimony by a defense handwriting expert exposed this fraud, the only plausible explanation for which was the desire of local officials to conceal race discrimination in jury selection. In an unprecedented moment of high drama, Supreme Court justices at oral argument examined local jury rolls through magnifying glasses.[68]

Norris was an appealing opportunity for the justices to reconsider precedent for another reason as well. By 1935, the innocence of the defendants seemed even clearer. At the first retrial in 1933, Ruby Bates had recanted, admitting that her rape allegations were fabricated. Yet the jury ignored her testimony, apparently crediting the prosecutor's claim that she had been bribed to perjure herself, and it imposed another death sentence. Leading white journalists in the South, such as Douglas Southall Freeman and Josephus Daniels, expressed outrage over the second round of convictions, given the defendants' probable innocence. The *Chattanooga News* declared, "[W]e cannot conceive of a civilized community taking human lives on the strength of the miserable affair." Another contemporary commentator noted the "widespread sympathy and indignation aroused by the [defendants'] plight." Thousands of protestors signed petitions and demonstrated at northern rallies. The mayor and prominent Democratic politicians supported protests in New York City. That newspapers throughout the country would applaud *Norris* is unsurprising, given that most people outside Alabama thought the Scottsboro defendants were innocent.[69]

Yet the justices had rejected jury discrimination claims in egregious cases before, and the probable innocence of the Scottsboro defendants was technically irrelevant to their appeal, as whatever subconstitutional rules the

Court embraced would have to be applied in subsequent cases regardless of the guilt or innocence of the defendants. Thus *Norris* probably cannot be explained simply on the basis of its compelling facts. Rather, the justices' turnabout on subconstitutional rules likely reflected incipient changes in social attitudes regarding black jury service.

Such attitudes are difficult to measure, but there is some evidence to support this speculation. Two important cases involving race discrimination in jury selection preceded *Norris* and helped focus public attention on the issue. In *Lee v. State* (1932), the Maryland Court of Appeals reversed the murder conviction of a black farmhand charged with killing a white family on Maryland's Eastern Shore. To secure a fair trial, the venue was changed to Baltimore County, but the presiding judge there had not allowed blacks on his juries for decades. The Maryland court, invoking the *Neal* dicta, ruled that the presumption that state officials had done their constitutional duty was overcome by a "long, unbroken absence" of blacks from juries. *Lee* was a landmark, departing from high-court precedent. Moreover, the decision came from a border state, which segregated blacks and had thrice tried to disfranchise them early in the century. If public and legal opinion regarding black jury service was changing in Maryland, it was almost certainly shifting elsewhere outside of the South.[70]

The other recent jury discrimination case was *Hale v. Crawford* (1933), which involved the question of whether a Massachusetts federal court could order the release of a black defendant being held for extradition on a Virginia indictment that charged him with murdering two white women. Crawford's argument against extradition was that blacks had been excluded from the Loudoun County grand jury that indicted him. Federal judge James Lowell ordered Crawford released on a writ of habeas corpus, but the First Circuit reversed on the ground that federal habeas proceedings were not the appropriate forum for determining race discrimination in jury selection. Although the Supreme Court declined review, *Crawford* attracted national attention. Southern congressmen demanded Lowell's impeachment, and the House appointed a committee to investigate him.[71]

Lee and *Crawford* seem to have had some effect. The *New York Times* reported after *Lee* that some Maryland counties were reconsidering jury selection practices. A conference of Virginia judges, which met after *Crawford*, agreed that blacks should sit on grand juries, and the NAACP found that as many as four or five states had begun placing blacks on juries for the first time in generations. These responses to judicial rulings apparently confirm what many contemporaries independently noted—that white resistance to black jury service had slightly eroded in the peripheral South. As blacks made economic, political, cultural, and educational progress, barring them from jury service increasingly seemed anomalous to progressive white southerners.[72]

The justices' willingness to change the law to curb race discrimination in jury selection is confirmed by *Norris*'s companion case. After *Powell*, Haywood Patterson was retried, reconvicted, and resentenced to death. Like Norris, he appealed his conviction on the ground of race discrimination in jury selection. Unlike Norris, however, it could be argued that he failed to raise his claim in a timely manner under Alabama's appellate procedure rules. The flaw was highly technical. Patterson's claim was untimely only if the ninety-day period in which to file a bill of exceptions commenced at the date of judgment rather than the date of sentencing, and if his new-trial motion, which would have tolled the ninety-day period, was nugatory because it was filed after the expiration of the trial court's term. Technical though it was, this procedural gaffe placed Patterson's life in jeopardy. The Alabama Supreme Court refused to consider the merits of his jury discrimination claim, which apparently meant that the U.S. Supreme Court could not either, even though Patterson raised almost precisely the same substantive claim that *Norris* had vindicated.[73]

In an unprecedented move, the justices, though acknowledging Alabama's right to apply its own appellate procedure rules and to dismiss federal claims not raised in compliance therewith, remanded Patterson's case to the state court to reconsider in light of *Norris*. The justices professed their unwillingness to believe that Alabama judges would have condemned Patterson to death because of procedural flaws in his appeal, had they foreseen that *Norris* would invalidate the jury selection procedures used in his case. The accuracy of this supposition is debatable. By the mid-1930s, southern judges were becoming sufficiently defensive that they sometimes grasped for independent state grounds with which to insulate their decisions from federal review. The Court's willingness to bend federal jurisdiction rules to prevent Patterson's execution indicates greater solicitude for the interests of mistreated black defendants than it had ever shown during the *Plessy* era.[74]

Brown v. Mississippi (1936) also required the justices to manufacture new constitutional law. The Court had never considered whether a confession extracted through torture would invalidate a state conviction. However, *Twining v. New Jersey* (1908) had denied that the Fourteenth Amendment extended the Fifth Amendment privilege against self-incrimination to the states. In *Brown*, the Mississippi Supreme Court relied on *Twining* to reject the federal constitutional claim. Moreover, even if the justices announced a new federal constitutional right, analogous precedent would have indicated that federal courts should defer to state court findings of fact regarding the voluntariness of confessions. The trial court in *Brown* found to be voluntary the confessions the defendants had made to the sheriff, which took place after their tortured confessions to the deputy sheriff.[75]

Yet, if the justices were going to make new constitutional law, *Brown* was as sympathetic a case as imaginable. The new federal right identified by the Court—a due process right not to be convicted on the basis of a confession obtained through torture—was already recognized by *every* state's law. There were only two states whose constitutions did not explicitly protect against forced self-incrimination, and in those two, courts had inferred such a right.

FIGURE 3.3
The defendants in *Brown v. Mississippi* (1936):
Henry Shields, Yank Ellington, and Ed Brown, in 1935.
(*Crisis Publishing Co.*)

Moreover, every state court that had considered the issue had excluded from evidence confessions extracted through force or threats of force, including Mississippi courts on several occasions in the 1920s. The state court refused to reverse the defendants' convictions in *Brown* because their state self-incrimination claim had not been properly raised at trial, and the federal right against self-incrimination had been construed not to apply in state courts.[76]

Brown also involved sympathetic facts for creating a new constitutional right. Incredibly, the deputy sheriff admitted torturing the defendants to confess, defending his actions on the candid though repulsive ground that the beatings were "not too much for a Negro." Moreover, the convictions of the defendants depended almost entirely on their confessions. Without them, the prosecution's case could not have gone to the jury. Thus, *Brown* created a new constitutional right in a case with possibly innocent defendants and undisputed facts regarding the violation.[77]

Finally, public opinion very likely supported *Brown*. In 1931, the Wickersham Commission report, *Lawlessness in Law Enforcement*, found that police chiefs generally condemned third-degree practices as uncivilized. Although psychological coercion, such as holding prisoners incommunicado, was still common, the commission found that physical torture was declining. By 1936, public revulsion against Nazi and Stalinist abuses of law enforcement further inclined most Americans to oppose confessions obtained by torture. Southern white liberals condemned such practices, as was shown by their support for the *Brown* appeal. Both newspapers in Jackson, Mississippi, endorsed the Court decision. Justice Griffiths of the state supreme court had written a scathing dissent, observing that the transcript of the trial "reads more like pages torn from some medieval account, than a record made within the confines of a modern civilization, which aspires to an enlightened constitutional government." Supreme Court justices easily distinguished between a prosecutor commenting on a defendant's refusal to take the stand (*Twining*) and "the rack and torture chamber" (*Brown*). Even McReynolds, who had little sympathy for blacks specifically or for criminal defendants generally and who had dissented in *Moore* and *Powell*, would not defend Mississippi's coercive practices. One wonders if the Court would not have reached the same result earlier had such a case presented itself. But many defendants like Brown would have been lynched a decade or two earlier, and those who were not generally lacked the resources for an appeal to the Supreme Court. *Brown* got there only because of financial support from the NAACP and southern liberal organizations.[78]

Thus far, we have considered how state judges and Supreme Court justices applied different paradigms in these criminal cases. State judges viewed any trial, regardless of how defective its procedures, as an improvement over lynching, while the justices thought criminal trials should determine guilt or innocence, not just substitute for a lynching. A second insight helps explain these decisions. Southern courts, after about 1920, became somewhat more committed to procedural justice for black criminal defendants. Indeed, state courts might have reversed convictions in these Supreme Court cases had the time and circumstances been slightly different. Yet, in publicized cases that apparently posed general challenges to Jim Crow and incited outside criticism of southern whites, state judges regressed in their treatment of black defendants.

Southern courts frequently bragged of the color-blind justice they dispensed to black defendants. In 1906, the Mississippi Supreme Court, reversing the murder conviction of a nonwhite defendant because of the prosecutor's improper racial appeal to the jury, boasted that in court everyone—black, white, and mulatto—is "on precisely the same exactly equal footing." Fifteen years later, the same court observed that "the humblest human being, be he white or black, red or yellow, is entitled to a fair and impartial trial on the sole issue of guilt or innocence." In one sense, these proud pretensions to nondiscriminatory justice were absurd. Everyone knew that blacks could not serve on southern juries, that black lawyers could not secure a fair hearing in court, that black witnesses were treated as less credible than whites, and that the death penalty in rape cases was reserved for black men convicted of victimizing white women. Yet many southern judges probably believed their own rhetoric. In 1933, one liberal white explained that "it is entirely possible for a southern white man to be uncompromisingly in favor of justice to the Negro and uncompromisingly against intermarriage." By the 1920s, southern courts frequently reversed convictions of black defendants charged with serious crimes against whites on a variety of procedural grounds—prejudicial appeals to juries, improper denial of change-of-venue motions, inadequate opportunity for defense counsel to prepare, and coerced confessions. One lawyer detected among southern state judges "a spirit abroad to assure the Nation as a whole that the courts will give the Negro 'a square . . . deal.'"[79]

Yet this liberal sentiment tended to evaporate in cases that were perceived to involve broader challenges to white supremacy or that generated outside criticism of white southerners. Perhaps human beings naturally respond defensively to external criticism. White southerners were especially sensitive, given their historical memories of the Civil War and Reconstruction.[80]

The Scottsboro cases best illustrate this phenomenon. The Alabama Supreme Court had previously reversed convictions in cases of mob domination because trial judges had failed to change venue. Other southern courts had reversed convictions because defense counsel was given inadequate opportunity to prepare, even where appointment had been a couple of days before trial. Yet in *Powell*, Alabama judges ruled that a fair trial was possible, despite the mob surrounding the courthouse, and that the right to counsel had been vindicated, despite the farcical appointment on the morning of the trial.[81]

The state jurists' implausible ruling may have been partly a defensive reaction to national criticism of Alabama's treatment of the Scottsboro defendants. The Communist organization International Labor Defense (ILD), which provided counsel in the initial Scottsboro appeals and retrials, made the episode a national and international cause célèbre, conducted mass protest meetings in northern cities, and orchestrated demonstrations at U.S. consulates overseas. The ILD consistently portrayed white Alabamans as "lynchers." Prickly about Yankee criticism in any context, Alabama whites were especially enraged at Communist castigation at a time when the party was having some success organizing rural Alabama farm workers in the midst of the depression. The governor and the justices of the state supreme court received thousands of abusive protest letters from around the world. The jurists were said to be "seething with anger at an avalanche of protests, demands, threats." When Chief Justice John C. Anderson opened his court's session in 1932, he criticized these inflammatory messages, made with "evident intent to bulldoze the court," and insisted, "This court will not be intimidated." After the state court rejected Powell's appeal, Anderson, the sole dissenter, explained to Walter White of the NAACP that his judicial colleagues had been influenced by a desire not to appear to be capitulating to ILD pressure.[82]

The Supreme Court's reversal simply exacerbated the defensiveness of white Alabamans. After the initial trials, some of them doubted whether the defendants had been treated fairly. After the Court's "stinging rebuke," however, doubts about the guilt of the defendants or the fairness of their trials could not be publicly expressed without repercussion. The Commission on Interracial Cooperation, which frequently supported black defendants' appeals of unjust convictions, declined to get involved in the Scottsboro cases because public opinion was so hostile. The defendants' few supporters in Alabama were squelched. A rabbi who was convinced of the defendants' innocence and attended a rally in their support was dismissed by his congregation and then hounded out of the state. A college professor who questioned the fairness of the Scottsboro trial proceedings had his contract terminated. The defense lawyer provided by the ILD, Samuel Leibowitz, compounded difficulties by calling white Alabamans "lantern jawed morons and lynchers" in publicized New York speeches. In the second and third rounds of trials, the chief issue was not the guilt or innocence of the defendants; it was loyalty to Alabama and to white supremacy. One prosecutor devoted most of his closing argument to attacking New York City. The jury foreman in Haywood Patterson's third trial, convinced of his innocence, explained that jurors felt they could not acquit and live peacefully in their communities, so instead they compromised on a seventy-five-year prison sentence. ILD verbal assaults had eliminated any chance of gubernatorial commutation.[83]

The refusal of the Arkansas court to reverse convictions in *Moore* may be similarly explained. That court's predicament was less the defensiveness of white Arkansans in the face of outside criticism than the impossibility of siding with blacks in a legal dispute that began with a bold challenge to white supremacy—black workers' efforts to organize a tenant farmers' union—and culminated in a racial massacre. The real issue in the *Moore* litigation was not whether the defendants were guilty of murder but whether to vindicate the white community's official story that the "race riot" had been instigated by blacks conspiring to murder white planters. Posed in those terms, how could an all-white jury of local citizens not have convicted? Although Arkansas Supreme Court justices enjoyed greater distance and independence from local opinion, they were unlikely to criticize whites in Phillips County who were struggling to maintain white supremacy. By contrast, in cases perceived to pose little threat to Jim Crow, many southern courts had reversed the convictions of blacks because of mob-dominated trials.[84]

The Mississippi court's refusal to reverse convictions in *Brown* makes sense only on this interpretation. In the 1910s and 1920s, that court reversed the convictions of several blacks because of objections to confessions that had been extracted with less brutality than that used in *Brown*, where one defendant had been twice strung up from a tree. Moreover, in one of those earlier cases, the court held that the conviction must be reversed, regardless of whether the defendant had protested the use of his coerced confession at the appropriate point of the trial. Yet in *Brown*, the court refused to consider the state constitutional claim because counsel had objected to the coerced confession at the wrong moment.[85]

Unlike the Scottsboro cases, *Brown* attracted little national attention. The NAACP deliberately avoided publicity, so as not to prejudice the defendants' chances of a reversal on appeal to the state supreme court or of a gubernatorial commutation. Mississippi was not vilified in the national press as Alabama had been. Thus, the state court's turnabout on coerced confessions must be attributable not to a backlash against specific outside criticism regarding *Brown*, but rather to a general shift in regional judicial outlook resulting from Scottsboro. After observing a neighboring state being pilloried by the nation for its treatment of black criminal defendants, a majority of Mississippi justices apparently was convinced of the desirability, where possible, of insulating judgments from federal scrutiny by invoking state procedural defaults. The court's shift was apparent in two decisions rendered between Scottsboro in 1931 and *Brown* in 1935. In *Perkins v. State* (1931), the court affirmed a murder conviction partly on the ground that defense counsel had failed to move for exclusion of an allegedly coerced confession at the appropriate point of the trial. In *Carraway v. State* (1934), that court refused to reverse a death sentence for rape, even though counsel had declined to seek a continuance or a change of venue out of fear that his client would be lynched. One cannot know for sure, but southern judges may have concluded after Scottsboro that if the North were set on criticizing their treatment of black defendants, despite what they saw as recent progress toward color-blind justice, they would provide no assistance.[86]

The Court's race-related criminal procedure decisions were almost certainly consonant with national opinion. Most Americans did not endorse farcical proceedings in which southern blacks, possibly or probably innocent of the charges against them, were tortured into confessing and sentenced to death after mob-dominated trials without the effective assistance of counsel. Northern blacks were not treated this way, though they were segregated in ghetto neighborhoods and discriminated against in employment and public accommodations. The biggest NAACP case of the 1920s illustrates the difference between northern and southern legal treatment of blacks charged with serious crimes against whites. Ossian Sweet was a black doctor in Detroit. He and numerous family members and friends were charged with murder for killing a member of a white mob that was besieging the Sweets' home in an effort to drive them out of a white neighborhood. The trial before Judge (later, Justice) Frank Murphy was "completely fair," according to contemporary NAACP testimonials, especially given the extent of Klan influence in Detroit in the mid-1920s. After the first trial ended with a deadlocked jury, Dr. Sweet's brother was acquitted in the only retrial that took place. A similar result in a southern courtroom at that time is difficult to imagine. Yet, even many southern whites did not condone the sort of treatment of black defendants condemned by the Court's decisions. As Gunnar Myrdal observed, discrimination in the legal system was near the bottom of the white supremacist hierarchy of preferences. Many southern whites intensely committed to segregation and opposed to interracial marriage did not endorse the unfair treatment of black criminal defendants. For that reason, eminent white lawyers represented black defendants such as Moore or Brown on appeal, when they never would have taken cases challenging school segregation or disfranchisement.[87]

Perhaps the justices would have been unwilling to intervene had the facts been less egregious. The paradox of these cases is that the facts made them easy but the law made them hard. Prior to *Moore*, scarcely any precedent existed for the intervention of federal courts in state criminal proceedings. *Moore* required a departure from *Frank*, and *Norris* implicitly repudiated precedents from the *Plessy* era. *Powell* and *Brown* involved no departure from precedent only because both were truly unprecedented. Never before had the justices broached reversing state convictions because of coerced confessions or denial of the right to counsel. For Court intervention in these areas to be effective, the justices had to be willing to accuse state courts and

FIGURE 3.4
Left to right: Dr. Ossian Sweet with his lawyers,
Perry, Chawke, and Clarence Darrow, circa 1925.
(*Crisis Publishing Co.*)

state officials of lying—something they were reluctant to do. *Moore* required the Court to disbelieve a state appellate court's determination that trial proceedings were not corrupted by mob domination. *Norris* required the justices to substitute their judgment for that of state judges on whether jury commissioners had lied when denying race discrimination in jury selection. For *Brown* to be effective, the Court would have to question sheriffs' denials that they had coerced confessions. The justices' willingness to blaze new trails probably depended on two factors: cases in which the injustices to black defendants and the dishonesty of state officials were manifest, and changes in the extralegal context that rendered the justices less tolerant of the egregious mistreatment of black defendants in the South.[88]

VOTING

White Primaries

The white primary was a principal mechanism for disfranchising southern blacks. Because Democrats completely dominated southern politics after the 1890s, excluding blacks from party primaries effectively nullified their political influence. Some county Democratic parties began excluding blacks by rule or custom in the 1870s and 1880s. State parties adopted the first rules that barred blacks in the 1890s. The first statutes that regulated primaries, enacted around 1900, placed restrictions on participation—for example, they allowed only persons qualified to vote in the general election—and authorized parties to adopt additional qualifications. In 1923, Texas became the first state to bar blacks from primaries by law. By 1930, blacks were excluded from Democratic primaries in almost all southern states by custom or party rule, though by law only in Texas.[89]

The interwar Court considered the constitutionality of white primaries three times, after dismissing an initial challenge as moot in 1924. The decision in *Nixon v. Herndon* (1927) invalidated the Texas statute barring blacks from party primaries. *Nixon v. Condon* (1932) struck down a revised Texas law authorizing party executive committees to set membership qualifications—an invitation that had been eagerly accepted by the Texas Democratic party's executive committee, which adopted a rule excluding blacks. *Grovey v. Townsend* (1935) rejected a constitutional challenge to the Texas Democrats' exclusion of blacks by a resolution of the party's annual convention.[90]

Herndon was the easiest of these cases, because state action was unquestionably present. As we have seen, the justices had long interpreted the Fourteenth and Fifteenth amendments to forbid race discrimination only by the state, not by private entities. For a political party to exclude blacks raised complicated questions regarding the scope of the state-action requirement: Was a party a public or a private entity? Were elections public functions for which states should be held accountable? Could a state be deemed responsible for "inviting" a private party to discriminate in its membership decisions? None of these complications existed in *Herndon*, however, where black participation in primaries was barred by statute, not party rule. Holmes, writing for the Court, thought the issue was easy. His two-page opinion declined to address the Fifteenth Amendment question because "it seems to us hard to imagine a more direct and obvious infringement of the 14th."[91]

Herndon was not as easy as Holmes imagined. Although the state had unquestionably acted, the Fourteenth Amendment does not clearly protect political rights. Holmes was disingenuous, or misinformed, when he declared, "[I]t is too clear for extended argument that color cannot be made the basis of a statutory classification affecting the right set up in this case." Most Republican proponents of the Fourteenth Amendment had not believed that they were protecting the political, as opposed to the civil, rights of blacks. Although the Fifteenth Amendment plainly safeguards the right to vote against race discrimination, whether it covered primary elections was uncertain. *Newberry v. United States* (1921) had ruled that Congress could not regulate campaign spending in House and Senate primaries, because they were not "elections" within the meaning of Article I, section 4's grant of power to Congress to regulate the time, place, and manner of federal elections. If primaries were not elections under Article I, then perhaps they did not implicate the right to "vote" under the Fifteenth Amendment. This is probably the reason that Holmes relied on the Fourteenth Amendment instead. Finally, Holmes's opinion in *Giles v. Harris* (1903) should have given him pause before the Court intervened in this "political" controversy. In *Herndon*, Holmes simply denied that because the subject matter of a case was political, it presented a nonjusticiable political question. He failed entirely to distinguish *Giles*.[92]

On the other hand, *Guinn v. Oklahoma* (1915), which invalidated the grandfather clause, had already rejected *Giles's* broadest implications by adjudicating a case involving the voting rights of blacks. Moreover, *Strauder* (1880) had repudiated the original understanding of the Fourteenth Amendment, which covered only civil rights, by protecting the right of blacks to serve on juries, which most of the amendment's sponsors had conceived to be a political right. Thus, although inconsistent with the original understanding of the Fourteenth Amendment, *Herndon* required only a mild extension of precedent. *Herndon* probably cannot be seen as minimalist constitutionalism. Yet by 1927, with the nation marginally more sensitized to race issues, the justices could not tolerate open race discrimination by the state. *Herndon* was unanimous, commanding support even from those justices least sympathetic to civil rights.[93]

Herndon was also a quintessential example of constitutional law's proclivity for suppressing outliers. Texas's white-primary law was the only one of its kind in the nation; other southern states excluded blacks by party rule. *Herndon* had nothing to say about the constitutionality of these schemes. Moreover, Texas's statute illustrates the tendency of Jim Crow laws to reflect, rather than create, white supremacy norms. Prior to the statute, most Texas counties already excluded blacks from Democratic primaries. The law at issue in *Herndon* was enacted at the behest of a politician from Bexar County, one of the few in Texas that permitted black participation in Democratic primaries, after an election in which black suffrage was a prominent issue. Jim Crow laws often originated in such anomalous circumstances. Thus, *Herndon* invalidated an outlier statute that itself suppressed an outlier practice. Even supporters of black disfranchisement could concede that the law had been a mistake.[94]

In all subsequent white-primary cases, the justices had to confront the intractable state-action issue. After *Herndon*, the Texas legislature immediately passed a law empowering the party executive committee to prescribe membership qualifications. As anticipated and intended, the Texas Democratic executive committee quickly passed a resolution excluding blacks. The issue in *Condon* was whether the state was constitutionally responsible for the party's discriminatory action. By the same 5–4 split that characterized many contemporaneous cases involving economic regulation, *Condon* found discriminatory state action on the ground that the Texas legislature, not the state Democratic party, had empowered the executive committee to prescribe membership qualifications. The majority declined to decide whether a party's exclusion of blacks would be state action in the absence of a statute specifying which entity within the party determined membership qualifications.

Condon seems a stretch. The Texas statute did nothing out of the ordinary; it simply restored state law to what it had been before the enactment of the 1923 statute, which barred blacks from primaries. Since Texas first regulated primaries in 1903, state law had authorized party executives to determine membership qualifications. In several other states, too, executive committees, not party conventions, excluded blacks from Democratic primaries. *Condon* found state action on the assumption that the 1927 statute altered the party's "natural" decision-making apparatus, but the legislature had probably intended only to confirm the party's inherent power to set membership qualifications through executive resolution.[95]

Condon's only effect was to defer for three years the more fundamental state-action question: Did the Constitution permit a political party to bar blacks from membership? Three weeks after *Condon*, the annual convention of the Texas Democratic party resolved to exclude blacks. *Condon*'s rationale for judicial intervention was now gone, as the state had not influenced the party's decision-making process. *Grovey v. Townsend* (1935) unanimously declined to find state action under these circumstances.

Grovey is a confused and confusing opinion. Justice Roberts conceded the ways in which Texas regulated primaries—requiring that they be held, that voter qualifications be the same as in general elections, that absentee voting be permitted, and that election judges enjoy certain powers. Roberts found two differences between primary and general elections dispositive on the issue of state action: Texas did not cover the expenses for primary elections; Texas did not furnish, nor did it count, the ballots for primary elections. Lower courts that adjudicated the constitutionality of white primaries often focused on these same factors. But neither Roberts nor the lower courts explained why certain forms of state involvement in primaries, but not others, constituted state action.[96]

State action is one of the hardest issues in constitutional law, and it arises in contexts across the constitutional spectrum. For present purposes, the question is: For what forms of race discrimination is the state constitutionally responsible? The reason the issue is so difficult is that this responsibility is not subject to objective measurement. State action is like causation. To say the state is responsible for race discrimination is to say that it caused that discrimination. Law employs two concepts of causation: but/for and proximate. X is a but/for cause of Y if Y would not have happened had X not been present. X is a proximate cause of Y if X is deemed legally responsible for bringing about Y. The key to understanding proximate cause is recognizing that it represents a legal conclusion, not an analytical tool. Any but/for cause can be deemed a proximate cause, depending on the goals of the inquiry.

Proximate-cause judgments tend to be made in one of two ways. The first is a consequentialist, forward-looking determination. From this perspective, efforts to shape future behavior by supplying appropriate incentives determine which but/for causes are deemed proximate. The second way is a backward-looking, intuitive judgment about moral responsibility. On this view, X is the proximate cause of Y if the decision maker feels that X is morally responsible for Y. Such judgments reflect culturally contingent background assumptions about the world. However, because these assumptions are deeply embedded and thus hidden from consciousness, they may seem to be rooted in nature rather than culture. For example, if a bicycle and a car collide, the determination of proximate cause, in this second sense, is informed by cultural assumptions regarding the more "natural" mode of transportation and the appropriate operating behavior of both vehicles. Different societies might well resolve such questions differently.[97]

State action is like proximate cause. Labeling something state action is making either a consequentialist judgment, which seeks to shape future behavior, or a deontological judgment, which is grounded in baseline assumptions about how the world operates (or should operate). In neither case, though, does determining the existence of state action involve objective measurement of degrees of causation. When a political party excludes blacks from membership, the state is a but/for cause if it had the power to forbid the exclusion but did not exercise it. Given how underdeveloped First Amendment doctrine was in 1935, Texas almost certainly had the power to bar a party from excluding blacks. Whether the state was a proximate cause of the exclusion of blacks depends on how one resolves the consequentialist and deontological questions noted above. The answer to the former obviously depends on whether one thinks that excluding blacks from party primaries is acceptable. That determination cannot be separated from one's general attitudes toward race discrimination.

For more complicated reasons, the deontological question yields a similar answer, even though that inquiry purports to be nonconsequentialist. Whether one deems government to be morally responsible for a situation involving race depends on one's general view of the state's proper role and one's particular views on race. Thus, determining state responsibility for the white primary cannot be divorced from one's attitudes toward race discrimination in the political process. Even hypothesizing a society with fixed views regarding government's appropriate sphere, the determination of government responsibility for a political party's racial exclusions will depend on the depth of that society's commitment to racial equality. Early in the twenty-first century, for example, a court might well deem the government's failure to prohibit private race discrimination in employment—a hypothetical repeal of Title VII of the 1964 Civil Rights Act—to be unconstitutional state action. Such a determination would depend on whether the society's assumption that the state forbids such discrimination has become as deeply ingrained as its assumption that the state punishes trespasses and physical assaults.

Grovey's consideration of the state-action issue occurred in largely uncharted waters. A handful of Court decisions had confirmed a state-action requirement in the Fourteenth and Fifteenth amendments. But the justices had also intimated that sometimes the state's *failure* to perform traditional governmental functions could constitute state action. In dicta, the Court had suggested that state failure to provide law enforcement protection to blacks or to enforce common-law rights of access to common carriers on behalf of blacks might violate the Fourteenth Amendment. *Truax v. Corrigan* (1921), which was not a race case, held that state withdrawal of traditional injunctive relief for property rights violations was unconstitutional. Beyond this, the Court had not explored the circumstances under which state *in*action could be unconstitutional. The uncertainty regarding state-action doctrine in the 1930s is illustrated by the unresolved debate over the constitutionality of federal antilynching legislation, which turned largely on whether the failure of the states to prosecute the lynchers of blacks amounted to unconstitutional state action. No consensus existed on that question.[98]

Grovey's unanimous holding of no state action reveals how little racial attitudes had changed by 1935, for two reasons. First, general conceptions of the appropriate spheres of public and private authority underwent dramatic change in the 1930s. The Great Depression and the New Deal led many Americans to deem the state responsible for economic arrangements that would have previously been considered private. Government's failure to regulate markets had seemed less of a choice warranting accountability when markets generally produced desirable results. As outcomes came to appear less favorable, government's failure to regulate began to seem more like a choice for which it should be held responsible. The Court's nonracial jurisprudence reflected such shifting perceptions of state responsibility. In 1934, the justices obliterated the public-private distinction in substantive due process, thereby enabling legislatures to regulate prices and wages in areas that had previously been deemed private and thus beyond legislative purview. This shift should have had implications for state action under the Fourteenth Amendment. If the private sphere was no longer constitutionally immune from government regulation, then the state's choice not to regulate it was one for which it could be held accountable. For the justices to fail to integrate changing conceptions of government responsibility into their equal protection jurisprudence says something about their racial attitudes.[99]

Second, the justices might easily have found state action in *Grovey* without ruling that inaction was tantamount to action. Texas regulated political parties in many ways. The more heavily the state regulated parties, the less difficult it would be to ascribe responsibility to it for areas not regulated. Texas law required parties to conduct primaries, dictated their date and time, specified the qualifications of election officials and the form and content of primary-election ballots, and determined the manner of challenging contested results. Indeed, Texas even restricted party membership decisions. For Texas to tell state Democrats that they could not exclude persons based on membership in social clubs but (implicitly) that they could exclude them based on race made the state seem much more responsible for Democrats' exclusion of blacks than if the state had not regulated membership at all. Instead, *Grovey* focused on the decision of Texas, unlike that of some other states, not to pay for primaries. But the justices failed to explain why this one facet of state noninvolvement in party affairs trumped numerous other aspects of state entanglement.[100]

Given changing general attitudes toward government responsibility for nonregulation and the numerous ways in which Texas did regulate political parties, the justices' determination that Texas Democrats' exclusion of blacks was not state action must indicate a relative indifference toward race discrimination in the political process. Indeed, public opinion regarding southern black suffrage probably had not changed much since 1900. Through the 1920s, prominent Republicans, such as Taft and Senator William Borah, continued to lament the Fifteenth Amendment "as one of the greatest mistakes ever made in this country." In 1927, a Republican congressman's appeal to enforce section 2 of the Fourteenth Amendment still fell on deaf ears. That same year, the *Washington Post* observed that "[t]he nation has tacitly consented to the arrangement" by which southern whites maintained political supremacy by disfranchising blacks. In the mid-1930s, the national Democratic party and the Roosevelt Justice Department showed no interest in interfering with southern white primaries, and administration officials "lost" affidavits sent to them by Texas blacks who complained of being excluded from such elections. Increases in southern black voter registration, which might have affected national opinion on white primaries, postdated the 1936 election, and thus came too late to influence the outcome in *Grovey*. Only World War II would fundamentally transform the nation's, and the justices', views regarding black suffrage. At that point, the Court overruled *Grovey*.[101]

Poll Taxes

Most southern states adopted poll taxes between 1890 and 1908. The amount was usually one or two dollars annually, though some states cumulated the tax over years of nonpayment. In most states, poll taxes were due six or nine months before elections, which deterred payment and increased the likelihood of misplacing the receipt, which had to be produced to vote. Just four southern states used the poll tax as the principal mechanism of disfranchisement; most combined it with literacy tests. The principal purpose of the tax was to disfranchise blacks, though poor whites were a subsidiary target. The poll tax did not contain built-in immunities for whites, unlike literacy tests with understanding or grandfather clauses.[102]

Constitutional challenges to the poll tax faced daunting legal hurdles. The Constitution explicitly authorizes states to set voter qualifications, including those for national elections. The Fifteenth Amendment qualifies this grant of power by providing that the right of U.S. citizens to vote "shall not be denied or abridged . . . on account of race." But that amendment does not clearly prohibit nonracial voter qualifications, simply because they have the purpose or effect of disfranchising disproportionate numbers of blacks. The Congress that approved the amendment contemplated forbidding property and education qualifications but lacked the votes to do so.

The decision in *Williams v. Mississippi* (1898) rejected a facial challenge to a literacy test adopted for the purpose of disfranchising blacks on the ground that legislative motive was irrelevant to constitutionality. To invalidate poll taxes on racial grounds would have required the Court to reconsider the relevance of legislative motive or to hold that voter qualifications that produced disparate racial impacts violated the amendment. Alternatively, the Court could have invalidated poll taxes, not because of racial ramifications, but because they disadvantaged poor people. As of the 1930s, however, the Court had never suggested that classifications based on wealth or those that produced disparate wealth effects raised serious constitutional questions.[103]

The poll-tax challenge that reached the Court in 1937, *Breedlove v. Suttles*, did not even raise the race issue. Breedlove was a poor white male from Georgia, who challenged the poll tax as arbitrary under the Equal Protection Clause, because it applied only to those aged twenty-one to sixty. In 1937, the justices were not prepared to invalidate age classifications under the Fourteenth Amendment. The Court did not take such challenges seriously until the 1970s, and even then it rejected them. *Breedlove* said nothing about the racial motivation or racial impact of the poll tax. Only after another thirty years of New Deal policies and a presidentially declared war on poverty would the Court begin to question the constitutionality of laws that disadvantaged the poor and invalidate the poll tax (in 1966).[104]

Only three southern states had abolished the poll tax on their own before *Breedlove*: North Carolina (1920), Louisiana (1934), and Florida (1937). The rest of the South continued to use the poll tax as a voter qualification. In the three abolishing states, the proponents of repeal had emphasized class and downplayed race. The number of black voters in these states did not increase appreciably after the tax was abolished. The national crusade against the poll tax, led by New Dealers seeking to enfranchise their natural political allies, did not commence until a year or two after *Breedlove*. President Roosevelt, although never formally endorsing federal anti–poll-tax legislation, criticized the tax as outmoded in September 1938. The liberal Southern Conference for Human Welfare called for repeal at the state and national levels at its inaugural conference two months later. The National Committee to Abolish the Poll Tax was most active in the 1940s, and the House did not pass the first of its five anti–poll-tax bills until 1942. For the justices to have invalidated the tax in 1937 would have placed them in the vanguard of a social reform movement—a position they rarely occupy. With traditional legal sources validating poll taxes, and national political opinion a couple of years away from mobilizing against them, *Breedlove* was easy.[105]

RESIDENTIAL SEGREGATION

The interwar Court confronted two sorts of challenges to residential segregation. The justices twice summarily invalidated residential segregation ordinances that were barely distinguishable from the Louisville law struck down in *Buchanan v. Warley*. The decision in *Corrigan v. Buckley* (1926) unanimously rejected a constitutional challenge to racially restrictive covenants.

Chapter 2 described the wave of residential segregation ordinances that swept cities of the border states and the peripheral South around 1910. *Buchanan* invalidated Louisville's ordinance in 1917. Yet many cities continued to pass such laws in the 1920s, including New Orleans, Dallas, Richmond, Norfolk, Atlanta, and Indianapolis. These ordinances generally differed in minor ways from Louisville's. A couple of them barred persons ineligible to marry each other under state law from purchasing homes in the same block, thus seeking to piggyback residential segregation laws on antimiscegenation statutes; the latter appeared to be clearly constitutional in the 1920s. Proponents may have doubted the constitutionality of these ordinances yet hoped that blacks lacked the resources or the fortitude to pursue legal challenges. Alternatively, some city councils may have genuinely believed that courts would distinguish these revised segregation ordinances from the law in *Buchanan*. Other supporters may have hoped that the justices would reconsider *Buchanan* in light of the growing northern support for residential segregation that resulted from interracial conflicts over housing spawned by the Great Migration. In addition, residential zoning had become more widespread and less controversial by the mid-1920s, as illustrated by the Court's landmark decision upholding general zoning ordinances, *Euclid v. Ambler Realty Co.* (1926). Most likely, city councils enacted these ordinances because doing so was politically profitable, regardless of whether courts ultimately sustained them. Arthur Spingarn of the NAACP saw the Indianapolis ordinance as little more than "a gesture to propitiate the White People's Protective League." Likewise, both leading Richmond newspapers understood that city's segregation ordinance as responsive to the political demands of lower-class whites who belonged to the Ku Klux Klan.[106]

Whatever explained their enactment, these ordinances did not survive legal challenge. With just one exception, lower courts invalidated them on the basis of *Buchanan*. A New Orleans judge, after opining that his city's ordinance was a reasonable police-power measure, struck it down anyway, as he found *Buchanan* indistinguishable. The only court to sustain such an ordinance, the Louisiana Supreme Court, followed *Plessy*, not *Buchanan*, criticized the latter as a "long step backwards in the march of civilization," and intimated that it had been rendered obsolete by recent zoning decisions, such as *Euclid*. The Supreme Court granted review in two such cases, in 1927 and 1930, each time summarily affirming *Buchanan*.[107]

Whether the justices would have reached the same result in the absence of *Buchanan* is an interesting question. The Great Migration fostered enormous racial tension over housing in northern industrial cities, and scores of black families were bombed or otherwise assaulted when they attempted to move into white neighborhoods. Northern opinion was probably as supportive of residential segregation as was southern, though perhaps not equally committed to using law to accomplish it. In any event, as *Buchanan* was limited to forbidding residential segregation *laws*, it had almost no impact on housing patterns and thus did not generate intense opposition. Moreover, the Court that reaffirmed *Buchanan* was as committed to the defense of property rights as any in American history. The justices' embrace of *Lochner*-ism had been tentative and inconsistent in the first two decades of the century, but in the 1920s they invalidated nearly 200 laws for interference with property or contract rights and entrepreneurial liberty. Despite their validation of residential zoning, these justices were probably offended by state laws that restricted people's rights to buy and sell property. Given clear precedent, the substantial interference with property rights, and the minimal consequences that invalidation of these ordinances had on residential patterns, the justices' reaffirmation of *Buchanan* is comprehensible, despite the strong support of whites throughout the nation for residential segregation.[108]

One reason the justices would have anticipated the limited impact of these rulings was that they had recently rejected a constitutional challenge to the popular substitute for segregation ordinances: racially restrictive covenants. As hundreds of thousands of southern blacks migrated to northern cities, urban ghettos overflowed, and some middle-class blacks sought admission to white neighborhoods. White property owners, often at the instigation of homeowners' associations, signed covenants not to sell to blacks (and often Jews and Asians as well), usually for a period of fifteen to fifty years, although occasionally in perpetuity. Some covenants forbade only black occupancy, but others covered ownership too. Such covenants first appeared in significant numbers around 1910, at the same time as residential segregation ordinances, but they did not become commonplace until the 1920s. By 1925, they had spread so rapidly, especially in northern cities, that the NAACP warned that *Buchanan* "will be practically nullified unless this manner of enforcing segregation is checked and defeated." The association at that time was fighting seventeen cases that involved restricted neighborhoods.[109]

Racial covenants were the private alternative to residential segregation ordinances, and it could be argued that they were immune from constitutional attack because state action was absent. The first Court challenge came in *Corrigan v. Buckley* (1926), which involved a racially restrictive covenant in the District of Columbia. The Court's appellate jurisdiction in cases from the District of Columbia courts was limited to adjudicating "substantial" federal claims. The appellant challenged the legality of the covenant itself, under the Constitution and the 1866 Civil Rights Act; the latter guaranteed blacks the same contract and property rights as whites. The decision in *Corrigan* dismissed as patently insubstantial the claim that the private covenant was itself state action. The justices further observed that the appeal petition did not challenge *judicial enforcement* of the covenant, but they indicated that such a claim would also have been insubstantial. The Court thus concluded that it lacked jurisdiction and declined to confront the further question of whether such covenants were void as against public policy, as some state courts had held. The NAACP chose to read *Corrigan* narrowly. As the inartfully drawn appeal petition had challenged only the covenants, the Court technically had not resolved the permissibility of judicial enforcement. Yet, *Corrigan*'s dicta had plainly sustained judicial enforcement of restrictive covenants, and many state courts so interpreted it. Repeated NAACP efforts over the next two decades to bring another restrictive covenant case to the Court failed.[110]

The constitutional question posed by restrictive covenants was analogous to the white-primary issue. Race discrimination was plainly present in both instances; the only question was whether it was fairly ascribable to the state. Arguing that restrictive covenants themselves implicated the state was difficult (though not impossible), and petitioners in *Corrigan* dropped that argument from their appeal. Yet judicial enforcement of covenants was plainly a type of state action. Precedent had established that judicial orders, just like executive orders or legislation, could constitute the state action necessary for a constitutional violation. Thus, the question was not whether the state had acted when it enforced covenants, but whether its action was discrimination that violated the Fourteenth Amendment (or, in the District of Columbia, the Due Process Clause of the Fifth Amendment). If courts enforced all private contracts regardless of their terms, then the enforcement of racially restrictive covenants would seem less like discrimination and more like neutral support for a regime of private contractual freedom. Indeed, the justices' enthusiasm for property and contract rights, which had made *Buchanan* easy, probably made *Corrigan* easy as well. For the state to refuse to enforce a contract limiting an owner's ability to sell his property might have appeared just as fundamental an interference with economic freedom as for the state itself to restrain the sale.[111]

However, the *Corrigan* issue was not that easy. Courts in the 1920s did not enforce a regime of universal contractual liberty. Common-law courts frowned on certain restraints on alienation. State courts were unpredictable as to which sorts of restrictive covenants they would enforce and which they would invalidate as against public policy. Although all courts enforced restrictions on use or occupancy, their response to restraints on sale varied, depending on the length of the restriction and the number of parties covered. If courts were unwilling to enforce certain restrictive covenants, then it could be argued that the choice to enforce others was one for which the state should be held accountable.[112]

As we saw with regard to white primaries, the state-action question is not whether the state *is* responsible for certain behavior, but whether it *should be deemed* responsible. Because states could have barred judicial enforcement of racially restrictive covenants, the choice not to do so was a but/for cause of the segregated housing that resulted from enforcement. Whether the state should also be deemed the proximate cause turns partly on general notions of government responsibility for private behavior and partly on how abhorrent one finds race discrimination. In the 1920s, government was generally deemed responsible for many fewer kinds of private behavior than it would be a decade or two later. Moreover, race discrimination in housing was less troublesome to most Americans than it would later become.

The Great Migration transformed residential segregation from a southern to a national issue. Northern blacks endured bombings, cross burnings, and mob assaults as they sought to escape ghettos by purchasing homes in white neighborhoods. The NAACP's 1925 annual report described "segregation by terrorism" and enumerated widespread bombings of black homes and churches over the previous year in several northern cities. The association sought to connect in the public mind contemporaneous challenges to restrictive covenants with its defense of Ossian Sweet, the black doctor from Detroit charged with murder for killing a member of a mob that was seeking to drive his family out of a white neighborhood. Yet the justices may have drawn a connection different from the one intended by the NAACP. If northern whites violently resisted residential integration, then perhaps peaceful means of segregating neighborhoods, such as restrictive covenants, should be encouraged. By the 1930s, the Federal Housing Agency's underwriting manual explicitly promoted restrictive covenants. The Works Progress Administration and the U.S. Housing Authority selected public housing projects with an eye toward preserving segregated housing patterns. With the political branches of the national government legitimizing restrictive covenants and residential segregation, the justices were naturally disinclined to interfere.[113]

Corrigan was easy for another reason as well: Precedent was strongly supportive of restrictive covenants. Although some state courts had invalidated particular restraints on alienation as contrary to public policy, only a single federal court decision, from the 1890s, had suggested that the Constitution barred judicial enforcement of restrictive covenants. A multitude of state and federal court rulings had held the contrary. So long as state judges construed state public policy to permit enforcement, precedents were virtually unanimous in rejecting constitutional challenges to judicial enforcement of restrictive covenants.[114]

PUBLIC EDUCATION

The interwar Court decided two constitutional cases that involved race and education. *Gong Lum v. Rice* (1927) rejected a Chinese American's challenge to Mississippi's decision to send her to a black school rather than to a white one. *Missouri ex rel. Gaines v. Canada* (1938) invalidated a statute that provided out-of-state scholarships for blacks who sought legal education that was denied them within the state.

Gong Lum was an unusual context for the justices' initial confrontation with public school segregation. In the Mississippi Delta, there was a small community of Chinese. They had come there during Reconstruction as replacements for black labor. Most of them ran grocery stores. Most whites in the delta displayed little animosity toward "pure" Chinese, in contrast with those of mixed Chinese-black ancestry. Local communities permitted Chinese-American children into white schools. It was the state of Mississippi, not the county school board, that had excluded Gong Lum. The state supreme court interpreted the state constitutional provision that mandated separate schools for "colored" children to include Chinese, and it sustained the reasonableness of that classification.[115]

We saw in chapter 1 that school segregation was nearly universal in the postbellum South. The text of the Fourteenth Amendment does not plainly bar it, and the original understanding pretty clearly permitted it. Dozens of lower court precedents almost unanimously sustained public school segregation. For the justices to reject a result so plainly indicated by the conventional legal sources would generally require a powerful social consensus in the opposite direction.[116]

Technically, Gong Lum did not challenge school segregation. The appellant's principal argument was that Mississippi denied equal privileges to Chinese by combining them with blacks, while whites enjoyed separate schools. Chief Justice Taft's opinion for a unanimous Court did not even address that argument. Instead, he understood the case to pose the question that lower court precedent had laid to rest: the constitutionality of public school segregation. Taft dismissed that challenge almost out of hand.[117]

For the Court to have invalidated school segregation in 1927 seems almost inconceivable. Although World War I had influenced national opinion on issues such as lynching and interracial violence, school segregation was as securely grounded as ever. In 1921, President Harding criticized race discrimination in the political and economic spheres but firmly rejected "every suggestion of social equality" and insisted that "racial amalgamation there cannot be." Northern opinion was more supportive of school segregation than previously, as the Great Migration had exacerbated racial prejudice. Many northern cities that had integrated schools before the war—New York, Philadelphia, Chicago, Cincinnati, and others—experienced increased segregation in the 1920s, partly because of growing residential segregation and partly because of gerrymandered attendance zones, discriminatory transfer policies, and other official segregating conduct. By 1927, school segregation was becoming a national phenomenon, not simply a southern one. The federal aid-to-education legislation that Congress seriously considered adopting in the mid-1920s would have implicitly sanctioned racial segregation in public schools.[118]

Northern blacks had "deep and passionate differences of opinion" over whether to challenge such segregation, which had advantages and disadvantages. Enforced separation connoted black inferiority and thus was stigmatic. In practice, black schools never received adequate funding. Moreover, school segregation removed a rare opportunity to promote interracial understanding among youngsters. On the other hand, segregated schools meant jobs for black teachers, whom white parents would not tolerate teaching their children. Black students in black schools could generally avoid the hostility, insults, and stereotyping they usually had to endure from white teachers and students in integrated schools. Finally, black schools offered more sympathetic portrayals of black history and culture. The NAACP's W. E. B. Du Bois launched a lively debate in 1934 with his qualified endorsement of segregated education. Du Bois thought it "idiotic simply to sit on the side lines and yell: 'No segregation' in an increasingly segregated world." He argued that blacks were "crucified" in integrated schools and that it was "suicidal" for blacks to concede the inferiority of their own schools by demanding integration.[119]

Southern blacks knew better than to challenge an aspect of Jim Crow so dear to whites. NAACP policy in the interwar period was to contest the spread of school segregation in the North, but not to challenge it where it was "so firmly entrenched by law that a frontal attack cannot be made." Contesting southern school segregation in the 1920s would have been fruitless and potentially suicidal. The NAACP conceded that "racial feeling [in the

South] is so strong that it would be impossible to carry on [mixed] schools." The association only brought suits it expected to win, and challenges to southern school segregation were not among them. *Gong Lum* was brought by Mississippi Chinese, not the NAACP. Because Gong Lum did not contest segregation and because Mississippi Chinese were not blacks, a prestigious local law firm took the case, and a respected trial judge granted relief, without alienating local opinion. Blacks who challenged school segregation in the South would have received very different treatment.[120]

Even southern white liberals did not question school segregation in the 1920s, fighting instead against lynching, police brutality, and the enormous racial disparities in educational funding, which continued to grow until roughly 1930. There were no public high schools for blacks in many Deep South cities until the 1920s and in hundreds of rural counties until after World War II. Ironically, a legal challenge to school segregation was all but unimaginable at a time when most southern blacks were being denied *any* secondary education.[121]

In this setting, Court invalidation of school segregation was inconceivable. The justices are rarely in the vanguard of social reform movements. If NAACP leaders doubted the wisdom of challenging southern school segregation in light of public opinion, the justices were not about to interfere with it, especially given that relevant legal sources strongly supported it.

Missouri ex rel. Gaines v. Canada (1938) challenged out-of-state tuition grants to blacks who sought graduate and professional education that was denied to them in Missouri. Before World War I, most southern blacks had been denied access even to high school education. As only minuscule numbers finished college, southern states provided no graduate or professional education for blacks. The issue first arose in the 1920s, as southern blacks graduated from high school and college in larger numbers. In 1921, Missouri became the first southern or border state to provide blacks with any advanced education. The legislature converted Lincoln Institute, an agricultural and industrial school for blacks, into Lincoln University. Until Lincoln achieved full university status, its board of curators was granted authority to provide blacks with tuition grants to attend integrated universities in neighboring states for courses not offered at Lincoln. The legislature did not actually appropriate funds for these grants until 1929. Maryland passed a similar law in 1933, which the legislature funded in 1935. Several border and upper South states—Kentucky, Oklahoma, Tennessee, Virginia, and West Virginia—enacted similar legislation soon afterward, apparently in response to threatened litigation. No southern or border state provided blacks with in-state professional education, and only two or three offered any graduate instruction. A couple of private institutions—Howard University in Washington, D.C., and Meharry Medical College in Nashville, Tennessee—offered some professional and graduate training.[122]

Most out-of-state tuition grant programs were patently inadequate, as they provided only tuition and did not cover travel and other living expenses. Moreover, legislatures usually appropriated fixed sums, allocated on a first-come, first-served basis, which meant that some applicants received nothing. Ironically, the initial legal challenges were brought in the two states that had been first to provide blacks with *anything* in regard to graduate and professional education. Such litigation was attractive to the NAACP, because inequalities were so stark and because advanced education was critical to black progress.[123]

Thomas Hocutt brought the first university equalization suit in 1933 when the University of North Carolina School of Pharmacy denied him admission based on race. The court dismissed that suit because Hocutt's undergraduate school failed to provide the transcript required for admission. In 1935, Donald Murray brought a similar suit against the University of Maryland Law School. Maryland had an out-of-state scholarship law, but the state's highest court ruled it inadequate and ordered Murray's admission. Lloyd Gaines sued next, after the University of Missouri Law School denied him admission based on race.[124]

None of this litigation directly challenged segregation, only the obvious inequality inherent in denying blacks the same in-state opportunities afforded to whites. Although the text of the Fourteenth Amendment need not be read to forbid all racial inequalities, by 1900 it was well established that separate must be equal to be constitutional, which presumably is why southern states bound themselves by law to provide blacks with equal-but-separate facilities. Dicta in *McCabe* (1914) confirmed that facial inequality was fatal to racial classifications, notwithstanding reasonable justifications for it, such as disparate per capita racial demand.

Yet in *Gaines*, Missouri purported to extend blacks equal treatment, by offering to subsidize their law school tuition just as it did for whites. To be sure, blacks would have to pursue their education outside the state, though whites would not. Yet segregated education inevitably offered somewhat different opportunities to blacks and whites. Blacks in segregated grade schools, especially in jurisdictions with low black population densities, frequently traveled longer distances to school. The legal question was when those differences rose to the level of unconstitutional inequality. Courts applying separate-but-equal principles had ruled that the Constitution required only "substantial equality" and that longer travel distances were insubstantial. By contrast, the decision in *Gaines* concluded that out-of-state travel was substantial inequality but did not explain why. The justices expressly disavowed reliance on obvious inequalities, such as Missouri's failure to subsidize travel and other living expenses, or the inability of out-of-state education to adequately prepare one for Missouri legal practice. Instead, they observed, "The basic consideration is not as to what sort of opportunities other States provide, . . . but as to what opportunities Missouri itself furnishes." This is

FIGURE 3.5
Thurgood Marshall (*standing*) with Donald Murray (*middle*),
circa 1935. (*Library of Congress, Prints and Photographs
Division, Visual Materials from the NAACP Records*)

unconvincing. Missouri, not some other state, provided Missouri blacks with
tuition grants. The Court failed to explain how that was an unconstitutional
deviation from what Missouri provided whites.[125]

Even reaching the merits in *Gaines* required a stretch. After Gaines had
applied for and been denied admission to law school, his lawyers made the
mistake of not asking the Lincoln Board of Curators to establish a separate
black law school, as Missouri law apparently empowered them to do if the
need arose among the state's black population. This procedural gaffe was
similar to McCabe's failure to request the service that he was being denied.
McCabe's lapse had proved fatal, in an opinion authored by Justice Hughes
in 1914. Twenty-four years later, Chief Justice Hughes circumvented the procedural problem by interpreting Missouri law to confer discretion, rather
than an obligation, on the Lincoln Board of Curators to establish a separate
black law school on request. Yet even on this interpretation, why did Gaines
not have to approach the curators before suing?[126]

FIGURE 3.6
Lloyd Gaines, 1936. (*Bettmann/CORBIS*)

Thus, one could argue that the Court should have dismissed *Gaines* as unripe, because the plaintiff had failed to pursue all available relief under state law. On the merits, *Gaines* was a case of first impression, requiring elucidation of the equality prong of separate but equal. The justices' willingness to finesse the procedural problem and their unconvincing focus on the sanctity of state boundaries in their discussion of the merits suggest a growing solicitude for civil rights litigants. The extralegal context of race relations had changed significantly by 1938. With black lawyers and economists playing unprecedented roles in federal administrative agencies and other black professionals earning novel cultural recognition, perhaps the justices found incongruous the wholesale exclusion of blacks from southern graduate and professional education. Ten years earlier, *Gaines* would not have been argued by a black lawyer such as Charles Hamilton Houston, who demonstrated through his Harvard legal pedigree and his forensic skills what blacks could achieve if afforded equal educational opportunities. Moreover, by 1938, several justices were becoming more attentive to the interests of racial and religious minorities—partly a reaction against the oppressive practices of foreign totalitarian regimes.[127]

Moreover, Maryland's highest court had invalidated a similar out-of-state scholarship scheme in 1936. (The rulings were distinguishable, as the

Maryland court relied on the inadequacies of out-of-state scholarships that *Gaines* purportedly deemed irrelevant.) If at least some border-state judges thought such laws unconstitutional, the issue must have been relatively easy for those Supreme Court justices who did not share the average Maryland jurist's sympathy for segregation. Southern newspaper reaction to *Gaines* was calm, compliant, and occasionally approving, which suggests that many educated southern whites no longer thought that shipping blacks out of state for education was morally acceptable. Some southern liberals proclaimed the ruling to be just. Even the Columbia, South Carolina, *State* did not "see how the supreme court could have decided the Missouri case except as it was decided." *Gaines* did not challenge segregation, as it required only that blacks be segregated within, not without, state boundaries. Such a ruling caused little consternation among white southerners.[128]

Interwar decisions reveal the justices' emerging sensitivity to racial injustice. In criminal procedure rulings for the first time, they scrutinized state court findings of fact regarding mob domination, the right to counsel, discrimination in jury selection, and the voluntariness of confessions. *Condon* stretched to find state action, and *Gaines* struggled to reach the merits and invalidate an out-of-state scholarship scheme on questionable grounds. Yet the justices showed no inclination to challenge core Jim Crow practices, such as segregation and disfranchisement. Nor did they significantly erode the state-action requirement, which ultimately proved among the most formidable barriers to securing racial justice. Not until World War II catalyzed fundamental shifts in U.S. racial attitudes and practices did the justices begin transforming the constitutional jurisprudence of race.

CONSEQUENCES

CRIMINAL PROCEDURE

Moore's reversal of convictions resulting from mob-dominated trials may have saved the lives of six black defendants. Given public opinion in Arkansas regarding the Phillips County race riot, the governor might have hesitated to commute sentences without the Court's intervention. Yet the governor did commute the sentences after *Moore*, rather than awaiting the federal habeas hearing and possible new trials, which suggests that the public clamor for executions had dissipated by 1923. Perhaps, then, the defendants would not have been executed regardless of the Court's intervention. One cannot know for sure.[129]

Measuring *Moore*'s broader impact is also difficult. The decision plainly did not end mob-dominated trials or even induce state appellate courts to consistently reverse guilty verdicts in such cases, as Scottsboro and other similar proceedings around 1930 make clear. Some lower courts construed *Moore* narrowly and refused to find mob domination on slightly less egregious facts. Moreover, even if fewer mob-dominated trials did take place after *Moore*, the reduction might have been attributable to changing social circumstances rather than to any Court decision. Urbanization, industrialization, better education, advances in communication and transportation, more professionalized law enforcement, and the greater threat of federal intervention eroded the background conditions that were conducive to lynchings. A reduction in threatened lynchings naturally translated into fewer mob-dominated trials. Southern lynchings declined steadily through the interwar years, except for a brief resurgence early in the depression. The reduction in lynchings was not attributable to the Court, which had no power to control them. Similarly, any reduction in mob-dominated trials may not have been the justices' doing.[130]

The Court likely saved the Scottsboro defendants from execution. Given white opinion in Alabama in the early 1930s, the governor would probably not have commuted their death sentences. Yet the Court's reversal of the first round of convictions in *Powell* and the second in *Norris* did not prevent Alabama from initiating a third, which resulted in one more death sentence and several lengthy prison terms. Indeed, the Court's reversals seemed only to further inflame local opinion, which ensured that prosecutors would not drop cases and that juries would continue to convict and impose draconian sentences. Eventually, the justices ran out of plausible federal grounds for reversing convictions. In 1937, they refused to review Haywood Patterson's fourth conviction, which carried a seventy-five-year sentence. That the justices probably believed the defendants were innocent was not, unfortunately, a sound constitutional basis for reversing their convictions. So, despite their innocence, the Scottsboro defendants each spent between five and twenty years in prison. The Court's two reversals may have saved their lives, but the Court could not prevent their unjust incarcerations. One possible lesson to learn is that state judges, if determined to have their way and prepared to lie and cheat, usually have sufficient means to frustrate federal court intervention.[131]

We have no way of measuring whether *Powell* produced better legal representation for southern black defendants. Even if representation did improve, the cause might have been increasing professionalization of the legal system or the growing belief among white southerners that preserving Jim Crow did not require sacrificing innocent black defendants. In addition, *Powell* was written as narrowly as possible, thus limiting its potential consequences. Not only did it cover only capital cases, but it seemed limited to the Scottsboro facts, including "the ignorance and illiteracy of the defendants, their youth, the circumstances of public hostility, the imprisonment and close surveillance of the defendants by the military forces."[132]

Even if *Powell* produced better legal representation for southern blacks, this may not have greatly affected case outcomes. The ILD criticized *Powell* for relying on the least significant ground of reversal. Indeed, Communists accused the Court of instructing Alabama on how to properly lynch the defendants. Even if appointed days before trial and afforded adequate opportunity to prepare, defense counsel was generally of little assistance to clients like these in a system heavily stacked against fair adjudication. The Scottsboro defendants enjoyed outstanding legal representation in their retrials, yet it made no difference to the results.

Placing blacks on southern juries would have had greater impact, which is why contemporaries thought the jury exclusion claim in Scottsboro more important than the right-to-counsel argument. In practice, however, *Norris* had little effect on southern jury selection. Southern newspaper reaction to the ruling was restrained, with predictions that *Norris* could be easily circumvented through lawful means. The Jackson, Mississippi, *Daily News* considered the ruling only a minor nuisance, as lawyers would have to invest time devising methods of evasion. In Mississippi and South Carolina, where jury service was tied to voter registration, *Norris* made no difference at all, as blacks remained almost universally disfranchised. In other states, *Norris* still permitted typical jury selection methods that vested enormous discretion in (white) jury commissioners. Proving race discrimination in the administration of such schemes was extremely difficult, *Norris* notwithstanding, especially because state courts made the initial factual determinations.[133]

Many southern whites concluded that *Norris* could be circumvented by placing a few blacks on jury rolls, where they would rarely be called, and even if they were, they might be intimidated out of serving. When a black college president in Texas refused to be excused from jury service in 1938, white hoodlums removed him from the jury room and threw him head first down the steps of a Dallas courthouse. Two other Dallas blacks summoned for jury service required protection from Texas Rangers. The presence of an occasional black on a grand jury could be nullified by requiring supermajorities, not unanimity, for indictment. The grand jury that reindicted the Scottsboro defendants after *Norris* consisted of thirteen whites and one black and operated under a rule requiring only two-thirds for indictment. The even rarer black called for service on trial juries could be excluded through challenges for cause, over which judges exercise enormous discretion, or through peremptory challenges, the number of which some states increased to nullify *Norris*'s impact. In Patterson's retrial, twelve blacks appeared on the venire of one hundred, but seven were excused on request and the other five were struck with peremptories.[134]

The most that *Norris* accomplished, and even then only in large cities in the peripheral South, was placing a single black on an occasional jury. As white racial opinion was beginning to soften in these areas anyhow, one can imagine their permitting occasional blacks to serve on juries regardless of the Court's intervention. Indeed, before *Norris*, black jurors were serving sporadically in parts of Maryland, Virginia, and Tennessee. In the Deep South and in most rural counties throughout the South, blacks did not serve on juries for another generation, despite *Norris*. A 1940 study found that the vast majority of rural counties in the Deep South "have made no pretense of putting Negroes on jury lists, much less calling or using them in trials." In a Louisiana case that reached the Supreme Court in 1939, a rural parish with a black population of nearly 50 percent had "complied" with *Norris* by placing three blacks, one of whom was dead, on a jury venire of three hundred.[135]

Brown v. Mississippi almost certainly saved three blacks from the death penalty but did not prevent possibly innocent defendants from spending three to seven years in jail. Doubtful of securing acquittals on retrial, defense lawyers thought it prudent to accept prison sentences rather than risk death penalties after a second trial.[136]

Measuring the amount of physical coercion used by southern sheriffs to extract confessions from blacks is impossible, and thus one cannot calculate *Brown*'s effect on such practices. Yet there are reasons to doubt that it had much effect. *Brown* was an easy case for Court intervention, as the deputy sheriff admitted the beatings. *Brown*'s likeliest effect was to reduce the candor of law enforcement officers. If sheriffs denied coercing blacks to confess and state courts believed them, federal judges were virtually powerless to intervene. Moreover, independently of *Brown*, physical torture seems to have been losing favor. The Wickersham Commission report in 1931 noted a reduction in extreme physical coercion, and public revulsion against Nazi and Stalinist law enforcement methods may have further discouraged such practices. Finally, *Brown*'s impact was limited because by the 1930s southern courts themselves generally reversed convictions based on confessions extracted through torture. Mississippi judges might well have reversed the *Brown* convictions had it not been for the Scottsboro backlash. Thus, at most, *Brown* held state courts to the standard they usually applied on their own.[137]

One reason these criminal decisions had so little impact was that southern black defendants could not ordinarily get to the Supreme Court. Their fate lay with less-sympathetic state judges, who did not necessarily agree with the constitutional rights identified by the justices. Most southern black defendants were poor and could not afford a lawyer, much less the several thousand dollars necessary for extensive appeals. The cases that reached the Court were atypical, as all depended on outside assistance. The NAACP financed the *Moore* litigation; the ILD bankrolled *Powell* and *Norris*; and the NAACP, the CIC, and the Association of Southern Women for the Prevention of Lynching underwrote *Brown*. The Phillips County race riot and the alleged rapes at Scottsboro captured national attention. Because these cases highlighted the worst excesses of Jim Crow, they provided outstanding fundraising opportunities. The NAACP and the ILD, respectively, got involved early and raised vast sums for appeals. *Brown* was more of a garden-variety murder case. Only the extraordinary efforts of appointed counsel, who covered costs from his own pocket, kept the case alive long enough for outside organizations to get involved and finance the high-court appeal.[138]

In run-of-the-mill criminal cases, indigent black defendants were represented not by elite lawyers hired by the NAACP or the ILD but by court appointees. These lawyers were generally white and could seldom be counted upon to aggressively defend their clients' rights, as doing so could be injurious to their careers or even hazardous to their health. A tacit agreement existed among many prosecutors and defense attorneys not to challenge the exclusion of blacks from juries. After two court-appointed white lawyers breached that understanding in a Maryland murder case in 1931, they were forced to withdraw under pressure, and the Communist lawyer who replaced them endured death threats and retaliatory disbarment proceedings. The ILD lawyer who represented the Scottsboro defendants in their initial retrials, Samuel Leibowitz, was besieged with death threats after he questioned the honesty of the jury commissioners and the alleged rape victims. The court-appointed white defense lawyer in *Brown* ruined a promising political career by pursuing the case so aggressively. In the wake of Scottsboro, two white ILD lawyers lost their lives while defending three blacks charged with raping and killing a white woman in Tuscaloosa, Alabama.[139]

Black lawyers, who might have been more aggressive in defending the rights of black clients, were scarce in the South. The number in Mississippi fell from twenty-one in 1910 to three in 1940, and in South Carolina during that time from seventeen to five. Outside of major cities, there were essentially none. Furthermore, the few black lawyers practicing were distinct liabilities in southern courtrooms, because of their generally inferior legal training and the racial prejudice of white judges and jurors. The NAACP, to preserve its credibility, would not take criminal cases unless it was convinced of the defendants' probable innocence. The general absence of rural branches hindered the NAACP's involvement in cases where abuses were likely to be greatest at the critical point in the litigation—when the trial record was being made. In addition, because of limited resources and the high cost of litigation, the association could take only a few of even the "good, clear cases . . . involving the fundamental rights of Negroes."[140]

NAACP involvement was a mixed blessing anyway for southern black defendants. The association provided essential financial backing and skilled lawyering, but its public involvement risked alienating local opinion, thereby reducing the chances of obtaining favorable jury verdicts, appellate reversals, or gubernatorial commutations. Thus, the NAACP faced a dilemma in these cases. The best way to win in state court was to maintain a low profile, hire eminent white defense counsel, and focus on narrow legal issues. But fundraising and political propagandizing required publicity, and the broadest and boldest attacks on Jim Crow attracted the most. Black lawyers were generally more reliable for raising fundamental challenges to white supremacy, and their courtroom presence provided valuable educational lessons to black audiences. Finally, although converting Scottsboro into a national and international event almost certainly reduced the chances of state appellate reversal or gubernatorial commutation—the NAACP criticized the ILD's tactics as "calculated to ensure . . . these lads [are] murdered"—it likely enhanced the prospects of success in the Supreme Court, where the justices cannot have been oblivious to national opinion that believed the defendants were innocent.[141]

Enlisting competent counsel on appeal was frequently too late, as inept or careless trial lawyering produced procedural defaults that insulated constitutional violations from appellate review. The coerced confession claims in *Brown* nearly failed to gain a Court hearing because defense counsel had challenged the voluntariness of confessions at the wrong point of the trial. Jury discrimination claims were procedurally defaulted in *Moore* and *Powell* and nearly so in *Patterson*. A similar lawyer's oversight in *Frank v. Mangum* cost the defendant appellate review of the question of whether his absence from the courtroom when the jury verdict was returned violated due process. Even skilled defense lawyers, as in *Frank*, could slip on the treacherous terrain of state criminal procedure. Until the Court in the civil rights era changed the rules regarding federal court deference to state procedural defaults, many valid federal constitutional claims were denied a hearing in any appellate court.[142]

Finally, white supremacy was so broadly and deeply rooted that compiling the trial record necessary for effective appellate review was difficult. In *Moore*, despite the wholesale slaughter of blacks in Phillips County, securing the affidavits necessary to support a change-of-venue motion proved nearly impossible, because blacks were intimidated by threats of economic and physical reprisal. When Walter White of the NAACP traveled to Arkansas to investigate the facts in preparation for litigation, he was nearly lynched. Blacks who testified to their qualifications in cases that challenged race discrimination in jury selection likewise risked retaliation. Rigorous cross-examination of white witnesses, especially women in rape cases, alienated white jurors and put defense counsel at risk. White witnesses who challenged Jim Crow norms were subject to intimidation as well. One of the physicians testifying in a Scottsboro trial privately confessed to the judge that he never believed a rape had occurred, but he refused to say so publicly, for fear that he could no longer live in the community in peace. Ruby Bates, who recanted her rape allegation in a Scottsboro retrial, refused to return to Alabama for subsequent proceedings after she received death threats.[143]

For these reasons—the inability of most southern black defendants to afford counsel, the limited availability of NAACP assistance, the morass of state procedural default rules, and the obstacles to compiling favorable trial records—cases such as *Moore*, *Powell*, *Norris*, and *Brown* were the exception, not the rule. The interwar Court probably heard only four such cases because similar ones failed to advance that far in the legal system. Many southern black defendants were denied their constitutional rights without any opportunity for appellate review.

VOTING

Herndon and *Condon* had almost no direct impact on black voting, because they were so easily circumvented. *Herndon* had no application outside of Texas, the only state to bar blacks by statute from party primaries. Even within Texas, public reaction to *Herndon* was nonchalant, because blacks could be excluded just as easily through party rule. Governor Dan Moody proposed legislation authorizing such exclusion on the same day *Herndon* was decided. *Condon* was also insignificant because it simply rerouted the exclusion decision from the party's executive committee to its annual state convention. Neither ruling induced southern Democratic parties to admit blacks.[144]

Assessing the significance of *Grovey*, which sustained black exclusion when the policy was adopted by party convention, requires speculating how effective a contrary ruling would have been. As we shall see, *Smith v. Allwright* (1944), which overruled *Grovey* and invalidated white primaries, appears to have had a dramatic effect on black voter registration in the South. Perhaps that means *Grovey* was significant. Yet, a great deal changed in the South between 1935 and 1944, creating a more receptive environment for a Court decision that invalidated white primaries. The best way of assessing *Grovey*'s significance may be to look not at the response to *Smith* but at the consequences of two lower court decisions in the early 1930s invalidating white primaries in Virginia and Florida. Those states paid for primary elections, unlike Texas, and lower courts considered that difference dispositive. Yet neither decision had much effect. Black voter registration increased little, and in rural counties the decisions were completely ignored. Charles Hamilton Houston drew the lesson that successful litigation had limited results unless local communities were prepared to act on it. In the 1930s, they generally were not. Indeed, had these lower court rulings led to more significant increases in black voter registration, legislatures would probably have tried to evade them by shifting financial responsibility for primaries from the government to political parties. Because the rulings were so inconsequential, nobody even bothered trying to circumvent them. By the time of *Smith*, blacks would be more insistent on voting, whites less resistant, the NAACP better situated to capitalize on the decision, and the federal government more supportive of enforcement.[145]

Breedlove rejected a constitutional challenge to the poll tax. How much impact would a contrary ruling have had on southern black suffrage? Experts have disagreed on whether poll taxes played a significant role in disfranchising blacks around 1900. This is a different question, however, from whether abolishing poll taxes in the 1930s would have enfranchised many blacks. Poll taxes may have had significant disfranchising effects when adopted, yet by the 1930s black disfranchisement was secured by many other methods as well. The poll tax was repealed in North Carolina in 1920, in Louisiana in 1934, and in Florida in 1937. After repeal, black voter registration in these states did not significantly increase, and in Louisiana, it actually declined. White voter registration, however, rose appreciably. Apparently, the poll tax had had a significant disfranchising effect on poor whites, while black disfranchisement depended more on discriminatory administration of literacy tests, white primaries, and the threat and reality of physical violence. In Alabama, 18,000 black men were exempted from the poll tax as World War I veterans, yet only 1,500 were registered to vote. Given white racial attitudes, these three southern states could not possibly have repealed poll taxes when they did, had substantial increases in black voter registration been a possible consequence. Opponents of poll-tax repeal often argued in racial terms, but supporters recognized this as a canard. The battle over repeal of the poll tax in the 1930s was over whether to enfranchise hundreds of thousands of poor whites. Blacks were not going to vote, no matter how that debate was resolved.[146]

RESIDENTIAL SEGREGATION

The *Buchanan* decision's invalidation of residential segregation ordinances had little or no effect on segregated housing patterns, and neither did the two summary affirmances in the interwar years. Too many alternative methods of segregating neighborhoods remained available. Most cities became much more segregated during this period, because of growing urbanization and the Great Migration. As late as 1910, no Chicago census tract was more than 61 percent black, and in 1920 none was more than 90 percent. By 1930, however, two-thirds of Chicago's blacks lived in tracts that were at least 90 percent black, and in 1940 three-fourths did. Residential segregation continued "as effectively without the law as with it."[147]

Corrigan rejected a challenge to racially restrictive covenants, so its significance partly depends on how effective a contrary decision would have been. *Shelley v. Kraemer* invalidated judicial enforcement of such covenants in 1948, with negligible effect on segregated housing patterns. Perhaps such a ruling would have been more efficacious at an earlier date, but probably not, given that enforcement resources would have been scarcer and the risk of violence for blacks testing their rights would have been greater. At a time when blacks who moved into white neighborhoods were regularly bombed or attacked by white mobs, and police rarely took steps to protect them, judicial enforcement of racially restrictive covenants was largely unnecessary to maintain segregated neighborhoods.

PUBLIC EDUCATION

The decision in *Gong Lum* affirmed the constitutionality of public school segregation, so its significance depends partly on how effective a contrary decision would have been at desegregating schools. Chapter 1 speculated that a *Plessy*-era decision invalidating school segregation would have been unenforceable, and we shall see in chapter 7 that *Brown v. Board of Education* (1954), which barred such segregation, was almost completely nullified by southern states for ten years, until Congress backed it up with effective enforcement legislation.

A contrary ruling in *Gong Lum* could not possibly have been more efficacious than *Brown* was. Presidents in the 1920s would have been even less supportive of school desegregation than Eisenhower was of *Brown*. The same is true of Congress, which in the 1920s failed to pass even the most rudimentary civil rights legislation—an antilynching law—but in 1957 would enact (weak) voting rights legislation. Federal government aid to public education was almost nonexistent in the 1920s, but by the 1960s it would prove the critical lever for enforcing desegregation. Northern opinion, which in the 1950s heavily favored *Brown*, would not have supported school desegregation in the 1920s. Southern whites would have been almost universally opposed to school desegregation in the 1920s, which was not *quite* true by the 1950s, and the intensity of their resistance would have been extraordinary. In the 1920s, southern NAACP branches were completely unequipped to take advantage of such a decision with follow-up litigation, and white violence would have been even more effective at suppressing such challenges than it was in the 1950s. Finally, the direct-action protest orchestrated by southern blacks in the early 1960s, which proved critical to the enforcement of *Brown* and to the enactment of the 1964 Civil Rights Act, was inconceivable in the 1920s. In 1927, the justices had no inclination to end public school segregation, but even if they had, the power to do so was lacking.[148]

Gaines, which invalidated out-of-state tuition grants for blacks to pursue graduate and professional education, had a greater effect on legislatures than most civil rights victories thus far considered. Yet its most direct consequence was perverse: Many states adopted the very scheme that the Court had invalidated.

When the NAACP began litigating graduate and professional school equalization cases in 1933, only the border states of Missouri and Maryland provided anything for advanced black education; both states had adopted out-of-state scholarship laws. In response to litigation, Maryland in 1935 began funding the scheme it had adopted two years earlier, and after losing the lawsuit in 1936, it tripled appropriations. Litigation or the threat thereof prompted several border and peripheral South states to adopt similar laws in the late 1930s.[149]

Gaines ruled such laws unconstitutional, which apparently left states with only two choices: provide equal but separate facilities for blacks within the state or integrate. Blacks in several states brought lawsuits challenging their exclusion from public universities, which led to "hurried conferences" among southern education officials to consider how to redress, consistent with *Gaines*, the virtually complete absence of public higher education for southern blacks. No state but West Virginia integrated its graduate or professional schools as the NAACP had been hoping, although Maryland had already integrated its law school in response to *Murray*. Missouri responded to *Gaines* by establishing a separate but obviously inferior law school for blacks. Maryland, Virginia, North Carolina, Kentucky, and Tennessee also began providing some rudimentary graduate and professional education for blacks in segregated institutions. Yet most southern states responded to *Gaines* by adopting the very out-of-state scholarship laws that the Court had invalidated. Only five states had such laws before *Gaines*, but by 1943 eleven did, and by 1948, seventeen. These laws were an improvement over what had previously been offered to blacks by way of advanced education—nothing—but they were a rather odd response to *Gaines*. Many southern white educators and politicians also began discussing the creation of regional universities for blacks, which would have been more efficient, given limited demand, than each state creating its own black graduate and professional schools. The only problem was that they, too, seemed plainly unconstitutional under *Gaines*. Not until after World War II did most southern states begin providing (segregated) higher education opportunities for blacks within their borders.[150]

Several commentators have ascribed more general significance to *Gaines* and claimed that it sounded "the death knell" for *Plessy* and "paved the way" for *Brown*. Looking backward from 1954, *Gaines* naturally appears to be a point of departure. Yet the notion that *Gaines* somehow doomed separate but equal is misconceived. The extralegal context of race relations was beginning to change by 1938, but not enough had happened since *Gong Lum* to erode the justices' support for school segregation. Commentators in the mid-1930s rightly observed that voluminous lower court precedent almost universally sustained school segregation. Writing in the same year as *Gaines*, one pair of experts predicted that if patterns of public education ever became uniform across regions, the North was much more likely to conform to the South's segregation practices than vice versa. *Gaines* only barred states from transporting black graduate and professional students out of state, while educating whites within. Nothing in the opinion intimated that a segregated black law school within the state was unconstitutional, and the NAACP read the decision only "as opening the way for legal action to compel equalization." The association had no plans to attack public school segregation any time soon. In 1936, Charles Houston observed, in connection with litigation challenging the exclusion of blacks from Baltimore County high schools, that "none of the Baltimore people believe that [integration] will be possible." If this were true in Baltimore, how much more so would it have been in the real South? All of the lower courts that confronted the issue interpreted

Gaines to authorize separate-but-equal black education. Federal aid-to-education legislation debated by Congress in 1937 still implicitly sanctioned public school segregation. The NAACP opposed that measure not because it would have permitted segregation but because it failed to guarantee an equal distribution of funds to black schools.[151]

Neither did *Gaines* indirectly undermine segregation by raising its costs. The NAACP had hoped that southern states would find the creation of separate-but-equal graduate and professional schools too expensive and thus integrate. Whether that hope would be realized depended on the intensity of southern whites' commitment to preserving segregation in higher education and the stringency of judicial interpretations of the equality requirement. The NAACP may have underestimated the determination of white southerners to preserve segregation in higher education. A more detached assessment after *Gaines* concluded that "those who are familiar with southern folkways realize that every other possible course will be exhausted before the color bar is taken down." A South Carolina newspaper predicted that no integration would occur "until public opinion changes radically," and a Virginia journal thought that "sentiment throughout the state is overwhelmingly against mixing the races." The border state of Oklahoma responded to *Gaines* by making it a crime to admit blacks to white schools or to teach in integrated classrooms.[152]

Moreover, *Gaines* did not disapprove of the "substantial equality" doctrine that had been used by lower courts applying separate but equal to sustain schemes in which blacks traveled farther to school than whites and in which black schools were denied certain facilities enjoyed by white ones. It is true that *Sweatt v. Painter* (1950) interpreted the equality requirement so stringently that segregation in higher education could not possibly survive in practice. But American race relations underwent enormous change between 1938 and 1950. One cannot assume that the justices in *Gaines* would have applied *Sweatt's* stringent conception of equality. *Gaines* provided no hint as to how inferior a black law school a state might have been able to get away with. The same Maryland court that in 1936 had invalidated out-of-state tuition grants for black law students sustained, in 1937, on a lenient reading of "substantial equality," Baltimore County's policy of sending its black children of high school age to segregated schools in the city of Baltimore, while paying tuition but not transportation costs. Had the justices approved a similarly permissive interpretation, *Gaines* would have put little indirect pressure on segregation.[153]

Some interwar litigation for racial equality lost in the Court. The justices declined to invalidate racially restrictive covenants, white primaries adopted by political parties, or public school segregation. Other civil rights litigation won, as the justices broadened constitutional protections for criminal defendants, invalidated white primaries imposed by the state, reaffirmed the invalidity of residential segregation ordinances, and barred out-of-state scholarship schemes for black graduate and professional education. But even Court victories produced little change in racial practices. Black service on southern juries did not increase appreciably after *Norris*, and housing segregation worsened, despite the reaffirmations of *Buchanan*. *Gaines* prompted legislative action, but neither integration nor the equalization of higher education ensued.

It is possible that civil rights litigation was more important for its intangible effects: convincing blacks that the racial status quo was malleable, educating them about their rights, providing focal points for organizing protest, and instructing oblivious northern whites about the egregiousness of Jim Crow conditions. Such intangible consequences are impossible to measure, but they may nonetheless have been real and perhaps even substantial.

A civil rights movement faced intimidating obstacles, especially in the South. One of the most formidable was simply convincing blacks that the status quo of racial subordination and oppression was not natural and inevitable but contingent and malleable. A black man in Louisa County, Virginia, confided to the NAACP in 1935 that our "worst enemy is ourselves." A southern branch officer told the national office in 1924, in connection with the fight against residential segregation, that "it is a very hard matter to convince the mass of our people that segregation is not the best thing for us." Walter White explained in 1937 that the NAACP's greatest difficulty was "getting over to the masses of our folks the significance of these fights." The civil rights movement not only had to overcome black hopelessness and fearfulness but also had to confront what Martin Luther King, Jr., later called the "ultimate tragedy of segregation"—the psychological damage that white supremacist ideology had inflicted on those blacks who had internalized its lessons.[154]

In theory, black protest could have assumed a variety of forms: migration, violent revolt, political mobilization, economic pressure, street demonstrations, or litigation. In practice, options were limited. Violent protest would have been suicidal—Du Bois called it "little less than idiotic"—given overwhelming white physical power and the will to use it. Political protest was unavailable to southern blacks, who remained almost universally disfranchised. Northern blacks did try to use their political power at the national level to benefit southern blacks, through measures such as federal antilynching legislation. Yet the political power of northern blacks was still minimal, and southern senators could block any civil rights legislation through filibuster. Few southern blacks commanded sufficient financial resources to leverage social change through economic pressure. Street demonstrations, which proved so effective in the 1960s, were not yet a realistic option. The South was still too violent, segregation and disfranchisement too deeply entrenched, and the threat of national intervention too remote. Black leaders observed, no doubt correctly, that a Gandhian strategy of nonviolent protest in the South would have led to "an unprecedented massacre of defenseless black men and women." In much of the region, blacks could not even protest against lynchings without incurring physical risk.[155]

There were only two protest options realistically available to southern blacks: migration, which the NAACP called "the most effective protest against Southern lynching, lawlessness, and general deviltry," and litigation. Hundreds of thousands pursued the former; many fewer chose the latter. Litigation had risks, though it was less risky than street protests or voter registration outside of major cities. In the 1930s, southern black teachers who filed pay-equalization lawsuits generally lost their jobs, even though they were not directly challenging segregation. In 1938, a black man who was contemplating filing suit for admission to the University of Georgia Medical School changed his plans after being advised that it "would, perhaps, place my family and me in a rather dangerous position." Charles Houston urged black teachers in Georgia to file their pay-equalization suit in Atlanta, where the risks of retaliatory violence would be lower. Most civil rights litigation in the 1930s took place in border states and the peripheral South, because challenging the racial status quo in the Deep South, even through the courts, remained too dangerous.[156]

Most civil rights leaders appreciated the limits of litigation, given prevailing racial mores. However, they differed as to whether litigation was the best option available. On the political Left, Ralph Bunche and Roger Baldwin, head of the American Civil Liberties Union (ACLU), criticized the NAACP's litigation strategy, because "forces that keep the Negro under subjection will find some way of accomplishing their purposes, law or no law." Bunche thought that the NAACP viewed the Constitution as "detached from the political and economic realities of American life," as a sort of "protective angel hovering above us." By contrast, he believed that the Constitution could not be "anything more than the controlling elements in the American society wish it to be." Like many political radicals of the 1930s, Bunche preferred interracial labor organization to litigation.[157]

Yet many blacks who advocated litigation appreciated its limited potential and acknowledged that judicial decisions are constrained by popular opinion. Charles Houston, the principal legal strategist of the NAACP in the 1930s, recognized that law "has certain definite limitations when it comes to changing the mores of a community." He conceded, "It is too much to expect the court to go against the established and crystallized social customs." Houston warned that "we cannot depend upon judges to fight . . . our battles" and urged that "the social and public factors must be developed at least along with and if possible before the actual litigation commences." Despite such constraints, litigation remained attractive to Houston and others, because alternative options were so bleak. In 1937, a liberal white sociologist in the South, Guy Johnson, wondered if the chief value of litigation "has not been to serve as a catharsis for those discontented, impatient souls who, while they see no hope for normal participation in American life, feel that they must never give in and admit that they are beaten down spiritually."[158]

Even if litigation could not "bring on a social revolution," as Bunche observed, it may have furthered several long-term goals. Litigation educated

FIGURE 3.7
Charles Hamilton Houston. (*Library of Congress, Prints and Photographs Division, Visual Materials from the NAACP Records*)

blacks about their rights and inspired them to challenge the racial status quo. The NAACP's national office wrote letters to southern blacks that explained their rights and the obligation of whites to abide by them. Some black communities in the South felt so hopeless and isolated that for the national office merely to make inquiries on their behalf would "do a lot of good." The 1930 Margold report, which formulated litigation strategy for the NAACP, stressed that lawsuits would "stir the spirit of revolt among blacks" and force whites to respect them. A memorandum by Charles Houston declared that a principal objective of litigation should be "to arouse and strengthen the will of local communities to demand and fight for their rights."[159]

Houston and Thurgood Marshall thought that organizing local communities in support of litigation was nearly as important as winning lawsuits. They frequently made speeches at mass rallies while visiting southern communities for court appearances. "On occasion," a recent biographer writes, Marshall "appears to have been brought to town nominally to work on pending litigation but actually to rally the troops." Because of the need "to back up our legal efforts with the required public support and social force," Houston referred to himself as "not only lawyer but evangelist and stump speaker." Marshall and Houston used their local appearances to link lawsuits with broader community concerns, such as voter registration or general political organizing.[160]

What happened to Ossian Sweet in Detroit or to the Scottsboro defendants in Alabama could happen to nearly any black American at almost any time. Because such cases demonstrated to blacks the importance of binding together in self-defense, they provided unparalleled fundraising and branch-building opportunities for the NAACP. The association raised more than $70,000 in connection with the Sweet case—a small fortune in the 1920s. Scottsboro provided a similar fundraising bonanza for the ILD, as the defendants' mothers undertook speaking tours in the North, drawing large crowds and raising vast sums. In less celebrated cases, such as challenges to residential segregation, five or ten thousand dollars was a more realistic fundraising objective—still more than was required to carry the cases to the Supreme Court. Lawsuits often provided occasions for organizing new NAACP branches. Many branches originated in residential segregation challenges around World War I. The branch in Meridian, Mississippi, grew out of the *Brown* litigation, which the NAACP saw as "an opening wedge into . . . Mississippi," the one state that it had previously been unable to penetrate.[161]

Litigation also provided salutary examples to southern black communities of the accomplishments and courage of black Americans. Watching a skilled black lawyer subject a white sheriff to a grueling cross-examination educated southern blacks, who virtually never witnessed such scenes of blacks confronting whites on an equal footing. Bold and capable performances by black lawyers in southern courtrooms seemed to contravene the very premises of white supremacy. A Marshall biographer notes that the most important audience on such occasions was neither the judge nor the jury, but rather "the African-American community observing the trial." The NAACP recognized the "moral effect" of using black lawyers. In 1933, Walter White observed that using a black lawyer in the Texas white-primary litigation would "have an excellent psychological effect upon colored people."[162]

Litigation may also have raised the salience of the race issue for whites. Houston observed, "The truth is there are millions of white people who have no real knowledge of the Negro's problems and who never give the Negro a serious thought." A major challenge for the civil rights movement was educating whites about oppressive conditions under Jim Crow. From its inception, the NAACP saw its principal functions as giving "the facts of the American Negro's situation to the civilized world" and "marshalling . . . an enlightened public sentiment in defence of the Negro's rights." Litigation furthered these objectives. Bunche observed, "Court decisions, favorable or unfavorable, serve to dramatize the plight of the race more effectively than any other recourse; their propaganda and educative value is great." William Hastie referred to the Supreme Court as "a forum for presenting the varied aspects of the race problem." With regard to the Sweet trial, Walter White noted that the NAACP might prefer not to have an early verdict directed in its favor, because that would truncate the educational process, "which gives the trial its greatest ultimate value." Criminal cases may have afforded the best educational opportunities, as they revealed Jim Crow at its worst: southern blacks, possibly or certainly innocent of the crimes charged, being rail-roaded to the death penalty through farcical trials. By highlighting the worst features of white supremacy, such litigation may have inspired a backlash against the system as a whole, much as millions of Americans turned against segregation and disfranchisement in the 1960s, after witnessing appalling scenes of brutality from Birmingham and Selma. Justices confronted with such egregious abuses may have begun to rethink their previously tolerant attitudes toward Jim Crow.[163]

Finally, litigation, when successful, provided blacks with one of the few reasons they had for optimism before 1940. During the first two decades of its existence, when the NAACP bragged of its victories, Supreme Court rulings almost always headed the list, because the association had so few triumphs in other arenas. One of the most formidable obstacles to creating a social protest movement under oppressive conditions is convincing potential par-ticipants that change is feasible. As black leader Kelly Miller observed in 1935, even if court victories produced little concrete change, at least they "keep open the door of hope to the Negro." Roscoe Dunjee, the NAACP's principal agent in Oklahoma, noted after one such court victory, "It is just such rifts in the dark clouds of prejudice which cause black folks to know that a better day is coming by and by."[164]

By the late 1930s, the extralegal context of race was becoming more progres-sive, albeit in minor ways. At the beginning of the interwar period, the federal government was investigating the NAACP for alleged subversive activities, and President Wilson was refusing to meet with its leaders to discuss the epi-demic of white-on-black violence spawned by the war. By the end of the period, the association's general secretary, Walter White, enjoyed unprece-dented access to the White House through the First Lady, and the federal government was sponsoring numerous race-relations conferences. In 1922, the Harding administration segregated the dedication ceremony for the Lin-coln Memorial, and in 1930, the Hoover administration segregated Gold Star widows and mothers who were traveling on ships to Europe to visit the graves of their husbands and sons killed in the war. By contrast, in 1939, 75,000 peo-ple—including cabinet members, congressmen, and a Supreme Court jus-tice—attended Marian Anderson's integrated concert at the Lincoln Memo-rial, after the Daughters of the American Revolution had refused to allow her into Constitution Hall because of her race.[165]

By the end of the 1930s, the NAACP detected "a new South . . . in the making." Several thousand blacks were registered to vote in large southern cities, and a few were sitting on state court juries, for the first time in decades. Racial disparities in educational funding were finally starting to decline, as even racial conservatives began to admit that "[n]eglect of Negro schools . . . has reached the point where it is a public disgrace." The annual number of blacks lynched, which had increased appreciably during and after World War I, fell to three by 1939. Southern branches of the NAACP, which had been decimated by the white supremacist backlash following the war, showed new signs of life in the 1930s, as the association's national membership grew by more than 150 percent. The cautious liberalism of the CIC, which focused on reducing inequalities within a segregated system and curtailing white-on-black violence, was challenged by the region's first significant interracial organization committed to abolishing segregation, the Southern Conference for Human Welfare (SCHW), which was founded in Birmingham in 1938. By the late 1930s, southern white liberals were supporting federal antilynching legislation, and soon they would endorse federal anti–poll-tax measures. An event indicative of incipient changes in black cultural status occurred in 1940: The national postal service issued a commemorative stamp of Booker T. Washington. He was the first black person to be so honored. In the late 1930s, Joe Louis, the black heavyweight boxing champion, "was greeted with sportsmanlike admiration in every corner of the land." This was a striking contrast to the reception of Jack Johnson, winner of the same title a quarter century earlier, when "Negroes hardly dared to whisper about it" and the federal government suppressed news of it by banning the interstate transportation of pictures from prize fights. The scientific community's understanding of racial difference was turned upside down during these years, as environment replaced biology as the dominant explanation. By the late 1930s, moreover, popular revulsion against Nazi fascism was making "the continued oppression of any minority group . . . an extremely unpopular pastime."[166]

These changes, though significant, must be kept in perspective. In Congress, the era ended much as it began—with a Senate filibuster of the most rudimentary civil rights legislation, the antilynching bill. Despite the liberalism of the Roosevelt administration, the president never endorsed antilynching or anti–poll-tax legislation, as he felt too politically beholden to the South. In 1940, blacks in the rural South remained almost completely disfranchised and excluded from jury service. Blacks in the urban South, just beginning to register to vote in significant numbers, often faced Klan intimidation when doing so. The political powerlessness of southern blacks was evident in the almost complete absence of black police officers. School segregation was as deeply entrenched as ever in the South and had become more prevalent in the North. Although racial disparities in educational funding in the South were beginning to decline, one commentator calculated that, at the existing pace, racial parity with regard to per capita pupil expenditures would take 29 years, with regard to the value of school property 129 years, and with regard to per capita transportation costs 230 years. In 1940, blacks who lived in northern cities, although they enjoyed greater political and economic power, were far more residentially segregated than they had been decades earlier and were twice as likely as whites to be unemployed.[167]

Although concrete changes in racial practices had been minor, the prospect of change seemed much greater by the late 1930s. As one historian observed, this was "a time of planting, not harvesting." In 1934, Du Bois's pessimism had led him to encourage blacks to "make the best of their life in a segregated world," while the astute observer H. L. Mencken had found himself "full of doubt that the American Negro will recover his constitutional rights on any near tomorrow." By 1940, however, black leaders such as Mary McLeod Bethune were predicting a brighter future for black Americans. Paul Robeson, returning to the United States in 1939 after years abroad, proclaimed that "change was in the air." That same year, William Hastie noted a growing commitment among southern whites to the fair treatment of blacks and a greater "aggressiveness and militancy" among southern blacks. In his magisterial study of American race relations, researched mostly in the late 1930s, Swedish social scientist Gunnar Myrdal contrasted the pessimism that characterized the early 1930s with the optimism that pervaded the end of the decade. Racial change appeared to be in the offing by 1940, but it was the cataclysmic events of World War II, not the Great Depression or the New Deal, that were responsible for fundamental changes in U.S. racial attitudes and practices.[168]

One cannot say whether the Supreme Court's race decisions of the interwar period were ahead of or behind the pace of extralegal change, but they certainly were not far out of step in either direction. As the racial attitudes of the country began to change, so did those of the justices. The criminal procedure decisions of this era cannot be understood as constitutional minimalism. These rulings did not involve transparent violations but rather required the justices to depart from precedent and to create new constitutional law. The justices imposed constitutional constraints on southern lynch law at practically the same moment that Congress was deliberating upon, and might have passed, were it not for the antimajoritarian filibuster rules of the Senate, statutory constraints on lynching. *Condon* and *Gaines* also required stretching existing constitutional law. These decisions apparently demonstrate a shift in the justices' sensitivity to racial injustice. Footnote 4 of *Carolene Products* (1938), which articulates a special role for the Court in protecting the rights of racial and religious minorities, marks the beginnings of such a shift at the level of constitutional theory.[169]

Yet interwar changes in the constitutional jurisprudence of race were not dramatic. Public school segregation seemed as secure in 1940 as in 1920. *Gong Lum* indicates that the justices still thought school segregation to be an easy constitutional issue in 1927, and nothing in *Gaines* suggests a change by 1938. Nor did the interwar Court cast doubt on the constitutionality of black disfranchisement, as shown by *Grovey* and *Breedlove*. *Corrigan*, which dismissed a constitutional challenge to racially restrictive covenants, and *Grovey*, which rejected a constitutional challenge to Texas's white primary, reveal how little the justices were prepared to budge on the critical issue of state action. Because that issue cannot be neatly separated from substantive views regarding particular policies, these rulings demonstrate how limited were the changes in the justices' racial attitudes. Even criminal procedure victories were rendered on rationales so narrow that the practical effects on

Jim Crow justice were minimal. *Norris*, for example, had almost no impact on black jury service, as it left broad discretion in the hands of white jury commissioners and did not restrict racially discriminatory uses of peremptory challenges. A couple of southern senators opposed Roosevelt's Court-packing plan in 1937 partly because they saw the Court as a bulwark of white supremacy.[170]

The justices, like their fellow citizens, were only beginning to rethink racial attitudes in the 1930s. As many black leaders voiced new confidence, so some Court watchers expressed optimism regarding the prospects of future civil rights litigation. These prognosticators could not have known how quickly and decisively their predictions would be vindicated. World War II would have transformative consequences, not only for the social and political context of race, but also for its constitutional jurisprudence. Within a decade, the justices would overrule racially regressive decisions and begin charting a new course for the constitutional law of race.[171]

CHAPTER FOUR

World War II Era: Context and Cases

A brutal triple murder took place near Hugo, Oklahoma, on New Year's Eve 1939. A white man, his wife, and their four-year-old son were shot, and their bodies were hacked with an axe and then burned. W. D. Lyons, a black man, was arrested several days later. According to the NAACP's account of what happened, prior to the arrest of Lyons, a white escapee from the state chain gang had confessed to the murders. But the governor's office, fearful of the political consequences of election-year allegations that lax supervision of the chain gang had resulted in a triple murder, decided to frame a black man. The governor sent a special investigator to Hugo. According to boastful statements the investigator made to several white witnesses, he assaulted Lyons for several hours with his "nigger beater" (a blackjack). He also made Lyons hold on his lap a pan containing the victims' bones. Many local whites, not to mention Lyons's lawyers, were convinced that Lyons was innocent. At the trial, which the judge called a "gala" event for the community, lawyers from the NAACP and the ACLU sowed enough doubts about Lyons's guilt that the all-white jury, after several hours of deliberation, sentenced him to life imprisonment rather than death. As Thurgood Marshall, who participated in the trial, stated: "You know that life for such a crime as that—three people killed, shot with a shotgun and cut up with an axe and then burned—shows clearly that they believed him innocent." Lyons appealed to the Supreme Court, arguing that a conviction based on a confession obtained by torture violated the Due Process Clause.[1]

FIGURE 4.1

W. D. Lyons, circa 1940. (*Library of Congress, Prints and Photographs Division, Visual Materials from the NAACP Records*)

The Court decided six kinds of race cases in the World War II era. With regard to voting, the justices invalidated Oklahoma's effort to grandfather its grandfather clause, struck down Texas's white primary, thereby overruling *Grovey v. Townsend* (1935), and condemned the exclusion of blacks from pre-primary elections conducted by a "private" political club in an East Texas county. With regard to graduate and professional education, the Court applied *Missouri ex rel. Gaines v. Canada* (1938) to require Oklahoma to provide qualified blacks with in-state legal education, ordered a black man admitted to the University of Texas School of Law because a recently created black law school was not equal, and forbade the education school of the University of Oklahoma from segregating a black student in dining, library, and classroom facilities. In the housing area, the justices ruled that court injunctions enforcing racially restrictive covenants were unconstitutional, and then they forbade enforcement of such agreements through damages suits as well.

In transportation, the justices decided two cases that involved segregation and two more that involved racial inequality. *Mitchell v. United States* (1941) and *Henderson v. United States* (1950) interpreted the Interstate Commerce Act to bar railroads from denying blacks equal luxury accommodations on account of their lower per capita demand. *Morgan v. Virginia* (1946) invalidated as an unconstitutional burden on interstate commerce the application of a bus segregation law to interstate passengers. Two years later, the justices ruled that a northern state's law forbidding race discrimination in public accommodations was not an unconstitutional burden on foreign commerce when it was applied to international travelers. With regard to criminal procedure, the Court extended earlier rulings that required the state to appoint counsel for indigent defendants, that barred race discrimination in jury selection, and that overturned convictions based on coerced confessions. Finally, two peonage decisions broadened the condemnation of phony false-pretenses laws in *Bailey v. Alabama* (1911).

Civil rights litigation enjoyed unprecedented success in the Court during this era. By 1950, the NAACP boasted a winning record of well over 90 percent in the high court. The justices overruled recent precedents on restrictive covenants and white primaries, and for the first time since *Buchanan v. Warley* (1917), they breached segregation barriers by ordering a black man admitted to a white law school. Many of these civil rights decisions were unanimous—a noteworthy accomplishment for a Court that rarely managed to avoid dissent. Only in criminal cases, which were no longer as obviously about race, was the Court's record mixed. In other contexts, the justices seemed willing to vindicate nearly any claim for progressive racial reform, even if doing so required considerable legal creativity.

The Court decided these cases against a social and political backdrop that was highly conducive to racial reform. World War II was a watershed event in the history of American race relations. Several factors connected with the war—its democratic ideology, the civil rights consciousness it fostered among blacks, the unprecedented political and economic opportunities it created for blacks, and the Cold War imperative for racial change that followed—combined to create a climate favorable to progressive racial change. By the mid-1940s, black leaders had good reason to be optimistic. In addition, civil rights litigants now faced a reconstituted Court that was in the process of carving out a new constitutional function for itself. Having repudiated their *Lochner*-era commitments to the protection of property and contract rights, the justices increasingly viewed themselves as playing a special role in protecting the rights of "discrete and insular minorities," of which blacks were a paradigmatic example.

CONTEXT

By the 1940s, long-term forces for racial change that had antedated World War II—urbanization, industrialization, the Great Migration, and educational advancement—were producing significant results. The war magnified these forces. In the 1940s, more than 1.5 million southern blacks, pushed by changes in southern agriculture and pulled by wartime industrial demand, migrated to northern cities. The political power of blacks grew, as they relocated from a region of nearly universal disfranchisement to one without significant suffrage restrictions and as they came to hold the balance of power between evenly matched Republican and Democratic parties in the North. Urbanization facilitated the creation of a black middle class, which possessed the inclination, capacity, and opportunity to engage in social protest. Even blacks who migrated to southern cities found less restrictive racial mores and better opportunities to coordinate social protest. Industrialization enhanced the economic opportunities of blacks and removed part of Jim Crow's original rationale: the maintenance of a subordinate class of agricultural laborers. Better education enabled blacks to envision different race relations and empowered them to pursue that vision. Better education for whites loosened their commitment to Jim Crow.[2]

Though these long-term forces were important, World War II's contribution to progressive racial change cannot be overstated. Earlier wars had had similarly egalitarian consequences. The American Revolution facilitated the abolition of slavery in the North and temporarily boosted manumissions in the South. The Civil War ultimately became a crusade against slavery; it generated dramatic changes in the legal status of northern blacks; and it culminated in postwar constitutional amendments that guaranteed a certain measure of civil and political equality to all blacks. Even World War I destabilized, without fundamentally undermining, the Jim Crow system, which was then at its historical apex.[3]

Several factors account for the egalitarian impact of war. Americans tend to define their war aims in democratic terms. The purpose of World War I was "to make the world safe for democracy" and that of World War II to defeat fascism. The democratic ideology of such conflicts forced Americans to confront, and sometimes to reform, their own contradictory practices, such as racial subordination. In addition, wars advance racial equality because of their dislocative effects. Total wars especially, such as the Civil War and World War II, undermine traditional patterns of status and behavior. Lincoln was driven first to emancipate and then to arm the slaves after a year-long effort to suppress disunionism without disrupting traditional racial patterns had proved unavailing. Finally, war usually involves common sacrifice for the general good and thus has inescapably egalitarian implications. Thus, sacrifices made by liberated slaves on Civil War battlefields paved the way for black enfranchisement after the war.[4]

World War II influenced racial attitudes and practices in many ways. The ideology of the war was antifascist and prodemocratic. Even before Pearl Harbor, revulsion against fascism had impelled many Americans to reconsider the meaning of democracy, with unavoidable racial implications. The commitment of Nazis to Aryan supremacy helped "give racism a bad name" in the United States. In 1939, a judge wrote to Justice Harlan Fiske Stone, noting the hypocrisy of Americans who criticized Nazi Germany for race discrimination, given Jim Crow. Likewise, the NAACP pointed out that "our government, raising its hands in horror over persecution on the other side of the world, might take a moment to glance at its own back yard," where it would see "Hitlerism . . . directed against citizens who happen not to be white." It is true that antifascist rhetoric produced little racial change in the short term and that white southerners became proficient at criticizing the anti-Semitism of the Nazis while overlooking the ramifications of that critique for white supremacy. Yet the disparity between American racial ideals and practices afforded valuable propaganda opportunities for the Nazis, who constantly assailed this double standard. For virtually the first time in U.S. history, domestic racial practices had acquired foreign-policy implications, and racially motivated lynchings "thr[ew] mud on the honor and dignity of the . . . country before the world."[5]

The entrance of the United States into the war deepened the contributions of this antifascist ideology to American culture. President Roosevelt urged Americans to "refut[e] at home the very theories which we are fighting abroad," while his Republican opponent in 1940, Wendell Willkie, observed that Americans could not honestly fight "the forces and ideas of imperialism abroad and maintain any form of imperialism at home." Frank Knox, the secretary of the navy, told civil rights leaders that "an army fighting allegedly for Democracy should be the last place in which to practice undemocratic segregation." A 1942 editorial in the New York Times urged America to curtail race discrimination in order to avoid "the sinister hypocrisy of fighting abroad for what it is not willing to accept at home." In 1943, Justice Frank Murphy told his colleagues that statutory racial distinctions are "at variance with the principles for which we are now waging war."[6]

Yet many blacks were cynical about the purportedly democratic objectives of the war. Before the United States entered the conflict, many blacks could perceive very little difference between the Axis nations and Great Britain, and they questioned why they should prefer an imperialist nation that exploited nonwhite peoples to Japan, which professed to be fighting against colonialism. Blacks wondered why the Four Freedoms celebrated by Churchill and Roosevelt seemed to apply only to European countries under Nazi domination and not to nonwhite peoples struggling to escape colonialism. Many blacks saw little sense in "a black man [being] killed fighting a yellow man for the protection of a white man." The Pittsburgh Courier, a leading black newspaper, observed a year before Pearl Harbor that "our war is not against Hitler in Europe, but against the Hitlers in America."[7]

The morale of blacks was generally low when the United States entered the war. According to a 1942 poll, most blacks in Harlem thought that they would be treated better, or at least no worse, under Japanese rule. Blacks saw a paradox in America's fighting against world fascism with a segregated army, and they complained of the "mock democracy" for which they were being asked to risk their lives. Many blacks agreed with the NAACP that the racism they were battling abroad and that which they confronted at home were "blood brothers." What was the difference between park benches in Berlin that were allocated to Jews and park benches in the American South that were allocated to blacks? The southern court system subjected blacks to injustices that "smack . . . strongly of the hideous crimes of Nazi rule." Blacks began demanding action instead of mere words, as they insisted that the war's democratic pretensions be translated into concrete racial reforms.[8]

The army's treatment of black soldiers compounded the cynicism of blacks. The *Pittsburgh Courier* complained that the War Department followed "the doctrine of white supremacy and racial separatism with a zeal that Dr. Joseph Goebbels would regard as commendable." Black soldiers protested their treatment in military camps (especially in the South), where they were segregated in accommodations, recreation, and transportation; forced to perform demeaning tasks from which whites were usually exempt; and subjected to constant abuse from white officers and military police. Black soldiers complained of being "treated like dogs," "wild animals," and "slaves"; they were forced to endure "a living hell." They were especially galled that German prisoners of war often received better treatment than they did. Many black soldiers were disappointed at the failure of the federal government to protect them from the abuse of white southerners. Some actually expressed indifference to the war's outcome. Such grievances were aired in public letters to black newspapers, which circulated widely among blacks.[9]

Blacks used their resentments constructively by adding a second front to the war, which became a fight against fascism at home as well as abroad. The war-related sacrifices of black people would be in the service of a better world, "which not only shall not contain a Hitler, but no Hitlerism." Blacks used the ideological underpinnings of the conflict "to prick the conscience of white America," as they highlighted the gap between the nation's democratic pretensions and its racist practices. When a black defendant was murdered during his retrial in a Texas courtroom after the Supreme Court had reversed his initial conviction, the NAACP observed that "much of the United States is no different from Hitler's Germany." In 1944, students at Howard University seeking to desegregate a restaurant in the District of Columbia carried signs that asked, "Are you for Hitler's way or the American way?" Many black newspapers compared the lynching of Cleo Wright in Sikeston, Missouri, in 1942 to Hitler's treatment of Jews. Traditional racial injustices became more difficult for whites to excuse and for blacks to bear during a "democratic" war in which blacks were dying on the battlefield. If blacks were "good enough to fight," then they were "good enough to vote" and "good enough for organized baseball."[10]

If the cognitive dissonance created by a Jim Crow army fighting Aryan supremacists was insufficient to induce most Americans to reconsider their racial practices, the opportunities afforded by American racial hypocrisy to Axis propagandists supplied more concrete incentives. Within forty-eight hours of the lynching of Cleo Wright, Axis radio had broadcast the details around the world, warning nonwhite listeners to expect similar treatment should the Allies win the war. When whites in Detroit rioted against blacks moving into public housing projects, Germany publicized the episode in South America and Japan did so in East Asia. Racial progressives in the United States used the potential for Axis exploitation of such racial incidents as an argument for reform. South Carolina whites who were trying to convince state Democrats to permit black participation in party primaries argued that doing so would help convince people in China, India, and elsewhere around the world that U.S. democracy respected human rights. Virginius Dabney, a Richmond newspaper editor, invoked similar arguments to urge Governor Colgate Darden to commute the death sentence of Odell Waller, a black sharecropper whose scheduled execution aroused national and international protest.[11]

Concern about such Axis propaganda impelled the federal government to act against the worst racial abuses. The Wright lynching proved a watershed. Before 1942, the federal government had disclaimed jurisdiction over private lynchings, reasoning that the Fourteenth Amendment applies only to state action. In the mid-1930s, the Roosevelt Justice Department had still been looking for excuses not to investigate even those lynchings that did seem to fall within the federal government's purview (because the responsible parties had crossed state boundaries). After the Wright lynching, Roosevelt ordered federal investigation of all lynchings, and the government tried to prosecute Wright's killers. The attorney general, Francis Biddle, explained that with the United States fighting to defend democracy around the world, lynchings had acquired international significance and thus came under federal control.[12]

During the war, blacks began more forcefully to demand their citizenship rights. Recalling with regret their willingness to "close ranks" and subordinate racial grievances during World War I, they resolved not to repeat that mistake. Southern blacks registered to vote in record numbers and demanded admission to Democratic primaries. James Hinton, head of the NAACP in South Carolina, reported that blacks were "aroused as never before, and we expect great things to come from this awakening." In 1943–1944, an NAACP voter registration campaign in Baltimore enrolled 9,000 blacks, and in Texas thousands more paid their poll taxes in order to be eligible to vote. Weary of Jim Crow indignities, many southern blacks refused to be segregated any longer on streetcars and buses, stood their ground when challenged, and thus provoked almost daily racial altercations. Blacks became less compliant with conventional rules of racial etiquette, finding small but symbolic ways to challenge the racial status quo. Black soldiers, frustrated by the constant racial abuse they suffered, began fighting back; the result was much interracial violence and many deaths. Hundreds of thousands of blacks channeled their militancy into NAACP membership, which increased ninefold during the war.[13]

The most organized manifestation of heightened black militancy was the March on Washington movement sponsored by A. Philip Randolph, the head of the Brotherhood of Sleeping Car Porters and the most prominent black labor union leader in the nation. Randolph's goal was to mobilize 100,000 blacks to march on the nation's capital in 1941 to protest race discrimination in the military and defense industries. No black protest of similar scale had occurred in U.S. history. Even relatively conservative black leaders were swept up in the rising tide of racial protest. In 1943, black author Rayford Logan asked a broad array of black leaders to contribute to a book that would examine "what the Negro wants." When the manuscript arrived at the publisher, the racially moderate white director of the University of North Carolina Press, W. T. Couch, was horrified to discover that even the least militant black contributors favored an immediate end to racial segregation—an enormous shift in opinion from the mid-1930s, for which Couch had been completely unprepared. Richmond newspaper editor Virginius Dabney observed that the war had "roused in the breasts of our colored friends hopes, aspirations, and desires which they formerly did not entertain, except in the rarest instances."[14]

Heightened black militancy occurred in a context of growing black political power. Even before the war ignited additional black migration to the North, northern politicians were seeking black votes, and Roosevelt was making symbolic racial concessions, including his appointment of Benjamin O. Davis, Sr., as the first black general and William Hastie, already the nation's first black federal judge, as civilian aide to the secretary of war. With Republicans criticizing the administration's policy of segregation in the armed forces and pundits predicting that 1940 would be the closest presidential election in decades, Roosevelt made further racial concessions: He promised more black combat units and the first black army aviators. Though the military did not desegregate during the war, black political pressure secured more black officers, the integration of officers' candidate schools in the air force, and as the 1944 election approached, an order from the War Department to desegregate most training-camp facilities.[15]

Black political clout was also partly responsible for the administration's decision to file a brief in the transportation discrimination case *Mitchell v. United States* (1941), and for the Justice Department's decision to assert jurisdiction over lynchings. The strategic importance of black voters in the North helped inspire the House to pass anti–poll-tax bills every two years in the 1940s, although southern Democratic senators killed them all. Fear of alienating northern blacks helped convince Democratic leaders to reject South Carolinian Jimmy Byrnes as the vice-presidential candidate in 1944. Harry S Truman, who received that nomination, had voted for antilynching and anti–poll-tax bills in the Senate as a faithful lieutenant of the Pendergast machine, which the many black voters of Kansas City generally supported. The Republican party adopted strong civil rights planks in 1940 and 1944, partly in an effort to win back black voters.[16]

World War II afforded unprecedented political opportunities for blacks to leverage concessions from the administration, which was determined to avoid divisive racial protest during wartime. As one black newspaper observed, "[E]ffective protest during emergency is infinitely more productive of results than ten times the efforts during periods of comparative normalcy." The prospect of a march on Washington, D.C., by 100,000 angry blacks "scared the government half to death." Desperate to avoid such a spectacle, Roosevelt issued an executive order banning employment discrimination in defense industries and in the federal government and establishing a Fair Employment Practices Commission (FEPC) to monitor compliance. Though the FEPC proved ineffective—it was underfunded and understaffed, lacked enforcement powers, and was constantly hounded by southern congressmen—it may have had symbolic significance, as a product of the first executive order on civil rights since Lincoln's Emancipation Proclamation. Blacks also used their political power to extract other fair-employment concessions. The War Labor Board outlawed racial wage differentials; the U.S. Employment Service began rejecting racially restricted job applications; and the National Labor Relations Board vowed to deny certification to discriminatory unions.[17]

World War II also created valuable economic opportunities for blacks. Military conscription produced labor shortages, which induced many war industries by 1942–1943 to relax their restrictions on hiring black workers. Unemployment among blacks fell from 937,000 in 1940 to 151,000 four years later, and the number of skilled black industrial workers doubled. The average income of urban black workers rose more than 100 percent during the war, a hefty increase even adjusting for inflation. Black soldiers, though still suffering rampant discrimination, received skills training, education, and, for many, the first semblance ever of economic security. War-related economic opportunities helped foster a black middle class, which proved instrumental to the postwar civil rights movement.[18]

Some facets of the war, it is true, retarded progressive racial reform. Black militancy and the concessions it elicited from the administration generated a backlash among southern whites, who noted, "Negroes were getting restless, sullen, uppity, out of line, and . . . something was going to have to be done about it." Assertive black passengers on streetcars who challenged segregation or other norms of racial etiquette often elicited violent—sometimes deadly—responses from whites. Black soldiers, tired of being segregated or otherwise humiliated, had frequent altercations with white military policemen and local law enforcement officers. In 1942, a white military policeman attempted to arrest a black soldier in Alexandria, Louisiana; in the ensuing race riot, 28 blacks were shot and nearly 3,000 were arrested. White leaders in New Iberia, Louisiana, orchestrated the beating and eviction from town of local NAACP officials who had helped establish an industrial welding school for blacks and needed to "be put in their place." Rumors of impending black uprisings swept the South. Riots in which thousands of whites attacked blacks erupted in Beaumont, Texas, and Mobile, Alabama, where white shipyard workers were anxious over FEPC interventions that threatened traditional racial prerogatives. The annual number of blacks lynched also increased during the war.[19]

Racially moderate white journalists in the South reacted to black demands for an end to segregation by warning of an impending racial holocaust. Mark Ethridge, publisher of the *Louisville Courier-Journal* and the first chairman of the FEPC, declared that "there is no power in the world—not even in all the mechanized armies of the earth, Allied and Axis—which could now force the southern white people to the abandonment of the principle of social segregation." The NAACP's Walter White acidly observed that "the highest casualty rate of the war seems to be that of Southern white liberals." As the administration made additional concessions to black demands, southern white Democrats expressed their displeasure and increased the volume of their white supremacist rhetoric.[20]

Even aside from the southern white backlash, black militancy and political power could accomplish only so much in the early 1940s. The civil rights consciousness of Americans emerged only gradually, and southern Democrats continued to exert disproportionate power in Congress. The military's treatment of black soldiers gradually improved during the war, but segregation remained essentially intact in army fighting units and on southern bases. Southern congressmen eviscerated the FEPC, blocked anti–poll-tax legislation, and deterred the administration from supporting the NAACP's challenge to the white primary or prosecuting those who obstructed the voting rights of southern blacks. The War Department ensured that defense housing was racially segregated. The North also experienced growing racial tension, especially over jobs and housing, and in 1943 deadly race riots erupted in Detroit and Harlem.[21]

Despite the tenacity of Jim Crow, World War II provided blacks with powerful ideological support, a renewed sense of mission, the political and economic resources with which to press for reform, and a broad array of white allies. Black voters became even more influential after the war. By 1946, hundreds of thousands of black voters lived in New York, Pennsylvania, Illinois, Michigan, Ohio, Maryland, and Missouri. In 1945–1946, in response to growing black political power and an emerging civil rights consciousness among whites, President Truman endorsed a permanent FEPC, appointed Irvin Mollison as the first black federal judge within the continental United States, and named William Hastie as governor of the Virgin Islands—the highest presidential appointment ever for a black man. After the 1946 congressional elections proved a debacle for the Democrats, Truman's political advisors determined that an appeal to black voters would be critical to his reelection in 1948. Blacks held the balance of power in several large industrial states in the North, and southern whites were thought to be too viscerally Democratic to bolt the party over civil rights.[22]

The competition for black votes was intense in 1948. The Republicans adopted a progressive civil rights plank, and their presidential nominee, Thomas Dewey, had a strong record on race as governor of New York, including signing into law the nation's toughest fair-employment measure. Truman's challenger from the Left was the Progressive party candidate, Henry Wallace, who was strongly committed to racial equality and impressed blacks by refusing to speak before segregated audiences in the South. Responding both to political imperatives and to the national revulsion against escalating white-on-black violence in the South, Truman became a civil rights enthusiast. In rapid succession, he appointed a landmark civil rights committee (December 1946), spoke on racial justice at the Lincoln Memorial to the NAACP's annual convention (June 1947), introduced wide-ranging civil rights legislation (February 1948), issued executive orders deseg-regating the military and the federal civil service (July 1948), and made the first ever presidential campaign appearance in Harlem (October 1948). In the summer of 1948, the Democratic National Convention had a floor fight over civil rights, which the progressives won. Though Truman's racial activism produced a Dixiecrat revolt, the president and his political advisors correctly calculated that southern losses—four Deep South states with thirty-eight electoral votes, plus one aberrant Tennessee elector—would be more than counterbalanced by northern gains. An inversion of the ratio of black support for the two major parties—that is, if blacks had voted roughly 2–1 for Dewey rather than for Truman—would have put the Republican in the White House.[23]

Black soldiers helped launch a new civil rights era by "return[ing] home fighting." Blacks serving overseas had frequently experienced novel free-doms. Foreign civilians often treated them as part of a liberation army, and many blacks enjoyed "their first experience in being treated as normal human beings." Black soldiers returning to the South often refused to quietly resume traditional racial patterns. A recently discharged black sailor in Columbia, Tennessee, reflecting the new mood, beat up a white radio repair-man who had cursed and struck his mother during a disagreement over a repair job. A race riot ensued. Thousands of black veterans tried to register to vote, and many expressed the view of one such veteran that "after having been overseas fighting for democracy, I thought that when we got back here we should enjoy a little of it." Thousands more joined the NAACP, and many became civil rights litigants, while others helped launch a postwar social movement for racial justice.[24]

Veterans were not the only blacks in a mood to fight for racial change. One white southerner observed with a sense of wonder that "it is as if some universal message had reached the great mass of Negroes, urging them to dream new dreams and to protest against the old order." Hundreds of thou-sands registered to vote and demanded access to Democratic primaries. The Alexandria, Louisiana, branch of the NAACP protested against the continuing obstruction of black voter registration and told a recalcitrant registrar that "you do not seem to realize that the social order [has] changed [now that] over ten thousand Negro men and women died in World War II for world democracy." Scores of blacks became plaintiffs in postwar lawsuits that demanded teacher pay equalization, nondiscriminatory administration of voter registration requirements, an end to racial exclusion from public facilities, admission to white graduate and professional schools, and equalization of grade school facilities. Northern blacks also became more militant. In several New Jersey counties, blacks boycotted segregated schools and demanded integration. Nationally, many blacks supported A. Philip Randolph's controversial threat—regarded by many whites as treasonous—to have blacks boycott universal military training until the army was desegregated.[25]

The Cold War, together with America's postwar emergence as an international superpower, also facilitated progressive racial change. American isolationism, which enjoyed deep roots and had been politically ascendant as recently as the late 1930s, was rendered increasingly obsolete by the technological, economic, and geopolitical developments of the 1940s. In an isolationist era, Americans did not have to worry about what foreigners thought of their racial practices. The Communist Party of America and the Soviet Union had bludgeoned Americans over the Scottsboro affair in the early 1930s, but the consequences were less serious at a time when Americans showed little interest in world leadership. After World War II, however, as Americans and Soviets competed for the allegiance of a predominantly nonwhite Third World, U.S. race relations acquired international significance. In the ideological contest with communism, U.S. democracy was on trial, and southern white supremacy was its greatest vulnerability, made all the more conspicuous by the postwar overthrow of colonial regimes throughout the world.[26]

The Soviet Union capitalized on American racial atrocities to trumpet the deficiencies of democratic capitalism. One State Department expert estimated that nearly half of all Soviet propaganda directed against the United States involved race issues. In 1946, Soviet foreign minister V. M. Molotov asked Secretary of State James Byrnes how Americans could justify pressing the Soviets to conduct free elections in Poland when America did not guarantee them in South Carolina or Georgia. Late in 1951, Secretary of State Dean Acheson was speaking to the UN General Assembly in Paris, demanding that the Soviets recognize the rights of Eastern European peoples, when word arrived that the sheriff of Lake County, Florida, had murdered Samuel Shepherd, whose conviction for raping a white woman had recently been reversed by the Supreme Court because of race discrimination in jury selection. The Soviet ambassador to the United Nations, Andrei Y. Vishinsky, promptly declared, "This is what human rights means in the United States." Later that year, America's delegates to the United Nations were held to account for the huge white mobs driving blacks out of an apartment building in Cicero, Illinois, and for the assassination of the NAACP's Florida leader, Harry Moore, in retaliation for his civil rights activities. These and other similar racial atrocities received front-page newspaper coverage in communist and nonwhite nations around the world.[27]

Black leaders became adept at using the Cold War imperative for racial change. In 1945, Walter White warned Americans and their allies that the race issue had acquired an international dimension and that Third World nations would gravitate toward the Soviet Union if America's democratic ideals were not translated into practice. Dr. Mordecai Johnson, the president of Howard University, warned that communists were using race to "tak[e] the world away from us right before our very eyes" and that every day's delay in reforming Jim Crow facilitated the spread of communism in Africa and Asia. In 1946–1947, the NAACP embarrassed the Truman administration by filing petitions with the United Nations that called for the investigation and redress of human rights violations in the South. In 1951, Ralph Bunche (who had won the 1950 Nobel Peace Prize) criticized Governor Jimmy Byrnes of South Carolina for threatening to close public schools if courts ordered them integrated, noting that a former secretary of state should have realized how such statements could harm America's international reputation. An NAACP official in Louisiana chided the chairman of the Caddo Parish Democratic executive committee for continuing to exclude blacks from party primaries and reminded him that the United States faced a grave international crisis and that its salvation depended on "convinc[ing] a great part of the rest of the world that democracy is the preferable way of life." Many letters sent to Governor John S. Battle of Virginia in 1951 urging him to commute the death sentences of seven black men convicted by all-white juries of raping a white woman warned that executing the Martinsville Seven would damage America's reputation in the Third World.[28]

The importance of the Cold War imperative for racial change is hard to overstate and probably difficult to fully appreciate in our post–Cold War era. Especially after the Soviets detonated an atomic bomb in 1949, and nuclear espionage by Klaus Fuchs and the Rosenbergs was publicly revealed, Americans became obsessed with the Cold War. Most of the era's domestic issues—the role of religion in public life, whether to build interstate highways, the public school curriculum (especially once the Soviets beat the Americans into space)—were debated in Cold War terms. In such an environment, supporting racial reform because of its international implications was perfectly natural.[29]

One cannot be certain, but the Cold War imperative for racial change seems to have been more than just rhetoric. The State Department, not known as a bastion of racial progressivism, strongly urged racial reform for Cold War reasons. In 1949, Secretary of Defense Louis Johnson defended the president's controversial order desegregating the military on the ground that segregation violated democratic principles and was "damaging to our country's reputation with millions of people around the world." Truman's civil rights committee invoked the Cold War imperative as one of its three arguments—the others were moral and economic—for racial reform: "[T]he United States is not so strong, the final triumph of the democratic ideal is not so inevitable, that we can ignore what the world thinks of us or our record." In embracing civil rights, Truman stressed "how closely our democracy is under observation," and he noted that "the top dog in a world which is half colored ought to clean his own house." The Cold War imperative was front and center when the administration began filing civil rights briefs in the late 1940s. Eisenhower and Kennedy, neither of whom was personally or politically inclined to support genuine racial reform, found Cold War arguments among the most convincing for ending segregation.[30]

The worldwide decolonization that began after World War II was important not only because it helped created a Cold War imperative for racial change but also because it provided an inspirational example to American blacks. The war sowed the seeds of destruction for colonial empires that had been created over centuries by white Europeans. A combination of the war's ideology—national self-determination and the Four Freedoms—practical military necessity, and the shattering of European economies ensured fundamental changes in how the Third World was governed. Black Americans realized that their country was not insulated from such international dislocations and that domestic racial reform was "part and parcel of the struggle against imperialism and exploitation in the Third World." Blacks hoped that if the principle of self-determination for colonized peoples could be established, "a tide of change would rush forth that the United States could not resist." Thus, civil rights leaders attended the inaugural UN session in San Francisco in April 1945 with a dual agenda: racial equality at home and colonial self-determination abroad. They criticized the UN charter as a "tragic joke," because it failed to guarantee self-determination, but they invoked its antidiscrimination provisions in legal briefs that challenged domestic racial practices.[31]

Forces for progressive racial reform did not induce white southerners to suddenly abandon racial practices that had developed over centuries. The white racial backlash ignited by wartime black militancy continued after the war. Its most horrific manifestation was the escalating white-on-black racial violence, including several lynchings, some of which claimed as victims black veterans still wearing their service uniforms. The Ku Klux Klan and other extremist racial groups enjoyed a postwar boom in membership. Yet another index of backlash was the more virulent race baiting engaged in by southern politicians, most notably, Senator Theodore Bilbo of Mississippi and Governor Eugene Talmadge of Georgia. The latter appealed to states' rights and white supremacy in opposition to "Yankee meddling and a federal civil rights program." Southern whites grew more disaffected with national Democrats, blaming them for the FEPC, the repeated anti–poll-tax bills, and even the justices' invalidation of the white primary. Disaffection turned into revolt in 1948, as the administration's embrace of civil rights drove millions of southern whites into the Dixiecrat fold.[32]

Turning back the clock proved impossible, however, as forces for progressive racial change that were inaugurated or accelerated by the war proved too powerful to stymie. Indeed, resistance efforts often backfired, unintentionally accelerating racial reform. A crescendo of white-on-black violence in 1946 — the race riot in Columbia, Tennessee, a quadruple lynching in Monroe, Georgia, and the maiming of black veteran Isaac Woodard in Batesburg, South Carolina — fostered the development of a national civil rights consciousness. The National Emergency Committee against Mob Violence was formed, and roughly 15,000 people in New York City and Washington, D.C., rallied to demand federal action against lynching. President Truman was personally horrified by what happened to Woodard: He was permanently blinded by a South Carolina sheriff after he argued with a white bus driver. Capitalizing on the public outrage, the NAACP took Woodard on a nationwide tour, hoping to educate northerners as to how white southerners treated black people. The increase in racially motivated violence helped inspire the creation of Truman's civil rights committee.[33]

The postwar social and political context of race was changing at all levels: national, southern, and northern. The national government's position on civil rights shifted dramatically during the 1940s, reflecting the increase in black political power, the antifascist ideology of the war, and the Cold War imperative for racial change. This shift in outlook was evident in numerous

FIGURE 4.2
Isaac Woodard after he was blinded by a sheriff in South Carolina, circa 1946.
(*Crisis Publishing Co.*)

federal actions: the creation of the FEPC, the Justice Department's investigation and prosecution of lynchings, its submission of briefs in civil rights cases, the passage of antilynching and anti–poll-tax bills by the House, the appointment of Truman's civil rights committee, civil rights legislation proposed by the president, and executive orders desegregating the military and the federal civil service. Changes in national racial practices also occurred outside of government. Perhaps of greatest symbolic significance was the desegregation of professional baseball, the national pastime, which took place in 1946–1947. By 1950, blacks were also playing in the National Football League and the National Basketball Association. In 1949, the American Medical Association accepted the first black into its House of Delegates; the American Nurses Association and the American Association of University Women also admitted blacks for the first time. By the late 1940s, church leaders of all denominations were condemning racial segregation, and Catholic parochial schools desegregated in many cities. For the first time, Hollywood began confronting racial issues, such as interracial marriage and lynching.[34]

Not only had the national government become more committed to civil rights, but it had also developed a greater capacity to enforce that commitment. During Reconstruction, all that was available to enforce national racial policy in recalcitrant southern states was a downsized army. The federal bureaucracy then was minuscule, and federal grant-in-aid programs that would later be used to influence southern racial policy did not exist. The vast spending programs of the New Deal and the postwar national-security state provided such leverage. As the South became increasingly dependent on national government spending, it became more vulnerable to federal edicts on race. Indeed, the southern states were the most dependent on national expenditures, from which they benefited disproportionately, because they made lower tax contributions and received larger benefits because of their poverty. The most impoverished southern states, which were also the most resistant to racial reform, were the most susceptible to federal fiscal control.[35]

The increased commitment of the national government to civil rights produced a backlash among southern whites, which culminated in the Dixiecrat revolt of 1948. Yet the most notable feature of that revolt may have been its failure. The Dixiecrats carried only the four Deep South states with the largest percentages of blacks, and even those were won only by seizing control of the Democratic party machinery. Outside of the Deep South, the New Deal/Fair Deal coalition held up well for Truman. The president won all of the other southern states, and in all of them but one, Dewey ran second. At the state level, with just a few exceptions, economically populist and racially moderate politicians continued to thrive by supporting expanded government services—education, roads, public health, old-age pensions—and downplaying race. Compared with the wave of racial reaction that would sweep the South after *Brown v. Board of Education* (1954), the white backlash of 1948 was tame.[36]

One reason that the Dixiecrats failed and that race-baiters such as Talmadge and Bilbo proved exceptional was the changing racial attitudes of whites. A contemporary political scientist concluded, "The failure of the Dixiecrats in 1948 and 1950 demonstrated that great masses of southerners would no longer be bamboozled by racist appeals." Though most white southerners remained adamantly opposed to school desegregation, their overall commitment to white supremacy was less intense than it had been. Many were prepared to accept some racial reforms, such as equalization of education spending, fairer legal treatment of blacks, greater black political participation, and occasionally even an end to segregation in contexts such as transportation. Forces that were operating at the national level, such as the democratic ideology of World War II and the Cold War imperative for racial change, also affected the racial attitudes of southern whites.[37]

Changes more specific to the South—the rising education levels of both whites and blacks, urbanization, industrialization, and demographic shifts—also helped liberalize white racial opinion. The gap between education spending in the North and that in the South decreased steadily in the middle decades of the twentieth century. As southern whites became better educated, their commitment to white supremacy gradually loosened. The level of education for blacks was rising even faster. In 1910, only 5,000 blacks attended college; in 1948, more than 88,000 did. By then, in Virginia, a slightly higher percentage of black high school graduates than of white high school graduates attended college. A better-educated black population undermined one of Jim Crow's original justifications: protecting whites from being dragged down by illiterate freedmen. Did whites need to be insulated from an "inferior" race that produced a Ralph Bunche, the Nobel Peace Prize winner? Higher education levels among blacks also undermined some of the legal aspects of Jim Crow. In 1947, Mississippi registrars reported that well-educated younger blacks were easily passing literacy tests. It is true that many whites were just as prejudiced against well-educated blacks as they were against ill-educated blacks; some whites were actually more resentful of the better-educated blacks. But for others, Jim Crow became harder to defend, both morally and legally, as blacks became better educated.[38]

Urbanization also ameliorated white racial attitudes, as racial mores in cities proved less restrictive than those in the countryside. World War II had helped erode southern insularity by exposing the South to novel external influences. Millions of southerners temporarily left the region for military service and confronted different racial norms for the first time in their lives. Army surveys found that whites who served in integrated combat units underwent profound changes in their racial attitudes. Some white veterans, tired of seeing their black comrades-in-arms "crap[ped] all over," enlisted in progressive racial causes, including support for black voter registration and the hiring of black police officers.[39]

Accelerating black migration to the North also influenced the racial attitudes of white southerners. Historically, whites who lived in heavily black counties manifested the staunchest commitments to white supremacy. As the number of majority-black counties fell—from 284 in 1900 to 180 in 1940—the number of white southerners who saw the preservation of white supremacy as a life-or-death matter declined. Another important demographic force for progressive racial change was the growing migration to the South of northern whites, who were in search of greater economic opportunity and a more favorable climate. These migrants, most of them natives of New England or the upper Midwest, were disproportionately well educated and brought more egalitarian racial mores with them. In Florida and Virginia, these relocated northern whites were already affecting the politics of race by the early 1950s and would have had even greater influence had it not been for the malapportioned legislatures in the southern states, which inflated the political power of rural native whites.[40]

A final factor contributing to the changing racial attitudes of whites was the gradual erosion of Jim Crow's basic premise: that the black and white races were fundamentally different. By the 1930s, most scientists had repudiated theories of biological racial differences. By the 1940s, this shift in scientific paradigms was filtering down to popular opinion, assisted by widespread revulsion against Nazism. The new racial paradigm was especially influential with youngsters, who imbibed it in school. Southern whites were resistant to the new understanding because of their heavy cultural investments in white supremacy. Still, by the 1940s, younger and better-educated whites in the South were having a harder time rationalizing Jim Crow.[41]

Even those white southerners whose commitment to white supremacy remained undiminished found it harder after the war to preserve traditional racial practices. Distinctive regional mores, such as Jim Crow, are difficult to maintain in a nation that watches the same movies and television programs and is densely interconnected by highways, airplanes, and long-distance telephone wires. A more integrated nation was likelier to evolve a single set of racial practices and beliefs, probably some combination of the northern and southern varieties. Moreover, the increasing social, economic, and cultural integration made it more costly to maintain aberrant regional practices. The South risked forfeiting industrial relocations, spring-training visits from the integrated Brooklyn Dodgers, and opportunities to host national conventions by resisting national trends toward greater racial equality. Finally, the expansion of mass media ensured that deviant southern racial practices received national—often international—attention. No longer could the news of southern racial atrocities be contained within the bounds of a generally sympathetic southern community.[42]

Changing white attitudes in the South translated into racial reform. Black voter registration in the South increased dramatically after the war, rising from roughly 250,000 in 1940 to 750,000 in 1948 and then to more than one million in 1952. In large cities such as New Orleans, Atlanta, and Memphis, blacks were able to qualify to vote almost as easily as in northern cities, and black voters occasionally held the balance of power in local elections.

Some observers concluded that even at the state level black voters were the deciding factor in the narrow election victories in 1948 of economically populist and racially moderate politicians, such as Lyndon Johnson in Texas, Sid McMath in Arkansas, and Fuller Warren in Florida. By 1950, black candidates were running for office in peripheral South cities and occasionally winning. By 1954, southern blacks served on eleven city councils and on fifteen boards of education.[43]

Southern blacks put to good use their newly secured suffrage rights and extracted concessions from increasingly responsive local governments. Protection against police brutality was a top priority for many blacks, and dozens of southern cities hired their first black police officers after the war. Southern cities also began providing black communities with better public services and recreational facilities, and states increased their spending on black education (a response not just to growing black political power but also to the threat of desegregation litigation). Some counties appointed black voter registrars for black precincts. In 1946, the *Pittsburgh Courier* went so far as to predict that "once Negroes start voting in large numbers . . . the jim crow laws will be endangered and the whole elaborate pattern of segregation threatened and finally destroyed." Though that prediction was exaggerated, growing black political power did threaten to eradicate the harsher manifestations of Jim Crow.[44]

Around 1950, cracks in the walls of segregation began to appear in the border states and in parts of the peripheral South. Catholic parochial schools in St. Louis, Washington, D.C., and other cities admitted their first black students in the late 1940s. St. Louis, Kansas City, and Washington, D.C., desegregated their public swimming pools. Medical societies in Baltimore and St. Louis admitted blacks for the first time. Ford's Theater in Baltimore and the National Theater in Washington, D.C., desegregated. In the early 1950s, many department stores and drugstores in Washington, D.C., desegregated their lunch counters. Maryland repealed its Jim Crow transportation law in 1951. Austin, Texas, desegregated its public library, and Mount Sinai Hospital in Miami Beach, Florida, appointed its first black staff physician.[45]

Other changes in racial practices penetrated even deeper into the South. Many southern cities desegregated their minor league baseball teams. Some blacks in the upper South began playing football for formerly white colleges, and integrated gridiron contests against northern schools that fielded black players became more common throughout the South. In 1952, the Southern Historical Association desegregated its inaugural meeting in Knoxville, Tennessee. In 1953, Ralph Bunche spoke in unsegregated public auditoriums in Raleigh, Miami, and Atlanta. In New Orleans, Catholic universities, public parks, and the public library were desegregated in the early 1950s, and the first black Catholic priest in the Deep South was ordained in 1953. Also in the early 1950s, Birmingham, perhaps the most racially repressive city in the South, desegregated elevators in downtown office buildings, and debates were taking place over desegregation of the city's police force and local bus transportation.[46]

Most of these changes in southern racial practices would have been unthinkable before the war. As the pace of change accelerated, expectations of further reform grew. By 1950, most black leaders were demanding the complete abolition of state-supported segregation, and a few southern white liberals joined the chorus. Though the vast majority of white southerners continued to demand the preservation of school segregation, they were beginning to recognize that even that citadel of Jim Crow might not be impervious to assault.[47]

Dramatic changes in racial attitudes and practices also occurred in the North. In the 1930s, liberals had usually had little to say about race, but after the war, civil rights headed the liberal reform agenda. Hubert Humphrey, the mayor of Minneapolis, had little concrete political incentive to promote civil rights reform, as he came from a city and a state with few black voters, yet it was he who introduced the landmark civil rights plank at the 1948 Democratic convention. Hundreds of organizations devoted to improving race relations and promoting civil rights reform were established in northern cities in the late 1940s. Religious organizations in the North condemned race discrimination, and foundations financed studies by social scientists into the origins and the means of eradicating racial and religious prejudice. Legal research in support of civil rights litigation became a favorite pro bono project of students at the Columbia University School of Law.[48]

Northern states and cities passed a barrage of civil rights legislation after the war. Though federal legislation promoting fair employment practices was defeated by a southern filibuster in the Senate in 1946, about a dozen northern states adopted their own fair employment measures by the early 1950s, and many cities did likewise. Though most of these laws had little practical effect, their passage symbolized the increased political power of northern blacks and the liberalization of white racial attitudes. Some northern states adopted far-reaching prohibitions on race discrimination in public accommodations, and a couple of them enacted novel constitutional or statutory provisions that threatened to terminate state aid for school districts that were in violation of prohibitions on segregation. These laws quickly desegregated schools in the southern counties of Illinois, Indiana, and New Jersey—before the Court had confronted school segregation in the South in *Brown v. Board of Education*. In 1946, California repealed its statutory authorization for the segregation of Asians in public schools, and a federal judge invalidated the state's policy of segregating Mexican Americans. Many northern states also sought to integrate national guard units, over the opposition of the army.[49]

It is true that some contemporaneous forces pushed against progressive racial change. Although many northern whites supported fair employment practices and opposed state-mandated school segregation, some drew the line at integrated housing. In 1944–1945, whites in the Detroit neighborhood of Oakwood opposed the construction of public housing for blacks there, noting that while they "have nothing against the colored" and "believe in the God-given equality of man," they "wouldn't want them [blacks] for a neighbor or growing up with [our] children." A 1942 poll revealed that 84 percent of Americans—in the North as well as the South—favored residential segregation. Housing authorities in northern cities made conscious decisions after the war to segregate public housing. Until at least 1950, the underwriting policy of the federal government explicitly encouraged residential segregation. Private real estate companies that developed enormous housing projects, such as Levittown or Stuyvesant Town, excluded blacks entirely. In 1951, blacks who dared to seek housing in the all-white suburb of Cicero, Illinois, encountered huge mobs of angry whites committed to keeping them out. In 1953, when a handful of black families moved into the Trumbull Park homes in Chicago, more than a thousand police officers had to provide protection. For several years, black homes in Trumbull Park were bombed, and blacks walking the neighborhood streets had to be accompanied by armed guards or risk being assaulted by white vigilantes. Segregated housing has proved to be one of the greatest obstacles to achieving racial equality in the United States. It was well entrenched before the nation developed its civil rights consciousness after the war, and the commitment of most whites to maintaining it has limited the transformative potential of the civil rights movement.[50]

McCarthyism proved to be another constraint on progressive racial change. The obsession of Americans with domestic subversion hindered the civil rights movement, as it did most social reform causes, by enabling opponents to brand reformers as communists. Liberal organizations, such as the American Civil Liberties Union, the American Jewish Committee, and the Congress of Industrial Organizations (CIO), devoted scarce resources to internal housecleaning, in order to insulate themselves from charges of communist complicity. The NAACP was no exception. In 1950, the association's annual convention passed overwhelmingly an anticommunist resolution and authorized the national executive to investigate alleged communist infiltration and to suspend branch charters where appropriate. Communists had indeed infiltrated a few branches, and NAACP leaders such as Thurgood Marshall were not as doggedly anticommunist as the professional redhunters would have wished. By and large, however, the association was strongly anticommunist, and its housecleaning was a costly diversion from more important matters, such as the legal assault on Jim Crow.[51]

The few white racial liberals in the South proved especially vulnerable to red-baiting. During the 1930s, communist organizations were the only predominantly white ones in the nation that were strongly committed to racial justice. Communists organized antilynching demonstrations and supported unjustly convicted southern blacks, such as the Scottsboro defendants and Angelo Herndon. During the Popular Front against fascism, from about 1935 to 1945, the lines between liberals, radicals, and communists became blurred, removing much of the stigma from communist affiliations. Such distinctions acquired greater significance after the dawn of the Cold War in 1946–1947, and this left white racial liberals in the South highly vulnerable. Their involvement with left-wing organizations, such as radical CIO unions, the Southern Conference for Human Welfare (SCHW), the Civil Rights Congress, and Henry Wallace's Progressive party, exposed them to vicious red-baiting. In 1947, the House Un-American Activities Committee labeled the integrationist SCHW a "deviously camouflaged communist-front organization." The left-wing unions that the CIO expelled in 1949 had the most black officers and organizers and the strongest commitment to fair employment practices. As the stock of anticommunism rose and that of white supremacy fell, segregationists repackaged themselves as anticommunists and subjected integrationist adversaries to a withering barrage of red-baiting. Anticommunism helped give racial segregation "a new lease on life."[52]

One other important factor worked against progressive racial change at this time. After 1948, the burgeoning political power of northern blacks was partially offset by the growing independence of southern white voters. Since the demise of Populism in the 1890s, southern whites had voted overwhelmingly Democratic. Roosevelt won more than 90 percent of the southern electoral vote in each of his four presidential victories. In 1948, Truman's political advisors had assumed that southern whites had nowhere else to turn, even if they were dissatisfied with the Democratic party's growing racial liberalism. However, the Dixiecrat revolt that year demonstrated that southern whites would not blindly follow the national Democratic party. Henceforth, the votes of southern whites, like those of northern blacks, were up for grabs, which meant that both parties had an incentive to offer racial policies that were attractive to them.[53]

The increased independence of southern white voters, together with the Cold War's general dampening of social reform impulses, led both major parties to adopt more conservative racial policies in the 1952 presidential election. Both party's candidates, Dwight David Eisenhower and Adlai Stevenson, were less progressive on race, in personal conviction and by political calculation, than Dewey and Truman had been in 1948. The decision of national Democrats to placate white southerners was evident not only in the nomination of Stevenson, who had a lukewarm racial record, but also in the vice-presidential nomination of Senator John Sparkman of Alabama. The Democratic convention also watered down the civil rights plank of 1948 — "a surrender to the southern wing of the party" — and offered an olive branch on the party loyalty issue to Dixiecrat bolters. The Republicans' civil rights plank also retreated from 1944 and 1948, and Eisenhower was tepid on race. His adult life had been spent in an army that was thoroughly segregated and disproportionately southern, and in 1948 he had testified against integrating the military. During the 1952 campaign, Eisenhower strongly opposed the creation of a permanent FEPC, which Stevenson reluctantly supported, and he courted southern voters by siding with Gulf Coast states in their dispute with the national government over tidelands oil. Eisenhower's southern strategy succeeded. He became the first Republican presidential candidate since Hoover in 1928 to win significant southern support, carrying four states—Texas, Florida, Virginia, and Tennessee—and winning 48.1 percent of the southern popular vote.[54]

The countervailing forces just noted restrained, but did not nullify, the powerful impulses for progressive racial change that had been ignited by the war. Although most northern whites opposed integrating their own neighborhoods, they increasingly favored suppressing the more extreme aspects of southern Jim Crow. Although concerns about domestic subversion retarded social reform in the early 1950s, the repressive influence of McCarthyism soon dissipated, while the Cold War imperative for racial change continued to promote civil rights. Although the increasing independence of southern white voters made both parties more conservative on race in 1952, the postwar momentum for racial reform could not be stopped, and bipartisan efforts by northern politicians in 1957 produced the first federal civil rights law in eighty-two years. Not all social and political forces favored progressive racial reform in the postwar years, but the overall extralegal context was as favorably disposed as it had ever been toward advances in civil rights.

Justices sitting on the high court during the World War II era proved remarkably supportive of progressive racial change. This development was largely fortuitous. By 1946, Presidents Roosevelt and Truman had entirely reconstituted the Court. In appointing new justices, both presidents had focused mainly on getting the Court to repudiate its *Lochner*-era commitments to constraining federal power and limiting government regulation of the economy. Neither president manifested any significant interest in the racial views of his prospective nominees. Roosevelt appointed a member of the NAACP's legal advisory committee, Felix Frankfurter, and a former Klansman, Hugo Black.[55] He appointed Frank Murphy, another NAACP advisor and a former governor of Michigan, who enjoyed the support of Catholics, Jews, blacks, and labor unions. Yet he also appointed Jimmy Byrnes, a typical white supremacist senator from South Carolina, who had filibustered against antilynching legislation and would later mount a last-ditch defense of school segregation as the governor of his state. Black Americans lauded the appointments of Frankfurter and Murphy and criticized those of Black and Byrnes. Roosevelt seems not to have cared either way.[56]

Truman appeared equally indifferent to the racial views of his Court nominees. He appointed the liberal former mayor of Cleveland, Harold Burton, who supported the NAACP and, as senator from Ohio, endorsed anti–poll-tax legislation and a permanent FEPC. But Truman also appointed southern politicians with conventional southern racial views: Fred Vinson of Kentucky and Tom Clark of Texas. Truman cared mainly about the willingness of his nominees to sustain the constitutionality of New Deal/Fair Deal economic policies (though political cronyism was also important). Race seems not to have entered the president's calculations, although by the mid-1940s, Truman probably would not have appointed a justice with the regressive racial views of Byrnes or the prior Klan affiliation of Black. But neither did he see any reason to appoint staunch racial progressives, such as Frankfurter or Murphy. How Truman's appointees would vote on civil rights issues was anybody's guess.[57]

Albeit not by design, the justices appointed by Roosevelt and Truman proved remarkably supportive of civil rights. Frankfurter and Murphy reflected the values and interests of core New Deal constituencies. Frankfurter, a Jewish immigrant from Austria who taught at the Harvard Law School, was so liberal on civil rights and civil liberties that his Court appointment had generated significant conservative opposition. During World War I, Frankfurter had defended the interests of the Bisbee miners—striking copper miners who were forcibly expelled by mine operators from Bisbee, Arizona, for their labor union activity and their left-wing political views. He had also encouraged President Wilson to pardon the West Coast radical Tom Mooney, who was convicted on slim evidence of planting a bomb that killed ten people at the Preparedness Day Parade in San Francisco in 1916. In the 1920s, Frankfurter had supported the commutation of the death sentences of the Massachusetts anarchists Nicola Sacco and Bartolomeo Vanzetti. The appointment of Frankfurter to the high court reflected the changing composition of the Democratic party; he represented the civil libertarian views of Jews, Catholics, blacks, labor unions, and liberal intellectuals. Murphy was a hero to many blacks because of his performance as the trial judge in the 1925 Sweet case, which he presided over with "absolute fairness," according to NAACP leaders. As a trial judge and later as the mayor of Detroit and the governor of Michigan, Murphy reflected the views of traditional New Deal constituencies. As Roosevelt's attorney general in 1939, he created the first civil liberties unit in the Justice Department.[58]

Roosevelt's other appointees from the North, such as Robert H. Jackson and William O. Douglas, were not career politicians like Murphy and thus may not have shared his visceral political predisposition in support of civil rights. Neither Jackson nor Douglas had had much occasion to think deeply about race issues before his appointment to the Court. Both men came from regions of the country where few blacks lived: Jackson from upstate New York and Douglas from the state of Washington. Both were staunch New Dealers and probably shared the tendency of prewar liberals to consider economic issues more important than racial ones. However, because they lacked strong racial preconceptions, Jackson and Douglas easily evolved in the same racially egalitarian direction as most well-educated, relatively affluent northerners in the 1940s.[59]

Truman made four Court appointments: two southerners (Vinson and Clark) and two northerners (Burton and Sherman Minton). All four were not only New Deal/Fair Deal devotees but also ardent Cold Warriors. Their voting records on civil liberties issues—such as freedom of speech, search and seizure, and coerced confessions—were reactionary compared to those of their colleagues. Yet their performances in race cases were progressive. The best explanation for these seemingly conflicting voting patterns may be the Cold War imperative for racial change. The predisposition of these justices to defer to the government in speech or criminal procedure cases may have inclined them to support racial equality claims, which came to the Court with the imprimatur of the federal government. In Court briefs, the Justice Department repeatedly invoked the Cold War imperative for racial change, which must have been music to these justices' ears.[60]

In the 1940s, the South remained an important Democratic constituency, which had to be acknowledged in appointments to the Court, yet the white southerners appointed by Roosevelt and Truman did not prove to be significant impediments to racial reform. Jimmy Byrnes, who might have proved to be such an obstacle, fortuitously retired after just one year's service (1941–1942) to help Roosevelt run the war. Black, who was initially derided as "Justice KKK Black," quickly proved an unlikely champion of racial equality. The other southern appointees of Roosevelt and Truman hailed from border states or the peripheral South—Reed and Vinson from Kentucky and Clark from Texas—and thus their commitment to white supremacy was probably somewhat attenuated. All three had served in important administration positions, which probably made them better attuned than most southern politicians to the critical role played by northern blacks in the New Deal coalition. As we shall see, in the 1950s, these three justices manifested varying degrees of sympathy for grade school segregation. On most other race issues—for example, white primaries, segregation in graduate and professional schools, and judicial enforcement of racially restrictive covenants—they showed little hesitation about joining or even authoring opinions in support of racial equality. Though their positions did not mirror those of most white southerners, they may have been consistent with those held by well-educated, relatively affluent, southern white lawyers.[61]

The new justices were personally more supportive of racial equality, and so were the Court's revised institutional commitments. As Roosevelt began reconstituting the Court in the late 1930s, the justices abandoned their protection of contract and property rights, granting legislatures a free hand in economic regulation. However, rather than extending across the board this newfound deference to legislatures, the justices began assuming a special role in protecting rights integral to the democratic process, such as voting and free speech, and the equality rights of "discrete and insular" minorities. The Court first explicitly articulated this new judicial role in a footnote to a 1938 opinion, *United States v. Carolene Products Co.* There, Justice Stone observed that the ordinary presumption of constitutionality applying to legislation was inoperable when a law "restricts those political processes which can ordinarily be expected to bring about repeal of undesirable legislation" or implicates "prejudice against discrete and insular minorities . . . which tends seriously to curtail the operation of those political processes ordinarily to be relied upon to protect minorities." In the following years, the justices incorporated this "political process" theory of judicial review into constitutional doctrine, rendering landmark decisions that expanded the equality rights of blacks and the First Amendment rights of political dissidents, religious minorities, and labor unions.[62]

This fundamental shift in the Court's constitutional commitments can be understood in several ways. One who shares Madisonian assumptions about the power-maximizing incentives of public officeholders might observe that judges are unlikely to broadly eviscerate their own power. Once they had abandoned their traditional function of protecting contract and property rights, the justices' natural ambition impelled them to lay claim to a new sphere of constitutional influence: civil rights and civil liberties. A political analyst might note that the new rights recognized under *Carolene Products* correlated neatly with the interests of the political constituencies that backed the New Deal. In the 1930s, free-speech rights were associated mainly with labor union organizing and picketing, and paradigmatic "discrete and insular" minorities included blacks, Jews, and Catholics. A sociologist might observe that the justices' increased attentiveness to the interests of racial and religious minorities coincided with the efforts of Americans to redefine democracy in opposition to the tenets of Nazi fascism and Soviet communism. The day after the *Carolene Products* decision came down, Stone noted to a friend, "I have been deeply concerned about the increasing racial and religious intolerance which seems to bedevil the world, and which I greatly fear may be augmented in this country." Lastly, a constitutional theorist might explain the new paradigm of judicial review as sound political and constitutional theory. On this view, politically accountable legislatures should generally make the value judgments that are controversial. But judicial deference makes less sense on issues that are constitutive of the democratic process, such as the right to vote or to engage in political speech, or on issues where one could argue that democratic procedures are susceptible to systematic malfunction, such as racial and religious discrimination. Whatever the correct explanation for its development, the *Carolene Products* paradigm put the Court's institutional weight, not just the justices' personal preferences, behind civil rights.[63]

CASES

VOTING

After *Guinn* (1915) invalidated Oklahoma's grandfather clause, the governor called a special legislative session to grandfather it. Under this 1916 statute, those who had voted in 1914, when the grandfather clause was in effect, were automatically registered to vote. Those who had not voted that year (a category that included all blacks) were given twelve days in which to register or else suffer permanent disfranchisement. In 1934, I. W. Lane tried to register in Wagoner County, Oklahoma, where only a few of the 7,000 black residents were registered. Lane was rejected because he had been eligible to register in 1916 but had missed the statutory window. The decision in *Lane v. Oklahoma* (1939) invalidated this transparent evasion of *Guinn*.[64]

On the merits, *Lane* was easy. If the grandfather clause was unconstitutional, then Oklahoma had no legitimate interest in grandfathering its effects. Indeed, the 1916 statute seems so obviously unconstitutional that the justices might have invalidated it, in a proper case, even before the incipient racial changes of the late 1930s made them more solicitous of black suffrage. The NAACP had planned an earlier challenge, but that litigation never materialized, thus illustrating how Court victories without subsequent enforcement litigation are unlikely to prove efficacious.[65]

The only debatable legal issue in *Lane* was whether litigants were required to exhaust state court challenges before suing in federal court. Lower federal courts had rejected Lane's lawsuit partly on this ground. An important Fifth Circuit ruling in a 1933 voting rights case, *Trudeau v. Barnes*, had likewise required federal litigants to exhaust their state court challenges. *Lane* rejected this approach, ruling that federal litigants need exhaust only their state *administrative* remedies, not *judicial* ones. The NAACP concluded, "More and more the supreme court can be depended upon to decide cases involving the rights of Negroes . . . without hairsplitting technicalities."[66]

The more significant suffrage issue for the Court during this period was the white primary. *Grovey v. Townsend* (1935) had unanimously ruled that the exclusion of blacks from Democratic primaries by party resolution did not qualify as state action under the Fourteenth or Fifteenth amendments. However, the NAACP did not regard *Grovey* as "completely fatal" and persisted in trying to persuade the Court to reconsider.[67]

Before the association could appeal another white primary case to the Court, however, an intervening decision on a related issue raised hopes that the justices might overrule *Grovey*. *United States v. Classic* (1941) involved the question of whether the federal government could constitutionally punish fraud in primary elections for national office. Article I, section 4 of the Constitution empowers Congress to regulate "Times, Places and Manner of holding Elections for Senators and Representatives." *Newberry v. United States* (1921), by a divided vote, had barred Congress from regulating Senate primaries, because they were deemed not to be "Elections" under this provision. *Classic* overruled *Newberry*, thereby sustaining federal authority to prosecute Louisiana election commissioners for fraud committed in a congressional primary.[68]

Classic was careful not to impeach the validity of *Grovey*. The government's brief in *Classic* distinguished *Grovey*, and Stone's majority opinion failed even to mention it. The cases are indeed distinguishable and in more than one way. First, Louisiana and Texas regulated primaries differently, thus making it possible to find state action in one case but not the other. Specifically, Louisiana paid the costs of primaries and required parties to conduct them in order for their candidates to appear on general-election ballots; Texas did neither. Second, *Grovey* involved the question of whether party regulation of primaries constituted state action under the Fifteenth Amendment, whereas *Classic* raised the question of whether primaries were elections under Article I, section 4. These questions need not yield the same answer. For example, the Court had long held that Article I, section 4 authorized Congress to regulate private action that interfered with voting rights in federal elections, while it had denied that Congress had power under the enforcement section of the Fifteenth Amendment to prohibit private interferences with black suffrage. Given that the justices had imposed a state-action requirement for congressional regulation under the Fifteenth Amendment but not under Article I, section 4, they might have easily treated primaries differently under the two provisions. Thus, *Classic* did not mandate the overruling of *Grovey*.[69]

Yet, much of *Classic*'s reasoning seemed relevant to the constitutionality of white primaries. In holding that primaries were elections under Article I, section 4, the Court emphasized factors that seemed equally pertinent to the state-action issue under the Fifteenth Amendment: Louisiana paid the costs of primaries; state law required candidates on general-election ballots to be selected through primaries; state law regulated the time, place, and manner of primaries; and, as a practical matter, primaries determined the outcome of general elections in these one-party states. Judges and justices had previously focused on these same factors in determining whether party rules excluding blacks from primaries amounted to unconstitutional state action. Assuming that the justices deemed *Classic* relevant to the white primary issue, the critical question was how to interpret this passage from the opinion: Constitutional rights were implicated in primary elections "where the state law has made the primary an integral part of the procedure of choice, or where in fact the primary effectively controls the choice." Throughout the one-party South, Democratic primaries "effectively control[led] the choice" at general elections. Yet, different states regulated primaries differently, and it was anybody's guess what it meant for state law to make primaries "an integral part of the procedure of choice."[70]

Most contemporaries assumed that *Classic* had implications for the white primary, and Stone later wrote that he considered *Grovey* doomed from the moment he wrote *Classic*. NAACP lawyers were confident that *Classic* would inter the white primary. Yet justices who had been inclined to do so could have easily reaffirmed *Grovey*, notwithstanding *Classic*, by distinguishing Texas law from Louisiana law or by distinguishing the Article I question from the Fifteenth Amendment one. Indeed, lower court judges did not believe that *Classic* had silently overruled *Grovey*.[71]

Yet in 1944, the justices voted 8–1 to overrule *Grovey* and invalidate the white primary, observing that stare decisis—the legal doctrine by which courts generally adhere to already decided cases—carries less weight in the constitutional arena. Noting that "the party takes its character as a state agency from the duties imposed upon it by state statutes," *Smith v. Allwright* emphasized the many ways in which Texas regulated parties and primaries, including setting the date of primary elections, requiring that they be conducted in certain ways, and subjecting them to state oversight. *Smith* also emphasized an apparently distinct point—that primaries had "become a part of the machinery for choosing officials" and that Texas could not escape responsibility by "casting its electoral processes in a form which permits a private organization to practice racial discrimination in the election." This latter language suggested that the justices might deem primaries to be state action, regardless of how state law regulated them.[72]

As we have seen, state action is like proximate cause. So long as the Constitution permitted Texas to forbid parties from discriminating based on race, the state's failure to do so was a but/for cause of black exclusion. Whether Texas should be deemed constitutionally responsible for that exclusion requires ascribing responsibility, not measuring it. That Texas regulated the Democratic party in some ways does not resolve whether it should be deemed responsible for failing to regulate it in others. Moreover, even if Texas did not regulate parties at all, it could still be deemed responsible for white primaries, because it had "cast . . . its electoral processes in a form which permits a private organization to practice racial discrimination in the election." Thus, the state-action determination inevitably required a judgment on the merits: For which forms of discrimination perpetrated by Texas Democrats *should* the state of Texas have been deemed responsible?

Answering this question is difficult, in part because political parties play vital roles in constituting the state, which makes it nonsensical to subject them to all the neutrality rules imposed by the Constitution on public actors. For example, although the First Amendment forbids government from favoring Republicans or Democrats, parties do that by their very nature. In constituting the government, parties require protection from government interference, including the judicial imposition of neutrality rules, such as those implied by the First Amendment. In addition, the First Amendment entitles parties to advocate controversial positions, such as white supremacy. Thus, cases such as *Smith* required the justices to explain why the Democratic party, which was free to exclude Republicans and to advocate white supremacy, was not free to exclude blacks. Moreover, even if Texas regulated the state Democratic party so intrusively that the Court deemed the state responsible for the party's exclusion of blacks, the justices would eventually have to decide whether the Constitution barred individuals from banding together in support of white supremacy.

In *Smith*, the justices had some inkling that they were confronting only the tip of the iceberg. The near-unanimous result is misleading. Jackson and Black initially voted with Roberts, who was ultimately the sole dissenter, to sustain Texas's white primary. Jackson noted that sooner or later the justices would have to determine whether individuals enjoyed constitutionally protected rights of political association. If individuals wished to mobilize in defense of white supremacy, how much would the Court constrain their associational rights in the service of racial equality?[73]

In 1944, however, that question could be postponed. Eight justices voted to overrule *Grovey* and bar the Texas Democratic party from excluding blacks. This shift, within the short span of nine years, from a unanimous decision sustaining white primaries to a near-unanimous ruling invalidating them, is unprecedented in U.S. constitutional history. One might attribute the turnabout to Roosevelt's nearly complete reconstitution of the Court. Only Stone changed his mind in the intervening years. The other justice remaining from the Court that decided *Grovey* was its author, Justice Owen Roberts, who bitterly dissented in *Smith* and assailed the Stone Court's propensity for overruling precedents, which "tends to bring adjudications of this tribunal into the same class as a restricted railway ticket, good for this day and train only."[74]

However, to focus on judicial turnover as the explanation for *Smith* is to miss the fundamental importance of World War II. Though the *Smith* opinion and the surviving conference notes do not explicitly refer to the war, the justices cannot have missed the contradiction between a war purportedly being fought for democratic ends and the pervasive disfranchisement of southern blacks. With black soldiers dying on battlefields around the world, the justices must have been tempted to help put America "a little nearer to a more perfect democracy, in which there will be but one class of citizens." Almost simultaneously with *Smith*, Congress was debating a bill to repeal poll taxes in federal elections as well as a more limited suspension of poll taxes for members of the armed services. The same democratic ideology that inspired Congress to consider these measures probably influenced judicial thinking about the white primary. The decisive difference between Congress and the Court was that southern Democrats had a stranglehold on the former. Poll-tax repeal failed in the Senate as the justices were interring the white primary.[75]

Another reason that *Smith* may have proved relatively easy for the justices—as a matter of politics, if not law—was that most Americans would have supported it. Northern opinion regarding poll-tax repeal supports this surmise; a 1940s Gallup poll revealed that nearly 70 percent of Americans favored repealing the tax, and northern congressmen voted overwhelmingly to abolish for federal elections this other peculiarly southern restriction on suffrage. Northerners had little reason to feel differently about white primaries and poll taxes, both of which restricted suffrage in only seven or eight southern states by the mid-1940s. Moreover, even southern whites were far less committed to preserving black disfranchisement than they were to maintaining school segregation. By the late 1940s, opinion polls showed a clear southern majority in favor of abolishing poll taxes. Thus, Kentuckian Stanley Reed apparently had no qualms about writing the opinion in *Smith*, whereas in *Brown v. Board of Education*, he planned to dissent until virtually the last minute.[76]

Smith did not definitively resolve the white primary issue. Thurgood Marshall was engaged in wishful thinking when he declared *Smith* to be "so clear and free of ambiguity" that it settled "once and for all" the right of blacks to participate in party primaries. The ambiguity in *Smith* virtually invited efforts at circumvention. To the extent that *Smith* turned on the extensive regulation of parties and primaries by the state of Texas, deregulation was a natural response. Within a fortnight, the governor of South Carolina, Olin Johnston, convened a special legislative session to repeal all 150 state statutes regulating parties. Other Deep South states watched and waited, as lower courts wrestled with South Carolina's efforts at circumventing *Smith*.[77]

In *Elmore v. Rice* (1947), Federal District Judge J. Waties Waring invalidated the exclusion of blacks from Democratic primaries in South Carolina, notwithstanding the legislature's efforts at political deregulation. *Classic* had focused on two factors in evaluating the permissibility of congressional regulation of primaries: whether "state law has made the primary an integral part of the procedure of choice" and whether "in fact the primary effectively controls the choice." Legislative deregulation of parties was relevant to the former but not to the latter. In seven of the previous eight presidential elections, Republican candidates had won less than 5 percent of the vote in South Carolina, illustrating the extent of Democratic party dominance. In striking down the white primary in South Carolina, Waring emphasized the dispositive nature of Democratic primaries and the extent to which state law had regulated parties prior to the recent deregulation. Waring thought it "pure sophistry" to suggest that legislative deregulation had altered political realities. He also denied that "the skies [would] fall," as predicted, if Democrats permitted blacks to participate in their primaries. The NAACP, which had found *Elmore* "terrifically tough" to prepare, exulted in Waring's "extraordinary" decision. After William Hastie had read the opinion three times, he "still [could not] believe it," and he congratulated Marshall on his "greatest legal victory." The Fourth Circuit Court of Appeals affirmed Waring in a less flamboyant opinion. Probably delighted to have southern judges running interference on a sensitive racial issue, the justices denied review. South Carolina's efforts at evasion had "received a complete and shattering defeat." Other Deep South states now abandoned their consideration of deregulation.[78]

Hastie and Marshall believed that *Elmore* had nailed down the lid on "the coffin of the white primary," but their celebration proved premature. One more variation remained for the justices' consideration. In Fort Bend County, Texas, the Jaybird Democratic Association had been excluding blacks from its pre-primary selection of candidates since 1889. The association, whose membership consisted of all whites who resided in the county, selected candidates who invariably became the Democratic nominees and then were elected to office. Similar schemes operated in other East Texas counties, some dating as far back as the late 1870s. Though the Jaybirds were not created to circumvent *Smith* and *Elmore*, it is easy to imagine much of the South following suit, had the Court sustained this scheme. Justices at the conference discussion of *Terry v. Adams* (1953) expressed concern that "[i]f this is approved it will be seized upon" and that approval "would practically overturn the previous cases."[79]

The difficulty for the justices, though, was that finding state action in the Jaybirds' scheme risked eliminating any protection for private political association—protection that many justices believed the First Amendment guaranteed. Several justices had worried in *Smith* that extending the ban on race discrimination from government to political parties would interfere with freedom of political association. In *Terry*, they were being asked to go further and forbid discrimination by a political club that state law did not regulate. Would they be asked next to prohibit individuals from mobilizing their friends in support of candidates who espoused white supremacy? Justice Jackson expressed a concern that others shared: Did not the "people have some rights" to political affiliation?[80]

The conflict felt by the justices over whether to protect associational rights or to safeguard their earlier white primary rulings from nullification is apparent in *Terry*'s seesaw history and its poorly reasoned opinions. The eventual 8–1 vote is misleading, as the justices found the case genuinely difficult. The initial conference vote was 5–4 to *reject* the constitutional challenge, on the ground that state action was absent. A second vote was 4-4, with Frankfurter passing. During the conference discussion, Frankfurter had said that he "can't see where [the] state comes in." He then changed his vote without explanation, thus creating a 5-4 majority to invalidate the Jaybirds' scheme. But four justices—Vinson, Reed, Minton, and Jackson—remained slated to dissent. Jackson, worried about infringing on private associational behavior and doubting whether the Jaybirds' electoral success was relevant to the state-action question, drafted a dissent that lambasted his colleagues for sacrificing "sound principle[s] of interpretation" in their haste to inter the "hateful little local scheme." Yet, when *Terry* was announced, only Minton dissented. Once their position no longer commanded a majority, Jackson, Reed, and Vinson apparently preferred subordinating "sound principle[s] of interpretation" to sustaining an abhorrent disfranchisement scheme.[81]

None of the three opinions for the majority in *Terry* is convincing. Black's plurality opinion emphasizes two points. First, Texas was responsible for establishing an electoral system in which private discriminatory groups could control the results. Second, the Jaybirds had long dominated politics in Fort Bend County, winning every office for the past half century. Clark's opinion emphasized these points and added unilluminating language about the Jaybirds being the "auxiliary" of the Democratic party and "part and parcel" of its operations.[82]

These analyses are not analytically flawed. So long as the state has constitutional authority to prohibit certain private behavior, one can easily ascribe constitutional responsibility to the state's decision to permit that behavior. Moreover, the likelihood that private behavior will produce certain disfavored results is a reasonable factor to consider in ascribing responsibility to the state for permitting it. Yet, Black and Clark would not have been willing to accept the broad implications of treating these considerations as determinative of the state-action issue. Under their approach, the state could have been deemed responsible for virtually every political outcome, and all results that disfavored blacks could have been ruled unconstitutional. For example, a legislature's choice to apportion seats on a geographical rather than a proportional basis often disadvantages minority groups. In the early 1950s, the justices were not about to invalidate geographic districting, yet under the analyses of Black and Clark, it is not clear why. The state chose the method of apportionment, and its consistent effect was to reduce the political influence of blacks. Frankfurter's concurring opinion in *Terry* is even less persuasive. He admitted that formal state action was "wholly wanting," and he refused to find it in the state's choice to tolerate private discrimination. Yet Frankfurter insisted that the participation of county officials, albeit as private citizens, in the selection of Jaybird candidates constituted state action. This reasoning is hard to follow. Did Frankfurter mean that the attendance of a public official at a private dinner that excluded blacks was unconstitutional? His rationale in *Terry* would suggest so, but this seems inconceivable.

Nobody in the *Terry* majority convincingly responded to Minton's dissent. The Jaybirds' scheme may have been "unworthy," Minton noted, but to condemn it required expanding state action to include private behavior that, one could argue, was entitled to First Amendment protection. Minton denied that the Jaybirds were a Democratic "auxiliary" and noted that successful Jaybird candidates got listed on Democratic primary ballots only through their own initiative and expense and without receiving formal acknowledgment as Jaybird candidates. He ridiculed Frankfurter's notion that public officials acting in their private capacities could convert private organizations into state actors. Regarding Texas's choice to permit the Jaybirds' scheme, Minton wondered how a state's refusal to regulate activity that was protected by the First Amendment could violate the Equal Protection Clause. He also expressed doubt that the success of the Jaybirds' scheme should be relevant to the state-action issue. Finally, Minton observed that successful northern politicians often had to secure endorsements from religious leaders or union officials. In the early 1950s—or even today—the justices could not conceivably have found such arrangements unconstitutional. Yet, according to the opinions of Black and Clark, it is not clear why. Minton's acerbic remark to Jackson seems justified: "When the Jaybird opinion comes down, there may be some question as to which election returns the Court follows! It will be damn clear they aren't following any law."[83]

In 1953, several justices subordinated their understanding of law to politics in order to protect black suffrage. Reed, who shared some of Minton's difficulties with *Terry*, went along with the majority, because the "[f]uture of [the] South depends on negro voting." Moreover, the justices were concerned that a contrary ruling would have nullified their earlier white primary decisions. That same year, the justices confronted a similar law/politics dilemma on the more explosive issue of school segregation. As in *Terry*, they agonized over the conflict before deciding to elevate politics over their understanding of the law.[84]

HIGHER EDUCATION

Southern states historically provided blacks with no graduate or professional education, a seemingly flagrant violation of separate but equal. Beginning mainly in the 1930s, several southern states established out-of-state scholarships to finance higher education for their black citizens in those northern universities that were willing to accept them. *Missouri ex rel. Gaines v. Canada* (1938) invalidated such programs on the ground that states were constitutionally obliged to provide equal services to blacks *within* their boundaries. As a result, a few border and peripheral South states began offering some graduate courses for blacks. Only Maryland and West Virginia integrated any programs. Most southern states continued to offer nothing. Ten years after *Gaines*, not a single southern state admitted blacks to a Ph.D. program, and only one accredited law school and one medical school in the South accepted blacks.[85]

The NAACP initially hoped that higher education litigation would pressure southern states to appropriate sufficiently large sums for equalizing black opportunities that they would eventually capitulate by integrating. Those hopes were quickly dashed, as southern legislatures after *Gaines* declined to significantly increase appropriations for black higher education. The small increase in funding that did occur was for out-of-state scholarships, which many states now adopted for the first time, even though *Gaines* had ruled them unconstitutional. Until the late 1940s, politicians and leading educators in the South also discussed the creation of regional universities to provide blacks with advanced education—proposals that also seemed to violate *Gaines*, which had ruled blacks to be entitled to equal treatment within state boundaries. Lower courts generally interpreted *Gaines* narrowly. Rather than ordering the immediate admission to white universities of black applicants who were being denied higher education, courts gave southern officials time to establish equal black facilities after a demand had been made for them.[86]

No more higher education cases reached the Court in the decade after *Gaines*. (Lloyd Gaines mysteriously disappeared, disrupting NAACP plans to challenge Missouri's evasive response to the Supreme Court's ruling.) The

NAACP had serious financial problems in the late 1930s; plaintiffs proved difficult to locate; and prospective suits were held in abeyance during World War II. A slew of higher education lawsuits were filed immediately after the war, however, as black veterans took advantage of the GI Bill of Rights to apply to white universities. Southern states, anticipating or reacting to such suits, enacted laws that required education officials to establish, on demand, separate-and-equal programs of advanced education for blacks, and they appropriated funds for these programs. For example, Texas allocated between two and three million dollars for black higher education, after recognizing the threat that litigation posed to racial segregation. State judges, impressed with such legislative efforts, generally found these separate black institutions to be adequate, though the NAACP called them "Jim Crow dumps."[87]

The justices did not reenter the fray until 1948. Two years earlier, Ada Lois Sipuel had sued for admission to the University of Oklahoma School of Law. Oklahoma offered legal education to whites but not to blacks. This was an obvious violation of *Gaines*, and thus the case was "simple and easy," as Jackson observed at conference. Acting with "unprecedented speed"—the order came just four days after oral arguments—the justices commanded Oklahoma to provide Sipuel with legal instruction, "as soon as it does for applicants of any other group."[88]

Though *Sipuel v. Board of Regents* (1948) was easy on the merits, a procedural snafu could have complicated matters had the justices been inclined to let it. When she applied to the University of Oklahoma, Sipuel had failed to demand that public officials establish a separate black law school. *McCabe* (1914) had found fatal a similar failure by plaintiffs to demand the sought-after facilities before suing. The Oklahoma Supreme Court rejected Sipuel's suit on this ground. By 1948, though, the justices were disdainful of such a ripeness objection. Vinson dismissively referred to it as "shadow boxing."[89]

Yet the justices stopped short of ordering Sipuel's admission to the University of Oklahoma. They reversed the state court decision, which had thrown out her suit, and remanded the case for further proceedings consistent with their ruling. At conference, only Murphy had flatly repudiated the separate-but-equal doctrine, favoring Sipuel's immediate admission. Other justices had left open the possibility that Oklahoma could satisfy the Constitution without desegregating. Leaping at this implicit invitation to equalize facilities, the state almost instantly opened a separate black law school. When Sipuel challenged it as an evasion of the Court's mandate, the justices denied relief, confirming that they had not yet interred separate but equal. The two most liberal justices, Murphy and Rutledge, dissented, protesting that an equal black law school could not possibly be created overnight.[90]

Two years later, the Court functionally overruled *Plessy* with regard to higher education. In 1946, Heman Sweatt had applied to the all-white University of Texas School of Law. During the litigation, Texas first set up an

FIGURE 4.3
Ada Lois Sipuel files her application to the University of
Oklahoma Law School, with (*left to right*) Dr. J. E. Fellows,
Thurgood Marshall, and Amos T. Hall, 1948. (*Library of
Congress, Prints and Photographs Division, Visual Materials
from the NAACP Records*)

interim black law school, and later a permanent one. The NAACP challenged the adequacy of this arrangement, and it also directly attacked the
constitutionality of segregation in higher education. The Court declined to
confront the latter question on the ground that the case could be more narrowly resolved. Yet the reasoning used by the justices to find the black law
school unequal essentially nullified segregation in higher education.[91]

The inferiority of Texas's black law school was not so obvious as to go
uncontested. The admissions requirements and curricula of the black and
white schools were the same; the three instructors at the black law school
also taught at the University of Texas; and the smaller student body of the
black law school afforded some pedagogical advantages. A former president
of the American Bar Association testified that the schools offered equal educational opportunities. The Court thought otherwise. The justices noted

FIGURE 4.4
Heman Sweatt in his mail
carrier uniform.
(*Bettmann*/CORBIS)

tangible features of the black school that *were* obviously inferior: the size of
the faculty, the number of books in the library, and the absence of opportunities for law review and moot court. They also emphasized intangible differences "incapable of objective measurement but which make for greatness in
a law school . . . [:] reputation of the faculty, experience of the administration, position and influence of the alumni, standing in the community, traditions and prestige." Finally, the justices observed that segregating Sweatt
denied him the opportunity to interact with whites, who were 85 percent of
the population in Texas and accounted for most of its lawyers, witnesses, and
judges. Equal legal education was impossible with "such a substantial and
significant segment of society excluded." Because equal protection rights are
"personal," the Court refused to tolerate the delay that creating an equal
black law school would require; instead, it ordered the immediate admission
of Sweatt to the University of Texas.[92]

Vinson's opinion for the unanimous Court in *Sweatt v. Painter* (1950)
refused to reconsider *Plessy*, and thus he technically complied with Frankfurter's admonition that the justices "not go beyond what is necessary." Yet, a
newly created black law school could not possibly have achieved equality

with regard to the intangible factors identified in *Sweatt*. Indeed, the justices' concern that attending the black law school would deny Sweatt interaction with Texas's numerically dominant whites was impossible to reconcile with segregation. Thus, most commentators thought that *Sweatt* had nullified segregation in higher education, and some believed that it had left the separate-but-equal doctrine generally "a mass of tatters."[93]

On the same day as *Sweatt*, the Court ordered the graduate education school of the University of Oklahoma to cease segregating—in classrooms, the library, and the cafeteria—the black man it had admitted pursuant to federal court order. *McLaurin v. Oklahoma* (1950) declared that segregation restrictions "impair and inhibit [McLaurin's] ability to study, to engage in discussions and exchange views with other students, and, in general, to learn his profession." As George McLaurin was receiving a tangibly equal education, the justices were apparently no longer prepared to accept segregation *within* an institution of higher education. *Sweatt* had proscribed segregation in *separate* institutions. That seemed to leave nowhere left for segregation to remain.[94]

Both *Sweatt* and *McLaurin* represented clear changes in the law. *Gaines* and *Sipuel* had simply insisted that blacks receive something, but the 1950 rulings interpreted "equality" so stringently that segregation in higher education became impossible. Had separate but equal always meant this, the South could not have constructed a social system around it. The briefs and lower court opinions in these cases confirm that existing law did not support the claims of Sweatt and McLaurin. Oklahoma and Texas simply urged the Court to follow precedent. The lower court decisions in these cases had insisted that tangible factors be equalized, but they had rejected on the basis of precedent the direct challenge posed to segregation. The Court's focus on intangibles in *Sweatt* and *McLaurin* was unprecedented.[95]

These rulings were not as easy for the justices as the unanimous outcomes might suggest. Several justices were troubled, especially in *Sweatt*, by the departures from precedent and original intent. The two Kentuckians, Reed and Vinson, were initially inclined to reject Sweatt's challenge, which is why the opinion was originally assigned to Black, with the chief justice provisionally in dissent. At conference, Vinson reviewed the original understanding of the Fourteenth Amendment and concluded that it did not cover public education. He also itemized a long list of precedents that sustained separate-but-equal education. For Vinson, vindicating Sweatt's claim required improvising a new meaning for the Fourteenth Amendment, one that was different from its original and historical interpretations. Reed likewise thought that it was "hard for me to say something that has been constitutional for years is suddenly bad. The 14th Amendment was not aimed at segregation." Jackson similarly observed that he could "find no basis for [the] idea that [the] Fourteenth [Amendment] reached schools." In correspondence, Jackson worried that *Sweatt* required the Court not merely to "fill gaps or construe the amendment to include matters which were unconsid-

George McLaurin segregated in his classroom at the
University of Oklahoma in 1948. (*Bettmann/*CORBIS)

ered" but "to include what was deliberately and intentionally excluded." Yet,
even though he believed that the Court was essentially "amending the Constitution," Jackson ultimately supported Sweatt's claim.[96]

 Sweatt and *McLaurin*, inconsistent with legal sources that were generally considered binding by these justices, are best explained in terms of social
and political change. By 1950, major league baseball had been desegregated
for three years—a salient development for several of the justices, who were
huge fans. The military was undergoing gradual desegregation, pursuant to
Truman's 1948 executive order. The Court's first black law clerk, William T.
Coleman, had served two terms earlier and authored a memo to Frankfurter
urging that *Plessy* be overruled. Coleman demonstrated by his very presence
at the Court that segregated legal education could no longer be defended on
the basis of black inferiority. Several justices probably shared Jackson's conviction that "the segregation system [in higher education] is breaking down
of its own weight and that a little time will end it in nearly all states." Clark

likewise stated that "the forces of progress in the South" were already eroding segregation in higher education. The assistant attorney general of Oklahoma conceded at oral argument in *McLaurin* that there might not be "much point" any longer to such segregation, which he predicted would be gone within a decade in his state.[97]

The Truman administration intervened in these cases to urge that *Plessy* be overruled, invoking the Cold War imperative for racial change. The Justice Department told the Court that "unless segregation is ended, a serious blow will be struck at our democracy before the world." Burton received a letter applauding his opinion in a 1950 case invalidating segregation in railroad dining cars (discussed below), because it "deprives communist agitators of one more weapon in their war upon our free society." The justices' unanimity in all three 1950 race cases—an impressive accomplishment for this ordinarily splintered Court—is most plausibly attributable to the Cold War imperative. The Truman appointees—Vinson, Burton, Clark, and Minton—rarely sided with civil liberties litigants. Perhaps it was sensitivity to Cold War arguments for racial reform that explains their greater solicitude for civil rights.[98]

Furthermore, the justices were aware that white southerners were no longer universally hostile to desegregation of higher education. In this sense, *Sweatt* and *McLaurin* were more like *Smith v. Allwright* than like *Brown v. Board of Education*. When Sipuel sought admission to the University of Oklahoma Law School, a thousand white students demonstrated in her support. Two thousand white students and faculty members rallied in support of Sweatt's suit against the University of Texas Law School, and white students there organized a college chapter of the NAACP—the only all-white branch in the country. Opinion polls conducted at these universities showed substantial—even majority—support among students for integration. Faculty members overwhelmingly supported it. Thus, the justices had no reason to expect violence or school closures in response to their decisions, which would certainly not be so with regard to *Brown*. Clark, a native Texan, dismissed as "groundless" the parade of horrors invoked in the brief of the southern attorneys general, and he predicted that there would be no violence or defiance as a result of *Sweatt*. Even Vinson, who was initially resistant to Sweatt's claim, observed that "no great harm would come from association in professional schools." In fact, the southern reaction to these rulings was almost entirely nonviolent, and many white students extended blacks a warm welcome. White reaction might have been rather different a decade earlier, when law students at the University of Missouri had predicted that Lloyd Gaines would be "treated like a dog" if admitted.[99]

Finally, the justices tend to reflect the opinions of a cultural elite more than those of the general public. By 1950, that elite, even in the South to a certain extent, had repudiated segregation in higher education. One amicus brief in *Sweatt*, which urged that *Plessy* be overruled, was signed by 187 law professors and deans—the sort of people whose opinions the justices were likely to share. Deans of some of the most prestigious law schools in the country had testified on the NAACP's behalf at trial, denying that separate black law schools could possibly be equal. The NAACP had also put into the trial record testimony by a prominent professor at the University of Chicago, who denied that scientists any longer believed in inherent racial differences. This had been true since at least the 1930s, but by 1950, the scientific consensus had trickled down to other members of the cultural elite, including the justices. Even the one justice most supportive of segregation in education, Reed, would not defend the notion of biological racial differences.[100]

The Court's functional overruling of *Plessy* in higher education did not necessarily doom other sorts of segregation. Specifically, *Brown v. Board of Education* was not foreordained in 1950. Real distinctions exist between education in grade schools and in graduate schools—distinctions that the justices could have invoked in *Brown* had they been so inclined. The intangible factors emphasized in *Sweatt*—"reputation of the faculty, experience of the administration, position and influence of the alumni, standing in the community, traditions and prestige"—are more important in law schools than in grade schools. In a 1950 memo, Clark pointed out to his colleagues that "it is entirely possible that Negroes in segregated grammar schools being taught arithmetic, spelling, geography, etc., would receive skills in these elementary subjects equivalent to those of segregated white students." Respected southern jurists highlighted these differences, rejecting challenges to segregation in grade schools and in other settings in the years between *Sweatt* and *Brown*.[101]

Notwithstanding such distinctions, many observers, then and since, have doubted whether the justices could have limited *Sweatt* and *McLaurin* to segregation in higher education. Yet the justices have frequently proved capable of limiting their rulings by fiat when logic has failed them. For example, the Court today requires that punishment be proportional to the crime where the death penalty is at issue but not elsewhere, on the unilluminating rationale that "death is different." The justices have applied seemingly random distinctions in deciding which forms of public assistance to religious schools are permissible and which are not. For most of the nineteenth century, the justices arbitrarily distinguished laws that unconstitutionally impaired contractual *rights* from those that permissibly interfered with contractual *remedies*. Four Court appointees of President Richard M. Nixon were confronted in the early 1970s with Warren Court precedents that had expanded the constitutional rights of indigents, and they resolved not to extend those rulings "an inch," while they also declined to overrule them. Thus, for the justices to have sustained separate but equal in some contexts, after functionally overruling it in higher education, would have been unexceptional.[102]

Moreover, the justices had strong practical, if not logical, reasons for declining to extend the 1950 rulings to grade schools. Southern white resistance to the desegregation of higher education was minimal outside of the

Deep South. Very few blacks were involved, and those whites most directly affected tended to be young adults, not impressionable children, and also were those with the most progressive racial attitudes (because they were the best educated). By contrast, grade school desegregation would involve huge numbers of blacks and whites, including the youngest, and would cut across class lines. The justices were fully aware that, however placid the reaction to the 1950 rulings, grade school desegregation "would involve a social revolution." Many commentators speculated that the prospects of fiercer white resistance might inhibit the justices from extending *Sweatt* and *McLaurin* to grade schools. Thurgood Marshall was not confident that they would take that leap any time soon. The solicitor general, Philip B. Perlman, who favored the administration's involvement in the 1950 cases, drew the line at grade school segregation.[103]

Internal deliberations in the 1950 cases reveal that the justices had yet to decide how far to go. Vinson, who was initially resistant to Sweatt's claim, worried "how [we] can draw the line there." Once he changed his mind about *Sweatt*, however, the distinction that initially eluded him became readily apparent, and in *Brown* he seemed inclined to sustain grade school segregation, though his sudden death prevented his participation in the final outcome. Black, who favored Sweatt's claim, thought it possible to distinguish between education in grade schools and in graduate schools. First, the custom of grade school segregation "extends far back," while law schools had no equivalent tradition of segregation (not because they were integrated but because blacks were completely excluded). Second, Black thought that segregation in higher education was "wholly unreasonable," while he left open the door to "reasonable segregation." Clark likewise distinguished the two sorts of educational segregation and opposed extending *Sweatt* "at that time." He said that he did not know how he would vote in grade school cases, and "[s]hould they arise tomorrow, I would vote to deny certiorari or dismiss the appeal." Minton, too, preferred to avoid that issue, noting, "[W]e can meet grade and high schools whenever we get to it." This internal evidence suggests that the result in *Brown* was anything but "a foregone conclusion in 1950."[104]

RESIDENTIAL SEGREGATION

Buchanan v. Warley (1917) invalidated residential segregation ordinances. *Corrigan v. Buckley* (1926) rejected a constitutional challenge to racially restrictive covenants on the ground that state action was absent, while it strongly hinted that even judicial enforcement of such agreements would not violate the Constitution. The NAACP persisted in treating the latter issue as unresolved, and several efforts over the next twenty years to secure clarification failed, as the justices refused to grant review in restrictive covenant cases.[105]

By the late 1940s, the justices may have felt that they could no longer responsibly evade the issue. The lack of new housing construction during the Great Depression and World War II, combined with the massive increases in urban populations that were a result of internal migration, had led to severe housing shortages. In some northern cities, a huge percentage of housing stock was covered by racially restrictive covenants. Black populations that had multiplied several times over were confined to ghetto neighborhoods that had barely expanded in space. Racial conflict over scarce housing was pervasive and helped cause a deadly race riot in Detroit in 1943. By the end of World War II, hundreds of lawsuits throughout the nation sought to enforce racially restrictive covenants, while defendants challenged the constitutionality of judicial enforcement.[106]

Shelley v. Kraemer (1948) was an injunction suit to keep a black family from taking possession of property covered by such a covenant. The defense was that judicial enforcement would violate the Equal Protection Clause. Precedent on this issue was about as clear as it ever gets. Not only had dicta in *Corrigan* denied that judicial enforcement of racially restrictive covenants was unconstitutional, but all nineteen state high courts that had considered the issue had reached the same conclusion, as had the District of Columbia courts. Only a single federal district judge had ruled to the contrary, and that was in 1892. It is true that a few state courts had refused to enforce such covenants on the ground that they were contrary to public policy. Even those decisions, however, were limited to covenants forbidding black *ownership*, not just use or occupancy. Moreover, the public policy ground was unavailable to the Supreme Court, as federal judges do not share the freedom of their state counterparts to impose extraconstitutional constraints on private contracting parties.[107]

In light of the clarity of precedent, lower courts in *Shelley* and two companion cases easily rejected the constitutional challenges. By 1946, the Court of Appeals for the District of Columbia Circuit had ruled seven times that the Constitution permitted judicial enforcement of racially restrictive covenants. Vinson had participated as a lower court judge in one of those cases, agreeing that judicial enforcement of private discriminatory contracts was not unconstitutional state action. Thurgood Marshall was reluctant to press the restrictive covenants issue, given the clarity of precedent and the number of NAACP defeats in lower courts, but the association was unable to control the litigation. William Hastie, too, opposed seeking certiorari in these cases and wondered whether the justices had granted review for the purpose of "slapp[ing]" down the association. Given hostile precedent, the NAACP relied mainly on sociological data regarding the inadequacy of ghetto housing and on vague and legally nonbinding sources, such as the Atlantic Charter and the UN charter. Only in the few years immediately before *Shelley* had even an incipient dissenting tradition developed on this issue.[108]

Precedent notwithstanding, *Shelley* barred injunctions to enforce racially restrictive covenants. Vinson's opinion treated the issue as one of first impression, observing that *Corrigan* had decided only that restrictive covenants themselves were not state action. This was technically true but disingenuous. *Corrigan's* statement that judicial enforcement of racially restrictive covenants would be permissible was dicta, but it was also unambiguous. Vinson did not even mention it. Yet many state courts had relied on it, treating as a settled matter the permissibility of judicial enforcement of such covenants.[109]

On the merits, Vinson explained that judicial orders, like legislation and executive action, can qualify as state action—a point that nobody disputed. The Court had ruled many times that judges engaged in jury selection or in devising common-law rules, such as restrictions on union picketing, were state actors bound by the Constitution. The question in *Shelley* was different: Did judicial enforcement of *private* racially discriminatory agreements violate the Fourteenth Amendment? Vinson failed to appreciate the difference between these issues: judges discriminating themselves and judges enforcing private discriminatory contracts just as they would any other agreement. Taken seriously, Vinson's rationale in *Shelley* threatens to obliterate the private sphere, as *all* behavior occurs against a backdrop of state-created common-law rules. For example, a discriminatory exclusion of certain people from one's home would be unconstitutional on this rationale, once the police were summoned or a trespass prosecution commenced to vindicate property rights. Thus, *Shelley* would have been a "truly revolutionary" decision, had subsequent cases taken it seriously, which they never did.[110]

Though Vinson failed to grasp the real issue, he may still have resolved it correctly, as one can sometimes be right by accident. That judges can generally enforce private contracts without violating the Constitution does not prove that judicial enforcement of racially restrictive covenants is permissible. One might conclude that racially discriminatory contracts are more objectionable than others, and therefore that the state should be held responsible for choosing to enforce them. Unless the Constitution affirmatively protected the right to make such agreements—something that few people seemed to believe in 1948—the state was free to prohibit their judicial enforcement. Failure to do so was a choice for which the state could be held accountable, if the choice were deemed sufficiently wrongful. Indeed, several state courts had refused to enforce certain racially restrictive covenants as a matter of public policy, thus highlighting the choice involved in the willingness of other states to enforce similar agreements. Whether that choice should have been ruled unconstitutional depends on how bad one deems "private" race discrimination to be and how responsible one considers the state for failing to eliminate it.[111]

By 1948, public attitudes toward race discrimination specifically and state responsibility for private wrongs generally had changed enough to enable the justices to decide *Shelley* as they did. The Great Depression and the New Deal had helped to alter conceptions of government responsibility for conduct occurring in the private sphere. The Four Freedoms of the

Atlantic Charter included freedom "from want" and "from fear"—not typical negative liberties against government interference, but affirmative rights to government protection from privately inflicted harms. A principal function of the Justice Department's civil liberties unit, which was created in 1939 under Frank Murphy, was to protect citizens—blacks, Jehovah's Witnesses, labor unionists—from private interferences with their rights. During the war, "freedom from fear" was translated into the novel federal protection of individuals from private lynchings. Truman invoked this notion of expanded government responsibility in his speech to the NAACP in June 1947, in which he declared that "the extension of civil rights today means not protection of the people against the government, but protection of the people by the government." Similar conceptions were implicit in the economic bill of rights touted by Roosevelt in the 1944 election, which asserted government responsibility for providing citizens with decent jobs, health care, housing, and education. The justices responded to such changed understandings of government responsibility by expanding the state-action concept, even outside of the race context. For example, *Marsh v. Alabama* (1946) ruled that a company town that imposed restrictions on employee speech was a state actor for purposes of the First Amendment.[112]

Perhaps even more important to *Shelley*'s outcome were changes in racial attitudes. Specifically, with regard to racially restrictive covenants, many Americans apparently shared one newspaper's view that "a nation that has poured out its blood and treasure in a war billed as a contest against racism can hardly afford the luxury of forcing its own citizens to live in ghettos." *Shelley* was decided in the same year that a national civil rights consciousness crystallized. Truman introduced landmark civil rights legislation earlier that year, and the issue played a significant role in the presidential election. Truman's civil rights committee had recommended legislation to prohibit racially restrictive covenants, and it successfully urged the administration to intervene in litigation challenging judicial enforcement. The Justice Department's brief in *Shelley* emphasized the Cold War imperative for racial change, possibly providing an important incentive for intervention by those justices not generally known for their constitutional activism. Moreover, restrictive covenants, unlike many racial issues, directly affected other minority groups—Jews, Asians, Latinos, and Native Americans, among others—whose collective interests were likely to command the attention of New Deal Democrats. Several minority groups filed amicus briefs in *Shelley*, thus clarifying the political valence of this issue for New Deal justices who dominated the Court at this time.[113]

In 1945, the justices had been so unconcerned about racially restrictive covenants that they would not even review such a case. In 1948, however, they unanimously ruled against judicial enforcement of such agreements.[114] Rarely have the justices changed their minds about an issue so swiftly and unanimously. But then, rarely has public opinion on any issue changed as rapidly as public opinion on race did in the postwar years. By the time of

Shelley, law review commentary, which generally reflects elite legal opinion, had turned overwhelmingly hostile toward the judicial enforcement of restrictive covenants.[115]

In *Shelley*, the personal values of the justices and the broader social and political context trumped the traditional legal sources. Before 1948, the constitutionality of judicial enforcement of racially restrictive covenants seemed certain. Nearly twenty state high courts had so ruled, and the justices would not even review such cases because the law seemed so clear. Yet *Shelley* unanimously jettisoned precedent because racially restrictive covenants struck the justices as egregious social policy. Numerous factors—the democratic ideology of the war, growing black political power, the Cold War imperative for racial change, and the urban housing crisis—had created a compelling sociopolitical case for legal change. The justices reversed themselves, in an opinion potentially revolutionizing state-action doctrine, in order to accomplish a just result.

Shelley was an injunction suit. Technically, it did not resolve the question of whether breachers of covenants could be sued for money damages. Lower courts split on this issue after *Shelley*. In *Barrows v. Jackson* (1953), the justices ruled that the Fourteenth Amendment also precluded damages actions to enforce such covenants. The vote was 6–1, with only Vinson dissenting.[116]

There was no question on the merits after *Shelley*: Judicial damages awards are no less state action than are injunctions. The only complication in *Barrows* was that both litigants were white, which left it unclear, as Vinson pointed out, who had standing to raise the equal protection rights of blacks. Minton's majority opinion conceded that the ordinary rule was against "third party" standing; litigants generally may not raise the rights of others. Yet Minton also noted precedents that departed from that rule under unusual circumstances. However, the cases he cited were inapposite. *Buchanan v. Warley* (1917), which invalidated residential segregation ordinances in a lawsuit brought by a white man, was easily distinguishable, as it vindicated the due process rights of white property owners, not the equal protection rights of blacks. Another case cited by Minton, *Pierce v. Society of Sisters* (1925), was also distinguishable. There, the Catholic school that challenged Oregon's prohibition on private schools alleged interference with its property rights, as well as with (third-party) parents' rights to control their children's upbringing. *Barrows* was apparently the first Court decision to allow standing based exclusively on third-party rights. Still, the justices' disinclination to reach a contrary result is easily understandable. Permitting damages actions for a breach of racially restrictive covenants would encourage enforcement as much as allowing injunctions would. To avoid circumvention of *Shelley*, the justices had little choice but to broaden third-party standing.[117]

On another residential segregation issue of possibly greater significance, however, the justices refused to get involved. The same day that *Sweatt* and *McLaurin* were decided, the Court, over dissents by Black and Douglas, denied certiorari in *Dorsey v. Stuyvesant Town Corporation*. There, a narrowly divided New York court of appeals had rejected a constitutional challenge to the racially exclusionary policies of a privately owned corporation, which had built apartments for 2,500 people on redeveloped Manhattan land. The argument for finding state action was that the city and the state had approved this specific project and that Stuyvesant Town Corporation had been formed only because state law authorized such redevelopment schemes. Moreover, the city had encouraged redevelopment through tax exemptions; it granted eminent domain power to developers; and it regulated the rental rates of apartments, though not the choice of tenants. The New York court observed that recent expansions of state-action doctrine, such as *Shelley*, plausibly suggested that the state was responsible for the exclusion of blacks in *Dorsey*. Yet the court refused to hold the state accountable, and the justices let that ruling stand. Larger development projects, such as Levittown, built housing for hundreds of thousands of people in the 1950s and excluded blacks entirely. Not until 1968 did the justices invalidate such policies, and they did so then by relying on an expansive reading of a civil rights statute from the Reconstruction era, not on the Constitution.[118]

TRANSPORTATION

During this period, the justices decided two sorts of cases involving segregation and discrimination in transportation. The decisions in *Mitchell v. United States* (1941) and *Henderson v. United States* (1950) both invalidated under the Interstate Commerce Act discrimination against black passengers in luxury railroad accommodations. These decisions are relevant to constitutional law, because the Court had long interpreted that statute to impose on private railroads the same equality rules that were mandated for states by the Constitution. *Morgan v. Virginia* (1946) and *Bob-Lo Excursion Co. v. Michigan* (1948) involved challenges under the Dormant Commerce Clause to state laws that, respectively, required and barred segregation of common carriers, including those transporting interstate or international passengers.[119]

Both of these sets of issues had generated legal rulings from as far back as the late nineteenth century. Soon after the enactment of the Interstate Commerce Act in 1887, the Interstate Commerce Commission (ICC) interpreted the statutory ban on "undue or unreasonable prejudice or disadvantage" to forbid racial inequality but not segregation. By the early 1900s, the ICC had become lax in enforcing the equality prong of separate but equal. Yet *McCabe* (1914), construing the Equal Protection Clause rather than the statute, denied that blacks could be excluded from luxury accommodations merely because of their lower per capita racial demand. *McCabe* arose under the Constitution, because Oklahoma law authorized the exclusion of blacks. In *Mitchell*, the same issue arose under the Interstate Commerce Act, because it was railroad policy, not state law, that authorized the discrimination. Yet the Court had long applied the same substantive standards under these different legal regimes, and the railroad's justification for excluding Mitchell from Pullman accommodations was precisely the same argument about disparate per capita racial demand that had been rejected in *McCabe*. Thus, *Mitchell* was easy for the justices, who unanimously invalidated the exclusionary policy. Indeed, the most surprising aspect of the case is that the ICC had ruled the other way.[120]

Even without *McCabe* on the books, the justices in 1941 might easily have invented its rationale. In other words, *Mitchell* was easy politically, not just legally. Though the justices were not yet ready to invalidate segregation, they would no longer turn a blind eye toward blatant racial inequality. *Gaines* (1938) had suggested as much, invalidating Missouri's out-of-state scholarships for blacks and rejecting the justification of disparate per capita racial demand. Similarly, lower federal courts at this time were invalidating facially discriminatory pay scales for teachers in the public schools. By 1941, the federal government had made several concessions to black political power, and Roosevelt was about to create the FEPC through the first executive order on race since the Emancipation Proclamation. Moreover, Arthur W. Mitchell was a congressman, which probably explains why the Justice Department intervened on his behalf. The justices would not have been eager to permit a southern railroad to exclude a black congressman from accommodations available to whites, as the nation became embroiled in a world conflict that redefined the meaning of democracy. The justices had rejected the per capita racial demand argument in the Progressive Era, when race relations had reached a post–Civil War nadir; they were not about to credit it as a new era of progressive racial change dawned. Even southern white newspapers were generally favorable to *Mitchell*, and one South Carolina journal observed that "plain justice" required equal service for blacks.[121]

Henderson (1950) raised a similar issue. When his case arose in 1941, the Southern Railway's practice was to set aside two tables for blacks behind a curtain in an eleven-table dining car, but to seat whites there if no blacks had yet appeared for service. Blacks who arrived while whites were occupying the "black" tables had to wait until they were completely empty to be seated, whereas whites continued to be accommodated at all tables. Henderson was unable to secure a dining-car seat during his entire journey. By the time the litigation reached the ICC, the railroad had changed its policy, and the commission ruled that, even though the old practices were discriminatory, Henderson was unlikely to suffer from them any more. Under the new rules, once a black person had requested dining-car service, the stewards were to cease placing whites at the "black" tables. The ICC found this practice substantially equal, but the district court disagreed, as blacks were still not guaranteed service on the same terms as whites, because whites could potentially sit at any table, and blacks could not. The railway then changed its policy again, this time allocating one table behind a wood partition exclusively to blacks. The ICC upheld this practice on the ground that blacks, though generating less than 5 percent of the dining-car demand, were receiving 9 percent of the seating space. The district court affirmed, but the Supreme Court reversed.[122]

Henderson did not involve the total exclusion of blacks from luxury services that *McCabe* and *Mitchell* had. Nor was the railroad's latest dining-car policy justified on the basis of disparate per capita racial demand, as blacks were receiving more space than their racial demand warranted. Yet the case was still relatively easy for the justices. Several high court precedents had insisted that equal protection rights are "personal"—that is, they belong to individuals, not groups. Thus, the relevant question in *Henderson* was not whether blacks received the same average benefits as whites, but whether particular blacks received the same benefits as particular whites. The answer was clearly not. If a black person entered the dining car when the "black" table was full, he would be denied service, while a white person arriving simultaneously might be served. This was racial inequality, as the justices had previously defined it.

Yet *Henderson* did not stop there. Though the justices declined to reconsider *Plessy*, as the Justice Department had invited them to do, the opinion implicitly condemned segregation. Relying on *McLaurin*, which was decided on the same day, Burton's opinion for the unanimous Court criticized the wood partition separating the "black" table because it highlighted "the artificiality of a difference in treatment which serves only to call attention to a racial classification of passengers." All forms of segregation would seem vulnerable to that objection, and thus *Henderson* hinted at broader implications.[123]

If *Henderson* was easy legally, it was a laugher politically. The justices had not hesitated to condemn railroad discrimination in 1941, before the war had crystallized a national civil rights consciousness. By 1950, public opinion was much less tolerant of race discrimination in transportation. In 1949, the administration actually proposed legislation to forbid segregation in interstate transportation. The attorney general, J. Howard McGrath, made a rare Court appearance in *Henderson* and asked the justices to overrule *Plessy*. Thus, *Henderson*'s claim plainly had the backing of the federal government. The facts made the case even more compelling. Henderson was an FEPC field representative, who was denied service while returning from Birmingham, Alabama, where he had helped to organize local hearings on employment discrimination. The justices cannot have been favorably disposed toward sustaining railroad discrimination against federal government employees, especially given the valuable propaganda opportunities it afforded the Soviets.[124]

Though law and politics made *Henderson* easy, the justices remained ambivalent about the broader segregation issue. As in *Sweatt* and *McLaurin*, they declined invitations to overrule *Plessy*. Yet the rationales of all three decisions raised doubts about the continuing validity of segregation. The best explanation for why the justices would articulate rationales inconsistent with segregation, while refusing to openly overrule *Plessy*, is that they were divided. At one pole, Douglas was so adamant that *Plessy* be overruled that until virtually the last minute he contemplated concurring separately in *Henderson*. By contrast, Reed stated at the *Henderson* conference that it was "impossible to say that segregation per se is prohibited by [the] constitution." Jackson likewise declared that "we must amend [the Constitution] if we ban segregation." Frankfurter thought it "inconceivable" that the authors of the 1887 Interstate Commerce Act had intended to bar segregation. Always eager to avoid "borrowing future trouble," Frankfurter not only wanted to avoid explicitly overruling *Plessy*, but also urged Burton to excise language from a draft opinion that condemned the "symbolic" separation produced by the wood partition. Such language, Frankfurter thought, was an "anti-segregation slogan." Moreover, this objection to symbolism was equally applicable to grade school segregation—an issue the justices had agreed they were not ready to confront. Burton removed the objectionable language, yet even so, his opinion is difficult to reconcile with segregation. Though the justices found *Henderson* easy, some of them remained reluctant to overrule *Plessy*, even with regard to transportation, where white southerners were less heavily invested in it.[125]

The justices actually did condemn segregation in transportation, but under the Dormant Commerce Clause, not the Equal Protection Clause. The decision in *Morgan v. Virginia* (1946) invalidated a state law requiring segregation on common carriers, as applied to an interstate bus passenger. As early as the 1820s, the Court had ruled that the Commerce Clause of the Constitution is not only an affirmative grant of power to Congress but also a negative constraint on state power. Determining which state laws so impair interstate commerce as to violate the Constitution has perplexed the justices for nearly two centuries. On the one hand, states have obvious and legitimate interests in regulating behavior that occurs within state boundaries and affects the lives of state citizens. On the other hand, inconsistent state laws regulating national commerce could potentially destroy it, and states have political incentives to engage in economic protectionism, which incites retaliation and could possibly ignite escalating trade wars, which would nullify the benefits of an economic union. By 1946, the Court's efforts to reconcile such competing considerations had produced scores of decisions under the Dormant Commerce Clause—rulings that had proved impossible for the justices or commentators to reconcile. Many of these involved state regulation of railroads.[126]

The application of state laws forbidding race discrimination in public accommodations to interstate railroads and ships had provoked constitutional challenges since the 1870s. *Hall v. DeCuir* (1878) invalidated under the Dormant Commerce Clause a Louisiana public accommodations law, as applied to a Mississippi River steamboat, which was carrying interstate travelers. Though the Court never invalidated inverse legislation—measures *requiring* segregation on interstate carriers—dicta in several decisions assumed that such laws would be equally unconstitutional, and the Court consistently construed ambiguous public accommodations laws to cover only *intra*state passengers. Thus, by the time of *Morgan*, the law seemed clear: The Dormant Commerce Clause permitted states to segregate intrastate, but not interstate, passengers. The justices could invalidate Virginia's law simply by invoking *DeCuir*.[127]

Yet constitutional law is rarely that simple. The complication in *Morgan* was that the Roosevelt Court had begun to transform doctrine under the Dormant Commerce Clause and was permitting states greater regulatory freedom. The same justices who objected to *Lochner*-era constraints on state economic regulation imposed under the guise of substantive due process tended to find pre-1937 Dormant Commerce Clause doctrine too restrictive. For example, in *South Carolina State Highway Department v. Barnwell Brothers* (1938), the Court sustained a state's stringent regulation on the size of trucks, despite the severe burden it imposed on interstate commerce by forcing large vehicles to circumvent the state's highways. The justices had previously invalidated many less burdensome regulations on railroads, which suggests that *Barnwell Brothers* represented a new departure under the Dormant Commerce Clause. Thus, although *DeCuir* clearly indicated that Virginia could not segregate interstate passengers, in 1946 *DeCuir* was not obviously still good law.[128]

By a 6–1 vote, the justices in *Morgan* ruled that Virginia could not segregate interstate bus passengers—a result apparently in tension with the Court's recent trend under the Dormant Commerce Clause toward easing regulatory constraints on states. The justices' growing solicitude for civil rights probably explains this doctrinal disjuncture. Although the justices were not yet ready to invalidate state-mandated segregation under the Equal Protection Clause, which would have been difficult to confine to transportation, they were willing to bend Dormant Commerce Clause doctrine to accomplish the same result—a ruling that was easily so limited.[129]

Justice Black's concurring opinion is the strongest evidence in support of this interpretation, as it seems flatly inconsistent with the position he had taken in recent cases under the Dormant Commerce Clause. Alone among the justices, Black seemed willing to completely jettison the Dormant Commerce Clause. In one recent case, *Southern Pacific Co. v. Arizona* (1945), he had vehemently dissented from an opinion invalidating Arizona's train-length statute—a law that had obvious and potentially severe disruptive effects on interstate commerce. If Black thought that the Dormant Commerce Clause permitted Arizona's law, which potentially required large freight trains to be disassembled at every state's borders, how could he have objected to Virginia's segregation statute, which at most required some passenger reshuffling as buses crossed state boundaries—and not even that when journeys traversed only southern states that had similar segregation laws? Black's concurrence in *Morgan* reiterated his objection to even relaxed

Dormant Commerce Clause constraints but then concluded that recent precedents required him to find the Virginia law invalid.[130]

Neither aspect of Black's reasoning is persuasive. The justices generally show little future deference to decisions from which they dissented, and Black's voting record displays no special fealty to such precedents. Thus, his insistence that precedent compelled his vote in *Morgan* rings hollow. (The implausibility of his position perhaps explains why Black was initially hesitant to support the outcome in *Morgan*.) If a justice rarely reverses his past positions out of deference to precedent, then stare decisis never compels him to do so, but rather he occasionally so chooses—a choice that is determined by politics, not law. Furthermore, recent precedents under the Dormant Commerce Clause, even if binding on Black, did not require the invalidation of Virginia's law. Arizona's train-length law imposed far more substantial burdens on interstate commerce than did Virginia's segregation statute—though Black implausibly claimed the opposite—and thus *Southern Pacific* did not compel the outcome in *Morgan*. Moreover, less than a decade earlier, *Barnwell Brothers* had sustained South Carolina's law regulating the size of trucks, which likewise imposed a far greater burden on interstate commerce than did Virginia's segregation statute. Thus, *Barnwell Brothers*, if it survived *Southern Pacific*, should have compelled a contrary result in *Morgan*.[131]

Because recent precedents under the Dormant Commerce Clause suggested that Virginia's segregation law was constitutional, *Morgan* is best explained in political, not legal, terms. By 1946, the justices had little sympathy for racial segregation in transportation. Extralegal forces that supported progressive racial change in other legal contexts were equally operative in the transportation field. The NAACP's brief in *Morgan* reminded the justices that the nation was just emerging from a "death struggle against the apostles of racism." A Gallup poll conducted in the late 1940s revealed that national opinion opposed racial segregation in interstate transportation by 49 percent to 43 percent. Perhaps more important, the justices appreciated that southern whites would be less resistant to ending segregation in interstate transportation than in public education or housing. As common carriers were one of the last southern institutions to be segregated in the nineteenth century, they would naturally be one of the first to be desegregated. Interracial contact on buses was transitory, impersonal, and generally involved adults, not children—all features distinguishing it from grade school education. Many white southerners who were adamantly opposed to desegregating grade schools easily accepted the end of transportation segregation. During the war, Virginius Dabney, the moderate editor of the *Richmond Times-Dispatch*, advocated desegregating local transportation in Virginia. A few years after *Morgan*, Armistead Boothe, a moderate Virginia legislator who believed that judicially compelled school desegregation would be "the keynote to tragedy," proposed a repeal of the statute that mandated segregation on common carriers. (*Morgan* had required ending segregation only for *inter*state travelers.) Several city newspapers in Virginia endorsed Boothe's proposal, as did a handful of legislators. One liberal white journalist who favored the measure observed that while public school desegregation "is not seriously considered" by most Virginians, many whites thought that forcing blacks, no matter how "distinguished," to the back of the bus was "idiotic and evil." The justices might well have predicted (rightly) that many southern whites would approve, or at least not condemn, the result in *Morgan*.[132]

The availability of a nonracial doctrine such as the Dormant Commerce Clause to achieve a result that the justices found politically appealing may have proved irresistible. Reliance on this doctrine enabled the justices to avoid direct criticism of southern racial policy—something that they continued to shy away from well into the 1950s. Concretely, the Dormant Commerce Clause rationale would also condemn the application to interstate transportation of northern laws forbidding segregation on common carriers. Perhaps more significant, this rationale forbade segregation only in interstate travel and thus did not directly threaten other forms of segregation. The NAACP appreciated that the justices were probably not ready to invalidate school segregation and thus did not raise the equal protection challenge in *Morgan*. That choice was probably wise, as Frankfurter later observed that he would not have supported a school segregation challenge in the mid-1940s.[133]

However, achieving racially progressive results through indirection had potential vices as well as virtues. As already noted, the Dormant Commerce Clause rationale for invalidating state laws that segregated interstate travelers would appear to apply equally to laws that barred such segregation; both types of statute potentially burdened commerce by subjecting carriers to conflicting requirements as they crossed state lines. In the late 1940s, northern state laws barring segregation on common carriers outnumbered southern state laws requiring it.

In 1948, the justices confronted a case that seemed to require them to swallow their own medicine; instead, they chose to have their cake and eat it too. Like most northern states, Michigan barred discrimination by common carriers. The Bob-Lo Excursion Company ran a boat service for Detroit daytrippers to Bois Blanc Island, located near the mouth of the Detroit River. Because the island belonged to Ontario, Canada, these expeditions technically qualified as foreign commerce. Bob-Lo excluded blacks, and Michigan prosecuted it under the state public accommodations law. Bob-Lo defended the suit on the ground that Michigan's law, as applied to international travelers, violated the Dormant Foreign Commerce Clause. *Morgan* seemed to provide compelling support for that argument, but the justices concluded otherwise.[134]

By a vote of 7–2, the decision in *Bob-Lo* rejected the constitutional challenge. Justice Wiley Rutledge's majority opinion distinguished the present case from *Morgan* on two grounds. First, although conceding that foreign commerce was involved, Rutledge insisted that it was not *very* foreign. Bois

Blanc Island was economically and socially a part of Michigan, and no established travel routes from Canada to the island existed. Second, both Ontario and Canada forbade race discrimination by common carriers, just as Michigan did. Thus, Bob-Lo faced no present, and little future, risk of conflicting legal obligations, though *Morgan* had not suggested that the constitutionality of Virginia's bus segregation law depended on whether passengers were traveling to states with conflicting legal requirements.[135]

No two cases are ever precisely alike. Thus, the justices usually have the option of distinguishing, rather than overruling, decisions that differ in seemingly minor ways. Such fine-grained distinctions are not necessarily illegitimate. So long as the justices can identify factual distinctions that bear some plausible legal significance—that parties have different names will not do—they have fulfilled the obligation to engage in "reasoned elaboration." Yet, in such cases, law has not compelled the outcome. With equal ease, the justices might have adhered to a legal principle stated at a higher level of generality, which would have rendered the precious factual distinctions irrelevant. Thus, *Bob-Lo* could have read *Morgan* to forbid state regulation of racial seating practices on common carriers that crossed state or national boundaries, which is how *Morgan* most naturally reads. One virtue of this interpretation would be clarity, which would discourage litigation over the question of how *foreign* commerce had to be to implicate the Constitution. But the justices in *Bob-Lo* chose to read *Morgan* more narrowly and rejected its application to pseudo-international travel, at least where the country of destination had no common-carrier regulations that conflicted with those of the state of origin. Two dissenters, Vinson and Jackson, objected to slicing *Morgan* this thinly.[136]

Because *Morgan* could be reconciled with either outcome in *Bob-Lo*, it was politics, not precedent, that determined the result in the latter case. It must have been tempting for the justices in *Bob-Lo* to read *Morgan* narrowly—even to distort it—in order to reach an antisegregation outcome. The justices decided *Bob-Lo* on the same day that President Truman introduced landmark civil rights legislation, including a bill to forbid segregation in interstate commerce. Fifteen years later, at another moment of unprecedented civil rights consciousness, the justices would engage in legal gymnastics that rated a much higher degree of difficulty, as they repeatedly stretched doctrine to overturn the convictions of sit-in demonstrators for trespass and breach of the peace.[137]

Mitchell and *Henderson* interpreted the Interstate Commerce Act to invalidate railroad policies of race discrimination as applied to interstate passengers, whereas *Morgan* interpreted the Dormant Commerce Clause of the Constitution to forbid state-imposed segregation of interstate passengers. Neither ruling applied to intrastate travel or to the carriers' policies of segregation (as opposed to discrimination), even as applied to interstate passengers. Until the justices changed their interpretation of the Equal Protection Clause, state-imposed segregation was permissible, unless it violated another constitutional provision, such as the Dormant Commerce Clause. More-over, neither the ICC nor the lower federal courts were likely to rule that practices deemed permissible under the Equal Protection Clause when imposed by states violated the statutory prohibition on "undue or unreason-able prejudice or disadvantage" when imposed by carriers.[138]

CRIMINAL PROCEDURE

In the 1940s and 1950s, the justices extended landmark rulings in three of the four criminal procedure contexts they had broached during the interwar period: race discrimination in jury selection, coerced confessions, and the right to counsel. Except for the jury discrimination case, *Norris v. Alabama* (1935), these earlier rulings—plus the one from the fourth criminal proce-dure context, mob-dominated trials—were not explicitly about race. Chap-ter 3 argued that only southern cases that involved allegations of serious black-on-white crime generated fact patterns that were sufficiently appalling to induce intervention by the high court. Yet none of these rulings had inti-mated that the new legal rights articulated—rights against mob-dominated trials and coerced confessions and in favor of state-appointed counsel in cap-ital cases—were limited to blacks. In the 1940s, Court cases that implicated these rights increasingly involved defendants who were white as well as black and northerners as well as southerners. Relatedly, the facts also became less egregious, and claims of factual innocence by defendants became more attenuated. As a result, the justices grew conflicted over whether to inter-vene, and unanimity became elusive. As criminal procedure issues ceased to be predominantly about race, they became harder to adjudicate.

Race discrimination in jury selection is, naturally, a racial issue. *Norris v. Alabama* altered the critical subconstitutional rules that determine whether such discrimination can be proved. *Norris* revitalized the presumption from *Neal* that the lengthy absence of blacks from juries in counties with substan-tial black populations was attributable to race discrimination, and the Court refused to defer to findings of fact by trial courts on matters that proved dis-positive of federal constitutional rights. Because southern states reformed their jury selection practices so little after *Norris*, the justices continued to find cases in which it was easy to reverse the convictions of southern blacks.[139]

Smith v. Texas (1940) reversed the rape conviction of a black man from Harris County, Texas. Blacks were 20 percent of the county's population and 10 percent of its poll-tax payers. Grand juries were selected from the poll-tax lists. Over the previous seven years, only 18 blacks had appeared on those lists, out of a total of 512 persons. Moreover, of those 18 only 5 had been called to serve, as compared with 379 of the 494 whites on the lists. Grand juries of 12 were selected by drawing 16 names from the lists. Each prospective juror was then assigned a number from 1 to 16, with those at the bottom rarely serving. Thirteen of the 18 blacks called were assigned the number 16. The justices found this to be an easy case of race discrimination. They insisted on examining the facts for themselves, even though Texas courts had found no discrimination. They also rejected the jury commissioners' defense that they had compiled the jury lists from personal acquaintances and that it was this practice, not discrimination, that explained the relative absence of blacks from juries. The justices responded that if jury commissioners did not know many blacks, then limiting prospective jurors to personal acquaintances *was* race discrimination.[140]

Hill v. Texas (1942) was another easy case of jury discrimination. Not a single black had served on a grand jury in Dallas County for decades, even though 8,000 had paid their poll taxes. Two of the three jury commissioners testified that they had chosen only personal acquaintances for grand jury service, and one explained, "I personally did not know of a qualified Negro." The Court unanimously reversed Hill's rape conviction.[141]

By the late 1940s, the justices were growing frustrated at how little their decisions had affected jury selection practices in the South. Justice Black voiced that irritation at a conference discussion in 1948: "[T]his rule [against race discrimination in jury selection] was announced 80 years ago—it is just getting to the point where there is a chance of it being carried out." The annoyance felt by the justices at southern nullification of *Norris* and its progeny may explain the unanimous reversals of several convictions on the ground of jury discrimination between 1947 and 1953—cases that were not quite so easy as *Smith* and *Hill*. For example, *Patton v. Mississippi* (1947) involved another complete exclusion of blacks from jury venires for a period of decades. However, in Lauderdale County, Mississippi, only an estimated twenty-five black males were qualified as electors—a statutory requirement for jury service in Mississippi. Without deciding whether blacks had suffered discrimination in voter registration, the Court ruled that, even though so few blacks were qualified as voters, the state still bore the burden of showing that the complete exclusion of blacks from jury venires was not attributable to race discrimination. Given that Mississippi had a somewhat stronger defense than Texas had had in *Smith* or *Hill*, the unanimous reversal in *Patton* probably indicates either growing irritation among the justices at southern evasion or a silent condemnation of race discrimination in voter registration.[142]

Still, the justices declined to take the steps necessary to actually place blacks on southern juries. *Patton* did not directly question the practice of limiting jury service to registered voters. No high court ruling cast doubt upon the common practice of conferring broad discretion on jury commissioners to select persons of "good intelligence, sound judgment, and fair character." The Court did not even flatly prohibit the insidious practice of commissioners limiting prospective jurors to their personal acquaintances, which meant white people. Perhaps most important, the justices refused even to review a case that challenged the discriminatory use of peremptory challenges by prosecutors to exclude all blacks from trial juries.[143]

Akins v. Texas (1945) was this Court's most extraordinary failure to intervene against race discrimination in jury selection. Akins was charged with murdering a white off-duty police officer in Dallas County. The sixteen-person grand jury that indicted him included a single black. All three commissioners admitted in testimony that they had refused to permit more than one black to sit on Akins's grand jury. Inexplicably, in light of that testimony, the Court found the commissioners' intentions unclear. Justice Reed explained for a majority of six that, given the factual uncertainty, the Court had to defer to the state court's findings of fact—an approach that was inconsistent with *Norris* and its progeny. As Akins had a strong self-defense claim to supplement his compelling jury discrimination challenge, the justices' lack of sympathy is puzzling.[144]

Perhaps the explanation is that the justices wished to commend, not condemn, a southern county that had taken some steps toward complying with *Norris*—by placing a black on a grand jury—at a time when most of the South was still defiant. Frankfurter praised Dallas County for having made a "conscientious effort to carry out the law." An alternative explanation is that the justices were so averse to requiring proportional black representation on juries that, perversely, they endorsed a racial quota. Reed's opinion noted that, given the percentage of blacks in Dallas County, an unbiased selection system would have produced an average of 1.8 blacks per grand jury. In light of this fact, Reed refused to hold that the presence of only one black on Akins's grand jury was evidence of discrimination. Yet Akins was not arguing for proportionality; he was challenging a quota. Given the commissioners' candid confessions that they had limited black representation to one, *Akins* should have been an easy case for reversal.[145]

The decision in *Brown v. Mississippi* (1936) overturned on due process grounds a conviction based on a confession that had been extracted through torture. High court decisions in the 1940s extended that prohibition to confessions obtained through lengthy questioning of suspects who were held incommunicado. Over time, these cases grew more difficult for the justices, as defendants who were white as well as those who were black challenged interrogation practices that were less barbaric and that were used in the North as well as the South.

The Court first extended *Brown* in *Chambers v. Florida* (1940). When a white man was killed near Fort Lauderdale in 1933, "the police instinctively reach[ed] for a Negro," rounding up for interrogation nearly forty black men without any particularized suspicion. Izell Chambers and three codefendants were held incommunicado for nearly a week, interrogated in all-night sessions, deprived of sleep, and threatened with lynching. Chambers also claimed that he had been beaten, though the police denied doing so, as they would in virtually all such cases after *Brown*. After being convicted and sentenced to death, Chambers appealed to the Supreme Court. The justices unanimously found that his confession had been unconstitutionally coerced, regardless of whether Chambers had been physically abused.[146]

Chambers was easy for the Court. Such interrogation practices were not only inhumane, they were unreliable. After a week of constant interrogation and sleep deprivation, suspects were likely to confess whether they were guilty or not. This is why Florida case law forbade such tactics, though the state courts had unaccountably failed to apply it here. Thus, *Chambers*, much like *Brown*, simply constitutionalized a standard that virtually all states already purported to employ. Further, the justices probably suspected that Chambers had been beaten, as "the third degree, particularly for Negroes in the south, does not confine itself to the classic form of the Socratic dialogue." Moreover, also as in *Brown*, the defendants' confessions were the only significant evidence that linked them to the crime, which thus raised doubts about their guilt. Finally, *Chambers* arose at a time when Americans generally, and the justices specifically, were trying to identify distinctions between U.S. democracy, on the one hand, and German fascism and Soviet communism, on the other. As Justice Black observed in his opinion for the Court in *Chambers*, "[T]yrannical governments had immemorially utilized dictatorial criminal procedure and punishment to make scapegoats of the weak, or of helpless political, religious or racial minorities and those who differed, who would not conform and who resisted tyranny." Americans aspired to do better, and they generally succeeded, except when southern blacks were accused of serious crimes against whites that aroused local passions.[147]

Over the next two years, the Court decided four more similar cases. Each involved the murder of a white man or the rape of a white woman, followed by a police roundup of numerous blacks, without any particularized suspicion. Each defendant was held incommunicado for up to a week and relentlessly interrogated until he confessed. In one case, law enforcement officers transported the defendant from county to county for several nights to avoid an actual or imagined lynch mob. In another case, the police took the defendant from jail into the woods for interrogation on several evenings. All of these defendants claimed that they had been beaten, which the police denied (in one case, the law enforcement officers insisted that they had "sweet talked" the defendant into confessing). Moreover, the confessions were the only direct evidence of the defendants' guilt. The justices found these cases to be easy. In two of them, they reversed convictions on the basis of *Chambers* without even bothering to hear oral arguments—a virtually unprecedented procedure at that time. The justices may have believed that these defendants were beaten into confessing in violation of *Brown*. But as they had no secure basis for rejecting findings by the trial courts to the contrary, it was easy enough to extend *Brown* to cover other coercive interrogation tactics.[148]

Then the cases got harder. Only black suspects in the South were routinely subjected to such brutal interrogation tactics. Northern blacks and whites throughout the nation might face tough questioning by the police, but nothing like this. As cases from the North and cases involving white defendants reached the Court, the consensus among the justices evaporated. Tough questions that could be avoided in *Brown* and *Chambers* now had to be faced: Did the Constitution ban coerced confessions because of a concern about their veracity or because of an aversion to state coercion? If only the former, then some fairly coercive but nonbrutal interrogation tactics might be permitted. Moreover, if the justices' concern was reliability, then the existence of evidence that independently corroborated guilt was relevant to whether a conviction based partly on a coerced confession should be overturned. This issue had not arisen in *Brown*, *Chambers*, or their progeny, because the prosecutions' cases without the defendants' confessions would have been clearly inadequate. Finally, regardless of the reasons that coerced confessions were suppressed, lines had to be drawn between permissible and impermissible interrogation. Reasonable people naturally disagreed over how to balance state interests in solving crimes with suspects' interests in avoiding coercive interrogation.[149]

The subsequent coerced confession cases involved suspects who had been detained without preliminary hearings in violation of state law. The police aggressively interrogated the defendants, usually for several hours at a time, sometimes over several days, but generally without denying them food and sleep. The defendants were secluded from friends, families, and lawyers. In some cases, additional circumstances relevant to the coercion issue were present. For example, one defendant was only fifteen years old, and another was made to answer questions while naked. Most defendants insisted that they had been beaten, though the police denied it, usually with greater plausibility than they had in *Chambers*. The justices sustained some of these convictions and reversed others; they were divided in every case. Commentators were unable to reconcile the results, which seemed to turn mainly on how Frankfurter reacted to the facts of a particular case. Several split decisions in 1948 and 1949 overturned convictions. However, after the two most liberal justices, Murphy and Rutledge, died in 1949, conservatives were able to assemble a majority that was less inclined to find unconstitutional coercion. Once the regional and the racial elements had been removed from coerced confession cases, they became more difficult for the justices to resolve because the level of coercion was reduced and the corroborating evidence of guilt was increased.[150]

This Court decided one other important coerced confession case, *Lyons v. Oklahoma* (1944). As noted at the beginning of this chapter, a black man, W. D. Lyons, was convicted in 1941 of a horrific triple murder near Hugo, Oklahoma. His claim that his confession had been coerced was strong. Several white witnesses testified that the state investigator who interrogated Lyons had bragged of beating him with a blackjack for six to seven hours before Lyons confessed. That confession was repeated roughly twelve hours later to a different officer in a different location. A divided Court ruled that the trial judge and jury could have reasonably concluded that Lyons's second confession was voluntary.[151]

This result is puzzling. The evidence of torture was stronger here than in any case since *Brown*, as several witnesses with no apparent incentive to lie corroborated Lyons's account of the beatings. Given the severity of the physical abuse, it seems odd to treat as voluntary the second confession made just hours later. Moreover, Lyons had a strong claim of innocence. Under a plausible alternative scenario constructed by the NAACP, the governor of Oklahoma had decided to frame a black man for the murders in order to cover up the possibility that the perpetrator was an escapee from a laxly supervised chain gang. The state's failure to prosecute Lyons for an entire year, even though he was taken into custody soon after the murders, was suspicious, given that southern black-on-white murder cases were generally prosecuted within weeks, if not days. Why a majority of the justices proved unsympathetic to Lyons's coerced confession claim is unclear. Perhaps they worried that reversing too many convictions risked inciting a public backlash against a Court that would be perceived as soft on crime.

The decision in *Powell v. Alabama* (1932) had interpreted the Due Process Clause to require states to provide counsel for indigent defendants in capital cases, and it had ruled that appointment of counsel on the morning of the trial was constitutionally inadequate. *Powell* was about race in the sense that only southern black defendants charged with serious crimes against whites would have had counsel appointed the morning of their trial. Yet white and black defendants, in the North as well as in the South, faced non-capital felony prosecutions without the aid of counsel. *Betts v. Brady* (1942) refused to extend *Powell* to all indigent defendants prosecuted for felonies. However, several subsequent decisions ruled that even if the Constitution did not entitle all such defendants to state-appointed counsel, particular circumstances—such as a defendant's age or intelligence—might make such an appointment mandatory. Most of these cases involved white defendants in the North. In the absence of the racial element, the facts were generally less egregious than in *Powell*, and the justices tended to divide.[152]

Post-*Betts* cases raised only the question of whether a particular felony defendant was entitled to state-appointed counsel. None of them addressed the question of how far in advance of the trial the lawyer had to be appointed. Only a single pre-*Betts* case, *Avery v. Alabama* (1940), considered that issue. *Avery* ruled that an appointment of counsel in a capital murder case three days before trial was acceptable, in the absence of a specific showing that the defendant had been prejudiced by the shortness of time that had been given counsel to prepare. *Avery*, too, is puzzling. Surely the justices, some of whom had experience in criminal litigation, understood that lawyers could not adequately prepare a defense in three days, especially when, as in *Avery*, they were simultaneously occupied with other cases. Likewise, the justices must have appreciated that defendants would be hard pressed to prove that the inadequate time given their lawyers to prepare had been prejudicial. The Court had not imposed similar "harmless error" obstacles with regard to claims of coerced confessions or race discrimination in jury selection, probably because the justices appreciated that such showings were almost impossible to make. Indeed, to the contrary, the Court had ruled that convictions must be reversed upon proof of race discrimination in jury selection, "no matter how strong the evidence of . . . guilt." Perhaps the justices in *Avery* were reluctant to impose specific time limits in defining the adequacy of defense counsel's appointment, because any numerical standard would seem arbitrary. If three days before trial was insufficient, what about four days or five? (A similar aversion to arbitrary numerical standards may explain why today's justices have been reluctant to engage in proportionality reviews of criminal sentences outside of the death penalty context.) Moreover, even after the Warren Court's criminal procedure revolution of the 1960s, the justices remained reluctant to recognize a constitutional right to *effective* assistance of counsel. Perhaps they were intimidated by the immense consequences for American criminal justice of identifying such a right. That the Court did not do so until 1984 is stunning, and even then the entitlement was minimal, and violations have been almost impossible to prove.[153]

During the World War II era, the justices were much more protective of civil rights than they had previously been. They overruled recent precedents such as *Corrigan* and *Grovey*, began to eviscerate *Plessy*, and potentially revolutionized state-action doctrine in *Smith*, *Shelley*, and *Terry*. Criminal procedure rulings extended earlier precedents involving race discrimination in jury selection, coerced confessions, and the right to counsel. Yet, the justices showed greater hesitancy in criminal cases than in other civil rights contexts and not simply when the issues ceased being predominantly about race. *Lyons* and *Avery* were still mainly about race. Not many white suspects were tortured with "nigger beaters" for several hours and forced to sit with pans of dead people's bones in their laps in an effort to extract confessions. Nor were many white capital defendants provided with defense counsel just three days before their trials. Yet the justices rejected challenges in both of these cases. Likewise, *Akins* unaccountably found the evidence conflicting on whether jury commissioners had deliberately limited the number of blacks on a grand jury to one, even though all three candidly admitted doing so.

One cannot know what explains these results. Yet, even as the justices later became more supportive of civil rights, they continued to show greater hesitancy at intervening against race discrimination in criminal cases than in others. In 1965, at the zenith of the civil rights movement, *Swain v. Alabama* refused to bar a prosecutor's use of peremptory challenges to exclude blacks entirely from a criminal jury. Nor did the 1960s Court grant review of constitutional challenges to racially discriminatory administration of the death penalty. Only in the 1970s did the justices vindicate such challenges, and not until 1986 did they overrule *Swain*. Yet, the very next year,

McCleskey v. Kemp again revealed the justices' limited commitment to pursuing racial justice in criminal cases: They narrowly rejected an equal protection challenge to the discriminatory administration of the death penalty in Georgia. Specifically, according to a study that the justices stipulated to be valid for purposes of the case, defendants who murdered whites were 4.3 times more likely to receive the death penalty than those who murdered blacks, controlling for all variables other than the race of the victims. The Court offered several justifications for the result in *McCleskey*. Race discrimination could not be entirely eliminated from the administration of the death penalty, so long as actors integral to the system, such as prosecutors and jurors, exercised significant discretion. Similar racial disparities existed throughout the criminal justice system; thus, to vindicate McCleskey's claim would have enormous consequences. McCleskey had not proven that race discrimination was a factor in his particular case—a showing that the Court had not required in its jury discrimination cases. Critics found these justifications lame, if not disturbing.[154]

More recently, the decision in *United States v. Armstrong* (1996) imposed a virtually impossible hurdle for defendants alleging racially selective prosecution. Before black defendants could gain discovery on such claims, *Armstrong* ruled, they must demonstrate that similarly situated whites had not been prosecuted. Yet this was the very point on which discovery was sought. Although the justices in cases that challenged the constitutionality of minority voting districts had frowned on the assumption that blacks and whites have different political preferences (which might warrant creating majority-black districts), *Armstrong* rejected the lower court's assumption that all crimes are equally likely to be committed by members of all races. Thus, the fact that this particular U.S. attorney's office had prosecuted in the preceding year twenty-four blacks and not a single white for crack distribution did not establish the prima facie case of selective prosecution necessary for discovery. Indeed, Chief Justice William H. Rehnquist went further and perversely reasoned that the disproportionate percentage of crack-distribution sentences received by blacks—as high as 90 percent in 1994—helped refute, rather than confirm, the selective prosecution claim.[155]

Thus, even the Warren Court, with its unparalleled support for civil rights, and the Rehnquist Court, with its ostensible commitment to constitutional color blindness, have tolerated race discrimination in criminal justice. This subsequent history helps explain why the postwar Court, which had yet even to condemn segregation, was so lax in its commitment to racial equality in criminal procedure. The relative timidity of the justices in this context probably reflects, as constitutional rulings usually do, public opinion. Most white Americans, even today, are reluctant to confront the troubling truths about the extent to which criminal justice remains color-coded.[156]

PEONAGE

The justices decided two peonage cases during World War II, *Taylor v. Georgia* (1942) and *Pollock v. Williams* (1944)—the first such decisions since the Progressive Era. Both were easy cases—so easy that perhaps, had similar cases presented themselves earlier, the justices would have reached the same results even before World War II had begun to transform U.S. race relations. Both decisions invalidated statutes that were patent evasions of *Bailey v. Alabama* (1911). They are less striking for their results than for the time that was necessary to bring the issue before the Court. These decisions confirm that Court rulings usually make little practical difference if beneficiaries lack the resources necessary to pursue follow-up litigation.[157]

To claim that these cases were easy is not to say that precedent compelled the outcomes, as both decisions required mild extensions of *Bailey*. Rather, they were easy for two other reasons. The justices were irritated at the continuing southern efforts to evade *Bailey* thirty years down the road, and by the 1940s, peonage practices seemed bizarrely anachronistic.

Bailey invalidated an Alabama law that criminalized entering into a labor contract that paid advance wages with the fraudulent intent to subsequently breach it. Critical to the decision was the statutory provision that authorized a presumption of fraudulent intent from the fact of the breach. *Bailey* did not suggest that the traditional offense of obtaining money under false pretenses was unconstitutional; the Court objected only to the statutory presumption, which effectively criminalized simple breaches of labor contracts, in violation of the Thirteenth Amendment. The presumption was especially objectionable, *Bailey* noted, because Alabama evidence law forbade defendants from testifying to uncommunicated motives for their behavior.

The Georgia statute in *Taylor* was virtually identical to the Alabama law in *Bailey*, including the objectionable presumption. Only two differences existed. Georgia criminalized the failure of workers to repay advance wages only if the breach was "without good and sufficient cause." Also, Georgia evidence law permitted defendants to make unsworn (but not sworn) statements regarding their motives, which was more than Alabama law had allowed in *Bailey*. *Taylor* found both of these differences inconsequential and invalidated the Georgia law.

Permitting defendants to escape punishment by demonstrating "good and sufficient cause" for their failure to repay advance wages was not, as *Taylor* observed, equivalent to requiring the prosecution to prove that defendants had fraudulent intent when signing the contracts. Taylor might have expected to repay the advance wages when he signed the contract, yet still lacked "good and sufficient cause" for his subsequent decision to breach it. Still, the "good cause" requirement did offer defendants a means of escaping liability that had not been available in *Bailey*. Thus, *Bailey* did not compel invalidation of the Georgia law. As to the difference in evidence law, *Taylor* simply noted that Alabama's prohibition on testimony regarding uncommunicated motives had been "far from controlling" in *Bailey*. But that is a controversial reading of precedent. Any time an opinion enumerates several factors in support of its holding, one cannot know which were essential to the result. Only subsequent rulings can clarify a precedent's scope, and they do so by choosing to broadly or narrowly construe it. Though *Taylor* is a plausible—perhaps even convincing—reading of *Bailey*, it was not compelled.[158]

Taylor was easy, not because *Bailey* logically mandated it, but because the justices were irritated at Georgia's having circumvented *Bailey* for three decades and because they were repulsed by peonage. As we saw in the white primary cases, the justices do not relish seeing their rulings evaded. Defining "evasion" is complicated, because judicial opinions that rely on multiple factors do not generate unambiguous holdings. Yet the justices probably think of their decisions as having "purposes" somewhat independent of the proffered rationales. The "purpose" of *Smith v. Allwright* apparently was to enable blacks to participate in Democratic party primaries. The purpose of *Bailey*, as clarified by *Taylor*, was to prevent the punishment of workers for simple breaches of labor contracts. The justices in *Taylor* plainly believed that Georgia was flouting *Bailey*, and this annoyed them.

That irritation was even more apparent in *Pollock*, which invalidated a Florida law nearly identical to the one in *Bailey*. Florida first enacted this law in 1919 and had reenacted it in 1943, a year after *Taylor*, which made the state appear to be thumbing its nose at the Court. The Florida Supreme Court rejected Pollock's appeal and distinguished *Taylor* on the ground that Pollock had pleaded guilty to the false-pretenses offense, and thus the objectionable statutory presumption may have played no role in his conviction—a plausible distinction in that defendants generally lack standing to challenge laws that did not affect their convictions. Yet Pollock could reasonably argue that the statutory presumption had induced his guilty plea, and thus he should be allowed to challenge it. Unfortunately, whether the presumption induced Pollock's plea is impossible to know, which means that whoever bore the burden of proof almost certainly would lose. The state court placed it on Pollock and then found that he had failed to meet it.[159]

Justice Jackson, writing for the majority, made the plausible, though hardly compelling, point that Florida had enacted and reenacted its law with the knowledge that the presumption was unconstitutional, and thus it should be barred from denying that the presumption had influenced Pollock's guilty plea. Jackson also plausibly noted that federal courts need not defer to the factual findings of state courts when they are dispositive of federal rights. He then found that the unconstitutional presumption had influenced Pollock's plea. Yet Jackson did not stop there. Displaying his irritation at Florida's evasion, Jackson denied that *Bailey* and *Taylor* had sustained all of the false-pretenses statute except for the presumption. Yet *Bailey* had certainly implied that. Venturing beyond the facts of *Pollock*, Jackson seemed to condemn—

while denying that he was doing so—all false-pretenses statutes involving laborers receiving advance wages. He noted that these laws invariably punished blacks for breaching labor agreements after receiving small advances, even without any evidence of fraudulent intent. Jackson plainly sought to preempt Florida's anticipated response to *Pollock*, which probably would have been to eliminate the objectionable presumption while continuing to prosecute under the false-pretenses statute, with the hope that all-white juries would infer fraud from the contractual breach even without the aid of the presumption. For the justices to essentially invalidate a law that was not before them is unusual; it contravenes their general preference for minimalist, case-by-case decision making. They clearly intended to convey a strong message condemning peonage.[160]

That the justices in the 1940s would be so hostile to peonage is unsurprising. During the Progressive Era, peonage had been one of the few racial practices that divided southern whites and drew criticism from northern whites. If elite opinion already condemned peonage in the 1910s, when most blacks lived in the South and performed agricultural labor, how anachronistic must it have seemed by 1940, when a couple of million blacks had migrated to the North and several million more to southern cities? Several forces—New Deal agricultural policies, technological advances in farming, and heightened wartime demand for industrial labor—were revolutionizing the southern economy in the 1940s. Peonage was nearly obsolete in this new economic order, and the justices must have been tempted to accelerate its extinction.

CHAPTER FIVE

World War II Era: Consequences

VOTING

Lane v. Oklahoma (1939) invalidated the Oklahoma statute that grandfathered the grandfather clause, but that decision had little effect on black voting. Despite the statute, blacks had been permitted to register and vote in most Oklahoma counties. Whites in Oklahoma viewed black suffrage in much the same way as did whites in border states, such as Maryland and Kentucky, where blacks had not suffered disfranchisement since the adoption of the Fifteenth Amendment in 1870. Oklahoma had a thriving two-party political system, and blacks made up only 7 percent of the population. Moreover, because Oklahoma's grandfathering statute was unique, *Lane* had no direct consequences elsewhere. All that it did was to invalidate an outlier statute that was already generally ignored.[1]

In contrast, *Smith v. Allwright* (1944), which struck down the white primary, may have been the most practically significant ruling thus far considered in this book. In 1940, just 3 percent of southern black adults were registered to vote, but by 1952, 20 percent were. Some of that increase preceded *Smith* and thus is attributable to factors associated with World War II, not to the Court. Nor can all of the post-1944 increase be reasonably attributed to *Smith*. Yet the Court's intervention was critical to this dramatic increase in the voting registration of southern blacks. That *Smith* should have had this effect, when lower court decisions invalidating white primaries in Virginia and Florida in the early 1930s did not, is interesting. It suggests that other factors made possible the enormous impact that *Smith* had on southern politics.[2]

Numerous changes in southern society and politics enabled *Smith* to be so efficacious. By the 1940s, many southern whites were less resistant than before to black participation in politics. Southern blacks had become more aggressive about demanding their rights. The proliferation of NAACP branches in the South facilitated challenges to legislative measures that were aimed at nullifying *Smith*. Those southern whites who continued to obstruct black suffrage faced a greater risk of federal prosecution. Finally, southern judges showed an unprecedented willingness to broadly construe the voting rights of southern blacks. These legal and extralegal factors created an environment in which it was possible for *Smith* to launch a political revolution in the urban South. In the absence of such background conditions, *Smith* would probably have been almost as inconsequential as earlier suffrage decisions, such as *Guinn* and *Herndon*. Each of these factors warrants a closer look, but first let us consider the immediate impact of *Smith* in the South.[3]

In Tennessee and North Carolina, which had never conducted statewide white primaries, and in Virginia, where federal courts had invalidated such elections many years earlier, the reaction of most whites to *Smith* was calm and collected. The two leading Richmond newspapers endorsed the decision, and one of them observed that blacks had voted in Virginia primaries for years, yet "the skies haven't fallen." In Arkansas and Texas, which *had* barred blacks from Democratic party primaries, many counties rescinded their racially exclusionary policies immediately after *Smith*. In the Deep South, however, Democratic party officials and public officeholders pledged resistance to *Smith* and continued to bar black participation in primaries in 1944. That year, only an estimated 200,000 blacks were registered to vote in the South, and they were overwhelmingly Republicans.[4]

Stunning changes quickly occurred. By 1946, black participation in primaries had dramatically increased in Georgia, Florida, and Texas; by 1948, in Louisiana and South Carolina; and by 1950, even in Mississippi. The number of blacks registered to vote in the South rose to roughly three-quarters of a million in 1948 and to a million in 1952. The quickest transformation occurred in Georgia, where black voter registration increased from roughly 20,000 in 1940 to 125,000 in 1947. Essentially no blacks had participated in Democratic primaries in South Carolina in 1946, but an estimated 35,000 did in 1948. The number of registered black voters in Louisiana increased from 8,000 to 43,000 within an eight-month period in 1948 and then rose to 107,000 by 1952. In Florida, there were roughly 20,000 registered black voters in 1944, 49,000 in 1947, and 116,000 in 1950. Even in Mississippi, where white resistance to black suffrage remained intense, black voter registration increased from 2,500 in 1946 to 20,000 in 1950.[5]

Reflecting on these numbers, the NAACP proclaimed *Smith* to be "a giant milestone in the progress of Negro Americans toward full citizenship." Without *Smith*, these changes would probably not have occurred when they did, but even with *Smith*, other supportive social and political conditions were critical to the changes. One important factor was the greater acceptance of black voting by southern whites. It is true that many whites, especially in the Deep South, remained adamantly opposed to black suffrage. Yet by 1944, many white newspapers in the South, especially but not exclusively in the peripheral South, endorsed *Smith* on the ground that blacks deserved "fair and just political . . . rights." An editorial in white Georgia newspapers that urged compliance with *Smith* elicited surprising statements of support rather than harassing midnight phone calls. When Deep South states adopted evasive measures, many white newspapers were critical. In 1946, Alabamans amended their constitution to empower registrars to administer vaguely worded literacy tests, which were designed to reduce black voter registration—the so-called Boswell amendment—but only 54 percent of whites voted in favor.[6]

Progressive white southerners, including those who supported organized labor's concurrent efforts to unionize the South, appreciated that black enfranchisement would probably benefit liberal politicians. Economically populist and racially moderate governors, such as Earl Long of Louisiana and Big Jim Folsom of Alabama, actively encouraged the surge in black voter registration that followed *Smith*. Folsom campaigned against the Boswell amendment and urged blacks who were unfairly denied registration to sue local officials. The white political establishment in Atlanta apparently also endorsed black suffrage. Fulton County registrars in 1948 not only permitted blacks to register but actually set up shop in black schools and churches to facilitate the process. Even in South Carolina, some white Democrats struggled to open their party to blacks, reasoning that many blacks were "now qualified in mind and character to take part in our form of government," that black soldiers were risking their lives in a war to defend democracy, and that black enfranchisement would help convince minority peoples around the world that U.S. democracy was not racist.[7]

By the late 1940s, many ordinary whites, who lacked any political incentive, were prepared to tolerate or even to support black suffrage, as disfranchisement increasingly appeared impossible to justify in a democratic age. Disfranchisement efforts were, according to one white newspaper, an effort "to turn the clock back, a failure to face up to facts." A white Democrat in South Carolina wrote to Thurgood Marshall to distance himself from his party's efforts to exclude blacks, which "profane[d] the Bill of Rights." A white Democrat in Alabama criticized her party's proscription of blacks as a "cruel and shameful thing." Other southern whites agreed that "[m]en who faced bullets overseas deserve ballots at home" and that black disfranchisement reflected "the [same] hateful ideologies" as the nation's enemies. Many whites defended the political participation of blacks while distinguishing school integration and interracial marriage, which they insisted must remain off limits.[8]

Another change in circumstance that enhanced *Smith*'s efficacy was the greater capacity of southern blacks to capitalize on it. Controversial court decisions generally have little impact unless they are energetically enforced. *Smith* was highly salient to southern blacks, who quickly began registering to vote and demanding access to Democratic party primaries. Thousands of returning black veterans took their release papers, which entitled them to exemption from the poll tax, and went directly to city hall to demand registration. Many expressed the view that after fighting abroad for democracy, they should be able to enjoy a little of it at home. Tens of thousands of nonveterans also sought to register after *Smith*. Southern blacks established progressive voters' leagues, which organized registration campaigns and conducted voter education classes to help applicants pass literacy tests. Record numbers of southern blacks tried to vote in Democratic primaries in 1944, notwithstanding publicized statements by party officials that blacks would remain barred. Many blacks who were rejected at the polls filed protests with the NAACP and the Justice Department.[9]

The greater militancy of southern blacks was apparent in the proliferation of lawsuits that challenged the continuing exclusion of blacks from Democratic primaries. Blacks brought such suits in Georgia in 1944, in several Florida counties in 1944–1945, and in South Carolina in 1947. Many more suits against recalcitrant party officials were threatened. Some blacks were so enthusiastic to sue that efforts by the NAACP's national office to coordinate litigation went for naught. Marshall and his legal staff favored deferring civil suits until the Justice Department had decided whether to criminally prosecute violations of *Smith*. Yet before the national office could communicate its preferences, the branch in Columbus, Georgia, had already gone too far down the litigation path to change course; the president explained, "[T]he people demanded that we continue the case." The branch in Jackson, Mississippi, was also reluctant to postpone litigation, as many members "are becoming impatient . . . and we are anxious to try to do something." Six months later, the president of the Jackson branch reminded Marshall that members "are very anxious to go to the courts with the case." Blacks who sought to vote in the 1946 Democratic primary in South Carolina were "expecting great things and are looking for a suit."[10]

Other blacks responded to *Smith* by filing another sort of lawsuit. Because *Smith* theoretically opened Democratic primaries to blacks, their right to vote suddenly acquired practical value in the one-party South. Southern blacks began demanding nondiscriminatory registration, and they sued registrars who refused to provide it. By 1945, blacks had brought such suits in Birmingham and Tuskegee, Alabama; St. John the Baptist Parish, Louisiana; Atlanta, Georgia; and Jacksonville, Florida. Many more blacks threatened to sue. When the voter registrar of Lake Charles, Louisiana, rejected black applicants through a variety of unlawful stratagems, they consulted a lawyer, who promptly threatened the registrar with litigation. Louisiana blacks were said to be "bursting with anxiety to knock out" discriminatory registration practices.[11]

The proliferation of NAACP branches in the South and the rising economic status of southern blacks—further consequences of the war—also facilitated an increase in litigation. NAACP membership grew from roughly 50,000 in 1940 to 450,000 in 1946, and the number of branches rose from 355 to 1,073. In one of the most racially recalcitrant states, South Carolina, membership in the association grew from about 800 in 1939 to 14,000 in 1948. Not only was the NAACP enrolling new members, but it was "pushing into areas where the name of this organization could hardly be whispered a few years ago," according to the head of its Florida branches, Harry T. Moore. More branches meant more communities able to support litigation. Branches also exchanged valuable information about local voting practices. Blacks in one community often became more determined to vote after discovering that blacks elsewhere had become enfranchised. Increased NAACP membership also translated into larger budgets, and the national office was finally able to hire several lawyers to supplement Marshall's heroic efforts. In the late 1930s and the early 1940s, the New York office had been too swamped to assist southern branches with their voting rights litigation. After the war, an expanded legal staff was better able to provide branches with advice and lawyering.[12]

Branches also had more money now with which to hire lawyers. The Shreveport branch, seeking advice from the national office about voter registration, announced that it was "ready with finances for anything." The branch in Jackson, Mississippi, eager to challenge the continuing exclusion of blacks from Democratic primaries, assured the national office that it could finance its own litigation. In addition, more white lawyers in the South were now willing to take voting rights cases in light of the diminishing resistance of southern whites to black suffrage. More black lawyers were now practicing in the South—an important development in that some white lawyers could not be trusted to press hard for the rights of blacks.[13]

Threats of litigation supplied government and party officials with direct incentives to comply with the Constitution. Although most of them probably opposed black suffrage, they were not willing to incur personal liability by illegally obstructing it. As threats of litigation flew in all directions, these officials began to comply with the law. Registrars in Spalding County, Georgia, saw little choice but to enroll blacks after Federal District Judge Frank Scarlett ordered them to and held the case open pending further complaint. In South Carolina, some local registrars, fearing litigation, defied orders from the state Democratic party by registering blacks. After Judge J. Waties Waring invalidated efforts by South Carolina Democrats to evade *Smith* and threatened them with contempt, 35,000 blacks were registered. In Washington Parish, Louisiana, blacks were denied registration until they formed an NAACP branch and filed suit before a sympathetic judge, J. Skelly Wright, who enjoined the registrar from further discrimination. As a result, Washington Parish registered its first black voter in 1950, and blacks in several other parishes filed suits that induced registrars to enroll them.[14]

By the mid-1940s, recalcitrant officials also had to worry about the prospect of criminal prosecution. NAACP branch officers constantly reminded them that willful violations of the voting rights of blacks could be prosecuted under federal civil rights statutes. Indeed, the Justice Department had recently prosecuted a few registrars in North and South Carolina for discrimination. One important consequence of the growing political power of northern blacks was that the department became more solicitous of the voting rights of southern blacks. Department officials frequently invited Marshall to Washington, D.C., to discuss voting issues, and they assured the NAACP that voting rights complaints were being thoroughly investigated. By contrast, in the mid-1930s, U.S. attorneys had barely gone through the motions of investigating such complaints and had been as likely to intimidate black complainants as to prosecute their cases.[15]

Immediately after *Smith*, Marshall wrote to Attorney General Francis Biddle requesting that U.S. attorneys be instructed to prosecute officials who persisted in excluding blacks from party primaries. NAACP lawyers bombarded the Justice Department with affidavits from southern blacks, which attested to persistent voting rights violations and demanded federal prosecutions. An NAACP officer in Birmingham bragged that he was sending "a bag of evidence almost daily" to the department. By the fall of 1944, Marshall was regularly conferring with department lawyers and negotiating over when and where to begin the prosecutions. In early 1945, the *New York Times* quoted Justice Department officials as contemplating immediate prosecutions in three states. A year later, the department publicly promised to prosecute any official who interfered with the voting rights of blacks.[16]

Despite such pronouncements, the department remained reluctant to prosecute. Yet it did launch investigations and dispatch agents of the Federal Bureau of Investigation (FBI) to southern communities to gather evidence, which offered food for thought to southern officials who might be contemplating interference with blacks' voting rights. Birmingham lawyer Arthur Shores reported that the U.S. attorney's visit to the board of registrars "had a very wholesome effect on helping us get . . . a large number [of black voters] registered." Harry T. Moore, founder of the Florida Progressive Voters' League, believed that a federal investigation of the incident in Greensboro, Florida, in which two black brothers were attacked and then run out of town in retaliation for their registration activities, would have "a healthy effect in all of those counties, where Negroes have been kept from the polls through intimidation." One of the brothers reported that the appearance of the FBI in Greensboro had the "crackers . . . looking very sick." Moreover, a heightened federal law enforcement presence in the South, even if it did not result in prosecutions, provided some physical security for blacks who ran risks by seeking to vote. Donald Jones, an NAACP official in the South, threatened the chairman of the Caddo Parish, Louisiana, Democratic executive committee with prosecution if he continued to endorse the exclusion of blacks from party primaries. Jones then quickly reminded Marshall to mention this case to the Justice Department, as "I threatened the gentleman and don't want to be caught with my breeches at half mast."[17]

Even apart from this greater federal presence, the South was safer for blacks by the mid-1940s than it had been a decade earlier—a change that contributed to the greater aggressiveness with which blacks pursued enforcement of their constitutional rights. It is important not to overstate this point. Southern whites lynched blacks more frequently during and after the war than they had immediately before it, and Marshall himself was nearly a victim of deadly violence while he was defending criminal cases that had arisen from the race riot in Columbia, Tennessee, in 1946. Still, various forces had made the South safer for blacks: urbanization, industrialization, improved education, reduced insularity, and the threat of federal prosecution for civil rights violations. Greater physical security was crucial to the enforcement of voting rights after *Smith* and to direct-action protests in the 1960s.[18]

Comparisons between the South in the interwar and postwar periods illustrate the greater physical security enjoyed by blacks over time. In Jacksonville, Florida, a Ku Klux Klan demonstration on election eve, 1920, drew a thousand participants and deterred most blacks from voting. That same year, election riots in Ocoee, Florida, killed as many as thirty blacks; witnesses to the slaughter were afraid to testify before an investigating committee in Washington, D.C. In 1932, police officers in Shreveport, Louisiana, who were armed with machine guns, suppressed the efforts of local blacks to organize a voters' league. City authorities warned that the streets would be drenched in blood before blacks would be permitted to vote. A black man who challenged Mississippi's white primary in 1927 was threatened and then run out of town. An average of roughly fifty southern blacks a year were lynched in the early 1920s and about twenty a year in the early 1930s.[19]

By the mid-1940s, the Klan, which was defending itself from state efforts to revoke its charter and from federal efforts to prosecute its leaders for tax evasion, was no longer in a position to intimidate many black voters. Hundreds of blacks flocked to Senate committee hearings that investigated Senator Theodore Bilbo's incitement of Mississippi whites to violence in the 1946 Senate primary—hearings that took place not in the relative safety of Washington, D.C., but in Jackson, Mississippi. In postwar Louisiana, tens of thousands of blacks registered to vote, even in some rural parishes, with the support of Governor Long and under the protective eye of the federal courts and the Justice Department. Though the number of lynchings briefly increased in the immediate aftermath of World War II, they had nearly disappeared by 1950, and the federal government aggressively investigated and prosecuted the few that occurred in the mid-1940s. Blacks attempting to vote in rural Deep South counties in the late 1940s still faced physical intimidation, but more often in the form of a beating than a lynching. Though the Deep South remained dangerous for blacks intent on exercising their rights, the degree of danger had decreased somewhat, thereby enabling blacks generally to exercise their rights without endangering their lives.[20]

Another important factor in the increased black voter registration of the 1940s was the generous interpretations of *Smith* and the Fifteenth Amendment offered by lower court judges. By contrast, black lawyers who had argued the Texas white primary cases before the Fifth Circuit in the early 1930s had faced insulting judges, who literally turned their backs on the lawyers during oral arguments. In correspondence with the NAACP's national office, these lawyers repeatedly doubted whether southern judges would ever vindicate blacks' voting rights, and they wondered whether even showing up for oral arguments was worthwhile, given that only an appeal to the Supreme Court held any hope of success. In the 1930s, southern judges rejected voting rights claims on technicalities and were willfully blind to racially discriminatory administration of facially neutral voter qualifications. Postwar judges proved much more supportive of blacks' voting rights. This judicial conversion was crucial to black voter registration in the 1940s, as southern white officials contrived numerous evasive strategies. Repeated appeals to the Supreme Court are expensive, and the justices cannot hear every case that alleges evasion of their earlier decisions. Thus, the posture of lower courts is critical to the implementation of Supreme Court edicts.[21]

Though many southern whites accepted black suffrage by the mid-1940s, most southern politicians and officeholders did not. Politicians are generally resistant to electoral change, given their vested interests in preserving the system that elected them. Whatever their motives, Democratic politicians and voter registrars defied and evaded *Smith*, as they sought to prevent the Court from "revolutioniz[ing] our southern customs and disrupt[ing] our peaceable existence." In most southern states, Democrats continued to exclude blacks from primaries for at least a year or two after *Smith*. The chairman of the Mississippi Democratic executive committee defiantly proclaimed that "the Supreme Court or no one else can control a democratic primary in Mississippi." Party officials elsewhere rightly noted that *Smith* did not necessarily invalidate all white primaries, as the decision relied on the way that Texas law treated parties and primaries, and other states regulated differently. For example, Texas required parties to conduct primaries, but Georgia did not. More important, to the extent that *Smith* turned on the fact that Texas regulated political parties, it might be possible to avoid the ruling by repealing all such regulations. South Carolina tried precisely this strategy after *Smith*, and other Deep South states contemplated following suit but waited to see first how lower courts responded.[22]

In fact, lower courts generally invalidated such evasions. The Fifth Circuit affirmed a district court ruling that rejected proffered distinctions between the white primaries of Georgia and Texas, and the Florida Supreme Court issued a similar decision. Judge Waring sternly rejected South Carolina's effort to evade *Smith* by deregulating the Democratic party, and the Fourth Circuit affirmed. These lower court decisions required extensions of *Smith*. The Fifth Circuit noted that *Smith* and *United States v. Classic* (1941) were not dispositive of the constitutionality of Georgia's white primary because of relevant differences in state regulations, but it nonetheless invalidated the exclusion of blacks by the Georgia Democratic party. Judges more hostile to black suffrage could have resolved these cases differently. But Waring insisted that "it is time for South Carolina to rejoin the Union." When party officials responded to his decision by adopting dual membership status based on race and a party loyalty oath designed to offend most blacks (it required support for segregation), an enraged Waring enjoined them, and the Fourth Circuit again affirmed.[23]

In the late 1940s, some southern states also tried to obstruct black voter registration. With Democratic primaries now theoretically open to blacks, tougher registration procedures and requirements became the favored method for impeding black suffrage. Alabama voters adopted the Boswell amendment, which required registrants to "understand and explain" a constitutional provision, not just to read it, and also required them to "understand the duties and obligations of good citizenship." Amendment supporters did not disguise their intention to confer broad discretion on registrars with which to preserve white political supremacy. Georgia also tightened its voter registration requirements, though it sought to avoid the legal pitfalls of the Boswell amendment by slightly constraining the discretion granted to registrars.[24]

With or without statutory authorization, registrars employed numerous stratagems for obstructing black suffrage. Some registration boards closed to prevent black enrollment, and others registered voters at undisclosed times in secret locations, contrary to statutory requirements. Whites discovered through word of mouth where and when to show up to register, while blacks were kept in the dark. When blacks were able to locate registrars, they were often forced to wait in line for hours, so that only a few at a time could register. Registrars required blacks to fill out their own forms and flunked them for trivial errors, while they filled out whites' forms for them. Blacks but not whites were asked to recite from memory the entire U.S. Constitution or to answer impossible and insulting questions, such as "How many bubbles are in a bar of soap?" Registrars required only blacks to produce registered voters to vouch for them. Some registrars did not even bother to indulge in the pretense of legality and informed blacks that they would not be registered regardless of their qualifications. Individual registrars often acted as a law unto themselves, ignoring even specific instructions from state officials to treat blacks fairly.[25]

For the first time ever, southern judges ruled such behavior unconstitutional. A three-judge federal court invalidated the Boswell amendment for delegating unconstitutionally broad discretion, which registrars had exercised in a discriminatory fashion. The court also objected to the discriminatory purpose that had animated the amendment. This condemnation of broad delegation and discriminatory legislative motive seemed to conflict with *Williams v. Mississippi* (1898) (discussed in chapter 1). Other southern judges also enjoined registrars from discriminating, suspending the customary presumption that public officials had fulfilled their duties in good faith. When registrars in roughly thirty Georgia counties began purging black voters at the behest of a former governor and current gubernatorial candidate, Eugene Talmadge, a federal judge quickly enjoined them. On a somewhat different issue, the Arkansas Supreme Court invalidated a law that was designed to evade *Smith* by separating state and federal elections (primary and general), barring discrimination only in federal ones, and thereby implicitly allowing it in state primaries.[26]

These lower court rulings made possible the postwar surge in southern black voter registration in the South. Democratic officials in Georgia and Florida did not allow blacks to participate in party primaries until lower courts had extended *Smith*. Blacks did not vote in significant numbers in Democratic primaries in South Carolina until Judge Waring had threatened to hold party officials in contempt if they continued to bar black participation even after he had clarified, "once and for all," that they would be required "to obey and carry out the orders of this court, not only in the technical respects but in the true spirit and meaning of the same." After Waring's rulings, 35,000 blacks voted in Democratic primaries in South Carolina in 1948. In Louisiana, two federal court decisions from the early 1950s that enjoined discriminatory voter registration facilitated a massive black enrollment.[27]

These lower court judges *chose* to extend *Smith* and to expand their interpretations of the Fifteenth Amendment. One contemporary commentator rightly observed that these decisions adopted "broad and discerning," rather than "narrow and literal" interpretations, as they nullified repeated efforts of white southerners "to find the magic combination of ambiguous wording, legalisms and technicalities which will allow them to make possible the impossible." These judges took seriously the admonition in *Classic* that the Constitution is "not to be read with such stultifying narrowness" and the proclamation in *Lane* that the Fifteenth Amendment "nullifies sophisticated as well as simple-minded modes of discrimination." Nor did all of these judges hold the relatively progressive racial views of a J. Waties Waring or a J. Skelly Wright (and such progressive judges simply did not exist before the war). By the late 1940s, even some less egalitarian jurists were willing to interpret the law to protect black suffrage. One of the Florida judges who invalidated the state's white primary was a "cracker," according to local NAACP officials. Southern judges almost certainly would not have interpreted an anti*segregation* Court decision with equal latitude, as experience after *Brown v. Board of Education* (1954) would confirm. Yet southern white judges apparently shared the general white hierarchy of racial preferences, which meant that they were much less resistant to black suffrage than to school desegregation.[28]

None of the conditions that enabled *Smith* to be efficacious—greater white acceptance of black voting, heightened black militancy in demanding rights, the greater physical security of southern blacks, the NAACP's broader presence, the increased threat of federal prosecution of rights violators, and the expansiveness of lower court interpretations of black suffrage rights—was itself a product simply of *Smith*. Thus, although *Smith* may have been critical to mobilizing black voter registration in the South, it would probably have been inefficacious in the absence of supportive social and political conditions.

Thus far, we have considered *Smith*'s contributions to black voter registration in the South. Two other points regarding the impact of *Smith* warrant discussion. First, although *Smith* inspired blacks to register and to vote, it also mobilized opposition among southern whites. As one NAACP branch official in Louisiana reported, "[T]he White South is sturred [*sic*] up to some extent and you may expect more of us killed down here than ever due to the . . . decision of the U.S. Supreme Court." Second, though black voter registration in the South had risen to roughly 20 percent in 1952, the large majority of southern blacks remained disfranchised. More than the Court's invalidation of the white primary would be necessary before most southern blacks could vote.[29]

The justices sought to cushion the blow of *Smith* by reallocating the opinion from Frankfurter, the Jewish Austrian immigrant from Harvard, to Reed, the native Kentuckian. That concession to the sensibilities of southern whites went largely for naught. Many southern Democrats shouted their defiance of *Smith*, warning that the elimination of the white primary would jeopardize segregation and racial purity. Senator John Holmes Overton of Louisiana thundered, "The South, at all costs, will maintain the rule of white supremacy." Even the liberal senator from Florida, Claude Pepper, breathed defiance after *Smith* was decided in the midst of his tough primary battle: "The South will allow nothing to impair white supremacy." Deep South Democrats insisted that *Smith* would not affect their exclusionary policies, and indeed it did not for the first couple of years. Southern newspapers predicted that *Smith*, which augured "a political and social revolution," would prove unenforceable. Private citizens warned, "[Y]ou can't push nigger equality on the south without a fight."[30]

In some southern states, *Smith* inspired efforts by legislatures and local officials to suppress black voter registration. Early in 1945, Emory Jackson, secretary of the NAACP's Birmingham branch, reported that registrars were "getting worse" since *Smith* and that the drive to register blacks did not "seem to be making much headway." Later that year, the branch secretary in Marion County, Florida, observed that southern whites were becoming resigned to black participation in Democratic primaries and were turning instead to other methods for preserving white political supremacy: fraud, economic reprisals, and physical violence. Late in 1947, the executive committee of the Caddo Parish, Louisiana, Democratic party ended its formal exclusion of blacks from primaries, but the local registrar refused to enroll blacks unless each could produce as character witnesses three whites who were personally known to the registrar and who resided in the same precinct as the would-be voter—virtually impossible requirements for blacks to satisfy.[31]

The most virulent political backlash against *Smith* came in Georgia, South Carolina, and Mississippi—the states with the highest percentages of blacks. In 1946, in Georgia, with a federal judge just having invalidated the state's white primary on the basis of *Smith*, Eugene Talmadge ran for governor on a platform of reinstating the white primary, preserving the county-unit system (which inflated the voting power of rural whites), and keeping blacks "in their place." He and his supporters raged against "'Negro lovers' in the Supreme Court," and they urged citizens to "Vote for Talmadge and a White Primary!" One Talmadge supporter noted that "the white primary is . . . the main and vital issue in this campaign." Talmadge himself warned that if blacks were permitted to vote in Democratic primaries, politicians would have to "kiss their babies if [they] want to be elected," and "[o]ur Jim Crow laws are gone, and our pretty white children will be going to school with Negroes." Talmadge urged whites to take advantage of a provision in Georgia electoral law that authorized challenges to registered voters, and he prophesied, "Wise Negroes will stay away from the white folks' ballot boxes on [election day]."[32]

In South Carolina, a few days after *Smith*, Senator Burnet Maybank warned that white southerners "will not accept these interferences" and that "we of the South will maintain our political and social institutions as we believe to be in the best interest of our people." Governor Olin Johnston called the legislature into special session a few days later. Proclaiming that "history has taught us that we must keep our white democratic primaries pure and unadulterated," he urged the repeal of all 150 state laws that regulated parties, in the hope that this would remove judicial objections to the white primary. Should such deregulation prove unavailing, though, Johnston warned, "We South Carolinians will use the necessary methods to retain white supremacy in all primaries and to safeguard the homes and happiness of our people." He concluded: "[W]hite supremacy will be maintained in our primaries. Let the chips fall where they may."[33]

Smith also mobilized Mississippi whites in defense of white political supremacy. The *Jackson Daily News* warned the justices that they were badly mistaken if they believed that blacks would vote in Democratic primaries in Mississippi. If anyone was foolish enough to think otherwise, "let them try." Aggressive efforts by Mississippi blacks to implement *Smith* created golden opportunities for demagogic politicians. Senator Theodore Bilbo, running for reelection in 1946, invoked the specter of "Negro domination" in a state that had just ceased having a black majority for the first time in a century. In a widely reported speech, Bilbo exhorted every "red blooded white man to use any means to keep the Niggers away from the polls." Declining to explicitly advocate violence, he slyly observed, "[Y]ou know and I know what's the best way to keep the Nigger from voting. You do it the night before the election. I don't have to tell you any more than that. Red blooded men know what I mean." Throughout Mississippi, enthusiastic supporters took the senator at his word. They burned crosses in Jackson. In Biloxi, a street sign warned blacks to "vote at your own risk." In Pucket, four whites beat and threatened to kill a black man for attempting to register. Whites brandishing pistols repulsed Medgar Evers and four other black veterans from the polls.[34]

Smith's backlash generated a counterbacklash. Mississippi Democrats could threaten and beat black voters without serious repercussion in 1875 or even 1935, but not any longer by 1945. Bilbo's thinly veiled exhortations to violence were too much for national opinion to bear. A white man from McAlester, Oklahoma, informed Bilbo that his speech was reminiscent of sentiments emanating from that "late departed and unlamented jerk in Germany," and he admonished the senator that "the time for this narrow-minded race hatred stuff is out." Bilbo had unwittingly challenged the federal government to prove that it could enforce a Court decision in the face of southern resistance. The Senate had little choice but to conduct investigative hearings, which were chaired by Senator Allen Ellender of Louisiana in Decem-

FIGURE 5.1
Senator Theodore Bilbo campaigns for reelection in Mississippi in 1946. (*Bettmann*/CORBIS)

FROM JIM CROW TO CIVIL RIGHTS

ber 1946. Those hearings educated northerners and motivated Mississippi blacks. Northern Republican senators on the committee appeared shocked by revelations of the force and fraud that had been used by white Mississippians to obstruct black suffrage. The *Washington Post* declared that it was impossible to read the committee report without "a sense of sickness" at the brutality. Roughly 150 Mississippi blacks—many of them war veterans and some displaying their good-conduct medals—volunteered to testify at committee hearings in Jackson about the violence they had endured while attempting to vote.[35] Many more Mississippi blacks expressed their determination to vote by visiting registrars' offices; black voter registration in Mississippi rose by 50 percent in the year following the hearings. White violence against southern blacks trying to vote also had "terrific publicity value" in the North. The use of obfuscation to impede the voting of southern blacks was one thing, the use of deadly force quite another.[36]

In the same way that northern opinion was repulsed by the violence used by Mississippi whites against black voters, judicial opinion was irritated by the evasive tactics used by South Carolina whites in response to *Smith*— tactics that one critic called "a shock to all decent people." Judge Waring was infuriated by the efforts of the state Democratic party to circumvent his rulings. When the South Carolina legislature repealed all the laws regulating parties, Waring decreed that it was time for the state to "rejoin the Union," and he ordered party officials to allow blacks to vote in primaries. When they responded by adopting dual membership status based on race and a loyalty oath designed to offend most blacks, an enraged Waring invalidated these party rules, declaring, "[T]he time has come when discrimination in political affairs [has] got to stop." Whether or not "there are any people who agree with me," Waring proclaimed, South Carolina was going to obey the law. He also warned that further violations of the letter or spirit of his order would be punished with imprisonment. One wonders if the justices, watching southern officials evade their constitutional rulings, did not share Waring's annoyance and his determination to expand legal interpretations if necessary to counter southern efforts at circumvention. The justices' willingness to find unconstitutional state action in *Terry v. Adams* (1953) supports this hypothesis.[37]

Notwithstanding the impressive postwar gains in black voter registration, for the most part southern blacks could still vote only in cities and large towns, especially in the Deep South. Though an estimated 22,000 blacks were registered to vote in Atlanta by 1946, in dozens of Deep South counties, many of them with black majorities, not a single black person was registered. Black voter registration in Louisiana rose from 8,000 to 43,000 in 1948, but roughly 50 percent of registered blacks lived in New Orleans, and in half of the state's 64 parishes not a single black person voted. By 1948, well over 100,000 blacks were registered in Georgia and 150,000 to 200,000 in Texas, while Mississippi and Alabama showed "no progress," with black voter registration there limited to a paltry 3,000 and 8,000, respectively.[38]

A formidable obstacle to black voting in rural areas was the threat and reality of physical violence. Though the South was less dangerous for blacks than it had been even a decade earlier, it was still violent. Large numbers of blacks registered to vote in Florida cities by the late 1940s, but in rural areas they faced Klan intimidation, letters warning those who dared to vote that they would "be floating up and down the river," and shots fired into their homes. Tens of thousands of blacks registered in Louisiana's urban parishes, but in rural areas they remained "afraid to even try to register because of repeated examples of brutality and threatened acts against their physical safety." Blacks in rural Louisiana received notes from the Klan threatening to put black voters "out of business" and warnings that whites were "figuring on raising Hell" if blacks tried to vote. In rural Alabama, sheriffs terrorized blacks who dared to register. By 1946, thousands of blacks voted with little resistance in Atlanta, Savannah, and Augusta, but blacks in rural Georgia had to endure Klan intimidation and threats that any black man who tried to vote would be "a dead Nigger." In Mississippi, even the cities remained dangerous. The editor of a black newspaper reported that fear was the reason that only 315 of 40,000 blacks in Jackson were registered in 1946. The *Jackson Daily News* published the names of blacks who were prominent in the Mississippi Progressive Voters' League and warned blacks to stay away from Democratic primaries "to prevent unhealthy and unhappy results."[39]

Blacks seeking to vote in the rural Deep South had good reason to be fearful. When war veteran Etoy Fletcher tried to register in rural Mississippi in 1946, the registrar informed him, "Niggers are not allowed to vote in Rankin County, and if you don't want to get into serious trouble, get out of this building." While waiting for a bus out of town, Fletcher was assaulted by four whites, who drove him several miles into the woods, "beat . . . and flogged [him] mercilessly," and warned him that he would be killed if he ever again attempted to vote. Many other aspiring black voters in Mississippi reported suffering similar assaults that summer, as "everything short of murder" was inflicted on them. In Gadsden County, Florida, in 1947–1948, two black half brothers, J. T. Smith and Harry Moody, helped mobilize 150 blacks to register to vote. Then, ignoring warnings from several whites, they tried to vote themselves. As a result, one of the brothers had his home blown up, crippling one of his children, and both were run out of town. In Montgomery County, Georgia, in 1946, D. V. Carter organized an NAACP branch, which consisted mainly of farmers and sharecroppers and was principally devoted to voter registration. Several hundred blacks registered as a result. After ignoring repeated Klan warnings to desist, Carter was severely beaten in 1948. Isaac Nixon, whom Carter had persuaded to vote, was murdered. An all-white jury acquitted the two whites who had killed him. In Louisiana in 1951, a white deputy sheriff killed, allegedly in self-defense, a black man who happened to be a plaintiff in an NAACP voting rights case. Harry Moore, founder of Florida's Progressive Voters' League, was assassinated (along with his wife) by a bomb planted in his home on Christmas night, 1951, possibly in retaliation for his suffrage activity.[40]

Although the Justice Department was more attentive to NAACP concerns by the late 1940s, it remained reluctant to prosecute officials who obstructed black voting. Democratic administrations in Washington, D.C., had political incentives not to prosecute southern Democrats, which might "translate impotent rumblings against the New Deal into actual revolt at the polls." Southern U.S. attorneys, especially those who were ambitious for elective office, were also unenthusiastic about prosecuting such cases. Even for those who were willing, these were difficult cases to win. Witnesses were hard to locate, as local communities protected culprits behind a veil of silence. White jurors generally would not convict officials for adhering to traditional mores rejecting black suffrage. Thus, NAACP pressure on the Justice Department to prosecute was unavailing—to the great frustration of the association, which had deferred numerous civil lawsuits on the view that criminal prosecutions should take priority. NAACP officials believed that they had reached a "distinct understanding" with the department to prosecute such cases and thus had some basis for concluding that they were victims of "double-dealing." Yet the department would not prosecute even egregious violations. Where prospective black voters were beaten or killed, the department would investigate but still not prosecute. Empty threats of fed-

FIGURE 5.2
Harry T. Moore.
(*Florida State Archives*)

FIGURE 5.3
The home of Harry and Henrietta Moore after the bombing
on Christmas night, 1951, which resulted in their deaths.
(*Florida State Archives*)

eral prosecution proved inadequate to deter the southern whites who were
most committed to obstructing black suffrage through force and fraud.[41]

Blacks who dared to exercise their suffrage rights also faced economic
reprisals, which were a special problem in rural areas, where nearly all blacks
were economically dependent on whites (unlike the situation in cities,
where the segregated economy had produced black professionals—doctors,
dentists, undertakers, ministers—who were largely independent of white
economic control). Public officials in Mobile, Alabama, pressured the U.S.
Postal Service to fire John LeFlore, the energetic chairman of the NAACP's
Regional Conference of Southern Branches, in retaliation for his suffrage
activity. Lawsuits to vindicate their voting rights were not a realistic option for
most rural blacks, who were indigent. Even the few who could afford to sue
might be unable to find a lawyer who was willing to take their case. Very few
black lawyers practiced in the rural South, and many white lawyers remained
reluctant to challenge black disfranchisement.[42]

Voting rights litigation in the rural Deep South entailed risks for both
clients and attorneys. Black lawyer Arthur Madison, who sued to compel
black voter registration in Montgomery County, Alabama, was arrested, con-

victed, and summarily disbarred for representing clients without authorization. The county sheriff had intimidated Madison's clients into withdrawing their consent. No white lawyers were willing to defend Madison at his trial. A black minister from Louisville, Mississippi, informed the NAACP of his unsuccessful effort to vote in the Democratic primary in 1946. He wanted the Justice Department informed, but because of "the social condition of the deep South," he did not want his name revealed until it was time to testify, as publicity would place his life in jeopardy. Even if such lawsuits could be safely brought, they were hardly a cinch to win. By the early 1950s, many federal judges were willing to enjoin discriminatory voter registration practices, but they would not yet invalidate vaguely worded literacy tests or command the registration of particular black applicants, for fear of usurping the authority of registrars.[43]

Blacks in the rural South would not vote in large numbers until after further interventions by the Court and, more important, by Congress and the president—developments that mainly did not take place until the 1960s. Only the federal executive could secure the physical safety of southern black voters. Only Congress could shift the burden of litigating suffrage cases from individual blacks to the federal government by empowering the attorney general to seek injunctions against registrars who practiced race discrimination—a remedy that also had the advantage of avoiding southern (white) juries. More important, only Congress could replace local registrars with federal officials where necessary to secure black voter registration. In 1966, the Court finally invalidated poll taxes in the few southern states that continued to use them as a restriction on the suffrage. Yet because the Court as late as 1959 continued to reject constitutional challenges to literacy tests, further congressional intervention was necessary to eliminate that substantial barrier to black suffrage.[44]

Smith v. Allwright, in conjunction with supportive social and political conditions, launched a racial revolution in southern politics. But *Smith* could not thwart the obstacles to black voting in the rural Deep South. Only the intervention of the national political branches could secure political equality for most southern blacks. That intervention was largely a product of the 1960s civil rights movement.

HIGHER EDUCATION

Sipuel v. Board of Regents (1948) and *Sweatt v. Painter* (1950) were instrumental to desegregating higher education in the border states and the peripheral South. Without these decisions, desegregation could not possibly have happened when it did. In the late 1940s, southern states still preferred to establish segregated regional universities for blacks in response to the 1938 *Gaines* decision, rather than to integrate. They tried to persuade Congress to enact legislation approving a compact among southern states to establish such schools.[45]

Supportive social and political conditions were critical to the efficacy of high court rulings that desegregated higher education. By 1950, many southern whites were less resistant to desegregating graduate and professional schools than they would have been even a decade earlier. In the Deep South, where white resistance remained intense, the Court's decisions were defied. Black litigants were available to implement *Sweatt* in most southern states only because many more blacks by 1950 had the credentials necessary for higher education and because the GI Bill of Rights and the greater prosperity of blacks in the postwar era made such education financially feasible. The expanded legal staff and budget of the NAACP—products of the membership explosion ignited by the war—enabled the state-by-state litigation that was necessary for implementing *Sweatt*.

Comparing the consequences of *Gaines* (1938) with those of *Sipuel* (1948) illustrates the importance of supportive social and political conditions to the efficacy of Court decisions. Both of these rulings held that blacks were entitled to equal educational facilities within a state. After *Gaines*, nothing happened except that more states adopted the very out-of-state scholarships that the Court had just invalidated. By contrast, after *Sipuel*, most southern states created separate programs of higher education for blacks and appropriated funds for them, and a couple of states integrated particular programs. Within six months of *Sweatt* (1950), roughly a thousand blacks were attending formerly white colleges and universities, mostly in Arkansas, Kentucky, Missouri, and Oklahoma.[46]

Outside of the Deep South, *Sipuel* and *Sweatt* were tolerated though hardly embraced. Only Arkansas and Delaware complied "voluntarily" by desegregating graduate and professional education without awaiting a lower court decision that specifically commanded action in these states. Officials in these states saw the writing on the wall after *Sipuel* and permitted a few blacks to matriculate at formerly white universities, though only in courses not being offered at the states' black colleges. Elsewhere in the South, public universities refused to desegregate until lower courts had specifically ordered them to do so. In Kentucky and Oklahoma, even before *Sweatt* had implied that segregation in higher education was no longer sustainable, federal courts had ordered white public universities to admit blacks where no comparable higher education was available to them. In 1950–1951, blacks brought lawsuits in most other southern states outside of the Deep South to compel compliance with *Sweatt*. Lower courts generally applied *Sweatt* in good faith, and university officials generally complied with federal court orders to desegregate. Yet blacks sometimes had to bring separate suits against recalcitrant departments within a university that had already desegregated some of its programs. Such dilatory action by university administrators was probably politically inspired, as they did not relish having to explain to segregationist politicians why they had dismantled segregation before a court had compelled them to do so. For example, the board of visitors of the University of Virginia refused to desegregate the law school until a federal court ordered it done, even though a legal opinion issued by the state attorney general had concluded that *Sweatt* required integration. After the federal court had spoken, though, the board eagerly complied with the ruling, not even bothering to appeal. This pattern repeated itself in Tennessee.[47]

Though these decisions made inroads into segregation in higher education in the South, their consequences were limited. Outside of the border states, a rigid distinction was maintained between graduate/professional and undergraduate education, with the latter remaining segregated until after *Brown v. Board of Education* (1954). Moreover, although significant numbers of blacks attended formerly white universities in border states after *Sweatt*, integration in Virginia, North Carolina, Tennessee, and Texas was merely token. As late as 1959, only eighteen blacks attended the University of Virginia, and only two were enrolled at Virginia Tech. Through the 1950s, most southern states with integrated public universities admitted blacks only to those courses not being offered at black colleges. Furthermore, university administrators tended to interpret judicial decrees narrowly; they permitted the admission of named plaintiffs only and continued to exclude those who were similarly situated. Finally, universities continued to discriminate in their administration of discretionary admission standards.[48]

In the Deep South, *Sweatt* was almost completely nullified. Except in Louisiana, not a single black attended a white public university in the Deep South for nearly a decade after *Sweatt*. Evasion and violence were the preferred methods of circumvention. South Carolina actually had little to evade. In 1946, John Wrighten sued the law school of the state university when his application was denied because of his race. That suit inspired the legislature to establish a black law school at the South Carolina State College for Negroes, which a federal court refused to rule unequal. Wrighten paid a price for daring to litigate; he reported that he "had stuck [his] neck out and . . . got it cut off." Whites in Charleston refused to employ him. Other blacks may have learned from Wrighten's experience, as no further suits challenging segregation in higher education were brought in South Carolina until 1958.[49]

Legal proceedings were more protracted in Georgia, but the ultimate result was the same. In 1951, the University of Georgia's law school rejected Horace Ward's application on account of his race and instead offered him an out-of-state scholarship. The legislature responded to Ward's suit by dramatically increasing appropriations for Georgia's three black colleges and for out-of-state scholarships. It also passed a law providing for the termination of public funding for any state university that desegregated even one department, whether voluntarily or under court order. The state board of regents responded to Ward's suit by requiring law school applicants to take admissions tests and to submit recommendations from two alumni and a superior-court judge, the latter of whom had to reside in the applicant's circuit—virtually impossible requirements for black applicants to satisfy. In 1952, Ward sued in federal court for admission, but the proceedings dragged on for five years (partly because he was inducted into the army) before his claim was dismissed on procedural grounds. In 1959, a federal court invalidated the alumni recommendation requirement as discriminatory—because the white university had no black alumni—but it refused to deprive university officials of the primary responsibility for admitting students. That year, the legislature adopted two more measures to preserve university segregation. One of them authorized the governor to close any part of the state university system if doing so was necessary to preserve public peace. The other measure imposed age limits on students, on the assumption that most black applicants were older. Higher education in Georgia remained entirely segregated until 1961.[50]

The most extraordinary legal obfuscation with regard to the desegregation of higher education occurred in Florida. For nine years, Virgil Hawkins tried to gain admission to the University of Florida School of Law. He appealed seven times to the state supreme court and four times to the U.S. Supreme Court. He was never admitted. Hawkins's odyssey began in 1949, when the law school denied his application on racial grounds. He sued in state court (inexplicably), and the Florida Supreme Court rejected his claim on the ground that the state's announced intention to create a black law school satisfied the Constitution—a reasonable reading of precedent had it not been for *Sweatt*, which was decided two months earlier. Rather than simply rejecting Hawkins's claim, however, the state court retained jurisdiction pending the trial judge's determination of whether the new black law school was substantially equal. Thus, Hawkins had no final state court judgment from which he could appeal to the Supreme Court. Relying on *Sweatt*, he refused to even try to show that the black law school was unequal. The state supreme court, after granting him a second opportunity to do so, dismissed his suit in 1952. The court cited *Sweatt* and *McLaurin* but acted as if they did not apply. The Supreme Court granted certiorari, then vacated and remanded "in light of the Segregation Cases . . . and conditions that now prevail."[51]

On remand, the Florida Supreme Court postponed further proceedings until the U.S. Supreme Court had resolved the remedial issue that it had deferred in *Brown*. In May 1955, *Brown II* required desegregation "with all deliberate speed," while it also authorized lower courts to consider local conditions in prescribing the pace of desegregation. Relying on *Brown II*, the Florida Supreme Court rejected Hawkins's demand for immediate admission and instead appointed a commissioner to take evidence on the likely consequences of admitting Hawkins to the University of Florida. The Florida jurists conceded their obligation to follow high-court edicts but insisted they were doing so. In a separate concurrence, Justice Glenn Terrell criticized *Brown*, observing that segregation had been "the unvarying law of the animal kingdom," not to mention God's will, and concluding that "closing cultural

FIGURE 5.4
Virgil Hawkins
(later photograph).
(*Florida State Archives*)

gaps is a long and tedious process and is not one for court decrees or legislative acts." Two dissenting judges thought it was their disagreeable duty to
order Hawkins's admission under controlling Supreme Court precedent,
which they believed, in the higher education context, was *Brown I*, not
Brown II. The Supreme Court granted certiorari again in May 1956 and then
vacated the state court judgment and remanded on the authority of *Brown I*.
The Court declared that "all deliberate speed" had no application to the
desegregation of higher education, and thus Hawkins was entitled to prompt
admission.[52]

Incredibly, the Florida Supreme Court on remand continued to deny
Hawkins's request for a writ of mandamus to compel his admission. The
court insisted that its prior refusal to admit Hawkins was based not only on its
interpretation of *Brown II* but also on traditional equitable principles governing the discretionary issuance of writs of mandamus. Though the justices had
now clarified that *Brown II* was inapplicable to higher education cases, the
Florida court refused to assume that they had intended to deprive state
judges of their traditional discretion over whether to issue such writs. The
Florida court then proceeded to exercise its discretion to deny the writ but
without prejudice to Hawkins's showing at some future date that he could be
admitted without causing great public mischief. A concurring judge, who

reiterated his willingness to comply with direct orders from above, insisted that the justices had been unaware of testimony taken by the commissioner that revealed the likelihood of violence if Hawkins were enrolled. Two dissenting judges chastised their colleagues for defying the Supreme Court.[53]

The justices now denied certiorari, without prejudice to Hawkins's seeking relief in federal court—an invitation he quickly accepted. In 1958, a federal judge rejected Hawkins's request for an injunction, but he was reversed on appeal. By now, though, the state board of control had raised the test score requirements for law school admission, and Hawkins was disqualified. On remand, the federal court enjoined the university from excluding applicants based on their race but declined to order the admission of Hawkins. Another black man desegregated the University of Florida that year. After nine years of litigation, Hawkins decided to pursue his education in friendlier climes, enrolling in a master's program at Boston University.[54]

The experiences of Ward and Hawkins illustrate the difficulties of implementing Court edicts in unreceptive lower courts. Both men ultimately lost their cases, but only after being bottled up in litigation for five and nine years, respectively. The lower court judges who rejected their claims were not, strictly speaking, defying the Supreme Court. Only Justice Terrell indicated a willingness to deny Hawkins's admission even in the face of a Court order directly mandating it. The other Florida judges took advantage of legal loopholes to deny Hawkins's admission. They capitalized on the failure of *Sweatt* to explicitly overrule *Plessy*, on the Court's invitation in its post–*Brown I* reversal in *Hawkins* to consider "conditions that now prevail," on *Brown II*'s failure to explicitly limit "all deliberate speed" to grade school desegregation, and on the Court's subsequent failure to directly command Hawkins's admission. Florida judges undoubtedly understood that they were contravening the justices' intentions, which is why the later Florida decisions in *Hawkins* generated dissents. Still, at no point did Florida judges defy a high-court edict. One possible lesson to draw is that opportunities for legal evasion are usually so plentiful that effective implementation of Court decisions generally requires that lower court judges be sympathetic to the enterprise or at least not overtly hostile.[55]

In Alabama and Mississippi, violence and intimidation were the chosen methods for evading *Sweatt*. In 1950, Autherine Lucy sued for admission after the University of Alabama rejected her application because of her race. After several years of procedural delay, federal judge Harlan Hobart Grooms ordered her admitted in 1955, and the university complied early in 1956. A race riot ensued. More than 1,000 students protested, and a cross was burned. The board of trustees promptly suspended Lucy from classes, insisting that it was for her own safety. She then began contempt proceedings against university officials, alleging that they had acted in bad faith in suspending her. The court dismissed the contempt motion but ordered Lucy reinstated. University officials then promptly expelled her, allegedly because she had filed "shocking and baseless" charges against them in the contempt proceedings.

Judge Grooms upheld the university's position, and early in 1957 Lucy abandoned her quest to attend the University of Alabama.[56]

Mississippi followed its characteristically unique path in evading *Sweatt*. When Medgar Evers applied to the University of Mississippi Law School early in 1954, the board of trustees added to its admissions standards a requirement that all applicants secure endorsements from five alumni who lived in the applicant's county. Evers dropped his efforts to gain admission, but four years later, Clennon King, a black history professor at Alcorn State, again tried to desegregate Ole Miss. State police officers ejected King from the campus and then took him to chancery court, where a lunacy warrant was sworn out against him, apparently on the theory that any black man who thought he could attend Ole Miss must be crazy. The judge ordered King committed to the state mental hospital for examination, and Governor James Coleman announced that King would be either committed as men-

tally ill or prosecuted for disturbing the peace and resisting arrest. King was ultimately declared sane and then released; he left Mississippi for Georgia the next day, reporting that he required a "change in scenery." Clyde Kennard apparently failed to learn from King's mistake and applied to the all-white Mississippi Southern College in September 1959. He was arrested immediately after leaving the administration building, charged with reckless driving and illegal possession of whiskey (he did not drink), found guilty, and fined six hundred dollars plus costs. A couple of years later, Kennard was sentenced to seven years at hard labor on possibly trumped-up charges of receiving twenty-five dollars' worth of stolen chicken feed. In 1962, James Meredith finally desegregated Mississippi higher education, but only after a race riot that killed two, injured hundreds, and required 15,000 federal troops to quell. White Mississippians evaded *Sweatt*, not through legal obfuscation, but by old-fashioned violence and intimidation.[57]

Deep South states were able to evade *Sweatt* for a decade or more. Florida did not begin to desegregate its public universities until 1958, Georgia until 1961, Mississippi until 1962, and South Carolina and Alabama until 1963. Though *Sweatt* had no immediate impact on Deep South practices, it had a noticeable effect on the region's politics by producing a minor backlash in white political opinion, which foreshadowed the repercussions that *Brown* would later have. The racially moderate *Atlanta Constitution* had warned that the Court's 1950 rulings would serve as "an open invitation to the KKK." That prediction was somewhat overstated, but the most avid of the South's race-baiting politicians reaped clear political benefits by highlighting the threat these rulings posed to white supremacy.[58]

This backlash effect was most evident in North Carolina, where a Democratic Senate primary of national significance was under way when the rulings came down. North Carolina's incumbent senator, Frank Porter Graham, was perhaps the most racially progressive southern politician of his era and thus was dangerously exposed on the race issue. Graham had served on Truman's civil rights committee, and he supported race-neutral suffrage qualifications, poll-tax repeal, and federal antilynching legislation. His challenger in 1950, Willis Smith, criticized Graham's liberal racial record, but in the first primary he principally assailed Graham's support for Truman's "socialistic" economic policies, such as national health insurance, and Graham's "softness" on communism and his past affiliations with allegedly subversive organizations ("Frank the Front"). Graham barely missed securing the first-primary majority that was necessary to avoid a runoff, but he did beat Smith by 48.9 percent to 40.5 percent. The *New York Times* treated Graham's near-victory as evidence of North Carolina's emergent racial liberalism.[59]

Smith nearly did not bother to contest the runoff election. The Court's higher education desegregation decisions, rendered on June 5, 1950, apparently changed his mind. Smith adroitly used the rulings to convert the runoff into a referendum on segregation. North Carolina's own university desegregation case was then pending in federal court, and public reaction in the state to the high court's rulings was "immediate and ominous." Smith blanketed the state with letters that emphasized their significance. The decisions also raised the salience of other racial issues for whites, such as the fair employment practices bill then pending in Congress and the alleged racial bloc vote for Graham in the first primary. A "full-blown racial panic" quickly ensued. Smith convinced enough eastern North Carolina farmers, who had allowed Graham's economic populism to trump his softness on race in the first primary, to alter their priorities and oust the incumbent. Graham had won eastern North Carolina by 16,000 votes in the first primary, but he lost it by 21,000 votes in the runoff. One must be careful not to overstate the extent of this backlash against *Sweatt* and *McLaurin*, as Graham still won 48 percent of the runoff vote. Yet the clear opinion shift in eastern North Carolina between the primaries demonstrated the backlash potential of Court decisions that interfered with "the southern way of life."[60]

Other extremist southern politicians also capitalized on the 1950 rulings. Governor Herman Talmadge of Georgia bragged a few days after the decisions that "as long as I am governor, Negroes will not be admitted to white schools." The Court's ruling in 1956 that Virgil Hawkins was entitled to prompt admission to the University of Florida School of Law became a principal issue in the pending gubernatorial primary. Challenged by extreme segregationists, racially moderate Governor Leroy Collins was pressured into taking a defiant stand. With candidates competing to occupy the most extreme segregationist position, the gubernatorial primary became, in the words of one newspaper, "a segregation surrey with a lunatic fringe on top."[61]

RESIDENTIAL SEGREGATION

Shelley v. Kraemer (1948) and *Barrows v. Jackson* (1953) barred the judicial enforcement of racially restrictive covenants, whether by injunction or damages action. There is no evidence that courts defied or evaded these decisions by continuing to enforce such agreements. Yet the rulings did not hold that the covenants themselves were unconstitutional, only that their judicial enforcement was. How much the continued existence of such agreements may have influenced private behavior is unknowable.[62]

The overall impact of these decisions is also difficult to measure. By the 1940s, racial covenants covered huge tracts of land in some northern cities, perhaps as much as 80 or 90 percent of white-owned housing in Chicago, Detroit, and Los Angeles. During the Great Depression and World War II, when relatively little new housing was built, restrictive covenants may have been instrumental in confining black ghettos to existing boundaries, even as the number of blacks living there increased dramatically, sometimes by as much as 200 or 300 percent. It is hard to say for sure, though, because many additional forces excluded blacks from white neighborhoods, including bank lending practices, federal government underwriting policies, real estate industry practices, the public housing and urban redevelopment decisions of local governments, and the fierce resistance of white homeowners to residential integration.[63]

In addition, as black neighborhoods burst at the seams during the war and blacks sought admission to white communities, litigation to enforce restrictive covenants often proved inadequate to exclude them. Many neighborhoods in which courts enforced restrictive covenants quickly turned overwhelmingly black anyway. *Shelley* may have been more important for eliminating doubts about title to land that was already held by blacks than for gaining blacks access to land that was held by whites. Restrictive covenant litigation generally proved too clumsy and expensive to frustrate powerful demographic and economic trends. Because blacks faced restricted housing opportunities, they would generally pay more than market value for housing located in changing neighborhoods, while whites would often sell at steep discounts to escape before neighborhoods turned black. Real estate agents known as "blockbusters" profited by buying discounted homes from whites and selling them at a premium to blacks. Occasional restrictive covenant litigation may have retarded such efforts. But most whites had little incentive to sue to enforce such agreements, given the substantial costs of litigation and the inability of individual plaintiffs to capture most of a lawsuit's gains, which flowed to all whites in the neighborhood, not just to those who sued. Moreover, once some blacks had entered a formerly white neighborhood, courts sometimes refused to enforce restrictive covenants on the remaining lots on the ground that changed circumstances had frustrated the purpose of the original agreement.[64]

The postwar housing boom rendered restrictive covenants almost completely obsolete. As millions of new homes were built in suburbs, whites had much less incentive to remain in urban neighborhoods that were in the path of expanding black ghettos or to litigate to preserve residential segregation. Whites had many reasons to leave cities for suburbs, even if judicial enforcement of racially restrictive covenants would have enabled them to keep blacks out of their neighborhoods: lower taxes, the desire to escape from urban vice and crime and to keep schools segregated, and pursuit of the American dream of owning land not too close to one's neighbors. The attractiveness of white suburbs might have rendered obsolete the judicial enforcement of restrictive covenants regardless of *Shelley*. One authority concludes that *Shelley* "simply delivered the final blow to a device that was already growing unequal to the task of preserving the racial homogeneity of white neighborhoods."[65]

Whether or not *Shelley* opened formerly white neighborhoods to blacks, it had essentially no impact on the amount of residential segregation. Indices measuring such segregation reveal no significant changes in large northern cities between 1940 and 1970. Urban whites moved to suburbs as blacks entered their neighborhoods, and blacks were generally not free to follow them there. Bank lending policies emphasized the racial stability of neighborhoods, which meant that blacks were denied loans to purchase homes in white areas. Incredibly, for two years after *Shelley*, the underwriting policy of the Federal Housing Administration (FHA) still encouraged racially restrictive covenants and discouraged black movement into white neighborhoods, because "inharmonious racial groups" rendered home mortgages too risky. The NAACP argued that *Shelley* barred the federal government from underwriting loans on property covered by restrictive covenants, but the FHA read the decision narrowly, to bar only judicial enforcement and not government encouragement of racial covenants.[66]

In addition, local governments building public housing after the war ensured that it was racially segregated, because "community attitudes" had to be accommodated. The few public housing authorities that tried to promote integration were overruled by local politicians who better reflected segregationist white opinion. In 1950, the U.S. Public Housing Authority disclaimed any interest in local decisions to segregate public housing, even if it was being built with federal funds. Courts did not bar such obviously unconstitutional behavior until the late 1960s, and subsequent remedial orders simply induced local governments to stop building public housing. In the 1950s, local urban renewal programs, which were also supported with federal funds, were consciously designed to maintain or even to increase the amount of residential segregation. Housing that was condemned under such programs was often somewhat integrated, whereas that replacing it was usually segregated. Private real estate developers who were building enormous suburban housing complexes tended to exclude blacks entirely. Levittown, Pennsylvania, was home to 60,000 whites, and not a single black, when it opened in the 1950s. Most real estate agents, through formal or informal agreement, refused to show blacks homes in white neighborhoods. Until 1950, doing so would have violated the code of professional standards of the National Association of Real Estate Brokers—a canon that most agents followed even after it was formally rescinded.[67]

The few blacks who successfully braved such barriers and bought homes in white neighborhoods often faced the threat and reality of mob violence. Blacks who moved into white neighborhoods in Miami after the war endured cross burnings, Klan bombings, police harassment, and arson. In the late 1940s, there were so many bombings of homes bought by black families in contested neighborhoods in Birmingham, Alabama, that one such area became popularly known as "Dynamite Hill." In 1951, a black family moved into a white apartment complex in the Chicago suburb of Cicero, and a mob consisting of thousands of angry whites, including the police chief and the chairman of the town council, drove them out. The police generally sided with whites over such incidents, and violence against blacks who sought homes in white neighborhoods was rarely prosecuted.[68]

Even as whites became more supportive of civil rights after the war, they still generally favored residential segregation. Moreover, both northern and southern whites supported residential segregation, which was not true of black disfranchisement or segregation in universities and in transportation. Racially restrictive covenants were just one of many methods available for maintaining housing segregation. During this era, the justices were disinclined to delve beneath the surface of residential segregation, refusing even to review a New York case that involved the exclusion of blacks from a large private housing development that had been constructed with public approval, tax breaks, and use of the eminent domain power. Thus, an isolated decision such as *Shelley* had almost no integrative effect. Even when the justices during the civil rights era proved more willing to challenge residential segregation, their rulings proved inefficacious. Early in the twenty-first century, the United States is nearly as residentially segregated as ever. The justices probably lack the capacity, and rarely have they shown much inclination, to contravene dominant public opinion on housing segregation.[69]

TRANSPORTATION

The decisions in *Mitchell v. United States* (1941) and *Henderson v. United States* (1950), which invalidated racial inequality in luxury railroad accommodations, had the effect of desegregating them. *Mitchell* ruled that blacks were entitled to equal access to Pullman accommodations, regardless of any disparate per capita racial demand. Because southern railways were unwilling to provide separate first-class cars for blacks, given the limited demand, many of them responded by integrating such facilities. Blacks were initially confined to separate compartments in Pullman cars and separate tables in dining cars (thus, the wooden partition in *Henderson*). Because *Mitchell* applied only to *inter*state passengers, southern railroads often continued to exclude blacks traveling within a single state from first-class facilities, at least where segregation proved impractical. But this regime of partial desegregation of luxury accommodations proved unstable during World War II, as railroad traffic quadrupled, and most such facilities then desegregated—a trend that continued after the war. In the Deep South, though, some railways continued to segregate Pullman cars. Segregation of the far more numerous second-class black passengers remained intact throughout the South, unaffected by *Mitchell*.[70]

Dining cars were the one first-class facility in which black passengers generally continued to be segregated even after the war. *Henderson* functionally barred such segregation, and almost all railroads immediately complied by removing segregation-enforcing partitions. Within a year, passengers reported that segregation had nearly disappeared from dining cars without incident.[71]

Why were *Mitchell* and *Henderson* so efficacious? One reason is that the most directly affected entities were profit-maximizing railroads. Some railroads had resisted segregation in the 1890s, fearing its costs. By the 1940s, however, railroads had adjusted to segregation and had little incentive to oppose it, unless they were required to provide blacks with separate first-class accommodations that were not cost-justified in light of the lower per capita demand of blacks. *Mitchell* and *Henderson* required precisely this and thus induced railroads to support the desegregation of luxury accommodations. Railroads continued to happily segregate second-class facilities, where the costs of segregation to them were minimal or nonexistent, given substantial black demand and the continuing practice of providing blacks with inferior treatment.

Another reason that *Mitchell* and *Henderson* were efficacious was the fact that railroads are supervised by a federal agency. Defiance of federal law by southern voter registrars had to be prosecuted in court before white jurors, but railroad companies that defied Court interpretations of the Interstate Commerce Act were subject to fines imposed by the Interstate Commerce Commission. The commission, though it was generally sympathetic toward railroads, would not countenance the nullification of federal law in the same way that white jurors in the South would.

Further, as with the desegregation of higher education, the integration of luxury railroad accommodations usually generated only minimal white resistance. Interracial contact in railroad travel was transitory and impersonal. Moreover, relatively few blacks could afford first-class facilities, and thus desegregating them produced little actual race mixing. Many of the upper-class whites who purchased such accommodations were more opposed to sharing them with lower-status whites than with higher-status blacks. Finally, blacks who could afford luxury accommodations were well positioned to litigate against those violating their rights.

The NAACP pronounced *Morgan v. Virginia* (1946) to be "the beginning of the end of Jim Crow transportation in this country." Yet, *Morgan's* invalidation of state laws that segregated interstate passengers had little impact on southern transportation practices. *Morgan* was based on the Dormant Commerce Clause, which early twentieth-century precedent had plainly established could be violated only by state laws, not carrier policies. Most bus companies and railroad companies did not need state compulsion to segregate passengers; they did so because of entrenched social custom and the preferences of their white passengers. Thus, the *Morgan* decision notwithstanding, most southern carriers continued to segregate interstate passengers. Much as segregation practices generally preceded the adoption of segregation laws in the late 1800s, so segregation practices continued largely unabated after the invalidation of those laws. With just one exception, federal courts ruled that *Morgan* permitted carrier policies of segregating interstate passengers. Until courts or the ICC construed the Interstate Commerce Act's prohibition on "undue or unreasonable prejudice or disadvantage" to bar segregation, carriers were free to segregate even interstate passengers. Nobody was likely to construe the statute that way until the justices had interpreted the Equal Protection Clause to forbid state-mandated segregation.[72]

The experience of freedom riders traveling on the Journey of Reconciliation in 1947 confirms that southern carriers continued to segregate blacks after *Morgan*. Members of the Congress on Racial Equality (CORE) spent two weeks traveling on Greyhound and Trailways buses in the upper South to test compliance with *Morgan*. They discovered that most people had never heard of the decision, that they were the only blacks who were protesting against segregation of bus transportation, and that their challenges were firmly rejected by bus drivers. Several of the freedom riders were arrested for resisting segregation, and they did not even dare to test their rights in the Deep South. Whether or not *Morgan* reached carrier policies of segregation, the threat of violence was enough to keep black travelers segregated in the Deep South.[73]

Though the dominant interpretation of *Morgan* did not bar carrier policies of segregation, by the early 1950s some carriers in the upper South and the border states were beginning to desegregate their interstate passengers. Fear of damages liability may have played a role in that decision, even though the law seemed to be on the carriers' side. In 1952, the NAACP announced that it would sue southern railroads that continued to segregate black interstate passengers. More important, some carriers outside of the Deep South concluded that ending segregation was the path of least resistance. With blacks manifesting increased resentment toward segregation in transportation and most whites in the upper South not intensely committed to preserving such segregation, many carriers in Arkansas, Kentucky, Tennessee, Texas, and Virginia quietly ceased enforcing it. Social practices changed because of shifting mores, not legal compulsion. Because racial mores in the Deep South had yet to change very much, the practice of segregation in transportation remained intact there. The few blacks in the Deep South who dared to protest against carrier segregation were evicted or worse. Even after the ICC in the wake of *Brown* ruled that segregation of interstate travelers violated the Interstate Commerce Act, many Deep South railroads continued for years to segregate blacks. Elsewhere, few carriers were inclined to resist the ICC's ruling.[74]

Morgan also did not apply to state laws segregating *intra*state passengers. Until the justices invalidated state-mandated segregation under the Equal Protection Clause, governments in the South were legally free to enforce segregation laws against local carriers. Thus, carriers that failed to segregate intrastate passengers risked prosecution under state and local segregation laws. Few companies were prepared to run that risk; most continued to segregate until coercive legislation was repealed or invalidated. Only a few cities in the peripheral South and the border states had voluntarily desegregated local transportation by the early 1950s. The justices finally invalidated state-mandated segregation in transportation in *Gayle v. Browder* (1956), a case that arose from the Montgomery bus boycott. Yet, in the post-*Brown* hysteria of southern politics, many Deep South cities defied that ruling for years. Thus, with regard to segregation in local transportation, some changes in practice occurred before court rulings had compelled them, and when those rulings finally materialized, they often proved powerless to compel further change in practices because of overwhelming white resistance. In the context of local transportation, the correlation between Court rulings and actual social practices was highly attenuated.[75]

In sum, Court decisions forbidding discrimination against black first-class passengers directly affected company segregation policies. Several factors—the economic incentives of railroads, the small number of blacks affected, and the higher socioeconomic status of both the blacks and the whites who were involved—produced desegregation even without direct judicial compulsion. By contrast, *Morgan*'s invalidation of state-mandated segregation of interstate travelers had little effect. The ruling did not implicate carrier policies of segregating interstate passengers; companies had no economic incentive to voluntarily desegregate all of interstate travel, as opposed to simply first-class accommodations; and white resistance to the desegregation of ordinary accommodations was much greater. It was changing racial mores, not judicial compulsion, that led many carriers outside of the Deep South to end segregation of interstate passengers by the early 1950s. Where state and municipal law required carriers to segregate local travelers and where white opinion supported continued enforcement, blacks remained segregated, even after favorable judicial rulings.

CRIMINAL PROCEDURE

Supreme Court decisions expanding criminal procedure rights had very little effect on southern criminal justice where serious black-on-white crime, such as rape or murder, was alleged. Southern juries remained almost entirely white, in spite of the Court's numerous reaffirmations of the right against race discrimination in jury selection. The Court's rulings refrained from directly interfering with the broad discretion of jury commissioners. Nor did the Court bar the popular practices of limiting prospective jurors to acquaintances of jury commissioners or to registered voters, both of which groups were disproportionately white. Even in counties where many blacks qualified for jury service, most (white) jury commissioners and judges still believed that blacks were biologically unequipped to serve responsibly. A Texas appellate judge, who had reluctantly reversed a conviction because of race discrimination in jury selection, noted that he "fully understood the sentiment that may have actuated the officers of the court below, and appreciate their disinclination to place the administration of the law, even in part, in the hands of the people assumed to be inferior to the white race." Similarly, in 1948, a Mississippi judge sarcastically observed that the state's jury selection statute required excluding those not possessing "good intelligence, sound judgment and fair character" and that he was aware of "no biological, mental, or psychological law" dictating that blacks qualified. Thus, the Court's jury discrimination cases did not impel jury commissioners and judges to select juries in color-blind fashion, but only to take the steps necessary to avoid reversal on appeal. As Justice Black warned in a 1955 conference discussion of a jury discrimination case, if local officials were afforded a second chance, they would simply "patch . . . up" the record and select another all-white jury to resentence the defendant to death.[76]

Even in the late 1940s, many Deep South counties continued to blatantly defy the Court by excluding blacks entirely from jury lists or by permitting the names of only one or two to appear. Some state supreme courts would reverse in egregious cases, where local officials had made no pretense of complying. In slightly less retrograde counties, a few blacks appeared on jury lists and venires, but they were never selected to serve. Such blacks were often superannuated, dead, disabled, or departed, and they never appeared in numbers approximating the black percentage of a county's population. In those counties that had been most influenced by the Court's jury discrimination rulings, one or two blacks now served on grand juries, where their presence could be nullified through supermajority voting rules or intimidation. A couple of state supreme courts followed an informal rule that treated the presence of a single black person on a grand jury as sufficient compliance with the Court's edict. After the extraordinary *Akins* decision, which affirmed a death sentence despite the jury commissioners' explicit admissions that they had imposed a quota of one black per grand jury, southern judicial officers had little incentive to do anything more.[77]

Well after blacks began regularly appearing on southern grand juries, trial juries remained entirely white. One method of exclusion was to carefully screen the blacks who were placed on jury lists and venires and to include only "Uncle Toms who begged to be excused," according to one NAACP branch president, referring to jury selection practices in Hinds County, Mississippi. More frequently, prosecutors used peremptory challenges to exclude the few blacks who appeared on trial venires by the 1940s. Confident that peremptories could preserve all-white juries, southern courts in explosive cases of black-on-white crime that were likely to attract appellate attention sometimes deliberately placed a black or two on the trial venire in order to secure against reversal. So long as blacks were not proportionately represented on venires, peremptory challenges could preserve all-white trial juries.[78]

The justices declined to take the steps that would have been necessary to place blacks on southern juries. In the 1940s, they refused to review a case that challenged the constitutionality of race-based peremptories and thus ensured several more decades in which blacks were almost universally excluded from trial juries in racially sensitive criminal cases. *Swain v. Alabama* finally took up that issue in 1965, only to sustain such a use of peremptory challenges by the prosecutor in Talladega County, Alabama, where every black person who had appeared on a jury venire since 1950 had been excluded. More than twenty years passed before the justices would overrule *Swain*. Thus, despite frequent Court interventions, blacks simply did not serve on trial juries in racially explosive criminal cases in the South. Every one of the fifteen black men executed by Kentucky between 1940 and 1962 had been convicted of a crime against a white by an all-white jury. Six separate juries, which consisted of a total of seventy-two white men, sentenced the Martinsville Seven to death in 1949 for raping a white woman in Southside, Virginia; the several blacks who appeared on the trial venires were all excluded for cause or through peremptories.[79]

The Supreme Court's expansions of the ban on coerced confessions do not appear to have been any more efficacious. It is impossible to measure the amount of physical coercion used by southern sheriffs against black suspects in spite of *Brown v. Mississippi* (1936) and *Chambers v. Florida* (1940). Yet such physical coercion probably did become less prevalent over time for several reasons, including the professionalization of southern police forces, the greater media scrutiny of interrogation practices, the postwar proliferation of NAACP branches, which monitored such abuses, the enhanced threat of federal prosecution, and growing black political power. Still, southern sheriffs continued to beat black suspects into confessing, especially in emotionally charged black-on-white criminal cases. High-court interventions did not end such coercion, though law enforcement officers learned from *Brown* to avoid excessive candor. Physical violence played an important role in sustaining white supremacy, and law enforcement officers felt more privileged than most whites in using it. Many southern sheriffs beat blacks not only to secure confessions, but because they enjoyed it and ran little risk of incurring sanctions for doing it.[80]

Court reversals of convictions on coerced confession grounds provided little incentive for southern sheriffs to cease extracting tortured confessions. Only the most unusual cases reached the Court. Lacking adequate resources, the NAACP declined to support even meritorious cases unless they presented a novel legal issue. Even though association lawyers were convinced that Willie Bryant had been illegally coerced into confessing—he was held incommunicado for twenty days—they opposed having the NAACP support an appeal to the Supreme Court because his case was not "extraordinary" or "dramatic." Most black defendants in the South were indigent and could not appeal even to state supreme courts, which were less fastidious than the justices about permissible interrogation methods. State courts, though willing to follow high-court rulings in clear cases, would not generally credit a coercion claim by a black defendant over the denial of a white sheriff. State appellate judges usually deferred to trial courts on the coercion issue, which meant that local white judges and jurors, who were generally sympathetic to the needs of sheriffs to coerce black suspects into confessing crimes, were usually the final arbiters of whether unconstitutional coercion had occurred. Moreover, after the extraordinary decision in *Lyons v. Oklahoma* (1944), even a concededly coerced confession remained potentially useful, because subsequent confessions, even if occurring as little as twelve hours later, might still qualify as "voluntary."[81]

Sheriffs who defied Court rulings that banned coerced confessions faced no significant risk of criminal liability. Because southern states declined to prosecute even the most egregious official violence against blacks, such as a sheriff's drunken murder of a black prisoner, they were not about to prosecute officers for extracting coerced confessions. Federal prosecutions were scarcely more likely. *Screws v. United States* (1945) required that federal-law violations be crystal clear in order for criminal liability to be imposed under federal civil rights statutes. Anything close to the line of permissibility did not qualify. Even in *Screws*, where the sheriff had wantonly murdered a black prisoner, several justices balked at applying the federal statute. Whether a majority of the Court in the 1940s would have imposed federal criminal liability on a sheriff for beating a suspect into confessing is uncertain.[82]

In any event, such cases were virtually impossible to win, even if southern U.S. attorneys had been eager to pursue them, which they rarely were. Defendants were frequently the only witnesses, other than the perpetrators, to beatings administered in the privacy of the jailhouse. White jurors were unlikely to believe the word of a black suspect over that of a white sheriff. Even if other witnesses existed, they were often reluctant to testify out of fear or social pressure. The FBI was disinclined to investigate such cases, because southern white agents usually shared their community's mores and because the bureau needed to maintain good working relationships with local police. Finally, the chances of convincing white jurors to indict and convict in such cases were remote. Defense lawyers would reargue the Civil War, harangue against the "outside interference" of the federal government, and appeal for an acquittal in order to cure the "meddlers' itch." In the 1940s, all-white southern juries still generally acquitted defendants of lynching or maiming blacks. They were not about to convict sheriffs who simply beat blacks into confessing. Thus, the Justice Department was reluctant to prosecute such cases.[83]

Suits seeking money damages against law enforcement officers who coerced defendants into confessing were equally unpromising. In the 1940s, it was unclear whether federal civil rights statutes permitted suits against state officials who violated state law, and every state forbade coerced confessions. White jurors were unlikely to sympathize with such plaintiffs: black criminal suspects. Such suits could also be dangerous, especially in those southern regions where coercion of black defendants was likely to be greatest. In 1940, a black man, Dave Reed, sued the sheriff of Leake County, Mississippi, for unlawfully shooting him. Reed was promptly kidnapped and never heard from again. Reinforced by a culture that condoned white violence against blacks and lacking any concrete incentives to desist, southern sheriffs continued beating black suspects into confessing, despite the Supreme Court's repeated condemnations of the practice.[84]

In the 1940s and the early 1950s, the Court extended *Powell v. Alabama* to require state appointment of counsel for indigent defendants in noncapital cases under certain circumstances. Yet the justices said almost nothing about the quality of that defense representation, except for ruling that an appointment of counsel three days before trial was permissible, unless the defendant could show that he had been prejudiced by the shortness of time. Thus, despite the Court's expansions of *Powell*, southern blacks could be woefully underrepresented without the Constitution being violated. And woefully underrepresented they were. Because the value of constitutional rights depends on having competent lawyers to raise them, most criminal procedure rulings mattered little to southern blacks, who were routinely denied adequate representation of counsel.[85]

Most southern black defendants could not afford lawyers, and thus their fate rested with court-appointed counsel. The NAACP financed occasional, highly meritorious cases. But the association rarely got involved in criminal litigation until after the trial. It possessed limited funds for such cases, and it did not regard itself as a legal aid bureau. Thus, the association limited its involvement to cases where "there is injustice because of race or color, and where there is a possibility of establishing a precedent for the benefit of Negroes in general." Given these restrictive ground rules, the NAACP often declined to take cases of obvious racial injustice.[86]

Even the rare black defendant in the South who was able to hire a lawyer could not be certain that he was getting his money's worth. Very few black lawyers practiced in the South in the 1940s. Those who did could be liabilities to their clients, as their mere presence in southern courtrooms could stimulate prejudice in the judge and jury. NAACP officials ransacked Mississippi in search of white lawyers to represent Albert Lee on charges of assault with intent to rape a (white) woman, not because the association was prejudiced against the "one or two Negro lawyers scattered over the state," but because "Red Neck" jurors were. The exclusion of blacks from southern law schools until the 1950s also affected the quality of black lawyers in the South.[87]

Yet at least black lawyers would generally have had the best interests of their clients at heart. Black defendants never knew what they were getting with white lawyers. Some proved genuinely committed to serving their clients' best interests—pursuing cases without adequate compensation, volunteering legal expenses out of their own pockets, and risking financial and occasionally physical injury for pursuing unpopular causes. Other white lawyers, however, shared the prejudices of their communities, assumed their clients deserved whatever sentences they received, and barely went through the lawyerly motions to collect a fee. These "shyster" lawyers, who "showed no more interest than was necessary for a perfunctory trial," failed to call witnesses, raise defenses, challenge the introduction of involuntary confessions, make new-trial motions, or appeal convictions. The failure of defense counsel, through incompetence or indifference, to make timely objections during trial precluded meaningful appellate review, given the stringency of state procedural default rules (to which the justices still deferred) and the refusal of appellate courts to monitor the adequacy of defense counsels' performance.[88]

Willie Francis, a sixteen-year-old Louisiana black who was sentenced to death for murdering a white man, was victimized by this sort of inept lawyering. Francis achieved national prominence in 1946–1947 when Louisiana sought to execute him "by installments," after the electric chair malfunctioned during the initial execution attempt. At his trial, Francis's two court-appointed lawyers had failed to challenge the all-white jury or to file a change-of-venue motion, despite the fact that Francis had been transferred to another county's jail for safekeeping. Defense counsel also failed to object to Francis's possibly coerced confession, which was the only direct evidence linking him with the crime. The lawyers made no opening argument, called no witnesses, may have failed to cross-examine prosecution witnesses, and neglected to inform the jury that the police had "lost" the alleged murder weapon.[89] Then they failed even to appeal his conviction, thus forfeiting any valid constitutional claims that he may have had. Francis may have been innocent of murder, yet no appellate court ever scrutinized his trial record. Francis's case was unique, however, not because of this inept lawyering—which was all too common for indigent southern blacks—but because of the bungled execution attempt. In 1947, the justices, by a 5–4 vote, rejected Francis's claim that a second execution attempt would constitute cruel and unusual punishment or violate due process. They did not even consider whether his trial representation had been adequate.[90]

Even white lawyers who were neither shysters nor incompetent did not invariably have the best interests of their black clients at heart. Forrest Jackson, a white lawyer whom the NAACP described as "our only effective agent in Mississippi, . . . in whom we put a great deal of reliance," turned out to be making white supremacist speeches in his Senate campaign. Jackson was no shyster. He secured Supreme Court reversal on coerced confession grounds of Albert Lee's conviction for assault with intent to rape. Still, blacks were entitled to wonder whether a white supremacist lawyer could reliably represent the interests of black clients.[91]

Indeed, white defense lawyers did not always aggressively represent black clients in emotionally charged criminal cases. Doing so would "lose friendship," as several white lawyers explained to the father of a black man charged with sexual assault on a white woman in Hinds County, Mississippi, in 1947. The white lawyer who eventually took this case dropped it before a second trial, after winning Court reversal of an initial conviction. After two recent high-court reversals of the convictions of Mississippi blacks in notorious criminal cases, "Mississippi white lawyers [were] afraid of their shadows." Southern white lawyers, due to personal conviction or social pressure, sometimes declined to challenge race discrimination in jury selection, as doing so "necessarily brings about ill feeling." Chief Justice Earl Warren explained at conference in a 1960s jury discrimination case that white lawyers "will not raise [this] question, for it will hurt their social standing." Thus, southern black defendants often lost their most promising ground for reversal on appeal.[92]

White lawyers risked severe social sanctions for defending black clients too vigorously when local communities were demanding blood. Most chose not to do so. Sonnie Dobbs, Jr., a black man charged with murdering a white man in Atalla County, Mississippi, in 1946, was defended by court-appointed whites, whom the NAACP thought did an excellent job under the circumstances. Still, they "lived in Mississippi and wanted to stay here" and thus dared not take the steps that were essential to Dobbs's defense, such as demanding a change of venue or challenging race discrimination in jury selection. White lawyers who refused to capitulate to such pressure often found their legal practices crippled and sometimes suffered physical violence. Joseph Murray, who admirably represented two blacks from McCormick, South Carolina, who were probably falsely accused of murder, reported that he had "incurred the ill will of so many people here that I am now unable to secure any practice and it looks as if I might have to move to some other place and begin over to try and again build up a practice." Stanley Belden, a white ACLU lawyer who ably represented W. D. Lyons against possibly trumped-up murder charges in Hugo, Oklahoma, in 1941, saw his legal practice ruined and was forced to leave the state. In the most explosive cases, where a black was charged with raping or murdering a white, it often proved difficult to find any white lawyer willing to take the case.[93]

Southern courts refused to extend *Powell* to require more able representation of indigent defendants. The justices had ruled that appointment of counsel on the morning of the trial was inadequate, so southern judges would appoint lawyers a few days before the trial. Black defendants whose lives were in jeopardy were routinely provided lawyers so near to trial that no serious investigation of facts or preparation of trial strategy was possible. In the most combustible cases, moreover, court-appointed counsel was strongly discouraged from seeking a continuance by threats to lynch their clients. Lawyers who persevered against such pressure generally saw their motions for a continuance rejected anyway, or else judges granted much shorter delays than they had sought. State supreme courts declined to find inadequate representation of counsel under such circumstances, and *Avery v. Alabama* (1940) had refused to find insufficient as a matter of law an appointment three days before trial.[94]

The other context in which the interwar Court had used Jim Crow justice as the occasion to create novel criminal procedure doctrine was mob domination of trials. *Moore v. Dempsey* (1923) had ruled that such trials violated the Due Process Clause and that federal courts were obliged to make the factual determination of mob domination for themselves, rather than defer to state court findings. The postwar Court did not elaborate on this right, though in one notorious case, *Shepherd v. Florida* (1951), Justice Jackson's concurring opinion objected to newspaper publicity that he thought precluded a fair trial for black defendants charged with raping a white woman. Extreme mob domination of trials, such as that involved in *Moore*, seems to have largely disappeared by World War II, probably for the same reasons that mass public lynchings had been rendered largely obsolete by then.[95]

Yet a sizable gap exists between mob-dominated trials and fair ones. Many blacks who were charged with murdering or raping whites in the postwar South were tried amid intense public agitation, threats of violence, and rumors of lynching. How could a black defendant receive a fair trial in a county from which sheriffs had to remove him for safekeeping until trial? Yet many such itinerant defendants received no change of venue. Their lawyers sometimes failed to even request one, either because of indifference or as a calculated judgment that asking for it might get their clients lynched. Other lawyers were unable to secure the affidavits that were necessary to support such a motion. Whites who wished to take matters into their own hands by dispensing "populist justice" strongly resisted the relocation of trials and exerted enormous pressure on those who contemplated signing change-of-venue affidavits. Blacks who filed such affidavits faced possible violence. Even when the venue was changed, it was usually only to an adjacent county, where public animosity toward the defendant was not noticeably reduced and where state militiamen were still required to secure his safety at trial. Not until 1961 did the justices rule that the Constitution requires a change of venue when there is strong evidence of community bias.[96]

Charles Trudell, a fifteen-year-old black charged with murdering a white man in Wilkinson County, Mississippi, in 1946, had to be transferred to another county's jail because of threatened mob violence. Defense counsel "were skating on thin ice in the trial of this case . . . in a court room packed with a vengeful community which over-flowed even into the courtyard." The lawyers made the record as strong as they could "without having [their] clients lynched on the spot," yet "even a motion for special [jury] venire would [have] result[ed] in immediate violence." Even in such extraordinary circumstances, which were reminiscent of the mob-dominated trials of the interwar period, it proved impossible to obtain the two affidavits necessary to support a change-of-venue motion.[97]

In 1939, Lee Lett and Hoyt Butler were indicted in Whitley City, Kentucky, for allegedly murdering two white men by ejecting them from a moving train. Only one black family lived in McCreary County, which had a reputation for extreme racial prejudice, and blacks were not even permitted to walk the streets of Whitley City. Four blacks were prosecuted for the murders, but Lett and Butler were northerners ("bad niggers"), and thus they aroused special hostility in the community. Their trial "took on the aspect of a county fair," as people came from all over "to see the niggers get tried." The appearance of a black NAACP lawyer who was investigating the case "caused quite a commotion" until he was run out of town. Some whites privately admitted that the defendants could not possibly secure a fair trial in Whitley City, yet nobody would sign an affidavit to that effect.[98]

Thus, in the most explosive cases where blacks were charged with raping or killing whites, Jim Crow justice had changed very little over the years. Mob domination had somewhat dissipated, but many trials were still conducted amid intense public hostility and threatened violence. Trial judges rarely granted changes of venue. Courts appointed defense counsel a few days before trial, rather than the morning thereof, but many of those lawyers barely went through the motions of conducting a defense, because of either indifference or community pressure. Southern sheriffs still routinely beat black suspects into confessing. Blacks rarely served on grand juries and almost never on trial juries.

The trial of the Groveland defendants, Samuel Shepherd and Walter Irvin, illustrates how racially biased criminal justice in the South still could be in the late 1940s. Four blacks were accused of raping a white woman in Lake County, Florida, in 1949. The defendants may have been innocent. The prosecution introduced no medical evidence to confirm that a rape had occurred. Under a plausible alternative scenario, the woman's estranged husband had concocted the rape allegation, with his wife's acquiescence, in order to protect himself from his in-laws' wrath, after he had ignored previous warnings not to physically abuse her again. Moreover, Lake County was experiencing severe racial tensions, as white citrus growers found black veterans, including Shepherd and Irvin, resistant to resuming prewar labor patterns. Shepherd's father, an independent black farmer, had also quarreled with white neighbors over their cows grazing on his property. Many whites believed that the Shepherds needed to be put in their place. After the defendants' arrest, a mob of more than a hundred whites surrounded the county jail and demanded that the suspects be turned over for lynching. When mob members were told that the defendants had been transferred out of Lake County for safekeeping, they vented their rage instead on Groveland's black community, destroying several homes and driving hundreds of blacks into the surrounding swamps in fear for their lives.

Medical testimony revealed that the defendants had been severely beaten before they confessed—a constitutional violation so transparent that prosecutors made no effort to introduce the confessions at trial. Yet word of the confessions reached the newspapers and thus possibly the jury as well. Pretrial newspaper coverage was extraordinary. The *Orlando Morning Sentinel* ran a front-page cartoon that pictured four electric chairs under the headline "Supreme Penalty" and over the caption "No Compromise!" In spite of such pervasive and prejudicial pretrial publicity, the trial judge denied the defendants' motion for a change of venue. Locating a white

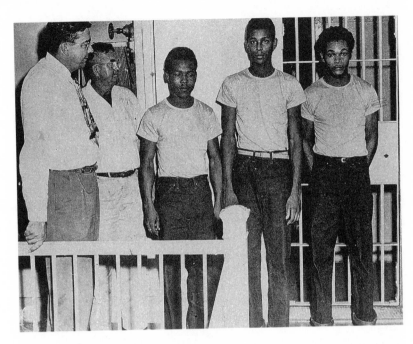

FIGURE 5.6

The Groveland defendants—(*left to right*) Walter Irvin,
Charlie Greenlee, and Samuel Shepherd—outside their
jail cell. *Far left*: Sheriff Willis McCall and jailer Reuben
Hatcher, 1949 or 1950. (*Library of Congress, Prints and
Photographs Division, Visual Materials from the
NAACP Records*)

lawyer who was willing to represent Shepherd and Irvin proved difficult
given the intense community hostility. When a willing lawyer was finally
found, his motion for a continuance in order to enable him to adequately
prepare for trial was denied. The trial took place in a mob atmosphere.
Defense lawyers needed police escorts and were instructed by the trial judge
to be ready to leave in a hurry when the verdict was announced. Blacks were
deliberately and unprecedentedly placed on the jury lists—an effort to guard
against reversal on appeal—but no blacks were allowed onto the trial jury.
The defendants were convicted and sentenced to death.[99] The state supreme
court affirmed, sustaining the trial judge's determination that a fair trial was
possible in Lake County, and rejecting the jury discrimination claim
because a black had served on the grand jury and several blacks had
appeared on the trial-jury lists. The Supreme Court unanimously reversed
on the ground of race discrimination in jury selection. Jackson and Frank-

furter concurred separately, denouncing prejudicial pretrial publicity and mob domination.[100]

On the way to a change-of-venue hearing before a second trial, the sheriff of Lake County, Willis McCall, suffered a flat tire on the lonely back road he was inexplicably taking and then was forced to shoot Irvin and Shepherd in self-defense as they allegedly attacked him (while handcuffed together). Somehow surviving, Irvin was forced to stand trial again for rape and received another death sentence, which the Florida Supreme Court affirmed. This time, the justices denied review. Governor Leroy Collins later commuted Irvin's sentence to life imprisonment. McCall emerged unscathed, as a coroner's jury determined that he had shot Shepherd and Irvin in self-defense.

Less publicized but no less outrageous was the murder trial of Sonnie Dobbs, Jr., in Atalla County, Mississippi, in 1946. Dobbs, a navy veteran, was charged with murdering a white man. The most plausible account of what really happened is that Dobbs, who was still wearing his service uniform, was harassed and then assaulted by rowdy, drunken whites. He fought back and killed, either accidentally or intentionally, one of his attackers. Had Dobbs been white, he would probably not have been charged at all, and he certainly could have successfully pled self-defense. Yet Mississippi blacks — especially if they were veterans in uniform — were apparently not permitted to defend themselves from white assaults. Dobbs was allowed just thirty min-

FIGURE 5.7
Shepherd and Irvin after they were shot by Sheriff McCall,
1951. (*Florida State Archives*)

utes with his court-appointed lawyers before the trial, which took place just ten days after the homicide. Defense counsel failed to request a change of venue, even though Dobbs had been transferred from the Atalla County jail amid rumors of a lynching. Angry whites packed the courtroom and menaced the jury, on which no blacks served—a fact that defense counsel somehow failed to protest. Because of either indifference or intimidation, counsel also neglected to raise a self-defense claim. The jury deliberated just minutes—one account said five, another twenty-five—before returning a death sentence. Dobbs's lawyers then failed to move for a new trial, which effectively forfeited any appellate review. The Mississippi Supreme Court affirmed his conviction without judging the merits of his appeal—a decision that the state's leading black lawyer called "one of the greatest miscarriages of justice in the history of [Mississippi]." No appeal was taken to the Supreme Court, and Dobbs was executed for committing what was at most the crime of manslaughter.[101]

Whether the trials of Dobbs and the Groveland defendants were representative of postwar criminal justice for black defendants in the Deep South is unknowable, though Francis, Lee, and Trudell—other blacks charged with serious crimes against whites—had broadly similar experiences. Many egregious cases may have disappeared entirely from the historical record, as greater mob influence made defense counsel less likely to object to trial errors or to appeal convictions. Judging from the appealed cases and the NAACP case files, farcical trials in which possibly innocent blacks were sentenced to death remained common, despite the justices' criminal procedure rulings.[102]

Criminal justice for blacks charged with similar crimes in peripheral South states was significantly different. The famous Martinsville Seven case illustrates those differences, though again it is impossible to determine how representative the case was. Seven young black men were charged with raping a white woman in Southside, Virginia, in 1949. The woman had indisputably been raped, and all seven defendants had indisputably engaged in forcible intercourse with her or been present as accomplices. No lynch mob attempted to execute the defendants, and the trial was conducted in a mob-free atmosphere. Not only were the defendants not beaten into confessing, but they were informed of their right not to answer police questions. The trials did not occur until five months after the crime, and defense counsel was appointed four months before trial. Both the judge and the prosecutor avoided references at trial to the defendants' race. Three blacks sat on the grand jury that indicted the defendants, and blacks appeared in each of the jury pools for the six separate trials. Although black newspapers and some radical journalists compared these proceedings to those at Scottsboro twenty years earlier, the dissimilarities are actually more striking. The Martinsville Seven had real trials with real lawyers that were conducted with relative dispassion before a fair judge.[103]

Yet the trials, convictions, and executions of the Martinsville Seven were fundamentally unjust for two reasons having to do with race. First, although blacks were in the jury pools for all of the defendants' trials, every one of the seventy-two jurors who tried and convicted them was white. Blacks were excluded from juries because of their opposition to the death penalty or through the use of peremptory challenges by prosecutors. Second, every death sentence imposed for rape or attempted rape in Virginia during the twentieth century involved a black man and a white woman. Before the Civil War, Virginia law had expressly reserved the death penalty in rape cases for black men who assaulted white women. That racial distinction was eliminated from the statute books in 1866, but in practice it continued to apply. Since 1908, when the state took over executions from localities, Virginia had executed forty-five blacks and not a single white for rape.[104] Thus, although the Martinsville Seven enjoyed ostensibly fair trials, their fate ultimately depended on their race. In Virginia rape cases, only blacks who assaulted whites ever received the death penalty, and only white jurors adjudicated their guilt and imposed sentence. Oliver Hill, the black Richmond lawyer who helped represent the Martinsville Seven for the NAACP, justifiably concluded that white Virginians knew that "we don't need to lynch the niggers. We can try them and then hang them." Virginia executed the Martinsville Seven in February 1951—the largest mass execution or lynching for rape in U.S. history.[105]

The continuing exclusion of blacks from juries, even in the peripheral South, ensured that southern criminal justice remained color conscious. Black jurors would probably have rejected the death penalty for black rape defendants as they knew that white rapists were never executed. Black jurors would probably have benefited black defendants in other cases as well, though this assumes that their independent judgment could have been guaranteed, which is quite possibly an unwarranted assumption in the South of this era.

Odell Waller was another black Virginian whose death sentence attracted national attention. He was a sharecropper who was convicted of murdering a white farmer, Oscar Davis, in Pittsylvania County, Virginia, in 1940. Waller had undeniably killed Davis, but he had a plausible self-defense claim. The two had an unpleasant history, including Davis's mutilation of Waller's dog. Immediately preceding Davis's death, they had quarreled over the distribution of crop shares. Waller claimed that Davis was known to carry a gun and that he was reaching for it when Waller shot him. Prosecution witnesses, however, denied that Davis usually carried a gun; he was clearly unarmed when Waller shot him; and at least one bullet entered his body from the back, which tended to undermine Waller's self-defense claim. The jury, limited to whites who had paid their poll taxes, rejected self-defense. But the defense was sufficiently plausible that a national crusade on Waller's behalf by the socialist Workers' Defense League persuaded not only national luminaries, such as Pearl Buck, John Dewey, and Eleanor Roosevelt, but also many prominent white Virginians to support commutation of his death sentence. How could having blacks on Waller's jury—and one-third of Pittsylvania County's population was black—not have made a difference? When the race of the defendant and decedent were reversed in another sharecropper homicide case in Pittsylvania County around the same time, the all-white jury deliberated just fifteen minutes before acquitting the defendant, apparently crediting his self-defense claim. Yet Governor Colgate Darden repulsed the efforts to commute Waller's death sentence, and he was executed in 1942.[106]

Other notorious criminal cases in the South in the 1940s involved similar facts. Rosa Ingram was a black sharecropper and the mother of twelve in Schley County, Georgia. In 1948, she and three of her sons were prosecuted for killing a white farmer, John Stratford, who lived on adjacent land. The Ingrams, too, had a plausible self-defense claim. They alleged that Stratford had come after them with a shotgun after repeated altercations over the Ingrams' livestock trespassing on his land. Only the defendants witnessed the killing. Circumstantial evidence suggested that Stratford may have been killed after two sequential struggles, which would have weakened the Ingrams' self-defense claims. Without any way of knowing for sure what happened, the all-white jury rejected self-defense, found the defendants guilty of

FIGURE 5.8
Odell Waller. (*Crisis Publishing Co.*)

murder, and sentenced them to death, which the trial judge then reduced to life imprisonment. The highly sympathetic facts helped convert the Ingrams' case into a leading story for black newspapers and into a successful fundraising vehicle. Yet because self-defense claims turn almost entirely on the credibility of witnesses and circumstantial evidence, jury determinations are largely insulated from reversal. The Ingrams lost their appeal in the Georgia Supreme Court and did not even bother attempting to carry the case further.[107]

L. C. Akins, whose jury discrimination claim did get to the Court, only to be rejected, also raised a self-defense claim, which his all-white jury likewise refused to credit. Akins got into an altercation with an off-duty, out-of-uniform white police officer, Leon Morris, when Akins apparently brushed against Morris's wife while boarding a Dallas streetcar in 1941. After Morris shot Akins, the latter grabbed the gun and killed Morris. This case also generated national publicity. The *Nation* plausibly speculated that had Akins been white, he would probably not even have been indicted. Yet because of his race, "Clarence Darrow himself could not save Akins in the Dallas County court," his lawyers informed Thurgood Marshall. Most southern whites apparently would not concede that blacks had a right to kill whites in self-defense. The average white policeman, prosecutor, or juror believed, according to the *Nation*, that "when a nigger kills a white man, death to him." In one typical black-on-white murder case in Mississippi, half of the members of the jury venire candidly admitted that they would not acquit a black man charged with killing a white, regardless of how compelling the evidence of self-defense. As most blacks surely felt as entitled to use self-defense as anyone else, the continuing exclusion of blacks from juries in the South almost certainly affected the outcome of such cases.[108]

Having blacks on juries would probably have made some difference in other categories of cases as well. Most white men in the South presumed that sex between a black man and a white woman was rape. Thus, black defendants who pleaded consent as a defense to charges of raping white women had essentially no chance before all-white juries. Even black defendants who pled mistaken identity might have benefited from having blacks on the jury. As late as the 1940s, some southern whites still believed that "you can't let a Nigger get off once you arrest him." A Birmingham physician explained that if a black man raped a white woman, "an example and a spectacle of punishment" was necessary. "If possible get the right Negro and string him up. String up one or two of his nearest relatives, at the same time. And if the right one can't be found, take some other Negro." It seems safe to assume that all blacks who might have sat on a jury would have disagreed with that sentiment.[109]

By the late 1940s, southern lynchings were nearly obsolete, and legal lynchings such as those involved in *Moore* and *Powell* had been tempered and confined to narrower portions of the Deep South. Yet nowhere in the South did blacks serve as jurors in inflammatory cases where serious black-on-white crime was alleged. All-white juries applied unwritten substantive liability rules according to which only black men could be executed for raping white women, and only whites were permitted to kill other whites in self-defense. Criminal justice outside of the rural Deep South may have acquired a veneer of legitimacy by the 1940s. The justices could find no constitutional error in cases such as those of the Martinsville Seven or that of Odell Waller, because the trials had ostensibly been fair. Yet black men were still being executed under circumstances where whites almost surely would not have been.

Given this state of affairs, one is entitled to wonder whether the Court's criminal procedure rulings were not insidious. In landmark decisions that protected the rights of southern black defendants, the justices employed some of their boldest rhetoric about the high court's heroic role in defending unpopular minorities from majoritarian oppression. An especially famous such statement appears in *Chambers v. Florida*, which extended *Brown v. Mississippi*'s bar on coerced confessions beyond physical violence. *Chambers* proudly proclaimed the obligation of judges to "stand against any winds that blow as havens of refuge for those who might otherwise suffer because they are helpless, weak, outnumbered or because they are non-conforming victims of prejudice and public excitement." This grandiose rhetoric was matched by the dramatic setting in which it was delivered: The *Chambers* opinion was read in full in open Court on Abraham Lincoln's birthday by former Klansman Hugo Black. An NAACP correspondent called this Court session "the most impressive . . . I have attended." Newspapers captured the event in banner headlines such as "Justices Rededicate Themselves as a Haven of Refuge for All Non-Conforming Victims of Public Prejudice." A glowing editorial in the *Nation* quoted some of Black's rhetoric and basked in the happy ending of *Chambers*, of which Americans "may be proud." The justices had freed "obscure and humble" black men, who lacked any political or economic issue around which to mobilize protest.[110]

Yet *Chambers* apparently had little effect on southern sheriffs who habitually coerced confessions from black suspects.[111] Nor did other criminal procedure rulings significantly alter Jim Crow justice. Were blacks clearly better off because of Court rulings that had little practical consequence for southern criminal justice but that enabled the justices to trumpet the vigilant defense that courts offered against racial prejudice in the law? Before the Court's interventions, at least everyone could see mob-dominated trials for what they were: farcical substitutes for lynchings. After such rulings, however, casual observers might have been misled into believing, along with the *New York Times*, that "the High Court stands on guard with flaming sword over the rights of every one of us."[112]

Blacks could be excused if they demurred from such sentiments. Even in states such as Virginia, where the formal requirements of due process were more attentively observed, blacks did not sit on juries in combustible cases where serious black-on-white crime was alleged. As a result, all-white juries continued to apply informal substantive liability rules that discriminated against blacks. The justices in the postwar period had opportunities to intervene against both of these racial flaws in the southern criminal justice system. Defendants appealed to the Court cases that challenged the racially motivated use of peremptory challenges by prosecutors and racial disparities in the administration of the death penalty. The justices refused even to grant review. Not until the 1970s would they become concerned about the discriminatory administration of the death penalty—mainly, but not exclusively, in the context of rape. Not until the 1980s would the justices forbid the race-conscious use of peremptories. Yet the rhetoric of *Chambers* suggests that the justices had convinced themselves, and perhaps others, that they had already taken enormous strides toward eliminating race discrimination from southern criminal justice. They had not. Their accomplishments were actually fairly trivial—more a change in form than in substance. To the extent that the justices and their admirers were deluded into thinking otherwise, these criminal procedure rulings may have caused actual harm to the interests of southern blacks.[113]

The Court's denial of review technically does not indicate that the justices approve of the lower court decision (though it may imply this, given the justices' self-proclaimed role as heroic defenders of minority rights). Yet this Court did not simply fail to intervene against certain racial inequalities in the criminal justice system of the South; it actually affirmed unjust convictions. In *Akins v. Texas* (1945), each of the jury commissioners had admitted his intention to limit the number of blacks per grand jury to one, yet somehow the justices found the record unclear on this point. Moreover, Akins had an especially appealing case for reversal, because his self-defense claim almost certainly would have prevailed had he been white. Yet the justices affirmed his death sentence, which the governor of Texas later commuted to life imprisonment after a nationwide protest campaign.

Lyons (1944) was the most compelling coerced confession case since *Brown v. Mississippi*—"a pretty bad miscarriage of justice," according to Justice Murphy's law clerk. The record contained convincing testimony by several whites that the governor's special deputy had admitted to savagely beating Lyons with a blackjack for several hours in an effort to obtain his confession. Lyons also had a strong claim of innocence. Yet the justices decided to defer to the jury's determination that Lyons's second confession, obtained just twelve hours after his brutal beatings had ended, was voluntary. For anyone convinced by the *Chambers* rhetoric, the force of the claims by Lyons and Akins that they had been unjustly treated was necessarily diminished. A Court serving as a "haven . . . of refuge for those who might otherwise suffer because they are helpless, weak, . . . or . . . non-conforming victims of prejudice" would surely have intervened on the behalf of these defendants had their claims been meritorious. But their claims were meritorious. The Court's failure to reverse their convictions is difficult to comprehend. Thus, not only did the *Chambers* rhetoric possibly legitimize an unjust system which the justices' occasional interventions were powerless to change, but by affirming particular convictions, the Court may have undermined the legitimacy of those defendants' claims that they had been unjustly treated.[114]

It is possible that these criminal procedure cases were more important for the litigation process that produced them than for the concrete changes they brought about in southern criminal justice. In the 1940s, criminal cases were still the type of litigation that proved most effective for mobilizing social protest, as they symbolized Jim Crow at its worst: the incarceration and execution of possibly innocent blacks after farcical trials. In previous chapters, we have seen how such cases afforded unparalleled opportunities for building NAACP branches and raising funds, as well as providing unique forums in which NAACP lawyers could educate southern blacks about the malleability of Jim Crow and northern whites about its barbarity.[115]

The extraordinary *Lyons* case from Oklahoma illustrates how criminal litigation could help mobilize social protest at a time when alternative reform strategies—political pressure, economic boycotts, street demonstrations, and physical resistance—remained largely unavailable to southern blacks. As described at the beginning of chapter 4, W. D. Lyons, a black man, was prosecuted for the brutal murder of a white couple and their four-year-old son near Hugo, Oklahoma, on New Year's Eve, 1939. The NAACP immediately grasped the splendid organizational opportunities that *Lyons* afforded. A black man had been savagely beaten into confessing and perhaps framed in a desperate effort to provide political cover for a governor. Lyons's ACLU lawyer, Stanley Belden, recognized the case as of "great importance" to the NAACP, and Roscoe Dunjee, the association's principal agent in Oklahoma, spotted a chance to "attract the attention of the entire nation." Dunjee worked hard to convince Thurgood Marshall to come to Hugo to participate in the trial and, along the way, to attend a half dozen organizational meetings across Oklahoma. Marshall consented and soon concluded that Lyons's case, if handled properly, could help raise a defense fund of ten thousand dollars. Between the beatings and the bones used to induce the confession, Marshall concluded that "this case has more appeal than any up to this time." In a letter from Oklahoma that described Lyons's trial, Marshall wrote: "We can raise money on these cases. We have been needing a good criminal case and we have it. Let's raise some real money."[116]

Not only did Marshall's visit to Oklahoma rally the troops, but his very presence in the Hugo courtroom offered important educational lessons to whites and blacks in attendance. Marshall reported that on the day of the trial, the courtroom was overflowing with a thousand spectators from around the county. No black lawyer had ever appeared in that courtroom before, and everyone was curious to see the NAACP litigator from New York. Marshall had wondered what the reaction would be when he arrived, but "the building did not fall and the world did not come to an end." He had expected to lose at trial, as he did, yet he still believed that vital educational lessons had been conveyed: "[O]ne thing this trial accomplished—the good citizens of that area have been given a lesson in constitutional law and the rights of Negroes which they won't forget for some time." Children, who had been released from school for the purpose of attending what the judge perversely called a "gala" event—in which a possibly framed black man was on trial for his life—received a lesson in constitutional law that they would never have learned in their classrooms. Marshall concluded: "I bet they have more respect for Negroes now." Moreover, "law enforcement officers now know that when they beat a Negro up they might have to answer for it on the witness stand."[117]

White spectators and law enforcement officers were not the only ones educated by the trial. Marshall and his co-counsel, Belden, had agreed that the former would cross-examine all of the police officers, "because we figured they would resent being questioned by a Negro and would get angry and this would help us. It worked perfect. They all became angry at the idea of a Negro pushing them into tight corners and making their lies so obvious." Marshall continued: "Boy, did I like that—and did the Negroes in the courtroom like it. . . . You can't imagine what it means to those people down there who have been pushed around for years to know that there is an organization that will help them. They are really ready to do their part now. They are ready for anything."[118]

Other contemporary criminal cases involving patent racial injustices—such as Waller's or Ingram's—also became vehicles for raising defense funds of tens of thousands of dollars and for mobilizing northern and occasionally international protest against the South's treatment of black criminal defendants. The national campaign against Louisiana's second attempt to execute young Willie Francis was supported by the former governor of New York, Herbert Lehman, the former mayor of New York City, Fiorello La Guardia, Congresswoman Helen Gahagan Douglas, and CIO leader Philip Murray. The governor of Texas, Coke Stevenson, commuted the death sentence of L. C. Akins to life imprisonment after a nationwide protest and the collection of 15,000 signatures from Dallas citizens on a clemency petition. By the time that Mississippi executed Willie McGee in 1951 for raping a white woman, the Civil Rights Congress had turned his case into an international cause célèbre, and several European newspapers protested his execution.[119]

The involvement of the NAACP (or the Civil Rights Congress or the Workers' Defense League) in these cases focused national attention on southern racial practices of which most northern whites had been ignorant. In 1945, the president of the NAACP's Baltimore branch urged the national office to get involved in the case of the Jones brothers, two black teenagers charged with murdering a white man in Somerset County, on Maryland's Eastern Shore. Blacks on the Eastern Shore, which was known as the "Mississippi of Maryland," were still treated like "slaves," and airing their grievances in court would focus outside attention on their plight. NAACP intervention in such cases also aroused interest among blacks in forming new branches and helped "build up the morale" of existing ones. Finally, whether or not Court victories changed southern criminal justice, they may have inspired southern blacks. *Chambers* may not have influenced the interrogation practices of southern sheriffs, but to many Florida blacks it nonetheless represented "a second emancipation."[120]

In spite of these organizational benefits, however, NAACP involvement in such cases remained a mixed blessing for southern black defendants. The NAACP's participation meant financial assistance, legal expertise, morale boosting, and the capacity to focus national attention on oppressive local practices, which might help spur their elimination. But to southern whites, the association represented "outside interference." Thus, the NAACP's involvement in a case inevitably raised the stakes from the fate of a particular black defendant to the capacity of southern whites to control their own race relations. For this reason, local defense counsel often preferred to exclude the NAACP altogether or at least to keep its involvement quiet. National agitation by the Revolutionary Workers' League and the Workers' Defense League against Virginia's planned execution of Odell Waller may have made it impossible for the governor to commute his sentence. The NAACP and other defense organizations needed to publicize the outrages of the southern criminal justice system in order to mold national opinion. Black defendants were chiefly interested in staying alive.[121]

PEONAGE

It is hard to believe that the Court's peonage rulings during World War II, *Taylor v. Georgia* (1942) and *Pollock v. Williams* (1944), had much effect on the amount of southern peonage. Few of the blacks who were likely candidates for prosecution under state peonage laws could have put their constitutional rights to effective use. Pollock could not afford to hire a lawyer, who might have informed him of his right under *Bailey* and *Taylor* not to be convicted under a phony false-pretenses law. As Pollock could not come up with the $5 necessary to buy himself out of debt, he was an unlikely candidate to produce the $500 bond necessary to appeal his conviction to a court beyond the control of local planters. Only the assistance of outside organizations enabled Pollock to appeal his conviction.[122]

Two Court rulings that invalidated state peonage laws were unlikely to have much effect, given that eradicating peonage depended less on shielding peons from state prosecution than on attacking the perpetrators of peonage via federal prosecution. Whites who were committed to holding blacks in peonage did not generally require the assistance of phony false-pretenses laws; they relied mainly on violence and the connivance of local sheriffs. In the 1930s, blacks who sought to organize sharecroppers and tenant farmers into a union in the Mississippi Delta could still be lynched or assassinated with impunity. Blacks who challenged a planter's distribution of crop shares or otherwise contested his authority likewise put their lives at risk. One southern planter was reported to have killed during his lifetime thirty black sharecroppers who had dared to challenge the injustice of their treatment; he was never even brought to trial. It was this sort of totalitarian control exercised by white planters that enabled peonage to survive. Yet, through the 1930s, the Roosevelt Justice Department showed little interest in prosecuting peonage. In 1935, Walter White of the NAACP observed that the department "seems to devote . . . most of its energy in trying to avoid taking action [in peonage cases]. One must have his facts in such incontrovertible shape that the Department cannot avoid acting, before it will proceed." Only after 1940 did the department change course, due to the black political leverage that resulted from World War II and the foreign-policy embarrassments caused by publicized peonage incidents. Even when federal prosecutors were willing to go forward with a case—as with allegations of peonage in Florida turpentine farms in the mid-1930s—the unwillingness of terrified black laborers to publicly support charges could undermine prosecutions. When cases did get off the ground, southern white jurors generally remained unwilling to convict their neighbors of violating federal antipeonage laws.[123]

The case of Walter Crayton reveals how little the maintenance of peonage depended on the enforcement of state coercive-labor laws. In 1937, Crayton, an elderly black Mississippian, got into trouble with his landlord for disputing the settlement he had been offered on that year's crops, which was less than $5. Crayton left the farm and moved into town. Several days later, his landlord spotted Crayton there, ordered him back to the farm, and warned him of trouble should he resist. After ignoring a second threat, Crayton was arrested and charged with forging the $4.50 check from the landlord found in his possession. When Crayton denied the forgery and told police that he had left the plantation because "I was tired of working for nothing," they beat him for disputing a white man's word. Crayton was then sent to the state penitentiary; his only crime was his effort to break free of peonage. He had no money with which to hire a lawyer, and the NAACP had no lawyers available in this part of Mississippi. Crayton's freedom was not constrained by peonage laws so much as by the totalitarian control that rural southern planters exercised over the lives of their black laborers. Crayton described his plight in a letter to the NAACP:

> You don't know how bad we colored farmers are treated. We are slaves. Work year [to] year for nothing. Charged for things we don't buy. Kept in debt to the plantation owners. The police is in cahoots. [I]f we leave we are arrested. Beaten [and] sent to the penitentiary.[124]

The number of peonage complaints filed with the Department of Justice dramatically declined between 1939 and 1945, which some have attributed partly to the Court's two peonage rulings in the early 1940s. Yet, it seems more likely that social and economic forces were eroding the conditions necessary for sustaining peonage. New Deal agricultural policies greatly reduced the demand for sharecroppers, and the war-related industrial boom of the early 1940s stimulated demand for black workers, which made coercive labor practices harder to sustain. Moreover, peonage, which had long been disfavored by the "better class" of white southerners, could survive only under insular conditions, which cloaked coercive labor practices from outside criticism and suppression. Such insularity was rapidly disappearing in a modernizing South, which featured better transportation and communication facilities. Telephone calls quickly alerted outsiders to the existence of peonage, and automobiles made it easier for peons to escape from planters' control. Finally, improvements in southern education made peonage harder to justify for whites and harder to impose on blacks.[125]

World War II was a watershed in U.S. race relations. The changes in racial attitudes and practices that occurred in the 1940s were more rapid and fundamental than any that had taken place since Reconstruction. In the early 1940s, the Roosevelt administration still allowed its racial policies to be shaped mainly by white southerners, but by the end of the decade, the Truman administration had embraced a civil rights agenda that drove Dixiecrats out of the party. The number of southern blacks registered to vote increased exponentially, and blacks in many southern cities began exerting real political influence. They elected the first black officeholders since the end of the nineteenth century, secured the appointments of the first black police officers since disfranchisement, and forced white politicians to take account of black interests. The first breaches in the walls of segregation occurred in the public universities of the peripheral South and in public accommodations in cities of the border states. In the North, a hot war against fascism and an incipient Cold War against communism, together with burgeoning black political power and the triumph of a scientific paradigm that attributed racial differences to environmental rather than biological causes, helped convert civil rights into a pressing concern of postwar liberals.

Black leaders in the postwar era evinced extraordinary optimism about the prospects for further racial reform. Ten years earlier, many blacks had doubted whether their grandchildren would live to see an end to segregation. Now, though, the question seemed to be whether segregation would meet its demise this year or next. Noting that racial changes had occurred far more rapidly than anyone could reasonably have predicted a decade earlier, black leaders now cautioned against conservative assumptions as to what was possible. In 1948, F. Palmer Weber, one of the South's most committed white racial reformers, was so impressed with the revolution that had recently occurred in black voter registration in the South—a quadrupling in just eight years—that he saw no reason why two million or more southern blacks could not be enrolled by 1950. In 1952, Lester Granger, executive director of the National Urban League, detected "a social malleability in the South today that has not been equaled since during the days of Reconstruction."[126]

The Court's race decisions of this era underwent the same extraordinary transformation as did society's racial attitudes and practices. *Smith v. Allwright* (1944), which invalidated the white primary, overruled by an 8–1 vote a unanimous decision from just nine years earlier. *Shelley v. Kraemer* (1948), which barred judicial enforcement of racially restrictive covenants, unanimously rejected dicta from another unanimous decision twenty-two years earlier and repudiated the position adopted by a score of state supreme courts. *Sweatt v. Painter* (1950) and *McLaurin v. Oklahoma* (1950) unanimously undermined, at least in the context of higher education, a separate-but-equal doctrine that had been almost universally endorsed by lower courts and by the justices for three-quarters of a century. *Smith*, *Shelley*, and *Terry v. Adams* (1953) suggested that the justices were no longer willing to permit state-action doctrine to obstruct the pursuit of racial equality.[127]

By 1950, black leaders were converging behind an all-out legal assault on segregation, which ten—even five—years earlier would have been inconceivable. Earlier, black leaders had disagreed among themselves over aims, tactics, and strategies. Some preferred to work for integration, others to seek genuine equality within a segregated system. Some believed that litigation was an effective method of achieving social change; others had grave doubts. Such disagreements were largely mooted by the integrationist ideology of the war and by the impressive legal victories of the NAACP. White southerners were beginning to recognize the looming threat posed to segregation, and they warned of dire consequences should legal challenges prove successful. Indeed, suits that challenged segregation in public grade schools were already under way in several southern and border states. How would the justices respond, and how would white southerners react should the Court vindicate those challenges?[128]

CHAPTER SIX

School Desegregation

In the spring of 1951, black students at segregated Moton High School in Prince Edward County, Virginia, commenced a strike against overcrowding and other unequal conditions in their school. This sort of youthful black militancy, though it was not uncommon in the postwar South, was a stunning departure from white expectations of black subservience in rural Southside, Virginia. Black teachers and parents implicitly supported the students' activism by not attempting to stifle it. NAACP leaders in Virginia initially tried to discourage the protest because Prince Edward County seemed like such an inhospitable environment in which to challenge Jim Crow education. When the students would not be dissuaded, however, the association's lawyers agreed to sponsor a lawsuit, but only on the condition that the students and their parents directly attack segregation, which had not been their initial intention. This lawsuit became one of the five consolidated cases that became known to history as *Brown v. Board of Education*.[1]

When cases that challenged the constitutionality of racial segregation in public schools reached the Supreme Court in 1951–1952, the social and political context had changed dramatically since 1927, when the justices had last (obliquely) considered the question. Several million blacks had migrated from southern farms to northern cities in search of greater economic opportunities and relative racial tolerance. One largely unintended consequence of this migration was black political empowerment, as blacks relocated from a region of pervasive disfranchisement to one of relatively unrestricted ballot access. Moreover, blacks in large northern cities frequently held the balance of power between the two major political parties.[2]

Demographic shifts, industrialization, and the dislocative impact of World War II had produced an urban black middle class with the education, disposable income, and lofty expectations conducive to involvement in social protest. Economic gains enabled blacks to challenge the racial status quo by freeing them from white control and by creating a powerful lever— the economic boycott—for extracting racial reforms. Economic progress also encouraged blacks to contest traditional racial practices by dramatizing the disparity between their economic and social status. Southern urbanization empowered blacks politically, because cities generally had looser restrictions on black suffrage. Urban blacks also found it easier to coordinate social protest, because of less-oppressive urban racial mores and the relative ease of overcoming collective-action problems in cities, given better transportation and communication facilities.

Ideological forces had also helped to transform American racial attitudes and practices. The war against fascism impelled many Americans to reconsider their racial preconceptions to clarify the differences between Nazi Germany and the Jim Crow South. The ensuing Cold War pressured Americans to reform their racial practices in order to convince nonwhite Third World nations that they should not equate democratic capitalism with white supremacy. Finally, developments in transportation and communication—television, interstate highways, the expansion of air travel—bound the nation into a more cohesive unit. The homogenization of the United States hindered the white South from maintaining deviant social practices such as Jim Crow.

Potent as these background forces for racial change were, by the early 1950s, they had yet to produce any dramatic changes in southern racial practices. Black voter registration in the South had increased from roughly 3 percent in 1940 to about 20 percent in 1952, but 80 percent of southern blacks remained voteless, and many Deep South counties with black majorities still disfranchised blacks entirely. Many southern cities had instituted less-offensive racial seating practices on buses, but none had desegregated them. Many other cities had desegregated their police forces and minor league baseball teams, and disparities in the public funding of black and white schools were rapidly diminishing. In large cities in the border states—Baltimore, Kansas City, St. Louis, Louisville, Wilmington—segregation in public accommodations was beginning to erode, and Catholic parochial schools were starting to integrate. Yet racial segregation in public grade schools remained completely intact in the southern and border states and in the District of Columbia. Segregation of public grade schools lay near the top of the white supremacist hierarchy of racial preferences. For the Court to invalidate it was certain to generate far greater controversy and resistance than had striking down the white primary or segregation in interstate transportation.

Five cases that challenged the constitutionality of segregation in public schools reached the Court in 1951–1952. The justices were unenthusiastic about confronting so quickly the issue that they had deliberately evaded in the 1950 university segregation cases, and the NAACP had not planned to force it this soon. The five cases were also quite unrepresentative of the southern school segregation issue. Three were from jurisdictions—Kansas, Delaware, and the District of Columbia—where whites were not deeply committed to segregation, and judicial invalidation would probably not cause great disruption. The other two cases, however, came from Clarendon County, South Carolina, and Prince Edward County, Virginia, where blacks were 70 percent and 45 percent of the populations, respectively. Broad forces for racial change had barely touched these counties, where judicial invalidation of school segregation might well jeopardize public education. The NAACP's executive secretary, Roy Wilkins, later confided that Clarendon County "would be the last place I'd pick" to integrate. Yet, ironically, the NAACP's 1950 decision to no longer accept equalization cases had pushed blacks in these counties to convert their grievances against inferior schools and lack of bus transportation into broad desegregation challenges. The association was not willing to abandon courageous blacks who were willing to challenge Jim Crow under oppressive conditions, but it did pressure them to attack segregation directly, which they would probably not have otherwise done. Some civil rights leaders questioned the wisdom of pushing a desegregation suit on the Court at this time, worrying that the strategy might backfire and produce a disastrous defeat. Why run the risk, they wondered, if narrower challenges to racial inequality were virtually certain to succeed? Even Thurgood Marshall had doubts as to whether the justices were prepared yet to invalidate school segregation. As we shall see, such concerns were well founded.[3]

BROWN V. BOARD OF EDUCATION: LAW OR POLITICS?

On May 17, 1954, the decision in *Brown v. Board of Education* unanimously invalidated racial segregation in public schools. The Court's opinion emphasized the importance of public education in modern life and refused to be bound by the views of the drafters of the Fourteenth Amendment or by those of late nineteenth-century justices, most of whom had held more benign views of segregation. Segregated public schools were "inherently unequal" and thus violated the Equal Protection Clause of the Fourteenth Amendment. Because a practice that the Court had just invalidated in the states could not possibly be permitted in the capital of the free world, the justices ruled in the companion case of *Bolling v. Sharpe* that the Due Process Clause of the Fifth Amendment imposed identical restrictions on the District of Columbia.[4]

Brown's unanimity can be misleading. Some scholars have concluded that the justices easily invalidated school segregation and that a contrary ruling in *Brown* was "scarcely imaginable" by 1954. This view is mistaken; the justices were deeply conflicted. When the School Segregation Cases were first argued in the fall of 1952, the outcome was uncertain. Before analyzing why many of the justices found *Brown* difficult, let us reconstruct the internal deliberations as the Court first considered the constitutionality of segregation in public schools.[5]

Fred M. Vinson began the discussion, as the chief justice traditionally does. Vinson was from Kentucky, a border state with southern leanings and a

FIGURE 6.1

The justices who deliberated on *Brown v. Board of Education* in the 1952 term. Standing (*left to right*): Tom C. Clark, Robert H. Jackson, Harold H. Burton, and Sherman Minton. Seated (*left to right*): Felix Frankfurter, Hugo L. Black, Chief Justice Fred M. Vinson, Stanley F. Reed, and William O. Douglas. (*Photograph by Fabian Bacrach, Collection of the Supreme Court of the United States*)

long tradition of segregated education. There is a "[b]ody of law [in] back of us on separate but equal," Vinson announced, and "Congress has not declared there should be no segregation." It is "[h]ard to get away from [the] long continued interpretation of Congress ever since the Amendments." Public schools in the District of Columbia "have long been segregated." Vinson was making two points in these introductory remarks. First, a long line of precedents upheld segregation as constitutional. Second, the same Congress that wrote the Fourteenth Amendment and was responsible for its enforcement had segregated schools in the District of Columbia for nearly one hundred years, which implied that it considered segregation to be constitutional. Vinson continued: "Harlan in his dissent in *Plessy* does not refer to schools." That the lone justice who had condemned railroad segregation in 1896 had implied that school segregation was acceptable was "significant." Vinson found it hard to "get away from that construction by those who wrote the amendments and those who followed." He also worried that the "complete abolition of public schools in some areas" was a "serious" possibility if the Court invalidated segregation. Though others "said we should not consider this," Vinson believed that "we can't close our eyes to [the] problem." He also thought it "would be better" if Congress acted. To maintain confidentiality and preserve fluidity, the justices decided not to take even a tentative vote at conference. Yet several of them kept informal tallies, and all but one of those recorded that Vinson would probably vote to reaffirm *Plessy*.[6]

As the senior associate justice, Hugo Black spoke next. He was the only justice from the Deep South—Alabama—and had briefly belonged to the Ku Klux Klan in the mid-1920s. Black predicted "violence if [the] court holds segregation unlawful," and he warned that "states would probably take evasive measures while purporting to obey." He thought that South Carolina "might abolish [its] public school system." Black worried that if the justices invalidated school segregation, district courts "would then be in the firing line for enforcement through injunctions and contempt." He did not believe in "law by injunction," perhaps because injunctions had undermined labor union organizing earlier in the century, and Black was a strong union supporter. Yet Black was certain that the intention of segregation laws was "to discriminate because of color," whereas the "basic purpose" of the Fourteenth Amendment was the "protection of the negro against discrimination." He was inclined to hold that "segregation per se is bad *unless* the long line of decisions bars that construction of the amendment." Black "would vote . . . to end segregation," but he expressed doubt about his colleagues: "If equal and separate prevails, [I would] give weight to findings in each state."

Stanley F. Reed, like Vinson, was from Kentucky. Of all the justices, he was the most supportive of segregation, in terms of both policy and constitutionality. Reed took a "different view" from Black, declaring that "state legislatures have informed views on this matter." "Negroes have not thoroughly assimilated," and states "are authorized to make up their minds." "[A] reasonable body of opinion in the various states [was] for segregation," which was "for [the] benefit of both [races]." After noting the "constant progress in this field and in the advancement of the interests of the negroes," Reed concluded that "states should be left to work out the problem for themselves." Because the Constitution's meaning was "not fixed," Reed asked, when are "the changes to be made?" He answered: When the "body of people think [segregation is] unconstitutional." He could not "say [that] time [has] come," when seventeen states still segregated schools. Reed predicted that "[s]egregation in the border states will disappear in 15 or 20 years." But in the Deep South, "separate but equal schools must be allowed." He thought that "10 years would make [the schools] really equal" in Virginia, and he urged his colleagues "to allow time for equalizing." Until then, he "would uphold separate and equal." Reed's statement was unambiguous: *Plessy* was good law and should be reaffirmed.

Felix Frankfurter was an Austrian Jew, who immigrated to the United States as a child. He taught law at Harvard for a quarter century before Roosevelt appointed him to the Court in 1939. Frankfurter and Black had feuded before over the meaning of the Fourteenth Amendment—specifically, whether it "incorporated" the Bill of Rights and made those guarantees applicable to the states, rather than simply to Congress, as intended at the founding. Reminiscent of that dispute, Frankfurter now wondered how Black could "know the purpose of the 14th amendment." Frankfurter had "read all of its history and he can't say it meant to abolish segregation." He also wanted "to know why what has gone before is wrong." He was reluctant to admit that "this court has long misread the Constitution." Moreover, he "can't say it's unconstitutional to treat a negro differently than a white." Yet Frankfurter also discussed the remedy that the Court might impose if it invalidated segregation: "These are equity suits. They involve imagination in shaping decrees. [I] would ask counsel on reargument to address themselves to problems of enforcement." Frankfurter appears not to have made up his mind, conceding that he "can't finish on [the] merits and would reargue all [the cases]."

Frankfurter had no similar doubts regarding the District of Columbia case, which he thought "raise[d] very different questions." To permit school segregation in the nation's capital was "intolerable," and Frankfurter was prepared "to vote today that [it] violates [the] due process clause." Paradoxically, Frankfurter was quicker to bar segregation where the legal argument against it was weaker. The Fourteenth Amendment binds states, not Congress, and the many slave owners who endorsed the Fifth Amendment, which does constrain Congress, presumably would not have condemned segregation in public schools, had such schools existed when the amendment was ratified in 1791. What Frankfurter found compelling was the moral, not the legal, argument against segregation in the nation's capital. In the end, he favored "put[ting] all the cases down for reargument," which he insisted was not "delaying tactics" but a "further maturing process." Even the D.C. case should be reargued to allow the Eisenhower administration time to fulfill the president's campaign promise to end racial segregation in areas under federal control through administrative action, which Frankfurter thought would produce "enormous . . . social gains" over judicial intervention.

William O. Douglas grew up in the state of Washington, where few black people lived. Then he traveled east to attend law school at Columbia University, after which he became a law professor, first at Columbia and then at Yale. In 1936, Roosevelt appointed him to the Securities and Exchange Commission, a position that afforded few opportunities to ponder racial issues. As a justice, Douglas often had little trouble resolving legal problems that vexed his colleagues, and segregation was no exception. "Segregation is an easy problem," Douglas stated, and the answer was "very simple." He explained:

> No classifications on the basis of race can be made. [The] 14th [A]mendment prohibits racial classifications. So does [the] due process clause of the 5th [Amendment]. A negro can't be put by the state in one room because he's black and another put in the other room because he's white. The answer is simple though the application of it may present great difficulties.

Nobody could have doubted where Douglas stood on *Brown*.

Robert H. Jackson was raised in upstate New York, another region with few blacks and no school segregation. Jackson admitted that his upbringing afforded him "little personal experience or firsthand knowledge by which to test many of the arguments advanced in these cases." He was "not conscious of the [race] problem" until he moved to Washington, D.C., in the 1930s to join the Roosevelt administration. Jackson's conference statement began bluntly:

> [There is] [n]othing in the text that says this is unconstitutional. [There is] nothing in the opinions of the courts that says it's unconstitutional. Nothing in the history of the 14th amendment [says it's unconstitutional]. On [the] basis of precedent [I] would have to say segregation is ok.

Jackson ridiculed the NAACP's brief as "sociology," not law. He noted that New York law mandated school segregation in the 1860s, when the Fourteenth Amendment was passed, and still did so in the 1890s, when *Plessy* was decided. Jackson thought that "it will be bad for the negros to be put into white schools" and doubted whether one can "cure this [race] situation by putting children [of different races] together." He would not "say it is unconstitutional to practice segregation tomorrow." Yet he predicted that "segregation is nearing an end. We should perhaps give them time to get rid of it and [I] would go along on that basis. There are equitable remedies that can be shaped to the needs." What Jackson meant by these final words is unclear, but he apparently could imagine joining a decision that invalidated segregation or that threatened to do so unless certain conditions were met. Jackson also wanted to invite the judiciary committees of the House and Senate to participate in the reargument, because "if stirred up . . . [,] they might abolish [segregation]." Still, the thrust of his remarks suggests that Jackson was dubious as to the legal basis for invalidating segregation.[7]

Harold H. Burton was the sole Republican justice in 1952, though he had been appointed by Democrat Harry Truman. Burton had been a senator from Ohio and, before that, the mayor of Cleveland, which is located in the Western Reserve, a region long known for its racial egalitarianism. Burton spoke briefly and to the point at conference: "*Sipuel* [and *Sweatt*] crossed the threshold of these cases. Education is more than buildings and faculties. It's a habit of mind." Burton continued: "With [the] 14th amendment, states do not have the choice. Segregation violates equal protection. [The] total effect is that separate education is not sufficient for today's problems. [It is] not reasonable to educate separately for a joint life." Though Burton "would give plenty of time in this decree," he plainly favored invalidating segregation in public education.

Tom C. Clark was from Texas, a peripheral South state. Few blacks lived in West Texas, where the commitment of whites to preserving segregation was relatively thin. East Texas, however, resembled the Deep South; many counties had majority or near-majority black populations, and most whites were deeply invested in Jim Crow. Clark declared that the "result must be the same in all the cases"—a statement that probably evinced the typical sensitivity of southern whites to perceived antisouthern prejudice. He meant that if the Court invalidated segregation in South Carolina and Virginia, it must do so as well in Delaware and Kansas. Clark observed that "the problem [in Texas] is as acute as anywhere. Texas also has the Mexican problem. [A] Mexican boy of 15 is in a class with a negro girl of 12. Some negro girls get in trouble" (read: pregnant). After this brief digression into Texas social history, Clark got to the point:

> If we can delay action it will help. [The] opinion should give lower courts the right to withhold relief in light of troubles. [I] would go along with that. Otherwise [I] would say we had led the states on to think segregation is OK and we should let them work it out.

Clark's statement is ambiguous. His willingness to "go along" with an opinion affording lower courts discretion to withhold relief indicates a possible vote against segregation. Yet his concern that the Court "had led the states on to think segregation is OK" and thus perhaps should "let them work it out" suggests an opposite vote. Clark, like Frankfurter and Jackson, was probably undecided.

Sherman Minton was from Indiana, a northern state with predominantly southern racial views. He and Truman had been cronies in the Senate—apparently an important criterion for Truman's Court appointments. Like Burton, Minton was brief and to the point at the conference: "[A] body of law has laid down [the] separate but equal doctrine. That however has been whittled away in these cases [referring to *Sweatt* and *McLaurin*]. Classification on the basis of race does not add up. It's invidious and can't be maintained." With regard to the District of Columbia case, Minton also observed: "Congress has authorized segregation but it's not legal. Our decree will cause trouble but the race carries trouble with it. The negro is oppressed and has been in bondage for years after slavery was abolished. Segregation is per se illegal." Minton left no doubt that he was voting to end school segregation.

This is approximately what the nine justices said as they first collectively considered the School Segregation Cases. Figuring out how these statements would have translated into votes requires speculation, as the justices decided, contrary to their usual practice, not to vote after speaking. In the absence of a formal tally, commentators have disagreed as to how the justices would have voted in December 1952. My view is that four of them—Black, Douglas, Burton, and Minton—thought that school segregation was plainly unconstitutional. But Court majorities require five, and no other justice was equally certain. Two of them—Vinson and Reed—probably leaned toward reaffirming *Plessy*. The other three—Frankfurter, Jackson, and Clark—were apparently ambivalent.

Before trying to explain how a 4–3–2 split became a 9–0 ruling against segregation, let us look more closely at each justice and speculate as to why he held the views that he did. Black's ready condemnation of segregation was perhaps the most surprising position taken by any of the justices. In 1952, he was the only member of the Court from the Deep South, and he had been a Klan member. Black appreciated better than his colleagues could how intensely resistant white southerners would be to judicial invalidation of school segregation. The consequences of that resistance would also be more personal for Black, whose immediate family members living in Alabama would feel the repercussions of his vote.

One cannot know for sure why Black concluded that school segregation was unconstitutional. He often claimed to be a textual literalist, but a constitutional injunction to states not to deny "equal protection of the laws" does not plainly forbid separate-but-equal schools. Nor does the legislative history of the Fourteenth Amendment clearly do so. Thus, the legal sources to which Black usually claimed allegiance seem to have better supported an opposite result in *Brown*. Accordingly, if he is to be taken at his word about his method of constitutional interpretation, Black's personal views about segregation, not his legal interpretation, must explain his vote. But why did Black personally condemn segregation at a time when few white Alabamans his age did so? Maybe Black was just idiosyncratic; he certainly had a contrarian personality. Another possibility is that Black was so chastened upon his appointment in 1937 by public criticism of his former Klan membership that he dedicated his judicial career to rebutting it. Soon after joining the Court, Black hired a Catholic secretary and a Jewish law clerk, apparently to dispel suspicions of religious prejudice flowing from his Klan affiliation. Not long thereafter, he wrote the landmark opinion in *Chambers v. Florida*, which reversed a black man's conviction because of a coerced confession and celebrated the Court's role as savior of oppressed minorities. Perhaps Black was like John Marshall Harlan, the former Kentucky slave owner who seems to have partially dedicated his judicial career to gainsaying Radical Republican criticism of his appointment by resisting the Court's post-Reconstruction retreat from racial equality.[8]

Douglas's vote may be the easiest to explain. He was less committed than the other justices to maintaining a distinction between the law and the judge's values, which is why Douglas frequently found to be easy issues that troubled his colleagues. For him, the immorality of segregation was the beginning and the end of the legal inquiry. If segregation was wrong, then it was unconstitutional. Douglas had revealed no special racial sensitivity in his pre-Court years, but he was a quintessential northern liberal. Before World War II, such people were generally more interested in economic issues than racial ones. By the late 1940s, however, racial egalitarianism had become a defining characteristic of theirs. By 1952, the immorality of segregation was no longer debatable for someone of Douglas's political ilk.[9]

The antisegregation votes of Burton and Minton are harder to explain. Neither was as liberal as Douglas. Their personal histories regarding race are thin. The little surviving evidence suggests that they shared neither Reed's support for segregation nor Frankfurter's passion for racial equality. On civil liberties issues generally, they were the most conservative justices, nearly always siding with the government and celebrating judicial restraint.[10]

Why would Burton and Minton, generally averse to civil liberties claims, have been so receptive to the civil rights claim in *Brown*? Perhaps the answer lies in a consideration that was emphasized in the briefs, the oral arguments, and the newspaper reactions but was never mentioned at conference: the Cold War imperative for racial change. Burton and Minton were fierce judicial Cold Warriors. Their enthusiasm for judicial restraint was most evident in cases challenging government loyalty and security programs, where they almost never found a constitutional violation. In *Brown*, the Cold War imperative put them in the unusual position of siding with individual-rights claimants and the federal government against state legislatures. The Justice Department's brief invoked the Cold War imperative as a principal justification for invalidating school segregation: "Racial discrimination furnishes grist for the Communist propaganda mills." Reed's law clerk recalled that his justice observed that he was hearing much on this subject and it was causing him to think, though he believed that it should be irrelevant. After *Brown*, supporters of the decision boasted that U.S. leadership of the free world "now rests on a firmer basis" and that U.S. democracy had been "vindicat[ed] . . . in the eyes of the world." Perhaps Burton and Minton, ever heedful of national security, concluded that barring segregation was service to that cause.[11]

Frankfurter and Jackson may have been the justices who were most conflicted over *Brown*, which posed for them a clash between law and poli-

tics. Both justices abhorred segregation, but both were committed to maintaining the distinction between the law and the personal values of judges.
Traditional legal sources to which they looked for guidance—text, original
intent, precedent, and custom—pointed more toward reaffirming than
overruling *Plessy*. Thus, as Jackson conceded, invalidating segregation
could be defended only in "political" terms. *Brown* required these justices
to choose between their aversion to segregation and their aversion to political decision making by judges. We shall further explore that conflict in a
moment.

Two justices, Vinson and Reed, were leaning toward reaffirming *Plessy*.
Both came from Kentucky, which legally mandated school segregation, and
Reed endorsed segregation as social policy. In 1947, he refused to attend a
Court party because black messengers were invited, and in 1952, he was
appalled that "a nigra" might sit down beside his wife at a restaurant after the
Court had interpreted an old civil rights statute to require the desegregation
of public accommodations in the District of Columbia. Less is known about
Vinson's racial views, though he was probably more ambivalent about segregation than northern justices, such as Burton and Minton, were. Thus,
although these Kentuckians were equally committed Cold Warriors, their
support for (or lesser aversion to) segregation may explain why they were less
influenced by the Cold War imperative. They were also less committed in
general to protecting individual rights than were Black or Douglas. School
segregation was not a vexing constitutional problem for Vinson or Reed
because their general inclination was to defer to legislatures; traditional legal
sources supported segregation; and the policy was congenial, or at least not
adverse, to their personal preferences. With law and politics aligned, Vinson
and Reed could readily reaffirm *Plessy*.[12]

In December 1952, only four justices were clearly prepared to invalidate
school segregation. Two were inclined to sustain it, and three appeared
undecided. The justices' informal head counts confirm that deep divisions
existed. In a memorandum to the files that he dictated the day *Brown* was
decided, Douglas observed:

> In the original conference, there were only four who voted that segrega-
> tion in the public schools was unconstitutional. Those four were Black,
> Burton, Minton and myself. Vinson was of the opinion that the *Plessy*
> case was right and that segregation was constitutional. Reed followed
> the view of Vinson, and Clark was inclined that way.

Frankfurter and Jackson, according to Douglas, "viewed the problem with
great alarm and thought that the Court should not decide the question if it
was possible to avoid it," though both believed that "segregation in the public schools was probably constitutional." Frankfurter distinguished between
school segregation in the District of Columbia, which he thought violated
the Due Process Clause, and in the states, where he thought that "history was
against the claim of unconstitutionality." In Douglas's estimation, in 1952,

"the vote would [have been] five to four in favor of the constitutionality of segregation in the public schools in the States with Frankfurter indicating he would join the four of us when it came to the District of Columbia case." Douglas's dislike of Frankfurter may have colored his perception of his colleague's likely vote, but his interpretation is consistent with the conference notes.[13]

Other justices who were counting heads reached roughly similar conclusions. In a letter written to Reed just days after *Brown* was decided, Frankfurter noted that he had "no doubt" that a vote taken in December 1952 would have invalidated segregation by five to four. The dissenters would have been Vinson, Reed, Jackson, and Clark, but not himself, and the majority would have written "several opinions." On another occasion, Frankfurter bragged that he had filibustered the decision in 1952–1953 "for fear that the case would be decided the other way under Vinson." After the initial conference, Reed reported to his law clerk that Vinson would probably join him in dissent, as would at least one other justice (Jackson or Clark). Burton and Jackson counted between two and four dissenters if the decision were rendered in 1952–1953. These roughly similar head counts confirm that the justices were deeply divided. Possibly, a bare majority existed to reaffirm *Plessy*.[14]

Worried about the "catastrophic" impact of a divided decision, Frankfurter suggested having the cases reargued on the pretense that the justices required further briefing on issues such as the original understanding of the Fourteenth Amendment and the remedial options that would be available should they invalidate segregation. The justices were far less interested in the answers to these questions than in securing additional time to resolve their differences. Five of them—Black, Frankfurter, Jackson, Burton, and Minton—voted for reargument, and on June 8, 1953, the cases were rescheduled for the next term.[15]

The principal difficulty with this interpretation, which emphasizes deep divisions and the possibility that no majority yet existed for overruling *Plessy*, is that the Court unanimously invalidated school segregation in the next term. If the justices were so conflicted in December 1952, how could they have achieved unanimity in May 1954? Perhaps my account treats the conference notes too literally. One commentator suggests, by contrast, that the justices were simply "talking through their concerns about what they knew they were going to do." Frankfurter and Jackson, on this view, were desperately seeking an acceptable path "to the decision that they wanted to reach." The justices' own head counts are dismissed as "seriously overstated." This interpretation, to its credit, more easily explains the unanimity of *Brown*. Its principal deficiencies are its strained reading of the conference notes and its dismissal of the justices' own head counts.[16]

Brown's unanimity does not disprove that deep divisions initially existed among the justices. Once a majority had agreed to invalidate segregation, potential dissenters faced strong pressures to conform. Yet, in December

1952, that majority had not yet materialized; only four justices had firmly indicated their willingness to overturn *Plessy*. Then, in September 1953, Vinson died suddenly. Frankfurter recorded his death as "the first indication I have ever had that there is a God." Eisenhower replaced Vinson with Earl Warren, the governor of California, to whom he had felt politically indebted since the 1952 Republican convention. Eisenhower did not appoint Warren to influence the outcome of *Brown*. Apparently, he briefly considered appointing instead John W. Davis, the lawyer who had defended segregation for South Carolina in the Supreme Court.[17]

Brown was reargued in December 1953. Warren opened the conference following the argument by proposing another informal discussion without a vote. On the merits, he declared that the "separate but equal doctrine rests on [the] basic premise that the Negro race is inferior. That is [the] only way to sustain *Plessy*." Yet the "argument of Negro counsel proves they are not inferior." He continued: "[W]e can't set one group apart from the rest of us and say they are not entitled to [the] same treatment as all others. [The] 13th, 14th and 15th Amendments were intended to make equal those who once were slaves." Acknowledging that this view "causes trouble perhaps," Warren could not "see how segregation can be justified in this day and age." Recognizing that the "time element is important in the deep south," Warren concluded, "we must act but we should do it in a tolerant way." Anyone counting heads—and all of the justices were—would have immediately recognized that the outcome in *Brown* was no longer in doubt. Warren, together with the four who had already indicated their support for overruling *Plessy*, made a majority. Many scholars have recognized Warren's role in securing unanimity in *Brown*, but few have identified the possibility that he may also have been instrumental to the outcome.[18]

With the result settled, two factors pushed toward unanimity. First, the justices appreciated that white southerners would receive *Brown* belligerently and perhaps violently. Resisters would be sure to exploit any hint of internal Court dissension. Justices who disagreed with the outcome thus felt pressure to suppress their convictions for the good of the institution. Warren and others persuaded Reed not to dissent, even though he remained convinced that *Brown* was wrong. Years earlier, Frankfurter had observed, "Reed was a soldier and glad to do anything that the interest of the Court might require." Three days after *Brown*, Frankfurter wrote to Reed to praise him for resolving the "hard struggle . . . involved in the conscience of your mind" in a manner that was conducive to the nation's "great good." Jackson left his hospital bed, where he was recovering from a heart attack, to be on the bench when *Brown* was announced, thus illustrating the importance that the justices attached to demonstrating their unanimity.[19]

A second factor may also have fostered unanimity. Let us recall that the more ambivalent justices, such as Frankfurter and Jackson, experienced *Brown* as a conflict between law and politics. They loathed segregation but doubted whether it was unconstitutional. After December 1953, they were irrelevant to the outcome, whereas a year earlier they had controlled it. Perhaps they could have endured a disjunction between their personal predilections and their constitutional views if it affected the outcome, but not for the sake of a dissent. If a majority was committed to invalidating segregation, they would acquiesce and suppress their legal doubts.

Though speculative, this interpretation draws support from the internal history of *Terry v. Adams* (1953), which was discussed in chapter 4. The issue there was whether the exclusion of blacks by the Jaybird Democratic Association qualified as "state action" under the Fourteenth or Fifteenth Amendments. The justices in *Terry* initially voted 5–4 to reject the constitutional challenge. Even after Frankfurter immediately switched sides, a closely divided decision seemed imminent. Vinson, Reed, Minton, and Jackson planned to dissent, and Jackson drafted an opinion that criticized the majority for sacrificing "sound principle[s] of interpretation." Yet when *Terry* came down, only Minton dissented. Apparently the other three prospective dissenters, once deprived of control over the outcome, were unwilling to subordinate their political preferences to their legal principles. Similar considerations may explain the unanimity in *Brown*.[20]

Brown was hard for justices who approached legal decision making as Frankfurter and Jackson did, because for them it posed a conflict between law and politics. The sources of constitutional interpretation that they usually invoked—text, original understanding, precedent, and custom—seemed to indicate that school segregation was permissible. The dearth of support in conventional legal sources for the position taken by the NAACP partially explains its reliance on controversial social science evidence, which led Jackson to contemptuously observe, "Marshall's brief starts and ends with sociology." By contrast, the personal values of these justices condemned segregation as "Hitler's creed." Their quandary was how to reconcile their legal and moral views.[21]

Frankfurter's self-identity as a judge required that he separate his personal views from the law. He preached that judges must decide cases on "the compulsions of governing legal principles," not "the idiosyncrasies of a merely personal judgment." In a memorandum he wrote with regard to the first flag-salute case, Frankfurter noted, "No duty of judges is more important nor more difficult to discharge than that of guarding against reading their personal and debatable opinions into the case." In another case, he declined to invalidate a death sentence, despite his personal opposition to capital punishment, because of "the disciplined thinking of a lifetime regarding the duty of this Court." Frankfurter scorned a former colleague, Frank Murphy— "Dear God," he called him—for his commitment to doing the right thing regardless of the law. Frankfurter was so averse to judges reading their personal values into the Constitution that he once favored treating the Due Process Clause "as raising 'political questions' . . . unfitted for the adjudicatory process," because its language was so "vague" and "open to subjective interpretation."[22]

Frankfurter undoubtedly abhorred racial segregation. More than that of any other justice, his personal behavior evinced egalitarian commitments. In the 1930s, he had served on the NAACP's National Legal Committee, and in 1948, he had hired the Court's first black law clerk, William Coleman. Yet in a memorandum he wrote while *Brown* was pending, Frankfurter insisted that his personal views on segregation were of limited relevance to the constitutional question:

> However passionately any of us may hold egalitarian views, however fiercely any of us may believe that such a policy of segregation as undoubtedly expresses the tenacious conviction of Southern States is both unjust and shortsighted[, h]e travels outside his judicial authority if for this private reason alone he declares unconstitutional the policy of segregation.

The Court could invalidate segregation, Frankfurter believed, only if it were legally as well as morally objectionable.[23]

Yet Frankfurter had difficulty finding a legal argument for striking down segregation that convinced him. His law clerk, Alexander Bickel, spent a summer reading the legislative history of the Fourteenth Amendment, and he reported to Frankfurter that "it is impossible to conclude that the 39th Congress intended that segregation be abolished; impossible also to conclude that they foresaw it might be, under the language they were adopting." Frankfurter was no doctrinaire originalist; he believed that the meaning of constitutional concepts changes over time. But this did not mean that judges were free to simply write their own moral views into the Constitution. In the early 1950s, twenty-one states and the District of Columbia still had mandatory or optional school segregation. Thus, Frankfurter could hardly maintain that "evolving standards of social decency" condemned segregation. Precedent strongly supported it. Of forty-four challenges to school segregation adjudicated by state appellate courts and lower federal courts between 1865 and 1935, not a single one had succeeded. Frankfurter ordinarily celebrated stare decisis, calling it "the most influential factor in giving a society coherence and continuity." He had recently reiterated that, although stare decisis had less force in constitutional law than elsewhere, he still "pause[d] long before overruling a prior line of constitutional adjudication." At conference, Frankfurter conceded that, based on legislative history and precedent, "*Plessy* is right."[24]

Brown presented a similar dilemma for Jackson. He too found segregation anathema. In a 1950 letter, Jackson, who had left the Court for a year in 1945–1946 to prosecute Nazis at Nuremberg, wrote to a law professor friend: "You and I have seen the terrible consequences of racial hatred in Germany. We can have no sympathy with racial conceits which underlie segregation policies." Yet, like Frankfurter, Jackson thought that judges were obliged to separate their personal views from the law, and he disfavored the frequent overruling of precedents.[25]

Jackson revealed his internal struggles in a draft concurring opinion which began: "Decision of these cases would be simple if our personal opinion that school segregation is morally, economically or politically indefensible made it legally so." But Jackson believed that judges must subordinate their personal preferences to the law, so this consideration was irrelevant. When he turned to the question of whether "existing law condemn[s] segregation," he had difficulty answering in the affirmative:

> Layman as well as lawyer must query how it is that the Constitution this morning forbids what for three-quarters of a century it has tolerated or approved. He must further speculate as to how [we can justify] this reversal of its meaning by the branch of the Government supposed not to make new law but only to declare existing law and which has exactly the same constitutional materials that so far as the states are concerned have existed since 1868 and in the case of the District of Columbia since 1791. Can we honestly say that the states which have maintained segregated schools have not, until today, been justified in understanding their practice to be constitutional?[26]

Jackson's constitutional analysis began with the text. As the Due Process Clause of the Fifth Amendment had been interpreted to permit (indeed, to protect) slavery, how could the identical provision in the Fourteenth Amendment be sensibly construed to bar segregation? Jackson concluded, "[T]here is no explicit prohibition of segregated schools and it can only be supplied by interpretation." Regarding the legislative history of the Fourteenth Amendment, Jackson observed that among the amendment's supporters

> may be found a few who hoped that it would bring about complete social equality and early assimilation of the liberated Negro into an amalgamated population. But I am unable to find any indication that their support was decision, and certainly their view had no support from the great Emancipator himself.

He summed up the legislative history: "It is hard to find an indication that any influential body of the movement that carried the Civil War Amendments had reached the point of thinking about either segregation or education of the Negro as a current problem, and harder still to find that the amendments were designed to be a solution."[27]

Turning from words to deeds, Jackson could "find nothing to show that the Congress which submitted these Amendments understood or intended to prohibit the practice here in question." The same Congress that passed the Fourteenth Amendment and every Congress since had supported school segregation in the District of Columbia. In the late 1860s, Congress had required southern states to ratify the Fourteenth Amendment as a condition of regaining their congressional representation, but it had never intimated that school segregation violated that condition of readmission. Jackson thought that the behavior of states ratifying the amendment was "equally impossible to reconcile with any understanding that the Amendment would prohibit segregation in schools." Eleven northern and border states ratifying the amendment had segregated schools, as did all of the reconstructed southern states. As to precedent, northern state courts, as well as a Supreme Court dominated by northerners, had concluded that the Fourteenth Amendment did not prohibit segregation: "Almost a century of decisional law rendered by judges, many of whom risked their lives for the cause that produced these Amendments, is almost unanimous in the view that the Amendment tolerated segregation by state action." Having canvassed the legal sources that he considered most relevant to constitutional interpretation—text, original intent, and precedent—Jackson concluded:

> Convenient as it would be to reach an opposite conclusion, I simply cannot find in the conventional material of constitutional interpretation any justification for saying that in maintaining segregated schools any state or the District of Columbia can be judicially decreed, up to the date of this decision, to have violated the Fourteenth Amendment.[28]

Jackson's draft opinion candidly admitted his difficulty in legally justifying a judicial ban on school segregation—a bit too candidly, in the estimation of his law clerk, E. Barrett Prettyman. Prettyman's memorandum responding to Jackson's draft noted that the nation must believe that *Brown* was "honestly arrived at, confidently espoused, and basically sound." If the country could "be made to feel . . . that it is a decision based upon *law*," then segregation "should die in relatively short order, no matter how many legal skirmishes ensue. On the other hand, if the country feels that a bunch of liberals in Washington has finally foisted off their social views on the public, it will not only tolerate but aid circumvention of the decision." Prettyman thought that Jackson's opinion should begin not with doubts and fears, but with a clear statement of his legal position. Yet Jackson's rationale for invalidating segregation occupied just two pages near the end of a twenty-three-page opinion, and it read as if it were "almost an afterthought." Prettyman advised that Jackson not "write as if you were ashamed to reach [this result]." He nicely captured Jackson's dilemma: The justice was, in a sense, "ashamed" of the result he reached. Jackson admitted to his colleagues his difficulty in "mak[ing] a judicial basis for a congenial political conclusion." Unable to "justify the abolition of segregation as a judicial act," he agreed to "go along with it" as "a political decision." Frankfurter did, too, but he was less candid about what he was doing.[29]

Jackson hesitated to invalidate segregation for another reason as well. He had become skeptical of judicial supremacy, not only because he thought it was inconsistent with democracy, but also because he feared that courts were bad at it. Jackson worried that unenforceable judicial decrees bred public cynicism about courts. In a posthumously published book, he wrote: "When the Court has gone too far, it has provoked reactions which have set back the cause it was designed to advance, and has sometimes called down upon itself severe rebuke." In 1954, Jackson wondered if the Court was up to the task of transforming southern race relations. His draft opinion asked why separate but equal has "remained a dead letter as to its equality aspect?" His answer was that the doctrine had been "declared and supported heartily only by the judicial department which has no power to enforce its own decrees." Blacks had to sue to enforce equality. But "[t]his was costly, it was time consuming and it was impossible for a disadvantaged people to accomplish on any broad scale." A judicial ban on segregation would be even harder to implement. Litigants would quickly discover "that devices of delay are numerous and often successful," especially as enforcement would require coercing "not merely individuals but the public itself." Because a ruling against one school district would not bind any other, every instance of recalcitrance would necessitate separate litigation. Individual blacks would bear this burden, as the Justice Department was unlikely to sue, and even if it wished to, Congress would probably not appropriate the necessary funds. Jackson preferred legislative action to judicial, not from "a mere desire to pass responsibility to others," but because it went "to the effectiveness of the remedy and to the use to be made of the judicial process over the next generation." As we shall see, Jackson's colleagues shared his concern that issuing unenforceable orders would damage the Court.[30]

Other justices shared Jackson's anxiety about invalidating a practice that was apparently sanctioned by traditional sources of constitutional interpretation. Clark conceded that he "always [had] thought that the 14th amendment covered the matter and outlawed segregation. But the history shows different." Vinson, like Jackson, observed that the same congressmen who passed the Fourteenth Amendment approved segregation in the District of Columbia's schools. Several justices worried about overruling an unbroken line of precedent that dated back to the 1860s. Clark thought that the Court had "led the states on to think segregation is OK," and even Black confessed that perhaps "the long line of decisions bars [the antisegregation] construction of the amendment."[31]

It is not surprising that the nine justices who were sitting in 1952—even those who drew the law/politics line differently than Frankfurter and Jackson did or who were less committed to maintaining any such distinction—would be uneasy about invalidating segregation. All of them were appointed by Presidents Roosevelt and Truman on the assumption that they supported, as Jackson put it, "the doctrine on which the Roosevelt fight against the old court was based—in part, that it had expanded the Fourteenth Amendment to take an unjustified judicial control over social and economic affairs." Or, as Black stated, Roosevelt had appointed him because "I was against using due process to force the views of judges on the country." For most of their professional lives, these men had criticized untethered judicial activism as undemocratic—the invalidation of the popular will by unelected officeholders who were inscribing their social and economic biases on the Constitution. This is how all nine of them understood the *Lochner* era, when the

Court had invalidated minimum wage, maximum hour, and protective labor legislation on a thin constitutional basis. The question in *Brown*, as Jackson's law clerk William H. Rehnquist noted, was whether invalidating school segregation would eliminate any distinction between this Court and the *Lochner*-era one, except for "the kinds of litigants it favors and the kinds of special claims it protects."[32]

Thus, several justices wondered if the Court was the right institution to forbid segregation. Several expressed views similar to Vinson's: If segregation was to be condemned, "it would be better if [Congress] would act." Even Black confessed that "[a]t first blush I would have said that it was up to Congress." In 1950, Jackson had observed that he "would support the constitutionality of almost any Congressional Act that prohibited segregation in education." Now he cautioned:

> However desirable it may be to abolish educational segregation, we cannot, with a proper sense of responsibility, ignore the question whether the use of judicial office to initiate law reforms that cannot get enough national public support to put them through Congress, is our own constitutional function. Certainly, policy decisions by the least democratic and the least representative of our branches of government are hard to justify.

"[I]f we have to decide the question," Jackson lamented, "then representative government has failed."[33]

In the end, even the most conflicted justices voted to invalidate segregation. How were they able to overcome their ambivalence? All judicial decision making involves elements of law and politics. Legal factors—text, original understanding, precedent, and custom—range along an axis from determinacy to indeterminacy. Political considerations—the judges' personal values, social mores, and external political pressure—array along a continuum from indifference to intense preference. When the law is clear, judges will generally follow it, unless they have very strong preferences to the contrary. When the law is relatively indeterminate, judges have no choice but to consult their own values and broader social mores. In *Brown*, the law—as understood by Frankfurter and Jackson—was reasonably clear: Segregation was constitutional. For justices to reject a result this clearly indicated by the legal sources suggests that they had very strong personal preferences to the contrary. Had they been more ambivalent about the morality of segregation, they might have followed the legal sources.

Why were these justices so repulsed by segregation at a time when national opinion was divided roughly down the middle? One possibility is fortuity: Integrationists just happened to dominate the Court in 1954. Had there been five Stanley Reeds, *Plessy* would probably have been reaffirmed. A more satisfying explanation emphasizes the systematic differences that exist between the justices and ordinary Americans. Two prominent ones are level of education and economic status. Justices are very well educated, having attended both college and law school—and often the most elite ones. (Jackson was a rare exception, having become a lawyer without attending law school.) They are also relatively wealthy. On many policy issues that become constitutional disputes, opinion correlates heavily with socioeconomic status, with elites tending to hold more liberal views on certain social issues, though not on economic ones. Early in the twenty-first century, such social issues include gay rights, abortion, and school prayer. In 1954, racial segregation was such an issue: 73 percent of college graduates approved of *Brown*, but only 45 percent of high school dropouts did so. Racial attitudes and practices were changing dramatically in postwar America. As members of the cultural elite, the justices were among the first to be influenced.[34]

As they deliberated over *Brown*, the justices expressed astonishment at the extent of the recent changes in racial attitudes and practices. Jackson treated such changes as constitutional justification for eliminating segregation. In his draft opinion, he wrote that segregation "has outlived whatever justification it may have had." Jackson noted, "Certainly in the 1860's and probably throughout the Nineteenth Century the Negro population as a whole was a different people than today. Lately freed from bondage, they had little opportunity as yet to show their capacity for education or even self-support and management." However, he continued, "Negro progress under segregation has been spectacular and, tested by the pace of history, his rise is one of the swiftest and most dramatic advances in the annals of man." This advance "has enabled him to outgrow the system and to overcome the presumptions on which it was based." Black progress had been sufficient for Jackson to conclude that race "no longer affords a reasonable basis for a classification for educational purposes."[35]

Other justices made similar observations. Frankfurter noted "the great changes in the relations between white and colored people since the first World War," and he remarked that "the pace of progress has surprised even those most eager in its promotion." Burton recorded the encouraging trend toward desegregation in restaurants and the armed forces, and Minton detected "a different world today." Southern justices were no less cognizant of change, though they were more inclined to treat it as a justification for staying their hand. Clark noted "much progress" in voting and education. Even Reed recorded the "constant progress in this field [public schooling] and in the advancement of the interests of the negros," and he observed that "segregation is gradually disappearing."[36]

The attitudes of the justices' law clerks may be the strongest evidence of this culturally elite bias favoring desegregation. With polls revealing a nation split down the middle, the clerks almost unanimously favored judicial invalidation of segregation, notwithstanding any difficulties in the legal justification for such a result. Of the fifteen to twenty young men clerking during the 1952 term, only Rehnquist seems to have favored reaffirming *Plessy*. Even those clerking for southern justices, some of whom had grown up with segregation, favored overturning it. Reed reported that he stopped discussing the issue with his clerks because they were so adamant that *Plessy* be overruled. By the 1950s, most highly educated, relatively privileged young adults—even those from the South—apparently had difficulty sympathizing with segregation.[37]

The justices did not possess the antisegregation youth bias of their clerks, but they did share the socioeconomic bias. Could Reed, who thought that segregation was constitutionally permissible and morally defensible, have been persuaded to join *Brown* had his culturally elite status not diminished the intensity of his segregationist sentiment? Even he had conceded that "of course" there was no "inferior race," though perhaps blacks had been "handicapped by lack of opportunity." It speaks volumes that an upper-crust Kentuckian who had spent much of his adult life in the nation's capital would have said such a thing. Most white southerners—less well educated, less affluent, and less exposed to the nation's cultural elite—would have demurred.[38]

The culturally elite biases of the justices increased the likelihood that they would invalidate segregation before national opinion had turned against it. Yet the potential gap between the attitudes of the justices and those of the public is limited; the justices are part of the larger culture and inhabit the same historical moment. As little as ten years before *Brown*, racial attitudes in the nation had probably not changed enough for even a culturally elite institution such as the Court to condemn segregation. The NAACP was wise not to push school desegregation challenges before 1950, as the justices would probably have rejected them. Frankfurter later noted that he would have voted to sustain school segregation in the 1940s, because "public opinion had not then crystallized against it."[39]

By the early 1950s, powerful political, economic, social, and ideological forces for progressive racial change had made judicial invalidation of segregation conceivable. Slightly more than half of the nation supported *Brown* from the day it was decided. Thus, *Brown* is not an example of the Court's resistance to majoritarian sentiment, but rather of its conversion of an emerging national consensus into a constitutional command. By 1954, the long-term trend against Jim Crow was clear. Justices observed that segregation was "gradually disappearing" and that it was "marked for early extinction." They understood that *Brown* was working with, not against, the current of history.[40]

Given the long-term trends in race relations and the Court's traditional constitutional role, perhaps it was inevitable that the justices would eventually invalidate school segregation. Jackson predicted, "Whatever we might say today, within a generation [segregation] will be outlawed by decision of this Court because of the forces of mortality and replacement, which operate upon it." If Reed was right that segregation would disappear in the border states within fifteen or twenty years even without judicial intervention, then the propensity of constitutional law to suppress isolated practices might have ensured an eventual ruling against segregation. A subsequent generation of justices, who probably would have found segregation even more abhorrent than their predecessors had, would have been sorely tempted to apply an ascendant national norm against segregation to shrinking numbers of hold-out states.[41]

But *Brown* was not inevitable in 1954, when seventeen states and the District of Columbia still segregated their schools and four more states permitted local communities to adopt segregation at their discretion ("local option"). *Brown* did not simply bring into line a few renegade states. Reed, who conceded that the Constitution's meaning was "not fixed," thought that the Court could invalidate an established practice only when the "body of people" had deemed it unconstitutional, which could not plausibly be said about school segregation in 1954. Lower courts were not blazing new trails on this issue, as they often do before the high court's momentous constitutional rulings. Prior to *Brown*, only a single California federal judge had repudiated the voluminous body of precedent that sanctioned separate but equal. As we have seen, significant legal hurdles confronted those justices who were personally inclined to invalidate segregation. The Court might easily have written an opinion that echoed John W. Davis's oral argument: "[S]omewhere, sometime, to every principle comes a moment of repose when it has been so often announced, so confidently relied upon, so long continued, that it passes the limits of judicial discretion and disturbance."[42]

Moreover, the probable consequences of invalidating segregation weighed heavily on the justices. The Court had never done anything like this before. Frankfurter observed that although individuals had brought these cases, the justices were effectively being asked "to transform state-wide school systems in nearly a score of States." He cautioned that a "declaration of unconstitutionality is not a wand by which these transformations can be accomplished." Jackson similarly noted that individual lawsuits were "a weak reed to rely on in initiating a change in the social system of a large part of the United States." Several justices worried that issuing unenforceable orders might "bring the court into contempt and the judicial process into discredit." Invalidating segregation would probably also produce violence and school closures. Vinson cautioned, "We can't close our eyes to [the] problem in various parts of [the] country. . . . When you force the complete abolition of public schools in some areas then it is most serious."[43]

In the early 1950s, several southern states were undertaking crash equalization programs that promised rapid redress of educational inequalities in black schools. Some justices were tempted to see if southern statesmen, such as their friend and former colleague Jimmy Byrnes, who had recently been elected governor of South Carolina, could deliver on such promises. Vinson observed that in Clarendon County, South Carolina, "you have equal facilities. [But it] took some time to make them equal." Reed pleaded with his colleagues to stay their hand, as "10 years would make [black schools] really

FIGURE 6.2
Left to right: George E. C. Hayes, Thurgood Marshall, and
James Nabrit, Jr., outside the Supreme Court on May 17, 1954,
after their victory in *Brown v. Board of Education*.
(*Bettmann*/CORBIS)

equal." Many southern white moderates likewise urged the Court to give
equalization a chance, while warning that invalidating school segregation
would jeopardize racial progress in the South.[44]

The justices were not oblivious to these arguments against invalidating
segregation. In December 1952, there was no secure majority yet for overruling *Plessy*. *Brown* was not inevitable in 1954. Roy Wilkins of the NAACP was
wise to prepare two different press releases as he awaited the ruling. The association could not be certain that it would win its case.[45]

BROWN II

The Court invalidated school segregation on May 17, 1954, but it ordered no
immediate remedy and deferred reargument on that issue until the following
term. Jackson's death in October, followed by delays over the confirmation of

his replacement, John M. Harlan (the grandson and namesake of the *Plessy* dissenter), postponed the reargument until April 1955.[46]

The justices confronted several issues with regard to the remedy in *Brown*. First, as to timing, should they order immediate desegregation or allow a gradual transition? Relatedly, should they impose a deadline for beginning and/or completing desegregation? Second, how detailed should the remedial decree be? The Court could dictate specifics about the desegregation process, remand to district courts to formulate decrees, or appoint a special master to take evidence and propose orders. Third, the Court could treat the lawsuits as class actions or limit relief to the named plaintiffs.

The justices chose vagueness and gradualism. They remanded the cases to district courts to issue decrees in accordance with "local conditions" while keeping in mind the "flexibility" of traditional "equitable principles." They required a "prompt and reasonable start toward full compliance," with additional time allowed if "consistent with good faith compliance at the earliest practicable date." District courts were to order the admission of "parties to these cases" to public schools on a nondiscriminatory basis "with all deliberate speed."[47]

The NAACP had pressed for immediate desegregation, with a completion deadline of the fall of 1956, which it called "generous in the extreme." Immediatists warned that gradualism would encourage resistance and that "the best way to integrate is to do it." The one law clerk who favored immediate relief emphasized "the extreme injustice of condemning half a generation of Negro school children to a segregated system," and he warned that delay "would greatly weaken the court's moral position." Yet the justices never seriously considered ordering immediate integration. Although Warren and Black stated at the outset of the *Brown II* conference that they had no "definite opinion" or "fixed views," in fact all of the justices had already decided in favor of gradualism and flexibility. Several considerations inclined them in this direction.[48]

Several justices noted that unanimity was "vital" and that it must be achieved if "humanly possible." In addition to the reasons that impelled unanimity in *Brown I*, the justices now had to provide clear guidance to district judges. The consensus behind unanimity ensured that the remedy would be flexible and gradualist. Vagueness cloaked differences of opinion. More important, several justices had insisted on gradualism as their price for voting to invalidate segregation in *Brown I*. The federal government had suggested this compromise between immediate desegregation and reaffirmation of *Plessy*, and it apparently worked. Jackson said that he would invalidate segregation but "won't be a party to immediate unconstitutionality," and Clark said that he would "go along" if the opinion "g[a]ve lower courts the right to withhold relief in light of troubles." Thus, an informal deal had enabled the Court to be unanimous in *Brown I*. The more ambivalent justices supported the result in exchange for a gradualist remedy. Yet even the less conflicted justices—Black, Douglas, and Burton—agreed to "give plenty of time" and to "put off enforcement awhile." Immediate desegregation was never in the cards if these justices did not favor it.[49]

Another factor in favor of gradualism was the perceived importance of avoiding unenforceable orders. Justice Black declared that "nothing could injure the court more than to issue orders that cannot be enforced," while Minton urged that the Court not "reveal its own weakness" with a "futile" decree. The unlikelihood that Congress would legislate in support of school desegregation heightened the justices' concern about issuing futile orders. President Eisenhower and the Justice Department were publicly backing gradualism. The more specific and immediate the relief ordered, the greater the chances of defiance. Vague commands are notoriously difficult to defy, because their meaning is so elusive.[50]

Were the justices valuing the Court's prestige—its dignity interest in avoiding the issuance of futile orders—over the plaintiffs' constitutional rights? Generally, once judges declare rights to exist, they immediately enforce them. The Court had previously followed this principle in other civil rights cases, such as *Sweatt v. Painter*. Departing from it troubled Vinson in *Brown I*, but he distinguished desegregation of grade schools from that of universities on the ground that the "problem [was] more serious when you have large numbers." Even those who found the legal argument for immediate enforcement "compelling" conceded that it was not "very practical, especially in the South Carolina and Virginia cases." Invoking precedents from the law of nuisance and antitrust, as well as the "practical flexibility" of equity, *Brown II* ruled that "the personal interest of the plaintiffs in admission to public schools . . . on a nondiscriminatory basis" had to be balanced against "the public interest" in desegregating "in a systematic and effective manner."[51]

The justices feared that immediate desegregation would cause violence and school closures. White southerners campaigned to convince them of this. Voters in South Carolina, Georgia, and Mississippi had sent messages by adopting constitutional amendments that authorized legislatures to end public education in response to court-ordered desegregation. In 1954–1955, Prince Edward County's board of supervisors refused to appropriate funds for public education—another warning to the justices. Public officials in Deep South states declined the Court's invitation to file amicus briefs in *Brown II*, thus signaling their intention not to be legally or morally bound by the decision, and they warned of the dire consequences of immediate desegregation. Those southern states that did participate in the *Brown II* argument likewise predicted that immediate desegregation would jeopardize public education and cause "prolonged social disorder." North Carolina's brief reported a poll of local police chiefs that found that 193 out of 199 predicted violence in response to immediate integration. Even southern racial moderates, whose advice the justices most valued, were publicly urging gradualism to reduce the risk of violence. By the time *Brown II* was decided, violence was no longer simply an abstract possibility. In September 1954, hundreds of angry white parents in Milford, Delaware, forced the closing of a desegregated school and the abandonment of integration; the episode received national publicity. Such ferocious resistance in a border state did not bode well for desegregation in the Deep South.[52]

NAACP lawyers responded to such warnings of violence by noting that southern officials had predicted similar outbreaks as a result of the 1950 desegregation rulings, but none had occurred. The justices were unpersuaded. Black noted that the Deep South "would never be a party to allowing white and negro to go to school together" and that there is "no more chance to enforce this in [the] deep south than prohibition in N[ew] Y[ork] City"— statements that made a "deep impression" on some of his colleagues. Reed also thought that "our order may result in public schools being abolished." Frankfurter, who was in direct contact with his "warm friend" Jimmy Byrnes, conveyed news of "chaotic" conditions in South Carolina.[53]

Sympathy with the plight of white southerners also inclined the justices toward gradualism: They felt guilty about undermining the expectations of those who had assumed the legitimacy of separate but equal based on past Court rulings. For example, Jackson had wondered in *Brown I* if "we honestly [can] say that the states which have maintained segregated schools have not, until today, been justified in understanding their practice to be constitutional." Even Black had worried that "the long line of decisions" might prevent the Court from overturning segregation. If they were going to reject "an almost universal understanding that segregation is not constitutionally forbidden," then "consideration of that in framing the decree would be just."[54]

Several justices also thought that they could reduce the resistance of southern whites by appearing sympathetic and accommodating. Frankfurter especially believed that "how we do what we do in the Segregation cases may be as important as what we do." He emphasized the "largely educational" effect of Court opinions and cautioned against their being "self-righteous." In *Brown I*, Warren had similarly urged that they act in a "tolerant way" and write a "non-accusatory" opinion. Jackson had warned that "it would retard acceptance of [*Brown I*] if the Northern majority of this Court should make a Pharisaic and self-righteous approach to this issue." On this subject, the justices' thinking mirrored that of President Eisenhower, who intervened in the brief writing in *Brown II* to urge that the feelings of white southerners be "met with understanding and good will."[55]

Some justices believed that accommodating the concerns of southern whites through a gradualist remedy might induce moderates to support *Brown*. Their law clerks almost unanimously thought so. Gradualism "would indicate to the South that the Court understands and is sympathetic to the problems which the decision raises in their states" and that it was "not trying to jam a new social order down their throats." By contrast, a "meat-ax decree ordering immediate integration" would be like "castor oil . . . forced on a child" and would probably produce "both confusion and lasting resentment." Frankfurter emphasized "the need to encourage moderate leadership," which might come especially from southern lawyers, many of whom he had taught at the Harvard Law School. Several clerks warned that a "clearly arbitrary and unreasonable" decree would probably be "ignored by almost all elements in the South." They urged the justices to heed the view of southern moderates, such as newspaper editors Harry Ashmore and Hodding Carter, who predicted that the immediate desegregation of schools would be disastrous.[56]

Among the justices, only Black seemed to appreciate that white southerners were "going to fight this" no matter what the Court said and thus "we can't undertake to settle the problem." Yet Black, too, endorsed a form of gradualism for fear of the Court's issuing a futile order. He and Douglas favored immediate integration but only for the named plaintiffs. They would refuse to treat the lawsuits as class actions and hope that few additional blacks would sue. Black was "not fond of class suits," nor was he "sure how many students would want their names in this litigation." If only "5 or 10" were admitted, most problems would "disappear." Though the other justices thought that these suits were obviously class actions and a draft order treated them as such, *Brown II* ultimately required the admission only of "parties to these cases." Reed apparently had persuaded a majority that "[t]hese are class suits but nothing should be said about it in the decree."[57]

Finally, racism may partially explain the gradualism of *Brown II*. The justices seemed to empathize more with white southerners, "who are to be coerced out of [segregation]," than with blacks, "who are coerced into [it]." How else can one explain Jackson's view that immediate enforcement of blacks' constitutional rights was "needlessly ruthless"? Furthermore, some justices paternalistically dismissed the NAACP's plea for immediate desegregation, because "only a reasonably considerate decree would be an expedient one for the persons it has sought to benefit." Lastly, not all of the justices were convinced that segregation could be casually dismissed as "Hitler's creed." Reed noted a "reasonable body of opinion" in support of segregation, and Jackson did not "deny the sincerity and passion with which many feel that their blood, lineage and culture are worthy of protection by enforced separatism of races." The justices decided *Brown* as a new epoch in U.S. race relations was dawning; it is hardly surprising that remnants of the preceding, less-egalitarian era would still infect their thinking.[58]

Whether the relief granted should be immediate or gradual was not the only issue to be resolved in *Brown II*. The justices also had to decide whether to impose deadlines for beginning and/or completing desegregation, which might embolden district judges who faced local pressure for delay. (Deadlines and gradualism are not the same issue, as deadlines can be immediate or delayed.) The NAACP urged immediate integration or at least a deadline of September 1956. The Justice Department suggested that district judges require school boards to submit desegregation plans within ninety days, but it opposed completion deadlines. The justices rejected deadlines altogether.

Warren began the conference by repudiating them. Reed thought that the Court should "[f]ix no definite time," and Douglas "[w]ould not suggest a date." One argument against deadlines was that they would become an excuse for failing to act earlier. Another was that precision enabled defiance, which the justices desperately wished to avoid. Frankfurter worried that any deadline would be "arbitrary"—a judicial fiat—which would "tend to alienate instead of enlist favorable or educable local sentiment." The justices also believed that administrative problems genuinely justified some delay. Desegregation required the redrawing of district lines and school attendance zones, consolidating schools, reassigning teachers and administrative staff, arranging student transportation, redesigning local finances, improving the conditions of ramshackle black schools, and accommodating students' disparate achievement levels. Thus, the justices had plausible reasons for eschewing deadlines. Yet by requiring desegregation with "all deliberate speed" and compliance "at the earliest practicable date," they invited delay by recalcitrant school boards and district judges and provided inadequate political cover for those who were willing to comply in good faith.[59]

Another issue for the justices was how much guidance to provide district judges in formulating their decrees. The president and the Justice Department, sources that were likely to influence the justices, urged decentralization—that is, returning cases to district judges with limited guidance. District judges were better informed about "local difficulties and variations." Also, they would not "be thought of as carpetbaggers." Their rulings would appear less "the mere imposition of a distant will"—a potentially significant benefit, given the traditional aversion of white southerners to outside dictation. Finally, the justices disapproved of federal courts—Supreme or otherwise—"operating as a super–school board." To the extent possible, elected officials and education experts should continue to assign students. A Burton clerk stated the prevalent view: "[W]e should not lose sight of the fact that this Court is a member of the judicial branch of the government."[60]

The justices were not completely naive. They understood that district judges would face enormous pressure to postpone and minimize desegregation. Justice Black noted that district courts would be "in the firing line," as states "took evasive measures while purporting to obey." Warren thought that to "let them flounder" without guidance would be "rather cruel." Frankfurter conceded that decentralizing the desegregation process "would unload responsibility upon lower courts most subject to community pressures without any guidance for them except our decision of unconstitutionality." This might result in "drawn-out, indefinite delay without even colorable compliance." If the Court gave them "something to rely on, they [could] better resist undesirable local pressures" by "point[ing] to a superior authority in undertaking what [would] often be unpopular action."[61]

Yet the justices disagreed over how much guidance to provide. Black doubted the need for any opinion to accompany the decree: "[T]he less we say the better off we are," because as "[t]here will be deliberate effort[s] to circumvent the decree, [i]t becomes desirable to write as narrowly as possible." Minton agreed, but the others felt obliged to offer lower courts some guidance. Yet none of them was prepared to impose the detailed rules that would have been necessary to constrain evasion or to insulate district judges from local pressure. Frankfurter wanted the impossible—an opinion that had "enough 'give' to leave room for variant local problems" but was not so "loose [as] to invite evasion." Warren, too, wished to give district courts "as much latitude as we can, but also as much support." These goals were irreconcilable.[62]

The justices ultimately adopted loose phraseology that could neither constrain evasion nor bolster compliance—"good faith" implementation, an order to begin "as soon as practicable," desegregation with "all deliberate speed." They said nothing about the permissibility of a wide array of desegregation policies that could be used to circumvent *Brown*: freedom-of-choice plans, which allowed parents to choose among several schools; pupil placement schemes, which assigned students to schools based on a long list of ostensibly race-neutral criteria; transfer options, which permitted parents to move their children out of desegregated schools; and grade-a-year plans, which started desegregation in the first or twelfth grade and then expanded it to one additional grade every year. The justices were aware of all of these issues, but they chose to allow the district courts to "carry the ball." Moreover, they did not take seriously the one reasonably clear instruction they did provide—that community disagreement with the constitutional principles announced by the Court could not justify delay. The justices thought that district courts *should* consider local resistance in determining the timing of desegregation, but they worried that saying so would "put a premium upon lawlessness." Justice Black thought that "attitudes should not be mentioned in [the] decree but they cannot be ignored." Frankfurter stated, "[The a]ttitude of the south is a fact to be taken into consideration as much as administrative difficulty." Can the justices have believed that district judges would take the instruction to ignore community sentiment more seriously than they took it themselves? Jackson had warned early in 1954, "I will not be a party to . . . casting upon the lower courts a burden of continued litigation under circumstances which subject district judges to local pressures and provide them with no standards to justify their decisions to their neighbors, whose opinions they must resist." With Jackson dead in 1955, his colleagues did just that.[63]

Brown II was a solid victory for white southerners. Although they did not convince the Court to repudiate *Brown I* or to explicitly authorize district judges to delay desegregation based on hostile community sentiment, they won on every other issue. The Court approved gradualism, imposed no deadlines for beginning or completing desegregation, issued vague guidelines, and entrusted (southern) district judges with broad discretion. Southern politicians lauded *Brown II* as a "very definite victory for the South," and newspapers called it "a distinct triumph for the southern viewpoint." Florida legislators broke into cheers when told of the decision. White reaction in Alabama was reported to be "restrained rejoicing." A Louisiana legislator declared, "It was the mildest decree the Supreme Court possibly could have handed down." A Mississippi politician celebrated the fact that a native Mississippi judge would determine what was "as soon as feasible." Other white southerners received the news with "an air of relief": Apparently the Court did not really intend to foist integration on them any time soon. Southern legislators opined that desegregation might be "feasible" in another fifty or one hundred years.[64]

Black leaders were disappointed with the decision, though they generally tried not to show it. One emphasized the "prompt and reasonable" start toward desegregation that the Court had required. Another rationalized that a fixed deadline would only have excused delay. A third opined that the Court had given "even the most recalcitrant southern states an honorable way to conform to the decision." The NAACP implausibly claimed to be "gratified" by the Court's "clear-cut determination" that blacks were to have their rights to nonsegregated education "'as soon as practicable.'" But some blacks could not hide their disappointment. An NAACP officer in Mississippi lamented, "It looks like the Supreme Court doesn't believe in our constitution." One prominent black journalist, James L. Hicks, noted that he was "deeply disappointed" and could not "fool [him]self into believing that we have won a great victory." Another black newspaperman, John H. McCray, admitted that he "can't find too much to cheer about in [the decision]," and he criticized the Court for "seek[ing] to do business" with diehard southern segregationists.[65]

The justices had conceived of gradualism partly as a peace offering to white southerners—an invitation to moderates to meet them halfway. Some southern politicians understood this, observing that the Court had "intended to appeal to the states to help work out this problem," "to correct an obnoxious decision," and to fix its "mistake." Many applauded the justices for their "moderate and reasonable" decision, which was "something to be thankful for," and they lauded the "lenien[t]" tone of Brown II. The Norfolk Virginian-Pilot called the ruling "a superb appeal to the wisdom, intelligence, and leadership of the Southern States." The Tampa Tribune predicted that it "will dissipate the thunderhead of turmoil and violence which had been gathering in Southern skies since the court held school segregation unconstitutional." Several legislatures suspended their consideration of bills to block desegregation, and other states canceled plans for special legislative sessions.[66]

Yet the same people who acknowledged the Court's conciliatory gesture often emphasized their undiminished commitment to preserving segregation. Others put a different spin on Brown II, perceiving it as weakness or "backtrack[ing]." A Florida segregationist thought the Court had "realized it made a mistake in May and is getting out of it the best way it can." A Texas legislator declared that the "Court got hold of a hot potato and didn't know what to do with it." A Virginia politician announced that "the court has not the courage of its previously avowed convictions." Some southern observers believed that the threats of school closures and violence had intimidated the justices, and they deduced that further pressure might persuade the Court to abandon *Brown* altogether. Over the following months, some white southerners predicted that patient determination on their part would convince the Court and the nation to abandon southern blacks as they had during Reconstruction.[67]

That *Brown II* was a mistake from the Court's perspective was quickly apparent. The justices' conciliatory gesture inspired defiance, not accommodation. Within months, public officials and private organizations were declaring their unmitigated opposition to desegregation. New organizations called "citizens' councils" were formed, and they endorsed all methods short of violence to preserve white supremacy. Several legislatures passed "interposition" resolutions, denouncing *Brown* as an "illegal encroachment" and declaring it "null, void and of no effect." Early in 1956, most southern congressmen signed the Southern Manifesto, which condemned *Brown* as "a clear abuse of judicial power" and pledged the South to all "lawful means" of resistance.[68]

To say that *Brown II* was misguided is not to say that the justices calculated foolishly. They operated without the aid of historical hindsight, and their prediction that conciliation on their part would strengthen southern moderates and encourage compliance was plausible. The mostly restrained southern reaction to *Brown I* and the early steps taken toward compliance in the border states may have induced the justices to underestimate the commitment of white southerners to preserving school segregation. Forecasts by contemporary commentators that *Brown II* would bolster moderates confirms that the justices' thinking was not implausible, simply wrong. Instead, the decision seems to have encouraged defiance and undermined those moderates who were already taking preliminary steps toward desegregation. In retrospect, the justices should have been firm and imposed deadlines and specific desegregation requirements. As Burton's law clerk pointed out, "A firm forceful policy . . . impresses people with the fact that you mean what you say." Yet in May 1955, correctly anticipating little support from the political branches and overestimating their ability to manage southern resistance, the justices opted for conciliatory vagueness.[69]

Did their miscalculation matter much? Probably not. For reasons explored in the next chapter, certain features of southern politics and the political dynamics of the segregation issue virtually ensured massive resistance. *Brown II*, by instilling hope among white southerners that *Brown I* could be overturned, did not help. But even an order for immediate integration would have been bitterly resisted. Most white southerners would oppose desegregation until they were convinced that resistance was futile and costly. The Court was powerless to make that showing on its own.[70]

The justices backed off after *Brown II*. With the notable exception of the Little Rock case, they distanced themselves from school desegregation for the next eight years. Their eagerness to avoid further racial controversy was quickly apparent. In 1955–1956, the Court faced challenges to state-mandated segregation outside of education: public beaches, golf courses, and local transportation. In barring school segregation, *Brown* had emphasized the importance of public education, rather than questioning the validity of all racial classifications. Thus, invalidating segregation in post-*Brown* cases seemed to require some further explanation. Yet the justices provided none; instead, they issued brief per curiam opinions that merely cited *Brown*. Those legal academics who were most committed to "reasoned elaboration" in judicial decision making were virtually apoplectic.[71]

In 1955–1956, the justices twice endured humiliation at the hands of southern state courts rather than further entangle themselves in racial controversy. First, they confronted a challenge to Virginia's antimiscegenation law. A Chinese man and a white woman had tried to circumvent the law by marrying in North Carolina. After returning to Virginia, the woman later sought an annulment under the antimiscegenation law, which her husband challenged as unconstitutional. The trial court granted the annulment, and the Virginia Court of Appeals affirmed and sustained the statute.[72]

Naim v. Naim was the last case the justices wished to see on their docket in 1955. Many southern whites had charged that the real goal of the NAACP's school desegregation campaign was "to open the bedroom doors of our white women to the Negro men" and "to mongrelize the white race." To strike down antimiscegenation laws so soon after *Brown* risked appearing to validate those suspicions. Moreover, opinion polls in the 1950s revealed that over 90 percent of whites, even outside the South, opposed interracial marriage. During oral arguments in one of the original school segregation cases, Frankfurter had seemed relieved when counsel denied that barring school segregation would necessarily invalidate antimiscegenation laws, as strong state interests could overcome even a presumptive ban on racial classifications. Frankfurter later explained that one reason *Brown* was written as it was—emphasizing the importance of public education rather than condemning all racial classifications—was to avoid the miscegenation issue. In 1954, Jackson's law clerk had noted the wisdom of not "hitting the South with so strong a punch at one time."[73]

The Court's problem was that *Naim v. Naim* seemed to fall within its mandatory jurisdiction. Today, the justices have almost complete discretion over their docket, but in the mid-1950s federal law still required them to grant appeals when state courts had rejected federal claims that were not "insubstantial." To say that antimiscegenation laws posed an insubstantial constitutional question would have been disingenuous. The importance was "obvious," law clerk William A. Norris told Justice Douglas, and "[f]ailure to decide the case would blur any distinction remaining between certiorari and appeal." Burton's clerk agreed that the Court could not honestly avoid the case, though he would have preferred to "give the present fire a chance to burn down." Both clerks underestimated the desperation and creativity of the justices. Though several of them wished to take jurisdiction, others searched for an escape route. Clark suggested one: The plaintiff should be estopped from invoking the miscegenation law because she knew of the defendant's race when they married and deliberately evaded the ban on interracial marriage. Burton suggested another: They could dismiss the case on the independent state ground that Virginia required residents to marry within the state—a plainly erroneous reading of Virginia law.[74]

Of all the justices, Frankfurter felt the gravest anxiety about the case. If this had been a certiorari petition, he would have rejected it, as "due consideration of important public consequences is relevant to the exercise of discretion in passing on such petitions." (Indeed, in 1954, the Court had denied certiorari in another southern miscegenation case.) But *Naim* was an appeal, and Frankfurter admitted that the challenge to antimiscegenation laws "cannot be rejected as frivolous." Still, the "moral considerations" for dismissing the appeal "far outweigh the technical considerations in noting jurisdiction." To thrust the miscegenation issue into "the vortex of the present disquietude" would risk "thwarting or seriously handicapping the enforcement of [*Brown*]." Frankfurter's proposed solution, which the justices adopted, was to remand the case to the Virginia Court of Appeals with instructions to return it to the trial court for further proceedings in order to clarify the parties' relationship to the commonwealth, which was said to be uncertain from the record; clarification might obviate the need to resolve the constitutional question. On remand, the Virginia jurists refused to comply with the Court's instructions; they denied that the record was unclear and that state law permitted returning final decisions to trial courts in order to gather additional evidence. Virginia newspapers treated the state court's response as an instance of nullification.[75]

The petitioner then filed a motion to recall the Court's mandate and to set the case for argument. Douglas's law clerk, Norris, now identified three options that were available. The Court could summarily vacate the state judgment to "punish" Virginia for its disobedience. Norris thought that this solution would be "intemperate and would unnecessarily increase the friction between this Court and the southern state courts." Second, the justices could circumvent the recalcitrant state high court and remand the case directly to the trial court. Finally, they could take the appeal, which would be a "tacit admission that the Court's original remand was unnecessary." Norris favored the last option and warned, "It will begin to look obvious if the case is not taken that the Court is trying to run away from its obligation to decide the case."[76]

Norris failed even to imagine the option chosen by a majority. Four justices—Warren, Black, Reed, and Douglas—voted to recall the Court's mandate and take the appeal. But the other five swallowed their collective pride and voted to dismiss the appeal on the ground that the Virginia court's response "leaves the case devoid of a properly presented federal question." A majority of the justices apparently preferred to be humiliated at the hands of truculent state jurists rather than to stoke further the fires of racial controversy. Once again, those academic commentators who were most committed to "reasoned elaboration" in judicial decision making criticized the Court for taking action that was "wholly without basis in the law."[77]

Georgia's turn to humiliate the justices came at about the same time. *Williams v. Georgia* (1955) raised an important question of federal courts doctrine: When does a state criminal defendant's failure to comply with state procedural rules, which leads the state court to refuse to consider his federal constitutional claim, constitute an "adequate and independent" state ground that bars Supreme Court review on the merits? Two years earlier, in *Avery v. Georgia*, the Court had overturned a black man's conviction because of possible race discrimination in jury selection. Jurors were supposed to be randomly selected by drawing tickets from a box, yet the names of whites were on tickets of a different color than those used for the names of blacks. *Avery* was decided by the justices after Williams's conviction, but the ruling of the state supreme court in *Avery*, which criticized the practice of differently colored tickets while declining to overturn Avery's conviction, had come down well before Williams's trial. Williams's lawyer, who was "guilty of almost criminal negligence," failed to raise the *Avery* challenge at trial or on the initial appeal, and the Georgia courts then ruled that the defendant had waived his right to have it considered.

Williams appealed his death sentence to the Supreme Court. Three justices—Warren, Black, and Douglas—voted to reverse his conviction outright: Georgia could not execute Williams based on the verdict of a jury that had been selected via obviously unconstitutional procedures simply because his lawyer had failed to object. To remand the case, Warren warned, was to invite the Georgia jurists to invent a different basis for denying Williams a new trial. The chief justice declared that he would not "have this man's life on my conscience" because of a "procedural dodge." Justice Black was likewise "afraid if [the case was] sent back it would be patched up," and Douglas "would not send it back for [Georgia] to take another crack." However, a majority did not support outright reversal. Harlan, who thought that "the aggravating facts of this case . . . call for our straining to vindicate the constitutional rights of the petitioner," suggested remanding the case to the Georgia court with a reminder that state law seemed to permit discretionary grants of new trials even after procedural defaults. Harlan believed that "on such remand there is some hope that the Georgia court would be constrained to reconsider its decision." Frankfurter said that he "would go beyond" Harlan's proposal and that he preferred to remand the case in a way that "would not give [Georgia] much room to stand pat." Frankfurter wrote the Court's opinion, observing that where state law grants courts discretion to order new trials in extraordinary cases, the Supreme Court had jurisdiction to ensure that that discretion was not exercised so as to frustrate constitutional rights. The Court declined to reverse outright, but it strongly hinted that it might do so if Georgia refused to order a new trial. The Court had jurisdiction, but it declined to exercise it—yet.[78]

On remand, the Georgia court declined to "supinely surrender [the] sovereign powers of this State," accused the Supreme Court of violating the Tenth Amendment by asserting jurisdiction in Williams, and reaffirmed its earlier ruling. The Georgia judges essentially told the justices "to go to hell." When Williams returned to the Court on a petition for certiorari in the winter of 1955–1956—the first ruling had been in June 1955—those justices who had previously favored outright reversal now reconsidered. Justice Black warned that challenging Georgia might precipitate a constitutional crisis. Nobody favored Frankfurter's suggestion that they at least respond to the insubordinate challenge made by the Georgia jurists to the Supreme Court's jurisdiction. All nine justices now voted to deny certiorari—and Georgia executed Williams shortly thereafter. The growing truculence of southern states over desegregation since Brown II must explain the justices' change of heart; they did not want to compound their desegregation difficulties by unnecessarily alienating southern courts. As in Brown II, the justices apparently discounted the possibility that by capitulating in Naim and Williams, they might encourage resistance by appearing craven rather than conciliatory.[79]

The justices also avoided further confrontation over school desegregation by denying full review in every case that was appealed until 1963, with the sole exception of the Little Rock case, Cooper v. Aaron (1958). Parties sought review in numerous cases—both where the lower court ruling was favorable to desegregation and where it was unfavorable—but the justices consistently denied it. They had apparently decided to say no more on the subject until they had received some signal of support from the political branches.[80]

That signal was not immediately forthcoming. President Eisenhower repeatedly refused to say whether he endorsed Brown. His duty, he insisted, was to enforce Court decisions, not to approve or disapprove of them. At Eisenhower's behest, the Republican party weakened its 1956 civil rights plank to "accept" rather than to "endorse" Brown, while it rejected forcible implementation. The president preached moderation and observed that Brown II had endorsed gradualism. Asked by reporters for a message to youngsters on desegregation, he repeated the mantra of southern whites that "it is difficult through law and through force to change a man's heart." Eisenhower urged that desegregation be resolved locally, and he denied a role for the federal government in "the ordinary normal case of keeping order and preventing rioting." The administration's failure in 1956 to enforce desegregation orders against local resistance in Clinton, Tennessee; Tuscaloosa,

Alabama; and Mansfield and Texarkana, Texas, encouraged similar violence elsewhere. Civil rights leaders beseeched Eisenhower to publicly condemn the "violence and terror in certain southern communities." Instead, he criticized "extremists on both sides," morally equating NAACP leaders, "who want to have the whole matter settled today," with the Klan. Critics noted "the painful injustice" in equating these groups—one seeking legal enforcement of *Brown* and the other violently defying it. Eisenhower privately noted that *Brown* was a foolish decision that "set back progress in the south at least 15 years." When rumors of his private views circulated, he refused to deny them. Not until 1959 did Eisenhower publicly declare that segregation was "morally wrong."[81]

Democrats who were seeking to replace Eisenhower as president in 1956 were not much more supportive of *Brown*. Senator Estes Kefauver of Tennessee allowed that he would be "very shy" about using federal troops to enforce desegregation and that he would do so only in a "very severe case." The most liberal Democratic presidential candidate, Governor Averell Harriman of New York, declared, "No responsible person could propose the use of federal troops." The eventual Democratic nominee, Illinois's former governor, Adlai Stevenson, urged cautious federal action in enforcing *Brown*. Stevenson preferred education and suasion to force, and he observed, "[You] do not upset habits and traditions that are older than the Republic overnight." Stevenson was no more willing than Eisenhower to condemn the Southern Manifesto, which repudiated *Brown* as "a clear abuse of judicial power"; instead, both men praised southern politicians for limiting themselves to support of "lawful resistance." When the chairman of the Democratic National Committee, Paul Butler, criticized Eisenhower early in 1956 for failing to show leadership on civil rights and contrasted his own party's proposals, he emphasized voting rights and the protection of citizens from violence but did not say a word about school desegregation.[82]

Congress did not support the Court either, showing "remarkably little effective interest in the whole fight for Negro rights." Throughout the 1950s, liberal congressmen failed in their efforts to pass symbolic statements affirming that *Brown* was the law of the land (not even that it was rightly decided). Southern Democrats dominated Senate committees, but the filibuster-free House was no champion of desegregation either. Congress did pass tepid civil rights legislation in 1957, but it covered only voting rights, and even that it did ineffectively. A proposal to empower the attorney general to bring desegregation suits was eliminated from the final bill with the president's assent. The clear implication of this excision, as Walter Lippmann noted, was that the right against school segregation was "not to be enforced by the executive power of the Federal Government." In the 1950s, Congress declined even to offer financial support to desegregating districts.[83]

The gradualism of politicians was mirrored by that of their constituents. Polls revealed that national majorities of nearly 4–1 preferred gradualism to immediate action, especially after desegregation had led to violence in

1955–1956. In the NAACP chapter of City College of New York—a strongly integrationist group, one would suppose—twice as many members favored gradualism as immediate integration. Indeed, many white liberals in the North strongly favored gradualism, because they assumed that southern blacks needed time to assimilate, and they feared the excessive centralization that federal coercion of white southerners would require. Early in 1956, *Life* ran an editorial entitled "Go Slow, Now," which urged southern blacks to be patient and to "avoid needless scraping of Southern sensitivities and emotions." Eleanor Roosevelt also defended gradualism, pointing out that "go slow doesn't mean, don't go." The *St. Louis Globe-Democrat*, another *Brown* supporter, suggested that the NAACP "make haste slowly," because racial tolerance must evolve gradually and traditional mores could not be changed overnight. Superintendent Omer Carmichael, whose leadership in peacefully desegregating Louisville schools in 1956 made him a national celebrity, blamed southern "chaos" on the NAACP's "push[ing] too fast."[84]

We have little direct evidence as to what the justices were thinking in 1955–1957. Desegregation orders were producing violent resistance, even in peripheral South states such as Tennessee and Texas. The political branches of the national government had done virtually nothing to support *Brown* or to intervene against violent resistance. Southern white moderates were urging a "cooling-off period" and warning that aggressive implementation of *Brown* "could set off violence and bloodshed." Even liberal northern Democrats supported gradualism. In this political environment, the justices may have calculated that further intervention on their part would prove harmful.[85]

The Court reentered the fray only after the Little Rock crisis. In September 1957, Governor Orval Faubus used the state militia to block enforcement of a court order desegregating Central High School. To avoid a contempt citation, Faubus later withdrew the state troops, but a white mob then filled the vacuum, forcing black students out of the integrated school. After enduring weeks of criticism from Democrats and civil rights leaders for being "wishy-washy" and refusing "to take a strong stand," Eisenhower nationalized the state militia and sent in the army's 101st Airborne Division. Ironically, Eisenhower had helped foment the crisis through his previous statements and inaction. In September 1956, when Governor Allan Shivers used Texas Rangers to block enforcement of a desegregation order as whites rioted in Mansfield, reporters asked Eisenhower how he planned to respond. The president pleaded ignorance of these events and of Shivers's defiant statements, while insisting that the federal government could not intervene in ordinary instances of rioting. During the summer of 1957, Eisenhower stated, "I can't imagine any set of circumstances that would ever induce me to send federal troops . . . into any area to enforce the orders of a federal court"; he had made a similar statement the preceding year. Faubus was justifiably surprised when the 101st Airborne appeared in Little Rock.[86]

An Arkansas national guardsman blocks four of the Little Rock
Nine from entering Central High School on September 4,
1957. The students are (*left to right*) Carlotta Walls, Gloria
Ray, Jane Hill, and Ernest Green. (*Arkansas History
Commission*)

Several blacks attended Central High under military guard during the
1957–1958 school year. The situation was chaotic. Hundreds of white students were suspended for harassing blacks, and there were more than twenty
bomb threats. Early in 1958, the Little Rock school board petitioned District
Judge Harry J. Lemley for a reprieve of two and a half years to allow community resistance to subside. Lemley acquiesced, stating that the court could
not "close its eyes and ears to the practical problem with which [the] board is
confronted." Noting the "chaos, bedlam, and turmoil" at Central High, the
"deep seated popular opposition in Little Rock to the principle of integration," and the view of many whites that the *Brown* decisions "do not truly represent the law," Lemley concluded that the right of black students to nondiscriminatory admission to public schools had to be balanced against the
public interest in a smoothly functioning educational system. The Eighth

Circuit Court of Appeals, sitting en banc, reversed by a vote of 6–1. The justices then convened in special session in the summer of 1958 to determine whether a district judge could delay desegregation, once it had begun, because of community resistance.[87]

Cooper v. Aaron was easy for the justices, who could appreciate as well as segregationists that if massive resistance "win[s] in Little Rock, integration is dead." To reward violent resistance by postponing desegregation would encourage similar behavior elsewhere. A Louisiana legislator had observed that Lemley's decision "shows that massive resistance really works. This gives us a powerful new weapon with which to protect our schools." Other southern officials evidently agreed, as reaction to Lemley's "wonderful" decision was "immediate and jubilant." The justices had to countermand this line of thought and demonstrate support for those who had ordered desegregation. A federal judge in Virginia announced that if the Court affirmed Lemley, he would permit Norfolk to continue segregating its schools, and another judge awarded Prince Edward County an extended deadline partly based on Lemley's ruling. The solicitor general intervened on the NAACP's side and warned that for the justices to approve delay in Little Rock would halt desegregation elsewhere. The justices also needed to demonstrate support for a

FIGURE 6.4
Federalized national guardsmen accompany the Little Rock
Nine as they leave school, October 9, 1957. (*Bettmann*/CORBIS)

president who had run political risks by dispatching troops to an American city. After *Brown*, they had anxiously awaited some sign of support from the political branches. Now that the president had finally provided it, the justices had no choice but to back him up.[88]

Cooper was more forceful and condemnatory than *Brown* had been—"judicial rhetoric that expressed displeasure amounting to anger," according to one astute contemporary. The justices blamed Faubus and the Arkansas legislature for the violence at Central High School. In dicta, they criticized the efforts not only to nullify *Brown* but also to evade it, such as allowing public school funds and buildings to be used by segregated private schools—precisely what the Arkansas legislature and governor were attempting to do at the time. Based on the vehemence of *Cooper*, one might have guessed that the justices would now aggressively monitor the desegregation process, but this was not so. The apparent boldness of the interventions by the president and the Court was misleading. Eisenhower had used federal troops only after the blatant defiance of a desegregation order by a governor whom he suspected of lying to his face. The justices had acted primarily to support the president. Neither party had abandoned gradualism.[89]

Justice Clark, who nearly dissented in *Cooper* because the Court had departed from its customary procedures in order to issue a quick ruling, reminded his colleagues that *Brown* had not contemplated desegregation "through push button action." Most of the other justices agreed. Justice William J. Brennan's draft opinion,[90] at Black's insistence, had required school boards to formulate deadlines for initiating and completing desegregation. Frankfurter objected to such rigidity, and a majority concurred; deadlines were removed. *Cooper* also referred to "desegregation" rather than "integration," because white southerners found the former "a shade less offensive." Even in the face of blatant defiance by the white South, a majority of the justices was inclined toward accommodation and gradualism.[91]

For several more years after *Cooper*, the justices continued to abstain as white southerners defied or evaded *Brown*. The Court denied review in virtually every post–Little Rock desegregation case, even where the circuit courts had split—usually an important consideration in favor of granting review. The NAACP "deplore[d]" the Court's refusal to grant review in cases challenging laws that were "designed to impede and frustrate full implementation of [*Brown*]."[92]

The Court took two noteworthy desegregation actions in 1958–1959. In December 1958, just months after *Cooper*, the justices in *Shuttlesworth v. Birmingham Board of Education* summarily affirmed a lower court decision that rejected a facial challenge to Alabama's pupil placement law. One year later, they denied review of a decision upholding Nashville's grade-a-year desegregation plan, which included a minority-to-majority transfer option.[93]

The summary affirmance in *Shuttlesworth* departed from the Court's usual pattern of denying review in school desegregation cases. Perhaps the justices felt obliged to grant review in this case because it was an appeal from a three-judge trial court, which falls within the Court's mandatory jurisdiction unless the constitutional issue is plainly insubstantial. A summary affirmance indicates agreement with the ruling below. By 1958, pupil placement had become a preferred method of avoiding desegregation; every southern state had adopted such a scheme. The justices carefully left open the possibility that plaintiffs could allege discriminatory administration of a pupil placement scheme, but they declined to invalidate it on its face. A contrary ruling would have been easy to defend. Alabama's placement law was part of a massive-resistance package that did not disguise the legislature's intention to defy *Brown*. The lower court had dismissed the legislature's interposition resolution as "an escape valve through which the legislators blew off steam." But one might easily have read it instead to indicate that the legislature had no intention of permitting any desegregation. Indeed, Alabama legislators had explicitly declared that if the pupil placement plan failed to block integration, they could then abolish the public schools. Just months earlier, Governor John Patterson had announced, "[W]e are going to maintain segregation in the public schools." The lower court in *Shuttlesworth* refused to "lightly reach . . . [the] conclusion" that Alabama was intent on nullification, but nothing had been left to inference.[94]

Even aside from the Alabama legislature's generally defiant purpose, the patent motive behind pupil placement was to frustrate desegregation by inviting surreptitious consideration of race by school boards and then confounding blacks who were dissatisfied with their placements in a maze of administrative appeals. The lower court in *Shuttlesworth* refused to consider legislative motive, but that position was debatable by 1958 and would be rejected by the Court in a school desegregation case a few years later. Another possible objection to pupil placement schemes was that they presumptively allocated students to their current (segregated) schools and placed the burden on them to request transfers. This was not an obviously sufficient remedy for past segregation. Federal courts in Louisiana and Virginia had invalidated placement schemes for such reasons, though the Fourth Circuit had sustained North Carolina's version. It is true that the placement laws of those states were not identical to Alabama's: The Louisiana law provided no criteria for constraining school board discretion, and Virginia's placement plan was even more clearly part of a legislative package designed to block all desegregation. But there were similarities too. Had they been so inclined, the justices could have written a persuasive opinion invalidating the Alabama law. Ironically, Alabama officials had worried that their law was in jeopardy after the lower court decisions that had invalidated placement plans in Louisiana and Virginia. After the latter ruling, Governor James Coleman of Mississippi had expressed a similar concern that his state was "legally naked and legally defenseless" against a desegregation suit, because its pupil placement law seemed doomed. As the battle over massive resistance climaxed in 1958–1959, however, the justices apparently had no desire to invalidate a scheme that was being used in some jurisdictions to achieve at least token desegregation.[95]

In a private memorandum, Douglas revealed that the justices were divided in *Shuttlesworth*. He and Warren thought the law "was a palpable device to avoid integration" and favored granting full review. Potter Stewart objected that "Alabama in good faith was seeking to comply with our decisions."[96] Douglas reported:

> That naive viewpoint so riled me that I prepared a memo for the court showing the purpose of the law. I also pointed out that this law, if not struck down, would be hard to knock out in its application. No purpose to discriminate on racial grounds would be shown in any application; it could be proved—as in the jury cases—only by showing a systematic discrimination that would be avoided by having token integration. I said that the case we could knock out would be a long time coming. The C[hief] J[ustice] spoke up and said, "not until we are long dead."

According to Douglas, Black "thought we were right; but he said nothing would be done anyway for a generation or more." The other justices were unwilling to invalidate the law on its face. Warren and Douglas chose not to dissent from the Court's summary affirmance, "for we felt that unanimity of the Court in the segregation cases was more important than anything else and that our dissent would underline the defeat or setback which school integration had suffered as a result of this decision." The setback was clear even without their dissent. Alabama officials were "jubilant" over *Shuttlesworth*, which Governor Patterson saw "as an indication that the Supreme Court is going to let us handle our own affairs." Senator Russell Long of Louisiana thought the decision was "the most encouraging thing for the South in some time," as it "shows a willingness of the court to settle for token integration." State senator Willie Rainach of Louisiana thought *Shuttlesworth* indicated that "[t]he court's position may well have deteriorated to the point that it would like to compromise," and Congressman James C. Davis of Georgia believed it showed that recent criticism of the Court "has jarred [the justices] into some common sense."[97]

The other important case around this time involved Nashville's desegregation plan, which was one of the first to adopt grade-a-year desegregation. School officials throughout the South closely followed this case and signaled their intention to follow suit if the Court endorsed the plan. Nashville's scheme also offered a transfer option to students who were assigned to schools where their racial group was in the minority. This ensured that no whites would be compelled to attend a majority-black school and encouraged blacks, through a variety of formal and informal pressures, to transfer out of racially mixed schools to which they had been assigned. By 1959, minority-to-majority transfer options were becoming a favored method of limiting desegregation. In *Kelley v. Board of Education of Nashville* (1959), the Court denied review of the Sixth Circuit decision upholding Nashville's plan—an action that ordinarily implies no view on the merits. Yet given the obvious importance of the case, and the unusual decision of three justices— Warren, Douglas, and Brennan—to publicly dissent from the Court's denial of review, the justices had plainly considered the issues carefully. The headline in the *Southern School News* read, "Court Backs Stairstep." White southerners generally concluded after *Kelley* that grade-a-year plans and minority-to-majority transfer options had been vindicated. Nashville's school superintendent announced that he was "immeasurably pleased" with the decision. A prominent southern journalist, John Temple Graves, wrote that the Court had given "clear hope that it begins to see that massive integration won't work," and he urged the white South now to endorse token desegregation in order to enable the justices to "save face." Martin Luther King, Jr., later observed that the Court "had granted legal sanction to tokenism."[98]

The justices' thinking in *Shuttlesworth* and *Kelley* can be reconstructed with some guesswork. Between 1957 and 1959, southern battle lines were drawn around outright defiance of *Brown* and token compliance. The extremism of post-*Brown* southern politics—discussed in the next chapter— had eliminated meaningful integration as an option. Eisenhower's use of troops at Little Rock demonstrated that schools could not remain segregated after courts had ordered them desegregated. But did they have to remain open? Massive resisters had been threatening to close schools as their "final resort" since 1954. Now they were put to the test. In 1958, Governor Faubus closed Little Rock's four high schools, and Governor Lindsay Almond of Virginia closed nine schools that courts had ordered desegregated in three localities: Charlottesville, Norfolk, and Warren County. Other states with similar school-closing legislation watched and waited as events in Arkansas and Virginia unfolded.[99]

In this struggle, "moderate" southern politicians fought to keep schools open by promising to restrict integration to token levels. In 1957, Republican Ted Dalton ran for governor of Virginia, repudiating massive resistance and school closures, and endorsing use of pupil placement for limited integration. That same year, Leroy Collins of Florida became the first Deep South governor to oppose massive resistance, condemning the legislature's interposition resolution as a "cruel hoax," insisting that some desegregation was inevitable, and promising that it could be delayed and controlled through the pupil placement law. Malcolm Seawell, the attorney general of North Carolina, endorsed similar policies in 1958; he acknowledged that *Brown* was the law of the land, criticized school closures, and lauded pupil placement as a mechanism for gradual change. These were risky positions for southern politicians to embrace at the time. Dalton was called "an integrationist." Collins was attacked for "surrendering" and called a "weakling," though northern liberals such as Eleanor Roosevelt applauded his "extremely courageous" stand. Seawell was attacked for "abject surrender" and compared to Judas Iscariot, even though only thirteen blacks attended desegregated schools in all of North Carolina—"eye-dropper integration," according to the NAACP. For the Court to have invalidated gradualist policies such as pupil placement, minority-to-majority transfer, and grade-a-year desegregation might have destroyed these moderate politicians, especially after the use of federal troops at Little Rock had already weakened them. Diehard segregationists would have seized upon such rulings as proof that no middle ground existed between massive resistance and massive integration. The justices closely followed southern politics, and since 1954 they had sought to bolster moderates, many of whom were explicitly appealing to the Court after Little Rock for a "cooling off" period. In 1959, Judge J. Skelly Wright, one of *Brown*'s staunchest defenders in the Deep South, proposed grade-a-year desegregation for New Orleans; he explained that another Little Rock must be avoided. Their decisions in *Shuttlesworth* and *Kelley* suggest that the justices were not deaf to such appeals.[100]

Internal Court documents indirectly support this interpretation. While the Little Rock case was pending, Frankfurter told Harlan that the justices' duty was to "serve as exemplars of understanding and wisdom and magnanimity" to southern moderates. He thought that the recent victory of moderate candidates in school board elections in Little Rock had "important implications ... which are relevantly to be kept in mind by us in the procedures we adopt, when choice is open, and in how we express what we do." Frankfurter viewed his concurring opinion in *Cooper*, which irked his colleagues by departing from the pattern of the justices speaking with a single voice on desegregation, as an appeal to moderate southern lawyers. A few months later, Frankfurter urged his colleagues to deny the NAACP a stay in a Florida case that required it to turn over its membership lists to a legislative investigating committee, because the state court had behaved moderately and refrained from "breathing ... defiance." So long as state jurists had produced "a creditable judicial document" and had deferred to high-court authority "in terms that ... are appropriately respectful," Frankfurter wanted to reward them. In a 1959 case that challenged Virginia's anti-NAACP laws, Black observed that "having originally adopted gradualism, I think we have to recognize the policy." He noted that even *Brown*'s defenders "mainly support gradualism" and that the recent victory of moderates in Little Rock counseled judicial restraint. Thus, Black wanted to give the Virginia Supreme Court a chance to construe these state laws before the Court decided whether to invalidate them.[101]

The words and the deeds of the executive branch may also have influenced the justices' reaffirmation of gradualism in 1958–1959. After sending troops into Little Rock, Eisenhower quickly clarified, and then periodically reiterated, that "they are not there to enforce desegregation; they are there to support our federal court system." In August 1958, Eisenhower denied a magazine report that he had privately criticized *Brown*, while admitting that he might have "said something about 'slower'." (Thurgood Marshall quipped in response, "If we slow down any more, we'll be going backward.") Editing a desegregation speech of his attorney general, William Rogers, Eisenhower urged that he avoid "the impression that the Federal government is looking for opportunities to intervene," refrain from suggestions that integration "will necessarily be permanent," and hint that an acceptable desegregation plan need not be completed within five or even ten years. The Justice Department resumed its policy of noninvolvement after Little Rock and declined to prosecute those who were accused of agitating disturbances at Central High School, thereby encouraging further resistance and undermining the school board.[102]

As massive resistance ended in Virginia early in 1959, the administration rushed to applaud the tokenism that ensued: twenty-one students were attending seven "integrated" schools in two cities. Eisenhower complimented Virginians on their "heartening" desegregation, which made him "very proud." Attorney General Rogers noted the "tremendous development in the thinking of the people" of Virginia over the past few months and explained that the administration would not press for "extreme" civil rights legislation—such as empowering the attorney general to bring desegregation suits—which "might do more harm than good." "In light of Virginia's experience," he noted, "we should keep our eyes open and wait." One year later, with fewer than one black school child in a thousand attending an integrated school in the South, Rogers made the extraordinary statement that the pace of desegregation is "surprisingly good when compared with the legal problems involved." Nothing that the administration said or did encouraged the Court to reject tokenism.[103]

The justices had one additional reason for not pressing desegregation in 1958–1959: They already faced withering assaults from several directions. The Court's "Red Monday" decisions of 1957—which limited congressional and state legislative investigations of alleged communists, as well as federal criminal prosecutions of them—were extremely controversial. Senator James Eastland of Mississippi, who had an ulterior motive, accused the justices of having "woven a web of protection around the Communist party." Yet even many people without segregationist impulses criticized these rulings. In 1958, Congress barely defeated bills that would have overturned several of these "procommunist" decisions and deprived the Court of jurisdiction over related issues—"the most bitter and violent [attack] the Court has sustained for a generation." That same year, the Conference of State Chief Justices voted 38–8 to criticize the Court for lacking self-restraint and invading the legislative field. Those members of the conference whose votes were not motivated by *Brown* may have been reacting partly to the Court's recent expansion of federal habeas corpus jurisdiction, which authorized federal trial judges to reverse the criminal rulings of state supreme courts—a development that was unlikely to win friends for the Court among the ranks of state chief justices. In addition, a couple of 1957 high-court decisions that reversed criminal convictions—harbingers of the Warren Court's criminal procedure revolution—had rankled the law enforcement lobby. White southerners, of course, had been after the Court since *Brown*. Rarely in U.S. history have the justices proved oblivious to sustained and powerful external criticism. The 1950s was no exception. In a pair of 1959 rulings, the justices appeared to back down on the communist issue. They may have chosen to acquiesce in token school desegregation for similar reasons.[104]

Although the justices were unwilling to accelerate the pace of school desegregation during these years, they proved somewhat readier to protect the NAACP's ability to conduct desegregation litigation. The justices understood that individual blacks could rarely litigate without the NAACP's assistance and that Congress was not about to authorize the Justice Department to bring desegregation suits. Thus, without an active NAACP to bring enforcement actions, *Brown* would have been doomed to irrelevance. Yet the white South's ferocious legal assault upon the association—described in greater detail in chapter 7—raised "the whole question of the future operation of the NAACP in the Southern states."[105]

In 1958 the Court ruled that the First Amendment forbade Alabama from requiring disclosure of NAACP membership lists in an action that challenged the association's failure to register under the state's foreign-corporation law. In 1960, the Court extended that ruling to cover efforts by Arkansas cities to obtain association membership lists through local tax ordinances. That year, the Court also invalidated under the First Amendment an Arkansas law that required public school teachers to disclose their organizational affiliations; the law was an indirect assault on black teachers who belonged to the NAACP. In 1963, the Court protected the association's membership lists from discovery by the Florida Legislative Investigation Committee, which was pursuing allegations of communist infiltration of NAACP branches. That year, the justices also intervened against Virginia's prosecution of the NAACP for violating a law that banned organizations from soliciting litigation for their own lawyers. None of the stricken laws was unique, as most southern states had adopted a variety of anti-NAACP measures after *Brown*.[106]

In 1963, an Arkansas jurist disparagingly referred to the Court as the "guardian for the NAACP." Yet the justices were ambivalent in that role. The NAACP cases got progressively harder for them, and they began to divide over how far to stretch the Constitution to protect the association from the harassment of southern states. None of the victories for the NAACP was automatic, as all of them required the Court to create new constitutional law.[107]

The justices probably found the first of these cases, *NAACP v. Alabama*, the easiest. Alabama sued to enjoin the NAACP from operating in the state because of its failure to register under the state's foreign-corporation law. During these proceedings, the NAACP was ordered to disclose its membership lists and then was ruled in contempt for failing to comply and fined $100,000. Under Alabama law, the NAACP could not obtain a hearing on its right to operate in the state until it purged itself of the contempt. The

Alabama Supreme Court affirmed the contempt judgment on a procedural default, and the NAACP appealed to the Supreme Court.

The justices saw the case as "part of the whole Segregation controversy" and "a rather transparent attempt to destroy the NAACP in Alabama." As Douglas's law clerk, William Cohen, pointed out, only "judicial blindness" could have prevented the Court from seeing that to allow Alabama to obtain the membership lists would be to destroy the NAACP by exposing its members to economic and physical reprisals. With other southern states pursuing similar tactics, the NAACP's very existence in the South hung in the balance, and with it the fate of the Court's school desegregation decisions. The Alabama court's effort to block Supreme Court review by invoking a procedural default—that the NAACP had sought the wrong writ for its appeal— was a transparent bait-and-switch, as state jurists had changed their minds during the proceedings as to which writ was appropriate. On the merits, the difficulty in reversing Alabama's judgment was that the Supreme Court had never before recognized a First Amendment right of organizations to keep their membership lists confidential. Only two years earlier, Thurgood Marshall had doubted whether the association could win these battles, as "it is pretty hard to say that filing of a membership list is in itself a violation of the Constitution." The only directly relevant precedent in the Supreme Court had *rejected* a constitutional challenge to New York's law from the 1920s that required the Ku Klux Klan to file its membership lists.

But the justices thought better of the NAACP than they did of the Klan, and judicial conceptions of the scope of the First Amendment had expanded since the 1920s. In 1958, the justices showed little hesitation at interpreting the constitutional guarantee of freedom of association to protect the confidentiality of group membership lists, though Clark briefly considered dissenting on the ground that the Alabama court was entitled to first crack at applying this newly identified First Amendment right. Balancing freedom of association against the state's interest in disclosure, the justices found no compelling need for the state to have access to NAACP membership lists in order to determine if the organization was "doing business" in Alabama. Because of the extraordinary recalcitrance of Alabama jurists, six years passed and three more trips to the Supreme Court were necessary before the NAACP was able to resume operations in the state. In the 1961 iteration of this case, the justices ordered the federal district court to give the NAACP a hearing on its right to operate in Alabama if the state court had not already done so within ten weeks. The justices repeatedly declined to impose similar deadlines in school desegregation cases.[108]

Bates v. Little Rock (1960) extended *NAACP v. Alabama* to cover city ordinances that required organizations seeking exemptions from a corporate-franchise tax to produce lists of dues payers. *Bates* was harder for the justices, because of the importance of the taxing power and because federal law uncontroversially required corporations that claimed tax-exempt status to list their sources of income and required lobbying organizations to list their members. Though a majority of the justices at conference found a clear First Amendment violation, others expressed doubts. Frankfurter thought that *NAACP v. Alabama* was not dispositive, as the "power of taxation is [the] ultimate power of gov[ernment]." Clark agreed that *Bates* "should be reasoned out." Harlan expressed the strongest reservations: "This is [a] rule for Negroes. If it were a white group, then there would be no constitutional right." As the Court gradually expanded constitutional protections that benefited the NAACP, other justices came to share Harlan's reservations. In *Bates*, though, the more dubious justices suppressed their doubts, and the decision was unanimous.[109]

Unanimity evaporated in the other 1960 case, *Shelton v. Tucker*. Arkansas and other southern states required public school teachers to disclose their recent organizational affiliations. National security rulings by the Court in the 1950s had acknowledged strong government interests in obtaining such information from public employees. The issue in *Shelton* was whether the Court would question the motive of southern states in seeking information to which recent precedents seemed to entitle them. The justices were deeply divided. The liberals thought that *NAACP v. Alabama*'s principle of associational privacy controlled the case and that Arkansas should not be permitted to circumvent it. The conservatives distinguished that case on the ground that governments had a more important interest in ascertaining the affiliations of public school teachers than in discerning the identity of NAACP branch members. Because the differences between the liberal and the conservative justices in *Shelton* mirrored those that existed in the national security cases, one cannot necessarily conclude that the justices had differential commitments to protecting the NAACP or to implementing *Brown*. Stewart, the swing vote, found the case "difficult." In contrast with *NAACP v. Alabama*, here he could see "a connection between [an] efficient school system and disclosure of information about the teachers." Stewart perceived no discrimination in the law's application because white and black teachers had to disclose the same information. Moreover, he was unwilling to "get into the climate of Arkansas or [the] motives of [the] legislature." Therein lay the rub. Unless the Court was willing to inquire into and possibly condemn the motives of Arkansas legislators, precedents plainly authorized the legislature to investigate the affiliations of public employees. Overcoming his doubts, Stewart provided the fifth vote to invalidate the law, and he then wrote the majority opinion, which distinguished between affiliations into which the state could legitimately inquire and those into which it could not. Harlan's dissent sensibly wondered how the state could tell the difference between the two before conducting its inquiry.[110]

The next year, the Court confronted two more NAACP cases, and a conservative majority was now prepared to abandon ship. The Virginia Supreme Court had construed a 1956 statute to bar agents of an organization that fomented litigation in which it lacked a pecuniary interest from urging parties to use the organization's lawyers. As a practical matter, this interpretation permitted NAACP members to encourage blacks to file desegregation suits but not to encourage them to use association lawyers. The justices faced a dilemma that was larger than this case. Standard NAACP practices violated several ethical rules governing lawyers' behavior. The NAACP encouraged people to bring lawsuits; it financially supported litigation; its agents urged parties to use association lawyers; and those lawyers frequently controlled litigation with little if any involvement from the parties. Southern states did not need to invent new rules to govern the ethical obligations of lawyers in order to harass the NAACP; the association violated the traditional rules. Yet without the NAACP and its methods, school desegregation litigation would have been nearly impossible. Black parents rarely thought to bring suit without the NAACP's advice and encouragement; few blacks had the money or the incentive to file desegregation suits on their own; and prospective litigants would have had difficulty locating NAACP lawyers unless someone directed them there.[111]

The justices had to choose between traditional legal principles that plainly authorized Virginia's action against the NAACP and their realization that the state was trying to impede the association's pursuit of school desegregation. They divided along the usual political lines. Justice Black, supporting the NAACP, thought that this law "was one of a group designed to thwart our segregation decision." The "NAACP is finished if this law stands." The state should not be permitted to "handicap and hobble those who are trying to enforce constitutional rights," and the association's support "is necessary if these Negro rights are to be enforced." Frankfurter took strong exception: "This court should not be [the] guardians of Negroes." As "colored people are now people of substance," and nothing in the record revealed that "this law is discriminatory" or "aimed at Negroes as such," the Court must sustain it. Clark agreed, noting that the Virginia law paralleled traditional restrictions on lawyers and concluding that in order to invalidate it "we would have to discriminate in favor of Negroes." Justice Charles Whittaker also thought that the law would be obviously permissible if applied to a white supremacy group, and he insisted, "[W]e should be color blind on this law."[112] In the November 1961 conference, the justices voted 5–4 to sustain Virginia's statute. Apparently, a majority of justices had reached the limit of their willingness to subordinate traditional legal principles to the imperative of protecting the NAACP from the harassment of southern states.[113]

Fortuity then intervened. Before the decision could be released in the spring of 1962, Whittaker abruptly retired and Frankfurter had to resign after a stroke. The change in the Court's composition then reversed the outcome. After reargument, the new appointees, Byron White and Arthur Goldberg, sided with the NAACP.[114] Most of the other justices adhered to their original positions. Black called the law "nothing but [a] legal contraption to put [the] NAACP out of business." By contrast, Harlan thought the law "plainly constitutional," as there was "no reason why [the] NAACP is immune from regular rules of champerty."[115] He also observed, *"Brown v. Board of Education* will never work out if it is left in the federal domain. The states must do it." Brennan's majority opinion in *NAACP v. Button* (1963) created a new First Amendment right of association for litigation purposes and noted that groups that litigated on behalf of white supremacy would be equally protected. Harlan's dissent accused the majority of applying different constitutional standards to racial problems, which he thought a terrible "setback . . . [to] the great principles established by *Brown v. Board of Education*."[116]

The Court's last important NAACP case, *Gibson v. Florida Legislative Investigation Committee* (1963), involved efforts by a committee of the Florida legislature to obtain association membership lists in order to determine whether communists had infiltrated the Miami branch. To the NAACP, this was simply another ruse for publicizing its membership and thus exposing individuals to reprisal. At stake was "the survival of the civil rights movement in Florida and the entire southeast." The president of the Miami branch, Theodore Gibson, defied legislative subpoenas to produce the membership lists, and he was jailed and fined. The Florida Supreme Court upheld the legislature's committee, and the NAACP appealed.[117]

In the autumn of 1961, the justices voted to sustain the committee, narrowly dividing along the same lines as they had initially in *Button*. The liberals urged realism. As Warren put it, "[I]f this stands *NAACP v. Alabama* is thwarted, for all legislatures will let loose on it." The conservatives argued that recent national security decisions that sustained legislative access to the membership lists of allegedly subversive groups were indistinguishable. Harlan thought that *Gibson* was different from *NAACP v. Alabama* because "states must have the power to ferret out communists." Less persuasively, he noted that "this is not harassment as in *NAACP v. Alabama*" and that there is "no invidious discrimination against [the] NAACP." The association was set to lose by 5–4. But, as in *Button*, the change in the Court's composition in 1962 reversed the outcome. After the case was reargued before the reconstituted Court, the liberals again insisted that Florida was attempting to circumvent *NAACP v. Alabama*, while the conservatives invoked precedents that established a legislature's right of access to membership lists when investigating alleged communists. The differences between the liberal and the conservative justices were not simply about race; they had divided along similar lines in subversion cases. As was true of Americans generally, conservative justices were more convinced than liberal ones of the seriousness of the communist threat. The newly appointed Goldberg provided the fifth vote for the NAACP, and he wrote the majority opinion in *Gibson*. Goldberg insisted that the legislative committee show some basis for suspecting communist infiltration of the NAACP before it could secure access to the membership lists, and he distinguished subversion precedents on the ground of the NAACP's conceded legitimacy. Harlan dissented, accusing the majority of requiring "an investigating agency to prove in advance the very things it is trying to find out."[118]

The Court's creativity in defending the NAACP from southern legal assault was duplicated in other areas. In 1960, the justices confronted a novel suffrage question. In 1957, the Alabama legislature, responding to the concerns of whites in Tuskegee about growing black voter registration, had redrawn the city's boundaries to fence out virtually all blacks while leaving whites unaffected. Given the racial residential patterns, the gerrymander had required some artistic imagination to succeed, and Tuskegee's new boundary had twenty-eight sides. The legislature had not hidden its racial purpose. But under existing constitutional law, the Court's authority to intervene was doubtful. In its entire history, the Court had never invalidated legislative districting. Just over a decade earlier, the justices had reaffirmed their unwillingness to resolve such "political questions." Moreover, in 1960, the weight of authority still rejected judicial inquiries into legislative motive. Accordingly, lower federal court judges, including some whose support for *Brown* was unquestioned, had dismissed the NAACP's challenge to the redistricting of Tuskegee. *Gomillion v. Lightfoot* (1960) thus presented the justices with a stark conflict between law and politics. The racial gerrymander was grotesque and abhorrent, but legal authority for invalidating it was weak.[119]

Undeterred, the justices struck down the gerrymander, manifesting a constitutional creativity that was absent from their post-*Brown* school desegregation jurisprudence. *Gomillion* ruled for the first time that a challenge to political districting was justiciable, and it found a violation of the Fifteenth Amendment right to vote without racial restriction, even though Tuskegee's former black residents were enfranchised in their new home, which was Macon County. Perhaps the greater creativity shown by the justices in *Gomillion* reflects the fact that black voting rights were much less controversial than school desegregation in 1960. An Alabama newspaper had warned that the state was "blundering dangerously" by confusing the right to vote with desegregation: Many Americans sympathized with school segregation, but few of them supported black disfranchisement.[120]

Notwithstanding the Court's aggressive defense of the NAACP and its willingness to creatively protect the suffrage rights of Tuskegee blacks, the justices would not reenter the school desegregation fray to express their impatience with the concept of "all deliberate speed" until 1963. By then, many lower court judges, responding to the explosion in direct-action protest that began in 1960, had already begun to reject gradualist methods that produced only token integration. National politicians were voicing dissatisfaction with glacial desegregation, and Congress was debating proposals to force quicker change in school districts that received federal funds. Late in 1962, Deputy Attorney General Nicholas Katzenbach criticized the "wide gulf" that lay between the Court's pronouncements and the social reality of continuing school segregation. In a special civil rights message to Congress in February 1963, President John F. Kennedy declared *Brown* "both legally and morally right" and criticized the pace of desegregation as "too slow, often painfully so." Reflecting this changed political and social climate, in the spring of 1963, the justices hinted at a new desegregation policy. In *Watson v. Memphis*, the Court rebuked a federal judge for applying "all deliberate speed" to the desegregation of public parks, and it warned that desegregation plans that "eight years ago might have been deemed sufficient" were no longer so. This was the justices' first commentary on the pace of desegregation since *Brown II*, and it came in the same month that Birmingham street demonstrations made civil rights the nation's top political priority. One week later, the decision in *Goss v. Board of Education* invalidated the same minority-to-majority transfer scheme that the justices had declined to review in 1959. *Goss* ruled that a one-way transfer option was a racial classification perpetuating segregation, and it observed that the context for construing "all deliberate speed" had been "significantly altered" since *Brown II*. The next year, the Court declared that "[t]he time for mere 'deliberate speed' has run out"; "[t]here has been entirely too much deliberation and not enough speed." The justices had previously voiced no objections to glacial desegregation, but the civil rights movement had apparently impelled a change of heart.[121]

The Court now intervened in the school desegregation process much more aggressively than would previously have been imaginable. In 1959, most of the justices apparently did not object to minority-to-majority transfer schemes, but in 1963 they did. Traditional constitutional doctrine required litigants to exhaust their state administrative remedies before suing in federal court, but in *McNeese v. Board of Education* (1963), the Court waived that requirement. In *Griffin v. County School Board* (1964), the justices strongly hinted that on the remand in the Prince Edward County case the district judge should order public schools reopened. In the mid-1950s, by contrast, there had been much doubt as to whether courts had the authority to forbid state officials from closing—for segregationist reasons—public facilities that the Constitution did not require the state to operate in the first place. For example, Reed had stated during *Brown II* deliberations that the Court "can't require public school systems." The principal rationale in *Griffin*—that the Equal Protection Clause barred one county from closing its public schools if other counties continued to operate them—was novel and unpersuasive. The justices failed to explain why intrastate disparities in public services violated the federal Constitution. They did no better at explaining why public tuition grants to attend private schools—grants that were equally available to blacks and to whites—violated the Equal Protection Clause simply because blacks were unwilling or unable to take advantage of them. In 1968, the justices unanimously invalidated a freedom-of-choice plan that they would probably have been delighted to sustain in the mid-1950s. Several years earlier, even the U.S. Civil Rights Commission, which was reliably more liberal on race issues than was the Court, had thought freedom of choice obviously constitutional. In *Swann v. Charlotte-Mecklenburg Board of Education* (1971), the justices sustained busing to achieve desegregation, and they approved a sweeping plan that effectively undid the effects of housing segregation. It is safe to say that in 1954 no justice had ever dreamed of such a thing.[122]

These decisions, though dramatic departures from 1950s constitutional doctrine, were consistent with the political climate that had developed by the time they were rendered (the 1971 decision in *Swann* may be an exception). The Justice Department urged the Court to invalidate minority-to-majority transfers in *Goss*. By 1964, Prince Edward County had become a national and international embarrassment, as 1,700 black youngsters went largely uneducated over several years. The Johnson administration urged the justices to reopen the county's public schools, and Attorney General Robert Kennedy called the situation "unnatural and unsatisfactory." The Court's invalidation of freedom of choice in *Green v. County School Board* (1968) on the ground that it produced insufficient integration tracked executive-branch guidelines that imposed a similar results-based test for determining whether school districts should forfeit their federal education funds.[123]

Although the success of the civil rights movement probably explains much of the justices' more aggressive posture on desegregation in the 1960s, they may also have simply become fed up with the intransigence and disingenuousness of southern whites. One cannot know for sure, but massive resistance may have come back to haunt white southerners. Moderate critics had predicted that massive resistance would eventually produce massive integration, and they may have been right. The justices eventually grew tired of the endless evasion and bad faith, and they adjusted constitutional and other doctrines in response. In an unprecedented 1961 ruling, *NAACP v. Gallion*, the justices, exasperated at the bad faith of Alabama jurists, ordered them to quickly hold a hearing on the NAACP's right to operate in the state or else forfeit jurisdiction to the federal district court. For similar reasons, *McNeese* abandoned the traditional requirement that federal litigants exhaust their state administrative remedies. In *Griffin*, the Court invalidated school closures partly because of the illicit motivation behind them: defiance of a federal court desegregation order. Traditional constitutional doctrine disfavored judicial inquiries into legislative motives, but years of massive resistance had changed the justices' minds. By 1964, they were so irritated by delays in Prince Edward County, where desegregation litigation had commenced in 1951, that they refused to afford state courts the usual opportunity to resolve state constitutional questions before the federal courts ruled on federal issues—the opposite of what they had done in an important NAACP case from Virginia in 1959. They also approved the district court's order to the county to levy taxes for the operation of public schools—a virtually unprecedented decision, about which several justices had doubts. Who knows whether they would have overcome those doubts, had it not been for the county's extraordinary defiance of *Brown*, which had lasted for an entire decade? Similarly, because the justices no longer trusted white southerners to do what they were told or to be honest about what they were doing, beginning in 1968 the Court evaluated desegregation plans based on actual results—how many blacks attended mixed schools. Contrast this with 1954, when many justices apparently believed that compliance with *Brown* need not require a great deal of integration. Burton, for example, had stated that "nonsegregation . . . may here and there result in some presence of more than one race." In *Green*, however, the justices explained that freedom of choice had to be evaluated against the backdrop of thirteen years of resistance and evasion.[124]

In 1954, the Court played a vanguard role in school desegregation. Half of the nation supported *Brown* from the day it was decided, but it was the justices who had put the issue on the map. Many of them had to overcome serious legal doubts to invalidate segregation, but fundamental changes in the extralegal context of race relations had rendered a contrary result too unpalatable to most of them. *Brown II* then authorized a relaxed transition. Gradualism appealed to the justices because it enabled them to maintain their unanimity, avoid issuing unenforceable orders, assuage their consciences, and appeal to southern moderates. White northerners generally endorsed gradualism, while many white southerners interpreted the Court's willingness to be accommodating as a sign of weakness. Southern politics moved far to the right as the region made a concerted effort at massive resistance. Given the intensity of white opposition to desegregation in the South and the president's indifference, the justices doubted that further intervention on their part to accelerate the process would prove constructive, and they feared that it might undermine southern moderates. Aside from their condemnation of outright defiance in the Little Rock case, the justices withdrew almost entirely from the school desegregation arena for nearly a decade. When they reentered in 1963–1964, they were following, not leading, national opinion. The civil rights movement had overtaken the school desegregation process, and the political branches of the national government were now playing the vanguard role. The contribution of *Brown* to these developments is the main topic of the next chapter.

CHAPTER SEVEN

Brown and the Civil Rights Movement

DIRECT EFFECTS

Many commentators have called *Brown* the most important Court decision of the twentieth century, perhaps the most important ever. Judicial decisions can matter in many different ways. This section considers *Brown's* direct consequences: How much school desegregation did it produce? The next section examines a variety of possible indirect effects.[1]

Even before *Brown*, some northern states that had many formally segregated school districts began to desegregate, in response to social and political forces emanating from World War II. In 1947, New Jersey passed a constitutional amendment that barred school segregation, and the governor ordered aggressive enforcement of it, including the withholding of state funds from districts that continued to segregate. In 1949, Illinois enacted a similar funds-withholding law. By the early 1950s—before *Brown*—officially sponsored segregation had largely disappeared from both states, showing that school desegregation could occur without a mandate from the Supreme Court.[2]

Four western states—Arizona, New Mexico, Kansas, and Wyoming—which permitted local communities to impose segregation at their discretion (local option), had similar experiences. These states had begun eradicating segregation before *Brown*, and the Court's intervention simply accelerated the process. The Arizona legislature replaced compulsory segregation with local option in 1952, but state trial courts invalidated the new law even before *Brown*. Tucson, which had never segregated high schools, desegregated its elementary schools several years before *Brown*, and Phoenix, with a black student population of 15 percent, allowed blacks to attend neighborhood schools in 1953. Smaller Arizona cities desegregated quickly and easily after *Brown*. In New Mexico, with a black population of only 1.2 percent, the few communities that segregated schools under local option desegregated the year before *Brown* or in the months following. In the fall of 1954, the state school superintendent reported that segregation "has been on the wane for many years." In the early 1950s, a couple of small Kansas cities that had segregated schools under local option voluntarily desegregated. The Topeka school board, which was the defendant in *Brown*, adopted a desegregation plan eight months before the decision, and the state's lawyer conceded at oral argument that the consequences of invalidating segregation in Kansas would not be serious. Even before *Brown II*, desegregation in Topeka was reported to be moving along "in fine shape," and Burton's law clerk predicted that the Court's decree "should have little or no effect on them."[3]

Border states, such as Delaware, Maryland, West Virginia, and Missouri, might have followed similar paths and desegregated even without Court intervention. Justice Reed's prediction that "segregation in the border states will disappear in 15 or 20 years" without judicial command was not absurd. *Brown* pushed against an open door in these states, where, as Jackson pointed out, segregation "lingers by a tenuous lease of life." Large cities in border states desegregated after *Brown* without waiting for follow-up litigation to coerce them. Baltimore, St. Louis, Wilmington, and Washington, D.C., began desegregating in the fall of 1954 or shortly thereafter, not even waiting for *Brown II*. Likewise, in Missouri, West Virginia, Arkansas, and West Texas, some counties with small black populations began desegregating shortly after *Brown I*. Some of these communities may have regarded *Brown* as a welcome "excuse to do what they wanted" but were not permitted to do under state law. A school superintendent in western Arkansas reported, "Segregation was a luxury we no longer could afford." Other counties may have preferred to maintain segregation but not so strongly that they were prepared to defy a Court ruling. Border-state governors refused to join their colleagues in the South in condemning *Brown*. Governor Theodore R. McKeldin of Maryland called the idea of resistance "fantastic nonsense."[4]

Although these border states had not begun desegregating their schools before *Brown*, other racial practices had changed, which smoothed the way for peaceful school desegregation. Baltimore teachers had served on interracial committees and projects; the association of public school teachers was integrated, as were adult education classes; and in 1952, thirty-five blacks had begun attending the white Baltimore Polytechnic Institute because black high schools in the city offered no equivalent advanced engineering courses. Also in 1952, Ford's Theater in Baltimore ended segregation, and the next year, the Lyric Theater allowed blacks to perform there for the first time. In

1953, the Baltimore Transit Company hired its first black employees, and some downtown department stores and drugstores desegregated their lunch counters. The readiness of city and state officials to comply with *Brown* is therefore less surprising, given how far segregation barriers had already been breached. A newspaper correspondent treated school desegregation in Baltimore as "one more step in the gradual emergence of Negroes in formerly all-white fields of human activity." Similarly, in St. Louis, black and white teachers already served together on committees; a citywide student council was integrated; and students competed in interracial sporting events. Most hotels had desegregated, as had some restaurants and theaters. The school superintendent in St. Louis pointed out that *Brown* "was consistent with rather than contrary to the pattern of thought and action which had characterized the progress of the city for a decade." By the time schools desegregated in Louisville in 1956, public transportation, city libraries, parks, swimming pools, the university, and the police and fire departments had already integrated. In Wilmington, Delaware, Catholic schools, schools for the deaf and blind, adult education classes, and committees of public school teachers had been integrated for years by the time that public schools desegregated in 1954. Black and white students performed together in city choruses and orchestras, and they competed against one another on sports teams. Movie theaters, hospitals, and the Delaware National Guard had recently integrated. Thus, Wilmington "was in a state of acceptance and readiness" by the time of *Brown*.[5]

Brown easily desegregated schools in border-state cities partly because most whites, even though opposed, were not intensely resistant. In 1954, these cities were less identifiably southern than they had been a decade or two earlier. Most border-state politicians endorsed *Brown* or at least expressed a willingness to comply, as did many newspapers, religious organizations, labor unions, and teachers' associations. The social and political conditions that prevailed in border-state cities enabled blacks to take better advantage of *Brown*. Blacks had substantial political power in these cities, which influenced the desegregation stance of politicians. Blacks in border-state cities often had money to litigate and could withstand economic pressure from whites. NAACP branches in these cities were strong, and violence against blacks seeking school desegregation was unlikely. Under such circumstances, *Brown* supplied the push that was necessary to induce public officials to do what they would not have undertaken voluntarily but were not strongly resistant to doing.[6]

Still, one should not overstate the ease with which border states complied with *Brown* or the amount of integration that occurred. In Baltimore, with roughly 60 percent of Maryland's black population, schools desegregated in the fall of 1954, but only 3 percent of black students chose to attend racially mixed schools under the city's open enrollment (freedom-of-choice) policy; this figure rose to 7.4 percent in 1955 and 13.8 percent in 1956. The percentage of blacks attending racially mixed schools increased to 31.3 percent by 1960, but this figure was misleading because it included blacks who had attended formerly white schools that had become almost entirely black as neighborhoods rapidly turned over. Desegregation came more slowly to the rest of the state. Counties in western and northern Maryland with tiny black populations desegregated the quickest, most of them beginning in 1955 and some saving money in the process. Counties with larger but still relatively small black percentages, such as Montgomery and Baltimore counties, steadily expanded their school desegregation through the 1950s. Yet in southern Maryland and on the Eastern Shore, where blacks constituted roughly 25–50 percent of the population and the racial attitudes of whites were "more hostile than in Mississippi," essentially no desegregation occurred until the early 1960s, as whites pressured blacks not to exercise their transfer rights. As of 1957, only 7 percent of blacks living in Maryland counties—that is, outside the city of Baltimore—attended desegregated schools, and in 1960 only 10 percent did. Not until 1962 did the state board of education begin to pressure counties to accelerate desegregation, and in the most recalcitrant areas, black attendance at formerly white schools remained token until after the 1964 Civil Rights Act.[7]

Similar patterns prevailed throughout the border region. Delaware politicians and school officials quickly announced after *Brown* that they would comply. In the fall of 1954, Wilmington desegregated without incident, and other school districts in northern Delaware followed gradually thereafter. In southern Delaware, however, polls showed that whites were almost unanimously opposed to desegregation, and in 1954, demonstrations by more than a thousand angry whites in Milford convinced the school board to reverse its earlier decision to desegregate. Virtually no desegregation took place in southern Delaware until nearly 1960. Kansas City and St. Louis, where the vast majority of Missouri's blacks lived, desegregated with "extraordinary calm" in 1954–1955, as did many counties in the state with small black populations. Half of the school districts in Missouri reported that they had desegregated to save money. But in the southeastern "boot-heel" counties along the Mississippi River, resistance was intense. High schools in that region remained segregated for several years after *Brown*, and elementary schools often did not desegregate until the early 1960s, when state officials finally began to pressure recalcitrant communities.

Soon after *Brown*, Kentucky politicians announced that they would "do whatever is necessary to comply with the law." Most Kentucky counties began desegregating in 1956, as did the state's largest city, Louisville, where peaceful desegregation earned national acclaim. But Kentucky's rural counties sometimes proved more resistant, some of them holding out until the early 1960s. In 1956, whites in two western Kentucky counties, Clay and Sturgis, rioted against desegregation. In Oklahoma, "southern in its traditions but western in its attitude," little overt opposition to *Brown* was expressed, and desegregation saved money because blacks in segregated schools had been receiving a third more per pupil than whites had. One education official estimated that the state saved a million dollars a year from desegregation. By the spring of 1956, Oklahoma was reported to be "far along the course" toward desegregation, but in the "Little Dixie" counties in the southeastern portion of the state, where black percentages were much higher, resistance proved intense, and little desegregation occurred for years. In West Virginia, where blacks were only about 5 percent of the population, public officials promised compliance with *Brown*, and nearly half of the state's counties began desegregating in the fall of 1954, with most of the others following in 1955. Yet in southern West Virginia, with the state's largest percentage of blacks, resistance proved more stalwart, desegregation was delayed, and racial disturbances occurred.[8]

Furthermore, even in those border-state cities where desegregation came quickly, the number of blacks attending racially mixed schools often remained small because of residential segregation, which led critics to deride urban school desegregation as "a mockery." St. Louis easily desegregated its elementary schools in 1955, but because of segregated housing patterns, only twelve such schools had racially mixed student bodies, while ninety-eight remained single race. For the same reason, desegregation in Oklahoma City placed only 15 percent of blacks in schools with whites; in Tulsa, where the school attendance zones were gerrymandered and a transfer option existed, the figure was just 3 percent. Even that minimal amount of desegregation proved difficult to sustain over time, as mixed schools resegregated because of demographic shifts. Baltimore neighborhoods turned over so quickly, as the black population increased and whites fled to the suburbs, that "integrated" schools went from having a handful of blacks to being nearly entirely black within a couple of years. By 1960, twenty-two formerly white Baltimore schools had student bodies that were majority black. In St. Louis, one high school that had been 74 percent white in 1955 was 99 percent black by 1963. Several formerly white schools in Oklahoma City became almost entirely black within just a few years.[9]

School segregation that resulted from a combination of residential segregation and neighborhood schools policies was not obviously a violation of *Brown*, and the NAACP did not challenge such arrangements until the early 1960s. On the contrary, even civil rights advocates tended to regard border-state desegregation as a success story in the 1950s.[10]

The eleven states of the former Confederacy responded to *Brown* very differently from the border states. No desegregation at all occurred until 1957, other than in two school districts in Tennessee (one of which, Oak Ridge, had federally operated schools), five in Arkansas with few blacks, and roughly one hundred in West and South Texas, which contained about 1 percent of the state's black schoolchildren. In the spring of 1957, a black congressman conceded that the South had won "the first round in the battle for compliance" with *Brown*. That fall, just thirteen black students entered formerly white schools in Nashville. In Little Rock, there were nine. Three North Carolina cities accounted for that state's total of eleven. The Little

Rock desegregation crisis, which culminated in President Eisenhower's use of federal troops, brought school desegregation nearly to a halt throughout the South. Other Arkansas districts that had planned to desegregate that fall now reconsidered. Texas passed a law that required cutting off state funds to districts that desegregated without conducting a referendum, and compliance with *Brown* then ground to a halt. No other southern state desegregated any schools until 1959, when Virginia ended its massive resistance by allowing twenty-one blacks into seven white schools in two cities, and Florida permitted Miami to desegregate two schools. On *Brown's* sixth anniversary in 1960, 98 of Arkansas's 104,000 black school students attended desegregated schools; 34 of North Carolina's 302,000; 169 of Tennessee's 146,000; and 103 of Virginia's 203,000. In the five Deep South states, not one of the 1.4 million black schoolchildren attended a racially mixed school until the fall of 1960. This is probably not exactly what the justices had in mind by "all deliberate speed."[11]

The pace of desegregation increased in the early 1960s, as burgeoning direct-action protest made blacks more aggressive in demanding school desegregation, lawsuits proliferated, and federal judges grew less tolerant of delay. Louisiana and Georgia experienced their first desegregation in 1960 and 1961, respectively, as New Orleans and Atlanta schools desegregated under court order. Houston and Dallas also desegregated in 1960–1961, and desegregation in Florida spread beyond Miami and the number of affected black students rose significantly. In North Carolina, Tennessee, and Virginia, the number of blacks attending desegregated schools doubled or tripled every year in the early 1960s. The largest increases in desegregation, in absolute numbers, came in Texas, where the state attorney general declared unconstitutional the 1957 law that required a referendum before desegregation, and in the border states of Maryland, Delaware, and Kentucky. Although by 1963 the increased pace of desegregation was unmistakable, only 1.06 percent of southern black students yet attended desegregated schools. In the Deep South states of Georgia and Louisiana, desegregation had yet to expand beyond a few large cities. In Alabama, South Carolina, and East Texas, desegregation had just begun that fall and was also restricted to the largest cities. In Mississippi, it would not commence until the following year. Nowhere in the South had desegregation penetrated far into rural areas.[12]

Justice Black had rightly predicted that "some counties won't have negroes and whites in the same school this generation." How could *Brown* have been so inefficacious for so long outside of the border states? The answer lies partly in the incentives of southern school boards and federal judges and partly in the constraints faced by southern blacks and the NAACP.[13]

Brown II explicitly noted that school boards would retain "primary responsibility" for placing students, subject to judicial oversight. Thus, the burden of implementing *Brown II* initially lay with school board members.

Most of them undoubtedly thought that *Brown* was wrongheaded, as did most white southerners, so their inclinations were to delay and evade as much as possible. Because *Brown II* supplied no clear mandate for action, it seemed to invite evasion, which made voluntary compliance politically difficult.[14]

For personal and political reasons, school board members resisted prompt and effective action toward desegregation. As we shall see, *Brown* radicalized southern politics, leading candidates for office to maneuver for the most extreme segregationist position, and turning "moderation" into a derisive term. Board members were elected officials, who could ill afford to ignore public opinion. Those who did often lost their jobs. School board members in Nashville, who were under intense local pressure to stall deseg-regation, defended a plan that a federal judge had already invalidated by not-ing that "we must represent the people." Board members were often caught in the cross fire between federal courts ordering desegregation and state politicians threatening to cut off funds or close schools if segregation laws were violated. School board members in Little Rock eventually resigned, having grown tired of being Governor Faubus's "whipping boys." Such offi-cials also had personal incentives to delay and evade compliance with *Brown*, as they had to live in communities that were staunchly opposed to desegregation. The school superintendent in Hoxie, Arkansas, and the high school principal in Clinton, Tennessee, resigned after desegregation riots had resulted in ordeals for their families. Board members who desegregated schools received harassing letters in Greensboro, North Carolina, suffered economic reprisals in New Orleans, had crosses burned on their lawns in Macon County, Alabama, and were physically assaulted in Springer, Okla-homa. They faced little pressure from the opposite direction. Until local liti-gation produced a desegregation order, they ran no risk of contempt sanc-tions. Criminal prosecution and civil damages actions were also unlikely, as defendants in such suits, unlike those in injunction cases, have a right to a jury trial, and white jurors would have been unlikely to convict officials for resisting desegregation. Thus, the incentives of school board members were heavily skewed toward delay and evasion. Moreover, they possessed an ample array of legitimate excuses for postponing desegregation: administra-tive complications in reassigning large numbers of students, overcrowded schools, community resistance, and the lower achievement levels and alleged immorality of blacks.[15]

School boards had strong reasons not to be the first in a state or region to desegregate, which would make them the focal point of segregationist pres-sure. The few boards that took or promised to take prompt steps toward good-faith compliance quickly reconsidered. The Chattanooga school board, believing that local opinion would support it, vowed after *Brown II* to make a "prompt and reasonable start" toward desegregation. Under criticism for its "cowardly and disloyal" action, the board quickly reconsidered and announced early in 1956 that community sentiment would not permit desegregation for at least five years. Governor Frank Clement soon announced that Tennessee schools would desegregate only under court order, and Chattanooga did not ultimately desegregate any schools until 1962. The Greensboro, North Carolina, school board announced the day after *Brown* that it would comply, which prompted harassing phone calls and threats to the school superintendent and the board chairman. Not until three years later did Greensboro begin desegregation, and even then it was merely token. School boards that acted first also ran heightened risks of violence, as itinerant troublemakers, such as John Kasper, a New Jersey segregationist who openly advocated forcible resistance to *Brown*, would come to town to rally the opposition. Clinton and Nashville—the second and third school districts in Tennessee to desegregate—had to endure extended visits from Kasper, which were followed by school bombings.[16]

Once a desegregation order had resulted in violence, school boards elsewhere became even more reluctant to end segregation. After a mob of angry whites closed a desegregated school in Milford, school boards elsewhere in southern Delaware refused to desegregate until compelled to do so by the courts. Facing hardening public reaction after Little Rock, most school boards chose the path of least resistance—delay and evasion—in order to avoid violence. Houston's school superintendent declared, "[T]he experiences of 1957 in some schools that tried integration show me that we are going to be slow to accept it." In 1958, the president of Baltimore's school board observed that Little Rock had made desegregation much more difficult than it had been four years earlier. As late as 1961, one Tennessee school board was still rejecting desegregation because it was "alarmed at the instances of violence, bloodshed and willful destruction of property which took place when efforts were made to integrate other areas of the South." Few school boards ultimately desegregated until courts had ordered it or at least until parties had threatened to litigate. The Knoxville school board, desperately seeking political cover, beseeched Judge Robert L. Taylor to command, not merely instruct, it to submit a desegregation plan. Even a court order was sometimes insufficient to prompt school board action. In Milton, Delaware, board members who had agreed to desegregate under court order resigned in the face of massive white protests, and their replacements vowed to fight on. A school board member in Houston declared that she would rather go to jail than vote to desegregate.[17]

Because school boards would generally not desegregate without a court order, the implementation of *Brown* depended on the ability of black parents to bring suits and on the willingness of federal judges to order desegregation. Neither condition was easily satisfied. *Brown* technically bound only school board defendants in five cases. Thus litigation was necessary in every southern school district—of which there were thousands—in which resistant boards declined to voluntarily desegregate. President Eisenhower declined to request, and Congress would not have granted anyway, authority for the attorney general to file desegregation suits on behalf of black parents.

Few blacks could afford the $10–15,000 necessary to litigate a case to the Supreme Court. They had little incentive to sue anyway, because litigation delays would probably prevent their children from reaping the benefits of a lawsuit. Only an organization that represented blacks as a group, such as the NAACP, could capture the benefits, and thus offset the costs, of desegregation litigation. Moreover, few white lawyers would have dared to take such cases. Not surprisingly, then, virtually all desegregation litigation involved the NAACP. Comprehending this, southern whites declared war on the association. No sooner had the Miami branch filed a school desegregation suit in 1956 then the state legislature began investigating it for alleged communist infiltration and demanded its membership lists—which, if publicized, would have invited reprisals against members. Virginia passed a law prohibiting organizations that lacked a pecuniary interest in litigation from soliciting suits for their lawyers—a measure that was clearly aimed at barring the NAACP from desegregation litigation and which would have effectively ended such suits. In Clarendon County, South Carolina, the citizens' council circulated the names of NAACP members, who then promptly lost their jobs, credit, and suppliers. Z. Alexander Looby and Arthur Shores, NAACP lawyers in Nashville and Birmingham who were responsible for school desegregation litigation, had their homes bombed. Alabama, Texas, and Louisiana temporarily shut down NAACP operations through litigation, thus severely hampering the organization's ability to bring desegregation suits. Even without this onslaught, the NAACP had limited resources and could not finance an infinite number of such suits. Further, the association remained weak in rural areas, where desegregation litigation rarely began until the mid-1960s.[18]

Even when the NAACP could finance litigation, individual blacks still had to enlist as plaintiffs. The association desperately solicited litigants, but in the Deep South, few blacks volunteered. Governor James Coleman of Mississippi thought the absence of desegregation suits indicated that "the thinking colored people . . . have paid no attention to outside agitators," and other state officials attributed it to the success of the school equalization campaign. Blacks were indeed divided over whether to pursue school desegregation—a 1955 Gallup poll found that only 53 percent of southern blacks supported *Brown*—given the fierce white resistance to desegregation, dramatic recent improvements in some black schools, the likely dismissals of black teachers after schools desegregated, and the ambivalence of the black community over black children attending predominantly white schools. But Mississippi blacks were also aware that "the KKK tries your case long before it can get before the Supreme Court." The three black men who had tried to desegregate Mississippi universities in the 1950s—Medgar Evers, Clennon King, and Clyde Kennard—were, respectively, subjected to death threats and ultimately murdered, forced into a lunacy hearing, and incarcerated on possibly trumped-up criminal charges. Hundreds of blacks signing school desegregation petitions in Deep South cities in 1954–1955 suffered swift and severe retribution. Newspapers published their names, which facilitated economic reprisals. Many of the petitioners had to relocate to find work. Texas police officers rounded up and interrogated petition signers, ostensibly to determine if the NAACP had duped them into participating. Some petitioners suffered violence, such as the president of the NAACP branch in Sulphur Springs, Texas, who had his home shot up and was driven out of the state. Neither the association nor the petitioners had expected quite so ferocious a response, and it clearly deterred prospective litigants, who could guess what would be in store for them and their children. The Reverend J. A. De Laine, who had helped to organize the original school desegregation suit in Clarendon County, was fired from his job as a public school teacher, had his life threatened by the Klan, saw his church burned down, and then had to flee South Carolina after being charged with assault for defending himself against vigilantes who were attacking his home. When the Reverend Fred Shuttlesworth escorted his children to a white Birmingham school to desegregate it, he was badly beaten by members of a mob who wielded brass knuckles and baseball bats, and his church was bombed three times in retaliation for his desegregation activities. Lacking other candidates, some NAACP officials volunteered themselves as plaintiffs and sued for the admission of their own children to white schools.[19]

Harassment of the NAACP and intimidation of prospective plaintiffs stymied desegregation litigation outside of the border states and the peripheral South. One of Justice Burton's law clerks had noted that "this Court cannot do anything to Miss[issippi] if it chooses to continue segregation unless a Negro chooses to try to enforce his rights there." None did so at the grade school level until 1963, despite repeated threats by the NAACP to sue in Mississippi beginning in 1955. In Georgia, the first desegregation suit outside of Atlanta was not filed until 1962. In Alabama, the first suit outside of Birmingham was not filed until 1963, even though beginning in the late 1950s blacks had sued several Alabama cities over segregation on buses and in parks. In 1959, Martin Luther King, Jr., and the Montgomery Improvement Association had threatened a school desegregation suit, which prompted Governor John Patterson to go on statewide radio to warn blacks "that if you follow a man like Martin Luther King, it is only going to lead to chaos and disorder and violence and the destruction of our public school system." No desegregation suit was brought in Montgomery until 1964. In South Carolina, threats to close desegregated schools and to fire black teachers apparently deterred the NAACP from pressing the Clarendon County case after an order to desegregate with "all deliberate speed" was issued on remand in 1955 but no steps were taken toward implementation. Blacks did not file suit in Charleston until 1962, and two years later that was still the only South Carolina city with any school desegregation. Even in the border state of Missouri, desegregation litigation did not begin in most boot-heel counties until 1963. Ironically, suits proliferated where desegregation was already furthest along. In 1956, the NAACP filed its eighth desegregation

FIGURE 7.1
The Reverend J. A. De Laine speaks at the NAACP
Legal Defense Fund's annual meeting in 1974.
(Photo courtesy *J. A. De Laine, Jr.*)

suit in Delaware and its ninth in West Virginia, while the first Deep South litigation was still years away. Desegregation litigation proved most feasible where resistance was the least intense and therefore litigation was least necessary, and vice versa.[20]

Litigation could only bring the issue before a judge, who would have to determine whether, when, and how schools would desegregate. Lower federal courts are the principal interpreters of Supreme Court opinions, and they would ultimately determine the meaning of *Brown II*. Justice Black had warned that "not one federal judge would favor [desegregation]"—a slight overstatement but not much of one. In 1954, all southern federal judges were white; the vast majority had been born and raised in the South; and their views on school desegregation did not deviate far from those of most white southerners. Many of them were openly disdainful of *Brown*, and almost none publicly endorsed it. Judge William H. Atwell of Dallas thought that segregation was "neither immoral nor unconstitutional," and he criticized *Brown* for its reliance on "modern psychological knowledge" rather than law. Judge T. Whitfield Davidson, born in East Texas though sitting on the bench in Dallas, insisted, "[T]he white man has a right to maintain his racial

FIGURE 7.2
The Reverend Fred Shuttlesworth
meets with the press after his release
from the hospital after he was
beaten by a mob while trying to
desegregate a Birmingham high
school in 1957. (*Birmingham Public
Library, Department of Archives and
Manuscripts, no. 829.1.1.61*)

integrity and it can't be done so easily in integrated schools." Judge George
Bell Timmerman of South Carolina believed that whites "still have the right
to choose their own companions and associates, and to preserve the integrity
of the race with which God Almighty has endowed them," and he insisted,
"The judicial power of the United States . . . does not extend to the enforcement of Marxist socialism as interpreted by Myrdal, the Swedish Socialist."
Judge R. Gordon West of Louisiana thought that *Brown* was "one of the truly
regrettable decisions of all times," and Judge Ashton H. Williams of South
Carolina contemplated recusing himself from a case involving desegregation
of public facilities, "since I cannot conscientiously support the 1954 ruling of
the Supreme Court." Even Judge Walter E. Hoffman, a Virginia Republican
who was the first judge to invalidate that state's massive-resistance legislation,
thought that the notion that *Brown* violated the Tenth Amendment was "meritorious . . . as an initial proposition." These were some of the judges who
were charged with enforcing *Brown*.[21]

Even judges who profoundly disagreed with desegregation might have
followed unambiguous Court orders to impose it, out of a sense of professional obligation. State and federal judges did nullify segregation laws after
Brown, revealing a willingness to follow clear Court edicts, "distasteful as it
might be," because they "had no right to reverse the rulings of the Supreme

Court." Some of these judges protested that they were not "free agent[s]," and others volunteered their personal opinions that *Brown* was wrong— "most unfortunate, and . . . entirely unconstitutional," according to one— but they did their duty to enforce it by invalidating segregation laws. *Brown II*, however, was hardly an order to do anything. Its indeterminacy invited judges to delay and evade, which they were inclined to do anyway.[22]

Lower court judges also faced political pressure not to order desegregation. As Black had observed, *Brown* put federal judges "on the battlefront" with precious little ammunition at their disposal. Politicians attacked judges who seemed overly eager to desegregate, and judges could point to no order from above commanding desegregation at any particular time or in any particular manner. Senator Harry Byrd of Virginia accused Judge Hoffman of "arrogance," "prejudice," and partisanship in his desegregation rulings. George Wallace repeatedly assailed Judge Frank Johnson for his "integrating, scallawagging, carpetbagging" ways. One Louisiana legislator questioned Judge J. Skelly Wright's mental soundness, and another called for his arrest.[23]

Lifetime job tenure provided federal judges with some insulation from political attack but not from the disapprobation of friends and colleagues. Just like school board members, federal judges had to live in the communities that they were being asked to desegregate against the wishes of most whites. An aide to Governor Wallace suggested, "These federal judges should be scorned and they and their families and their friends should be ostracized by responsible Southerners." And so they were. Judges endured hate mail, harassing midnight phone calls, and occasional cross burnings. The grave of the son of Judge Richard Rives of the Fifth Circuit was desecrated. The home of the mother of Judge Frank Johnson of Montgomery was bombed. After Judge Waring voted to desegregate Clarendon County schools, shots were fired into his home. Soon thereafter, having tired of being "the lonesomest man in town," he retired from the bench and moved to New York. Waring was such an outcast in Charleston that fewer than a dozen whites (but two hundred blacks) attended his funeral service there in 1968. The district judge whose firmness on desegregation spawned the Little Rock crisis was Ronald N. Davies of North Dakota, who was sitting by designation and thus relatively immune from local pressure. His successor, long-time Arkansan Harry J. Lemley, proved more accommodating of delay.[24]

Lower court judges had little incentive to press desegregation where it was likely to produce school closures or violence. On remand from the Supreme Court in the Clarendon County and Prince Edward County cases, three-judge courts refused to impose desegregation deadlines when faced with threats of school closures, and they expressed annoyance at the NAACP's insistence on immediate desegregation. Judge Frank Hooper in Atlanta deferred enforcement of his desegregation order for two years in order to give the state legislature a "last chance" to repeal school closure laws; he reasoned that "all deliberate speed" was "consistent . . . with the preservation if possible of our common school system." After some desegregation orders resulted in riots, most judges were determined to avoid similar chaos in their own backyards. One federal judge, citing the violence in Milford and Little Rock, concluded that "total and immediate integration of the Delaware school system is out of the question." Judge Hooper refused to order desegregation in Atlanta "so speedily that there will be violence." Judge Taylor, acknowledging his failure to foresee the "frightful lawlessness" and "terrorism" at Clinton, where he had ordered desegregation in 1956, justified a grade-a-year plan for Knoxville as necessary to avoid a repetition. Although *Brown II* instructed courts not to consider community resistance in fashioning desegregation orders, the justices had not taken that instruction seriously, and neither did most district judges, who thought that the size of the local black population, the intensity of white resistance, and the likelihood of violence were obviously relevant considerations.[25]

Personal and political incentives not to press desegregation, together with a legal standard that conferred broad discretion, led most federal judges to countenance delay. So long as school boards "studied" the problem, judges were generally satisfied for at least a couple of years after *Brown*. The first judicial desegregation orders generally required ending segregation with "all deliberate speed" but without imposing any deadline; such orders proved nearly worthless in practice. By the time that judges were ready to impose deadlines, southern political opinion had become so extreme that most of them were reluctant to order anything beyond token integration and some not even that. In light of the indeterminate legal standard, it was predictable that a great deal would depend on the inclination of particular judges and on the environment in which they operated. Northern judges on the Eighth Circuit construed *Brown II* more stringently than did a southern judge in Little Rock, whose decisions they reviewed, and northern and southern judges on the Sixth Circuit had different opinions regarding desegregation in Tennessee. In the border state of Kentucky, some federal judges construed "all deliberate speed" to mean "now," and they imposed desegregation orders soon after *Brown II* and were less inclined to accept grade-a-year plans than were judges sitting farther south. In upper South states, such as Arkansas, Tennessee, and Virginia, some judges issued desegregation orders with deadlines as early as 1956 or 1957. But in recalcitrant districts, which were usually those with large black populations, judges were disinclined to impose early deadlines. Although each of his Virginia colleagues had already issued desegregation orders, in 1957 Judge Sterling Hutcheson refused to set a deadline for Prince Edward County, because the "present state of unrest and racial tension in the county" counseled "patience, time, and a sympathetic approach." When the Fourth Circuit ordered him to set a deadline, Hutcheson chose 1965, which got him reversed again. In Dallas, protracted jousting between segregationist trial judges and an increasingly impatient Fifth Circuit, combined with years of legal uncertainty over the constitutionality of Texas's 1957 referendum requirement, delayed desegregation until 1961. In Louisiana, even the progressive-minded J. Skelly Wright, who issued a desegregation order without a deadline in 1956, permitted delays until 1960 in light of hostile opinion, which he conceded would not permit desegregation "overnight." Segregationist judges in Alabama dragged their feet for years, until in 1963 the Fifth Circuit finally commanded action.[26]

When judges eventually ordered desegregation, the same incentives just noted inclined most of them to endorse gradualism and tokenism. In an early interpretation, Judge John Parker of the Fourth Circuit insisted that *Brown* "forbids the use of governmental power to enforce segregation"; it "does not require integration." In other words, the remedial obligation of school districts was to dismantle state-sponsored segregation, not to produce racial balance in the schools. Parker's interpretation may seem like a bad-faith distortion of *Brown's* meaning, but he was no nullifier. One of Burton's pro-*Brown* clerks had stated an identical view during *Brown II* deliberations—a perspective that Burton apparently voiced as his own during the justices' conference: "The mere admission of colored children to white schools, or vice versa, is not in itself justifiable. The Constitution does not call for that." Lower court judges frequently cited Parker's dictum, which rapidly became the conventional interpretation. Even compliant judges thought that *Brown* "may well not necessitate such extensive changes in the school system as some anticipate."[27]

In the 1950s, most judges sustained proposals for even minimal desegregation, relieved to have avoided outright defiance and convinced that *Brown* had not authorized courts to substitute their judgment regarding pupil allocation for that of school boards. The only desegregation plan that courts consistently ruled unconstitutional provided for three types of schools within a district—black, white, and racially mixed—and allowed parents to choose among them. Courts sustained every other school board proposal for delay and evasion: grade-a-year, pupil placement, minority-to-majority transfer, and freedom of choice. *Brown II* had not plainly required more, and judges had powerful incentives not to push harder than the Court was mandating. With the justices indicating no disapproval, the evasive techniques of school boards were "confined more by the limits of personal ingenuity than by judicial restraint."[28]

Pupil placement and freedom of choice became the preferred methods of limiting desegregation. The former drew on a long tradition of white southerners evading federal constitutional constraints by granting local officials "practically unreviewable discretion." Placement laws, which were adopted by all southern states, authorized administrators to place students according to a long list of racially neutral factors, such as students' residence, psychological fitness, scholastic aptitude, health and moral standards, suitability of curriculum, and availability of space and transportation. Although race was not an enumerated criterion, the purpose and effect of these plans was to enable administrators to maintain segregation, while insulating the system from legal challenge because of the difficulty of proving that a multi-factor decision was racially motivated. Such plans also delayed litigation in federal court, because parents who were dissatisfied with their children's placement could not sue until they had exhausted time-consuming and burdensome administrative appeals, which themselves afforded ample opportunity for procedural errors that would forfeit litigation rights. Placement plans also presumptively maintained the segregationist status quo, as petitioners bore the burden of requesting placements other than to their current (segregated) schools. Finally, because the plans purported to extend individualized treatment, it was nearly impossible to bring class-action suits to challenge them, because plaintiffs could not demonstrate sufficient commonality of circumstance. To avoid judicial invalidation, placement boards had to eventually permit some integration, but the numbers of blacks admitted were invariably token. In North Carolina, which pioneered pupil placement, twelve black students attended desegregated schools in three cities in 1957 — enough race mixing to withstand an initial judicial challenge. Refusing to presume discriminatory administration, lower courts declined to invalidate pupil placement plans on their face, so long as they were disassociated from other legislation that mandated segregation or school closures, and the Supreme Court concurred.[29]

School districts that eschewed pupil placement in favor of neighborhood schools generally offered liberal transfer options that curtailed desegregation. Broad transfer rights were consistent with Judge Parker's view that *Brown* required states to stop segregating but did not require them to integrate. Before 1954, southern whites had demanded compulsory segregation, but within a few years of *Brown* they were treating freedom of association as a "God-given right." In 1962, Georgia voters wrote that principle into their constitution. The vast majority of whites exercised minority-to-majority transfer options to leave desegregated schools to which they had been assigned. Most blacks who were eligible for desegregation opted out as well. In 1958 in Nashville, all but 4 percent did so. In Texas that year, only 1 black out of 1,229 who were eligible attended a desegregated school in Amarillo; 6 out of 2,111 in Lubbock; and 31 out of 1,100 in Austin. Counties on Maryland's Eastern Shore technically desegregated soon after *Brown*, but until the 1960s, most did not have a single black who exercised the right to transfer to a white school. An NAACP leader in West Virginia thought it "disgraceful" that so few blacks took advantage of *Brown*. But black parents justifiably feared economic reprisals, mistreatment of their children, and even violence. In 1957, every black parent in Nashville who registered a child in a white school received a threatening call from the Klan. Black students who pioneered desegregation suffered taunting, threats, and physical abuse. Many of them ultimately capitulated to the pressure and returned to black schools, while those who endured often sacrificed good education in the service of integration.[30]

In the late 1950s, the Court did nothing to condemn this tokenism and was widely perceived to have endorsed it. The Eisenhower administration appeared to celebrate it, relieved at having avoided a repetition of Little Rock in Virginia in 1958–1959. Some school districts—mainly outside of the Deep South—that had been awaiting resolution of school closure battles before beginning desegregation now implemented the tokenist measures that courts had validated. The number of blacks admitted to white schools was minuscule, yet courts generally declined to interfere. State attorney general Seawell told a congressional committee in 1959, when 40 of North Carolina's 300,000 black students were attending desegregated schools, that his state was gradually adjusting to *Brown*, and editors of the *New Republic* called the state a "Model for the South." The chairman of the U.S. Civil Rights Commission thought that Nashville's progress was "very encouraging," even though only 42 of the district's 12,000 black students were attending desegregated schools in 1960. With good reason, Thurgood Marshall complained that massive resistance had given way to "token compliance," yet courts were acquiescing in the "unbelievably slow" pace. In 1961, he warned, "[A]n atmosphere has been created whereby pupil assignment and stairstep integration is becoming acceptable as a legitimate compromise for constitutional rights." Another civil rights leader worried that a "bored and disgusted nation might leave the South to handle the race problem in its own way." In the Deep South, aside from Atlanta and New Orleans, where nine and twelve black students, respectively, attended desegregated schools in the fall of 1961, nothing at all had happened.[31]

The pace of school desegregation accelerated primarily because of the civil rights movement. Beginning with sit-in demonstrations in 1960 and Freedom Rides in 1961, direct-action protest swept the South. In response, the NAACP began demanding more effective desegregation policies, more blacks brought suits, and some federal judges rejected tokenist strategies that had previously been deemed acceptable. These changes preceded by two or three years the justices' first expressions of impatience with the glacial pace of desegregation.

Soon after the sit-ins began, the NAACP's secretary reported, "Students who participated in protest demonstrations have been stimulated to move toward more desegregation in education." The association encouraged that development. In May 1960, the NAACP's leader in Florida announced a mass campaign to enroll blacks in racially mixed schools. That summer and fall, both the number of blacks who petitioned for transfers to white schools under placement schemes and the number who declined to transfer out of racially mixed schools under neighborhood plans increased dramatically. This campaign expanded in 1961. Marshall made speeches across the South, denouncing token integration, which he called an insult to the intelligence of black people, and urging blacks to commence a massive assault on segregated schools. Civil rights rallies in Atlanta urged blacks to apply for transfers to white schools. The Florida NAACP called for an all-out campaign against school segregation, in which thousands of blacks would demand transfers under placement plans, which the association now denounced as subterfuges. The association organized several black families in Polk County, Florida, to seek admission to white schools after hundreds of blacks were arrested during direct-action protests. In 1962, school desegregation finally came to the county of Wicomico on Maryland's Eastern Shore as an indirect consequence of student lunch-counter demonstrations. Desegregation suits in Albany, Georgia, and Charleston, Missouri, also grew out of such protests.[32]

In 1960, the annual race-relations report of the Tuskegee Institute observed that sit-in demonstrations had "encouraged a country-wide reexamination of the moral consequences of the continuing delays in implementing desegregation." Many judges also seemed to be reexamining their positions. In the summer of 1960, the Third Circuit rejected grade-a-year desegregation for Delaware, notwithstanding the justices' recent refusal to review the Sixth Circuit ruling sustaining that policy for Nashville. Shortly thereafter, Judge Albert V. Bryan threw out the grade-a-year plan of Fairfax County, Virginia, reasoning that Fairfax, with its 4 percent black population, could move more quickly than Nashville, with its 37 percent. In 1961–1962, several Tennessee judges rejected grade-a-year plans, ordering counties to desegregate several grades at once or, in some instances, all grades simultaneously. Late in 1960, the Fifth Circuit invalidated as discriminatory the minority-to-majority transfer option in the Dallas desegregation plan, disagreeing with the Sixth Circuit's resolution of that issue in the Nashville case. In 1962, the Fourth Circuit followed suit, and so did several district judges. Many courts now rejected certain features of pupil placement plans, such as the requirement for achievement tests, which applied only to blacks. Some judges went even further, ruling that placement schemes were inadequate as desegregation plans so long as they presumptively placed students in the same segregated schools—a clear departure from earlier decisions.[33]

Even courts that still tolerated placement plans began to look more closely at their administration, found discrimination, and ordered large increases in the number of blacks assigned to desegregated schools. Early in 1961, the Eighth Circuit ruled discriminatory the Little Rock school board's administration of its pupil placement plan and demanded "affirmative action" to produce "integration on more than a token fashion." The number of blacks attending desegregated schools in Little Rock quadrupled the next year. In 1962, the Fourth Circuit began invalidating the discriminatory administration of placement plans in North Carolina and Virginia. That year, the school board in Charlotte-Mecklenburg, North Carolina, radically revised its placement policy to assign students primarily on the basis of geography rather than requiring blacks to petition for admittance to white schools; the number of blacks attending racially mixed schools promptly increased from 27 to 413. Desegregation also began to penetrate into new areas—eastern North Carolina, East Texas, the Florida panhandle—as some school boards saw the writing on the wall, and others were compelled by courts to act. Border states that had tolerated segregation in recalcitrant districts—rural Kentucky, Maryland's Eastern Shore, Missouri's boot-heel—began exerting pressure to eliminate it. Yet, some intensely resistant districts and segregationist judges still refused to accelerate the pace; they continued to practice and permit the discriminatory administration of placement plans, which yielded only token desegregation.[34]

The altered social climate affected the politics of desegregation. In the fall of 1961, the U.S. Civil Rights Commission issued sweeping recommendations for accelerating desegregation, including requiring all districts to file desegregation plans with the federal government within six months and withholding 50 percent of federal education money from segregated districts. The Kennedy administration, which in the fall of 1961 had praised token desegregation in Dallas and Atlanta, pressed for more aggressive action in 1962. For the first time, the administration threatened to litigate against, and to cut off funds for, segregated districts that received federal money to educate the children of military personnel. Southern officials expressed alarm at the prospect of losing millions of federal education dollars. The Justice Department filed the first such suits in 1962–1963, and many districts desegregated rather than run the "disastrous" risk of losing federal funds.[35]

After the epic Birmingham street demonstrations in the spring of 1963 (described below) and the administration's introduction of landmark civil rights legislation in response, the pace of school desegregation accelerated significantly. That summer, Attorney General Robert Kennedy told the Senate Judiciary Committee that desegregation must speed up, and the Justice Department intervened in an NAACP desegregation suit to tell the justices the same thing. The chairman of the House Judiciary Committee, Emanuel Celler, warned that he was keeping "a watchful eye" on federal judges who were responsible for "unconscionable delay" in handling civil rights cases—a thinly veiled threat of impeachment. There were 161 school districts that desegregated in the fall of 1963, by far the largest number since 1956, and three and a half times the number of the preceding fall. The NAACP, making a "big push" to end segregation, now demanded "total and complete" desegregation, and a few judges ordered it. Pupil placement plans were increasingly abandoned in favor of freedom-of-choice plans. Many districts announced the desegregation of all grades at once, as they had become convinced that courts would order it if they did not voluntarily implement it. For the first time, some judges barred school boards from making teacher assignments based on race. All of these developments occurred before the Supreme Court declared, "[T]he time for mere 'deliberate speed' has run out."[36]

Notwithstanding this accelerated desegregation pace, when Congress passed the 1964 Civil Rights Act, only one black child in a hundred in the South attended a racially mixed school. The federal judiciary, acting without any congressional or much presidential backing, had proved powerless to accomplish more. Most of that 1 percent, moreover, had resulted from lower court decisions of the early 1960s, which had increased the pace of desegregation in response to broad social currents. Those decisions would not have happened without *Brown*, but they also would not have happened without the civil rights movement.[37]

In supporting the 1964 act, Senator Paul Douglas of Illinois observed that desegregation would take one thousand years to complete in the Deep South if the current pace continued. Because of the statute, it did not. The attorney general exercised his newly granted authority to bring desegregation suits, and the Department of Health, Education, and Welfare (HEW) threatened to withhold federal education funds from districts that continued to segregate. The percentage of southern black children in desegregated schools shot up from 1.18 percent in 1964 to 6.1 percent in 1966, 16.9 percent in 1967, 32 percent in 1969, and roughly 90 percent in 1973. (These figures do not distinguish between blacks attending school with many whites and with few whites.) HEW's imposition of more stringent desegregation guidelines in 1966—rejecting freedom of choice in favor of actual integration—accelerated the process, especially as lower courts incorporated these guidelines into their desegregation decrees. The 1964 Civil Rights Act, not *Brown*, was plainly the proximate cause of most school desegregation in the South. The remainder of this chapter investigates the linkage between the Court decision and the statute.[38]

INDIRECT EFFECTS

Counting the number of black children attending desegregated schools is only one way—and perhaps a rather poor one—of evaluating *Brown's* importance. Countless scholars have asserted *Brown's* broader significance, calling the decision "the most important political, social, and legal event in America's twentieth-century history" and "the foundation of our quest for equal justice in the United States." More specifically, observers have claimed that *Brown* "launched the public debate over racial equality," "raised the issue [of racial equality] a few notches on the national agenda," "raised black awareness," "stimulated black hope," "gave a great boost to black expectations," and "awoke a new activism within the black community."[39]

This section considers several possible indirect effects of *Brown*: How much did the decision increase the salience of the segregation issue and thus force people to take a position? How much did the Court's moral authority educate people into condemning segregation? Did *Brown* inspire southern blacks to launch more aggressive legal challenges to Jim Crow? Did the decision motivate blacks to engage in alternative forms of protest, such as boycotts, sit-ins, Freedom Rides, and street demonstrations? Did *Brown*, by cultivating faith in legal action, possibly *discourage* direct-action tactics? Did desegregation developments after *Brown*, by revealing the limits of litigation-induced social change, encourage a shift to direct-action tactics in the 1960s? To what extent did desegregation rulings mobilize southern white resistance, radicalize southern politics, and encourage violence, which ultimately produced a national backlash in favor of civil rights legislation? How much did *Brown* create concrete opportunities for violent confrontation, which influenced national opinion in favor of civil rights?

Unfortunately, none of these indirect effects can be measured with precision. History is not science; one cannot repeat experiments and control for particular variables. Still, one can make a plausible case that *Brown* mattered more in some of these ways than in others. Specifically, I shall argue that *Brown* was less directly responsible than is commonly supposed for the direct-action protests of the 1960s and more responsible for ensuring that those demonstrations were brutally suppressed by southern law enforcement officers. That violence, when communicated through television to national audiences, transformed racial opinion in the North, leading to the enactment of landmark civil rights legislation.[40]

SALIENCE AND EDUCATION

Supreme Court rulings can direct public attention to previously ignored issues. Americans were not preoccupied with flag burning until the Court issued two controversial rulings on the subject in 1989–1990. Within six months of a 1990 decision on the right to die, a half million Americans drafted living wills.[41]

Brown surely had this sort of impact. News coverage was extraordinary. Major newspapers heralded the decision in front-page, banner headlines. The *New York Times* assigned fifty staff members to cover the story, and they produced seven pages of information related to the ruling. A 1955 poll conducted in small towns in North Carolina and Georgia revealed that 60 percent of respondents had discussed *Brown* within the preceding week. The corresponding numbers in the North were lower—17 percent—but still impressive. Four days after *Brown*, a twelve-year-old girl from Brooklyn wrote to Justice Douglas to praise the "wonderful" decision, which represented a "beginning for the negro people." Most Court decisions may escape the attention of most Americans, but *Brown* did not.[42]

Brown forced many people to take a position on school segregation (President Eisenhower was an exception, as he refused to offer an opinion when asked two days after the ruling). Before *Brown*, desegregation of the military and major league baseball had been salient issues; school segregation was not. In 1947, Truman's civil rights committee took a position on nearly all salient race issues; school segregation was not among them. *Brown* changed this. In 1952, neither the Democratic nor the Republican national party took a position on school segregation, but in 1956 both of them did.

Civil rights generally, and school segregation particularly, played a large role at both parties' national conventions that year. During the presidential election campaign, all of the Democratic candidates for the nomination made several statements regarding school desegregation, and so did Eisenhower and Vice President Richard Nixon. From the 1920s to the 1950s, civil rights bills in Congress had dealt with lynching, the poll tax, and job discrimination. School desegregation—in the context of the attorney general's authority to bring injunction suits—first became the subject of proposed legislation in 1956–1957.[43]

Brown also dramatically increased the importance of race in southern politics. In the postwar years, populist politicians had won many victories throughout the South by supporting expanded public services and downplaying race. *Brown* rendered this strategy obsolete. By 1955–1956, school desegregation had become the dominant issue in most southern elections. Outside of politics, church groups, labor unions, and debating societies in the South resolved their support for *Brown* or, more frequently, their opposition to it. Segregation also became a more salient issue in the North. In New York's 1956 Senate race, Republican Jacob Javits and Democrat Robert Wagner accused each other of "aiding segregation"—a debate that they would not have had but for *Brown*.[44]

That *Brown* forced people to take a position on school segregation is not to say that it influenced the position they took. Some endorsed it and others condemned it—and Eisenhower said that he would enforce it, while refusing to endorse or condemn it. Southern politicians, forced to take a position on an issue that many of them would have preferred to avoid, overwhelmingly denounced *Brown*. By contrast, northern liberals, who may not have had much previous occasion to consider school segregation, now condemned it as a moral evil. Most national religious organizations responded similarly. They had not previously expressed an opinion on school segregation, but once forced to do so, the only conceivable one they could take was to condemn it. Even the organizations of Southern Baptists and Methodists endorsed *Brown* as consistent with Christian principles, leading many of their local affiliates to violently dissent. In the mid-1950s, any serious Democratic presidential candidate had to endorse *Brown*.[45]

Being forced to take a position in favor of *Brown* did not equate to being strongly committed to implementing the ruling. One could endorse *Brown* without supporting the use of federal troops to enforce it, or cutting off federal education funds to districts that defied it, or breaking a southern filibuster in the Senate over legislation to implement it. An early 1957 poll showed that 72 percent of Americans were opposed to cutting off federal education funds to districts that continued to segregate their schools. According to 1956 Gallup polls, more than 70 percent of whites outside of the South thought that *Brown* was right, but only a small percentage (less than 6 percent) considered civil rights the nation's most important issue. In the South, where over 40 percent thought that civil rights was the leading issue, only 16 percent of whites agreed with *Brown*. In the mid-1950s, the whites with the strongest feelings about *Brown* generally disagreed with it the most vehemently. Only the 1960s civil rights movement would equalize the intensity of commitment of those whites who supported segregation and those who opposed it.[46]

The passage of the 1957 Civil Rights Act illustrates these points about salience and relative intensity of preference. Without *Brown*, Congress most likely would not have enacted civil rights legislation when it did. No such bill had passed since 1875, and since the 1920s many proposed measures had succumbed to the threat or reality of Senate filibuster. After *Brown* raised the salience of race, many northerners—white and black—demanded civil rights legislation. Liberals in both parties endorsed the concept as the 1956 elections approached.[47]

Although heightened attention to race after *Brown* made civil rights legislation possible, the relatively tepid preferences of northern whites ensured that any statute would be limited in scope and largely ineffectual. In an extraordinary display, Eisenhower publicly confessed that he "didn't completely understand" his administration's own bill. Title III, which would have authorized the attorney general to sue for injunctions over any civil rights violation, including school segregation, was stricken from the bill after the president appeared dismayed by Senator Richard Russell's charge that the measure would force desegregation with "federal bayonets." The bill's scope was then restricted to voting rights, with liberal senators protesting that "the rug is [being] pulled from under our feet by the administration." Yet even thus limited, the bill proved unacceptable to white southerners, who further sabotaged it with an amendment that guaranteed jury trials for those who were charged with criminal contempt for violating an injunction. Because few southern whites would convict public officials for disfranchising blacks, the jury-trial provision essentially nullified the statute's impact. The crucial votes for narrowing its scope came from western Democrats, who traded their votes on civil rights legislation in exchange for southern support for federal water projects. Seven years later, when commitments to civil rights were stronger, even the longest filibuster in Senate history could not induce northern and western senators to abandon their support.[48]

Brown increased the salience of the segregation issue, and in 1954 many Americans, if forced to take a position, could only be integrationists. Yet, endorsing a position and being strongly committed to it are very different things. Set against the intense preferences of southern whites for preserving segregation, the weak endorsement of *Brown* by many northerners was ineffectual.

Conventional wisdom holds that one of *Brown*'s most important consequences was to educate white Americans to condemn racial segregation. Yet, surprisingly little evidence supports this view. Americans have generally felt free to disagree with the Supreme Court and to make up their own minds about moral controversies. *Dred Scott v. Sandford* (1857), which barred the federal government from prohibiting slavery in the territories, did not convince many Americans that slavery should be permitted there. *Engel v. Vitale* (1962) ruled that the Constitution prohibits state-sponsored prayer in public schools, yet polls indicate that a solid majority of Americans still favor that practice today. Rather than educating people to oppose the death penalty, *Furman v. Georgia* (1972), which ruled capital punishment to be unconstitutional under certain circumstances, seems to have mobilized support for it. Opinion polls suggest that *Roe v. Wade* (1973), which invalidated most statutes criminalizing abortion, has not changed many minds on that subject. Nor does *Bowers v. Hardwick* (1986), which upheld the constitutionality of criminal sodomy laws as applied to consenting homosexual adults, seem to have convinced many Americans that government should treat homosexuality as immoral. If none of these landmark decisions educated many people to agree with the Court, why should *Brown* have?[49]

Of course, it is possible that *Brown* was simply different. The fact that other famous rulings had little educational impact does not prove that *Brown* did not. The educational influence of *Brown* must be analyzed on its own. Yet one should not discount the possibility that most Americans ultimately agreed with *Brown*, not because the Court influenced their thinking, but because other developments, such as the civil rights movement, did.

Opinion poll data suggest that *Brown* did not educate many southern whites. A 1959 Gallup poll showed that only 8 percent of southern whites supported *Brown*, down from 15 percent in earlier polls. Rather than persuading southern whites to support desegregation, *Brown* inspired them to ridicule the Court, to criticize its "shocking, outrageous, and reprehensible" decision, to support curbs on its jurisdiction, to recommend impeaching its justices, and to propose investigating its members for communist influence. Southern whites were not educated by a decision that they believed ignored precedent, transgressed original intent, indulged in sociology, infringed on the reserved rights of states, and usurped Congress's authority. Newspaper editor James J. Kilpatrick stated a typical view: "[I]n May of 1954, that inept fraternity of politicians and professors known as the United States Supreme Court chose to throw away the established law. These nine men repudiated the Constitution, sp[a]t upon the tenth amendment, and rewrote the fundamental law of this land to suit their own gauzy concepts of sociology." Another prominent southern journalist, John Temple Graves, wrote, "The Supreme Court . . . has tortured the Constitution. The South will torture the Supreme Court decision." Those who were inclined to criticize the Constitution rather than the Court denied the lawfulness of the Fourteenth Amendment, arguing that southern states had been coerced into ratifying it. The attorney general of Georgia, Eugene Cook, proposed making it a capital offense to assist federal authorities in the enforcement of *Brown*. Citizens' councils, far from being educated by

Brown, celebrated its anniversary by holding protest rallies, at which they told the Supreme Court to "go to Hell."[50]

Most northern whites did not ridicule *Brown* in this way, and many of them strongly endorsed it. Senator Hubert Humphrey of Minnesota called *Brown* "another step in the forward march of democracy," and Senator Herbert H. Lehman of New York said the decision was "news which all free men throughout the world must hail with joy." Yet to observe that most northerners applauded *Brown* is not necessarily to say that they were educated by it. Powerful political, economic, social, and ideological forces were impelling Americans toward more egalitarian racial views, quite independently of the Court's pronouncements. Revulsion against Nazi theories of Aryan supremacy and the Holocaust probably educated northern opinion at least as much as *Brown* did. Moreover, poll data reveal no large shift in northern attitudes toward school segregation in the years after *Brown*, as one might have expected if its educational influence was significant. One opinion poll showed that 5 percent more Americans agreed with *Brown* in 1959 than in 1954—an increase in antisegregation sentiment of 1 percent a year, which might easily have been attributable to extralegal forces as much as to the Court's ruling. *Brown* may have had a marginal impact on those who were undecided and thus most susceptible to the Court's influence, but it did not fundamentally transform the racial attitudes of most Americans.[51]

Brown changed the minds of few southern whites, who generally ridiculed the decision rather than being educated by it. *Brown* may have had more influence on northern whites, but many of them condemned segregation independently of the Court, and many others would not do so until southern resistance to the civil rights movement in the 1960s had dramatized for them the brutality of Jim Crow. Black Americans, of course, did not need the Court's moral instruction to convince them that racial segregation was evil. In the postwar period, black leaders had become overwhelmingly integrationist—far more so than they had been in earlier eras.[52]

MOTIVATIONAL EFFECT

Although *Brown* was unnecessary for educating blacks to condemn segregation, it unquestionably motivated them to challenge it. After both *Brown* rulings, the NAACP urged southern blacks to petition school boards for immediate desegregation on threat of litigation. Blacks filed such petitions in hundreds of southern localities, including in the Deep South. In a few cities, such as Baton Rouge and Montgomery, blacks even showed up in person to try to register their children at white schools. In the mid-1950s, but for *Brown*, such challenges would have been inconceivable in the Deep South, where race relations had been least affected by broad forces for racial change. One might have predicted that a campaign for racial reform there would have begun with voting rights or the equalization of black schools, not with school desegregation, which was hardly the top priority of most blacks and was more likely to incite violent white resistance. Merely signing one's name to a school desegregation petition was an act of courage for blacks in the Deep South, and it frequently incited economic reprisals and occasionally physical violence. The petition campaign contributed significantly to the rise of massive resistance in the mid-1950s; black efforts to implement *Brown* stimulated more resistance than did the decision itself. As the *Jackson Daily News* editorialized, "[T]here is only one way to meet the attack of the NAACP. Organized aggression must be met by organized resistance."[53]

Southern blacks took other, mostly litigation-based action as well "to strike while the iron is hot." Four days after *Brown*, Jo Ann Robinson, the president of the Women's Political Council in Montgomery, warned the mayor that blacks would boycott city buses if segregation did not end. In Columbia, South Carolina, blacks filed lawsuits challenging segregation in city parks and on city buses. In Birmingham, *Brown* inspired the Reverend Fred Shuttlesworth and his Alabama Christian Movement for Human Rights to seek out litigation opportunities, and suits were brought challenging segregation on city buses and in parks, the railroad terminal, and public employment. Mississippi blacks mounted voter registration campaigns in 1954–1955. Blacks in Greensboro, North Carolina, demanded desegregation of the public golf course and improvements in black schools.[54]

Brown prompted southern blacks to challenge Jim Crow more aggressively than they might otherwise have done in the mid-1950s. As we shall see, such challenges inspired southern whites to make a more vigorous defense of the racial status quo than they might otherwise have undertaken.

Brown motivated litigation, but what about direct-action protest? What is the connection between *Brown* and the Montgomery bus boycott or the 1960s sit-ins, Freedom Rides, and street demonstrations? Some scholars have treated *Brown* as the "spiritual father" of direct-action protest, occasionally even suggesting that, without *Brown*, the 1960s civil rights movement would not have taken place when it did. Evidence for this causal connection is weak.[55]

There is no denying *Brown*'s symbolic importance to African Americans. One black newspaper stated a widely shared view: *Brown* was "the greatest victory for the Negro people since the Emancipation Proclamation." One black leader called *Brown* "a majestic break in the dark clouds," and another later recalled that blacks "literally got out and danced in the streets." A black journalist subsequently noted, "[I]t would be impossible for a white person to understand what happened within black breasts on that Monday." Blacks celebrated *Brown*'s anniversary, May 17, which attested to its symbolic importance. For the Court to have vindicated their cause, especially when few other important institutions were doing so, provided blacks with "moral support." Because a principal obstacle for any social reform movement is convincing potential participants that success is feasible, *Brown* must have facilitated the mobilization of civil rights protest.[56]

Yet neither the symbolism of *Brown* nor the hopefulness it inspired were tantamount to putting black demonstrators on the streets. One cannot know for sure, but the evidence that *Brown* directly inspired such protests is thin.

What was the connection between *Brown* and the Montgomery bus boycott? The boycott began in December 1955 and lasted for an entire year. It was the first major direct-action protest of the modern civil rights era—a "decisive turning point in the life of southern Negroes." It demonstrated—to Montgomery, the South, the nation, and the world—that tens of thousands of ordinary black southerners, united across class lines, were fed up with the racial status quo and were prepared to fight it, even at the cost of extreme personal hardship, incarceration, and threatened injury and death. The boycott both fostered and featured black agency, as Montgomery blacks became convinced that through collective action they could transform social conditions. In the words of its organizers, the Montgomery movement marked "the passage of southern Negroes from an attitude of servility and passivity to a spirit of solidarity, fearlessness and hope." The executive secretary of the NAACP, Roy Wilkins, thought that the boycott was important because it "demonstrates before all the world that Negroes have the capacity for sustained collective action." The skill, fortitude, and courage with which blacks organized and executed the boycott contravened southern white stereotypes of black ineptitude, laziness, and timidity. Montgomery whites had never seen blacks "organize and discipline themselves, to carry something out to a finish," and they were consequently "very much impressed by their determination and courage." Blacks, not immune from being influenced by white stereotypes, were impressed as well.

Moreover, this obviously indigenous action flew in the face of southern white protestations that blacks were satisfied with the racial status quo and that "outside agitators," such as communists or the NAACP, were responsible for all racial discord in the South. Alabama whites could write off Autherine Lucy, who was attempting to desegregate the University of Alabama, as "just one unfortunate girl who doesn't know what she is doing, but in Montgomery it looks like all the niggers have gone crazy." The boycott also demonstrated the tactical value of nonviolent protest. The "quiet courage, dignity, and magnanimity" with which Montgomery blacks protested their racial oppression virtually ensured that white opponents, who used economic reprisals, trumped-up criminal charges, and even bombings, would face a "damning indictment" in the eyes of observers. The boycott attracted national and international attention. Thousands of dollars in financial support (as well as many shoes) poured in from around the country, and supporters participated in a national "deliverance day of prayer" to demonstrate solidarity with Montgomery blacks. The boycott also revealed the growing intransigence of southern whites toward even minimal black demands for reform, thus increasing the stakes of the burgeoning racial controversy in the South. Finally, Montgomery created and brought to national prominence a new black leader, Martin Luther King, Jr., who would play an instrumental role in the civil rights movement.[57]

Based on its timing—the boycott began just eighteen months after *Brown*—and a few statements by participants, some scholars have concluded that *Brown* was instrumental to the boycott. One cannot know for certain, but this seems unlikely. *Brown* may have induced Jo Ann Robinson of the Women's Political Council to complain about bus segregation to Montgomery's mayor, but it does not appear to have inspired tens of thousands of blacks to boycott the buses.[58]

If *Brown* had directly inspired the boycott, it is puzzling why protestors for the first two months did not include integration among their demands. Rather, they principally sought an end to the humiliating practices of white bus drivers, including verbal insults—"Nigger," "black bastard"—physical abuse, and an enraging proclivity to drive off before black passengers, who had to pay the fare at the front of the bus, had boarded again at the rear. The boycott leaders also demanded black drivers for predominantly black routes and seating practices that would fill buses on a first-come, first-served basis— whites from the front, blacks from the rear, and nobody forced to stand over empty seats or to relinquish her own. At the outset of the boycott, black leaders repeatedly stressed that they were not seeking an end to segregation, which would have been the logical goal had *Brown* been their primary inspiration. Indeed, the NAACP initially refused to support the boycott, because its leaders sought only "more polite segregation." The fact that boycott leaders did not originally contemplate litigation further weakens claims regarding *Brown*'s causal influence.[59]

A similar bus boycott had taken place the year before *Brown* in Baton Rouge, Louisiana, thus proving that direct-action protest did not require the inspiration of the Court. In June 1953, Baton Rouge blacks boycotted city buses for a week, after drivers had refused to comply with a new city ordinance that required that passengers be seated on a first-come, first-served basis. Several thousand blacks attended mass meetings; the boycott was nearly 100 percent effective; and the city council quickly offered a compromise that was accepted by black leaders. Montgomery's black ministers knew of the Baton Rouge boycott, were in touch with its leaders, and adopted some of its tactics. That Baton Rouge blacks conducted a successful bus boycott in 1953 does not prove that *Brown* had nothing to do with the Montgomery boycott, but it is suggestive.[60]

Brown's most significant contribution to the events in Montgomery may have been its impact on whites rather than on blacks. The Baton Rouge episode suggests that blacks in the Deep South did not need the inspiration of *Brown* to protest offensive bus practices. But why did public officials in Baton Rouge capitulate to black protest, while those in Montgomery refused to accept the same seating practices that already prevailed in many Deep South cities, including Mobile? Rather than making minimalist concessions,

Montgomery officials became intransigent, adopting a "get tough" policy, arresting boycott organizers on fabricated charges, joining the citizens' council, and failing to suppress violence against boycott leaders. The greater resistance of whites explains why the Montgomery boycott lasted a year, while the one in Baton Rouge was over in a week, and why the initially minimalist demands of Montgomery blacks turned into a federal court challenge to segregation. In the post-*Brown* South, whites tended to view all racial issues against the backdrop of school desegregation. Thus, Montgomery mayor W. A. Gayle thought that what blacks really wanted was "to destroy our social fabric," and another local segregationist called the bus demands "piddling stuff," as compared with the NAACP's real objectives: complete integration and interracial marriage. In such an environment, whites refused to make any concessions to black demands, no matter how reasonable. "If we granted the Negroes these demands," a white lawyer for the bus company privately explained, "they would go about boasting of a victory that they had won over the white people; and this we will not stand for." As public officials in Montgomery debated how to respond to the bus demands of blacks in January 1956, four southern governors were announcing that their states would defy *Brown* through interposition resolutions. Had it not been for the crystallization of southern white resistance that resulted from *Brown*, events in Montgomery might have taken a very different course.[61]

None of this is to deny that the Supreme Court's decision in *Gayle v. Browder* (1956), which extended *Brown* to invalidate bus segregation laws, was critical to desegregating Montgomery buses. The same day that *Gayle* was decided, November 13, 1956, city officials secured a state court injunction against the car pools of the Montgomery Improvement Association—a ruling that could have destroyed the boycott. Yet to focus on *Gayle's* contribution to desegregating Montgomery buses is to risk fundamentally misunderstanding the significance of the boycott to the modern civil rights movement. The Montgomery bus boycott demonstrated black agency, resolve, courage, resourcefulness, and leadership. The boycott revealed the power of nonviolent protest, deprived southern whites of their illusions that blacks were satisfied with the racial status quo, challenged other southern blacks to match the efforts of those in Montgomery, and enlightened millions of whites around the nation and the world about Jim Crow. A less satisfactory outcome would have been disappointing to Montgomery blacks, but it hardly would have negated, or even greatly tarnished, the momentous accomplishments of the movement.[62]

After Montgomery, surprisingly little direct-action protest took place in the South until 1960. The Montgomery Improvement Association undertook no further direct action. City parks and other public facilities, including schools, remained segregated. Blacks in a few other southern cities conducted bus boycotts that were patterned after Montgomery's—most notably, in Rock Hill, South Carolina, and in Tallahassee, Florida—but these proved less successful. On *Brown's* third anniversary in 1957, Martin Luther King,

Jr., led a prayer pilgrimage to Washington, D.C., in support of black voting rights, but the turnout was disappointing—only 15–25,000 people, as compared with the 50–60,000 that had been predicted. The prayer pilgrimage was part of the voter registration drive of the Southern Christian Leadership Conference (SCLC), the "Crusade for Citizenship," which floundered in the late 1950s. In 1957–1958, blacks in Tuskegee, Alabama, protested the state legislature's gerrymandering them out of the city with an effective boycott of white merchants; mass rallies in support of the boycott attracted thousands. Blacks in Orangeburg, South Carolina, also conducted a boycott in response to the economic reprisals taken by whites against black parents who had signed school desegregation petitions. In 1958–1959, small sit-in demonstrations that protested lunch-counter segregation took place in several cities in the southern and border states—Oklahoma City, Wichita, St. Louis, Miami, Nashville, and others—but they attracted little attention and generated no ripple effect. Thus, whether or not *Brown* inspired the Montgomery bus boycott, it produced no general outbreak of direct-action protest in the 1950s.[63]

In 1960, however, the South exploded with direct-action protests against race discrimination. On February 1, four black college students sat in at the segregated lunch counter in the Woolworth's drugstore in Greensboro, North Carolina. Within days, similar demonstrations had spread to other cities in North Carolina; within weeks, to surrounding states; and within months, to much of the urban South. Hundreds of youngsters participated in most cities, and scores were arrested. One NAACP official called the demonstrations "the most inspiring, and most dramatic appeals for citizenship of anything I've seen in all my 49 years." Those cynics who had expected the demonstrations quickly to "fizzle out, panty-raid style" were disappointed. The sit-ins "caught the imagination of the entire nation" and received extensive and generally favorable coverage in national newspapers and on television. They were endorsed by many northern, and a few southern, politicians of both parties, including President Eisenhower, Vice President Nixon, and the leading Democratic presidential contenders. (Former president Truman was the principal exception; he briefly disparaged the demonstrations as communist-inspired, but later retracted his embarrassing statement.) Supportive northerners raised funds to assist jailed southern protestors and conducted their own sympathy demonstrations in hundreds of cities at the local outlets of chain stores whose southern branches discriminated. Over the next year, southern black youngsters, together with sympathetic whites, sat in at restaurants, lunch counters, and libraries; "stood in" at movie theaters; "kneeled in" at churches; and "waded in" at beaches. All told, an estimated 70,000 people participated in such demonstrations, and roughly 4,000 were arrested. More than a hundred southern localities desegregated some public accommodations as a result.[64]

In the spring of 1961, black and white "freedom riders" traveled on buses through the South to enforce a Supreme Court decision forbidding segregation in interstate bus terminals. The initial demonstrators were severely beaten in Birmingham and Montgomery, Alabama, and their successors were incarcerated by the hundreds in Jackson, Mississippi. The Freedom Rides were a huge fundraising and public relations success for the Congress on Racial Equality (CORE), which sponsored them. Most northerners were appalled at the violence that was perpetrated upon peaceful demonstrators who were exercising federally guaranteed rights. Beginning in late 1961, the SCLC commenced mass demonstrations against segregation in Albany, Georgia, which lasted for nearly a year. The Student Nonviolent Coordinating Committee (SNCC) began projects to register black voters in some of the most retrograde parts of Mississippi. In the spring of 1963, massive street demonstrations by blacks in Birmingham, Alabama, resulted in hundreds of arrests and produced televised scenes of violence by law enforcement officers against peaceful demonstrators that sickened northern audiences and impelled national politicians to support landmark civil rights legislation. In the months after Birmingham, spin-off demonstrations occurred in hundreds of southern cities and towns; more than 100,000 people participated, and nearly 15,000 were arrested.[65]

What, if any, was the connection between *Brown* and the direct-action protests of the early 1960s? The nearly six-year gap between *Brown* and the Greensboro sit-ins suggests that any such connection must be indirect and convoluted. If *Brown* was a direct inspiration, why did the protests not begin until 1960?

The outbreak of direct-action protest can be explained independently of *Brown*. Background political, economic, social, and ideological forces had created conditions that were ripe for racial protest. As southern blacks moved from farms to cities, they became easier to organize as a result of superior urban communication and transportation facilities. The growth of black institutions in southern cities—social, political, civic, educational, and religious—provided the organizational framework from which a civil rights movement could emerge. Most notably, the black church provided leadership, funding, and a mass following, and black colleges produced aggressive young leaders and a corps of willing foot soldiers. The rising economic status of southern blacks enabled the financing of protest activities as well as boycotts to leverage social change. Greater black prosperity also highlighted the indignities of enforced social subordination. Better education for blacks created leaders who could direct social protest and college students who could participate in it. A better-educated white population meant that there were fewer diehard segregationists who were prepared to use violence in defending a lost cause. Greater restraints on violence, especially in southern cities, also facilitated direct-action protest. Those restraints were both internal and external: Modern city dwellers in the South did not generally countenance violence, and businesspeople positively despaired of it, while by 1960 the federal government was less willing to permit southern whites to maim or kill blacks with impunity. The increasing political power of northern blacks made the national government more supportive of the civil rights protests of southern blacks. The growing political power of southern blacks made local officeholders more responsive to black concerns and less willing to countenance the brutal suppression of racial protest. The explosive growth of national media, especially television, ensured that news of black protest spread quickly to other southern communities, where it could be duplicated, and to the North, where sympathetic audiences rallied in support of its goals. In addition, southern whites who were exposed to the media were less likely to be hard-core segregationists. The ideology of racial equality that had flowed from World War II broadened and deepened after the war and left in its wake fewer white Americans who were prepared to endorse Jim Crow. A generation of black soldiers who served during and after the war were not easily intimidated by the threats of white supremacists, and they often found insufferable the incongruity between their former role as soldiers for democracy and their continuing racially subordinate status. Many of them became civil rights leaders.[66]

That conditions for a mass racial protest movement were ripe does not explain why the explosion came in 1960 rather than, say, five years earlier. Two factors may help explain the precise timing of the modern civil rights movement. The first has to do with the Cold War and McCarthyism. Americans' concern over spreading international communism and the threat it posed to national security had peaked in the early 1950s. Within the space of a year, beginning in 1949, the Soviets had detonated their first nuclear bomb; communists had won control over mainland China; and North Korea had invaded South Korea, which put the United States at war again. With the threat of nuclear holocaust looming on the horizon, Americans became preoccupied with foreign policy concerns, which made the time inopportune for a crusade for domestic racial reform. Anxiety over domestic subversion peaked simultaneously, as Americans became transfixed by Senator Joseph McCarthy's allegations of communist infiltration of the State Department and by the trials of alleged Soviet spies, including Alger Hiss, Klaus Fuchs, and Julius and Ethel Rosenberg. Fear of communists was rampant, and any protest movement that challenged the established political, social, or economic order was susceptible to charges of being communist-inspired. Moreover, many of the white Americans who were most sympathetic to racial equality belonged to left-wing organizations, some of which were linked, either openly or covertly, with communists or fellow-travelers. Integrationist groups such as the Southern Conference on Human Welfare, the Civil Rights Congress, the Southern Negro Youth Congress, and radical labor unions were devastated by the reactionary politics of McCarthyism. Southern segregationists deftly turned this dynamic to their advantage. They constantly charged—and for the most part seem genuinely to have believed—that racial reformers were communist-inspired. Liberal groups, such as the NAACP, which were especially vulnerable to charges of communist infiltration, devoted much of their time and energy in the early 1950s to purging left-wingers. To launch large-scale direct-action protests in such an environment would have been difficult. By 1960, however, fear of domestic subversion had subsided—the issue played essentially no role in the presidential election that year—and the threat of nuclear holocaust had receded, if only slightly. Perhaps these developments opened space for the emergence of a mass racial protest movement. On this view, the civil rights revolution of the 1960s had little to do with *Brown* and much to do with the demise of McCarthyism and the slight easing of Cold War tensions, which had proven temporary impediments to a protest movement that was mainly spawned by World War II.[67]

The decolonization of Africa may also help to explain why direct-action protest broke out in 1960 rather than a few years earlier. In 1957, Ghana became the first black African nation to win its independence from colonial rule. Within a half-dozen years, more than thirty other African countries had followed suit, seventeen of them in 1960 alone. American civil rights leaders identified the African independence movements as an important motivation for their own. They saw American civil rights protests as "part of the revolt of the colored peoples of the world against old ideas and practices of white supremacy." African freedom movements demonstrated to American blacks the feasibility of racial change through collective action, while heightening their frustration with the domestic status quo. As James Baldwin explained, American blacks who observed African independence movements lamented that "all of Africa will be free before we can get a lousy cup of coffee." In 1960, Roy Wilkins observed that Africans were electing prime ministers and sending delegates to the United Nations, while Mississippi blacks still could not vote. The decolonization of Africa possibly provided the spark that was necessary to detonate a social protest movement that was already set to explode.[68]

Conditions were ripe in the United States for a mass racial protest movement, and factors such as the decolonization of Africa and the demise of McCarthyism may help to explain why it exploded in 1960 rather than a few years earlier. Alternatively, the precise timing of the Greensboro sit-ins and the extraordinary spin-off responses they produced may simply have been fortuitous. Compelling background circumstances did not dictate that the movement begin at a particular time and place. One cannot tell why the scattered sit-in demonstrations of 1958–1959 failed to produce the volcanic response of the Greensboro sit-ins in 1960. Once the latter attracted media attention, though, their repetition elsewhere was virtually guaranteed. Moreover, once sit-ins began to achieve some success at desegregating public accommodations, thus making racial reform seem feasible, new volunteers were certain to appear.[69]

Brown was an important symbol to blacks, and it furthered a growing perception that fundamental racial reform was possible. Yet there is little evidence to directly connect *Brown* with the Montgomery bus boycott or with the direct-action protests of the early 1960s. Deep background forces set the stage for mass racial protest. *Brown* was not the spark that ignited it.

Indeed, in the short term, *Brown* may have *discouraged* direct-action protest. The NAACP's enormous Court victory encouraged blacks to litigate, not to protest in the streets. *Brown* also elevated the stature of the NAACP among blacks, and the association favored litigation and lobbying, not direct-action protest. How could anyone argue with the NAACP's litigation strategy after *Brown*? In 1955, the association reported a large increase in its income, which it attributed to *Brown* "and the hope and expectation that the Supreme Court decision had provided the bases for successful action through [the] courts."[70]

One cannot measure the extent to which *Brown* may have discouraged direct-action protest, so this claim is speculative. But it does have the virtue of explaining the relative absence of such protest in the middle to late 1950s. Before World War II, sit-ins and street demonstrations were probably impractical in most of the South, because they would have incited violent suppression. In such an environment, litigation was the most viable means of racial protest and possibly the only one. The Montgomery bus boycott demonstrated that conditions had changed by the mid-1950s: Direct-action protest had become a viable alternative means of pursuing racial reform. Yet, even after Montgomery, little direct action occurred until 1960. After the NAACP's inspiring victory in *Brown*, perhaps most blacks were inclined to see what litigation could deliver, especially given the reservations that most Americans had about direct-action protest, which for many of them called to mind the fascist street demonstrations of the 1930s. Many of the black activists who would participate in direct-action protests in the early 1960s were busy in the mid- to late 1950s organizing black families to sign school desegregation petitions and file lawsuits.[71]

After Montgomery, a group of prominent black ministers in the South launched a direct-action organization, the SCLC, with which the NAACP had strained relations from the start. This tension was partly attributable to institutional jealousy. The NAACP saw itself as *the* civil rights organization, and it was not favorably disposed toward an upstart group that might compete for funding, membership, and headlines. The two organizations also had different theories of how to achieve social reform. The Montgomery ministers who led the boycott had been slow to litigate in part because this was not their preferred method of pursuing social change. The extraordinary success of the boycott further convinced them of the virtues of direct-action protest. Though they did not denigrate the NAACP's past contributions of "brilliant" legal representation, they believed that after Montgomery "a new stage has been set." Court decisions had to be implemented at the community level, and "direct action is our most potent political weapon."[72]

The NAACP drew a different lesson from Montgomery. The association was convinced that its victory in *Gayle* was "how the Montgomery buses *really* got desegregated," and it hoped that "some smart newspaper-man will finally catch on." To NAACP leaders, such as Marshall, King was a "first-rate rabble-rouser." The association did not actively support the SCLC's prayer pilgrimage in 1957 or its other voter registration activities. When the SCLC tried to move into Jackson, Mississippi, in 1958, with the NAACP under legal assault, the association's field secretary there "naturally discouraged" it. Montgomery notwithstanding, the NAACP remained com-mitted to the same litigation tactics of the previous half-century and discour-aged direct action. By the late 1950s, some branches were suggesting that "the time-tested and eminently successful legal, legislative and educational approach of the NAACP be supplemented and supported by direct mass action." But the NAACP leadership would not budge. The association had a vested interest in discouraging alternative strategies of protest that it could not monopolize. Moreover, the NAACP was "composed of lawyers and they don't march in the streets." In the late 1950s, the association's national office tried to prevent the Oklahoma City youth council from conducting sit-in demonstrations. The national office also refused to support a direct-action challenge to segregation in the public library by the Petersburg, Virginia, branch. Thus, the chairman of the NAACP branch in Greensboro, North Carolina, had good reason for turning to CORE, rather than to his own national office, when student sit-in demonstrators asked for his assistance in February 1960.[73]

Into the 1960s, NAACP officials continued "to question the applicability of passive resistance to the American scene." The association's traditional aversion to direct-action protest, as well as its commitment to avoiding legal violations, led it to initially criticize the sit-in demonstrations. When those protests proved enormously popular and successful, the NAACP became "eager to identify the organization with this protest movement." The associa-tion hoped to respond to "the many ill-informed hints from outside that we may have outlived our usefulness" by demonstrating that it was not "purely a 'legal' agency," but rather "a multi-weapon action organization." NAACP officials, indulging in some creative historical revisionism, emphasized the association's involvement in sit-ins "since the very beginning," noting with pride that its youth branches in Oklahoma City and Wichita had first adopted the tactic in 1958, that the four initial Greensboro demonstrators belonged to an NAACP youth chapter, and that other youth members were sitting in throughout the South. The association also assumed responsibility for representing arrested demonstrators at trial and for financing their bail bonds.[74]

Although the NAACP claimed, in relation to "the new spirit of protest," to be "the responsible generator, . . . the chief sustainer and guide, . . . and . . . the principal custodian of [its] working out," in fact the association contin-ued to misunderstand the significance of direct action. While King was urg-ing students to go to jail "to arouse the dozing conscience of our nation," the NAACP was telling them to take bail and trying to convert the sit-ins into "one or two" test cases. The association discouraged mass participation and arrests, because excessive bail obligations were causing an "unfortunate dissipation" of NAACP resources and because its leaders believed that litigation challenging the legality of arrests was equally effective regardless of the number of defendants. For the NAACP, then, the principal purpose of sit-in demonstrations was to test the constitutionality of laws that protected a shopkeeper's right to racially segregate his customers. The association failed to grasp the fundamental significance of sit-in demonstrations: that they enhanced the agency of blacks through collective protest; that they made it "absolutely clear that the Negro is not satisfied with segregation"; and that they provoked vigilantes and law enforcement officers to use "fascist-like tactics," including tear gas, police dogs, and fire hoses. Converting sit-in demonstrations into test cases, as the NAACP advocated, would have effectively nullified such contributions.[75]

In 1961, the association's opposition to direct action led it to discourage the Freedom Rides, which at the time Wilkins called "a big mistake." When CORE asked the NAACP's field secretary in Mississippi, Medgar Evers, to help organize a mass meeting around the bus demonstrators' arrival in Jackson, Evers demurred. The NAACP feared that the Freedom Rides would "possibly hinder some of [its] efforts already in progress" in Jackson. Only after these demonstrations proved enormously successful at exposing "the viciousness, crudity and disregard of law characteristic of Southern segregationists"—hardly a surprising accomplishment, given that this had been their purpose—did the NAACP change its tune and urge its college chapter members who were traveling home for the summer to insist on nonsegregated transportation.

NAACP officials were also slow to support other forms of direct-action protest in the early 1960s. As a result, the association increasingly had to compete with other organizations for the loyalty of its own members, who wished to partake in the spirit of the times. When the president of the Mississippi state conference of branches, Aaron Henry, evinced too much enthusiasm for cooperating with direct-action organizations, NAACP national officials took a dim view of his "belie[f] that whosoever frees him and his people should be used."[76]

The NAACP's predominant focus on litigation was myopic. In earlier decades, litigation had helped to mobilize black protest, build branches, raise funds, and educate northern whites and judges about Jim Crow. But the capacity of litigation to transform race relations was limited. Litigation did not foster black agency—the belief among individual blacks that they could meaningfully contribute to racial change. Rather, it taught the lesson that individual blacks should sit back—as "passive spectator[s]," in King's words—and allow elite lawyers and white judges to transform race relations for them. Litigation could not "involve the Negro masses" in the same way that boycotts, sit-ins, and street demonstrations could. Only direct-action protest could enable individuals to make personal, "daily rededications" to changing their world and foster "community spirit through community sacrifice." By contrast, NAACP leaders doubted the ability of ordinary black citizens to effect social change: "[H]owever much people are aroused over an issue, in the final analysis correction of the wrong must occur via the established agencies and procedures." The NAACP tried to help people by litigating and lobbying for them, but the Highlander Folk School and the Student Nonviolent Coordinating Committee tried to teach them how to help themselves. Moreover, litigation was limited in its capacity to generate conflict and violence—conditions that proved indispensable to transforming northern opinion on race. By contrast, white supremacist vigilantes and law enforcement officers had difficulty restraining themselves when confronted with black street demonstrators. Finally, Court decisions such as *Brown* could significantly alter social practices only if lower courts aggressively implemented them, Congress and the president enforced them, and local officials could be prevented from nullifying them. Each of these conditions depended on educating public opinion, which direct action accomplished better than litigation could. As King stated, "Only when the people themselves begin to act are rights on paper given life blood." The accelerated pace of school desegregation that accompanied the outburst of direct-action protests in the early 1960s proves his point.[77]

Litigation and direct action can complement each other to a certain extent. For example, direct-action protests can enforce court decisions, as the freedom riders were attempting to do. Thus, an optimal allocation of resources within a broad social protest movement might distribute some to both litigation and direct action. King and the SCLC tended to emphasize ways in which direct action complemented litigation, perhaps seeking to defuse the NAACP's visceral defensiveness toward potential competitors. But the civil rights movement had no unitary oversight board to allocate scarce resources to their optimal uses. Rather, the NAACP and direct-action organizations competed for limited money and personnel. In the late 1950s, the NAACP's greater prestige, which was only enhanced by *Brown*, probably attracted more resources to litigation than was desirable from the perspective of those seeking to promote progressive racial change.[78]

Brown may have indirectly discouraged direct-action protest for another reason. The extraordinary violence that *Brown* unleashed in the South made direct action dangerous. Mississippi blacks were killed for voting in 1955, which they had not been in the late 1940s. One reason that SCLC founders initially shied away from further direct action after Montgomery was their fear of eliciting violence; the bus boycott itself had incited numerous bombings and shootings.[79]

Thus, although *Brown* probably contributed to the belief among blacks that Jim Crow was vulnerable, it did not foster the view that they could personally help to end it. Rather, the high court's ruling encouraged additional investment in litigation, as elite NAACP lawyers tried to convince white judges to end segregation. *Brown* possibly discouraged direct-action tactics, which had the capacity to enhance individual agency and to generate transformative conflict. Further, by elevating the NAACP's stature, *Brown* solidified control over the civil rights agenda by an organization that was profoundly skeptical of direct-action protest.

In the short term, *Brown* may have delayed direct action by encouraging litigation. But this aspect of the decision was self-correcting, as *Brown* either would or would not produce school desegregation. Within a few years, it had become clear that litigation without a social movement to support it could not produce significant social change. Thus, over the long term, *Brown* may have encouraged direct action by raising hopes and expectations, which litigation then proved incapable of fulfilling. Alternative forms of protest arose to fill the gap.[80]

Generalizing about what most blacks expected to happen after *Brown* is difficult. Some predicted that implementation would be "a long and laborious process" and that "the months that lie ahead will be ones that will try our very souls." But others were optimistic about enforcement, and few could have predicted the nearly complete nullification that took place in the South over the next half decade. White southerners had earlier warned that desegregation of higher education could not happen without bloodshed, yet it had, leading many blacks to discount the threats of violence and school closures made by southern whites after *Brown*. In 1955, NAACP officials insisted that their goal was school desegregation "in most areas of the South not later than September 1956," and they predicted that all forms of segregation would be eliminated by 1963 (whereas, in fact, three Deep South states had yet to desegregate a single grade school by then). They may have privately been less confident, but NAACP officials seem to have believed that rapid desegregation of urban schools, even in the Deep South, was feasible. Such expectations were not completely naive, as one would have had difficulty predicting the ferocity of resistance among southern whites or the tepid commitment to enforcement of the Eisenhower administration.[81]

That litigation alone could not desegregate schools was clear by 1960, if not earlier. Through a campaign of massive defiance, fraud, and evasion, southern states had almost completely nullified *Brown*. One cannot precisely measure the connection between black frustration over the pace of court-ordered desegregation and the explosion of direct-action protest, but many contemporaries explicitly identified such a linkage. King attributed direct-action protest to black "disappoint[ment] over the slow pace of school desegregation." The NAACP's 1960 convention declared the youth protests "symptomatic of the growing impatience of Negro Americans with the injustices of segregation and [the] snail-like pace of desegregation." Roy Wilkins thought that blacks were tired of "this foolishness"—the white South's nullification of *Brown*—and were "in a hurry for their rights." They were no longer "so particular" about whether to use "mass demonstration" or litigation. James Farmer of CORE defended the Freedom Rides on the ground that "we've had test cases and we've won them all and the status remains quo."[82]

By the early 1960s, many blacks were seeking not only faster methods of change but also extralegal ones. White southerners' nullification of *Brown* through legal machinations, extralegal violence, and economic reprisals disillusioned many blacks about the capacity of law to secure racial justice. Some southern officials and judges had proved willing to lie in their efforts to evade *Brown*. In response to desegregation suits, a Birmingham school board member denied that city schools were segregated, and the chancellor of the University of Mississippi insisted that the exclusion of James Meredith had nothing to do with his "being a Negro." Astonishingly, federal district judge Sidney Mize agreed, dismissing Meredith's suit on the ground that Ole Miss "is not a racially segregated institution"—news that "may startle some people in Mississippi," Judge John Minor Wisdom pointed out in reversing Mize's judgment. State judges were sometimes even worse. One ran for reelection declaring, "I speak for the white race," and he promised to deal the NAACP "a blow from which [it] shall never recover." The chief justice of the Alabama Supreme Court volunteered that he "would close every school from the highest to the lowest before I would go to school with colored people." A few state jurists actually declared the Fourteenth Amendment to be unconstitutional. Others engaged in extraordinary chicanery to evade desegregation or otherwise deny justice to blacks. Thus, direct action had the virtue not only of being quicker but also of being extralegal while remaining nonviolent. Those blacks who were even more profoundly disillusioned by massive resistance abandoned the hope of peaceful change and the goal of racial integration, and they turned instead to black nationalism and violence as methods of racial betterment. The rapid growth of the Black Muslims in the 1960s was the most extreme manifestation of the black revolt against litigation as a method of social reform.[83]

Brown contributed to direct-action protest in another way as well. As southern states moved to suppress the NAACP, southern blacks had no choice but to support alternative protest organizations. Before *Brown*, most white southerners thought the NAACP "at worst was a bunch of Republicans." But afterward, it "became an object of consuming hatred." According to four black ministers in South Carolina, "The business of fighting the NAACP is to many Southern white men today as necessary as breathing." Because many white southerners thought that "integration is the southern expression of communism," they saw the NAACP as a communist agent or stooge. The South Carolina legislature asked the U.S. attorney general to list the association as subversive, and the attorney general of Georgia alleged that "two-thirds of the officers of the NAACP have subversive or communist backgrounds." Southern whites so overwhelmingly despised the NAACP that many politicians successfully ran for office by attacking it. In 1958, the attorney general of Alabama, John Patterson, won the governorship by bragging that he had shut down NAACP operations in the state. That year, Governor Faubus won reelection by ignoring his opponents and promising never to allow Arkansas to become a colony run by Sherman Adams (Eisenhower's chief of staff) with Daisy Bates (head of the NAACP in Arkansas) as colonial governor.[84]

Southern states proved enormously creative at translating white hatred of the NAACP into legal mechanisms for shutting it down. The most popular initiative sought to obtain association membership lists, which could be publicized and used "to intimidate and persecute [members], often to the point of bombing and personal violence." States sought to compel disclosure of membership lists via corporate-registration statutes, lobbyist-registration laws, state income tax laws, corporate-franchise tax ordinances, legislative antisubversion investigations, and laws that required public school teachers to list their organizational memberships. Another popular anti-NAACP measure barred members from public employment, especially as school-teachers, on the ground that affiliation was "wholly incompatible with the peace, tranquillity, and progress that all citizens have a right to enjoy." Many states harassed the NAACP and its lawyers with criminal prosecutions and bar association disciplinary proceedings, charging offenses such as stirring up lawsuits, financially supporting litigation, taking control of litigation, and the unauthorized practice of law. Citizens' councils used economic pressure against NAACP members, denying them jobs, credit, and access to goods and services. Where legal methods failed, violence sometimes succeeded. Whites in Belzoni, Mississippi, shot Gus Courts, the president of the local NAACP branch, for his voter registration activity. The home of Daisy Bates was the target of repeated cross burnings, shootings, and bombings. The NAACP saw itself as engaged in "a bitter cold war," where "no holds are barred."[85]

This anti-NAACP crusade took its toll. Alabama shut down operations for eight years (1956–1964), and Louisiana and Texas did so for briefer periods. In 1957, Wilkins reported that "the future operation of the NAACP in the Southern states" was at risk. Southern membership fell from 128,000 in 1955 to 80,000 in 1957, and nearly 250 branches shut down. Most of the losses came in the Deep South, where the assault was sharpest. Membership in Louisiana fell from more than 13,000 to 1,700 and in South Carolina from 8,200 to 2,200. Mississippi field secretary Medgar Evers reported that "economic pressures and violence" were so prevalent that many members "are not with us any more" and that only the "pure of heart" were sticking with the association. The NAACP had to divert scarce resources from challenging school segregation to fending off legal attack. Association members also suffered psychologically. The national director of branches reported "an atmosphere of gloom . . . pervading" the annual Texas meeting, as injunction proceedings "succeed in arresting our activities and have a traumatic effect on

FIGURE 7.3
Gus Courts recovers in the
hospital after he was shot,
1955. (*Library of Congress,
Prints and Photographs
Division, Visual Materials
from the NAACP Records*)

our leadership." Something had to be done "to regain the confidence of the Negroes in the southern branches." Even though courts eventually invalidated most of the anti-NAACP legal measures, the litigation dragged on for years. While such suits were pending, membership fell, spirits sagged, and resources were diverted.[86]

As the NAACP struggled to survive in the South, blacks turned elsewhere for leadership. Black ministers, many of whom held prominent positions in NAACP branches, formed new organizations, such as the Alabama Christian Movement for Human Rights in Birmingham, the United Christian Movement in Shreveport, the Inter-Civic Council in Tallahassee, and the SCLC. The leadership vacuum created by the anti-NAACP assault also facilitated the expansion into the South of an older organization, CORE. These other groups used the NAACP's base of supporters, but they deployed their resources differently. By inciting massive retaliation against the NAACP, *Brown* ironically fostered new organizations that lacked the association's institutional and philosophical biases against direct action.[87]

With school desegregation litigation achieving paltry results, and the chief litigators under withering assault, southern blacks had little choice but to explore alternative methods and organizations of social protest. By revealing the limits of litigation as an engine of social change and by provoking massive retaliation against the NAACP, *Brown* may have indirectly accelerated the transition to direct action.

BROWN'S BACKLASH

Whatever its connection to *Brown*, a powerful direct-action protest movement had exploded in the South by the early 1960s. Sit-ins, Freedom Rides, and street demonstrations became a regular feature of southern life. When law enforcement officers responded to such protests with restraint and (even unlawful) arrests, media attention quickly waned, and demonstrators usually failed to accomplish their objectives. This is how Sheriff Laurie Pritchett defeated mass demonstrations in Albany, Georgia, in 1961–1962 and how Mississippi officials defused the Freedom Rides in the summer of 1961. By contrast, when southern sheriffs violently suppressed demonstrations with beatings, police dogs, and fire hoses, media attention escalated and northerners reacted with horror and outrage.

This section explores the connection between *Brown* and the violent suppression of civil rights demonstrations. My claim is that *Brown* radicalized southern politics, as voters elected candidates who espoused extreme segregationist positions. A few public officials openly advocated violent resistance to desegregation, and others passively tolerated it. Many more spouted fire-breathing rhetoric that encouraged such violence. *Brown* also created concrete occasions—court-ordered desegregation—upon which violent confrontation was likely. It was the brutality of southern whites resisting desegregation that ultimately rallied national opinion behind the enforcement of *Brown* and the enactment of civil rights legislation.

Brown's Impact on Southern Politics

One of *Brown's* principal effects was to radicalize southern politics. By encouraging extremism, *Brown* increased the likelihood that once direct-action protest developed, it would incite a violent response. In the early 1960s, civil rights demonstrators often sought racial reforms that were less controversial than school desegregation, including voting rights, desegregated lunch counters, and more jobs for blacks. If not for the retrogression that *Brown* produced in southern politics, such demands might have been received sympathetically or at least without unrestrained violence. *Brown* ensured that when street demonstrations came, politicians such as Bull Connor, Jim Clark, Ross Barnett, and George Wallace were there to meet them.

Pre-*Brown*

Before *Brown*, racial moderates generally controlled southern politics: Big Jim Folsom, John Sparkman, and Lister Hill in Alabama; Lyndon Johnson in Texas; Earl Long in Louisiana; Kerr Scott in North Carolina; Sid McMath, William Fulbright, and the early Orval Faubus in Arkansas; and Albert Gore (the future vice president's father), Estes Kefauver, and Frank Clement in Tennessee. These politicians were economically populist and, although segregationist, they downplayed race while accommodating gradual racial reform. Coalitions composed of less-affluent whites and the growing number of enfranchised blacks elected candidates who supported increased government spending on education, roads, public health, and old-age pensions. Many of these politicians defeated opponents who warned that white supremacy was in danger.[88]

Big Jim Folsom was perhaps the leading exemplar of this phenomenon. In 1946 and 1954, he won gubernatorial elections in Alabama, running on populist platforms of expanded public services, abolition of the poll tax, and reapportionment of the legislature. With regard to race, Folsom stated that "all men are just alike"; he urged "fellowship and brotherly love"; and he declared that blacks were entitled to their fair share of Alabama's wealth. Folsom urged the liberalization of voter qualifications, appointed registrars who were committed to the nondiscriminatory administration of registration requirements, favored equalizing the salaries of black teachers, and supported the creation of more state parks for blacks. When pressed during the 1954 campaign for his views on *Brown*, which had just been decided, Folsom joked, "I don't intend to make the good colored people of Alabama . . . go to school with us white folks." That year, he easily defeated candidates who emphasized the importance of preserving white supremacy—a striking contrast with the racial fanaticism that would characterize Alabama politics within a year or two.[89]

Exceptions do exist to this general rule that racial moderates prospered in southern politics between World War II and *Brown*. The most obvious exception is the Dixiecrat revolt of 1948. But Dixiecrats carried only four states—those with the largest black percentages—and even those victories depended on having secured control of the Democratic party machinery, which enabled Dixiecrats to capitalize on the traditional party loyalties of southern voters by running slates of electors pledged to Strom Thurmond and Fielding Wright under the Democratic label. Thus, in the one Deep South state where Dixiecrats were kept off the Democratic ticket—Georgia—they won only 20.3 percent of the vote, as compared with 79.8 percent and 72 percent in neighboring Alabama and South Carolina. Outside of the Deep South, the New Deal/Fair Deal coalition held up well for President Truman, and Thurmond usually ran third, trailing the Republican candidate, Thomas Dewey, as well. In Arkansas and Virginia, states that would lead massive resistance in the mid-1950s, Dixiecrats won only 16.5 percent and 10.3 percent of the vote, respectively. In 1950, Dixiecrats suffered additional defeats at the polls, most notably Thurmond's loss to Olin Johnston in South Carolina's Senate race. Rather than viewing the Dixiecrat revolt as evidence of a powerful pre-*Brown* racial backlash, a contemporary political scientist concluded from its defeat that "the great masses of southerners would no longer be bamboozled by racist appeals."[90]

Victories by the race-baiting Talmadges, father and son, in Georgia gubernatorial elections in 1946, 1948, and 1950 confirm that politicians could manipulate the race issue to their advantage even before *Brown* had

FIGURE 7.4
Big Jim Folsom towers over the crowd at a campaign rally.
(*Birmingham Public Library, Department of Archives and Manuscripts, no. 98.45 H*)

increased its salience. But the lesson should not be overdrawn. Georgia's unique county-unit system for electing statewide officials inflated the voting power of rural whites, who were the most committed to preserving white supremacy. This is why Georgia consistently produced some of the region's most demagogic governors. Moreover, both Talmadges used recent Court decisions—*Smith v. Allwright* in the 1946 election, *Sweatt v. Painter* in 1950—to exaggerate the threat being posed to white supremacy.[91]

The famous defeats in the 1950 primaries of Senators Frank Porter Graham in North Carolina and Claude Pepper in Florida are also weaker evidence of the existence of a pre-*Brown* racial backlash than is often supposed. Both incumbents were "soft" on race, but the defeat of neither should be seen as a referendum victory for racial reaction. Pepper's opponent, George Smathers, focused his attack less on the senator's racial liberalism and more on his support for New Deal/Fair Deal redistributive policies, his close labor union ties, and his moderate stance toward the Soviet Union ("Red Pepper"). Similarly, in the initial North Carolina primary that year, Willis Smith mainly criticized Graham's past affiliations with allegedly subversive organizations ("Frank the Front") and his present support for the allegedly socialist policies of Truman's Fair Deal, such as national health insurance and repeal of the Taft-Hartley labor law. In short, the tactics of Smathers and Smith duplicated those of Republicans throughout the nation in 1950: antisocialism attacks on Truman's domestic policies and McCarthyite challenges to his alleged softness on communism, foreign and domestic. The defeats of these racial moderates had more to do with Truman's unpopularity and the potency of McCarthyism as an electoral weapon than with any incipient racial backlash in the South.[92]

Race was more important to Graham's defeat in the runoff primary, though even here the lesson is uncertain. Graham was probably more exposed on the race issue than any other southern politician. Widely identified as his generation's foremost southern liberal, Graham was a member of Truman's civil rights committee, the first president of the interracial and integrationist Southern Conference on Human Welfare, and one of only three southern senators to oppose the filibuster against fair employment practices legislation. Graham was almost unique among southern office-holders in endorsing the eventual abolition of racial segregation. Thus, rather than treating his defeat as evidence of a pre-*Brown* racial backlash, perhaps one should be struck that a southern politician who was this liberal on race nearly won the first primary—earning 48.9 percent of the vote—and barely lost the runoff with 48 percent. Graham could not possibly have done this well in the racial fanaticism that characterized southern politics after *Brown*. Moreover, as we saw in chapter 5, only the intervention of the Supreme Court's 1950 decisions that invalidated segregation in graduate and professional schools enabled Smith to make race the dominant issue in the runoff, thus demonstrating the backlash potential of the Court's race rulings.[93]

Thus, neither the Dixiecrat revolt, nor the defeats of Senators Graham and Pepper, nor the Talmadges' gubernatorial victories are convincing evidence of a pre-*Brown* racial backlash. On the contrary, populist southern politicians who supported expanded public services while downplaying race prospered between World War II and *Brown*. In such a political environment, gradual racial reform could be accomplished without inciting a white backlash. Black voter registration in the most regressive states, Mississippi and Alabama, increased tenfold in the decade following World War II, and in Louisiana it increased more than twentyfold. Dozens of urban police forces in the South, including those of Indianola and Biloxi, Mississippi, hired their first black officers. Minor league baseball teams, even in places such as Montgomery and Birmingham, signed their first black players. Most southern states, including Louisiana, peacefully desegregated their graduate and professional schools under court order. Blacks began serving again on southern juries, even in places such as Natchez and Greenville, Mississippi. In Louisiana and in most states outside of the Deep South, the first blacks since Reconstruction were elected to urban political offices, and the walls of segregation were occasionally breached in public facilities and public accommodations. None of these racial changes generated any significant white backlash.[94]

None of this is to suggest that the South was moving gradually but inexorably toward peaceful school desegregation. In the absence of *Brown*, southern states almost certainly would *not* have desegregated their schools within a decade or two. Southern whites were much more intensely resistant to school desegregation than to allowing blacks to vote, to become police officers, or to play on integrated baseball teams. Moreover, most southern blacks were more interested in improving black education, reducing police brutality, and securing access to decent jobs than in desegregating grade schools. Yet, before *Brown* focused attention on school desegregation, southern politics was generally controlled by moderates, who downplayed race while accommodating gradual racial change. *Brown* turned that political world upside down.

Brown and the Radicalization of Southern Politics

Politicians outside of the Deep South reacted to *Brown I* with restraint, even in states that would quickly become leaders of massive resistance. Governor Francis Cherry of Arkansas promised that his state would "obey the law. It always has." The governor of Virginia, Thomas B. Stanley, guaranteed a "calm" and "dispassionate" response to *Brown*, and the state's superintendent of public education predicted "no defiance." Governor Frank Clement of Tennessee observed that the ruling was "handed down by a judicial body which we, the American people, . . . recognize as supreme." That spring and summer, *Brown* attracted little attention in Democratic primaries in Arkansas, Alabama, Florida, and Texas. Throughout most of the South, newspaper editors urged calm and avoided talk of defiance. The *Nashville Tennessean* declared that southerners "have learned to live with change. They can learn to live with this one." Ralph McGill of the *Atlanta Constitution* was reported to have said, "Segregation is on the way out . . . and he who tries to tell the people otherwise does them great disservice." Even the *Clarion-Ledger* of Jackson, Mississippi, was surprisingly evasive, adopting a wait-and-see attitude. The day after *Brown*, the school board of Greensboro, North Carolina, voted 6–1 to instruct the superintendent to study means of compliance, and within a week the Little Rock school board had followed suit.[95]

Some political reaction in the Deep South was more defiant. Governor Herman Talmadge declared, "Georgia is going to resist mixing the races in the schools if it is the sole state of the nation to do so," and eight of the nine candidates competing in Georgia's pending gubernatorial primary favored preserving school segregation. Senator Eastland of Mississippi announced that "the South will not abide by or obey this legislative decision by a political court," and Mississippi officials warned that they would abolish public education before integrating. That fall, voters in Georgia and Mississippi passed constitutional amendments that authorized legislatures to close schools rather than desegregate them. In Louisiana, "it would seem that the Supreme Court opinion never really happened." The legislature, in session when *Brown* was decided, overwhelmingly resolved to censure the Court's "usurpation of power" and used its police power to adopt a new school segregation law. South Carolina officials called for restraint but gave no hint that they intended to abandon segregation. Statements from some Deep South politicians quickly became even shriller. In September, Talmadge declared, "[N]o amount of force whatever can compel desegregation of white and Negro schools," while Governor-elect Marvin Griffin announced, "[C]ome hell or high water, races will not be mixed in Georgia schools."[96]

Would the rest of the region fall in line behind the defiant proclamations of the Deep South? The answer became apparent over the next eighteen months, as white opinion throughout the South grew more extreme. Citizens' councils, new organizations that were committed to preserving white supremacy by all means short of violence—the "uptown" Klan, according to critics—began forming in Mississippi in the summer of 1954, quickly spread to Alabama, and then expanded across the South, achieving a maximum membership of perhaps 250,000. Whites flocked to the councils as southern blacks began filing desegregation petitions with school boards, many of them reasoning that "[w]e must make certain that Negroes are not allowed to force their demands on us." *Brown II* fueled further resistance, as many southern whites detected weakness in the justices' efforts to be conciliatory. When lower courts began ordering desegregation, violence erupted, which further radicalized white opinion. The admission of Autherine Lucy to the University of Alabama in February 1956 produced a race riot, and Alabama whites, already riled over the Montgomery bus boycott, now joined citizens' councils in droves. That month, a segregationist rally in Montgomery drew 10,000 people, and the newly formed citizens' council in Tuscaloosa enrolled 3,000 members. Early in 1956, several state legislatures in the South adopted interposition resolutions that purported to nullify *Brown*. They also passed dozens of laws designed to avoid desegregation—measures that authorized school closures, repealed compulsory attendance requirements, cut off public funding for integrated schools, provided public money for private schools, empowered school boards to place pupils in schools that were still segregated, and attacked the NAACP. In March 1956, most southern congressmen signed the Southern Manifesto, which assailed the Court's "clear abuse of judicial power" and pledged all "lawful means" of resistance.[97]

Political contests in southern states quickly assumed a common pattern: Candidates tried to show that they were the most "blatantly and uncompromisingly prepared to cling to segregation at all costs." "Moderation" became "a term of derision," as the political center collapsed, leaving only "those who want to maintain the Southern way of life or those who want to mix the races." Moderate critics of massive resistance were labeled "double crossers," "sugar-coated integrationists," "cowards," "traitors," and "burglars . . . [who] want to rob us of our priceless heritage." Most moderates either joined the segregationist bandwagon or they were retired from service. A Virginia politician observed that it "would be suicide to run on any other platform [than segregation]." A liberal southern editor explained, "[I]t takes guts not to come out for segregation every day."[98]

Brown radicalized southern politics, whereas earlier racial changes had not, for three principal reasons. First, *Brown* was harder to ignore than earlier changes. Most white southerners did not see black jurors or black police officers, who policed black neighborhoods only, and they would have been largely unaware of the dramatic increases in black voter registration. Even some instances of integration—such as on city buses or golf courses—would have gone unnoticed by many white southerners. But they could not miss *Brown*, which received front-page coverage in virtually every newspaper in the country and was a constant topic of southern conversations. A northern white visitor found after *Brown* that segregation "is the foremost preoccupation of the Southern mind. . . . [It] intrudes into almost every conversation. It nags, it bothers and it will not be ignored." A citizens' council leader credited the Court with "awaken[ing] us from a slumber of about 30 years," and an Alabama official noted that white southerners owed the justices "a debt of gratitude" for "caus[ing] us to become organized and unified."[99]

Second, *Brown* represented federal interference in southern race relations—something that white southerners, who "harbor[ed] in historical memory, with deep resentment, the program of reconstruction and the deep humiliation of carpetbag government imposed by conquest," could not tolerate. Some earlier racial changes—such as the hiring of black police officers and the desegregation of minor league baseball teams—flowed from choices made by white southerners. Other changes—such as the increased public funding of black education and the growing number of blacks registered to vote—had been influenced by federal court decisions, but they still depended on choices made by southern whites. *Brown* was different; it left southern whites no choice but to desegregate their schools. Accordingly, *Brown* was "viewed by many white Southerners as federal intervention designed to destroy their way of life."[100]

Third and perhaps most important, *Brown* commanded that racial change take place in a different order than might otherwise have occurred. By the early 1950s, many southern cities had relaxed Jim Crow in public transportation, police department employment, athletic competition, and voter registration. White southerners were more intensely committed to preserving school segregation, which lay near the top of the white supremacist hierarchy of preferences. Blacks, conversely, were often more interested in voting, ending police brutality, securing decent jobs, and receiving a fair share of public education funds than in desegregating grade schools. These partially inverse hierarchies of preference among whites and blacks opened space for political negotiation—to the extent that blacks had the power to compel whites to bargain. *Brown* mandated change in an area where whites were most resistant, thus virtually ensuring a backlash. Had the Court first decided a case such as *Gayle v. Browder*, desegregating local bus transportation, the reaction of white southerners would probably have been more restrained.[101]

For these reasons, *Brown* provoked greater white resistance than did earlier racial changes. This is not a criticism of *Brown*. The justices neither are bound by the hierarchy of preferences of white supremacists, nor are they required to accommodate the visceral resistance of white southerners to externally coerced change. Explaining the reasons that *Brown* radicalized southern politics does not entail endorsing an alternative path to racial reform as preferable.

The post-*Brown* backlash in the South was manifested in at least two different ways. First, there were clear instances of racial retrogression—reversal of racial reforms that had occurred before *Brown*. Second, politics in every southern state moved significantly to the right.

One dramatic racial retrogression in the post-*Brown* South was the resurgence of the Ku Klux Klan, which had earlier seemed set to "disappear permanently from the American scene." After *Brown*, the Klan reappeared in states such as South Carolina, Florida, and Alabama, where it had rarely been observed in recent years. The legal assault of southern states on the NAACP was another racial retrogression. For decades, southern whites had grudgingly tolerated the association, but after *Brown* they declared war on it. For example, Septima Clark had taught in South Carolina public schools for forty years, but in 1956 she was dismissed because of her NAACP affiliation. The association's southern membership, which had been steadily rising after the war, plummeted in the wake of *Brown* as affiliation became too dangerous.[102]

With school desegregation lurking in the background, Deep South whites suddenly could no longer tolerate black voting. Dramatic postwar expansions of black suffrage in Mississippi, Alabama, and Louisiana were halted and then reversed. Late in 1954, Mississippi voters adopted by a 5–1 margin a more stringent literacy test, which they had rejected just two years earlier. Registrars in Mississippi and Louisiana purged thousands of blacks from the voter rolls under laws that granted them discretion to expunge names for technical registration flaws. Black voter registration in Mississippi declined from 22,000 in 1954 to 8,000 in 1956. Alabama, Georgia, and Virginia passed new laws making voter registration more difficult. A regional trend toward eliminating the poll tax ended with *Brown*, and five southern states continued to impose that suffrage qualification until the Court ruled it unconstitutional in 1966. In 1955, two Mississippi blacks, the Reverend George Lee and Lamar Smith, were murdered for encouraging blacks to vote. Mississippi whites had beaten and threatened blacks who tried to vote in the late 1940s after *Smith v. Allwright,* but they had not killed anybody.[103]

    Brown also retarded progress in university desegregation. In the early 1950s, most southern states had peacefully desegregated graduate and professional schools under lower court orders that enforced *Sweatt v. Painter.* By 1955, roughly 2,000 blacks attended desegregated universities in southern and border states—a "quiet revolution" from 1950. Even in the Deep South, four of Louisiana's seven public universities had desegregated. One might have predicted that other Deep South universities would soon follow. Indeed, in 1953, the president of the University of South Carolina confided to a colleague that he expected to desegregate within two or three years. *Brown* changed all of that. The University of Texas quickly reversed a decision to extend desegregation to undergraduates. Universities in the Deep South used extraordinary legal maneuvers to resist desegregation, sometimes dragging out litigation for nearly a decade. After court orders finally compelled desegregation, race riots erupted at the University of Alabama in 1956, the University of Georgia in 1961, and Ole Miss in 1962. Most public universities in the Deep South did not ultimately desegregate until more than a decade after *Sweatt.* Meanwhile, the Louisiana legislature tried to undo the university desegregation that had occurred in that state before *Brown.* State legislators passed a measure that was designed to exclude blacks from formerly white universities by requiring all applicants to produce "good character" certificates from their high school principals, who could be fired for providing them for blacks under another state law that prohibited promoting integration. Segregationists then insisted that the law be applied retroactively to blacks who were already attending integrated universities. In 1956, Louisiana blacks largely ceased applying to such institutions, and the number of them already enrolled fell dramatically. Federal courts quickly enjoined the enforcement of these statutes, but black enrollment at Louisiana's desegregated universities nonetheless declined from 650 to fewer than 200.[104]

    The post-*Brown* backlash also reversed progress that had been made in desegregating sports. Early in 1954, the Birmingham city commission, eager to encourage a spring-training visit from Jackie Robinson's Brooklyn Dodgers, repealed the city's ban on interracial sporting competitions. Within two weeks of *Brown,* voters in a referendum reversed that decision by a 3–1 margin. A couple of years later, Montgomery likewise abandoned its policy of permitting integrated minor league baseball games. Deep South states also reversed a trend toward allowing college basketball and football teams to compete against integrated squads, at least in games played outside of the South. In 1955, a college football team from Mississippi had squared off against a school with black players in the Little Rose Bowl, but legislative threats to cut off funding induced state football and basketball teams to decline similar invitations the next year. As late as 1962, the Mississippi State basketball team had to reject an invitation to the National Collegiate Athletic Association (NCAA) tournament because of the state's informal ban on interracial sporting competitions. In the early 1950s, the University of Georgia football team had competed several times against squads with black players, but Governor Griffin asked the university board of regents to bar Georgia Tech from playing in the 1956 Sugar Bowl because its scheduled opponent had a black player. Griffin reasoned that competing against blacks on the gridiron was no different from attending school with them. The regents rebuffed Griffin after 2,500 Tech students marched on the state capital, but they insisted that no integrated collegiate sporting events take place within the state. It was the integrated Sugar Bowl in New Orleans in 1956 that helped persuade the Louisiana legislature to forbid future interracial sporting events in the state. Until a federal court invalidated that law, several Louisiana universities had to abandon their policies permitting interracial competition, and Texas League baseball teams that played in Shreveport had to leave their black players behind.[105]

Even minor interracial courtesies and interactions that were uncontroversial before 1954 often had to be suspended in the post-*Brown* racial hysteria. In 1959, Governor John Patterson of Alabama barred black marching bands from the inaugural parade, where they had previously been warmly received. Mississippi's state sovereignty commission, charged with preserving segregation, pressured the state board of education to ban a previously unobjectionable film promoting racial toleration that was sponsored by the Anti-Defamation League. Since its founding in 1942, Koinonia Farm, an interracial religious cooperative in Americus, Georgia, had experienced little harassment, but after *Brown* its products were boycotted and its roadside produce stands were shot at. Interracial unions that had thrived in the South for years self-destructed after *Brown*. The white supremacist film *Birth of a Nation*, which had largely disappeared from movie theaters in the 1930s, resurfaced in several southern cities in the mid-1950s. After *Brown*, many whites stopped contributing to the Urban League, which was not even involved with school desegregation, and many white audiences ceased inviting singing groups from black colleges to perform.[106]

The radicalization of political opinion throughout the South in the mid-1950s also illustrates *Brown*'s backlash effect. In 1954, Arkansans had elected Orval Faubus governor on a populist platform of increased spending on public education and old-age pensions. Neither Faubus nor his opponent highlighted race, and Governor Cherry promised that Arkansas would obey *Brown*. In his inaugural address in January 1955, Faubus again ignored race, and later that year he became the first Arkansas governor to appoint blacks to the state Democratic Central Committee. In 1954–1955, three Arkansas school districts with small black populations desegregated without interference from Faubus, who disclaimed authority to intervene in local school matters. Meanwhile, school boards in the state's largest cities were considering early implementation of desegregation plans. Legislative debate in 1955 focused on whether to comply with *Brown* or to circumvent it, but few endorsed outright defiance. By 1956, though, polls registered a rightward shift in public opinion, and Faubus's principal opponent for reelection was Jim Johnson, chief organizer of the state's citizens' councils. With Johnson calling him "pussy-footing" and demanding a special legislative session to consider resistance measures, Faubus moved to the right, endorsing an interposition resolution and a pupil placement plan. Though Johnson proposed closing schools that had already desegregated, Faubus won an easy victory by promising that no school district would have to integrate against its will.[107]

Public opinion in Arkansas continued to become more extreme, however, and the following year, Faubus reconsidered his position on local control over desegregation. In the summer of 1957, with the Little Rock citizens' council pressuring him to intervene against court-ordered desegregation, Faubus declared that no city with as large a black population as Little Rock's was ready for even token integration. Late in August, Governor Griffin of Georgia came to town to denounce desegregation, further riling local opinion. Faubus testified before a state judge that he had evidence that racial mixing would produce violence, and the court enjoined desegregation, only to be quickly overturned by a federal judge. Invoking the need to protect lives and property, Faubus then used the state militia to block desegregation. He withdrew the state troops after being threatened with contempt sanctions, leaving in their place only a city police force that proved inadequate to fend off the angry white mob that surrounded Central High School. Eisenhower then dispatched federal troops to protect the black students. Faubus's motives in the Little Rock crisis are uncertain: Did he deliberately foment a riot to bolster his candidacy for a third term as governor, or did he stumble into a situation that he proved unable to control? Whatever his intentions, though, there is no denying that Faubus's position on desegregation had become much more extreme since 1955.[108]

White opinion in Virginia also moved significantly to the right after 1954. Public officials had counseled restraint after *Brown*, and a "general air of calm resignation" existed in the state's largest cities. In November 1955, the Gray Commission, appointed by the governor to recommend desegregation policy, endorsed local option, which would permit desegregation in willing communities, and public tuition grants for students who wished to attend private, segregated schools. Governor Stanley seemed to support the plan. But James J. Kilpatrick, editor of the *Richmond News Leader*, launched a campaign to have southern state legislatures nullify *Brown*, and Senator Harry Byrd organized regionwide massive resistance. The Virginia legislature then rejected local option and instructed the Gray Commission to consider other proposals. In the summer of 1956, as federal district courts ordered desegregation in Charlottesville and Norfolk, the governor endorsed massive resistance and called the legislature into special session to implement it. In August, the Gray Commission also approved massive resistance. The special legislative session enacted laws that provided for state pupil placement (thus rejecting local option), the closing of integrated schools, the termination of public funding for integrated schools, and the authorization of public tuition grants for private education.[109]

In Florida, Governor Leroy Collins tried to pursue a moderate course, warning that the "state cannot afford an orgy of race conflict and discord," avoiding defiant talk, and criticizing interposition as serving "no useful purpose." But in 1956, extremist Sumter Lowry challenged Collins for the governorship, insisting that "segregation is the only issue." Collins and other candidates were forced "to hop on the segregation train." In the midst of the gubernatorial primary, the Supreme Court's latest ruling in the *Hawkins* case, rejecting further delay in desegregating the University of Florida School of Law, helped to radicalize public opinion. Previous pleas by Collins for "moderation" and "understanding" now became promises to preserve segregation by "every lawful means." He appointed a commission to study methods of preserving segregation, and he spoke for the first time of calling a special legislative session. Richard Ervin, the state attorney general, previously known as "one of the most level-headed and far-sighted" politicians in the state, likewise adopted in his reelection bid most of his opponent's extreme segregationist views. Two months into the spring electioneering, one state official reported "a great deterioration of race relations all over the state." During the campaign, Florida's only black assistant state attorney lost his job for being "too outspoken" on segregation; he had stated in a radio interview that his work was "not necessarily confined to Negro cases." Collins won a decisive victory in the gubernatorial primary, which moderates portrayed as "a crashing rebuke to the criers of race hatred," but in fact Florida's racial politics had moved far to the right.[110]

The most stunning defeat for moderation came in Alabama, where Big Jim Folsom was destroyed by the post-*Brown* racial hysteria. Folsom had refused to join other southern governors in a statement condemning *Brown*, vetoed several pieces of massive-resistance legislation, ridiculed a nullification resolution as "just a bunch of hogwash," lambasted the citizens' councils as "haters and baiters," and invited the black congressman from Harlem, Adam Clayton Powell, to the governor's mansion for a drink, which was later described as "the most expensive scotch and soda in the history of Alabama politics." By the fall of 1955, some legislators and the citizens' councils were denouncing the governor. Early in 1956, Folsom began to move to the right, as the race riot resulting from the admission of Autherine Lucy to the University of Alabama crystallized extremist sentiment in the state. With citizens' council rallies drawing mass participation, for the first time Folsom declared his support for preserving segregation, and he signed several bills designed to do so. As he traveled around the state in his campaign to become a Democratic national committeeman, Folsom defended himself from charges of moderation. His opponent was a little-known state representative, Charles McKay, who had authored the legislature's nullification resolution and now accused Folsom of being one of the "foremost supporters of the NAACP." Political commentators treated the contest as a bellwether of Alabama public opinion on race. Folsom was annihilated, losing by a margin of 3–1. After his defeat, he moved further right, promising that schools would not integrate so long as he was governor, and promoting segregationist legislation. By the summer of 1957, he was signing a nullification resolution and denying that he had ever opposed the concept. But Folsom's change of heart came too late. In the 1958 gubernatorial election, all leading candidates distanced themselves from the governor's "moderate" racial views, and the most extreme segregationist won.[111]

In 1955–1956, political opinion also became more extreme in North Carolina, Tennessee, and Texas. Running for reelection in 1956, the governor of North Carolina, Luther Hodges, was attacked for his "very lukewarm stand" on segregation. In response, he called the legislature into special session to enact segregationist measures, such as proposed constitutional amendments that would authorize local referenda on school closures and public tuition grants to attend private schools—measures that he had opposed just a year earlier. Two of the three North Carolina congressmen who refused to sign the Southern Manifesto early in 1956 were defeated for reelection that spring. The manifesto issue clearly caused the lopsided defeat of Congressman Charles B. Deane, as he had not even faced competition in the previous two elections, and no opponent had come forward in 1956 until Deane took his rebellious stand. Also in the spring of 1956, two Tennessee education boards made "rather sudden and unexpected reversals of desegregation policies." The University of Tennessee's board of trustees, which had approved a gradual desegregation plan for undergraduates, now decided to indefinitely postpone its implementation. The Chattanooga board of education, which had agreed to comply with *Brown*, now opposed desegregation for at least five more years. One newspaper reported that recent developments made it "increasingly difficult for Tennessee's politicians to steer a middle course on the subject of desegregation." Governor Frank Clement, who had previously resisted legislative action on this issue, now proposed several segregationist measures. In Texas, the policy of local option had enabled more than one hundred districts, mostly in western counties with minuscule black populations, to desegregate after *Brown*. Governor Allan Shivers had voiced no opposition to communities choosing for themselves to desegregate. But in 1956, Texas opinion polls registered growing public opposition to desegregation, and voters overwhelmingly approved an interposition resolution and stronger segregationist measures. In the summer of 1956, the governor twice used state troops to block court-ordered desegregation, and in 1957 the legislature cut off funds to school districts that desegregated without first conducting a referendum. Desegregation in Texas ground to a halt.[112]

That Mississippi, Louisiana, South Carolina, and Georgia would massively resist *Brown* was never seriously in doubt. That the border states would desegregate with relative ease was equally certain. How the rest of the South would respond was unclear. Until *Brown II*, and in some cases for months afterward, these states pursued a wait-and-see strategy. Massive resistance would have played out very differently had they decided not to follow the Deep South's lead. But by early 1956, the South was "marching in close order along the same resistance road." A nearly united white South had enlisted in the campaign to overturn or defy *Brown*.[113]

The Little Rock crisis of September 1957 further radicalized southern politics. Even moderate opponents of massive resistance criticized the use of federal troops to enforce desegregation orders. In North Carolina, Governor Hodges called the use of troops "a tragic mistake" and declared, "I have to associate myself with the people of my section," while Senator W. Kerr Scott compared Little Rock to the carpetbagger invasion of Reconstruction and deplored this "blow at the sovereignty of the states." Southern state legislatures called on Congress to censure the president, and they enacted "Little Rock" laws, which required the automatic closure of schools that were forced to integrate by federal troops. Governor Faubus became a regional hero, and other southern politicians drew the lesson that aggressive defiance of federal authority translated into political gain.[114]

The 1957 gubernatorial election in Virginia, which took place just one month after federal troops entered Little Rock, was a bellwether of southern political opinion. Virginia was one of the few southern states with a significant Republican presence. In 1953, the GOP's gubernatorial candidate, Theodore Dalton, won roughly 45 percent of the vote on a platform of increased state services and poll-tax repeal. *Brown* weakened Virginia Republicans, as the Democratic Byrd machine championed white supremacy and minimized the significance of other issues. Even before Little Rock, school segregation dominated the 1957 gubernatorial race. Democrat Lindsay Almond endorsed massive resistance, while Dalton favored token integration through pupil placement. Little Rock destroyed whatever slim chance Dalton may have had. White Virginians who were angry with Eisenhower for using federal troops to coerce desegregation delivered a message to the president by rejecting Dalton, whose share of the vote fell by nearly ten percentage points from 1953. Commentators agreed that Little Rock was devastating to southern Republicans. Dalton concluded, "Little Rock knocked me down to nothing. It wasn't a little rock, it was a big rock." Republican congressman Joel T. Broyhill of Virginia declared, "[A]ny Republican in the South who supports integration is a dead duck."[115]

Faubus parlayed his defiance of federal authority into a landslide victory in his 1958 quest for a third term as governor in a state with a tradition of two-term chief executives. During the summer and fall of 1958, political opinion in Arkansas moved even further to the right, as the Supreme Court rejected the Little Rock school board's request to postpone desegregation, and Faubus then closed the city's high schools—a decision that was promptly vindicated by Little Rock voters in a referendum. That fall, Faubus's political clout peaked when his implicit opposition to the reelection of Congressman Brooks Hays enabled a politically unknown opponent, who conducted an eight-day write-in campaign attacking Hays's racial moderation, to defeat this nationally prominent, eight-term congressman. Faubus subsequently won three more consecutive gubernatorial elections for a grand total of six. Throughout the South, huge and wildly enthusiastic crowds attended Faubus's speeches; in 1960, the States' Rights party ran him as their presidential candidate; and a national Gallup poll identified him as one of the world's ten most admired statesmen, along with Eisenhower, Truman, and Winston Churchill.[116]

Elsewhere in the South, post–Little Rock political contests featured militant segregationists competing for the most extreme positions and bragging of their willingness to defy federal authority. In Alabama's 1958 gubernatorial primary, all of the candidates repudiated Folsom's racial moderation and touted their segregationist credentials. George Wallace, who was tainted by his past affiliations with Folsom and an early reputation for "softness" on race, bragged of his own defiance of federal authority. In 1956, as circuit judge in Barbour County, Wallace had threatened to arrest FBI agents if they came into his county seeking access to jury selection records to verify charges of race discrimination. In his 1958 gubernatorial campaign, Wallace promised to close schools rather than see them integrated by federal troops. His principal opponent was the state attorney general, John Patterson, who bragged of having shut down NAACP operations in the state. The Klan endorsed Patterson, whom Wallace criticized for not repudiating the endorsement. Patterson was so extreme that Wallace unwittingly became the candidate of moderation and won heavy black support. Patterson easily won the runoff primary, leaving Wallace to ruminate that "they out-niggered me that time, but they will never do it again."[117]

Other election contests in the Deep South that year were similar. In Georgia, Lieutenant Governor Ernest Vandiver, who was running for governor, declared, "There is not enough money in the federal treasury to force us to mix the races in the classrooms of our schools," and he promised to use the national guard to block integration. In response, his opponent called Vandiver "weak" on segregation and accused him of being the NAACP's candidate. In South Carolina, gubernatorial candidates competed over who could best maintain segregation. In Florida, the more extreme candidate won the Senate race over an opponent who emphasized his "two Confederate grandfathers," and the only state legislator to oppose segregation bills in the past lost his congressional reelection bid in a campaign that was devoted entirely to segregation issues, in which he was portrayed as "a member and tool of the NAACP."[118]

The radicalizing political effect of Little Rock was ironic. Eisenhower's use of troops should have demonstrated the futility of massive resistance, but instead it undermined moderates and bolstered extremists. The only way to maintain segregation after Little Rock was to close schools that had been ordered integrated. Governors Almond and Faubus did this in 1958, thus altering the calculus of segregationist politics. Before school closures, most whites were prepared to experiment with massive resistance. Afterward, they had to compare the costs and benefits of school closures against those of token integration. Different states resolved this trade-off differently. In 1959, Virginia and Arkansas ended their massive resistance, and Texas, Tennessee, and Florida also charted courses toward token compliance, following the path chosen by North Carolina from the outset. In the Deep South, however, massive resisters continued to dominate politics for a few more years.[119]

Virginia's massive resistance ended abruptly. On January 19, 1959, federal and state courts invalidated key components of the state's massive-resistance legislation. Governor Almond, after one final defiant outburst, did a volte-face, condemned further resistance as futile, and called for legislative changes that would permit token desegregation. Two weeks later, twenty-one black students entered seven formerly white schools. In April, the general assembly, by the margin of a single vote in the senate, substituted local option for massive resistance. Popular and legislative support for defiance steadily declined thereafter. By 1961, both leading gubernatorial candidates preferred freedom of choice to massive resistance.[120]

Arkansas likewise ended its massive resistance in 1959. The legislature denied Governor Faubus's request to expand the size of the Little Rock school board, which would have enabled him to pack it with segregationists. That spring, moderates regained control of the board, as voters rejected Faubus's entreaties and evicted segregationist board members who had attempted to purge scores of moderate teachers and administrators. In June, a federal court invalidated the state's school-closing legislation, and later that summer, Little Rock high schools reopened for the first time in a year. In an effort to save face, Faubus continued to condemn the Court, criticize integration, and predict violence, but he ceased interfering with school desegregation, and he urged segregationists to fight their battles at the polls, not on the streets. Voters continued to reward Faubus politically for his past defiance of federal authority, but a majority no longer supported his massive-resistance policies. Over the following year, desegregation of Little Rock schools expanded without incident, and by 1960 even the eastern Arkansas black belt was beginning to peacefully desegregate, as citizens' councils decided to abandon forcible resistance. That year, Arkansas voters overwhelmingly rejected a state constitutional amendment that would have authorized local school closures.[121]

Florida, Texas, and Tennessee, states that had never fully embraced massive resistance, further distanced themselves from it in 1958–1959. The month after massive resistance ended in Virginia, the school board in Dade County, Florida, became the first in the Deep South to announce that it would desegregate a grade school, in the fall of 1959. Governor Collins endorsed the move, though many legislative leaders denounced it as "outrageous." For the rest of the year, the governor battled with segregationist legislators over anti-integration proposals, but the legislature eventually authorized pupil placement, and in September, Dade County desegregated two schools without incident. Although a segregationist won the Florida governor's race in 1960, he opposed school closures. The governor of Tennessee, Buford Ellington, who had won a typical post–Little Rock contest in 1958 by calling himself an "old-fashioned segregationist" and promising to close schools if necessary to avoid integration, declared in February 1959 that he was no smarter than Governor Almond, who "threw in the towel" in Virginia. The following year, Senator Kefauver won a sweeping victory over an opponent who assailed his racial moderation and his refusal to sign the Southern Manifesto. The segregation issue was essentially dead in Tennessee politics. Texas seems to have avoided the Little Rock effect entirely. In 1958, racial moderates won gubernatorial and Senate races, and that fall an opinion poll showed that two-thirds of Texans believed segregation in the state would be abolished. By 1960, the issue had largely disappeared from state politics, and an opinion poll revealed that 54 percent of Texans favored some integration, and only 31 percent endorsed defiance or evasion to maintain complete segregation.[122]

In the Deep South, however, massive resisters continued to dominate politics. In the months following *Cooper v. Aaron*, the Little Rock case, politicians from that region declared that the South would never "surrender" and that "if we stand determined and united, there is no power on earth that can force us to mix the races in our schools." At the end of 1959, one newspaper publisher concluded, "Deep South convictions . . . are unchanged by recent developments," and another thought that it would be "many, many years before we have integration even on a limited scale." Gubernatorial contests in Mississippi and Louisiana demonstrated that the collapse of massive resistance in Arkansas and Virginia had not weakened the resolve of diehard segregationists in the Deep South. The 1959 gubernatorial primary in Mississippi featured four candidates, all of whom agreed on banning the NAACP and maintaining complete segregation. Representative John Bell Williams, who contemplated entering the race, declared that Mississippi's next governor must be prepared "to rot in a federal prison for contempt of a court order . . . forcing integration." Lieutenant Governor Carroll Gartin promised "never [to] weaken in my stand for total and complete segregation," and another candidate declared that "the will of the people, and not the decisions of the United States Supreme Court, is the law of the land." Ross Barnett, the extremist in the field, had previously traveled to Tennessee to help defend those who faced criminal charges in connection with the desegregation riot in Clinton. Barnett sought to tie Gartin to the relatively moderate racial policies of Governor Coleman, who had criticized nullification as "foolish" and "legal poppycock" and had promised to maintain segregation without "keep[ing] ourselves in a daily uproar over it." By contrast, Barnett assailed moderation as "the foot in the door for integration," and he bragged of his membership in the citizens' council. Barnett promised to avoid school integration during his governorship, attributed the downfall of Egyptian culture to the "mongrelization" of the races, and proclaimed that "the good Lord was the original segregationist." In a landslide, Mississippi whites preferred Barnett's extremism to Gartin's "sane and sensible" approach to maintaining segregation. In his inaugural address, Barnett reiterated, "[O]ur schools at all levels must be kept segregated at all costs."[123]

Louisiana's gubernatorial primary in 1959–1960 confirmed that much of the Deep South was oblivious to the end of massive resistance elsewhere. The racial hysteria that swept Louisiana after Little Rock destroyed the Long machine's coalition of poor whites and blacks. Governor Long had previously criticized citizens' council members as "hotheads," declined to lead the legislative drive toward massive resistance, and opposed the purges of black voters. On the defensive after Little Rock, Long now insisted that he was "1,000 percent for segregation," while he continued to criticize the dean of Louisiana segregationists, Willie Rainach, for "scar[ing] everybody in the state to death . . . [e]very time you say Nigger." All eleven Democratic candidates for governor affirmed their commitment to preserving segregation. For the first time in a generation, no Long candidate made the runoff. The winner, Jimmie Davis, promised "no retreat, no compromise." Several months after the election, a poll showed that parents of white schoolchildren in New Orleans—almost certainly the most moderate whites in the state—favored school closures over token integration by more than 4–1. Political leaders remained united behind the policy of maintaining complete segregation, and that fall the legislature went to war against Judge J. Skelly Wright, as it fought to block the desegregation of New Orleans schools.[124]

Georgia, South Carolina, and Alabama showed few signs of retreat either. In his inaugural address in January 1959, Georgia governor Vandiver proclaimed, "[W]e have only just begun to fight," and he sharply criticized token integrationists as "fomenters of division and discord." Admitting that the defeat of massive resistance in Virginia was "a blow to our cause," Vandiver reiterated his commitment to maintaining complete segregation. Early in 1959, he proposed and received legislation that authorized the governor to close a single school within a system if it was ordered integrated—a response to the pending desegregation suit in Atlanta. In his state-of-the-state address in 1960, Vandiver promised that Georgia would resist "again and again and again" and use every lawful means to preserve segregation. In his 1959 inaugural address, the governor of South Carolina, Ernest Hollings, similarly vowed to maintain school segregation, and he later criticized Governor Almond for abandoning massive resistance in Virginia. Lieutenant Governor Burnet R. Maybank promised that South Carolina would not "yield one inch," and a leading newspaper in the state urged citizens to begin seriously considering private education.[125]

Alabama, which had reacted to *Brown* with restraint under Folsom, now became the most defiant southern state under Governor Patterson. In his 1959 inaugural address, Patterson denounced the notion of "a little integration" and promised to use "every ounce of energy" to block desegregation. He also urged the enactment of school closure legislation modeled on Virginia's. When that state's massive-resistance legislation was invalidated on the same day as Patterson's inaugural, he warned that Alabama might have to abandon public education altogether. A few months later, the state's chief justice declared that he would close every school in the state before he would accept integration. The *Montgomery Advertiser* thought that school closures were inevitable. Over the next year, Patterson reiterated his promise to close integrated schools, denounced token integration as a "sign of weakness," and predicted violence if integration occurred.[126]

The Deep South's desegregation crisis loomed near, as federal courts in the summer of 1959 ordered school boards in New Orleans and Atlanta to present desegregation plans with an eye toward action in the fall of 1960. In both states, rural-dominated legislatures seemed inclined to close schools rather than to desegregate them. But in both cities, groups of parents and, to a lesser extent, businessmen, and in New Orleans leaders of the Catholic church as well, began mobilizing behind open schools and token desegregation. Such groups were stronger and quicker to act in Georgia, and the New Orleans crisis culminated first, which allowed Georgia to learn from it.[127]

The desegregation crisis in New Orleans in the fall of 1960 illustrates how fanatical Deep South politics had become. The earlier Little Rock episode had clearly established that court orders could not be defied indefinitely and that efforts to do so entailed potentially enormous costs, including school closures, an end to business relocations, and the tarnishing of a city's national image. Under heavy political pressure in the summer of 1960, the Orleans Parish school board asked the governor to block Judge Wright's desegregation order. But if schools could not be kept open and segregated, a majority of board members preferred token integration to school closures. However, the rural-dominated legislature and a governor elected on a platform of diehard resistance would not permit New Orleans to desegregate without a fight. In August, Governor Davis seized control of the schools but was quickly enjoined by a federal court, which invalidated laws enabling the governor and the legislature to maintain segregated schools; the court restored control over New Orleans schools to the parish school board. Governor Davis then called the legislature into special session, where it enacted more than twenty segregation measures, including an interposition law that directed the arrest of any federal judge or marshal who implemented desegregation orders, statutes that authorized the legislature to take over New Orleans schools and the governor to close them, and a law that empowered the governor to appoint a new school board. Wright promptly enjoined all of these measures and then issued a restraining order against the governor, the legislature, and hundreds of other state and local officials. In November, four black first-graders integrated two schools, which prompted nearly all whites to boycott them. For months, segregationist legislators continued to meddle in the city's educational affairs, but within a year of this "Second Battle of New Orleans," state officials had retreated from massive resistance and substituted local option, pupil placement, and public tuition grants to attend private schools.[128]

With court-ordered desegregation in Atlanta set for the fall, early in 1960 the Georgia legislature appointed the Sibley Commission to canvass public opinion and to recommend whether to abandon massive resistance in favor of local option. Opinion in the state generally divided along urban-rural lines, but also between north and south Georgia, the latter possessing the state's largest black populations and the most diehard whites. Dominant opinion in Atlanta favored keeping schools open, and had the state legislature not been so malapportioned, massive resistance might have died easier. Atlanta businessmen, ministers, politicians, and a parents' group, Help Our Public Education, worked furiously to shift opinion in favor of open schools. Former governor Ellis Arnall entered the 1962 gubernatorial race early, on a platform of open schools, and former governor M. E. Thompson declared, "[I]t is absurd to close all state schools just to keep one Negro from going to school with white pupils in Atlanta." Other politicians, however, pledged resistance to the bitter end. In April, the Sibley Commission submitted a sharply divided report: A slender majority had approved local option, pupil placement, and a liberal transfer policy. Whether the legislature would approve this recommendation was far from clear. Federal judge Hooper now extended the desegregation deadline by a year to give legislators a final opportunity to repeal massive-resistance laws, which he urged them to do. Hooper also made it clear that if schools closed in Atlanta, they would have to shut down in the rest of the state as well to avoid an equal protection violation.[129]

Two intervening events helped tilt the balance in favor of keeping Atlanta schools open. First, New Orleans exploded in violence as two schools desegregated there in November 1960. Atlanta businessmen and politicians cringed at the thought of such violence being replicated in the "city too busy to hate." Second, time ran out on the University of Georgia before Judge Hooper's deadline for Atlanta expired. In January 1961, Judge William A. Bootle ordered two blacks admitted to the Athens campus, and when the Fifth Circuit overturned his stay, they entered immediately. After rioting by whites led to the black students being suspended for their own safety, Judge Bootle ordered them reinstated and the university complied, bringing Georgia its first desegregation at any educational level. Most legislators preferred admitting two black students to closing the university, which was the alma mater of many of them. Governor Vandiver then quickly abandoned massive resistance, calling for legislation to enable him to keep desegregated schools open. Diehards such as Roy Harris and Marvin Griffin criticized the governor's capitulation, but the legislature replaced mandatory school closures with local option, pupil placement, and public tuition grants to attend private schools. The desegregation of the University of Georgia thus paved the way for Atlanta's school desegregation that fall, which took place without incident.[130]

With token grade school desegregation accomplished in New Orleans and Atlanta, the collapse of massive resistance elsewhere seemed inevitable. Only South Carolina, Mississippi, and Alabama remained completely segregated, and their ability to hold out much longer was doubtful. Opinion polls revealed that most southerners now regarded desegregation as inevitable: 76 percent in 1961, compared with only 43 percent in 1957. One former diehard segregationist explained, "I was for segregation as long as it had a chance to win, but there's no use beating a dead cat." Early in 1961, Governor Almond of Virginia told a Montgomery audience that he had fought to preserve segregation "to the end of the road," but he would not abandon public education.[131]

With Atlanta schools desegregated, a majority of Georgia voters in 1962 apparently abandoned massive resistance by electing as governor the moderate Carl Sanders—"moderate means that I am a segregationist but not a damned fool"—over the rabid segregationist, former governor Griffin. During the campaign, Griffin had urged that words such as "compromise" and "inevitable" be stricken from the vocabulary, attacked Sanders as Martin Luther King, Jr.'s candidate, and issued a joint call with George Wallace for Deep South unity against integration. Sanders, who criticized both King and Wallace, promised that Georgia would not close its schools. With the aid of a federal court decision invalidating the county-unit system, which vastly overrepresented rural voters in statewide elections, Sanders won handily, leading political observers to note the end of an era in Georgia. Sanders emphasized that violence would not be tolerated as school desegregation spread to cities beyond Atlanta. Even the diehard segregationist attorney general, Eugene Cook, now proclaimed that "99 percent of the people of Georgia have abandoned the feeling that we should close every school in the state rather than admit one Negro." The first black elected to the state legislature since Reconstruction, Leroy Johnson, reported, "[T]here's a new look in Georgia."[132]

There was still a distinctively old look to Alabama and Mississippi, where politicians seemed to prefer embracing "embattled martyrdom" to acknowledging the inevitability of desegregation. Even after New Orleans and Atlanta had desegregated, Governor Patterson of Alabama left no doubt that he would close schools rather than see them integrated, and he warned of violence if integrationists persisted in their efforts. Candidates seeking to succeed Patterson as governor in 1962 launched a typical post–Little Rock campaign, vying for the most extreme segregationist position. Reflecting the tenor of the times in Alabama, former governor Folsom abandoned the moderation of his earlier campaigns, promised to preserve school segregation during his constituents' lifetimes, criticized Patterson for not jailing the freedom riders, and frequently used the word "nigger" in his speeches, which political observers could not recall his ever before doing. Bull Connor attacked "weak-kneed" integrationists and ran for governor on the record of diehard resistance to racial change that he had compiled as Birmingham's police commissioner. State senator Albert Boutwell emphasized his sponsorship of massive-resistance legislation. Attorney General MacDonald Gallion touted his success at keeping the NAACP out of business. George Wallace denied that desegregation was inevitable and campaigned mainly against federal judicial tyranny, bragging that he had defied a 1958 court order to turn over voting records to the U.S. Civil Rights Commission. Wallace called Judge Frank Johnson a liar for suggesting that Wallace had secretly released the records to avoid a contempt citation. He also promised to defy any integration order, "even to the point of standing at the school house door in person." His opponent in the runoff primary, state senator Ryan deGraffenried, criticized as irresponsible Wallace's "running around, daring the federal government to throw him in jail," but Alabama voters apparently preferred Wallace's extremism, awarding him an easy victory.[133]

At least Wallace's defiant threats subjected him to criticism. In Mississippi, where whites simply hoped "to put [up] a good fight before losing," political extremism went mostly unchallenged. The legislature continued to pass massive-resistance measures after other states had stopped doing so. The state attorney general, Joe T. Patterson, instructed state officers to enforce segregation laws, notwithstanding contrary federal authority. As a crisis loomed over court-ordered desegregation of Ole Miss in September 1962, Governor Barnett reiterated, "[N]o school will be integrated in Mississippi while I am your governor." He planned to interpose his authority against that of the federal courts, and he announced that all officeholders should resign unless they were prepared to go to jail. Business and professional leaders remained silent until it was too late.[134]

The race riot at Ole Miss, which brought federal troops back into the South, turned the massive-resistance tide in South Carolina. Even before Ole Miss, South Carolina politicians had been quieter about segregation than were their counterparts in Alabama, and the issue attracted less attention than it previously had in the 1962 races for governor and senator. Public officials began hinting that flexibility could preserve the most segregation, and Governor Hollings declined to criticize such statements, noting that South Carolina had a "firm policy of flexibility." In August, a well-connected journalist wrote that politicians realized the state would have to integrate soon, though they would not publicly admit it. The Ole Miss crisis produced a "very significant change of mood," as South Carolina's "vicarious suffering" yielded a conviction that "it must not happen here." With a court order to integrate Clemson University looming late in 1962, the departing governor, Hollings, promised that South Carolina would not duplicate Little Rock or Ole Miss and implicitly criticized Barnett and Wallace for their last-ditch stands. Even the strongly segregationist Columbia *State* conceded, "[T]he issue is no longer one of whether there shall be integration, but of how reasonably it will be brought about." Clemson alumni, many of whom held powerful political positions, insisted that they "had too much sense" to close the university to prevent integration, and they promised to avoid "any tragedy like Mississippi." Business leaders closed ranks behind a call to preserve law and order even in the face of a judicial command to integrate. When Harvey

Gantt (who later became mayor of Charlotte, North Carolina, and a candidate for the U.S. Senate) entered Clemson in January 1963—the first desegregation at any educational level in South Carolina since Reconstruction—a formidable law enforcement presence ensured that no disturbances occurred.[135]

Alabama politicians were more divided over what lesson to learn from Ole Miss. Governor Patterson telegrammed his support to Governor Barnett and criticized the "tyrannical" use of troops, which would "mark the end of our existence as a democratic republic." The state's entire congressional delegation also supported Barnett, declaring, "Mississippi's fight is Alabama's fight." Governor-elect Wallace likewise endorsed Mississippi's resistance and dared the federal government to throw Barnett in jail. Wallace continued railing against "lousy, no-account judges," and he promised to keep the University of Alabama segregated. Yet dissenting voices were now heard in Alabama. Prominent business and civic leaders, the *Birmingham News*, Lieutenant Governor–elect James Allen, and Attorney General–elect Richmond Flowers all condemned Wallace's "bravado," urged against school closures, and insisted that "another Oxford" must be avoided at all costs. But Wallace would have none of it, refusing to "take back one single utterance," and he informed those who passed resolutions urging him to stand down that they were "wasting paper." In his inaugural address in January 1963, Wallace reaffirmed his defiant stand: "In the name of the greatest people that have ever trod this earth, I draw the line in the dust and toss the gauntlet before the feet of tyranny and I say segregation now, segregation tomorrow, segregation forever." By contrast, Attorney General Flowers, in his inaugural statement, urged Alabamans to distinguish between "a fighting chance and a chance to fight," and warned that defiance of federal court orders "can only bring disgrace to our state." Business leaders criticized "indecent and irresponsible" political elements for creating a national image of Alabama as a place of "reaction, rebellion and riots, of bigotry, bias and backwardness." In April 1963, Attorney General Robert Kennedy met with Wallace in Montgomery but was unable to budge him, as Wallace reaffirmed his pledge to maintain segregation forever. In June, in a carefully orchestrated charade, Wallace physically blocked desegregation of the University of Alabama, before standing down in the face of superior federal force. That fall, he obstructed court-ordered desegregation of grade schools in several Alabama cities before capitulating there as well.[136]

Although Deep South politicians continued to fulminate against integration, massive resistance came to an end. In Louisiana, parochial schools desegregated in 1962, and by the following year, citizens' councils were largely a spent force. In the gubernatorial primary of 1963–1964, race continued to dominate, but the loser, deLesseps S. Morrison, referred to himself as a segregationist "within the rule of reason," and the more avidly segregationist victor, John McKeithen, pointedly rejected school closures. In Mississippi's 1963 gubernatorial race, school segregation dominated, and Lieutenant Governor Paul Johnson emphasized his role in physically blocking James Meredith's admission to Ole Miss—"Stand Tall with Paul"—while promising, if necessary, to again interpose his body between the forces of federal tyranny and the people of Mississippi. He urged that the state "fight harder next time" and pledged to "resist the integration of any school anywhere in Mississippi." But the disaster at Ole Miss had finally liberated dissenters, and for virtually the first time in a decade, voices of "moderation" were heard in Mississippi, calling for open schools and peaceful compliance with court orders. In March 1963, Mississippi State participated in the racially mixed NCAA basketball tournament, and another "impregnable barrier" to desegregation fell. After running a defiant campaign, Governor Johnson's inaugural address sang a different tune. He declared that "hate, or prejudice, or ignorance will not lead Mississippi while I sit in the governor's chair," and he seemed to acknowledge the inevitability of desegregation, insisting that he would not fight "a rear-guard defense of yesterday" but rather would pursue Mississippi's "share of tomorrow." In the fall of 1964, Mississippi became the last state to desegregate its grade schools.[137]

Explaining Massive Resistance

Why did *Brown* so radicalize southern politics in the short term, leading politicians to compete for the most extreme segregationist positions? Politics does not usually work this way. Rather, politicians generally strive for the middle, seeking to assemble majority coalitions by appealing to median voters who, by definition, are moderates rather than extremists. There *were* white racial moderates in the South—people who favored compliance with court orders, opposed school closures, and would have tolerated gradual desegregation. *Brown II* had consciously appealed to such moderates and sought to empower them. Why did that strategy fail so abysmally? Why were so few moderate voices heard in the South after *Brown*?

One explanation focuses on southern politicians. Either because they miscalculated their constituents' preferences or because they demagogically capitalized on their constituents' fears, politicians became extremists and created an environment that chilled the expression of moderate sentiment. On this view, massive resistance was not inevitable, at least outside of the Deep South. Politicians could have espoused more moderate positions without losing office, as shown by electoral results in Tennessee and Texas. Had they chosen this route, politicians might have mobilized more vocal support from the large bloc of moderates, who instead fell silent.[138]

It is true that some politicians had incentives for extremism, regardless of their constituents' preferences. In Virginia, the Byrd machine had reason to emphasize race issues, which could distract voters from debates over public services, which were gradually weakening its political position. But in most of the South, it was not politicians who were primarily responsible for massive resistance. The political dynamics of the segregation issue combined with certain features of southern politics to propel public debate toward extremism, independently of the machinations of politicians. Most officials, including those who were ordinarily inclined toward racial moderation, became more extremist to survive, and those few who resisted were generally destroyed.[139]

Several factors helped foster massive resistance. Diehard segregationists had stronger preferences than did most moderates. They also had the capacity and the inclination to use repressive tactics to create the appearance that southern whites were united behind massive resistance. Diehard states similarly exerted pressure on more moderately inclined neighbors to support massive resistance. Further, legislative malapportionment exaggerated the political power of extremists. Perhaps most important, the desire of nearly all whites to preserve segregation if possible virtually ensured an attempt at massive resistance. Differences among whites concerned the burdens that they were willing to bear to preserve segregation, not their preference for it. Finally, the use of federal troops, which proved necessary to suppress massive resistance, ironically bolstered it in the short term.

Although many white southerners were prepared to comply with *Brown*, and a few actually agreed with it, hard-core segregationists tended to be more intensely committed. Some white moderates came from regions with small black populations, so that school desegregation would not greatly affect them. Ardent segregationists tended to come from rural areas with large black populations or from working-class urban neighborhoods without rigid residential segregation. Those who were most committed on the segregation issue tended to be most adamantly opposed to *Brown*. By virtue of their strong preferences, they were also likely to control southern racial policy. Legislative commissions that were appointed to recommend responses to *Brown* were generally dominated by black-belt segregationists. The legislator who chaired Virginia's commission, Garland Gray, came from Southside, and he had already recorded his "unalterable opposition" to the Court's "monstrous" decision. All five members of the Arkansas legislative committee that recommended policy on school segregation represented the delta region, which had the state's largest black populations.[140]

Diehard segregationists were not only more intensely committed than their adversaries were, but they also had the inclination and the capacity to silence dissent. Massive resisters wanted to suppress opposition because they believed that only by presenting a united front could they induce the Court and the nation to retreat from *Brown*. This issue arose mainly in the context of whether to allow local-option desegregation. If given a choice, portions of many southern states—northwestern Arkansas, West Texas, northern and western Virginia, eastern Tennessee, the city of Atlanta—were prepared to comply with *Brown*. But massive resisters in state government were determined to eliminate that choice for fear that any deviation from universal segregation would make integration appear inevitable, embolden the NAACP, and undermine the campaign to convince northern integrationists that the South would never tolerate *Brown*. Thus, the Virginia legislature revoked Arlington County's right to elect school board members as punishment for the board's 1956 vote to desegregate, and it rejected the Gray Commission's initial proposal for local-option desegregation. In 1957, the Texas legislature required local communities to conduct referenda before desegregating or else lose their state education funds. More than 120 school districts in Texas had desegregated before this law was passed, but almost none did so for several years thereafter. Governor Faubus used state troops to prevent racially moderate Little Rock from complying with a desegregation order that had broad support in the local white community. Massive resisters in Georgia worried that Atlanta, with its "wrecking crew of extremists, ultra-liberals and renegade politicians," could prove to be the "Achilles' heel in the fight to keep segregation." When Mayor William B. Hartsfield asked the state legislature to adopt local option, Governor Griffin declared that the mayor "cannot throw in the towel for me or any other Georgian," and Senator Richard Russell warned against "surrender" talk. The Southern Manifesto was a highly successful effort by senators such as Russell and Harry Byrd to coerce moderates—Lister Hill, John Sparkman, William Fulbright, Brooks Hays—into maintaining a united front. The political rhetoric of massive resisters, denying any middle ground and portraying moderates as integrationists and NAACP sympathizers, was similarly motivated and similarly effective.[141]

Their incentive to suppress dissent is clear, but why were massive resisters so effective at doing so? The answer, in short, is that the South was not an open society characterized by robust debate on racial issues. In 1960, a law school dean in Mississippi pointed out that "[f]riends won't argue among themselves" about segregation, and "you can't think out loud hardly." James Silver, a history professor at Ole Miss, charged that Mississippi had "erected a totalitarian society which has eliminated the ordinary processes through which change can come about." A South Carolina minister, noting that people were afraid even to protest the beating of a local band teacher for his allegedly integrationist statements, observed, "[F]ear covers South Carolina like the frost." Newspaper editor Hodding Carter warned that the First Amendment was in great danger in the South. In such an environment, white moderates were "immobilized by confusion and fear," and they mostly went into hiding.[142]

In the mid-1950s, massive resisters were a majority in much of the South, and thus they could use the levers of government to suppress dissent. Public school teachers and university professors lost their jobs or were harassed by legislative investigating committees for daring to support integration or even for urging obedience to the law and criticizing mob violence. Unwilling to tolerate such assaults on academic freedom, many of them resigned and moved elsewhere, which only exacerbated the problem of the closed society. Integrationist university students faced similar harassment and expulsion. Hundreds of them, both black and white, were suspended or expelled for participating in direct-action protests in the 1960s.

Some southern states targeted speech as well as speakers, removing offensive books from circulation. When the Georgia board of education banned textbook statements that charged whites with discrimination against blacks, the chairman explained, "There is no place in Georgia schools at any time for anything that disagrees with our way of life." An Alabama legislator sparked a national controversy by demanding that public libraries ban a popular children's book about the marriage of two rabbits, one white and one black. Even the staunchly segregationist *Montgomery Advertiser* thought this was "idiocy," but the legislator defended himself on the ground that "the South has room for only one viewpoint."[143]

Private suppression of dissent supplemented public suppression, if that distinction even makes sense given the blending of the two spheres in the Deep South, where citizens' councils received public funding and their members dominated public office. The councils applied economic pressure to blacks who pursued integration and to whites who were deemed insufficiently committed to segregation. The U.S. Civil Rights Commission had difficulty enlisting Mississippi whites to serve on the state's advisory committee after a citizens' council editor warned, "[A]ny scalawag southerner who fronts for our mortal enemies will face the well-deserved contempt and ostracism that any proud people would feel for a traitor." White students who initially befriended the Little Rock Nine were condemned as "Nigger lovers," and Ole Miss faculty and administrators who were civil to James Meredith were frequently harassed. The few whites who publicly supported the Montgomery bus boycott received threatening phone calls. When a few white families refused to boycott desegregated schools in New Orleans in 1960, they received death threats, homes were vandalized, parents were fired from jobs, and one family gave up and moved north. Violence was the last resort for compelling white conformity. When a white woman contributed an essay to the moderate publication *South Carolinians Speak*, in which she urged gradual desegregation, her home was bombed. A mob beat up a white minister in Clinton, Tennessee, for escorting black students to the desegregated school. A northern white minister attending the University of Alabama was kidnapped and beaten for inviting a black minister and his congregants to attend a meeting with white students.[144]

Such pressure suppressed the traditional organs of moderate racial opinion. Newspapers that advocated desegregation or simple compliance with the law were boycotted and sometimes shut down. The editor of the only South Carolina newspaper that urged compliance with *Brown* was driven out of the state, as was the editor of one of the few Mississippi newspapers that criticized Governor Barnett's antics at Ole Miss. A student editor at Auburn University had a cross burned on his lawn for supporting the Freedom Rides. Southern ministers who advocated integration, or simply protested against extremist resistance, were usually evicted by their congregations. In 1963, twenty-eight Methodist ministers in Mississippi signed a statement supporting school desegregation, and all but seven of them were gone within a year. Many other ministers simply suppressed their private convictions that segregation was immoral. Under pressure from public officials, some southern universities stopped inviting integrationist speakers. Citizens' councils harassed social clubs that expressed interest in hearing opposing viewpoints. Some television stations refused to air national programs that discussed integration, explaining that they were not "running a propaganda machine for the NAACP."[145]

If southern society was closed for whites, it was hermetically sealed for blacks. Because blacks were the most integrationist of southerners, suppressing their viewpoint was critical to maintaining the veneer of solid support for segregation. Blacks were subject to the same forms of segregationist pressure as whites, but the coercion was often more intense. Citizens' councils announced, "We intend to make it difficult, if not impossible, for any Negro who advocates desegregation to find and hold a job, get credit, or renew a mortgage." Police harassed integrationist blacks, broke up their meetings, arrested them on fraudulent charges, and sometimes beat them. During the Montgomery bus boycott, public officials who were pursuing a "get tough" policy arrested scores of blacks on phony traffic charges and tried to disbar the black lawyer who filed the bus desegregation suit and to alter his draft classification. A black man in Bessemer, Alabama, was sentenced to six months in jail for breach of the peace and inciting to riot for reproducing a picture from a northern newspaper of a black man praying to God that equal rights would be extended to all. The president of the NAACP branch in Yazoo City, Mississippi, who had earlier circulated a school desegregation petition, received a life sentence for killing a prowler trespassing on his property, when prosecutors belonging to the citizens' council and an all-white jury refused to credit his self-defense claim. The most aggressive black integrationists were targets of extraordinary white violence. Daisy Bates, leader of Little Rock's desegregation forces, had her home fire-bombed seven times within two years.[146]

Southern society was closed, but Mississippi verged on totalitarianism. The state sovereignty commission spied on civil rights workers and channeled public funds to citizens' councils. The legislature made it a crime to incite a breach of the peace by urging "nonconformance with the established traditions, customs, and usages of the State of Mississippi," and Governor Coleman threatened to prosecute speakers who entered Mississippi to agitate the race issue. A white newspaper editor, who was sued for libel for criticizing law enforcement officers who mistreated blacks, observed, "[I]n much of Mississippi, we live in an atmosphere of fear." When the long-time Ole Miss history professor James Silver criticized the state as a "closed society" in 1963, public officials, failing to perceive the irony, announced that "it is time to get rid" of Silver and "to stifle his degrading activities." Mississippi officials concocted phony charges against blacks who pursued integration. Clyde Kennard, who tried to desegregate Mississippi Southern University, was later sentenced to seven years at hard labor for allegedly trying to buy twenty-five dollars' worth of stolen chicken feed. When Medgar Evers called Kennard's sentence "a mockery of judicial justice," he received thirty days in jail for contempt. Nobody ruled Senator Eastland in contempt, though, when he told white Mississippians, "You are not required to obey any court which passes out such a ruling [*Brown*]. In fact, you are obligated to defy it." In many parts of Mississippi, blacks still faced "systematic racial terrorism." A visitor to Jefferson County reported, "It is all but unbelievable to see the fear that is shown by the Negro people." In many counties, not a single black person dared to register to vote. In the early 1960s, civil rights workers in Mississippi were routinely beaten, bombed, shot at, and occasionally killed. Local officials permitted the Klan to operate virtually without restraint.[147]

Racial moderates had neither the inclination nor the capacity to use such methods. They did not control state or local governments, and thus they could not fire segregationist teachers, expel segregationist students, or use law enforcement apparatus to harass citizens' council members. Nor did moderates make harassing phone calls to segregationists, burn crosses on their lawns, or blow up their homes. When Robert Williams, the president of the NAACP branch in Union County, North Carolina, advocated that blacks meet "violence with violence" in the wake of Mack Parker's lynching

FIGURE 7.5
Medgar Evers, the NAACP's field secretary in Mississippi, was murdered in 1963 for his civil rights activity. (*Library of Congress, Prints and Photographs Division, New York World-Telegram & Sun Collection*)

in Mississippi in 1959, the national office immediately suspended him. Thus, hard-core segregationists were not only more intensely committed to their position than were moderate whites, but they were also more willing to use coercive measures to achieve victory. The suppression of moderate opinion had a cascading effect: As some people were intimidated into silence, the pressure on others to conform intensified.[148]

Just as within one state diehard segregationists could pressure moderates by denying the inevitability of desegregation, so could extremist states pressure their moderate neighbors. Politicians had difficulty explaining to constituents why they had to desegregate when neighboring states were not doing so. This dynamic partially explains Governor Faubus's dilemma over school desegregation in Little Rock in 1957. Alabama and Texas had flouted desegregation orders the previous year, and the segregationist governor of Georgia, Marvin Griffin, had visited Little Rock two weeks before schools were scheduled to open, expressing shock that any governor with troops at his disposal would allow integration. Citizens approached Faubus on the street, demanding to know, "[I]f Georgia doesn't have integration, why does Arkansas?" On other occasions, citizens' councils asked why Faubus remained silent, while governors in South Carolina and Georgia were denouncing Court decisions that banned segregation in public parks, playgrounds, and golf courses. Alabama citizens' councils pressured their congressmen "to join us in this fight, so we won't have to go to Mississippi, Georgia or South Carolina" to find real segregationists.[149]

Comprehending this dynamic and the importance of maintaining regional unity, diehard states in the Deep South pressured their more moderate neighbors to conform to massive resistance. The Columbia *State* criticized states that were abandoning segregation without a fight, because "surrender of some states makes it harder for the others to hold the line." Mississippi citizens' councils sent money and literature to Hoxie, Arkansas, to incite resistance after the school board voluntarily desegregated in 1955. Soon after he had fomented violent resistance to desegregation in Clinton, Tennessee, John Kasper, the South's leading peripatetic troublemaker, told Birmingham segregationists, "We want trouble and we want it everywhere we can get it." When sixteen Clintonians were arrested in connection with Kasper's disturbances, several attorneys general from southern states agreed to defend them—an expression of regional solidarity. Senator Eastland also traveled through the South, speaking to mass segregationist rallies, warning against efforts "to pick [us] off one by one under the damnable doctrine of gradualism," and criticizing "border states [that] have weak-kneed politicians in the capital . . . [and] weak governors." Both the interposition movement and the Southern Manifesto were partially aimed at pressuring moderate states to support massive resistance. The perceived importance of maintaining regional unity led Virginians to criticize North Carolina's token integrationism as "abject surrender" and Alabamans to regard Virginia's abandonment of massive resistance as a "crippling blow."[150]

Extremists also benefited from legislative malapportionment, which in every state favored rural districts that contained the most committed white supremacists. In Alabama and Georgia, black-belt counties enjoyed nearly twice the representation that their populations warranted, meaning that whites in those counties, where blacks were generally disfranchised, exercised even more disproportionate political power. Moreover, such counties tended to reelect the same representatives for decades, which enhanced their legislative seniority and thus further augmented the political power of diehard segregationists. Moderate racial opinion in cities was often nullified by malapportionment. For example, Atlanta had little clout in the rural-dominated Georgia legislature. Georgia's unique county-unit system, which extended malapportionment to elections for state executive office, explains the extremism of governors such as Talmadge and Griffin. Roy Harris conceded, "The county unit system is absolutely essential in order to maintain the pattern of segregation in Georgia." In other states, which elected executive officers on the principle of one person, one vote, governors often tried to force legislative reapportionment, but their efforts came to naught. When Governors Folsom and Collins called special legislative sessions in Alabama and Florida in the mid-1950s to consider reapportionment, legislators instead enacted massive-resistance measures. Had *Brown* been decided after *Reynolds v. Sims* (1964) invalidated malapportionment in state legislatures, rather than before, massive resistance might have played out rather differently.[151]

Yet the most important explanation for the temporary triumph of massive resistance may be this: Many southern whites—perhaps a majority outside of the Deep South—preferred token integration to school closures, but very few favored token integration over segregation. Thus, opinion polls on *Brown* revealed minimal support among southern whites, but referenda on school closures showed substantial white opposition. Consequently, until it became clear that preserving segregation entailed school closures, moderate whites had every reason to allow massive resistance to run its course, as they too preferred to avoid desegregation. The difference between white "moderates" and "extremists" was not in their preference for segregation, but in the sacrifices they were prepared to make to maintain it.[152]

From this perspective, the crucial development of the mid-1950s was the growing conviction among white southerners that *Brown* could be successfully defied and segregation preserved. Massive resisters may have been emboldened by the fierce and successful opposition to desegregation put up by whites in Milford, Delaware, in the fall of 1954. If border-state whites could frustrate desegregation, how could it possibly be imposed on the real South? *Brown II* furthered this conviction, as many southern whites sensed the beginnings of a judicial retreat. President Eisenhower's obvious lack of enthusiasm for *Brown*, his statements rejecting the use of federal troops to enforce desegregation orders, and his refusal to intervene against violent resistance to desegregation in Texas, Alabama, and Tennessee in 1956 encouraged southern whites to question the inevitability of integration. Historical memories of the first Reconstruction, when southern whites had worn down the (never intense) commitment of northern whites to protecting the political and civil rights of southern blacks, inspired hope that determined resistance could nullify *Brown*. One segregationist editor, urging white southerners to "shape their destiny and control their way of life, just as they did in the far more dangerous period of Reconstruction," triumphantly concluded: "Our forefathers saved white men's civilization. We can do it again." Senator Eastland similarly noted, "Southern people have been tested in the past and have not been found wanting," and he predicted "a new golden hour of Southern history." Analogies to Prohibition also offered solace to southern whites: Many Americans, in the North as well as the South, had drawn the lesson from that historical episode that national efforts to coerce social reform against strong resistance were doomed to failure.[153]

One cannot know how many white southerners genuinely believed that *Brown* could be nullified and segregation preserved. But many southern politicians spoke this way, and constituents may well have believed what they wanted to. Governor Almond of Virginia had "faith that the decision ultimately will be reversed," and Senator Byrd thought that "if people are firm enough and determined enough," the justices might change their minds. The segregation czar of Louisiana, Willie Rainach, promised that school closures would be unnecessary because the mere threat of them would be sufficient to block desegregation, and he predicted that the Court would reverse itself within a decade. Another Louisiana legislator observed: "When those birds in the Supreme Court realize we mean business, we'll find we won't have to change our entire school system." A South Carolina judge expressed confidence that "this decision will be eventually reversed, though it may take years." Countless other politicians, without explicitly suggesting that the Court would change its mind, insisted that desegregation would not come "in a thousand years" or in their "lifetime," thereby encouraging the belief that it was not inevitable. The principal purposes of the Southern Manifesto included convincing white southerners that desegregation was not inevitable and convincing northerners that the South would not capitulate. Efforts at undermining the perceived inevitability of desegregation also had a cascading effect: The fewer people who accepted desegregation as inevitable, the less so it became.[154]

Such political rhetoric convinced at least some people. A circular from a white supremacist organization declared, "The fact that the Supreme Court has ruled as it has, in favor of the black man, is no sign that the whole thing is settled. Many times in the past the Supreme Court has reversed itself, and many other times it has merely overlooked enforcing its rulings." A reporter from Norfolk, Virginia, noted that after the "general air of calm resignation" following *Brown I*, the notion had developed "that the fatal day would be delayed for many years," and "in some quarters there was actual belief that integration would never come." The Little Rock school board, petitioning in 1958 for a delay in the desegregation process, told the federal court that massive resisters had convinced many people that desegregation was not inevitable and that Faubus had bolstered that belief by using the state militia to block it. Political journalist Samuel Lubell, who was interviewing white southerners during this period, reported, "By the spring of 1957 the segregationists, emboldened by the lack of opposition to their efforts, had come to believe that nullification of the Supreme Court's decision was in sight." According to Gallup polls, the number of white southerners who believed that school desegregation was inevitable fell from 55 percent early in 1956 to 43 percent in August 1957.[155]

Once Eisenhower used federal troops at Little Rock, however, only school closures could prevent desegregation. As several schools closed in Virginia and in Little Rock in 1958, white southerners had to confront a previously avoided question: What costs were they prepared to incur in order to preserve segregation? Many had supported massive resistance as a bluff or as an initial response but were unwilling to pursue it to its logical conclusion: the abolition of public schools. Parents' groups that were dedicated to saving public education sprang up across the South, and some local chambers of commerce mobilized against school closures.[156]

The speed with which massive resistance crumbled outside of the Deep South after schools were closed suggests one of two possibilities: Either many whites had endorsed school closures only as a bluff to induce a retreat by the Court and by integrationist northerners, or they had genuinely supported closures but without carefully calculating the costs. Once the bluff was called, and the costs of school closures were made concrete, the attitudes of white southerners toward school desegregation changed rapidly.[157]

A post–Little Rock poll revealed that two out of three whites in Virginia would rather close schools than integrate them. Reflecting that opinion, in 1958, Governor Almond closed schools in Charlottesville, Norfolk, and Warren County, while continuing to give fiery speeches that endorsed massive resistance. But private school arrangements quickly proved unsatisfactory, especially in Norfolk, where a federal judge enjoined public employees from teaching in private schools and thousands of children went uneducated. Public opinion in Virginia changed rapidly as a result. By November, newspapers that had formerly supported massive resistance were calling for "speedy abandonment" of that "futile" strategy and the adoption of "a new approach." James J. Kilpatrick, editor of the *Richmond News Leader* and the principal force behind the interposition movement three years earlier, now called for "new weapons and new tactics" and endorsed token integration. Public officials soon reflected that opinion shift. Although Southside politicians continued to endorse "massive resistance all the way," Governor Almond changed his tune virtually overnight. After federal and state courts invalidated school closures in January 1959, Almond repudiated massive resistance in favor of local option and token integration. He criticized proposals to abandon public education as "going back to the dark ages" and warned that Virginia "cannot secede from the Union [or] overthrow the federal government." An opinion poll showed that two out of three Virginians now supported the governor's new policy.[158]

Attitudes toward school desegregation also changed quickly in Little Rock. Governor Faubus had promised an easy transition from public to private education, and in September 1958, Little Rock voters supported school closures in a referendum by a margin of greater than 5–2. But the white private school quickly proved unsatisfactory, especially after a federal court blocked its use of public money and public school buildings. In December, school board elections showed that voters were evenly divided between candidates of the citizens' council and those of more moderate businesspeople. In February 1959, the 2,000 members of the Little Rock Chamber of Commerce voted by a margin of better than 3–1 to reopen high schools with token integration. The business community could easily count the costs of school closures: Ten businesses had relocated to Little Rock in the two years before September 1957, but not a single one had done so since. In May 1959, voters narrowly recalled segregationist school board members in retaliation for their purges of moderate teachers and replaced them with token integrationists. By the time that Little Rock public high schools reopened with a few blacks that fall, the private school corporation had gone bankrupt. In 1960, Samuel Lubell discovered that the same Little Rock whites who two years earlier had preferred to see Central High burned down rather than "infested with niggers" now favored token integration over school closures.[159]

Because their moment of truth arrived later, Georgians were able to learn vicariously from the tribulations of others. Little Rock officials and business leaders visited Atlanta to warn of the economic and social costs entailed by diehard segregationism. In his 1958 gubernatorial campaign and then repeatedly over the next two years, Governor Vandiver rejected local option and token integration in favor of school closures. Yet public opinion began to shift as school closures loomed once Judge Hooper ordered Atlanta to desegregate in 1960, which he later postponed until 1961. Parents' organizations, business leaders, and most newspapers preferred token integration to school closures. Reflecting this opinion shift, Vandiver encouraged the legislature to appoint the Sibley Commission, which searched for an honorable means of retreat. By early 1961, as the desegregation crisis hit the University of Georgia, Vandiver was declaring that "[w]e cannot abandon public education" and urging the repeal of statutes that required integrated schools to close and their replacement with provisions for local option and public tuition grants for students to attend private schools. Henceforth, Vandiver insisted that federal court orders must be obeyed, and he bragged that his administration had kept the schools open.[160]

These dramatic turnabouts in Virginia, Arkansas, and Georgia help explain the political dynamics of massive resistance. Until attempted, nobody knew whether it could succeed. School closures were a cheap threat, and the costs, if implemented, were hard to calculate in advance. After Little

Rock, however, only school closures could preserve segregation. Once they were tried, public opinion turned rapidly against them because of the harm to education and to business development. Moderates, who had previously possessed little incentive to oppose massive resistance, now asserted themselves, and the debate rapidly swung in their favor. Token integration, though "still . . . objectionable," was "not intolerable," and it was preferable to school closures. Moreover, this dynamic, which favored moderation, was as self-reinforcing as the earlier one, which had supported extremism. As the first moderates asserted themselves and demanded open schools, others found it easier to follow.[161]

Yet the realism that was impelled by Little Rock, New Orleans, and Ole Miss had little immediate effect on Governors Patterson, Wallace, and Barnett. In the late 1950s, diehard resisters may genuinely have believed that desegregation could be avoided and the Court induced to back down. Explaining their behavior in 1962–1963 is more difficult, as they surely understood by then that they could not preserve "segregation forever" and that to "fight harder next time" was no formula for success. The reason that politicians continued to make such pledges is probably that voters in Alabama and Mississippi continued to reward them for doing so. For example, Wallace plainly anticipated political gain from fomenting a desegregation fight with the federal government, even though his stand in the schoolhouse door in Tuscaloosa was a carefully orchestrated charade. The real question is why voters rewarded such irresponsible pledges once desegregation had become inevitable. Perhaps they were so embittered at the prospect of externally coerced racial change that they preferred, in the best southern tradition, to fight futile battles rather than to capitulate. Many whites in Mississippi and Alabama, though conceding that "you can't fight the Federal government and win," still insisted, "[W]e'll never accept it voluntarily" and "they'll have to force it on us." As William Faulkner pointed out, Mississippi whites "will accept another civil war, knowing they're going to lose."[162]

Finally and ironically, massive resistance could end only after Eisenhower had proved his willingness to use federal troops to enforce desegregation orders, yet the deployment of these forces bolstered massive resistance in the short term. As a general rule, external threats tend to unify a polity. When NATO forces bombed Serbia in 1999, even critics of President Slobodan Milosevic temporarily rallied behind him in opposition to the outside attacks. Historically, white southerners have been especially sensitive to outside interference with their "way of life." Thus, when Eisenhower sent federal troops into Little Rock, moderate white southerners united with extremists in assailing the president. Ironically, though Little Rock should have discouraged extremism by demonstrating the futility of massive resistance, its immediate effect was to further radicalize southern opinion and to empower politicians who promised defiance of "federal tyranny."[163]

On statewide television, Faubus referred to Little Rock as an "occupied" city, implicitly appealing to the bitter historical memories that Arkansas whites had of the Civil War and of Reconstruction, when federal troops had invaded the South. Southern political opinion overwhelmingly supported Faubus and condemned Eisenhower. A North Carolina congressman asserted, "The issue of integrated schools is dwarfed by the precipitous and dictatorial stab at the rights of an individual state." Several southern politicians compared the use of federal troops at Little Rock to the Soviet Union's invasion of Hungary in 1956. Governor George Timmerman of South Carolina criticized the president for "trying to set himself up as a dictator," and he resigned his commission in the naval reserves. Senator Russell condemned the use of "storm troopers." Circuit judge George Wallace compared Eisenhower to Hitler and accused the president of substituting "military dictatorship for the Constitution of the United States."[164]

President Kennedy's use of federal forces to desegregate Ole Miss in the fall of 1962 had a similar, albeit less dramatic, effect on southern politics. Political leaders in Arkansas rallied behind Mississippi governor Barnett,

FIGURE 7.6
Governor Orval Faubus holds up the front page of the
Manchester (N.H.) *Union Leader* after President Dwight
Eisenhower sent federal troops into Little Rock, September 28,
1957. (*Bettmann*/CORBIS)

even though their state's public universities had desegregated nearly fifteen years earlier. Texas whites condemned the use of troops by 58 percent to 33 percent, even though the segregation issue by then had virtually disappeared from Texas politics. After Ole Miss, the Republican candidate for the U.S. Senate in Alabama, James Martin, urged voters to "go to the polls with a Rebel yell," and he tried to associate his opponent, Senator Lister Hill, with the Kennedy administration. Martin came within one percentage point of becoming the state's first Republican senator since Reconstruction. In 1963, Paul Johnson won the governorship of Mississippi by denouncing the use of federal troops to desegregate Ole Miss.[165]

These are the reasons that *Brown* radicalized southern politics and induced candidates for public office to adopt extreme segregationist positions. Fire-breathing resistance to federal authority translated into political gain. Politicians calculated that white voters would reward stalwart resistance to racial change, even if it resulted in violence.

Brown, Violence, and Civil Rights Legislation

Before the Freedom Rides, Birmingham, Freedom Summer, and Selma, some of the most violent racial episodes in the South involved school desegregation. Virtually every year after *Brown*, school desegregation generated violent resistance somewhere: Milford, Delaware, in 1954; Hoxie, Arkansas, in 1955; Tuscaloosa, Alabama; Clinton, Tennessee; Mansfield, Texas; and Clay and Sturgis counties, Kentucky, in 1956; Little Rock, Arkansas, and Nashville, Tennessee, in 1957; Clinton (again) in 1958; New Orleans, Louisiana, in 1960; Athens, Georgia, in 1961; Oxford, Mississippi, in 1962; and Birmingham, Alabama, in 1963. Thus, in addition to radicalizing southern politics in ways that enhanced the likelihood of racial violence, *Brown* created concrete occasions for such outbreaks.[166]

Violent episodes involving school desegregation tarnished the national image of white southerners. Resisting court orders to desegregate inevitably placed them on the wrong side of the law. Most Americans believed that judicial rulings should be obeyed, even by those who strongly disagreed with them; the alternative was anarchy. Eisenhower capitalized on this widespread conviction, insisting that the federal troops he had sent to Little Rock were there "to support our federal court system—not to enforce desegregation." When Kennedy sent federal troops into Oxford, Mississippi, he likewise emphasized his duty "to implement the orders of the court," which was necessary to preserve "a government of laws, and not of men." For individuals to violate court orders was bad enough, but mob resistance was even worse. Few things offended national opinion more than substituting the rule of the mob for that of the law. In addition, violent confrontations over school desegregation tended to reveal blacks at their best and whites at their worst. The few blacks who had been handpicked as desegregation pioneers were almost always middle class, bright, well dressed, well mannered, and nonviolent. The mobs that sought to exclude them from white schools tended to be lower class, vicious, obscene, unruly, and violent. Photographic images of these confrontations, according to a *New York Post* editorial, showed "quiet, resolute Negro children defying jeers and violence and sadism." To the extent that Americans formed their opinions on school desegregation and Jim Crow from watching televised scenes of mob violence from Little Rock or New Orleans, southern whites were in a lot of trouble.[167]

Some violent outbreaks over desegregation were brief, as it did not take long to bomb schools in Clinton and Nashville. Other episodes were protracted, such as Little Rock and New Orleans. Lengthy desegregation confrontations attracted media attention, especially from television reporters, and bombings provided graphic photographs. Confrontation and violence play well on television, and extended conflict gives photographers and reporters time to assemble. Few Americans owned television sets in 1950. By the time of Little Rock, most of them did, and by the time of New Orleans

FIGURE 7.7
A white man kicks black newspaper reporter Alex Wilson as a mob watches outside of Little Rock's Central High School, September 23, 1957. Wilson said, "I fought for my country, and I'm not running from you," as he was attacked. (*Arkansas History Commission*)

and Oxford, the vast majority did. Live footage of white mobs assailing black students affected national opinion more profoundly than did still images of bombed buildings.[168]

Desegregation riots at Tuscaloosa, Little Rock, and New Orleans helped to shape national opinion on race. In February 1956, a mob numbering more than a thousand, throwing rocks and eggs and threatening a lynching, drove Autherine Lucy out of the University of Alabama. One northern newspaper condemned mob violence in opposition to court decisions and proclaimed, "Shame Falls on Alabama." Adlai Stevenson, not known for his strong statements on civil rights, denounced the mob violence as "deplorable" and "intolerable." A South Carolina newspaper called the riot "a public disgrace," which "has given the South another black eye" and "played right into the hands of professional South-baiters." Compared with the mob, blacks had been models "of discipline, patience, and understanding." The *Washington Post* predicted that the incident would "outrage opinion even in areas where extreme views against integration prevail." Roy Wilkins cited the riot as evidence of the need for civil rights legislation to protect against mob violence and to withhold federal funds from defiant educational institutions in the South.[169]

Little Rock was a much larger event; it lasted for weeks and culminated in the use of federal troops to protect black students from an enormous mob surrounding Central High School. Outside of the South, public opinion overwhelmingly condemned the mob violence and supported the president, "who had no choice" but to act as he did. Governor Faubus was widely ridiculed — "the sputtering sputnik from the Ozarks," according to Maryland governor Theodore McKeldin. The NAACP's Gloster Current "thank[ed] God for Governor Faubus. He has hastened integration five years by opening the eyes of the country to the kind of thinking that will call out the National Guard to keep nine Negro students out of Little Rock High School." Wilkins similarly labeled Faubus "a valuable enemy, [who] has aided in many ways in clarifying the issue of segregation" and "aroused and educated to our point of view millions of people in America." Ironically, though Faubus alienated northern opinion, southern whites hailed him as a hero, thus ensuring that other southern politicians would mimic his behavior and further repulse northern opinion. Little Rock influenced attitudes around the world, not just in the United States. But whereas nonsoutherners criticized the South, non-Americans tended to condemn the entire nation for tolerating such behavior.[170]

In November 1960, similarly ugly scenes were repeated in New Orleans. But this time, the targets of the mob were six-year-olds. Night after night, nationwide television audiences watched hundreds of vicious protestors, their faces contorted by hate, spitting, snarling, and yelling obscenities — such as "kill them niggers" — at first-graders walking to school in their Sunday best. The author John Steinbeck, who happened to be traveling through New Orleans at the time, called the mob's rantings "bestial and filthy and degenerate," and he compared them to "the vomitings of demoniac humans." The *New York Times*, which thought that the effort of "a racist rabble . . . to subvert the Constitution and substitute anarchy for law" was "degrading and dangerous," warned that "[t]he conscience of America" would not tolerate the "mobsters" or the "insurrectionary histrionics" of the state's elected officials. A Miami woman reported that "the appalling sight and sound . . . [made her] sick—almost physically ill," while a German-born doctor compared the scenes from New Orleans to those enacted in Nazi Germany in the 1930s.[171]

Much of the southern white-on-black violence of the 1950s occurred in the context of court-ordered school desegregation. To the extent that such violence helped transform national opinion on race, *Brown* was directly responsible.

Brown helped foment violence in other ways as well. Though it is hard to know for sure, the simple existence of *Brown* may have fostered violence against blacks by white vigilantes. It is more nearly certain that *Brown* induced extremist politicians to use inflammatory rhetoric that may have indirectly incited violence. *Brown* also led some officeholders to calculate the political benefits of violently suppressing civil rights protest. One cannot prove that *Brown*, or the extremism that it encouraged in southern politics, caused whites to beat or kill blacks, but such causal inferences are plausible, perhaps even probable.

Polls revealed that 15–25 percent of southern whites favored violence, if necessary, to resist school desegregation. The post-*Brown* rebirth of the Ku Klux Klan in the South suggests a greater willingness among whites to use violence. One Klan leader reported that *Brown* created "a situation loaded with dynamite" and "really gave us a push." In 1956, Klan rallies drew hundreds, even thousands, in parts of South Carolina, Georgia, Alabama, and Florida—states where the Klan had recently been deemed defunct. Such gatherings condemned the Court and the NAACP and threatened forcible resistance to desegregation. Now that the justices "have abolished the Mason-Dixon line," Klansmen vowed "to establish the Smith and Wesson line." In 1957, six Birmingham Klansmen castrated a randomly selected black man after taunting him for "think[ing] nigger kids should go to school with [white] kids."[172]

In the late 1940s, Mississippi whites had threatened and beaten blacks for their suffrage activities, but in 1955, the Reverend George Lee in Belzoni and Lamar Smith in Brookhaven were killed for voting or encouraging other blacks to do so. The annual number of reported lynchings in Mississippi had dropped to zero in the years before *Brown*, but in 1955, in addition to the Lee and Smith murders, fourteen-year-old Emmett Till was killed for allegedly whistling at a white woman in Money, Mississippi. That year, the NAACP published a pamphlet entitled "M Is for Mississippi and Murder." Connecting these killings to *Brown* is speculative, but the timing suggests a possible linkage, and some contemporaries inferred a causal connection. The *Herald* of Yazoo City, Mississippi, declared that the blood of Till was on the hands of the justices. The unwillingness of white jurors to indict or convict the clearly guilty white murderers of blacks is even more plausibly linked to *Brown's* impact on southern white opinion. One Mississippi white declared, "There's open season on the Negroes now. They've got no protection, and any pecker-wood who wants can go out and shoot himself one, and we'll free him." Till's funeral in Chicago attracted thousands of mourners, and a photograph of his mutilated body in *Jet* seared the conscience of northerners. Segregating black schoolchildren was one thing, lynching them quite another. Wilkins condemned Mississippi's "political murders" and the "system that permits the shooting down of little boys," and demanded federal civil rights legisla-tion. Republican representative Hugh Scott of Pennsylvania itemized the Mississippi brutalities and also called for legislation to "eliminate this kind of horror from American life."[173]

Mississippi was not the only southern state to become more racially vio-lent after *Brown*. Birmingham, Alabama, where civic leaders in the early 1950s had tried to clean up the city's image by suppressing violence, once again became "Bombingham" after *Brown*. Between 1955 and 1963, Birming-ham blacks were the targets of twenty-one bombings, none of which the police were able to solve. In Montgomery, the homes and churches of sev-eral black ministers and other civil rights leaders were bombed during and after the bus boycott. One study counted more than 100 violent incidents in the South connected to civil rights activity between January 1, 1955, and May 1, 1958. Most of these involved the bombing of homes, schools, and churches, but some Jewish synagogues were also targeted. The victims were usually black, but moderate whites were occasionally attacked as well. After listening to a judge denounce the Supreme Court's "asinine" decisions for an hour, a grand jury in Camden, South Carolina, declined to indict six men who were charged with beating the white director of a school band for allegedly making integrationist statements. Synagogue bombings attracted special attention and condemnation in the North. Both New York senators visited Atlanta after a temple was bombed in late 1958, and they demanded legislation that would authorize federal intervention in such cases.[174]

The lynching of Mack Parker in April 1959, which captured front-page headlines in major newspapers as well as the attention of President Eisen-hower, "revolted and stunned" Americans. Whites had seized Parker, who was scheduled to stand trial for raping a white woman, from the jail in Poplarville, Mississippi, and killed him—the state's first old-style lynching since World War II. One cannot say whether *Brown's* radicalizing effect on southern whites contributed to the lynching, though a Mississippi newspa-per blamed the Court and drew the lesson that "force must not be used in pushing revolutionary changes in social custom. Every such action pro-duces equal and opposite reaction." Moreover, the judge who presided over the grand jury that was investigating the lynching urged its members to "have the backbone to stand against any tyranny . . . [even including] the Board of Sociology setting [sic] in Washington, garbed in Judicial Robes, and 'dishing out' the 'legal precedents' of Gunnar Myrdal." Southern congressmen worried that Parker's lynching would prompt efforts to pass civil rights legislation. Governor Coleman condemned the murder and hoped that Mississippians "won't be punished by civil rights legislation for what a handful have done." Citizens' council guru Judge Tom Brady predicted that the NAACP would "rejoice in this highly regrettable incident" and "will urge passage of vicious civil rights measures." He was right. Wilkins declared that Parker's murder proved that "mob violence is not dead in the South," and it demonstrated "the necessity of further and stronger protection of civil rights . . . by the federal government." He also called the lynching "the natural consequence of an organized campaign of law defiance" by southern politicians. Constituents wrote to their congressmen to express horror and to demand federal legislation to curb such atrocities. Attorney General Rogers announced that he was studying the need for new legislation in light of Parker's lynching and the unwillingness of a local grand jury to indict known participants, which he thought "as flagrant and calculated a misjustice as I know of." Prominent liberals, such as Senators Hubert Humphrey, Paul Douglas, and Jacob Javits, made forceful calls for federal civil rights legislation.[175]

It is speculative to attribute to *Brown* incidents of white vigilante violence against blacks, but diehard segregationists identified and promoted precisely that linkage. In 1956, John Kasper traveled through Alabama, attacking Governor Folsom's moderation, and calling for "marching bands" and "roving forces" to converge on any area threatened with desegregation. Mississippi citizens' councils, which claimed to repudiate violence, conceded that "there is a point beyond which even the most judicious restraint becomes cowardice." A Dallas minister told a large citizens' council rally that if public officials would not block integration, plenty of people were prepared "to shed blood if necessary to stop this work of Satan." A member of the Tuskegee citizens' council warned, "We will stop integration if it takes bloodshed." A handbill that was circulated at a huge citizens' council rally in Montgomery denounced desegregation and declared, "When in the course of human events it becomes necessary to abolish the Negro race, proper methods should be used," including guns and knives. When extremists blew up a Jewish community center in Nashville in 1958, a caller to a rabbi's home explicitly made the connection to desegregation by threatening any other "nigger-loving place" in town.[176]

White southerners could hardly be collectively blamed for random acts of violence committed by white vigilantes against blacks. However, when public officials incited such violence, which they did both directly and indirectly, many northerners responded by demanding civil rights legislation. Southern politicians fomented violence by explicitly encouraging it, by predicting it, and by using extremist rhetoric that inspired it.[177]

Most southern politicians avoided explicit exhortations to violence, and many affirmatively discouraged it, either to immunize themselves from criticism when violence occurred or because they rightly understood that violence would "do irreparable harm to our cause and turn public opinion against us." A southern congressman warned that the gains made in convincing northerners that *Brown* was lawless "can be swept away by one shotgun blast, by one explosion of dynamite touched off in the heat of passion." Still, a few politicians could not restrain themselves. An Alabama legislator declared that whites must leave the state, "stay here and be humiliated, or take up our shotguns." A Mississippi legislator stated that "a few killings" now could "save a lot of bloodshed later on." Others promoted violence more discreetly. A few days after a raging mob had driven Autherine Lucy out of Tuscaloosa, Senator Eastland told an enormous citizens' council rally that he knew "you good people of Alabama don't intend to let the NAACP run your schools." On other occasions, Eastland told audiences that they were "obligated to defy [*Brown*]" and that southern whites, when previously tested, had "not been found wanting." Such indirect exhortations to violence were scarcely more subtle than those of Senator Bilbo in 1946.[178]

Rather than explicitly promoting violence, many southern politicians simply predicted it, which King pointed out was "a conscious or unconscious invitation to it." The attorney general of South Carolina warned, "[O]ur patience may become exhausted, and when that happens, God knows what the results will be." Roy Harris predicted that integrationist efforts would produce "hatred and bloodshed," and Judge Tom Brady endorsed the view of the *Jackson Daily News* that "[h]uman blood may stain Southern soil in many places because of [*Brown*]." Diehard segregationists, after hearing enough of such predictions, were likely to make good on them. The failure of public officials to condemn violence also had the effect of encouraging it. Rather than denouncing a Mansfield mob that blocked court-ordered desegregation and called for the blood of black students, Governor Shivers commended the "orderly protests against a situation instigated and agitated by the [NAACP]."[179]

Other officials repudiated violence, while using extremist rhetoric that probably encouraged it. Governor Griffin condemned violence but also insisted that "no true Southerner feels morally obliged to recognize the legality of this act of tyranny [*Brown*]," and he proclaimed that the South "stands ready to battle side-by-side for its sacred rights, . . . but not with guns." Senator Talmadge likened *Brown* to a coup d'état by a foreign dictator, and he called it "judicial tyranny" and "the greatest single blow ever . . . struck against constitutional government." After the temple bombing in Atlanta, Griffin and Talmadge called for severe punishment of the perpetrators— probably "communists," they said—yet in the same breath they denied that *Brown* was the law of the land and vowed that the South would never "surrender." Eastland condemned *Brown* as "illegal, immoral, dishonest, and a disgrace," and he proclaimed, "[R]esistance to tyranny is obedience to God."

Though he did not explicitly endorse violence, handbills distributed at meetings at which he spoke called for abolishing the black race. In another speech, Eastland cautioned, "Acts of violence and lawlessness have no place," and he insisted, "The fight we wage must be a just and legal fight." But this was immediately after he had incited his audience with reminders that "[t]here is no law that a free people must submit to a flagrant invasion of their personal liberty" and that "[n]o people in all the history of Government have been forced to integrate against their will." Congressman James Davis of Georgia likewise insisted, "There is no place for violence or lawless acts," right after he had called *Brown* "a monumental fraud which is shocking, outrageous and reprehensible," warned against "meekly accept[ing] this brazen usurpation of power," and denied any obligation on "the people to bow the neck to this new form of tyranny." These politicians either knew that such rhetoric was likely to incite violence, or they were criminally negligent for not knowing it.[180]

In terms of influencing national opinion, whether political demagoguery produced violence was less important than the perception that it did. The NAACP constantly asserted such a linkage, for example, blaming southern politicians for fostering a climate that was conducive to the lynching of Mack Parker. Wilkins insisted that the bombers of southern synagogues "were made bold by groups of so-called respectable people which have urged publicly that the courts be defied." James Meredith blamed the assassination of Medgar Evers in 1963 on "governors of the Southern states and their defiant and provocative actions." Others drew similar connections. A lawyer in Clinton, Tennessee, blamed school desegregation violence on the congressmen who signed the Southern Manifesto: "What the hell do you expect these people to do when they have 90 some odd congressmen from the South signing a piece of paper that says you're a southern hero if you defy the Supreme Court." The Honolulu *Star-Bulletin* attributed the desegregation riot in Tuscaloosa to the "fiery . . . language" of public officials. After Atlanta's temple bombing, Mayor Hartsfield declared, "Whether they like it or not, every rabble-rousing politician is the godfather of the cross-burners and the dynamiters who are giving the South a bad name"—a judgment with which Attorney General Rogers concurred.[181]

The general connection between extremist politicians and violence is plausible, but the linkage between particular public officials and the brutality that inspired civil rights legislation is compelling. The principal players were Bull Connor, John Patterson, Ross Barnett, George Wallace, and Jim Clark. The violence that they cultivated, condoned, or unintentionally fomented proved critical to transforming national opinion on race.

Though the increased violence of southern whites against blacks in the late 1950s influenced national racial opinion, it was neither sufficiently sustained nor frequently enough captured on television to generate the widespread outrage that would be necessary to the enactment of transformative civil rights legislation. As of 1960, southern whites still tended to care more about preserving segregation than northern whites did about eliminating it. In the early 1960s, civil rights leaders consciously evolved a new strategy for turning northern racial opinion in their favor. In the 1950s, Martin Luther King, Jr., was still trying to convince southern whites that racial segregation was wrong—to "awaken a sense of moral shame in the[m]." Within a few years, however, he had largely abandoned such efforts in favor of trying to win support from northern whites, most of whom already thought that segregation was wrong but were disinclined to do much about it. Lynchings, such as those of Till in 1955 or Parker in 1959, had educated and energized northern whites by unveiling the violence at the core of white supremacy and belying the claims of southern whites that blacks endorsed the racial status quo. In 1961, a white New Yorker told the NAACP that he had sympathized with the association's cause for years but that it took the murders of Till and Parker "to crystallize my rage." Wilkins put the point more bluntly: Whenever "some outrage occurs, white people send the NAACP checks." To transform northern opinion, then, southern civil rights leaders concluded that they had to provoke violence against themselves, especially in settings that were likely to attract national media attention. Direct-action protest would probably incite brutal repression, and if the conflict lasted long enough, the national media would pay attention and so would the nation.[182]

The success of this strategy of "creative tension" depended on the presence of certain conditions. In 1960, most white Americans disapproved of direct-action protest. Many shared former President Truman's view that "[i]f anyone came into my store and tried to stop business, I'd throw him out." To win public support, then, protestors had to be unambiguously in the right and their adversaries in the wrong. Their behavior had to be impeccable and their objectives clearly legitimate. The contrast they sought to portray was between well-dressed, polite, studious blacks peacefully protesting and "a ragtail rabble, slackjawed, black jacketed, grinning fit to kill" assaulting them. The demonstrators' success also required the "cooperation" of law enforcement officers, either by countenancing private violence or perpetrating their own. Peaceful arrests, even if illegal, dampened protest without generating violent confrontation; the media got bored, the demonstrators grew tired, and the Kennedy administration failed to intervene. Such was the lesson of Albany, Georgia, in 1961–1962, as Laurie Pritchett, the "nonviolent police chief," arrested hundreds of demonstrators and outlasted the movement. Violent assaults on protestors, by contrast, captured media attention, forced the administration to intervene, and outraged northerners. Thus, the freedom riders "count[ed] upon the racists of the South to create a crisis," and SCLC leaders "calculated for the stupidity of a Bull Connor."[183]

T. Eugene "Bull" Connor was first elected to the Birmingham city commission in 1937 on a pledge to crush the communist/integrationist threat posed by the CIO's unionization efforts. In 1938, he broke up the inaugural meeting of the Southern Conference for Human Welfare in Birmingham because it violated a local segregation ordinance. In the late 1940s, Connor's police department failed to take action in response to a wave of bombings that were directed at black families moving into contested neighborhoods. By 1950, however, civic leaders had come to view Connor as an embarrassment. A committee to encourage business relocations was hampered by the city's racial violence and the extremism of politicians such as Connor. Businessmen orchestrated his public humiliation through an illicit sexual encounter, and Connor retired from politics in 1953. Birmingham then saw some racial progress, including the establishment of the first hospital for blacks, the desegregation of elevators in downtown office buildings, and serious efforts toward desegregating the police force.[184]

After *Brown*, however, Birmingham's racial progress ground to a halt. In 1955, the city council rejected proposals to hire black police officers, which it said might lead to "serious racial trouble" in light of *Brown*. An interracial committee disbanded in 1956; consultation between the races largely ceased; and Connor resurrected his political career. In 1957, he regained his seat on the city commission by promising that he would not permit "professional agitators and radicals to come into Birmingham and stir up racial strife" and attacking his opponent, who insisted that "it doesn't take agitation to maintain segregation," as weak on the race issue. In the late 1950s, a powerful Klan element wreaked havoc in Birmingham with a wave of unsolved bombings and brutality. The police, under Connor's control, declined to interfere and may well have covered up evidence of the crimes.

FIGURE 7.8
Bull Connor at a press conference, May 10, 1963.
(*Bettmann*/CORBIS)

Standing for reelection in 1961, Connor cultivated extremists by offering the Klan fifteen minutes of "open season" on the freedom riders as they rolled into town. Promising the Klansmen through an intermediary that he would keep officers away from the scene, Connor reportedly beseeched them: "By God, if you are going to do this thing, do it right!" After horrific beatings were administered to media representatives as well as demonstrators, the *Birmingham News* wondered, "Where were the police?" Voters may have been less curious, having handed a landslide victory just two weeks earlier to Connor, who had invited the violence.[185]

When the freedom riders traveled on to Montgomery, the police again mysteriously disappeared, and the demonstrators were savagely beaten once more. Governor Patterson had promised safe passage, and thus he bore considerable responsibility for the violence. Patterson was one of the most extreme southern politicians of the 1950s; he had won the governorship in 1958 while predicting that integration would cause "violence, disorder, and bloodshed" and refusing to repudiate the Klan's endorsement. As governor, Patterson frequently reiterated his diehard opposition to desegregation, and he warned that southern "enemies" were launching "an all-out war to completely destroy our customs, traditions and way of life." After New Orleans erupted in violence over school desegregation in 1960, Patterson promised that the violence there would be nothing as compared with the consequences of forced integration in Alabama, where there would be "hell to pay." Patterson vowed that when the federal showdown came, "I'll be one of the first ones stirring up trouble, any way I can." He blamed the freedom riders themselves—"professional agitators," he called them—for the violence they suffered. But Klansmen may have taken their lead from the governor, who could probably have prevented the violence had he been so inclined. Whether Patterson, Connor, and Montgomery police commissioner L. B. Sullivan had incited violence against the freedom riders or merely failed to prevent it, public opinion generally deemed them responsible. Federal judge Frank Johnson, Attorney General Robert Kennedy, Senator Kefauver, and former governor Folsom all blamed state and local officials for the brutality. *Time* wrote that Alabama officials, from "Governor John Patterson on down, abdicated their duties of maintaining law and order." The *Birmingham News* singled out Patterson specifically for blame, noting that he had "talk[ed] for months in a manner that could easily say to the violent, the intemperate . . . that they were free to do as they pleased when it came to the hated integrationists."[186]

Alabama politicians had handed the civil rights movement an important victory on a silver platter. Reflecting a visceral opposition to direct action, only about 24 percent of Americans had supported the Freedom Rides, while 64 percent disapproved. Critics viewed the demonstrators as "provocateurs, or inciters to disorder." David Brinkley of NBC television thought that the freedom riders, though within their legal rights, should cease their "exhibition," which was "doing positive harm" by "inflam[ing] . . . Southern opin-

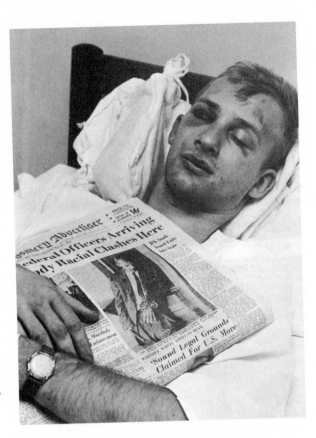

FIGURE 7.9
Freedom rider Jim Zwerg after
he was beaten in Montgomery,
May 21, 1961.
(*Bettmann*/CORBIS)

ion" and making "advances even more difficult than they already were." But
the freedom riders were behaving nonviolently, exercising rights recently
declared by the Supreme Court, and enduring vicious beatings. This was
southern white supremacy at its ugliest—"the violent brutality of mobsters,"
as the NAACP described it. Even in Montgomery and Birmingham,
Alabama, leading newspapers criticized the "savage scene," the "howling
mobs," and the "raging attack." Most Americans condemned Alabama for its
treatment of the freedom riders. Roughly two-thirds of all Americans now
supported desegregation of public transportation, and overwhelming majorities endorsed Kennedy's decision to use federal marshals to protect the freedom riders in Montgomery. Influenced by "horrified" constituents, northern
congressmen began discussing civil rights legislation—a topic that had previously been considered dead. Senator Javits of New York stated, "[T]he whole
country must be deeply shocked, appalled and . . . ashamed by the . . . violence," while Senate majority leader Mike Mansfield declared that the
Alabama disorders "should cause us—as a nation—to hang our heads in
shame."[187]

The fall of 1962, when James Meredith integrated Ole Miss, was the first time that people were killed in a desegregation riot. Governor Barnett did not openly advocate violence, and he probably hoped to avoid it. But his defiant rhetoric likely contributed to the bloodshed in Oxford, Mississippi, and it certainly fostered the perception that he was responsible. Barnett had been elected governor in 1959 on an extreme segregationist platform. As a candidate, he implicitly endorsed violence: "We can stop this integration fight if we have the blood and guts of our forefathers." In a speech to the citizens' council after his nomination, Barnett declared: "Physical courage is a trait sadly lacking in altogether too many of the South's so-called leaders. We must separate the men from the boys. We must identify the traitors in our midst. We must eliminate the cowards from our front lines." In his inaugural address, Barnett promised, "[O]ur schools at all levels must be segregated at all costs."[188]

As court-ordered desegregation became imminent at Ole Miss in the summer of 1962, Barnett was trapped. His defiant vows made retreat politically unpalatable. Rather than preparing Mississippians for the inevitable, he continued to breathe defiance, planned to "interpose" his authority against that of the federal courts, threatened to arrest federal officers who interfered with state officials in the performance of their duties, and called for the resignation of all state officials who were unwilling to go to jail for defying federal authority in this "righteous cause." One state senator went even further, demanding resistance "regardless of the cost in human life." After twice physically blocking Meredith's entrance to the university, Barnett privately negotiated an agreement with the Justice Department that would enable him to avoid contempt sanctions by retreating after a public display of federal force. Yet his defiant ravings had created a frenzied atmosphere in which Barnett could not prevent violence. A race riot involving as many as 3,000 people broke out in Oxford on September 30, 1962, killing two and injuring several hundred. Barnett blamed federal marshals for the fiasco, but most commentators and national politicians pinned the responsibility on him. Whether or not Barnett had sought the violence, he reaped political benefits from it and became "the dominant political figure in Mississippi as long as he live[d]." Barnett was ineligible to succeed himself in office, but in 1963 voters rewarded the futile defiance that had caused deadly violence by electing Paul Johnson, who campaigned on the role that he had played as lieutenant governor in blocking Meredith's admission.[189]

Meanwhile, after the failed demonstrations of Albany, Georgia, in 1961–1962, the leadership of the SCLC was searching for a city with a police chief who was unlikely to duplicate Laurie Pritchett's restraint. They selected Birmingham, perhaps the South's most violent city, where Bull Connor, as commissioner of public safety, had already achieved notoriety by allowing the Klan to beat freedom riders in 1961. King was much criticized for refusing to defer the Birmingham demonstrations until after he had attempted to negotiate with the new mayor, Albert Boutwell, who had recently defeated Connor for the post. But Reverend Shuttlesworth was urging King to act quickly, while Connor remained police commissioner—a position that would be eliminated under the city's new form of government once the mayoralty results had survived legal challenge. King's lieutenant Wyatt Walker later explained: "We knew that when we came to Birmingham that if Bull Connor was still in control, he would do something to benefit our movement. We didn't want to march after Bull was gone." The strategy worked brilliantly. After some initially uncharacteristic restraint, Connor unleashed police dogs and fire hoses against demonstrators, many of whom were children. Television and newspaper coverage featured images of police dogs attacking unresisting demonstrators, including one that President Kennedy reported made him "sick." Congressmen condemned the "shocking episodes of police brutality." Newspaper editorials called the violence "a national disgrace." Citizens voiced their "sense of unutterable outrage and shame" and demanded that politicians take "action to immediately put to an end the barbarism and savagery in Birmingham." Within ten weeks, spin-off demonstrations spread to more than 100 cities, as Birmingham "detonated a revolution."[190]

FIGURE 7.10
One of Bull Connor's police dogs attacks a black bystander during street demonstrations. President John Kennedy said this photograph made him "sick." (*Birmingham News*)

Televised brutality against peaceful civil rights demonstrators in Birmingham dramatically altered northern opinion on race and enabled the passage of the 1964 Civil Rights Act. Comparing the Kennedy administration's civil rights policy before and after Birmingham demonstrates the transformative effect of that episode. When Kennedy was elected president in 1960, he was not a civil rights enthusiast, and his victory depended on the support of southern whites. At the outset of the Kennedy administration, the NAACP was not expecting legislation to accelerate the pace of school desegregation. The administration warned against congressional efforts to condition the receipt of federal education funds on progress being made toward school desegregation, and polls showed that Americans were opposed to such measures by a 3–1 margin. Critics called the administration "timid and reluctant" and accused it of "dragging its feet" on civil rights, but polls showed that two-thirds of Americans thought the pace of desegregation was "too fast" or "about right," and only 11 percent thought it "not fast enough." When Kennedy finally proposed civil rights legislation in February 1963—two months before the Birmingham demonstrations began—it focused on voting rights. With regard to school desegregation, the administration proposed only technical and financial assistance to desegregating districts—a proposal that even Eisenhower had supported in the late 1950s. Kennedy did not endorse the proposals of liberals to grant the attorney general authority to institute desegregation suits or to empower the president to terminate federal education funds for school districts that remained segregated. Administration critic William F. Buckley rightly observed that the landmark civil rights bill proposed by Kennedy in the summer of 1963 "was not even conceived of as recently as a year ago."[191]

Outside of the school desegregation context, the administration had also been cautious on civil rights before Birmingham. After promising during the 1960 campaign that civil rights legislation would be his first priority, during his first two years in office Kennedy repeatedly declared that he would not seek such legislation because Congress would not pass it. For those two years, Kennedy also delayed fulfilling a campaign pledge to eliminate race discrimination in federally assisted housing with the "stroke of a pen." When he finally did issue the housing order, it was limited in scope and prospective only. Kennedy placated southern Democrats with atrocious judicial appointments, including William Harold Cox, Senator Eastland's college roommate, who later referred to blacks from the bench as "niggers" and "chimpanzees." The Kennedy Justice Department negotiated the resolution of racial conflict with white southerners behind the scenes, rather than confronting it openly, prosecuting wrongdoers, and compelling the enforcement of civil rights. Rather than supporting the freedom riders' exercise of federal rights to nonsegregated transportation, the administration privately authorized Mississippi officials to illegally jail them in exchange for promises to avoid violence. After convincing civil rights workers in Mississippi to redirect their energies toward voter registration, which was assumed to be less provocative than freedom rides or street demonstrations, the administration broke its apparent promise to protect them from violence. By 1962, congressional liberals and black leaders were regularly criticizing the administration for failing to take a vigorous stand on civil rights. Birmingham changed everything.[192]

Opinion polls revealed that the percentage of Americans who deemed civil rights to be the nation's most urgent issue rose from 4 percent before Birmingham to 52 percent afterward. A majority of Americans now favored expansive civil rights legislation. Denouncing the Birmingham violence, congressmen introduced measures to end federal aid to segregated schools. Kennedy overhauled his earlier civil rights proposals to include broader voting rights protections, the desegregation of public accommodations, authority for the attorney general to bring school desegregation suits, and the termination of federal funding for programs that engaged in race discrimination. Only after the police dogs and fire hoses of Birmingham did Kennedy announce on national television that civil rights was a "moral issue as old as the scriptures and as clear as the American Constitution." Bishops now announced that the nation's 45 million Catholics had a "strict moral duty" to support civil rights. That fall, after a quarter of a million Americans had marched on Washington, D.C., in support of civil rights and four black youngsters had been blown up in Birmingham's Sixteenth Street Baptist Church, congressmen toughened the administration's bill, adding prohibitions on employment discrimination and broadening the attorney general's authority over desegregation suits. Just five days after Kennedy's assassination on November 22, 1963, President Lyndon Johnson told a joint session of Congress that "no memorial oration or eulogy could more eloquently honor President Kennedy's memory than the earliest possible passage of the civil rights bill for which he fought so long." With Johnson's strong backing, the bill became law in the summer of 1964, after withstanding the longest filibuster in Senate history.[193]

Alabama's governor, George Wallace, had played a minor role in suppressing the Birmingham demonstrations and would play a more substantial role in the violence that lay ahead. Perhaps more than any other individual, Wallace personified the post-*Brown* racial fanaticism of southern politics. Early in his political career, in the late 1940s and early 1950s, Wallace had been criticized as "soft" on segregation. Unlike Connor, he was in the half of the Alabama delegation that did not walk out of the 1948 Democratic National Convention over the civil rights plank, and in 1954 he had been Folsom's campaign manager for southern Alabama. By the mid-1950s, however, Wallace felt the changing political winds, broke with Folsom, and cultivated conflict with federal authorities over race issues in his position as Barbour County circuit judge. After his defeat in the 1958 gubernatorial election, Wallace vowed never to be "out-niggered" again, and in 1962 he made good on that promise. Though some Alabama officials repudiated massive resistance after Ole Miss, Wallace continued to denounce federal "tyranny" and to promise "segregation forever." Like most southern politicians, he publicly condemned violence. Yet Wallace's actions from 1963 to 1965 directly and indirectly encouraged the brutality that helped transform national opinion on race.[194]

During the Birmingham demonstrations in the spring of 1963, Wallace dispatched several hundred state troopers to the city, and they supplemented Bull Connor's brutality with some of their own. He also publicly praised Connor for forcefully suppressing the demonstrations. That summer in Tuscaloosa, Wallace fulfilled his pledge to stand in the schoolhouse door, physically blocking the university's entrance before, in a carefully planned charade, stepping aside in the face of superior federal force—more than 15,000 federalized national guardsmen. Learning from Ole Miss, Wallace had warned that he would not "tolerate mob action," and massive security measures kept Tuscaloosa "peaceful and serene."[195]

Yet Wallace, like Barnett, had grown overconfident in his ability to spout defiant rhetoric without provoking violence. After Tuscaloosa, Wallace continued to promise a "forceful stand" against grade school desegregation, which federal courts had ordered in Alabama for the fall. In September, Wallace used state troopers to block school desegregation in Birmingham, Mobile, Huntsville, and Tuskegee—action that was contrary to the wishes of most local officials, who called Wallace a "dictator" for preventing them from complying with court orders to desegregate. In Birmingham, white mobs demonstrated outside the schools that were scheduled to desegregate; the home of a black lawyer who was heavily involved in school desegregation litigation was bombed; and a minor race riot erupted, in which police killed a black man and roughly twenty others were injured. Wallace had encouraged extremist groups to wage "a boisterous campaign" against school desegregation, and now he defended the rioters, who he insisted are "not thugs—they are good working people who get mad when they see something like this happen." Threatened with contempt citations by all five Alabama district judges, and overmatched by President Kennedy's federalization of the state national guard, Wallace relented. The schools desegregated, but Wallace had "stirred up a devil's brew of racial hatred that [could] erupt any minute into further violence." Within a week, tragedy had struck. Birmingham Klansmen, possibly inspired by the governor's protestations that "I can't fight federal bayonets with my bare hands," dynamited the Sixteenth Street Baptist Church, killing four black schoolgirls. Within hours of the bombing, two other black teenagers were killed, one by white hoodlums and the other by the police. It was the largest death toll of the civil rights era, and Wallace received much of the blame, though he denied any "blood on his hands" and attributed responsibility instead to some "demented fool." Wilkins charged Wallace with encouraging a "deliberate mass murder," while King blamed the governor for "creat[ing] the climate that made it possible for someone to plant that bomb." Alabama attorney general Flowers linked the carnage to Wallace's defiance: "The individuals who bombed the Sixteenth Avenue [*sic*] Church in their way were standing in the schoolhouse door." President Kennedy noted "a deep sense of outrage and grief" and thought it "regrettable that public disparagement of law and order has encouraged violence which has fallen on the innocent." Senator Javits of New York declared that Wallace "cannot escape some responsibility" for the bombing. Senator Sam Ervin of North Carolina decried Wallace as "the chief aider and abettor of those who would attempt to pass foolish [civil rights] laws." Wallace may not have sought the violence, but his provocative rhetoric probably contributed to it, and he certainly took no measures to prevent it, as had South Carolina officials, whose public schools peacefully desegregated that same month.[196]

Most of the nation was appalled by the murder of innocent schoolchildren, which even the Alabama congressional delegation condemned as a "heartless criminal atrocity." One week after the bombing, tens of thousands of people across the United States participated in memorial services and marches. Northern whites wrote to the NAACP to join, to condemn, and to apologize. One white woman asked the association to "[p]lease enlist me in an army of protest or help me to find a way to express my feelings." A white lawyer from Los Angeles wrote, "Today I am joining the NAACP; partly, I think, as a kind of apology for being caucasian, and for not being in Birmingham to lend my physical support." Another white woman in the North con-

FIGURE 7.11

The Sixteenth Street Baptist Church in Birmingham after it was bombed on September 15, 1963. (*Birmingham Public Library, Department of Archives and Manuscripts, no. 85.1.22*)

demned those Birmingham whites who were involved in the bombing or who condoned it as "the worst barbarians," and she said that she was "ashamed to think that I bear their color skin." She also declared that the bombing had "certainly changed my attitude," which previously had been "somewhat lukewarm" on civil rights. A white man from New Rochelle wrote: "How shall I start? Perhaps to say that I am white, sorry, ashamed, and guilty. . . . Those who have said that all whites who, through hatred, intolerance, or just inaction are guilty are right." A black veteran of World War I from South Carolina, who had "seen many things that have been irksome" in his seventy years, including the lynchings of Till and Parker and the murders of Moore and Evers, told the NAACP that "nothing in my life has had the effect upon me [that] the bombing of the Church and the Murder of the six Negroes in Birmingham [had]." He prayed that God would not "let these children die in vain," and he enclosed money to be divided among the families of the murdered youngsters. The NAACP urged its members to "flood Congress with letters in support of necessary civil rights legislation to curb such outrages," and Wilkins demanded that the federal government "cut off every nickel" going to Alabama. Northern congressmen reflected the outrage of their constituents by introducing amendments to strengthen the administration's pending civil rights bill.[197]

Wallace's critics in Alabama attacked his schoolhouse-door routine at Tuscaloosa as "the greatest production since Cleopatra," and they accused him of making "a monkey of himself" and "a mockery of Alabama." But most voters apparently disagreed. Wallace remained enormously popular, and in January 1964 he won an important victory when the state Democratic executive committee instructed the Alabama delegation to the 1964 national convention to support Wallace as a favorite-son candidate for president. Meanwhile, Wallace continued to rail against the "shocking" pronouncements of federal "judicial tyrant[s]" and to urge local authorities to resist desegregation, though he refrained from any more schoolhouse-door stands. But the linkage between Wallace and civil rights violence had not ended, with Selma still in the future.[198]

Before Selma, though, the civil rights stage shifted back to Mississippi, where movement leaders during the summer of 1964 successfully repeated the Birmingham strategy. Civil rights activists in Mississippi, after struggling for years against horrific violence to organize the state, decided to import hundreds of mostly white northern college students for a Freedom Summer of civil rights activity. They understood that bringing "outside agitators" to Mississippi would probably elicit a deadly response, and they calculated that the national media and the Johnson administration would lavish attention on relatively affluent whites from the nation's most prestigious universities. The strategy worked even more effectively and more tragically than they had anticipated. Within days, three civil rights workers had disappeared. For much of the summer, FBI agents and national media representatives blanketed the state searching for them. Their murders, combined with dozens of church bombings, shootings, beatings, and other atrocities taught an attentive nation unforgettable lessons about Jim Crow, Mississippi-style. The groundwork was laid for further civil rights legislation. Selma brought it to fruition.[199]

Situated in the heart of Alabama's black belt, Selma was home to the state's first citizens' council, which had quickly enrolled nearly a quarter of Dallas County's white males. Selma was also home to Sheriff Jim Clark, one of the South's most notorious racial hotheads. Indeed, in the spring of 1963, at Wallace's instigation, Clark had traveled to Birmingham to assist Bull Connor in forcibly suppressing street demonstrations. Early in 1965, the SCLC brought its voter registration campaign to Selma, in search of another Birmingham-style victory.[200]

In Selma, King and his colleagues refined the already successful tactics of Birmingham. They chose Selma as the site of their voter registration campaign partly because of the presence there of a law enforcement officer with Bull Connor–like proclivities. Sheriff Clark had a temper which "could be counted on to provide vivid proof of the violent sentiments that formed white supremacy's core." Moreover, in contrast with Birmingham, the Selma demonstrators had a more defined objective—voting rights—and were better able to maintain strict nonviolence. The result was another resounding success for the civil rights movement. After initially displaying restraint that "disappoint[ed]" SCLC workers, Clark finally returned to form and brutalized nonresisting demonstrators. The violence culminated in Bloody Sunday, March 7, 1965, when county and state law enforcement officers viciously assaulted marchers as they crossed the Edmund Pettus Bridge on the way to Montgomery. Governor Wallace had promised that the march would be broken up by "whatever measures are necessary," and Colonel Al Lingo, Wallace's chief law enforcement lieutenant, insisted that the governor himself had given the order to attack. That evening, ABC television interrupted its broadcast of *Judgment at Nuremberg* for a lengthy film report of peaceful demonstrators being assailed by stampeding horses, flailing clubs, and tear gas. Two white volunteers from the North were killed in the events surrounding Selma: a Unitarian minister from Boston and a mother of five from Detroit.[201]

Most of the nation was repulsed by the "ghastly scenes" from Selma that they watched on television. *Time* reported, "Rarely in history has public opinion reacted so spontaneously and with such fury." President Johnson "deplored the brutality." Over the following week, huge sympathy demonstrations took place across the country. Hundreds of clergymen from around the nation flocked to Selma to show their solidarity with King and his comrades. Citizens demanded remedial action from their congressmen, scores of whom condemned the "deplorable" violence and the "shameful display" of Selma and now endorsed voting rights legislation. On March 15, 1965, President Johnson proposed such legislation before a joint session of Congress. Seventy million Americans watched on television as the president beseeched them to "overcome this crippling legacy of bigotry and injustice" and declared his faith that "we shall overcome." Prior to Selma, administration officials had been divided over whether to pursue voting rights legislation in the near term, but national revulsion at the brutalization of peaceful protestors prompted immediate action.[202]

Although most Americans were appalled by the violence of vigilantes and law enforcement officers at Birmingham and Selma, the politicians who were partly responsible for it calculated—usually correctly—that Alabama voters would reward them for their role in fostering it. Contemporaries speculated that Connor's violent suppression of civil rights demonstrations in Birmingham was calculated to earn him support among segregationist voters should he run for state office. Indeed, the following year, Connor was elected state public service commissioner, as he capitalized on the name recognition he had achieved during the Birmingham demonstrations. Wallace remained enormously popular among whites in Alabama, in spite of—or perhaps because of—his partial responsibility for the violence at Birmingham and Selma. When he provoked a showdown with the Kennedy administration over the desegregation of grade schools in several Alabama cities in the fall of 1963 (the episode that culminated in the bombing of Birmingham's Sixteenth Street Baptist Church), Wallace was apparently anticipating political gain—specifically, a change in the state constitution that would enable him to serve a second consecutive term as governor. Sheriff Clark calculated that his brutality against demonstrators in Selma would translate into a viable gubernatorial candidacy in 1966. He withdrew from that race only after Wallace, who was barred from succeeding himself, announced the candidacy of his wife, Lurleen, who then won the election. Clark rightly appreciated that nobody could outflank Wallace as a symbol of resistance to racial change.[203]

The violence used by white law enforcement officers in the South against peaceful black demonstrators repulsed national opinion and led directly to the passage of landmark civil rights legislation. *Brown* was less directly responsible than is commonly supposed for putting those demonstrators on the street, but it was more directly responsible for the violent reception they encountered.

The post-*Brown* racial fanaticism of southern politics produced a situation that was ripe for violence, while *Brown* itself created concrete occasions on which violent opposition to school desegregation was likely. Some of the ensuing violence was mainly attributable to white vigilantes, but much of it was encouraged, directly or indirectly, by extremist politicians, whom voters rewarded for the irresponsible rhetoric that fomented atrocities. Even before the violent outbreaks of the 1960s, most white northerners had agreed with *Brown* in the abstract, but they were disinclined to push hard for its enforcement; many of them agreed with Eisenhower that the NAACP should rein in its demands for immediate desegregation. It was televised scenes of officially sanctioned brutality against peaceful black demonstrators that transformed northern opinion on race. By helping to lay bare the violence at the core of white supremacy, *Brown* accelerated its demise. President Eisenhower, Justice Black, and many southern moderates had foreseen that *Brown* would retard southern racial progress and destroy southern political liberalism. Justice Jackson, too, had warned, "When the Court has gone too far, it has provoked reactions which have set back the cause it was designed to advance." Though these individuals rightly anticipated *Brown*'s backlash, they failed to foresee the ensuing counterbacklash that would develop as northerners were repulsed by the violence of southern whites against peaceful black demonstrators and endorsed landmark civil rights legislation in response. The harder that southern whites fought to maintain Jim Crow, the more they seemed to accelerate its demise.[204]

Would the same violence have confronted civil rights demonstrators without *Brown*? One cannot know for certain. But without *Brown*, school desegregation would probably not have been a pressing issue in the 1950s. Southern blacks generally had other priorities, including ending police brutality, securing voting rights, gaining access to decent jobs, and equalizing public funding of black schools. Moreover, before *Brown*, southern whites had proved willing to make small concessions on racial issues that were less important to them than school segregation. Without *Brown*, negotiation might have continued to produce gradual change without inciting white violence. How southern whites in this counterfactual universe would have responded if and when black street demonstrations erupted is impossible to tell. In the absence of post-*Brown* political fanaticism, however, one can imagine freedom riders arriving in Birmingham and Montgomery without police commissioners inviting Klansmen to beat them, and one can imagine blacks demonstrating for voting rights in Selma without law enforcement officers brutalizing them. By the early 1960s, most southern whites could probably have tolerated desegregated transportation and black suffrage, had *Brown* not converted all racial challenges, in their minds, into fundamental assaults on Jim Crow. Whether and how southern schools would have desegregated in this counterfactual scenario is anybody's guess, but it almost certainly would not have happened as quickly as it did under the 1964 Civil Rights Act. Only the violence that resulted from *Brown*'s radicalization of southern politics enabled transformative racial change to occur as rapidly as it did.

CONCLUSION

In 1896, most white Americans approved of racial segregation, and most of the justices of the Supreme Court thought that it was plainly constitutional. In 1954, the justices unanimously invalidated segregation, and about half of all Americans agreed with that ruling. How should we understand this dramatic shift in popular and legal opinion? How much was it attributable to extralegal factors and how much to law?

Clearly, changes in the social and political context of race relations preceded and accounted for changes in judicial decision making. This is not to say that the Court decisions did not matter, only that they reflected social attitudes and practices more than they created them. The justices in *Brown* understood this, commenting on the "spectacular" advances, the "great changes," and the "constant progress" being made in race relations. In the absence of such changes, *Brown* would not have been decided as it was, as the justices themselves observed.

What caused these fundamental changes in the racial attitudes and practices of U.S. society? This book has identified a wide variety of political, economic, social, demographic, ideological, and international causes of racial change. They cannot be ranked in terms of importance, because history is not science, and repeat experiments controlling for particular variables are impossible. Still, one may be able to say something useful, even if it cannot be scientifically verified, about the long-term causes of racial change. It is helpful to divide causal factors into those that were internal to the South and those that were external to it. Both sorts of factors played important roles in producing racial change. Because southern whites were generally resistant to changes in racial practices, pressure was required to effect them. Southern blacks supplied some of that pressure, aided by improvements in education, the growth of a black middle class, greater militancy resulting from World War II, and the more tolerant racial norms that existed in the urban, as opposed to the rural, parts of the South. But Jim Crow was so ruthless and pervasive that internally generated change was difficult to accomplish. Because southern whites did not permit blacks to become very well educated, there were few black lawyers available to challenge the system in court. Because southern blacks were generally not permitted to vote, internal change through politics was nearly impossible. Because whites controlled the livelihood of most blacks, protest generally resulted in severe economic reprisals. The system was ultimately secured by the threat and the reality of physical violence against those blacks (and whites) who dared to challenge it. As the NAACP noted in the mid-1930s, "[I]t is the fear of lynching and physical violence, which more than anything else cripples our progress and prevents our taking a more active part in the fight against the injustices heaped upon us."[1]

It is nearly impossible to change such a system without external pressure. That was supplied by the NAACP and, eventually, by national public opinion and the intervention of the federal government. NAACP political campaigns for federal antilynching legislation induced southern states to take action against lynching. During and after World War II, lawsuits and the threats of them induced southern states to begin equalizing spending on black education and permitting blacks to register to vote. Pressure by the national government helped to create an environment in which southern blacks could engage in racial protest with some measure of physical security. Ultimately, landmark civil rights legislation in the 1960s supplied coercive mechanisms that accelerated the downfall of formal Jim Crow. External pressure was produced by a combination of factors: the Great Migration, the rising prosperity and political clout of northern blacks, the ideology of World War II, and the Cold War imperative for racial change.

Wars have proved instrumental in advancing progressive racial change. The Civil War emancipated slaves and inspired postwar constitutional amendments that protected the civil and political rights of blacks. Though these amendments were notoriously unenforced in the South for decades, they did enfranchise northern blacks, which had important long-term consequences. NAACP membership increased tenfold during both the First and the Second World Wars—conflicts that fostered greater civil rights militancy among blacks. These wars created political and economic opportunities for black advancement and had egalitarian ideological implications, which induced some whites to reconsider long-held racial assumptions. Though southern whites were able to squelch black militancy after World War I, conditions had changed too much by the time of World War II to permit a repeat performance.[2]

The Second World War proved to be a watershed in the history of U.S. race relations. Returning black veterans became the vanguard of the modern civil rights movement. The ideological ramifications of the war against fascism, combined with the ensuing Cold War imperative for racial change, profoundly influenced the racial views of millions of white Americans. As huge numbers of blacks migrated to the North to take advantage of novel economic opportunities, northern blacks began to exert considerable influence over national racial policy.

Apart from war, long-term forces such as urbanization, industrialization, and better education fostered progressive racial change. Urbanization enabled blacks to become better educated, thus ensuring eventual challenges to Jim Crow. Urban blacks commanded greater economic resources, which provided more funds for social protest, dramatized the disparities between the economic and the social status of blacks, and created a weapon—economic boycotts—with which to extract changes in racial practices. Urban blacks created institutions, such as churches and colleges, which helped to overcome collective-action barriers to social protest, which better urban transportation and communication also facilitated. More relaxed racial mores in cities opened space for black protest by reducing the threat of physical violence. Most southern cities had NAACP branches, which shared information about racial conditions elsewhere, offered legal expertise for challenging rights violations, and spread the risks and the costs of racial protest. The relatively open access to voting enjoyed by urban blacks created a modicum of political influence, which helped foster the physical security that was necessary for social protest to occur. No civil rights movement was possible at a time when most blacks picked cotton on southern plantations.

Better-educated whites in the South were less intensely committed to preserving traditional racial practices. Moreover, as the South became less insular, racial change became harder to resist. World War II exposed millions of southerners, white and black, to novel racial attitudes and practices. The growth of the mass media exposed millions more to outside influences, which tended to erode traditional racial (and other) mores. Media penetration also prevented white southerners from limiting outside scrutiny of their treatment of blacks. Northerners had not seen southern lynchings on television, but Bull Connor's brutalization of peaceful black demonstrators came directly into their living rooms. The spread of NAACP branches into more remote parts of the South also made it more difficult to insulate racial atrocities from media attention.

Long-term international trends also advanced the cause of progressive racial change in the United States. The decolonization of Africa inspired American blacks to demand their political and civil rights. Postwar competition with the Soviet Union for the allegiance of nonwhite Third World nations forced Americans to improve their domestic racial practices in order to demonstrate that democratic capitalism was not synonymous with white supremacy. This Cold War imperative influenced the racial policies of presidential administrations from the 1940s to the 1960s and may have influenced the justices who were most preoccupied with national security concerns.

Finally, a decrease in white-on-black violence in the South was critical to progressive racial change. The heightened black militancy that grew out of World War I was crushed by a crescendo of white violence, including scores of lynchings and several racial massacres. In 1919, Texas whites could maim the NAACP's national secretary, John Shillady, and go unpunished. A southern civil rights movement was almost inconceivable in such an environment, and even litigation challenging racial injustice was difficult to sustain. By contrast, in 1959, state officials in Mississippi intervened to keep local segregationists from arresting Roy Wilkins, the NAACP's executive secretary, on trumped-up charges; the officials feared negative publicity and the likely intervention of the national government. In the 1960s, demonstrators could generally engage in direct-action protest in the South without risking serious physical violence, at least in most southern cities and towns. School desegregation litigants incurred economic reprisals and threats, but usually not actual violence.[3]

Ironically, the relative decline in white-on-black violence, which made civil rights protest possible, ensured that any residual violence would stand out, especially with the assistance of the national media. White southerners lynched a hundred blacks a year around 1900, yet most northerners showed little concern. But isolated lynchings in the 1950s—Emmett Till's in 1955, Mack Parker's in 1959—appalled most northerners (and many southerners too) and rallied support for civil rights legislation. Street demonstrations were possible in Birmingham in 1963 partly because greater constraints on white violence had created a more secure physical environment. As Martin Luther King, Jr., put it, "The striking thing about the nonviolent crusade of 1963 was that so few felt the sting of bullets or the clubbing of billies and nightsticks." Yet law enforcement brutalization of peaceful protestors, piped directly into American homes by television, profoundly influenced national opinion and led directly to the enactment of transformative civil rights legislation.[4]

What does the Court's racial jurisprudence from *Plessy* to *Brown* tell us about the nature of judicial decision making? How much is it a product of legal factors, such as text, original intent, and precedent, and how much of political factors, such as the values of judges, social and political context, and external political pressure? We have seen that all judicial decisions are products of the intersection between the legal and the political axes. When the legal sources are relatively determinate, the justices tend to adhere to them, unless their political preferences to the contrary are very strong. The justices invalidated the grandfather clause in *Guinn* (1915) and the phony false-pretenses law that supported peonage in *Bailey* (1911) because these were transparent evasions of constitutional constraints, because the justices had no personal inclination to reach contrary results, and probably because they believed that public opinion supported the outcomes. Had the Fourteenth Amendment explicitly barred segregation, *Plessy* might well have come out the other way.

Yet constitutional clarity is itself an ambiguous concept. Whether the traditional sources of constitutional law are thought to plainly forbid a particular practice depends on the personal values of the interpreter and on the social and political context. Oklahoma judges, who were committed to black disfranchisement, did not regard the grandfather clause as an obvious violation of the Fifteenth Amendment, because it was not an express racial classification and some blacks qualified to vote under it. To justices who were less invested in black disfranchisement, however, the grandfather clause was about as obvious a constitutional violation as was imaginable. Because constitutional clarity lies in the eye of the beholder, no judicial interpretation can ever be a result simply of the legal axis; rather, all such interpretations are inevitably a product of the intersection of both axes.

Brown illustrates the same point. To the justices who were most committed to traditional legal sources, such as text, original intent, precedent, and custom, *Brown* should have been an easy case—for *sustaining* school segregation. Jackson candidly conceded that barring segregation could be defended only in political, not legal, terms.* Thus, the legal axis alone can never determine a constitutional interpretation, as judges always have to choose whether to adhere to that axis. When their preferences are strong, the justices may reject even relatively determinate law, because they are unable to tolerate the result it indicates. In 1954, most of the justices considered racial segregation—the doctrine that Hitler had preached—to be evil, and they were determined to forbid it, regardless of whether conventional legal sources sanctioned that result.

Cases in which subconstitutional rules determine outcomes also illustrate how the legal and the political axes intersect. *Strauder v. West Virginia* (1880), which barred race discrimination in jury selection, was effectively nullified in later cases, as the justices applied stringent subconstitutional rules that governed standards of proof, rules of access to federal court, and standards of appellate review of trial court findings of fact. One may be tempted to say that the justices applied these particular subconstitutional rules because they were insufficiently committed to protecting the right of blacks to serve on juries. But subconstitutional rules are part of the law, and they may exist for reasons that have nothing to do with race. Thus, the justices' adherence to them in the race context cannot be dismissed as simple

---

*I emphasize again that my claim is not that *Brown* cannot be defended in legal terms, only that it cannot be so defended given Jackson's understanding of permissible legal sources. I have tried to show that *Brown* was a product of judicial values and sociopolitical context. I have not argued that this makes *Brown* an illegitimate judicial decision.

racism. On the other hand, subconstitutional rules are not written in stone. They can, and they did, change as the justices became more supportive of racially egalitarian results. Thus, Court decisions that failed to protect black jury service based on the application of subconstitutional rules must be understood as products of the interplay between the political and the legal axes. In the absence of these particular subconstitutional rules, the results might have been more egalitarian, which means that the legal axis mattered. But had the justices been more committed to black jury service, they might have changed the subconstitutional rules earlier, which means that the political axis mattered too.

Guinn and *Bailey* are unusual in that constitutional violations are rarely that transparent. The text of the Constitution fails to supply dispositive answers to most questions. "Equal protection" does not plainly forbid separate but equal, and "state action" under the Fourteenth and Fifteenth amendments is hardly self-defining. Precedent could supply greater clarity, yet the justices feel free to overrule past decisions, and they lack any clear legal standard that prescribes when to do so. The justices seem to overrule decisions that strike them as *really* wrong, which is obviously more of a political criterion than a legal one. *Grovey* (1935), which sustained the constitutionality of white primaries, proved unpalatable to the justices in 1944, not because its legal reasoning was faulty, but because during World War II they found black disfranchisement offensive.[5]

Another reason that constitutional law is generally indeterminate is the absence of consensus regarding which sources of interpretation are legitimate. For example, Justice Black claimed to be a textualist and an originalist, but Reed expressly defended the notion of a living Constitution, and Murphy seems to have thought that the justices must take account of morality. That justices who disagreed about the permissible sources of interpretation would reach different interpretive results seems inevitable. Moreover, even if consensus did exist regarding the permissible sources of interpretation, in the absence of an accepted hierarchy for resolving conflicts between them, interpretive disagreement would be unavoidable. The upshot is that justices engaged in constitutional interpretation have substantial room to maneuver; they cannot help but be influenced by their personal values and the social and political contexts of their times. Thus, we should not be surprised that the justices in the early twenty-first century divide 5–4, along consistent political lines, over most interesting and important constitutional issues, including federalism, abortion, affirmative action, minority voting districts, school prayer, religious-school vouchers, campaign finance reform, picking presidents, and others. These divisions are indicative not of bad faith, but of constitutional law's indeterminacy. On such issues, where personal preferences tend to be strong, only very determinate law could be constraining, and constitutional law is rarely that.[6]

Because of constitutional law's indeterminacy, social and political context matters greatly to constitutional interpretation, as the Court's decisions in the race area demonstrate. Between *Plessy* (1896) and *Brown* (1954), the conventional constitutional sources that were pertinent to the segregation issue did not change. Nor was *Plessy* an obviously wrong legal interpretation. The Equal Protection Clause does not plainly bar segregation, and the original understanding of the Fourteenth Amendment probably permitted it. Abundant legal precedents and deeply entrenched social customs supported segregation. On the conventional legal materials, *Plessy* was at least plausible, and it was arguably right. As the justices in 1896 almost certainly thought that segregation was good policy, the case was easy. Fifty-eight years later, the Court came out the other way—unanimously—despite the doubts of several justices as to whether invalidating segregation could be legally justified. The social and political context of race had changed so dramatically, as had the personal racial attitudes of the justices, that even a relatively weak legal case could not deter them from invalidating segregation. Similarly, *Smith's* overruling of *Grovey* on white primaries and *Shelley's* overruling of *Corrigan* on the judicial enforcement of racially restrictive covenants illustrate the importance of social and political context to constitutional interpretation. As World War II altered the racial attitudes of the populace and of the judiciary, the Court easily overruled recent unanimous decisions.

Whether social and political context *should* play such a large role in constitutional interpretation is beyond the scope of this book. That the justices have behaved a certain way in the past does not make it right, nor does it necessarily suggest that they will continue to behave that way in the future. On the other hand, if the Court's constitutional interpretations have always been influenced by the social and political contexts of the times in which they were rendered, perhaps it is impossible for them not to be. If that is so, then arguing against the inevitable seems pointless.

Because social and political context does play such a substantial role in the justices' constitutional decision making, the romantic image of the Court that was sketched by Justice Black in *Chambers v. Florida*—rescuing from oppression the "helpless, weak, . . . or . . . non-conforming victims of prejudice"—is probably unrealistic. The justices reflect dominant public opinion too much for them to protect truly oppressed groups. Not only did the Court fail to intervene against slavery before the Civil War, but it extended positive constitutional protection to the institution. The justices validated the exclusion of Japanese Americans from the West Coast during World War II and the persecution of political leftists during the McCarthy era. And, as we have seen, during the heyday of Jim Crow, the justices approved segregation and disfranchisement.[7]

Constitutional law generally has sufficient flexibility to accommodate dominant public opinion, which the justices have little inclination, and limited power, to resist. For example, the conventional sources of constitutional law did not plainly bar segregation, which in 1896 seemed like progressive racial policy given escalating white-on-black violence and the strong commitment of most whites to preserving "racial purity." The upshot is that courts are likely to protect only those minorities that are favorably regarded by majority opinion. Ironically, when a minority group suffering oppression is most in need of judicial protection, it is least likely to receive it. Groups must command significant social, political, and economic power before they become attractive candidates for judicial solicitude. The justices would not have dreamed of protecting women or gays under the Equal Protection Clause before the women's movement and the gay rights movement. Similarly, segregation and disfranchisement began to seem objectionable to the justices only as blacks became a vital New Deal constituency, achieved middle-class status and professional success, and earned federal judgeships, a Nobel Prize, a military generalship, and a prestigious clerkship with a Supreme Court justice.

None of this is to suggest that the justices perfectly reflect national opinion. Many famous cases confirm that they do not. When the Court invalidated school prayer or criminal prohibitions on flag burning, and when the justices protected certain procedural rights of criminal defendants, they were plainly frustrating dominant opinion. When this happens, it is usually a product of the culturally elite values of the justices. On certain issues, differences of opinion correlate with socioeconomic status. All of the justices are very well educated, and most of them are reasonably affluent. This may explain why, on issues such as school prayer and flag burning, their views seem systematically more liberal than those of average Americans. In the middle of the twentieth century, race was an issue on which popular and elite opinion significantly diverged. Perhaps this explains why the justices in the early 1970s supported busing and school desegregation in the North despite strong public opposition.[8]

But during the time period covered by this book, not a single Court decision involving race clearly contravened national public opinion. *Brown* was the closest to doing so, but half of the country supported it from the day it was decided. Because of their culturally elite biases, the justices may have found *Brown* (politically) easier than most Americans did, but by 1954, background forces for racial change had already altered public opinion enough so that half the nation endorsed *Brown* from the outset. Because the justices found *Brown* so difficult to justify legally, perhaps they would not have decided it as they did had it not been so easy politically. By 1954, segregation seemed like such an egregious evil to the nation's cultural elite that the justices simply could not make themselves sustain it.

Though the justices generally reflect elite opinion, there are some obvious exceptions. Correlations exist between high socioeconomic status and liberal political positions on certain cultural issues, but they are not perfect. On the Court in the early twenty-first century, Justices Antonin Scalia and Clarence Thomas, although members of the cultural elite, certainly do not share its liberal political propensities. Thus, constitutional rulings always reflect some element of fortuity in the composition of the Court. Had there been five Justice Reeds, *Brown* almost certainly would not have been decided as it was. Nor is it inconceivable that there could have been five justices in 1954 whose views were like Reed's, given that President Roosevelt had been virtually oblivious to the racial attitudes of his appointees to the Court.

This suggests another element of fortuity in Court decision making. Important constitutional issues often change across generations, and sometimes unpredictably so. Few could have forecast in the late 1930s, when Roosevelt began reconstituting the Court, that school segregation would become the biggest constitutional issue of the twentieth century. Yet it did, and within just fifteen years. Because Roosevelt and, to a lesser extent, Truman were largely indifferent to the racial views of their nominees and because the South remained an important component of the New Deal coalition, more Reeds could easily have been serving in 1954. Yet even Reed was not impervious to broad forces for racial change. Had he been so, he would probably have stood his ground and dissented in *Brown*. Yet Reed authored opinions invalidating the white primary and segregation in interstate travel, which suggests that he shared some culturally elite values, though of the southern variety.[9]

Congressional representatives are presumably members of the cultural elite as well, yet they lagged far behind the justices in achieving progressive racial results. Why? First, members of Congress have to respond to their constituents in order to be reelected, while the justices enjoy lifetime tenure. Of course, justices are not completely removed from public influence, but their relative insulation affords them some leeway to respond to their own culturally elite values, whereas representatives have to attend more closely to popular opinion or risk early retirement. Second, the U.S. Congress—especially the Senate—is far from majoritarian. Though national opinion plainly supported antilynching legislation in the 1930s and anti–poll-tax legislation in the 1940s, Senate filibusters regularly defeated such measures, as well as all other civil rights proposals until 1957.

The antimajoritarianism of the Senate raises the interesting possibility that the Court's race decisions from the 1920s onward may have reflected national opinion better than did Congress's (in)action. In the 1920s and 1930s, the justices intervened several times against southern lynch law, while southern Democrats in the Senate thrice killed antilynching bills that had passed the House. The Court invalidated the white primary in the 1940s. In that same decade, the House passed an anti–poll-tax bill every two years, and the Senate killed them all. Opinion polls revealed that half the nation supported *Brown* at a time when Congress would not have dreamed of legislating against school segregation.[10]

Southern politics was even more absurdly antimajoritarian. It is ironic that during their deliberations in *Brown*, the justices expressed anxiety about usurping the functions of representative government, given how unrepresentative southern legislatures were in the 1950s. Eighty percent of southern blacks were still disfranchised in 1952, and legislatures were badly malapportioned in favor of rural whites, who were the most committed to maintaining white supremacy. Thus, *Brown* was not only consistent with what half of all Americans thought about segregation, but it was not drastically inconsistent with what a properly functioning southern political system might have produced. This raises the interesting question of whether *Brown* might have been unnecessary had southern blacks been fully enfranchised and had one-person, one-vote principles been in operation. One cannot know for sure, but most southern whites were so committed to preserving school segregation that they would probably have outvoted blacks favoring integration. Equalization of black schools would have been a likelier scenario than legislative desegregation. But the question is hypothetical because southern whites would not permit most blacks to vote until Congress forced them to do so. And Congress would not act until national opinion demanded it, which happened only after *Brown* had elicited and exposed the most brutal aspects of Jim Crow, to the horror of national television audiences.[11]

Even if *Brown* were possible in 1954 only because the justices held culturally elite values, one must keep in mind that the potential gap between the justices' values and those of the general public is limited. In 1954, *Brown* was politically easier for the justices than it was for average Americans because they held culturally elite values. But as few as ten years earlier, the justices would probably have lacked the inclination to invalidate school segregation. At a time when the vast majority of white Americans believed in white supremacy, so did most justices. *Plessy* had been an easy case for them. In 1896, the justices were just as culturally elite as they would be in 1954, but at the turn of the century even well-educated, relatively affluent whites generally supported segregation and disfranchisement. Though the culturally elite values of the justices open space for them to deviate from popular opinion in their constitutional interpretations, that space is limited. The fact that the justices live in the same historical moment and share the same culture as the general population is probably more important to their constitutional interpretations than the fact that they occupy a distinct socioeconomic subculture.

The hesitancy shown by the Court in its race rulings of the 1940s and 1950s confirms that the gap between the racial attitudes of the public and of the cultural elite is limited. Though the justices changed the relevant subconstitutional rules in an effort to place blacks on juries, they declined to even hear a case that sought the invalidation of race-based peremptory challenges, thus ensuring that blacks would remain excluded from juries for several more decades. The justices invalidated residential segregation ordinances and the judicial enforcement of racially restrictive covenants, but they refused to even grant review in a case that raised momentous questions of state responsibility for "private" residential segregation. The justices invalidated school segregation, but they tolerated and even approved evasive measures that ensured that virtually no desegregation would actually occur. Not until popular opinion mobilized behind *Brown* did the Court become more interventionist. Though the justices in the 1940s and 1950s were more supportive of racial equality than were average Americans, they were not so committed to it that they were willing to reconsider traditional postulates of the legal system, such as limited judicial power, federalism, and presumptions that public officials act in good faith. As a result, determined white southerners were able to effectively nullify the Court's progressive race rulings.

The personal values of judges and the broader social and political context within which they decide cases are important components of the political axis, but one must not neglect more direct external political constraints, which occasionally influence judicial decision making. *Brown II* was plainly shaped by the justices' awareness that their power is limited. They did not wish to issue an unenforceable ruling, and they were dubious, with good reason, as to whether Congress and the president would enforce orders for immediate desegregation. The justices were also consciously appealing to southern moderates for support. Such strategic considerations not only shaped *Brown II*, but they almost certainly influenced the justices' decision to vacate the school desegregation field for nearly a decade thereafter.[12]

Brown was an atypical constitutional ruling in that only half the nation supported it. Most of the Court's race decisions considered in this book imposed a national consensus on a handful of southern outliers. Reading dominant public opinion into the Constitution is a natural temptation for any interpreter. When people strongly favor a particular policy about which the Constitution offers no determinate guidance, they are understandably inclined to construe the document to support that policy. Because the justices broadly reflect society, if most people feel strongly about a particular policy, it is likely that most justices will as well. They will then face the same temptation to constitutionalize the position that they support as a policy matter.

More constitutional law than is commonly supposed reflects this tendency to constitutionalize consensus and suppress outliers. Extreme examples include *Pierce v. Society of Sisters* (1925) and *Griswold v. Connecticut* (1965), where the Court created new constitutional rights, respectively, to attend private school and to use contraceptives and in the process invalidated the laws of only one or two states. Many of the race decisions canvassed in this book reflect this same tendency. *Guinn* invalidated the only grandfather clause still in operation, and *Nixon v. Herndon* (1927) struck down the only state law mandating white primaries. *McCabe* (1914) indicated that the railroad accommodation laws of just four southern states were unconstitutional, and even *Smith v. Allwright* had implications for how primary elections were conducted in just nine southern states. Landmark criminal procedure decisions, such as *Powell v. Alabama* (1932) and *Brown v. Mississippi* (1936), are even more extreme examples of the Court suppressing isolated practices, as these rulings held southern states to norms to which they themselves generally adhered. National opinion overwhelmingly favored such rulings. Thus, these earlier criminal procedure interventions were unlike subsequent land-marks, such as *Miranda v. Arizona* (1966), which plainly contravened public opinion. Constitutional law much more frequently involves the Court sup-pressing outliers than rescuing powerless minorities from majoritarian oppression.[13]

What lessons shall we draw from this study about the consequences of Court rulings? To begin, one should be humble in one's convictions: We have no way of precisely measuring the impact, direct or indirect, of Court decisions. However, although this is not science, something useful can still be said on the subject.[14]

Both polar positions in the scholarly debate should be rejected. *Brown* did not "change . . . the whole course of race relations in the United States," nor did it create the civil rights movement. But neither was *Brown* irrelevant. The Court's ruling plainly raised the salience of school segregation, encour-aged blacks to litigate against it, changed the order in which racial practices would otherwise have been contested, mobilized extraordinary resistance to racial change among southern whites, and created concrete occasions for street confrontations and violence.[15]

As to direct effects, some Court decisions plainly matter more than do others. *Smith v. Allwright* launched a revolution in politics in the urban South, while *Buchanan v. Warley* (1917) had absolutely no impact on racial residential patterns. *Sipuel* (1948) and *Sweatt* (1950) integrated public uni-versities outside of the Deep South, whereas roughly contemporaneous criminal procedure decisions had almost no effect on the southern criminal justice system in explosive cases of alleged black-on-white crime. *Brown* immediately desegregated schools in border-state cities, but it was almost completely nullified for a decade in the Deep South. The efficaciousness of Court decisions depends on certain social and political conditions: the unity and the determination of beneficiaries in enforcing newly declared rights; the relative physical security with which rights can be exercised; the intensity of opponents' resistance; the geographic concentration of opposition; the ease with which particular rights can be evaded; the extent to which the vin-dication of rights turns on disputed facts, which appellate courts find difficult to review; the availability of sanctions for violators; the presence of lawyers with the inclination and the capacity to support litigation; the type of court in which litigation is likely to occur; the existence of organizations that are able to spread the risks and the costs of litigation while capturing the benefits; the availability of market mechanisms to facilitate the implementation of rights; and the extent to which the enforcement of rights depends on the law as opposed to customs and social norms.

One reason that *Smith* had more dramatic short-term consequences for black voter registration than *Brown* had for school desegregation is that blacks were more united behind and more intensely committed to voting rights than they were to integrated schools. Voting protects other rights, and in the postwar period many black leaders insisted that if southern blacks could win genuine protection for their voting rights, they could secure other rights for themselves through politics. The right to vote was also more directly implicated by the democratic ideology of World War II than was the right to nonsegregated education. How could one possibly justify denying suffrage rights to soldiers who had just risked their lives fighting to defend democracy? Black servicemen returning to the South in the mid-1940s often took their discharge papers straight to city hall to register to vote. They did not proceed directly to local school boards to demand integrated education for their children. Moreover, blacks were historically far more divided over whether to pursue integrated education than whether to pursue the right to vote. The prospect of genuinely equal though separate schools appealed to many blacks. Segregated schools offered several advantages to blacks: job opportunities for black teachers in an era when few white-collar occupations were open to blacks; an educational environment that was relatively free from the stereotyping, insults, and humiliation that characterized the experience of black children in integrated schools; and sympathetic portrayals of black history and culture. None of this is to deny that by the late 1940s most black Americans had become enthusiastic integrationists. But blacks were plainly more united behind and intensely committed to voting rights than they were to integrated education.[16]

Blacks were more divided over some rights than others, but they were more militant about enforcing all of their rights after World War II than before. This greater militancy was partly a product of greater physical security. Constitutional rights are not worth much when asserting them is likely to get one beaten or killed. Had *Plessy* come out the other way, southern railroads would likely have remained segregated. Blacks who tested such a right to nonsegregated travel would have jeopardized their lives in an era of rampant lynching. If Texas whites in 1919 could maim the national secretary of the NAACP and suffer no consequences, how grave a risk of physical violence were most black litigants in the South facing? By contrast, in 1950, lynchings were nearly obsolete, and postwar black litigants were far more likely to face economic reprisal than physical violence. The national government now monitored and occasionally intervened against violence directed toward blacks exercising their constitutional rights, and most southern whites no longer countenanced lynchings or extreme violence. Even in the 1950s, it took great courage to litigate against Jim Crow in the Deep South, but the reduced risk of reprisal in the form of physical violence enabled blacks to assert rights more aggressively than would have been conceivable in earlier decades.

The intensity of opponents' resistance may be as important a factor in whether Court decisions prove efficacious as is the aggressiveness with which beneficiaries pursue their rights. Southern whites were much less resistant to black suffrage or the desegregation of higher education than they were to black jury service or integrated grade school education. Black disfranchisement has always occupied a lower rung on the hierarchy of preferences of white supremacists than has school segregation, which is one reason that many southern blacks were not disfranchised until the 1890s, whereas southern public schools were almost universally segregated even during Reconstruction. By the 1940s, many moderate white southerners explicitly supported removing barriers to black political participation, while they insisted that schools must remain segregated. Whites had a harder time justifying black disfranchisement to themselves in light of improved black education and the democratic ideology of World War II. Many southern whites thought that white primaries "profane[d] the Bill of Rights" and were a "cruel and shameful thing." Similarly, many southern whites supported black efforts to desegregate professional and graduate schools, and in the 1940s, southern school boards frequently capitulated without much resistance to teacher-pay equalization suits. By contrast, most white southerners ferociously resisted grade school desegregation, which involved the race mixing of young children, male and female, and thus for most whites had inevitable connotations of miscegenation. Most southern whites were also probably more resistant to black jury service than to black suffrage. Even if blacks were fully enfranchised, whites would retain secure political majorities in most southern counties and in all southern states. But criminal juries generally operated on the basis of unanimity, not simple majority rule. Thus, the presence of a single black on a criminal jury could block the conviction of a black man charged with raping a white woman or killing a white man. Whites who sought to maintain effective social control over blacks cared more about keeping them off of juries than they cared about keeping them out of polling places.[17]

Some constitutional rights are easier to circumvent than others partly because alleged denials turn on facts that are relatively difficult to establish. Early on, white southerners discovered that the most effective means of evading federal constitutional constraints was to delegate unfettered discretion to local administrators, who could maintain white supremacy without openly violating the Constitution. This was the means by which southern blacks were excluded from jury service, disfranchised, and cheated out of their fair share of public education funds. Over time, however, some of these administrative schemes for perpetuating white supremacy became more difficult to sustain than others. As blacks became better educated, registrars had a harder time seriously maintaining that black voter applicants had flunked literacy tests that less well educated whites were generally passing. The same was true of blacks getting onto jury venires, but in that context, peremptory challenges enabled prosecutors to exclude even qualified blacks from jury service through the 1980s. The peremptory challenge had no analogue in voting. By contrast, a black defendant who crossed swords at trial with a white sheriff over whether his confession was voluntarily given or induced by a beating had a much harder time convincing white fact finders that his account was true. Thus, the disparate evidentiary burdens inherent in establishing violations of particular rights may help explain why Court decisions protecting black suffrage were more efficacious than those forbidding coerced confessions. Then too, judges and jurors are likely to find some rights bearers more sympathetic than others. Black criminal defendants— indigent, often illiterate, frequently guilty of some crime even if not the one charged—were less attractive rights bearers than were the middle-class, well-educated blacks endeavoring to vote or seeking admission to public universities from which blacks were excluded.

The efficacy of rights also depends on the subconstitutional rules that are applicable to their enforcement: burdens of proof, including the willingness of courts to infer purposeful discrimination from disparate impact; rules of access to federal court; and standards of appellate review. Subconstitutional rules were especially critical in the race context, because southern whites generally chose to evade constitutional constraints by entrusting local administrators with broad discretion. Whether such administrative discrimination could be successfully challenged in court depended almost entirely on the subconstitutional rules. Thus, blacks would not sit on southern juries until the justices approved of inferring deliberate discrimination from the long-term absence of blacks from juries and until they ceased deferring entirely to state court findings of fact on the issue of discrimination. Similarly, southern schools remained largely segregated despite *Brown* until the Court began questioning the good faith of school officials, easing the access of desegregation litigants to federal court, and presuming that student bodies that failed to reflect the racial composition of the local population were illegally segregated. Because the justices determine the content of subconstitutional rules, they have greater control over this variable than over some others.

This point about the importance of subconstitutional rules may yield a lesson about the limitations of constitutional formalism. Constitutional interpretation that is limited to form and is unwilling to delve into substance is vulnerable to nullification by determined resistance. Southern whites were so creative and persistent that they almost completely eliminated black suffrage despite the existence of a constitutional amendment that forbids disfranchisement based on race. Much of this disfranchisement resulted from extralegal methods—force and fraud. But some of it simply took advantage of the evasive opportunities afforded by constitutional formalism. So long as the justices refused to inquire into legislative motive or to closely examine the discriminatory exercise of administrative discretion, southern whites were able to disfranchise blacks without violating the Constitution. Similar evasive techniques made it possible to exclude blacks from southern juries and to create enormous racial disparities in education funding despite clear substantive constitutional norms prohibiting such discrimination.

The relative availability of sanctions against violators also influences the efficacy of the Court decisions that articulate particular rights. In the 1940s, law enforcement officers and jury commissioners had little direct incentive to abide by the constitutional rights of black defendants, because civil and criminal sanctions were generally unavailable. After *Screws v. United States* (1945), it was far from certain that the justices would approve the imposition of federal criminal liability on sheriffs who beat defendants into confessing. Nor was it clear in the 1940s that courts would authorize the imposition of monetary liability under federal civil rights statutes against public officers who contravened state law as well as the federal Constitution; and every state barred the use of physical force to obtain confessions.

By contrast, voter registrars and party officials who interfered with the voting rights of blacks were more vulnerable to federal legal sanctions. After *Smith v. Allwright*, officials who refused to allow blacks to participate in party primaries were committing clear constitutional violations, which would probably qualify for federal criminal prosecution even under the restrictive standard of *Screws*. The NAACP constantly threatened registrars and party officials with criminal liability if they defied *Smith*, and the Justice Department publicly announced that it would prosecute such cases, although it eventually decided not to do so. Civil suits for damages were also more realistic in voting rights cases. The Court's first two white primary decisions sustained damages actions under federal statute against public officials who refused to allow blacks to participate in Democratic primaries. One reason that southern school boards were able to resist *Brown* for so long is that the first school desegregation lawsuits never sought money damages. One reason that they did not was the well-founded supposition that white jurors in the South would never impose liability on public officials for resisting school desegregation. Indeed, the constitutional guarantee of a jury trial before the imposition of criminal or civil liability was a huge impediment to the enforcement of any civil right, so long as blacks were excluded from southern juries and most whites opposed blacks' civil rights.

On a related matter, the public enforcement of civil rights is likely to be more efficacious than private enforcement. The Justice Department commanded far greater resources than did the NAACP or individual black litigants; it monopolized criminal enforcement; and it did not bear the same risks of economic reprisal and physical retaliation for challenging traditional racial practices. One reason that *Smith* proved so efficacious is that the Justice Department made credible threats to enforce it. Similarly, the pace of school desegregation accelerated dramatically after the 1964 Civil Rights Act authorized federal enforcement. Public action also offers enforcement mechanisms that are unavailable to private litigants, such as threats to terminate public funds for rights violators and the appointment of federal administrators to replace recalcitrant state officials. Yet, public enforcement generally depends on public support for the underlying right. Congress and the president did little to back *Brown* until the civil rights movement transformed national opinion on race. It is banal but true that rights are likely to be better enforced when they enjoy broad public support. This observation surely explains why the Court is better at suppressing outliers than at supplying definitive resolutions to issues that genuinely rend the nation, such as abortion and the death penalty in the 1970s, school segregation in the 1950s, and slavery in the federal territories in the 1850s. The political branches of the national government do not tend to support Court decisions simply because the justices have spoken. Rather, they respond to public opinion, which may or may not endorse the Court's handiwork. Congress and the president ultimately got behind *Brown*, not because of *Brown*, but because the civil rights movement had altered public opinion on school segregation.[18]

The availability and the quality of lawyers also plays a role in the enforcement of rights. One underappreciated reason that civil rights victories had such disappointing results before World War II is that there were few black lawyers practicing in the South and those who were frequently were badly educated and poorly trained. Most white lawyers would not take civil rights cases because of the "personal odium" that attached to those who challenged "the venerable system." The NAACP had limited resources; it was absent from much of the South until the 1940s; and it could not intervene without the assistance of local counsel. Constitutional rights are worth little without effective lawyers to raise them. Black criminal defendants were usually poor, and the court-appointed lawyers they received in capital cases often simply went through the motions of representing them, failing to challenge even clear violations of their clients' constitutional rights. By contrast, blacks who challenged voting rights violations hired their own lawyers. After World War II, they found that white lawyers were more willing to take such cases and that there were more and better-trained black lawyers practicing in the South.[19]

The nature of the court in which rights violations are litigated also affects enforceability. State appellate and federal judges were more likely than state trial judges to vindicate the constitutional rights of southern blacks, because they were better educated, more professionalized, and more independent of local opinion, which often proved hostile to the rights. Cases of black criminal defendants usually did not proceed beyond trial courts, mainly because state provision of counsel did not generally extend to appeals, but also because procedural defaults frequently insulated trial errors from appellate review. Many black criminal defendants suffered egregious violations of their rights that were never reviewed by any court that was likely to be sympathetic toward enforcement. By contrast, blacks litigating voting rights violations were free to choose their forum—usually federal court. They also frequently commanded the resources that were necessary to pursue appeals to courts that were more likely to sympathize with their claims. Moreover, judges themselves were influenced by the traditional hierarchy of white supremacist values. Southern judges were far more likely to sympathize with, and thus to liberally construe, *Smith v. Allwright* or *Sweatt v. Painter* than *Brown v. Board of Education*. The willingness of lower court judges to apply *Smith* in a "broad and discerning" manner, rather than in a "narrow and literal" one, proved critical to its implementation, given the multiple evasions attempted by southern officials.[20]

The clarity of legal instructions also influences lower court implementation. Even though most federal judges in the South thought that *Brown* was wrongheaded, their sense of professional obligation generally deterred them from defying it. Almost all of them acknowledged that formal school segregation had to end, whether or not they agreed with *Brown*. Yet *Brown II* was so vague as to be meaningless. It provided southern judges with no political cover, which made it difficult for them to adopt broad constructions even if they were inclined to do so, which few of them were, given their personal opposition to school desegregation. Instead, most judges countenanced delay and evasion.

The existence of an organization able to capture the benefits of litigation, while spreading the costs and the risks, also proved critical to the effective implementation of civil rights. Isolated Court rulings in favor of civil rights made essentially no difference, as is shown by the nonexistent consequences of decisions such as *Bailey* and *Guinn*. Follow-up litigation was invariably required to implement rights, and in the absence of a robust NAACP, it proved impossible to sustain. Individual blacks could rarely afford the thousands of dollars necessary to litigate cases through the appeals process. Nor did individuals have much incentive to sue, as litigation generally dragged on for years, disrupting the lives of the litigants. Virgil Hawkins spent an entire decade trying to attend the University of Florida School of Law before he finally gave up, and many named plaintiffs in school desegregation suits never attended a racially mixed school. Criminal defendants, who had ample incentive to litigate violations of their rights, rarely had the required resources and thus were usually dependent on the assistance of outside organizations. This may explain why the Court's landmark criminal procedure rulings did not take place until the interwar period, when such organizations first acquired the presence necessary for involvement in such litigation. In addition, civil rights plaintiffs risked devastating economic reprisals and, occasionally, physical violence. Only the NAACP, which represented blacks generally, across generations, could capture the benefits of litigation, while spreading the risks and the costs. Without the vast expansion of the association during and after World War II, the dramatic increases in black voter registration after *Smith* and the widespread assaults on school desegregation after *Brown* would not have been possible.[21]

The NAACP's virtual monopolization of civil rights litigation was a mixed blessing. With nearly all school desegregation suits being channeled through the association, white southerners had an easy target to attack. Their withering assault on the NAACP in the mid-1950s nearly put it out of business in the Deep South and impeded desegregation litigation. Moreover, the NAACP and its clients did not have identical interests. Black criminal defendants wanted their convictions reversed or their death sentences commuted, which often required raising the narrowest possible objections, hiring eminent white counsel, and appealing for benevolent racial paternalism. By contrast, the NAACP wanted to publicize racial injustice, rally public opinion, build branches, raise funds, and use black lawyers for educational and symbolic reasons. Similarly, in the early 1950s, blacks in Prince Edward County and in Clarendon County wanted bus transportation and equalization of grade school facilities. The NAACP gave them a choice between suing for integration or going it alone. Integration was not the obviously right strategy to pursue, given the extraordinary resistance of whites to racial mixing and the increased willingness of southern states after World War II to equalize school facilities in order to avoid court-ordered desegregation. Despite such conflicts of interest, the NAACP was usually the only game in town for civil rights litigants.

Constitutional litigation can only redress those problems that are grounded in law. Because white supremacy depended less on law than on entrenched social mores, economic power, ideology, and physical violence, the amount of racial change that litigation could produce was inevitably limited. Invalidating white primaries could enroll only so many voters at a time when in many Deep South counties blacks still risked economic and physical reprisals for attempting to vote. Invalidating residential segregation ordinances and barring the judicial enforcement of racially restrictive covenants had little effect on segregated housing patterns, which had numerous extralegal causes. Even school desegregation litigation ultimately had limited integrative effect, because of segregated housing patterns and white flight to suburbs and to private segregated academies. At most, courts can implement the rights that they identify. But constitutional rights are generally limited to negative constraints on government. They do not ordinarily entitle beneficiaries to positive government assistance or to protection against private power. Because white supremacy ultimately depended more on extralegal forces than on law, the Court's ability to uproot it was limited.[22]

The Court's civil rights decisions were difficult to enforce for another reason specific to race: Resistance was geographically concentrated. *Roe v. Wade*, which invalidated most criminal prohibitions on abortion, divided national opinion in approximately the same way that *Brown* did. But opposition to *Roe* was spread throughout the nation, not concentrated in one region, as it was with *Brown*. Virtually all white southerners disagreed with *Brown*, and opponents of other race decisions, such as *Smith* or *Sweatt*, were likewise concentrated in the South. In the 1950s, whites still held most of the political, economic, social, and physical power in the South. This meant that virtually all officials who were responsible for enforcing *Brown* — school board members, judges, jurors, politicians, and law enforcement officers — disagreed with it. Those southerners who endorsed *Brown* — mainly blacks — held little power. Under such circumstances, the enforcement of rights is necessarily quite difficult. Very few other Court decisions have produced such stark regional patterns of agreement and disagreement. Thus, progressive race rulings may have been uniquely difficult to implement.

Brown was more difficult to enforce than *Roe* for another reason as well. Regardless of how much opposition existed to abortion, capitalism ensured the development of a market to supply what those exercising the *Roe* right demanded: abortion services. By contrast, *Brown* created no favorable market opportunities to facilitate enforcement, because essentially no southern whites wanted grade school desegregation. Anyone who established private integrated schools after *Brown*, performing a market function analogous to that of abortion clinics after *Roe*, would have done a very poor business indeed.[23]

As we have seen, the efficacy of Court decisions depends on many social and political factors. Such factors ensured that *Brown* would be difficult to enforce. Most power holders in an entire region thought the decision was wrong and were intensely mobilized against it; this included the actors who were initially responsible for its enforcement. Black beneficiaries of the ruling were neither united behind the right nor as intensely committed to its enforcement as they were with regard to some other rights. Congress and the president were unenthusiastic about implementing the decision. The effective monopolization of enforcement resources by the NAACP created a precarious situation, in which opposition forces could effectively nullify the ruling simply by shutting down a single organization. A multitude of techniques for evading the right were available, and sanctions against violators were mostly unobtainable.

One great irony of twentieth-century U.S. history is that, after *Brown*, southern whites abandoned the tried-and-true evasive techniques that for decades had successfully nullified the constitutional rights of blacks, in favor of outright defiance. Southern whites had eschewed open confrontation with the Court over black jury service and black suffrage, while completely sabotaging those rights through administrative discrimination. But rather than follow North Carolina's lead and use similarly fraudulent mechanisms to circumvent school desegregation, the white South declared war on the Court, nullified *Brown*, and used state troops and vigilante mobs to block the enforcement of desegregation orders. Such open defiance forced President Eisenhower's hand, alienated national opinion, radicalized southern politics, fostered violence, and irritated the justices. One cannot know how long token school desegregation might have persisted had white southerners played their hand differently, but in retrospect, massive resistance almost certainly proved a mistake from their perspective. The nature of southern politics may have impelled that mistake. Southern politicians reaped rewards for adopting extremist positions. Governor Faubus won four more terms in office because he called out the militia to block the desegregation of Little Rock schools, and state legislators across the South saw political profit in passing interposition resolutions. The electoral incentives of southern politicians led them to respond to *Brown* in ways that ultimately facilitated its enforcement.[24]

One lesson to draw from this history regarding the consequences of Court decisions is ironic: Litigation is unlikely to help those most desperately in need. We have already seen that the justices, reflecting broader social mores, are unlikely to side with litigants who lack significant social standing. Even once litigants secure Court victories, they must have a certain amount of power in order to enforce them. When southern blacks were most oppressed, they could not even bring equalization suits to challenge the enormous, and obviously unconstitutional, racial disparities that existed in education funding. Challenges to legal lynching reached the Court only in the 1920s and 1930s, when racial conditions in the South had ameliorated enough for liberal organizations to support such cases. Almost all of the civil rights litigation during the Progressive Era (the 1910s) came from the border states, not the more oppressive South. Not a single school desegregation suit was brought in Mississippi until nine years after *Brown*, whereas many were filed in border states that were already desegregating. Litigation requires lawyers, economic resources, and some security from physical danger. Those most in need of racial justice from the courts were least likely to get it, because conditions were too oppressive to permit legal challenges. This lesson may not be applicable outside of the race context, as few social reform movements in the United States confront regimes that are as totalitarian as was Jim Crow Mississippi.[25]

What can be said about the indirect consequences of litigation: raising the salience of issues, educating people, and motivating them? Such indirect effects are even harder to measure than are direct effects, though they may be just as real. It seems indisputable that *Brown* raised the salience of school segregation. People, social organizations, and political parties and candidates were forced to take a position on the issue, which they had previously been able to avoid doing. For northern liberals and for many religious organizations, taking a position on school segregation in 1954 inevitably meant opposing it. *Brown* also forced southern politicians to take a position on the issue, which many of them would have preferred to avoid doing. Given dominant public opinion in the South, however, the only conceivable position that they could take was to support segregation and to condemn *Brown*. By shifting racial debate from other issues to school segregation, *Brown* clearly had an effect.

Brown also plainly inspired blacks. To have the Court declare segregation to be unconstitutional was symbolically important, and it furthered the hope and the conviction that fundamental racial change was possible. *Brown* directly inspired southern blacks to file petitions and lawsuits seeking school desegregation—something that almost certainly would not have happened in the mid-1950s, at least in places such as Mississippi or South Carolina, had it not been for *Brown*. Thus, *Brown* shaped the agenda of southern blacks and shifted the focus to school desegregation and away from other issues that had preoccupied them before the Court's ruling: voting rights, school equalization, police brutality, and employment discrimination. This agenda-setting effect mattered, because southern whites were much more resistant to school desegregation than to many of the other reforms on the agenda of blacks.

Brown's educational effect, as distinguished from its motivational consequences, is probably overstated. There is little evidence to suggest that many Americans changed their position on school segregation because of the justices' moral influence. White southerners bitterly denounced *Brown*. Most white northerners supported it, but more because they already agreed with its principles than because they were educated by the decision. Moreover, in the mid-1950s, their endorsement was fairly tepid. Few white northerners were prepared to support aggressive enforcement of *Brown* until the early 1960s. Northern opinion on race was educated far more by the civil rights movement than by *Brown*.

The limited educational influence of *Brown* is consistent with that of other landmark Court rulings. *Roe v. Wade* (1973) apparently did not educate many Americans to support abortion rights, as the country remains divided roughly down the middle three decades later. *Bowers v. Hardwick* (1986), which upheld the application of state criminal sodomy laws to consenting adult homosexuals, apparently has not educated many Americans to agree with the Court; rather, a robust gay rights movement has developed over the ensuing years. *Furman v. Georgia* (1972), which invalidated the arbitrary enforcement of the death penalty, plainly has not educated many Americans to oppose capital punishment, given opinion polls showing public support at 70 percent or higher. *Engel v. Vitale* (1962), which invalidated voluntary, nondenominational prayer in public schools, has consistently been opposed by 60–70 percent of the American public. Apparently, relatively few Americans take moral instruction on pressing policy questions from the justices.[26]

Indeed, to the contrary, many landmark Court rulings seem to have generated backlashes rather than support. *Dred Scott v. Sandford* (1857), which essentially declared the Republican party to be unconstitutional by forbidding the federal regulation of slavery in national territories, seemed to help the party politically rather than annihilate it. *Furman* apparently mobilized support for the death penalty, as thirty-five states responded to the Court's ruling within four years by amending their death penalty statutes in the hope of satisfying the constitutional qualms of the justices. *Roe* mobilized antiabortion activists who had not previously played a significant role in American politics. In 1993, the Hawaii Supreme Court ruled that marriage could not be limited to heterosexuals; within a few years, thirty states and Congress had passed "defense of marriage" acts in opposition.[27]

Brown produced precisely this sort of backlash. As southern blacks, inspired by the Court's ruling, filed school desegregation petitions and lawsuits, southern whites mobilized extraordinary resistance in response. Politics moved dramatically to the right, moderates collapsed, and extremists prospered. In the mid-1950s, racial retrogression characterized the South, as progress that had been made in black voting, university desegregation, and the integration of athletic competitions was halted and then reversed. Politicians used extremist rhetoric that encouraged violence, and some of them, such as Bull Connor and Jim Clark, correctly calculated that the violent suppression of civil rights protest would win votes. Court-ordered desegregation also created concrete occasions for violence, usually in settings that ensured that white supremacists would come off badly.[28]

One should not be surprised that landmark Court decisions would produce such backlashes. When the justices resolve controversies that rend the nation in half, their rulings naturally arouse opposition among those who lost in the Court. Perhaps more important, Court decisions can disrupt the order in which social change might otherwise have occurred by dictating reform in areas where public opinion is not yet ready to accept it. In the early 1950s, most southern blacks were more intent on securing voting rights, curbing police brutality, improving black schools, and winning access to decent jobs than they were on integrating grade schools. Most southern whites shared a partially inverse hierarchy of racial preferences: They were far more resistant to desegregating schools than they were to making concessions on black voting, school equalization, and so forth. Given these preferences, political negotiation between blacks and whites, assuming that blacks had sufficient clout to compel negotiation, would certainly not have focused immediately on school desegregation. Yet courts respond to the agendas set by litigants not by political negotiation. By demanding change first on an issue on which whites were most recalcitrant, *Brown* encouraged massive resistance.

The Hawaii Supreme Court's decision to protect gay marriages illustrates the same phenomenon. By the early 1990s, public opinion on homosexuality had changed dramatically, with majorities now supporting a ban on discrimination with regard to sexual orientation in employment and public accommodations. But the one issue on which heterosexuals were most resistant to change was marriage. Political negotiation would probably have left reform on that issue for last. By advancing it prematurely, *Baehr v. Lewin* ensured a political backlash against gay marriage.[29]

Roe v. Wade produced a similar effect by imposing an abortion regime that was much more permissive than the one being politically negotiated at the time in numerous state legislatures. *Roe* effectively invalidated the abortion laws of forty-six states by forbidding most regulation of abortion in the first trimester of pregnancy. Though in the preceding years, abortion-rights reformers had made significant progress in state legislatures, they had not generally secured rights as unrestricted as those declared in *Roe*. Naturally, a Court ruling that dictated a result significantly different from the one that was simultaneously being negotiated in legislatures generated a strong backlash. None of this is to criticize such rulings, only to explain their effects.[30]

Yet backlashes themselves may have unpredictable ramifications, which further complicates efforts to assess the importance of Court decisions. *Brown* created a massive backlash among southern whites, radicalized politics, and fomented violence. But that violence, especially when directed at peaceful protestors and broadcast on television, produced a counterbacklash. In 1954, most northerners agreed with *Brown* in the abstract, but their preferences were not strong enough to make them willing to face down the resistance of southern whites. It was southern violence against civil rights demonstrators that transformed national opinion on race. By the early 1960s, northerners were no longer prepared to tolerate the brutal beatings of peaceful black demonstrators, and they responded to such scenes by demanding civil rights legislation that attacked Jim Crow at its core.

From the Civil War through the civil rights movement, it has been easiest to mobilize northern white opinion in support of the rights of southern blacks in response to brutality, violence, and lynching. When southern whites quietly segregated or disfranchised blacks, northern whites often remained indifferent. They have sometimes, though, refused to countenance brutality and violence. Thus, during Reconstruction, Klan violence induced a Republican Congress in 1870 and 1871 to stretch constitutional boundaries by enacting far-reaching civil rights legislation. Appreciating this dynamic, the NAACP made federal antilynching legislation its first political priority between the two world wars. The association recognized that lynching was the easiest issue around which to mobilize national opinion in support of federal intervention in southern race relations. The New York branch once complained that it "labor[ed] under a peculiar difficulty . . . [because] it has no violent outrages confronting it; it can present no picturesque wrongs to arouse public opinion or to inflame the popular imagination." Likewise, the Court's criminal procedure decisions of the interwar period indicate that southern lynch law was the most compelling racial issue around which to mobilize national *judicial* opinion. A postwar resurgence in lynchings, maimings, and race riots prompted President Truman in 1946 to appoint his civil rights committee, which inaugurated a chain of events that culminated in 1948 with the Democratic party's adoption of a landmark civil rights platform and Truman's issuance of executive orders desegregating the military and the federal civil service. This counterbacklash dynamic culminated at Birmingham and Selma, as northerners demanded transformative civil rights legislation after watching televised scenes of law enforcement officers brutalizing peaceful black demonstrators.[31]

Apart from the consequences of Court victories, litigation can itself perform important educational, motivational, and organizational functions. NAACP lawyers educated blacks about their constitutional rights and instilled hope that racial conditions were malleable. Many branches formed around litigation, which also proved to be an excellent fundraising tool. Black lawyers served as role models to black audiences in courtrooms, as they jousted with whites in the only southern forum that permitted racial interactions on a footing of near-equality, and they demonstrated forensic skills that belied conventional white stereotypes of black inferiority. Criminal litigation afforded especially valuable opportunities for educating northern whites and judges about the barbarities of Jim Crow, as possibly innocent blacks faced death sentences that had been imposed on the basis of tortured confessions and farcical trials. It is impossible to measure any of these intangible consequences of litigation, but NAACP lawyers such as Charles Hamilton Houston and Thurgood Marshall considered them nearly as important as Court victories themselves. Thus, to judge the success or failure of a litigation campaign based solely on the concrete consequences of Court decisions is mistaken, given the capacity of litigation to mobilize social protest.[32]

Before World War II, alternative forms of protest—political mobilization, economic boycotts, street demonstrations, and physical resistance— were largely unavailable to southern blacks, who lived under a ruthlessly repressive regime of Jim Crow. At that time, litigation did not compete with alternative protest strategies for scarce resources, and it offered the advantages of not requiring large-scale participation to succeed and of taking place in the relative safety of courthouses rather than on the streets. Yet there was a risk of exaggerating the contributions that litigation could make to social reform. In the 1930s, civil rights leaders appreciated that court decisions required social support to be efficacious. Charles Houston warned, "[W]e cannot depend upon judges to fight . . . our battles," and he urged that "the social and public factors must be developed at least along with and if possible before the actual litigation commences." By the 1950s, though, litigation had secured such impressive Court victories and the NAACP was riding so high on its success that direct-action protest may have been discouraged, even though it had now become a viable option given the greater physical security enjoyed by southern blacks. Litigation and direct action now competed for scarce resources, and litigation seemed to have the edge in the 1950s, until the effective nullification of *Brown* by white southerners demonstrated the limited capacity of lawsuits alone to produce social change.[33]

Though litigation had performed valuable service in mobilizing racial protest and securing Court victories, some of which concretely advanced progressive racial change, it could not fulfill all of the functions of direct action. Sit-ins, Freedom Rides, and street demonstrations fostered black agency much better than did litigation, which encouraged blacks to place faith in elite black lawyers and white judges rather than in themselves. That litigation does not require mass participation to succeed in court was its virtue in the 1910s and 1920s but its vice by the 1950s and 1960s. In addition, direct-action protest more reliably created conflict and incited opponents' violence, which ultimately proved critical to transforming national opinion on race.[34]

Brown played a role both in generating direct action and in shaping the response it received from white southerners. *Brown* made Jim Crow seem more vulnerable, and any social protest movement must overcome a formidable hurdle in convincing potential participants that change is feasible. *Brown* raised the hopes and expectations of black Americans, which were then largely dashed by massive resistance; this demonstrated that litigation alone could not produce meaningful social change. *Brown* inspired southern whites to try to destroy the NAACP, with some temporary success in the Deep South, and this unintentionally forced blacks to support alternative protest organizations, which embraced philosophies more sympathetic to direct action. Finally, the southern white backlash that was ignited by *Brown* increased the chances that once civil rights demonstrators appeared on the streets, they would be greeted with violence rather than with gradualist concessions. It is impossible to precisely measure any of these consequences of *Brown*, but the ruling plainly influenced the way in which America's racial transformation occurred.

Court decisions do matter, though often in unpredictable ways. But they cannot fundamentally transform a nation. The justices are too much products of their time and place to launch social revolutions. And, even if they had the inclination to do so, their capacity to coerce change is too heavily constrained. The justices were not tempted to invalidate school segregation until a time when half the nation supported such a ruling. They declined to aggressively enforce the *Brown* decision until a civil rights movement had made northern whites as keen to eliminate Jim Crow as southern whites were to preserve it. And while *Brown* did play a role in shaping both the civil rights movement and the violent response it received from southern whites, deep background forces ensured that the United States would experience a racial reform movement regardless of what the Supreme Court did or did not do.

NOTES

INTRODUCTION

1. Buck, *Road to Reunion*, 282.

2. United States v. Butler, 297 U.S. 1, 62 (1936); Holmes, *Common Law*, 1. For classic statements of the realist view, see Frank, *Law and the Modern Mind*; Hutcheson, "The Judgment Intuitive." For leading modern variants of the realist view, see Segal & Spaeth, *Supreme Court and the Attitudinal Model*, esp. 208–60; Segal & Cover, "Ideological Values and the Votes of U.S. Supreme Court Justices"; Tushnet, "Following the Rules Laid Down." For law professors adopting the moderate formalist position, see, for example, Dworkin, "Hard Cases"; Schauer, "Easy Cases." For political scientists emphasizing the importance of the legal component in judicial decision making, see Clayton & Gillman, *Supreme Court Decision Making*; see also Epstein & Kobylka, *The Supreme Court and Legal Change*, 299–312. For an excellent summary of the current status of the debate within the political science community, see Gillman, "What's Law Got to Do with It?"

3. On the elite biases of judges, see Klarman, "What's So Great about Constitutionalism?" 189–91. For the view that the Court's constitutional interpretations tend to reflect the broader social and political climate of the era, see McCloskey, *American Supreme Court*; Dahl, "Decision Making in a Democracy"; Friedman, "Dialogue and Judicial Review"; Klarman, "Rethinking the Civil Rights and Civil Liberties Revolutions." Cf. Marshall, *Public Opinion and the Supreme Court*, 78–98, 192.

4. On the importance of *Brown* specifically, compare Rosenberg, *Hollow Hope*, 71, 169, 338, and Rosenberg, "*Brown* Is Dead!" 171, with Greenberg, *Crusaders in the Courts*, 12, 116, and Owen Fiss, "A Life Twice Lived," *Yale Law Journal* 100 (Mar.

1991): 1117–18. See also chapter 7. On the general question of the impact of Supreme Court decisions, see, in addition to Rosenberg, Wasby, *Impact of the United States Supreme Court*; Schultz, *Leveraging the Law*; Handler, *Social Movements and the Legal System*, esp. 192–209; Segal & Spaeth, *Supreme Court and the Attitudinal Model*, 333–55; Canon, "Supreme Court and Policy Reform"; Schuck, "Public Law Litigation and Social Reform"; McCann, "Reform Litigation on Trial"; Dolbeare & Hammond, *School Prayer Decisions*, 133–53.

5. See Handler, *Social Movements and the Legal System*, 214–22; McCann, *Rights at Work*, 10, 56–57, 279. But cf. Rosenberg, *Hollow Hope*, 107–56; Rosenberg, "Positivism, Interpretivism, and the Study of Law."

CHAPTER 1

1. Kelley, "*Plessy*," 1, 6, 18–29 (quotes at 18, 22, 29). See also Woodward, "Case of the Louisiana Traveler," 148–54; Lofgren, Plessy, 28–32.

2. Perry, *Constitution in the Courts*, 145; Baer, *Equality under the Constitution*, 112; Oberst, "*Plessy v. Ferguson*," 417; Olsen, *Thin Disguise*, 1; Jones, "The Harlan Dissent," 951–54. See generally Klarman, "Rethinking the Civil Rights and Civil Liberties Revolutions."

3. "Redemption" refers to the replacement of Reconstruction governments controlled by Republicans and supported by most blacks with Democratic regimes supported by most southern whites and seldom committed to protecting the rights of blacks.

4. Woodward, *Origins of the New South*, 78–81, 209, 321; Anderson, *Race and Politics in North Carolina*, ix, 130, 137, 159, 319–20, 331–32; Tindall, *South Carolina Negroes*, 12, 20–30, 38–39, 61–64, 66–67, 306; Wharton, *Negro in Mississippi*, 181, 202–3; Cartwright, *Triumph of Jim Crow*, 49–50, 175–76, 198; Cresswell, *Multi-Party Politics in Mississippi*, 17, 89; Fischer, *Segregation Struggle in Louisiana*, 134–36; Lewinson, *Race, Class, and Party*, 37–39; Woodward, *Strange Career of Jim Crow*, 32–44; Hackney, *Populism to Progressivism in Alabama*, 180–84; Somers, "Black and White in New Orleans," 20–21; Wright, *Life behind a Veil*, 7, 50–51; Wynes, *Race Relations in Virginia*, 149; Dephloff & Jones, "Race Relations in Louisiana," 322. Cf. Rabinowitz, *Race Relations in the Urban South*, 331–34; Williamson, *After Slavery*, chap. 10; Cell, *Highest Stage of White Supremacy*, chap. 4; McMillen, *Dark Journey*, 3–5. See also Rabinowitz, "More than the Woodward Thesis," 849; Cohen, *At Freedom's Edge*, 202, 246; Woodward, "*Strange Career* Critics," 862.

5. Brundage, *Lynching in the New South*, 7–8; Tindall, *South Carolina Negroes*, chap. 12; Anderson, *Race and Politics in North Carolina*, 146, 245–47, 252–79; Cartwright, *Triumph of Jim Crow*, 52, 60; Cohen, *At Freedom's Edge*, 211 table 9, 246; Novak, *Wheel of Servitude*, 36; McPherson, *Abolitionist Legacy*, 138, 300–306; Somers, "Black and White in New Orleans"; Arnesen, *Waterfront Workers of New Orleans*, 74, 83–84, 88–89, 91–98, 114, 118–21, 123–49; Fischer, *Segregation Struggle in Louisiana*, 148–51; Wright, *Life behind a Veil*, 50, 59–62, 70–74; Wharton, *Negro in Mississippi*, 230–33; Gilmore, *Gender and Jim Crow*, 9–10.

6. Miller, "A Negro's View," 1060; Kelley, "*Plessy*," 29; Meier, *Negro Thought in America*, 100–118, 146–48, 218–19; McMillen, *Dark Journey*, 186–90; Dittmer, *Black Georgia*, 168–69, 172, 175–79; Meier & Rudwick, *Along the Color Line*, chap. 9; Woodward, *Origins of the New South*, 350, 355–60; McPherson, *Abolitionist Legacy*, chap. 19; Cecelski & Tyson, *Democracy Betrayed*, 4–5. See also Woodward, *Origins of the New South*, 337–38; Meier, *Negro Thought in America*, 38–40, 109, 111–14, 173, 196,

214–15; Mabry, "Disfranchisement of the Negro in Mississippi," 329; Ayers, *Promise of the New South*, 289; McMillen, *Dark Journey*, 50–51.

7. Compare Woodward, *Origins of the New South*, chaps. 8, 9, 12, and Woodward, *Strange Career of Jim Crow*, 69–82, with Rabinowitz, *Race Relations in the Urban South*, 135–36, 167, and Rabinowitz, *First New South*, 140.

8. Kantrowitz, *Ben Tillman*, 110–47, 156, 168–69 (quotation), 175–76; Woodward, *Origins of the New South*, 185–204, 209–11, 235–62; Ayers, *Promise of the New South*, chaps. 9–10; Cresswell, *Multi-Party Politics in Mississippi*, chaps. 4–5; Lewinson, *Race, Class, and Party*, chap. 4; Anderson, *Race and Politics in North Carolina*, 171–72, 193; Fredrickson, *Black Image in the White Mind*, 90–92, 226, 262; Baker, *Following the Color Line*, 84, 87, 252; Tindall, *South Carolina Negroes*, 20–21, 306; Woodward, *Strange Career of Jim Crow*, 48–50; Rabinowitz, *First New South*, 109, 118, 169–70; Cartwright, *Triumph of Jim Crow*, 166–68.

9. Anderson, *Race and Politics in North Carolina*, 145, 214–17, 222, 239, 252–79; Cantrell & Barton, "Texas Populists," 683; Fredrickson, *Black Image in the White Mind*, 202–3, 264, 266; Goodwyn, "Populist Dreams and Negro Rights," 1447; Ogden, *Poll Tax in the South*, 11, 17; Woodward, *Strange Career of Jim Crow*, 76–80; Hart, *Redeemers, Bourbons & Populists*, 194–95.

10. Charles Edward Russell, "Leaving It to the South," *Crisis* 1 (Apr. 1911): 24.

11. Mary White Ovington, "How the National Association for the Advancement of Colored People Began," *Crisis* 8 (Aug. 1914): 184; Cohen, *At Freedom's Edge*, 92–93; Spear, *Black Chicago*, 7–8, 12 table 1, 23, 44–45, 201; Osofsky, *Harlem*, 35, 40–42; McPherson, *Abolitionist Legacy*, 309–11; Gerber, *Black Ohio*, 28–29, 249–63, 276, 295; Thornbrough, *Negro in Indiana*, 184–91, 206, 207 n. 2, 265, 279–82, 332, 392; Katzman, *Before the Ghetto*, 93; Kusmer, *A Ghetto Takes Shape*, 30–31; Baker, *Following the Color Line*, chap. 6; Fishel, "The North and the Negro," 57, 363, 396–424, 489–90; Meier & Rudwick, "Alton, Illinois, Case"; Meier & Rudwick, "East Orange, New Jersey, Experience"; Bassett, "Stirring Up the Fires," 298; *Nation* 58 (14 June 1894): 439; *New York Age*, 1 Oct. 1908, p. 1.

12. Degler, *In Search of Human Nature*, 48–49; Kraditor, *Woman Suffrage Movement*, 201–2; Lofgren, *Plessy*, 98–99; Higham, *Strangers in the Land*, chaps. 3, 4, 6; Olsen, *Thin Disguise*, 21; McPherson, *Abolitionist Legacy*, 125, 322–23.

13. Hackney, *Populism to Progressivism in Alabama*, 159–61; Perman, *Struggle for Mastery*, 238; Poe, "Suffrage Restrictions," 542; Woodward, *Origins of the New South*, 324–26; Lauren, *Power and Prejudice*, 64–70; Downes v. Bidwell, 182 U.S. 244 (1901); Woodward, *Strange Career of Jim Crow*, 70–74; Stone, *American Race Problem*, 379–80; Gatewood, "Negro Troops in Florida," 15.

14. Buck, *Road to Reunion*, 67–68, 102–3, 123–25, 134–35; Woodward, *Strange Career of Jim Crow*, 70; Gillette, *Retreat from Reconstruction*, 72; Foner, *Reconstruction*, 500–505, 567, 580–82; DeSantis, *Republicans Face the Southern Question*, 32–33, 54–56, 74.

15. Buck, *Road to Reunion*, 282; Letter to the Editor, *Nation* 54 (24 Mar. 1892): 227; *Nation* 62 (21 May 1896): 391–92; Somers, "Black and White in New Orleans," 40; Fishel, "The North and the Negro," 411–12, 415–16; Kraditor, *Woman Suffrage Movement*, 170–72, 199–200, 213; McPherson, *Abolitionist Legacy*, 319–22; Stone, *American Race Problem*, 293.

16. Ayers, *Promise of the New South*, 329–33; Gatewood, "Negro Troops in Florida," 10; Gerber, *Black Ohio*, 361–62, 364; Gleijeses, "African Americans and the War against Spain," 199, 204–6; Buck, *Road to Reunion*, 118, 283, 306–7; Miller,

"Negro's View," 1060; *New York Times* (hereafter *NYT*), 13 Nov. 1898, p. 18; Stone, *American Race Problem*, 293–97; Gilmore, *Gender and Jim Crow*, 56–57; William McKinley, "Second Inaugural Address" (4 Mar. 1901), in *Presidents Speak*, ed. Lott, 207–12.

17. DeSantis, *Republicans Face the Southern Question*, 19–132, 158, 168, 196; Buck, *Road to Reunion*, chap. 4; Cox & Cox, "Negro Suffrage and Republican Politics"; Foner, *Reconstruction*, 228–31, 282–307; Gillette, *Right to Vote*, 46–49; Wang, *Trial of Democracy*, 91–92, 105–6, 109, 134–79; Benedict, "Politics of Reconstruction," 80–81, 86; Goldman, "A Free Ballot and a Fair Count," 65–108, 190.

18. Buck, *Road to Reunion*, chap. 4; Gillette, *Retreat from Reconstruction*, 1–16, 179–85, 230–35, 366–70, 374–75; Wang, *Trial of Democracy*, 138–40, 163–215; Goldman, "A Free Ballot and a Fair Count," chaps. 3, 4, 6; DeSantis, *Republicans Face the Southern Question*, chaps. 1–5; "Republican Platform of 1880," in *National Party Platforms*, ed. Johnson & Porter, 62; "Republican Platform of 1884," in ibid., 74; "Republican Platform of 1888," in ibid., 80; James A. Garfield, "Inaugural Address" (4 Mar. 1881), in *Inaugural Addresses*, 163–70; Symposium, "Ought the Negro to Be Disfranchised? Ought He to Have Been Enfranchised?" *North American Review* 268 (1879): 225–31 (James Blaine); ibid., 244–50 (James Garfield).

19. DeSantis, *Republicans Face the Southern Question*, 19–181, 190–93, 246, 261–62; Gillette, *Retreat from Reconstruction*, 335–62; Wang, *Trial of Democracy*, chaps. 4–5; Goldman, "A Free Ballot and a Fair Count," chaps. 3–4; Kousser, *Shaping of Southern Politics*, 12 table 1.1, 92–93; *Nation* 59 (27 Dec. 1894): 475.

20. Buck, *Road to Reunion*, chap. 11; Wang, *Trial of Democracy*, 224–27, 242–52, 263; Welch, "Federal Elections Bill"; DeSantis, *Republicans Face the Southern Question*, chap. 5; Perman, *Struggle for Mastery*, 38–41; *Nation* 61 (5 Sept. 1895): 162; ibid. (21 Aug. 1890): 141, 144; ibid. (28 Aug. 1890): 161, 164.

21. DeSantis, *Republicans Face the Southern Question*, 21; Gerber, *Black Ohio*, 338; Gillette, *Retreat from Reconstruction*, 372–76; Goldman, "A Free Ballot and a Fair Count," 254–55; Callcott, *Negro in Maryland Politics*, chap. 4; Burnham, "American Political Universe," 12–14, 23–24; McAdam, *Development of Black Insurgency*, 70; *Nation* 61 (5 Sept. 1895): 162; ibid. 62 (14 May 1896): 370–71; Welch, *Presidencies of Grover Cleveland*, 40–41, 97, 110–11, 212.

22. *Nation* 62 (21 May 1896): 391–92; ibid. 61 (5 Sept. 1895): 162; Gerber, *Black Ohio*, 338, 361–62; Kousser, *Shaping of Southern Politics*, 22 n. 12, 31; DeSantis, *Republicans Face the Southern Question*, 231, 255; Gilmore, *Gender and Jim Crow*, 115; Fishel, "Negro in Northern Politics," 475; Wang, *Trial of Democracy*, 261–62; Thornbrough, *Negro in Indiana*, 315; "Republican Party Platform of 1892," in *National Party Platforms*, ed. Johnson & Porter, 93; "Republican Party Platform of 1896," in ibid., 109; William McKinley, "First Inaugural" (4 Mar. 1897), in *Inaugural Addresses*, 198–207.

23. Highsaw, *Edward Douglass White*, 19, 23–24; Schmidt, "Principle and Prejudice, Part III," 883–84; McCaul, *Black Struggle for Public Schooling*, 61–63; Ely, *Chief Justiceship of Melville W. Fuller*, 7–8; Board of Education v. Tinnon, 26 Kans. 1, 23 (1881) (Brewer, J., dissenting); Brodhead, *David J. Brewer*, 107. See also Glennon, "Henry Billings Brown," 553; Hylton, "The Judge Who Abstained in *Plessy v. Ferguson*," 323–32.

24. Yarbrough, *Judicial Enigma*, 55–59, 62, 77–78, 84, 109–10, 138–39; Beth, *John Marshall Harlan*, chap. 5; Civil Rights Cases, 109 U.S. 3, 26 (1883) (Harlan, J., dissent-

ing); Plessy v. Ferguson, 163 U.S. 537, 552 (1896) (Harlan, J., dissenting); Berea College v. Kentucky, 211 U.S. 45, 58 (1908) (Harlan, J., dissenting).

25. Minter, "Codification of Jim Crow," 9–14; McFeely, *Frederick Douglass*, 92–93; Litwack, *North of Slavery*, 106–9; Singer, "No Right to Exclude," 1374; Stephenson, *Race Distinctions*, 112; page 20.

26. Fischer, *Segregation Struggle in Louisiana*, 31–41, 62–63, 69, 78–79; Barnes, *Journey from Jim Crow*, 2–3; Stephenson, *Race Distinctions*, 115, 208–10; Somers, "Black and White in New Orleans," 23–24, 28; Wharton, *Negro in Mississippi*, 175, 230–31; Lofgren, Plessy, 18–19; Foner, *Reconstruction*, 369–71, 421–22; page 49.

27. Woodward, *Strange Career of Jim Crow*, 23–24, 27–29, 38–41; Wynes, *Race Relations in Virginia*, 69, 71–73, 150; Minter, "Codification of Jim Crow," 90–91, 136–37, 171, 193–95; Riegel, "Persistent Career of Jim Crow," 27; Welke, "When All the Women Were White," 266–67, 276 n. 40; Cartwright, *Triumph of Jim Crow*, 168, 185; Somers, "Black and White in New Orleans," 28; Fischer, *Segregation Struggle in Louisiana*, 31–41, 148–49; Williamson, *After Slavery*, 281–83; Heard v. Georgia Railroad, 1 I.C.C. 719, 720–22 (1888); Letter to the Editor, *Nation* 50 (13 Mar. 1890): 219; *Charleston News & Courier*, 5 Nov. 1883, p. 2; "South Carolina Society," *Atlantic Monthly* 39 (June 1877): 670, 676; Meier & Rudwick, *Along the Color Line*, 268–69, 309–10; Wright, *Life behind a Veil*, 52–54. But cf. Williamson, *After Slavery*, 283–85; Rabinowitz, *First New South*, 133–34, 138; Rabinowitz, *Race Relations in the Urban South*, 182. See also Lofgren, Plessy, 9–17; Cell, *Highest Stage of White Supremacy*, chap. 4; Woodward, "*Strange Career* Critics," 862.

28. Somers, "Black and White in New Orleans," 29, 38; Woodward, *Strange Career of Jim Crow*, 31–35, 97–105; Lofgren, Plessy, 17, 22; Mangum, *Legal Status of the Negro*, chap. 8; Stephenson, *Race Distinctions*, chap. 9; Cartwright, *Triumph of Jim Crow*, 103–7; Flomsbee, "First 'Jim Crow' Law," 235–47; Minter, "Codification of Jim Crow," 51–67, 161; Barnes, *Journey from Jim Crow*, 7–11; Meier & Rudwick, *Along the Color Line*, chap. 12; Roback, "Political Economy of Segregation," 893–917. See also page 50. An 1881 Tennessee segregation law was an aberration.

29. Riegel, "Persistent Career of Jim Crow," 27; Woodward, *Strange Career of Jim Crow*, 48–50; Wharton, *Negro in Mississippi*, 231–32; Lofgren, Plessy, 24–26; Baker, *Following the Color Line*, 29–30; Woodward, *Origins of the New South*, 211–12; Hart, *Redeemers, Bourbons & Populists*, 164–65; Minter, "Codification of Jim Crow," 62, 83, 114–15, 128, 132, 144, 193; Bacote, "Negro Proscriptions, Protests, and Proposed Solutions," 472–73; Welke, "When All the Women Were White," 277, 295, 312; Rabinowitz, *Race Relations in the Urban South*, 333–39; Ayers, *Promise of the New South*, 140–41, 145, 247, 520 n. 74; Kantrowitz, *Ben Tillman*, 143; Perman, *Struggle for Mastery*, 245–69; Cobb, "Segregating the New South," 1018–19, 1022–23; Bassett, "Stirring Up the Fires," 300–301; Cell, *Highest Stage of White Supremacy*, 55–58, 103–4, 131–35, 142–43; Weaver, "Failure of Civil Rights," 370.

30. Kull, *Color-Blind Constitution*, 3–4, 58–87 (quotation at 64); Maltz, *Civil Rights, the Constitution and Congress*, 6, 82–92; Berger, *Government by Judiciary*, 143–44; Bickel, "Original Understanding and the Segregation Decision," 42–45, 60.

31. Bond, "Original Understanding of the Fourteenth Amendment," 435–67; Fishel, "The North and the Negro," 56–57, 66, 97–100; Litwack, *North of Slavery*, chap. 3; Foner, *Reconstruction*, 25–26, 226–27, 244–45; Maltz, *Civil Rights, the Constitution, and Congress*, 6, 71, 74–76; Kull, *Color-Blind Constitution*, 60, 76–77, 85–86; *Congressional Globe*, 39th Cong., 1st sess., 1866, 541 (Rep. John L. Dawson); ibid.,

App. 183 (Sen. Garrett Davis); Bickel, "Original Understanding and the Segregation Decision," 11–29; Grossman, *Democratic Party and the Negro*, 1–14; Avins, "Social Equality and the Fourteenth Amendment," 640–56; Berger, *Government by Judiciary*, chaps. 3, 4, 9; Gillette, *Right to Vote*, 21–45; Fairman, *Reconstruction and Reunion*, chap. 20.

32. Barnes, *Journey from Jim Crow*, 2; Gerber, *Black Ohio*, 46; Strauss, "The Irrelevance of Constitutional Amendments," 1462–63, 1480–82, 1491–92, 1496–1503, 1505; Klarman, "What's So Great about Constitutionalism?" 171.

33. Lofgren, *Plessy*, 65, 124, 146; Maltz, "'Separate but Equal'," 558–68; McConnell, "Originalism and the Desegregation Decisions," 982–84, 1117–19; Railroad Company v. Brown, 84 U.S. 445 (1873); Kull, *Color-Blind Constitution*, 91–93; Maltz, *Civil Rights, the Constitution, and Congress*, 124; Foner, *Reconstruction*, 437–39.

34. Compare McConnell, "Originalism and the Desegregation Decisions," 1120–31, with Klarman, "*Brown*, Originalism, and Constitutional Theory," 1884–1914, and Maltz, "Originalism and the Desegregation Decisions," 223–31.

35. Lofgren, *Plessy*, 47, 67, 79; Maltz, "'Separate but Equal'," 568; Kull, *Color-Blind Constitution*, 88–89, 96, 116; Riegel, "Persistent Career of Jim Crow," 20, 39–40; Welke, "When All the Women Were White," 296; Minter, "Codification of Jim Crow," 23. But see Bernstein, "Case Law in *Plessy*," 192–98.

36. Day v. Owen, 5 Mich. 520 (1858); West Chester and Philadelphia v. Miles, 55 Pa. 209 (1867); Gray v. Cincinnati Southern Railroad, 11 F. 683 (C.C.S.D. Ohio 1882); Murphy v. Western & Atlantic Railroad, 23 F. 637 (C.C.E.D. Tenn. 1885); Houck v. Southern Pacific Railway, 38 F. 226 (C.C.W.D. Tex. 1888); Cooley, *Law of Torts*, 282–84; Lofgren, *Plessy*, chap. 6; Maltz, "'Separate but Equal'," 553–58; Minter, "Codification of Jim Crow," 14–23, 31–33, 41–42, 74–83, 107–8; Welke, "When All the Women Were White"; Pingrey, "Racial Discrimination," 92; Stephenson, *Race Distinctions*, 211–14.

37. United States v. Dodge, 25 F. 882 (W.D. Tex. 1877); Smoot v. Kentucky Central Railway, 13 F. 337 (C.C.D. Ky. 1882) (dicta); United States v. Washington, 20 F. 630 (C.C.W.D. Tex. 1883) (dicta); Hall v. DeCuir, 95 U.S. 485, 504 (1878) (Clifford, J., concurring); Council v. Western & Atlantic Railroad, 1 I.C.C. 638 (1887); Lofgren, *Plessy*, 134–35, 141–44, 238 n. 45; Riegel, "Persistent Career of Jim Crow," 25, 30–35; Singer, "No Right to Exclude," 1384; Minter, "Codification of Jim Crow," 42–45, 112. But cf. McConnell, "Originalism and the Desegregation Decisions," 990–97, 1002–4, 1013–14, 1022–23, 1073–77, 1099–1100.

38. The rights-privileges distinction permits government to place otherwise unconstitutional restrictions on benefits that it provides as a matter of discretion, not right. In Holmes's famous dictum, the state can restrain a police officer's speech in otherwise unconstitutional ways because, though he may have a right to free speech, he has no right to be a police officer.

39. Maltz, "Only Partially Color Blind," 992; Pace v. Alabama, 106 U.S. 583 (1883); Kull, *Color-Blind Constitution*, 116; Lofgren, *Plessy*, 78; page 26.

40. Holden v. Hardy, 169 U.S. 366, 398 (1898); Collins, *Fourteenth Amendment*, 109; Lofgren, *Plessy*, 79–80, 84–88, 92, 94, 183–84; Fiss, *Troubled Beginnings of the Modern State*, 363–64; Lund, "Constitution, the Supreme Court, and Racial Politics," 1137, 1143–44; Gillman, *Constitution Besieged*, chap. 2; Nelson, *Fourteenth Amendment*, 121–22, 150–51, 175–96.

41. *Plessy*, 163 U.S. at 544; Riegel, "Persistent Career of Jim Crow," 20, 37–40; Lofgren, Plessy, 92, 145, 200, 242 n. 68; Kull, *Color-Blind Constitution*, 88–89, 116; Cobb, "Segregating the New South," 1035. But see Schmidt, "Principle and Prejudice, Part I," 461; Olsen, *Thin Disguise*, 5–7, 17; Harris, *Quest for Equality*, 101; Oberst, "Strange Career of *Plessy*," 410–11.

42. Plessy v. Ferguson, 163 U.S. 537, 544, 551 (1896).

43. Stone, *American Race Problem*, 64; Fishel, "The North and the Negro," 396–97; Baker, *Following the Color Line*, 305; Brundage, *Lynching in the New South*, 126–27, 156, 200, 209; Cell, *Highest Stage of White Supremacy*, 19, 30–31, 174–80; Ayers, *Promise of the New South*, 432; Fredrickson, *Black Image in the White Mind*, 293–94; Baker, "Segregation of White and Colored Passengers on Interstate Trains," 445; Woodward, "Case of the Louisiana Traveler," 153–54; pages 12–15.

44. Allen v. Davis, 10 Weekly Notes of Cases 156 (Crawford County, Pa., 1881); Coger v. North Western Union Packet Co., 37 Iowa 145 (1873); King v. Gallagher, 93 N.Y. 438, 457 (1883) (Danforth, J., dissenting); Kull, *Color-Blind Constitution*, 99–100, 108. Brewer was absent, but independent evidence suggests he would have voted with the majority. But cf. Hylton, "The Judge Who Abstained in *Plessy v. Ferguson*," 329–32, 336–44.

45. Mangum, *Legal Status of the Negro*, chap. 3; Stephenson, *Race Distinctions*, 121–24, 129–30, 132; Grossman, *Democratic Party and the Negro*, 63–106; Gerber, *Black Ohio*, 41, 45, 49, 57–58, 236, 459; Thornbrough, *Negro in Indiana*, 259–66; Katzman, *Before the Ghetto*, 91, 96–97; Fishel, "The North and the Negro," 4, 278–79, 380–84, 433 n. 268, 501; Singer, "No Right to Exclude," 1374–77; Weaver, "Failure of Civil Rights," 374–77; McCoy, "False Promises"; Avins, "De Facto and De Jure School Segregation," 236–37; McPherson, *Abolitionist Legacy*, 115–16. But see Olsen, *Thin Disguise*, 8.

46. McPherson, *Abolitionist Legacy*, 314; Stone, *American Race Problem*, 5–10, 13, 52, 346–48; Fishel, "Negro in Northern Politics," 466; Grossman, *Democratic Party and the Negro*, 154–55; Gerber, *Black Ohio*, 235–36; Thornbrough, *Negro in Indiana*, 302.

47. Lofgren, Plessy, 197; Schmidt, "Principle and Prejudice, Part I," 469; Ely, *Melville W. Fuller*, 158. But see Olsen, *Thin Disguise*, 25, 123–30.

48. Berea College v. Kentucky, 211 U.S. 45 (1908); Blakeman, "Berea College," 4–5, 26 n. 45; Nelson, "Experiment in Interracial Education at Berea College," 23.

49. *Plessy*, 163 U.S. at 544, 551; Munn v. Illinois, 94 U.S. 113 (1877); Ribnik v. McBride, 277 U.S. 350 (1928); Tyson & Brother v. Banton, 273 U.S. 418 (1927); Gillman, *Constitution Besieged*, 68–69, 180; Cushman, *New Deal Court*, 48–52, 57; Brief for Plaintiff in Error, *Berea College v. Kentucky*, 9–10, 24–26; Berea College v. Kentucky, 211 U.S. 45, 68–69 (1908) (Harlan, J., dissenting); Schmidt, "Principle and Prejudice, Part I," 447–49; Stephenson, *Race Distinctions*, 154–59; Fiss, *Troubled Beginnings of the Modern State*, 370–72; Bernstein, "Philip Sober Controlling Philip Drunk: *Buchanan v. Warley*," 830–32; Bernstein, "*Plessy* versus *Lochner*," 100–101; Seidman, "*Brown* and *Miranda*," 695–97; Blakeman, "Berea College"; Heckman & Hall, "Berea College"; Nelson, "Experiment in Interracial Education at Berea College"; McPherson, *Abolitionist Legacy*, chap. 14.

50. Schmidt, "Principle and Prejudice, Part I," 449–51; Stephenson, *Race Distinctions*, 159–64, 184; Gerber, *Black Ohio*, 266–67; Douglas, "Limits of Law," 684–97, 701–4; Meier & Rudwick, "Alton, Illinois, Case"; Meier & Rudwick, "East Orange,

New Jersey, Experience"; Meier & Rudwick, *Along the Color Line*, 310; Jelks, "Struggle against Jim Crow in Grand Rapids"; Spear, *Black Chicago*, 23, 45, 85–86; Baker, *Following the Color Line*, 123, 229; Gould, *Theodore Roosevelt*, 257–61; Blakeman, "Berea College," 21, 23–24; *Indianapolis Freeman*, 5 Dec. 1908, p. 6; Bernstein, "*Plessy* versus *Lochner*," 106–7.

51. Ely, *Melville W. Fuller*, 159; Ho Ak Kow v. Nunan, 5 Saw. 562 (C.C.D. Calif. 1879) (Justice Field on circuit); *Berea College*, 211 U.S. at 62–67 (Harlan, J., dissenting); Gillman, *Constitution Besieged*, 106–9; Bernstein, "Philip Sober Controlling Philip Drunk: *Buchanan v. Warley*," 832–33; Bernstein, "*Plessy* versus *Lochner*," 102–4, 107; Kull, *Color-Blind Constitution*, 134; Fiss, *Troubled Beginnings of the Modern State*, 370–71; Schmidt, "Principle and Prejudice, Part I," 447, 452.

52. Scheiner, "Theodore Roosevelt and the Negro," 181; Muller v. Oregon, 208 U.S. 412 (1908); Holden v. Hardy, 169 U.S. 366 (1898); Lofgren, Plessy, 110; Mangum, *Legal Status of the Negro*, 239–40; Brief for the Defendant in Error, *Berea College v. Kentucky*, 2, 4, 6–12, 39; Berea College v. Kentucky, 94 S.W. 623, 624–27 (Ky. Ct. App. 1906); Note, "Color Line in Private Schools," 218.

53. Kousser, *Dead End*, 21; Reynolds v. Board of Education, 72 P. 274, 281 (Kans. 1903).

54. Thornbrough, *Negro in Indiana*, 161–66, 317–23; Ment, "Racial Segregation in the Public Schools," 1, 12–16, 19, 82–200; Litwack, *North of Slavery*, chap. 4; Levy, *Chief Justice Shaw*, 116; Fishel, "The North and the Negro," 169–255; Gerber, *Black Ohio*, 190–91; Berwanger, "Reconstruction on the Frontier," 318, 326; Mabee, "Long Island's Black 'School War'"; Price, "School Segregation in Nineteenth-Century Pennsylvania"; Bridges, "Equality Deferred," 87, 96; Kousser, *Dead End*, 20, 38 n. 28; McConnell, "Originalism and the Desegregation Decisions," 967–71.

55. Foner, *Reconstruction*, 96, 320–22, 332, 365–68, 553–54, 592–93; Harlan, "Desegregation in New Orleans Public Schools"; Fischer, *Segregation Struggle in Louisiana*, chaps. 5, 6; Vaughn, *Schools for All*, 55, 57, 85–102; Franklin, "Jim Crow Goes to School," 230–31, 233–34; Tindall, *South Carolina Negroes*, 211; Wingo, "Race Relations in Georgia," 194–95; Cartwright, *Triumph of Jim Crow*, 18, 107, 182; Wright, *Blacks in Louisville*, 65; Anderson, *Race and Politics in North Carolina*, 329; Homel, "Two Worlds of Race?" 239–40.

56. McConnell, "Originalism and the Desegregation Decisions," 960, 962, 965–67, 1036–40; Kelly, "Congressional Controversy over School Segregation"; Fairman, *Reconstruction and Reunion*, 1177–79, 1193; Berger, *Government by Judiciary*, chap. 7; Bickel, "Original Understanding and the Segregation Decision," 56, 59; Avins, "De Facto and De Jure School Segregation," 244–46; Maltz, "'Separate but Equal'," 567; Maltz, "Civil Rights Act," 616; Maltz, "Originalism and the Desegregation Decisions," 228–31; *Congressional Globe*, 39th Cong., 1st sess., 1866, 500 (Edgar Cowan); ibid., 1117, 1118 (James Wilson); ibid., 1121–22 (Andrew Rogers); ibid., 1268 (Michael Kerr). But cf. McConnell, "Originalism and the Desegregation Decisions," 1120–31.

57. Bertonneau v. Board of Education, 3 F. Cas. 294 (C.C.D. La. 1878); United States v. Buntin, 10 F. 730 (1882); King v. Gallagher, 93 N.Y. 438 (1883); Garnes v. McCann, 21 Ohio State 198 (1871); Cory v. Carter, 48 Ind. 327 (1874); Lehew v. Brummell, 103 Mo. 551 (1891); Stoutmeyer v. Duffy, 7 Nev. 342 (1872); Ward v. Flood, 48 Calif. 36 (1874); Kousser, *Dead End*; Kull, *Color-Blind Constitution*, 95–112; McConnell, "Originalism and the Desegregation Decisions," 971–77; Mangum, *Legal Status of the Negro*, 78–119; Stephenson, *Race Distinctions*, 177–90.

58. Allen v. Davis, 10 Weekly Notes of Cases 156 (Crawford County, Pa., 1881); Tinnon v. Board of Education, 26 Kans. 1 (1881); Clark v. Board of Directors, 24 Iowa 266 (1868); Workman v. Detroit, 18 Mich. 399 (1869); Longress v. Board of Education of Quincy, 101 Ill. 308 (1882); Going, "Blair Education Bill"; Gatewood, "North Carolina and Federal Aid to Education." But cf. Kousser, *Dead End*, 10–12.

59. Fishel, "The North and the Negro," chaps. 4, 5, 7; Grossman, *Democratic Party and the Negro*, 66, 70, 75, 81, 87–92; Gerber, *Black Ohio*, 45, 56–57, 190–244; Douglas, "Limits of Law," 684–97. But cf. McConnell, "Originalism and the Desegregation Decisions," 970; Ment, "Racial Segregation in the Public Schools," 145–46.

60. People v. City of Alton, 54 N.E. 421, 428 (Ill. 1899); Foner, *Reconstruction*, 31–32; Gerber, *Black Ohio*, 26–30, 41; Thornbrough, *Negro in Indiana*, 184–91; Fredrickson, *Black Image in the White Mind*, 133–34; Bridges, "Equality Deferred," 84; Crew, *Black Life in Secondary Cities*, 125–27; Grossman, *Democratic Party and the Negro*, 100–101; page 12.

61. Gerber, *Black Ohio*, 211–12, 230–31, 235–43, 331, 333–34, 338; Grossman, *Democratic Party and the Negro*, chap. 3; Katzman, *Before the Ghetto*, 180; Bridges, "Equality Deferred," 104–8; Meier & Rudwick, "East Orange, New Jersey, Experience," 25, 31; Meier & Rudwick, "Alton, Illinois, Case," 395; Portwood, "Alton School Case," 3; pages 14–15.

62. Douglas, "Limits of Law," 687–89, 694–95; Fishel, "The North and the Negro," chaps. 4, 5; Gerber, *Black Ohio*, 41, 53, 56, 190–97, 271, 274–76; Hendrick, "Equality of Educational Opportunity in California," 24–25; Ment, "Racial Segregation in the Public Schools," 78–81, 99–101, 136–37, 158; *Cleveland Gazette*, 16 Feb. 1884, p. 2; ibid., 7 June 1884, p. 2; Chase v. Stephenson, 71 Ill. 383 (1874).

63. Price, "School Segregation in Nineteenth-Century Pennsylvania," 135–37; Ment, "Racial Segregation in the Public Schools," 149, 153, 169–70, 180, 183, 282, 286; Douglas, "Limits of Law," 684–97; Gerber, *Black Ohio*, 57, 265–66; Fishel, "The North and the Negro," 183–84, 317–25; Meier & Rudwick, "East Orange, New Jersey, Experience," 29; Meier & Rudwick, "Alton, Illinois, Case," 395; Du Bois, *Philadelphia Negro*, 349; Homel, "Two Worlds of Race?" 242; *Nation* 58 (15 Feb. 1894): 112.

64. *Crisis* 3 (Dec. 1911): 58; Yarbrough, *Judicial Enigma*, 228; Schmidt, "Principle and Prejudice, Part I," 472; Fiss, *Troubled Beginnings of the Modern State*, 369; Berea College v. Kentucky, 211 U.S. 45, 58 (1908) (Harlan, J., dissenting); Maltz, "Only Partially Color Blind," 990–91. But see Kull, *Color-Blind Constitution*, 124–29. See also Yarbrough, *John Marshall Harlan*, 121–23; Bernstein, "*Plessy* versus *Lochner*," 105–6; Frankfurter to Harlan, 6 July 1956, Box 485, Harlan Papers, Princeton University Library; Frankfurter to Harlan, 18 July 1956, ibid.; Frankfurter to Harlan, 31 July 1956, ibid.

65. Litwack, *North of Slavery*, 75, 263; Grossman, *Democratic Party and the Negro*, 16; Woodward, *Strange Career of Jim Crow*, 20.

66. Gillette, *Right to Vote*, chap. 1; Mathews, *Fifteenth Amendment*, 11–14, 17–18, 22; Bond, "Original Understanding of the Fourteenth Amendment," 445–53; Fishel, "Northern Prejudice and Negro Suffrage"; Fredrickson, *Black Image in the White Mind*, 183–86; Gerber, *Black Ohio*, 35–37; Thornbrough, *Negro in Indiana*, 239–41; Berwanger, "Reconstruction on the Frontier"; Hiller, "Disfranchisement of Delaware Negroes," 125–27; Foner, *Reconstruction*, 223–24; McMillen, *Dark Journey*, 36–37; Amar, "Jury Service as Political Participation," 223–26.

67. Foner, *Reconstruction*, 251–69; Maltz, *Civil Rights, the Constitution and Congress*, 36–37, 50, 122–23; James, *Ratification of the Fourteenth Amendment*, 24,

42–43, 47–48; Fairman, *Reconstruction and Reunion*, 253–58; Fishel, "Northern Prejudice and Negro Suffrage."

68. Fairman, *Reconstruction and Reunion*, 259–309; Maltz, *Civil Rights, the Constitution and Congress*, 124–41; Foner, *Reconstruction*, 271–80.

69. "Republican Platform of 1868," in *National Party Platforms*, ed. Johnson & Porter, 39; Foner, *Reconstruction*, 315, 445–49; Fishel, "The North and the Negro," 104–24; Gerber, *Black Ohio*, 38–40; Thornbrough, *Negro in Indiana*, 241–49; Gillette, *Right to Vote*, 92, 101–3, 113–47; Maltz, *Civil Rights, the Constitution and Congress*, 121–56; Cox & Cox, "Negro Suffrage and Republican Politics"; Mathews, *Fifteenth Amendment*, 20–21, 60–63, 73; Bridges, "Equality Deferred," 90–93. See also Goldman, "*A Free Ballot and a Fair Count*," 6–10.

70. Foner, *Reconstruction*, 291, 294, 351–58; Wharton, *Negro in Mississippi*, 167–69, 176, 179; McMillen, *Dark Journey*, 37; Tindall, *South Carolina Negroes*, 8–9; Williamson, *After Slavery*, 330; Rabinowitz, *First New South*, 75–76.

71. Foner, *Reconstruction*, 422–44, 550–63; Gillette, *Retreat from Reconstruction*, 104–65, 306–23; Wharton, *Negro in Mississippi*, chap. 13; Williamson, *South Carolina Negroes*, 266–73, 343, 357, 360; Williams, *Ku Klux Klan Trials*, 127–30; Cresswell, *Multi-Party Politics in Mississippi*, 14–17; Kantrowitz, *Ben Tillman*, 64–76; Benedict, "Politics of Reconstruction," 57, 70–71.

72. Anderson, *Race and Politics in North Carolina*, 4–5, 43, 64, 66, 106–7, 187, 238, 245, 247, 250–51, 276, 333, 340–41; Cartwright, *Triumph of Jim Crow*, 65–66, 71–72, 78–80, 83, 101; Rice, *Negro in Texas*, chap. 6; Kousser, *Shaping of Southern Politics*, 15 table 1.2, 28, 106–7, 130; Woodward, *Strange Career of Jim Crow*, 32–33; Cresswell, *Multi-Party Politics in Mississippi*, 17, 42–43; Tindall, *South Carolina Negroes*, 54, 58–59; Wharton, *Negro in Mississippi*, 202; Fischer, *Segregation Struggle in Louisiana*, 152–53; Wynes, *Race Relations in Virginia*, 42–43; Meier, *Negro Thought in America*, 37; Nieman, "Black Political Power and Criminal Justice," 395–96.

73. Kousser, *Shaping of Southern Politics*, 36, 99, 107–8, 153–54, 157; Wynes, *Race Relations in Virginia*, 41; DeSantis, *Republicans Face the Southern Question*, 191; Anderson, *Race and Politics in North Carolina*, 145; Cartwright, *Triumph of Jim Crow*, 95–97, 199–202, 216, 237; Cresswell, *Multi-Party Politics in Mississippi*, 215.

74. *Crisis* 2 (June 1911): 60; Kousser, *Shaping of Southern Politics*, 3, 39–40, 50, 99, 127, 147, 161–62, 174–75, 189–90, 203, 243, 246; Perman, *Struggle for Mastery*, 5–6, 11–12; Anderson, *Race and Politics in North Carolina*, 185, 296; Cresswell, *Multi-Party Politics in Mississippi*, 220; Tindall, *South Carolina Negroes*, 68–71, 88–89; Rice, *Negro in Texas*, 113–14, 130–39; Cell, *Highest Stage of White Supremacy*, 185. See also pages 54–55.

75. Rose, "Negro Suffrage," 18, 26–32; Ratliff v. Beale, 74 Miss. 247, 266 (1896); Stephenson, *Race Distinctions*, chap. 11; Kousser, *Shaping of Southern Politics*, chaps. 2–3; Perman, *Struggle for Mastery*, esp. 19–20, 321–24; Ogden, *Poll Tax in the South*, chaps. 1–2; Hackney, *Populism to Progressivism in Alabama*, chap. 9; Tindall, *South Carolina Negroes*, chap. 5; Woodward, *Origins of the New South*, 330–38; Callcott, *Negro in Maryland Politics*, chap. 5; Lewinson, *Race, Class, and Party*, chaps. 4–5.

76. Kousser, *Shaping of Southern Politics*, 32, 41–42, 67 table 3.2, 91 table 4.3, 196–97, 210–11, 238, 239 table 9.1; Perman, *Struggle for Mastery*, chaps. 3–5, 7–10, 13; Cohen, *At Freedom's Edge*, 205, 209 table 8; Tindall, *South Carolina Negroes*, 69–70.

77. Kousser, *Shaping of Southern Politics*, 32, 140, 152, 238; Wharton, *Negro in Mississippi*, 182, 197–98, 208–9; Lewinson, *Race, Class, and Party*, 86–87; Cresswell, *Multi-Party Politics in Mississippi*, 102; Anderson, *Race and Politics in North Car-*

olina, 145, 165; Cartwright, *Triumph of Jim Crow*, 91 n. 69, 208; Fredrickson, *Black Image in the White Mind*, 262; Welch, "Federal Elections Bill," 512, 526; Perman, *Struggle for Mastery*, 38–41; Goldman, "A Free Ballot and a Fair Count," 190; Ogden, *Poll Tax in the South*, 29–30; Dephloff & Jones, "Race Relations in Louisiana," 321; *Nation* 51 (31 July 1890): 86–87.

78. Populism was a political movement rooted primarily in the South and the West, which championed the interests of poor farmers by supporting inflationary monetary policies, government regulation of railroads, and subsidies for agriculture.

79. Woodward, *Origins of the New South*, 261–62, 275–77, 322, 343–44; Kousser, *Shaping of Southern Politics*, 16–17, 36–37, 40, 43, 68–70, 91, 131, 157–59, 175, 203, 215–16; Anderson, *Race and Politics in North Carolina*, chaps. 11, 12, 14; Hackney, *Populism to Progressivism in Alabama*, 22, 36, 42–43, 47, 62–63, 151–52, 177; Rice, *Negro in Texas*, chap. 5; Goodwyn, "Populist Dreams and Negro Rights"; Cantrell & Barton, "Texas Populists," 660, 683, 687–91; Ogden, *Poll Tax in the South*, chap. 1; Cell, *Highest Stage of White Supremacy*, 119–22, 152–54, 170; Ayers, *Promise of the New South*, 269–76, 304; Lewinson, *Race, Class, and Party*, 74–76; Rabinowitz, *First New South*, 101–12; Mabry, "Louisiana Politics and the 'Grandfather Clause'," 291–92; Taylor, "Populism and Disfranchisement in Alabama," 410, 414–20; Mabry, "Ben Tillman Disfranchised the Negro," 171–73, 182; Stone, *American Race Problem*, 261–71.

80. Lewinson, *Race, Class, and Party*, 81, 104, 106, 123, 144; Kousser, *Shaping of Southern Politics*, 101 table 4.10, 145 table 6.3, 163 table 6.6, 223; Rabinowitz, *First New South*, 114–15; Woodward, *Strange Career of Jim Crow*, 342–44; Grantham, "Georgia Politics and the Disfranchisement of the Negro," 20; Lewis, *In Their Own Interests*, 21; Cresswell, *Multi-Party Politics in Mississippi*, 109, 220; Ogden, *Poll Tax in the South*, 115–17.

81. Klarman, "Political Process Theory," 789–807; Wharton, *Negro in Mississippi*, 134, 176; Tindall, *South Carolina Negroes*, 58–59; Cresswell, *Multi-Party Politics in Mississippi*, 142; Anderson, *Race and Politics in North Carolina*, 4–5, 54, 187, 245, 248–51, 315–19; Foner, *Reconstruction*, 355–57, 362–63, 590–92, 595; Rabinowitz, *Race Relations in the Urban South*, 36–42, 266, 277; Rice, *Negro in Texas*, 86–112, 240–41; Nieman, "Black Political Power and Criminal Justice"; Wharton, *Negro in Mississippi*, 167–68; Wynes, *Race Relations in Virginia*, 25–26, 29–30; Cartwright, *Triumph of Jim Crow*, 119, 128–30, 147–50; Pincus, *Virginia Supreme Court*, 47; pages 42–47.

82. U.S. Constitution, Amend. XV, § 1; *Nation* 90 (7 Apr. 1910): 334; Tindall, "South Carolina Constitutional Convention of 1895," 283; Kousser, *Shaping of Southern Politics*, 45–46; Stephenson, *Race Distinctions*, 319–20; Callcott, *Negro in Maryland Politics*, 130–32; Porter v. Commissioners of Kingfisher County, 51 P. 741 (Okla. 1898); Howell v. Pate, 119 Ga. 537 (1904).

83. Eaton, "Suffrage Clause in the New Constitution of Louisiana," 281–82, 288, 289; Rose, "Negro Suffrage," 19; Buck, *Road to Reunion*, 287; Ratliff v. Beal, 74 Miss. 247, 266 (1896); Poe, "Suffrage Restrictions," 534–37; Callcott, *Negro in Maryland Politics*, 122; Collins, *Fourteenth Amendment*, 141–44; Hackney, *Populism to Progressivism in Alabama*, 190–91; Mabry, "Disfranchisement of the Negro in Mississippi," 329; Tindall, *South Carolina Negroes*, 85–86; Perman, *Struggle for Mastery*, 28; Mabry, "Louisiana Politics and the 'Grandfather Clause'," 309; *Baltimore Sun*, 3 Feb. 1908, p. 12; *Nation* 61 (19 Sept. 1895): 199; ibid. 8 (18 Feb. 1869): 124.

84. *Congressional Globe*, 40th Cong., 3d sess., 1869, 863; Maltz, *Civil Rights, the Constitution and Congress*, 142–56; Gillette, *Right to Vote*, 46–78; Mathews, *Fifteenth*

Amendment, 24, 32–36, 41–46; Rose, "Negro Suffrage," 23–24; Stone v. Smith, 34 N.E. 521 (Mass. 1893).

85. Brief of Plaintiff in Error, *Williams v. Mississippi*, 4–6, 15–17; Brief for Appellant, *Giles v. Harris*, 10–13; Yick Wo v. Hopkins, 118 U.S. 356, 373–74 (1886).

86. Williams v. Mississippi, 170 U.S. 213 (1898); Fletcher v. Peck, 6 Cranch 87, 130 (1810); Barbier v. Connolly, 113 U.S. 27 (1885); *Congressional Globe*, 40th Cong., 3d sess., 1869, 863 (Oliver P. Morton); ibid., 1009 (Jacob M. Howard and William M. Stewart). See also McCray v. United States, 195 U.S. 27, 56 (1904); Ex parte McCardle, 7 Wall. 506, 514 (1868); Cooley, *Constitutional Limitations*, 257–59.

87. McCulloch v. Maryland, 4 Wheat. 316, 422 (1819); Cummings v. State of Maryland, 4 Wall. 277 (1866); Ex parte Garland, 4 Wall. 333 (1866); Ho Ah Kow v. Nunan, 12 Fed. Cas. 252 (C.C.D. Calif. 1879); McClain, *In Search of Equality*, 47, 53–54, 73–76. See also Hammer v. Dagenhart, 247 U.S. 251 (1918); Powell v. Pennsylvania, 127 U.S. 678, 695 (1887) (Field, J., dissenting).

88. Yick Wo v. Hopkins, 118 U.S. 356 (1886).

89. Mabry, "Louisiana Politics and the 'Grandfather Clause'," 300, 304, 309; Williams v. Mississippi, 170 U.S. at 223–25; McMillen, *Dark Journey*, 42; *Nation* 51 (4 Sept. 1890): 183–84; Kousser, *Shaping of Southern Politics*, 58 n. 29, 59 n. 31; Woodward, *Origins of the New South*, 332–33, 341; Mabry, "Ben Tillman Disfranchised the Negro," 180; Schmidt, "Juries, Jurisdiction, and Race Discrimination," 1469; Kantrowitz, *Ben Tillman*, 227–28.

90. *Williams*, 170 U.S. at 225; *Yick Wo*, 118 U.S. at 373–74; Mangum, *Legal Status of the Negro*, 395.

91. Giles v. Harris, 189 U.S. 475, 486–88 (1903); Giles v. Teasley, 193 U.S. 146, 164–66 (1904).

92. Fiss, *Troubled Beginnings of the Modern State*, 376–79; Rose, "Negro Suffrage," 39; Schmidt, "Principle and Prejudice, Part III," 847, 849–50; Ex parte Milligan, 71 U.S. (4 Wall.) 2, 109 (1866); Korematsu v. United States, 323 U.S. 214, 242 (1944) (Jackson, J., dissenting).

93. *Nation* 90 (7 Apr. 1910): 334; ibid. 87 (19 Nov. 1908): 480–81; *Crisis* 9 (Feb. 1915): 177–78; Blakeman, "Berea College," 23–24; Mills v. Green, 159 U.S. 651 (1895); Jones v. Montague, 194 U.S. 147 (1904); Selden v. Montague, 194 U.S. 154 (1904); Mangum, *Legal Status of the Negro*, 400.

94. James v. Bowman, 190 U.S. 127 (1903); United States v. Cruikshank, 92 U.S. 542 (1875); Civil Rights Cases, 109 U.S. 3 (1883); United States v. Harris, 106 U.S. 629 (1883).

95. Given v. United States, 25 F. Cas. 1324 (C.C.D. Del. 1873); United States v. Canter, 25 F. Cas. 281 (C.C.S.D. Ohio 1870); United States v. Hall, 26 F. Cas. 701 (C.C.S.D. Ala. 1871) (Judge Woods); United States v. Crosby, 25 F. Cas. 701 (1871) (by implication); United States v. Cruikshank, 25 F. Cas. 707, 713–14 (C.C.D. La. 1874), 92 U.S. 542, 556 (1875); Mathews, *Fifteenth Amendment*, 104–14; Mangum, *Legal Status of the Negro*, 381; Benedict, "Preserving Federalism," 71–75; Ex parte Yarbrough, 110 U.S. 651 (1884); Ex parte Siebold, 100 U.S. 371 (1880); Karem v. United States, 121 F. 256 (6th Cir. 1903); United States v. Amsden, 6 F. 819 (D.C.D. Ind. 1881).

96. Poe, "Suffrage Restrictions," 537–41; "The Grandfather Clause," *NYT*, 23 June 1915, p. 10; Cecelski & Tyson, *Democracy Betrayed*, 4–5; Prather, "'We Have Taken a City'," 31–39; Kousser, *Shaping of Southern Politics*, 258, 262–63; Fiss, *Troubled Beginnings of the Modern State*, 379; Stone, *American Race Problem*, 420; Mangum, *Legal Status of the Negro*, 388, 394; Gleijeses, "African Americans and the

War against Spain," 199–200; Meier, *Negro Thought in America*, 35–36, 214–15; Hackney, *Populism to Progressivism in Alabama*, 175–77, 186; Dittmer, *Black Georgia*, 99–101; Mabry, "Disfranchisement of the Negro in Mississippi," 319–20; Woodward, *Origins of the New South*, 326–27, 347–48; Lewinson, *Race, Class, and Party*, 88–89; Gilmore, *Gender and Jim Crow*, 123–24; *Nation* 61 (19 Sept. 1895): 199.

97. *Nation* 66 (26 May 1898): 398–99; ibid. 53 (16 July 1891): 46–47; ibid. 61 (31 Oct. 1895): 302; Kousser, *Shaping of Southern Politics*, 251–54; Kraditor, *Ideas of the Woman Suffrage Movement*, 126–32; McPherson, *Abolitionist Legacy*, 125; Hackney, *Populism to Progressivism in Alabama*, 159–60; Woodward, *Origins of the New South*, 324–25; Stone, *American Race Problem*, 412–13; Perman, *Struggle for Mastery*, 238; Poe, "Suffrage Restrictions," 542; pages 12–15.

98. Stone, *American Race Problem*, 351 (quotation), 353, 415–20; Baker, *Following the Color Line*, 240, 302–3; Keller, *Regulating a New Society*, 255–56; McPherson, *Abolitionist Legacy*, 112, 313, 354–55; Wang, *Trial of Democracy*, 254–57, 261; Perman, *Struggle for Mastery*, 30, 43–47, 224–31, 234–44; "Republican Platform of 1904," in *National Party Platforms*, ed. Johnson & Porter, 139; Bayer, "Apportionment Section of the Fourteenth Amendment," 965–66, 974; Garner, "Fourteenth Amendment and Southern Representation"; "The Fourteenth Amendment," *Crisis* 10 (May 1915): 28.

99. Mathews, *Fifteenth Amendment*, 126; Cobb, "Segregating the New South," 1030; Garner, "Commentary," 831.

100. Litwack, *North of Slavery*, 94, 96; Rabinowitz, *Race Relations in the Urban South*, 38–39; McCaul, *Black Struggle for Public Schooling*, 100; Thornbrough, *Negro in Indiana*, 271; Gerber, *Black Ohio*, 40; Mangum, *Legal Status of the Negro*, 311; Wharton, *Negro in Mississippi*, 135–37; Nieman, "Black Political Power and Criminal Justice," 399 table 1; Wynes, *Race Relations in Virginia*, 25–26; Tindall, *South Carolina Negroes*, 263–64; Callcott, *Negro in Maryland Politics*, 61–63; Strauder v. West Virginia, 100 U.S. 303 (1880); Bush v. Kentucky, 107 U.S. 110 (1883).

101. Anderson, *Race and Politics in North Carolina*, 317–19; Stephenson, *Race Distinctions*, 253–71; Cartwright, *Triumph of Jim Crow*, 176–77; Wynes, *Race Relations in Virginia*, 138; Rice, *Negro in Texas*, 255–57; Gilmore, *Gender and Jim Crow*, 84; Nieman, "Black Political Power and Criminal Justice," 400–401.

102. Bickel, "Original Understanding and the Segregation Decision," 62; Schmidt, "Juries, Jurisdiction, and Race Discrimination," 1423–24; Maltz, *Civil Rights, the Constitution and Congress*, 67–68, 147–55; Bond, "Original Understanding and the Fourteenth Amendment," 446–47; Maltz, "Civil Rights Act," 623–25; Gillette, *Right to Vote*, 50, 60–61, 68, 71, 77–78; Foner, *Reconstruction*, 423–24; *Congressional Globe*, 40th Cong., 3d sess., 1869, 1296 (Henry Wilson); Ex parte Virginia, 100 U.S. 339, 365–68 (1880) (Field, J., dissenting); NYT, 15 Feb. 1869, p. 4. But see Amar, "Jury Service as Political Participation," 228–34.

103. Maltz, "Originalism and the Desegregation Decisions," 227–28; McConnell, "Originalism and the Desegregation Decisions," 1024 n. 365; Schmidt, "Juries, Jurisdiction, and Race Discrimination," 1427–28; *Congressional Globe*, 42d Cong., 2d sess., 1872, 843 (Sen. Carpenter); ibid., 844 (Sen. Sherman).

104. Strauder v. West Virginia, 100 U.S. 303, 306–10 (1880); Schmidt, "Juries, Jurisdiction, and Race Discrimination," 1414, 1422–29, 1450–54; Bickel, "Original Understanding and the Segregation Decision," 64–65. See also Cresswell, "Case of Taylor Strauder."

105. Mississippi Code Ann. § 2358 (1892), reproduced in Williams v. Mississippi, 170 U.S. 213, 218–19 (1898); Eastling v. Arkansas, 62 S.W. 584, 587 (Ark. 1901); Neal v.

Delaware, 103 U.S. 370, 397 (1881); Schmidt, "Juries, Jurisdiction, and Race Discrimination," 1457–58.

106. Anderson, *Race and Politics in North Carolina*, 168–69, 242–48, 310–11; Wynes, *Race Relations in Virginia*, 45; Tindall, *South Carolina Negroes*, 58–67, 255; West, "Race War in North Carolina," 581–82, 590; Mabry, "North Carolina Suffrage Amendment," 2, 17; Cresswell, *Multi-Party Politics in Mississippi*, 142, 185; Gould, *Theodore Roosevelt*, 118–22; Stone, *American Race Problem*, chap. 7.

107. Thornbrough, *Negro in Indiana*, 395; Gerber, *Black Ohio*, 215–17, 338, 365; Crew, *Black Life in Secondary Cities*, 136–37; Katzman, *Before the Ghetto*, 204; Kusmer, *A Ghetto Takes Shape*, 64–65; Meier, *Negro Thought in America*, 163, 165; Scheiner, "Theodore Roosevelt and the Negro," 175–78; Dittmer, *Black Georgia*, 94, 106–7; Woodward, *Origins of the New South*, 462; NYT, 22 Nov. 1898, p. 6; *Nation* 76 (8 Jan. 1903): 21.

108. Mississippi Code Ann. § 2358 (1892), quoted in Schmidt, "Juries, Jurisdiction, and Race Discrimination," 1462–63, 1469–71; Smith v. Mississippi, 162 U.S. 592 (1896); Carter v. Texas, 177 U.S. 442 (1900); Rogers v. Alabama, 192 U.S. 226 (1904); Collins, *Fourteenth Amendment*, 76; Gibson v. Mississippi, 162 U.S. 565 (1896); Tarrance v. Florida, 188 U.S. 519 (1903); Brownfield v. South Carolina, 189 U.S. 426 (1903); Martin v. Texas, 200 U.S. 316 (1906); Thomas v. Texas, 212 U.S. 278 (1909); Franklin v. South Carolina, 218 U.S. 161 (1910).

109. Smith v. State, 77 S.W. 453, 454 (Tex. Crim. App. 1903); Royals v. State, 75 So. 199 (Fla. 1917); Thomas v. Texas, 212 U.S. 278 (1909); Virginia v. Rives, 100 U.S. 313 (1880); Schmidt, "Juries, Jurisdiction, and Race Discrimination," 1430–40, 1455, 1462–75, 1498; Mangum, *Legal Status of the Negro*, chap. 12; Stephenson, *Race Distinctions*, chap. 10; Collins, *Fourteenth Amendment*, 73–75; Thompson v. State, 74 S.W. 914 (Tex. Crim. App. 1903); Tarrance v. Florida, 30 So. 685 (Fla. 1901); State v. Daniels, 46 S.E. 743 (N.C. 1904); Haynes v. State, 72 So. 180 (Fla. 1916).

110. Schmidt, "Juries, Jurisdiction, and Race Discrimination," 1413, 1458, 1476–81; Eastling v. State, 62 S.W. 584 (Ark. 1901); State v. Baptiste, 30 So. 147 (La. 1901); Welch v. State, 236 P. 68 (Okla. 1925); Commonwealth v. Johnson, 78 Ky. 509 (1880); Gillespie, "Constitution and the All-White Jury," 68–71, 74–75; Norris v. Alabama, 294 U.S. 587 (1935); Pierre v. Louisiana, 306 U.S. 354, 358 (1939). But cf. Schmidt, "Juries, Jurisdiction, and Race Discrimination," 1482–95.

111. Callcott, *Negro in Maryland Politics*, 135; Barnes, *Journey from Jim Crow*, 15; Thomas, "Public Education and Black Protest in Baltimore," 387–88; Mangum, *Legal Status of the Negro*, 221–22; Minter, "Codification of Jim Crow," 144.

112. Westin, "The State and Segregated Schools," 5, 32–33, 39; Fischer, *Segregation Struggle in Louisiana*, 13, 27–28, 44; Howard, "Struggle for Equal Education in Kentucky," 307, 309, 315; Vaughn, *Schools for All*, 27–37; Rice, *Negro in Texas*, 211–12, 214; Wharton, *Negro in Mississippi*, 245; Wright, *Life behind a Veil*, 35; Foner, *Reconstruction*, 207–8; Callcott, *Negro in Maryland Politics*, 63–64.

113. Page 25.

114. Kousser, "Progressivism: For Middle-Class Whites Only," 173, 178–79; Franklin, "Jim Crow Goes to School," 227–28, 235; Tindall, *South Carolina Negroes*, 210–14; Homel, "Two Worlds of Race?" 247, 249; Rabinowitz, *Race Relations in the Urban South*, 170, 176, 178–81; Dailey, "Deference and Violence in the Postbellum Urban South," 568; Harris, "Stability and Change in Discrimination," 378; Vaughn, *Schools for All*, 43–48; Mangum, *Legal Status of the Negro*, 133; Anderson, *Education of Blacks in the South*, 22, 25, 96–97; Baker, *Following the Color Line*, 84–86, 247–48;

Harlan, *Separate and Unequal*, 40, 69–70; Westin, "The State and Segregated Schools," 100, 208.

115. Wingo, "Race Relations in Georgia," 185–92, 199–203 (quotation at 202); *Crisis* 1 (Jan. 1911): 7; Woodward, *Strange Career of Jim Crow*, 93–94; Wynes, *Race Relations in Virginia*, 122, 132, 134; Tindall, *South Carolina Negroes*, 213–14, 223; Wharton, *Negro in Mississippi*, 246; Harlan, *Separate and Unequal*, 40, 137–38; Haller, *Scientific Attitudes of Racial Inferiority*, chap. 2; Fredrickson, *Black Image in the White Mind*, chap. 8; Anderson, *Education of Blacks in the South*, 100–101.

116. Puitt v. Commissioners, 94 N.C. 709, 715 (1886); Riggsbee v. Town of Durham, 94 N.C. 800 (1886); Claybrook v. Owensboro, 16 F. 297 (D. Ky. 1883); Dawson v. Lee, 83 Ky. 49 (1885); Anderson, *Race and Politics in North Carolina*, 329; Howard, "Struggle for Equal Education in Kentucky," 321–23; Stephenson, *Race Distinctions*, 196–99; Westin, "The State and Segregated Schools," 61–66; Logan, "Public School Education for Negroes in North Carolina," 348, 352, 354–55.

117. Sisk, "Negro Education in the Alabama Black Belt," 128; Harlan, *Separate and Unequal*, 15–16, 61, 102–8, 139–44, 158–59, 174–75, 201, 228–29, 235–36; Westin, "The State and Segregated Schools," 67–71, 116–17, 138, 182, 192–93, 201–4; Wingo, "Race Relations in Georgia," 206–8, 215–16; Dittmer, *Black Georgia*, 116, 142–43; Tindall, *South Carolina Negroes*, 212; McMillen, *Dark Journey*, 75–76; Woodward, *Origins of the New South*, 405; Gilmore, *Gender and Jim Crow*, 158–59; Mangum, *Legal Status of the Negro*, 127–28; Logan, "Public School Education for Negroes in North Carolina," 352; *Crisis* 1 (Dec. 1910): 6. For denials of the claim that black education received more than the proportionate share of taxes paid by blacks, see Harlan, *Separate and Unequal*, 19; McMillen, *Dark Journey*, 77–79; Ayers, *Promise of the New South*, 419–20; Kousser, "Separate but *Not* Equal," 25–27.

118. Harlan, *Separate and Unequal*, 11, 14–15, 69, 74, 95, 106, 130–32 (quotation at 131), 162, 166–67, 176, 204–7, 246, 248–50, 254–55, 265, 269 table 17; Westin, "The State and Segregated Schools," chap. 4; Tindall, *South Carolina Negroes*, 221–23; McMillen, *Dark Journey*, 72–74; Franklin, "Jim Crow Goes to School," 235; Sisk, "Negro Education in the Alabama Black Belt," 129; Dittmer, *Black Georgia*, 143; Wingo, "Race Relations in Georgia," 212–15; Lowery v. Board of Graded School Trustees, 52 S.E. 267, 272 (N.C. 1905); Smith v. Board of Trustees, 53 S.E. 524, 530 (N.C. 1906).

119. Cumming v. Richmond County Board of Education, 29 S.E. 488 (Ga. 1898); aff'd, 175 U.S. 528, 544–45 (1899); Kousser, "Separate but *Not* Equal"; Schmidt, "Principle and Prejudice, Part I," 470–72.

The Court also disapproved of the remedy requested by the plaintiffs: the termination of public funding for the white high school. The justices professed themselves unable to see how reducing educational opportunities for whites would benefit blacks who were alleging discrimination.

120. Kull, *Color-Blind Constitution*, 3–4, 81–82, 114–15; King v. Gallagher, 93 N.Y. 437, 448–50 (1883); Tussman & tenbroek, "Equal Protection of the Laws," 343–44; *Cumming*, 29 S.E. at 490–91; Lofgren, *Plessy*, 190; Schmidt, "Principle and Prejudice, Part I," 468–70; Tushnet, *NAACP's Legal Strategy*, 22; Kousser, *Dead End*, 27–28; Seidman, "*Brown* and *Miranda*," 692.

121. *Cumming*, 175 U.S. at 542; Schmidt, "Juries, Jurisdiction, and Race Discrimination," 1497–98; *Congressional Globe*, 39th Cong., 1st sess., 1866, App. 219 (Sen. Timothy O. Howe); Mangum, *Legal Status of the Negro*, 89; Kousser, "Separate but *Not* Equal," 35–36; pages 21, 44, 76–79.

122. Anderson, *Education of Blacks in the South*, 33–78, 186, 188, 196–98; Harlan, *Separate and Unequal*, 133, 247, 256; Meier, *Negro Thought in America*, chap. 6; Westin, "The State and Segregated Schools," 196, 198; Homel, "Two Worlds of Race?" 251; Dittmer, *Black Georgia*, 146; Ayers, *Promise of the New South*, 322–23; Connally, "*Cumming v. Richmond County Board of Education*," 75–77.

123. Anderson, *Education of Blacks in the South*, 92–94, 226–29 (quotation at 226); Hackney, *Populism to Progressivism in Alabama*, 163; *Crisis* 2 (June 1911): 49; Baker, *Following the Color Line*, 304; Harlan, *Separate and Unequal*, chap. 3; Meier, *Negro Thought in America*, 85–99, 164–65; William Howard Taft, "Southern Democracy and Republican Principles," in Taft, *Present-Day Problems*, 225–26.

124. Olsen, *Thin Disguise*, 1, 17, 25; Wynes, *Race Relations in Virginia*, 76; Jones, "The Harlan Dissent," 951–54; Wasby, *Impact of the United States Supreme Court*, 171; Schmidt, "Principle and Prejudice, Part I," 470; Ely, *Melville W. Fuller*, 158; Fischer, *Segregation Struggle in Louisiana*, 154; Glasrud, "Jim Crow's Emergence in Texas," 52; Frank, "Can Courts Erase the Color Line?" 305; *Crisis* 8 (June 1914): 69; Lofgren, *Plessy*, 203; Mathews, "Keeping Down Jim Crow," 119–24; Tindall, *South Carolina Negroes*, 300; Minter, "Codification of Jim Crow," 174–75; Perman, *Struggle for Mastery*, 249–56.

125. Ayers, *Promise of the New South*, 327; pages 366–68, 464.

126. Gillette, *Retreat from Reconstruction*, chaps. 10–11; Foner, *Reconstruction*, 550–52; Valone, "Prejudice and Politics," 66, 81; Avins, "De Facto and De Jure School Segregation," 218–21, 226, 231; page 20.

127. McPherson, *Abolitionist Legacy*, 21–22; Valone, "Prejudice and Politics," 88–94, 105; Weaver, "Failure of Civil Rights," 368; Fischer, *Segregation Struggle in Louisiana*, 69–70, 81–85, 145; Fishel, "The North and the Negro," 373, 376–77; Gerber, *Black Ohio*, 48–49; Wright, *Life behind a Veil*, 56–59; Wynes, *Race Relations in Virginia*, 77–78; Wharton, *Negro in Mississippi*, 230–31; Foner, *Reconstruction*, 370–72; Williamson, *After Slavery*, 287; Mangum, *Legal Status of the Negro*, 33; *Charleston News & Courier*, 5 Nov. 1883, p. 2.

128. Gerber, *Black Ohio*, 258–62; Thornbrough, *Negro in Indiana*, 260–65; Fishel, "The North and the Negro," 378–82; Weaver, "Failure of Civil Rights," 374–77; *NYT*, 30 June 1895, p. 20; page 8; Lofgren, *Plessy*, 32; Riegel, "Persistent Career of Jim Crow," 21 n. 19, 24 n. 31; Fischer, *Segregation Struggle in Louisiana*, 69–71, 82–87; Somers, "Black and White in New Orleans," 25; Kelley, "*Plessy*," 22, 25; Dittmer, *Black Georgia*, 166–67, 172–74, 206–7; Mangum, *Legal Status of the Negro*, 113. See also Palmore, "Race, Transportation and the Dormant Commerce Clause," 1803–4.

129. Williamson, *After Slavery*, 274–99, esp. 298–99; Somers, "Black and White in New Orleans," 38; Woodward, *Origins of the New South*, 212; Stephenson, *Race Distinctions*, 5, 214–15, 238, 350–51; Mangum, *Legal Status of the Negro*, 57, 206–7, 215; Wharton, *Negro in Mississippi*, 232; McMillen, *Dark Journey*, 8–9; Rabinowitz, *Race Relations in the Urban South*, 182; Lofgren, *Plessy*, 9–17, 201; Doyle, *Etiquette of Race Relations in the South*, 146–49, 153; Chiles v. Chesapeake & Ohio Railway, 218 U.S. 71 (1910); Barnes, *Journey from Jim Crow*, 12; Palmore, "Race, Transportation, and the Dormant Commerce Clause," 1804–7. But cf. Jones, "Harlan Dissent," 955; Roback, "Political Economy of Segregation," 903–4, 912; Campbell, "Jim Crow Streetcars in Savannah," 202–3.

The Commerce Clause of the Constitution, which serves primarily as a grant of power to Congress, has long been interpreted by courts to also restrain states from legislating in ways that are deemed overly burdensome on interstate commerce.

130. "A Matter of Manners," *Crisis* 40 (Dec. 1933): 292–93; McMillen, *Dark Journey*, 23–28; Dailey, "Deference and Violence in the Postbellum Urban South," 558–61, 565, 572–75, 589; Doyle, *Etiquette of Race Relations in the South*, chap. 10; Dollard, *Caste and Class*, chap. 8; Powdermaker, *After Freedom*, 44–50.

131. Ayers, *Promise of the New South*, 432; Somers, "Black and White in New Orleans," 41–42; Schmidt, "Principle and Prejudice, Part III," 866; Garner, "Commentary," 830; Bassett, "Stirring Up the Fires," 302–4; Baker, *Following the Color Line*, 246, 254–59, 266; Wynes, "Evolution of Jim Crow Laws," 417, 420; Moore, "Jim Crow in Georgia," 561.

132. Heckman & Hall, "Berea College," 47.

133. Blakeman, "Berea College," 10; Heckman & Hall, "Berea College," 37–38, 42–43; Nelson, "Experiment in Interracial Education at Berea College," 17–24; *Nation* 87 (19 Nov. 1908): 480–81.

134. Williamson, *After Slavery*, 217–18, 290; Wynes, *Race Relations in Virginia*, 124–25; *Nation* 19 (17 Sept. 1874): 180; Kousser, *Dead End*, 5; Somers, "Black and White in New Orleans," 20; Brundage, *Lynching in the New South*, 25, 111–13; Wharton, *Negro in Mississippi*, 225; pages 351–54.

135. Kousser, *Dead End*; Douglas, "Limits of Law," 681–704; Price, "School Segregation in Nineteenth-Century Pennsylvania," 135; Longress v. Quincy, 101 Ill. 308 (1882); Dove v. Keokuk, 41 Iowa 689 (1875); Pierce v. Burlington, 46 N.J.L. 76 (1884); McConnell, "Originalism and the Desegregation Decisions," 975–76; Meier & Rudwick, "Alton, Illinois, Case," 400; Portwood, "Alton School Case," 19; Fishel, "The North and the Negro," 193–94, 207–8; Gerber, *Black Ohio*, 200–202, 205–6, 265; Meier, *Negro Thought in America*, 48–49; Ment, "Racial Segregation in the Public Schools," 156–58, 172, 282–83; Bustard, "The New Jersey Story," 275–76.

136. People ex rel. Bibb v. Alton, 179 Ill. 616 (1899), 193 Ill. 309 (1901), 209 Ill. 461 (1904), 221 Ill. 275 (1906), 233 Ill. 542 (1908); Meier & Rudwick, "Alton, Illinois, Case"; Portwood, "Alton School Case"; Kousser, *Dead End*, 36–37 n. 23; Douglas, "Limits of Law," 702–4; *New York Age*, 1 Oct. 1908, p. 1; page 25.

137. Miller, "A Negro's View," 1061; Mangum, *Legal Status of the Negro*, 394; pages 38–39. But see Pildes, "Democracy, Anti-Democracy, and the Canon," 311–17.

138. Perman, *Struggle for Mastery*, 21–22, 45–47; Goldman, "A Free Ballot and a Fair Count," 88; Wang, *Trial of Democracy*, 93–133; Rose, "Negro Suffrage," 41; Williams, *Ku Klux Klan Trials*, 2, 43–48, 100–102, 108, 112, 113, 122–27; Swinney, "Enforcing the Fifteenth Amendment"; Hall, "South Carolina Ku Klux Klan Trials"; Cresswell, "Enforcing the Enforcement Acts"; Lyons, "Ku Klux Klan Trials in North Carolina"; Schmidt, "Juries, Jurisdiction and Race Discrimination," 1408–9, 1417–18, 1450–54, 1495–96; Gillette, *Retreat from Reconstruction*, 42–45; Tindall, *South Carolina Negroes*, 72, 256–57.

139. Lewinson, *Race, Class, and Party*, 67; Wynes, *Race Relations in Virginia*, 56; Gilmore, *Gender and Jim Crow*, 110–14, 121–24; *Crisis* 10 (Aug. 1915): 175; Cecelski & Tyson, *Democracy Betrayed*, 4–5; Ogden, *Poll Tax in the South*, 8, 29–31; Perman, *Struggle for Mastery*, 12, 15, 18; Coleman, "Constitution of 1890," 81–82; Cohen, *At Freedom's Edge*, 207; McMillen, *Dark Journey*, 8, 39; Kelley, "Plessy," 14; *Nation* 51 (31 July 1890): 87; ibid. 61 (19 Sept. 1895): 199.

140. Cohen, *At Freedom's Edge*, 205 table 8. Compare Key, *Southern Politics*, 535–36, with Kousser, *Shaping of Southern Politics*, 3, 41, 43, 83, 139, 151, 208, 211, 218 table 7.13, 241 table 9.2. See also Perman, *Struggle for Mastery*, 18–19, 271, 285, 297–98;

Ayers, *Promise of the New South*, 309; Anderson, *Race and Politics in North Carolina*, 185; Cartwright, *Triumph of Jim Crow*, 239; Cresswell, *Multi-Party Politics in Mississippi*, 19–20, 108–9; Woodward, *Origins of the New South*, 343; Ogden, *Poll Tax in the South*, chap. 5; Wynes, *Race Relations in Virginia*, 53–54; Rabinowitz, *First New South*, 115–16; Grantham, "Georgia Politics and the Disfranchisement of the Negro," 6, 9–11, 16, 21; Lewinson, *Race, Class, and Party*, 92–93; Dittmer, *Black Georgia*, 94; Tindall, *South Carolina Negroes*, chap. 5.

141. DeSantis, *Republicans Face the Southern Question*, chap. 1; Gillette, *Retreat from Reconstruction*, chaps. 5, 7; Goldman, "A Free Ballot and a Fair Count," xxiv–xxv; Foner, *Reconstruction*, 603; Mangum, *Legal Status of the Negro*, 393–94; McMillen, *Dark Journey*, 44, 47–48.

142. Warren, *Supreme Court in United States History*, 1:729–36; Norgren, "Cherokee Nation Cases," 70–71; pages 327, 365.

143. Curriden & Phillips, *Contempt of Court*, 41–44, 59, 62, 69–70, 73, 82, 84, 88, 122–23, 146–59, 167–68, 216–18, 232–33, 249–50, 306, 310, 318; United States v. Shipp, 203 U.S. 563 (1906), 214 U.S. 386 (1909), 215 U.S. 580 (1909). See also Webb, "Lynching of Ed Johnson."

144. Pages 125–28; Batson v. Kentucky, 476 U.S. 79 (1986).

145. Mangum, *Legal Status of the Negro*, 78, 121; Anderson, *Race and Politics in North Carolina*, 329; Harlan, *Separate and Unequal*, 47; Connally, "*Cumming v. Richmond County Board of Education*," 80; Douglas, *Desegregation of the Charlotte Schools*, 11, 15–16; Trustees of Colored Schools v. Trustees of White Schools, 203 S.W. 520 (Ky. 1918); Crosby v. City of Mayfield, 117 S.W. 316 (Ky. 1909); Thompson, "Negro Separate School," 230.

146. *Crisis* 1 (Feb. 1911): 19–20; ibid. 6 (Aug. 1913): 175; Wendell Phillips Stafford, "The Civil Rights Act," ibid. 7 (Mar. 1914): 253; ibid. 9 (Apr. 1915): 293. See also "The Grandfather Clause," ibid. 10 (Sept. 1915): 231–32; "Victory," ibid. (May 1927): 106; Harlan, *Booker T. Washington*, 1:246–47.

147. Schmidt, "Juries, Jurisdiction, and Race Discrimination," 1440, 1472, 1475; Glennon, "Jurisdictional Legacy of the Civil Rights Movement."

148. Schmidt, "Juries, Jurisdiction, and Race Discrimination," 141; Foner, *Reconstruction*, 603; Gillette, *Retreat from Reconstruction*, 363; Skowronek, *Building a New American State*, 46, 161–62.

149. Williamson, *After Slavery*, 298–99; McMillen, *Dark Journey*, 4, 9–10, 23–32; Stephenson, *Race Distinctions*, 351–52; Wharton, *Negro in Mississippi*, 216–33, 274; Gerber, *Black Ohio*, 49; Glasrud, "Jim Crow's Emergence in Texas," 56; Moore, "Jim Crow in Georgia," 554–57. But cf. Woodward, *Strange Career of Jim Crow*, 68–69, 97, 102, 105. See also pages 91–92.

CHAPTER 2

1. Baker, "Struggle for Freedom"; Daniel, *Shadow of Slavery*, 69–78; Harlan, *Booker T. Washington*, 2:250–51.

2. Bailey v. Alabama, 219 U.S. 219 (1911); United States v. Reynolds, 235 U.S. 133 (1914); McCabe v. Atchison, Topeka & Santa Fe Railway Co., 235 U.S. 151 (1914); Guinn v. Oklahoma, 238 U.S. 347 (1915); Myers v. Anderson, 238 U.S. 368 (1915); Buchanan v. Warley, 245 U.S. 60 (1917).

3. "The Supreme Court," *Crisis* 9 (Dec. 1914): 77; Schmidt, "Principle and Prejudice, Part I," 446. But cf. Howard, *Shifting Wind*, 156–94.

4. McMillen, *Dark Journey*, 302–6; Cohen, *At Freedom's Edge*, 297–98; Kirby, *Race and Reform in the Progressive South*, 155; Keller, *Regulating a New Society*, 257–68; Schmidt, "Principle and Prejudice, Part I," 452, 455–56.

5. Oswald Garrison Villard, "Color Hysteria," *Crisis* 1 (Apr. 1911): 25.

6. *Crisis* 1 (Mar. 1911): 5; ibid. 8 (June 1914): 78; ibid. 1 (Nov. 1910): 10; ibid. 2 (June 1911): 51, 56; ibid. 3 (Nov. 1911): 34; ibid. (Mar. 1912): 204; ibid. 5 (Mar. 1913): 220; ibid. 6 (May 1913): 15; ibid. 9 (Nov. 1914): 11; ibid. (Dec. 1914): 64; ibid. 10 (July 1915): 136; pages 12, 23–24; Baker, *Following the Color Line*, 111, 123–24; Evans, *Black and White in the Southern States*, 212–15; Gerber, *Black Ohio*, 261–62, 268–70; Spear, *Black Chicago*, 88; Douglas, "Limits of Law," 701–10; Wiseman, "Racism in Democratic Politics," 46–47; LePore, "Prelude to Prejudice," 99–104; Stephenson, *Race Distinctions*, 159–62.

7. *Crisis* 1 (Mar. 1911): 5; John Haynes Holmes, letter to the editor, ibid. (Oct. 1911): 251; ibid. 9 (Dec. 1914): 64; ibid. 14 (Sept. 1917): 221; Cohen, *At Freedom's Edge*, 96–102; Gerber, *Black Ohio*, 62, 66 n. 14, 74–78, 254–57, 298–99, 302–3, 306; Spear, *Black Chicago*, 31, 34, 36–40, 111, 159; Thornbrough, *Negro in Indiana*, 284–87, 350–57; Katzman, *Before the Ghetto*, 116, 124–25; Kusmer, *A Ghetto Takes Shape*, 70, 75–76; Osofsky, *Harlem*, 46–52; Baker, *Following the Color Line*, 126–28, 131–34, 201–2; Chicago Commission, *Negro in Chicago*, chaps. 1–2; Senechal, *Race Riot*; Tuttle, *Race Riot*; Rudwick, *Race Riot*.

8. *Crisis* 3 (Dec. 1911): 57; Litwack, *Black Southerners in the Age of Jim Crow*, 295–96, 301–3; Lewis, *In Their Own Interests*, 18; Lamon, *Black Tennesseans*, 37–40; Baker, *Following the Color Line*, 252; Perman, *Struggle for Mastery*, chaps. 9–11, 13; pages 30–33.

9. Pages 44–45; Pillsbury, "A Federal Remedy for Lynching," 707–8; *Crisis* 10 (May 1915): 21; ibid. 1 (Feb. 1911): 6; ibid. (Apr. 1911): 9, 12; ibid. 3 (Apr. 1912): 229; ibid. 4 (July 1912): 116; ibid. 7 (Dec. 1913): 63; ibid. (Feb. 1914): 175–76, 189–90; ibid. (Apr. 1914): 278–80; ibid. 8 (June 1914): 69; ibid. (Oct. 1914): 272; Walter White, "The Work of a Mob," ibid. 17 (Sept. 1918): 221–23; Mangum, *Legal Status of the Negro*, 55, 57, 62–63, 65, 67, 73, 175; Baker, *Following the Color Line*, 36, 252, 266; Callcott, *Negro in Maryland Politics*, 133–37; Cohen, *At Freedom's Edge*, 245–46, 256, 274–75, 291; Meier & Rudwick, *Along the Color Line*, 267–306; Perman, *Struggle for Mastery*, 264–69; Lamon, *Black Tennesseans*, chap. 2; Dittmer, *Black Georgia*, 16–21; McMillen, *Dark Journey*, 8–9, 293–95; Woodward, *Strange Career of Jim Crow*, 97–102; Kirby, "Clarence Poe's Vision," 31–38.

10. Anderson, *Education of Blacks in the South*, 230–34; Dittmer, *Black Georgia*, 29–33, 37–38; McMillen, *Dark Journey*, 159–60, 164–69; Lamon, *Black Tennesseans*, 134, 141, 158–59, 174–75; Evans, *Black and White in the South*, chap. 24; Arnesen, "Race Question and the American Railroad Brotherhoods"; Matthews, "Georgia Race Strike of 1909"; Meier & Rudwick, *Along the Color Line*, 130; *Crisis* 2 (May 1911): 15; ibid. 10 (May 1915): 17; ibid. (July 1915): 128.

11. "The Grandfather Clause," *NYT*, 23 June 1915, p. 10; "The Birth of a Nation," *Crisis* 10 (June 1915): 69–71; Fishel, "The North and the Negro," 472–73; Allen et al., "Negro Rights in the Senate"; Wiseman, "Racism in Democratic Politics," 55–56; Keller, *Regulating a New Society*, 259–60; Meier & Rudwick, *Along the Color Line*, 164 n. 31; Kraditor, *Ideas of the Woman Suffrage Movement*, 213; Mead, *Joe Louis*, 31–32, 38; Kirby, *Race and Reform in the Progressive South*, 91–94; Cripps, "*Birth of a Nation*"; *Crisis* 1 (Feb. 1911): 5; ibid. (Mar. 1911): 5; ibid. 3 (Apr. 1912): 236–37; ibid. 6

(Aug. 1913): 191; "The Bar Association," ibid. 9 (Dec. 1914): 82; "To Your Tents, O Nordics!" ibid. 28 (July 1924): 104.

12. Stone, *American Race Problem*, chap. 7; Sherman, *Republican Party and Black America*, 23–51; Gould, *Theodore Roosevelt*, 22–24, 118–22; Scheiner, "Theodore Roosevelt and the Negro," 171–80; Woodward, *Origins of the New South*, 463–65; Harlan, *Booker T. Washington*, 2:20–23.

13. Theodore Roosevelt, "The Negro Problem," in *The Works of Theodore Roosevelt*, vol. 16, *American Problems* (New York: Scribner's, 1926), 346–47; "The Education of the Negro," in ibid., 351–55; "Sixth Annual Message to Congress," in ibid., vol. 15, *State Papers as Governor and President*, 351–54; Scheiner, "Theodore Roosevelt and the Negro," 180–82; Wiseman, "Racism in Democratic Politics," 45–47; Woodward, *Origins of the New South*, 465–66.

14. Sherman, *Republican Party and Black America*, 52–82; Gould, *Theodore Roosevelt*, 236–44; Lane, *Brownsville Affair*; Thornbrough, "Brownsville Episode and the Negro Vote."

15. *Crisis* 8 (May 1914): 11; William Howard Taft, "Inaugural Address," 4 Mar. 1909, in Taft, *Presidential Addresses and State Papers*, 1:64–66; Sherman, *Republican Party and Black America*, chap. 4; Harlan, *Booker T. Washington*, 2:338–49; Dittmer, *Black Georgia*, 94, 106–7; McMillen, *Dark Journey*, 62–63; Meier, "Negro and the Democratic Party," 184–85; Wiseman, "Racism in Democratic Politics," 52; Woodward, *Origins of the New South*, 467–68; Schmidt, "Principle and Prejudice, Part III," 851–56; *Crisis* 1 (Dec. 1910): 13; ibid. (Apr. 1911): 16; ibid. (July 1911): 100, 111; ibid. 4 (Aug. 1912): 167, 181.

16. "Mr. Taft," *Crisis* 2 (Oct. 1911): 243; Weiss, "Fighting Wilsonian Segregation," 62–63; Gavins, "Urbanization and Segregation," 270; Taft, "Southern Democracy and Republican Principles" (22 Aug. 1907), in Taft, *Present-Day Problems*, 228; "Republican Platform of 1912," in *National Party Platforms*, ed. Johnson & Porter, 183–88; Sherman, *Republican Party and Black America*, 92, 101–12; Casdorph, *Republicans, Negroes, and Progressives*, 145; Mowry, "Progressive Lily White Party," 241–42; Villard, *Segregation in Baltimore and Washington*, 13; Meier, "Negro and the Democratic Party," 185–89; *Crisis* 4 (Sept. 1912): 216; "The Last Word in Politics," ibid. (Nov. 1912): 29; "The Election," ibid. 5 (Dec. 1912): 75; ibid. (Jan. 1913): 122.

17. *Crisis* 6 (Oct. 1913): 298; "The President," ibid. 9 (Feb. 1915): 181; Sosna, "South in the Saddle"; Wolgemuth, "Federal Segregation"; Wolgemuth, "Wilson's Appointment Policy"; Weiss, "Fighting Wilsonian Segregation"; Sherman, *Republican Party and Black America*, chap. 5; Heckscher, *Woodrow Wilson*, 292; Dittmer, *Black Georgia*, 181–82; *Crisis* 5 (Apr. 1913): 270; ibid. 6 (May 1913): 11; "Another Open Letter to Woodrow Wilson," ibid. 6 (Sept. 1913): 232–34; ibid. 7 (Nov. 1913): 333–34, 343; ibid. (Jan. 1914): 125–26; ibid. (Apr. 1914): 284; ibid. 9 (Apr. 1915): 289, 290.

18. Sosna, "South in the Saddle," 35, 36; Woodward, *Origins of the New South*, 456–57, 480; Wiseman, "Racism in Democratic Politics," 54, 57–58; Kirby, *Race and Reform in the Progressive South*, 14–15, 36, 56; Grantham, *Southern Progressivism*, 126, 351–52, 359–60; Schmidt, "Principle and Prejudice, Part I," 455; "Theodore Roosevelt and the South," *Raleigh News and Observer*, 1 Oct. 1912, p. 4.

19. Lewinson, *Race, Class, and Party*, 92–94; Monnet, "Negro Disfranchisement," 43; Mabry, "Louisiana Politics and the 'Grandfather Clause'," 299–300; Mabry, "Ben Tillman Disfranchised the Negro," 179; Mabry, "North Carolina Suffrage Amendment," 4; Rose, "Negro Suffrage," 29–30; Stephenson, *Race Distinctions*, 305–8; Perman, *Struggle for Mastery*, 29–30.

20. Mabry, "Louisiana Politics and the 'Grandfather Clause'," 301, 304, 306, 309; Woodward, *Origins of the New South*, 334–35, 340; Callcott, *Negro in Maryland Politics*, 127–28; Grantham, "Georgia Politics and the Disfranchisement of the Negro," 6–7, 9; Hackney, *Populism to Progressivism in Alabama*, 194–98, 228; Poe, "Suffrage Restrictions," 542; Eaton, "Suffrage Clause in the New Constitution of Louisiana," 289–90; Mabry, "North Carolina Suffrage Amendment," 4, 15, 20; Gilmore, *Gender and Jim Crow*, 121; Rose, "Negro Suffrage," 29–30; Stephenson, *Race Distinctions*, 307, 315–16; *Crisis* 9 (Dec. 1914): 74.

21. "The Right to Vote," *Washington Post* (hereafter *Wash. Post*), 23 June 1915, p. 6; Monnet, "Negro Disfranchisement," 57; *Guinn*, 238 U.S. at 363; Schmidt, "Principle and Prejudice, Part III," 862; Brief for the NAACP, *Guinn v. United States*, 3–4; *Crisis* 1 (Dec. 1910): 12. See also Ayers, *Promise of the New South*, 299.

22. Atwater v. Hassett, 27 Okla. 292 (1910).

23. *Crisis* 2 (July 1911): 104; "The Grandfather Clause," *NYT*, 23 June 1915, p. 10; Taft, "Inaugural Address" (4 Mar. 1909), in Taft, *Presidential Addresses and State Papers*, 64–65; Taft, "Southern Democracy and Republican Principles," in Taft, *Present-Day Problems*, 226–27; Callcott, *Negro in Maryland Politics*, 129–30; Wiseman, "Racism in Democratic Politics," 53; Monnet, "Negro Disfranchisement," 62. See also Eaton, "Suffrage Clause," 293.

24. Higgs, *Competition and Coercion*, 38; Cohen, *At Freedom's Edge*, 8–12, 28–34, 222; Novak, *Wheel of Servitude*, chaps. 1–3; Foner, *Reconstruction*, 199–201, 208–9; McMillen, *Dark Journey*, chap. 4; Wilson, *Black Codes of the South*, chaps. 3, 5.

25. Cohen, *At Freedom's Edge*, chap. 8; Daniel, *Shadow of Slavery*; Novak, *Wheel of Servitude*; Dittmer, *Black Georgia*, 82–86; McMillen, *Dark Journey*, 140–47; Ayers, *Vengeance and Justice*, chap. 6; Mancini, *Convict Leasing*; Bernstein, "Restrictions on Interstate Migration of African Americans"; Lichtenstein, "Chain Gangs."

26. Civil Rights Cases, 109 U.S. 3, 28–32 (1883); Williams v. Fears, 179 U.S. 270 (1900); Joseph v. Randolph, 71 Ala. 499 (1882); State v. Moore, 113 N.C. 697 (1893); In re Turner, 1 Abbott's U.S. Reporter 84 (C.C.D. Md. 1867) (Chase, C.J.); United States v. Hodges, 203 U.S. 1 (1906); Clyatt v. United States, 197 U.S. 207 (1905).

27. Peonage Cases, 123 F. 671, 680 (M.D. Ala. 1903); State v. Armstead, 103 Miss. 790 (1912); Ex parte Hollman, 79 S.C. 9 (1908); Toney v. State, 141 Ala. 120 (1904); Ex parte Drayton, 153 F. 986 (D.S.C. 1907); Robertson v. Baldwin, 165 U.S. 275 (1897); Note, "Criminal Enforcement of Contracts for Labor as 'Involuntary Servitude'," *Columbia Law Review* 11 (Apr. 1911): 363–65.

28. Cohen, *At Freedom's Edge*, 230–31; Novak, *Wheel of Servitude*, 37–38, 56–60; Schmidt, "Peonage Cases," 651, 675–77; Bailey v. Alabama, 219 U.S. 219, 234 (1911).

29. Schmidt, "Peonage Cases," 665, 668–69, 674 n. 104, 675 n. 106, 714.

30. *Bailey*, 219 U.S. at 246–47 (Holmes, J., dissenting). See also Buck v. Bell, 274 U.S. 200 (1927); Meyer v. Nebraska, 262 U.S. 390, 403 (1923) (Holmes, J., dissenting); Weems v. United States, 217 U.S. 349, 382 (1910) (White, J., dissenting); Giles v. Harris, 189 U.S. 475 (1903).

31. Mancini, *Convict Leasing*, 41, 134–35; United States v. Reynolds, 235 U.S. 133 (1914); Daniel, *Shadow of Slavery*, 26 n. 15; Cohen, *At Freedom's Edge*, 225–26, 242–43; Novak, *Wheel of Servitude*, 32, 52–53; Baker, *Following the Color Line*, 50, 96–98, 105; Dittmer, *Black Georgia*, 72–74, 87–88; Harris, "Government Control of Negroes," 578–82; *Crisis* 4 (Aug. 1912): 182.

32. Brief for Defendants in Error, *United States v. Reynolds*, 14–15; Schmidt, "Peonage Cases," 698–99.

33. *Reynolds*, 235 U.S. at 139–40, 146–47, 150 (Holmes, J., concurring); Schmidt, "Peonage Cases," 699; Brief for the United States, *United States v. Reynolds*, 3, 26–27.

34. Schmidt, "Peonage Cases," 658–59, 671–73, 694, 718; Cohen, *At Freedom's Edge*, 4–5, 228, 233–38; Harris, "Government Control of Negroes," 569, 578–81, 585–88; Holmes, "Labor Agents," 436–48; Lichtenstein, "Chain Gangs," 89; Novak, *Wheel of Servitude*, 46; Russell, *Report on Peonage*; United States v. McClellan, 127 F. 971, 978–79 (S.D. Ga. 1904); Ex parte Drayton, 153 F. 986, 996 (D.S.C. 1907); page 72.

35. Cohen, *At Freedom's Edge*, 293; United States v. McClellan, 127 F. 971, 973, 977 (S.D. Ga. 1904); United States v. Clement, 171 F. 974, 976 (D.S.C. 1909); Russell, *Report on Peonage*, 4–6, 32; Daniel, *Shadow of Slavery*, 112–13, 121. See also "To the People of Georgia," *Zebulon Journal* (Georgia), 2 June 1921, NAACP, part 10, reel 16, fr. 861.

36. *Crisis* 9 (Feb. 1915): 177; "Georgia's Reputation," *New York Globe*, 18 May 1921, NAACP, part 10, reel 15, fr. 988; Schmidt, "Peonage Cases," 658–59, 663–64, 671, 677; Daniel, *Shadow of Slavery*, 65; Harlan, *Booker T. Washington*, 2:249–51; Aucoin, "Thomas Goode Jones," 263–65; Baker, "Struggle for Freedom"; Brief of the Attorney General of the United States as Amicus Curiae, *Bailey v. Alabama*; *Crisis* 1 (Dec. 1910): 7; ibid. (Feb. 1911): 11. See also A. J. Galloway to NAACP, 11 July 1924, NAACP, part 10, reel 16, frs. 241–42.

37. Mancini, *Convict Leasing*, 98, 129–30, 140–43, 149–50, 230.

38. Barnes, *Journey from Jim Crow*, 10; Mangum, *Legal Status of the Negro*, 192.

39. *McCabe*, 235 U.S. 151, 161, 162–64; Brief for Appellees, *McCabe v. Atchison, Topeka & Santa Fe Railway Co.*, 20–21.

40. Fenton, *Constitutional Law*, 279; Note, "Statutory Discriminations against Negroes with Reference to Pullman Cars," *Harvard Law Review* 28 (Feb. 1915): 417–19; pages 44–46.

41. Schmidt, "Jim Crow," 488–91, 493; Kull, *Color-Blind Constitution*, 136–37; Cumming v. Richmond County Board of Education, 175 U.S. 528 (1899); pages 43–47.

42. Gong Lum v. Rice, 275 U.S. 78 (1927); State of Missouri ex rel. Gaines v. Canada, 305 U.S. 337 (1938).

43. Kellogg, "Negro Urban Clusters"; Cell, *Highest Stage of White Supremacy*, 134–35; Dittmer, *Black Georgia*, 9–13; Harris, "Government Control of Negroes," 571; Gerber, *Black Ohio*, 98–106, 288–89; Katzman, *Before the Ghetto*, 69; Kusmer, *A Ghetto Takes Shape*, 12, 42; Spear, *Black Chicago*, 14–15; Osofsky, *Harlem*, 12.

44. Power, "Apartheid Baltimore Style"; Rice, "Residential Segregation by Law"; Wright, "Residential Segregation in Louisville"; Stephenson, "Segregation of the White and Negro Races"; Christensen, "Race Relations in St. Louis," 129; Vose, *Caucasians Only*, 51; Hott, "Municipal Zoning and Segregation Ordinances," 342; Brief for Defendant in Error, *Buchanan v. Warley*, 20–23, 32–35, 47–48, 86–90; *Crisis* 1 (Nov. 1910): 6; ibid. 2 (May 1911): 31; ibid. 7 (Jan. 1914): 117.

45. *Buchanan*, 245 U.S. at 79–81; S. S. Field, "The Constitutionality of Segregation Ordinances," *Virginia Law Review* 5 (Nov. 1917): 81–91; Note, "Constitutionality of Segregation Ordinance," *Michigan Law Review* 16 (Dec. 1917): 109–11; Note, "Race Segregation Ordinance Invalid," *Harvard Law Review* 31 (Jan. 1918): 475–79; James F. Minor, "Constitutionality of Segregation Ordinances," *Virginia Law Register* 18 (Dec. 1912): 561–76; Comment, "Unconstitutionality of Segregation Ordinances," *Yale Law Journal* 27 (Jan. 1918): 393–97; Warren B. Hunting, "The Constitutionality

of Race Distinctions and the Baltimore Negro Segregation Ordinance," *Columbia Law Review* 11 (Jan. 1911): 24–35; Rice, "Residential Segregation by Law," 195–96; Bernstein, "Philip Sober Controlling Philip Drunk: *Buchanan v. Warley*," 836–39, 856, 858; Tushnet, "Progressive Era Race Relations Cases," 999.

46. Berger, *Government by Judiciary*, 18–19, 22–23, 163–65, 169, 173, 239; Maltz, *Civil Rights, the Constitution and Congress*, 109, 113, 117; Bickel, "Original Understanding and the Segregation Decision," 12–13, 16–17, 46–47, 56–58; Harrison, "Privileges or Immunities Clause," 1389, 1409; Foner, *Reconstruction*, 198–200; Wilson, *Black Codes of the South*, 66, 79; In re Lee Sing, 43 F. 359 (N.D. Calif. 1890); McClain, *In Search of Equality*, chap. 9.

47. *Buchanan*, 245 U.S. at 74, 78–79; Schmidt, "Jim Crow," 504–5, 517–21; Schmidt, "Principle and Prejudice, Part III," 901; Kull, *Color-Blind Constitution*, 139; Brief for the Plaintiff in Error, *Buchanan v. Warley*, 15–16, 29–30; Missouri ex rel. Gaines v. Canada, 305 U.S. 337, 353 (1938) (McReynolds, J., dissenting); Powell v. Alabama, 287 U.S. 45, 77 (1932) (McReynolds, J., dissenting); Nixon v. Condon, 286 U.S. 73, 89 (1932) (McReynolds, J., dissenting); Moore v. Dempsey, 261 U.S. 86, 92 (1923) (McReynolds, J., dissenting). But see Brown v. Mississippi, 297 U.S. 278 (1936); Nixon v. Herndon, 273 U.S. 536 (1927). See also Cushman, "Secret Lives of the Four Horsemen," 571–84.

48. Carey v. City of Atlanta, 84 S.E. 456 (Ga. 1915); State v. Gurry, 88 A. 546 (Md. Ct. App. 1913); State v. Darnell, 81 S.E. 338 (N.C. 1914); Higginbotham, "De Jure Housing Segregation," 808–20; Hott, "Municipal Zoning and Segregation Ordinances," 343–46; Schmidt, "Principle and Prejudice, Part I," 501–2; Mangum, *Legal Status of the Negro*, 140–41. But see Harris v. City of Louisville, 177 S.W. 472 (Ky. 1915); Hopkins v. City of Richmond, 86 S.E. 139 (Va. 1915); Harden v. City of Atlanta, 93 S.E. 401 (Ga. 1917).

49. Bunting v. Oregon, 243 U.S. 426 (1917); Hadacheck v. Sebastian, 239 U.S. 394 (1915); Reinman v. Little Rock, 237 U.S. 171 (1915); Euclid v. Ambler Realty Co., 272 U.S. 365 (1926); Schmidt, "Principle and Prejudice, Part I," 520–21; Bernstein, "Philip Sober Controlling Philip Drunk: *Buchanan v. Warley*," 841–42; Brief for Defendant in Error, *Buchanan v. Warley*, 96–100; Hott, "Municipal Zoning and Segregation Ordinances," 349.

50. Adams v. Tanner, 244 U.S. 590 (1917); Wilson v. New, 243 U.S. 332, 364 (1917) (Day, J., dissenting).

51. Brief for the Plaintiff in Error, *Buchanan v. Warley*, 14; Brief Amicus Curiae for the Baltimore Branch of the NAACP, *Buchanan v. Warley*, 27–28; Pennsylvania Coal Co. v. Mahon, 260 U.S. 393, 413, 415 (1922) (Holmes, J.); Rideout v. Knox, 148 Mass. 368, 372–73 (1889) (Holmes, J.); Harris v. City of Louisville, 177 S.W. 472, 476 (Ky. 1915); *Euclid*, 272 U.S. at 390–91; Hott, "Municipal Zoning and Segregation Ordinances," 334–38.

52. Epstein, *Forbidden Grounds*, 91–115 (quotation at 99); Epstein, "*Buchanan v. Warley*"; Bernstein, "Restrictions on Interstate Migration of African Americans," 831–39; Bernstein, "Philip Sober Controlling Philip Drunk: *Buchanan v. Warley*," 875–81; Roback, "Political Economy of Segregation"; Ely, "*Buchanan v. Warley*." See also Schmidt, "Principle and Prejudice, Part I," 456.

53. Robert Bork, "Civil Rights: A Challenge," *New Republic*, 31 Aug. 1963, p. 21; Avins, "Thirteenth Amendment Limitations," 252–56.

54. *Crisis* 7 (Nov. 1913): 335; ibid. (Dec. 1913): 169; "A Momentous Decision," *Nation*, 15 Nov. 1917, p. 526.

55. Schmidt, "Principle and Prejudice, Part III," 899; Schmidt, "Principle and Prejudice, Part I," 460.

56. Mary White Ovington, "How the National Association for the Advancement of Colored People Began," *Crisis* 8 (Aug. 1914): 185; ibid. 10 (Aug. 1915): 171; Giles v. Harris, 189 U.S. 475 (1903); Schmidt, "Principle and Prejudice, Part III," 865; Monnet, "Negro Disfranchisement," 59; pages 36–37. See also *Crisis* 9 (Dec. 1914): 74.

57. United States v. Mosley, 238 U.S. 383, 388–93 (1915) (Lamar, J., dissenting); United States v. Reese, 92 U.S. 214 (1875); Act of 8 Feb. 1894, 28 Stat. 36 (1894); Schmidt, "Principle and Prejudice, Part III," 837–41, 870–75, 878.

58. "In Court," *Crisis* 9 (Jan. 1915): 134; Schmidt, "Principle and Prejudice, Part I," 492–93. See also Carle, "Race, Class, and Legal Ethics in the Early NAACP," 123–24.

59. Rice, "Residential Segregation by Law," 185–86; Schmidt, "Principle and Prejudice, Part I," 498, 512–13; Baker, *Oliver Wendell Holmes*, 499–500.

60. *Crisis* 9 (Feb. 1915): 177–78; pages 24, 36–37.

61. Schmidt, "Principle and Prejudice, Part III," 852, 861, 879; "The Grandfather Clause," *Crisis* 10 (Sept. 1915): 231; Callcott, *Negro in Maryland Politics*, 127; Mangum, *Legal Status of the Negro*, 399–400; *Crisis* 10 (Aug. 1915): 171–76, 197.

62. Schmidt, "Principle and Prejudice, Part III," 845, 861, 879, 880, 898 (quotations at 879–80); *Crisis* 10 (Aug. 1915): 172; *NYT*, 22 June 1915, p. 8; *Guinn*, 238 U.S. at 366, 367; Norrell, *Civil Rights Movement in Tuskegee*, 112.

63. Carle, "Race, Class, and Legal Ethics in the Early NAACP," 129; Lane v. Wilson, 307 U.S. 268 (1939); Schmidt, "Principle and Prejudice, Part III," 880–81; *Crisis* 3 (Feb. 1912): 158; ibid. 6 (June 1913): 90.

64. Schmidt, "Peonage Cases," 646, 648, 688–89, 718; Novak, *Wheel of Servitude*, 63 n. 1.

65. Wilson v. State, 75 S.E. 619 (Ga. 1912); Phillips v. Bell, 94 So. 699 (Fla. 1922); Taylor v. State, 191 Ga. 682 (1941), rev'd, 315 U.S. 25 (1942); Pollock v. Williams, 322 U.S. 4 (1944); 1919 Fla. Laws c. 7917, § 2; Cohen, *At Freedom's Edge*, 190, 290; Novak, *Wheel of Servitude*, 64–68, 78–83; Daniel, *Shadow of Slavery*, 180–85; Schmidt, "Peonage Cases," 689–90.

66. State v. Armstead, 60 So. 778 (Miss. 1913); State v. Griffin, 70 S.E. 292 (N.C. 1911); Thomas v. State, 69 So. 908 (Ala. 1915); Pollock v. Williams, 322 U.S. 4, 18–20 (1944); Cohen, *At Freedom's Edge*, 292–93; Novak, *Wheel of Servitude*, 63–64, 68; Schmidt, "Peonage Cases," 689.

67. Johns v. Patterson, 211 S.W. 387 (Ark. 1919); Williams v. Fears, 179 U.S. 270 (1900); Schmidt, "Peonage Cases," 648–49, 716–17; Novak, *Wheel of Servitude*, 63–64, 69, 109 n. 25; Cohen, *At Freedom's Edge*, 238, 273; Lichtenstein, "Chain Gangs," 93–94, 109; "Crime," *Crisis* 32 (May 1926): 9.

68. Clyatt v. United States, 197 U.S. 207 (1905); Daniel, *Shadow of Slavery*, 26, 112–13, 144; McMillen, *Dark Journey*, 123–27; Schmidt, "Peonage Cases," 672; Cohen, *At Freedom's Edge*, 279–80, 285–86; Novak, *Wheel of Servitude*, 63, 76–77; Russell, *Report on Peonage*, 27.

69. State v. Armstead, 60 So. 778, 780–81 (Miss. 1912); Frank Jones to James Weldon Johnson, 5 Feb. 1927, NAACP, part 10, reel 16, fr. 304; Daniel, *Shadow of Slavery*, 23, 32–33, 52–64, 110–18, 124, 129, 132–39, 145–47; Novak, *Wheel of Servitude*, 44–45, 64, 86–87, 89; Baker, *Following the Color Line*, 80; Schmidt, "Peonage Cases," 648, 654–55, 663, 667–68, 715; Dittmer, *Black Georgia*, 75, 78–79; McMillen, *Dark Journey*, 145–46; *Crisis* 2 (July 1911): 96; ibid. 7 (Jan. 1914): 116–17; W. R. R. Rogers to John-

son, 16 June 1921, NAACP, part 10, reel 16, fr. 16; Peonage Report on Mississippi (1921), ibid., fr. 54; Anonymous to NAACP, 8 Oct. 1928, ibid., frs. 183–86; Sallie Miller to William Andrews, 26 Aug. 1931, p. 3, ibid., fr. 396; W. B. Lyens to Roy Wilkins, 1 Sept. 1932, ibid., frs. 418–24; Wilkins to Wallace Townsend, 2 Feb. 1933, ibid., frs. 430–31; NYT, 27 Mar. 1921, ibid., fr. 600; NYT, 28 Mar. 1921, ibid., fr. 610; Walter White to Brown, 10 June 1929, ibid., fr. 912; Anonymous to NAACP, 3 Sept. 1930, ibid., fr. 917; Anonymous to NAACP, 25 Apr. 1921, ibid., reel 15, fr. 963. See also United States v. Clement, 171 F. 974, 979 (D.S.C. 1909); Ex parte Hollman, 79 S.C. 9, 26 (1908).

70. "Slavery," Crisis 22 (May 1921): 6; "The Flood, the Red Cross and the National Guard," ibid. 35 (Jan. 1928): 5–7; ibid. (Feb. 1928): 41–43; Cohen, At Freedom's Edge, 24–25, 290, 292, 296–98; Daniel, "Alonzo Bailey Case," 655; Higgs, Competition and Coercion, 59, 76–77, 119, 130–31; Daniel, Shadow of Slavery, 110, 132, 138–40, 148–49, 153–57; Dittmer, Black Georgia, 77, 80–81; Schmidt, "Peonage Cases," 648, 717; Novak, Wheel of Servitude, 64; Woodman, "Economic Reconstruction," 273–74; J. Henderson to W. E. B. Du Bois, 26 May 1921, NAACP, part 10, reel 16, fr. 6; Anonymous to Johnson, 8 July 1921, ibid., frs. 18–20; W. S. Larkin to NAACP, 6 Sept. 1921, ibid., frs. 33–34; Peonage Report on Georgia (1921), ibid., frs. 47–49; Peonage Report on Florida (1921), ibid., fr. 50; Peonage Report on Texas (1921), ibid., fr. 51; Peonage Report on South Carolina (1921), ibid., fr. 52; Peonage Report on Tennessee (1921), ibid., fr. 55; Report on Three Peonage Cases in Georgia (1921), ibid., frs. 56–62; W. H. Booker to NAACP, 2 Feb. 1922, ibid., frs. 68–72; H. L. Henderson to Spingarn, 26 Aug. 1922, ibid., fr. 125; Anonymous to J. E. Spingarn, 2 July 1923, ibid., fr. 156; R. L. Thornton to Johnson, 16 Oct. 1923, ibid., frs. 187–94; E. Parker to NAACP, 30 Oct. 1923, ibid., frs. 195–97; Pensacola Journal, 19 May 1925, ibid., fr. 281; Mosley to Bagnall, 19 Feb. 1927, ibid., fr. 307; affidavit of James Felton, 30 May 1927, ibid., frs. 316–18; Wilkins to C. H. Myers, 28 Apr. 1932, ibid., fr. 408; New York Call, 9 Dec. 1921, ibid., fr. 877; statement of James Felton (1931), ibid., reel 17, frs. 336–41; L. W. Washington to Johnson, 2 May 1921, ibid., reel 15, frs. 978–80.

71. Minter, "Codification of Jim Crow," 71–72, 79–83, 107–8, 112, 144, 206–7; Barnes, Journey from Jim Crow, 13, 211 n. 32; Schmidt, "Principle and Prejudice, Part I," 463 n. 69, 486 n. 153; Lamon, Black Tennesseans, 7–8; Sherman, Republican Party and Black America, 68–69; page 20.

72. Crisis 1 (Feb. 1911): 29; ibid. 6 (July 1913): 120; ibid. 7 (Jan. 1914): 117; ibid. 9 (Dec. 1914): 75; "Jim Crow," ibid. (Feb. 1929): 65–66; "'Jim-Crow' Travel," ibid. 37 (Mar. 1930): 88, 103–5; Barnes, Journey from Jim Crow, 15.

73. Schmidt, "Principle and Prejudice, Part I," 477, 492–93, 523 (quotation); Kull, Color-Blind Constitution, 132–38 (quotation at 135); Shelley v. Kraemer, 334 U.S. 1, 22 n. 29 (1948); Missouri ex rel. Gaines v. Canada, 305 U.S. 337, 350–51 (1938). See also Long, "Segregation in Interstate Railway Coach Travel."

74. McCabe, 235 U.S. at 160; Gong Lum v. Rice, 275 U.S. 78 (1927). But cf. Schmidt, "Principle and Prejudice, Part I," 487, 493 n. 165.

75. "A Momentous Decision," Nation 105 (15 Nov. 1917): 526; "Victory," Crisis 16 (Dec. 1917): 61; William H. Baldwin III, "Erasing the Color Line: The Supreme Court Decision on Negro Segregation," Survey 39 (24 Nov. 1917): 185–86; Schmidt, "Principle and Prejudice, Part I," 501, 508–9, 523; Higginbotham, "De Jure Housing Segregation," 769–70, 873–74; Bernstein, "Philip Sober Controlling Philip Drunk: Buchanan v. Warley," 800; Ely, "Buchanan v. Warley," 955; Fischel, "Judicial Reversal of Apartheid," 990; Howard, Shifting Wind, 15, 191–92.

76. *Crisis* 7 (Apr. 1914): 283; *Richmond News Leader*, 6 Nov. 1917, pp. 4–5; Harris, "Government Control of Negroes," 571; McMillen, *Dark Journey*, 12–14; Lewis, *In Their Own Interests*, 78–79; Wright, *Life behind a Veil*, 236; Power, "Apartheid Baltimore Style," 314–20; Spear, *Black Chicago*, 14–17, 142, 145 table 11; Gosnell, *Negro Politicians*, 19–21; Marshall, "*Buchanan v. Warley*," 99; Irvine v. City of Clifton Forge, 97 S.E. 310 (Va. 1918); Jackson v. State, 103 A. 910 (Md. 1918); Glover v. City of Atlanta, 96 S.E. 562 (Ga. 1918); Liberty Annex Corp. v. City of Dallas, 289 S.W. 1067 (Tex. Civ. App. 1926).

77. Booker T. Washington, "My View of Segregation Laws," *New Republic* 5 (4 Dec. 1915): 113–14; Dittmer, *Black Georgia*, 13; W. Ashbie Hawkins, "A Year of Segregation in Baltimore," *Crisis* 3 (Nov. 1911): 28–29; ibid. 10 (Aug. 1915): 199; pages 50–51, 54–55. See also Harlan, *Booker T. Washington*, 2:430–31.

78. Grossman, *Great Migration*, 127; Katzman, *Before the Ghetto*, 55; Vose, *Caucasians Only*, 5, 9, 19, 28, 66–67, 100, 106–7, 156, 223–26; Wright, *Life behind a Veil*, 236; DeGraaf, "Los Angeles Ghetto," 349; Power, "Apartheid Baltimore Style," 318–19, 325; Spear, *Black Chicago*, 26, 209–10; Bayor, *Twentieth-Century Atlanta*, chap. 3; Silver, "Racial Origins of Zoning"; Bernstein, "Philip Sober Controlling Philip Drunk: *Buchanan v. Warley*," 862–66; Lamon, *Black Tennesseans*, 137; Hirsch, *Making the Second Ghetto*, 9–10; Jackson, *Crabgrass Frontier*, 198–214; Sugrue, *Origins of the Urban Crisis*, 43–51.

79. Dittmer, *Black Georgia*, 14; Lewis, *In Their Own Interests*, 77–78; Spear, *Black Chicago*, 20–22, 201, 208, 211–12, 219–20; Wright, *Life behind a Veil*, 237; Bayor, *Twentieth-Century Atlanta*, 59; DeGraaf, "Los Angeles Ghetto," 336, 346, 348; Grossman, *Great Migration*, 174, 178; Tuttle, *Race Riot*, 159, 178; Chicago Commission, *Negro in Chicago*, 3, 34, 46, 122–35; *Crisis* 2 (Nov. 1911): 6–7; ibid. 4 (June 1912): 64; ibid. (Oct. 1912): 272; ibid. 7 (Nov. 1913): 323; ibid. 8 (Sept. 1914): 219; ibid. 9 (Apr. 1915): 289.

80. Ely, "*Buchanan v. Warley*," 955; Higginbotham, "De Jure Housing Segregation," 862; Bernstein, "Philip Sober Controlling Philip Drunk: *Buchanan v. Warley*," 869–70; Schmidt, "Principle and Prejudice, Part I," 523; Moore, "Jim Crow in Georgia," 558–61; Bayor, *Twentieth-Century Atlanta*, 54–55; Dittmer, *Black Georgia*, 14, 20–21; Glasrud, "Jim Crow's Emergence in Texas," 55; Lewis, *In Their Own Interests*, 77; Vose, *Caucasians Only*, 51–52; Woodward, *Strange Career of Jim Crow*, 116–18; McMillen, *Dark Journey*, 8–9; Wynes, "Evolution of Jim Crow Laws," 419–21; Barnes, *Journey from Jim Crow*, 14; Mangum, *Legal Status of the Negro*, 217; pages 69–70.

81. Schmidt, "Principle and Prejudice, Part I," 445, 459; Hixson, "Moorfield Storey," 551 n. 77; *Crisis* 1 (Feb. 1911): 11; ibid. 10 (Sept. 1915): 226; Wright, "Residential Segregation in Louisville," 50–52; Bernstein, "Philip Sober Controlling Philip Drunk: *Buchanan v. Warley*," 874; Chong, *Collective Action and the Civil Rights Movement*, chaps. 5–6; McAdam, *Development of Black Insurgency*, 105–6, 111. See also *Crisis* 1 (Feb. 1911): 19–20; Editorial, "Victory," ibid. 15 (Dec. 1917): 61.

82. Wright, "Residential Segregation in Louisville," 52; Wright, *Life behind a Veil*, 197–98, 238; Bernstein, "Philip Sober Controlling Philip Drunk: *Buchanan v. Warley*," 871–72.

83. W. E. B. Du Bois, "Violations of Property Rights," *Crisis* 2 (May 1911): 31; Dittmer, *Black Georgia*, 22; Tushnet, *Thurgood Marshall*, vii; Cell, *Highest Stage of White Supremacy*, 15, 240–41; Brundage, *Lynching in the New South*, 204; McMillen, *Dark Journey*, 285–88, 294; Meier & Rudwick, *Along the Color Line*, 279, 309–10, 348. See also Kelley, "Black Working-Class Opposition."

84. "Protest," *Crisis* 37 (Oct. 1930): 353; Dittmer, *Black Georgia*, 206; McMillen, *Dark Journey*, 314–16; Evans, *Black and White in the Southern States*, 198.

85. Schmidt, "Peonage Cases," 677–79; Daniel, "Alonzo Bailey Case," 659, 662; Aucoin, "Thomas Goode Jones," 264–65.

86. Balkin, "Agreements with Hell," 1729, 1732; Seidman, "*Brown* and *Miranda*," 717; Rosenberg, *Hollow Hope*, 340; Scheingold, "Constitutional Rights and Social Change," 75–76.

87. Bell v. Maryland, 378 U.S. 227 (1964). See also Klarman, "Modern Equal Protection," 272–76.

88. Rosenberg, *Hollow Hope*, 50, 97–100; Halpern, *Limits of the Law*, chap. 3; Garrow, *Protest at Selma*, 19 table 1-3, 189 table 6-1 (1978). See also Spann, *Race against the Court*, chaps. 6–7.

89. Compare Schmidt, "Principle and Prejudice, Part I," 445–46, 460, 523–24, and Schmidt, "Principle and Prejudice, Part III," 898–905, with Kennedy, "Race Relations Law," 1647–48, 1651–52, and Tushnet, "Progressive Era Race Relations Cases," 1000–1001.

90. Griffin v. County School Board, 377 U.S. 218, 231 (1964); Brown v. Mississippi, 297 U.S. 278 (1936); Moore v. Dempsey, 261 U.S. 86 (1923); Shelley v. Kraemer, 334 U.S. 1 (1948); Smith v. Allwright, 321 U.S. 649 (1944); Green v. County School Board, 391 U.S. 430 (1968); NAACP v. Button, 371 U.S. 415, 435 (1963); ibid., 445 (Douglas, J., concurring); NAACP v. Alabama, 357 U.S. 449, 462 (1958).

CHAPTER 3

1. Cortner, *Mob Intent on Death*, 7–23; "The Real Causes of Two Race Riots," *Crisis* 19 (Dec. 1919): 56–62.

2. Grossman, *Great Migration*, 3–4, 13–18, 28–30; Cohen, *At Freedom's Edge*, 103–8; Dittmer, *Black Georgia*, 186–91; McAdam, *Development of Black Insurgency*, 74–81; McMillen, *Dark Journey*, chap. 8; Johnson, "Negro Migration," 404–8; Sherman, *Republican Party and Black America*, 126; Gerber, *Black Ohio*, 470; Trotter, *Black Milwaukee*, 40; Chicago Commission, *Negro in Chicago*, 79–80, 106; Kusmer, *A Ghetto Takes Shape*, 157, 160; Myrdal, *American Dilemma*, 1:183–85.

3. *Crisis* 28 (Aug. 1924): 153; McAdam, *Development of Black Insurgency*, 79–80; Berman, *Civil Rights in the Truman Administration*, 80–81; Lawson, *Black Ballots*, 346; Moon, *Balance of Power*, 10, 35, 198; Weiss, *Farewell to the Party of Lincoln*, 181–83; Burnham, "American Political Universe," 12; Gosnell, *Negro Politicians*, 37, 40–41, 55–56, 80–81, 200, 204, 213, 237, 250–51, 367–68; Spear, *Black Chicago*, 35–36, 120–25, 187–91; Tuttle, *Race Riot*, 184–207; Osofsky, *Harlem*, 159–78; "Black Rulers of White Folk," *Crisis* 37 (Jan. 1930): 14–15; Francis E. Rivers, "Negro Judges for Harlem," ibid. (Nov. 1930): 377, 393. See also Cox, *Blacks in Topeka*, 189–90; Kusmer, *A Ghetto Takes Shape*, 245–47, 252, 271–74; Trotter, *Blacks in Southern West Virginia*, 217–37; Bunche, *Political Status of the Negro*, 572–606.

4. *Christian Science Monitor*, quoted in W. E. B. Du Bois, "The Defeat of Judge Parker," *Crisis* 37 (July 1930): 225–27, 248; *Time*, 17 Aug. 1936, p. 10; Zangrando, *NAACP Crusade against Lynching*, 42–43, 51–71; Rable, "Politics of Antilynching Legislation," 203–4; Gosnell, *Negro Politicians*, 80–81; pages 111, 116.

5. Gerber, *Black Ohio*, 297–300, 309–15, 318–19; Thornbrough, *Negro in Indiana*, 360–66, 393; Spear, *Black Chicago*, 181–84; Trotter, *Blacks in Southern West Virginia*, 145–69; McAdam, *Development of Black Insurgency*, 135; Myrdal, *American Dilemma*, 1:72, 75–78, 2:1065–70; Meier & Rudwick, *Along the Color Line*, 315–32;

Greenberg, *Black Harlem*, 114–39; "Buying and Selling," *Crisis* 40 (Nov. 1931): 393. But cf. Kirby, *Black Americans in the Roosevelt Era*, 232–33.

6. Anderson, *Education of Blacks in the South*, 22, 25, 95–97, 197–98; Grossman, *Great Migration*, 246–51; Homel, "Two Worlds of Race?" 251–53; Myrdal, *American Dilemma*, 2:879–80; Sitkoff, *New Deal for Blacks*, 31.

7. Chicago Commission, *Negro in Chicago*, 98–100, 176–77; Myrdal, *American Dilemma*, 2:723, 777–79; Grossman, *Great Migration*, 75, 78, 166–67; pages 105, 107.

8. "The Riots," *Crisis* 18 (Sept. 1919): 243; Grossman, *Great Migration*, 164–66, 171–72; Spear, *Black Chicago*, 129–30; Tuttle, *Race Riot*, 32–66; Rudwick, *Race Riot*, 27–57; Chicago Commission, *Negro in Chicago*, 1–78; Tindall, *New South*, 151–55; *NYT*, 27 Oct. 1921, p. 1; Sherman, *Republican Party and Black America*, 148–51.

9. Mordecai Wyatt Johnson, "The Faith of the American Negro," *Crisis* 24 (Aug. 1922): 156; Cohen, *At Freedom's Edge*, 233–37, 249–50, 298; Brundage, *Lynching in the New South*, 209, 229–30; Dittmer, *Black Georgia*, 189–91; Grossman, *Great Migration*, 50–54, 60–61; McMillen, *Dark Journey*, 85, 278–81; "Dawn," *Crisis* 13 (Apr. 1917): 267; Mary White Ovington, "Revisiting the South," ibid. 34 (Apr. 1927): 42.

10. Grantham, *Southern Progressivism*, 5; Tindall, *New South*, 94–95; Myrdal, *American Dilemma*, 1:183–85. See also McMillen, *Dark Journey*, 267–69; Dittmer, *Black Georgia*, 27; Hackney, *Populism to Progressivism in Alabama*, xv.

11. McAdam, *Development of Black Insurgency*, 97–98; Bullock, "Urbanization and Race Relations," 215–16; Myrdal, *American Dilemma*, 1:304–10, 2:895, 950; Wright, *Life behind a Veil*, 220–28; Brundage, "Black Resistance and White Violence," 278; Harlan, *Separate and Unequal*, 15–16, 262–63; Anderson, *Education of Blacks in the South*, 186. See also Hine, *White Primary in Texas*, 56–57, 74–75, 130.

12. Lewinson, *Race, Class, and Party*, 128, 132–38, 146–52; Bunche, *Political Status of the Negro*, 258, 300–303, 307, 309–12, 317; Toppin, "Atlanta NAACP's Fight for Equal Schools, 1916–1917"; Myrdal, *American Dilemma*, 2:614–15, 776; Harris, "Government Control of Negroes," 570–71; Bullock, "Urbanization and Race Relations," 220–21; Brundage, *Lynching in the New South*, 104, 124, 126–27, 159; Ayers, *Promise of the New South*, 156–57; McMillen, *Dark Journey*, 230, 314–16; Dittmer, *Black Georgia*, 206–7; Lamon, *Black Tennesseans*, 266; Chong, *Collective Action and the Civil Rights Movement*, 167–69; McAdam, *Development of Black Insurgency*, 77, 88–90, 97–100, 128–32; Cell, *Highest Stage of White Supremacy*, 131–32; *Crisis* 10 (Oct. 1915): 273; ibid. 18 (Aug. 1919): 181; "Education," ibid. 29 (Nov. 1924): 9. But cf. Cell, *Highest Stage of White Supremacy*, 133–35, 169, 232; Woodward, "Strange Career Critics," 858–60.

13. Schmidt, "Principle and Prejudice, Part I," 458; Arthur P. Davis, "The Negro College Student," *Crisis* 37 (Aug. 1930): 270; "Education and Work," ibid., 280; Margo, *Race and Schooling in the South*, 7 table 2.1; Hine, *White Primary in Texas*, 56; McMillen, *Dark Journey*, 88 table 3.7; Wynes, *Race Relations in Virginia*, 132; Cell, *Highest Stage of White Supremacy*, 30–31; Sitkoff, *New Deal for Blacks*, 31; Anderson, *Education of Blacks in the South*, 274; W. E. B. Du Bois, "The Negro Citizen," *Crisis* 36 (May 1929): 155; "The Year of Education, 1929," ibid. (Aug. 1929): 263; "Colleges," ibid. 39 (Sept. 1932): 298; E. A. Schaal, "Will the Negro Rely upon Force?" ibid. 40 (Jan. 1933): 8–9; McAdam, *Development of Black Insurgency*, 97–98; Myrdal, *American Dilemma*, 2:744, 879–82, 910–11; Grossman, *Great Migration*, 74–75, 80, 82–88; Spear, *Black Chicago*, 134–36; Dollard, *Caste and Class*, 190, 201–3.

14. *Crisis* 6 (July 1913): 128; Benj. Griffith Brawley, "Atlanta Striving," ibid. 8 (May 1914): 29; "The Forward-Looking South," ibid. 37 (Apr. 1930): 137–38; Zan-

grando, NAACP *Crusade against Lynching*, 6–7 table 2, 46; Brundage, *Lynching in the New South*, 9, 20, 36–37, 70, 104, 126–27, 210–11, 242; Dittmer, *Black Georgia*, 208–9; Grantham, *Southern Progressivism*, 234–35, 374–85, 407–9, 413; Myrdal, *American Dilemma*, 2:842–50; Tindall, *New South*, 177–79; Lamon, *Black Tennesseans*, 256–64; Sullivan, *Days of Hope*, 32; Chatfield, "Southern Sociological Congress," 336–37, 347. But cf. Cell, *Highest Stage of White Supremacy*, 4–5, 133–34, 232.

15. *Crisis* 18 (May 1919): 14; Jordan, "Damnable Dilemma," 1574; Kennedy, *First World War*, 41–42; Reich, "Soldiers of Democracy," 1482; Kellogg, *NAACP*, 264; Myrdal, *American Dilemma*, 1:421–22; Hemmingway, "Prelude to Change," 216–18; Lewis, *In Their Own Interests*, 33–34; "Democracy," *Crisis* 14 (July 1917): 114–15; ibid. 18 (June 1919): 65. But cf. Cell, *Highest Stage of White Supremacy*, 249.

16. "Close Ranks," *Crisis* 16 (July 1918): 111; ibid. 18 (May 1919): 14; Gavins, "Urbanization and Segregation," 270–71; "The Ballot," *Crisis* 17 (Dec. 1918): 62; ibid. 18 (Aug. 1919): 180; ibid. (Oct. 1919): 288; Reich, "Soldiers of Democracy," 1482–85, 1493–98; Jordan, "Damnable Dilemma," 1562; Haynes, *Houston Riot*, 65–66, 71, 83, 318–23; Smith, "Houston Riot," 88–94; Hemmingway, "Prelude to Change," 222; Chicago Commission, *Negro in Chicago*, 481, 488; Tuttle, *Race Riot*, 216–22, 262; Norwood, "Bogalusa Burning," 610–11, 614, 627.

17. Kellogg, *NAACP*, 135, 137, 145. See also Tindall, *New South*, 159; Autrey, "Can These Bones Live?" 1–2; Brundage, *Lynching in the New South*, 184, 230; Dittmer, *Black Georgia*, 206; Jordan, "Damnable Dilemma," 1575; Sherman, *Republican Party and Black America*, 123–24; Barnes, *Journey from Jim Crow*, 17; Reich, "Soldiers of Democracy," 1494; Zangrando, *NAACP Crusade against Lynching*, 35; Morton to Shillady, Memorandum on Negro Suffrage and Disfranchisement, 26 May 1929, p. 9, NAACP, part 4, reel 1, fr. 180; Chas. A. J. McPherson to NAACP, 18 Nov. 1920, ibid., fr. 483.

18. "The Ku Klux Are Riding Again!" *Crisis* 17 (Mar. 1919): 230; ibid. 21 (Feb. 1921): 165; Mordecai Wyatt Johnson, "The Faith of the American Negro," ibid. 24 (Aug. 1922): 156–57; Myrdal, *American Dilemma*, 2:999; Grantham, *Southern Progressivism*, 276–77; Rabinowitz, *First New South*, 49; Reich, "Soldiers of Democracy," 1485, 1488, 1502; Dittmer, *Black Georgia*, 203–5; Norwood, "Bogalusa Burning," 611, 615–17; McMillen, *Dark Journey*, 306; Lamon, *Black Tennesseans*, 272.

19. "School Segregation," *Crisis* 31 (Mar. 1926): 230; Kusmer, *A Ghetto Takes Shape*, chap. 8; Spear, *Black Chicago*, 201–22; Trotter, *Black Milwaukee*, 66–72, 202; Duncan, "Changing Race Relationships in the Border and Northern States," chaps. 3–4; Douglas, "Limits of Law," 705–8, 712; Hixon, "Moorfield Storey," 543; Henry M. Bates to Oscar W. Baker, 24 Nov. 1926, NAACP, part 5, reel 3, frs. 772–73; Baker to Walter White, 2 Dec. 1926, ibid., frs. 780–81; Herbert Seligman, report, 18 Apr. 1930, ibid., reel 2, frs. 143–44; Chicago Commission, *Negro in Chicago*, 3, 46, 122–35; Myrdal, *American Dilemma*, 2:602; Moore, *Ku Klux Klan in Indiana*, 140–45; Meier & Rudwick, *Along the Color Line*, 290–306; Sherman, *Republican Party and Black America*, 205–6; W. E. B. Du Bois, "The Tragedy of 'Jim Crow'," *Crisis* 26 (Aug. 1923): 169–72; "Inter-Marriage," ibid. 29 (Apr. 1925): 251; "The Chicago Conference," ibid. 32 (May 1926): 23–24; "Victory in Gary," ibid. 35 (Jan. 1928): 13; "Schools," ibid. (Feb. 1928): 50; "Concubinage," ibid. 41 (Feb. 1934): 51–53.

20. Myrdal, *American Dilemma*, 1:293–96, 304–6; Spear, *Black Chicago*, 151–55; Trotter, *Black Milwaukee*, 47, 53–55, 61–64, 73; Chicago Commission, *Negro in Chicago*, 403–35; Greenberg, *Black Harlem*, 18–28, 71–73; Northrup, *Organized Labor and the Negro*; "To the American Federation of Labor," *Crisis* 28 (Aug. 1924): 153.

21. Tindall, *New South*, 111–42, 161–64; Myrdal, *American Dilemma*, 1:230–50, 281–84, 287; McMillen, *Dark Journey*, 112–13 tables 4.1 and 4.2, 159–60, 164–65; Northrup, *Organized Labor and the Negro*, 19–21, 38–40, 119–20; Bernstein, "Licensing Laws"; Lamon, *Black Tennesseans*, 160, 162–64; Arnesen, "Race Question and American Railroad Brotherhoods," 1629–30; Anderson, *Education of Blacks in the South*, 229–34; Norwood, "Bogalusa Burning"; "Augusta and Atlanta," *Crisis* 36 (Feb. 1929): 66; "Our Economic Peril," ibid. 37 (Mar. 1930): 101; "Industry Comes to the South," ibid. 38 (Dec. 1931): 431.

22. Houston, "Educational Inequalities Must Go!" 300–301; Harlan, *Separate and Unequal*, 259; Tindall, *New South*, 175–79, 272; Boykin, "White and Negro Teachers' Salaries," 41 table 1; "Politics and Power," *Crisis* 23 (Feb. 1922): 153; "Mississippi," ibid. 24 (July 1922): 104; "Education," ibid. 29 (Nov. 1924): 8; "High Schools," ibid. 34 (Aug. 1927): 201–2; "South Carolina," ibid. 35 (Jan. 1928): 24; Lewis, *In Their Own Interests*, 83–84; Kneebone, *Southern Liberal Journalists*, 74, 90–91; Sosna, *Southern Liberals and the Race Issue*, 1–19, 24–27, 38–40; Eagles, *Jonathan Daniels and Race Relations*, 23–46; Kirby, *Black Americans in the Roosevelt Era*, 9–11; Woodward, *Strange Career of Jim Crow*, 116; Wynes, "Evolution of Jim Crow Laws," 416, 419; Moore, "Jim Crow in Georgia," 560–61; Wright, *Life behind a Veil*, 62; McKay, "Segregation and Public Recreation," 703–6.

23. "Shillady and Texas," *Crisis* 18 (Oct. 1919): 283; Autrey, "Can These Bones Live?" 3–6; Walter White, memorandum, 26 Feb. 1929, NAACP, part 5, reel 2, fr. 806; Smith, "Black Attorneys and the NAACP in Virginia," 5–6; Reich, "Soldiers of Democracy," 1500–1503; Kellogg, NAACP, 239–41; Fairclough, *Civil Rights Struggle in Louisiana*, 20; Brundage, *Lynching in the New South*, 230; Tindall, *New South*, 569; Lamon, *Black Tennesseans*, 19, 267–69; McMillen, *Dark Journey*, 314–16. See also "Klan Rule," *Crisis* 35 (Jan. 1928): 12–13; Robert W. Bagnall, "The Present South," ibid. 36 (Sept. 1929): 303; William Pickens, "Re-Visiting the South," ibid. 37 (Apr. 1930): 127.

24. "The Dyer Bill," *Crisis* 27 (Jan. 1924): 123; "Vote," ibid. 28 (July 1924): 104; "La Follette," ibid. (Aug. 1924): 154; "On the Fence," ibid. 35 (Nov. 1928): 381; "Whispers," ibid.; "The Campaign of 1928," ibid. (Dec. 1928): 418; W. E. B. Du Bois, "Herbert Hoover," ibid. 362–63; "President Harding and Social Equality," ibid. 23 (Dec. 1921): 53–56; "The Harding Political Plan," ibid. (Jan. 1922): 105–6; "Kicking Us Out," ibid. 24 (May 1922): 11; ibid. 28 (Aug. 1924): 152; "The NAACP and Parties," ibid. (Sept. 1924): 199–200; William Pickens, "Progressive Political Action," ibid. 211; "Where We Stand," ibid. (Oct. 1924): 247–48; Symposium, "How Shall We Vote?" ibid. 29 (Nov. 1924): 12–14; "The Acceptance Speeches," ibid. 35 (Oct. 1928): 346; "How Shall We Vote?" ibid.; "Color Discrimination in Government Service," ibid. (Nov. 1928): 369, 387–90; "Segregation," ibid. (Dec. 1928): 418; "Mr. Hoover and the Negro," ibid. 38 (June 1931): 207–8; Lester A. Walton, "Vote for Roosevelt," ibid. 39 (Nov. 1932): 343–44; Sherman, *Republican Party and Black America*, chaps. 6, 8, 9; Weiss, *Farewell to the Party of Lincoln*, 5–8, 15–17; Zangrando, *NAACP Crusade against Lynching*, 63, 76; *NYT*, 27 Oct. 1921, p. 1; Reagan, "Presidential Election of 1928 in Alabama"; McCarthy, "Smith vs. Hoover"; Tindall, *New South*, 245–51; Bunche, *Political Status of the Negro*, 193–98.

25. Myrdal, *American Dilemma*, 2:754; Sitkoff, *New Deal for Blacks*, 34; Fairclough, *Civil Rights Struggle in Louisiana*, 20; Goldfield, *Black, White, and Southern*, 23.

26. Sitkoff, *New Deal for Blacks*, 35–38, 252–53, 269; Kirby, *Black Americans in the Roosevelt Era*, 97–105; Lewis, *In Their Own Interests*, 111–17; Fairclough, *Civil Rights Struggle in Louisiana*, 41–42; Greenberg, *Black Harlem*, 74–75; Sullivan, *Days of Hope*, 20–21; Myrdal, *American Dilemma*, 1:289, 354–56, 2:1106; Tindall, *New South*, 571; *Crisis* 39 (Nov. 1932): 362–63; Trotter, *Black Milwaukee*, 147–50; Wolters, *Negroes and the Great Depression*, 90–92; Lamon, *Black Tennesseans*, 193; Wright, *Life behind a Veil*, 225–26; Miller, "Ladies and the Lynchers," 265; McGovern, *Anatomy of a Lynching*, 39–41.

27. Report of the Legal Committee, p. 2, Minutes of the Board of Directors Meeting, 14 Nov. 1932, NAACP, part 1, reel 2, fr. 1523; Roy Wilkins to Alonzo P. Holly, 25 May 1932, ibid., part 4, reel 1, fr. 994; Kirby, *Black Americans in the Roosevelt Era*, 152–217; Sitkoff, *New Deal for Blacks*, 245–46, 250–51, 254–57; Bunche, "Tactics and Programs of Minority Groups," 308–20; Myrdal, *American Dilemma*, 2:788–92; Tushnet, *NAACP's Legal Strategy*, 10–14; Lewis, *Du Bois*, 2:301–2; Bates, "Agenda of the Old Guard," 368–77; Robert W. Bagnall, "N.A.A.C.P. Branch Activities," *Crisis* 41 (Jan. 1932): 457, 473; unsigned memorandum, 21 Oct. 1937, NAACP, part 3, series A, reel 2, frs. 880–82; "Funds," *Crisis* 37 (Nov. 1930): 389. See also Roy Wilkins to C. H. Myers, 28 Apr. 1932, NAACP, part 10, reel 16, frs. 408–9.

28. Sitkoff, *New Deal for Blacks*, 39–46, 51; Sherman, *Republican Party and Black America*, 252–53, 255; "Democratic Platform of 1932," in *Party Platforms*, ed. Porter & Johnson, 331–33; "Republican Platform of 1932," in ibid., 349; Weiss, *Farewell to the Party of Lincoln*, 19–20, 29–31, 38–40, 244–45, 250–51; Gosnell, *Negro Politicians*, 30–31; Moon, *Balance of Power*, 30, 36–37; "Is Lynching a Crime?" *Crisis* 41 (Nov. 1934): 341; "The Best of the Anti-Lynching Fights," ibid. 42 (June 1935): 177; Walter White, "U.S. Department of (White) Justice," ibid. (Oct. 1935): 309–10. See also "When a Kidnapping Is Not a Kidnapping," ibid. 41 (Dec. 1934): 368.

29. Oswald Garrison Villard, "The Plight of the Negro Voter," *Crisis* 41 (Nov. 1934): 323; Wolters, *Negroes and the Great Depression*, 98–155; Sitkoff, *New Deal for Blacks*, 34–57; Abrams, *North Carolina and the New Deal*, 161–89; Kirby, *Black Americans in the Roosevelt Era*, 34, 128, 148, 150, 162–63, 179; Tindall, *New South*, 412–14, 480, 545–49; Myrdal, *American Dilemma*, 1:256–59, 343, 360–62; John P. Davis, "What Price National Recovery?" *Crisis* 40 (Dec. 1933): 271–72; Charles H. Houston & John P. Davis, "TVA: Lily-White Reconstruction," ibid. 41 (Oct. 1934): 290–91, 311; John P. Davis, "The Plight of the Negro in the Tennessee Valley," *Crisis* 42 (Oct. 1935): 294–95, 314–15.

30. Sitkoff, *New Deal for Blacks*, 77–82; Kirby, *Black Americans in the Roosevelt Era*, 16–23, 30–33, 39–42, 54, 59, 106–51, 210, 214, 218–19; Tindall, *New South*, 547, 549–50; Myrdal, *American Dilemma*, 1:74; Schulman, *Cotton Belt to Sunbelt*, 46–47; Weiss, *Farewell to the Party of Lincoln*, 136–56, 174, 209–10; Bunche, *Political Status of the Negro*, 98–100; Sullivan, *Days of Hope*, 44, 53–55.

31. Weiss, *Farewell to the Party of Lincoln*, 40–42, 100–101, 120–35; Cooke, *Eleanor Roosevelt*, 2:3–5, 153–54, 160–61, 185–86; Sitkoff, *New Deal for Blacks*, 59–64; Kirby, *Black Americans in the Roosevelt Era*, 76–96; Fishel, "Negro in the New Deal Era," 111–12; *Crisis* 41 (Jan. 1934): 20.

32. Weaver, "Racial Policy in Public Housing"; Wolters, *Negroes and the Great Depression*, 196–98, 202–5; Sitkoff, *New Deal for Blacks*, 66–68, 72–73, 76–77, 107, 272; Kirby, *Black Americans in the Roosevelt Era*, 22–23; Bunche, *Political Status of the Negro*, 505–15; Fishel, "Negro in the New Deal Era," 115; Tindall, *New South*, 644;

Fairclough, *Civil Rights Struggle in Louisiana*, 44; Sosna, *Southern Liberals and the Race Issue*, 66–67, 87; Patterson, "Failure of Party Realignment in the South," 611.

33. Editorial, *Charleston News & Courier*, 24 Mar. 1936, p. 4, in *Negro Suffrage*, ed. Logan, 58–59; Sitkoff, *New Deal for Blacks*, 91–101; Fishel, "Negro in the New Deal Era," 111–12; Weiss, *Farewell to the Party of Lincoln*, 185–87, 192, 206, 218–21; Tindall, *New South*, 556; Editorial, *Crisis* 43 (Dec. 1939): 369; McAdam, *Development of Black Insurgency*, 81–82; Myrdal, *American Dilemma*, 1:505–7; Sullivan, *Days of Hope*, 93; *Time*, 17 Aug. 1936, p. 10; Bunche, *Political Status of the Negro*, 83.

34. Fishel, "Negro in the New Deal Era," 116–17; Sitkoff, *New Deal for Blacks*, 107–11, 119, 131, 135, 169, 173, 175–83, 188, 332; Brinkley, *Liberalism and Its Discontents*, 76–77; Barone, *Our Country*, 77–78; Klarman, "Rethinking the Civil Rights and Civil Liberties Revolutions," 39–46; James Weldon Johnson to Louis Marshall, 24 Sept. 1927, NAACP, part 5, reel 4, fr. 351; pages 120–21.

35. Sitkoff, *New Deal for Blacks*, 70, 74, 118 (quotation), 287–88, 293; Fishel, "Negro in the New Deal Era," 115; Kluger, *Simple Justice*, 205; Kirby, *Black Americans in the Roosevelt Era*, 208; Myrdal, *American Dilemma*, 1:361–62; *Crisis* 45 (Mar. 1938): 84.

36. "In Court," *Crisis* 9 (Jan. 1915): 133–34; Sitkoff, *New Deal for Blacks*, 75, 217–18; Charles H. Thompson, "75 Years of Negro Education," *Crisis* 45 (July 1938): 204; Meier & Rudwick, *Along the Color Line*, 128–73; Tushnet, *NAACP's Legal Strategy*, 30–33; Houston, "Need for Negro Lawyers," 52; Carle, "Race, Class, and Legal Ethics in the Early NAACP," 118–19; page 166.

37. Sitkoff, *New Deal for Blacks*, 169–89; Northrup, *Organized Labor*, 8–16, 159–71, 237–38; Tindall, *New South*, 572–73; Myrdal, *American Dilemma*, 1:402–3, 2:1099, 1110–11; Bates, "Agenda of the Old Guard," 372.

38. Degler, *In Search of Human Nature*, 173–86; Sitkoff, *New Deal for Blacks*, 190–215; Myrdal, *American Dilemma*, 1:91–97, 2:1002–3; Fredrickson, *Black Image in the White Mind*, 329–31; Hovenkamp, "Social Science and Segregation."

39. Robert W. Bagnall, "N.A.A.C.P. Branch Activities," *Crisis* 40 (May 1931): 170; "North Carolina Breaks the Tradition," ibid. 43 (Dec. 1936): 369; "Press Comment on Anti-Lynching Bill," ibid. 44 (May 1937): 143, 153; "Virginia Dailies on Lynching," ibid. 145; David Cartwright, "Political Futures and the Negro," ibid. (June 1937): 171; "North Carolina Does It Again," ibid. (Nov. 1937): 337; "Gallup Poll Shows People Favor Bill," ibid. (Dec. 1937): 372; "Dallas," ibid. 45 (June 1938): 177; "Duke Joins Up," ibid. (Nov. 1938): 361; "Football Honor Roll," ibid. 46 (Nov. 1939): 337; Bunche, *Political Status of the Negro*, 71–72, 300, 438, 445, 451–52, 462, 547–71; Moon, *Balance of Power*, 175–78; Sitkoff, *New Deal for Blacks*, 75, 98–99; Bayor, *Twentieth-Century Atlanta*, 18–20; McMillen, *Dark Journey*, 314; Hoffman, "Modern Movement for Equal Rights in South Carolina," 363; Lau, "Clarendon County," 6; J. L. LeFlore to Marshall, 13 Mar. 1937, NAACP, part 3, series A, reel 2, fr. 67; Marshall to Walter White, 28 Nov. 1938, ibid., frs. 126–27; Tushnet, *NAACP's Legal Strategy*, 58–65, 77–81; Tindall, *New South*, 501; Boykin, "White and Negro Teachers' Salaries"; Kneebone, *Southern Liberal Journalists*, 142–43; Fairclough, *Civil Rights Struggle in Louisiana*, 50–51; Sullivan, *Days of Hope*, 93; Dollard, *Caste and Class*, 198; Norrell, "Labor at the Ballot Box," 205–6.

40. Editorial, *Fayette Chronicle*, 26 Sept. 1937, p. 4, in *Negro Suffrage*, ed. Logan, 46; Editorial, *Charleston News & Courier*, 12 June 1936, p. 41, in ibid., 61–63; Charles H. Houston to Roy Wilkins, 16 Sept. 1938, NAACP, part 4, reel 1, frs. 882–83; *Birmingham News*, 11 July 1936, p. 4, in *Negro Suffrage*, ed. Logan, 3; Editorial, *Augusta*

Chronicle, 27 Aug. 1938, p. 4, in ibid., 34–35; Editorial, *Charleston News & Courier*, 24 Mar. 1936, p. 4, in ibid., 58–59; Editorial, *Charleston News & Courier*, 28 Apr. 1936, p. 4, in ibid., 59–60; Editorial, *Charleston News & Courier*, 3 Aug. 1938, p. 4, in ibid., 71–73; *Greenville News*, 8 Aug. 1938, p. 4, in ibid., 77–78; Sitkoff, *New Deal for Blacks*, 102–23, 292–93; Freidel, *FDR and the South*, 77–81, 92; Martin, *Civil Rights and the Crisis of Liberalism*, 56–58; Patterson, "Failure of Party Realignment in the South," 602–4, 610, 617; Schulman, *Cotton Belt to Sunbelt*, 47; Barone, *Our Country*, 121–22; Sullivan, *Days of Hope*, 65–66; Brinkley, *Liberalism and Its Discontents*, 77–78; "Senator George Uses Race-Hatred Argument," *Crisis* 45 (Sept. 1938): 303.

41. *NYT*, 25 June 1936, p. 12; *Birmingham News*, 11 July 1936, p. 4, in *Negro Suffrage*, ed. Logan, 3; Letter to the Editor, *Charleston News & Courier*, 24 June 1936, p. 4, in ibid., 65; Editorial, *State* (Columbia, S.C.), 2 July 1936, p. 4a, in ibid., 74–75; Editorial, *State*, 8 Aug. 1936, p. 41, in ibid., 75–76.

42. Sitkoff, *New Deal for Blacks*, 89–91, 100, 262–67; Greenberg, *Black Harlem*, 96–97, 116–26, 137–39; Bunche, *Political Status of the Negro*, 584–85, 596–97; Homel, "Two Worlds of Race?" 253–54; Thornbrough, "Breaking Racial Barriers," 303–4; Mangum, *Legal Status of the Negro*, 76–77; *Time*, 17 Aug. 1936, p. 11; Meier & Rudwick, *Along the Color Line*, 307–404; Skotnes, "Buy Where You Can Work"; "Battle Renewed for Civil Rights," *Crisis* 42 (Oct. 1935): 311; Homel, *Black Chicagoans and the Public Schools*, 164–72; I. Maximilian Martin, "The Pennsylvania Civil Rights Act," *Crisis* 42 (Nov. 1935): 341, 350; Victor R. Daly, "Washington's Minority Problem," ibid. 46 (June 1939): 171; "The Catholics Speak," ibid. (Dec. 1939): 369. See also "Race Superiority Theory Lashed," ibid. 45 (Nov. 1938): 361.

43. Jones, "Negro before the Court during 1930," 230; Nelson, *Fourteenth Amendment*, 100–101; Post, "Substantive Due Process in the Taft Court Era"; Murphy, *Constitution in Crisis Times*, 41–67; Cushman, *New Deal Court*; Nixon v. Herndon, 273 U.S. 536 (1927); Brown v. Mississippi, 297 U.S. 278 (1936); Gong Lum v. Rice, 275 U.S. 78 (1927); Grovey v. Townsend, 295 U.S. 45 (1935); Corrigan v. Buckley, 271 U.S. 323 (1926); Nixon v. Condon, 286 U.S. 73 (1932); Herndon v. Lowry, 301 U.S. 242 (1937). See also Cushman, "Secret Lives of the Four Horsemen"; pages 193–96.

44. Higginbotham, *Shades of Freedom*, 156–58; "Mr. Harding," *Crisis* 22 (July 1921): 101; "The World Last Month," ibid. 13 (Dec. 1916): 59; Carter, "Charles Hamilton Houston," 2153–54; Kruse, "Gaines Case," 121; Ross, *Muted Fury*, 185; White, *Oliver Wendell Holmes*, 342–43, 353; Baskerville, *Louis D. Brandeis*, 54–55; Strum, *Brandeis*, 141–42, 164; Bracey, "Louis Brandeis and the Race Question," 863–64, 868, 873, 878, 883–85, 909; Pusey, *Charles Evans Hughes*, 1:110–11, 216, 2:622; Hutchinson & Garrow, *Memoir of John Knox*, 51, 160.

45. Goings, *Defeat of Judge John J. Parker*; Watson, "Defeat of Judge Parker"; Sherman, *Republican Party and Black America*, 239–46; Kluger, *Simple Justice*, 141–44; Sitkoff, *New Deal for Blacks*, 84–86; W. E. B. Du Bois, "The Defeat of Judge Parker," *Crisis* 37 (July 1930): 225; *NYT*, 8 May 1930, p. 1; Newman, *Hugo Black*, 89–100, 102–4, 112–17, 126–29, 239–49, 254–62; Ball & Cooper, *Of Power and Right*, 16, 20–25, 141; Robertson, *James F. Byrnes*, 298–99.

46. Cortner, *Mob Intent on Death*, 5–23; Rogers, "Elaine Race Riots of 1919"; "The Real Causes of Two Race Riots," *Crisis* 19 (Dec. 1919): 56–62.

47. Carter, *Scottsboro*, 3–50; Goodman, *Scottsboro*, 3–23.

48. Cortner, "*Scottsboro*" *Case in Mississippi*, 5–13, 15–31, 131–36.

49. Carter, *Scottsboro*, chaps. 1–2; Goodman, *Scottsboro*, chaps. 1–2; Cortner, *Mob Intent on Death*, chap. 1; Cortner, "*Scottsboro*" *Case in Mississippi*, chaps. 1–2.

The Scottsboro defendants were certainly innocent of the crimes charged, as revealed by a subsequent recantation by one of the alleged victims. Their innocence should have been reasonably clear at the trial, both from medical evidence and from the conflicting testimony of the prosecution witnesses. See Brief for Petitioners, *Powell v. Alabama*, 28–30, reprinted in *Landmark Briefs*, ed. Kurland & Casper, 27:324–26; Carter, *Scottsboro*, 27–30, 227–28, 232. The defendants in *Brown* were possibly innocent, and the state surely lacked sufficient evidence to convict them apart from their confessions, which had been obtained through torture. See Brown v. State, 161 So. 465, 471 (Miss. 1935) (Griffith, J., dissenting). The defendants in *Moore* were at most guilty of being present when lethal shots were fired, and not even clearly of this. See Cortner, *Mob Intent on Death*, 124–25. See also Downer v. Dunaway, 53 F. 2d 586 (5th Cir. 1931); Emanuel, "Lynching and the Law in Georgia"; Bass, *Unlikely Heroes*, 35–37.

50. The Bill of Rights, enacted in 1791, constrains only the federal government. One of the largest questions surrounding adoption of the Fourteenth Amendment in 1866–1868 was whether it would make the provisions in the Bill of Rights applicable to the states. The answer was not clear. For most of the next hundred years, the Supreme Court refused to apply the Bill of Rights to the states through the Fourteenth Amendment, though beginning in the 1920s and the 1930s the Court did apply some of its most important provisions, such as freedom of speech, to the states. Only in the 1960s did the justices apply most of the remaining provisions to the states.

51. Hurtado v. California, 110 U.S. 516 (1884); Maxwell v. Dow, 176 U.S. 581 (1900); Twining v. New Jersey, 211 U.S. 78 (1908); Stephens, *Supreme Court and Confessions of Guilt*, 42.

52. John Gould Fletcher, "Is This the Voice of the South?" *Nation* 137 (27 Dec. 1933): 734; Tom Tippett, "Short Cut to a Lynching," *Crisis* 43 (Jan. 1936): 9; Miller, *Race Adjustment*, 79; Carter, *Scottsboro*, 133–35, 241; Baker, *Following the Color Line*, 198–99; Miller, "Ladies and the Lynchers," 270; Wright, "Legal Executions of Kentucky Blacks," 251, 257; Raper, *Tragedy of Lynching*, 50; McMillen, *Dark Journey*, 206–7; Litwack, *Black Southerners in the Age of Jim Crow*, 299–301; Emanuel, "Lynching and the Law in Georgia," 246; *Crisis* 7 (Nov. 1913): 328; ibid. (Feb. 1914): 169; "The Athens of Texas," ibid. 37 (July 1930): 245–46. See also Smead, *Lynching of Mack Charles Parker*, 28–29, 33–34. But cf. Dorr, "Black-on-White Rape and Retribution in Twentieth-Century Virginia," 713–15, 736, 739–43.

53. *Crisis* 8 (July 1914): 116; Carter, *Scottsboro*, 105, 189. See generally Brundage, *Lynching in the New South*; Brundage, *Lynching in the South*; Wright, *Racial Violence*; Raper, *Tragedy of Lynching*, chaps. 1–3; Hale, *Culture of Segregation*, chap. 5; Litwack, *Black Southerners in the Age of Jim Crow*, chap. 6; McMillen, *Dark Journey*, chap. 7; Ayers, *Vengeance and Justice*, 238–55; Baker, *Following the Color Line*, chap. 9; Myrdal, *American Dilemma*, 2:558–69; Tindall, *South Carolina Negroes*, chap. 12; *Crisis* 10 (June 1915): 71; "The Waco Horror," ibid. 12 Supp. (July 1916): 1–8.

54. Raper, *Tragedy of Lynching*, 25, 46–47; Kellogg, *NAACP*, 210; Brundage, *Lynching in the New South*, 209, 238; Myrdal, *American Dilemma*, 2:565; Miller, "Ladies and the Lynchers," 277; Phillips, "Lynching and the Execution of Blacks in North Carolina"; Tindall, *New South*, 174, 554; Lewis, "'Judge Lynch' in Arkansas"; Wright, "Legal Executions in Kentucky"; McMillen, *Dark Journey*, 206–17; Carter, *Scottsboro*, 115; Ayers, *Vengeance and Justice*, 246; Mangum, *Legal Status of the Negro*, 298; Tindall, *South Carolina Negroes*, 252; Rice, *Negro in Texas*, 253; Bettis v.

State, 261 S.W. 46 (Ark. 1924); Emanuel, "Lynching and the Law in Georgia," 229; Cortner, *"Scottsboro" Case in Mississippi*, 3–4, 8; *Moore*, 261 U.S. at 88–90; Brief for Petitioners, *Powell v. Alabama*, 36–37, reprinted in *Landmark Briefs*, ed. Kurland & Casper, 27:332–33; Wright, *Racial Violence in Kentucky*, 251, 255; Curriden & Phillips, *Contempt of Court*, 49, 59, 62; Graham v. State, 82 S.E. 282, 285 (Ga. 1914); Harris v. State, 50 So. 626 (Miss. 1909); Williams v. State, 84 So. 8 (Miss. 1919); Thompson v. State, 26 S.W. 987 (Tex. Crim. App. 1894); Cleveland v. State, 94 S.W. 2d 746 (Tex. 1936); Cortner, *Mob Intent on Death*, 101; Downer v. Dunaway, 1 F. Supp. 1001, 1003 (M.D. Ga. 1932).

55. "Playing with Fire," *Forum* (Washington, Ga.), 25 June 1931, quoted in Emanuel, "Lynching and the Law in Georgia," 246 n. 161; Carter, *Scottsboro*, 105–7, 111–13 (quotation at 113); Cortner, *"Scottsboro" Case in Mississippi*, 11; Goodman, *Scottsboro*, 55–57; *Powell*, 141 So. at 211. See also McGuinn, "Fair Trials in Maryland," 164; Owsley, "Scottsboro," 285; Green, *Harry T. Moore*, 43–47.

56. *Brown*, 161 So. at 472 (Miss. 1935) (Griffith, J., dissenting); McMillen, *Dark Journey*, 208. See also Fairclough, *Civil Rights Struggle in Louisiana*, 26–29; "The Aiken Lynching," *Crisis* 34 (Sept. 1927): 222; "The Costigan-Wagner Bill," ibid. 42 (Feb. 1935): 55. On rare occasions, lynch mobs actually constituted themselves into extralegal adjudicative bodies, taking evidence and sometimes freeing a wrongly accused suspect. See McMillen, *Dark Journey*, 226–27, 239–44; Wright, "Legal Executions in Kentucky," 252.

57. *Wash. Post*, 22 June 1915, p. 3; Frank v. Mangum, 237 U.S. 309 (1915); Dinnerstein, *Leo Frank Case*, esp. 32, 127–28; MacLean, "Leo Frank Case Revisited"; Appellant's Argument, *Frank v. Mangum*, 3–8, reprinted in *Landmark Briefs*, ed. Kurland & Casper, 17:476–81; *Frank*, 237 U.S. at 345–50 (Holmes, J., dissenting).

58. *Moore*, 261 U.S. at 91–92; Hicks v. State, 220 S.W. 308, 309–10 (Ark. 1920); Fay v. Noia, 372 U.S. 391, 420–21 (1962); ibid., 457–58 (Harlan, J., dissenting); Paul Bator, "Finality in Criminal Law and Federal Habeas Corpus for State Prisoners," *Harvard Law Review* 76 (Jan. 1963): 441, 488–91; Cortner, *Mob Intent on Death*, 185–88; Eric M. Freedman, "Milestones in Habeas Corpus, Part II. Leo Frank Lives: Untangling the Historical Roots of Meaningful Habeas Corpus Review of State Convictions," *Alabama Law Review* 51 (Summer 2000): 1467, 1530–35; Note, *Yale Law Journal* 33 (1923): 82–84; Note, *Harvard Law Review* 37 (1925): 247–50; Brief for the Appellants, *Moore v. Dempsey*, 35–37, 40, reprinted in *Landmark Briefs*, ed. Kurland & Casper, 21:230–32, 235.

59. Cortner, *Mob Intent on Death*, 144–46.

60. "President Harding," *Crisis* 22 (June 1921): 68; Kellogg, *NAACP*, chap. 10; Sherman, *Republican Party and Black America*, 123–24, 174–99; Zangrando, *NAACP Crusade against Lynching*, 22–71 (esp. 35, 38); Note, *Harvard Law Review* 37 (1925): 250; Walter White, "The Work of a Mob," *Crisis* 16 (Sept. 1918): 221; ibid. 18 (June 1919): 59; "Anti-Lynching Legislation," ibid. 22 (May 1921): 8–9; "The Dyer Bill," ibid. (Sept. 1921): 212; "The Dyer Bill," ibid. 23 (Apr. 1922): 262–63; "Attention! Aim!" ibid. 24 (June 1922): 59.

61. Carter, *Scottsboro*, 50; Brief of Petitioners, *Powell v. Alabama*, 3–4, 34–62, reprinted in *Landmark Briefs*, ed. Kurland & Casper, 27:299–300, 330–58.

62. Brief for Respondent, *Powell v. Alabama*, 27–28, reprinted in *Landmark Briefs*, ed. Kurland & Casper, 27:399–400; Nelson, *Fourteenth Amendment*, 69; Carter, *Scottsboro*, 163–64; Sitkoff, *New Deal for Blacks*, 224–25; Cilella & Kaplan, "Discrimination against Negroes in Jury Service," 505–6.

63. Otto M. Bowman, "Comment," *Oregon Law Review* 12 (Apr. 1933): 229–33; Brief for Petitioners, *Powell v. Alabama*, 48–49, reprinted in *Landmark Briefs*, ed. Kurland & Casper, 27:344–55.

64. Carter, *Scottsboro*, 17–50; Brief for Petitioners, *Powell v. Alabama*, 9–14, 51–59, reprinted in *Landmark Briefs*, ed. Kurland & Casper, 27:305–10, 347–55; *Powell*, 287 U.S. at 56–57; State v. Collins, 29 So. 180 (La. 1900); Stroud v. Commonwealth, 169 S.W. 1021 (Ky. 1914). See also McDaniel v. Commonwealth, 205 S.W. 915 (Ky. 1918).

65. "The Scottsboro Case," *Wash. Post*, 8 Nov. 1932, p. 6; "The Scottsboro Case," *New York Herald-Tribune*, 8 Nov. 1932, p. 20; "The Scottsboro Cases," *Baltimore Sun*, 9 Nov. 1932, p. 10; "Righteously Remanded," *Richmond News Leader*, 8 Nov. 1932, p. 8; "The Scottsboro Case," *Richmond Times-Dispatch*, 9 Nov. 1932, p. 10.

66. Norris v. State, 156 So. 556 (Ala. 1934); Brief in Opposition to Petition for Writ of Certiorari, *Norris v. Alabama*, 7.

67. *Norris*, 294 U.S. at 589–91, 598; Schmidt, "Juries, Jurisdiction, and Race Discrimination," 1476–83; Eckhardt, "Comment," 233–35; Jefferson, "Race Discrimination in Jury Service," 424.

68. Carter, *Scottsboro*, 282–83, 319–20; *Norris*, 294 U.S. at 593 n. 1; *NYT*, 16 Feb. 1935, p. 2.

69. *Chattanooga News*, reprinted in "The South Split over the Scottsboro Verdict," *Literary Digest* 115 (22 Apr. 1933): 4; "Recent Decision," *Columbia Law Review* 35 (May 1935): 776, 777; Carter, *Scottsboro*, 232, 243–45, 252–53, 270, 322; Goodman, *Scottsboro*, 132, 148–49, 152–53; "Justice for Negroes," *NYT*, 2 Apr. 1935, p. 20; "The Scottsboro Decision," *Wash. Post*, 3 Apr. 1935, p. 8; "Comment on the Scottsboro Ruling," ibid.; "New Scottsboro Opinion," *Baltimore Sun*, 3 Apr. 1935, p. 12; "The Scottsboro Decision," *New York Herald-Tribune*, 2 Apr. 1935, p. 18; "Scottsboro Again," *Crisis* 42 (Feb. 1935): 48.

70. Lee v. State, 161 A. 284, 288 (Md. 1932); Nelson, *Fourteenth Amendment*, 76–77; McGuinn, "Fair Trials in Maryland," 154–64; *NYT*, 27 July 1932, p. 16.

71. Hale v. Crawford, 65 F. 2d 739 (1st Cir.), cert. denied, 290 U.S. 674 (1933); Nelson, *Fourteenth Amendment*, 77–79; Kluger, *Simple Justice*, 147–53; Tushnet, *NAACP's Legal Strategy*, 39–42; Lewis, *Du Bois*, 2:332–33; White, "George Crawford," 15; Richard W. Hale, "Justice and Law: A Dissertation on the Crawford Case," *Crisis* 41 (May 1934): 142–44; Charles H. Houston & Leon A. Ransom, "The Crawford Case," *Nation* 139 (4 July 1934): 17–19. Crawford was later tried and convicted in Loudoun County but received a life sentence rather than the death penalty, which the NAACP deemed a moral victory.

72. Myrdal, *American Dilemma*, 2:828; Nelson, *Fourteenth Amendment*, 79; White, "Crawford," 15; Jones, "Negro before the Court during 1932," 230; *NYT*, 27 July 1932, p. 16; Cilella & Kaplan, "Discrimination against Negroes in Jury Service," 498, 505; White to the American Fund–N.A.A.C.P. Joint Committee of Negro Work, memorandum, 13 Sept. 1934, p. 5, NAACP, part 3, series A, reel 2, fr. 214; John Temple Graves, "Scottsboro Ruling Disturbs the South," *NYT*, 7 Apr. 1935, sec. 5, p. 6.

73. Carter, *Scottsboro*, 303–8.

74. Patterson v. Alabama, 294 U.S. 600 (1935); "Recent Decision," *Columbia Law Review* 35 (May 1935): 776, 778; "Comment," *Columbia Law Review* 35 (June 1935): 941–42.

75. Brown v. Mississippi, 297 U.S. 278 (1936); Twining v. New Jersey, 211 U.S. 78 (1908); Brown v. State, 161 So. 465, 468 (Miss. 1935); Brief of Respondent, *Brown v. Mississippi*, 6–7, reprinted in *Landmark Briefs*, ed. Kurland & Casper, 31:104–5.

76. Wickersham Commission, *Lawlessness in Law Enforcement*, 11:3–4, 25, 28; Stephens, *Supreme Court and Confessions of Guilt*, 38–39; pages 132–33.

77. *Brown*, 297 U.S. at 279, 284; 161 So. at 471 (Griffith, J., dissenting).

78. *Brown*, 161 So. at 470; 297 U.S. at 285–86; Wickersham Commission, *Lawlessness in Law Enforcement*, 11:43–46, 91; Cortner, *"Scottsboro" Case in Mississippi*, 90–102, 120–21, 145–46; Klarman, "Rethinking the Civil Rights and Civil Liberties Revolutions," 65–66; Raymond, "Rejecting Totalitarianism," 1198–99; Stephens, *Supreme Court and Confessions of Guilt*, 40–42.

79. Hampton v. State, 40 So. 545, 546 (Miss. 1906); Funches v. State, 87 So. 487, 488 (Miss. 1921); Kneebone, *Southern Liberal Journalists*, 91; Jones, "Negro before the Court during 1930," 230; Clark v. State, 59 So. 887, 888 (Miss. 1912); Morehead v. State, 151 P. 1183, 1190 (Okla. Crim. App. 1915); Jones v. State, 109 So. 189, 190–91 (Ala. 1926); *Crisis* 1 (Dec. 1910): 7; Mangum, *Legal Status of the Negro*, 343–49, 356–63; McMillen, *Dark Journey*, 197–223; State v. Jones, 53 So. 959 (La. 1911); Williams v. State, 146 So. 422 (Ala. 1933); Tannehill v. State, 48 So. 662 (Ala. 1909); Sykes v. State, 42 So. 875 (Miss. 1907); Story v. State, 97 So. 806 (Miss. 1923); Byrd v. State, 123 So. 867 (Miss. 1929); Graham v. State, 82 S.E. 282 (Ga. 1914); Bell v. State, 20 S.W. 2d 618 (Ark. 1929); "In Texas," *Crisis* 26 (Aug. 1923): 165. See also Myrdal, *American Dilemma*, 2:552, 555.

80. Carter, *Scottsboro*, 109–10; Owsley, "Scottsboro"; Klarman, "*Brown*, Racial Change and the Civil Rights Movement," 109–11. For exceptions, see Powell v. State, 141 So. 201, 214 (Ala. 1932) (Anderson, C.J., dissenting); *Brown*, 158 So. at 343 (Anderson, J., dissenting); ibid., 161 So. at 471 (Griffith, J., dissenting); Carter, *Scottsboro*, 223–34, 266, 273.

81. Powell v. State, 141 So. 201 (Ala. 1932); Thompson v. State, 23 So. 676 (Ala. 1898); Seay v. State, 93 So. 403, 405 (Ala. 1922); page 125.

82. Carter, *Scottsboro*, 109–10, 119–36, 141–45, 152–53, 156 (quotation), 159–60, 174–78, 180–81, 243–45, 250–51; Goodman, *Scottsboro*, 27–31, 47–50; Owsley, "Scottsboro"; John Temple Graves, "Alabama Resents Outside Agitation," *NYT*, 21 June 1931, sec. 3, p. 5; ibid., 8 Nov. 1932, pp. 1, 13; Clarence Darrow, "Scottsboro," *Crisis* 41 (Mar. 1932): 81. See also Dinnerstein, *Leo Frank*, 105–6, 116–17.

83. Carter, *Scottsboro*, 100, 113, 118–20, 136, 153, 190 (quotation), 244–46, 253–61, 348, 372, 389–97; Owsley, "Scottsboro," 284; "The Affirmation of the Scottsboro Cases," *Birmingham News*, 25 Mar. 1932, p. 52; Cortner, *"Scottsboro" Case in Mississippi*, 37, 90–102; Emanuel, "Lynching and the Law in Georgia," 234–36; Goodman, *Scottsboro*, 152.

84. Newman v. State, 84 S.E. 597 (Ga. 1915); Graham v. State, 82 S.E. 282 (Ga. 1914); State v. Weldon, 74 S.E. 43 (S.C. 1912); Browder v. Commonwealth, 123 S.W. 328 (Ky. 1909); Brown v. State, 36 So. 73 (Miss. 1904); Collier v. State, 42 S.E. 226 (Ga. 1902); Thompson v. State, 23 So. 676 (Ala. 1898); Massey v. State, 20 S.W. 758 (Tex. Crim. App. 1892); Mangum, *Legal Status of the Negro*, 278, 282–85. The fact that the Arkansas Supreme Court twice reversed the death sentences of another set of six black defendants, who were also charged with murder arising from the Phillips County riot, may appear to undermine this interpretation. However, the state judges may have regarded these as compromise verdicts: So long as some of the Phillips County defendants were executed, the state's interest in vindicating white supremacy was satisfied. See Ware v. State, 252 S.W. 934 (Ark. 1923), 225 S.W. 626 (Ark. 1920); Walter F. White, "The Defeat of Arkansas Mob Law," *Crisis* 25 (Apr. 1923): 259–61; "Victory in Arkansas," *Crisis* 26 (Aug. 1923): 163–64; Waterman & Overton, "Aftermath of *Moore v. Dempsey*"; Cortner, *Mob Intent on Death*, 84–105.

85. Fisher v. State, 110 So. 361 (Miss. 1926); Whip v. State, 109 So. 697 (Miss. 1926); White v. State, 91 So. 903 (Miss. 1922); Mathews v. State, 59 So. 842 (Miss. 1912); McMillen, *Dark Journey*, 213; *Brown*, 158 So. at 342–43, 161 So. at 466–67. See also Bell v. State, 9 S.W. 2d 238 (Ark. 1928); Enoch v. Commonwealth, 126 S.E. 222 (Va. 1925); Butler v. State, 112 So. 685 (Miss. 1927).

86. Cortner, *"Scottsboro" Case in Mississippi*, 95–96, 103; Perkins v. State, 135 So. 357 (Miss. 1931); Carraway v. State, 154 So. 306 (Miss. 1934). See also Patterson v. State, 156 So. 567 (Ala. 1934).

87. Walter White, "The Sweet Trial," *Crisis* 31 (Jan. 1926): 125–29; James Weldon Johnson, "Detroit," ibid. 32 (July 1926): 117–20; Press Release, 28 Nov. 1935, NAACP, part 5, reel 3, fr. 164; White to Judge Frank Murphy, 4 Dec. 1925, ibid., frs. 230–31; Baker to White, 8 Mar. 1926, ibid., frs. 462–63; Myrdal, *American Dilemma*, 1:60–61, 2:526–29, 534, 555–56; McGuinn, "Fair Trials in Maryland," 145; Pincus, *Virginia Supreme Court*, 247–48; Emanuel, "Lynching and the Law in Georgia," 234–36; Cortner, *"Scottsboro" Case in Mississippi*, 64–69; Cortner, *Mob Intent on Death*, 43–44; Meier & Rudwick, *Along the Color Line*, 134.

88. "Recent Case," *George Washington Law Review* 1 (Nov. 1932): 116–17; Nelson, *Fourteenth Amendment*, 103–5.

89. Hine, *White Primary in Texas*, chaps. 1–2; Weeks, "White Primary," 135–53; Bunche, *Political Status of the Negro*, 30–32, 130, 150–54; Kousser, *Shaping of Southern Politics*, 73–77; Lamon, *Black Tennesseans*, 40–42; Dittmer, *Black Georgia*, 94–97.

90. Love v. Griffith, 266 U.S. 32 (1924); Nixon v. Herndon, 273 U.S. 536 (1927); Nixon v. Condon, 286 U.S. 73 (1932); Grovey v. Townsend, 295 U.S. 45 (1935); Hine, *White Primary in Texas*; Kluger, *Simple Justice*, 137–39, 233–39; Nelson, *Fourteenth Amendment*, 34–41, 85–106; Mangum, *Legal Status of the Negro*, 405–22; Lawson, *Black Ballots*, chap. 2; Hainsworth, "The Negro and the Texas Primaries."

91. *Herndon*, 273 U.S. at 541.

92. Ibid.; Lawson, *Black Ballots*, 27; Weeks, "White Primary," 145; Brief of Texas, *Nixon v. Herndon*, 5–6, 12–13; Schmidt, "Principle and Prejudice, Part III," 887–96; pages 36–37.

93. Pages 40, 69–71; Reply Brief for Plaintiff in Error, *Nixon v. Herndon*, 27; *Herndon*, 273 U.S. at 540–41.

94. "The Negro's Right to Vote," *Wash. Post*, 8 Mar. 1927, p. 6; Hine, *White Primary in Texas*, 47–49; Nelson, *Fourteenth Amendment*, 36–37; Alilunas, "Legal Restrictions on the Negro in Politics," 167, 172–73; Weeks, "White Primary," 138; Lawson, *Black Ballots*, 24–25. See also *Crisis* 8 (Aug. 1914): 172.

95. *Condon*, 286 U.S. at 105–6 (McReynolds, J., dissenting); Respondent's Brief, *Nixon v. Condon*, 5–6, 10–11, 13; Hainsworth, "Texas Primaries," 426; Alilunas, "Legal Restrictions on the Negro in Politics," 164–67; Weeks, "White Primary," 138–39.

96. Grovey v. Townsend, 295 U.S. 40 (1935); White v. Lubbock, 30 S.W. 2d 722 (Tex. Civ. App. 1930); West v. Blilely, 33 F. 2d 177 (E.D. Va. 1929), aff'd, 33 F. 2d 177 (4th Cir. 1929); Robinson v. Holman, 26 S.W. 2d 66 (Ark. 1930); Nixon v. Condon, 34 F. 2d 464 (W.D. Tex. 1929), aff'd, 49 F. 2d 1012 (5th Cir. 1931). See also Hine, *White Primary in Texas*, chap. 5; Editorial, *Richmond Times-Dispatch*, 3 Apr. 1935, p. 8, in *Negro Suffrage*, ed. Logan, 111; Weeks, "White Primary," 144–45, 153; Mangum, *Legal Status of the Negro*, 414–16; Lewinson, *Race, Class, and Party*, 155–56.

97. Seidman & Tushnet, *Remnants of Belief*, 49–71; Tushnet, *"Shelley v. Kraemer and Theories of Equality"*; Brest, "State Action and Liberal Theory."

98. Civil Rights Cases, 109 U.S. 3, 19 (1883); United States v. Harris, 106 U.S. 629, 639–40 (1883); Truax v. Corrigan, 257 U.S. 312, 328–30 (1921). On federal antilynching bills, see "The Federal Anti-Lynching Bill," *Columbia Law Review* 38 (Jan. 1938): 199–207; David O. Walter, "Proposals for a Federal Anti-Lynching Law," *American Political Science Review* 28 (June 1934): 436, 440–42; L. C. Dyer & George C. Dyer, "The Constitutionality of a Federal Anti-Lynching Bill," *St. Louis Law Review* 13 (1927–1928): 186–99.

99. West Coast Hotel v. Parrish, 300 U.S. 379, 391–400 (1937); Nebbia v. New York, 291 U.S. 502, 523–25, 534–39 (1934); Cushman, *New Deal Court*, 79–83; Seidman & Tushnet, *Remnants of Belief*, 66–67.

100. Petitioner's Reply Brief, *Nixon v. Condon*, 3–5, 8; Brief for Respondents, *Grovey v. Townsend*, 11, 15.

101. "Borah," *Crisis* 32 (Aug. 1926): 165; "The Negro's Right to Vote," *Wash. Post*, 8 Mar. 1927, p. 6; "Discourtesy," *Crisis* 41 (Oct. 1934): 308; Walter White, "U.S. Department of (White) Justice," ibid. 42 (Oct. 1935): 309; Chairman of National Legal Committee of NAACP to James A. Farley, 12 Mar. 1934, NAACP, part 4, reel 1, frs. 647–50; White to Farley, 16 July 1934, ibid., frs. 656–57; White to Sen. Robert Wagner, 25 July 1934, ibid., frs. 661–62; White to Emil Hurja, 23 Aug. 1934, ibid., frs. 697–98; Hurja to White, 7 Sept. 1934, ibid., fr. 737; White to R. D. Evans, 4 Sept. 1934, ibid., fr. 724; White to Joseph B. Kennan, 4 Sept. 1934, ibid., frs. 725–26; White to Keenan, 20 Sept. 1934, ibid., frs. 747–48; Sherman, *Republican Party and Black America*, 221–23; Nelson, *Fourteenth Amendment*, 50–55; Smith v. Allwright, 321 U.S. 649 (1944), discussed on pages 198–201.

102. Ogden, *Poll Tax in the South*, chaps. 1–2; Bunche, *Political Status of the Negro*, chap. 11. See also Kousser, *Shaping of Southern Politics*, 68–72.

103. Pages 34–35.

104. Breedlove v. Suttles, 302 U.S. 277 (1937); Massachusetts Board of Retirement v. Murgia, 427 U.S. 307 (1976); Harper v. Virginia State Board of Elections, 383 U.S. 663 (1966); Klarman, "Rethinking the Civil Rights and Civil Liberties Revolutions," 64.

105. Sitkoff, *New Deal for Blacks*, 132–34; Ogden, *Poll Tax in the South*, 123–28, 178–85, 199, 244–45, 252–54, 286–87; Bunche, *Political Status of the Negro*, 336–37, 364; Lawson, *Black Ballots*, 55–85; *Daily Clarion-Ledger* (Jackson, Miss.), 12 Sept. 1938, p. 4, in *Negro Suffrage*, ed. Logan, 45–46.

106. Arthur Spingarn to Walter White, 19 Mar. 1926, NAACP, part 5, reel 2, fr. 539; "Council Limits Home Residence," undated and unidentified press clipping, ibid., fr. 529; NAACP Press Release, 14 Feb. 1929, ibid., fr. 786; undated and unidentified press clippings, ibid., fr. 871; *New York Herald-Tribune*, 15 Mar. 1927, ibid., fr. 778; Walter White, memorandum, 25 Feb. 1929, p. 2, ibid., fr. 807; NAACP Press Release, 26 Mar. 1926, ibid., frs. 549–50; Robert W. Bagnall to Johnson, 24 Sept. 1924, ibid., frs. 629–30; Nelson, *Fourteenth Amendment*, 24–29; Moore, *Ku Klux Klan in Indiana*, 140–41; Lewis, *In Their Own Interests*, 69, 77–78; Bayor, *Twentieth-Century Atlanta*, 54–55; "A City Violates Law," *Crisis* 36 (Apr. 1929): 121.

107. Tyler v. Harmon, 104 So. 202, 208 (La. 1925), rev'd, 273 U.S. 668 (1927); City of Richmond v. Deans, 281 U.S. 704 (1930); Press Release, n.d., NAACP, part 5, reel 2, fr. 585; "Race Zoning Law Is Ruled against in District Case," undated and unidentified press clipping, ibid., fr. 646; Jos. R. Pollard to W. T. Andrews, 23 May 1929, ibid., fr. 842; NAACP Press Release, 23 July 1926, ibid., reel 4, fr. 888.

108. Pages 80–82, 105–6; Semonche, *Supreme Court Responds to a Changing Society*, 422–26; Murphy, *Constitution in Crisis Times*, 41–67.

109. Extracts from 1925 annual report, p. 4, NAACP, part 5, reel 1, fr. 951; *Detroit Independent*, 23 Oct. 1925, ibid., reel 2, fr. 1008; undated and unidentified press clipping, ibid., fr. 186; NAACP Press Release, 27 Feb. 1925, ibid., reel 4, fr. 389; Vose, *Caucasians Only*, 9–10; *Crisis* 4 (Sept. 1912): 222.

110. Corrigan v. Buckley, 271 U.S. 328 (1926); Herbert J. Seligman, "The Negro Protest against Ghetto Conditions," *Current History* 25 (Mar. 1927): 831, 832; Press Release, 18 June 1926, NAACP, part 5, reel 4, fr. 539; Johnson to Louis Marshall, 3 Feb. 1928, ibid., reel 2, fr. 100; William T. Andrews, circular, 20 Feb. 1928, ibid., fr. 106; Vose, *Caucasians Only*, 19; Cornish v. O'Donoghue, 30 F. 2d 98 (D.C. Cir.), cert. denied, 279 U.S. 871 (1929); Russell v. Wallace, 30 F. 2d 781 (D.C. Cir.), cert. denied, 279 U.S. 871 (1929); Grady v. Garland, 89 F. 2d 817 (D.C. Cir.), cert. denied, 302 U.S. 694 (1937).

111. Brief for Appellee, *Corrigan v. Buckley*, 7.

112. Appellant's Points, *Corrigan v. Buckley*, 42–46; Vose, *Caucasians Only*, 20–21; Nelson, *Fourteenth Amendment*, 148–51; Bruce, "Racial Zoning by Private Contract"; Los Angeles Investment Co. v. Gary, 186 P. 596 (Calif. 1919); Queensborough Land Co. v. Cazeaux, 67 So. 641 (La. 1915); Koehler v. Rowland, 205 S.W. 217 (Mo. 1918); Parmalee v. Morris, 188 N.W. 330 (Mich. 1922); White v. White, 150 S.E. 531 (W.Va. 1929).

113. Extract from 1925 annual report, p. 6, NAACP, part 5, reel 1, fr. 953; White to Lieutenant James F. Gegan, 4 Dec. 1924, ibid., fr. 576; "The Case of Dr. Sweet," *Afro-American Presbyterian*, 8 Oct. 1925, ibid., reel 2, fr. 984; "Residential Segregation," *Public Journal* (Philadelphia), 10 Oct. 1925, ibid., fr. 985; *Pittsburgh Courier*, 18 July 1925, ibid., fr. 962; James Weldon Johnson, letter to the editor, *Philadelphia Ledger*, 16 Nov. 1925, ibid., reel 4, fr. 43; Roy Wilkins to Stewart McDonald, 12 Oct. 1948, ibid., frs. 929–30; White to E. P. Lovett, 26 Oct. 1925, ibid., reel 3, frs. 19–20; NAACP Press Release, 14 May 1926, ibid., frs. 658–59; Myrdal, *American Dilemma*, 2:622–27; Miller, "Causes of Segregation"; *Crisis* 31 (Nov. 1925): 9–10; "Segregation," ibid. (Mar. 1926): 229–30; Tindall, *New South*, 546; Sitkoff, *New Deal for Blacks*, 50, 67; Jackson, *Crabgrass Frontier*, 198–214.

114. Nelson, *Fourteenth Amendment*, 29; Brief for Appellee, *Corrigan v. Buckley*, 9, 12. But see Gandolfo v. Hartman, 49 F. 181 (9th Cir. 1892).

115. Loewen, *Mississippi Chinese*, chaps. 1–2; Rhee, "Chinese in the Mississippi Delta"; Rice v. Gong Lum, 104 So. 105 (Miss. 1925).

116. Peterson, "Negro Separate School," 366–67.

117. Brief and Argument for Plaintiff in Error, *Gong Lum v. Rice*, 9–10; Brief for Defendants in Error, *Gong Lum v. Rice*, 36; Gong Lum v. Rice, 275 U.S. 78, 85–87 (1927).

118. NYT, 27 Oct. 1921, p. 1; Homel, *Black Chicagoans and the Public Schools*, 27–36; Meier & Rudwick, *Along the Color Line*, chap. 13; Kusmer, *A Ghetto Takes Shape*, 183, 187–89; Homel, "Two Worlds of Race?" 241–42; Du Bois, "Tragedy of 'Jim Crow'," 169–72; "The Victory of Springfield," *Crisis* 26 (Sept. 1923): 200; "The Sterling Discrimination Bill," ibid. (Oct. 1923): 252–55; "School Segregation," ibid. 31 (Mar. 1926): 230; Oak & Oak, "Separate Education in New Jersey"; "Follow Up," *Philadelphia Tribunal*, 26 Sept. 1925, NAACP, part 5, reel 2, fr. 979.

119. Du Bois, "Tragedy of 'Jim Crow'," 170; *Crisis* 41 (Feb. 1934): 52–53; Du Bois, "Does the Negro Need Separate Schools?" *Crisis* 41 (Jan. 1934): 20; ibid. (Apr. 1934):

115–17; "Segregation: A Symposium," ibid. (Mar. 1934): 79–82; Lewis, *Du Bois*, 2:335–44; Sitkoff, *New Deal for Blacks*, 251–52; Kirby, *Black Americans in the Roosevelt Era*, 189–202; Tushnet, *NAACP's Legal Strategy*, 8–10; Sullivan, "Prelude to *Brown*," 17–20; Thompson, "Court Action the Only Reasonable Alternative," 427–34; "The Negro and the Northern Public Schools," *Crisis* 25 (Mar. 1923): 205–8; Douglas, "Limits of Law," 712–19; Homel, "Two Worlds of Race?" 242–43; Myrdal, *American Dilemma*, 2:900–902; Editorial, *Pittsburgh Courier*, 30 Nov. 1929, NAACP, part 5, reel 2, fr. 893.

120. Houston, "Educational Inequalities Must Go!" 300–301; "Mixed Schools," *Crisis* 22 (Aug. 1921): 150; ibid. 41 (Feb. 1934): 51–53; Du Bois, "Tragedy of 'Jim Crow'," 170; Myrdal, *American Dilemma*, 2:796–97; McNeil, *Charles Hamilton Houston*, 34–36; Hoffman, "Modern Movement for Equal Rights in South Carolina," 356; McMillen, *Dark Journey*, 290–93; Nelson, *Fourteenth Amendment*, 162–63; Brief for Plaintiff in Error, *Gong Lum v. Rice*, 6, 16, 18; Rhee, "Chinese in the Mississippi Delta," 122, 125.

121. Kneebone, *Southern Liberal Journalists*, 12, 74–75, 149–50; Tindall, *New South*, 181; Houston, "Educational Inequalities Must Go!" 301; Report of Educational Inequalities in Arkansas, NAACP, part 3, series A, reel 2, frs. 172–73; Charles H. Houston, Memorandum concerning the Fight for Equality of Educational Opportunity, 19 Dec. 1936, ibid., frs. 611–12; National Educational Program of the NAACP, 27 Oct. 1936, ibid., reel 3, frs. 70–73; Anderson, *Education of Blacks in the South*, 188, 193; Myrdal, *American Dilemma*, 2:950–51; Tindall, *New South*, 270–71; "Education," *Crisis* 36 (Apr. 1929): 132.

122. Houston, "Cracking Closed University Doors," 370; Nelson, *Fourteenth Amendment*, 113–14; State ex rel. Gaines v. Canada, 113 S.W. 2d 783 (Mo. 1937); Brief in Support of Petition for Writ of Certiorari, *Missouri ex rel. Gaines v. Canada*, 12–13; Note, "Exclusion of Negroes from State-Supported Professional Schools"; "Comment," *North Carolina Law Review* 17 (Apr. 1939): 280–85; Elsa Kievits, "Comment," *Southern California Law Review* 13 (Nov. 1939): 68–74; Mangum, *Legal Status of the Negro*, 135; Smith, "Black Attorneys and the NAACP in Virginia," 8; "Professional Training," *Crisis* 38 (Jan. 1931): 11.

123. Houston, "Cracking Closed University Doors," 364; Houston to K. Norman Diamond, 14 Apr. 1936, NAACP, part 3, series A, reel 2, frs. 489–93; University of Maryland v. Murray, 169 Md. 478 (Ct. App. 1935); McNeil, *Charles Hamilton Houston*, 116, 133–34; Tushnet, *NAACP's Legal Strategy*, 34–36; Houston, "Educational Inequalities Must Go!" 301.

124. Kluger, *Simple Justice*, 155–58, 187–95, 202–4, 212–13; Tushnet, *NAACP's Legal Strategy*, 52–53, 56–58, 70–77; Burns, "Graduate Education for Blacks in North Carolina," 195–201; Seawright, "Desegregation at Maryland," 63–71; McGuinn, "Courts and Equality of Educational Opportunity," 159–62; Kruse, "Gaines Case."

125. *Gaines*, 305 U.S. at 349; King v. Gallagher, 93 N.Y. 438 (1883); Lehew v. Brummell, 103 Mo. 551 (1891); Williams v. Zimmerman, 192 A. 355 (Md. 1937); Brief of the Respondent, *Missouri ex rel. Canada v. Gaines*, 40–43; Brief of the Petitioner, ibid., 14–15; Kull, *Color-Blind Constitution*, 142–43; Tushnet, *NAACP's Legal Strategy*, 72–73. See also Seidman, "*Brown* and *Miranda*," 701.

126. Brief for Respondent, *Missouri ex rel. Canada v. Gaines*, 25, 35–37, 50, 60–64; *Gaines*, 305 U.S. at 353.

127. Mason, *Harlan Fiske Stone*, 515; "James W. Johnson and Louis T. Wright," *Crisis* 41 (Nov. 1934): 332–33; pages 195–96.

128. "Press Comment on the Gaines Case," 52–53, 61; Kruse, "Gaines Case," 124; R. B. Atwood to White, 14 Mar. 1939, NAACP, part 3, series A, reel 4, frs. 244–45; McGuinn, "Courts and Equality of Educational Opportunity," 163; Seawright, "Desegregation at Maryland," 69–70; "A New Note," *Crisis* 44 (Feb. 1937): 49.

129. "Victory in Arkansas," *Crisis* 26 (Aug. 1923): 163–64; "The Arkansas Cases Nearly Ended," ibid. 27 (Jan. 1924): 124–25; "The End of the Arkansas Cases," ibid. 29 (Apr. 1925): 272–73; Waterman & Overton, "Aftermath of *Moore v. Dempsey*," 5; Cortner, *Mob Intent on Death*, 182–83.

130. Powell v. State, 141 So. 201, 208–9 (Ala. 1932); Downer v. Dunaway, 1 F. Supp. 1001 (M.D. Ga. 1932); Ex parte Hollins, 14 P. 2d 243 (Okla. Crim. App. 1932); State v. Wilson, 158 So. 621 (La. 1935); Bard v. Chilton, 20 F. 2d 906 (6th Cir. 1927).

131. Carter, *Scottsboro*, 181, 189–90, 329, 341–48, 369–79. See also Dickson, "State Court Defiance"; Paulson & Hawkes, "Virgil Hawkins"; Tushnet, *Thurgood Marshall*, 283–89.

132. 287 U.S. at 71.

133. Carter, *Scottsboro*, 326–27; Nelson, *Fourteenth Amendment*, 82–83; *Birmingham News*, 5 Apr. 1935, p. 8; *Charleston News and Courier*, 13 Apr. 1935, p. 4; Mangum, *Legal Status of the Negro*, 333; Barbour, "Exclusion of Negroes from Jury Service," 200–204; State v. Grant, 19 S.E. 2d 638 (S.C. 1942); *Birmingham News*, 30 Apr. 1935, p. 1, in *Negro Suffrage*, ed. Logan, 2.

134. "Federal Action Sought in Texas Jury Case," *Crisis* 45 (Nov. 1938): 366; Carter, *Scottsboro*, 338–41, 369–70; Schmidt, "Juries, Jurisdiction, and Race Discrimination," 1482; Jefferson, "Race Discrimination in Jury Service," 433–34, 447; Nelson, *Fourteenth Amendment*, 82–83; Eckhardt, "Comment," 233–35.

135. Myrdal, *American Dilemma*, 2:549–50; Nelson, *Fourteenth Amendment*, 82 n. 96; page 127; Fairclough, *Civil Rights Struggle in Louisiana*, 63–64; Sitkoff, *New Deal for Blacks*, 231; *Pittsburgh Courier*, 29 Jan. 1943, p. 3; Pierre v. Louisiana, 306 U.S. 354 (1939); Martin, "Jess Hollins Rape Case," 187.

136. Cortner, *"Scottsboro" Case in Mississippi*, 153, 159.

137. Tushnet, *Thurgood Marshall*, 57; pages 129–30, 132–33.

138. Nelson, *Fourteenth Amendment*, 45; Walter White, "The Defeat of Arkansas Mob Law," *Crisis* 25 (Apr. 1923): 259–61; Press Release, 12 Sept. 1924, NAACP, part 5, reel 4, frs. 335–36; *Afro American* (national ed., Baltimore, Md.), 22 Feb. 1936, pp. 1–2; Carter, *Scottsboro*, 143–44, 170 n. 98; Cortner, *"Scottsboro" Case in Mississippi*, 40, 43–49; Kellogg, *NAACP*, 243; "Snatched from Mississippi Gallows," *Crisis* 42 (Mar. 1935): 79.

139. Houston, "Need for Negro Lawyers"; William Pickens to NAACP, 11 Apr. 1926, NAACP, part 5, reel 2, fr. 753; G. W. Lucas to James Weldon Johnson, 24 Apr. 1926, ibid., fr. 755; Cilella & Kaplan, "Discrimination against Negroes in Jury Service," 503 n. 17; Carter, *Scottsboro*, 75, 79–80, 179, 199–202, 205–10, 276 n. 7; Tushnet, *Thurgood Marshall*, 57; McGuinn, "Fair Trials in Maryland," 156–57; In re Ades, 6 F. Supp. 467 (1934). See also McMillen, *Dark Journey*, 217; Emanuel, "Lynching and the Law in Georgia," 237 n. 115; Browder v. Commonwealth, 123 S.W. 328 (Ky. 1909); Cortner, *"Scottsboro" Case in Mississippi*, 46, 59–60, 105–6, 155–56; Curriden & Phillips, *Contempt of Court*, 69–71.

140. "NAACP Funds," *Crisis* 33 (Dec. 1926): 63; Myrdal, *American Dilemma*, 2:550; Houston, "Need for Negro Lawyers," 49, 50 table 1; Meier & Rudwick, *Along the Color Line*, 130; McMillen, *Dark Journey*, 215; Kellogg, *NAACP*, 293; Sitkoff, *New*

Deal for Blacks, 217–18; Tushnet, *Thurgood Marshall*, 28–29; Litwack, *Black Southerners in the Age of Jim Crow*, 249–52; Editorial, *Crisis* 9 (Jan. 1915): 133–34.

141. "Communist Strategy," *Crisis* 40 (Sept. 1931): 314; "Herndon and the Scottsboro Cases," ibid. 42 (Dec. 1935): 369; Cortner, *"Scottsboro" Case in Mississippi*, 41–42, 90, 96; Cortner, *Mob Intent on Death*, 44–45, 49–50; Carter, *Scottsboro*, 53, 61–62, 75, 84–85; Walter White to "Jim," 17 Sept. 1925, p. 2, NAACP, part 5, reel 2, fr. 1032; White to Ira W. Jayne, 21 Sept. 1925, ibid., frs. 1056–57; White to Oscar W. Baker, 5 Oct. 1925, ibid., frs. 1115–18; White to O. O. Sweet, 6 Oct. 1925, ibid., frs. 1126–27; McNeil, *Charles Hamilton Houston*, 109–10.

142. Powell v. State, 141 So. 201, 210 (Ala. 1932); Patterson v. State, 156 So. 567 (Ala. 1934); Hicks v. State, 220 S.W. 308, 309 (Ark. 1920); *Frank*, 237 U.S. at 343; Fay v. Noia, 372 U.S. 391 (1962).

143. Cortner, *Mob Intent on Death*, 26, 91–92; Emanuel, "Lynching and the Law in Georgia," 240; Carter, *Scottsboro*, 205–10, 214–15, 223–24, 291. See also Browder v. Commonwealth, 123 S.W. 328 (Ky. 1909); Curriden & Phillips, *Contempt of Court*, 84, 88, 98.

144. Nelson, *Fourteenth Amendment*, 39, 85–86; NYT, 8 Mar. 1927, pp. 1, 6; *Wash. Post*, 8 Mar. 1927, pp. 1, 4.

145. Bliley v. West, 42 F. 2d 101 (4th Cir. 1930); Goode v. Johnson, 149 So. 736 (Fla. 1933); Bunche, *Political Status of the Negro*, 442; Hine, *White Primary in Texas*, 95–96, 101. But cf. Lewinson, *Race, Class, and Party*, 156; Burch, "NAACP before and after *Grovey v. Townsend*," 72–73; pages 236–53.

146. Kousser, *Shaping of Southern Politics*, 65–66, 71; Key, *Southern Politics*, 535, 579, 597–98, 603–6, 617–18; Ogden, *Poll Tax in the South*, 118, 125–26, 129, 174–75; Fairclough, *Civil Rights Struggle in Louisiana*, 24; Bunche, *Political Status of the Negro*, 54–55, 58–59, 330–31, 337–38, 342, 382–83; Myrdal, *American Dilemma*, 1:515; Farris, "Re-Enfranchisement of Negroes in Florida," 268; Editorial, *Jackson Daily Clarion Ledger*, 12 Sept. 1938, p. 4, in *Negro Suffrage*, ed. Logan, 45–46; Robert Smith, "The Poll Tax: Enemy of Democracy," *Crisis* 46 (Apr. 1939): 106.

147. Nelson, *Fourteenth Amendment*, 29; Spear, *Black Chicago*, 14–17; Hirsch, *Making the Second Ghetto*, 4; Sugrue, *Origins of the Urban Crisis*, 23–24. See also Miller, "Causes of Segregation," 829–30; Fairclough, *Civil Rights Struggle in Louisiana*, 18.

148. Hyman & Sheatsley, "Attitudes toward Desegregation," 36; chapter 7.

149. Note, "Exclusion of Negroes from State-Supported Professional Schools," 1298–99; McGuinn, "Courts and Equality of Educational Opportunity," 162; Kluger, *Simple Justice*, 189, 195; Seawright, "Desegregation at Maryland," 62–63, 65; White to K. Norman Diamond, 14 Apr. 1936, NAACP, part 3, series A, reel 2, frs. 489–93; Thurgood Marshall to George Snowden, 4 June 1937, ibid., fr. 761.

150. Kruse, "Gaines Case," 124; Nelson, *Fourteenth Amendment*, 123 n. 58, 124 n. 63, 125–26, 168; U.S. Civil Rights Commission, *Public Higher Education*, 19–22; Tindall, *New South*, 562–63; "Educational Equality Fight," *Crisis* 46 (Oct. 1939): 310; ibid. (Nov. 1939): 339, 341; Bluford v. Canada, 32 F. Supp. 707 (W.D. Mo. 1940); Mangum, *Legal Status of the Negro*, 135–36; R. B. Atwood to White, 14 Mar. 1939, NAACP, part 3, series A, reel 4, frs. 244–45; Glenn Hutchinson, "Jim Crow Challenged in a Southern University," *Crisis* 46 (Apr. 1939): 103; Houston, "Cracking Closed University Doors"; Sitkoff, *New Deal for Blacks*, 222; Lucile Bluford, "Missouri 'Shows' the Supreme Court," *Crisis* 46 (Aug. 1939): 231–32, 242; Myrdal, *Ameri-*

can Dilemma, 2:629, 833, 904; Barksdale, "The Gaines Case," 309–13; Burns, "Graduate Education for Blacks in North Carolina," 204–7; Minutes of the NAACP Board of Directors Meeting, 11 Sept. 1939, NAACP, part 1, reel 2, fr. 990; Jenkins, "Availability of Higher Education for Negroes," 462, 464, 470; *NYT*, 12 Nov. 1939, sec. 4, p. 10; pages 253–55.

151. Higginbotham & Smith, "Hughes Court," 1124, 1125; "University of Missouri Case Won," *Crisis* 46 (Jan. 1939): 10; Charles H. Houston to Yolanda Barnett, 1 Apr. 1936, NAACP, part 3, series A, reel 4, fr. 205; Sitkoff, *New Deal for Blacks*, 241–42; Tindall, *New South*, 562; Kruse, "Gaines Case," 126; Carter, "Charles Hamilton Houston," 2153; *Portland* (Maine) *Herald*, in "Press Comment on the Gaines Case," 52–53, 61; Peterson, "Present Status of the Negro Separate School," 354, 366; Risen, "Separation of Races in the Public Schools," 50–51, 66, 133; Oak & Oak, "Development of Separate Education in New Jersey," 109–10; Houston, "Cracking Closed University Doors"; State v. Canada, 153 S.W. 2d 12 (Mo. 1941); Bluford v. Canada, 32 F. Supp. 707 (W.D. Mo. 1940); Wrighten v. Board of Trustees, 72 F. Supp. 948 (E.D.S.C. 1947); Sweatt v. Painter, 210 S.W. 2d 442 (Tex. Civ. App. 1948); "Dangerous Federal School Aid," *Crisis* 44 (Feb. 1937): 41–42, 50, 60.

152. Glenn Hutchinson, "Jim Crow Challenged in Southern Universities," *Crisis* 46 (Apr. 1939): 103; "Press Comment on the Gaines Case," 53; Editorial, *Charleston News and Courier*, quoted in "Sense and Nonsense from South Carolina," *Crisis* 48 (Sept. 1941): 287; Levy, "Racial Integration of American Higher Education," 303.

153. Peterson, "Present Status of the Negro Separate School," 369; Marshall, "Racial Integration in Education," 319; Risen, "Separation of Races in the Public Schools," 73–74; Dameron v. Bayless, 14 Ariz. 180 (1912); State ex rel. Cheeks v. Wirt, 177 N.E. 441 (Ind. 1931); Williams v. Zimmerman, 192 A. 353 (Md. 1937); pages 205–8. But cf. Kull, *Color-Blind Constitution*, 143.

154. J. Rice Perkins to Walter White, 7 May 1935, NAACP, part 3, series A, reel 4, fr. 367; Jasper E. Gayle to Robert W. Bagnall, 27 Nov. 1924, part 5, reel 2, fr. 645; White to Edward S. Lewis, 8 Sept. 1937, part 3, series A, reel 2, frs. 818–19; King, *Stride toward Freedom*, 37; King, *Why We Can't Wait*, 65, 111; Myrdal, *American Dilemma*, 2:758–59, 825; Cell, *Highest Stage of White Supremacy*, 240–41; Kellogg, *NAACP*, 131; Fairclough, *Civil Rights Struggle in Louisiana*, 47; Kluger, *Simple Justice*, 157; McAdam, *Development of Black Insurgency*, 106; Brundage, "Black Resistance and White Violence," 272; Dollard, *Caste and Class*, 182–84; Sullivan, "Prelude to Brown," 11. See also Scott, *Contempt and Pity*, 24–26, 82–83; *Crisis* 34 (Sept. 1927): 224; George S. Schuyler, "Do We Really Want Equality?" ibid. 44 (Apr. 1937): 102–3.

155. "Violence," *Crisis* 41 (May 1934): 147–48; "The Negro and Non-Resistance," ibid. 28 (June 1924): 58; ibid. 46 (July 1939): 211; Thompson, "Court Action the Only Reasonable Alternative"; Bunche, "Tactics and Programs of Minority Groups," 312; Myrdal, *American Dilemma*, 2:558–69; Fairclough, *Civil Rights Struggle in Louisiana*, 25–26; Brundage, "Black Resistance and White Violence," 272–73; Howard & Howard, "Early Years of the NAACP in Tampa," 51–52; Meier & Rudwick, *Along the Color Line*, 348; Dollard, *Caste and Class*, 290–91. See also Hine, *White Primary in Texas*, 45–46; Cortner, *Mob Intent on Death*, 26.

156. "Migration and Help," *Crisis* 13 (Jan. 1917): 115; Clarence M. Wigfall to Marshall, 2 May 1938, NAACP, part 3, series A, reel 3, fr. 503; J. L. LeFlore to Marshall, 13 Mar. 1937, ibid., reel 2, fr. 67; Houston to B. T. Harvey, 29 Apr. 1938, ibid., reel 3, frs. 496–98; Kluger, *Simple Justice*, 215; Nelson, *Fourteenth Amendment*, 131; Tushnet,

NAACP's Legal Strategy, 59–62, 72–73; Green, Harry T. Moore, 35–40; Peterson, "Present Status of the Negro Separate School," 362; Dollard, Caste and Class, 302. See also Kelley, "Black Working-Class Opposition," 75–112; Brundage, "Black Resistance and White Violence," 271–85.

157. Kluger, Simple Justice, 132; Bunche, "Tactics and Programs of Minority Groups," 315. See also Bates, "Agenda of the Old Guard"; Meier & Rudwick, Along the Color Line, 321, 325, 331, 339–40, 344; Walker, ACLU, 89.

158. Houston & Ransom, "Crawford Case," 18–19; McNeil, Charles Hamilton Houston, 135 (quotation), 139, 223; Sullivan, Days of Hope, 91; Nelson, Fourteenth Amendment, 62–63. See also Thompson, "Court Action the Only Reasonable Alternative," 422–26; Charles H. Thompson, "The Negro Separate School," Crisis 42 (Aug. 1935): 230–31; Sitkoff, New Deal for Blacks, 221–22.

159. Bunche, Political Status of the Negro, 108; J. Rice Perkins to Walter White, 7 May 1935, NAACP, part 3, series A, reel 4, fr. 367; Greenberg, Crusaders in the Courts, 59, 212; Charles H. Houston, memorandum, 26 Oct. 1934, part 3, series A, reel 1, frs. 859–60; Marshall to Roy L. Ferguson, 19 Aug. 1937, ibid., reel 2, frs. 789–90. See also Zangrando, NAACP Crusade against Lynching, 38–39, 214; Sherman, Republican Party and Black America, 198; McGuinn, "Fair Trials in Maryland," 163–65; Sitkoff, New Deal for Blacks, 242–43; "Protest," Crisis 37 (Oct. 1930): 352–53; Jones, "Negro before the Court during 1930," 230; Hainsworth, "Negro and the Texas Primaries," 433–34, 441–42; Smith, "Black Attorneys and the NAACP in Virginia," 27.

160. Tushnet, Thurgood Marshall, 30; McNeil, Charles Hamilton Houston, 145. See also ibid., 216–18; Sullivan, Days of Hope, 83–84, 91; Carle, "Race, Class, and Legal Ethics in the Early NAACP," 121–22, 126–27; Smith, "Black Attorneys and the NAACP in Virginia," 3–4, 19; Symposium, "Courts and Racial Integration in Education," 336 (Thurgood Marshall).

161. "Snatched from Mississippi Gallow [sic]," Crisis 42 (Mar. 1935): 79; Press Release, 15 Jan. 1926, NAACP, part 5, reel 3, fr. 415; "Dr. Sweet," Florida Sentinel, 14 Nov. 1925, ibid., reel 4, fr. 34; "A Hopeful Sign," St. Louis Argus, 1 Jan. 1926, ibid., fr. 210; "Sweet Case," unidentified press clipping, 29 May 1926, ibid., fr. 291; "Nation Wide Defense Fund a Success," Crisis 31 (Feb. 1926): 187; Carter, Scottsboro, 143–44; Kellogg, NAACP, 184–86; Schmidt, "Principle and Prejudice, Part I," 503, 514; Wright, Life behind a Veil, 231, 238; Martin, "Jess Hollins Rape Case," 181; Sullivan, "Prelude to Brown," 9–10; Legal Defense Report on Residential Segregation (1926), NAACP, part 5, reel 1, fr. 955; Bagnall to Johnson, 24 Sept. 1924, ibid., reel 2, frs. 629–30; G. W. Lucas to Bagnall, 19 Nov. 1924, ibid., fr. 644; Lucas to Bagnall, 9 Mar. 1925, ibid., fr. 716; A. V. Dunn to Bagnall, 9 Nov. 1924, ibid., reel 4, frs. 820–21; Cortner, "Scottsboro" Case in Mississippi, 72–73; Kluger, Simple Justice, 195, 199. See also Crisis 21 (Feb. 1921): 165–66; "Victory," ibid. 26 (Aug. 1923): 151; "In Texas," ibid. 165.

162. Tushnet, Thurgood Marshall, 62–63, 66; Oscar W. Baker to White, 8 Mar. 1926, NAACP, part 5, reel 3, frs. 462–63; Meier & Rudwick, Along the Color Line, 149–52; Hainsworth, "The Negro and the Texas Primaries," 435–36; Kluger, Simple Justice, 150–53. See also Sullivan, Days of Hope, 91; Martin, Angelo Herndon, 58; Green, "Memphis Freedom Movement," 22–23; White, "George Crawford"; Minutes of NAACP Board of Directors Meeting, 11 June 1951, pp. 2–3, NAACP, part 1, reel 3, frs. 380–81.

163. Charles Hamilton Houston, "Don't Shout Too Soon," Crisis 43 (Mar. 1936): 79; "A 20th Anniversary Year," Crisis 36 (Mar. 1929): 83; Bunche, Political Status of the

Negro, 108; White to Johnson, 15 Nov. 1925, NAACP, part 5, reel 3, fr. 92; Minutes of the NAACP Board of Directors Meeting, 14 Nov. 1938, p. 3, part 1, reel 2, fr. 918; Schmidt, "J. Waties Waring," 13; Sitkoff, *New Deal for Blacks*, 243, 278, 296–97; Myrdal, *American Dilemma*, 1:48; Zangrando, *NAACP Crusade against Lynching*, 18; *Crisis* 3 (Feb. 1912): 157; ibid. 9 (Dec. 1914): 86; "The Lynching Fund," ibid. 13 (Dec. 1916): 62; "Publicity," ibid. 24 (May 1922): 9. See also "Everybody's Fight," ibid. 44 (June 1937): 177.

164. Nelson, *Fourteenth Amendment*, 106 n. 177; Martin, "Jess Hollins Rape Case," 179; Chong, *Collective Action and the Civil Rights Movement*, chaps. 5–6; McAdam, *Development of Black Insurgency*, 105–6, 111; "N.A.A.C.P.," *Crisis* 26 (Sept. 1923): 199. See also "The Indianapolis Conference," ibid. 34 (July 1927): 155; "Three Achievements and Their Significance," ibid. (Sept. 1927): 222; "A 20th Anniversary Year," ibid. 36 (Mar. 1929): 83; Carle, "Race, Class and Legal Ethics in the Early NAACP," 118.

165. Sitkoff, *New Deal for Blacks*, 81–82, 326–35; Myrdal, *American Dilemma*, 2:660–61, 998–1000; Fishel, "Negro in the New Deal Era," 121; Reich, "Soldiers of Democracy," 1502; Rudwick, *Race Riot*, 134; Sherman, *Republican Party and Black America*, 165–66, 247; Weiss, *Farewell to the Party of Lincoln*, 260–66; "Lincoln, Harding, James Crow and Taft," *Crisis* 24 (July 1922): 122; "We Are Ashamed for Them," ibid. 46 (Feb. 1939): 49; "The Real D.A.R.," ibid. (May 1939): 145.

166. "A New South in the Making," *Crisis* 46 (Apr. 1939): 113; "Miracle," ibid. 47 (May 1940): 145; Victor R. Daly, "Washington's Minority Problem," ibid. 46 (June 1939): 171; "America Moves Up a Notch," ibid. 42 (Nov. 1935): 337; Fairclough, *Civil Rights Struggle in Louisiana*, 37, 47; Mangum, *Legal Status of the Negro*, 307; Sitkoff, *New Deal for Blacks*, 261, 272, 289, 291–92; Hoffman, "Modern Movement for Equal Rights in South Carolina," 367; Smith, "Black Attorneys and the NAACP in Virginia," 6; Kneebone, *Southern Liberal Journalists*, 105, 148, 170–71; Tindall, *New South*, 636–37; Sullivan, *Days of Hope*, 99–100; Editorial, *Richmond Times-Dispatch*, 2 Feb. 1937, p. 6; Lawson, *Black Ballots*, chap. 3; *Crisis* 47 (Apr. 1940): 115; Mead, *Joe Louis*, 115–16, 158–59; *Crisis* 6 (Aug. 1913): 177.

167. Weiss, *Farewell to the Party of Lincoln*, 247; Bunche, *Politial Status of the Negro*, 75, 307, 388–437, 560, 563; Myrdal, *American Dilemma*, 2:1000; Fairclough, *Civil Rights Struggle in Louisiana*, 25; Sitkoff, *New Deal for Blacks*, 98; Sullivan, *Days of Hope*, 144–45; Daniel, "Education for Negroes in the Secondary School," 458; Edith Stern, "Jim Crow Goes to School in New York," *Crisis* 44 (July 1937): 201; "The Masquerade Is Over," ibid. 46 (June 1939): 179; "Klan Threats to Voters," ibid. (Aug. 1939): 241; "Brownsville, Tenn., U.S.A., 1940," ibid. 47 (Aug. 1940): 232.

168. Sitkoff, *New Deal for Blacks*, ix, 58, 82–83, 244, 328, 335; *Crisis* 41 (May 1934): 148; H. L. Mencken, "Notes on Negro Strategy," ibid. (Oct. 1934): 304; William H. Hastie, "A Look at the NAACP," ibid. 46 (Sept. 1939): 263–64, 274; Kirby, *Black Americans in the Roosevelt Era*, 114; *Crisis* 41 (Apr. 1934): 115–17; Du Bois, "Does the Negro Need Separate Schools?" 330, 332; Cell, *Highest Stage of White Supremacy*, 274–75; Myrdal, *American Dilemma*, 2:754; Lewis, *Du Bois*, 2:331.

169. Note, "Negro Citizen," 831–32; Nelson, *Fourteenth Amendment*, 159–60, 162; United States v. Carolene Products Co., 304 U.S. 144, 152–53 n. 4 (1938); Cover, "Origins of Judicial Activism"; Klarman, "Modern Equal Protection," 221–26; Lusky, "Carolene Products Reminiscence."

170. Freidel, *FDR and the South*, 92–94.

171. Nelson, *Fourteenth Amendment*, 160, 168.

CHAPTER 4

1. Thurgood Marshall to Walter White, 2 Feb. 1941, NAACP, part 8, series B, reel 8, frs. 886–88; Roscoe Dunjee to Marshall, 26 Dec. 1940, ibid., frs. 849–50; Stanley D. Belden to Marshall, 7 Jan. 1941, ibid., fr. 852; Dunjee to Marshall, 13 Jan. 1941, ibid., fr. 855; NAACP Press Release, 31 Jan. 1941, ibid., fr. 876; Belden to Marshall, 31 Mar. 1941, ibid., frs. 932–33; Belden to Marshall, 6 May 1941, ibid., frs. 951–52; "Tortured with Charred Bones," *Crisis* 48 (Mar. 1941): 85; Tushnet, *Thurgood Marshall*, 61–64.

2. Schulman, *Cotton Belt to Sunbelt*, 16–20, 82, 102–3; Wynn, *Second World War*, 61; Bartley, *New South*, 10–11, 123–24; McAdam, *Development of Black Insurgency*, 74–81; Daniel, "Transformation of the Rural South," 232, 236, 242–43; pages 100–104.

3. Foner, *American Freedom*, 97, 219–47; Klinker with Smith, *Rise and Decline of Racial Equality*, 3–4, 16–23, 51–71, 161–201; Dalfiume, "'Forgotten Years' of the Negro Revolution," 90–106; Fairclough, *Civil Rights Struggle in Louisiana*, chap. 4; Dittmer, *Struggle for Civil Rights in Mississippi*, chap. 1; McCoy & Ruetten, *Minority Rights and the Truman Administration*, chap. 1; Litwack, *North of Slavery*, 6–12, 14–15; Zilversmit, *Abolition of Slavery in the North*, 109–12, 117–19, 126–27, 137–38, 146, 169–70, 227–29; Foner, *Reconstruction*, 66–67, 114–15, 223, 244–45, 255; Gillette, *Right to Vote*, 81, 85; McPherson, *Battle Cry of Freedom*, 494–97, 840–41; Isaacs, *New World of Negro Americans*, 37–38; McMillen, *Dark Journey*, 316–17; pages 28, 104. But see Polenberg, "The Good War?" 321.

4. Klarman, "History of American Freedom," 272–76.

5. Norrell, "One Thing We Did Right," 68; "Charity Begins at Home," *Crisis* 45 (Apr. 1938): 113; "Refugees and Citizens," ibid. (Sept. 1938): 301; "Negroes, Nazis, and Jews," ibid. (Dec. 1938): 393; "A New Fight for Democracy," ibid. 46 (Jan. 1939): 17; "Lily White Democracy," ibid. (Feb. 1939): 49; "Lynching and Liberty," ibid. 47 (July 1940): 209; ibid. 40 (Dec. 1933): 269; *Pittsburgh Courier*, 22 Jan. 1938, sec. 1, p. 1; *Atlanta Constitution*, 5 Feb. 1939, p. 6b, in *Negro Suffrage*, ed. Logan, 31–32; Kneebone, *Southern Liberal Journalists*, 181; Sitkoff, *New Deal for Blacks*, 298–301, 324; Klinkner with Smith, *Rise and Decline of Racial Equality*, 136–43; Weiss, "Ethnicity and Reform," 566, 571; Kellogg, "Civil Rights Consciousness in the 1940s," 30–31; Bixby, "Roosevelt Court," 763; Grill & Jenkins, "Nazis and the American South," 669–70, 676; *Atlanta Constitution*, 17 Jan. 1939, p. 7; ibid., 24 Mar. 1939, p. 10.

6. Wynn, *Second World War*, 28, 45, 107; Willkie, *One World*, 190; Barone, *Our Country*, 160; Isaacs, *New World of Negro Americans*, 41–42; Hirabayashi v. United States, 320 U.S. 81, 110 (1943) (Murphy, J., concurring); Kellogg, "Civil Rights Consciousness in the 1940s," 18, 23–24, 31; Foner, *American Freedom*, chap. 10; Dudziak, "Desegregation as a Cold War Imperative," 68–70.

7. Wynn, *Second World War*, 102; Dalfiume, *Fighting on Two Fronts*, 109–10; Garfinkle, *March on Washington Movement*, 22–24; Blum, *V Was for Victory*, 182–83; Sitkoff, "Racial Militancy and Interracial Violence," 664–65; Wilkins, "Negro Wants Full Equality," 113–15; Randolph, "March on Washington Movement," 134; Wesley, "Four Freedoms," 111; *Crisis* 47 (June 1940): 180.

8. McGuire, *Taps for a Jim Crow Army*, 134–39; Editorial, *Crisis* 39 (Jan. 1942): 7; Anne Wakefield to Gov. Earl Warren, 6 May 1943, NAACP, part 8, series B, reel 2, frs. 180–81; Garfinkle, *March on Washington Movement*, 26; Dalfiume, *Fighting on Two Fronts*, 107–14, 123–24, 127; Wilkerson, "Freedom," 196–97; Finkle, "Conservative

Aims of Militant Rhetoric," 701, 707; Wilkins, "Negro Wants Full Equality," 130; *Crisis* 49 (Mar. 1942): 79.

9. Dalfiume, *Fighting on Two Fronts*, 66–81; McGuire, *Taps for a Jim Crow Army*, 16, 18, 23–24, 41–44, 50–52, 64–65, 67–69, 72–74, 85–87, 173, 184–85, 191, 196–99, 201–3, 222, 236; Bethune, "Certain Unalienable Rights," 250–51; Sitkoff, "Racial Militancy and Interracial Violence," 667–69; Blum, *V Was for Victory*, 190–91.

10. Editorial, *Crisis* 49 (Jan. 1942): 7; Dalfiume, *Fighting on Two Fronts*, 96–97, 106, 113; *Crisis* 48 (July 1941): 215; Blum, *V Was for Victory*, 217–18; Jessie Myles to NAACP, 30 July 1945, NAACP, part 4, reel 9, frs. 11–12; Tygiel, *Baseball's Great Experiment*, 69, 74; Rogosin, *Baseball's Negro Leagues*, 19, 199; Lamb, "Jackie Robinson's Journey to Integrate Baseball," 182; Fairclough, *Civil Rights Struggle in Louisiana*, 76; Capeci, "Lynching of Cleo Wright," 868–70; *Crisis* 49 (Mar. 1942): 79; Coleman, "Freedom from Fear on the Home Front," 416; Isaacs, *New World of Negro Americans*, 42–44; Grill & Jenkins, "Nazis and the American South," 668, 688–93; Hoyt Butler to Marshall, 19 Apr. 1943, NAACP, part 8, series B, reel 2, frs. 445–46; unsigned letter from Gurdon, Arkansas, to NAACP, 16 July 1944, part 4, reel 6, frs. 682–83; Earl S. Horton to NAACP, 9 Feb. 1942, ibid., reel 7, fr. 232; Marshall to Francis Biddle, 5 July 1944, ibid., reel 8, fr. 133; James Lee to Wilkins, 22 May 1944, ibid., reel 9, frs. 205–6.

11. Isaacs, *New World of Negro Americans*, 27–31; Wynn, *Second World War*, 112–13; Dudziak, "Cold War Imperative," 66–68; Hughes, "My America"; *Crisis* 47 (Mar. 1940): 84–85; Rotnem, "Right 'Not to Be Lynched'," 57; Coleman, "Freedom from Fear on the Home Front," 415; Capeci, "Lynching of Cleo Wright," 871; *NYT*, 13 May 1941, quoted in *Crisis* 48 (June 1941): 183; NAACP to Congressman Rudolph G. Tenerowicz, 23 Apr. 1942, NAACP, part 5, reel 5, frs. 279–80; *Detroit Free Press*, 7 Mar. 1942, ibid., fr. 289; undated and unidentified press clipping, part 4, reel 10, fr. 729; "To Vindicate Virginia Justice," *Richmond Times-Dispatch*, 14 June 1942, sec. 4, p. 6; Sherman, *Odell Waller*, 126, 142.

12. *Crisis* 49 (May 1942): 166–67; "When a Kidnapping Is Not a Kidnapping," ibid. 41 (Dec. 1934): 368; Walter White, "U.S. Department of (White) Justice," ibid. 42 (Oct. 1935): 309–10; Carr, *Federal Protection of Civil Rights*, 164, 168–70; Belknap, *Federal Law and Southern Order*, 19; McGovern, *Anatomy of a Lynching*, 119–23; Coleman, "Freedom from Fear on the Home Front," 425–27; Rotnem, "Right 'Not to be Lynched'," 57–59.

13. "Close Ranks," *Crisis* 16 (July 1918): 111; James Hinton to Marshall, 21 July 1942, NAACP, part 4, reel 10, fr. 735; Hinton to Marshall, 4 Aug. 1942, ibid., fr. 739; Hinton to Marshall, 20 Aug. 1942, ibid., fr. 740; W. J. Durham to Marshall, 8 Feb. 1944, ibid., reel 11, frs. 382–83; Fairclough, *Civil Rights Struggle in Louisiana*, 76–78, 82–83; Finkle, "Conservative Aims of Militant Rhetoric," 704–5; McCoy & Ruetten, *Minority Rights and the Truman Administration*, 17; Sancton, "Trouble in Dixie"; Sancton, "Race Fear Sweeps the South"; Sitkoff, "Racial Militancy and Interracial Violence," 662, 670–71; Wynn, *Second World War*, 25, 48–49, 100; Dalfiume, *Fighting on Two Fronts*, 46, 111, 112 n. 27, 123; Garfinkle, *March on Washington Movement*, 26, 32; Kelley, "Black Working-Class Opposition," 86; Barnes, *Journey from Jim Crow*, 38–40; Mormino, "G.I. Joe Meets Jim Crow," 26–28, 33–34, 37; Nelson, "Struggle for Black Equality in Mobile," 963, 966–69; Tushnet, *NAACP's Legal Strategy*, 135.

14. Bartley, *New South*, 14; Garfinkle, *March on Washington Movement*; Dalfiume, *Fighting on Two Fronts*, 36–42, 115–24; Logan, *What the Negro Wants*, introduction, 27–29; Janken, "*What the Negro Wants* Controversy," 156–59, 163–65, 167–68, 172.

15. McCoy & Ruetten, *Minority Rights and the Truman Administration*, 9–10; Dalfiume, *Fighting on Two Fronts*, 31–37, 40–43, 84–88; Wynn, *Second World War*, 30, 38; Blum, *V Was for Victory*, 185, 208–9; Klinker with Smith, *Rise and Decline of Racial Equality*, 153–54; Sitkoff, "Racial Militancy and Interracial Violence," 664; "What Is the Negro Voter Offered?" *Crisis* 47 (May 1940): 145; "Salute to General Davis," ibid. (Dec. 1940): 375.

16. Mitchell v. United States, 313 U.S. 80 (1941); Barnes, *Journey from Jim Crow*, 27; Lawson, *Black Ballots*, 67–70; Berman, *Civil Rights and the Truman Administration*, 8–10, 15; McCullough, *Truman*, 234, 323; Ferrell, *Choosing Truman*, 12–13, 27–30; Barone, *Our Country*, 212; Kellogg, "Civil Rights Consciousness in the 1940s," 24; "Republican Platform of 1940," in *National Party Platforms*, ed. Porter & Johnson, 393; "Republican Platform of 1944," in ibid., 412.

17. Wynn, *Second World War*, 42–44, 46, 48–51, 100–101; Foner, *American Freedom*, 242; Garfinkle, *March on Washington Movement*, 37–96, 103–6, 111, 149; Dalfiume, *Fighting on Two Fronts*, 115–24; Blum, *V Was for Victory*, 188, 196–98, 213–15; Reed, *Seedtime of the Civil Rights Movement*, 1–10, 73–76, 90–101, 345–46; Burk, *Eisenhower Administration and Black Civil Rights*, 90; Schulman, *Cotton Belt to Sunbelt*, 76–77.

18. Wynn, *Second World War*, 28, 39, 55–58; Blum, *V Was for Victory*, 196–97; DeGraaf, "Impact of World War II," 26–28; Sitkoff, *Struggle for Black Equality*, 14–15, 18; McCoy & Ruetten, *Minority Rights and the Truman Administration*, 350; Sugrue, *Origins of the Urban Crisis*, 26–28.

19. Sancton, "Trouble in Dixie," 11–14; Johnson, "Race Relations in the South," 27–29; Logan, preface, in *What the Negro Wants*, ed. Logan; Wilkins, "Negro Wants Full Equality," 113; Odum, "Social Change in the South," 244; Mormino, "G.I. Joe Meets Jim Crow," 26–29, 33–34, 38; McGuire, *Taps for a Jim Crow Army*, esp. 183–88; Dalfiume, *Fighting on Two Fronts*, 72–73; *Crisis* 51 (Oct. 1944): 323–24; Sitkoff, "Racial Militancy and Interracial Violence," 668–69, 672; Fairclough, *Civil Rights Struggle in Louisiana*, 80, 85, 89–98; Sancton, "Race Fear Sweeps the South," 81–83; Nelson, "Struggle for Black Equality in Mobile," 952, 969–82; Blum, *V Was for Victory*, 191; Bartley, *New South*, 12; Capeci, "Lynching of Cleo Wright," 883; Coleman, "Freedom from Fear on the Home Front," 426–27.

20. Garfinkle, *March on Washington Movement*, 103; Foner, *American Freedom*, 245; Finkle, "Conservative Aims of Militant Rhetoric," 695; Graves, "Southern Negro and the War Crisis," 500–502, 504–5, 516–17; Sullivan, *Days of Hope*, 156–58, 164; John Temple Graves, unidentified newspaper, 30 June 1944, NAACP, part 4, reel 6, fr. 269; Bartley, *New South*, 79–80; Fairclough, *Civil Rights Struggle in Louisiana*, 80.

21. Blum, *V Was for Victory*, 200–206, 214–15; Dalfiume, *Fighting on Two Fronts*, 44–63, 82–104; Reed, *Seedtime of the Civil Rights Movement*, 72–76, 90–91; Lawson, *Black Ballots*, 69–70, 73–75, 79–80; *Crisis* 50 (Apr. 1943): 116; NAACP open letter, 14 Feb. 1943, part 5, reel 5, fr. 345; Federal Public Housing Authority to NAACP, telegram, 16 Feb. 1943, ibid., frs. 353–54; Capeci & Wilkerson, *Detroit Rioters of 1943*, 3–18; Sugrue, *Origins of the Urban Crisis*, 29; Sitkoff, "Black Militancy and Interracial Violence," 673–75; *Crisis* 50 (June 1943): 183.

22. "Report on the Black Vote in Southern States in 1946," NAACP, part 4, reel 8, frs. 862–75 (hereafter, "Report on the Black Vote"); Dalfiume, *Fighting on Two Fronts*, 142–46; Berman, *Civil Rights in the Truman Administration*, 24–39, 80–82; McCoy & Ruetten, *Minority Rights and the Truman Administration*, 13–33, 97–98, 100, 134–35; Bartley, *New South*, 78.

23. Berman, *Civil Rights in the Truman Administration*, 16–19, 27–29, 76–77, 87, 103, 116–18, 240; McCoy & Ruetten, *Minority Rights and the Truman Administration*, 43, 98–100, 113, 122–26, 143–44; Plummer, *Rising Wind*, 188–89; Sitkoff, "Truman and the Election of 1948," 597, 608; Ferrell, *Truman*, 165–68, 292–99; Martin, *Civil Rights and the Crisis of Liberalism*, 70–72, 78–81; Lawson, *Black Ballots*, 77–79, 120, 127; McCullough, *Truman*, 569–70, 586–89, 702; Truman, *Memoirs*, 2:179–84; Barone, *Our Country*, 215–21; McAdam, *Development of Black Insurgency*, 81, 158; Kirkendall, "Election of 1948," 3139–40.

24. Dittmer, *Struggle for Civil Rights in Mississippi*, 68; Wynn, *Second World War*, 28–29, 34–35, 106; Norrell, *Civil Rights Movement in Tuskegee*, 44–46, 60–61; Dalfiume, *Fighting on Two Fronts*, 132–33; *Crisis* 53 (Aug. 1946): 250–51; Fairclough, *Civil Rights Struggle in Louisiana*, 105; Brooks, "Winning the Peace," 564, 568–69; O'Brien, *Color of the Law*, 7–33; Jessie Myles to NAACP, 30 July 1945, NAACP, part 4, reel 9, frs. 11–12; affidavit of World War II veterans denied registration in Greenville, Mississippi, 25 June 1946, ibid., fr. 37; James F. Estes to "Sir," 13 June 1946, part 3, series C, reel 23, fr. 431; "Mississippi Sees Negro Votes Rise," *NYT*, n.d., ibid., fr. 103; Lawson, *Black Ballots*, 103; Plummer, *Rising Wind*, 151; *Crisis* 57 (Nov. 1950): 648–49; Baker, "Ambiguous Legacies," 102; Walker, *Sit-Ins in Atlanta*, 4.

25. Odum, "Social Change in the South," 247; G. M. Johnson to Nora Windon, 18 Aug. 1948, NAACP, part 4, reel 8, fr. 592; Tushnet, *Thurgood Marshall*, chap. 8; Tushnet, *NAACP's Legal Strategy*, chap. 6; Kluger, *Simple Justice*, chaps. 10–12; Levy, "Racial Integration of American Higher Education," 311; Lawrence v. Hancock, 76 F. Supp. 1004 (D. W.Va. 1948); Carter v. School Board, 182 F. 2d 531 (4th Cir. 1950); Corbin v. County School Board, 177 F. 2d 924 (4th Cir. 1949); *Crisis* 56 (Jan. 1949): 10–13, 29; Dalfiume, *Fighting on Two Fronts*, 122, 163–66, 169; *Crisis* 55 (July 1948): 212.

26. Dudziak, *Cold War Civil Rights*; McAdam, *Development of Black Insurgency*, 82–83; Isaacs, *New World of Negro Americans*, 6–20; Berman, *Civil Rights and the Truman Administration*, 63, 77–78, 85, 240; Lefberg, "Chief Justice Vinson," 297–302; Carter, *Scottsboro*, 59, 167–69, 172.

27. Green, *Harry T. Moore*, 10, 142, 177; Dalfiume, *Fighting on Two Fronts*, 139; Lawson, *Black Ballots*, 122–23; *To Secure These Rights*, 101; "Answer to Vishinsky," *Crisis* 58 (Dec. 1951): 666–67, 674; Lawson et al., "Groveland," 20; Plummer, *Rising Wind*, 202, 219; *Afro American* (Baltimore), 22 Mar. 1952, p. 21; McCoy & Ruetten, *Minority Rights and the Truman Administration*, 293; Dudziak, *Cold War Civil Rights*, 4–6, 26–39.

28. Symposium, "Courts and Racial Integration," 263, 264; Donald Jones to E. Wayles Browne, 13 Oct. 1947, NAACP, part 4, reel 8, fr. 520; White, *Rising Wind*, 145–55; Dudziak, "Desegregation as a Cold War Imperative," 95; Berman, *Civil Rights in the Truman Administration*, 65–66; McCoy & Ruetten, *Minority Rights and the Truman Administration*, 67; Plummer, *Rising Wind*, 171, 178–79, 182; *NYT*, 1 Apr. 1951, p. 1; Rise, *Martinsville Seven*, 107.

29. Dudziak, "Desegregation as a Cold War Imperative," 65–66, 103–13; Fried, *McCarthy Era*, 164–66; Whitfield, *Cold War*, 77–91.

30. Dalfiume, *Fighting on Two Fronts*, 138–39, 183, 185; *To Secure These Rights*, 95, 101, 146–48; McCoy & Ruetten, *Minority Rights and the Truman Administration*, 100; Plummer, *Rising Wind*, 179–80, 199, 201; Dudziak, *Cold War Civil Rights*, 27, 29, 45–61, 79–112, 118–19, 130–36, 164–65, 167–69.

31. Harris, "Racial Equality and the United Nations Charter," 130–31; Isaacs, *New World of Negro Americans*, 4, 36–37; Plummer, *Rising Wind*, 77, 84–85, 89–93, 123–24, 132–33, 138, 149, 164; Wilkerson, "Freedom"; Marshall to Wilkins, 20 Feb. 1946, NAACP, part 4, reel 8, fr. 24; Symposium, "Courts and Racial Integration," 260 (Robert Weaver); King, "Current Crisis in Race Relations," 9.

32. Bernd, "Georgia," 314–15; McCoy & Ruetten, *Minority Rights and the Truman Administration*, 43–54; Dalfiume, *Fighting on Two Fronts*, 132–33; Wynn, *Second World War*, 109, 116; Norrell, *Civil Rights Movement in Tuskeegee*, 55–57; Odum, "Social Change in the South," 242, 244; McAdam, *Development of Black Insurgency*, 89 table 5.5; Bartley, *New South*, 76, 78–80; Fairclough, *Civil Rights Struggle in Louisiana*, 113; Green, *Harry T. Moore*, 69–71; Brooks, "Winning the Peace," 582–85; *To Secure These Rights*, 20; Frederickson, "Racial Violence in South Carolina," 178–81, 188; Egerton, *Generation before the Civil Rights Movement*, 361–75; Bernd, "Disfranchisement of Blacks in Georgia," 494–98; Sullivan, *Days of Hope*, 211; "Trouble in Dixie," *New Republic* 108 (Jan. 1943): 50; *Mobile Press*, 11 Apr. 1944, NAACP, part 4, reel 6, fr. 295; John Temple Graves, *Birmingham Age Herald*, 8 July 1944, ibid., reel 7, fr. 416.

33. Frederickson, "Racial Violence in South Carolina," esp. 184–85; Bartley, *New South*, 76–77; McCoy & Ruetten, *Minority Rights and the Truman Administration*, 43–46; Ferrell, *Truman*, 293–95; McCullough, *Truman*, 588–89.

34. Carr, *Federal Protection of Civil Rights*, chap. 4; Capeci, "Lynching of Cleo Wright," 859–60, 875–76, 886; Coleman, "Freedom from Fear on the Home Front," 425–26; *To Secure These Rights*, 18–19, 124; Fairclough, *Civil Rights Struggle in Louisiana*, 91–92, 115–16; Marshall to E. Norman Lacey, 16 Dec. 1941, NAACP, part 4, reel 7, frs. 200–203; Memorandum for the United States, *Mitchell v. United States*, 313 U.S. 80 (1941); Brief for the United States as Amicus Curiae, *Shelley v. Kraemer*; Memorandum for the United States as Amicus Curiae, *Sweatt v. Painter*; McCoy & Ruetten, *Minority Rights and the Truman Administration*, 92–94, 161–70, 181–88; *New Republic* 122 (19 June 1950): 5–6; Tygiel, *Baseball's Great Experiment*, chaps. 8–10; Rampersad, *Jackie Robinson*, 135–87; Rogosin, *Baseball's Negro Leagues*, 218, 220.

35. Schulman, *Cotton Belt to Sunbelt*, 112–20.

36. McCoy & Ruetten, *Minority Rights and the Truman Administration*, 101, 125–28; Bartley & Graham, *Southern Politics*, 25, 33, 51–52, 85–86; Heard, *Two-Party South?* 20–33, 251–79; Berman, *Civil Rights in the Truman Administration*, 100–102, 107–15, 125, 132–33; Martin, *Civil Rights and the Crisis of Liberalism*, 81–88; Ader, "Why the Dixiecrats Failed," 366–69; Frederickson, *Dixiecrat Revolt*, 184–85; Kirkendall, "Election of 1948," 3140–41; Black, *Southern Governors and Civil Rights*, 41–45; Dallek, *Lyndon Johnson*, 1:288–89, 367–70.

37. Heard, *Two-Party South?* 148; Goldfield, *Black, White, and Southern*, 40, 48–49, 52; Odum, "Social Change in the South," 242–58.

38. McKinney & Bourque, "Changing South," 406–8; Caffrey, Anderson, & Garrison, "Change in Racial Attitudes," 556; Hyman & Sheatsley, "Attitudes toward Desegregation," 37–39; Matthews & Prothro, "Southern Racial Attitudes," 113–17; Du Bois, "Negro since 1900"; Benjamin Muse, "State Adjusting to Non-Segregation," *Wash. Post*, 17 Sept. 1950, sec. 2, p. 6b; *NYT*, 2 Feb. 1947, NAACP, part 4, reel 9, fr. 103.

39. Brooks, "Winning the Peace," 572–73, 576–77, 580, 590–93; Goldfield, *Black, White, and Southern*, 43–44; Skates, "World War II as a Watershed," 135–36; McKinney & Bourque, "Changing South," 411; Odum, "Social Change in the South," 244; Dalfiume, *Fighting on Two Fronts*, 100; Wilkins, "Negro Wants Full Equality," 131–32.

40. Black, *Southern Governors and Civil Rights*, 57–59; Key, *Southern Politics*, 5, 544; Blalock, "Discrimination in the South," 680; Pettigrew, "Desegregation and Its Chances for Success," 342–43; Pettigrew & Campbell, "Faubus and Segregation," 443–44, 446–47; Heard, *Two-Party South?* 149; McMillen, *Citizens' Council*, 98–100; Dauer, "Florida," 119–23; Wilkinson, *Harry Byrd*, 157–69.

41. Du Bois, "Negro since 1900"; Johnson, "Race Relations in the South," 30; Hyman & Sheatsley, "Attitudes toward Desegregation," 38–39; Erskine, "Race Relations," 138; page 113. After *Brown*, social scientists who sympathized with white supremacy tried to reinvigorate older theories of black biological inferiority. See McMillen, *Citizens' Council*, 164–71; Newby, *Social Scientists and Defense of Segregation*, 185–212.

42. Klarman, "*Brown*, Racial Change, and the Civil Rights Movement," 47–51; McKinney & Bourque, "Changing South," 399, 409–11; Cobb, *Selling of the South*, 131, 135–36; Tygiel, *Baseball's Great Experiment*, 110, 225–26, 268, 313–16; McMillen, *Citizens' Council*, 238; Garrow, *Protest at Selma*, 163–66.

43. McCoy & Ruetten, *Minority Rights and the Truman Administration*, 159–61; Garrow, *Protest at Selma*, 7 table 1-1, 11 table 1-2; Hornsby, "City That Was Too Busy to Hate," 123–24; Bayor, *Twentieth-Century Atlanta*, 134–35, 175; Editorial, *Afro*, 14 Aug. 1948, NAACP, part 4, reel 7, frs. 542–43; *Chicago Defender*, 14 Aug. 1948, p. 1, ibid., fr. 530; Weber, "Citizenship in the South," 8 Nov. 1948, part 4, reel 7, frs. 549–53; Chafe, *Civilities and Civil Rights*, 35, 58; Heard, *Two-Party South?* 218; Moon, *Balance of Power*, 164, 188; Johnson, *Best Practices in Race Relations*, 42–43; Dabney, *Below the Potomac*, 198–99; "Report on the Black Vote"; John Popham, "The Southern Negro: Change and Paradox," *NYT Mag.*, 1 Dec. 1957, pp. 27, 132–33; Bartley, *New South*, 175; Fairclough, *Civil Rights Struggle in Louisiana*, 106; Green, *Harry T. Moore*, 73–74.

44. Lawson, *Black Ballots*, 128; Chafe, *Civilities and Civil Rights*, 32; Goldfield, *Black, White, and Southern*, 45–47; Heard, *Two-Party South?* 208–19; Bartley, *New South*, 175; McCoy & Ruetten, *Minority Rights and the Truman Administration*, 160–61; Johnson, *Best Practices in Race Relations*, 43; Fairclough, *Civil Rights Struggle in Louisiana*, 106; Hornsby, "City That Was Too Busy to Hate," 123; Mormino, "G.I. Joe Meets Jim Crow," 40–41; Brooks, "Winning the Peace," 571; "Report on the Black Vote," 9, fr. 870. See also Klarman, "Political Process Theory," 788–814.

45. Symposium, "Courts and Racial Integration," 403–5; McCoy & Ruetten, *Minority Rights and the Truman Administration*, 60, 162, 336; *Crisis* 54 (Nov. 1947): 342–44; Draper v. City of St. Louis, 92 F. Supp. 546 (E.D. Mo. 1950); Williams v. Kansas City, 104 F. Supp. 848 (W.D. Mo. 1952); McKay, "Segregation and Public Recreation," 719; *Crisis* 59 (Mar. 1952): 178–79; ibid. 60 (Jan. 1953): 34–35; Kluger, *Simple Justice*, 432; Barnes, *Desegregation of Public Transit*, 82.

46. Adelson, *Brushing Back Jim Crow*, 35, 39, 47–48, 56, 63, 65–67, 74; Tygiel, *Baseball's Great Experiment*, 225–26, 265–76; Benjamin Muse, "Segregation Losing Popularity," *Wash. Post*, 19 Feb. 1950, sec. B, p. 8b; Guy Johnson, "Segregation versus Integration," *Crisis* 60 (Dec. 1953): 591; Sheldon Hackney, "C. Vann Woodward, 1908–1999: In Memoriam," *Journal of Southern History* 66 (May 2000): 207–14; Fairclough, *Civil Rights Struggle in Louisiana*, 106, 171; Thornton, "Municipal Politics," 45, 48; Eskew, *But for Birmingham*, 104–6.

47. Symposium, "Courts and Racial Integration," 239, 333, 349, 407, 414, 419–20, 435; Fairclough, *Civil Rights Struggle in Louisiana*, 165; Goldfield, *Black, White, and Southern*, 49–51; Sosna, *Southern Liberals and the Race Issue*, 140, 204–11.

48. Foner, *American Freedom*, 247; Brock, *Americans for Democratic Action*, 75–76, 95–99, 103; Solberg, *Hubert Humphrey*, 11–20, 125–26; Jackson, *Gunnar Myrdal and America's Conscience*, 236–37, 274–76, 281–93; McCoy & Ruetten, *Minority Rights and the Truman Administration*, 65; Broussard, *Black San Francisco*, 192–204; Brinkley, *Liberalism and Its Discontents*, 99–100; Robert L. Carter to David Kagon, 20 Aug. 1946, NAACP, part 4, reel 10, fr. 840; Carter to Francis Levenson, 16 Jan. 1947, ibid., fr. 846.

49. McCoy & Ruetten, *Minority Rights and the Truman Administration*, 20–24, 32–33, 62, 158–59; Garfinkle, *March on Washington Movement*, 171; Wynn, *Second World War*, 54–55; Capeci, "Fiorello H. La Guardia and Employment Discrimination," 51–61; Wunderlich, "New York's Anti-Discrimination Law," 247 n. 71; Phillip Greenwood, "How History Was Made in State of New Jersey," *Crisis* 57 (May 1950): 277; Douglas, "Limits of Law," 719–43; Thornbrough, "Breaking Racial Barriers," 311; Brener, "Public School Desegregation through Political Process"; Cohen, "Dilemma of School Integration in the North"; Bustard, "New Jersey Story," 277–85; Ming, "Segregation in the Public Schools of the North and West"; Gloster Current, "Exit Jim Crow Schools in New Jersey," *Crisis* 56 (Jan. 1949): 10–13, 29; ibid. 57 (Mar. 1950): 172–73; ibid. 58 (Dec. 1951): 677; ibid. 59 (Nov. 1952): 586–87; Cooke, "Segregation of Mexican-American Children in Southern California," 419–21; Mendez v. Westminster School Dist., 64 F. Supp. 544 (S.D. Calif. 1946), aff'd, 161 F. 2d 774 (9th Cir. 1947); Dalfiume, *Fighting on Two Fronts*, 159–61.

50. Sugrue, *Origins of the Urban Crisis*, 73–88 (quotation at 79); McCoy & Ruetten, *Minority Rights and the Truman Administration*, 159, 293; Broussard, *Black San Francisco*, 167–68; Massey & Denton, *American Apartheid*, 49; Hirsch, "Massive Resistance in the Urban North," 522–23, 527–37, 546–48; pages 262–64.

51. Fried, *McCarthy Era*, 29–36, 164–65; Foner, *American Freedom*, 257–59; Fairclough, *Civil Rights Struggle in Louisiana*, 136–37, 143; McCoy & Ruetten, *Minority Rights and the Truman Administration*, 353; Honey, "Labor and Civil Rights in the Postwar South," 439–52; Sitkoff, *Struggle for Black Equality*, 17–18; Plummer, *Rising Tide*, 167–69, 173–74, 183–84, 190–92, 197–98, 214–15; Record, *Race and Radicalism*, 32, 132–68, 193; Herbert Hill, "The Communist Party: Enemy of Negro Equality," *Crisis* 58 (June–July 1951): 365–71, 421–24; "The NAACP and the Communists," *Crisis* 56 (Mar. 1949): 72; Tushnet, *Thurgood Marshall*, 44–46.

52. Bartley, *New South*, 55–56, 60–61, 64; Honey, "Labor and Civil Rights in the Postwar South," 448; Record, *Race and Radicalism*, 57–131, 166–68; Martin, "International Labor Defense"; Martin, *Angelo Herndon*, 10–16, 44, 64–65; Carter, *Scottsboro*, 51–103; Foner, *American Freedom*, 211–15, 258; Krueger, *Southern Conference for Human Welfare*, 67–69, 139–43, 152–58, 167–68; Fairclough, *Civil Rights Struggle in Louisiana*, 137–47; Martin, "Civil Rights Congress"; McCoy & Ruetten, *Minority Rights and the Truman Administration*, 180; Dudziak, *Cold War Civil Rights*, 11–13.

53. McCoy & Ruetten, *Minority Rights and the Truman Administration*, 147; Bartley, *New South*, 103.

54. Bernstein, "Election of 1952," 3215, 3234, 3238–40, 3247, 3251–52; Martin, *Civil Rights and the Crisis of Liberalism*, 93–97, 105–13; Berman, *Civil Rights in the Truman Administration*, 200–208, 211–18; McCoy & Ruetten, *Minority Rights and the Truman Administration*, 114, 319, 323–26; Bartley, *New South*, 99–101; Ambrose, *Eisenhower*, 1:531, 555, 567, 2:125, 531, 567; Burk, *Eisenhower Administration and Black Civil Rights*, 15–20, 23, 28, 152–53; Stern, "Presidential Strategies and Civil Rights," 772–77; *Crisis* 59 (Oct. 1952): 518–19; Bartley & Graham, *Southern Politics*, 86–87, 90.

55. Black's former Klan affiliation was suspected, though not proven, prior to his appointment. When it became public knowledge after Senate confirmation, Roosevelt disingenuously feigned ignorance.

56. Nelson, *Fourteenth Amendment*, 109–10; Newman, *Hugo Black*, 240; Robertson, *James F. Byrnes*, 76, 85–86, 251–52, 282–86, 298–99; Abraham, *Supreme Court Appointments*, 160, 175; "Hugo Black, Justice of the Supreme Court," *Opportunity* 15 (1937): 292–93; *Crisis* 48 (Apr. 1941): 136; "Mr. Justice Black Should Resign," ibid. 59 (Oct. 1937): 305; Sitkoff, *New Deal for Blacks*, 66.

57. McCoy & Ruetten, *Minority Rights and the Truman Administration*, 24; Berry, *Mr. Justice Burton*, 20–21; Gugin & St. Clair, *Sherman Minton*, 115, 247, 311; Rudko, *Truman's Court*, chap. 3; Pritchett, *Vinson Court*, 1–2, 19–20; Urofsky, *Supreme Court under Stone and Vinson*, 143–45, 148–58; Abraham, *Supreme Court Appointments*, 181–88.

58. White to Frank Murphy, 4 Dec. 1925, NAACP, part 5, reel 3, fr. 164; Sitkoff, *New Deal for Blacks*, 331; Tushnet, *Thurgood Marshall*, 67–70; Parrish, *Felix Frankfurter*, chaps. 5, 10; Urofsky, *Felix Frankfurter*, 19–21; Howard, *Mr. Justice Murphy*, 26–30, 58, 168, 203–4; Bixby, "Roosevelt Court," 771–73; Press Release, 28 Nov. 1925, NAACP, part 5, reel 3, fr. 164.

59. Chernack, "Robert H. Jackson," 85; Simon, *William O. Douglas*, 201; Jackson, *Gunnar Myrdal and America's Conscience*, 236–37, 274.

60. Rudko, *Truman's Court*, chaps. 3–6; Pritchett, *Vinson Court*, 47–49, 57–79, 146–66, 188–92; Kluger, *Simple Justice*, 269–71; Urofsky, *Supreme Court under Stone and Vinson*, 157–58; St. Clair & Gugin, *Fred M. Vinson*, 170; Dudziak, *Cold War Civil Rights*, 90–107.

61. Kruse, "Gaines Case," 120; Sitkoff, *New Deal for Blacks*, 229; chapter 6.

62. United States v. Carolene Products Co., 304 U.S. 144, 152–53 n. 4 (1938); Lusky, "Carolene Products Reminiscence"; Powell, "Carolene Products Revisited"; Cover, "Origins of Judicial Activism in the Protection of Minorities"; Ely, *Democracy and Distrust*; Pritchett, *Roosevelt Court*, chaps. 4–5; Mason, *Harlan Fiske Stone*, chap. 31; Howard, *Mr. Justice Murphy*, chaps. 11–12; West Virginia School Board v. Barnette, 319 U.S. 624 (1943); Thornhill v. Alabama, 310 U.S. 88 (1940); Schneider v. State, 308 U.S. 147 (1939); Waite, "Debt of Constitutional Law to Jehovah's Witnesses"; Barber, "Jehovah's Witnesses"; Rotnem & Folsom, "Recent Restrictions upon Religious Liberty."

63. Mason, *Harlan Fiske Stone*, 515; "The Federalist No. 51," in *The Federalist*, ed. Jacob E. Cooke (Middletown, Conn.: Wesleyan University Press, 1961), 347–53; Klarman, "Rethinking the Civil Rights and Civil Liberties Revolutions," 31–62; Berman, "New Deal for Free Speech"; Pritchett, *Roosevelt Court*, 136; Bixby, "Roosevelt Court"; West Virginia School Board v. Barnette, 319 U.S. 624, 640–42 (1943); Skinner v. Oklahoma, 316 U.S. 535, 541, 546 (1942) (Jackson, J., concurring); Chambers v. Florida, 309 U.S. 227, 241 (1940); Ely, *Democracy and Distrust*, chaps. 4–6; Klarman, "Political Process Theory," 788–819.

64. Page 86; NAACP, part 4, reel 3, frs. 422–24; unidentified and undated press clipping, ibid., frs. 440–41; Charles A. Chandler to Houston, 8 Apr. 1937, ibid., fr. 203.

65. Undated opinion in the matter of the Oklahoma election law by lawyer Barbour, NAACP, part 4, reel 1, frs. 423–24; Ethelbert T. Barbour to A. B. Whitby, n.d., ibid., frs. 303–4.

66. *Crisis* 46 (July 1939): 211; Lane v. Wilson, 98 F. 2d 980 (10th Cir. 1938); Trudeau v. Barnes, 1 F. Supp. 453 (E.D. La. 1932), aff'd, 65 F. 2d 563 (5th Cir.), cert. denied, 290 U.S. 659 (1933); Brief of Respondents, *Lane v. Wilson*, 38–46.

67. Houston to R. D. Evans, 9 Mar. 1938, NAACP, part 4, reel 3, fr. 366.

68. United States v. Classic, 313 U.S. 299 (1941); Newberry v. United States, 256 U.S. 232 (1921); Carr, *Federal Protection of Civil Rights*, chap. 4; Bixby, "Roosevelt Court," 792–812; Schmidt, "Principle and Prejudice, Part III," 888–98.

69. Ex parte Yarbrough, 110 U.S. 651 (1884); Lawson, *Black Ballots*, 40; Brief for the United States, *United States v. Classic*, 10–11, 26 n. 12, 34–35.

70. *Classic*, 313 U.S. at 318; Bixby, "Roosevelt Court," 804–5.

71. Mason, *Harlan Fiske Stone*, 617; Dabney, *Below the Potomac*, 197; Folsom, "White Primary," 1027–28, 1032; Bixby, "Roosevelt Court," 803–4; Hine, *White Primary in Texas*, 205, 206–7, 213–14; Smith v. Allwright, 131 F. 2d 593 (5th Cir. 1942) (per curiam).

72. 321 U.S. at 652, 663, 664; Hine, *White Primary in Texas*, chap. 10; Lawson, *Black Ballots*, chap. 2.

73. Bixby, "Roosevelt Court," 812–13; Howard, *Mr. Justice Murphy*, 356; Tushnet, *Thurgood Marshall*, 106.

74. *Smith*, 321 U.S. at 669 (Roberts, J., dissenting); Pritchett, *Roosevelt Court*, 23, 25 table 1.

75. "Primaries Are Not Private," *NYT*, 5 Apr. 1944, p. 18; Lawson, *Black Ballots*, 65–66, 72–73; *Time* 43 (17 Apr. 1944): 20–21; Klinker with Smith, *Rise and Decline of Racial Equality*, 193. See also Arthur Krock, "In the Nation," *NYT*, 4 Apr. 1944, NAACP, part 4, reel 11, fr. 226; NAACP Press Release, 20 Mar. 1944, ibid., fr. 404.

76. Myrdal, *American Dilemma*, 1:60–61, 2:587–88; Lawson, *Black Ballots*, 22; Krueger, *Southern Conference for Human Welfare*, 128; Ogden, *Poll Tax in the South*, 185–201; Gallup, *Gallup Poll*, 2:783, 810; Kluger, *Simple Justice*, 595–96, 655–56, 680, 698.

77. Lawson, *Black Ballots*, 46, 49–50; Note, *Columbia Law Review* 47 (1947): 76, 81; James D. Barnett, Note, *Oregon Law Review* 23 (June 1944): 264, 267; Sullivan, *Days of Hope*, 169–70; *NYT*, 18 Apr. 1944, p. 13; "Negro Vote Battle Looms in Alabama," ibid., 3 Mar. 1947, p. 44; "Democratic Vote of Negroes Upheld," ibid., 28 July 1945, p. 24; *Tampa Times*, 27 Mar. 1946, NAACP, part 4, reel 6, fr. 870; Baskin to Gov. Talmadge, 16 May 1947, ibid., reel 9, frs. 983–84; McCray to NAACP, 18 Jan. 1947, ibid., reel 10, fr. 850; Marshall to Thurman Arnold, 7 Apr. 1947, ibid., fr. 875.

78. Elmore v. Rice, 72 F. Supp. 516, 527 (E.D.S.C.), aff'd, 165 F. 2d 387 (4th Cir. 1947), cert. denied, 333 U.S. 875 (1948); Marshall to John McCray, 22 Jan. 1947, NAACP, part 4, reel 10, fr. 848; White to unnamed editors, 14 July 1947, ibid., reel 9, fr. 899; William Hastie to Marshall, 19 July 1947, ibid., frs. 900–901; "The Right to Vote," *New South* 4 (Feb. 1949): 3; Note, "Negro Disenfranchisement," 80–90; Preliminary Memorandum re: Primaries in South Carolina and Georgia, 10 Feb. 1947, NAACP, part 4, reel 10, fr. 470; Marshall to C. A. Scott, 23 Sept. 1947, ibid., reel 8, fr. 209.

79. Hastie to Marshall, 19 July 1947, NAACP, part 4, reel 9, frs. 900–901; Marshall to Hastie, 22 July 1947, ibid., frs. 902–3; Burton conference notes, *Terry v. Adams*, 17 Jan. 1953, Box 244, Burton Papers; Dickson, *Supreme Court in Conference*, 839–40; Hine, *White Primary in Texas*, 27–29; Rice, *Negro in Texas*, 118; Austin Burkhart, "The White Man's Primary," *Crisis* 56 (Mar. 1949): 81–82; ibid. 58 (Mar. 1951): 191–92.

80. Burton conference notes, *Terry v. Adams*, 17 Jan. 1953, Box 244, Burton Papers.

81. Ibid.; Jackson, draft dissent, *Terry v. Adams*, 3 Apr. 1953, pp. 1, 9, Box 179, Jackson Papers; Berry, *Mr. Justice Burton*, 126; Hutchinson, "Unanimity and Desegregation," 38; Tushnet, *Thurgood Marshall*, 110–11.

82. *Terry*, 345 U.S. 461, 482–83 (1953).

83. *Terry*, 345 U.S. at 484 (Minton, J., dissenting); Tushnet, *Thurgood Marshall*, 112.

84. Burton conference notes, *Terry v. Adams*, 17 Jan. 1953, Box 244, Burton Papers; Tushnet, *Thurgood Marshall*, 110–11.

85. U.S. Civil Rights Commission, *Public Higher Education*, 19–23; Kluger, *Simple Justice*, 257; pages 148–52, 160–62.

86. Marshall, "Racial Integration in Education," 319; U.S. Civil Rights Commission, *Public Higher Education*, 15, 18–23, 26–28; Dabney, *Below the Potomac*, 216, 220–30; McCoy & Ruetten, *Minority Rights and the Truman Administration*, 117; Levy, "Racial Integration of American Higher Education," 303; McCready v. Byrd, 73 A. 2d 8 (Md. 1950); State ex rel. Bluford v. Canada, 153 S.W. 2d 12 (Mo. 1941); State ex rel. Michael v. Witham, 165 S.W. 2d 378 (Tenn. 1942); Sipuel v. Board of Regents, 180 P. 2d 135 (Okla. 1947); Bluford v. Canada, 32 F. Supp. 707 (W.D. Mo. 1940); pages 160–62.

87. Baker, "Ambiguous Legacies," 108, 112–13, 115, 124; Tushnet, *NAACP's Legal Strategy*, 82, 135; Tushnet, *Thurgood Marshall*, 122–23; unidentified author to White & Houston, Memorandum re: the Garland Fund, 7 Oct. 1936, NAACP, part 3, reel 1, fr. 1052; *Crisis* 54 (Feb. 1947): 51; Kluger, *Simple Justice*, 257–58; Sweatt v. Painter, 210 S.W. 2d 442 (Tex. Civ. App. 1948); Wrighten v. Board of Trustees, 72 F. Supp. 948 (E.D.S.C. 1947); Wilson v. Board of Supervisors, 92 F. Supp. 986 (E.D. La. 1950); State ex rel. Michael v. Witham, 165 S.W. 2d 378 (Tenn. 1942); U.S. Civil Rights Commission, *Public Higher Education*, 22–25; Marshall, "Racial Integration in Education," 319; Burns, "Graduate Education for Blacks in North Carolina," 210, 212.

88. Hutchinson, "Unanimity and Desegregation," 7; *Crisis* 55 (Feb. 1948): 54–55; Tushnet, *NAACP's Legal Strategy*, 120; Tushnet, *Thurgood Marshall*, 129. See also Fisher, *Autobiography of Ada Lois Sipuel Fisher*, 122.

89. Dickson, *Supreme Court in Conference*, 636; Sipuel v. Board of Regents of University of Oklahoma, 180 P. 2d 135 (Okla. 1947). See also Tushnet, *NAACP's Legal Strategy*, 121.

90. Hutchinson, "Unanimity and Desegregation," 7–9; Fisher v. Hurst, 333 U.S. 147 (1948). See also Tushnet, *NAACP's Legal Strategy*, 121–22; Kluger, *Simple Justice*, 260; Fisher, *Autobiography of Ada Lois Sipuel Fisher*, 126, 132.

91. Sweatt v. Painter, 339 U.S. 629, 631 (1950); Entin, "*Sweatt v. Painter*," 3–71; Tushnet, *Thurgood Marshall*, 126–47; Kluger, *Simple Justice*, 260–66, 275–78, 280–82.

92. *Sweatt*, 339 U.S. at 634; Sweatt v. Painter, 210 S.W. 2d 442 (Tex. Civ. App. 1948); Entin, "*Sweatt v. Painter*," 34; Brief of Respondents, *Sweatt v. Painter*, 108–12, 117–18.

93. Hutchinson, "Unanimity and Desegregation," 23–24; Arthur Krock, "An Historic Day in the Supreme Court," NYT, 6 June 1950, p. 28; *Crisis* 57 (July 1950): 444–45. See also NYT, 11 June 1950, sec. 4, p. 1; *New Republic* 122 (19 June 1950): 5–6; Frank, "United States Supreme Court: 1949–50," 35–36; Ransmeier, "Fourteenth Amendment," 241.

94. McLaurin v. Oklahoma State Regents, 339 U.S. 637, 641 (1950); NYT, 11 June 1950, sec. 4, p. 1; Levy, "Racial Integration of American Higher Education," 309–10.

95. Sweatt v. Painter, 210 S.W. 2d 442 (Tex. Civ. App. 1948); McLaurin v. Oklahoma State Regents, 87 F. Supp. 528 (W.D. Okla. 1949); Brief for Respondents,

Sweatt v. Painter, 10–44; Brief for Appellees, *McLaurin v. Oklahoma State Regents*, 10–20; Entin, "*Sweatt v. Painter*," 58–59.

96. Clark conference notes, *McLaurin* and *Sweatt*, Box A2, Clark Papers; Burton conference notes, *McLaurin* and *Sweatt*, Box 204, Burton Papers; Dickson, *Supreme Court in Conference*, 637–44; Hutchinson, "Unanimity and Desegregation," 19–27; St. Clair & Gugin, *Fred M. Vinson*, 311–12; Jackson to Charles Fairman, 5 Apr. 1950, quoted in Tushnet, *Thurgood Marshall*, 143.

97. Hutchinson, "Unanimity and Desegregation," 15, 27 n. 215, 89–90; Tushnet, *Thurgood Marshall*, 140, 143; Frank, "United States Supreme Court: 1949–50," 37 n. 141.

98. Frank, "United States Supreme Court: 1949–50," 34; Berry, *Mr. Justice Burton*, 69, 95, 150; Memorandum for the United States as Amicus Curiae, *Sweatt v. Painter*, 1–2, 11–12; Tushnet, *Thurgood Marshall*, 139–40; Pritchett, *Truman Court*, 25 table 1, 129–30, 162 table 18, 254 table 23; Lefberg, "Chief Justice Vinson," 297–302.

99. Clark, Memorandum to Conference (handwritten draft), Apr. 1950, p. 3, Box A2, Clark Papers; Burton conference notes, *McLaurin* and *Sweatt*, Box 204, Burton Papers; *Crisis* 46 (Feb. 1930): 51; ibid. 55 (Mar. 1948): 84–85; ibid. 54 (May 1947): 149; Kluger, *Simple Justice*, 259–60, 262; Urofsky, *Supreme Court under Stone and Vinson*, 250–51; Krueger, *Southern Conference for Human Welfare*, 189; Fisher, *Autobiography of Ada Lois Sipuel Fisher*, 107, 114, 122, 130, 146; Levy, "Racial Integration of American Higher Education," 306–7; Edna Kerin, "Separate Is Not Equal," *Crisis* 57 (May 1950): 288–92, 332; Tushnet, *NAACP's Legal Strategy*, 129; *NYT*, 23 Oct. 1950, p. 29; ibid., 29 Oct. 1950, sec. 4, p. 9; *New Republic* 122 (19 June 1950): 5–6; Marshall, "Racial Integration in Education," 320; Brief for the Texas Council of Negro Organizations as Amicus Curiae, *Sweatt v. Painter*, 14–17, 28–32. See also P. D. W. & L. T. [law clerks] to "Boss" [Clark], 1 Apr. 1950, Box A2, Clark Papers.

100. Emerson, "Segregation and the Equal Protection Clause"; Kluger, *Simple Justice*, 275; Entin, "*Sweatt v. Painter*," 45–51; Levy, "Racial Integration of American Higher Education," 305. See also Brief of Respondents, *Sweatt v. Painter*, 231ff.

101. Clark, Memorandum to Conference (handwritten draft), Apr. 1950, pp. 2–3, Box A2, Clark Papers; Marshall, "Racial Integration in Education," 322; Lefberg, "Chief Justice Vinson," 279; Briggs v. Elliott, 98 F. Supp. 529 (E.D.S.C. 1951); Davis v. County School Board, 103 F. Supp. 337 (E.D. Va. 1952). See also Boyer v. Garrett, 183 F. 2d 582 (4th Cir. 1950); Camp v. Recreation Board for District of Columbia, 104 F. Supp. 10 (D.D.C. 1952); McKay, "Segregation and Public Recreation," 706, 717.

102. Hutchinson, "Unanimity and Desegregation," 21; Tushnet, *NAACP's Legal Strategy*, 134–36; Tushnet, *Thurgood Marshall*, 145–47; Entin, "*Sweatt v. Painter*," 69 n. 354; Harmelin v. Michigan, 501 U.S. 957 (1991); Wallace v. Jaffree, 472 U.S. 38, 110–11 (1985) (Rehnquist, J., dissenting); Mason v. Haile, 25 U.S. (12 Wheat.) 370, 378 (1827); Douglas conference notes, *United States v. Kras*, 20 Oct. 1972, Box 1594, Douglas Papers.

103. Ashmore, "Racial Integration," 252; Symposium, "Courts and Racial Integration," 261 (Ashmore); Boothe, "Civil Rights in Virginia," 969–70; Hyman, "Segregation and the Fourteenth Amendment," 560; Frank, "United States Supreme Court: 1949–50," 37; Arthur Krock, "An Historic Day in the Supreme Court," *NYT*, 6 June 1950, p. 28; Fairclough, *Civil Rights Struggle in Louisiana*, 155; Kluger, *Simple Justice*, 291; Elman, "Solicitor General's Office," 825–26. The Truman administration did file a brief in *Brown* but only after Perlman resigned, over an unrelated issue. His successor, Robert Stern, favored involvement.

104. Burton conference notes, *McLaurin* and *Sweatt*, Box 204, Burton Papers; Clark, Memorandum to Conference (handwritten draft), Apr. 1950, p. 6, Box A2, Clark Papers; Clark conference notes, *McLaurin* and *Sweatt*, Box A2, Clark Papers; Douglas conference notes, *McLaurin*, 8 Apr. 1950, Box 192, Douglas Papers; Hutchinson, "Unanimity and Desegregation," 3, 19–27, 87, 89–90; Tushnet, *Thurgood Marshall*, 145.

105. Pages 79–83, 142–46; Cornish v. O'Donoghue, 30 F. 2d 98 (D.C. Cir.), cert. denied, 279 U.S. 871 (1929); Grady v. Garland, 89 F. 2d 817 (D.C. Cir.), cert. denied, 302 U.S. 694 (1937); Mays v. Burgess, 147 F. 2d 969 (D.C. Cir.), cert. denied, 325 U.S. 868 (1945); Vose, *Caucasians Only*, 156.

106. Crisis 54 (Oct. 1947): 308–10; Vose, *Caucasians Only*, 56–57; Capeci & Wilkerson, *Detroit Rioters of 1943*, 25, 63, 146; pages 261–62.

107. Vose, *Caucasians Only*, 20–21, 100–121, 177–210; Kluger, *Simple Justice*, 248–49, 251–55; Crisis 55 (June 1948): 179–81; Fassett, *Stanley Reed*, 445; McGovney, "Racial Residential Segregation," 10–11; Respondent's Brief, *Shelley v. Kraemer*, 47–48, 50–51, 53; Gandolfo v. Hartmann, 49 F. 181 (C.C.S.D. Calif. 1892).

108. Hastie to Marshall, 19 July 1947, NAACP, part 4, reel 9, frs. 900–901; Kraemer v. Shelley, 198 S.W. 2d 679 (Mo. 1946); Sipes v. McGhee, 25 S.W. 2d 638 (Mich. 1947); Hurd v. Hodge, 162 F. 2d 233, 235 (D.C. Cir. 1947) (Edgerton, J., dissenting); Hundley v. Gorewitz, 132 F. 2d 23 (D.C. Cir. 1942); Kluger, *Simple Justice*, 248–49, 253; Vose, *Caucasians Only*, 24, 59, 93–98, 137–38, 162–63; Tushnet, *Thurgood Marshall*, 88–91; Fairchild v. Raines, 151 P. 2d 260, 267 (Calif. 1944) (Traynor, J., concurring); *To Secure These Rights*, 69–70; Petition for Writ of Certiorari and Petitioner's Brief, *Shelley v. Kraemer*, 19, 23, 34–39, 53–56. See also Respondent's Brief, ibid., 12–13.

109. Ridgway v. Cockburn, 296 N.Y.S. 936 (N.Y. Sup. Ct. 1937); United Cooperative Realty Co. v. Hawkins, 108 S.W. 2d 507 (Ky. 1937), Meade v. Dennistone, 196 A. 330 (Md. 1938); Doherty v. Rice, 3 N.W. 2d 734 (Wis. 1942); Thornhill v. Herdt, 130 S.W. 2d 175 (Mo. App. 1939); Vose, *Caucasians Only*, 19, 28.

110. Kurland, *Warren Court*, 89; Tushnet, "*Shelley v. Kraemer*," 388; Henkin, "*Shelley v. Kraemer*," 476–77; Respondent's Brief, *Shelley v. Kraemer*, 21–43.

111. Tushnet, "*Shelley v. Kraemer*," 384–91; Henkin, "*Shelley v. Kraemer*," 483–87, 496–97; Respondent's Brief, *Shelley v. Kraemer*, 57–59.

112. Vose, *Caucasians Only*, 171; Coleman, "Freedom from Fear on the Home Front," 425–27; Carr, *Federal Protection of Civil Rights*, chap. 1; Foner, *American Freedom*, chap. 10; Patterson, *Grand Expectations*, 55–56; Marsh v. Alabama, 326 U.S. 501 (1946).

113. DeGraaf, "Impact of World War II," 30; *To Secure These Rights*, 168–69; Brief of the United States as Amicus Curiae, *Shelley v. Kraemer*, 19–20, 38; Consolidated Brief in Behalf of American Jewish Committee et al., as Amici Curiae, *Shelley v. Kraemer*, 4–5; Brief of the American Civil Liberties Union, Amicus Curiae, *Shelley v. Kraemer*, 27–30; Kluger, *Simple Justice*, 252; Vose, *Caucasians Only*, 194–95; Tushnet, *Thurgood Marshall*, 91–92; "Washington Segregation Cases," Crisis 29 (Dec. 1924): 69.

114. The vote in *Shelley* was 6–0. Three justices—Reed, Jackson, and Rutledge—did not participate, apparently because they owned property that was covered by racially restrictive covenants.

115. Mays v. Burgess, 147 F. 2d 869 (D.C. Cir.), cert. denied, 325 U.S. 868 (1945); Vose, *Caucasians Only*, 175, 248–49, 275 nn. 44–45; McGovney, "Racial Residential

Segregation," 18–19; Kahen, "Validity of Anti-Negro Restrictive Covenants," 207–13; Groner & Helfeld, "Race Discrimination in Housing," 451–58; Kluger, *Simple Justice*, 254; Tushnet, *Thurgood Marshall*, 96.

116. Barrows v. Jackson, 346 U.S. 249 (1953). Compare Correll v. Earley, 237 P. 2d 1017 (Okla. 1951) and Weiss v. Leaon, 225 S.W. 2d 127 (Mo. 1949), with Phillips v. Naff, 52 N.W. 2d 158 (Mich. 1952) and Roberts v. Curtis, 93 F. Supp. 604 (D.C.D.C. 1950).

117. Brief for Petitioners, *Barrows v. Jackson*, 8–9, 19; Brief of Amici Curiae, *Barrows v. Jackson*, 8–10; Pritchett, *Vinson Court*, 143; Buchanan v. Warley, 245 U.S. 60 (1917); Pierce v. Society of Sisters, 268 U.S. 510 (1925).

118. Dorsey v. Stuyvesant Town Corp., 87 N.E. 2d 541 (N.Y. 1949), cert. denied, 339 U.S. 981 (1950); *New Republic* 122 (19 June 1950): 5–6; *NYT*, 6 June 1950, p. 17; Jones v. Alfred Mayer, 392 U.S. 409 (1968).

119. Mitchell v. United States, 313 U.S. 80 (1941); Henderson v. United States, 339 U.S. 816 (1950); Morgan v. Virginia, 328 U.S. 373 (1946); Bob-Lo Excursion Co. v. Michigan, 333 U.S. 28 (1948).

120. Mitchell v. Chicago, Rock Island & Pacific Railway Co., 229 I.C.C. 703 (1938); Barnes, *Journey from Jim Crow*, 23–24; pages 20, 76–79, 89.

121. Barnes, *Journey from Jim Crow*, 30–31; Tushnet, *NAACP's Legal Strategy*, 58–65, 68–69, 77–81, 89–99, 102–4; "Everybody's Fight," *Crisis* 44 (June 1937): 177.

122. Henderson v. Southern Railway Co., 269 I.C.C. 73 (1947); 80 F. Supp. 32 (D. Md. 1948); Barnes, *Journey from Jim Crow*, 66–71; Tushnet, *Thurgood Marshall*, 135–36.

123. Henderson v. United States, 339 U.S. 816, 825 (1950).

124. Barnes, *Journey from Jim Crow*, 66, 73; Kluger, *Simple Justice*, 277.

125. Burton conference notes, *Henderson v. United States*, Box 204, Burton Papers; Douglas conference notes, *Henderson v. United States*, 8 Apr. 1950, Box 196, Douglas Papers; Frankfurter to Conference, memorandum, 31 May 1950, ibid.; Hutchinson, "Unanimity and Desegregation," 23 n. 190, 27–30; Tushnet, *Thurgood Marshall*, 145; P. D. W. & L. T. to "Boss," 1 Apr. 1950, Box A2, Clark Papers.

126. Gibbons v. Ogden, 22 U.S. (9 Wheat.) 1 (1824); Brown v. Maryland, 25 U.S. (12 Wheat.) 419 (1827); Morgan v. Virginia, 328 U.S. 373 (1946); Cushman, "Formalism and Realism in Commerce Clause Jurisprudence."

127. Palmore, "Race, Transportation, and the Dormant Commerce Clause," 1773, 1776, 1779–92, 1799–1801, 1810–15; Hall v. DeCuir, 95 U.S. 485 (1878); Barnes, *Journey from Jim Crow*, 52–53, 56–57, 59–60; Chesapeake & Ohio Railway v. Kentucky, 179 U.S. 388 (1900); Louisville, New Orleans & Texas Railway Co. v. Mississippi, 133 U.S. 587 (1890). Cf. South Covington & Cincinnati Street Railway Co. v. Kentucky, 252 U.S. 399 (1920).

128. South Carolina State Highway Department v. Barnwell Bros., 303 U.S. 177 (1938); Tushnet, *Thurgood Marshall*, 73–74; Gardbaum, "New Deal Constitutionalism," 489–90, 509, 520–29. See also Milk Control Board v. Eisenberg Farm Products, 306 U.S. 346 (1939); Duckworth v. Arkansas, 314 U.S. 390 (1941); Brief of Appellee, *Morgan v. Virginia*, 15, 20.

129. Barnes, *Journey from Jim Crow*, 47–48. But see Palmore, "Race, Transportation and the Dormant Commerce Clause," 1810–15.

130. *Morgan*, 328 U.S. at 386–88 (Black, J., concurring); Southern Pacific Co. v. Arizona, 325 U.S. 761, 784–95 (Black, J., dissenting); Pritchett, *Roosevelt Court*, 128–29; Brief of Appellee, *Morgan v. Virginia*, 26.

131. Douglas conference notes, *Morgan v. Virginia*, 30 Mar. 1946, Box 123, Douglas Papers. Compare Betts v. Brady, 316 U.S. 455, 474 (1942) (Black, J., dissenting), with

Adamson v. California, 332 U.S. 46, 68 (1947) (Black, J., dissenting), and Colegrove v. Green, 328 U.S. 549 (1946) (Black, J., dissenting), with Baker v. Carr, 369 U.S. 186 (1962). See Spaeth & Segal, *Majority Rule or Minority Will*, 286–315, esp. 291 table 9-1.

132. Gallup, *Gallup Poll*, 2:782–83; Boothe, "Civil Rights in Virginia," 958–63; Benjamin Muse, "Segregation Losing Popularity," *Wash. Post*, 19 Feb. 1950, sec. B, p. 8b; Brief for Appellant, *Morgan v. Virginia*, 28; Barnes, *Journey from Jim Crow*, 61–62, 102; Sherman, *Odell Waller*, 184; *Crisis* 53 (July 1946): 201.

133. Douglas memorandum, 25 Jan. 1960, reprinted in *Douglas Letters*, ed. Urofsky, 169; Barnes, *Journey from Jim Crow*, 41–42; Greenberg, *Crusaders in the Courts*, 110; Brief of Appellee, *Morgan v. Virginia*, 4.

134. Bob-Lo Excursion Co. v. Michigan, 333 U.S. 28 (1948); Pritchett, *Vinson Court*, 127–28.

135. 333 U.S. at 34–40.

136. 333 U.S. at 43–45 (Jackson, J., dissenting).

137. Klarman, "Modern Equal Protection," 272–76; Barnes, *Journey from Jim Crow*, 48–50, 54.

138. Barnes, *Journey from Jim Crow*, 78–85, 97–102; Keys v. Carolina Coach Co., 64 M.C.C. 769 (1955).

139. Pages 125–28.

140. Smith v. Texas, 311 U.S. 128 (1940).

141. Hill v. Texas, 316 U.S. 400 (1942). See also Hale v. Kentucky, 303 U.S. 613 (1938); Boskey & Pickering, "State Criminal Procedure," 279–82.

142. Berry, *Mr. Justice Burton*, 70; Patton v. Mississippi, 332 U.S. 463 (1947); Brunson v. North Carolina, 333 U.S. 851 (1948); Shepherd v. Florida, 341 U.S. 50 (1951); Avery v. Georgia, 345 U.S. 559 (1953).

143. Akins v. Texas, 325 U.S. 398, 402–3 (1945); Smith v. Texas, 311 U.S. 128, 130–31 (1940); People v. Roxborough, 12 N.W. 2d 466 (Mich. 1943), cert. denied, 323 U.S. 749 (1944). See also Swain v. Alabama, 380 U.S. 202 (1965).

144. *Daily Times Herald* (Dallas), 16 Sept. 1941, NAACP, part 8, series B, reel 8, frs. 35–37; *Dallas Morning News*, 16 Sept. 1941, ibid., frs. 39–40; NAACP Press Release, 26 Sept. 1941, ibid., fr. 42; *Akins*, 325 U.S. at 406; Tushnet, *Thurgood Marshall*, 61. See also page 281.

145. Murphy conference notes, *Akins v. Texas*, Murphy Papers, Box 69, reel 131, fr. 36; Fine, *Murphy*, 391; *Akins*, 325 U.S. at 405–6. See also *Swain*, 380 U.S. at 202, 208–9. A few years later, the Court in *Cassell v. Texas* (1951) made it clear that proportionality caps on the number of blacks sitting on a jury were unconstitutional.

146. "Four Negroes," *Nation* 150 (24 Feb. 1940): 269–70; NAACP Press Release, 16 Feb. 1940, NAACP, part 8, series B, reel 2, frs. 833–36; Chambers v. Florida, 309 U.S. 227 (1940); Wilson, "*Chambers v. Florida*," esp. 5–15.

147. "Four Negroes," *Nation* 150 (24 Feb. 1940): 269–70; *Chambers*, 309 U.S. at 236; 187 So. 156, 157 (Fla. 1939); Deiterle v. State, 124 So. 47 (Fla. 1929); Mathieu v. State, 133 So. 550 (Fla. 1931). See also Ashcraft v. Tennessee, 322 U.S. 143, 155 (1944); Malinski v. New York, 324 U.S. 401, 433 (1945) (Murphy, J., dissenting).

148. White v. Texas, 310 U.S. 530 (1940); Canty v. Alabama, 309 U.S. 629 (1940); Ward v. Texas, 316 U.S. 547, 552 (1942); Lomax v. Texas, 313 U.S. 544 (1941); *Crisis* 47 (May 1940): 149–50; "Notice to Alabama," ibid. (Apr. 1940): 113, 116; ibid. 49 (July 1942): 227; Tushnet, *Thurgood Marshall*, 57. See also Alex C. Birch to Marshall, 11 July 1939, NAACP, part 8, series B, frs. 541–43; Birch to Leon A. Ransom, 14 Feb. 1940, ibid., frs. 606–7; Ransom to Marshall, 12 Mar. 1940, ibid., fr. 610.

149. Watts v. Indiana, 338 U.S. 49, 59–61 (1949) (Jackson, J., dissenting); Stein v. New York, 346 U.S. 156, 203 (1953) (Douglas, J., dissenting).

150. Lisenba v. California, 314 U.S. 219 (1941); Malinski v. New York, 324 U.S. 401 (1945); Ashcraft v. Tennessee, 322 U.S. 143 (1944); Watts v. Indiana, 338 U.S. 49 (1949); Turner v. Pennsylvania, 338 U.S. 62 (1949); Harris v. South Carolina, 338 U.S. 68 (1949); Haley v. Ohio, 332 U.S. 596 (1948); Stroble v. California, 343 U.S. 181 (1952); *Stein,* 346 U.S. 156; Stephens, *Supreme Court and Confessions of Guilt,* 90–113; Case & Van Etten, "Criminal Confessions in Capital Cases"; Boskey & Pickering, "State Criminal Procedure," 286–95; Pritchett, *Truman Court,* 159–63.

151. Lyons v. Oklahoma, 322 U.S. 596 (1944), discussed further on pages 284–85.

152. Powell v. Alabama, 287 U.S. 45 (1932), which was discussed on pages 123–25; Betts v. Brady, 316 U.S. 455 (1942); De Meerleer v. Michigan, 329 U.S. 663 (1947); Uveges v. Pennsylvania, 335 U.S. 437 (1948); Wade v. Mayo, 334 U.S. 672 (1948); Gibbs v. Burke, 337 U.S. 773 (1949); Pritchett, *Roosevelt Court,* 138–41; Pritchett, *Vinson Court,* 156–59.

153. Avery v. Georgia, 345 U.S. 559, 561 (1953); Avery v. Alabama, 308 U.S. 444 (1940); Strickland v. Washington, 466 U.S. 668 (1984); Cole, *No Equal Justice,* 64–65, 77–86, 91–95; Note, "*Gideon's* Promise Unfulfilled," 2062–69.

154. Swain v. Alabama, 380 U.S. 202 (1965); Furman v. Georgia, 408 U.S. 238 (1972); Coker v. Georgia, 433 U.S. 584 (1977); Batson v. Kentucky, 476 U.S. 79 (1986); McCleskey v. Kemp, 481 U.S. 279, 315 (1987); Cole, *No Equal Justice,* 119, 133–40; Kennedy, "*McCleskey v. Kemp*"; Carter, "When Victims Happen to Be Black."

155. United States v. Armstrong, 517 U.S. 456 (1996); Shaw v. Reno, 509 U.S. 630, 647 (1993); Karlan, "Race, Rights, and Remedies," 2024–25; McAdams, "Race and Selective Prosecution"; Cole, *No Equal Justice,* 158–60.

156. Cole, *No Equal Justice;* Kennedy, *Race, Crime, and the Law.*

157. Pollock v. Williams, 322 U.S. 4 (1944); Taylor v. Georgia, 315 U.S. 25 (1942); pages 71–74, 86–87. See also United States v. Gaskin, 320 U.S. 527 (1944).

158. *Taylor,* 315 U.S. at 31.

159. Williams v. Pollock, 14 So. 2d 700 (Fla. 1943).

160. *Pollock,* 322 U.S. at 13–25; Bailey v. Alabama, 219 U.S. 219, 235–38 (1911). Jackson also denied the significance of differences among Florida's evidence law, which allowed defendants to testify regarding uncommunicated motives, Alabama's law, which did not, and Georgia law, which permitted only unsworn statements.

CHAPTER 5

1. Opinion by lawyer Barbour in the matter of the Oklahoma Election Law, undated, NAACP, part 4, reel 1, frs. 423–24; Committee of Editors and Writers of the South, "Voting Restrictions in the 13 Southern States," part 4, reel 7, frs. 459–60 (hereafter, "Voting Restrictions").

2. Garrow, *Protest at Selma,* 7 table 1-1, 11 table 1-2; Lawson, *Black Ballots,* 85 table 1; Donald Jones to Marshall, 10 Aug. 1942, NAACP, part 4, reel 8, fr. 387; Bennett B. Ross to Walter White, 22 Aug. 1942, ibid., fr. 389; Carsie A. Hall to Marshall, 26 Aug. 1942, ibid., fr. 797; W. R. Saxon to Marshall, 15 Mar. 1941, ibid., reel 9, fr. 151.

3. Pages 85–86, 158.

4. Hine, *White Primary in Texas,* 224; NYT, 4 Apr. 1944, p. 15; "Dixie Vote," unidentified and undated press clipping, NAACP, part 4, reel 7, fr. 583. See also Editorial, *Atlanta Constitution,* 5 Apr. 1944, ibid., fr. 585; B. R. Edmunds to NAACP, 2 Dec. 1944, ibid., fr. 424; Marshall to A. T. Walden, 26 July 1944, ibid., frs. 620–21;

Palmer Weber to Thurgood Marshall et al., memorandum, "Citizenship in the South," 8 Nov. 1948, ibid., frs. 549–53 (hereafter, Weber, "Citizenship in the South").

5. Weber, "Citizenship in the South," 1–2 (frs. 549–50); Bartley, *New South*, 171; Hine, *White Primary in Texas*, 238; Lawson, *Black Ballots*, 114, 134 table 1; *Crisis* 55 (Sept. 1948): 274–75; Fairclough, *Civil Rights Struggle in Louisiana*, 106, 131; Lawson et al., "Groveland," 2; Emmons, "Harry T. Moore," 242; Green, *Harry T. Moore*, 117.

6. Editorial, *Crisis* 53 (July 1946): 201; "Time Bomb," *Time* 43 (17 Apr. 1944): 20–21; Weber, "Citizenship in the South," 1 (fr. 549); Fairclough, *Civil Rights Struggle in Louisiana*, 102; Hine, *White Primary in the South*, 222–23; Moon, *Balance of Power*, 178; Editorial, *Crisis* 51 (May 1944): 136, 164–65; "Voting Restrictions," frs. 451–67; "White Supremacy," *Dallas News*, 7 Jan. 1948, NAACP, part 4, reel 8, fr. 211; "Mississippi Mud," *Birmingham World*, 7 Aug. 1947, ibid., reel 9, fr. 126; "An Expected Decision," *Atlanta Constitution*, 4 Mar. 1946, ibid., reel 7, fr. 713. See also NYT, 3 Mar. 1947, p. 44; Key, *Southern Politics*, 635; Lawson, *Black Ballots*, 91–92.

7. NAACP Press Release, 5 May 1942, NAACP, part 4, reel 10, fr. 715; Weber, "Citizenship in the South," 1–2 (frs. 549–50); Lawson, *Black Ballots*, 91; Norrell, *Civil Rights Movement in Tuskegee*, 72–74, 88–89; Sims, *James E. Folsom*, 163–65, 168, 171–72; unidentified and undated press clipping, part 4, reel 6, fr. 241; O. H. Finney, Jr., to Willie Louis Dick, 6 Dec. 1949, ibid., fr. 248; Fairclough, *Civil Rights Struggle in Louisiana*, 132; Kurtz & Peoples, *Earl K. Long*, 151, 197–98, 209–10, 268; NYT, 5 Apr. 1944, p. 12; flyer encouraging blacks to register, 26 June 1944, part 4, reel 6, fr. 267; Arnall, *Shore Dimly Seen*, 59–60; Emmons, "Harry T. Moore," 235; *Atlanta Daily World*, 13 Apr. 1948, part 4, reel 8, fr. 228; James M. Hinton to Marshall, 22 Apr. 1942, ibid., reel 10, frs. 709–10; unidentified and undated press clipping, ibid., fr. 729.

8. "Mississippi Mud," *Birmingham World*, 7 Aug. 1947, NAACP, part 4, reel 9, fr. 126; John M. Lofton, Jr., to Marshall, n.d., ibid., fr. 957; Dorothy Q. Rainey to J. Lon Duckworth, 20 June 1944, ibid., reel 7, frs. 592–93; "Qualified to Vote but Denied the Chance" (political advertisement), *Birmingham Post*, 17 June 1946, ibid., reel 6, frs. 263–66. See also *Arkansas Labor Journal*, 28 Feb. 1945, p. 1, ibid., fr. 697; B. R. Edmunds to NAACP, 2 Dec. 1944, ibid., reel 7, fr. 424; Brooks, "Winning the Peace," 602.

9. Norrell, *Civil Rights Movement in Tuskegee*, 60–61; Fred James to NAACP, 11 Apr. 1944, NAACP, part 4, reel 6, frs. 845–47; Houston Dutton to NAACP, 10 Aug. 1944, ibid., reel 8, frs. 396–97; Benjamin James Pittman to NAACP, 2 July 1946, ibid., reel 10, frs. 820–23; Fairclough, *Civil Rights Struggle in Louisiana*, 89, 111; Dittmer, *Struggle for Civil Rights in Mississippi*, 1–9; Lawson, *Black Ballots*, 101–2, 126; Eskew, *But for Birmingham*, 70; Brooks, "Winning the Peace," 568–70; Emory O. Jackson to J. B. Vines, 29 June 1944, NAACP, part 4, reel 6, frs. 76–77; Jackson to Legal Redress and Registration Committee, 18 Aug. 1944, ibid., frs. 83–84; unidentified press clipping, 13 Feb. 1945, ibid., fr. 274; Arthur A. Madison to Marshall, 8 May 1944, ibid., frs. 325–26; flyer encouraging blacks to register, ibid., fr. 267; statement by the Progressive Voters League of Florida, 20 June 1945, ibid., reel 7, frs. 42–43; newsletter from NAACP, 4 May 1944, ibid., fr. 414; John H. McCray, "The Progressive Party in South Carolina," *Southern Frontier* (Aug. 1944), ibid., reel 9, frs. 397–99; Green, *Harry T. Moore*, 54, 59; Sullivan, *Days of Hope*, 170, 212; *Atlanta Constitution*, 1 July 1944, NAACP, part 4, reel 7, fr. 610; Hinton to Marshall, 22 Apr. 1942, ibid., reel 10, frs. 709–10; Letter from E. M. Cams, 15 May 1942, ibid., fr. 721; Mary Moore, affidavit, 9 Feb. 1945, ibid., reel 6, fr. 120; Enna Pope, affidavit, n.d., ibid., fr. 121; Ida Lee Rodgers, affidavit, 10 Feb. 1945, ibid., fr. 122.

10. W. M. Thomas to Marshall, 28 Aug. 1944, NAACP, part 4, reel 8, fr. 90; J. Wesley Dixon to Marshall, 28 Aug. 1944, ibid., reel 7, fr. 420; Carsie A. Hall to Marshall, 16 Feb. 1945, ibid., reel 9, fr. 8; Harold B. Boulware to Marshall, 5 July 1946, ibid., reel 10, frs. 825–27; King v. Chapman, 62 F. Supp. 639 (M.D. Ga. 1945), aff'd, 154 F. 2d 460 (5th Cir. 1946), cert. denied, 327 U.S. 800 (1946); *Atlanta Constitution*, 14 June 1945, NAACP, part 4, reel 7, fr. 676; *NYT*, 28 July 1945, p. 24; Elmore v. Rice, 72 F. Supp. 516 (E.D.S.C.), aff'd, 165 F. 2d 387 (4th Cir. 1947), cert. denied, 333 U.S. 875 (1948); Daniel E. Byrd to H. J. Levy, 20 Oct. 1947, NAACP, part 4, reel 8, frs. 514–15; Donald Jones to Marshall, 22 Oct. 1947, ibid., fr. 526; James M. Hinton to Marshall, 21 Dec. 1945, ibid., reel 10, fr. 807; Marshall to Arthur D. Shores, 5 May 1944, ibid., reel 6, fr. 70; Marshall to Edward D. Davis, 2 May 1944, ibid., fr. 851; Farris, "Re-Enfranchisement of Negroes in Florida," 272–73.

11. A. P. Tureaud, Memorandum on Registrars' Practices in Various Louisiana Parishes, 1 Sept. 1944, NAACP, part 4, reel 8, frs. 407–9 (hereafter, Tureaud Memorandum); Hall v. Nagel, 154 F. 2d 931 (5th Cir. 1946); Mitchell v. Wright, 154 F. 2d 924 (5th Cir. 1946); *Crisis* 51 (Aug. 1945): 231; NAACP Press Release, 21 June 1945, part 4, reel 6, fr. 151; Harry T. Moore to Marshall, 23 Apr. 1946, ibid., reel 7, fr. 365; Emory O. Jackson to J. B. Vines, 29 June 1944, ibid., reel 6, frs. 76–77; E. K. McIlrath to Jacksonville City Commissioners, 3 May 1945, ibid., reel 7, frs. 22–23; Daniel E. Byrd to Jackson Parish Registrar of Voters, 21 Oct. 1947, ibid., reel 8, frs. 518–19.

12. Green, *Harry T. Moore*, 76; Editorial, *Shreveport Sun*, 30 Apr. 1949, NAACP, part 4, reel 7, fr. 563; Dalfiume, *Fighting on Two Fronts*, 123; Bartley, *New South*, 29; Tushnet, *Thurgood Marshall*, 28, 33–35; William Henry Samuel to NAACP, 7 Sept. 1948, part 4, reel 8, fr. 600; Norman Lacey to White, 26 May 1940, ibid., reel 7, frs. 121–25; D. H. Malloy to NAACP, 22 Nov. 1941, ibid., frs. 177–78; Frank D. Reeves to Lacey, 26 Nov. 1941, ibid., fr. 176; J. L. LeFlore to White, 29 Nov. 1941, ibid., frs. 179–82; LeFlore to Marshall, 22 May 1938, ibid., reel 1, fr. 837; Marshall to LeFlore, 11 June 1938, ibid., fr. 852. See also Smith, "Black Attorneys and the NAACP in Virginia," 25–26.

13. Donald Jones to Marshall, 10 Dec. 1947, NAACP, part 4, reel 8, fr. 544; Carsie Hall to Marshall, 16 Feb. 1945, ibid., reel 9, fr. 8; Hall to Marshall, 27 Aug. 1945, ibid., fr. 13; Fairclough, *Civil Rights Struggle in Louisiana*, 134; Houston Dutton to Marshall, 28 Sept. 1944, part 4, reel 8, frs. 418–19; Louis Thompson to Marshall, 23 Dec. 1944, ibid., reel 9, fr. 257; Chas. A. J. McPherson to NAACP, 9 Nov. 1920, ibid., reel 1, frs. 445–46; Carter W. Wesley, "Texans Seek the Right to Vote," *Crisis* 47 (Oct. 1940): 313. See also Memorandum re: Telephone Conversation with C. H. Tobias, 21 Oct. 1920, NAACP, part 4, reel 1, fr. 346.

14. *Atlanta Constitution*, 20 Aug. 1948, NAACP, part 4, reel 6, fr. 218; Harold R. Boulware to Marshall, 5 July 1946, ibid., reel 10, frs. 825–27; Harold R. Boulware, Memorandum on Problem Presented by South Carolina: *Brown v. Baskin*, 21 June 1946, pp. 1, 6, ibid., reel 9, frs. 476, 481 (hereafter, Boulware Memorandum); Fairclough, *Civil Rights Struggle in Louisiana*, 133–34; Dean v. Thomas, 93 F. Supp. 129 (E.D. La. 1950); Byrd v. Brice, 104 F. Supp. 442 (W.D. La. 1952); Joseph A. Berry & Daniel L. Beasley to White, 20 July 1948, NAACP, part 4, reel 6, frs. 208–14; Charles A. Chandler to Charles H. Houston, 8 Apr. 1937, ibid., reel 3, fr. 203. See also Marshall to Arthur D. Shores, 18 Apr. 1945, ibid., reel 6, fr. 136.

15. Byrd to Levy, 20 Oct. 1947, NAACP, part 4, reel 8, frs. 514–15; Chair of Alexandria, Louisiana, Branch Legal Committee to NAACP, 30 Sept. 1944, ibid., fr. 424; G. M. Johnson to Nora Windon, Aug. 1948, ibid., frs. 592–93; Marshall to Tom Clark, 11

Sept. 1944, ibid., reel 9, frs. 236–37; Marshall to W. R. Saxon, 14 May 1942, ibid., fr. 180; Saxon to Marshall, 20 May 1942, ibid., frs. 190–91; *Greenville News*, 27 Nov. 1941, ibid., reel 10, fr. 633; Lottie P. Gaffney to Marshall, 28 Feb. 1942, ibid., frs. 644–45; Francis Biddle to Marshall, 8 Aug. 1944, ibid., reel 7, fr. 418; Biddle to C. A. Scott, 1 Dec. 1944, ibid., frs. 628–29; Marshall to Clark, 9 May 1944, ibid., reel 6, fr. 327; White to Homer S. Cummings, 30 Aug. 1935, ibid., reel 2, frs. 220–21; Houston to Attorney General, 16 Oct. 1935, ibid., frs. 231–32; Houston to Attorney General, 18 Nov. 1935, ibid., fr. 259; John Marshall to Robert W. Bagnall, 23 Oct. 1928, ibid., fr. 347.

16. Emory O. Jackson to Marshall, 16 Feb. 1945, NAACP, part 4, reel 6, fr. 131; Marshall to Francis J. Biddle, 3 Apr. 1944, ibid., reel 11, fr. 395; *Crisis* 51 (May 1944): 164–65; "Time Bomb," *Time* 43 (17 Apr. 1944): 20–21; Lawson, *Black Ballots*, 47; Milton R. Konvitz to Victor Rotnem, 17 Apr. 1944, NAACP, part 4, reel 6, fr. 309; Marshall to Biddle, 5 July 1944, ibid., reel 8, frs. 133–34; Marshall to Biddle, 19 July 1944, ibid., frs. 138–40; Marshall to Scott, 27 Oct. 1944, ibid., fr. 104; Marshall to LeFlore, 23 Nov. 1945, ibid., reel 6, fr. 548; *NYT*, 14 Mar. 1945, ibid., reel 8, fr. 141; *Charleston Evening Post*, 6 Apr. 1946, ibid., reel 7, fr. 430.

17. Arthur Shores to Marshall, 16 Sept. 1939, NAACP, part 4, reel 3, fr. 182; Moore to Marshall, 12 July 1948, ibid., reel 6, fr. 791; J. T. Smith to NAACP, 20 Aug. 1948, ibid., fr. 798; Donald Jones to Marshall, 22 Oct. 1947, ibid., reel 8, fr. 526. See also Marshall to S. M. Coleman, 29 June 1950, ibid., fr. 613.

18. Tushnet, *Thurgood Marshall*, 52–55.

19. Zangrando, *NAACP Crusade against Lynching*, 6–7 table 2; James Floyd to White, 7 Dec. 1920, NAACP, part 4, reel 1, fr. 936; Alexander Akerman to Sen. William C. Kenyon, 5 Nov. 1920, ibid., frs. 925–27; *Houston Defender*, 23 July 1932, ibid., reel 4, fr. 114; Mack Holiman to NAACP, 3 Dec. 1927, ibid., reel 2, frs. 103–4; James Weldon Johnson to Nathaniel B. Bond, 30 Dec. 1927, ibid., fr. 111; S. R. Redmond to Johnson, 5 Jan. 1928, ibid., fr. 118; Walter White, "Election Day in Florida," in NAACP, *Disfranchisement of Colored Americans in the Presidential Election of 1920*, 9–10, 12–13, ibid., reel 1, frs. 540–41, 543–44; *Crisis* 21 (Feb. 1921): 165; Green, *Harry T. Moore*, 23–24; Howard, *Shifting Wind*, 197.

20. *New York Post*, 3 June 1946, NAACP, part 4, reel 8, fr. 175; *NYT*, 18 Feb. 1951, p. 48; pages 249–53; Capeci, *Cleo Wright*, chap. 3; Lawson, *Black Ballots*, 107–8; Fairclough, *Civil Rights Struggle in Louisiana*, 113.

21. Fred C. Knollenberg & Frank Cameron to NAACP, 17 Nov. 1930, NAACP, part 4, reel 3, fr. 549; Knollenberg & Cameron to Arthur B. Spingarn, 2 Sept. 1930, ibid., frs. 527–28; Cameron & Knollenberg to Nathan R. Margold, 13 Nov. 1930, ibid., frs. 550–51; Spingarn to White, 28 Jan. 1930, ibid., fr. 452; Trudeau v. Barnes, 65 F. 2d 563 (5th Cir. 1933); Lane v. Wilson, 98 F. 2d 980 (10th Cir. 1938), rev'd, 307 U.S. 268 (1939); Nixon v. Condon, 49 F. 2d 1012 (5th Cir. 1931), rev'd, 286 U.S. 73 (1932).

22. Editorial, *Alabama* 10 (6 July 1945), p. 1, NAACP, part 4, reel 6, fr. 155; unidentified press clipping, 4 Apr. 1944, ibid., reel 7, fr. 583; Klarman, "Majoritarian Judicial Review"; Issacharoff & Pildes, "Partisan Lockups of the Democratic Process"; *NYT*, 4 Apr. 1944, p. 1; ibid., 8 June 1944, p. 38; Cushman, "*Smith v. Allwright*," 75; Farris, "Re-Enfranchisement of Negroes in Florida," 273–83; pages 246–48.

23. Elmore v. Rice, 72 F. Supp. 516, 528 (E.D.S.C.), aff'd, 165 F. 2d 387 (4th Cir. 1947), cert. denied, 333 U.S. 875 (1948); King v. Chapman, 62 F. Supp. 639 (M.D. Ga. 1945), aff'd, 154 F. 2d 460 (5th Cir. 1946), cert. denied, 327 U.S. 800 (1946); Davis v. Florida ex rel. Cromwell, 23 So. 2d 85 (Fla. 1945); Brown v. Baskin, 78 F. Supp. 933 (E.D.S.C. 1948), aff'd, 174 F. 2d 391 (4th Cir. 1949). See also T. B. Wilson to White, 14

July 1947, NAACP, part 4, reel 9, fr. 117; Key, *Southern Politics*, 640–41; Lewis, "Negro Voter in Mississippi," 341.

24. Editorial, *Alabama* 10 (6 July 1945), p. 1, NAACP, part 4, reel 6, fr. 155; unidentified and undated press clipping, ibid., fr. 280; unidentified and undated press clipping, ibid., fr. 281; Key, *Southern Politics*, 632–33; Lawson, *Black Ballots*, 90–93; Marshall to Col. A. T. Walden, 17 Mar. 1949, NAACP, part 4, reel 8, fr. 240; Marshall to James Nabrit, 13 Apr. 1949, ibid., fr. 241; Franklin v. Harper, 55 S.E. 2d 221 (Ga. 1949).

25. Lawson, *Black Ballots*, chap. 4; Norrell, *Civil Rights Movement in Tuskegee*, 36–40, 44–46, 59–78; Note, "Negro Disenfranchisement," 90–97; Report of the Legislative Committee of the Tuskegee Branch of the NAACP, 20 July 1948, NAACP, part 4, reel 6, frs. 208–14; Joseph A. Berry to Wilkins & Marshall, 10 Dec. 1948, ibid., frs. 357–65; Tureaud Memorandum; *Crisis* 59 (June–July 1952): 378–80; Jackson to editor of the *Birmingham News-Age-Herald*, part 4, reel 6, frs. 110–11; E. D. Nixon to White, 11 Aug. 1943, ibid., fr. 42; affidavit of a group of veterans, 25 June 1946, ibid., reel 9, fr. 37; group denied registration in Rutherfordton, North Carolina, to White, 31 Oct. 1944, ibid., fr. 247; McCray, "Progressive Party in South Carolina," *Southern Frontier* (Aug. 1944), ibid., frs. 397–99; Boulware Memorandum; Moore to Marshall, 15 Dec. 1945, part 4, reel 6, fr. 993; Moore to Marshall, 30 May 1946, ibid., fr. 1007; Jackson to Marshall, 13 Dec. 1949, ibid., frs. 253–54.

26. Davis v. Schnell, 81 F. Supp. 872 (S.D. Ala.), aff'd, 336 U.S. 933 (1949); pages 34–36; Note, "Negro Disenfranchisement," 95; Francis Collopy, Comment, *Notre Dame Lawyer* 24 (Summer 1949): 571, 573; Byrd v. Brice, 104 F. Supp. 442 (W.D. La. 1952); Dean v. Thomas, 93 F. Supp. 129 (E.D. La. 1950); Mitchell v. Wright, 154 F. 2d 924 (5th Cir.), cert. denied, 329 U.S. 733 (1946); Marshall to Biddle, 3 Oct. 1944, NAACP, part 4, reel 8, frs. 433–34; Florida ex rel. Graham v. Bowden, No. 16237-L (Fla. Cir. Ct. 1945), ibid., reel 7, frs. 13–14; Lawson, *Black Ballots*, 89; Sullivan, *Days of Hope*, 213; Bernd, "Disfranchisement of Blacks in Georgia," 494–500; *NYT*, 12 July 1946, p. 15; ibid., 14 July 1946, p. 29; Robert L. Carter, memorandum, 10 July 1947, part 4, reel 7, fr. 725; Adams v. Whittaker, 195 S.W. 2d 634 (Ark. 1946). The reason that the Arkansas legislature thought that *Smith* applied only to *federal* primaries is unclear, as the Fifteenth Amendment does not distinguish between state and federal elections.

27. Brown v. Baskin 78 F. Supp. 933, 942 (E.D.S.C. 1948), aff'd, 174 F. 2d 391 (4th Cir. 1949); letter to Walter White, 16 Feb. 1946, NAACP, part 4, reel 7, fr. 711; Hine, *White Primary in Texas*, 239; Attorney General Watson to Harry Moore, 19 Feb. 1946, part 4, reel 6, fr. 900; C. B. Motley to Miss Karin, Memorandum re: *Brown v. Baskin*, 7 Apr. 1949, ibid., reel 9, frs. 465–66; Boulware Memorandum, 7 (fr. 482); Lawson, *Black Ballots*, 54; Fairclough, *Civil Rights Struggle in Louisiana*, 133–34.

28. "The Right to Vote," *New South* 4 (Feb. 1949): 1, 4; United States v. Classic, 313 U.S. 299, 320 (1941); Lane v. Wilson, 307 U.S. 268, 275 (1939); Theodore Redding to Edward R. Dudley, 3 Apr. 1945, NAACP, part 4, reel 6, fr. 974; Yarbrough, *J. Waties Waring*; Schmidt, "J. Waties Waring," esp. 5, 11; Bass, *Unlikely Heroes*, chap. 7. Compare Brown v. Baskin, 174 F. 2d 391 (4th Cir. 1949), with Briggs v. Elliot, 132 F. Supp. 776 (E.D.S.C. 1955). See also Egerton, *Generation before the Civil Rights Movement*, 406–7; pages 354–59.

29. Georgia M. Johnson to National Legal Committee, 4 Apr. 1944, NAACP, part 4, reel 11, fr. 298.

30. *Time* 43 (17 Apr. 1944): 20–21; "Theory versus Condition," clipping from unidentified Georgia newspaper, 4 Apr. 1944, NAACP, part 4, reel 7, fr. 585; H. L. Hunnicutt to Claude Dempsey, 21 Feb. 1945, ibid., reel 6, fr. 693; Frankfurter, Mem-

orandum on *Smith v. Allwright*, n.d., Frankfurter Papers, part 1, reel 10, frs. 165–68; Mason, *Harlan Fiske Stone*, 614–15; *NYT*, 5 Apr. 1944, p. 12; ibid., 4 Apr. 1944, pp. 1, 15; undated clipping from *Arkansas Gazette*, part 4, reel 6, fr. 676; *Augusta Chronicle*, 13 Apr. 1946, ibid., reel 7, frs. 433–36; Mormino, "G.I. Joe Meets Jim Crow," 39–40; unidentified press clipping, 4 Apr. 1944, part 4, reel 7, fr. 583; Malcolm E. Lafargue to Byrd, 23 Oct. 1947, ibid., reel 8, fr. 529; LeFlore to Konvitz, 12 Apr. 1944, ibid., reel 6, frs. 302–3; Shores to Marshall, 3 May 1944, ibid., fr. 67; Farris, "Re-Enfranchisement of Negroes in Florida," 271. See also Frederickson, *Dixiecrat Revolt*, 40–41. But cf. Lawson, *Black Ballots*, 46; Tushnet, *Thurgood Marshall*, 107.

31. Jackson to Marshall, 16 Feb. 1945, NAACP, part 4, reel 6, fr. 131; Jackson to Marshall, 8 Feb. 1945, ibid., fr. 116; unidentified press clipping, 13 Feb. 1945, ibid., fr. 274; John A. Buggs to Marshall, 18 Dec. 1945, ibid., fr. 892; Byrd to Marshall, 6 Nov. 1947, ibid., reel 8, fr. 531; Jones to Tom Clark, 24 Nov. 1947, ibid., fr. 535. See also Chair of Alexandria, Louisiana, Branch Legal Committee to NAACP, 30 Sept. 1944, ibid., reel 8, fr. 424; Marshall to Biddle, 3 Oct. 1944, ibid., frs. 433–34.

32. Brooks, "Winning the Peace," 585–87, 600–601 n. 99; Sullivan, *Days of Hope*, 211. See also Bernd, "Disfranchisement of Blacks in Georgia," 494–96; Anderson, *Eugene Talmadge*, 219–33.

33. Cushman, "*Smith v. Allwright*," 75; *NYT*, 14 Apr. 1944, p. 1; Olin T. Johnston, Speech to Joint Assembly and General Assembly of South Carolina, 14 Apr. 1944, NAACP, part 4, reel 10, frs. 481–82; Elmore v. Rice, 72 F. Supp. 516, 520 (E.D.S.C. 1947).

34. *Crisis* 51 (May 1944): 164–65; Dittmer, *Struggle for Civil Rights in Mississippi*, 1–3; Lawson, *Black Ballots*, 99–100, 103; Lewis, "Negro Voter in Mississippi," 329, 332; Fairclough, *Civil Rights Struggle in Louisiana*, 136; Sullivan, *Days of Hope*, 7, 211; NAACP, "Negro Vote in Southern States, 1946," 7–8, NAACP, part 4, reel 8, frs. 862, 868–69 (hereafter, "Negro Vote"); Rev. George T. J. Strype to Lamarr Caudley, 2 July 1946, ibid., reel 9, frs. 57–58; "Tinder for Talmadge," *Newsweek*, 1 July 1946, p. 22; *NYT*, 15 July 1946, p. 1; Heard, *Two-Party South?* 192; Bernd, "Disfranchisement of Blacks in Georgia," 494–98.

35. Southern Democrats, who enjoyed a majority on the Ellender committee, refused to hold Bilbo responsible for the violence that pervaded his 1946 campaign. The minority Republicans dissented. However, Republicans controlled the new Congress, which convened in 1947, and they refused to seat Bilbo. A compromise was negotiated that laid Bilbo's credentials on the table, while he took a leave of absence owing to ill health. Bilbo died later that year, thus mooting the issue of whether to seat him.

36. H. W. Polson to Sen. Bilbo, 23 June 1946, NAACP, part 4, reel 9, fr. 31; "Bilboism," *Wash. Post*, 6 Dec. 1946, p. 18; Franklin H. Williams to A. T. Walden, 25 Oct. 1948, NAACP, part 4, reel 8, fr. 316; Byrd to Marshall, 3 July 1946, ibid., reel 9, frs. 49–50; Byrd to Marshall, 6 July 1946, ibid., fr. 60; "Probes: Votes and the Man," *Newsweek*, 16 Dec. 1946, pp. 33–34; Dittmer, *Struggle for Civil Rights in Mississippi*, 3–9; Lawson, *Black Ballots*, 105–14; Lewis, "Negro Voter in Mississippi," 332–39. See also Wilkins to White, memorandum, 3 Nov. 1948, NAACP, part 4, reel 8, fr. 320.

37. Mrs. Allan Knight Chalmers to Marshall, 1 May 1944, NAACP, part 4, reel 11, fr. 357; transcript of statement by Judge Waring in *Brown v. Baskin*, 16 July 1948, pp. 1, 3, ibid., reel 9, frs. 636–38; Key, *Southern Politics*, 631.

38. Weber, "Citizenship in the South," 2, 4 (frs. 550, 552); Fairclough, *Civil Rights Struggle in Louisiana*, 123–24, 129–30; Key, *Southern Politics*, 522; Lawson, *Black Ballots*, 129–30; Emmons, "Harry T. Moore," 237; "Negro Vote," 6, 11 (frs. 867,

872); Tureaud Memorandum; Edward R. Dudley to John Allum, 9 Feb. 1948, NAACP, part 4, reel 8, fr. 581; Harry T. Moore to Marshall, 15 Dec. 1945, ibid., reel 6, fr. 993; Elbridge G. Brooks to NAACP, 19 July 1948, ibid., fr. 946; Garrow, *Protest at Selma*, 9; Bernd, "Georgia," 500; Lewis, "Negro Voter in Mississippi," 334.

39. Anonymous letter from Milton, Florida, to NAACP, 14 Apr. 1948, NAACP, part 4, reel 6, fr. 936; Tureaud Memorandum, fr. 409; Tureaud to Justice Department, 17 Jan. 1948, part 4, reel 8, fr. 569; Rev. John Allum to NAACP, 4 Feb. 1948, ibid., frs. 579–80; C. L. Jordan to NAACP, 29 Jan. 1948, ibid., fr. 215; *Jackson Daily News*, n.d., ibid., fr. 892; Deacon Smith, undated statement, ibid., reel 6, frs. 910–11; Moore to Gov. Willard F. Caldwell, 20 Apr. 1948, ibid., fr. 941; Eldridge G. Brooks to NAACP, 19 July 1948, ibid., fr. 946; Tureaud to Justice Department, 23 Jan. 1948, ibid., reel 8, fr. 573; Tureaud to J. Skelly Wright, 29 July 1948, ibid., fr. 590; Herbert Monte Levy to Marshall, 30 June 1950, ibid., fr. 615; Jackson to Marshall, 13 Dec. 1949, ibid., reel 6, frs. 253–54; Clayborn Williams et al. to "Whom It May Concern," 7 Dec. 1949, ibid., frs. 250–51; "Negro Vote," 6 (fr. 867); *Newsweek*, 16 Dec. 1946, pp. 33–34; Green, *Harry T. Moore*, 54, 59; Sullivan, *Days of Hope*, 213.

40. Etoy Fletcher, affidavit, 15 June 1946, NAACP, part 4, reel 8, fr. 894; V. R. Collier, statement, 2 July 1946, ibid., reel 9, fr. 61; ibid., frs. 51–56; Carter to Clark, 1 July 1946, ibid., fr. 47; J. T. Smith to White, 11 May 1948, ibid., reel 6, frs. 762–65; D. H. Spencer to Mrs. Black, 12 May 1948, ibid., frs. 767–68; Smith, affidavit, 1 June 1948, ibid., frs. 779–81; Moore to Marshall, 12 July 1948, ibid., fr. 791; Emmons, "Harry T. Moore," 241; Green, *Harry T. Moore*, 1–5, 168–69; Dr. Ralph Mark Gilbert to Williams, 14 Oct. 1948, ibid., reel 7, fr. 867; Williams to Henry Lee Moon, Memorandum re: D. V. Carter, 26 Nov. 1948, ibid., frs. 883–86; *NYT*, 12 Sept. 1948, ibid., reel 8, fr. 288; Walden to Williams, 21 Oct. 1948, ibid., frs. 312–13; *Crisis* 58 (Dec. 1951): 674; Fairclough, *Civil Rights Struggle in Louisiana*, 130–31. See also Green, "Memphis Freedom Movement," 23.

41. Lawson, *Black Ballots*, 46, 48–49, 119; Marshall to Scott, 6 Dec. 1944, NAACP, part 4, reel 7, fr. 630; Byrd to Carter, 30 July 1946, ibid., reel 9, fr. 80; Carter to Clark, 16 July 1946, ibid., fr. 74; Marshall to Clark, 11 Sept. 1944, ibid., frs. 236–37; Emmons, "Harry T. Moore," 240–41; Lafargue to Byrd, 23 Oct. 1947, ibid., reel 8, fr. 529; V. R. Collier, statement, 2 July 1946, ibid., reel 9, frs. 51–56; Marshall to Wendell Burge, telegram, 21 May 1941, ibid., reel 10, fr. 600; unidentified and undated press clipping, ibid., fr. 609; *To Secure These Rights*, 121; Alexander M. Campbell to Williams, 30 Nov. 1948, NAACP, part 4, reel 6, fr. 794; Campbell to Marshall, 22 May 1949, ibid., reel 7, frs. 1038–39; Gaffney to Marshall, 28 Feb. 1942, ibid., reel 10, frs. 644–45; unidentified and undated press clipping, ibid., reel 9, fr. 609; Carr, *Federal Protection of Civil Rights*, 149, 178; Marshall to Walden, 25 Sept. 1944, part 4, reel 7, fr. 625; Marshall to LeFlore, 11 Dec. 1945, ibid., reel 6, fr. 550; Scott & Wallace Van Jackson to Marshall, 26 Aug. 1944, ibid., reel 8, frs. 83–84; Scott to Marshall, 29 Apr. 1945, ibid., reel 9, fr. 648; Marshall to Scott, 14 Dec. 1944, ibid., fr. 633; Walden to Biddle, 13 Mar. 1945, ibid., fr. 637; Walden to Marshall, 1 Sept. 1944, ibid., reel 8, frs. 91–92; Tushnet, *Thurgood Marshall*, 105, 107.

42. LeFlore to Marshall, 5 Feb. 1946, NAACP, part 4, reel 6, frs. 551–52; "Schnell Accuses Negro Leader," *Mobile Press*, 1 Feb. 1946, ibid., fr. 553; Gaffney to NAACP, 4 June 1942 ibid., reel 10, frs. 666–69; Byrd to Carter, 6 July 1947, ibid., reel 9, frs. 115–16.

43. Rev. C. N. Eiland to White, 16 July 1946, NAACP, part 4, reel 9, fr. 73; Moore to C. A. Smith, 26 May 1948, ibid., reel 6, frs. 942–43; Byrd to T. Vincent Quinn, 16

Dec. 1947, ibid., reel 8, frs. 551–52; LeFlore to Marshall, 9 Apr. 1944, ibid., reel 6, fr. 293; Marshall to Clark, 1 May 1944, ibid., fr. 321; Shores to Marshall, 22 Apr. 1944, ibid., fr. 315; *NYT*, 10 Apr. 1944, p. 21; Marshall to Smith, 11 Feb. 1947, part 4, reel 9, fr. 108; Byrd v. Brice, 104 F. Supp. 442, 443 (W.D. La. 1952).

44. Civil Rights Act of 1957, Pub. L. No. 85-315, § 131 (c), 71 Stat. 634, 637–38 (codified as amended at 42 U.S.C. § 1971 [c] [1994]); Civil Rights Act of 1965, Pub. L. No. 89-110, § 3 (a)-(b), 79 Stat. 437, 437 (codified as amended at 42 U.S.C. § 1973a [a]-[b] [1994]); Harper v. Virginia Board of Elections, 383 U.S. 663 (1966); Lassiter v. Northampton County Board of Elections, 360 U.S. 45 (1959); Lawson, *Black Ballots*, 120–21, 349; Key, *Southern Politics*, 608; Ogden, *Poll Tax in the South*, 135–36; Handler, *Social Movements and the Legal System*, 118–29.

45. *NYT*, 9 Feb. 1948, p. 15; Minutes of NAACP Board of Directors Meeting, 8 Mar. 1948, pp. 1–2, part 1, reel 3, frs. 790–91; ibid., 12 Apr. 1948, pp. 5–6, frs. 803–4; ibid., 13 Dec. 1948, pp. 2–3, frs. 872–73.

46. Pages 160–62; *NYT*, 23 Oct. 1950, p. 29; ibid., 29 Oct. 1950, sec. 4, p. 9; Roy Wilkins, "Undergirding the Democratic Ideal," *Crisis* 58 (Dec. 1951): 647–49; Marshall, "Racial Integration in Education," 319; Atwood, "Public Negro College," 354–56.

47. U.S. Civil Rights Commission, *Public Higher Education*, 27–36; *NYT*, 1 Feb. 1948, p. 14; 15 July 1950, p. 15; 10 Sept. 1950, sec. 4, p. 10; 5 Dec. 1950, p. 29; Johnson v. Board of Trustees, 83 F. Supp. 707 (E.D. Ky. 1949); McLaurin v. Oklahoma State Regents, 87 F. Supp. 526 (W.D. Okla. 1948); McKissick v. Carmichael, 187 F. 2d 949 (4th Cir. 1951); McCready v. Byrd, 73 A. 2d 8 (Md. 1950); *NYT*, 11 June 1950, sec. 4, p. 1; Benjamin Muse, "State Adjusting to Non-Segregation," *Wash. Post*, 17 Sept. 1950, sec. 2, p. 6b; *Crisis* 59 (Feb. 1952): 115–19; Burns, "Graduate Education for Blacks in North Carolina," 215–18.

48. U.S. Civil Rights Commission, *Public Higher Education*, 28–30, 56–63, 70–72, 79, 82, 87, 90–95; *NYT*, 29 May 1949, p. 4; 3 Sept. 1950, p. 25; 23 Oct. 1950, p. 29; Parker v. Delaware, 75 A. 2d 225 (Del. 1950); Roger B. Farquhar, "Bland Assurances Solve No Problem," *Wash. Post*, 23 May 1954, sec. 2, p. 2b; Kluger, *Simple Justice*, 289–90; Atwood, "Public Negro College"; *NYT*, 24 Oct. 1958, p. 34; *Crisis* 60 (Mar. 1953): 168–69; *NYT*, 5 Feb. 1956, p. 60.

49. Baker, "Ambiguous Legacies," 123–24; Wilson v. Board of Supervisors, 92 F. Supp. 986 (E.D. La. 1950); U.S. Civil Rights Commission, *Public Higher Education*, 17, 70–71, 82–84; *Crisis* 58 (Nov. 1951): 605; ibid. (May 1951): 333; Wrighten v. Board of Trustees, 72 F. Supp. 948 (E.D.S.C. 1947); Tushnet, *NAACP's Legal Strategy*, 87–88.

50. U.S. Civil Rights Commission, *Public Higher Education*, 89–94; *Crisis* 60 (Mar. 1953): 168–69; Ward v. Regents of the University of Georgia, 191 F. Supp. 491 (N.D. Ga. 1957); Hunt v. Arnold, 172 F. Supp. 847 (N.D. Ga. 1959); *NYT*, 18 Feb. 1951, p. 48; ibid., 22 Apr. 1951, p. 58.

51. U.S. Civil Rights Commission, *Public Higher Education*, 75–80; Paulson & Hawkes, "Virgil Hawkins," 59–71; Durbin, "Virgil Hawkins," 916, 922–42; State ex rel. Hawkins v. Board of Control, 47 So. 2d 608 (Fla. 1950), 53 So. 2d 116 (Fla. 1951), 60 So. 2d 162 (Fla. 1952), rev'd, 347 U.S. 971 (1954).

52. 83 So. 2d 20 (Fla. 1955), rev'd, 350 U.S. 413 (1956).

53. 93 So. 2d 254 (Fla. 1957).

54. 355 U.S. 839 (1957); *Hawkins*, 253 F. 2d 752 (5th Cir. 1958), on remand, 162 F. Supp. 851 (N.D. Fla. 1958).

55. U.S. Civil Rights Commission, *Public Higher Education*, 250–53.

56. *Newsweek*, 12 Mar. 1956, pp. 38–40; Clark, *Schoolhouse Door*, 19–20, 37–90, 96–102; Adams v. Lucy, 228 F. 2d 619, 620 (5th Cir. 1955), aff'g, 134 F. Supp. 235 (N.D. Ala.); U.S. Civil Rights Commission, *Public Higher Education*, 84–89; NYT, 5 Feb. 1956, p. 60.

57. *NYT*, 20 June 1958, p. 24; U.S. Civil Rights Commission, *Public Higher Education*, 81–82; *NYT*, 6 June 1958, p. 25; 7 June 1958, p. 10; 19 June 1958, p. 31; 30 Sept. 1959, p. 16; *Southern School News* (hereafter SSN), Oct. 1962, pp. 1, 10–13; Silver, *Closed Society*, 93–95.

58. U.S. Civil Rights Commission, *Public Higher Education*, 96–97; *New Republic*, 19 June 1950, pp. 5–6.

59. Pleasants & Burns, *1950 Senate Race in North Carolina*, 12, 24–30, 41–43, 85, 89–100, 122, 129–32, 144–87; Lubell, *Future of American Politics*, 101–2; Edsall & Williams, "North Carolina," 373–75.

60. Pleasants & Burns, *1950 Senate Race in North Carolina*, 189–246, 259–63, 268–69 (quotations at 195, 226); Chafe, *Civilities and Civil Rights*, 77–78.

61. *NYT*, 11 June 1950, sec. 4, p. 1; Paulson & Hawkes, "Virgil Hawkins," 64–66; Durbin, "Virgil Hawkins," 933–35; Pleasants & Burns, *1950 Senate Race in North Carolina*, 248, 250, 254–55; Lubell, *Future of American Politics*, 104–8, 120; *Crisis* 57 (Nov. 1950): 648–49.

62. Vose, *Caucasians Only*, 211–12, 228–29; Sugrue, *Origins of the Urban Crisis*, 45.

63. *To Secure These Rights*, 68; Vose, *Caucasians Only*, 5, 9; Sugrue, *Origins of the Urban Crisis*, 44; DeGraaf, "Impact of World War II," 29, 31; *Crisis* 54 (Oct. 1947): 308–10; Brief of the United States as Amicus Curiae, *Shelley v. Kraemer*, 10–11, 31–33; Kluger, *Simple Justice*, 255; Massey & Denton, *American Apartheid*, 37.

64. Loren Miller, "Covenants in the Bear Flag State," *Crisis* 53 (May 1946): 138–40, 155; unidentified newspaper clipping, 16 Jan. 1926, NAACP, part 5, reel 4, fr. 575; Kluger, *Simple Justice*, 247; Massey & Denton, *American Apartheid*, 37–38, 43, 188; Hirsch, *Making the Second Ghetto*, 29–31; Sugrue, *Origins of the Urban Crisis*, 45–46, 194–97; Mohl, "Making the Second Ghetto in Metropolitan Miami," 412–21; Hansberry v. Lee, 311 U.S. 32 (1940).

65. Hirsch, *Making the Second Ghetto*, 16; Massey & Denton, *American Apartheid*, 43–45; Jackson, *Crabgrass Frontier*, 231–35; Sugrue, *Origins of the Urban Crisis*, 41–42, 245–46.

66. NAACP, Memorandum on Racial Discrimination in Federal Housing, 28 Oct. 1944, part 5, reel 5, frs. 555–67 (quotation at fr. 559); Tushnet, *Thurgood Marshall*, 96–98; Vose, *Caucasians Only*, ix, 225–26; DeGraaf, "Impact of World War II," 31; Massey & Denton, *American Apartheid*, 46, 47 table 2.3, 51–54; Jackson, *Crabgrass Frontier*, 198–203, 208–15; Sugrue, *Origins of the Urban Crisis*, 43–44, 46–47, 183–90; Memorandum on Racial Discrimination by the Federal Housing Administration, 1948, NAACP, part 5, reel 5, frs. 574–86; Franklin Richards to Raymond Foley, 21 May 1948, ibid., fr. 645; Loren Miller to White, memorandum, 7 July 1948, ibid., frs. 651–54; *Crisis* 55 (Dec. 1948): 372–73; ibid. 56 (May 1949): 146–47; McCoy & Ruetten, *Minority Rights and the Truman Administration*, 213–15.

67. Mary Simkhovitch to James H. Hubert, 21 Nov. 1939, NAACP, part 5, reel 4, fr. 1078; Hirsch, *Making the Second Ghetto*, 223–24, 254–55; Massey & Denton, *American Apartheid*, 36–37, 50, 55–57, 90–91; Sugrue, *Origins of the Urban Crisis*, 34, 43–51, 72–88; Broussard, *Black San Francisco*, 177–79; White to Nathan Straus, 25 Sept. 1939, NAACP, part 5, reel 4, fr. 1058; *Crisis* 57 (Mar. 1950): 172–73; Gautreaux v. Romney, 363 F. Supp. 690 (N.D. Ill. 1973); Mohl, "Making of the Second Ghetto in

Metropolitan Miami," 401–2; Foner, *American Freedom*, 267; *Crisis* 58 (Jan. 1951): 39–40; Vose, *Caucasians Only*, 223–25, 250.

68. Mohl, "Making of the Second Ghetto in Metropolitan Miami," 395, 405–10; Green, *Harry T. Moore*, 132–33; Eskew, *But for Birmingham*, 53–61, 68, 81–82; *Crisis* 59 (Jan. 1952): 40–45; Hirsch, "Massive Resistance in the Urban North," 522–41.

69. Jones v. Alfred Mayer, 392 U.S. 409 (1968); Hills v. Gautreaux, 425 U.S. 284 (1976); Massey & Denton, *American Apartheid*, chaps. 3–4, 7–8.

70. Barnes, *Journey from Jim Crow*, 32–34; Long, "Segregation in Interstate Railway Coach Travel."

71. Barnes, *Journey from Jim Crow*, 78–79.

72. *Crisis* 53 (July 1946): 201; Chiles v. Chesapeake & Ohio Railway, 218 U.S. 71 (1910); Barnes, *Journey from Jim Crow*, 52–53, 63–65, 79–80; Whiteside v. Southern Bus Lines, 177 F. 2d 949 (6th Cir. 1949); Day v. Atlantic Greyhound Corp., 171 F. 2d 59 (4th Cir. 1948); Simmons v. Atlantic Greyhound Corp. 75 F. Supp. 166 (W.D. Va. 1947); Pridgen v. Carolina Coach Co., 47 S.E. 2d 609 (N.C. 1948); Frank, "Color Line," 312; Mays v. Southern Railway, 268 I.C.C. 352 (1947); Jackson v. Seaboard Air Line Railway Co., 269 I.C.C. 399 (1947); Brown v. Southern Railway, 269 I.C.C. 711 (1948); Palmore, "Race, Transportation, and the Dormant Commerce Clause," 1815–16.

73. Barnes, *Journey from Jim Crow*, 58–60, 84; Meier, *CORE*, 33–39.

74. Barnes, *Journey from Jim Crow*, 83–84, 101–2; *Crisis* 58 (May 1951): 333; ibid. 59 (Dec. 1952): 655–56.

75. Barnes, *Journey from Jim Crow*, 85, 120–31.

76. Brief of Petitioner, *Hill v. Texas*, 9, in NAACP, part 8, series B, reel 6, fr. 494 (quoting *Smith v. State*); McGee v. State, 40 So. 2d 160, 164 (Miss. 1949); Berry, *Mr. Justice Burton*, 174; G. F. Porter to Marshall, 20 Oct. 1941, NAACP, part 8, series B, reel 1, frs. 47–48; State v. Perkins, 31 So. 2d 188 (La. 1947).

77. Smith v. Texas, 311 U.S. 128 (1940); Patton v. Mississippi, 332 U.S. 463 (1947); Avery v. Georgia, 345 U.S. 559 (1953); Reece v. Georgia, 350 U.S. 85 (1955); motion for new trial, *Mississippi v. Dobbs*, Apr. 1946, NAACP, part 8, series B, reel 4, frs. 299–305; NAACP Press Release, 21 Jan. 1948, ibid., reel 7, frs. 592–93; McGee v. State, 26 So. 2d 680 (Miss. 1946); Holland v. State, 67 P. 2d 58 (Okla. Crim. App. 1937); Akens v. State, 167 S.W. 2d 758 (Tex. Crim. App. 1943); Edwards, "White Justice in Dallas," 253–55; State v. Perkins, 31 So. 2d 188 (La. 1947); Fairclough, *Civil Rights Struggle in Louisiana*, 128; Sherman, *Odell Waller*, 90; Lawson et al., "Groveland," 10; Claudius A. Turner to Department of Justice, 24 Nov. 1941, part 8, series B, reel 6, frs. 125–27; Shepherd v. State, 46 So. 2d 880 (Fla. 1950).

78. W. A. Bender to Marshall, 2 June 1948, NAACP, part 8, series B, reel 7, frs. 981–82; Swain v. Alabama, 380 U.S. 202 (1965); Whitus v. Georgia, 385 U.S. 545 (1967); McGee v. State, 40 So. 2d 160 (Miss. 1948); State v. Perkins, 31 So. 2d 188 (La. 1947); Edna B. Kerin, "Another Chance for the Groveland Victims," *Crisis* 58 (May 1951): 317–21, 350; NAACP Press Release, 21 Jan. 1948, part 8, series B, reel 7, frs. 592–93; Haraway v. State, 153 S.W. 2d 161 (Ark. 1941); Fairclough, *Civil Rights Struggle in Louisiana*, 128; Rise, *Martinsville Seven*, 36; Sherman, *Odell Waller*, 90.

79. Swain v. Alabama, 380 U.S. 202 (1965), overruled by Batson v. Kentucky, 476 U.S. 79 (1986); Wright, "Legal Executions of Kentucky Blacks," 266; Rise, *Martinsville Seven*, 36–37, 47, 128–30.

80. Canty v. Alabama, 309 U.S. 629 (1940); Lyons v. Oklahoma, 322 U.S. 596 (1944); Shepherd v. Florida, 341 U.S. 50 (1951); Fairclough, *Civil Rights Struggle in*

Louisiana, 121; Green, *Harry T. Moore*, 90–96; McCullogh to NAACP, telegram, 31 Jan. 1948, part 8, series B, reel 4, fr. 631; William Henry Huff, circular, 25 Feb. 1946, ibid., fr. 751; Jimmie Gordon, affidavit, 30 May 1954, ibid., reel 5, fr. 676.

81. Konvitz to Marshall, 25 Apr. 1944, NAACP, part 8, series B, reel 2, frs. 151–52; undated memorandum (probably 1942) regarding Willie Bryant, ibid., frs. 106–11; Huff, circular, 25 Feb. 1946, ibid., reel 4, fr. 751; Boskey & Pickering, "State Criminal Procedure," 298–99; State v. Wilson, 37 So. 2d 804 (La. 1948); Lyons v. Oklahoma, 322 U.S. 596 (1944).

82. Screws v. United States, 325 U.S. 91 (1945); ibid., 157–61 (Roberts, Frankfurter, and Jackson, JJ., dissenting); Carr, *Federal Protection of Civil Rights*, 105–15. See also Tushnet, *Thurgood Marshall*, 50.

83. Frederickson, "Racial Violence in South Carolina," 194; Carr, *Federal Protection of Civil Rights*, chaps. 5–6; *To Secure These Rights*, 122–26; Belknap, *Federal Law and Southern Order*, 20, 25; Coleman, "Freedom from Fear on the Home Front," 423–24; Fairclough, *Civil Rights Struggle in Louisiana*, 93–94, 116–18; Lawson et al., "Groveland," 14–15; Kerin, "Another Chance for the Groveland Victims." But see United States v. Sutherland, 37 F. Supp. 344 (N.D. Ga. 1940).

84. Monroe v. Pape, 365 U.S. 167 (1961); O. H. Barnett, Jr., to NAACP, 24 Oct. 1940, part 8, series B, reel 7, frs. 867–68; Barnett to Benj. A. Green, 5 Jan. 1941, ibid., fr. 874.

85. Pages 230–31.

86. Marshall to John Henry Joseph, 10 July 1941, NAACP, part 8, series B, reel 7, fr. 426; Marshall to James H. Kimmel, 22 Dec. 1941, ibid., reel 1, fr. 754; Marshall to W. A. Bootle, 25 Feb. 1941, ibid., reel 2, fr. 97; Robert L. Carter to Marshall, memo, 28 Feb. 1950, ibid., reel 6, fr. 996; Konvitz to Marshall, memo, 25 Apr. 1944, ibid., reel 2, frs. 151–52; Frank D. Reeves to Prentice Thomas, 19 Apr. 1941, ibid., fr. 428.

87. Bender to Marshall, 2 June 1948, part 8, series B, reel 7, frs. 981–82.

88. Bender to Williams, 9 Feb. 1948, NAACP, part 8, series B, reel 7, fr. 979; William Huff, circular, 25 Feb. 1946, ibid., reel 4, frs. 751–52; Joseph Murray to Marshall, 29 Dec. 1939, ibid., reel 1, frs. 463–64; Murray to Marshall, 13 Jan. 1940, ibid., frs. 465–66; Roscoe Dunjee to Marshall, 13 Jan. 1941, ibid., reel 8, fr. 855; J. A. Williams to Georgia M. Johnson, 13 May 1944, ibid., reel 1, frs. 303–6; J. A. Williams to Spencer Bradley, 11 June 1945, ibid., frs. 357–58; motion for new trial, *Mississippi v. Dobbs*, Apr. 1946, ibid., reel 4, frs. 299–305; NAACP Press Release, 16 Feb. 1940, ibid., reel 2, fr. 833; Marian Wynn Perry to Walter D. Coleman, 2 Dec. 1946, ibid., reel 8, frs. 44–45; Michel v. Louisiana, 350 U.S. 91 (1955); Williams v. Georgia, 349 U.S. 375 (1955).

89. As no transcript was made of the trial proceedings, we cannot know whether defense counsel cross-examined prosecution witnesses.

90. Miller, *Willie Francis*, 23–27; Fairclough, *Civil Rights Struggle in Louisiana*, 119. The leading authority on Francis concludes that there is no way of knowing whether he was guilty. See Miller, chap. 2.

91. Carter to Paul W. Hudgins, 1 June 1946, NAACP, part 8, series B, reel 8, fr. 15; Bender to Marshall, 10 Nov. 1947, ibid., fr. 969. See also Horne, *Civil Rights Congress*, 79.

92. F. W. Lee to NAACP, 27 Feb. 1947, NAACP, part 8, series B, reel 7, frs. 966–68; Bender to Marshall, 2 June 1948, ibid., frs. 981–82; Jas. S. McConnell to Marshall, 19 Mar. 1941, ibid., reel 6, fr. 113; Dickson, *Supreme Court in Conference*, 565. See also Horne, *Civil Rights Congress*, 79; Utillus R. Phillips to Roy Wilkins, 4 Mar. 1940, part 8, series B, reel 8, frs. 688–89.

93. Supplementary Brief for Appellant, *Dobbs v. Mississippi*, 22, NAACP, part 8, series B, reel 4, fr. 398; Murray to Marshall, 9 Feb. 1940, ibid., reel 1, frs. 494–96; Turner to White, 28 Feb. 1941, ibid., reel 6, frs. 97–98; Turner to White, 12 Mar. 1941, ibid., frs. 102–3; J. A. Williams to Georgia M. Johnson, 13 May 1944, ibid., reel 1, frs. 303–6; Stanley D. Belden to Marshall, 26 Apr. 1941, ibid., reel 8, fr. 947; Prentice Thomas, Report on Case of Lett and Butler, 12 Apr. 1941, ibid., reel 2, frs. 421–25; Lawson et al., "Groveland," 10; Tushnet, *Thurgood Marshall*, 65; motion for new trial, *Mississippi v. Dobbs*, Apr. 1946, part 8, series B, reel 4, frs. 299–305; Horne, *Civil Rights Congress*, 80.

94. Miller, *Willie Francis*, 23; Sherman, *Odell Waller*, 15, 21–22, 178; Lawson et al., "Groveland," 10; McGee v. State, 26 So. 2d 680 (Miss. 1946); Kimel to NAACP, 2 Dec. 1941, NAACP, part 8, series B, reel 1, frs. 749–50; J. C. Bird to Wilkins, 22 Jan. 1940, ibid., reel 2, frs. 276–78; motion for new trial, *Mississippi v. Dobbs*, Apr. 1946, ibid., reel 4, fr. 305; Wilkins to White, memo, 26 Feb. 1940, ibid., reel 2, fr. 305; Avery v. Alabama, 308 U.S. 444 (1940).

95. Pages 117–23, 153; Shepherd v. Florida, 341 U.S. 50 (1951).

96. Motion for new trial, *Mississippi v. Dobbs*, Apr. 1946, NAACP, part 8, series B, reel 4, frs. 299–305; McGee v. State, 26 So. 2d 680 (Miss. 1946); ibid., 33 So. 2d 843 (Miss. 1948); Green, *Harry T. Moore*, 100; Murray to Marshall, 13 Jan. 1940, part 8, series B, reel 1, frs. 465–66; Coleman to Perry, 17 Feb. 1947, ibid., reel 8, frs. 121–22; Lillie M. Jackson to Wilkins, 28 Mar. 1945, ibid., reel 7, frs. 283–84; G. F. Porter to Marshall, 14 Mar. 1942, ibid., reel 1, fr. 57; Irvin v. Dowd, 366 U.S. 717 (1961).

97. Coleman to Perry, 17 Feb. 1947, NAACP, part 8, series B, reel 8, frs. 121–22; Perry to Marshall, 4 Feb. 1947, ibid., fr. 111.

98. Prentice Thomas, Report on the Lett & Butler Cases, 12 Apr. 1941, NAACP, part 8, series B, reel 2, frs. 421–25; Marshall to Branches in Kentucky, Ohio, West Virginia, Memorandum regarding Lee C. Lett and Hoyt Butler, 16 Apr. 1940, ibid., frs. 266–68; Bird to Wilkins, 22 Jan. 1940, ibid., frs. 276–78; Bird to Marshall, 10 Apr. 1940, ibid., frs. 320–21. See also Jas. S. McConnell to Marshall, 19 Mar. 1941, ibid., reel 6, frs. 110–15.

99. One of the four, Ernest Thomas, was killed by the sheriff's posse. A second, Charlie Greenlee, was only sixteen years old, and the prosecutor chose not to pursue the death penalty against him. Only Shepherd and Irvin received death sentences.

100. Lawson et al., "Groveland," 2–5, 9–10; Green, *Harry T. Moore*, 81–108, 115–16, 127–28, 134–53, 191, 206–7; "Florida's Little Scottsboro: Groveland," *Crisis* 56 (Oct. 1950): 266–68, 285–86; "Florida Shooting," ibid. 58 (Nov. 1951): 598; "The Lake County Shooting," ibid. (Dec. 1951): 637–40; "Walter Irvin's Story of the Shooting," ibid. 641–44; Kerin, "Another Chance for the Groveland Victims," 317–21, 350; Shepherd v. Florida, 46 So. 2d 880 (Fla. 1950), rev'd, 341 U.S. 50 (1951), on remand, 66 So. 2d 288 (Fla. 1953), cert. denied, 346 U.S. 927 (1954).

101. S. D. Redmond to Perry, 12 Feb. 1947, NAACP, part 8, series B, reel 4, frs. 439–40; motion for new trial, *Mississippi v. Dobbs*, Apr. 1946, ibid., frs. 299–305; undated and unidentified press clippings, ibid., fr. 320; Petition for Certiorari to Mississippi Supreme Court, *Dobbs v. Mississippi*, Sept. 1946, ibid., frs. 342–49; Supplementary Suggestions of Error, ibid., frs. 360–75; Supplementary Brief for Appellant, ibid., frs. 377–403; Perry to Carter, Memorandum re: Sonnie Dobbs, Jr., 10 Mar. 1947, ibid., frs. 449–50; Dobbs v. State, 29 So. 2d 84 (Miss.), cert. denied, 331 U.S. 787 (1947).

102. Lyons v. Oklahoma, 322 U.S. 596 (1944); Martin, "Civil Rights Congress," 45–50; Richard H. J. Hanley to "Tom," 22 June 1946, NAACP, part 8, series B, reel 3, frs. 141–42; Lillie M. Jackson to Wilkins, 28 Mar. 1945, ibid., reel 7, frs. 283–84; press clippings, *Afro-American* (Baltimore), Mar. 1945, ibid., frs. 285–86; *Somerset News*, 29 Mar. 1945, ibid., fr. 295.

103. Rise, *Martinsville Seven*, chaps. 1–2, esp. pp. 53–54. See also Dorr, "Black-on-White Rape and Retribution in Twentieth-Century Virginia," 714, 722, 724–27, 745–46.

104. Similarly, between 1925 and 1950, Florida executed thirty-three blacks and only one white for rape. In its entire history, Mississippi had executed no whites for rape.

105. Rise, *Martinsville Seven*, 3, 85, 93, 102, 126, 156–57. See also Dorr, "Black-on-White Rape and Retribution in Twentieth-Century Virginia," 717; Martin, "Civil Rights Congress," 47.

106. Sherman, *Odell Waller*, 1–14, 25–31, 99–115, 123–28, 155–65; Waller v. Virginia, 16 S.E. 2d 808 (1941), cert. denied, 316 U.S. 679 (1942). See also Turner to Justice Department, 24 Nov. 1941, NAACP, part 8, series B, reel 6, frs. 125–27.

107. Ingram v. State, 48 S.E. 2d 891 (Ga. 1948); Martin, "Rosa Lee Ingram Case," 251–68; *Crisis* 55 (Apr. 1948): 123; ibid. (Nov. 1948): 338–40.

108. Akins v. Texas, 325 U.S. 398 (1945); G. F. Porter to Marshall, 20 Oct. 1941, NAACP, part 8, series B, reel 1, frs. 47–48; *Dallas Daily Times Herald*, 16 Sept. 1941, ibid., frs. 35–36; Edwards, "White Justice in Dallas," 254–55; motion for new trial, *Mississippi v. Dobbs*, Apr. 1946, part 8, series B, reel 4, fr. 300. See also ibid., frs. 1–141; *Crisis* 59 (Dec. 1952): 655–56.

109. Hanley to "Tom," 22 June 1946, NAACP, part 8, series B, reel 3, frs. 141–42; Dabney, *Below the Potomac*, 189–90; Hollins v. Oklahoma, 295 U.S. 394 (1935); McGee v. State, 26 So. 2d 680 (Miss. 1946); ibid., 33 So. 2d 843 (Miss. 1948); ibid., 40 So. 2d 160 (Miss. 1949); Martin, "Jess Hollins Rape Case," 175, 186; Martin, "Civil Rights Congress," 47; Horne, *Civil Rights Congress*, 78–79; Dollard, *Caste and Class*, 323–24. See also Dorr, "Black-on-White Rape and Retribution in Twentieth-Century Virginia," 737–39.

110. *Chambers*, 309 U.S. at 241; Gertrude B. Stone to White, memo, 12 Feb. 1940, NAACP, part 8, series B, reel 2, fr. 854; *Washington Daily News*, 12 Feb. 1940, ibid., fr. 810; "Four Negroes," *Nation*, 24 Feb. 1940, pp. 269–70; *NYT*, 13 Feb. 1940, part 8, series B, reel 2, fr. 813; "Rebuke to Torture," *Crisis* 47 (Mar. 1940): 81.

111. Nor did the ruling do Chambers himself much good, as he apparently lapsed into mental illness after his seven-year ordeal in the Florida criminal justice system and had to be committed to an insane asylum.

112. "Due Process," *NYT*, 12 Mar. 1940, p. 22; *Tampa Tribune*, 1 Sept. 1940, NAACP, part 8, series B, reel 2, fr. 894; S. D. McGill to Leon A. Ransom, 10 May 1940, ibid., fr. 892.

113. People v. Roxborough, 12 N.W. 2d 466 (Mich. 1943), cert. denied, 323 U.S. 749 (1944); Hampton v. Commonwealth, 58 S.E. 2d 288 (Va.), cert. denied, 339 U.S. 989 (1950); Furman v. Georgia, 408 U.S. 238 (1972); Coker v. Georgia, 433 U.S. 584 (1977); Batson v. Kentucky, 476 U.S. 79 (1986); Balkin, "Agreements with Hell," 1729, 1732; Seidman, "*Brown* and *Miranda*," 717; Spann, *Race against the Court*, 110, 150–51; Rise, *Martinsville Seven*, 158–60. Cf. Cole, *No Equal Justice*, 80–81, 108–9.

114. Certiorari memorandum, *Lyons v. Oklahoma*, Box 67, Murphy Papers, reel 129, frs. 14–15; page 171. See also E. B. to Justice Douglas, certiorari memorandum, *Lyons v. Oklahoma*, Box 94, Douglas Papers.

115. Green, *Harry T. Moore*, 110–11; pages 93–95, 163–67.

116. Belden to Marshall, 7 Jan. 1941, NAACP, part 8, series B, reel 8, fr. 852; Dunjee to Marshall, 13 Jan. 1941, ibid., fr. 855; Marshall to White, 2 Feb. 1941, ibid., frs. 886–88; Dunjee to Marshall, 26 Dec. 1940, ibid., frs. 849–50.

117. Marshall to office, Memorandum re: W. D. Lyons Trial, 29 Jan. 1941, NAACP, part 8, series B, reel 8, frs. 877–78; Marshall to White, 2 Feb. 1941, ibid., frs. 886–88; Marshall to White, 29 Jan. 1941, ibid., fr. 881; Dunjee to Marshall, 18 Jan. 1941, ibid., fr. 855.

118. Marshall to White, 2 Feb. 1941, NAACP, part 8, series B, reel 8, frs. 886–88. See also Fairclough, *Civil Rights Struggle in Louisiana*, 129.

119. Sherman, *Odell Waller*, 174; *Crisis* 55 (May 1948): 146–47; Martin, "Rosa Lee Ingram Case," 254–63; "The Shape of Things," *Nation*, 6 Oct. 1945, p. 327; Martin, "Civil Rights Congress," 49–50; Green, *Harry T. Moore*, 107, 116; Marshall to Otis Milner, 25 Mar. 1947, NAACP, part 8, series B, reel 5, fr. 591; Milner to NAACP, 11 Mar. 1947, ibid., fr. 592; Marshall to Bertrand deBlanc, 15 Apr. 1947, ibid., fr. 608; deBlanc to NAACP, 31 Mar. 1947, ibid., fr. 609; NAACP Press Release, 9 May 1946, ibid., fr. 431; Horne, *Civil Rights Congress*, 74–76, 84–98.

120. Lillie M. Jackson to Wilkins, 28 Mar. 1945, NAACP, part 8, series B, reel 7, frs. 283–84; Carter to Marshall, memo, 28 Feb. 1950, ibid., reel 6, fr. 996; S. D. McGill to Murphy, 15 Feb. 1940, ibid., reel 2, fr. 830. See also N. W. Griffin to Marshall, 2 Feb. 1950, ibid., reel 6, frs. 1001–2.

121. Tureaud to Marshall, 11 May 1946, NAACP, part 8, series B, reel 5, fr. 407; Tureaud to White, 6 May 1946, ibid., frs. 357–58; Sherman, *Odell Waller*, 141, 155. See also Horne, *Civil Rights Congress*, 77.

122. *Pollock*, 322 U.S. at 15–16; Brodie, "Right to Be Free from Bondage," 381–83.

123. White to Mother Philip Neri, 2 Aug. 1935, NAACP, part 10, reel 16, fr. 448; "Can the States Stop Lynching?" *Crisis* 43 (Jan. 1936): 7; "Frank Weems Case," ibid. (Oct. 1936): 295; Norman Thomas, "Socialism's Appeal to Negroes," ibid. 43 (Oct. 1936): 294; ibid. 47 (Feb. 1940): 44–45; Daniel, *Shadow of Slavery*, 174, 178–80; Marshall to Corine Sanders, 14 Dec. 1937, NAACP, part 10, reel 16, fr. 557. See also Alfred Edgar Smith to White, 12 Nov. 1937, ibid., fr. 548; "Report of Forced Labor in Warren County, Georgia" (1937), ibid., frs. 563–69; Statement by James Felton (1931), ibid., reel 17, frs. 336–41.

124. Walter Crayton to George Harvey, 27 Mar. 1940, NAACP, part 8, series B, reel 3, frs. 586–92. See also Thurgood Marshall to C. Herbert Marshall, Jr., 5 Jan. 1940, ibid., fr. 602.

125. Carr, *Federal Protection of Civil Rights*, 180–82; Daniel, *Shadow of Slavery*, 185–86. On remaining peonage, see *Crisis* 50 (July 1943): 212; Daniel, *Shadow of Slavery*, 186–88. See also W. A. Lynk to NAACP, 15 May 1937, part 10, reel 16, fr. 453; Charles Hamilton Houston, "Peonage and Forced Labor" (draft newspaper article), 30 Sept. 1937, ibid., frs. 466–67; Houston to Homer Cummings, 23 Sept. 1937, ibid., fr. 495; "Report of Forced Labor in Warren County, Georgia" (1937), ibid., frs. 563–69; *NYT*, 16 Sept. 1937, ibid., fr. 570.

126. Granger, "Achieving Racial Integration in Education," 347; Symposium, "Courts and Racial Integration," 383–84, 393, 407; Jenkins, "Problems Incident to Racial Integration," 414, 419–20; *NYT*, 26 June 1951, p. 27; Weber, "Citizenship in the

South," 3 (fr. 551); "Integration," *Crisis* 41 (Apr. 1934): 117. See also Bartley, *New South,* 35–36; *Shreveport Sun,* 30 Apr. 1949, NAACP, part 4, reel 7, fr. 563.

127. Schwartz, "Negro and the Law," 448–49.

128. Jenkins, "Problems Incident to Racial Integration," 420; Nabrit, "Appraisal of Court Action," 422; Symposium, "Courts and Racial Integration," 435; Benjamin Muse, "Abrupt Halt of Segregation Feared," *Wash. Post,* 3 June 1951, sec. 2, p. 6b; "Color Line Cracking in the South," *NYT,* 23 Oct. 1950, p. 29.

CHAPTER 6

1. Turner, "Black Schooling and Protest in Prince Edward County," esp. 1, 33–38; Kluger, *Simple Justice,* 466–71, 475–78; Smith, *They Closed Their Schools,* 31–69. See also Lau, "Clarendon County," 12–18.

2. Pages 100–104, 173–93.

3. Unidentified and undated press clipping (probably 1958), NAACP, part 20, reel 11, fr. 27; Tushnet, *Thurgood Marshall,* 150–51, 165; Kluger, *Simple Justice,* 290–94, 475–76, 523–24, 531, 535–36; Muse, *Ten Years of Prelude,* 9; Elman, "Solicitor General's Office," 837; Southern, "Judge Waring's Fight against Segregation," 219–20; Minutes of the NAACP Board of Directors Meeting, 9 Oct. 1950, p. 2, part 1, reel 3, fr. 1117. See also Frank, "Can Courts Erase the Color Line?" 314–15; Symposium, "Courts and Racial Integration," 328–29 (Will Maslow), 329–30 (Marjorie McKenzie).

4. Brown v. Board of Education, 347 U.S. 483, 495 (1954); Bolling v. Sharpe, 347 U.S. 497 (1954).

5. Patterson, Brown, 116; Tushnet, *Thurgood Marshall,* 194; Kurland, *Warren Court,* 89.

6. I have consulted and am quoting from the conference notes of Burton, Clark, Douglas, and Jackson. The conference notes are broadly similar, but they are not transcriptions. I am quoting from the notes, but one should not assume that they perfectly captured what was said at the conferences. On the whole, however, they appear to be quite accurate. Burton conference notes, Segregation Cases, 13 Dec. 1952, Box 244, Burton Papers, Library of Congress; Clark conference notes, *Brown v. Board of Education,* Box A27, Clark Papers, Tarlton Law Library, University of Texas; Douglas conference notes, *Brown v. Board of Education* and *Bolling v. Sharpe,* 13 Dec. 1952, case file: Segregation Cases, Box 1150, Douglas Papers, Library of Congress; Jackson conference notes, 12 Dec. 1952, Box 184, Jackson Papers, Library of Congress. See also Dickson, *Supreme Court in Conference,* 646–54; Kluger, *Simple Justice,* chap. 23; Tushnet, "What Really Happened in *Brown*"; Hutchinson, "Unanimity and Desegregation," 34–44.

7. In addition to the conference notes, see Jackson draft concurrence, 6 Jan. 1954, Box 184, Jackson Papers. See also Chernack, "Robert H. Jackson," 85 n. 162.

8. Newman, *Hugo Black,* 91–100, 249–61, 267; Powe, *Warren Court,* 5; pages 17, 116, 227–28. On Harlan, see Frankfurter to Harlan, 31 July 1956, Box 485, Harlan Papers, Princeton University Library.

9. Kluger, *Simple Justice,* 602; White, "Anti-Judge," 46–48, 65–86; pages 190, 194.

10. Berry, *Mr. Justice Burton,* 59–69, 94–120, 145–46; Gugin & St. Clair, *Sherman Minton,* 215, 220–44, 265, 293–94, 310–11; Kluger, *Simple Justice,* 612; Frank, "United States Supreme Court: 1951–1952," 50; Wallace, "Mr. Justice Minton," 147–57, 179–88; Atkinson, "Justice Sherman Minton," 101.

11. Brief for the United States as Amici Curiae, *Brown v. Board of Education,* 6, in *Landmark Briefs,* ed. Kurland & Casper, 49:121; Tushnet, *Thurgood Marshall,*

172–73; *Chicago Defender*, 22 May 1954, p. 5; Fassett, *Stanley Reed*, 571; Brief on Behalf of ACLU et al., *Brown v. Board of Education*, 28–31, in *Landmark Briefs*, ed. Kurland & Casper, 49:183–86; Neier, *Limits of Litigation in Social Change*, 31–32, 38; Powe, *Warren Court*, 35–37; Dudziak, *Cold War Civil Rights*, 104–10.

12. Fassett, *Stanley Reed*, 555–56, 559–61; Kluger, *Simple Justice*, 588–89, 595.

13. Douglas, memorandum for the file, Segregation Cases, 17 May 1954, Box 1149, Douglas Papers.

14. Frankfurter to Reed, 20 May 1954, Reed Papers; Douglas conference notes, *Brown II*, 16 Apr. 1955, Box 1150, Douglas Papers; Fassett, *Stanley Reed*, 567; Kluger, *Simple Justice*, 614; Elman, "Solicitor General's Office," 829.

15. Frankfurter to Reed, 20 May 1954, Reed Papers; docket sheet, *Brown v. Board of Education*, Box 1150, Douglas Papers; Frankfurter, Memorandum for the Conference re: Segregation Cases, 27 May 1953, Box A27, Clark Papers; Kluger, *Simple Justice*, 614–16; Tushnet, *Thurgood Marshall*, 194–95.

16. Tushnet, *Thurgood Marshall*, 194, 215.

17. Kluger, *Simple Justice*, 656; Elman, "Solicitor General's Office," 840; Ambrose, *Eisenhower*, 2:128; Young, "Eisenhower's Federal Judges," 557 n. 77.

18. Douglas conference notes, *Briggs v. Elliott*, 12 Dec. 1953, case file: Segregation Cases, Box 1149, Douglas Papers; Douglas, memorandum for the file, Segregation Cases, 17 May 1954, ibid.; Kluger, *Simple Justice*, 679, 683, 698–99; Ball & Cooper, *Of Power and Right*, 177–79; Schwartz, *Warren*, 82, 106; Patterson, *Brown*, 60, 64–65; White, *Earl Warren*, 163–69; Powe, *Warren Court*, 28.

19. Frankfurter, memorandum on *Smith v. Allwright*, n.d., 3, Frankfurter Papers, part 1, reel 10, fr. 167; Frankfurter to Reed, 20 May 1954, Reed Papers; Douglas memorandum, Segregation Cases, 17 May 1954, Box 1149, Douglas Papers; Kluger, *Simple Justice*, 685, 698; Fassett, *Stanley Reed*, 569–73; Schwartz, *Earl Warren*, 89–90, 94, 102; White, *Earl Warren*, 167–68.

20. Terry v. Adams, 345 U.S. 461 (1953); pages 201–4.

21. Clark conference notes, *Brown v. Board of Education*, Box A27, Clark Papers; Dickson, *Supreme Court in Conference*, 639; Douglas conference notes, *McLaurin v. Oklahoma*, 8 Apr. 1950, Box 192, Douglas Papers; Tushnet, *Thurgood Marshall*, 188–191; Powe, *Warren Court*, 23; Burt, "*Brown's* Reflection," 1486–87.

22. Urofsky, *Supreme Court under Stone and Vinson*, 34, 109 n. 112, 130, 217, 223; Adamson v. California, 332 U.S. 46, 68 (1947) (Frankfurter, J., concurring); Minersville School District v. Gobitis, 310 U.S. 586, 596 (1940); Haley v. Ohio, 332 U.S. 596, 602–3 (1947); Frankfurter to Hand, 13 Feb. 1958, Frankfurter Papers, part 3, reel 27, frs. 565–68; Frankfurter, "Red Terror of Judicial Reform."

23. Frankfurter, memorandum (first draft), n.d., 1, Frankfurter Papers, part 2, reel 4, fr. 378; Kluger, *Simple Justice*, 598; Urofsky, *Felix Frankfurter*, 128–29; Urofsky, *Supreme Court under Stone and Vinson*, 260.

24. Alexander M. Bickel to Frankfurter, 22 Aug. 1953, Frankfurter Papers, part 2, reel 4, frs. 212–14; Berry, *Mr. Justice Burton*, 142; Douglas conference notes, *Briggs v. Elliott*, 12 Dec. 1953, case file: Segregation Cases, Box 1149, Douglas Papers; Note, "Constitutionality of Educational Segregation," 214 n. 20; Urofsky, *Supreme Court under Stone and Vinson*, 217–18, 222; Kluger, *Simple Justice*, 598–99.

25. Jackson to Charles Fairman, 13 Mar. 1950, Fairman file, Box 12, Jackson Papers; Chernack, "Robert H. Jackson," 52; United States v. South-Eastern Underwriters' Ass'n, 322 U.S. 533, 589–95 (1944) (Jackson, J., dissenting); Helvering v. Griffiths, 318 U.S. 371, 403 (1943); Simpson, "Robert H. Jackson," 326–29, 338–41.

26. Jackson draft concurrence, School Segregation Cases, 15 Mar. 1954, pp. 1–2, case file: Segregation Cases, Box 184, Jackson Papers. Whether Jackson ever intended to publish this opinion is unclear; a heart attack in March 1954 probably disabled him from doing so, even had he been so inclined.

27. Ibid., 5–7.

28. Ibid., 7–10.

29. EBP [E. Barrett Prettyman] to Jackson, n.d., 1, 3, Box 184, Jackson Papers; Burton conference notes, School Segregation Cases, 12 Dec. 1953, Box 244, Burton Papers; Kluger, *Simple Justice*, 603–4; Tushnet, *Thurgood Marshall*, 211–14.

30. Jackson, *Supreme Court*, 80; Jackson draft concurrence, School Segregation Cases, 7 Dec. 1953, pp. 8–10, case file: Segregation Cases, Box 184, Jackson Papers; Chernack, "Robert H. Jackson," 53–54, 59–63, 73–75, 88–89.

31. Clark in Douglas conference notes, *Briggs v. Elliott*, 12 Dec. 1953, case file: Segregation Cases, Box 1149, Douglas Papers; other statements cited above.

32. Jackson to Fairman, 13 Mar. 1950, Fairman file, Box 12, Jackson Papers; Newman, *Hugo Black*, 277; WHR [William H. Rehnquist], "A Random Thought on the Segregation Cases," Box 184, Jackson Papers; Jackson, *Struggle for Judicial Supremacy*, 321–23; Parrish, *Felix Frankfurter*, 20–21, 58–59, 165–68; Balkin, *What Brown v. Board of Education Should Have Said*, 15.

33. Burton conference notes, School Segregation Cases, 12 Dec. 1953, Box 244, Burton Papers; Clark conference notes, *Brown v. Board of Education*, Box A27, Clark Papers; Jackson to Fairman, 13 Mar. 1950, Fairman file, Box 12, Jackson Papers; Jackson draft concurrence, School Segregation Cases, 7 Dec. 1953, pp. 7–8, case file: Segregation Cases, Box 184, Jackson Papers; Douglas conference notes, *Briggs v. Elliott*, 12 Dec. 1953, case file: Segregation Cases, Box 1149, Douglas Papers. The justices seem to have ignored the fact that in the early 1950s southern legislatures were hardly representative, given the extent of black disfranchisement and legislative malapportionment. See Klarman, "Political Process Theory," 788–819.

34. Klarman, "What's So Great about Constitutionalism?" 189–91; Tushnet, *Thurgood Marshall*, 187–88; Gallup, *Gallup Poll*, 2:1250; Tumin, "Readiness and Resistance to Desegregation," 260–62; Tumin, Barton, & Burrus, "Readiness for Desegregation," 46; Greeley & Sheatsley, "Attitudes toward Racial Integration," 15–16; Killian & Haer, "Attitudes regarding School Desegregation," 161; Peltason, *Fifty-Eight Lonely Men*, 34–35.

35. Jackson draft concurrence, School Segregation Cases, 15 Mar. 1954, pp. 1, 19–21, case file: Segregation Cases, Box 184, Jackson Papers.

36. Frankfurter memorandum, n.d., p. 2, Frankfurter Papers, part 2, reel 4, fr. 379; Kluger, *Simple Justice*, 684; Douglas conference notes, *Briggs v. Elliott*, 12 Dec. 1953, case file: Segregation Cases, Box 1149, Douglas Papers; Burton conference notes, School Segregation Cases, 12 Dec. 1953, Box 244, Burton Papers; Douglas conference notes, *Brown v. Board of Education*, 13 Dec. 1952, case file: Segregation Cases, Box 1150, Douglas Papers.

37. Gallup, *Gallup Poll*, 2:1249–50; Kluger, *Simple Justice*, 614; Fassett, "Reed and *Brown v. Board of Education*," 53; LCG to Reed, certiorari memorandum, *Brown v. Board of Education*, Reed Papers; RLR to Reed, certiorari memorandum, *Davis v. School Board of Prince Edward County*, ibid.; SSN, Apr. 1956, p. 3; June 1956, p. 13; Oct. 1956, p. 10.

38. Burton conference notes, School Segregation Cases, 12 Dec. 1953, Box 244, Burton Papers.

39. Douglas memorandum, 25 Jan. 1960, in *Douglas Letters*, ed. Urofsky, 169. See also Tushnet, *Thurgood Marshall*, 126–27; Greenberg, *Crusaders in the Courts*, 110.

40. Douglas conference notes, *Brown v. Board of Education*, 13 Dec. 1952, case file: Segregation Cases, Box 1150, Douglas Papers; Jackson draft concurrence, School Segregation Cases, 15 Mar. 1954, p. 1, case file: Segregation Cases, Box 184, Jackson Papers; Gallup, *Gallup Poll*, 2:1249–50; Patterson, *Brown*, 72; Rosenberg, *Hollow Hope*, 169. See also Schmidt, "J. Waties Waring," 28.

41. Jackson draft concurrence, School Segregation Cases, 15 Mar. 1954, p. 1, case file: Segregation Cases, Box 184, Jackson Papers; Peltason, *Fifty-Eight Lonely Men*, 249.

42. Bell, "*Brown v. Board of Education*," 172; Jackson conference notes, Segregation Cases, 12 Dec. 1952, Box 184, Jackson Papers; Mendez v. Westminster School District, 64 F. Supp. 544 (S.D. Calif. 1946), aff'd on other grounds, 161 F. 2d 774 (9th Cir. 1947).

43. Frankfurter, memorandum to justices, 15 Jan. 1954, p. 1, Reed Papers; Jackson draft concurrence, 15 Mar. 1954, p. 13, case file: School Segregation Cases, Box 184, Jackson Papers; Clark conference notes, *Brown v. Board of Education*, Box A27, Clark Papers.

44. Clark conference notes, *Brown v. Board of Education*, Box A27, Clark Papers; Jackson conference notes, School Segregation Cases, 12 Dec. 1952, Box 184, Jackson Papers; Kluger, *Simple Justice*, 336, 345, 481, 499–500, 531–33, 591, 600–601; Ashmore, "Racial Integration," 252–55; Bolton, "Mississippi's School Equalization Program," 807–8.

45. Tushnet, *Thurgood Marshall*, 216.

46. SSN, Dec. 1954, p. 1; Hutchinson, "Unanimity and Desegregation," 52. President Eisenhower nominated Harlan to the Court late in 1954, but his confirmation was delayed for several months, partly by white southerners who were concerned about how he would vote on school segregation. Once confirmed, Harlan proved to be an extremely able justice and the leader of the conservative group that dissented from many Warren Court landmarks.

47. Brown v. Board of Education (*Brown II*), 349 U.S. 294, 298–301 (1955).

48. SSN, Jan. 1955, p. 5; Brief of American Veterans' Committee, Amicus Curiae, *Brown v. Board of Education* (*Brown II*), 34; "Law Clerks' Recommendations for Segregation Decree" (hereafter, "Clerks' Recommendations"), 10 Apr. 1955, p. 6, Box 337, Burton Papers; Douglas conference notes, *Brown II*, 16 Apr. 1955, case file: Segregation Cases, Box 1149, Douglas Papers. My account of the internal deliberations in *Brown II* relies on the conference notes of Burton, Douglas, Frankfurter, and Warren. See also Dickson, *Supreme Court in Conference*, 663–69.

49. Warren conference notes, *Brown II*, case file: Segregation Cases, Box 574, Warren Papers (Burton); Burton conference notes, Segregation Cases, 16 Apr. 1955, Box 244, Burton Papers (Black); Burton conference notes, School Segregation Cases, 13 Dec. 1952, Box 244, Burton Papers (Jackson); Douglas conference notes, *Brown v. Board of Education*, 13 Dec. 1952, case file: Segregation Cases, Box 1150, Douglas Papers (Clark and Burton); Douglas conference notes, *Briggs v. Elliott*, 12 Dec. 1953, case file: Segregation Cases, Box 1149, Douglas Papers (Douglas); Elman, "Solicitor General's Office," 827–29; Hutchinson, "Unanimity and Desegregation," 40–41, 87; Brief for the United States as Amicus Curiae, *Brown v. Board of Education*, 27–31, in *Landmark Briefs*, ed. Kurland & Casper, 49:142–46; WBM to Burton, memorandum, *Brown II*, 38–39, Box 248, Burton Papers.

50. Warren conference notes, *Brown II*, case file: Segregation Cases, Box 574, Warren Papers (Black); Burton conference notes, Segregation Cases, 16 Apr. 1955, Box 244, Burton Papers (Minton); Leflar & Davis, "Segregation in the Public Schools," 429.

51. Clark conference notes, *Brown v. Board of Education*, Box A27, Clark Papers; E.P. [E. Barrett Prettyman] to Warren, bench memorandum, Segregation Cases, 17, case file: Segregation Cases, Box 574, Warren Papers; *Brown II*, 349 U.S. at 300; "Clerks' Recommendations," 5; Hutchinson, "Unanimity and Desegregation," 36–37.

52. SSN, Dec. 1954, p. 15; Sept. 1954, pp. 5, 12; Oct. 1954, pp. 2, 4, 7, 16; Nov. 1954, pp. 6–7, 14; Dec. 1954, pp. 5, 6, 11; Jan. 1955, p. 6; "Segregation Research Report" (by law clerks), 17 Nov. 1954, pp. 20–24, 65–68, Box 1151, Douglas Papers; Talmadge, *You and Segregation*, 59–60; Kee, "*Brown* Decision and Milford, Delaware," 206, 211–34.

53. Burton conference notes, Segregation Cases, 16 Apr. 1955, Box 244, Burton Papers (Black); Douglas conference notes, *Brown II*, 16 Apr. 1955, case file: Segregation Cases, Box 1149, Douglas Papers (Harlan and Reed); Frankfurter to Warren, 8 July 1954, Box 184, Jackson Papers; Tushnet, *Thurgood Marshall*, 177; Kluger, *Simple Justice*, 504; SSN, Dec. 1954, p. 6.

54. Douglas conference notes, *Brown v. Board of Education*, 13 Dec. 1952, case file: Segregation Cases, Box 1150, Douglas Papers; Jackson draft concurrence, School Segregation Cases, 15 Mar. 1954, pp. 2, 5, 22, case file: Segregation Cases, Box 184, Jackson Papers.

55. Frankfurter to Brethren, 14 Apr. 1955, Box 337, Burton Papers; Douglas conference notes, *Brown II*, 16 Apr. 1955, case file: Segregation Cases, Box 1149, Douglas Papers; Burton conference notes, Segregation Cases, 16 Apr. 1955, Box 244, Burton Papers; Douglas conference notes, *Briggs v. Elliott*, 12 Dec. 1953, case file: Segregation Cases, Box 1149, Douglas Papers; Warren to the Court, 7 May 1954, Box 184, Jackson Papers; Jackson draft concurrence, School Segregation Cases, 15 Mar. 1954, p. 4, case file: Segregation Cases, Box 184, Jackson Papers; Brief for the United States on the Further Argument of the Questions for Relief, *Brown v. Board of Education*, 8 (hereafter, "U.S. brief, *Brown II*"); Young, "Eisenhower's Federal Judges," 558; Peltason, *Fifty-Eight Lonely Men*, 18; Burk, *Eisenhower Administration and Black Civil Rights*, 148–49.

56. "Clerks' Recommendations," 5, 9; EBP [Prettyman] to Jackson, Note re: Segregation Cases, 4, Box 184, Jackson Papers; Prettyman to Warren, bench memorandum, Segregation Cases, 17, case file: Segregation Cases, Box 574, Warren Papers.

57. Douglas conference notes, *Brown II*, 16 Apr. 1955, case file: Segregation Cases, Box 1149, Douglas Papers; Frankfurter conference notes, *Brown II*, 16 Apr. 1955, File 4044, Box 219, Frankfurter Papers, Library of Congress; Warren conference notes, *Brown II*, case file: Segregation Cases, Box 574, Warren Papers; Tushnet, *Thurgood Marshall*, 229–31; Hutchinson, "Unanimity and Desegregation," 57–58.

58. Jackson draft concurrence, School Segregation Cases, 15 Mar. 1954, pp. 2, 4, 22–23, case file: Segregation Cases, Box 184, Jackson Papers; Douglas conference notes, *Brown I*, 13 Dec. 1952, case file: Segregation Cases, Box 1150, Douglas Papers. See also RST to Burton, supplemental memo, 6 Dec. 1953, p. 5, Box 244, Burton Papers.

59. Douglas conference notes, *Brown II*, 16 Apr. 1955, case file: Segregation Cases, Box 1149, Douglas Papers; Frankfurter conference notes, *Brown II*, 16 Apr. 1955, File 4044, Box 219, Frankfurter Papers; Warren conference notes, *Brown II*, case file: Segregation Cases, Box 574, Warren Papers; Frankfurter, Memorandum on the

Segregation Decree, 14 Apr. 1955, p. 2, file: Segregation Cases, Box 574, Warren Papers; U.S. brief, *Brown II*, 24–25, 27–28. See also WBM to Burton, memorandum, *Brown II*, 35, Box 248, Burton Papers; Frankfurter, "Segregation Considerations," n.d., Frankfurter Papers, Library of Congress; Frankfurter to Brethren, 15 Jan. 1954, pp. 1–2, Box 263, Burton Papers.

60. Frankfurter, Memorandum on the Segregation Decree, 14 Apr. 1955, file: Segregation Cases, Box 574, Warren Papers; JDF to Reed, n.d. (probably summer 1954), Reed Papers; WBM to Burton, memorandum, *Brown II*, 28, 31, 35–36, Box 248, Burton Papers; SSN, Dec. 1954, p. 1; U.S. brief, *Brown II*, 8–27; NYT, 24 Nov. 1954, p. 12; Frankfurter, "Segregation Considerations," n.d., Frankfurter Papers, Library of Congress; "Clerks' Recommendations," 1–4; EP to Warren, bench memorandum, Segregation Cases, 18, case file: Segregation Cases, Box 574, Warren Papers; Warren conference notes, *Brown II*, case file: Segregation Cases, Box 574, Warren Papers (Burton); Burton notes for conference, 16 Apr. 1955, Box 337, Burton Papers.

61. Douglas conference notes, *Brown I*, 13 Dec. 1952, case file: Segregation Cases, Box 1150, Douglas Papers; Frankfurter conference notes, *Brown II*, 16 Apr. 1955, File 4044, Box 219, Frankfurter Papers; Frankfurter, Memorandum on the Segregation Decree, 14 Apr. 1955, p. 1, file: Segregation Cases, Box 574, Warren Papers; Frankfurter, "Segregation Considerations," n.d., 2, Frankfurter Papers, Library of Congress; "Clerks' Recommendations," 2.

62. Warren conference notes, *Brown II*, case file: Segregation Cases, Box 574, Warren Papers; Frankfurter conference notes, *Brown II*, 16 Apr. 1955, File 4044, Box 219, Frankfurter Papers; Burton conference notes, Segregation Cases, 16 Apr. 1955, Box 244, Burton Papers; Frankfurter Memorandum on the Segregation Decree, 14 Apr. 1955, pp. 2–3, file: Segregation Cases, Box 574, Warren Papers. See also "Clerks' Recommendations," 2–3.

63. WBM to Burton, memorandum, *Brown II*, 35–38, Box 248, Burton Papers; Warren conference notes, *Brown II*, case file: Segregation Cases, Box 574, Warren Papers; Douglas conference notes, *Brown II*, 16 Apr. 1955, case file: Segregation Cases, Box 1149, Douglas Papers; Jackson draft concurrence, School Segregation Cases, 15 Mar. 1954, p. 17, case file: Segregation Cases, Box 184, Jackson Papers; JRR to Burton, Box 263, Burton Papers; "Clerks' Recommendations"; Leflar & Davis, "Segregation in the Public Schools," 404–17; Tushnet, *Thurgood Marshall*, 217.

64. SSN, June 1955, pp. 1–10; *Richmond Times-Dispatch*, 1 June 1955, p. 10; Woodward, "New Reconstruction," 504.

65. SSN, June 1955, pp. 1, 3, 4; Report of Secretary to NAACP Board of Directors, May 1955, p. 2, NAACP, part 1, reel 2, fr. 766; James L. Hicks, "Voters Vineyard," *Afro-American* (Baltimore), 11 June 1955, p. 4; John H. McCray, "Need for Changing," ibid. See also Thurgood Marshall & Roy Wilkins, "Interpretation of Supreme Court Decision & the NAACP Program," *Crisis* 62 (June–July 1955): 329–33; "A Clear-Cut Victory," *Afro-American* (Baltimore), 11 June 1955, p. 4.

66. SSN, June 1955, pp. 1–9.

67. SSN, June 1955, pp. 1, 3, 5, 7, 9; July 1955, p. 14; Aug. 1955, p. 15.

68. SSN, Feb. 1956, pp. 1, 4; Apr. 1956, pp. 1, 2; Aug. 1955, pp. 1, 4, 5; Sept. 1955, pp. 1, 5, 6–7, 9; Oct. 1955, pp. 1, 3, 4; Jan. 1956, p. 1. For scholarly criticism of *Brown II*, see Hochschild, *New American Dilemma*, 47–49, 148; Wilkinson, Brown *to* Bakke, 63–68, 80–81; Morris, *Civil Rights Movement*, 28–29; Peltason, *Fifty-Eight Lonely Men*, 245; Horwitz, *Warren Court*, 29–30; Powe, *Warren Court*, 56–57; Balkin, *What*

Brown v. Board of Education *Should Have Said*, 40–41; Kirk, "Little Rock School Crisis," 73–74.

69. WBM to Burton, memorandum, *Brown II*, 34, Box 248, Burton Papers; Leflar, "What the Court Really Said," *SSN*, June 1955, p. 1; *NYT*, 19 May 1954, p. 20; Roche, "*Plessy v. Ferguson*," 54–56; Kirk, "Little Rock School Crisis," 73–74; Jackson, "White Liberal Intellectuals, Civil Rights, and Gradualism," 99; Woodward, "New Reconstruction," 503–4. See also "Equal Education for All," *Wash. Post*, 19 May 1954, p. 14; Bass, *Unlikely Heroes*, 15.

70. Greenberg, *Crusaders in the Courts*, 389–90; Muse, *Ten Years of Prelude*, 25–26.

71. Hutchinson, "Unanimity and Desegregation," 60–61 n. 505; Klarman, "Modern Equal Protection," 247–48; Wilkinson, Brown *to* Bakke, 78–79; Hart & Sacks, "The Legal Process," 164–70; Wechsler, "Neutral Principles," 11–12, 15–17.

72. Naim v. Naim, 87 S.E. 2d 749 (1955).

73. *SSN*, Jan. 1955, p. 2; Nov. 1955, p. 9; oral argument in *Bolling v. Sharpe*, 10–11, in *Landmark Briefs*, ed. Kurland & Casper, 49:405–6; Prettyman to Jackson, n.d., 8, Box 184, Jackson Papers; Judge Walter Jones, "I Speak for the White Race," *Montgomery Advertiser*, 4 Mar. 1957, NAACP, part 20, reel 4, fr. 436; Brady, *Black Monday*, 64–67; Talmadge, *You and Segregation*, 42–44; Greenberg, *Crusaders in the Courts*, 172; Elman, "Solicitor General's Office," 845–47; Gunther, *Learned Hand*, 664–70; Gallup, *Gallup Poll*, 2:1572.

74. WAN [William Norris] to Douglas, certiorari memorandum, *Naim v. Naim*, 24 Oct. 1955, office memos, nos. 350–99, Box 1164, Douglas Papers; WAN to Douglas, supplemental memorandum, *Naim v. Naim*, n.d., ibid.; Hutchinson, "Unanimity and Desegregation," 63; docket sheet, file: Administrative Docket Book 201–400, Box 1162, Douglas Papers; Clark to Jackson, handwritten note, n.d., Box A47, Clark Papers; 28 U.S.C. § 1257 (1952); Dorr, "*Naim v. Naim*," 149–50.

75. Frankfurter memorandum, *Naim v. Naim*, Frankfurter Papers, part 2, reel 17, frs. 588–90; Frankfurter to Clark, handwritten note, n.d., Box A47, Clark Papers; Jackson v. Alabama, 72 So. 2d 116 (Ala.), cert. denied, 348 U.S. 888 (1954); Naim v. Naim, 350 U.S. 891 (1955), on remand, 90 S.E. 2d 849 (Va. 1956); Hutchinson, "Unanimity and Desegregation," 64–66; Dorr, "*Naim v. Naim*," 149–50, 153–54, 156.

76. WAN to Douglas, certiorari memorandum, *Naim v. Naim*, 1 Mar. 1956, case file: office memos, numbers 350–99, Box 1164, Douglas Papers.

77. Naim v. Naim, 350 U.S. 985 (1956); docket sheet, file: Administrative Docket Book 201–400, Box 1162, Douglas Papers; Dorr, "*Naim v. Naim*," 158; Paul Bator et al., Hart & Wechsler's *The Federal Courts and the Federal System*, 2d ed. (Mineola, N.Y.: Foundation, 1973), 660–62; Gerald Gunther, "The Subtle Vices of the 'Passive Virtues': A Comment on Principle and Expediency in Judicial Review," *Columbia Law Review* 64 (Jan. 1964): 11–12. But see Bickel, *Least Dangerous Branch*, 174.

78. TON to Justice Burton, certiorari memo, Box 270, Burton Papers; Burton conference notes, *Williams v. Georgia*, Box 270, Burton Papers; Harlan, Memorandum for the Conference, 23 Apr. 1955, folder 412, Box 2, Harlan Papers; Dickson, *Supreme Court in Conference*, 241–44; Williams v. State, 82 S.E. 2d 217 (Ga. 1954), remanded, 349 U.S. 375 (1955); Avery v. State, 70 S.E. 2d 716 (Ga. 1952), rev'd, 345 U.S. 559 (1953); Dickson, "State Court Defiance," 1426–52; Prettyman, *Death and the Supreme Court*, 264–67, 273–89.

79. Williams v. State, 88 S.E. 2d 376, 377 (Ga. 1955), cert. denied, 350 U.S. 950 (1956); Prettyman, *Death and the Supreme Court*, 290; Dickson, "State Court Defi-

ance," 1466–81; Frankfurter, Memorandum to the Conference, 10 Jan. 1956, folder 328, Box 11, Harlan Papers. But cf. Burt, *"Brown's* Reflection," 1494.

80. SSN, Apr. 1957, pp. 3, 14; July 1957, p. 1; Feb. 1958, pp. 1–2; July 1958, p. 5; Nov. 1958, p. 11; May 1959, p. 1.

81. SSN, Apr. 1956, p. 1; Sept. 1956, p. 1; Oct. 1956, p. 6; Aug. 1959, p. 1; NYT, 15 Mar. 1956, p. 1; 20 Aug. 1956, pp. 1, 8; statement by Roy Wilkins to *New York Post*, 1 Feb. 1957, NAACP, part 21, reel 13, fr. 7; Ernest Calloway to Eisenhower & Brownell, telegram, 7 Feb. 1956, part 20, reel 6, fr. 113; Young, "Eisenhower's Federal Judges," 555, 560–61; Peltason, *Fifty-Eight Lonely Men*, 46–51, 138–46; Muse, *Ten Years of Prelude*, 73–75, 87–102; Burns, *Montgomery Bus Boycott*, 308, 341–42; Marvin M. Karpatkin, "The Real Extremists," *Congress Weekly*, 14 Apr. 1958, pp. 9–10, NAACP, part 22, reel 3, frs. 243–44; Ambrose, *Eisenhower*, 2:190–91, 305–6, 327–28, 336–37; Burk, *Eisenhower Administration and Black Civil Rights*, 134–35, 142, 144, 154, 159, 161–63, 165–67, 192.

82. SSN, Mar. 1956, p. 13; Apr. 1956, p. 2; July 1956, p. 4; Jackson, "White Liberal Intellectuals, Civil Rights, and Gradualism," 104; NYT, 15 Mar. 1956, pp. 1, 16; 13 Feb. 1956, pp. 1, 14, 15; *Time*, 20 Feb. 1956, pp. 18–19; Muse, *Ten Years of Prelude*, 64; Martin, *Civil Rights and the Crisis of Liberalism*, 137–43; Collier, "Segregation and Politics," 119; speech of Paul Butler to Leadership Conference on Civil Rights, 6 Mar. 1956, pp. 9–10, NAACP, part 21, reel 12, frs. 221–22.

83. Woodward, "The South and the Law of the Land," 374; Woodward, "Great Civil Rights Debate," 287, 291; SSN, Dec. 1956, p. 1; Sept. 1959, p. 8; Feb. 1960, p. 3; Apr. 1960, p. 1; May 1960, p. 16.

84. "Go Slow, Now," *Life*, 12 Mar. 1956, p. 37; "The Autherine Lucy Case," *St. Louis Globe-Democrat*, 4 Mar. 1956, NAACP, part 20, reel 6, fr. 237; SSN, Mar. 1957, p. 12; Gallup, *Gallup Poll*, 2:1420; Jackson, "White Liberal Intellectuals, Civil Rights, and Gradualism," 98–100, 103–5; Results of Survey by City College of New York Chapter of NAACP, part 20, reel 6, fr. 345. See also Walter Lippmann, "The Miss Lucy Case," *Wash. Post*, 9 Feb. 1956, p. A15; Muse, "Moderates and Militants," 8–9.

85. Muse, "Moderates and Militants," 8–9; Muse, "When and How the South Will Integrate," 55; Tushnet, "Comment," 122.

86. SSN, Oct. 1956, p. 6; Oct. 1957, pp. 1–3, 11, 15; Dec. 1957, p. 2; NYT, 18 July 1957, p. 12; Muse, *Ten Years of Prelude*, 90–92, 140–41; Peltason, *Fifty-Eight Lonely Men*, 51, 142–46; Freyer, *Little Rock Crisis*, 98–109; Powell, "Massive Resistance in Arkansas," 39–40; Burk, *Eisenhower Administration and Black Civil Rights*, 167, 172–73, 185–86; Ambrose, *Eisenhower*, 2:336–37, 409–10; Kutler, "Eisenhower," 90–91; Lewis, "Origins and Causes of the Civil Rights Movement," 14–16; speech by Sen. George Smathers, 10 Oct. 1957, p. 1, NAACP, part 20, reel 6, fr. 826.

87. Aaron v. Cooper, 163 F. Supp. 13, 21, 29 (E.D. Ark. 1958); SSN, Mar. 1958, p. 2; July 1958, pp. 8–9; Sept. 1958, p. 3; Peltason, *Fifty-Eight Lonely Men*, 183–87.

88. SSN, Nov. 1957, p. 11; Jan. 1958, p. 6; July 1958, pp. 3, 11, 12, 16; Aug. 1958, pp. 10–11; Sept. 1958, pp. 1, 3, 6, 7; June 1959, p. 6; *Virginian-Pilot* (Norfolk), 23 Aug. 1958, p. 1; "A Historic Court Session," NYT, 27 Aug. 1958, p. 28; "The Rule of Law," ibid., 14 Sept. 1958; Wilkinson, *Brown to Bakke*, 92. See also Gallup, *Gallup Poll*, 2:1563.

89. Woodward, "The South and the Law of the Land," 370; Cooper v. Aaron, 358 U.S. 1, 15–16, 19 (1958); Peltason, *Fifty-Eight Lonely Men*, 192, 199; Muse, *Ten Years of Prelude*, 158; Wilkinson, *Brown to Bakke*, 93–94; Burk, *Eisenhower Administration and Black Civil Rights*, 185–86; Ambrose, *Eisenhower*, 2:416–17.

90. William J. Brennan was appointed to the Court by Eisenhower in 1956 to replace Sherman Minton. He became one of the great liberal justices in the Court's history, and Eisenhower reportedly referred to Brennan's appointment in retrospect as a foolish mistake.

91. Clark draft dissent, Box A73, Clark Papers; Brennan to Clark, 23 May 1963, Box 97, Brennan Papers; Hutchinson, "Unanimity and Desegregation," 76 n. 644; typewritten notes for conference on *Cooper*, 3, Box 14, Brennan Papers; Tushnet, *Thurgood Marshall*, 260, 263–64.

92. Minutes of the NAACP Board of Directors Meeting, Oct. 1959, p. 6, part 1, Supp. 1956–1960, reel 2, fr. 200.

93. SSN, Dec. 1958, p. 3; May 1959, p. 1; Nov. 1959, p. 1; Jan. 1960, pp. 1, 3; Feb. 1961, p. 1; June 1961, p. 11; Nov. 1962, p. 13; Wilkinson, *Brown to Bakke*, 79, 85–86.

94. Shuttlesworth v. Birmingham Board of Education, 162 F. Supp. 372, 381 (N.D. Ala.), aff'd, 358 U.S. 101 (1958); Douglas memorandum, *Shuttlesworth v. Birmingham Board of Education*, 17 Nov. 1958, pp. 3–7, Box 1211, Douglas Papers; SSN, May 1964, p. 5B; July 1955, p. 2; Aug. 1955, p. 13.

95. SSN, Dec. 1957, p. 11; Apr. 1957, p. 13; Nov. 1957, p. 11; Mar. 1960, p. 12; Orleans Parish School Board v. Bush, 242 F. 2d 156 (5th Cir.), cert. denied, 354 U.S. 921 (1957); School Board of City of Newport News v. Atkins, 246 F. 2d 325 (4th Cir.), cert. denied, 355 U.S. 855 (1957); Carson v. Warlick, 238 F. 2d 724 (4th Cir. 1956), cert. denied, 353 U.S. 910 (1957); Davis v. Schnell, 81 F. Supp. 852 (S.D. Ala.), aff'd, 336 U.S. 933 (1949); Ludley v. Board of Supervisors of Louisiana State University, 150 F. Supp. 900 (E.D. La. 1957), aff'd, 252 F. 2d 372, 376 (5th Cir. 1958); NAACP v. Patty, 159 F. Supp. 503, 516 n. 6 (E.D. Va. 1958) (three-judge court), vacated sub nom. Harrison v. NAACP, 360 U.S. 167 (1959); Griffin v. County School Board, 377 U.S. 218, 231 (1964); Douglas memo, *Shuttlesworth*, 17 Nov. 1958, pp. 1–7, Box 1211, Douglas Papers; Tushnet, *Thurgood Marshall*, 244–46; Peltason, *Fifty-Eight Lonely Men*, 83–92.

96. Stewart was appointed by Eisenhower in 1958 to replace Harold Burton. Southern segregationists in the Senate delayed and then voted against his confirmation, suspecting (rightly) that Stewart was personally supportive of *Brown*. Stewart proved to be a moderate conservative on nonracial issues; he frequently dissented from Warren Court landmarks and helped form a more conservative majority on the Burger Court in the 1970s.

97. Douglas, handwritten memo to the file regarding *Shuttlesworth*, Box 1211, Douglas Papers; SSN, Dec. 1958, pp. 3, 10; Jan. 1959, p. 10; *Richmond Times-Dispatch*, 25 Nov. 1958, p. 11. See also SSN, Feb. 1959, p. 15; Nov. 1959, p. 13; *Time*, 8 Dec. 1958, p. 18; Meador, "Assignment of Pupils to the Public Schools," 542–43.

98. SSN, Jan 1960, pp. 1, 3; Mar. 1960, p. 6; July 1958, p. 6; July 1959, p. 11; Aug. 1959, pp. 10, 12; Aug. 1961, p. 11; Kelley v. Board of Education of Nashville, 270 F. 2d 209 (6th Cir.), cert. denied, 361 U.S. 924 (1959) (Warren, Douglas, and Brennan dissenting); King, *Why We Can't Wait*, 19; Graham, "Desegregation in Nashville," 153; pages 358–59.

99. SSN, Oct. 1958, pp. 1–3; Aug. 1958, p. 6; Lassiter, "Rise of the Suburban South," 45–46, 108.

100. SSN, Feb. 1957, p. 7; Mar. 1957, p. 16; Apr. 1957, p. 3; May 1957, p. 4; Nov. 1958, p. 15; July 1957, p. 3; Oct. 1957, p. 7; Nov. 1957, p. 14; Feb. 1958, p. 15; Mar. 1958, p. 5; Apr. 1958, pp. 4–5; July 1958, pp. 12, 15; Aug. 1958, p. 16; Dec. 1958, pp. 5, 10; Aug. 1959, p. 8; Ely, *Crisis of Conservative Virginia*, 56–69; Lassiter, "Rise of the Suburban South," 213–14, 222–24, 235–36.

101. Frankfurter to Harlan, 2 Sept. 1958, Box 492, Harlan Papers; Hutchinson, "Unanimity and Desegregation," 76–77, 84; Frankfurter to conference, memorandum, 20 Feb. 1959, Box 1200, Douglas Papers; Black to Douglas, handwritten note, *In re Harrison*, Box 1208, Douglas Papers. See also Frankfurter to Black, 6 May 1963, Box 485, Harlan Papers.

102. SSN, Nov. 1957, p. 5; Sept. 1958, p. 5; Young, "Eisenhower's Federal Judges," 564; NYT, 28 Aug. 1958, p. 10; SSN, Dec. 1957, pp. 2–3; Apr. 1958, p. 5; June 1958, p. 9; Clarence Laws to Wilkins, 18 Dec. 1957, NAACP, part 20, reel 6, frs. 541–43; Peltason, *Fifty-Eight Lonely Men*, 179–81; Freyer, "Little Rock Crisis Reconsidered," 367; Ambrose, *Eisenhower*, 2:420–21.

103. SSN, Mar. 1959, p. 16; Apr. 1959, p. 6; Mar. 1960, p. 16; Feb. 1959, p. 1; July 1959, p. 4. See also Jackson, "White Liberal Intellectuals, Civil Rights, and Gradualism," 109.

104. SSN, Aug. 1956, p. 13; Sept. 1958, p. 5; Aug. 1960, p. 8; NYT, 24 Aug. 1958, p. 1; Woodward, "The South and the Law of the Land," 371–72; Watkins v. United States, 354 U.S. 178 (1957); Sweezy v. New Hampshire, 354 U.S. 234 (1957); Yates v. United States, 354 U.S. 298 (1957); Mallory v. United States, 354 U.S. 449 (1957); Jencks v. United States, 353 U.S. 657 (1957); Brown v. Allen, 344 U.S. 443 (1953); Uphaus v. Wyman, 360 U.S. 72 (1959); Barenblatt v. United States, 360 U.S. 109 (1959); Murphy, *Congress and the Court*, 99–268; Pritchett, *Congress versus the Supreme Court*, 3–71, 117–33; Ross, "Attacks on the Warren Court," 497–528; Klarman, "*Bush v. Gore*," 1757–60. See also "How U.S. Judges Feel about the Supreme Court," *U.S. News & World Report*, 24 Oct. 1958, pp. 36–37.

105. Wilkins to Board of Directors, memo, 7 May 1957, NAACP, part 20, reel 12, fr. 296.

106. NAACP v. Alabama, 357 U.S. 449 (1958); Bates v. Little Rock, 361 U.S. 516 (1960); Shelton v. Tucker, 364 U.S. 479 (1960); Gibson v. Florida Legislative Investigation Committee, 372 U.S. 539 (1963); NAACP v. Button, 371 U.S. 415 (1963); pages 382–83.

107. SSN, July 1963, p. 9.

108. Frankfurter to Clark, 25 June 1958, Box A66, Clark Papers; W. C. [William Cohen] to Douglas, bench memo, 20 May 1957, *NAACP v. Alabama*, Box 1186, Douglas Papers; Minutes of Board of Directors Meeting, 9 Apr. 1956, p. 5, NAACP, part 20, reel 12, fr. 782; Douglas conference notes, *NAACP v. Alabama*, 17 Jan. 1958, Argued Cases Folder 85–99, Box 1186, Douglas Papers; Klarman, "*Bush v. Gore*," 1738–39; *NAACP v. Alabama*, 357 U.S. at 458; Bryant v. Zimmerman, 278 U.S. 63 (1928); Clark draft dissent, 30 June 1958, Box A66, Clark Papers; Tushnet, *Thurgood Marshall*, 284–89; Hutchinson, "Unanimity and Desegregation," 70–72; Glennon, "Jurisdictional Legacy of the Civil Rights Movement," 887–90; NAACP v. Gallion, 368 U.S. 16 (1961).

109. Douglas conference notes, *Bates v. Little Rock*, 20 Nov. 1959, Box 1222, Douglas Papers; CM to Douglas, certiorari memorandum, 22 Apr. 1959, ibid.; Stewart to Brethren, 19 Jan. 1960, ibid.

110. Douglas conferences notes, *Shelton v. Tucker*, 11 Nov. 1960, Box 1234, Douglas Papers; SD to Douglas, certiorari memorandum, 4 Jan. 1960, ibid.; *Shelton*, 364 U.S. at 487–88, 496, 497–98 (Harlan, J., dissenting); Garner v. Board of Public Works, 341 U.S. 716 (1951); Adler v. Board of Education, 342 U.S. 485 (1952); Beilan v. Board of Education, 357 U.S. 399 (1958); Tushnet, *Thurgood Marshall*, 294–95.

111. NAACP v. Button, 371 U.S. 415 (1963); *SSN*, Dec. 1958, pp. 6–7; Carter to Wilkins & Gloster Current, memo, 13 June 1958, NAACP, part 22, reel 9, frs. 106–7; Carter to Henry Moon, memo on *NAACP v. Gray*, 27 Oct. 1961, ibid., frs. 385–88; Report of the Committee on Offenses against the Administration of Justice, Commonwealth of Virginia, 1957, part 20, reel 12, frs. 1012–48; Tushnet, *Thurgood Marshall*, 128, 274–75. See also Carle, "Race, Class, and Legal Ethics in the Early NAACP," esp. 121–24, 130–31, 133–44.

112. Whittaker was appointed by Eisenhower in 1957 to replace Stanley Reed. He served only until 1962 and had little influence on the Court or the law.

113. Douglas conference notes, *NAACP v. Gray*, 10 Nov. 1961, Box 1287, Douglas Papers.

114. White was appointed by President John F. Kennedy to replace Whittaker. "Whizzer" White had been a star football player in college and in the National Football League, as well as a Rhodes scholar and a stellar law student at Yale. He served on the Court for thirty years and proved to be a predictable ally of neither the liberal nor the conservative wings of the Court. Though some have argued that White grew more conservative, as the rest of the Court did, in the 1970s and 1980s, he remained generally liberal on race issues.

Goldberg was appointed by Kennedy to replace Frankfurter in the "Jewish seat" on the Court, which had existed since the appointment of Brandeis in 1916. Goldberg served only three years. President Johnson pressured him to resign in 1965 to become ambassador to the United Nations, so the president could appoint as successor his personal favorite, Abe Fortas. During Goldberg's brief tenure, he proved to be a staunch liberal. His appointment is often characterized as critical to the formation of the liberal majority that dominated the Court until President Nixon's conservative appointments of 1969–1972.

115. *Champerty* involves a third party without a direct stake in litigation subsidizing it in exchange for a share of the recovery.

116. Douglas conference notes, *NAACP v. Gray*, 12 Oct. 1962, Box 1287, Douglas Papers; Tushnet, *Thurgood Marshall*, 279–82; *Button*, 371 U.S. at 429–31, 444–45, 448 (Harlan, J., dissenting).

117. Lawson, "Florida Legislative Investigation Committee," 299–317 (quotation at 311).

118. Douglas conference notes, *Gibson v. Florida Legislative Investigation Committee*, 8 Dec. 1961, 12 Oct. 1962, 14 Dec. 1962, Box 1287, Douglas Papers; *Gibson*, 372 U.S. at 546–50, 579, 580 (Harlan, J., dissenting); Carter to Moon, memo, 7 Dec. 1961, NAACP, part 22, reel 9, fr. 450; Lusky, "Nullification," 1174; Tushnet, *Thurgood Marshall*, 295–300; Lawson, "Florida Legislative Investigation Committee," 312–15.

119. Gomillion v. Lightfoot, 167 F. Supp. 405 (M.D. Ala. 1958), aff'd, 270 F. 2d 594 (5th Cir. 1959), rev'd, 364 U.S. 339 (1960); Colegrove v. Green, 328 U.S. 549 (1946); Norrell, *Civil Rights Movement in Tuskegee*, 91–92, 123–24; *SSN*, Dec. 1960, p. 13; Yarbrough, *Judge Frank Johnson*, 73–75; Bass, *Unlikely Heroes*, chap. 6.

120. *SSN*, Oct. 1959, p. 7.

121. *SSN*, Dec. 1962, p. 16; Mar. 1963, p. 1; Watson v. Memphis, 373 U.S. 526, 530 (1963); Goss v. Board of Education, 373 U.S. 683, 689 (1963); Griffin v. County School Board, 377 U.S. 218, 229, 234 (1964); *SSN*, Jan 1963, p. 1; Apr. 1963, p. 2; May 1963, pp. 1, 16; June 1963, p. 5; Muse, *Ten Years of Prelude*, 271, 274–75; pages 360–63.

122. *Goss*, 373 U.S. 683; McNeese v. Board of Education, 373 U.S. 668 (1963); *Griffin*, 377 U.S. at 230–31, 233–34; Burton conference notes, Segregation Cases, 16 Apr. 1955, Box 244, Burton Papers; *SSN*, Aug. 1955, p. 11; May 1959, pp. 6, 7; Oct. 1961, pp. 8–9; Green v. County School Board, 391 U.S. 430 (1968); Swann v. Charlotte-Mecklenburg Board of Education, 402 U.S. 1 (1971); Tonkins v. City of Greensboro, 162 F. Supp. 549 (M.D.N.C. 1958).

123. *SSN*, June 1964, p. 10; May 1962, p. 20; Brief for the United States as Amicus Curiae, *Goss v. Board of Education*, 15–41; Brief for the United States as Amicus Curiae, *Griffin v. County School Board*, 16–40; Dunn, "School Desegregation in the South," 44–45, 61–64; Wilkinson, Brown *to* Bakke, 99, 107–18.

124. Burton, Memorandum as to Segregation Cases for Conference, 16 Apr. 1955, Box 337, Burton Papers; *SSN*, Dec. 1957, p. 10; July 1960, p. 2; NAACP v. Gallion, 368 U.S. 16 (1961); *McNeese*, 373 U.S. 668; *Griffin*, 377 U.S. at 228–29, 231–32, 233; Harrison v. NAACP, 360 U.S. 167 (1959); Douglas conference notes, *Griffin v. County School Board*, 3 Apr. 1964, Box 1304, Douglas Papers; WBM to Burton, memorandum, *Brown II*, 30, Box 248, Burton Papers; Wilkinson, Brown *to* Bakke, 100–101; *Green*, 391 U.S. at 437–38. See also Prettyman to Jackson, n.d., 7, Box 184, Jackson Papers.

CHAPTER 7

1. Greenberg, *Crusaders in the Courts*, 197; Wilkinson, Brown *to* Bakke, 6; Douglas, *Desegregation of the Charlotte Schools*, 25; Dudziak, "Desegregation as a Cold War Imperative," 62; Gill, "*Brown v. Board of Education*: Twenty-Five Years After," 99.

2. Douglas, "Limits of Law," 719–27, 737–43.

3. *Southern School News* (hereafter SSN), Oct. 1954, pp. 15, 16; WBM to Burton, Memo on Supplemental Material Filed, 12 Apr. 1955, Box 244, Burton Papers, Library of Congress; *SSN*, Dec. 1955, pp. 1, 2; Tushnet, *Thurgood Marshall*, 174–75, 217–18; Wilson, *Time to Lose*, 146–47, 167.

4. Douglas conference notes, *Brown v. Board of Education* and *Bolling v. Sharpe*, 13 Dec. 1952, case file: Segregation Cases, Box 1150, Douglas Papers, Library of Congress; Jackson draft concurrence, School Segregation Cases, 15 Mar. 1954, pp. 1–2, case file: Segregation Cases, Box 184, Jackson Papers, Library of Congress; *SSN*, Oct. 1954, pp. 1, 3, 4–5, 8, 10, 14; Dec. 1954, pp. 4, 5; Aug. 1958, p. 11; Sept. 1954, pp. 2–4, 6–7, 9, 11, 14; Apr. 1963, p. 2; Lasch, "Along the Border," 60–61.

5. *SSN*, Oct. 1954, pp. 8, 10; Aug. 1955, p. 19; Mar. 1958, p. 12; Sept. 1954, pp. 6–7, 9; Feb. 1955, p. 8; Feb. 1959, p. 9; Palumbos, "Baltimore Civil Rights Movement," 453; Kluger, *Simple Justice*, 432; Meier, "Successful Sit-Ins in a Border City," 231.

6. *SSN*, Sept. 1954, pp. 3, 6, 7, 14; Nov. 1954, pp. 6–7; July 1955, p. 7; Aug. 1955, p. 19; *NYT*, 18 May 1954, pp. 1, 20; Lasch, "Along the Border," 61; James, "South's Own Civil War," 33; Jones, "City Limits," 75–77, 80–82; Muse, *Ten Years of Prelude*, 18, 30–31.

7. Palumbos, "Baltimore Civil Rights Movement," 472; *SSN*, Sept. 1954, pp. 6–7; Oct. 1954, p. 8; Apr. 1955, p. 6; July 1955, pp. 10–11; July 1956, p. 5; Feb. 1957, p. 4; Nov. 1957, p. 4; Dec. 1957, p. 6; Aug. 1958, p. 7; Sept. 1958, pp. 8–9; Feb. 1959, p. 9; Mar. 1959, pp. 6–7; Aug. 1959, p. 5; Oct. 1959, p. 11; Feb. 1960, p. 10; Apr. 1960, p. 12; May 1960, p. 9; Jan. 1961, p. 13; Mar. 1961, p. 11; May 1961, p. 7; Sept. 1961, p. 15; Dec. 1961, pp. 10–11; Feb. 1962, pp. 1–2; May 1962, p. 14; June 1962, p. 14; Aug. 1962, p. 14; Sept. 1962, p. 13; Dec. 1963, pp. 8–9.

8. *SSN*, Oct. 1955, pp. 5, 6, 7, 10, 11; Oct. 1954, pp. 4, 7, 16; Apr. 1956, pp. 15, 16; June 1956, pp. 11, 15, 16; Sept. 1954, pp. 3, 7, 9, 11, 14; Nov. 1954, pp. 6–7, 16; Dec. 1954, pp. 9, 10; Jan. 1955, p. 4; May 1955, pp. 3, 4; June 1955, p. 5; July 1955, p. 7; Aug. 1955, p. 5; Sept. 1955, pp. 1, 2, 5, 11, 15; Dec. 1955, p. 10; Mar. 1956, p. 16; May 1956, p. 10; Aug. 1956, pp. 2, 3, 8, 15; Sept. 1956, pp. 5, 7, 10, 16; Oct. 1956, pp. 3, 5, 10; Apr. 1957, p. 10; May 1957, p. 12; June 1957, p. 3; July 1957, p. 8; Sept. 1957, pp. 11, 12, 13; Oct. 1957, p. 12; Nov. 1957, p. 12; June 1958, p. 12; Sept. 1958, pp. 12, 15, 16; Jan. 1959, p. 12; Feb. 1959, p. 7; Oct. 1959, p. 6; Aug. 1960, p. 2; Apr. 1961, p. 13; Aug. 1961, p. 13; Oct. 1961, pp. 5, 10; Dec. 1961, p. 11; Jan. 1962, p. 16; Apr. 1962, p. 7; June 1962, p. 15; Nov. 1962, p. 8; Mar. 1963, p. 7; Lasch, "Along the Border," 56–70; Muse, *Ten Years of Prelude*, 30–33; Kee, "*Brown* Decision and Milford, Delaware," 211–34, 236–37, 242.

9. *SSN*, July 1959, pp. 1, 3; July 1955, p. 7; Oct. 1955, p. 5; Nov. 1955, p. 14; June 1956, pp. 15, 16; Oct. 1956, p. 12; Aug. 1959, p. 5; Apr. 1960, p. 12; May 1960, p. 9; June 1960, p. 11; Mar. 1961, p. 11; Aug. 1961, p. 10; Sept. 1961, p. 16; Oct. 1961, p. 10; Nov. 1961, pp. 1, 3, 15; July 1962, pp. 1, 15; Jan. 1963, p. 16; Mar. 1964, p. 9; May 1964, p. 2B; Jones, "City Limits," 80–82.

10. Tushnet, *Thurgood Marshall*, 234; *SSN*, May 1958, p. 1; Jan. 1962, pp. 1, 6; Apr. 1962, pp. 10–11; June 1962, pp. 5, 9; Wilkins to Hon. Robert Whitehead, n.d. (probably 1959), NAACP, part 22, reel 5, frs. 706–10; Muse, *Ten Years of Prelude*, 36–37.

11. *SSN*, June 1957, pp. 1, 8; Sept. 1954, p. 2; Oct. 1954, p. 3; Aug. 1955, p. 15; Sept. 1955, pp. 1, 9; Oct. 1955, pp. 12, 14; Apr. 1956, p. 3; Sept. 1956, pp. 3, 12, 15; July 1957, p. 10; Aug. 1957, pp. 1, 3; Sept. 1957, pp. 1, 3, 6, 10, 15; Oct. 1957, pp. 3, 5, 6; Apr. 1958, p. 12; Sept. 1958, pp. 10, 13, 14; Oct. 1958, p. 5; Jan. 1959, p. 3; Feb. 1959, pp. 1, 4; Mar. 1959, p. 3; May 1959, p. 6; Sept. 1959, pp. 1, 3, 4, 9, 10; Oct. 1959, pp. 4, 5; Apr. 1960, pp. 1, 5, 6, 8, 11, 13; June 1960, p. 11; Aug. 1963, p. 15; Lasch, "Along the Border," 58, 70; Woodward, "The South and the Law of the Land," 369.

12. *SSN*, Sept. 1960, pp. 1, 7; Oct. 1960, pp. 1, 6, 9; Dec. 1960, pp. 1, 8–10; Sept. 1961, pp. 1, 4, 6, 7, 11, 14, 15; Oct. 1961, pp. 1, 4, 12; Dec. 1961, p. 7; Sept. 1962, pp. 1, 3, 5; Dec. 1962, pp. 1, 9, 15; Jan. 1963, pp. 2, 4; Apr. 1963, p. 2; June 1963, pp. 3, 15; July 1963, p. 12; Aug. 1963, pp. 1, 17; Sept. 1963, pp. 1–3, 7, 8, 12; Oct. 1963, pp. 3, 5, 13–16, 18; Dec. 1963, pp. 1, 5, 13; May 1964, pp. 2B, 14B, 15B; Muse, *Ten Years of Prelude*, 187, 210–11, 228, 231–32, 275.

13. Douglas conference notes, *Brown II*, 16 Apr. 1955, Box 1150, Douglas Papers.

14. *Brown II*, 349 U.S. at 299; Peltason, *Fifty-Eight Lonely Men*, 99.

15. *SSN*, Jan. 1958, p. 3; Dec. 1958, p. 13; Feb. 1956, p. 11; Aug. 1956, p. 3; Dec. 1956, pp. 8–9; July 1957, p. 2; Sept. 1957, p. 15; Oct. 1957, p. 9; Mar. 1958, p. 3; Sept. 1958, p. 15; Feb. 1960, p. 14; Apr. 1962, p. 6; Feb. 1964, p. 12; *Newsweek*, 9 Sept. 1957, pp. 35–36; *NYT*, 20 Sept. 1960, p. 4E; Peltason, *Fifty-Eight Lonely Men*, 54–55, 96; Robinson, "No Man's Land," 184–88; Leflar & Davis, "Segregation in the Public Schools," 425–26.

16. *SSN*, June 1956, pp. 6–7; Sept. 1954, p. 10; Aug. 1955, p. 16; Oct. 1955, p. 12; Jan. 1956, p. 2; Apr. 1956, p. 4; May 1956, p. 11; July 1956, p. 7; Sept. 1956, p. 3; Jan. 1957, pp. 6–7; Aug. 1957, p. 6; Sept. 1957, p. 3; Oct. 1957, pp. 1, 5, 6; July 1960, p. 7; Sept. 1962, p. 10; George Barrett, "Study in Desegregation: The Clinton Story," *NYT Mag.*, 16 Sept. 1956, pp. 11ff; Chafe, *Civilities and Civil Rights*, 16; Wolff, *Greensboro Sit-Ins*, 77; Workman, "Deep South," 94–95; Peltason, *Fifty-Eight Lonely Men*, 30–31, 158–59; Kirk, "Little Rock School Crisis," 74–75; Belknap, *Federal Law and Southern Order*, 29–30.

17. SSN, Aug. 1958, p. 4; Oct. 1961, p. 12; Sept. 1955, p. 10; May 1956, p. 10; Aug. 1956, p. 9; July 1957, p. 11; Oct. 1957, p. 3; Apr. 1958, p. 12; June 1958, p. 12; July 1958, pp. 5, 10; Sept. 1958, p. 10; Jan. 1959, p. 7; Mar. 1960, p. 2; Apr. 1960, p. 3; Peltason, *Fifty-Eight Lonely Men*, 96–97, 110; Patterson, Brown, 75; Muse, *Ten Years of Prelude*, 77–78.

18. Leflar & Davis, "Segregation in the Public Schools," 417, 423; Muse, *Ten Years of Prelude*, 78; Peltason, *Fifty-Eight Lonely Men*, 57–58, 64–65, 100–101; NAACP v. Button, 371 U.S. 415 (1963); background information on *NAACP v. Gray*, 2, NAACP, part 20, reel 13, fr. 197; Carter to Henry Lee Moon, memo, *NAACP v. Gray*, 27 Oct. 1961, part 22, reel 9, frs. 385–88; background material on Gibson case, part 20, reel 7, frs. 109–10; Wilkins to Ross L. Malone, telegram, 29 Apr. 1959, ibid., reel 1, frs. 149–50; Statement of Billie S. Fleming before the Senate Subcommittee on Constitutional Rights, 16 Apr. 1959, pp. 2–6, ibid., reel 11, frs. 45–49; SSN, Apr. 1956, p. 12; Feb. 1958, p. 15; June 1958, p. 12; Apr. 1959, p. 5; May 1959, p. 11; May 1960, p. 5; Apr. 1961, p. 3. See also George C. Hickerson to Wilkins, 24 Apr. 1958, NAACP, part 22, reel 2, fr. 859; *Texarkana Gazette*, 28 Sept. 1956, part 20, reel 12, fr. 159; pages 382–84.

19. SSN, Oct. 1956, p. 2; Lomax, *Negro Revolt*, 30, 114; SSN, Nov. 1954, p. 16; June 1955, p. 15; Oct. 1955, pp. 4, 8–9, 16; Nov. 1955, pp. 1–2, 11; Sept. 1956, p. 6; Oct. 1957, p. 4; Aug. 1958, p. 11; June 1959, p. 15; July 1959, p. 11; Oct. 1959, p. 7; Apr. 1961, p. 3; Oct. 1961, p. 14; Feb. 1963, p. 15; Mar. 1963, p. 6; Apr. 1963, p. 10; Sept. 1963, p. 2; June 1964, p. 15; Gallup, *Gallup Poll*, 2:1402; Statement of Mrs. Gussie P. Young, Feb. 1956, NAACP, part 20, reel 1, frs. 344–45; Nathan Stewart to Wilkins, 8 Apr. 1957, ibid., frs. 412–18; NAACP Press Release, 8 Apr. 1961, ibid., frs. 556–57; NAACP Press Release, 9 Feb. 1956, ibid., reel 2, fr. 22; C. R. Darden to Ronald Moskowitz, 4 Mar. 1958, ibid., frs. 121–24; NAACP Press Release, 4 Oct. 1956, ibid., reel 12, fr. 152; McMillen, *Citizens' Council*, 210–11; Payne, *Mississippi Freedom Struggle*, 42–43; Dittmer, *Struggle for Civil Rights in Mississippi*, 50–52; Cobb, *Most Southern Place on Earth*, 215; Peltason, *Fifty-Eight Lonely Men*, 60; Kluger, *Simple Justice*, 525; Patterson, Brown, xxv–xxvi; Baker, "Ambiguous Legacies," 137, 162–63, 168, 178–80; Greenberg, *Crusaders in the Courts*, 226; Lau, "Clarendon County," 18–24; Manis, *Fred Shuttlesworth*, 107–12, 148–59, 170–73, 328; Eskew, *But for Birmingham*, 131–32, 140–42.

20. WBM to Burton, memorandum, *Brown II*, 29, Box 248, Burton Papers; SSN, Oct. 1959, pp. 3, 7; Dec. 1955, p. 11; Mar. 1956, p. 10; May 1956, p. 15; June 1956, p. 13; July 1956, pp. 2, 3; Nov. 1956, p. 10; Mar. 1957, p. 1; June 1959, p. 12; Aug. 1959, p. 16; Sept. 1959, p. 6; May 1960, p. 3; June 1960, pp. 14–15; Oct. 1960, p. 7; Feb. 1962, p. 5; July 1962, pp. 10–11; Sept. 1962, p. 14; Jan. 1963, p. 2; Mar. 1963, pp. 6, 7; Apr. 1963, pp. 1, 8, 10; July 1964, pp. 15–16; Sept. 1964, p. 10; Peltason, *Fifty-Eight Lonely Men*, 99–100; Baker, "Ambiguous Legacies," 170–71.

21. Douglas conference notes, *Brown II*, 16 Apr. 1955, case file: Segregation Cases, Box 1149, Douglas Papers; SSN, Jan. 1958, p. 6; Jan. 1957, p. 10; Aug. 1960, p. 8; Sept. 1959, p. 10; Feb. 1958, p. 7; Mar. 1963, p. 14; Oct. 1960, p. 7; Dec. 1960, p. 6; June 1960, p. 3; July 1961, p. 3. See also SSN, Aug. 1955, p. 6; May 1958, p. 6; July 1958, pp. 8–9; Mar. 1959, p. 2; June 1963, p. 18; Peltason, *Fifty-Eight Lonely Men*, 5–8, 21, 73–74; Muse, *Ten Years of Prelude*, 77; Vines, "Federal District Judges," 343–47, 352; Rosenberg, *Hollow Hope*, 90–91.

22. SSN, Mar. 1964, p. 14; Oct. 1956, p. 8; June 1963, p. 6; May 1959, p. 7; Nov. 1955, p. 1; June 1956, p. 6; July 1956, p. 4; Nov. 1956, p. 6; Mar. 1964, p. 1; Leflar, "Law

of the Land," 10–11; Muse, *Ten Years of Prelude*, 99–100; Peltason, *Fifty-Eight Lonely Men*, 10–13, 129–30, 246; Sanders, "*Brown v. Board of Education*, " 734. Cf. Vines, "Southern State Supreme Courts and Race Relations," 9–10, 13.

23. Burton conference notes, Segregation Cases, 13 Dec. 1952, Box 244, Burton Papers; *SSN*, June 1957, p. 4; Apr. 1962, p. 3; *NYT*, 15 Nov. 1960, pp. 1, 42; Peltason, *Fifty-Eight Lonely Men*, 9, 43, 244–45.

24. *SSN*, Nov. 1962, p. 11; Schmidt, "J. Waties Waring," 3; *SSN*, May 1958, p. 6; Mar. 1962, p. 13; Peltason, *Fifty-Eight Lonely Men*, 9–10, 162, 170, 207; Patterson, *Brown*, 91–92; Yarbrough, *J. Waties Waring*, 192, 210–11, 241; Fairclough, *Civil Rights Struggle in Louisiana*, 213, 245; Baker, *Second Battle of New Orleans*, 423–24; Bass, *Unlikely Heroes*, 79–82, 115.

25. *SSN*, June 1960, p. 16; July 1959, p. 2; May 1959, p. 12; Jan. 1960, p. 16; Sept. 1960, pp. 2, 3; Aug. 1955, pp. 1, 6–8, 10–13; Feb. 1957, p. 11; July 1958, pp. 8–9; Sept. 1958, p. 7; Aug. 1959, p. 8; Oct. 1960, pp. 11, 15; Mar. 1962, p. 8.

26. *SSN*, Feb. 1957, pp. 6, 8, 11, 12; Aug. 1955, pp. 6, 10; Jan. 1956, pp. 8–9; Feb. 1956, p. 8; Mar. 1956, p. 5; Apr. 1956, p. 4; Aug. 1956, pp. 6, 12; Sept. 1956, p. 15; Jan. 1957, p. 11; Mar. 1957, p. 14; May 1957, p. 2; Aug. 1957, p. 8; Sept. 1957, p. 10; Dec. 1957, p. 10; May 1958, p. 16; June 1958, p. 5; July 1958, pp. 10, 14; Sept. 1958, pp. 1, 5, 7; Oct. 1958, p. 3; Mar. 1959, p. 8; June 1959, pp. 6, 14; July 1959, p. 12; Aug. 1959, pp. 1, 8; Nov. 1959, p. 10; Feb. 1960, p. 4; Mar. 1960, p. 10; Apr. 1960, p. 11; May 1960, p. 12; June 1960, p. 1; July 1960, p. 1; Sept. 1960, p. 16; Oct. 1960, p. 1; Jan. 1961, p. 14; July 1962, pp. 10–11; Sept. 1962, p. 15; Armstrong v. Board of Education, 323 F. 2d 333 (5th Cir. 1963); Nelson v. Grooms, 307 F. 2d 76 (N.D. Ala. 1962); Peltason, *Fifty-Eight Lonely Men*, 18–21, 110–11, 114–22, 126–27, 134, 210–13, 218–19; Vines, "Federal District Judges," 347–49; Leflar, "Law of the Land," 13–14.

27. Briggs v. Elliott, 132 F. Supp. 776, 777 (E.D.S.C. 1955); *SSN*, Aug. 1957, p. 16; Burton, Memorandum as to Segregation Cases for Conference, 16 Apr. 1955, p. 1, Box 337, Burton Papers; *SSN*, Aug. 1955, p. 6; Feb. 1957, pp. 7, 8; Jan. 1958, p. 6; May 1959, p. 1; July 1959, p. 2; WBM to Burton, memorandum, *Brown II*, 30, Box 248, Burton Papers; Patterson, *Brown*, 85; Wilkinson, *Brown to Bakke*, 81–82.

28. Leflar & Davis, "Segregation in the Public Schools," 416; *SSN*, Sept. 1956, p. 15; Dec. 1957, p. 10; Jan. 1958, p. 6; Mar. 1958, p. 14; July 1958, p. 6; Sept. 1960, pp. 1–2; Jan. 1961, p. 14; Peltason, *Fifty-Eight Lonely Men*, 127–32.

29. *SSN*, Apr. 1964, p. 2; Meador, "Assignment of Pupils to the Public Schools," 526–71; Peltason, *Fifty-Eight Lonely Men*, 78–92; McCauley, "Be It Enacted," 136–39; Carson v. Warlick, 232 F. 2d 724 (4th Cir. 1956), cert. denied, 353 U.S. 910 (1957); Hood v. Board of Trustees, 232 F. 2d 626 (4th Cir.), cert. denied, 352 U.S. 870 (1956); Shuttlesworth v. Birmingham Board of Education, 162 F. Supp. 372 (N.D. Ala.) (three-judge court), aff'd, 358 U.S. 101 (1958); *SSN*, Feb. 1957, pp. 1–2; Aug. 1957, pp. 3, 14; Apr. 1959, p. 4; May 1959, p. 1; Sept. 1959, pp. 3, 10; Nov. 1959, pp. 1, 7; Jan. 1960, p. 14; Feb. 1960, p. 5; June 1960, p. 6; Aug. 1960, p. 10; Sept. 1960, p. 10; Oct. 1960, p. 12; Oct. 1961, p. 1; June 1962, p. 1; Mar. 1964, pp. 1, 11; May 1964, pp. 5B, 8B.

30. *SSN*, Feb. 1961, pp. 8, 15; Oct. 1958, p. 9; Sept. 1957, pp. 2, 10; Oct. 1957, pp. 3, 5; Nov. 1957, pp. 3, 13; Feb. 1958, p. 12; July 1958, p. 10; Sept. 1958, p. 10; Jan. 1959, p. 3; Oct. 1959, p. 12; Nov. 1960, pp. 1, 5; Sept. 1961, p. 15; Nov. 1961, pp. 1, 5; Dec. 1961, p. 14; Oct. 1962, pp. 3, 5; Nov. 1962, p. 3; Sept. 1963, pp. 22, 24; Oct. 1963, p. 13; Apr. 1964, p. 3; Graham, "Desegregation in Nashville," 145–46; Wilkinson, *Brown to Bakke*, 87, 108–9; Greene, "School Desegregation," 21–23; Daniel, *The South in the 1950s*, 270–81; transcript of conversation between Mrs. L. C. Bates and Gloster Current, 13

Nov. 1957, p. 1, NAACP, part 20, reel 6, fr. 530; Clarence Laws, statement, 14 Nov. 1957, p. 1, ibid., fr. 532.

31. SSN, Apr. 1960, pp. 2, 5, 7; "Six Years Later," *New Republic*, 7 Sept. 1959, pp. 3–4; SSN, Aug. 1959, pp. 6, 8, 10, 13, 14; Nov. 1960, pp. 1, 12, 15; Aug. 1961, pp. 11, 14, 16; Mar. 1959, p. 3; May 1959, pp. 10–11; June 1959, pp. 6–7; July 1959, pp. 1, 2, 6; Sept. 1959, pp. 1, 9, 10; Oct. 1959, pp. 2, 6, 13, 14; Nov. 1959, p. 7; Dec. 1959, p. 16; Jan. 1960, pp. 1, 16; Feb. 1960, p. 16; Mar. 1960, p. 12; May 1960, pp. 7, 8; June 1960, p. 6; July 1960, pp. 2, 5; Aug. 1960, pp. 6, 10; Sept. 1960, pp. 1, 8, 10; Oct. 1960, pp. 1, 5, 9, 11; Dec. 1960, pp. 1–2, 11; Jan. 1961, p. 1; June 1961, p. 13; Sept. 1961, pp. 1, 3; Oct. 1961, pp. 1, 2, 3; Virginius Dabney, "Next in the South's Schools: 'Limited Integration'," *U.S. News & World Report*, 18 Jan. 1960, pp. 92–94; Muse, *Ten Years of Prelude*, 178, 197, 231; Peltason, *Fifty-Eight Lonely Men*, 245; pages 333–34.

32. Report of Secretary to the NAACP Board of Directors, Apr. 1960, NAACP, part 1, supp. 1956–60, reel 2, fr. 357; SSN, Apr. 1960, pp. 13, 14; June 1960, pp. 5, 13; Aug. 1960, p. 6; Nov. 1960, p. 6; Oct. 1960, p. 5; June 1961, pp. 1, 5, 8, 10; July 1961, pp. 1, 4, 11, 16; Feb. 1962, pp. 3, 5, 7; June 1962, pp. 4, 14; July 1962, p. 12; Aug. 1962, p. 7; Sept. 1962, pp. 5, 14; Nov. 1962, pp. 7, 8; Oct. 1962, p. 19; June 1963, p. 13; July 1963, p. 12; Dec. 1963, pp. 4–5.

33. SSN, Mar. 1961, p. 3; Aug. 1960, pp. 1–2; Oct. 1960, pp. 6–7; Nov. 1960, p. 7; Jan. 1961, p. 14; Apr. 1961, p. 11; May 1961, p. 3; Nov. 1961, pp. 2, 7; Dec. 1961, p. 6; Jan. 1962, pp. 8, 12; Mar. 1962, p. 8; Apr. 1962, pp. 1, 12, 13, 20; May 1962, pp. 2, 8; June 1962, p. 10; Aug. 1962, p. 13; Sept. 1962, p. 1; Oct. 1962, pp. 1, 2, 19; Jan. 1963, p. 1; Morland, *Token Desegregation and Beyond*, 7–14; Muse, *Ten Years of Prelude*, 231–32; Gellhorn, "Decade of Desegregation," 6 n. 16; U.S. Civil Rights Commission, *Public Schools*, 4–14.

34. SSN, Apr. 1961, pp. 10–11, 14; June 1961, p. 13; Sept. 1961, pp. 1, 4, 6, 7; Oct. 1961, p. 6; Dec. 1961, pp. 6, 8, 11; June 1962, pp. 1, 5, 6, 10; Aug. 1962, pp. 4, 7, 16; Sept. 1962, pp. 1, 3, 4, 8, 10–11, 13, 17, 19; Oct. 1962, pp. 2, 19; Nov. 1962, pp. 3, 4, 9; Dec. 1962, p. 4; Jan. 1963, pp. 1, 7, 12–14; Feb. 1963, p. 12; Mar. 1963, p. 12; Apr. 1963, pp. 4, 14; May 1963, p. 15; June 1963, pp. 3, 18; July 1963, pp. 2, 4, 11; Aug. 1963, pp. 1, 17, 18; Apr. 1964, p. 12; May 1964, p. 7A; U.S. Civil Rights Commission, *Public Schools*, 14–16.

35. SSN, Apr. 1962, pp. 1–4, 20; Oct. 1961, p. 1; May 1962, p. 4; Aug. 1962, p. 16; Sept. 1962, pp. 8, 9, 16; Oct. 1962, pp. 2, 16; Nov. 1962, p. 7; Dec. 1962, p. 2; Feb. 1963, pp. 2, 3, 10, 13, 16, 18; Mar. 1963, pp. 1, 2, 8; Apr. 1963, p. 5; June 1963, pp. 2, 7; July 1963, p. 12; Dec. 1963, p. 7.

36. SSN, July 1963, pp. 10, 17; Jan. 1964, pp. 2, 10; Aug. 1963, pp. 4, 8, 15, 19; *Griffin*, 377 U.S. at 234; SSN, June 1963, p. 13; Oct. 1963, pp. 1, 5, 13; Nov. 1963, p. 9; Feb. 1964, pp. 1, 14; Mar. 1964, pp. 4, 8; Apr. 1964, pp. 1, 2, 8, 12; May 1964, p. 4A; June 1964, pp. 1, 3.

37. SSN, May 1964, p. 1A; Dunn, "School Desegregation in the South," 42; Rosenberg, *Hollow Hope*, 52.

38. SSN, May 1964, p. 1A; Rosenberg, *Hollow Hope*, 50 table 2.1; Wilkinson, *Brown to Bakke*, 102–14; Singleton v. Jackson Municipal Separate School District, 348 F. 2d 729 (5th Cir. 1965), 355 F. 2d 865 (5th Cir. 1966); United States v. Jefferson County Board of Education, 372 F. 2d 836 (5th Cir. 1966); Note, "Courts, HEW, and Southern School Desegregation," 335–39.

39. Wilkinson, *Brown to Bakke*, 6; Glickstein, "Impact of *Brown*," 55; Neier, *Limits of Litigation in Social Change*, 241–42; Canon, "Supreme Court as a Cheerleader," 648; Goldfield, *Black, White, and Southern*, 91–92; Sitkoff, *Struggle for*

Black Equality, 37–38; Norrell, "One Thing We Did Right," 70; Eskew, "Alabama Christian Movement for Human Rights," 11. See also Jones, "Desegregation of Urban Schools," 553; Pritchett, "Equal Protection and the Urban Majority," 869; Bains, "Birmingham, 1963," 159; Dittmer, "Politics of the Mississippi Movement," 67; Zalman, "Juricide," 303.

40. On the difficulty of measuring such indirect effects, see Rosenberg, *Hollow Hope*, 108; Handler, *Social Movements and the Legal System*, 210.

41. Goldstein, *Flag Burning and Free Speech*, 109–19; "A Slow Death amid Doctor-Family Conflict," *Wash. Post*, 16 June 1991, p. A1; Flemming, Bohte, & Wood, "Supreme Court's Influence on Attentiveness to Issues," 22, 32, 46, 52–53. See also McCann, *Rights at Work*, 59–60; Cain, *Rainbow Rights*, 179, 193.

42. Pettigrew, "Desegregation and Its Chances for Success," 341 table 3; Muse, *Ten Years of Prelude*, 16–17; Geraldine Gardner to Justice Douglas, 21 May 1954, Box 1150, Douglas Papers; *NYT*, 18 May 1954, p. 1; *Wash. Post*, 18 May 1954, p. 1; *Time*, 24 May 1954, pp. 21–22; Fleming, Bohte, & Wood, "Supreme Court's Influence on Attentiveness to Issues," 41–42; Canon, "Supreme Court as a Cheerleader," 648; Pritchett, "Equal Protection and the Urban Majority," 869. But see Rosenberg, *Hollow Hope*, 111–17.

43. *SSN*, Mar. 1956, p. 13; Apr. 1956, p. 1; Sept. 1956, pp. 1, 2; pages 324–25; *National Party Platforms*, ed. Porter & Johnson, 487, 504, 542; *NYT*, 13 Feb. 1956, p. 1; 3 Apr. 1956, p. 18; 26 Apr. 1956, p. 1; 16 Aug. 1956, p. 1; 20 Aug. 1956, pp. 1, 8; 21 Aug. 1956, pp. 1, 8, 15; *To Secure These Rights*, 65, 151–71; Martin, *Civil Rights and the Crisis of Liberalism*, 137–55.

44. *SSN*, Dec. 1956, p. 2; Sept. 1954, pp. 10, 12; Nov. 1954, p. 15; Feb. 1955, p. 14; Mar. 1955, p. 13; July 1955, pp. 3, 4, 11; Sept. 1955, p. 12; Oct. 1955, p. 12; Feb. 1956, p. 14; Mar. 1956, p. 16; Apr. 1956, p. 3; *NYT*, 21 Oct. 1956, p. 74.

45. James, "South's Own Civil War," 23–24; McMillen, *Citizens' Council*, 172–74; Daniel, *The South in the 1950s*, 184; Alvis, *Religion and Race*, 56–57; Manis, *Southern Civil Religions in Conflict*, 64–66; *SSN*, Apr. 1956, p. 1; Sept. 1956, p. 5; Oct. 1956, p. 13; *Wash. Post*, 19 May 1954, p. A8; pages 390–91, 394–97. See also Caro, *Lyndon Johnson*, 3:832, 837, 849–50.

46. Gallup, *Gallup Poll*, 2:1401, 1426; *SSN*, Apr. 1957, p. 5; Patterson, Brown, 80, 119; Pettigrew, "Desegregation and Its Chances for Success," 341 table 3; Thornbrough, "Breaking Racial Barriers," 327–30, 336–39; Woodward, *Strange Career of Jim Crow*, 149.

47. Anderson, *Eisenhower, Brownell, and the Congress*, 2–4, 24–25; Lawson, *Black Ballots*, 148–58; Woodward, "Great Civil Rights Debate," 284–85. See also James Reston, "Politics and Civil Rights," *NYT*, 24 July 1957, p. 13. But see Rosenberg, *Hollow Hope*, 117–19.

48. *SSN*, Aug. 1957, p. 10; *NYT*, 3 July 1957, pp. 1, 10; 4 July 1957, pp. 1, 20; 9 July 1957, pp. 1, 19; 10 July 1957, pp. 1, 14; 12 July 1957, pp. 1, 13; James Reston, "A Southern Victory," ibid., p. 13; 17 July 1954, pp. 1, 14; 19 July 1957, pp. 1, 5; 21 July 1957, pp. 1, 37; 25 July 1957, pp. 1, 12; 27 July 1957, pp. 1, 9; 2 Aug. 1957, pp. 1, 8; 3 Aug. 1957, pp. 1, 6; *Time*, 22 July 1957, p. 12; Woodward, "Great Civil Rights Debate," 286–91; Ambrose, *Eisenhower*, 2:406–12; Burk, *Eisenhower Administration and Black Civil Rights*, 222–26; Fite, *Richard B. Russell*, 336–43; Caro, *Lyndon Johnson*, 3:870–1012.

49. Gellhorn, "Decade of Desegregation," 16; Tushnet, "Significance of *Brown*," 177; Greenberg, "Supreme Court, Civil Rights, and Civil Dissonance," 1522–24; Patterson, *Grand Expectations*, 390; Dred Scott v. Sandford, 60 U.S. (19

How.) 393 (1857); Engel v. Vitale, 370 U.S. 421 (1962); Furman v. Georgia, 408 U.S. 238 (1972); Roe v. Wade, 410 U.S. 113 (1973); Bowers v. Hardwick, 478 U.S. 186 (1986); Fehrenbacher, Dred Scott *Case*, 561–67; Jeffries, *Lewis F. Powell*, 354–59; Rosenberg, *Hollow Hope*, 188, 341–42; Klarman, "What's So Great about Constitutionalism?" 176–78.

50. Speech of Rep. James C. Davis of Georgia, 31 Mar. 1956, in "Extension of Remarks of Rep. John Bell Williams," *Congressional Record*, 23 Apr. 1956, NAACP, part 20, reel 13, fr. 347; SSN, June 1955, p. 9; Jacobstein, *Segregation Factor in the Florida Democratic Gubernatorial Election of 1956*, 7–8; Citizens' Council Member to Charles Gomillion, 26 Feb. 1959, NAACP, part 20, reel 6, fr. 11; Sen. James Eastland, "The South Will Fight!" *Arkansas Faith* (Dec. 1955): 6–10, 13, 27, ibid., reel 13, frs. 301–5, 308, 322; speech by Sen. George Smathers, 10 Oct. 1957, ibid., reel 6, frs. 826–29; SSN, Oct. 1954, p. 9; Mar. 1955, p. 14; Apr. 1955, p. 5; July 1955, p. 4; Aug. 1955, p. 13; Dec. 1955, pp. 11, 14; June 1956, pp. 11, 16; Aug. 1956, p. 10; Feb. 1957, p. 3; Mar. 1957, p. 3; Apr. 1957, p. 13; Aug. 1957, p. 13; June 1958, p. 10; Dec. 1960, p. 9; Peltason, *Fifty-Eight Lonely Men*, 107–8; Brady, *Black Monday*, 39–40; Rosenberg, "African-American Rights after *Brown*," 214; Scheingold, "Constitutional Rights and Social Change," 79.

51. *Wash. Post*, 18 May 1954, pp. 1, 2; Muse, *Ten Years of Prelude*, 16, 18–19; SSN, Sept. 1956, pp. 1–2; Gallup, *Gallup Poll*, 2:1249, 3:1616; Burk, *Eisenhower Administration and Black Civil Rights*, 202; Jenkins, "Problems Incident to Racial Integration," 412; LaFarge, "Cooperative Acceptance of Racial Integration," 431.

52. Gallup, *Gallup Poll*, 2:1526–27; Jenkins, "Problems Incident to Racial Integration," 420; Nabrit, "Appraisal of Court Action," 422; Symposium, "Courts and Racial Integration in Education," 435 (Dent).

53. Report of Secretary to NAACP Board of Directors, Sept. 1955, p. 5, part 1, reel 2, fr. 786; "Directives to the Branches Adopted by Emergency South-Wide NAACP Conference," *Crisis* 62 (June–July 1955): 339–40, 381; Opotowsky, "Dixie Dynamite," 12–13 (frs. 679–80); SSN, Sept. 1954, pp. 8, 10–12; Oct. 1954, pp. 2, 3, 7; Nov. 1954, p. 13; June 1955, p. 5; July 1955, pp. 6, 11; August 1955, p. 17; Sept. 1955, pp. 1, 5, 6, 10, 16; Oct. 1955, pp. 3, 8; Nov. 1955, pp. 6, 12; *Chicago Defender*, 18 Sept. 1954, p. 3; Dittmer, *Struggle for Civil Rights in Mississippi*, 44–45, 50–52; McMillen, *Citizens' Council*, 28–30, 41–44, 74–77, 208–11; Fairclough, *Civil Rights Struggle in Louisiana*, 188; Thornton, "Montgomery Bus Boycott," 194 n. 33; Bolton, "Mississippi's School Equalization Program," 809–10.

54. SSN, Sept. 1954, p. 7; June 1955, p. 11; Burns, *Montgomery Bus Boycott*, 58; Garrow, *Bearing the Cross*, 15; Manis, *Fred Shuttlesworth*, 104, 121–22, 125; Jones, "Fred L. Shuttlesworth," 136; Eskew, "Alabama Christian Movement for Human Rights," 14–16, 21, 38, 43–45; Dittmer, *Struggle for Civil Rights in Mississippi*, 53; Chafe, *Civilities and Civil Rights*, 84.

55. SSN, June 1964, p. 2; Greenberg, *Crusaders in the Courts*, 12; Wilkinson, *Brown to Bakke*, 49; Kluger, *Simple Justice*, 710; Clark, "Racial Justice in Education," 95; Kizer, "Impact of *Brown v. Board of Education*," 18. Cf. Patterson, Brown, 221. But see Rosenberg, *Hollow Hope*, 131–34.

56. Muse, *Ten Years of Prelude*, 1, 19; *Chicago Defender*, 22 May 1954, p. 5; Morris, *Civil Rights Movement*, 81; Lomax, *Negro Revolt*, 73–74; Tushnet, "Comment," 122–23; Fairclough, *Southern Christian Leadership Conference*, 40; Patterson, Brown, xiv, 70–71, 119; Hampton & Fayer, *Oral History of the Civil Rights Movement*, 76; King, *Stride toward Freedom*, 191; Manis, *Fred Shuttlesworth*, 79; Daniel, *The South in*

the 1950s, 180–81; *SSN*, June 1959, p. 15; June 1960, p. 16. See also Canon, "Supreme Court and Policy Reform," 224.

57. Burns, *Montgomery Bus Boycott*, xii, 4, 14, 16, 25, 95–96, 117–18, 124–27, 134–35, 137, 152–53, 161–62, 169, 177, 186, 195, 199, 201–4, 209, 213, 218, 230, 243–44, 246, 256–57, 281–82, 314, 316, 318, 320, 329–31; Muriel Symington, letter to the editor, *New York Post*, 9 Apr. 1956, NAACP, part 20, reel 5, fr. 274; Wilkins to Branches, telegram, 23 Feb. 1956, ibid., fr. 130; NAACP Press Release, 28 Feb. 1956, ibid., fr. 163; NAACP Press Release, 5 Mar. 1956, ibid., fr. 176; Protestant Council of the Five Towns and Rockaways, resolution, 1 Mar. 1956, ibid., frs. 220–21; Women's International League for Peace and Freedom, resolution, June 1956, ibid., fr. 401; Morris, *Civil Rights Movement*, 51–63, 130, 159–60; Garrow, *Bearing the Cross*, 78; King, *Stride toward Freedom*, 184, 187; Thornton, "Montgomery Bus Boycott," 230–34.

58. Burns, *Montgomery Bus Boycott*, 58; Garrow, "Revisionist Devaluing of Brown," 154–57; Garrow, *Bearing the Cross*, 15; Hampton & Fayer, *Oral History of the Civil Rights Movement*, xxvii; Weisbrot, *Freedom Bound*, 14; McMahon & Paris, "Politics of Rights Revisited," 67–78. But cf. Patterson, Brown, 119; Rosenberg, *Hollow Hope*, 134–38.

59. Burns, *Montgomery Bus Boycott*, 19, 26, 61–73, 82, 92–93, 97–99, 100–101, 106–9, 110, 229–30; Branch, *Parting the Waters*, 144, 151; Garrow, *Bearing the Cross*, 21–22, 25–26, 31, 52; Rosenberg, *Hollow Hope*, 137; Thornton, "Montgomery Bus Boycott," 211 n. 49, 229. See also Glennon, "Montgomery Bus Boycott," 70.

60. Morris, *Civil Rights Movement*, ix–x, 17–25, 58; Fairclough, *Civil Rights Struggle in Louisiana*, 156–61; King, *Stride toward Freedom*, 75; Sinclair, "Civil Rights Struggle in Baton Rouge," 349–56.

61. Burns, *Montgomery Bus Boycott*, 19, 78–80, 99, 113–14, 128, 147, 180–81, 188, 208, 246; Fairclough, *Civil Rights Struggle in Louisiana*, 161–62; King, *Stride toward Freedom*, 126–27, 151; Thornton, "Montgomery Bus Boycott," 213–15, 230–33.

62. Gayle v. Browder, 352 U.S. 903 (1956); Burns, *Montgomery Bus Boycott*, 27, 299–300; Morris, *Civil Rights Movement*, 62–63; King, *Stride toward Freedom*, 64, 158–60; Tushnet, *Thurgood Marshall*, 304–5; Glennon, "Montgomery Bus Boycott," 60–61, 89, 93; Thornton, "Montgomery Bus Boycott," 229; Garrow, "Revisionist Devaluing of *Brown*," 157.

63. Fairclough, *Southern Christian Leadership Conference*, 39–40, 48–49; Fairclough, "Preachers and the People," 433, 437; Garrow, *Bearing the Cross*, 93, 103–4, 120–21; Eskew, *But for Birmingham*, 27–28, 37; Morris, *Civil Rights Movement*, 63–68, 100, 111, 177, 188–94; Oppenheimer, *Sit-In Movement*, 33–35, 125; Laue, *Direct Action and Desegregation*, 70–71; Norrell, *Civil Rights Movement in Tuskegee*, 93–110; Rosenberg, *Hollow Hope*, 133–34; *SSN*, May 1957, p. 5; June 1957, p. 16; Sept. 1957, p. 2; Sept. 1958, p. 15; Aug. 1959, p. 3; Nov. 1959, pp. 5, 11; Apr. 1960, p. 10; *Crisis* 65 (Dec. 1958): 612–13; "Role of the NAACP in the 'Sit-Ins'," May 1960, p. 1, NAACP, part 21, reel 22, fr. 113. See also Palumbos, "Baltimore Civil Rights Movement," 454–56, 463–64. This is not to say that important local organizing did not continue. It clearly did, and it laid the groundwork for massive direct-action protest in the 1960s. See Morris, *Civil Rights Movement*, 40–76, 100–119, 174–95; Payne, *Mississippi Freedom Struggle*, 60, 113; Dittmer, *Struggle for Civil Rights in Mississippi*, 85.

64. *SSN*, June 1960, p. 10; Apr. 1960, pp. 1, 2, 3–6, 10, 13–16; Report of the Secretary to NAACP Board of Directors, Feb. 1960, p. 4, NAACP, part 1, supp. 1956–1960, reel 2, fr. 309; Oppenheimer, *Sit-In Movement*, 36–59, 117–81; Lomax, *Negro Revolt*, 121–31; Morris, *Civil Rights Movement*, 195–213; Dittmer, *Struggle for Civil Rights in*

Mississippi, 86–89; Laue, *Direct Action and Desegregation*, 76–77; "Lunch Counter Protests Spread," SSN, Mar. 1960, pp. 1–5; May 1960, pp. 4–5, 10–12, 14; Sept. 1960, p. 11; Nov. 1960, p. 15; May 1961, p. 15; *Time*, 14 Mar. 1960, p. 21; *Newsweek*, 22 Feb. 1960, pp. 27–28; NYT, 21 Apr. 1960, p. 23; *Crisis* 67 (May 1960): 313–19; "Role of the NAACP in the 'Sit-Ins'," May 1960, p. 1, NAACP, part 21, reel 22, fr. 113; NAACP Press Release, 3 Mar. 1960, ibid., fr. 223; NAACP Press Release, 17 Mar. 1960, ibid., frs. 229–30; NAACP Press Release, 24 Mar. 1960, ibid., frs. 234–36; List of NAACP Branch, Youth Councils, and College Chapters Participating in Picketing Demonstrations, 25 May 1960, ibid., frs. 272–82.

65. Garrow, *Bearing the Cross*, 154–61, 173–219, 231–64; Branch, *Parting the Waters*, 412–561, 601–32, 725–802; Eskew, *But for Birmingham*, 217–97; Payne, *Mississippi Freedom Struggle*, 104–31; Dittmer, *Struggle for Civil Rights in Mississippi*, chs. 5–8; Weisbrot, *Freedom Bound*, 55–76; Farmer, *Lay Bare the Heart*, 195–210; Manis, *Fred Shuttlesworth*, 343–90.

66. Morris, *Civil Rights Movement*, 4, 8, 12, 19, 44, 47–50, 74–79, 87, 196–205, 211–13; Payne, *Mississippi Freedom Struggle*, 40–41, 66, 124, 202–3, 416–17; Oppenheimer, *Sit-In Movement*, 12–13, 16, 21, 53, 86, 94–97, 118, 120–24, 129; Lomax, *Negro Revolt*, 4–5, 130–31; Sitkoff, *Struggle for Black Equality*, 84–85; Fairclough, "Historians and the Civil Rights Movement," 396–97; Fairclough, "Preachers and the People," 440; Von Eschen, Kirk, & Pinard, "Conditions of Direct Action," 312–15, 322; Lewis, "Origins and Causes of the Civil Rights Movement," 3, 7; Walker, *Sit-Ins in Atlanta*, 1–5; Chafe, *Civilities and Civil Rights*, 22–23, 115–17, 212; Eskew, "Alabama Christian Movement for Human Rights," 68–69, 77; Laue, *Direct Action and Desegregation*, 73–76; Wynn, *Second World War*, 122, 127; Searles & Williams, "Negro College Students' Participation in Sit-Ins," 216–28; *Time*, 21 Mar. 1960, p. 21.

67. Fried, *McCarthy Era*, 29–36, 164–65, 175–78, 193–94; Norrell, "One Thing We Did Right," 69, 71; Bartley, *Massive Resistance*, 185–89; McMillen, *Citizens' Council*, 195–98, 269; Norrell, *Civil Rights Movement in Tuskegee*, 105; Sullivan, "Southern Reformers," 98–99; Laue, *Direct Action and Desegregation*, 81; Fairclough, "Historians and the Civil Rights Movement," 389–90; Fairclough, *Civil Rights Struggle in Louisiana*, 136–37; Sitkoff, *Struggle for Black Equality*, 17; Smith, "America's Most Important Problem," 166–67; Marable, *Race, Reform, and Rebellion*, 18–32; Horne, *Civil Rights Congress*, 99–130.

68. Burns, *Montgomery Bus Boycott*, 256, 343; Lomax, *Negro Revolt*, 76–77; Carson, *SNCC*, 16; Isaacs, *New World of Negro Americans*, 50–54, 290–93; Sitkoff, *Struggle for Black Equality*, 83; Plummer, *Rising Wind*, 285, 289, 315; Rosenberg, *Hollow Hope*, 144–45; Payne, *Mississippi Freedom Struggle*, 49–50; Garrow, *Bearing the Cross*, 54, 63, 71; King, *Why We Can't Wait*, 21–22, 83; Roy Wilkins, press conference transcript, pp. 7–8, NAACP, part 21, reel 13, frs. 65–66.

69. Oppenheimer, *Sit-In Movement*, 36–37, 40–43; Von Eschen, Kirk, & Pinard, "Conditions of Direct Action," 318; "Lunch Counter Protests Spread," SSN, Mar. 1960, pp. 1–5; Apr. 1960, p. 6; Hampton & Fayer, *Oral History of the Civil Rights Movement*, 56–57; Farmer, *Lay Bare the Heart*, 192; Sitkoff, *Struggle for Black Equality*, 91; Laue, *Direct Action and Desegregation*, 75–76, 81. Cf. Burns, *Montgomery Bus Boycott*, 18.

70. Answer to interrogatory, *NAACP v. Almond*, 13 Aug. 1957, pp. 1–2, NAACP, part 20, reel 12, frs. 958–59; Lomax, *Negro Revolt*, 109; Payne, *Mississippi Freedom Struggle*, 87. See also *Crisis* 63 (Feb. 1956): 105–6.

71. Morris, *Civil Rights Movement*, 38; Fairclough, "Preachers and the People," 437–40; Greene, "School Desegregation," 3, 13–15, 30–31, 36–37. See also King, *Why We Can't Wait*, 41.

72. "The Role of Law in Our Struggle: Its Advantages and Limitations," working paper no. 7, in Burns, *Montgomery Bus Boycott*, 339–41; Fairclough, *Southern Christian Leadership Conference*, 44–47; Morris, *Civil Rights Movement*, 38, 120–24; Garrow, "Commentary," 60–62; Dittmer, "Politics of the Mississippi Movement," 71–72; Garrow, *Bearing the Cross*, 78, 91–92, 103, 134.

73. John A. Morsell, Memorandum on Program for 1960 Convention, 2 May 1960, p. 2, NAACP, part 22, reel 9, fr. 216; Tushnet, *Thurgood Marshall*, 305; Dittmer, "Politics of the Mississippi Movement," 72; Patricia Simon to Gloster Current, 24 Apr. 1958, p. 2, NAACP, part 22, reel 9, fr. 624; Morris, *Civil Rights Movement*, 35–37, 124–25, 186–87; Garrow, "Commentary," 56; Morsell to Mary McLucas, 28 Sept. 1960, part 20, reel 11, fr. 706; *Amsterdam News* (New York), 1 June 1957, ibid., part 21, reel 13, fr. 8; Lomax, *Negro Revolt*, 101–5, 121–23; Farmer, *Lay Bare the Heart*, 189–92, 216. See also Greene, "School Desegregation," 25.

74. Morsell to Moon, memo, 3 May 1960, p. 3, NAACP, part 22, reel 9, fr. 213; Carter to Wilkins, memo, 2 Mar. 1960, p. 2, ibid., fr. 179; Morsell, Memorandum on Program for 1960 Convention, 2 May 1960, pp. 1–2, ibid., frs. 215–16; Wilkins to Hon. Theodore Spaulding, 28 Mar. 1961, part 21, reel 22, fr. 19; Carter to Morsell, 5 May 1960, part 22, reel 9, frs. 209–10; Wilkins to Kivie Kaplan, 24 Apr. 1961, part 21, reel 22, frs. 8–9; NAACP, Special Report on Sitdowns, ibid., frs. 69–104; Wilkins, transcript of press conference, p. 5, ibid., reel 13, fr. 63; Patterson, Brown, 121–22; Morris, *Civil Rights Movement*, 198, 216, 317 n. 64; Payne, *Mississippi Freedom Struggle*, 61–62; Tushnet, *Thurgood Marshall*, 309–10.

75. Morsell, Memorandum on Program for 1960 Convention, 2 May 1960, p. 2, NAACP, part 22, reel 9, fr. 215; SSN, Mar. 1960, p. 3; undated and unidentified memorandum (probably fall 1961), part 22, reel 3, frs. 374–76; SSN, May 1960, pp. 5, 6; NAACP Press Release, 17 Mar. 1960, part 21, reel 22, fr. 229; SSN, Apr. 1960, pp. 3, 4, 9; May 1961, p. 15; Wilkins, press conference transcript, part 21, reel 13, fr. 65; NAACP Press Release, 10 Mar. 1960, part 20, reel 12, frs. 101–2; Robert W. Saunders to Wilkins, memo, 16 June 1961, part 21, reel 22, frs. 47–48; Oppenheimer, *Sit-In Movement*, 120, 142–43, 170–71, 178; Lomax, *Negro Revolt*, 96–97; Dittmer, *Struggle for Civil Rights in Mississippi*, 163–65; Wolf, *Greensboro Sit-Ins*, 150–52.

76. Farmer, *Lay Bare the Heart*, 13–14; Medgar Evers to Gordon Carey, 4 May 1961, pp. 2–3, NAACP, part 21, reel 12, frs. 230–31; Wilkins to Presidents and Advisors of NAACP College Chapters, memo, 26 May 1961, ibid., fr. 242; Dittmer, "Politics of the Mississippi Movement," 81; Clarence A. Laws to Mrs. D. A. Combre, 3 Oct. 1961, part 21, reel 12, frs. 279–80; Dittmer, *Struggle for Civil Rights in Mississippi*, 99; Weisbrot, *Freedom Bound*, 55–56; Fairclough, *Civil Rights Struggle in Louisiana*, 282–83; SSN, July 1961, p. 6.

77. Morris, *Civil Rights Movement*, 123–24; Lomax, *Negro Revolt*, 112–13, 115, 152; Burns, *Montgomery Bus Boycott*, 329–31, 335–36; Morsell to McLucas, 28 Sept. 1960, NAACP, part 20, reel 11, fr. 706; Branch, *Parting the Waters*, 598; Payne, *Mississippi Freedom Struggle*, 67–72, 87–88, 235, 281–83, 332–33, 404; Spann, *Race against the Court*, 88; *Daily Oklahoman*, 8 May 1964, NAACP, part 21, reel 22, fr. 57.

78. SSN, June 1964, p. 2; King, *Why We Can't Wait*, 42; King, *Stride toward Freedom*, 33–34; Garrow, *Bearing the Cross*, 78, 91–92, 134; Fairclough, *Southern Christian Leadership Conference*, 44, 47, 64–65.

79. Pages 424–26; Burns, *Montgomery Bus Boycott*, 31–32.

80. Patterson, Brown, 121; Sitkoff, *Struggle for Black Equality*, 37–38, 69–70, 83–84; Oppenheimer, *Sit-In Movement*, 25; Walker, *Sit-Ins in Atlanta*, 3–4; Dunbar, "Latest Reform of the South," 252; Scheingold, "Constitutional Rights and Social Change," 80.

81. "A Clear-Cut Victory," *Afro-American* (Baltimore), 11 June 1955, p. 4; James L. Hicks, "Voters Vineyard," ibid.; SSN, Sept. 1955, p. 1; July 1955, p. 16; Aug. 1955, pp. 6–9; July 1956, p. 7; *Crisis* 62 (Aug.–Sept. 1955): 395; Lomax, *Negro Revolt*, 74–75; Tushnet, *Thurgood Marshall*, 232, 267–68; Fairclough, *Civil Rights Struggle in Louisiana*, 165–67; Dittmer, "Politics of the Mississippi Movement," 69; Patterson, Brown, 71. Cf. Southern, "Judge Waring's Fight against Segregation," 219.

82. King, *Why We Can't Wait*, 18–19; SSN, Apr. 1960, pp. 2, 13; Sept. 1960, p. 12; Wilkins to Presidents of NAACP Branches et al., memo, 2 Feb. 1961, NAACP, part 21, reel 22, fr. 6; Wilkins, press conference transcript, pp. 7–8, ibid., reel 13, frs. 65–66; Farmer, *Lay Bare the Heart*, 13.

83. SSN, Nov. 1962, pp. 1, 17; Feb. 1961, p. 1; July 1962, p. 1; Walter Jones, "I Speak for the White Race," *Montgomery Advertiser*, 4 Mar. 1957, NAACP, part 20, reel 4, fr. 436; NAACP Press Release, 11 Aug. 1961, p. 2, ibid., reel 5, fr. 48; SSN, Apr. 1959, p. 3; Rosenberg, *Hollow Hope*, 91; Lomax, *Negro Revolt*, 75–80, 155, 164–77; Lusky, "Nullification," 1163, 1166; Manis, *Fred Shuttlesworth*, 129; Dittmer, "Politics of the Mississippi Movement," 72; pages 354–59.

84. Wilkins to W. Lester Banks, 20 Aug. 1957, NAACP, part 20, reel 12, fr. 982; Muse, *Ten Years of Prelude*, 39, 40; open letter from four black ministers, n.d., p. 2, part 20, reel 11, fr. 185; Talmadge, *You and Segregation*, 34–36; SSN, July 1958, p. 16; Dec. 1956, p. 8; Morris, *Civil Rights Movement*, 26, 35; Bartley, *Massive Resistance*, 185–88, 212–13; SSN, Nov. 1955, p. 15; Mar. 1956, p. 9; Aug. 1958, p. 8; Eugene Cook, "The Ugly Truth about the NAACP," part 20, reel 13, frs. 838–45; Resolution of Mississippi State Senate, 6 Mar. 1958, ibid., reel 3, fr. 611; Associated Press news story, 16 Jan. 1959, ibid., reel 6, fr. 637; Tushnet, *Thurgood Marshall*, 305; page 392.

85. Wilkins to Texas Branches, 12 Dec. 1957, NAACP, part 20, reel 12, frs. 504–5; SSN, Apr. 1956, pp. 12, 14; Wilkins to Carter Wesley, 31 May 1957, part 20, reel 12, frs. 364–68; Wilkins, affidavit, n.d., ibid., reel 4, frs. 635–37; NAACP Press Release, 25 July 1956, ibid., frs. 639–40; Carter, memo, 6 Jan. 1960, part 22, reel 9, frs. 163–64; *Wash. Post*, 22 Dec. 1959, part 20, reel 13, frs. 220–21; NAACP Press Release, 7 Jan. 1960, ibid., fr. 224; Wilkins to Evers, 31 July 1956, ibid., reel 1, frs. 579–80; *Pittsburgh Courier*, 21 June 1956, ibid., fr. 668; S. W. Boynton, affidavit, 28 July 1956, ibid., reel 4, frs. 425–26; open letter from four black ministers, n.d., p. 2, part 20, reel 11, fr. 185; Daisy Bates to William Rogers, telegram, 8 July 1959, ibid., reel 6, fr. 372; Mrs. L. C. Bates, Statement to Press Conference, 1 Nov. 1957, ibid., frs. 498–99; SSN, Nov. 1956, p. 8; Dec. 1956, pp. 8, 10; Jan. 1957, pp. 1–2, 16; July 1957, p. 9; Dec. 1957, p. 2; Jan. 1958, p. 9; Feb. 1958, p. 12; Jan. 1959, p. 14; Aug. 1959, pp. 6, 13; Feb. 1962, p. 14; Murphy, "Anti-NAACP Laws," 371–90; Peltason, *Fifty-Eight Lonely Men*, 65–78; Tushnet, *Thurgood Marshall*, 272–300; Bartley, *Massive Resistance*, 212–20; Payne, *Mississippi Freedom Struggle*, 41–42; Dittmer, *Struggle for Civil Rights in Mississippi*, 46–47.

86. Wilkins to Board of Directors, memo, 7 May 1957, NAACP, part 20, reel 12, fr. 296; Evers to Current, 2 Oct. 1956, ibid., reel 14, fr. 96; Current to Wilkins, memorandum, 18 June 1957, ibid., reel 12, frs. 410–14; Francis L. Williams to Current, 20 June 1958, part 22, reel 9, fr. 650; SSN, May 1956, p. 12; Nov. 1956, p. 15; Jan. 1957, pp. 1–2;

June 1957, p. 2; Dec. 1959, p. 15; NAACP Press Release, 25 Oct. 1956, part 20, reel 12, fr. 198; Tushnet, *Thurgood Marshall*, 284–91, 300; Wilkins to NAACP Members, June 1957, part 20, reel 12, fr. 525; Wilkins to Texas Branch Presidents, 12 Dec. 1957, ibid., frs. 504–5; Carter to Wilkins, memorandum, 18 July 1957, ibid., frs. 462–65; *Arkansas Gazette*, 28 Feb. 1958, ibid., reel 6, fr. 573; Morris, *Civil Rights Movement*, 33–34; Fairclough, *Civil Rights Struggle in Louisiana*, 209–11, 225–26; Greenberg, *Crusaders in the Courts*, 220–21; Peltason, *Fifty-Eight Lonely Men*, 76–77; Lau, "Clarendon County," 25; Baker, "Ambiguous Legacies," 179–80; Lawson, "Florida Legislative Investigation Committee," 316.

87. Morris, *Civil Rights Movement*, 34, 38, 40–76, 87, 132–34, 178–79; Fairclough, *Southern Christian Leadership Conference*, 22–23, 45–46; Fairclough, *Civil Rights Struggle in Louisiana*, 297–98; Manis, *Fred Shuttlesworth*, 94–99; Carter to Wilkins, Memo re: Cooperating with Southern Christian Leadership Conference, 3 Feb. 1960, NAACP, part 22, reel 9, fr. 175; *Montgomery Advertiser*, 28 Nov. 1957, part 21, reel 13, frs. 9, 11.

88. Goldfield, *Black, White, and Southern*, 48–49; Dallek, *Lyndon Johnson*, 1:368–70; Black, *Southern Governors and Civil Rights*, 37–39, 41–45; Bartley & Graham, *Southern Politics*, 25, 33–37, 50; Howard, "Louisiana," 546–47; Sherrill, *Gothic Politics in the Deep South*, 77–78; Pleasants & Burns, *1950 Senate Race in North Carolina*, 6; Edsall & Williams, "North Carolina," 370–71, 373.

89. Sims, *James E. Folsom*, 26, 30, 58, 154, 163–66, 168, 171; SSN, Sept. 1955, p. 3; Feb. 1955, p. 2; Frady, *Wallace*, 102–5; Norrell, *Civil Rights Movement in Tuskegee*, 64, 72–74, 86; Sherrill, *Gothic Politics in the Deep South*, 275; Strong, "Alabama," 446–49.

90. Heard, *Two-Party South?* 20–28, 148, 164, 246; Bartley & Graham, *Southern Politics*, 85–86; Bartley, *Massive Resistance*, 32–37; Ader, "Why the Dixiecrats Failed," 366–69; Kirkendall, "Election of 1948," 3140–41; Key, *Southern Politics*, 339–42, 671. But cf. Frederickson, *Dixiecrat Revolt*, 167, 184–85, 198–216.

91. Pages 247, 261; Brooks, "Winning the Peace," 586–87; Bartley, *Massive Resistance*, 40–43.

92. Pleasants & Burns, *1950 Senate Race in North Carolina*, 24, 42–43, 76, 89, 91, 96, 98–99, 122, 129–32, 147–48, 171, 218–19, 263; Sherrill, *Gothic Politics in the Deep South*, 147–51; Dauer, "Florida," 133; Bartley & Graham, *Southern Politics*, 52; Edsall & Williams, "North Carolina," 373–74; Frederickson, *Dixiecrat Revolt*, 202–3; Crispell, *George Armistead Smathers*, 54–74; Ambrose, *Nixon*, 1:213–23; Fried, *McCarthy Era*, 129–30.

93. Pleasants & Burns, *1950 Senate Race in North Carolina*, 12, 25–27, 41–42, 56–57, 85, 151, 189, 216, 219–24, 226–28, 244, 255, 263, 268–69; Lubell, *Future of American Politics*, 101–6; Edsall & Williams, "North Carolina," 375; pages 260–61.

94. SSN, Jan. 1955, p. 12; Wright, "Desegregation of Public Accommodations in Louisville," 192; Chafe, *Civilities and Civil Rights*, 32–40; Lewis, *In Their Own Interests*, 193–97; Korstad & Lichtenstein, "Early Civil Rights Movement," 793; Freyer, *Little Rock Crisis*, 20–21; Norrell, *Civil Rights Movement in Tuskegee*, 60–62, 73–76, 86; Thornton, "Montgomery Bus Boycott," 175, 180 n. 17; Thornton, "Municipal Politics," 45, 48; Dittmer, *Struggle for Civil Rights in Mississippi*, 28, 34; Payne, *Mississippi Freedom Struggle*, 26–27; Fairclough, *Civil Rights Struggle in Louisiana*, 106, 165, 171; Adelson, *Brushing Back Jim Crow*, 136–37; Woodward, "New Reconstruction," 503; "Deep in Dixie: Race Progress," *U.S. News & World Report*, 26 Feb. 1954, pp. 53–54.

95. SSN, Sept. 1954, pp. 2, 5, 10, 13, 14; McCain, "Segregation Decision," 371–72, 376, 378; Woodward, "New Reconstruction," 503; Statement of Dr. Chester C. Travelstead to Delegate Assembly for Civil Rights, 4 Mar. 1956, p. 2, NAACP, part 21, reel 12, fr. 198 (hereafter, Travelstead Statement); Workman, "Deep South," 94; Muse, *Ten Years of Prelude*, 17, 20–21, 124; Chafe, *Civilities and Civil Rights*, 16; Peltason, *Fifty-Eight Lonely Men*, 31–32; Dittmer, *Struggle for Civil Rights in Mississippi*, 37; Fairclough, *Civil Rights Struggle in Louisiana*, 167; Kluger, *Simple Justice*, 711; Tomberlin, "*Brown* Decision," 24–29, 32, 35; NYT, 18 May 1954, pp. 1, 20; 19 May 1954, pp. 1, 18, 20.

96. *Chicago Defender*, 25 Sept. 1954, p. 3; SSN, Sept. 1954, pp. 5, 8, 12, 13; Oct. 1954, p. 6; Dec. 1954, p. 6; Jan. 1955, p. 10; NYT, 18 May 1954, pp. 1, 20; Workman, "Deep South," 97; Muse, *Ten Years of Prelude*, 20–22, 24; Patterson, Brown, 78; McCain, "Segregation Decision," 381–83.

97. Geyer, "'New' Ku Klux Klan," 139; SSN, Feb. 1956, p. 6; Jan. 1955, p. 2; July 1955, p. 1; Aug. 1955, p. 17; Sept. 1955, p. 6; Oct. 1955, p. 3; Nov. 1955, p. 11; Jan. 1956, pp. 1, 2; Mar. 1956, pp. 1, 6–7, 9, 10, 14; Apr. 1956, pp. 1, 5, 9, 14; June 1956, p. 10; Sept. 1956, p. 15; Oct. 1956, p. 2; May 1964, pp. 1B, 5B; Halberstam, "Citizens' Councils," 293–302; Opotowsky, "Dixie Dynamite," 1–19 (frs. 670–86); McMillen, *Citizens' Council*, 19–31, 42–50, 59–68, 74–77, 268–69; Workman, "Deep South," 99–102; McCauley, "Be It Enacted," 130–46; Dittmer, *Struggle for Civil Rights in Mississippi*, 50–51; Carter, *George Wallace*, 83–84; Muse, *Ten Years of Prelude*, 62–72; Lubell, *White and Black*, 89–92.

98. Muse, *Ten Years of Prelude*, 161, 168; SSN, Feb. 1959, p. 11; Nov. 1954, p. 15; July 1956, p. 3; Oct. 1959, p. 3; July 1957, p. 3; James, "South's Own Civil War," 23; Opotowsky, "Dixie Dynamite," 18 (fr. 685); SSN, Jan. 1956, p. 12; Mar. 1956, p. 13; Apr. 1956, p. 11; May 1956, p. 1; June 1956, pp. 1, 2; Aug. 1956, p. 5; Apr. 1957, pp. 3, 4; May 1957, p. 12; Aug. 1957, p. 2; June 1961, p. 4; May 1964, pp. 1B, 5B; "Able and Willing," *Montgomery Advertiser*, 8 July 1956, NAACP, part 20, reel 13, frs. 373–74; Bartley, *Massive Resistance*, 68, 192, 247.

99. Hamilton Basso, letter to the editor, NYT, 10 Apr. 1955, p. 10E; SSN, Apr. 1955, p. 3; Nov. 1959, p. 16; May 1958, p. 5; Fairclough, *Civil Rights Struggle in Louisiana*, 153; Pettigrew, "Desegregation and Its Chances for Success," 341 table 3.

100. Jackson draft concurrence, School Segregation Cases, 15 Mar. 1954, p. 3, case file: Segregation Cases, Box 184, Jackson Papers; Burns, *Montgomery Bus Boycott*, 208.

101. Tumin, "Readiness and Resistance to Desegregation," 256; Greeley & Sheatsley, "Attitudes toward Racial Integration," 14; Brink & Harris, *Negro Revolution*, 148, 161–63; Lawson, *Black Ballots*, 148, 179–80, 345; Peltason, *Fifty-Eight Lonely Men*, 246–47; Lubell, *White and Black*, 108 table VI; SSN, May 1958, p. 5; July 1959, p. 7; Mar. 1960, p. 5.

102. Rice, *Ku Klux Klan in American Politics*, 118–20; Muse, *Ten Years of Prelude*, 45–46; Morris, *Civil Rights Movement*, 139; Payne, *Mississippi Freedom Struggle*, 114; pages 382–84, 424.

103. SSN, Dec. 1954, p. 8; Mar. 1956, p. 14; Nov. 1956, p. 15; Jan. 1957, p. 12; Dec. 1957, p. 8; Mar. 1958, p. 13; Apr. 1958, p. 5; May 1958, p. 10; Aug. 1958, p. 13; Dec. 1959, p. 8; Apr. 1960, p. 8; Harper v. Virginia, 383 U.S. 663 (1966); McMillen, *Citizens' Council*, 216–17, 219, 223–26, 320; Dittmer, *Struggle for Civil Rights in Mississippi*, 52–54, 70–71; Payne, *Mississippi Freedom Struggle*, 35–39; Fairclough, *Civil Rights Struggle in Louisiana*, 198, 206–7, 226–27; Vines, "Wholesale Purge," 39–46; Ogden, *Poll Tax in the South*, 215, 229–30, 235–38, 289; NAACP Press Release, 1 Nov. 1956,

part 20, reel 3, frs. 358–59; Memorandum on the Possibility of Unseating the Mississippi Congressional Delegation, Jan. 1956, pp. 1–2, ibid., frs. 577–78; "Are You Curious about Mississippi?" 20 Jan. 1961, pp. 2–3, ibid., reel 2, frs. 173–74.

104. SSN, Jan. 1956, p. 15; Oct. 1954, p. 13; July 1956, p. 8; Aug. 1956, p. 11; Oct. 1956, pp. 1, 5; Dec. 1956, p. 15; Feb. 1957, pp. 1–3, 16; Mar. 1957, p. 8; May 1957, p. 13; Nov. 1957, p. 16; Dec. 1958, p. 8; Travelstead Statement, 2 (fr. 198); Parham, "Halls of Ivy," 170–72; Muse, *Ten Years of Prelude*, 53–54; pages 254–55.

105. Tygiel, *Baseball's Great Experiment*, 275–78; Eskew, *But for Birmingham*, 105–6; Henderson, "Mississippi State University Basketball Controversy," 831; SSN, Jan. 1956, pp. 6, 10; Mar. 1956, p. 5; May 1956, p. 12; July 1956, p. 8; Aug. 1956, p. 11; Dec. 1956, p. 7; Feb. 1957, p. 13; Apr. 1957, p. 13; Dec. 1958, p. 8; Mar. 1959, p. 12; Apr. 1961, p. 15; *Newsweek*, 12 Dec. 1955, p. 104; Parham, "Halls of Ivy," 179–80; Adelson, *Brushing Back Jim Crow*, 121–27, 131, 154–55, 177–78, 188–94, 204.

106. SSN, Feb. 1959, p. 16; Nov. 1959, p. 8; Price, "Violence and Intimidation," 51–52 (frs. 388–89); Opotowsky, "Dixie Dynamite," 16–17 (frs. 683–84); Muse, *Ten Years of Prelude*, 38–39, 41; Fairclough, *Civil Rights Struggle in Louisiana*, 204–5; Belknap, *Federal Law and Southern Order*, 31.

107. Jim Johnson, "Let's Build a Private School at Hoxie," *Arkansas Faith* (Dec. 1955): 12, NAACP, part 20, reel 13, fr. 307; SSN, Feb. 1955, p. 2; June 1955, p. 2; July 1955, p. 3; Mar. 1956, p. 4; Apr. 1956, p. 8; May 1956, pp. 10–11; June 1956, p. 2; Aug. 1956, p. 3; May 1964, p. 4B; Freyer, *Little Rock Crisis*, 74–82; McCain, "Segregation Decision," 376–78; Badger, "White Reaction to *Brown*," 85–86; Kirk, "Little Rock School Crisis," 67–70, 76–77; Reed, *Faubus*, 169–81; Powell, "Massive Resistance in Arkansas," 14–19; Black, *Southern Governors and Civil Rights*, 100; Goldfield, *Black, White, and Southern*, 107; Sherrill, *Gothic Politics in the Deep South*, 77–78, 83–85; Bartley, *Massive Resistance*, 142, 260–61.

108. SSN, June 1957, p. 9; July 1957, p. 10; Sept. 1957, pp. 6–7; Oct. 1957, pp. 1–3; Aug. 1958, p. 8; Muse, *Ten Years of Prelude*, 122–37; Wilkinson, *Brown to Bakke*, 88–90; Freyer, *Little Rock Crisis*, 98–109; Reed, *Faubus*, 181–232; Jacoway, "Little Rock," 6–9; Bartley, *Massive Resistance*, 252–53, 263–69; Sherrill, *Gothic Politics in the Deep South*, 89, 100–108; Powell, "Massive Resistance in Arkansas," 42–47.

109. Dick Mansfield, "Local Report from Norfolk," 22 May 1958, p. 3, NAACP, part 22, reel 1, fr. 520; SSN, Sept. 1954, p. 13; Oct. 1954, p. 14; Feb. 1955, p. 10; Dec. 1955, p. 3; Jan. 1956, p. 14; June 1956, p. 13; July 1956, p. 10; Aug. 1956, p. 12; Sept. 1956, p. 8; Oct. 1956, p. 16; Wilkinson, *Harry Byrd*, 123–33; Ely, *Crisis of Conservative Virginia*, 37–46; Muse, *Virginia's Massive Resistance*, 15–34.

110. SSN, Mar. 1956, p. 13; letter to the editor, *Tampa Morning Tribune*, n.d., NAACP, part 20, reel 7, fr. 217; Saunders to Wilkins, 7 May 1956, ibid., fr. 198; SSN, June 1956, pp. 2, 12; undated press clipping, *Florida Sentinel*, part 20, reel 13, fr. 429; SSN, May 1956, p. 4; *Tampa Morning Tribune*, 10 May 1956, part 20, reel 7, fr. 200; undated press clipping, *Tampa Morning Tribune*, ibid., fr. 212; SSN, Apr. 1956, p. 9; Collier, "Segregation and Politics," 121–22; Jacobstein, *Florida Democratic Gubernatorial Primary of 1956*, 25–40, 71–74.

111. SSN, Feb. 1956, p. 4; July 1958, p. 11; June 1956, p. 10; Dec. 1954, p. 2; Apr. 1955, p. 2; July 1955, p. 2; Sept. 1955, p. 3; Oct. 1955, p. 8; Nov. 1955, p. 9; Dec. 1955, p. 4; Mar. 1956, p. 6; Apr. 1956, p. 5; May 1956, p. 5; Oct. 1956, p. 9; Feb. 1957, p. 15; July 1957, p. 11; "Able and Willing," *Montgomery Advertiser*, 8 July 1956, NAACP, part 20, reel 13, frs. 373–76; Sims, *James E. Folsom*, 173–77, 183–86; Bartley, *Massive Resistance*, 281–86; Strong, "Alabama," 449–50.

112. SSN, Apr. 1956, p. 11; May 1956, p. 11; June 1955, p. 15; July 1955, p. 12; Feb. 1956, p. 8; June 1956, pp. 1, 4; July 1956, pp. 6, 7; Aug. 1956, p. 14; Sept. 1956, p. 12; Dec. 1956, p. 5; Jan. 1957, p. 4; June 1957, p. 2; Aug. 1957, p. 8; Sept. 1957, p. 10; Collier, "Segregation and Politics," 124–25; Douglas, *Desegregation of the Charlotte Schools*, 32–33, 36; Badger, "Southern Manifesto," 528–32; Graham, "Desegregation in Nashville," 147–49; Bartley, *Massive Resistance*, 275.

113. "Able and Willing," *Montgomery Advertiser*, 8 July 1956, NAACP, part 20, reel 13, frs. 373–76; SSN, Feb. 1955, p. 11; Mar. 1955, pp. 6, 16; June 1955, p. 8; July 1955, p. 1; June 1956, p. 1; *Chicago Defender*, 18 Sept. 1954, p. 3.

114. SSN, Oct. 1957, pp. 8, 15; Nov. 1957, pp. 3, 8, 11, 14, 15, 16; Dec. 1957, p. 5; Feb. 1958, p. 1; Muse, *Ten Years of Prelude*, 144–45; Black, *Southern Governors and Civil Rights*, 103, 172–76, 302–4; Bartley, *Massive Resistance*, 277–78; pages 419–20.

115. SSN, Dec. 1957, p. 10; Oct. 1957, p. 7; Nov. 1957, pp. 5, 9–11, 14; Oct. 1958, p. 20; Dec. 1958, p. 3; Eisenberg, "Virginia," 39–40, 46, 50–53; Wilkinson, *Harry Byrd*, 102–5, 112, 137–38; Ely, *Crisis of Conservative Virginia*, 56–69; Bartley, *Massive Resistance*, 270–71.

116. SSN, Apr. 1958, pp. 12–13; Aug. 1958, p. 8; Sept. 1958, pp. 1–2; Oct. 1958, pp. 1–3, 7; Nov. 1958, p. 8; Dec. 1958, pp. 5, 9, 12, 13; Mar. 1960, p. 12; Aug. 1960, p. 5; Jan. 1961, p. 12; Day, "Congressman Brooks Hays and the Election of 1958," 241–64; Reed, *Faubus*, 246–51, 263–65; Sherrill, *Gothic Politics in the Deep South*, 106–9; Powell, "Massive Resistance in Arkansas," 57; Gallup, *Gallup Poll*, 2:1584.

117. SSN, Dec. 1957, p. 15; Feb. 1958, p. 9; Mar. 1958, p. 12; May 1958, p. 9; June 1958, p. 8; July 1958, p. 11; Carter, *George Wallace*, 90–96; Frady, *Wallace*, 121–31; Bartley & Graham, *Southern Politics*, 67.

118. SSN, June 1958, p. 3; Aug. 1958, p. 16; Oct. 1958, pp. 17, 18; Apr. 1958, p. 13; July 1958, p. 14; Sept. 1958, p. 12; Nov. 1958, p. 11; Black, *Southern Governors and Civil Rights*, 66–68, 80–82; Roche, *Sibley Commission*, 72–73.

119. Muse, *Ten Years of Prelude*, 178; McMillen, *Citizens' Council*, 361–62; Lubell, *White and Black*, 97–102; Kirk, "Little Rock School Crisis," 81–82.

120. SSN, Feb. 1959, pp. 1, 4, 5; May 1959, p. 2; Aug. 1959, p. 13; Apr. 1960, p. 8; Aug. 1960, p. 15; Feb. 1961, p. 5; Muse, *Ten Years of Prelude*, 178, 181–87; Muse, *Virginia's Massive Resistance*, 122–43, 160–66; Ely, *Crisis of Conservative Virginia*, 122–35.

121. SSN, Mar. 1959, p. 2; Apr. 1959, pp. 10, 12; June 1959, pp. 1–3; Sept. 1959, pp. 1, 2, 15; Oct. 1960, pp. 11–12; Nov. 1960, p. 13; Dec. 1960, p. 11; Mar. 1961, p. 6; July 1962, p. 7; Peltason, *Fifty-Eight Lonely Men*, 203–7; Muse, *Ten Years of Prelude*, 194–96; Freyer, *Little Rock Crisis*, 160–63.

122. SSN, Mar. 1959, p. 3; Sept. 1958, p. 10; Mar. 1959, p. 12; Feb. 1958, p. 10; Aug. 1958, p. 4; Oct. 1958, p. 14; Apr. 1959, p. 14; July 1959, p. 6; Sept. 1959, p. 4; Oct. 1959, p. 5; June 1960, pp. 3, 5; Aug. 1960, pp. 14, 15; Sept. 1960, p. 2; Oct. 1960, p. 16; Feb. 1961, p. 4; Apr. 1961, p. 3; July 1962, p. 3; Aug. 1962, p. 10; Jan. 1963, p. 11.

123. SSN, Nov. 1958, p. 10; Dec. 1958, pp. 5, 15; Sept. 1958, p. 4; Mar. 1959, p. 13; Sept. 1959, p. 5; Johnston, *I Rolled with Ross*, 78–87; SSN, Jan. 1956, p. 6; May 1956, p. 15; Feb. 1960, p. 7; May 1958, p. 4; Oct. 1958, p. 16; Dec. 1958, p. 11; Feb. 1959, p. 11; June 1959, p. 15; July 1959, p. 11; Aug. 1960, pp. 1, 14–15; Bartley, *Massive Resistance*, 136; Black, *Southern Governors and Civil Rights*, 60, 63; McMillen, *Citizens' Council*, 323, 326.

124. SSN, June 1956, p. 3; Aug. 1958, p. 3; Dec. 1959, p. 15; Apr. 1958, p. 14; June 1959, p. 5; Oct. 1959, p. 11; Nov. 1959, p. 13; Jan. 1960, p. 11; Feb. 1960, p. 14; June 1960, pp. 1–2; Aug. 1960, p. 14; Sept. 1960, pp. 1–15; Oct. 1960, pp. 2–3; Nov. 1960, pp. 1, 14;

Dec. 1960, pp. 1, 8–10; Fairclough, *Civil Rights Struggle in Louisiana*, 231–32, 234–54; Fairclough, "Political Coup d'Etat"; Bartley & Graham, *Southern Politics*, 59–60; Howard, "Louisiana," 556–59.

125. Lassiter, "Rise of the Suburban South," 217–18; SSN, Mar. 1959, p. 7; Feb. 1960, pp. 1–2; June 1959, p. 9; Jan. 1959, p. 10; Feb. 1959, pp. 8, 10; July 1959, p. 1; Nov. 1959, p. 12; Aug. 1960, pp. 14, 15.

126. SSN, Feb. 1959, p. 16; Apr. 1959, p. 3; Mar. 1960, p. 6; May 1959, p. 4; June 1959, pp. 3, 12; Oct. 1959, p. 7; Dec. 1959, p. 1; Feb. 1960, p. 9; Aug. 1960, pp. 11, 14; Jan. 1961, pp. 1, 5; Feb. 1961, p. 14; page 431.

127. SSN, Jan. 1959, p. 5; Apr. 1959, p. 7; Aug. 1959, pp. 1, 4, 8; Apr. 1960, p. 1; June 1960, p. 2; July 1960, pp. 1, 12; Aug. 1960, pp. 7–8; Jan. 1961, p. 10; Sept. 1961, p. 1; Muse, *Ten Years of Prelude*, 216–25; Lassiter, "Rise of the Suburban South," 204–40.

128. SSN, Feb. 1960, p. 14; June 1960, pp. 1–2; July 1960, pp. 1, 12; Aug. 1960, p. 7; Sept. 1960, pp. 1, 15–16; Oct. 1960, pp. 2–3; Nov. 1960, pp. 1, 14; Dec. 1960, pp. 1, 8–10; Jan. 1961, pp. 8–9; Feb. 1961, pp. 6–7; Mar. 1961, pp. 1, 8–9; May 1961, pp. 1, 8; Feb. 1962, pp. 8–9; June 1962, p. 9; Bush v. Orleans Parish School Board, 5 R.R.L.R. 666, 1023 (1960), aff'd, 364 U.S. 500 (1960); Peltason, *Fifty-Eight Lonely Men*, 221–43; Fairclough, *Civil Rights Struggle in Louisiana*, 234–54; Baker, *Second Battle of New Orleans*, 327–452.

129. SSN, Jan. 1960, pp. 1, 16; Feb. 1960, pp. 1–2; Mar. 1960, p. 15; Apr. 1960, p. 3; May 1960, pp. 1–2; June 1960, p. 16; Aug. 1960, p. 14; Oct. 1960, p. 3; Nov. 1960, p. 2; Lassiter, "Rise of the Suburban South," 241–61; Roche, *Sibley Commission*, 78–175.

130. SSN, May 1961, p. 15; Dec. 1960, p. 1; Jan. 1961, p. 3; Feb. 1961, pp. 1, 8–11; Mar. 1961, pp. 1–2; June 1961, pp. 1, 8; Sept. 1961, pp. 1, 6; Lassiter, "Rise of the Suburban South," 263–93; Roche, *Sibley Commission*, 178–88.

131. SSN, Dec. 1962, p. 10; Mar. 1961, pp. 1–3; July 1961, pp. 13, 15; Brink & Harris, *Negro Revolution*, 150; Gallup, *Gallup Poll*, 2:1507, 3:1705. See also Brauer, *John F. Kennedy and the Second Reconstruction*, 200.

132. Lassiter, "Rise of the Suburban South," 297; SSN, Mar. 1962, p. 12; Mar. 1963, p. 4; Apr. 1963, p. 15; Apr. 1962, p. 11; May 1962, p. 16; June 1962, p. 12; Aug. 1962, p. 7; Oct. 1962, p. 9; Dec. 1962, pp. 4, 7; Oct. 1963, p. 7.

133. SSN, Feb. 1962, pp. 12, 13; Mar. 1962, pp. 1, 2, 12; Feb. 1959, p. 16; Apr. 1962, pp. 3, 12; May 1962, pp. 1, 6; Jan. 1961, pp. 1, 5; Feb. 1961, p. 14; Oct. 1961, pp. 5, 16; June 1962, pp. 1, 8; Jan. 1963, p. 1; Muse, *Ten Years of Prelude*, 230–31; Carter, *George Wallace*, 98–109; Frady, *Wallace*, 135–39; Norrell, *Civil Rights Movement in Tuskegee*, 114–17; Sherrill, *Gothic Politics in the Deep South*, 278–80.

134. SSN, Dec. 1963, p. 10; Doyle, *American Insurrection*, 65–66; SSN, Jan. 1962, p. 3; May 1962, p. 9; Oct. 1962, pp. 1, 10, 12–13; Muse, *Ten Years of Prelude*, 244–46.

135. SSN, Jan. 1962, p. 15; May 1963, p. 14; Jan. 1963, pp. 1, 11, 15; June 1962, p. 5; July 1962, p. 12; Sept. 1962, pp. 9, 11; Nov. 1962, p. 14; Feb. 1963, pp. 1, 8–9; Muse, *Ten Years of Prelude*, 242, 256–59; George McMillan, "Integration with Dignity," *Saturday Evening Post*, 9 Mar. 1963, pp. 16–21.

136. SSN, Oct. 1962, pp. 13–14; Nov. 1962, pp. 10–11; Dec. 1962, p. 3; Feb. 1963, pp. 10–11; Apr. 1963, p. 9; July 1962, p. 10; Jan. 1963, p. 10; May 1963, p. 2; June 1963, pp. 1, 6–7; July 1963, pp. 1, 5–6; Sept. 1963, pp. 1–3; May 1964, p. 3A; Carter, *George Wallace*, 110–14, 117–23, 133–51, 162–83; Muse, *Ten Years of Prelude*, 261, 266–68.

137. Johnston, *I Rolled with Ross*, 102; SSN, Feb. 1964, pp. 1, 2; Aug. 1963, p. 20; Nov. 1963, pp. 1, 6; Mar. 1963, p. 6; NYT, 22 Jan. 1964, pp. 1, 28; Rowe-Sims, "Mississippi State Sovereignty Commission," 45; Fairclough, *Civil Rights Struggle in*

Louisiana, 261; SSN, Dec. 1963, pp. 15–16; Jan. 1964, p. 5; Apr. 1963, p. 10; Sept. 1963, p. 14; McMillen, *Citizens' Council*, 348–49; Black, *Southern Governors and Civil Rights*, 63–64, 208–11; Silver, *Closed Society*, 62–63; Henderson, "Mississippi State University Basketball Controversy," 831–40.

138. Badger, "Southern Manifesto," 528, 532–33; Badger, "Arkansas and the Southern Manifesto," 356–58; Powell, "Massive Resistance in Arkansas," 102–9.

139. Wilkinson, *Harry Byrd*, 112–14, 151–54; Muse, *Virginia's Massive Resistance*, 46–47, 168, 176; Muse, *Ten Years of Prelude*, 61; pages 391–92, 394–97.

140. SSN, Oct. 1954, p. 14; Nov. 1954, p. 15; Sept. 1954, p. 13; Mar. 1956, p. 4; Killian & Haer, "Attitudes regarding School Segregation," 161 table 1; Bartley, *Massive Resistance*, 13–14, 253–54, 337; Ely, *Crisis of Conservative Virginia*, 30, 34–37; McMillen, *Citizens' Council*, 6–7, 45–46, 93–94, 103–5, 292–93; Pettigrew & Campbell, "Faubus and Segregation," 442–45; Bartley & Graham, *Southern Politics*, 53, 80, 186–187; Peltason, *Fifty-Eight Lonely Men*, 33–35; Abbott, "Norfolk Business Community," 108. See also Gallup, *Gallup Poll*, 2:1281.

141. SSN, June 1958, p. 3; June 1956, p. 16; Dec. 1958, p. 15; Oct. 1955, p. 13; Feb. 1956, p. 14; Mar. 1956, p. 14; Apr. 1956, p. 1; Sept. 1956, p. 8; Oct. 1956, p. 16; Mar. 1957, p. 14; Apr. 1957, p. 15; June 1957, p. 2; Aug. 1957, p. 8; Sept. 1957, pp. 4, 10; July 1958, p. 13; Jan. 1959, p. 5; July 1959, pp. 1–2; Feb. 1960, p. 2; Apr. 1960, p. 11; Sen. James Eastland, "The South Will Fight!!" *Arkansas Faith* (Dec. 1955): 13, 27, NAACP, part 20, reel 13, frs. 308, 322; McMillen, *Citizens' Council*, 250; Muse, *Ten Years of Prelude*, 147–48, 214; Lassiter, "Rise of the Suburban South," 241, 253; Peltason, *Fifty-Eight Lonely Men*, 43–45, 130; Badger, "Southern Manifesto," 517–18; Wilkinson, *Harry Byrd*, 132–33, 151–52.

142. SSN, Mar. 1960, p. 7; Dec. 1963, p. 10; Opotowsky, "Dixie Dynamite," 12 (fr. 679); Burns, *Montgomery Bus Boycott*, 168, 208, 303; Price, "Violence and Intimidation," 65–66 (frs. 402–3); SSN, May 1957, p. 7; Silver, *Closed Society*, 151–55; Muse, *Ten Years of Prelude*, 48–49, 161, 168.

143. SSN, June 1955, p. 18; June 1959, p. 12; Dec. 1955, p. 6; Mar. 1956, pp. 7, 9; Apr. 1956, pp. 7, 12; June 1956, p. 13; Aug. 1956, p. 11; Oct. 1956, p. 10; Feb. 1957, p. 7; Aug. 1957, p. 15; May 1958, p. 9; July 1958, p. 16; Nov. 1958, p. 8; Sept. 1959, pp. 5, 6; Dec. 1959, p. 5; June 1960, p. 10; Jan. 1961, p. 11; Nov. 1961, p. 13; Sept. 1962, pp. 2–3; Dec. 1963, p. 10; Jan. 1964, pp. 9, 11; Press Release, 8 May 1958, NAACP, part 20, reel 11, frs. 270–72; Travelstead Statement, 2–3 (frs. 198–99); Parham, "Halls of Ivy," 178–79; Robinson, "No Man's Land," 197; Muse, *Ten Years of Prelude*, 160–61, 168–72; Dittmer, *Struggle for Civil Rights in Mississippi*, 60–61, 142; McMillen, *Citizens' Council*, 240–42; Bartley, *Massive Resistance*, 227–33; Silver, *Closed Society*, 81–82, 111–12.

144. SSN, Mar. 1960, p. 7; Jan. 1958, p. 8; Dec. 1963, p. 10; McMillen, *Citizens' Council*, 246–47, 290, 313–15, 319, 326–28, 334, 336–37; Rowe-Sims, "Mississippi State Sovereignty Commission," 34, 39; SSN, July 1956, p. 11; Jan. 1957, pp. 3, 6; Dec. 1957, pp. 2, 6–7; Jan. 1961, p. 10; Mar. 1961, p. 9; James D. Fackler, statement, 17 Mar. 1961, NAACP, part 20, reel 4, fr. 474; Opotowsky, "Dixie Dynamite," 11 (fr. 678); Halberstam, "Citizens' Councils," 300; Price, "Violence and Intimidation," 14–36, 54, 65–66 (frs. 351–73, 398, 401–2); Burns, *Montgomery Bus Boycott*, 117–18, 141–42; Peltason, *Fifty-Eight Lonely Men*, 241–42; Muse, *Ten Years of Prelude*, 50, 161–62; Fairclough, *Civil Rights Struggle in Louisiana*, 249–50; Daniel, *The South in the 1950s*, 239–42.

145. *Birmingham Post-Herald*, 22 Dec. 1960, NAACP, part 21, reel 22, fr. 399; SSN, Oct. 1955, p. 3; Dec. 1955, pp. 7, 11; Mar. 1956, p. 3; Aug. 1957, p. 13; Nov. 1957, p. 11; Jan.

1958, p. 9; Mar. 1958, p. 3; Apr. 1958, p. 5; May 1959, p. 15; July 1960, p. 10; July 1961, p. 9; Sept. 1962, p. 3; Dec. 1962, p. 2; H. L. Mitchell, Preliminary Report on the Rise of the White Citizens' Council Movement, 30 Jan. 1956, pp. 2–3, NAACP, part 20, reel 13, frs. 325–26; "Editor Says Councils Try to Destroy Paper," unidentified and undated press clipping, ibid., fr. 742; "Bilbo's Ghost Haunts a Mississippi Educator," unidentified press clipping, 14 Mar. 1958, ibid., reel 2, fr. 118; Opotowsky, "Dixie Dynamite," 18 (fr. 685); Dittmer, *Struggle for Civil Rights in Mississippi*, 61–69, 463–64 n. 62; Price, "Violence and Intimidation," 22 (fr. 359); Muse, *Ten Years of Prelude*, 164–66; Silver, *Closed Society*, 37–39, 57–58; Daniel, *The South in the 1950s*, 235–38.

146. Press Release, 25 July 1956, pp. 1–2, NAACP, part 20, reel 4, frs. 639–40; Asbury Howard, Jr., statement, n.d., ibid., frs. 468–69; M. M. Jones, statement, n.d., ibid., fr. 48; Current to NAACP Officials, memo, 31 Jan. 1956, ibid., reel 5, frs. 120–21; unidentified document, ibid., frs. 157–59; Orzell Billingsley, Jr., to Carter, 26 Nov. 1958, part 22, reel 1, frs. 296–97; Evers to Carter, 22 May 1959, ibid., fr. 595; Mahalie Berry, statement, 22 May 1959, ibid., frs. 596–97; Evers to Carter, 16 Sept. 1959, ibid., reel 2, frs. 212–13; Burns, *Montgomery Bus Boycott*, 42, 125, 287–89; Manis, *Fred Shuttlesworth*, 162–63, 232–34; SSN, Oct. 1960, p. 13; Dec. 1958, p. 12; Price, "Violence and Intimidation," 37–84 (frs. 374–421).

147. Bartley, *Massive Resistance*, 211; SSN, Jan. 1959, p. 13; Dec. 1963, p. 10; Apr. 1964, p. 14; NYT, 3 Dec. 1960, NAACP, part 20, reel 1, fr. 611; "Are You Curious about Mississippi?" 20 Jan. 1961, p. 2, ibid., reel 2, fr. 173; Payne, *Mississippi Freedom Struggle*, 7, 36–40, 205, 298–300, 316, 396–97; Robert L. T. Smith, "Visit to Jefferson County, [Mississippi]," part 20, reel 2, fr. 166; Silver, *Closed Society*, esp. xix–xx, 37–39, 41–42, 65–67, 79–80, 86–87, 92–95, 101–2; Rowe-Sims, "Mississippi State Sovereignty Commission," 34, 38; SSN, Apr. 1957, p. 14; Nov. 1961, p. 13; Jan. 1964, p. 11; Carter to "Lawrence," 30 Apr. 1962, NAACP, part 22, reel 1, fr. 170; NAACP Press Release, 8 Apr. 1961, part 20, reel 1, frs. 556–57; Monthly Report of Mississippi Field Secretary, 5 Oct. 1962, p. 3, ibid., reel 15, fr. 50; Dittmer, *Struggle for Civil Rights in Mississippi*, 53–60, 107–10, 122, 142; Cobb, *Most Southern Place on Earth*, 222–26; Cagin & Dray, *Civil Rights Campaign for Mississippi*, 326, 328; Lawson, *Black Ballots*, 130.

148. SSN, June 1959, p. 11; Peltason, *Fifty-Eight Lonely Men*, 136–37; Minutes of the NAACP Board of Directors Meeting, 11 May 1959, pp. 3–4, part 1, supp. 1956–1960, reel 2, frs. 100–101; ibid., Aug. 1959, fr. 127. See also Manis, *Fred Shuttlesworth*, 194, 235; Tyson, *Robert F. Williams*, 149–65.

149. SSN, Sept. 1957, pp. 6, 7; Nov. 1955, p. 9; June 1956, p. 10; "Faubus Silent Again," *Arkansas Faith* (Dec. 1955): 23, NAACP, part 20, reel 13, fr. 318; Muse, *Ten Years of Prelude*, 125; Peltason, *Fifty-Eight Lonely Men*, 53–54, 163–64; Freyer, *Little Rock Crisis*, 95, 100; McMillen, *Citizens' Council*, 272–74; Bartley, *Massive Resistance*, 258; Sherrill, *Gothic Politics in the Deep South*, 98–99, 207–8; Longenecker, *Selma's Peacemaker*, 170–71; Powell, "Massive Resistance in Arkansas," 37–39.

150. SSN, Oct. 1955, p. 3; May 1956, p. 15; McMillen, "Organized Resistance to School Desegregation in Tennessee," 318–19; SSN, Nov. 1958, p. 15; Mar. 1959, p. 15; Sept. 1955, p. 10; Jan. 1956, p. 5; Feb. 1956, p. 16; Mar. 1956, pp. 4, 7; Jan. 1957, p. 7; McMillen, *Citizens' Council*, 40; Handlin, "Civil Rights after Little Rock," 395; Thorndike, "James J. Kilpatrick," 56–57, 60–61; Sherrill, *Gothic Politics in the Deep South*, 207–8.

151. SSN, Apr. 1962, p. 11; McCauley, "Be It Enacted," 134–36; Tumin, "Readiness and Resistance," 259; Lassiter, "Rise of the Suburban South," 184–88, 192–95, 199;

SSN, Jan. 1956, p. 13; Feb. 1956, p. 6; Aug. 1957, p. 7; Nov. 1957, p. 14; May 1962, p. 7; Saunders to Wilkins, 7 May 1956, NAACP, part 20, reel 7, fr. 198; Muse, *Ten Years of Prelude*, 66, 149, 216; McMillen, *Citizens' Council*, 99–101; Peltason, *Fifty-Eight Lonely Men*, 43–44; Bartley, *Massive Resistance*, 18–19, 42, 94, 144, 278–79, 283; Key, *Southern Politics*, 119–22, 666; Bernd, "Georgia," 296–97; Jacobstein, *Florida Democratic Gubernatorial Election of 1956*, 14–16, 19, 24. See also Burt, "Brown's Reflection," 1490 n. 32.

152. SSN, Nov. 1954, p. 11; Dec. 1954, pp. 6, 8; Jan. 1955, p. 10; Feb. 1956, p. 11; Sept. 1956, p. 3; Aug. 1958, p. 6; Workman, "Deep South," 98–99; Peltason, *Fifty-Eight Lonely Men*, 33; Muse, *Virginia's Massive Resistance*, 58, 69–70; Tumin, "Readiness and Resistance," 256, 258 table 1; Chappell, "Divided Mind of Southern Segregationists," 46, 48; Lassiter, "Rise of the Suburban South," 93, 173, 195–200, 216, 222; Lassiter & Lewis, "Massive Resistance Revisited," 3–4, 14–15; Lubell, *White and Black*, 97; Gallup, *Gallup Poll*, 2:1401, 1526–27, 3:1616.

153. SSN, Dec. 1959, p. 14; Eastland, "The South Will Fight!!" *Arkansas Faith* (Dec. 1955): 8, 27, NAACP, part 20, reel 13, frs. 303, 322; Lubell, *White and Black*, 93, 96; Peltason, *Fifty-Eight Lonely Men*, 48–49, 95–96; Handlin, "Civil Rights after Little Rock," 393, 395–96; Woodward, "'New Reconstruction,'" 502–3, 507; SSN, Nov. 1954, p. 3; Jan. 1957, p. 16; Dec. 1957, p. 14; Aug. 1960, p. 8; unidentified and undated press clipping, NAACP, part 20, reel 13, fr. 454; McMillen, *Citizens' Council*, 358–59; Patterson, *Grand Expectations*, 394–95; Bartley, *Massive Resistance*, 127–28, 249; Kirk, "Little Rock School Crisis," 73–74, 81; pages 319–20, 324–25.

154. Ely, *Crisis of Conservative Virginia*, 61, 100–102; SSN, July 1958, p. 16; July 1957, p. 4; Sept. 1957, p. 16; Aug. 1956, p. 9; Oct. 1956, p. 10; Jan. 1956, p. 5; Feb. 1956, p. 15; Apr. 1957, p. 3; June 1957, p. 7; July 1957, p. 5; Sept. 1957, pp. 4, 8; Nov. 1957, p. 14; June 1958, p. 3; Oct. 1958, p. 16; Jan. 1959, p. 10; Apr. 1962, p. 20; Brady, *Black Monday*, 19; Talmadge, *You and Segregation*, 76, 78; Lassiter, "Rise of the Suburban South," 78; Badger, "Southern Manifesto," 517–18; Badger, "Arkansas and the Southern Manifesto," 355, 360; Peltason, *Fifty-Eight Lonely Men*, 95–96, 194; Dabney, "Virginia's 'Peaceable, Honorable Stand'," 56.

155. Daniel Broom of White People's Association to "All White People," n.d., NAACP, part 20, reel 13, fr. 483; Mansfield, "Local Report from Norfolk," 22 May 1958, part 22, reel 1, fr. 518; Lubell, *White and Black*, 96; Bartley, *Massive Resistance*, 276–77; SSN, Mar. 1958, p. 3; Brief for the Petitioners, *Cooper v. Aaron*, 27–29.

156. Lubell, *White and Black*, 97–98; Fairclough, *Civil Rights Struggle in Louisiana*, 205; Bartley, *Massive Resistance*, 320; Kirk, "Little Rock School Crisis," 81–82; Dabney, "Virginia's 'Peaceable, Honorable Stand'," 55; Lassiter, "Rise of the Suburban South," 114–16, 157–60; Muse, *Ten Years of Prelude*, 151, 178–79, 185, 191–92, 215–17; Peltason, *Fifty-Eight Lonely Men*, 195; Hershman, "Massive Resistance Meets Its Match," 105–13; SSN, Jan. 1959, p. 5; Feb. 1959, p. 16; Apr. 1959, pp. 7, 14; May 1959, p. 14; Mar. 1961, p. 8; Aug. 1961, p. 9.

157. Muse, *Ten Years of Prelude*, 150–51; Tumin, Barton, & Burrus, "Education, Prejudice and Discrimination," 49.

158. SSN, Dec. 1958, p. 6; July 1959, p. 6; Nov. 1959, p. 9; Dec. 1957, pp. 10–11; Aug. 1958, p. 6; Sept. 1958, pp. 1, 6; Jan. 1959, p. 9; Feb. 1959, pp. 1, 4–5; June 1959, p. 7; Dec. 1959, p. 2; NYT, 16 Nov. 1958, pp. 1, 48; "80 Days without Public Schools," *Newsweek*, 1 Dec. 1958, pp. 23–26; Muse, *Ten Years of Prelude*, 156–57, 178–80, 183–85; Peltason, *Fifty-Eight Lonely Men*, 214–18; Jeffries, *Lewis F. Powell*, 150–53; Ely, *Crisis of Conservative Virginia*, 83–89; Lubell, *White and Black*, 98.

159. Lubell, *White and Black*, 100; SSN, Oct. 1958, pp. 5, 7; Nov. 1958, pp. 8–9; Dec. 1958, pp. 12–13; Jan. 1959, p. 14; Apr. 1959, pp. 10, 12; June 1959, pp. 2, 3; Aug. 1959, pp. 6, 12; Sept. 1959, p. 15; Aaron v. McKinley, 4 R.R.L.R. 543 (1959); Muse, *Ten Years of Prelude*, 153–56, 191–97; Peltason, *Fifty-Eight Lonely Men*, 195–205; Bartley, *Massive Resistance*, 328–31; Freyer, *Little Rock Crisis*, 154–63; Cobb, "Lesson of Little Rock," 114–15; Powell, "Massive Resistance in Arkansas," 68, 77–79.

160. SSN, Feb. 1961, pp. 1, 8–11; June 1958, p. 3; Sept. 1958, p. 12; Dec. 1958, p. 15; July 1959, pp. 1, 2; Dec. 1959, p. 16; Jan. 1960, pp. 1, 16; Feb. 1960, pp. 1, 2; Mar. 1960, p. 15; May 1961, pp. 14–15; June 1961, p. 8; July 1961, p. 5; Nov. 1961, p. 8; Feb. 1962, p. 5; Lassiter, "Rise of the Suburban South," 225–75; Roche, *Sibley Commission*, 80–95, 162–88.

161. SSN, Mar. 1960, p. 6; Oct. 1958, p. 2; Feb. 1959, p. 13; June 1959, p. 3; Jan. 1960, p. 9; Oct. 1962, p. 8; May 1963, p. 6; Muse, *Ten Years of Prelude*, 156–57, 211, 214; Peltason, *Fifty-Eight Lonely Men*, 193–95; Cobb, "Lesson of Little Rock," 114–15, 117; Lubell, *White and Black*, 97–102; "Six Years Later," *New Republic*, 7 Sept. 1959, pp. 3–4.

162. SSN, Feb. 1963, p. 10; Aug. 1963, p. 20; Lubell, *White and Black*, 106–7; "What of the Law?" *New Republic*, 2 Apr. 1956, p. 9; SSN, July 1963, pp. 1, 5–7; Nov. 1963, p. 6; May 1964, p. 3A; Carter, *George Wallace*, 109.

163. Dabney, "Virginia's 'Peaceable, Honorable Stand'," 55; Bartley, *Massive Resistance*, 270, 277–78, 287; Sherrill, *Gothic Politics in the Deep South*, 107–8; Jacoway, "Little Rock Business Leaders and Desegregation," 24; Powell, "Massive Resistance in Arkansas," 9–10, 53; Ely, *Crisis of Conservative Virginia*, 59; Goldfield, *Black, White, and Southern*, 22, 71; Sosna, *Southern Liberals and the Race Issue*, 31, 158–59, 199–200; Dollard, *Caste and Class*, 49.

164. SSN, Oct. 1957, pp. 4, 5, 8, 9, 13, 15, 16; Nov. 1957, pp. 7, 9, 11, 15, 16; Dec. 1957, p. 2; Freyer, "Little Rock Crisis Reconsidered," 369; Ambrose, *Eisenhower*, 2:420–21; Bartley, *Massive Resistance*, 277.

165. SSN, Dec. 1962, pp. 2–3; Oct. 1962, p. 8; Feb. 1963, p. 3; pages 407–8.

166. SSN, Oct. 1960, p. 1; June 1962, pp. 1, 7; May 1964, pp. 12B–13B; Price, "Violence and Intimidation," 71 (fr. 408); Westfeldt, "Communities in Strife."

167. SSN, Nov. 1957, p. 5; Oct. 1962, p. 12; *New York Post*, 24 Sept. 1956, NAACP, part 20, reel 12, fr. 151; *Charlotte News & Observer*, 7 Feb. 1956, ibid., reel 6, fr. 118; Muse, *Ten Years of Prelude*, 114–15; Peltason, *Fifty-Eight Lonely Men*, 239; Jackson, "White Liberal Intellectuals, Civil Rights, and Gradualism," 106, 108.

168. SSN, Feb. 1961, p. 13; Patterson, Brown, 110–11. See also Garrow, *Protest at Selma*, 163–66.

169. "Shame Falls on Alabama," *Worcester* (Massachusetts) *Telegram*, 8 Feb. 1956, NAACP, part 20, reel 6, fr. 121; *NYT*, 12 Feb. 1956, p. 57; "A Riot: A Public Disgrace," *Cheraw* (South Carolina) *Chronicle*, 9 Feb. 1956, part 20, reel 6, fr. 122; "Failure in Alabama," *Wash. Post*, 8 Feb. 1956, p. A12; *Charlotte News & Observer*, 7 Feb. 1956, part 20, reel 6, fr. 118; Autherine Lucy, "Recounting of Events," ibid., frs. 167–70; Paris Office of American Jewish Committee to Edwin J. Lukas, memo, 5 Mar. 1956, ibid., frs. 282–84; Herbert L. Wright to Wilkins, memo, 24 May 1956, ibid., fr. 315; NAACP Press Release, 9 Feb. 1956, ibid., fr. 140; SSN, Mar. 1956, p. 6; "Mob Rule at Tuscaloosa," *NYT*, 8 Feb. 1956, p. 32; Clark, *Schoolhouse Door*, 71–81.

170. SSN, Oct. 1957, pp. 10, 15; Nov. 1957, pp. 4, 15; Dec. 1958, p. 12; Hackney, "Little Rock and the Promise of America," 25; Muse, *Ten Years of Prelude*, 122, 138, 142; Dudziak, *Cold War Civil Rights*, 115–51; Gallup, *Gallup Poll*, 2:1517; Burk, *Eisen-*

hower Administration and Black Civil Rights, 190; Carter to Michael M. Nisselson, 22 Sept. 1958, NAACP, part 22, reel 4, fr. 121; Nisselson to Carter, 26 Aug. 1958, ibid., fr. 122.

171. "Economic Lynching," *NYT*, 19 Nov. 1960, p. 20; Inger, *New Orleans School Crisis*, 57–58; Fairclough, *Civil Rights Struggle in Louisiana*, 247–48, 252; SSN, Dec. 1960, pp. 1, 8–10; Jan. 1961, pp. 1, 8–10; *NYT*, 15 Nov. 1960, pp. 1, 42; 16 Nov. 1960, pp. 1, 22; *Newsweek*, 28 Nov. 1960, pp. 19–20; Muse, *Ten Years of Prelude*, 220–21.

172. N. K. Perlow, "KKK Leader Warns: 'We Mean Business'," *Police Gazette* (Aug. 1956): 7, NAACP, part 20, reel 13, fr. 444; Opotowsky, "Dixie Dynamite," 15 (fr. 682); Manis, *Fred Shuttlesworth*, 147; Eskew, *But for Birmingham*, 115; Belknap, *Federal Law and Southern Order*, 28–29; Tumin, "Readiness and Resistance," 258 table 1; Killian & Haer, "Attitudes regarding School Desegregation," 161 table 1; "The Ku Klux Klan Revival," *Facts* (Nov.–Dec. 1956): 91–94, NAACP, part 20, reel 13, frs. 467–70; transcript of conference between Herbert Hill and Klan informant, 10 Oct. 1960, ibid., frs. 862–70; SSN, Apr. 1956, p. 13; May 1956, pp. 4, 5; July 1956, pp. 9, 11; Sept. 1956, pp. 5, 13; Oct. 1956, pp. 4, 9; Nov. 1956, pp. 9, 13; Feb. 1957, p. 7; Price, "Violence and Intimidation," 4–9 (frs. 341–46).

173. "M Is for Mississippi and Murder," NAACP, part 20, reel 2, frs. 656–58; Dittmer, *Struggle for Civil Rights in Mississippi*, 53–58; Cobb, *Most Southern Place on Earth*, 214–22; Wilkins, Keynote Address to National Delegate Assembly for Civil Rights, 4 Mar. 1956, p. 6, NAACP, part 21, reel 12, fr. 193 (hereafter, Wilkins, Keynote Address); Rep. Hugh Scott, Speech before the National Assembly on Civil Rights, 5 Mar. 1956, p. 3, ibid., fr. 203; Payne, *Mississippi Freedom Struggle*, 36–40, 53–54, 138–39; Whitfield, *Emmett Till*, 15–42; Hampton & Fayer, *Oral History of the Civil Rights Movement*, 7; Brady, *Black Monday*, 63–64; Patterson, *Grand Expectations*, 395–96; Belknap, *Federal Law and Southern Order*, 31–32.

174. Price, "Violence and Intimidation," 37–70 (frs. 374–407) (quotation at fr. 403); *NYT*, 16 Sept. 1963, p. 26; Eskew, *But for Birmingham*, 53, 131–32, 300–302, 322; Manus, *Fred Shuttlesworth*, 107–9, 170–73, 402–4; Rev. U. J. Fields to "Dear Friend," 21 Jan. 1957, NAACP, part 20, reel 5, fr. 814; King, *Stride toward Freedom*, 174–78; Burns, *Montgomery Bus Boycott*, 341; Belknap, *Federal Law and Southern Order*, 28–29, 53–54; SSN, Feb. 1958, p. 9; Apr. 1958, pp. 9, 10; May 1958, p. 5; Nov. 1958, p. 10; Dec. 1958, p. 15; *NYT*, 13 Oct. 1958, pp. 1, 29; Harrison E. Salisbury, "Fear and Hatred Grip Birmingham," *NYT*, 12 Apr. 1960, pp. 1, 28.

175. *NYT*, 29 Apr. 1959, pp. 1, 23; Smead, *Lynching of Mack Charles Parker*, esp. 68–70, 74–75, 95–96, 101, 105, 163–68, 175, 180–81 (quotations at 95, 175, 181); SSN, May 1959, pp. 4, 8; June 1959, pp. 8, 15; Wilkins to Ross L. Malone, telegram, 29 Apr. 1959, NAACP, part 20, reel 1, frs. 149–50; Wilkins to "Friends," 29 Apr. 1959, ibid., fr. 154; I. J. Jilbert to Rep. John J. McFall, 7 May 1959, ibid., fr. 176; Catherine D. Browne, "Civil Rights Law Needs Some Teeth," unidentified and undated press clipping, ibid., fr. 188; *Wash. Post*, 18 Nov. 1959, ibid., fr. 229; Dittmer, *Struggle for Civil Rights in Mississippi*, 83–84; Belknap, *Federal Law and Southern Order*, 61–62; *NYT*, 26 Apr. 1959, pp. 1, 46; 27 Apr. 1959, pp. 1, 14; *Time*, 4 May 1959, p. 16; *Newsweek*, 4 May 1959, pp. 31–32.

176. SSN, Oct. 1956, p. 9; Feb. 1963, p. 17; Aug. 1957, p. 7; Anonymous to Charles Gomillion, 26 Feb. 1959, NAACP, part 20, reel 6, fr. 11; handbill circulated at Montgomery citizens' council meeting, 10 Feb. 1956, ibid., reel 5, fr. 126; SSN, Apr. 1958, p. 10; Dec. 1960, p. 13; Price, "Violence and Intimidation," 18 (fr. 355).

177. Lusky, "Nullification," 1174.

178. Speech of Rep. James C. Davis, 31 Mar. 1956, in "Extension of Remarks of Rep. John Bell Williams," *Congressional Record*, 23 Apr. 1956, NAACP, part 20, reel 13, fr. 351; SSN, Mar. 1957, pp. 6, 16; NAACP Press Release, 1 Mar. 1956, part 20, reel 5, fr. 168; Cobb, *Most Southern Place on Earth*, 214; SSN, Mar. 1956, p. 7; "Are You Curious about Mississippi?" p. 2, part 20, reel 2, fr. 173; Eastland, "The South Will Fight!!" *Arkansas Faith* (Dec. 1955): 27, ibid., reel 13, fr. 322; SSN, June 1958, p. 13; May 1961, p. 3; June 1964, p. 15.

179. King, *Stride toward Freedom*, 174; SSN, Jan. 1960, p. 9; Jan. 1956, p. 5; Mar. 1956, p. 10; Brady, *Black Monday*, 41; Statement by Gov. Alan Shivers, 31 Aug. 1956, in 1 R.R.L.R. 885 (1956).

180. SSN, Nov. 1954, p. 10; June 1956, p. 3; Aug. 1956, p. 5; July 1955, p. 1; Aug. 1956, p. 5; Nov. 1958, p. 10; Burns, *Montgomery Bus Boycott*, 153–54; Eastland, "The South Will Fight!!" *Arkansas Faith* (Dec. 1955): 8–9, NAACP, part 20, reel 13, frs. 303–4; speech of Rep. James C. Davis, 31 Mar. 1956, in "Extension of Remarks of Rep. John Bell Williams," *Congressional Record*, 23 Apr. 1956, ibid., frs. 346, 347, 351; SSN, Aug. 1956, p. 16; Nov. 1958, p. 15; July 1963, p. 9; Peltason, *Fifty-Eight Lonely Men*, 138.

181. NAACP Press Release, 21 Mar. 1958, part 20, reel 12, fr. 6; SSN, Aug. 1963, p. 20; Peltason, *Fifty-Eight Lonely Men*, 138; "Incited by Others," *Star-Bulletin*, 13 Feb. 1956, NAACP, part 20, reel 6, fr. 217; Robert E. Bundy to Executives of Voluntary Affiliate Organizations, Circular re: Recent Bombing Incidents, 20 Oct. 1958, ibid., fr. 723; SSN, June 1959, p. 16; Wilkins, Keynote Address, 3–4 (frs. 190–91); Minutes of Board of Directors Meeting, 9 Apr. 1956, p. 2, part 20, reel 12, fr. 779; Wilkins to "Friends," 29 Apr. 1959, ibid., reel 1, fr. 154; SSN, Nov. 1958, p. 10; Dec. 1958, p. 7; July 1963, p. 9; Belknap, *Federal Law and Southern Order*, 28.

182. King, *Stride toward Freedom*, 87, 102–4 (quotation), 216–18; John P. Kavanagh to NAACP, 14 May 1961, part 20, reel 3, frs. 119–20; Wilkins to H. D. Monteith, 15 Nov. 1956, p. 2, ibid., reel 11, fr. 177; Fairclough, "Preachers and the People," 430–31; Fairclough, "Historians and the Civil Rights Movement," 397; Von Eschen, Kirk, & Pinard, "Conditions of Direct Action," 322; Garrow, *Protest at Selma*, 2–3, 220–232; Payne, *Mississippi Freedom Struggle*, 393–94; Sitkoff, *Struggle for Black Equality*, 29. But cf. Eskew, *But for Birmingham*, 213.

183. SSN, Apr. 1960, p. 14; Wolff, *Greensboro Sit-Ins*, 152; Morris, *Civil Rights Movement*, 242, 249–50; Hampton & Fayer, *Oral History of the Civil Rights Movement*, 75; Garrow, *Bearing the Cross*, 187–88, 201, 209, 216–17, 251; Garrow, *Protest at Selma*, 2, 155, 159–60, 221, 225; Brink & Harris, *Negro Revolution*, 145; Von Eschen, Kirk, & Pinard, "Conditions of Direct Action," 319–22; Fairclough, "Historians and the Civil Rights Movement," 397; Payne, *Mississippi Freedom Struggle*, 394; Branch, *Parting the Waters*, 631; Fager, *Selma*, 19; McAdam, *Development of Black Insurgency*, 174–79; Sitkoff, *Struggle for Black Equality*, 125–26; Bains, "Birmingham, 1963," 220, 239; Oates, "Week the World Watched Selma," 50–51; Ely, "Negro Demonstrations and the Law," 941, 943, 947, 951, 957, 965, 967–68; Daniel, *The South in the 1950s*, 285.

184. Eskew, *But for Birmingham*, 91–92, 104–5; Thornton, "Municipal Politics," 47–48; Manis, *Fred Shuttlesworth*, 82; Nunnelley, *Bull Connor*, 4, 30, 34, 36–37, 40–44, 67.

185. Nunnelley, *Bull Connor*, 4, 51–60, 67, 74–75, 78, 98–101, 107–9; Manis, *Reverend Fred Shuttlesworth*, 84, 86, 137, 161, 170–73, 265, 267; Eskew, *But for Birmingham*, 118, 153, 157, 160, 165–66, 175–76; Thornton, "Municipal Politics," 48–49.

186. SSN, Mar. 1958, p. 13; Dec. 1959, p. 1; Jan. 1961, p. 1; July 1961, pp. 9, 13; *Time*, 26 May 1961, p. 16; 107 *Congressional Record* 9216 (29 May 1961); *Time*, 2 June 1961, pp.

14–18; NYT, 21 May 1961, p. 78; SSN, June 1958, p. 8; Oct. 1959, p. 7; Feb. 1961, p. 14; Mar. 1962, p. 2; 107 *Congressional Record* 8603 (23 May 1961) (Sen. Estes Kefauver); Oppenheimer, *Sit-In Movement*, 167; Lomax, *Negro Revolt*, 138–40; Branch, *Parting the Waters*, 441–50; Yarbrough, *Judge Frank Johnson*, 82–83; Manis, *Fred Shuttlesworth*, 278; Clabaugh, "Newspaper Coverage of the Freedom Rides," 51, 54.

187. Wilkins to Branch Officers, memo, 25 May 1961, NAACP, part 21, reel 12, fr. 241; David Brinkley, statement, 25 May 1961, ibid., fr. 240; Clabaugh, "Newspaper Coverage of the Freedom Rides," 50–51; Alice Cahn to NAACP, 16 May 1961, part 20, reel 3, fr. 271; 107 *Congressional Record* 8027 (16 May 1961) (Sen. Javits); ibid. 8498 (22 May 1961) (Sen. Mansfield); ibid. 8506, 8509–10, 8532–33, 8568–69, 8712; SSN, July 1961, p. 4; Lusky, "Nullification," 1170; Sitkoff, *Struggle for Black Equality*, 105, 112; Laue, *Direct Action and Desegregation*, 107–9; Gallup, *Gallup Poll*, 3:1723–24.

188. SSN, Sept. 1957, p. 16; Oct. 1959, p. 3; Feb. 1960, p. 7; Doyle, *American Insurrection*, 52–53; pages 401–2, 406.

189. SSN, Oct. 1962, pp. 1, 10–12; Nov. 1962, pp. 1, 16–18; Jan. 1963, p. 13; Sherrill, *Gothic Politics in the Deep South*, 185–86; *Newsweek*, 14 Oct. 1963, p. 36; *Time*, 12 Oct. 1962, pp. 21–24; Greenberg, *Crusaders in the Courts*, 326; Dittmer, *Struggle for Civil Rights in Mississippi*, 138–42; Doyle, *American Insurrection*, 65–66, 70; Muse, *Ten Years of Prelude*, 246–55; Black, *Southern Governors and Civil Rights*, 63, 208–11; Johnston, *I Rolled with Ross*, 89–113; Brauer, *John F. Kennedy and the Second Reconstruction*, 180–204; Branch, *Parting the Waters*, 647–53, 659–70.

190. Garrow, *Bearing the Cross*, 227–28, 231–64; Garrow, *Protest at Selma*, 138–41, 166–68; King, *Why We Can't Wait*, 65–66, 69, 79, 114; Rose V. Russell to Pres. Kennedy, 8 May 1963, NAACP, part 20, reel 4, fr. 307; Nubar Esaian to Pres. Kennedy, 8 May 1963, ibid., frs. 313–15; Remarks by Mayor Robert F. Wagner of New York at NAACP rally, 8 May 1963, ibid., frs. 295–97; Rep. James H. Gilbert to Pres. Kennedy, 8 May 1963, ibid., fr. 323; 109 *Congressional Record* 8125 (9 May 1963) (Rep. Lindsay); ibid. 8616 (15 May 1963) (Rep. Gallagher); Manis, *Fred Shuttlesworth*, 331–32, 345, 348–49, 365–66, 369–72; Eskew, *But for Birmingham*, 3–7, 17, 217–99; SSN, May 1963, p. 2; Oct. 1963, p. 15; Morris, *Civil Rights Movement*, 250–58, 274; Dittmer, *Struggle for Civil Rights in Mississippi*, 160–69; Bains, "Birmingham, 1963," 175–83, 189–90, 217, 219, 222–25; Eskew, "Alabama Christian Movement for Human Rights," 73–74, 77–78, 80–83; Branch, *Parting the Waters*, 710, 725–26, 758–65; Lentz, "News Magazine Coverage of the 1963 Birmingham Civil Rights Crisis," 7–10, 12, 16; Brauer, *John F. Kennedy and the Second Reconstruction*, 232–38; Stern, *Kennedy, Johnson, and Civil Rights*, 84–90; Sitkoff, *Struggle for Black Equality*, 148–49; *Newsweek*, 13 May 1963, pp. 27–29. But cf. Eskew, *But for Birmingham*, 208–16.

191. SSN, June 1961, p. 11; Mar. 1963, p. 1; excerpts from various articles by William Buckley in *National Review*, p. 4, NAACP, part 21, reel 1, fr. 154; Gallup, *Gallup Poll*, 3:1769; SSN, Apr. 1961, pp. 1, 5; May 1961, p. 13; Feb. 1962, p. 7; Mar. 1962, p. 1; June 1962, p. 16; Apr. 1963, p. 2; NYT, 1 Mar. 1963, pp. 1, 5; J. Francis Polhaus to Clarence Mitchell, memorandum, 6 Jan. 1961, part 22, reel 4, frs. 229–31; NAACP Press Release, 26 Apr. 1963, part 20, reel 3, fr. 377; Stern, *Kennedy, Johnson, and Civil Rights*, 79–80.

192. SSN, Oct. 1960, p. 4; June 1961, p. 11; Aug. 1961, p. 14; Jan. 1962, p. 1; Feb. 1962, p. 7; June 1962, p. 15; Aug. 1962, p. 9; Apr. 1963, p. 2; NYT, 2 Sept. 1960, pp. 1, 11; Clarence Mitchell to Wilkins, 8 Mar. 1961, NAACP, part 22, reel 3, frs. 643–45; Lomax, *Negro Revolt*, 229–30; Brauer, *John F. Kennedy and the Second Reconstruction*, 32–44, 61–64, 84–85, 105–6, 110, 129–31, 205–9; Stern, *Kennedy, Johnson, and*

Civil Rights, 40–48, 51–52, 58–60, 63–69; Branch, *Parting the Waters*, 382–83, 405–6, 469–77, 480, 586–87, 682–83; Garrow, *Bearing the Cross*, 161–62, 169–70; McMillen, "Black Enfranchisement in Mississippi," 357–60; Payne, *Mississippi Freedom Struggle*, 107–11, 123–24, 173–74; Dittmer, *Struggle for Civil Rights in Mississippi*, 92–95, 119–20, 153–57, 169; Eskew, *But for Birmingham*, 299, 310–12.

193. Brauer, *John F. Kennedy and the Second Reconstruction*, 246–47, 259–62; SSN, Sept. 1963, pp. 5, 23; Dec. 1963, p. 1; June 1963, p. 5; July 1963, pp. 1, 16; Oct. 1963, pp. 1, 8; Feb. 1964, pp. 1, 13; Mar. 1964, p. 1; NYT, 17 Sept. 1963, pp. 1, 25; "The Blame—and Beyond," ibid., p. 34; 19 Sept. 1963, p. 17; Gallup, *Gallup Poll*, 3:1812, 1837–38, 1842; Garrow, *Protest at Selma*, 141–44; Orfield, *Reconstruction of Southern Education*, 33–36; Bains, "Birmingham, 1963," 195, 222–23, 238–39; Sitkoff, *Struggle for Black Equality*, 127–28, 148–53; Branch, *Parting the Waters*, 808–9; Stern, *Kennedy, Johnson, and Civil Rights*, 106–7, 160–70; Garrow, *Bearing the Cross*, 267–69; Eskew, *But for Birmingham*, 4, 17, 299, 310–12; Loevy, *Civil Rights Act of 1964*, 24, 38, 53, 78–80, 154; Dallek, *Lyndon Johnson*, 2:60, 111–21.

194. SSN, June 1962, p. 8; June 1963, p. 5; Carter, *George Wallace*, 76, 82, 84–87, 96; Strong, "Alabama," 448–49, 451–52; Frady, *Wallace*, 97–98, 106–8, 116, 121–22; pages 399, 405–6.

195. SSN, June 1963, pp. 1, 5, 6; Apr. 1963, p. 8; July 1963, pp. 1, 5; *Newsweek*, 20 May 1963, pp. 25–27; Carter, *George Wallace*, 110–14, 116–17, 119, 126–27, 133–51; Eskew, *But for Birmingham*, 6, 228, 282; Muse, *Ten Years of Prelude*, 267; Bains, "Birmingham, 1963," 192, 199.

196. SSN, July 1963, p. 5; Sept. 1963, pp. 1–3, 17, 22; Carter, *George Wallace*, 162–83 (quotes at 166, 172, 173); "Wallace's Defeat in 'Victory'," NYT, 11 Sept. 1963, p. 42; 16 Sept. 1963, p. 26; SSN, Oct. 1963, pp. 1, 8, 10–11; Nov. 1963, p. 2; NYT, 6 Sept. 1963, pp. 1, 14; 7 Sept. 1963, pp. 1, 9; 9 Sept. 1963, pp. 1, 16; 10 Sept. 1963, pp. 1, 27; 11 Sept. 1963, pp. 1, 31; 16 Sept. 1963, pp. 1, 26; "New Outrage in Birmingham," ibid., p. 34; 17 Sept. 1963, pp. 1, 24, 25; 19 Sept. 1963, pp. 1, 17; 23 Sept. 1963, pp. 1, 23; *Time*, 27 Sept. 1963, pp. 17–18; Muse, *Ten Years of Prelude*, 276–78; Lusky, "Nullification," 1174 n. 49; Henry Lee Moon to Pres. Kennedy, telegram, 16 Sept. 1963, NAACP, part 20, reel 3, fr. 748; Laura Valdes to Pres. Kennedy, telegram, n.d., ibid., fr. 749; Manis, *Fred Shuttlesworth*, 401–4.

197. NYT, 18 Sept. 1963, p. 27; Grace M. Graham to NAACP, telegram, 15 Sept. 1963, part 20, reel 3, fr. 926; Donald B. Brown to Wilkins, 18 Sept. 1963, ibid., fr. 941; Elouise May to NAACP, 16 Sept. 1963, ibid., fr. 947; Robert E. Feir to Wilkins, 23 Sept. 1963, ibid., fr. 959; Manzie Ridgill to Wilkins, 17 Sept. 1963, ibid., frs. 919–20; NAACP Press Release, 21 Sept. 1963, ibid., fr. 986; SSN, Oct. 1963, p. 11; NYT, 17 Sept. 1963, p. 26. See also Robert Smith, "Birmingham's Real Horror Is Ghastly White Silence," *Pittsfield* (Massachusetts) *Berkshire Eagle*, 23 Sept. 1963, part 20, reel 3, fr. 954; Organizers of March on Washington to Pres. Kennedy, telegram, 16 Sept. 1963, ibid., frs. 989–91; NAACP Press Release, 26 Sept. 1963, ibid., frs. 811–12; assorted press clippings, ibid., frs. 785, 792, 978.

198. NYT, 9 Sept. 1963, p. 16; SSN, Nov. 1963, p. 2; Jan. 1964, pp. 1, 12; Feb. 1964, pp. 1, 12–13; Mar. 1964, p. 13; Lubell, *White and Black*, 112–13.

199. SSN, Apr. 1964, p. 14; Payne, *Mississippi Freedom Struggle*, 297–301, 396; Dittmer, *Struggle for Civil Rights in Mississippi*, 199–200, 208–10, 244–52; Cagin & Dray, *Civil Rights Campaign for Mississippi*, 218–20, 330–32, 349–50, 386, 412; McAdam, *Freedom Summer*, 39, 81, 96–101, 103, 118, 150–54; Holt, *Summer That Didn't End*, 20–26, 28–29; Rachal, "Mississippi Response to Freedom Summer," 315,

321–22, 324; Stern, *Kennedy, Johnson, and Civil Rights*, 188–90; Sitkoff, *Struggle for Black Equality*, 171, 176–77.

200. Fairclough, *Southern Christian Leadership Conference*, 225–29; Garrow, *Protest at Selma*, 2–3, 32–34; Thornton, "Municipal Politics," 55, 60; McMillen, *Citizens' Council*, 43; Fager, *Selma*, 18–19; Eskew, *But for Birmingham*, 281, 301–2; Carter, *George Wallace*, 240.

201. Thornton, "Municipal Politics," 60; Garrow, *Protest at Selma*, 2–3, 32–34, 42–45, 60–61, 73–80, 135, 146–49, 159 table 4-1, 223, 230–31; Longnecker, *Selma's Peacemaker*, 23–24, 36, 112–13, 123–24, 127, 129–30, 139–42, 162–64, 174–77; Fairclough, *Southern Christian Leadership Conference*, 229–43; Carter, *George Wallace*, 246–49; Fager, *Selma*, 18, 22–98; Branch, *Parting the Waters*, 779–80, 794–96; Garrow, *Bearing the Cross*, 250–52; Sitkoff, *Struggle for Black Equality*, 186–90; Sherrill, *Gothic Politics in the Deep South*, 266; Oates, "Week the World Watched Selma," 56.

202. *Time*, 19 Mar. 1965, pp. 23–28; 26 Mar. 1965, pp. 19–23; "Special Message to the Congress: The American Promise" (15 Mar. 1965), in *Public Papers of the Presidents of the United States: Lyndon B. Johnson, 1965*, vol. 1 (Washington, D.C., 1966): 281, 284; 111 *Congressional Record* 4984–89, 5014–15 (15 Mar. 1964); Carter, *George Wallace*, 250, 254–55; Garrow, *Protest at Selma*, 78–108; Fairclough, *Southern Christian Leadership Conference*, 247, 249–51; Fager, *Selma*, 208–9; Stern, *Kennedy, Johnson, and Civil Rights*, 215–17; Sitkoff, *Struggle for Black Equality*, 186–87; Dallek, *Lyndon Johnson*, 2:212, 215–20; Gallup, *Gallup Poll*, 3:1933.

203. Garrow, *Bearing the Cross*, 251; SSN, June 1963, p. 6; July 1957, p. 11; Nunnelley, *Bull Connor*, 169–70; Thornton, "Municipal Politics," 48–49; Bains, "Birmingham, 1963," 167–68, 187–88; Eskew, "Alabama Christian Movement for Human Rights," 23–28, 35–36; Branch, *Parting the Waters*, 420–22; Fager, *Selma*, 208–9; Longenecker, *Selma's Peacemaker*, 217; NYT, 6 Sept. 1963, pp. 1, 14; 10 Sept. 1963, pp. 1, 27; *Time*, 13 Sept. 1963, p. 26.

204. Jackson, *Supreme Court*, 80; Burk, *Eisenhower Administration and Black Civil Rights*, 192; Whitfield, *Emmett Till*, 72; Tushnet, "What Really Happened in Brown," 1928; Brady, *Black Monday*, 31–33.

CONCLUSION

1. Louis T. Wright, "The 26th Year of the N.A.A.C.P.," *Crisis* 43 (Aug. 1936): 244.

2. Klinker with Smith, *Rise and Decline of Racial Equality*, 3–4, 16–23, 51–71, 161–201.

3. "Shillady and Texas," *Crisis* 18 (Oct. 1919): 283; SSN, June 1959, p. 15; *Jackson Daily News*, 18 May 1959, NAACP, part 20, reel 2, fr. 135; Smead, *Lynching of Mack Charles Parker*, 149–50; Marable, *Race, Reform, and Rebellion*, 62.

4. King, *Why We Can't Wait*, 39–40; Fairclough, "Historians and the Civil Rights Movement," 396–97.

5. See generally Spaeth & Segal, *Majority Rule or Minority Will*, 287–315; cf. Schauer, "Easy Cases."

6. Segal & Spaeth, *Supreme Court and the Attitudinal Model*, 32–73; Klarman, "Fidelity, Indeterminacy, and the Problem of Constitutional Evil"; Tushnet, "Critique of Interpretivism and Neutral Principles."

7. Dred Scott v. Sandford, 60 U.S. (19 How.) 393 (1857); Korematsu v. United States, 323 U.S. 214 (1944); Dennis v. United States, 341 U.S. 494 (1951); Klarman,

"Rethinking the Civil Rights and Civil Liberties Revolutions." See generally McCloskey, *American Supreme Court*; Dahl, "Supreme Court as a National Policy Maker"; Friedman, "Dialogue and Judicial Review." In the race context specifically, see Spann, *Race against the Court*, 2–5, 19–26, 81–82. Cf. Marshall, *Public Opinion and the Supreme Court*, 78–98, 192; Feeley & Rubin, *Judicial Policy Making and the Modern State*, 332.

8. Klarman, "What's So Great about Constitutionalism?" 189–91; Swann v. Charlotte-Mecklenburg Board of Education, 402 U.S. 1 (1971); Keyes v. School District No. 1, Denver, Colorado, 413 U.S. 189 (1973); Ryan & Heise, "Political Economy of School Choice," 2052–58. Cf. Schauer, "Incentives, Reputation, and the Inglorious Determinants of Judicial Behavior," 628–29.

9. Cf. Jeffries, "Art of Judicial Selection," 598–99.

10. Zangrando, *NAACP's Crusade against Lynching*, 19, 64, 143, 162; Lawson, *Black Ballots*, chap. 3.

11. Klarman, "Political Process Theory," 788–819.

12. For scholarship that emphasizes the strategic aspect of Supreme Court decision making, see Murphy, *Elements of Judicial Strategy*, 171–75, 186–97, 204–10; Maltzman, Spriggs, & Wahlbeck, "Strategy and Judicial Choice"; Knight & Epstein, "Struggle for Judicial Supremacy"; Epstein & Walker, "Role of the Supreme Court"; Graber, "Marshall Court and Party Politics"; Graber, "Problematic Establishment of Judicial Power"; Klarman, "'Great' Marshall Court Decisions," 1157–64; Klarman, "Bush v. Gore," 1757–60.

13. Powe, *Warren Court*, 489–94; Marshall, *Public Opinion and the Supreme Court*, 84–85, 188; Klarman, "Rethinking the Civil Rights and Civil Liberties Revolutions," 16–17. See also Feeley & Rubin, *Judicial Policy Making and the Modern State*, 367.

14. Rosenberg, *Hollow Hope*, 108; Handler, *Social Movements and the Legal System*, 210; Schuck, "Public Law Litigation and Social Reform," 1786.

15. Compare Elman, "Solicitor General's Office," 837, and Greenberg, *Crusaders in the Courts*, 12, with Rosenberg, *Hollow Hope*, 71, 169, 338.

16. Harper v. Virginia Board of Elections, 383 U.S. 663, 667 (1966); Reynolds v. Sims, 377 U.S. 533, 562 (1964); Lawson, *Black Ballots*, 102, 128, 147, 166, 238; Moon, *Balance of Power*, 9; Klarman, "Political Process Theory," 788–819; Dittmer, *Local People*, 1–9; Fairclough, *Civil Rights Struggle in Louisiana*, 111; Norrell, *Civil Rights Movement in Tuskegee*, 60–61; Brooks, "Winning the Peace," 564, 568–70; Douglas, "Limits of Law," 697–701, 712–19; Tushnet, *NAACP's Legal Strategy*, 8–10.

17. John M. Lofton, Jr., to Marshall, n.d., NAACP, part 4, reel 9, fr. 957; Dorothy Q. Rainey to J. Lon Duckworth, 20 June 1944, ibid., reel 7, frs. 592–93; Lawson, *Black Ballots*, 148–49, 179–80, 345; Arnall, *Shore Dimly Seen*, 59–60; Myrdal, *American Dilemma*, 1:60–61.

18. Rosenberg, *Hollow Hope*, 31–32, 336–37. See also Handler, *Social Movements and the Legal System*, 111–29; Galanter, "Why the 'Haves' Come Out Ahead," 136–37.

19. W. G. Cornett to Arthur Garfield Hays, 30 Aug. 1938, NAACP, part 4, reel 1, fr. 867. Cf. Epp, *Rights Revolution*, 20, 56–58.

20. "The Right to Vote," *New South* 4 (Feb. 1949): 1, 4, NAACP, part 4, reel 7, frs. 554, 557.

21. Cf. Epp, *Rights Revolution*, 17–22, 197–200, 205; Galanter, "Why the 'Haves' Come Out Ahead," 98–104, 138–39, 140–44.

22. Cf. Scheingold, "Constitutional Rights and Social Change," 82–83.

23. Rosenberg, *Hollow Hope*, 33, 195–201. See also Canon, "Supreme Court and Policy Reform," 235–36, 242.

24. Lusky, "Nullification," 1167. Cf. Woodward, "The South and the Law of the Land," 374. See also Douglas, *Desegregation of the Charlotte Schools*, 39–40, 43–49.

25. Cf. Galanter, "Why the 'Haves' Come out Ahead"; Scheingold, "Constitutional Rights and Social Change," 83–84; Epp, *Rights Revolution*, 203, 205.

26. Cf. Marshall, *Public Opinion and the Supreme Court*, 132–56, 189–90, 193; Rosenberg, *Hollow Hope*, 338; McCann, *Rights at Work*, 89; Canon, "Supreme Court and Policy Reform," 229; Franklin & Kosaki, "Republican Schoolmaster," 753–54, 768. But cf. Hoekstra, "Supreme Court and Opinion Change," 122–23.

27. Fehrenbacher, *Dred Scott Case*, 561–67; Steiker & Steiker, "Constitutional Regulation of Capital Punishment," 410–12; Jeffries, *Lewis Powell*, 354–59, 414; Rosenberg, *Hollow Hope*, 188, 341–42; Hanna Rosin & Pamela Ferdinand, "Gays Achieve Breakthrough in Vermont," *Wash. Post*, 17 Mar. 2000, p. A1. Cf. Marshall, *Public Opinion and the Supreme Court*, 146–47, 189–90; Epstein & Kobylka, *Supreme Court and Legal Change*, 84–90, 207; Franklin & Kosaki, "Republican Schoolmaster," 763, 767–68.

28. Cf. Scheingold, "Constitutional Rights and Social Change," 80; Rosenberg, *Hollow Hope*, 155–56.

29. Hanna Rosin & Richard Morin, "As Tolerance Grows, Acceptance Remains Elusive," *Wash. Post*, 26 Dec. 1998, p. A1; Baehr v. Lewin, 852 P. 2d 44 (Haw. 1993).

30. Rosenberg, *Hollow Hope*, 182–95, 235–38, 258–65.

31. *Crisis* 3 (Feb. 1912): 159; "Three Achievements and Their Significance," ibid. 34 (Sept. 1927): 222; "Press Comment on Anti-Lynching Bill," ibid. 44 (May 1937): 153, 163; Foner, *Reconstruction*, 425–44, 454–49; Trelease, *White Terror*, chap. 24; Williams, *Ku Klux Klan Trials*, 40–43; Zangrando, *NAACP Crusade against Lynching*, 77; McCoy & Ruetten, *Truman Administration*, 42–54; *To Secure These Rights*, 20–27; Frederickson, "Racial Violence in South Carolina," 177–85, 198.

32. Cf. McCann, *Rights at Work*, 10, 56–57, 89, 279.

33. McNeil, *Charles Hamilton Houston*, 135; Sullivan, *Days of Hope*, 91. Cf. Rosenberg, *Hollow Hope*, 338–41.

34. Cf. Lomax, *Negro Revolt*, 162–63.

BIBLIOGRAPHY

NEWSPAPERS AND PERIODICALS

Crisis (journal of the National Association for the Advancement of Colored People)
Nation
New Republic
Newsweek
New York Times
Southern School News
Time
Washington Post

MANUSCRIPT COLLECTIONS

Papers of the National Association for the Advancement of Colored People. Edited by August Meier. Frederick, Md.: University Publications of America, 1982. Microfilm.

Part 1 (Meetings of Boards of Directors, Records of Annual Conferences, Major Speeches, Special Reports)

Part 3 (Campaign for Educational Equality)

Part 4 (Voting Rights Campaign)

Part 5 (Campaign against Residential Segregation)

Part 8 (Discrimination in the Criminal Justice System)

Part 10 (Peonage, Labor, and the New Deal)

Part 20 (White Resistance and Reprisals)

Part 21 (NAACP Relations with the Modern Civil Rights Movement)

Papers of Supreme Court Justices

Brennan, William J. Papers. Manuscripts Division, Library of Congress.

Burton, Harold H. Papers. Manuscripts Division, Library of Congress.

Clark, Tom C. Papers. Tarleton Law Library, University of Texas.

Douglas, William O. Papers. Manuscripts Division, Library of Congress.

Frankfurter, Felix. Papers. Frederick, Md.: University Publications of America, 1986. Microfilm.

Harlan, John Marshall. Papers. Princeton University Library, Princeton, N.J.

Jackson, Robert H. Papers. Manuscripts Division, Library of Congress.

Murphy, Frank. Papers. Bentley Historical Library, University of Michigan.

Reed, Stanley F. Papers. Special Collections and Archives, University of Kentucky Libraries.

Warren, Earl. Papers. Manuscripts Division, Library of Congress.

BOOKS

Abraham, Henry J. *Justices, Senators and Presidents: A History of the U.S. Supreme Court Appointments from Washington to Clinton*. Rev. ed. New York: Oxford University Press, 1999.

Abrams, Douglas. *Conservative Constraints: North Carolina and the New Deal*. Jackson: University Press of Mississippi, 1992.

Adelson, Bruce. *Brushing Back Jim Crow: The Integration of Minor-League Baseball in the American South*. Charlottesville: University of Virginia Press, 1999.

Alvis, Joel, Jr. *Religion and Race: Southern Presbyterians, 1946–83*. Tuscaloosa: University of Alabama Press, 1994.

Ambrose, Stephen E. *Eisenhower*. Vol. 1, *Soldier, General of the Army, President-Elect, 1880–1952*. New York: Simon & Schuster, 1983.

——. *Eisenhower*. Vol. 2, *The President*. New York: Simon & Schuster, 1984.

Anderson, Eric. *Race and Politics in North Carolina 1872–1901: The Black Second*. Baton Rouge: Louisiana State University Press, 1981.

Anderson, J. W. *Eisenhower, Brownell, and the Congress: The Tangled Origins of the Civil Rights Bill of 1956–1957*. University: University of Alabama Press, 1964.

Anderson, James D. *The Education of Blacks in the South, 1860–1935*. Chapel Hill: University of North Carolina Press, 1988.

Anderson, William. *The Wild Man from Sugar Creek: The Political Career of Eugene Talmadge*. Baton Rouge: Louisiana State University Press, 1975.

Arnall, Ellis. *The Shore Dimly Seen*. Philadelphia: Lippincott, 1946.

Arnesen, Eric. *Waterfront Workers of New Orleans: Race, Class, and Politics, 1863–1923*. New York: Oxford University Press, 1991.

Ayers, Edward L. *Vengeance and Justice: Crime and Punishment in the 19th-Century South*. New York: Oxford University Press, 1984.

——. *Promise of the New South: Life after Reconstruction*. New York: Oxford University Press, 1992.

Baer, Judith. *Equality under the Constitution: Reclaiming the Fourteenth Amendment*. Ithaca, N.Y.: Cornell University Press, 1983.

Baker, Liva. *The Justice from Beacon Hill: The Life and Times of Oliver Wendell Holmes*. New York: HarperCollins, 1991.

———. *The Second Battle of New Orleans: The Hundred-Year Struggle to Integrate the Schools*. New York: HarperCollins, 1996.

Baker, Ray Stannard. *Following the Color Line: American Negro Citizenship in the Progressive Era*. New York: Harper & Row, 1908.

Balkin, Jack, ed. *What* Brown v. Board of Education *Should Have Said*. New York: New York University Press, 2001.

Ball, Howard, & Phillip J. Cooper. *Of Power and Right: Hugo Black, William O. Douglas, and America's Constitutional Revolution*. New York: Oxford University Press, 1992.

Barnes, Catherine A. *Journey from Jim Crow: The Desegregation of Southern Transit*. New York: Columbia University Press, 1983.

Barone, Michael. *Our Country: The Shaping of America from Roosevelt to Reagan*. New York: Free Press, 1990.

Bartley, Numan V. *The Rise of Massive Resistance: Race and Politics in the South during the 1950s*. Baton Rouge: Louisiana State University Press, 1969.

———. *The New South, 1945–80: The Story of the South's Modernization*. Baton Rouge: Louisiana State University Press, 1995.

Bartley, Numan V., & Hugh D. Graham. *Southern Politics and the Second Reconstruction*. Baltimore, Md.: Johns Hopkins University Press, 1975.

Baskerville, Steven W. *Of Laws and Limitations: An Intellectual Portrait of Louis D. Brandeis*. Rutherford, N.J.: Fairleigh Dickinson University Press, 1994.

Bass, Jack. *Unlikely Heroes*. Tuscaloosa: University of Alabama Press, 1981.

Bayor, Ronald H. *Race and the Shaping of Twentieth-Century Atlanta*. Chapel Hill: University of North Carolina Press, 1996.

Belknap, Michal R. *Federal Law and Southern Order: Racial Violence and Constitutional Conflict in the Post-Brown South*. Athens: University of Georgia Press, 1987.

Berger, Raoul. *Government by Judiciary: The Transformation of the Fourteenth Amendment*. Cambridge, Mass.: Harvard University Press, 1977.

Berman, William C. *The Politics of Civil Rights in the Truman Administration*. Columbus: Ohio State University Press, 1970.

Berry, Mary Frances. *Stability, Security, and Continuity: Mr. Justice Burton and Decision Making in the Supreme Court 1945–1958*. Westport, Conn.: Greenwood, 1978.

Beth, Loren P. *John Marshall Harlan: The Last Whig Justice*. Lexington: University Press of Kentucky, 1992.

Bickel, Alexander. *The Least Dangerous Branch*. Indianapolis, Ind.: Bobbs-Merrill, 1962.

Black, Earl. *Southern Governors and Civil Rights: Racial Segregation as a Campaign Issue in the Second Reconstruction*. Cambridge, Mass.: Harvard University Press, 1976.

Blum, John Morton. *V Was for Victory: Politics and American Culture during World War II*. New York: Harcourt Brace Jovanovich, 1976.

Brady, Tom. *Black Monday*. Winona, Miss.: Association of Citizens' Councils, 1954.

Branch, Taylor. *Parting the Waters: America in the King Years 1954–63*. New York: Simon & Schuster, 1988.

Brauer, Carl M. *John F. Kennedy and the Second Reconstruction*. New York: Columbia University Press, 1977.

Brink, William, & Louis Harris. *The Negro Revolution in America*. New York: Simon & Schuster, 1964.

Brinkley, Alan. *Liberalism and Its Discontents*. Cambridge, Mass.: Harvard University Press, 1998.

Brock, Clifton. *Americans for Democratic Action: Its Role in National Politics*. Washington, D.C.: Public Affairs Press, 1962.

Brodhead, Michael J. *David J. Brewer: The Life of a Supreme Court Justice, 1837–1910*. Carbondale: Southern Illinois University Press, 1994.

Broussard, Albert S. *Black San Francisco: The Struggle for Racial Equality in the West 1900–1954*. Lawrence: University Press of Kansas, 1993.

Brundage, W. Fitzhugh. *Lynching in the New South: Georgia and Virginia, 1880–1930*. Urbana: University of Illinois Press, 1993.

Brundage, W. Fitzhugh, ed. *Under Sentence of Death: Lynching in the South*. Chapel Hill: University of North Carolina Press, 1997.

Buck, Paul H. *The Road to Reunion, 1865–1900*. Boston: Little, Brown, 1937.

Bunche, Ralph J. *The Political Status of the Negro in the Age of FDR*. Edited by Dewey W. Grantham. Chicago, Ill.: University of Chicago Press, 1973.

Burk, Robert Fredrick. *The Eisenhower Administration and Black Civil Rights*. Knoxville: University of Tennessee Press, 1984.

Burns, Stewart, ed. *Daybreak of Freedom: The Montgomery Bus Boycott*. Chapel Hill: University of North Carolina Press, 1997.

Cagin, Seth, & Philip Dray. *We Are Not Afraid: The Story of Goodman, Schwerner and Chaney and the Civil Rights Campaign for Mississippi*. New York: Macmillan, 1988.

Cain, Patricia A. *Rainbow Rights: The Role of Lawyers and Courts in the Lesbian and Gay Civil Rights Movement*. Boulder, Colo.: Westview, 2000.

Callcott, Margaret Law. *The Negro in Maryland Politics 1870–1912*. Baltimore, Md.: Johns Hopkins University Press, 1969.

Capeci, Dominic. *The Lynching of Cleo Wright*. Lexington: University Press of Kentucky, 1998.

Capeci, Dominic J., Jr., & Martha Wilkerson. *Layered Violence: The Detroit Rioters of 1943*. Jackson: University Press of Mississippi, 1991.

Caro, Robert A. *The Years of Lyndon Johnson*. Vol. 3, *Master of the Senate*. New York: Knopf, 2002.

Carr, Robert K. *Federal Protection of Civil Rights: Quest for a Sword*. Ithaca, N.Y.: Cornell University Press, 1947.

Carson, Clayborne. *In Struggle: SNCC and the Black Awakening of the 1960s*. Cambridge, Mass.: Harvard University Press, 1981.

Carter, Dan T. *Scottsboro: A Tragedy of the American South*. Rev. ed. Baton Rouge: Louisiana State University Press, 1979.

——. *The Politics of Rage: George Wallace, the Origins of the New Conservatism, and the Transformation of American Politics*. New York: Simon & Schuster, 1995.

Cartwright, Joseph H. *Triumph of Jim Crow: Tennessee Race Relations in the 1880s*. Knoxville: University of Tennessee Press, 1976.

Casdorph, Paul D. *Republicans, Negroes, and Progressives in the South, 1912–1916*. University: University of Alabama Press, 1981.

Cecelski, David, & Timothy Tyson, eds. *Democracy Betrayed: The Wilmington Race Riot of 1898 and Its Legacy*. Chapel Hill: University of North Carolina Press, 1998.

Cell, John W. *The Highest Stage of White Supremacy: The Origins of Segregation in South Africa and the American South*. Cambridge: Cambridge University Press, 1982.

Chafe, William H. *Civilities and Civil Rights: Greensboro, North Carolina, and the Black Struggle for Freedom*. New York: Oxford University Press, 1980.

Chicago Commission on Race Relations. *The Negro in Chicago: A Study of Race Relations and a Race Riot in 1919*. Chicago, Ill.: University of Chicago Press, 1922.

Chong, Dennis. *Collective Action and the Civil Rights Movement*. New York: Oxford University Press, 1991.

Clark, E. Culpepper. *The Schoolhouse Door: Segregation's Last Stand at the University of Alabama*. New York: Oxford University Press, 1993.

Clayton, Cornell W., & Howard Gillman. *Supreme Court Decision Making: New Institutionalist Approaches*. Chicago, Ill.: University of Chicago Press, 1999.

Cobb, James C. *The Selling of the South: The Southern Crusade for Industrial Development, 1936–1980*. Urbana: University of Illinois Press, 1982.

——. *The Most Southern Place on Earth: The Mississippi Delta and the Roots of Regional Identity*. New York: Oxford University Press, 1992.

Cohen, William. *At Freedom's Edge: Black Mobility and the Southern White Quest for Racial Control, 1861–1915*. Baton Rouge: Louisiana State University Press, 1991.

Cole, David. *No Equal Justice: Race and Class in the American Criminal Justice System*. New York: New Press, 1999.

Collins, Charles Wallace. *The Fourteenth Amendment and the States*. Boston: Little, Brown, 1912.

Cook, Blanche Wiesen. *Eleanor Roosevelt*. Vol. 2, 1933–1938. New York: Viking, 1999.

Cooley, Thomas M. *A Treatise on the Law of Torts*. Chicago, Ill.: Callaghan, 1880.

——. *A Treatise on the Constitutional Limitations Which Rest upon the Legislative Power of the States of the American Union*. 7th ed. Boston: Little, Brown, 1903.

Cortner, Richard C. *A "Scottsboro" Case in Mississippi: The Supreme Court and Brown v. Mississippi*. Jackson: University Press of Mississippi, 1986.

——. *A Mob Intent on Death: The NAACP and the Arkansas Riot Cases*. Middletown, Conn.: Wesleyan University Press, 1988.

Cox, Thomas C. *Blacks in Topeka, Kansas, 1865–1915: A Social History*. Baton Rouge: Louisiana State University Press, 1982.

Cresswell, Stephen. *Multi-Party Politics in Mississippi, 1877–1902*. Jackson: University Press of Mississippi, 1995.

Crew, Spencer R. *Black Life in Secondary Cities: A Comparative Analysis of the Black Communities of Camden and Elizabeth, New Jersey, 1860–1920*. New York: Garland, 1993.

Crispell, Brian Lewis. *Testing the Limits: George Armistead Smathers and Cold War America*. Athens: University of Georgia Press, 1999.

Curriden, Mark, & Leroy Phillips, Jr. *Contempt of Court: The Turn-of-the-Century Lynching That Launched a Hundred Years of Federalism*. New York: Faber and Faber, 1999.

Cushman, Barry. *Rethinking the New Deal Court: The Structure of a Constitutional Revolution*. New York: Oxford University Press, 1998.

Dabney, Virginius. *Below the Potomac: A Book about the New South*. New York: Appleton-Century, 1942.

Dalfiume, Richard M. *Desegregation of the U.S. Armed Forces: Fighting on Two Fronts, 1939–53*. Columbia: University of Missouri Press, 1969.

Dallek, Robert. *Lyndon Johnson and His Times.* Vol. 1, *Lone Star Rising, 1908–1960.* New York: Oxford University Press, 1991.

———. *Lyndon Johnson and His Times.* Vol. 2, *Flawed Giant, 1961–1973.* New York: Oxford University Press, 1998.

Daniel, Pete. *The Shadow of Slavery: Peonage in the South, 1901–1969.* Urbana: University of Illinois Press, 1972.

———. *Lost Revolutions: The South in the 1950s.* Chapel Hill: University of North Carolina Press, 2000.

Degler, Carl. *In Search of Human Nature: The Decline and Revival of Darwinism in American Social Thought.* New York: Oxford University Press, 1991.

DeSantis, Vincent P. *Republicans Face the Southern Question: The New Departure Years, 1877–1897.* New York: Greenwood, 1959.

Dickson, Del, ed. *The Supreme Court in Conference (1940–1985): The Private Discussions behind Nearly 300 Supreme Court Decisions.* New York: Oxford University Press, 2001.

Dinnerstein, Leonard. *The Leo Frank Case.* New York: Columbia University Press, 1968.

Dittmer, John. *Black Georgia in the Progressive Era, 1900–1920.* Urbana: University of Illinois Press, 1977.

———. *Local People: The Struggle for Civil Rights in Mississippi.* Urbana: University of Illinois Press, 1994.

Dolbeare, Kenneth M., & Phillip E. Hammond. *The School Prayer Decisions: From Court Policy to Local Practice.* Chicago, Ill.: University of Chicago Press, 1971.

Dollard, John. *Caste and Class in a Southern Town.* New Haven, Conn.: Yale University Press, 1937; Madison: University of Wisconsin Press, 1988.

Douglas, Davison M. *Reading, Writing & Race: The Desegregation of the Charlotte Schools.* Chapel Hill: University of North Carolina Press, 1995.

Doyle, Bertram Wilbur. *The Etiquette of Race Relations in the South: A Study in Social Control.* Chicago, Ill.: University of Chicago Press, 1937.

Doyle, William. *An American Insurrection: The Battle of Oxford, Mississippi, 1962.* New York: Doubleday, 2001.

Du Bois, W. E. B. *The Philadelphia Negro: A Social Study.* Philadelphia: University of Pennsylvania, 1899.

Dudziak, Mary. *Cold War Civil Rights: Race and the Image of American Democracy.* Princeton, N.J.: Princeton University Press, 2000.

Eagles, Charles W. *Jonathan Daniels and Race Relations: The Evolution of a Southern Liberal.* Knoxville: University of Tennessee Press, 1982.

Eagles, Charles W., ed. *The Civil Rights Movement in America.* Jackson: University Press of Mississippi, 1986.

Egerton, John. *Speak Now against the Day: The Generation before the Civil Rights Movement in the South.* Chapel Hill: University of North Carolina Press, 1994.

Ely, James W., Jr. *The Crisis of Conservative Virginia: The Byrd Organization and the Politics of Massive Resistance.* Knoxville: University of Tennessee Press, 1976.

———. *The Chief Justiceship of Melville W. Fuller, 1888–1910.* Columbia: University of South Carolina Press, 1995.

Ely, John Hart. *Democracy and Distrust.* Cambridge, Mass.: Harvard University Press, 1980.

Epp, Charles R. *The Rights Revolution: Lawyers, Activists, and Supreme Courts in Comparative Perspective.* Chicago, Ill.: University of Chicago Press, 1998.

Epstein, Lee, ed. *Contemplating Courts*. Washington, D.C.: CQ Press, 1995.

Epstein, Lee, & Joseph F. Kobylka. *The Supreme Court and Legal Change: Abortion and the Death Penalty*. Chapel Hill: University of North Carolina Press, 1992.

Epstein, Richard A. *Forbidden Grounds: The Case against Employment Discrimination Laws*. Cambridge, Mass.: Harvard University Press, 1992.

Eskew, Glenn T. *But for Birmingham: The Local and National Movements in the Civil Rights Struggle*. Chapel Hill: University of North Carolina Press, 1997.

Evans, Maurice S. *Black and White in the Southern States*. London: Longmans, 1915.

Fager, Charles E. *Selma, 1965*. New York: Scribner's, 1974.

Fairclough, Adam. *To Redeem the Soul of America: The Southern Christian Leadership Conference and Martin Luther King, Jr.* Athens: University of Georgia Press, 1987.

———. *Race and Democracy: The Civil Rights Struggle in Louisiana, 1915–1972*. Athens: University of Georgia Press, 1995.

Fairman, Charles. *Reconstruction and Reunion, 1864–1888*. Part 1. New York: Macmillan, 1971.

Farmer, James. *Lay Bare the Heart: An Autobiography of the Civil Rights Movement*. New York: Arbor House, 1985.

Fassett, John D. *New Deal Justice: The Life of Stanley Reed of Kentucky*. New York: Vantage, 1994.

Feeley, Malcolm M., & Edward L. Rubin. *Judicial Policy Making and the Modern State*. Cambridge: Cambridge University Press, 1998.

Fehrenbacher, Don E. *The Dred Scott Case: Its Significance in American Law and Politics*. New York: Oxford University Press, 1978.

Fenton, H. A. *Constitutional Law*. Annapolis, Md.: U.S. Naval Institute, 1914.

Ferrell, Robert H. *Choosing Truman: The Democratic Convention of 1944*. Columbia: University of Missouri Press, 1994.

———. *Harry S Truman: A Life*. Columbia: University of Missouri Press, 1994.

Fine, Sidney. *Frank Murphy: The Washington Years*. Ann Arbor: University of Michigan Press, 1984.

Fischer, Roger A. *The Segregation Struggle in Louisiana 1862–1877*. Urbana: University of Illinois Press, 1974.

Fisher, Ada Lois Sipuel, with Danney Goble. *A Matter of Black and White: The Autobiography of Ada Lois Sipuel Fisher*. Norman: University of Oklahoma Press, 1996.

Fiss, Owen M. *Troubled Beginnings of the Modern State, 1888–1910*. Vol. 8 of *History of the Supreme Court of the United States*. New York: Macmillan, 1993.

Fite, Gilbert C. *Richard B. Russell, Jr.: Senator from Georgia*. Chapel Hill: University of North Carolina Press, 1991.

Foner, Eric. *Reconstruction: America's Unfinished Revolution 1863–1877*. New York: Perennial, 1988.

———. *The Story of American Freedom*. New York: Norton, 1998.

Frady, Marshall. *Wallace*. New York: World, 1968.

Frank, Jerome. *Law and the Modern Mind*. New York: Coward-McCann, 1930.

Frederickson, Kari. *The Dixiecrat Revolt and the End of the Solid South, 1932–1968*. Chapel Hill: University of North Carolina Press, 2001.

Fredrickson, George M. *The Black Image in the White Mind: The Debate on Afro-American Character and Destiny 1817–1914*. New York: Harper & Row, 1971.

Freidel, Frank. *F. D. R. and the South*. Baton Rouge: Louisiana State University Press, 1965.

Freyer, Tony. *The Little Rock Crisis: A Constitutional Interpretation.* Westport, Conn.: Greenwood, 1984.

Fried, Richard M. *Nightmare in Red: The McCarthy Era in Perspective.* New York: Oxford University Press, 1990.

Gallup, George H. *The Gallup Poll: Public Opinion 1935–1971.* 3 vols. New York: Random House, 1972.

Garfinkle, Herbert. *When Negroes March: The March on Washington Movement in the Organizational Politics for FEPC.* Glencoe, Ill.: Free Press, 1959.

Garrow, David J. *Protest at Selma: Martin Luther King, Jr., and the Voting Rights Act of 1965.* New Haven, Conn.: Yale University Press, 1978.

———. *Bearing the Cross: Martin Luther King, Jr., and the Southern Christian Leadership Conference.* New York: Vintage, 1988.

Garrow, David J., ed. *Birmingham, Alabama, 1956–1963: The Black Struggle for Civil Rights.* Brooklyn, N.Y.: Carlson, 1989.

Gerber, David A. *Black Ohio and the Color Line, 1860–1915.* Urbana: University of Illinois Press, 1976.

Gillette, William. *Right to Vote: Politics and the Passage of the Fifteenth Amendment.* Baltimore, Md.: Johns Hopkins University Press, 1965.

———. *Retreat from Reconstruction, 1869–1879.* Baton Rouge: Louisiana State University Press, 1979.

Gillman, Howard. *The Constitution Besieged: The Rise and Demise of Lochner Era Police Powers Jurisprudence.* Durham, N.C.: Duke University Press, 1993.

Gilmore, Glenda Elizabeth. *Gender and Jim Crow: Women and the Politics of White Supremacy in North Carolina, 1896–1920.* Chapel Hill: University of North Carolina Press, 1996.

Goings, Kenneth W. *"The NAACP Comes of Age": The Defeat of Judge John J. Parker.* Bloomington: Indiana University Press, 1990.

Goldfield, David. *Black, White, and Southern: Race Relations and Southern Culture, 1940 to the Present.* Baton Rouge: Louisiana State University Press, 1990.

Goldman, Robert M. *"A Free Ballot and a Fair Count": The Department of Justice and the Enforcement of Voting Rights in the South, 1877–1893.* New York: Garland, 1990.

Goldstein, Robert Justice. *Flag Burning and Free Speech: The Case of Texas v. Johnson.* Lawrence: University of Kansas Press, 2000.

Goodman, James. *Stories of Scottsboro.* New York: Pantheon, 1994.

Gosnell, Harold F. *Negro Politicians: The Rise of Negro Politics in Chicago.* 1935. Reprint, Chicago, Ill.: University of Chicago Press, 1967.

Gould, Lewis L. *The Presidency of Theodore Roosevelt.* Lawrence: University Press of Kansas, 1991.

Graham, Hugh Davis. *The Civil Rights Era: Origins and Development of National Policy, 1960–1972.* New York: Oxford University Press, 1990.

Grantham, Dewey W. *Southern Progressivism: The Reconciliation of Progress and Tradition.* Knoxville: University of Tennessee Press, 1983.

Green, Ben. *Before His Time: The Untold Story of Harry T. Moore.* New York: Free Press, 1999.

Greenberg, Cheryl Lynn. *Or Does It Explode?: Black Harlem in the Great Depression.* New York: Oxford University Press, 1991.

Greenberg, Jack. *Crusaders in the Courts: How a Dedicated Band of Lawyers Fought for the Civil Rights Revolution.* New York: Basic, 1994.

Grossman, James R. *Land of Hope: Chicago, Black Southerners, and the Great Migration*. Chicago, Ill.: University of Chicago Press, 1989.

Grossman, Lawrence. *The Democratic Party and the Negro: Northern and National Politics, 1868–92*. Urbana: University of Illinois Press, 1976.

Gugin, Linda C., & James E. St. Clair. *Sherman Minton: New Deal Senator, Cold War Justice*. Indianapolis: Indiana Historical Society, 1997.

Gunther, Gerald. *Learned Hand: The Man and the Judge*. New York: Knopf, 1994.

Hackney, Sheldon. *Populism to Progressivism in Alabama*. Princeton, N.J.: Princeton University Press, 1969.

Hale, Grace Elizabeth. *Making Whiteness: The Culture of Segregation in the South, 1890–1940*. New York: Pantheon, 1998.

Haller, John S., Jr. *Outcasts from Evolution: Scientific Attitudes of Racial Inferiority, 1859–1900*. Urbana: University of Illinois Press, 1971.

Halpern, Stephen C. *On the Limits of the Law: The Ironic Legacy of Title VI of the 1964 Civil Rights Act*. Baltimore, Md.: Johns Hopkins University Press, 1995.

Hampton, Henry, & Steve Fayer, eds. *Voices of Freedom: An Oral History of the Civil Rights Movement from the 1950s through the 1980s*. New York: Bantam, 1990.

Handler, Joel F. *Social Movements and the Legal System: A Theory of Law Reform and Social Change*. New York: Academic, 1978.

Harlan, Louis R. *Separate and Unequal: Public School Campaigns and Racism in the Southern Seaboard States, 1901–1915*. Chapel Hill: University of North Carolina Press, 1958.

——. *Booker T. Washington*. Vol. 2, *The Wizard of Tuskegee 1901–1915*. New York: Oxford University Press, 1983.

Harris, Robert. *The Quest for Equality: The Constitution, Congress and the Supreme Court*. Baton Rouge: Louisiana State University Press, 1960.

Hart, Henry, & Albert Sachs. *The Legal Process: Basic Problems for the Making and Application of Law*. Westbury, N.Y.: Foundation, 1994.

Hart, Roger L. *Redeemers, Bourbons & Populists: Tennessee 1870–1896*. Baton Rouge: Louisiana State University Press, 1975.

Havard, William C., ed. *The Changing Politics of the South*. Baton Rouge: Louisiana State University Press, 1972.

Haynes, Robert V. *A Night of Violence: The Houston Riot of 1917*. Baton Rouge: Louisiana State University Press, 1976.

Heard, Alexander. *A Two-Party South?* Chapel Hill: University of North Carolina Press, 1952.

Heckscher, August. *Woodrow Wilson*. New York: Scribner's, 1991.

Higginbotham, A. Leon, Jr. *Shades of Freedom: Racial Politics and Presumptions in the American Legal Process*. New York: Oxford University Press, 1996.

Higgs, Robert. *Competition and Coercion: Blacks in the American Economy 1865–1914*. Cambridge: Cambridge University Press, 1977.

Higham, John. *Strangers in the Land: Patterns of American Nativism 1860–1925*. New Brunswick, N.J.: Rutgers University Press, 1955.

Highsaw, Robert B. *Edward Douglass White: Defender of the Conservative Faith*. Baton Rouge: Louisiana State University Press, 1981.

Hine, Darlene Clark. *Black Victory: The Rise and Fall of the White Primary in Texas*. Millwood, N.Y.: KTO Press, 1979.

Hirsch, Arnold R. *Making the Second Ghetto: Race and Housing in Chicago, 1940–1960*. Cambridge: Cambridge University Press, 1983.

Hochschild, Jennifer L. *The New American Dilemma: Liberal Democracy and School Desegregation*. New Haven, Conn.: Yale University Press, 1984.

Holmes, Oliver Wendell, Jr. *The Common Law*. 1881. Reprint, Boston: Little, Brown, 1948.

Holt, Len. *The Summer That Didn't End*. New York: Morrow, 1965.

Homel, Michael W. *Down from Equality: Black Chicagoans and the Public Schools, 1920–41*. Urbana: University of Illinois Press, 1984.

Horne, Gerald. *Communist Front? The Civil Rights Congress, 1946–1956*. Rutherford, N.J.: Fairleigh Dickinson University Press, 1988.

Horwitz, Morton. *The Warren Court and the Pursuit of Justice*. New York: Hill & Wang, 1998.

Howard, J. Woodford, Jr. *Mr. Justice Murphy: A Political Biography*. Princeton, N.J.: Princeton University Press, 1968.

Howard, John R. *The Shifting Wind: The Supreme Court and Civil Rights from Reconstruction to Brown*. Albany: State University of New York Press, 1999.

Hutchinson, Dennis J., & David J. Garrow, eds. *The Forgotten Memoir of John Knox: A Year in the Life of a Supreme Court Clerk in FDR's Washington*. Chicago, Ill.: University of Chicago Press, 2002.

Inaugural Addresses of the Presidents of the United States: From George Washington, 1789, to George Bush, 1989. Washington, D.C.: U.S. Government Printing Office, 1989.

Inger, Morton. *Politics and Reality in an American City: The New Orleans School Crisis*. New York: Center for Urban Education, 1969.

Isaacs, Harold. *The New World of Negro Americans*. New York: Viking, 1963.

Jackson, Kenneth T. *Crabgrass Frontier: The Suburbanization of the United States*. New York: Oxford University Press, 1985.

Jackson, Robert H. *The Struggle for Judicial Supremacy: A Study of a Crisis in American Power Politics*. New York: Knopf, 1941.

———. *The Supreme Court in the American System of Government*. Cambridge, Mass.: Harvard University Press, 1955.

Jackson, Walter A. *Gunnar Myrdal and America's Conscience: Social Engineering and Racial Liberalism, 1938–1987*. Chapel Hill: University of North Carolina Press, 1990.

Jacobstein, Helen L. *The Segregation Factor in the Florida Democratic Gubernatorial Election of 1956*. Gainesville: University of Florida Press, 1972.

Jacoway, Elizabeth, & David R. Colburn, eds. *Southern Businessmen and Desegregation*. Baton Rouge: Louisiana State University Press, 1982.

Jacoway, Elizabeth, & C. Fred Williams, eds. *Understanding the Little Rock Crisis: An Exercise in Remembrance and Reconciliation*. Fayetteville: University of Arkansas Press, 1999.

James, Joseph. *The Ratification of the Fourteenth Amendment*. Macon, Ga.: Mercer University Press, 1984.

Jeffries, John C., Jr. *Justice Lewis F. Powell, Jr*. New York: Scribner's, 1994.

Johnson, Charles. *Into the Mainstream: A Survey of Best Practices in Race Relations in the South*. Chapel Hill: University of North Carolina Press, 1947.

Johnson, Donald Bruce, & Kirk H. Porter, eds. *National Party Platforms, 1840–1972*. 5th ed. Urbana: University of Illinois Press, 1975.

Johnston, Erle. *I Rolled with Ross: A Political Portrait*. Baton Rouge, La.: Moran, 1980.

Kantrowitz, Stephen. *Ben Tillman & the Reconstruction of White Supremacy*. Chapel Hill: University of North Carolina Press, 2000.

Katzman, David M. *Before the Ghetto: Black Detroit in the Nineteenth Century*. Urbana: University of Illinois Press, 1973.

Keller, Morton. *Regulating a New Society: Public Policy and Social Change in America, 1900–1933*. Cambridge, Mass.: Harvard University Press, 1994.

Kellogg, Charles Flint. *NAACP: A History of the National Association for the Advancement of Colored People*. Vol. 1, 1909–1920. Baltimore, Md.: Johns Hopkins University Press, 1967.

Kennedy, David. *Over There: The First World War and American Society*. New York: Oxford University Press, 1980.

Kennedy, Randall. *Race, Crime, and the Law*. New York: Pantheon, 1997.

Key, V. O., Jr. *Southern Politics in State and Nation*. New York: Knopf, 1949.

King, Martin Luther, Jr. *Stride toward Freedom: The Montgomery Story*. New York: Harper & Row, 1958.

———. *Why We Can't Wait*. New York: Penguin, 1964.

Kirby, Jack Temple. *Darkness at the Dawning: Race and Reform in the Progressive South*. Philadelphia: Lippincott, 1972.

Kirby, John B. *Black Americans in the Roosevelt Era: Liberalism and Race*. Knoxville: University of Tennessee Press, 1980.

Klinnker, Philip A., & Rogers M. Smith. *The Unsteady March: The Rise and Decline of Racial Equality in America*. Chicago, Ill.: University of Chicago Press, 1999.

Kluger, Richard. *Simple Justice: The History of* Brown v. Board of Education *and Black America's Struggle for Equality*. New York: Knopf, 1976.

Kneebone, John T. *Southern Liberal Journalists and the Issue of Race, 1920–1944*. Chapel Hill: University of North Carolina Press, 1985.

Kraditor, Aileen. *The Ideas of the Woman Suffrage Movement, 1890–1920*. New York: Columbia University Press, 1965.

Kousser, J. Morgan. *The Shaping of Southern Politics: Suffrage Restriction and the Establishment of the One-Party South, 1880–1910*. New Haven, Conn.: Yale University Press, 1974.

———. *Dead End: The Development of 19th-Century Litigation on Racial Discrimination in Schools*. Oxford: Clarendon, 1986.

Krueger, Thomas A. *And Promises to Keep: Southern Conference for Human Welfare, 1938–1948*. Nashville, Tenn.: Vanderbilt University Press, 1967.

Kull, Andrew. *The Color-Blind Constitution*. Cambridge, Mass.: Harvard University Press, 1992.

Kurland, Philip B. *Politics and the Constitution and the Warren Court*. Chicago, Ill.: University of Chicago Press, 1970.

Kurland, Philip B., & Gerhard Casper, eds. *Landmark Briefs and Arguments of the Supreme Court of the United States*. Washington, D.C.: University Publications of America, 1975–.

Kurtz, Michael L., & Morgan D. Peoples. *Earl K. Long: The Saga of Uncle Earl and Louisiana Politics*. Baton Rouge: Louisiana State University Press, 1990.

Kusmer, Kenneth. *A Ghetto Takes Shape: Black Cleveland, 1870–1930*. Urbana: University of Illinois Press, 1976.

Lamon, Lester C. *Black Tennesseans, 1900–1930*. Knoxville: University of Tennessee Press, 1976.

Lane, Ann J. *The Brownsville Affair: National Crisis and Black Reaction.* Port Washington, N.Y.: Kennikat, 1971.

Lassiter, Matthew D., & Andrew B. Lewis. *The Moderates' Dilemma: Massive Resistance to School Desegregation in Virginia.* Charlottesville: University Press of Virginia, 1998.

Laue, James H. *Direct Action and Desegregation, 1960–1962: Toward a Theory of the Rationalization of Protest.* Brooklyn, N.Y.: Carlson, 1989.

Lauren, Paul Gordon. *Power and Prejudice: The Politics and Diplomacy of Racial Discrimination.* Boulder, Colo.: Westview, 1988.

Lawson, Steven F. *Black Ballots: Voting Rights in the South 1944–1969.* New York: Columbia University Press, 1976.

Levy, Leonard. *The Law of the Commonwealth and Chief Justice Shaw.* Cambridge, Mass.: Harvard University Press, 1956.

Lewinson, Paul. *Race, Class, and Party: A History of Negro Suffrage and White Politics in the South.* London: Oxford University Press, 1932.

Lewis, David Levering. *W. E. B. Du Bois.* Vol. 2, *The Fight for Equality and the American Century 1919–1963.* New York: Holt, 2000.

Lewis, Earl. *In Their Own Interests: Race, Class, and Power in Twentieth-Century Norfolk Virginia.* Berkeley: University of California Press, 1991.

Litwack, Leon. *North of Slavery: The Negro in the Free States, 1790–1860.* Berkeley: University of California Press, 1961.

———. *Trouble in Mind: Black Southerners in the Age of Jim Crow.* New York: Vintage, 1998.

Loevy, Robert D., ed. *The Civil Rights Act of 1964: The Passage of the Law That Ended Racial Segregation.* Albany: State University of New York Press, 1997.

Loewen, James W. *Mississippi Chinese: Between Black and White.* Cambridge, Mass.: Harvard University Press, 1971.

Lofgren, Charles A. *The Plessy Case: A Legal-Historical Interpretation.* New York: Oxford University Press, 1987.

Logan, Rayford W., ed. *The Attitude of the Southern White Press toward Negro Suffrage, 1932–1940.* Washington, D.C.: Foundation, 1940.

———. *What the Negro Wants.* Chapel Hill: University of North Carolina Press, 1944; New York: Agathon, 1969.

Lomax, Louis E. *The Negro Revolt.* New York: Harper, 1962.

Longenecker, Stephen L. *Selma's Peacemaker: Ralph Smeltzer and Civil Rights Mediation.* Philadelphia: Temple University Press, 1987.

Lott, Davis Newton, ed. *The Presidents Speak: The Inaugural Addresses of the American Presidents, from Washington to Clinton.* New York: Holt, 1994.

Lubell, Samuel. *The Future of American Politics.* New York: Harper, 1952.

———. *White and Black: Test of a Nation.* New York: Harper & Row, 1964.

Maltz, Earl M. *Civil Rights, the Constitution and Congress, 1863–1869.* Lawrence: University Press of Kansas, 1990.

Mancini, Matthew. *One Dies, Get Another: Convict Leasing in the American South, 1866–1928.* Columbia: University of South Carolina Press, 1996.

Mangum, Charles S., Jr. *The Legal Status of the Negro.* Chapel Hill: University of North Carolina Press, 1940.

Manis, Andrew Michael. *Southern Civil Religions in Conflict: Black and White Baptists and Civil Rights, 1947–1957.* Athens: University of Georgia Press, 1987.

——. *A Fire You Can't Put Out: The Civil Rights Life of Birmingham's Reverend Fred Shuttlesworth*. Tuscaloosa: University of Alabama Press, 1999.

Marable, Manning. *Race, Reform, and Rebellion: The Second Reconstruction in Black America, 1945–1990*. Jackson: University Press of Mississippi, 1991.

Margo, Robert A. *Race and Schooling in the South, 1880–1950: An Economic History*. Tuscaloosa: University of Alabama Press, 1990.

Marshall, Thomas R. *Public Opinion and the Supreme Court*. Boston: Unwin Hyman, 1989.

Martin, Charles. *The Angelo Herndon Case and Southern Justice*. Baton Rouge: Louisiana State University Press, 1976.

Martin, John Frederick. *Civil Rights and the Crisis of Liberalism: The Democratic Party, 1945–1976*. Boulder, Colo.: Westview, 1979.

Mason, Alpheus. *Harlan Fiske Stone: Pillar of the Law*. New York: Viking, 1956.

Massey, Douglas S., & Nancy A. Denton. *American Apartheid: Segregation and the Making of the Underclass*. Cambridge, Mass.: Harvard University Press, 1993.

Mathews, John N. *Legislative and Judicial History of the Fifteenth Amendment*. Baltimore, Md.: Johns Hopkins University Press, 1909.

McAdam, Doug. *Political Process and the Development of Black Insurgency*. Chicago: University of Chicago Press, 1982.

——. *Freedom Summer*. New York: Oxford University Press, 1988.

McCann, Michael. *Rights at Work: Law and Politics of Pay Equity*. Chicago: University of Chicago Press, 1994.

McCaul, Robert L. *The Black Struggle for Public Schooling in Nineteenth-Century Illinois*. Carbondale: Southern Illinois University Press, 1987.

McClain, Charles J. *In Search of Equality: The Chinese Struggle against Discrimination in Nineteenth-Century America*. Berkeley: University of California Press, 1994.

McCloskey, Robert G. *The American Supreme Court*. 2d ed., revised by Sanford Levinson. Chicago: University of Chicago Press, 1994.

McCoy, Donald R., & Richard T. Ruetten. *Quest and Response: Minority Rights and the Truman Administration*. Lawrence: University Press of Kansas, 1973.

McCullough, David. *Truman*. New York: Simon & Schuster, 1992.

McFeely, William S. *Frederick Douglass*. New York: Norton, 1991.

McGovern, James R. *Anatomy of a Lynching: The Killing of Claude Neal*. Baton Rouge: Louisiana State University Press, 1982.

McGuire, Phillip. *Taps for a Jim Crow Army: Letters from Black Soldiers in World War II*. Santa Barbara: ABC-Clio, 1983.

McMillen, Neil R. *The Citizens' Council: Organized Resistance to the Second Reconstruction*. Urbana: University of Illinois Press, 1971.

——. *Dark Journey: Black Mississippians in the Age of Jim Crow*. Urbana: University of Illinois Press, 1989.

McNeil, Genna Rae. *Groundwork: Charles Hamilton Houston and the Struggle for Civil Rights*. Philadelphia: University of Pennsylvania Press, 1983.

McPherson, James M. *The Abolitionist Legacy: From Reconstruction to the NAACP*. Princeton: Princeton University Press, 1975.

——. *The Battle Cry of Freedom: The Civil War Era*. New York: Oxford University Press, 1988.

Mead, Chris. *Champion: Joe Louis, Black Hero in White America*. New York: Scribner's, 1985.

Meier, August. *Negro Thought in America 1880–1915*. Ann Arbor: University of Michigan Press, 1963.

Meier, August, & Elliot Rudwick. *CORE: A Study in the Civil Rights Movement, 1942–1968*. New York: Oxford University Press, 1973.

——. *Along the Color Line: Explorations in the Black Experience*. Urbana: University of Illinois Press, 1976.

Miller, Arthur S., & Jeffrey H. Bowman. *Death by Installments: The Ordeal of Willie Francis*. New York: Greenwood, 1988.

Miller, Kelly. *Race Adjustment: Essays on the Negro in America*. New York: Neale, 1908.

Moon, Henry Lee. *Balance of Power: The Negro Vote*. Garden City, N.Y.: Doubleday, 1948.

Moore, Leonard J. *Citizen Klansmen: The Ku Klux Klan in Indiana, 1921–1928*. Chapel Hill: University of North Carolina Press, 1991.

Morland, J. Kenneth. *Southern Schools: Token Desegregation and Beyond*. Atlanta, Ga.: Southern Regional Council, 1963.

Morris, Aldon D. *The Origins of the Civil Rights Movement: Black Communities Organizing for Change*. New York: Free Press, 1984.

Morris, Thomas D. *Free Men All: The Personal Liberty Laws of the North, 1780–1861*. Baltimore, Md.: Johns Hopkins University Press, 1974.

Murphy, Paul L. *The Constitution in Crisis Times, 1918–1969*. New York: Harper & Row, 1972.

Murphy, Walter F. *Congress and the Court: A Case Study in the American Political Process*. Chicago, Ill.: University of Chicago Press, 1962.

——. *Elements of Judicial Strategy*. Chicago, Ill.: University of Chicago Press, 1964.

Muse, Benjamin. *Virginia's Massive Resistance*. Bloomington: Indiana University Press, 1961.

——. *Ten Years of Prelude: The Story of Integration since the Supreme Court's 1954 Decision*. New York: Viking, 1964.

Myrdal, Gunnar. *An American Dilemma: The Negro Problem and Modern Democracy*. 2 vols. New York: Harper, 1944.

Neier, Aryeh. *Only Judgment: The Limits of Litigation in Social Change*. Middletown, Conn.: Wesleyan University Press, 1982.

Nelson, William E. *The Fourteenth Amendment: From Political Principle to Judicial Doctrine*. Cambridge, Mass.: Harvard University Press, 1988.

Newby, I. A. *Challenge to the Court: Social Scientists and Defense of Segregation, 1954–1966*. Baton Rouge: Louisiana State University Press, 1967.

Newman, Roger K. *Hugo Black: A Biography*. New York: Pantheon, 1994.

Norrell, Robert J. *Reaping the Whirlwind: The Civil Rights Movement in Tuskegee*. New York: Knopf, 1985.

Northrup, Herbert. *Organized Labor and the Negro*. New York: Harper, 1944.

Novak, Daniel A. *The Wheel of Servitude: Black Forced Labor after Slavery*. Lexington: University Press of Kentucky, 1978.

Nunnelley, William A. *Bull Connor*. Tuscaloosa: University of Alabama Press, 1991.

O'Brien, Gail. *The Color of Law: Race, Violence and Justice in the Post–World War II South*. Chapel Hill: University of North Carolina Press, 1999.

Ogden, Frederic D. *The Poll Tax in the South*. University: University of Alabama Press, 1958.

Olsen, Otto H., ed. *The Thin Disguise: Turning Point in Negro History*, Plessy v. Ferguson: *A Documentary Presentation (1864–1896)*. New York: Humanities Press, 1967.

Oppenheimer, Martin. *The Sit-In Movement of 1960*. Brooklyn, N.Y.: Carlson, 1989.

Orfield, Gary. *The Reconstruction of Southern Education: The Schools and the 1964 Civil Rights Act*. New York: Wiley-Interscience, 1969.

Osofsky, Gilbert. *Harlem: The Making of a Ghetto. Negro New York, 1890–1930*. New York: Harper & Row, 1966.

Parrish, Michael E. *Felix Frankfurter and His Times: The Reform Years*. New York: Free Press, 1982.

Patterson, James T. *Grand Expectations: The United States, 1945–1974*. New York: Oxford University Press, 1996.

——. Brown v. Board of Education: *A Civil Rights Milestone and Its Troubled Legacy*. New York: Oxford University Press, 2001.

Payne, Charles M. *I've Got the Light of Freedom: The Organizing Tradition and the Mississippi Freedom Struggle*. Berkeley: University of California Press, 1995.

Peltason, J. W. *Fifty-Eight Lonely Men: Southern Federal Judges and School Desegregation*. New York: Harcourt, Brace & World, 1961.

Perman, Michael. *Struggle for Mastery: Disfranchisement in the South, 1888–1908*. Chapel Hill: University of North Carolina Press, 2001.

Perry, Michael. *The Constitution in the Courts: Law or Politics?* New York: Oxford University Press, 1994.

Pincus, Samuel N. *The Virginia Supreme Court, Blacks and the Law*. New York: Garland, 1990.

Pleasants, Julian M., & Augustus M. Burns III. *Frank Porter Graham and the 1950 Senate Race in North Carolina*. Chapel Hill: University of North Carolina Press, 1990.

Plummer, Brenda Gayle. *Rising Wind: Black Americans and U.S. Foreign Affairs, 1935–1960*. Chapel Hill: University of North Carolina Press, 1996.

Powdermaker, Hortense. *After Freedom: A Cultural Study in the Deep South*. New York: Viking, 1939.

Powe, Lucas A., Jr. *The Warren Court and American Politics*. Cambridge, Mass.: Harvard University Press, 2000.

Prettyman, Barrett, Jr. *Death and the Supreme Court*. New York: Harcourt, Brace & World, 1961.

Pritchett, C. Herman. *The Roosevelt Court: A Study in Judicial Politics and Values 1937–1947*. New York: Macmillan, 1948.

——. *Civil Liberties and the Vinson Court*. Chicago, Ill.: University of Chicago Press, 1954.

——. *Congress versus the Supreme Court 1957–1960*. Minneapolis: University of Minnesota Press, 1961.

Pusey, Merlo J. *Charles Evans Hughes*. 2 vols. New York: Macmillan, 1951.

Rabinowitz, Howard N. *Race Relations in the Urban South, 1865–1890*. New York: Oxford University Press, 1978.

——. *The First New South 1865–1920*. Arlington Heights, Ill.: Harlan Davidson, 1992.

Rampersad, Arnold. *Jackie Robinson: A Biography*. New York: Knopf, 1997.

Raper, Arthur. *The Tragedy of Lynching*. Chapel Hill: University of North Carolina Press, 1933.

Record, Wilson. *Race and Radicalism: The NAACP and the Communist Party in Conflict*. Ithaca, N.Y.: Cornell University Press, 1964.

Reed, Merl. *Seedtime of the Modern Civil Rights Movement: The President's Committee on Fair Employment Practice, 1941–1946*. Baton Rouge: Louisiana State University Press, 1991.

Reed, Roy. *Faubus: The Life and Times of an American Prodigal*. Fayetteville: University of Arkansas Press, 1997.

Rice, Arnold. *The Ku Klux Klan in American Politics*. Washington, D.C.: Public Affairs Press, 1962.

Rice, Lawrence D. *The Negro in Texas 1874–1900*. Baton Rouge: Louisiana State University Press, 1971.

Rise, Eric W. *The Martinsville Seven: Race, Rape, and Capital Punishment*. Charlottesville: University Press of Virginia, 1995.

Robertson, David. *Sly and Able: A Political Biography of James F. Byrnes*. New York: Norton, 1994.

Robinson, Armstead L., & Patricia Sullivan, eds. *New Directions in Civil Rights Studies*. Charlottesville: University Press of Virginia, 1991.

Roche, Jeff. *Restructured Resistance: The Sibley Commission and the Politics of Desegregation in Georgia*. Athens: University of Georgia Press, 1998.

Rogosin, Donn. *Invisible Men: Life in Baseball's Negro Leagues*. New York: Atheneum, 1983.

Rosenberg, Gerald N. *The Hollow Hope: Can Courts Bring about Social Change?* Chicago, Ill.: University of Chicago Press, 1991.

Ross, William. *A Muted Fury: Populists, Progressives, and Labor Unions Confront the Courts, 1890–1937*. Princeton, N.J.: Princeton University Press, 1994.

Rudko, Frances Howell. *Truman's Court: A Study in Judicial Restraint*. New York: Greenwood, 1988.

Rudwick, Elliott M. *Race Riot at East St. Louis, July 2, 1917*. Carbondale: Southern Illinois University Press, 1964.

Russell, Charles W. *Report on Peonage*. n.p., 1908.

St. Clair, James E., & Linda C. Gugin. *Chief Justice Fred M. Vinson of Kentucky*. Lexington: University Press of Kentucky, 2002.

Schlesinger, Arthur M., & Fred L. Israel, eds. *History of American Presidential Elections, 1789–1968*. 4 vols. New York: Chelsea House, 1971.

Schulman, Bruce J. *From Cotton Belt to Sunbelt: Federal Policy, Economic Development, and the Transformation of the South, 1938–1950*. New York: Oxford University Press, 1991.

Schultz, David A. *Leveraging the Law: Using the Courts to Achieve Social Change*. New York: Lang, 1998.

Schwartz, Bernard. *Super Chief: Earl Warren and His Supreme Court: A Judicial Biography*. New York: New York University Press, 1983.

Scott, Daryl Michael. *Contempt and Pity: Social Policy and the Image of the Damaged Black Psyche, 1880–1996*. Chapel Hill: University of North Carolina Press, 1997.

Segal, Jeffrey A., & Harold J. Spaeth. *The Supreme Court and the Attitudinal Model*. New York: Cambridge University Press, 1993.

Seidman, Louis Michael, & Mark V. Tushnet. *Remnants of Belief: Contemporary Constitutional Issues*. New York: Oxford University Press, 1996.

Semonche, John E. *Charting the Future: The Supreme Court Responds to a Changing Society, 1890–1920.* Westport, Conn.: Greenwood, 1978.

Senechal, Roberta. *The Sociogenesis of a Race Riot: Springfield, Illinois, in 1908.* Urbana: University of Illinois Press, 1990.

Sherman, Richard B. *The Republican Party and Black America: From McKinley to Hoover, 1896–1933.* Charlottesville: University Press of Virginia, 1973.

———. *The Case of Odell Waller and Virginia Justice, 1940–1942.* Knoxville: University of Tennessee Press, 1992.

Sherrill, Robert. *Gothic Politics in the Deep South: Stars of the New Confederacy.* New York: Grossman, 1968.

Shoemaker, Don, ed. *With All Deliberate Speed: Segregation-Desegregation in Southern Schools.* New York: Harper, 1957.

Silver, James W. *Mississippi: The Closed Society.* New York: Harcourt, Brace & World, 1963.

Simon, James F. *Independent Journey: The Life of William O. Douglas.* New York: Harper & Row, 1980.

Sims, George E. *The Little Man's Big Friend: James E. Folsom in Alabama Politics, 1946–1958.* University: University of Alabama Press, 1985.

Sitkoff, Harvard. *A New Deal for Blacks: Emergence of Civil Rights as a National Issue.* Vol. 1, *The Depression Decade.* New York: Oxford University Press, 1978.

———. *The Struggle for Black Equality 1954–1992.* Rev. ed. New York: Hill & Wang, 1993.

Skowronek, Stephen. *Building a New American State: The Expansion of National Administrative Capacity, 1877–1920.* Cambridge: Cambridge University Press, 1982.

Smead, Howard. *Blood Justice: The Lynching of Mack Charles Parker.* New York: Oxford University Press, 1986.

Smith, Bob. *They Closed Their Schools: Prince Edward County, Virginia, 1951–1964.* Chapel Hill: University of North Carolina Press, 1965.

Solberg, Carl. *Hubert Humphrey: A Biography.* New York: Norton, 1984.

Sosna, Morton. *In Search of the Silent South: Southern Liberals and the Race Issue.* New York: Columbia University Press, 1977.

Spaeth, Harold J., & Jeffrey A. Segal. *Majority Rule or Minority Will: Adherence to Precedent on the U.S. Supreme Court.* New York: Cambridge University Press, 1999.

Spann, Girardeau A. *Race against the Court: The Supreme Court and Minorities in Contemporary America.* New York: New York University Press, 1993.

Spear, Allan H. *Black Chicago: The Making of a Negro Ghetto, 1890–1920.* Chicago, Ill.: University of Chicago Press, 1967.

Stephenson, Gilbert Thomas. *Race Distinctions in American Law.* New York: Appleton, 1910.

Stern, Mark. *Calculating Visions: Kennedy, Johnson, and Civil Rights.* New Brunswick, N.J.: Rutgers University Press, 1992.

Stone, Alfred Holt. *Studies in the American Race Problem.* New York: Doubleday, Page, 1908.

Strum, Philippa. *Brandeis: Beyond Progressivism.* Lawrence: University Press of Kansas, 1993.

Sugrue, Thomas J. *The Origins of the Urban Crisis: Race and Inequality in Postwar Detroit.* Princeton, N.J.: Princeton University Press, 1996.

Sullivan, Patricia. *Days of Hope: Race and Democracy in the New Deal Era.* Chapel Hill: University of North Carolina Press, 1996.

Taft, William Howard. *Present Day Problems: A Collection of Addresses Delivered on Various Occasions by William H. Taft.* New York: Dodd, Mead, 1908.

———. *Presidential Addresses and State Papers of William Howard Taft.* Vol. 1. New York: Doubleday, Page, 1910.

Talmadge, Herman. *You and Segregation.* Birmingham, Ala.: Vulcan, 1955.

Thornbrough, Emma Lou. *The Negro in Indiana before 1900: A Study of a Minority.* Indianapolis: Indiana Historical Bureau, 1957.

Tindall, George Brown. *South Carolina Negroes 1877–1900.* Columbia: University of South Carolina Press, 1952.

———. *The Emergence of the New South 1913–1945.* Vol. 10 of *A History of the South.* Baton Rouge: Louisiana State University Press, 1967.

To Secure These Rights: The Report of the President's Committee on Civil Rights. New York: Simon & Schuster, 1947.

Trelease, Allen W. *White Terror: The Ku Klux Klan Conspiracy and Southern Reconstruction.* New York: Harper & Row, 1971.

Trotter, Joe W. *Black Milwaukee: The Making of an Industrial Proletariat, 1915–45.* Urbana: University of Illinois Press, 1985.

———. *Coal, Class, and Color: Blacks in Southern West Virginia 1915–32.* Urbana: University of Illinois Press, 1990.

Truman, Harry S. *Memoirs.* Vol. 2, *Years of Trial and Hope.* Garden City, N.Y.: Doubleday, 1956.

Tushnet, Mark V. *The NAACP's Legal Strategy against Segregated Education, 1925–1950.* Chapel Hill: University of North Carolina Press, 1987.

———. *Making Civil Rights Law: Thurgood Marshall and the Supreme Court, 1936–1961.* New York: Oxford University Press, 1994.

Tuttle, William M., Jr. *Race Riot: Chicago in the Red Summer of 1919.* New York: Atheneum, 1970.

Tygiel, Jules. *Baseball's Great Experiment: Jackie Robinson and His Legacy.* New York: Oxford University Press, 1983.

Tyson, Timothy B. *Radio Free Dixie: Robert F. Williams and the Roots of Black Power.* Chapel Hill: University of North Carolina Press, 1999.

U.S. Commission on Civil Rights. *Equal Protection of the Laws in Public Higher Education.* 1960.

———. *Civil Rights U.S.A./Public Schools, Southern States.* 1962.

Urofsky, Melvin I. *Felix Frankfurter: Judicial Restraint and Individual Liberties.* Boston: Twayne, 1991.

———. *Division and Discord: The Supreme Court under Stone and Vinson, 1941–1953.* Columbia: University of South Carolina Press, 1997.

Urofsky, Melvin I., ed. *The Douglas Letters: Selections from the Private Papers of Justice William O. Douglas.* Bethesda, Md.: Adler & Adler, 1987.

Vaughn, William Preston. *Schools for All: The Blacks and Public Education in the South, 1865–1877.* Lexington: University Press of Kentucky, 1974.

Villard, Oswald Garrison. *Segregation in Baltimore and Washington.* New York: n.p., 1913.

Vose, Clement V. *Caucasians Only: The Supreme Court, the NAACP, and the Restrictive Covenant Cases*. Berkeley: University of California Press, 1959.

Walker, Jack. *Sit-Ins in Atlanta: A Study in the Negro Revolt*. New York: McGraw-Hill, 1964.

Walker, Samuel. *In Defense of American Liberties: A History of the ACLU*. New York: Oxford University Press, 1990.

Wang, Xi. *The Trial of Democracy: Black Suffrage and Northern Republicans, 1860–1910*. Athens: University of Georgia Press, 1997.

Warren, Charles. *The Supreme Court in United States History*. Vol. 1, *1789–1835*. Boston: Little, Brown, 1922.

Wasby, Stephen L. *The Impact of the United States Supreme Court: Some Perspectives*. Homewood, Ill.: Dorsey, 1970.

Weisbrot, Robert. *Freedom Bound: A History of America's Civil Rights Movement*. New York: Norton, 1990.

Weiss, Nancy J. *Farewell to the Party of Lincoln: Black Politics in the Age of FDR*. Princeton, N.J.: Princeton University Press, 1983.

Welch, Richard E., Jr. *The Presidencies of Grover Cleveland*. Lawrence: University Press of Kansas, 1988.

Wharton, Vernon Lane. *The Negro in Mississippi 1865–1890*. Chapel Hill: University of North Carolina Press, 1947.

White, G. Edward. *Earl Warren: A Public Life*. New York: Oxford University Press, 1982.

———. *Justice Oliver Wendell Holmes: Law and the Inner Self*. New York: Oxford University Press, 1993.

White, Walter. *A Rising Wind*. Garden City, N.Y.: Doubleday, Doran, 1945.

Whitfield, Stephen J. *A Death in the Delta: The Story of Emmett Till*. Baltimore, Md.: Collier Macmillan, 1988.

———. *The Culture of the Cold War*. Baltimore, Md.: Johns Hopkins University Press, 1991.

Wickersham Commission. *Report*. Vol. 11, *Report on Lawlessness in Law Enforcement*. 1931.

Wilkinson, J. Harvie. *Harry Byrd and the Changing Face of Virginia Politics 1946–1966*. Charlottesville: University Press of Virginia, 1968.

———. *From Brown to Bakke: The Supreme Court and School Integration, 1954–1978*. New York: Oxford University Press, 1979.

Williams, Lou Falkner. *The Great South Carolina Ku Klux Klan Trials, 1871–1872*. Athens: University of Georgia Press, 1996.

Williamson, Joel. *After Slavery: The Negro in South Carolina during Reconstruction, 1861–1877*. Chapel Hill: University of North Carolina Press, 1965.

Willkie, Wendell. *One World*. New York: Simon & Schuster, 1943.

Wilson, Paul E. *A Time to Lose: Representing Kansas in Brown v. Board of Education*. Lawrence: University Press of Kansas, 1995.

Wilson, Theodore B. *The Black Codes of the South*. University: University of Alabama Press, 1965.

Wolff, Miles. *Lunch at the Five and Ten: The Greensboro Sit-Ins: A Contemporary History*. New York: Stein & Day, 1970.

Wolters, Raymond. *Negroes and the Great Depression: The Problem of Economic Recovery*. Westport, Conn.: Greenwood, 1971.

Woodward, C. Vann. *Origins of the New South 1877–1913*. Baton Rouge: Louisiana State University Press, 1951.

———. *The Strange Career of Jim Crow*. 3d ed. New York: Oxford University Press, 1974.

Wright, George C. *Life behind a Veil: Blacks in Louisville, Kentucky, 1865–1920*. Baton Rouge: Louisiana State University Press, 1990.

———. *Racial Violence in Kentucky, 1865–1940: Lynchings, Mob Rule and "Legal Lynchings."* Baton Rouge: Louisiana State University Press, 1990.

Wynes, Charles E. *Race Relations in Virginia 1870–1902*. Charlottesville: University of Virginia Press, 1961.

Wynn, Neil A. *The Afro-American and the Second World War*. New York: Holmes & Meier, 1976.

Yarbrough, Tinsley E. *Judge Frank Johnson and Human Rights in Alabama*. University: University of Alabama Press, 1981.

———. *A Passion for Justice: J. Waties Waring and Civil Rights*. New York: Oxford University Press, 1987.

———. *John Marshall Harlan: Great Dissenter of the Warren Court*. New York: Oxford University Press, 1992.

———. *Judicial Enigma: The First Justice Harlan*. New York: Oxford University Press, 1995.

Zangrando, Robert L. *The NAACP Crusade against Lynching, 1909–1950*. Philadelphia: Temple University Press, 1980.

Zilversmit, Arthur. *The First Emancipation: The Abolition of Slavery in the North*. Chicago, Ill.: University of Chicago Press, 1967.

ARTICLES

Abbott, Carl. "The Norfolk Business Community: The Crisis of Massive Resistance." In *Southern Businessmen and Desegregation*, edited by Elizabeth Jacoway & David R. Colburn, 98–119. Baton Rouge: Louisiana State University Press, 1982.

Ader, Emile B. "Why the Dixiecrats Failed." *Journal of Politics* 15 (Aug. 1953): 356–69.

Alilunas, Leo. "Legal Restrictions on the Negro in Politics." *Journal of Negro History* 25 (Apr. 1940): 153–60.

Allen, Howard W., et al. "Political Reform and Negro Rights in the Senate, 1909–1915." *Journal of Southern History* 37 (May 1971): 191–212.

Amar, Vikram David. "Jury Service as Political Participation Akin to Voting." *Cornell Law Review* 80 (Jan. 1995): 203–59.

Arnesen, Eric. "'Like Banquo's Ghost, It Will Not Down': The Race Question and the American Railroad Brotherhoods, 1880–1920." *American Historical Review* 99 (Dec. 1994): 1601–33.

Ashmore, Harry S. "Racial Integration with Especial Reference to Education in the South." *Journal of Negro Education* 21 (Summer 1952): 250–55.

Atkinson, David N. "Justice Sherman Minton and the Protection of Minority Rights." *Washington & Lee Law Review* 34 (Winter 1977): 97–117.

Atwood, R. B. "The Public Negro College in a Racially Integrated System of Higher Education." *Journal of Negro Education* 21 (Summer 1952): 352–63.

Aucoin, Brent J. "Thomas Goode Jones and African-American Civil Rights in the South." *Historian* 60 (Winter 1998): 257–72.

Autrey, Dorothy. "'Can These Bones Live?': The National Association for the Advancement of Colored People in Alabama, 1918–1930." *Journal of Negro History* 82 (Winter 1997): 1–12.

Avins, Alfred. "Freedom of Choice in Personal Service Occupations: Thirteenth-Amendment Limitations on Antidiscrimination Legislation." *Cornell Law Quarterly* 49 (Winter 1964): 228–56.

———. "De Facto and De Jure School Segregation: Some Reflected Light on the Fourteenth Amendment from the Civil Rights Act of 1875." *Mississippi Law Journal* 38 (Mar. 1967): 179–247.

———. "Social Equality and the Fourteenth Amendment: The Original Understanding." *Houston Law Review* 4 (Spring 1967): 640–56.

Bacote, Clarence A. "Negro Proscriptions, Protests, and Proposed Solutions in Georgia, 1880–1908." *Journal of Southern History* 25 (Nov. 1959): 471–98.

Badger, Anthony J. "The Forerunner of Our Opposition: Arkansas and the Southern Manifesto of 1956." *Arkansas Historical Quarterly* 56 (Autumn 1997): 353–60.

———. "The White Reaction to *Brown*: Arkansas, the Southern Manifesto, and Massive Resistance." In *Understanding the Little Rock Crisis*, edited by Elizabeth Jacoway & C. Fred Williams, 83–97. Fayetteville: University of Arkansas Press, 1999.

———. "Southerners Who Refused to Sign the Southern Manifesto." *Historical Journal* 42 (June 1999): 517–34.

Bains, Lee E., Jr. "Birmingham, 1963: Confrontation over Civil Rights." In *Birmingham, Alabama*, edited by David J. Garrow, 151–292. Brooklyn, N.Y.: Carlson, 1989.

Baker, J. Newton. "The Segregation of White and Colored Passengers on Interstate Trains." *Yale Law Journal* 19 (Apr. 1910): 445–52.

Baker, Ray Stannard. "A Pawn in the Struggle for Freedom." *American Magazine* 72 (Sept. 1911): 608–10.

Balkin, J. M. "Agreements with Hell and Other Objects of Our Faith." *Fordham Law Review* 65 (Mar. 1997): 1703–38.

Barber, Hollis W. "Religious Liberty v. the Police Power: Jehovah's Witnesses." *American Political Science Review* 41 (Apr. 1947): 226–47.

Barbour, J. F., Jr. "The Exclusion of Negroes from Jury Service." *Mississippi Law Journal* 9 (Dec. 1935): 196–204.

Barksdale, Norval P. "The Gaines Case and Its Effect on Negro Education in Missouri." *School & Society* 51 (Mar. 1940): 309–13.

Bassett, John S. "Stirring Up the Fires of Race Antipathy." *South Atlantic Quarterly* 2 (Oct. 1903): 297–98.

Bates, Beth Tomkins. "A New Crowd Challenges the Agenda of the Old Guard in the NAACP, 1933–1941." *American Historical Review* 102 (Apr. 1997): 340–77.

Bayer, Eugene Sidney. "The Apportionment Section of the Fourteenth Amendment: A Neglected Weapon for Defense of the Voting Rights of Southern Negroes." *Case Western Law Review* 16 (June 1965): 965–94.

Bell, Derrick. "*Brown v. Board of Education*: Forty-five Years after the Fact." *Ohio Northern University Law Review* 26, no. 2 (2000): 171–82.

Benedict, Michael Les. "Preserving Federalism: Reconstruction and the Waite Court." *Supreme Court Review* (1978): 39–79.

———. "The Politics of Reconstruction." In *American Political History: Essays on the State of the Discipline*, edited by John F. Marszalek & Wilson D. Miscambel, 54–107. Notre Dame, Ind.: University of Notre Dame Press, 1997.

Berman, Geoff. "A New Deal for Free Speech: Free Speech and the Labor Movement in the 1930s." *Virginia Law Review* 80 (Feb. 1994): 291–322.

Bernd, Joseph L. "Georgia: Static and Dynamic." In *Changing Politics of the South*, edited by William C. Havard, 294–365. Baton Rouge: Louisiana State University Press, 1972.

——. "White Supremacy and the Disfranchisement of Blacks in Georgia, 1946." *Georgia Historical Quarterly* 66 (Winter 1982): 492–513.

Bernstein, Barton J. "Case Law in *Plessy v. Ferguson.*" *Journal of Negro History* 47 (July 1962): 192–98.

——. "Election of 1952." In *American Presidential Elections*, edited by Arthur M. Schlesinger & Fred L. Israel, 4:3215–37. New York: Chelsea House, 1971.

Bernstein, David. "Licensing Laws: A Historical Example of the Use of Government Regulatory Power against African Americans." *San Diego Law Review* 31 (Feb.–Mar. 1994): 89–104.

——. "The Law and Economics of Post–Civil War Restrictions on Interstate Migration of African Americans." *Texas Law Review* 76 (Mar. 1998): 781–847.

——. "Philip Sober Controlling Philip Drunk: *Buchanan v. Warley* in Historical Perspective." *Vanderbilt Law Review* 51 (May 1998): 799–879.

——. "*Plessy* versus *Lochner*: The Berea College Case." *Journal of Supreme Court History* 25 (2000): 93–111.

Berwanger, Eugene H. "Reconstruction on the Frontier: The Equal Rights Struggle in Colorado, 1865–1867." *Pacific Historical Review* 44 (Aug. 1975): 313–30.

Bestor, Arthur. "State Sovereignty and Slavery: A Reinterpretation of Proslavery Constitutional Doctrine, 1846–1860." *Journal of the Illinois Historical Society* 54 (Summer 1961): 122–80.

Bethune, Mary McLeod. "Certain Unalienable Rights." In *What the Negro Wants*, edited by Rayford W. Logan, 248–58. Chapel Hill: University of North Carolina Press, 1944; New York: Agathon, 1969.

Bickel, Alexander M. "The Original Understanding and the Segregation Decision." *Harvard Law Review* 69 (Nov. 1955): 1–65.

Bixby, David M. "The Roosevelt Court, Democratic Ideology and Minority Rights: Another Look at *United States v. Classic.*" *Yale Law Journal* 90 (Mar. 1981): 741–815.

Blakeman, Scott. "Night Comes to Berea College: The Day Law and African-American Reaction." *Filson Club Historical Quarterly* 70 (Jan. 1996): 3–26.

Blalock, H. M., Jr. "Percent Non-White and Discrimination in the South." *American Sociological Review* 22 (Dec. 1957): 677–82.

Bolton, Charles C. "Mississippi's School Equalization Program, 1945–1954: A Last Gasp to Try to Maintain a Segregated Educational System." *Journal of Southern History* 66 (Nov. 2000): 781–814.

Bond, James E. "The Original Understanding of the Fourteenth Amendment in Illinois, Ohio, and Pennsylvania." *Akron Law Review* 18 (Winter 1985): 435–67.

Boothe, Armistead L. "Civil Rights in Virginia." *Virginia Law Review* 35 (Nov. 1949): 928–70.

Boskey, Bennett, & John H. Pickering. "Federal Restrictions on State Criminal Procedure." *University of Chicago Law Review* 13 (Apr. 1946): 266–99.

Boykin, Leander. "The Status and Trends of Differentials between White and Negro Teachers' Salaries in the Southern States, 1940–1946." *Journal of Negro Education* 18 (Winter 1949): 40–47.

Bracey, Christopher A. "Louis Brandeis and the Race Question." *Alabama Law Review* 52 (Spring 2001): 859–910.

Brest, Paul. "State Action and Liberal Theory: A Casenote on *Flagg Bros. v. Brooks.*" *University of Pennsylvania Law Review* 130 (June 1982): 1296–1330.

Bridges, Roger D. "Equality Deferred: Civil Rights for Illinois Blacks, 1865–1885." *Journal of the Illinois State Historical Society* 74 (Summer 1981): 83–108.

Brodie, Sydney. "The Federally Secured Right to Be Free from Bondage." *Georgetown Law Journal* 40 (Mar. 1952): 367–98.

Brooks, Jennifer E. "Winning the Peace: Georgia Veterans and the Struggle to Define the Political Legacy of World War II." *Journal of Southern History* 66 (Aug. 2000): 563–604.

Bruce, Drew A. "Racial Zoning by Private Contract." *Virginia Law Register* 13 (Jan. 1928): 526–41.

Brundage, W. Fitzhugh. "The Roar on the Other Side of Silence: Black Resistance and White Violence in the American South, 1880–1940." In *Under Sentence of Death*, edited by W. Fitzhugh Brundage, 271–91. Chapel Hill: University of North Carolina Press, 1997.

Bullock, Henry Allen. "Urbanization and Race Relations." In *The Urban South*, edited by Rupert B. Vance & Nicholas J. Demerath, 207–29. Chapel Hill: University of North Carolina Press, 1954.

Bunche, Ralph J. "A Critical Analysis of the Tactics and Programs of Minority Groups." *Journal of Negro Education* 4 (July 1935): 308–20.

Burnham, Walter D. "The Changing Shape of the American Political Universe." *American Political Science Review* 59 (Mar. 1965): 7–28.

Burns, Augustus M., III. "Graduate Education for Blacks in North Carolina, 1930–1951." *Journal of Southern History* 46 (May 1980): 195–218.

Burt, Robert A. "*Brown*'s Reflection." *Yale Law Journal* 103 (Apr. 1994): 1483–94.

Bustard, Joseph L. "The New Jersey Story: The Development of Racially Integrated Public Schools." *Journal of Negro Education* 21 (Summer 1952): 275–85.

Caffrey, Bernard, Simms Anderson, & Janet Garrison. "Change in Racial Attitudes of White Southerners after Exposure to the Atmosphere of a Southern University." *Psychological Reports* 25 (Oct. 1969): 555–58.

Campbell, Walter E. "Profit, Prejudice, and Protest: Utility Competition and the Generation of Jim Crow Streetcars in Savannah, 1905–1907." *Georgia Historical Quarterly* 70 (Summer 1986): 197–231.

Canon, Bradley C. "The Supreme Court as a Cheerleader in Politico-Moral Disputes." *Journal of Politics* 54 (Aug. 1992): 637–53.

———. "The Supreme Court and Policy Reform: The Hollow Hope Revisited." In *Leveraging the Law*, edited by David A. Schultz, 215–49. New York: Lang, 1998.

Cantrell, Greg, & D. Scott Barton. "Texas Populists and the Failure of Biracial Politics." *Journal of Southern History* 55 (Nov. 1989): 659–92.

Capeci, Dominic J., Jr. "Fiorello H. La Guardia and Employment Discrimination, 1941–43." *Italian Americana* 7 (Spring–Summer 1983): 49–67.

———. "The Lynching of Cleo Wright: Federal Protection of Constitutional Rights during World War II." *Journal of American History* 72 (Mar. 1986): 859–87.

Carle, Susan. "Race, Class, and Legal Ethics in the Early NAACP (1910–1920)." *Law & History Review* 20 (Spring 2002): 97–146.

Carter, Robert L. "Tribute [to Charles Hamilton Houston]." *Harvard Law Review* 111 (June 1998): 2149–55.

Carter, Stephen. "When Victims Happen to Be Black." *Yale Law Journal* 97 (Feb. 1988): 420–47.

Case, Lewis H., & John A. Van Etten. "Due Process Criminal Confessions in Capital Cases Arising in the State Courts." *Albany Law Review* 14 (Jan. 1950): 149–72.

Chappell, David. "The Divided Mind of Southern Segregationists." *Georgia Historical Quarterly* 82 (Spring 1998): 45–72.

Chatfield, E. Charles. "The Southern Sociological Congress: Organization of Uplift." *Tennessee Historical Quarterly* 19 (Dec. 1960): 328–47.

Chernack, Gregory S. "The Clash of Two Worlds: Justice Robert H. Jackson, Institutional Pragmatism, and *Brown*." *Temple Law Review* 72 (Spring 1999): 51–109.

Christensen, Lawrence O. "Race Relations in St. Louis, 1865–1916." *Missouri Historical Review* 78 (Jan. 1984): 123–36.

Cilella, Alfred J., & Irwin J. Kaplan. "Discrimination against Negroes in Jury Service." *Illinois Law Review* 29 (Dec. 1934): 498–519.

Clabaugh, Jason Paul. "Reporting the Rage: An Analysis of Newspaper Coverage of the Freedom Rides of May, 1961." *Southern Historian* 14 (Spring 1993): 41–57.

Clark, Kenneth B. "Racial Justice in Education: Continuing Struggle in a New Era." Reprinted in *Howard Law Journal* 23, no. 1 (1980): 93–124.

Cobb, James C. "Segregating the New South: The Origins and Legacy of *Plessy v. Ferguson*." *Georgia State University Law Review* 12 (June 1996): 1017–36.

———. "The Lesson of Little Rock: Stability, Growth, and Change in the American South." In *Understanding the Little Rock Crisis*, edited by Elizabeth Jacoway & C. Fred Williams, 107–22. Fayetteville: University of Arkansas Press, 1999.

Cohen, Ronald D. "The Dilemma of School Integration in the North: Gary, Indiana, 1945–1960." *Indiana Magazine of History* 82 (June 1986): 161–84.

Coleman, Frank. "Freedom from Fear on the Home Front." *Iowa Law Review* 29 (Mar. 1944): 415–29.

Coleman, James P. "The Origin of the Constitution of 1890." *Journal of Mississippi History* 19 (Apr. 1957): 69–92.

Collier, Bert. "Segregation and Politics." In *With All Deliberate Speed*, edited by Don Shoemaker, 110–29. New York: Harper, 1957.

Connally, C. Ellen. "Justice Harlan's 'Great Betrayal'? A Reconsideration of *Cumming v. Richmond County Board of Education*." *Journal of Supreme Court History* 25 (2000): 72–92.

Cooke, W. Henry. "The Segregation of Mexican-American School Children in Southern California." *School & Society* 67 (June 1948): 417–21.

Cover, Robert. "The Origins of Judicial Activism in the Protection of Minorities." *Yale Law Journal* 91 (June 1982): 1287–1316.

Cox, LaWanda, & John Cox. "Negro Suffrage and Republican Politics: The Problem of Motivation in Reconstruction Historiography." *Journal of Southern History* 33 (Aug. 1967): 303–30.

Cresswell, Stephen. "The Case of Taylor Strauder." *West Virginia History* 44 (Spring 1983): 193–211.

———. "Enforcing the Enforcement Acts: The Department of Justice in Northern Mississippi, 1870–1890." *Journal of Southern History* 53 (Aug. 1987): 421–40.

Cripps, Thomas. "The Reaction of the Negro to the Motion Picture *Birth of a Nation*." *Historian* 25 (May 1963): 344–62.

Cushman, Barry. "The Secret Lives of the Four Horsemen." *Virginia Law Review* 83 (Apr. 1997): 559–645.

——. "Formalism and Realism in Commerce Clause Jurisprudence." *University of Chicago Law Review* 67 (Fall 2000): 1089–1150.

Cushman, Robert E. "The Texas 'White Primary' Case: *Smith v. Allwright.*" *Cornell Law Quarterly* 30 (Sept. 1944): 66–76.

Dabney, Virginius. "Virginia's 'Peaceable, Honorable Stand'." *Life*, 22 Sept. 1958, pp. 51–52, 55–56.

Dahl, Robert A. "Decision Making in a Democracy: The Supreme Court as a National Policy Maker." *Journal of Public Law* 6 (Fall 1957): 279–95.

Dailey, Jane. "Deference and Violence in the Postbellum Urban South: Manners and Massacres in Danville, Virginia." *Journal of Southern History* 63 (Aug. 1997): 553–90.

Dalfiume, Richard M. "The 'Forgotten Years' of the Negro Revolution." *Journal of American History* 55 (June 1968): 90–106.

Daniel, Pete. "Up from Slavery and Down to Peonage: The Alonzo Bailey Case." *Journal of American History* 57 (Dec. 1970): 654–70.

——. "The Transformation of the Rural South: 1930 to the Present." *Agricultural History* 55 (July 1981): 231–48.

Daniel, Walter G. "Availability of Education for Negroes in the Secondary School." *Journal of Negro Education* 16 (Summer 1947): 450–58.

Dauer, Manning J. "Florida: The Different State." In *Changing Politics of the South*, edited by William C. Havard, 92–164. Baton Rouge: Louisiana State University Press, 1972.

Day, John Kyle. "The Fall of a Southern Moderate: Congressman Brooks Hays and the Election of 1958." *Arkansas Historical Quarterly* 59 (Autumn 2000): 241–64.

DeGraaf, Lawrence B. "The City of Black Angels: Emergence of the Los Angeles Ghetto, 1890–1930." *Pacific Historical Review* 34 (Aug. 1970): 323–52.

——. "Significant Steps on an Arduous Path: The Impact of World War II on Discrimination against African Americans in the West." *Journal of the West* 35 (Jan. 1996): 24–33.

Dephloff, Henry C., & Robert R. Jones. "Race Relations in Louisiana, 1877–98." *Louisiana History* 9 (Fall 1968): 301–24.

Dickson, Del. "State Court Defiance and the Limits of Supreme Court Authority: *Williams v. Georgia* Revisited." *Yale Law Journal* 103 (Apr. 1994): 1423–81.

Dittmer, John. "The Politics of the Mississippi Movement." In *Civil Rights Movement*, edited by Charles W. Eagles, 65–93. Jackson: University Press of Mississippi, 1986.

Dorr, Gregory Michael. "Principled Expediency: Eugenics, *Naim v. Naim* and the Supreme Court." *American Journal of Legal History* 42 (Apr. 1998): 119–59.

Dorr, Lisa Lindquist. "Black-on-White Rape and Retribution in Twentieth-Century Virginia: 'Men, Even Negroes, Must Have Some Protection'." *Journal of Southern History* 66 (Nov. 2000): 711–48.

Douglas, Davison M. "Limits of Law in Accomplishing Racial Change: School Segregation in the Pre-*Brown* North." *UCLA Law Review* 44 (Feb. 1997): 677–744.

Du Bois, W. E. B. "The Tragedy of 'Jim Crow'." *Crisis* 26 (Aug. 1923): 169–72.

——. "Does the Negro Need Separate Schools?" *Journal of Negro Education* 4 (July 1935): 328–35.

——. "The Negro since 1900: A Progress Report." *New York Times Magazine*, 21 Nov. 1948, pp. 24, 54–59.

Dudziak, Mary. "Desegregation as a Cold War Imperative." *Stanford Law Review* 41 (Nov. 1988): 61–120.

Dunbar, Leslie W. "Reflections on the Latest Reform of the South." *Phylon* 22 (Third Quarter 1961): 249–57.

Dunn, James R. "Title VI, the Guidelines, and School Desegregation in the South." *Virginia Law Review* 53 (Dec. 1967): 42–88.

Durbin, Lawrence A. "Virgil Hawkins: A One-Man Civil Rights Movement." *Florida Law Review* (Dec. 1999): 913–56.

Dworkin, Ronald. "Hard Cases." *Harvard Law Review* 88 (Apr. 1975): 1057–1109.

Eaton, Amasa M. "The Suffrage Clause in the New Constitution of Louisiana." *Harvard Law Review* 13 (Dec. 1899): 278–93.

Eckhardt, Willard. "Comment." *Illinois Bar Journal* 24 (1936): 233–35.

Edsall, Preston W., & J. Oliver Williams. "North Carolina: Bipartisan Paradox." In *Changing Politics of the South*, edited by William C. Havard, 366–423. Baton Rouge: Louisiana State University Press, 1972.

Edwards, George Clifton. "White Justice in Dallas." *Nation*, 15 Sept. 1945, pp. 253–55.

Eisenberg, Ralph. "Virginia: The Emergence of Two-Party Politics." In *Changing Politics of the South*, edited by William C. Havard, 39–91. Baton Rouge: Louisiana State University Press, 1972.

Eisgruber, Christopher L. "Is the Supreme Court an Educative Institution?" *New York University Law Review* 67 (Nov. 1992): 961–1032.

Elman, Philip. "The Solicitor General's Office, Justice Frankfurter, and Civil Rights Litigation, 1946–1960: An Oral History." *Harvard Law Review* 100 (Feb. 1987): 817–52.

Ely, James W., Jr. "Negro Demonstrations and the Law: Danville as a Test Case." *Vanderbilt Law Review* 27 (Oct. 1974): 927–68.

———. "Reflections on *Buchanan v. Warley*, Property Rights and Race." *Vanderbilt Law Review* 51 (May 1998): 953–73.

Emanuel, Anne S. "Lynching and the Law in Georgia, circa 1931: A Chapter in the Legal Career of Judge Elbert Tuttle." *William & Mary Bill of Rights Journal* 5 (Winter 1996): 215–48.

Emerson, Thomas I., et al. "Segregation and the Equal Protection Clause: Brief for the Committee of Law Teachers against Segregation in Legal Education." *Minnesota Law Review* 34 (Mar. 1950): 289–329.

Emmons, Caroline. "'Somebody Has Got to Do That Work': Harry T. Moore and the Struggle for African-American Voting Rights in Florida." *Journal of Negro History* 82 (Spring 1997): 232–43.

Entin, Jonathan L. "*Sweatt v. Painter*, the End of Segregation, and the Transformation of Education Law." *Review of Litigation* 5 (Winter 1986): 3–71.

Epstein, Lee, & Thomas G. Walker. "The Role of the Supreme Court in American Society: Playing the Reconstruction Game." In *Contemplating Courts*, edited by Lee Epstein, 315–46. Washington, D.C.: CQ Press, 1995.

Epstein, Richard A. "Lest We Forget: *Buchanan v. Warley* and Constitutional Jurisprudence of the 'Progressive Era'." *Vanderbilt Law Review* 58 (May 1998): 787–96.

Erskine, Hazel G. "The Polls: Race Relations." *Public Opinion Quarterly* 26 (Spring 1962): 134–48.

Eskew, Glenn T. "The Alabama Christian Movement for Human Rights and the Birmingham Struggle for Civil Rights, 1956–1963." In *Birmingham, Alabama*, edited by David J. Garrow, 3–114. Brooklyn, N.Y.: Carlson, 1989.

Fairclough, Adam. "The Preachers and the People: The Origins and Early Years of the Southern Christian Leadership Conference, 1955–1959." *Journal of Southern History* 52 (Aug. 1986): 403–40.

———. "State of the Art: Historians and the Civil Rights Movement." *Journal of American Studies* 24 (Dec. 1990): 387–98.

Farris, Charles D. "The Re-Enfranchisement of Negroes in Florida." *Journal of Negro History* 39 (Oct. 1954): 259–83.

Fassett, John D. "Mr. Justice Reed and *Brown v. Board of Education.*" *Yearbook of the Supreme Court Historical Society* (1986): 48–63.

Finkelman, Paul. "*Prigg v. Pennsylvania* and Northern State Courts: Anti-Slavery Use of a Pro-Slavery Decision." *Civil War History* 25 (Mar. 1979): 5–35.

Finkle, Lee. "The Conservative Aims of Militant Rhetoric: Black Protest during World War II." *Journal of American History* 60 (Dec. 1973): 692–713.

Fischel, William A. "Why Judicial Reversal of Apartheid Made a Difference." *Vanderbilt Law Review* 51 (May 1998): 975–91.

Fishel, Leslie H., Jr. "Northern Prejudice and Negro Suffrage, 1865–1870." *Journal of Negro History* 39 (Jan. 1954): 8–26.

———. "The Negro in Northern Politics, 1870–1900." *Mississippi Valley Historical Review* 42 (Dec. 1955): 466–89.

———. "The Negro in the New Deal Era." *Wisconsin Magazine of History* 48 (Winter 1964–1965): 111–26.

Flemming, Roy B., John Bohte, & B. Dan Wood. "One Voice among Many: The Supreme Court's Influence on Attentiveness to Issues in the United States, 1947–1992." In *Leveraging the Law*, edited by David A. Schultz, 21–61. New York: Lang, 1998.

Flomsbee, Stanley J. "The Origin of the First 'Jim Crow' Law." *Journal of Southern History* 15 (May 1949): 235–47.

Folsom, Fred, Jr. "Federal Elections and the White Primary." *Columbia Law Review* 43 (Nov.–Dec. 1943): 1026–35.

Frank, John P. "The United States Supreme Court: 1949–50." *University of Chicago Law Review* 18 (Autumn 1950): 1–54.

———. "Can Courts Erase the Color Line?" *Journal of Negro Education* 21 (Summer 1952): 304–16.

———. "The United States Supreme Court: 1951–52." *University of Chicago Law Review* 20 (Autumn 1952): 1–68.

Frankfurter, Felix. "The Red Terror of Judicial Reform." In *Felix Frankfurter on the Supreme Court: Extrajudicial Essays on the Court and the Constitution*, edited by Philip B. Kurland, 158–68. Cambridge, Mass.: Belknap, 1970.

Franklin, Charles H., & Liane C. Kosaki. "Republican Schoolmaster: The U.S. Supreme Court, Public Opinion, and Abortion." *American Political Science Review* 83 (Sept. 1989): 751–71.

Franklin, John Hope. "Jim Crow Goes to School: The Genesis of Legal Segregation in Southern Schools." *South Atlantic Quarterly* 58 (Spring 1959): 225–35.

Frederickson, Kari. "'The Slowest State' and 'Most Backward Community': Racial Violence in South Carolina and Federal Civil Rights Legislation, 1946–1948." *South Carolina Historical Magazine* 98 (Apr. 1997): 177–202.

Freyer, Tony A. "The Little Rock Crisis Reconsidered." *Arkansas Historical Quarterly* 56 (Autumn 1997): 360–70.

Friedman, Barry. "Dialogue and Judicial Review." *Michigan Law Review* 91 (Feb. 1993): 577–682.

Galanter, Marc. "Why the 'Haves' Come Out Ahead: Speculations on the Limits of Legal Change." *Law & Society Review* 9 (Winter 1975): 95–160.

Gardbaum, Stephen. "New Deal Constitutionalism and the Unshackling of the States." *University of Chicago Law Review* 64 (Spring 1997): 483–566.

Garner, James Wilford. "The Fourteenth Amendment and Southern Representation." *South Atlantic Quarterly* 4 (July 1905): 209–16.

———. "Commentary." *American Journal of Sociology* 13 (1907–1908): 828–31.

Garrow, David J. "Commentary." In *Civil Rights Movement*, edited by Charles W. Eagles, 55–64. Jackson: University Press of Mississippi, 1986.

———. "Hopelessly Hollow History: Revisionist Devaluing of *Brown v. Board of Education*." *Virginia Law Review* 80 (Feb. 1994): 151–60.

Gatewood, Willard B., Jr. "North Carolina and Federal Aid to Education: Public Reaction to the Blair Bill, 1881–1890." *North Carolina Historical Review* 40 (Oct. 1963): 465–88.

———. "Negro Troops in Florida, 1898." *Florida Historical Quarterly* 49 (July 1970): 1–15.

Gavins, Raymond. "Urbanization and Segregation: Black Leadership Patterns in Richmond, Virginia, 1900–1920." *South Atlantic Quarterly* 79 (Summer 1980): 259–73.

Gellhorn, Walter. "A Decade of Desegregation: Retrospect and Prospect." *Utah Law Review* 9 (1964): 3–17.

Geyer, Elizabeth. "The 'New' Ku Klux Klan." *Crisis* 63 (Mar. 1956): 139–48.

Gill, Robert L. "The Impact, Implications and Prospects of *Brown v. Board of Education*: Twenty-five Years After." *Negro Education Review* 30 (Apr.–July 1979): 64–109.

Gillespie, John R. "The Constitution and the All-White Jury." *Kentucky Law Journal* 39 (Nov. 1950): 65–78.

Gillman, Howard. "What's Law Got to Do with It? Judicial Behavioralists Test the 'Legal Model' of Judicial Decision Making." *Law and Social Inquiry* 26 (Spring 2001): 465–504.

Glasrud, Bruce A. "Jim Crow's Emergence in Texas." *American Studies* 15 (Spring 1974): 47–60.

Gleijeses, Piero. "African Americans and the War against Spain." *North Carolina Historical Review* 73 (Apr. 1996): 184–214.

Glennon, Robert J. "Justice Henry Billings Brown: Values in Tension." *University of Colorado Law Review* 44 (1972–1973): 553–604.

———. "The Role of Law in the Civil Rights Movement: The Montgomery Bus Boycott, 1955–1957." *Law and History Review* 9 (Spring 1991): 59–112.

———. "The Jurisdictional Legacy of the Civil Rights Movement." *Tennessee Law Review* 61 (Spring 1994): 869–932.

Glickstein, Howard A. "The Impact of *Brown v. Board of Education* and Its Progeny." *Howard Law Journal* 23, no. 1 (1980): 51–55.

Going, Allen J. "The South and the Blair Education Bill." *Mississippi Valley Historical Review* 44 (Sept. 1957): 267–90.

Goodwyn, Lawrence C. "Populist Dreams and Negro Rights: East Texas as a Case Study." *American Historical Review* 76 (Dec. 1971): 1435–56.

Graber, Mark A. "The Passive-Aggressive Virtues: *Cohens v. Virginia* and the Problematic Establishment of Judicial Power." *Constitutional Commentary* (Spring 1995): 67–92.

——. "Federalist or Friends of Adams: The Marshall Court and Party Politics." *Studies in American Political Development* 12 (Oct. 1998): 229–66.

Graham, Hugh Davis. "Desegregation in Nashville: The Dynamics of Compliance." *Tennessee Historical Quarterly* 25 (Spring–Winter 1966): 135–54.

Granger, Lester B. "Some Tactics Which Should Supplement Resort to the Courts in Achieving Racial Integration in Education." *Journal of Negro Education* 21 (Summer 1952): 344–49.

Grantham, Dewey W., Jr. "Georgia Politics and the Disfranchisement of the Negro." *Georgia Historical Quarterly* 32 (Mar. 1948): 1–21.

Graves, John Temple. "The Southern Negro and the War Crisis." *Virginia Quarterly Review* 18 (Autumn 1942): 500–517.

Greeley, Andrew M., & Paul B. Sheatsley. "Attitudes toward Racial Integration." *Scientific American* 225 (Dec. 1971): 13–19.

Greenberg, Jack. "The Supreme Court, Civil Rights, and Civil Dissonance." *Yale Law Journal* 77 (July 1968): 1520–44.

Grill, Johnpeter H., & Robert L. Jenkins. "The Nazis and the American South in the 1930s: A Mirror Image?" *Journal of Southern History* 58 (Nov. 1992): 667–94.

Groner, Isaac N., & David M. Helfeld. "Race Discrimination in Housing." *Yale Law Journal* 57 (Jan. 1948): 426–58.

Hackney, Sheldon. "Little Rock and the Promise of America." In *Understanding the Little Rock Crisis*, edited by Elizabeth Jacoway & C. Fred Williams, 23–28. Fayetteville: University of Arkansas Press, 1999.

Hainsworth, Robert Wendell. "The Negro and the Texas Primaries." *Journal of Negro History* 18 (1933): 426–50.

Halberstam, David. "The White Citizens' Councils." *Commentary* 22 (Oct. 1956): 293–302.

Hall, Kermit. "Political Power and Constitutional Legitimacy: The South Carolina Ku Klux Klan Trials, 1871–1872." *Emory Law Journal* 33 (Fall 1984): 921–51.

Handlin, Oscar. "Civil Rights after Little Rock: The Failure of Moderation." *Commentary* 24 (Nov. 1957): 392–96.

Harlan, Louis. "Desegregation in New Orleans Public Schools during Reconstruction." *American Historical Review* 67 (Apr. 1962): 663–75.

Harris, Carl V. "Reforms in Government: Control of Negroes in Birmingham, Alabama, 1890–1920." *Journal of Southern History* 38 (Nov. 1972): 567–600.

——. "Stability and Change in Discrimination against Black Public Schools: Birmingham, Alabama, 1871–1931." *Journal of Southern History* 51 (Aug. 1985): 375–416.

Harris, Robert L., Jr. "Racial Equality and the United Nations Charter." In *New Directions in Civil Rights Studies*, edited by Armstead L. Robinson & Patricia Sullivan, 126–48. Charlottesville: University Press of Virginia, 1991.

Harrison, John. "Reconstructing the Privileges and Immunities Clause." *Yale Law Journal* 101 (May 1992): 1385–1474.

Havard, William C. "The South: A Shifting Perspective." In *Changing Politics of the South*, edited by William C. Havard, 3–36. Baton Rouge: Louisiana State University Press, 1972.

Heckman, Robert Allen, & Betty Gene Hall. "Berea College and the Day Law." *Register of the Kentucky Historical Society* 66 (Jan. 1968): 35–52.

Hemmingway, Theodore. "Prelude to Change: Black Carolinians in the War Years, 1914–20." *Journal of Negro History* 65 (Summer 1980): 212–27.

Hendrick, Irving G. "Approaching Equality of Educational Opportunity in California: The Successful Struggle of Black Citizens, 1880–1920." *Pacific History* 25 (Winter 1981): 22–29.

Henkin, Louis. "*Shelley v. Kraemer*: Notes for a Revised Opinion." *University of Pennsylvania Law Review* 110 (Feb. 1962): 473–505.

Hershman, James H., Jr. "Massive Resistance Meets Its Match." In *Moderates' Dilemma*, edited by Matthew D. Lassiter & Andrew B. Lewis, 104–33. Charlottesville: University Press of Virginia, 1998.

Higginbotham, A. Leon, Jr., & William C. Smith. "The Hughes Court and the Beginning of the End of the 'Separate but Equal' Doctrine." *Minnesota Law Review* 76 (May 1992): 1099–1131.

Higginbotham, A. Leon, Jr., et al. "De Jure Housing Segregation in the United States and South Africa: The Difficult Pursuit of Racial Justice." *University of Illinois Law Review* 4 (1990): 763–877.

Hiller, Amy H. "The Disfranchisement of Delaware Negroes from the Late Nineteenth Century." *Delaware History* 13 (Oct. 1968): 124–53.

Hirsch, Arnold R. "Massive Resistance in the Urban North: Trumbull Park, Chicago, 1953–1966." *Journal of American History* (Sept. 1995): 522–50.

Hixson, William B., Jr. "Moorfield Storey and the Struggle for Equality." *Journal of American History* 55 (Dec. 1968): 533–54.

Hoekstra, Valerie J. "The Supreme Court and Opinion Change: An Experimental Study of the Court's Ability to Change Opinion." *American Political Science Quarterly* 23 (Jan. 1995): 109–29.

Hoffman, Edwin D. "The Genesis of the Modern Movement for Equal Rights in South Carolina, 1930–39." *Journal of Negro History* 44 (Oct. 1959): 346–69.

Holmes, William F. "Labor Agents and the Georgia Exodus, 1899–1900." *South Atlantic Quarterly* 79 (Autumn 1980): 436–48.

Homel, Michael W. "Two Worlds of Race? Urban Blacks and the Public Schools, North and South, 1865–1940." In *Southern Cities, Southern Schools: Public Education in the Urban South*, edited by David N. Plank & Rick Ginsberg, 237–61. New York: Greenwood, 1990.

Honey, Michael. "Operation Dixie: Labor and Civil Rights in the Postwar South." *Mississippi Quarterly* 45 (Fall 1992): 439–52.

Hornsby, Alton, Jr. "A City That Was Too Busy to Hate." In *Southern Businessmen and Desegregation*, edited by Elizabeth Jacoway & David R. Colburn, 121–36. Baton Rouge: Louisiana State University Press, 1982.

Hott, George D. "Constitutionality of Municipal Zoning and Segregation Ordinances." *West Virginia Law Quarterly* 33 (June 1927): 332–49.

Houston, Charles H. "The Need for Negro Lawyers." *Journal of Negro Education* 4 (Jan. 1935): 49–52.

——. "Educational Inequalities Must Go!" *Crisis* 42 (Oct. 1935): 300–301, 316.

——. "Cracking Closed University Doors." *Crisis* 42 (Dec. 1935): 364.

Houston, Charles H., & Leon A. Ransom. "The Crawford Case." *Nation* 139 (4 July 1934): 17–19.

Hovenkamp, Herbert. "Social Science and Segregation before *Brown*." *Duke Law Journal* (1985): 624–72.

Howard, Perry H. "Louisiana: Resistance and Change." In *Changing Politics of the South*, edited by William C. Havard, 525–87. Baton Rouge: Louisiana State University Press, 1972.

Howard, Victor B. "The Struggle for Equal Education in Kentucky, 1866–1884." *Journal of Negro Education* 46 (Summer 1977): 305–28.

Howard, Walter T., & Virginia M. Howard. "The Early Years of the NAACP in Tampa, 1915–1930." *Tampa Bay History* 16 (Fall–Winter 1994): 41–56.

Hughes, Langston. "My America." In *What the Negro Wants*, edited by Rayford W. Logan, 299–307. Chapel Hill: University of North Carolina Press, 1944; New York: Agathon, 1969.

Hutcheson, Joseph C. "The Judgment Intuitive: The Function of the 'Hunch' in Judicial Decisions." *Cornell Law Quarterly* 14 (Apr. 1929): 274–88.

Hutchinson, Dennis J. "Unanimity and Desegregation: Decision Making in the Supreme Court, 1948–1958." *Georgetown Law Journal* 68 (Oct. 1979): 1–87.

Hylton, J. Gordon. "The Judge Who Abstained in *Plessy v. Ferguson*: Justice David Brewer and the Problem of Race." *Mississippi Law Journal* 61 (Fall 1991): 315–64.

Hyman, Herbert H., & Paul B. Sheatsley. "Attitudes towards Desegregation." *Scientific American*, Dec. 1956, pp. 35–39.

Hyman, J. D. "Segregation and the Fourteenth Amendment." *Vanderbilt Law Review* 4 (Apr. 1951): 555–73.

Issacharoff, Samuel, & Richard H. Pildes. "Politics as Markets: Partisan Lockups of the Democratic Process." *Stanford Law Review* 50 (Feb. 1998): 643–717.

Jackson, Walter A. "White Liberal Intellectuals, Civil Rights and Gradualism, 1954–60." In *The Making of Martin Luther King and the Civil Rights Movement*, edited by Brian Ward & Tony Badger, 96–114. New York: New York University Press, 1996.

Jacoway, Elizabeth. "Taken by Surprise: Little Rock Business Leaders and Desegregation." In *Southern Businessmen and Desegregation*, edited by Elizabeth Jacoway & David R. Colburn, 15–41. Baton Rouge: Louisiana State University Press, 1982.

———. "Introduction: Understanding the Past: The Challenge of Little Rock." In *Understanding the Little Rock Crisis*, edited by Elizabeth Jacoway & C. Fred Williams, 1–22. Fayetteville: University of Arkansas Press, 1999.

James, Weldon. "The South's Own Civil War: Battle for the Schools." In *With All Deliberate Speed*, edited by Don Shoemaker, 15–35. New York: Harper, 1957.

Janken, Kenneth R. "African-American Intellectuals Confront the 'Silent South': The *What the Negro Wants* Controversy." *North Carolina Historical Review* 70 (Apr. 1993): 153–79.

Jefferson, Bernard S. "Race Discrimination in Jury Service." *Boston University Law Review* 19 (June 1939): 413–47.

Jeffries, John C., Jr. "Lewis F. Powell, Jr., and the Art of Judicial Selection." *Harvard Law Review* 112 (Jan. 1999): 597–602.

Jelks, Randal M. "Making Opportunity: The Struggle against Jim Crow in Grand Rapids, Michigan, 1890–1927." *Michigan Historical Review* 19 (Fall 1993): 23–48.

Jenkins, Martin D. "The Availability of Higher Education for Negroes in the Southern States." *Journal of Negro Education* 16 (Summer 1947): 459–73.

———. "Problems Incident to Racial Integration and Some Suggested Approaches to These Problems: A Critical Summary." *Journal of Negro Education* (Summer 1952): 411–21.

Johnson, Charles S. "The Present Status of Race Relations in the South." *Social Forces* 23 (Oct. 1944): 27–32.

Johnson, Guy B. "The Negro Migration and Its Consequences." *Journal of Social Forces* 2 (Mar. 1924): 404–8.

Jones, Edgar. "City Limits: Segregation-Desegregation in the Cities." In *With All Deliberate Speed*, edited by Don Shoemaker, 71–87. New York: Harper, 1957.

Jones, Harry H. "The Negro before the Court during 1930." *Crisis* 40 (Oct. 1933): 230.

Jones, Lewis W. "Fred L. Shuttlesworth: Indigenous Leader." In *Birmingham, Alabama*, edited by David J. Garrow, 115–50. Brooklyn, N.Y.: Carlson, 1989.

Jones, Nathaniel R. "The Desegregation of Urban Schools Thirty Years after *Brown*." *University of Colorado Law Review* 55 (Summer 1984): 515–57.

———. "The Harlan Dissent: The Road Not Taken: An American Tragedy." *Georgia State University Law Review* 12 (June 1996): 951–1016.

Jordan, William. "'The Damnable Dilemma': African-American Accommodations and Protest during World War I." *Journal of American History* 81 (Mar. 1995): 1562–83.

Kahen, Harold I. "Validity of Anti-Negro Restrictive Covenants: A Reconsideration of the Problem." *University of Chicago Law Review* 12 (Feb. 1945): 198–213.

Karlan, Pamela S. "Race, Rights, and Remedies in Criminal Adjudication." *Michigan Law Review* 96 (June 1998): 2001–30.

Kee, Ed. "The *Brown* Decision and Milford, Delaware, 1954–1965." *Delaware History* 27 (Fall–Winter 1997): 205–44.

Kelley, Robin D. G. "'We Are Not What We Seem': Rethinking Black Working-Class Opposition in the Jim Crow South." *Journal of American History* 80 (June 1993): 75–112.

Kellogg, John. "Negro Urban Clusters in the Postbellum South." *Geographical Review* 67 (July 1977): 310–21.

Kellogg, Peter J. "Civil Rights Consciousness in the 1940s." *Historian* 42 (Nov. 1979): 18–41.

Kelly, Alfred H. "The Congressional Controversy over School Segregation, 1867–1875." *American Historical Review* 64 (Apr. 1959): 537–63.

Kennedy, Randall. "Race Relations Law and the Tradition of Celebration: The Case of Professor Schmidt." *Columbia Law Review* 86 (Nov. 1986): 1622–61.

———. "*McCleskey v. Kemp*: Race, Capital Punishment, and the Supreme Court." *Harvard Law Review* 110 (May 1988): 1388–1443.

Kerin, Edna B. "Another Chance for the Groveland Victims." *Crisis* 58 (May 1951): 317–21, 350.

Killian, Lewis M., & John L. Haer. "Variables Related to Attitudes regarding School Desegregation among White Southerners." *Sociometry* 21 (June 1958): 159–64.

King, Martin Luther, Jr. "The Current Crisis in Race Relations." *New South* 13 (Mar. 1958): 8–12.

Kirby, Jack Temple. "Clarence Poe's Vision of a Segregated 'Great Rural Civilization'." *South Atlantic Quarterly* 68 (Winter 1969): 27–38.

Kirk, John A. "Arkansas, the *Brown* Decision, and the 1957 Little Rock School Crisis." In *Understanding the Little Rock Crisis*, edited by Elizabeth Jacoway & C. Fred Williams, 67–82. Fayetteville: University of Arkansas Press, 1999.

Kirkendall, Richard S. "Election of 1948." In *American Presidential Elections*, edited by Arthur M. Schlesinger & Fred L. Israel, 4:3099–3145. New York: Chelsea House, 1971.

Kizer, Benjamin H. "The Impact of *Brown v. Board of Education*." *Gonzaga Law Review* 2 (Mar. 1967): 1–18.

Klarman, Michael J. "The Puzzling Resistance to Political Process Theory." *Virginia Law Review* 77 (May 1991): 747–832.

——. "An Interpretative History of Modern Equal Protection." *Michigan Law Review* 90 (Nov. 1991): 213–318.

——. "*Brown*, Racial Change, and the Civil Rights Movement." *Virginia Law Review* 80 (Feb. 1994): 7–150.

——. "*Brown*, Originalism, and Constitutional Theory: A Response to Professor McConnell." *Virginia Law Review* 81 (Oct. 1995): 1881–1936.

——. "Rethinking the Civil Rights and Civil Liberties Revolutions." *Virginia Law Review* 82 (1996): 1–67.

——. "Majoritarian Judicial Review: The Entrenchment Problem." *Georgetown Law Journal* 85 (Feb. 1997): 491–553.

——. "Fidelity, Indeterminacy, and the Problem of Constitutional Evil." *Fordham Law Review* 65 (Mar. 1997): 1739–56.

——. "What's So Great about Constitutionalism?" *Northwestern University Law Review* 93 (Fall 1998): 145–94.

——. "Rethinking the History of American Freedom." *William & Mary Law Review* 42 (Oct. 2000): 265–88.

——. "How Great Were the 'Great' Marshall Court Decisions?" *Virginia Law Review* 87 (Oct. 2001): 1111–84.

——. "*Bush v. Gore* through the Lens of Constitutional History." *California Law Review* 89 (Dec. 2001): 1721–65.

Knight, Jack, & Lee Epstein. "On the Struggle for Judicial Supremacy." *Law & Society Review* 30, no. 1 (1996): 87–120.

Korstad, Robert, & Nelson Lichtenstein. "Opportunities Found and Lost: Labor, Radicals, and the Early Civil Rights Movement." *Journal of American History* 75 (Dec. 1988): 786–811.

Kousser, J. Morgan. "Separate but *Not* Equal: The Supreme Court's First Decision on Racial Discrimination in Schools." *Journal of Southern History* 46 (Feb. 1980): 17–44.

——. "Progressivism: For Middle-Class Whites Only. North Carolina Education, 1880–1910." *Journal of Southern History* 46 (May 1980): 169–94.

Kruse, Kevin M. "Personal Rights, Public Wrongs: The Gaines Case and the Beginning of the End of Segregation." *Journal of Supreme Court History* (1997): 113–30.

Kutler, Stanley. "Eisenhower, the Judiciary and Desegregation: Some Reflections." In *Eisenhower: A Centenary Assessment*, edited by Gunter Bischof & Stephen E. Ambrose, 87–100. Baton Rouge: Louisiana State University Press, 1995.

LaFarge, John. "The Development of Cooperative Acceptance of Racial Integration." *Journal of Negro Education* 21 (Summer 1952): 430–33.

Lamb, Chris. "'I Never Want to Take Another Trip Like This One': Jackie Robinson's Journey to Integrate Baseball." *Journal of Sports History* 24 (Summer 1997): 177–91.

Lasch, Robert. "Along the Border: Desegregation at the Fringes." In *With All Deliberate Speed*, edited by Don Shoemaker, 56–70. New York: Harper, 1957.

Lassiter, Matthew D., & Andrew B. Lewis, "Introduction: Massive Resistance Revisited: Virginia's White Moderates and the Byrd Organization." In *Moderates' Dilemma*, edited by Matthew D. Lassiter & Andrew B. Lewis, 1–21. Charlottesville: University Press of Virginia, 1998.

Lawson, Steven F. "The Florida Legislative Investigation Committee and the Constitutional Readjustment of Race Relations, 1956–1963." In *An Uncertain Tradition: Constitutionalism and the History of the South*, edited by Kermit L. Hall & James W. Ely, Jr., 296–325. Athens: University of Georgia Press, 1989.

Lawson, Steven F., et. al. "Groveland: Florida's Little Scottsboro." *Florida Historical Quarterly* 65 (July 1986): 1–26.

Lefberg, Irving F. "Chief Justice Vinson and the Politics of Desegregation." *Emory Law Journal* 24 (1975): 243–312.

Leflar, Robert A. "'Law of the Land': The Courts and the Schools." In *With All Deliberate Speed*, edited by Don Shoemaker, 1–14. New York: Harper, 1957.

Leflar Robert A., & Wylie H. Davis. "Segregation in the Public Schools, 1953." *Harvard Law Review* 67 (Jan. 1954): 377–435.

Lentz, Richard. "The Prophet and the Citadel: News Magazine Coverage of the 1963 Birmingham Civil Rights Crisis." *Communication* 10 (Dec. 1987): 5–30.

LePore, Herbert P. "Prelude to Prejudice: Hiram Johnson, Woodrow Wilson, and the California Alien Land Law Controversy of 1913." *Southern California Quarterly* 61 (Spring 1979): 99–110.

Levy, David W. "Before *Brown*: The Racial Integration of American Higher Education." *Journal of Supreme Court History* 24 (1999): 298–313.

Lewis, David Levering. "The Origins and Causes of the Civil Rights Movement." In *Civil Rights Movement*, edited by Charles W. Eagles, 3–17. Jackson: University Press of Mississippi, 1986.

Lewis, Earl M. "The Negro Voter in Mississippi." *Journal of Negro Education* 26 (Summer 1957): 329–50.

Lewis, Todd E. "Mob Justice in the 'American Congo': 'Judge Lynch' in Arkansas during the Decade after World War I." *Arkansas Historical Quarterly* 52 (Summer 1993): 156–84.

Lichtenstein, Alex. "Good Roads and Chain Gangs in the Progressive South: The Negro Convict as a Slave." *Journal of Southern History* 59 (Feb. 1993): 85–110.

Logan, Frenise A. "The Legal Status of Public School Education for Negroes in North Carolina, 1877–1894." *North Carolina Historical Review* 32 (July 1955): 346–57.

Lund, Nelson. "The Constitution, the Supreme Court, and Racial Politics." *Georgia State University Law Review* 12 (June 1996): 1129–50.

Lusky, Louis. "Racial Discrimination and the Federal Law: A Problem in Nullification." *Columbia Law Review* 63 (Nov. 1963): 1163–91.

——. "Footnote Rudux: A Carolene Products Reminiscence." *Columbia Law Review* 82 (Oct. 1982): 1093–1105.

Mabee, Carleton. "Long Island's Black 'School War' and the Decline of Segregation in New York State." *New York History* 58 (Oct. 1977): 385–411.

Mabry, William Alexander. "'White Supremacy' and the North Carolina Suffrage Amendment." *North Carolina Historical Review* 13 (Jan. 1936): 1–24.

———. "Louisiana Politics and the 'Grandfather Clause'." *North Carolina Historical Review* 13 (Oct. 1936): 290–310.

———. "Ben Tillman Disfranchised the Negro." *South Atlantic Quarterly* 37 (Apr. 1938): 170–83.

———. "Disfranchisement of the Negro in Mississippi." *Journal of Southern History* 4 (Aug. 1938): 318–33.

MacLean, Nancy. "Gender, Sexuality, and the Politics of Lynching: The Leo Frank Case Revisited." *Journal of American History* 77 (Dec. 1991): 917–48.

Maltz, Earl M. "'Separate but Equal' and the Law of Common Carriers in the Era of the Fourteenth Amendment." *Rutgers Law Journal* 17 (Spring–Summer 1986): 553–68.

———. "The Civil Rights Act and the Civil Rights Cases: Congress, Court, and Constitution." *Florida Law Review* 44 (Sept. 1992): 605–35.

———. "Only Partially Color Blind: John Marshall Harlan's View of Race and the Constitution." *Georgia State University Law Review* 12 (June 1996): 973–1016.

———. "Originalism and the Desegregation Decisions: A Response to Professor McConnell." *Constitutional Commentary* 13 (Winter 1996): 223–31.

Maltzman, Forrest, James F. Spriggs II, and Paul J. Wahlbeck. "Strategy and Judicial Choice: New Institutionalist Approaches to Supreme Court Decision Making." In *Supreme Court Decision Making*, edited by Cornell W. Clayton & Howard Gillman, 43–63. Chicago, Ill.: University of Chicago Press, 1999.

Marshall, Thurgood. "An Evaluation of Recent Efforts to Achieve Racial Integration in Education through Resort to the Courts." *Journal of Negro Education* 21 (Summer 1952): 316–27.

Martin, Charles H. "Oklahoma's 'Scottsboro' Affair: The Jess Hollins Rape Case, 1931–1936." *South Atlantic Quarterly* (Spring 1980): 175–88.

———. "The International Labor Defense and Black America." *Labor History* 26 (Spring 1985): 165–94.

———. "Race, Gender, and Southern Justice: The Rosa Lee Ingram Case." *American Journal of Legal History* 29 (July 1985): 251–68.

———. "The Civil Rights Congress and Southern Black Defendants." *Georgia Historical Quarterly* 71 (Spring 1987): 25–52.

Mathews, Linda M. "Keeping Down Jim Crow: The Railroads and the Separate Coach Bill in South Carolina." *South Atlantic Quarterly* 73 (Winter 1974): 117–29.

Matthews, Donald R., & James W. Prothro. "Southern Racial Attitudes: Conflict, Awareness, and Political Change." *Annals* 344 (Nov. 1962): 108–21.

Matthews, John Michael. "The Georgia Race Strike of 1909." *Journal of Southern History* 40 (Nov. 1974): 613–30.

McAdams, Richard. "Race and Selective Prosecution: Discovering the Pitfalls of *Armstrong*." *Chicago-Kent Law Review* 73, no. 2 (1998): 605–67.

McCain, R. Ray. "Reactions to the United States Supreme Court Segregation Decision of 1954." *Georgia Historical Quarterly* 52 (Dec. 1968): 371–87.

McCann, Michael W. "Reform Litigation on Trial." *Law & Social Inquiry* 17 (Fall 1992): 715–43.

McCarthy, G. Michael. "Smith vs. Hoover: The Politics of Race in West Tennessee." *Phylon* 39 (June 1978): 154–68.

McCauley, Patrick E. "'Be It Enacted': The Legislative Record." In *With All Deliberate Speed*, edited by Don Shoemaker, 130–46. New York: Harper, 1957.

McConnell, Michael W. "Originalism and the Desegregation Decisions." *Virginia Law Review* 81 (May 1995): 947–1140.

McGovney, D. O. "Racial Residential Segregation by State Court Enforcement of Restrictive Agreements, Covenants or Conditions in Deeds Is Unconstitutional." *California Law Review* 33 (Mar. 1945): 5–39.

McGuinn, Henry J. "Equal Protection of the Law and Fair Trials in Maryland." *Journal of Negro History* 24 (Apr. 1939): 143–66.

——. "The Courts and Equality of Educational Opportunity." *Journal of Negro Education* 2 (Apr. 1939): 150–63.

McKay, Robert B. "Segregation and Public Recreation." *Virginia Law Review* 40 (Oct. 1954): 697–731.

McKinney, John C., & Linda B. Bourque. "The Changing South: National Incorporation of a Region." *American Sociological Review* 36 (June 1971): 399–412.

McMahon, Kevin J., & Michael Paris. "The Politics of Rights Revisited: Rosenberg, McCann, and the New Institutionalism." In *Leveraging the Law*, edited by David A. Schultz, 63–134. New York: Lang, 1998.

McMillen, Neil R. "Organized Resistance to School Desegregation in Tennessee." *Tennessee Historical Quarterly* 30 (Fall 1971): 315–28.

——. "Black Enfranchisement in Mississippi: Federal Enforcement and Black Protest in the 1960s." *Journal of Southern History* 43 (Aug. 1977): 351–72.

Meador, Dan. "The Constitution and the Assignment of Pupils to the Public Schools." *Virginia Law Review* 45 (May 1959): 517–71.

Meier, August. "The Negro and the Democratic Party, 1875–1915." *Phylon* 17 (Second Quarter 1956): 173–91.

——. "The Successful Sit-Ins in a Border City: A Study in Social Causation." *Journal of Intergroup Relations* 2 (Summer 1961): 230–37.

Meier, August, & Elliott M. Rudwick. "Early Boycotts of Segregated Schools: The East Orange, New Jersey, Experience, 1899–1906." *History of Education Quarterly* 7 (Spring 1967): 22–35.

——. "Early Boycotts of Segregated Schools: The Alton, Illinois, Case, 1897–1908." *Journal of Negro Education* 36 (Autumn 1967): 394–402.

Miller, Kathleen Atkinson. "The Ladies and the Lynchers: A Look at the Association of Southern Women for the Prevention of Lynching." *Southern Studies* 17 (Fall 1978): 261–80.

Miller, Kelly. "A Negro's View." *Outlook*, 31 Dec. 1898, pp. 1059–63.

——. "The Causes of Segregation." *Current History* 25 (Mar. 1927): 827–33.

Ming, William R., Jr. "The Elimination of Segregation in the Public Schools of the North and West." *Journal of Negro Education* 21 (Summer 1952): 265–75.

Mohl, Raymond A. "Making the Second Ghetto in Metropolitan Miami, 1940–1960." *Journal of Urban History* 21 (Mar. 1995): 395–427.

Monnet, Julian C. "The Latest Phase of Negro Disfranchisement." *Harvard Law Review* 26 (Nov. 1912): 42–63.

Moore, John Hammond. "Jim Crow in Georgia." *South Atlantic Quarterly* 66 (Autumn 1967): 554–65.

Mormino, Gary R. "G.I. Joe Meets Jim Crow: Racial Violence and Reform in World War II, Florida." *Florida Historical Quarterly* 73 (July 1994): 23–42.

Mowry, George. "The South and the Progressive Lily White Party of 1912." *Journal of Southern History* 6 (May 1940): 237–47.

Murphy, Walter. "The South Counterattacks: The Anti-NAACP Laws." *Western Political Quarterly* 12 (June 1959): 371–90.

Muse, Benjamin. "Moderates and Militants." *New Republic*, 2 Apr. 1956, pp. 8–9.

———. "When and How the South Will Integrate." *Harpers* 214 (Apr. 1957): 51–55.

Nabrit, James M. "An Appraisal of Court Action as a Means of Achieving Racial Segregation [*sic*] in Education." *Journal of Negro Education* 21 (Summer 1952): 421–30.

Nelson, Bruce. "Organized Labor and the Struggle for Black Equality in Mobile during World War II." *Journal of American History* 80 (Dec. 1993): 952–88.

Nelson, Paul David. "Experiment in Interracial Education at Berea College, 1858–1905." *Journal of Negro History* 59 (Jan. 1974): 13–27.

Nieman, Donald G. "Black Political Power and Criminal Justice: Washington County, Texas, 1868–1884." *Journal of Southern History* 55 (Aug. 1989): 391–420.

Norgren, Jill. "The Cherokee Nation Cases of the 1830s." *Yearbook of the Supreme Court Historical Society* (1994): 65–82.

Norrell, Robert J. "Labor at the Ballot Box: Alabama Politics from the New Deal to the Dixiecrat Movement." *Journal of Southern History* 57 (May 1991): 201–34.

———. "One Thing We Did Right: Reflections on the Movement." In *New Directions in Civil Rights Studies*, edited by Armstead L. Robinson & Patricia Sullivan, 65–80. Charlottesville: University Press of Virginia, 1991.

Norwood, Stephen H. "Bogalusa Burning: The War against Biracial Unionism in the Deep South, 1919." *Journal of Southern History* 63 (Aug. 1997): 591–628.

Note. "Constitutionality of a Statute Compelling the Color Line in Private Schools." *Harvard Law Review* 22 (Jan. 1909): 217–18.

Note. "Exclusion of Negroes from State-Supported Professional Schools." *Yale Law Journal* 45 (May 1936): 1296–1301.

Note. "The Negro Citizen in the Supreme Court." *Harvard Law Review* 52 (Mar. 1939): 823–32.

Note. "Negro Disenfranchisement: A Challenge to the Constitution." *Columbia Law Review* 47 (Jan. 1947): 76–98.

Note. "Constitutionality of Educational Segregation." *George Washington Law Review* 17 (Feb. 1949): 208–25.

Note. "The Courts, HEW, and Southern School Desegregation." *Yale Law Journal* 77 (Dec. 1967): 321–65.

Note. "*Gideon's* Promise Unfulfilled: The Need for Litigated Reform of Indigent Defense." *Harvard Law Review* 113 (June 2000): 2062–79.

Oak, Eleanor H., & Vishnu V. Oak. "The Development of Separate Education in New Jersey." *Education* 59 (Oct. 1938): 109–12.

Oak, Vishnu V., & Eleanor H. Oak. "The Illegal Status of Separate Education in New Jersey." *School & Society* 47 (May 1938): 671–73.

Oates, Stephen B. "The Week the World Watched Selma." *American Heritage* 33 (June–July 1982): 48–63.

Oberst, Paul. "The Strange Career of *Plessy v. Ferguson*." *Arizona Law Review* 15 (1973): 389–413.

Odum, Howard W. "Social Change in the South." In *The Southern Political Scene 1938–1948*, edited by Taylor Cole & John H. Hallowell, 242–58. Gainesville, Fla.: Journal of Politics, 1948.

Opotowsky, Stan. "Dixie Dynamite: The Inside Story of White Citizens' Councils" (Jan. 1957). In NAACP Papers, part 20, reel 13, frs. 670–86.

Owsley, Frank L. "Scottsboro: The Third Crusade." *American Review* 1 (June 1933): 257–85.

Palmore, Joseph R. "The Not-So-Strange Career of Interstate Jim Crow: Race, Transportation, and the Dormant Commerce Clause, 1878–1946." *Virginia Law Review* 83 (Nov. 1997): 1773–1817.

Palumbos, Robert M. "Student Involvement in the Baltimore Civil Rights Movement, 1953–63." *Maryland Historical Magazine* 94 (Winter 1999): 449–92.

Parham, Joseph B. "Halls of Ivy: Southern Exposure: In the Colleges." In *With All Deliberate Speed*, edited by Don Shoemaker, 163–82. New York: Harper, 1957.

Patterson, James T. "The Failure of Party Realignment in the South, 1937–1939." *Journal of Politics* 27 (Aug. 1965): 602–17.

Paulson, Darryl, & Paul Hawkes. "Desegregating the University of Florida Law School: *Virgil Hawkins v. the Florida Board of Control.*" *Florida State University Law Review* 12 (Summer 1984): 59–71.

Peterson, Gladys Tignore. "The Present Status of the Negro Separate School as Defined by Court Decisions." *Journal of Negro Education* 4 (July 1935): 351–74.

Pettigrew, Thomas F. "Desegregation and Its Chances for Success: Northern and Southern Views." *Social Forces* 35 (May 1957): 339–44.

Pettigrew, Thomas F., & Ernest Q. Campbell. "Faubus and Segregation: An Analysis of Arkansas Voting." *Public Opinion Quarterly* 24 (Autumn 1960): 436–47.

Phillips, Charles. "Exploring Relations among Forms of Social Control: The Lynching and Execution of Blacks in North Carolina, 1889–1918." *Law & Society Review* 21 (1987): 361–74.

Pillsbury, Albert E. "A Brief Inquiry into a Federal Remedy for Lynching." *Harvard Law Review* 15 (May 1902): 707–13.

Pingrey, D. H. "A Legal View of Racial Discrimination." *American Law Register* 30 (Feb. 1891): 69–105.

Poe, Clarence H. "Suffrage Restrictions in the South: Its Causes and Consequences." *North American Review* 175 (July 1902): 534–43.

Polenberg, Richard. "The Good War? Reappraisal of How World War II Affected American Society." *Virginia Magazine of History and Biography* 100 (July 1992): 295–322.

Portwood, Shirley J. "The Alton School Case and African-American Community Consciousness, 1897–1908." *Illinois Historical Journal* 91 (Spring 1998): 2–20.

Post, Robert. "Defending the Lifeworld: Substantive Due Process in the Taft Court Era." *Boston University Law Review* 78 (Dec. 1998): 1489–1545.

Powell, Lewis F., Jr. "Carolene Products Revisited." *Columbia Law Review* 82 (Oct. 1982): 1087–92.

Power, Garrett. "Apartheid Baltimore Style: The Residential Segregation Ordinances of 1910–1913." *Maryland Law Review* 42 (1983): 289–328.

Prather, H. Leon, Sr. "We Have Taken a City." In *Democracy Betrayed*, edited by David Cecelski & Timothy Tyson, 15–41. Chapel Hill: University of North Carolina Press, 1998.

"Press Comment on the Gaines Case." *Crisis* 45 (Feb. 1939): 52–53, 61.

Price, Edward J., Jr. "School Segregation in Nineteenth-Century Pennsylvania." *Pennsylvania History* 43 (Apr. 1976): 121–37.

Pritchett, C. Hermann. "Equal Protection and the Urban Majority." *American Political Science Review* 58 (Dec. 1964): 869–75.

Rabinowitz, Howard N. "More than the Woodward Thesis: Assessing *The Strange Career of Jim Crow*." *Journal of American History* 75 (Dec. 1989): 842–56.

Rable, George C. "The South and the Politics of Antilynching Legislation, 1920–1940." *Journal of Southern History* 51 (1985): 201–20.

Rachal, John R. "'The Long Hot Summer': The Mississippi Response to Freedom Summer, 1964." *Journal of Negro History* 84 (Fall 1999): 315–39.

Randolph, A. Philip. "March on Washington Movement Presents Program for the Negro." In *What the Negro Wants*, edited by Rayford W. Logan, 133–62. Chapel Hill: University of North Carolina Press, 1944; New York: Agathon, 1969.

Ransmeier, Joseph S. "The Fourteenth Amendment and the 'Separate but Equal' Doctrine." *Michigan Law Review* 50 (Dec. 1951): 203–60.

Raymond, Margaret. "Rejecting Totalitarianism: Translating the Guarantees of Constitutional Criminal Procedure." *North Carolina Law Review* 76 (Apr. 1998): 1193–1263.

Reagan, Hugh D. "Race as a Factor in the Presidential Election of 1928 in Alabama." *Alabama Review* 19 (Jan. 1966): 5–19.

Reich, Steven A. "Soldiers of Democracy: Black Texans and the Fight for Citizenship, 1917–1921." *Journal of American History* 82 (Mar. 1996): 1478–1504.

Rhee, Jeannie. "In Black and White: Chinese in the Mississippi Delta." *Journal of Supreme Court History* (1994): 117–32.

Rice, R. L. "Residential Segregation by Law, 1910–1917." *Journal of Southern History* 34 (May 1968): 179–99.

Riegel, Stephen J. "The Persistent Career of Jim Crow: Lower Federal Courts and the 'Separate but Equal' Doctrine, 1865–1896." *American Journal of Legal History* 28 (Jan. 1984): 17–40.

Roback, Jennifer. "The Political Economy of Segregation: The Case of Segregated Streetcars." *Journal of Economic History* 46 (Dec. 1986): 893–917.

Robinson, Glen. "Man in No Man's Land: The School Administrator." In *With All Deliberate Speed*, edited by Don Shoemaker, 183–201. New York: Harper, 1957.

Roche, John P. "*Plessy v. Ferguson*: Requiescat in Pace?" *University of Pennsylvania Law Review* 103 (Oct. 1954): 45–58.

Rogers, O. A., Jr. "The Elaine Race Riots of 1919." *Arkansas Historical Quarterly* 19 (Summer 1960): 142–50.

Rose, John C. "Negro Suffrage: The Constitutional Point of View." *American Political Science Review* 1 (Nov. 1906): 17–46.

Rosenberg, Gerald N. "*Brown* Is Dead! Long Live *Brown*!: The Endless Attempt to Canonize a Case." *Virginia Law Review* 80 (Feb. 1994): 161–71.

——. "Positivism, Interpretivism, and the Study of Law." *Law & Social Inquiry* 21 (Spring 1996): 435–56.

——. "African-American Rights after *Brown*." *Journal of Supreme Court History* 24 (1999): 201–25.

Ross, William G. "Attacks on the Warren Court by State Officials: A Case Study of Why Court-Curbing Movements Fail." *Buffalo Law Review* 50 (Spring–Summer 2002): 483–612.

Rostow, Eugene V. "The Democratic Character of Judicial Review." *Harvard Law Review* 66 (Dec. 1952): 193–224.

Rotnem, Victor W. "The Federal Civil Right 'Not to Be Lynched'." *Washington University Law Quarterly* 28 (Feb. 1943): 57–73.

Rotnem, Victor W., & F. G. Folsom, Jr. "Recent Restrictions upon Religious Liberty." *American Political Science Review* 36 (Dec. 1942): 1053–68.

Rowe-Sims, Sarah. "The Mississippi State Sovereignty Commission: An Agency History." *Journal of Mississippi History* 61 (Spring 1999): 29–58.

Ryan, James E., & Michael Heise. "The Political Economy of School Choice." *Yale Law Journal* 111 (June 2002): 2043–2136.

Sancton, Thomas. "Race Fear Sweeps the South." *New Republic* 108 (Jan. 1943): 81–83.

——. "Trouble in Dixie." *New Republic* 108 (Jan. 1943): 11–14.

Sanders, Francine. "*Brown v. Board of Education*: An Empirical Reexamination of Its Effects on Federal District Courts." *Law & Society Review* 29 (1995): 731–56.

Schauer, Frederick. "Easy Cases." *Southern California Law Review* 58 (Jan. 1985): 399–440.

——. "Incentives, Reputation, and the Inglorious Determinants of Judicial Behavior." *University of Cincinnati Law Review* 68 (Spring 2000): 615–36.

Scheiner, Seth M. "President Theodore Roosevelt and the Negro, 1901–1908." *Journal of Negro History* 47 (July 1962): 169–82.

Scheingold, Stuart. "Constitutional Rights and Social Change: Civil Rights in Perspective." In *Judging the Constitution: Critical Essays on Judicial Lawmaking*, edited by Michael W. McCann & Gerald L. Houseman, 73–91. Glenview, Ill.: Scott, Foresman, 1989.

Schmidt, Benno C., Jr. "Principle and Prejudice: The Supreme Court and Race in the Progressive Era. Part I: The Heyday of Jim Crow." *Columbia Law Review* 82 (Apr. 1982): 444–524.

——. "Principle and Prejudice: The Supreme Court and Race in the Progressive Era. Part II: The Peonage Cases." *Columbia Law Review* 82 (May 1982): 646–718.

——. "Principle and Prejudice: The Supreme Court and Race in the Progressive Era. Part III: Black Disfranchisement from the KKK to the Grandfather Clause." *Columbia Law Review* 82 (June 1982): 835–905.

——. "Juries, Jurisdiction, and Race Discrimination: The Lost Promise of *Strauder v. West Virginia*." *Texas Law Review* 61 (May 1983): 1401–99.

Schuck, Peter. "Public Law Litigation and Social Reform." *Yale Law Journal* 102 (May 1993): 1763–86.

Schwartz, Bernard. "The Negro and the Law in the United States." *Modern Law Review* 14 (Oct. 1951): 446–61.

Searles, Ruth, & J. Allen Williams, Jr. "Negro College Students' Participation in Sit-Ins." *Social Forces* 40 (Mar. 1962): 215–20.

Seawright, Sally. "Desegregation at Maryland: The NAACP and the Murray Case in the 1930s." *Maryland Historian* 1 (Spring 1970): 59–74.

Segal, Jeffrey A., & Alfred D. Cover. "Ideological Values and the Votes of U.S. Supreme Court Justices." *American Political Science Review* 83 (June 1989): 557–65.

Seidman, Louis Michael. "*Brown* and *Miranda*." *California Law Review* 80 (May 1992): 673–753.

Silver, Christopher. "The Racial Origins of Zoning: Southern Cities from 1910–40." *Planning Perspectives* 6 (1991): 189–205.

Simpson, Dwight J. "Robert H. Jackson and the Doctrine of Judicial Restraint." *UCLA Law Review* 3 (Apr. 1956): 325–59.

Sinclair, Dean. "'Equal in All Places': The Civil Rights Struggle in Baton Rouge, 1953–1963." *Louisiana History* 39 (1998): 347–66.

Singer, Joseph William. "No Right to Exclude: Public Accommodations and Private Property." *Northwestern University Law Review* 90 (Summer 1996): 1283–1497.

Sisk, Glenn N. "Negro Education in the Alabama Black Belt, 1875–1900." *Journal of Negro Education* 22 (Spring 1953): 126–35.

Sitkoff, Harvard. "Harry Truman and the Election of 1948: The Coming of Age of Civil Rights in American Politics." *Journal of Southern History* 37 (Nov. 1971): 597–616.

——. "Racial Militancy and Interracial Violence in the Second World War." *Journal of American History* 58 (Dec. 1971): 661–81.

Skates, John R. "World War II as a Watershed in Mississippi History." *Journal of Mississippi History* 37 (May 1975): 131–42.

Skotnes, Andor. "'Buy Where You Can Work': Boycotts for Jobs in African-American Baltimore, 1933–1934." *Journal of Social History* 27 (Summer 1994): 735–61.

Smith, C. Calvin. "The Houston Riot of 1917, Revisited." *Houston Review* 13 (1991): 85–102.

Smith, Tom W. "America's Most Important Problem: A Trend Analysis, 1946–1976." *Public Opinion Quarterly* 44 (Summer 1980): 164–80.

Somers, Dale A. "Black and White in New Orleans: A Study in Urban Race Relations." *Journal of Southern History* 19 (Feb. 1974): 19–42.

Sosna, Morton. "The South in the Saddle: Racial Politics during the Wilson Years." *Wisconsin Magazine of History* 54 (Autumn 1970): 30–49.

Southern, David W. "Beyond Jim Crow Liberalism: Judge Waring's Fight against Segregation in South Carolina, 1942–52." *Journal of Negro History* 66 (Autumn 1981): 209–27.

Steiker, Carole S., & Jordan M. Steiker. "Sober Second Thoughts: Reflections on Two Decades of Constitutional Regulation of Capital Punishment." *Harvard Law Review* 109 (Dec. 1995): 355–438.

Stephenson, Gilbert T. "The Segregation of the White and Negro Races in Cities." *South Atlantic Quarterly* 13 (Jan. 1914): 1–18.

Stern, Mark. "Presidential Strategies and Civil Rights: Eisenhower, the Early Years, 1952–54." *Presidential Studies Quarterly* 19 (Fall 1989): 769–95.

Strauss, David. "The Irrelevance of Constitutional Amendments." *Harvard Law Review* 114 (Mar. 2001): 1457–1505.

Strong, Donald S. "Alabama: Transition and Alienation." In *Changing Politics of the South*, edited by William C. Havard, 427–71. Baton Rouge: Louisiana State University Press, 1972.

Sullivan, Patricia. "Southern Reformers, the New Deal and the Movement's Foundation." In *New Directions in Civil Rights Studies*, edited by Armstead L. Robinson & Patricia Sullivan, 81–104. Charlottesville: University Press of Virginia, 1991.

Swinney, Everette. "Enforcing the Fifteenth Amendment, 1870–1877." *Journal of Southern History* 28 (May 1962): 202–18.

Symposium. "The Courts and Racial Integration in Education." *Journal of Negro Education* 21 (Summer 1952): 229–444.

Taylor, Joseph H. "Populism and Disfranchisement in Alabama." *Journal of Negro History* 34 (Oct. 1949): 410–27.

Thomas, Bettye C. "Public Education and Black Protest in Baltimore 1865–1900." *Maryland Historical Magazine* 71 (Fall 1976): 381–91.

Thompson, Charles H. "Court Action: The Only Reasonable Alternative to Remedy Immediate Abuses of the Negro Separate School." *Journal of Negro Education* 4 (July 1935): 419–34.

———. "The Negro Separate School." *Crisis* 42 (Aug. 1935): 230–52.

Thornbrough, Emma Lou. "The Brownsville Episode and the Negro Vote." *Mississippi Valley Historical Review* 44 (Dec. 1957): 469–93.

———. "Breaking Racial Barriers to Public Accommodations in Indiana, 1935–1963." *Indiana Magazine of History* 83 (Dec. 1987): 300–343.

Thorndike, Joseph J. "'The Sometimes Sordid Level of Race and Segregation': James J. Kilpatrick and the Virginia Campaign against *Brown*." In *Moderates' Dilemma*, edited by Matthew D. Lassiter & Andrew B. Lewis, 51–71. Charlottesville: University Press of Virginia, 1998.

Thornton, J. Mills. "Challenge and Response in the Montgomery Bus Boycott of 1955–1956." *Alabama Review* 33 (July 1980): 163–235.

———. "Municipal Politics and the Course of the Movement." In *New Directions in Civil Rights Studies*, edited by Armstead L. Robinson & Patricia Sullivan, 38–64. Charlottesville: University Press of Virginia, 1991.

Tindall, George B. "The Question of Race in the South Carolina Constitutional Convention of 1895." *Journal of Negro History* 37 (July 1952): 277–303.

Tomberlin, Joseph A. "Florida Whites and the *Brown* Decision of 1954." *Florida Historical Quarterly* 51 (1972): 22–36.

Toppin, Edgar A. "Walter White and the Atlanta NAACP's Fight for Equal Schools, 1916–1917." *History of Education Quarterly* 7 (Spring 1967): 3–21.

Tumin, Melvin M. "Readiness and Resistance to Desegregation: A Social Portrait of the Hard Core." *Social Forces* 36 (Mar. 1958): 256–63.

Tumin, Melvin, Paul Barton, & Bernie Burrus. "Education, Prejudice and Discrimination: A Study in Readiness for Desegregation." *American Sociological Review* 23 (Feb. 1958): 41–49.

Tushnet, Mark. "Following the Rules Laid Down: A Critique of Interpretivism and Neutral Principles." *Harvard Law Review* 96 (Feb. 1983): 781–827.

———. "Comment." In *Civil Rights Movement*, edited by Charles W. Eagles, 117–25. Jackson: University Press of Mississippi, 1986.

———. "*Shelley v. Kraemer* and Theories of Equality." *New York Law Review* 33 (1988): 383–408.

———. "What Really Happened in *Brown v. Board of Education*." *Columbia Law Review* 91 (Dec. 1991): 1867–1930.

———. "The Significance of *Brown v. Board of Education*." *Virginia Law Review* 80 (Feb. 1994): 173–84.

———. "Progressive Era Race Relations Cases in Their 'Traditional' Context." *Vanderbilt Law Review* 51 (May 1998): 993–1002.

Tussman, Joseph, & Jacobus tenBroek. "Equal Protection of the Laws." *California Law Review* 37 (Sept. 1949): 341–81.

Urofsky, Melvin I. "Myth and Reality: The Supreme Court and Protective Legislation in the Progressive Era." *Yearbook of the Supreme Court Historical Society* (1983): 53–72.

Vines, Kenneth N. "A Louisiana Parish: Wholesale Purge." In *The Negro and the Ballot in the South*, edited by Margaret Price, 34–46. Atlanta, Ga.: Southern Regional Council, 1959.

——. "Federal District Judges and Race Relations Cases in the South." *Journal of Politics* 26 (May 1964): 337–57.

——. "Southern State Supreme Courts and Race Relations." *Western Political Quarterly* 18 (Mar. 1965): 5–18.

Von Eschen, Donald, Jerome Kirk, & Maurice Pinard. "The Conditions of Direct Action in a Democratic Society." *Western Political Quarterly* 22 (June 1969): 309–25.

Waite, Edward. "The Debt of Constitutional Law to Jehovah's Witnesses." *Minnesota Law Review* 28 (Mar. 1944): 209–46.

Wallace, Harry L. "Mr. Justice Minton: Hoosier Justice on the Supreme Court." *Indiana Law Journal* 34 (Winter 1959): 145–205.

Waterman, J. S., & E. E. Overton. "The Aftermath of *Moore v. Dempsey*." *Arkansas Law Review & Bar Association Journal* 6 (Winter 1951–1952): 1–7.

Watson, Richard L., Jr. "The Defeat of Judge Parker: A Study in Pressure Groups and Politics." *Mississippi Valley Historical Review* 50 (Sept. 1963): 213–34.

Weaver, Robert C. "Racial Policy in Public Housing." *Phylon* 1 (Second Quarter 1940): 149–61.

Weaver, Valeria. "The Failure of Civil Rights 1875–1883 and Its Repercussions." *Journal of Negro History* 54 (Oct. 1969): 368–82.

Webb, Michael D. "'God Bless You All, I Am Innocent': Sheriff Joseph F. Shipp, Chattanooga, Tennessee, and the Lynching of Ed Johnson." *Tennessee Historical Quarterly* 58 (Summer 1999): 156–79.

Wechsler, Herbert. "Toward Neutral Principles of Constitutional Law." *Harvard Law Review* 73 (Nov. 1959): 1–35.

Weeks, O. Douglas. "The White Primary." *Mississippi Law Journal* 8 (Dec. 1935): 135–53.

Weiss, Nancy J. "The Negro and the New Freedom: Fighting Wilsonian Segregation." *Political Science Quarterly* 84 (Mar. 1969): 61–79.

Weiss, Richard. "Ethnicity and Reform: Minorities and the Ambience of the Depression Years." *Journal of American History* 66 (Dec. 1979): 566–85.

Welch, Richard E., Jr. "The Federal Elections Bill of 1890: Postscripts and Prelude." *Journal of American History* 52 (Dec. 1965): 511–26.

Welke, Barbara Y. "When All the Women Were White, and All the Blacks Were Men: Gender, Class, Race, and the Road to *Plessy*, 1855–1914." *Law & History Review* 13 (Fall 1995): 261–316.

Wesley, Charles H. "The Negro Has Always Wanted the Four Freedoms." In *What the Negro Wants*, edited by Rayford W. Logan, 90–112. Chapel Hill: University of North Carolina Press, 1944; New York: Agathon, 1969.

West, Henry Litchfield. "The Race War in North Carolina." *Forum* 26 (Jan. 1899): 578–91.

Westfeldt, Wallace. "Communities in Strife: Where There Was Violence." In *With All Deliberate Speed*, edited by Don Shoemaker, 36–55. New York: Harper, 1957.

White, G. Edward. "The Anti-Judge: William O. Douglas and the Ambiguities of Individuality." *Virginia Law Review* 74 (Feb. 1988): 17–86.

White, Walter. "George Crawford: Symbol." *Crisis* 41 (Jan. 1934): 15.

Wilkerson, Doxey A. "Freedom: Through Victory in War and Peace." In *What the Negro Wants*, edited by Rayford W. Logan, 193–216. Chapel Hill: University of North Carolina Press, 1944; New York: Agathon, 1969.

Wilkins, Roy. "The Negro Wants Full Equality." In *What the Negro Wants*, edited by Rayford W. Logan, 113–32. Chapel Hill: University of North Carolina Press, 1944; New York: Agathon, 1969.

Wiseman, John B. "Racism in Democratic Politics, 1904–1912." *Mid-America* 51 (Jan. 1969): 38–58.

Wolgemuth, Kathleen Long. "Woodrow Wilson's Appointment Policy and the Negro." *Journal of Southern History* 24 (Nov. 1958): 457–71.

——. "Woodrow Wilson and Federal Segregation." *Journal of Negro History* 44 (Apr. 1959): 158–73.

Woodman, Harold D. "Economic Reconstruction and the Rise of the New South, 1865–1900." In *Interpreting Southern History: Historiographical Essays in Honor of Sanford W. Higginbotham*, edited by John B. Boles & Evelyn Thomas Nolen, 254–307. Baton Rouge: Louisiana State University Press, 1987.

Woodward, C. Vann. "The 'New Reconstruction' in the South: Desegregation in Historical Perspective." *Commentary* 21 (June 1956): 501–8.

——. "The Great Civil Rights Debate: The Ghost of Thaddeus Stevens in the Senate Chamber." *Commentary* 24 (Oct. 1957): 283–91.

——. "The South and the Law of the Land." *Commentary* 26 (Nov. 1958): 369–74.

——. "The Case of the Louisiana Traveler." In *Quarrels That Have Shaped the Constitution*, edited by John A. Garraty, 145–58. New York: Harper & Row, 1962.

——. "*Strange Career* Critics: Long May They Persevere." *Journal of American History* 75 (Dec. 1989): 857–68.

Workman, W. D., Jr. "The Deep South: Segregation Holds Firm." In *With All Deliberate Speed*, edited by Don Shoemaker, 88–109. New York: Harper, 1957.

Wright, George C. "The NAACP and Residential Segregation in Louisville, Kentucky, 1914–1917." *Register of the Kentucky Historical Society* 78 (Winter 1980): 39–54.

——. "Desegregation of Public Accommodations in Louisville." In *Southern Businessmen and Desegregation*, edited by Elizabeth Jacoway & David R. Colburn, 191–210. Baton Rouge: Louisiana State University Press, 1982.

——. "By the Book: The Legal Executions of Kentucky Blacks." In *Under Sentence of Death*, edited by W. Fitzhugh Brundage, 250–70. Chapel Hill: University of North Carolina Press, 1997.

Wunderlich, Frieda. "New York's Anti-Discrimination Law." *Social Research* 17 (June 1950): 219–47.

Wynes, Charles E. "The Evolution of Jim Crow Laws in Twentieth-Century Virginia." *Phylon* 28 (Fourth Quarter 1960): 416–25.

Young, Jeffrey R. "Eisenhower's Federal Judges and Civil Rights Policy: A Republican 'Southern Strategy' for the 1950s." *Georgia Historical Quarterly* 78 (Fall 1994): 536–65.

Zalman, Marvin. "Juricide." In *Leveraging the Law*, edited by David A. Schultz, 293–318. New York: Lang, 1998.

UNPUBLISHED THESES, DISSERTATIONS, AND STUDENT AND ACADEMIC PAPERS

Baker, R. Scott. "Ambiguous Legacies: The NAACP's Legal Campaign against Segregation in Charleston, South Carolina, 1935–1975." Ph.D. diss., Columbia University, 1993.

Brener, Jason. "'Upon Our Own Strong Arms': Public School Desegregation through Political Process: A Case Study of New Jersey." Student paper, University of Virginia School of Law, Spring 1992.

Burch, Alan Robert. "The NAACP before and after *Grovey v. Townsend*." Master's thesis, University of Virginia, 1994.

Duncan, Hannibal Gerald. "The Changing Race Relationship in the Border and Northern States." Ph.D. diss., University of Pennsylvania, 1922.

Fairclough, Adam. "A Political Coup d'Etat? How the Enemies of Earl Long Overwhelmed Racial Moderation in Louisiana." Paper presented at the Conference on Massive Resistance at the University of Suffolk in Brighton, England, March 2002.

Fishel, Leslie H., Jr. "The North and the Negro, 1865–1900." Ph.D. diss., Harvard University, 1953.

Green, Laurie B. "The Urban-Rural Two-Way Road: The Memphis Freedom Movement in the Era of *Brown v. Board of Education*." Paper presented at the conference on *Brown v. Board of Education* at the Institute for Southern Studies at the University of South Carolina, June 2002.

Greene, Christina. "'If You Want Anything Done, Tell the Women and the Children': School Desegregation, Direct Action and the 'Backlash Theory' in North Carolina, 1954–1963." Paper presented at the conference on *Brown v. Board of Education* at the Institute for Southern Studies at the University of South Carolina, June 2002.

Kelley, Blair. "*Plessy* and Early Challenges to the Doctrine of 'Separate, but Equal'." Paper presented at the conference on *Brown v. Board of Education* at the Institute for Southern Studies at the University of South Carolina, June 2002.

Lassiter, Matthew David. "The Rise of the Suburban South: The 'Silent Majority' and the Politics of Education, 1945–75." Ph.D. diss., University of Virginia, 1999.

Lau, Peter F. "From the Periphery to the Center: Clarendon County, South Carolina, *Brown*, and the Struggle for Democracy and Equality in America." Paper presented at the conference on *Brown v. Board of Education* at the Institute for Southern Studies at the University of South Carolina, June 2002.

Long, Herman H. "Segregation in Interstate Railway Coach Travel" (Dec. 1952). In Box A27, Tom Clark Papers, Tarleton Law Library, University of Texas.

Lyons, David. "Federal Enforcement of Civil Rights: *United States v. Shotwell* and the Ku Klux Klan Trials in North Carolina, 1871." Student paper, University of Virginia School of Law, 1991.

McCoy, Stanford K. "False Promises: Public Accommodations Statutes in the North after the Civil Rights Cases." Student paper, University of Virginia School of Law, 1998.

Marshall, Wesley G. "The Dawn Is Breaking: *Buchanan v. Warley* and the Fight against Residential Segregation." Master's thesis, University of Virginia, 1985.

Ment, David Martin. "Racial Segregation in the Public Schools of New England and New York, 1840–1940." Ph.D. diss., Columbia University, 1975.

Minter, Patricia. "The Codification of Jim Crow: The Origins of Segregated Railroad Transit in the South, 1865–1910." Ph.D. diss., University of Virginia, 1994.

Powell, Lee Riley. "Massive Resistance in Arkansas: A Tale of Race Relations and an Undemocratic Political System in the 1950s." Student paper, University of Virginia School of Law, 1992.

Price, Margaret. "Joint Interagency Fact-Finding Project on Violence and Intimidation" (draft). In NAACP Papers, part 20, reel 11, frs. 338–442.

"Report on the Black Vote in Southern States in 1946." In NAACP Papers, part 4, reel 8, frs. 862–75.

Risen, Maurice L. "Legal Aspects of Separation of Races in the Public Schools." Ph.D. diss., Temple University, 1935.

Schmidt, Christopher W. "J. Waties Waring and the Making of Liberal Jurisprudence in Post–World War II America." Paper presented at the conference on *Brown v. Board of Education* at the Institute for Southern Studies at the University of South Carolina, June 2002.

Smith, Larissa M. "Black Attorneys and the NAACP in Virginia: Creating a Civil Rights Vanguard." Paper presented at the conference on *Brown v. Board of Education* at the Institute for Southern Studies at the University of South Carolina, June 2002.

Sullivan, Patricia. "Prelude to *Brown*: Education and the Struggle for Racial Justice during the NAACP's Formative Years, 1909–34." Paper presented at the conference on *Brown v. Board of Education* at the Institute for Southern Studies at the University of South Carolina, June 2002.

Turner, Kara Miles. "Black Schooling and Protest in Prince Edward County, Virginia." Paper presented at the conference on *Brown v. Board of Education* at the Institute for Southern Studies at the University of South Carolina, June 2002.

Valone, James S. "Prejudice and Politics: The Civil Rights Act of 1875." Master's thesis, Pennsylvania State University, 1958.

Westin, Richard Barry. "The State and Segregated Schools: Negro Public Education in North Carolina, 1863–1923." Ph.D. diss., Duke University, 1966.

Wilson, Rai. "The Forms of Citizenship: *Chambers v. Florida*." Student paper, University of Virginia School of Law, 2000.

Wingo, Horace Calvin. "Race Relations in Georgia, 1872–1908." Ph.D. diss., Emory University, 1962.

INDEX

Italicized page numbers refer to illustrations.

Belden, Stanley, 273, 284–85
Berea College, 23–24
Berea College v. Kentucky, 9, 23–24, 28, 51, 80–82, 85
Bethune, Mary McLeod, 110, 169
Betts v. Brady, 230
Bibles, 48, 65
Bickel, Alexander, 304
Biddle, Francis, 177, 241
Bilbo, Theodore, 184, 187, 242, 247–48, 248, 427, 534n35
Bill of Rights, 118, 295, 502n50
Binghamton (N.Y.) *Press*, 86
Birmingham Board of Education, Shuttlesworth v., 329–33
Birmingham church bombing, 436–39, 438, 441
Birmingham News, 407, 431
Birmingham street demonstrations, 362, 433–37, 434
Birth of a Nation, 66, 104, 394
Black, Hugo L.
  antimiscegenation laws and, 323
  anti-NAACP measures and, 338
  appointment of, 116, 193–95, 522n55
  coerced confessions and, 228
  constitutional interpretation of, 448–49
  criminal procedure and, 282
  gradualism and, 333
  higher education segregation and, 212
  jury discrimination and, 226, 268, 323–24
  racial violence and, 441
  residential segregation and, 216
  school desegregation and, 293, 294–95, 298, 300, 307–8, 313–18, 329, 331, 349, 354, 356
  transportation segregation and, 221–22
  white primaries and, 199, 203
black agency, 370, 372, 379, 381
black cabinet, 110, 115
Black Codes, 17, 71–72, 80
black labor. *See also* agricultural laborers, black
  in interwar period, 105, 108, 112

in Progressive era, 61, 63–65, 71–76, 86–88
  in Reconstruction era, 71–72
  in World War II era, 178–79
black migration. *See* migration, black
black militancy
  in interwar period, 101, 104
  in World War II era, 178–80, 184, 239, 246
Black Muslims, 382
black nationalism, 382
Blaine, James G., 14
Blair bill, 26
Blease, Cole, 44, 64
blockbusters, 262
bloody-shirt tactics, 14–15
Bloody Sunday, 440–41
Bob-Lo Excursion Co. v. Michigan, 217, 223–24
Bolling v. Sharpe, 292
bombings
  in *Brown* era, 327, 351–53, 356, 383, 411–12, 422–23, 425, 428, 430
  civil rights movement and, 436–39, 438, 440
  in interwar period, 105, 143, 145, 430
  in Progressive era, 92
  in World War II era, 191, 250–51, 252, 263
Bonaparte, Charles, 83
Boothe, Armistead, 222–23
Bootle, William A., 404
Borah, William, 116, 140
Boston University, 258
Boswell amendment, 238, 244
Boutwell, Albert, 405, 433
Bowers v. Hardwick, 367, 464
Bowman, James v., 37
boxing, 63, 66, 168
boycotts, economic
  in *Brown* era, 291, 369–73, 376
  in interwar period, 101, 108, 115
  in *Plessy* era, 58
  in Progressive era, 94
  in World War II era, 267, 284
boycotts, military, 182
Bradley, Joseph P., 37
Brady, Betts v., 230
Brady, Tom, 426, 427

Carmichael, Omer, 326
Carolene Products Co., United States v., 169, 195–96
Carraway v. State, 133
Carter, D. V., 250
Carter, Hodding, 316, 410
Carter v. Texas, 42
Catholics, 111, 189, 193, 194, 196, 298
Catholic schools, 115, 186, 189, 216, 291, 346
CCC (Civilian Conservation Corps), 109
Celler, Emanuel, 362
Central High School (Little Rock, Ark.), 326–29, 327, 334, 395, 418, 422, 423
certiorari, 212–13, 216, 256, 258, 322, 324
chain gangs, 61, 71, 87, 171, 230
Chambers, Izell, 227–28, 541n111
Chambers v. Florida, 227–29, 269, 282–83, 286, 298, 541n111
champerty, 338, 553n115
Charleston News & Courier, 114
Charlotte-Mecklenburg Board of Education, Swann v., 341–42
Chattanooga News, 126
Cherokee removal, 56
Cherry, Francis, 389, 394
Chicago Defender, 101
Chinese aliens, 34–35, 80
Chinese-American students, 99, 146–48
church bombings, 436–39, 438, 440, 441
Churchill, Winston, 175, 399
CIC (Commission of Interracial Cooperation), 104, 131, 155, 168
CIO (Congress of Industrial Organizations), 108, 111, 112, 114, 191–92, 285, 429
citizens' councils, 400, 402, 406–7, 411–14, 418, 426, 440
civil liberties, 36, 111, 194–96, 210, 215, 299
Civil Rights Act (1866), 10, 17, 19, 40, 80, 144
Civil Rights Act (1870), 84
Civil Rights Act (1875), 17, 19–20
  invalidation of, 18, 22, 49

Civil Rights Act (1957), 366
Civil Rights Act (1964), 95, 139, 160, 347, 362–63, 435, 441, 458
Civil Rights Cases (1883), 50, 72
Civil Rights Congress, 192, 285, 375
civil rights consciousness, 94, 180, 185, 191, 215, 219, 224
civil rights movement
  bombings and, 436–39, 438, 440
  Brown v. Board of Education and, 6–7, 363–442
  direct-action protests and, 360–61, 373–84, 385, 410, 433–37, 439–42
  federal intervention and, 55, 260, 432, 437
  racial violence and, 364, 374, 380, 385, 421–42, 432
  street demonstrations and, 341, 362, 369, 374, 433–37, 434
civil service, 68, 97, 100, 181, 186
Civil Service Commission, 68
Civil War, 13–14, 23, 36, 66, 174, 444
Clarion-Ledger (Jackson, Miss.), 389
Clark, Jim, 385, 428, 440–41
Clark, Septima, 392
Clark, Tom C.
  anti-NAACP measures and, 336–38
  appointment of, 193, 195
  higher education segregation and, 209–12
  school desegregation and, 293, 297, 298, 300–301, 307, 309, 313, 329
  white primaries and, 202–3
class actions, 52, 313, 316, 359
Classic, United States v., 197–98, 201, 245
class segregation, 11, 18, 30, 265
Clement, Frank, 351, 385, 389, 397
Clemson University, 406
Cleveland, Grover, 13
closed society, 410–12
Clyatt v. United States, 72
coerced black labor, 72–76, 87–88, 96, 287–88
Cohen, William, 336
Cold War imperative, 182–84, 187, 192–95, 210, 215–16, 219, 291, 299–300, 375–76

Dalton, Ted, 332, 398
Daniels, Josephus, 68–69, 126
Darden, Colgate, 177, 280
Darrow, Clarence, 134, 281
Daughters of the American Revolution, 167
Davidson, T. Whitfield, 354
Davies, Ronald N., 356
Davis, Benjamin O., Sr., 178
Davis, James C., 331, 427
Davis, Jimmie, 402, 403
Davis, John W., 302, 311
Davis, Oscar, 279
Day, William, 80, 81
deadlines, judicial, 313, 316–18, 329, 357–58
Deane, Charles B., 397
death sentences
    in *Brown* era, 323–24
    in interwar period, 99, 117–21, 125–26, 131, 133, 153, 155
    in World War II era, 177, 183, 211, 231–32, 268, 272, 275–80, 283, 540n99
decolonization, 184, 376
DeCuir, Hall v., 220–21
deGraffenried, Ryan, 406
De Laine, J. A., 353, 354
democratic capitalism, 182–84, 291
Democrats
    in *Brown* era, 325–26, 364–65, 394, 396, 398, 402, 435
    civil rights movement and, 373, 439
    in interwar period, 99, 100, 107, 109, 111–12, 114, 116, 135, 137, 140
    in *Plessy* era, 38, 49
    in post-Reconstruction era: disfranchisement, 10–12, 14–16, 30–32, 53–54, 470n3; jury service, 40; railroad segregation, 17, 22; school segregation, 27
    in Progressive era, 67, 68
    in Reconstruction era, 19, 28–29, 40
    in World War II era, 386: anti—poll-tax legislation and, 178, 200; conventions in, 181, 190, 192; Dixiecrats and, 186; elections in, 174, 180, 201, 251; residential segregation and, 215; U.S. Supreme

Court and, 195; voter registration and, 240; white primaries and, 183, 199–203, 237–39, 243–45, 248, 534n35
Dempsey, Moore v. See Moore v. Dempsey
deontological judgments, 138–39
DePriest, Oscar, 101
desegregation. *See also Brown v. Board*
    in World War II era, 189–90: of federal civil service, 181, 186; of higher education, 209–12, 254–59; of military, 181–83, 186, 192, 209; of transportation, 222–23, 264–67
Dewey, John, 280
Dewey, Thomas, 181, 186, 192, 386
dining-car accommodations, 217–20, 264
direct-action protests
    in *Brown* era, 340, 349, 363–64, 369–73, 429–31
    in civil rights movement, 360–61, 373–84, 385, 410, 433–37, 439–42
    in World War II era, 242
discretion, administrative
    in *Brown* era, 330, 358–59
    in interwar period, 154
    in *Plessy* era, 33–37, 44–46, 53, 55, 57, 59, 69, 456
    in post-Reconstruction era, 35, 41
    in Progressive era, 78, 85–86
    in World War II era, 226, 232, 244
discretion, judicial, 318, 321, 323–24
discretionary admission standards, 255–56, 258–59
disfranchisement, black
    in *Brown* era, 291, 340
    in interwar period, 99–101, 105, 107–10, 135–42, 154, 158–59
    in *Plessy* era, 9, 13, 28–39, 42, 45, 52–55, 59–60
    in post-Reconstruction era, 10–11, 30–34, 43
    in Progressive era, 69–71, 75, 85–86, 91–92, 96
    in Reconstruction era, 18–19
    in World War II era, 197, 200, 238
disfranchising amendments, 31
disfranchising conventions, 31, 52, 69

northern states
in *Brown* era, 365–66, 368, 423–25,
428–29
civil rights movement and, 373–74,
380, 385, 432, 435, 438–39
in interwar period, 100, 105–6, 111,
115, 143, 145, 147
in *Plessy* era, 13, 22–23, 27, 38, 41, 47,
51–53, 57
in post-Reconstruction era, 12
in Progressive era, 63–64, 70–71
in Reconstruction era, 18–19, 22
in World War II era, 180, 182, 190
nuclear espionage, 183
nuclear holocaust, 183, 375–76
nullification
in *Brown* era, 322, 330, 355–56, 366,
381–82, 416–17
in interwar period, 154
in *Plessy* era, 51, 55–56, 59, 64
in Progressive era, 70–71, 73, 96
in World War II era, 202, 204, 206,
208, 226, 245, 255, 265
Nuremberg Trial, 304

oaths, 35, 54, 249
Oberlin College, 105
officeholders, black
in *Brown* era, 389, 405
in interwar period, 113, 115
in *Plessy* era, 41, 64
in post-Reconstruction era, 10, 15,
30, 32
in Reconstruction era, 10, 29, 40
in World War II era, 189
Oklahoma Supreme Court, 70, 205
Ole Miss. *See* University of Mississippi
organized labor. *See also* labor unions;
unionism, interracial
in interwar period, 98, 106, 111, 112
in Progressive era, 64–65, 75–76
in World War II era, 238
original understanding, 9, 15, 59
in *Brown* era, 300, 303–6, 308, 367
disfranchisement and, 33–34
higher education segregation and,
208
jury service and, 40
in Progressive era, 62

public school segregation and,
25–26, 146
railroad segregation and, 19–20
Orlando Morning Sentinel, 275
outliers, 78–79, 85, 136–37, 236, 453–54
Overton, John Holmes, 246

Pace v. Alabama, 21, 77
Painter, Sweatt v. See Sweatt v. Painter
Parker, John, 101, 108, 116, 358–59
Parker, Mack, 413, 425–26, 428, 429,
439, 446
party platforms, 14–15, 109, 122–23, 190,
192
party primaries. *See* white primaries
paternalism, 11, 17–18
patronage, federal, 41, 66–68, 107, 112
Patterson, Haywood, 127–28, 132, 153
Patterson, Joe T., 406
Patterson, John
elections and, 383, 399
on King, 353
racial violence and, 428, 431
school desegregation and, 330–31,
402–3, 405, 407, 419
white backlash and, 394
Patton v. Mississippi, 226
pay-equalization suits, 113, 164, 182, 218
Peabody fund, 47
Pearl Harbor, 174–75
Peck, Fletcher v., 34–35
Pendergast machine, 178
peonage
in interwar period, 100, 108
in Progressive era, 61, 71–76, 86–88,
95–96
in World War II era, 173, 233–35,
286–89
Peonage Act (1867), 73–74, 87
Pepper, Claude, 246, 387–88
per curiam opinions, 321
Perkins v. State, 133
Perlman, Philip B., 212, 525n103
personal rights, 77–78, 89–90
petition signers, 352–53, 368–69, 373,
377, 390
petty larceny, 72, 74–75
Phagan, Mary, 120–21
Pierce v. Society of Sisters, 216, 453

ripeness objection, 84, 205
Rives, Richard, 356
Roberts, Owen, 115, 137–38, 199, 200
Robertson v. Baldwin, 73
Robeson, Paul, 169
Robinson, Jackie, 393
Robinson, Jo Ann, 369, 371
Robinson, Spotswood, 112
Roddy, Stephen, 125
Roe v. Wade, 367, 462, 464–65
Rogers, William, 334, 426, 428
Roosevelt, Eleanor, 110, 115, 280, 326, 332
Roosevelt, Franklin D., 15
  civil rights legislation and, 115, 140, 142, 168, 177, 179, 218, 287–88
  New Deal and, 109–12, 114, 215
  U.S. Supreme Court and, 115–16, 170, 193–95, 200, 295–96, 307, 451, 522n55
  World War II and, 175, 192
Roosevelt, Theodore, 24, 39, 41, 66–67, 122
Roosevelt Court, 221
Rosenberg, Ethel, 183, 375
Rosenberg, Julius, 183, 375
Rosenwald fund, 47
Russell, Charles, 76
Russell, Richard, 366, 410, 420
Rutledge, Wiley, 205, 223, 229, 526n114

Sacco, Nicola, 194
Sanders, Carl, 405
Scalia, Antonin, 450
Scarlett, Frank, 240
scholarships, out-of-state, 99, 146, 148–52, 160–63, 204, 218, 254–55
school-closing measures, 332, 341–42, 350, 356, 360, 382, 398, 399–403, 415–19
school desegregation. *See* desegregation
school prayer, 309
school segregation. *See also* higher education segregation
  in *Brown* era, 389–421
  in interwar period, 99, 105, 146–52, 160–70
  in *Plessy* era, 25–27, 43–45, 51, 57

in post-Reconstruction era, 10, 15–16, 25
in Progressive era, 63, 90
in Reconstruction era, 10–11, 18–19, 43
in World War II era, 195, 200, 210–12, 222–23, 239
School Segregation Cases, 292–93, 298
SCHW (Southern Conference for Human Welfare), 142, 168, 192
"scientific" theories, 113, 116, 168, 188, 211
SCLC (Southern Christian Leadership Conference), 373, 374, 377–78, 380, 384, 429, 433, 440
Scott, Hugh, 425
Scott, W. Kerr, 385, 398
Scottsboro defendants, 117–20, 123–27, 124, 131–33, 153–57, 166, 278, 501–2n49
Screws v. United States, 270, 458
Seawell, Malcolm, 332, 360
secret-ballot laws, 30–31, 54
sectional reconciliation, 13–14, 23, 38
Securities and Exchange Commission, 296
segregation. *See also* desegregation
  in *Brown* era, 389–408
  civil rights movement and, 374–75, 379
  in interwar period, 99, 105–7, 110, 112, 134, 142–52, 159–70
  in *Plessy* era, 8–9, 17–28, 20–23, 25, 43–45, 48–52
  in post-Reconstruction era, 10–11, 13, 16, 25, 39
  in Progressive era, 62–65, 68, 75, 78, 79–85, 90–97
  in Reconstruction era, 18–20, 43
  in World War II era, 288–89: Cold War and, 184; in higher education, 172–73, 195, 204–12; in military, 176, 178, 180; in residential housing, 212–17; in transportation, 217–25
self-defense claims, 277–83, 412
Selma march, 440–41
separate and *unequal*
  in interwar period, 106

Spencer, Herbert, 82
Spingarn, Arthur, 143
sporting competitions, 11, 113, 186, 346, 393–94. *See also* baseball; boxing
Stalinist abuses, 130, 155
standards of proof, 36, 41–42
Stanley, Thomas B., 389, 395
Star-Bulletin (Honolulu), 428
stare decisis, 198, 304
state-action doctrine
  in *Brown* era, 303, 306
  in interwar period, 99, 135–40, 144–45
  in *Plessy* era, 37
  in Progressive era, 95
  in World War II era, 177, 197–99, 201–3, 214–17, 231
state-appointed counsel. *See* court-appointed counsel
States' Rights party, 399
status quo, racial
  in *Brown* era, 291, 359, 369, 370, 372, 376, 429
  in interwar period, 163–64
  in World War II era, 177
steamboat segregation, 50, 220
Steinbeck, John, 423
Stern, Robert, 525n103
Stevenson, Adlai, 192, 325, 423
Stevenson, Coke, 285
Stewart, Potter, 331, 337, 551n96
St. Louis Globe-Democrat, 326
Stone, Harlan Fiske, 174, 195–98, 200
Stone Court, 200
Storey, Moorfield, 90, 91, 93, 103, 112
Stratford, John, 280
Strauder v. West Virginia, 9, 40–43, 55, 59, 91, 123, 136, 447
streetcar segregation
  in interwar period, 108
  in post-Reconstruction era, 18
  in Progressive era, 64–65, 68, 94
  in Reconstruction era, 10
  in World War II era, 177, 179
street demonstrations
  in civil rights movement, 341, 362, 369, 374, 433–37, 434
  in interwar period, 163–64
  in *Plessy* era, 58

in Progressive era, 94–95
  in World War II era, 284
Stuyvesant Town Corporation, Dorsey v., 216–17
subconstitutional rules, 42–43, 55, 59, 99, 126–27, 225, 457
subordination, black, 101, 163, 174, 374–75
subversion cases, 339, 376
suffrage, black. *See* voting, black
suffrage, women's, 63
Sugar Bowl, 394
Sullivan, L. B., 431
Sutherland, George, 121, 123
Suttles, Breedlove v., 99, 141, 158–59, 169
Swain v. Alabama, 231, 269
Swann v. Charlotte-Mecklenburg Board of Education, 341–42
Sweatt, Heman, 205, 207, 207–10, 212
Sweatt v. Painter, 454, 459
  in *Brown* era, 297, 314, 387, 393
  in interwar period, 162
  in World War II era, 207–12, 216, 219, 253–56, 258–61, 289
Sweet, Ossian, 105, 133, 134, 145, 166, 194
symbolic legislation
  in interwar period, 110–11
  in *Plessy* era, 50, 60
  in Progressive era, 82, 93, 96
  in World War II era, 190
symbolism of *Brown*, 369–70, 376
synagogue bombings, 425, 428

Taft, William Howard, 41, 47, 67–68, 71, 116, 121–22, 140, 147
Taft-Hartley labor law, 388
Talmadge, Eugene, 184, 187, 245, 247, 261, 386–88
Talmadge, Herman E., 386–88, 389–90, 415, 427
Tampa Tribune, 319
Taney, Roger, 68
Tanner, Adams v., 81
Taylor, Robert L., 351, 357
Taylor v. Georgia, 233–34, 286
teachers, 113, 335, 337, 345–46, 352–53, 400, 410, 418

University of Oklahoma Law School, 205, 206, 210
University of South Carolina, 393
University of Tennessee, 397
University of Texas, 172, 205–7, 210, 393
upper-class whites, 11, 18
urbanization, 445
  in *Brown* era, 291
  in interwar period, 102–3, 105, 115, 159
  in World War II era, 174, 187, 242
Urban League, 288, 394
U.S. Civil Rights Commission, 341, 360, 362, 406, 411
U.S. Congress
  in *Brown* era, 294–95, 298, 307–8, 314, 325, 335, 340, 351, 366–67
  in interwar period, 123, 160
  in *Plessy* era, 26, 37–39, 49–50, 53
  in post-Reconstruction era, 30–31, 44, 54
  in Reconstruction era, 18–20, 28–29, 40
  in World War II era, 200, 253, 253–54
U.S. Employment Service, 179
U.S. Health, Education, and Welfare Department (HEW), 363
U.S. Housing Authority, 145
U.S. Interior Department, 110
U.S. Justice Department
  in *Brown* era, 299, 307, 314, 316–17, 334, 335, 342
  civil rights movement and, 362, 433, 435
  in interwar period, 109, 140, 177, 287
  in *Plessy* era, 56, 59
  in Reconstruction era, 54
  in World War II era: black voting rights and, 239, 241, 251, 253; civil liberties unit in, 194, 215; Cold War and, 195, 210; lynchings and, 178, 186; transportation segregation and, 218–19
U.S. Postal Service, 252
U.S. Public Housing Authority, 263
U.S. State Department, 182–83, 375
U.S. Supreme Court. *See also specific case names*
  civil rights movement and, 364

constitutional interpretation and, 446–68
  in interwar period, 101, 108, 112, 113, 115–16
  in *Plessy* era, 9–10, 16–17, 21, 25–27, 47–48, 58–60
  in post-Reconstruction era, 12–13, 18
  in Progressive era, 62–63, 70
  in Reconstruction era, 19
  in World War II era, 172–73, 193–96, 243, 256–58, 263–64, 282–84
U.S. War Department, 176, 178, 180

vagrancy laws, 65, 71–72, 74, 87
Vandiver, Ernest, 399, 402, 404, 418
Vanzetti, Bartolomeo, 194
Vardaman, James, 11–12, 64, 68
venue, change of
  in interwar period, 125, 127, 131, 157
  in World War II era, 272–75, 277–78
veterans, black, 205, 239, 248–50, 275, 277, 445, 454–55
veterans, white, 187
vigilantes, white, 191, 353, 379–80, 424, 426, 441
Villard, Oswald Garrison, 68, 93
Vinson, Fred M.
  appointment of, 193, 195
  higher education segregation and, 205, 207–8, 210, 212
  residential segregation and, 213–14, 216
  school desegregation and, 293, 293–94, 298, 300–303, 307–8, 311, 314
  transportation segregation and, 224
  white primaries and, 202
violence, racial. *See also* lynchings; murders
  in *Brown* era: gradualism and, 324–26; Little Rock crisis and, 327–29, 422; massive resistance and, 350–53; school desegregation and, 314–15, 356–57, 383, 390, 404, 411–13
  civil rights movement and, 364, 374, 380, 385, 421–42, 432
  in interwar period, 98, 101, 103, 105, 122–23